In accordance with the latest syllabus prescribed by the
Central Board of Secondary Education, New Delhi

MOST LIKELY
CBSE QUESTION BANK

CLASS XII
CHEMISTRY

Category Wise & Chapter Wise

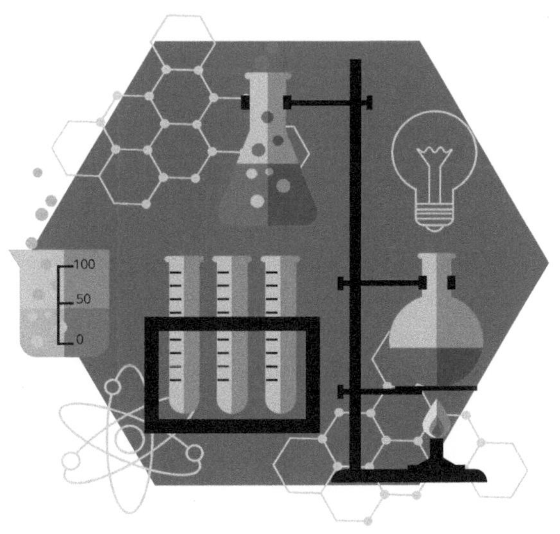

By

A PANEL OF AUTHORS

EDITION
YEAR 2021

ISBN : 978-93-91184-27-8

PUBLISHED BY

 **GURUKUL BOOKS & PACKAGING**
(Unit of Oswal Printers & Publishers Pvt. Ltd.)

 1/12, Sahitya Kunj, M.G. Road, Agra - 282002

 (0562) 2527771-4, +91 7534077222

 info@oswalpublishers.in

 www.oswalpublishers.com

The cover of this book has been designed using resources from Freepik.com

PREFACE

Gurukul's CBSE Most Likely Question Bank series is updated as per the latest syllabus given by the Central Board of Secondary Education.

This title highlights the knowledge-based and skill-based goals of the Bloom's Taxonomy by making the students acquainted with relevant facts and concepts and also teaching them ways to apply their subjective knowledge into practise for desired academic results.

This book provides ample practice questions arranged section-wise so that the students can revise the whole syllabus in a comparatively lesser time and develop the ability of prioritising and categorising topics for effective learning. It covers all probable types of questions asked in the exams. The solutions have been prepared by eminent subject experts with explanations. Solutions follow the standard Marking Scheme of the CBSE Board.

In addition, questions from compartment paper, foreign paper and latest board paper have also been incorporated in the chapters.

The series is an attempt to instil confidence in students to face the board examination. The language used is simple, to the point and questions cover all the important topics as per the weightage given to them by the board.

We hope this book will be a valuable asset for the students. All further suggestions towards improving the series are welcome and would be incorporated in the future editions.

Note : Questions marked with :

'★' are board exam questions from previous years

'★★' are frequently asked board exam questions

—The Publishers

How to Prepare for Board Exams Using Gurukul's
Most Likely Question Bank

The Most Likely Question Bank is a great learning tool for CBSE Examinations as it is the most comprehensive and concisely composed set of questions for students. In order to prepare well for their exams, students may follow the following approach.

- **Step 1 :** Prepare Your Theory

  Students must go through the theory of the chapters, from their textbooks covering the syllabus as per the Board Guidelines.

- **Step 2 :** Understand the Categories

  The contents have been arranged as per different 'Category' of Questions. Each category in turn covers topics from all the chapters of the syllabus. e.g., Short Answers category will cover the short answer type questions from all the chapters of the syllabus in that subject.

- **Step 3 :** Complete Syllabus Revision

  When students revise questions from any single category, they are revising the entire syllabus in different assemblages.

- **Step 4 :** Customised Learning

  Students with different learning calibers can customize their preparations. They can refer the objective questions first to get a basic understanding of the chapters and topics, and then they can take up the most complex categories.

- **Step 5 :** Check Your Progress

  Students can check their answers against the solutions given next to the questions. This will save time and help in faster revisions. Students can benefit tremendously from this series by using them optimally for their exam preparations.

FINDING THE RIGHT BIN FOR MASKS?

 Masks are a powerful shield against virus. The purpose behind wearing is to stop the spread of saliva and nasal discharge from infecting the other person.

 Global use of disposable face masks and gloves is estimated to have been 100 billion pieces every month.

 Masks are made up of a synthetic material called, TNT which takes more than 400 years to decompose.

 Also masks come in a myriad of shades. The first step towards its healthy disposal is to choose which one to wear at the first place.

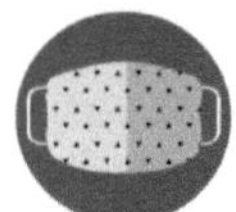 For casual use, choose tight cloth masks which can be reused over and over again. However, wearing it in vicinity of an infected person can be a wrong choice.

 When visiting hospitals and other contaminated zones, choose loose fitting surgical masks which blocks droplets and splashes of saliva. However, they are ineffective against very small particles that come off sneezing and coughing in close vicinity.

 N95 Masks are not for routine use and must be spared for medical experts who are in direct contact with the patient.

 When it comes to disposing a mask, the very first step is to wash your hands before removing it from your face.

 Wash your hands for atleast 20 seconds, using either an alcohol based sanitizer (having 60% alcohol) or using soap and water.

 Remove your mask either using the mask strings or downside up. Don't touch the center of mask.

 If you are wearing a cloth mask, put it separately into wash without mixing it with other clothes.

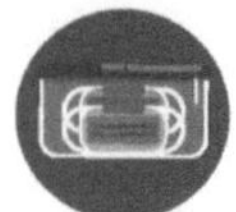 In case of a surgical mask, fold it inwards such that the droplets are not exposed to the air. Make it into a roll and wrap it up in two polythene bags or tissue bag, one inside the other.

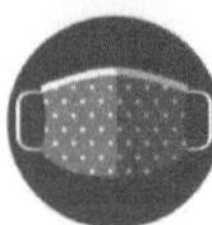 Prefer cloth masks for casual use and avoid one time used masks.

CONTENTS

Note: Questions marked with :
'★' are board exam questions from previous years
'★★' are frequently asked board exam questions

CLASS XII
(THEORY)

Total Period (Theory 160 + Practical 60)

Max. Marks : 70

Time : 3 Hours

Unit No.	Title	No. of Periods	Marks
Unit – I	Solid State	10	
Unit – II	Solutions	10	
Unit – III	Electrochemistry	12	23
Unit – IV	Chemical Kinetics	10	
Unit – V	Surface Chemistry	08	
Unit – VI	General Principles and Processes of Isolation of Elements	08	
Unit – VII	p-Block Elements	12	19
Unit – VIII	d-and f-Block Elements	12	
Unit – IX	Coordination Compounds	12	
Unit – X	Haloalkanes and Haloarenes	10	
Unit – XI	Alcohols, Phenols and Ehters	10	
Unit – XII	Aldehydes, Ketones and Carboxylic Acids	10	28
Unit – XIII	Amines	10	
Unit – XIV	Biomolecules	12	
Unit – XV	Polymers	08	
Unit – XVI	Chemistry in Everyday Life	06	
	Total	**160**	**70**

SYLLABUS

Unit I   **:**   **Solid State**   **10 Periods**

Classification of solids based on different binding forces: molecular, ionic, covalent and metallic solids, amorphous and crystalline solids (elementary idea). Unit cell in two dimensional and three dimensional lattices, calculation of density of unit cell, packing in solids, packing efficiency, voids, number of atoms per unit cell in a cubic unit cell, point defects, electrical and magnetic properties.

Band theory of metals, conductors, semiconductors and insulators and n and p type semiconductors.

Unit II   **:**   **Solutions**   **10 Periods**

Types of solutions, expression of concentration of solutions of solids in liquids, solubility of gases in liquids, solid solutions, colligative properties - relative lowering of vapour pressure, Raoult's law, elevation of boiling point, depression of freezing point, osmotic pressure, determination of molecular masses using colligative properties, abnormal molecular mass, Van't Hoff factor.

Unit III   **:**   **Electrochemistry**   **12 Periods**

Redox reactions, EMF of a cell, standard electrode potential, Nernst equation and its application to chemical cells, Relation between Gibbs energy change and EMF of a cell, conductance in electrolytic solutions, specific and molar conductivity, variations of conductivity with concentration, Kohlrausch's Law, electrolysis and law of electrolysis (elementary idea), dry cell-electrolytic cells and Galvanic cells, lead accumulator.

Unit IV   **:**   **Chemical Kinetics**   **10 Periods**

Rate of a reaction (Average and instantaneous), factors affecting rate of reaction: concentration, temperature, catalyst; order and molecularity of a reaction, rate law and specific rate constant, integrated rate equations and half-life (only for zero and first order reactions), concept of collision theory (elementary idea, no mathematical treatment). Activation energy, Arrhenious equation.

Unit V   **:**   **Surface Chemistry**   **08 Periods**

Adsorption - physisorption and chemisorption, factors affecting adsorption of gases on solids, catalysis, homogenous and heterogenous activity and selectivity; enzyme catalysis colloidal state distinction between true solutions, colloids and suspension; lyophilic, lyophobic multi-molecular and macromolecular colloids; properties of colloids; Tyndall effect, Brownian movement, electrophoresis, coagulation, emulsion - types of emulsions.

Unit VI   **:**   **General Principles and Processes of Isolation of Elements**   **08 Periods**

Principles and methods of extraction - concentration, oxidation, reduction - electrolytic method and refining; occurrence and principles of extraction of aluminium, copper, zinc and iron.

Unit VII **:**   **Some p-Block Elements**   **12 Periods**

Group-15 Elements : General introduction, electronic configuration, occurrence, oxidation states, trends in physical and chemical properties; Nitrogen preparation properties and uses; compounds of Nitrogen: preparation and properties of Ammonia and Nitric Acid, Oxides of Nitrogen (Structure only); Phosphorus - allotropic forms, compounds of Phosphorus: Preparation and properties of Phosphine, Halides and Oxoacids (elementary idea only).

Group-16 Elements : General introduction, electronic configuration, oxidation states, occurrence, trends in physical and chemical properties, dioxygen: Preparation, Properties and uses, classification of Oxides, Ozone,. Sulphur -allotropic forms; compounds of Sulphur: Preparation Properties and uses of Sulphur-dioxide, Sulphuric Acid: industrial process of manufacture, properties and uses; Oxoacids of Sulphur (Structures only).

Group-17 Elements : General introduction, electronic configuration, oxidation states, occurrence, trends in physical and chemical properties; compounds of halogens, Preparation, properties and uses of Chlorine and Hydrochloric acid, interhalogen compounds, Oxoacids of halogens (structures only).

Group-18 Elements : General introduction, electronic configuration, occurrence, trends in physical and chemical properties, uses.

| Unit VIII : | **"d" and "f" Block Elements** | **12 Periods** |

General introduction, electronic configuration, occurrence and characteristics of transition metals, general trends in properties of the first row transition metals - metallic character, ionization enthalpy, oxidation states, ionic radii, colour, catalytic property, magnetic properties, interstitial compounds, alloy formation, preparation and properties of $K_2Cr_2O_7$ and $KMnO_4$.

Lanthanoids— Electronic configuration, oxidation states, chemical reactivity and lanthanoid contraction and its consequences.

Actinoids—Electronic configuration, oxidation states and comparison with lanthanoids.

| Unit IX : | **Coordination Compounds** | **12 Periods** |

Coordination compounds—Introduction, ligands, coordination number, colour, magnetic properties and shapes, IUPAC nomenclature of mononuclear coordination compounds. Bonding, Werner's theory, VBT, and CFT; structure and stereoisomerism, importance of coordination compounds (in qualitative inclusion, extraction of metals and biological system).

| Unit X : | **Haloalkanes and Haloarenes.** | **10 Periods** |

Haloalkanes : Nomenclature, nature of C-X bond, physical and chemical properties, optical rotation, mechanism of substitution reactions.

Haloarenes : Nature of C-X bond, substitution reactions (Directive influence of halogen in monosubstituted compounds only).

Uses and environmental effects of - dichloromethane, trichloromethane, tetrachloromethane, iodoform, freons, DDT.

| Unit XI : | **Alcohols, Phenols and Ethers** | **10 Periods** |

Alcohols : Nomenclature, methods of preparation, physical and chemical properties (of primary alcohols only), identification of primary, secondary and tertiary alcohols, mechanism of dehydration, uses with special reference to methanol and ethanol.

Phenols : Nomenclature, methods of preparation, physical and chemical properties, acidic nature of phenol, electrophillic substitution reactions, uses of phenols.

Ethers : Nomenclature, methods of preparation, physical and chemical properties, uses.

| Unit XII : | **Aldehydes, Ketones and Carboxylic Acids** | **10 Periods** |

Aldehydes and Ketones : Nomenclature, nature of carbonyl group, methods of preparation, physical and chemical properties, mechanism of nucleophilic addition, reactivity of alpha hydrogen in aldehydes, uses.

Carboxylic Acids : Nomenclature, acidic nature, methods of preparation, physical and chemical properties; uses.

| Unit XIII : | **Amines** | **10 Periods** |

Amines : Nomenclature, classification, structure, methods of preparation, physical and chemical properties, uses, identification of primary, secondary and tertiary amines.

Diazonium salts : Preparation, chemical reactions and importance in synthetic organic chemistry.

| Unit XIV : | **Biomolecules** | **12 Periods** |

Carbohydrates : Classification (aldoses and ketoses), monosaccharides (glucose and fructose), D-L configuration oligosaccharides (sucrose, lactose, maltose), polysaccharides (starch, cellulose, glycogen); Importance of carbohydrates.

Proteins : Elementary idea of - amino acids, peptide bond, polypeptides, proteins, structure of proteins - primary, secondary, tertiary structure and quaternary structures (qualitative idea only), denaturation of proteins; enzymes. Hormones - Elementary idea excluding structure.

Vitamins : Classification and functions.

Nucleic Acids : DNA and RNA.

| Unit XV : | **Polymers** | **08 Periods** |

Classification - natural and synthetic, methods of polymerization (addition and condensation), copolymerization, some important polymers: natural and synthetic like polythene, nylon polyesters, bakelite, rubber. Biodegradable and non-biodegradable polymers.

| Unit XVI : | **Chemistry in Everyday life** | **06 Periods** |

Chemicals in medicines - analgesics, tranquilizers antiseptics, disinfectants, antimicrobials, antifertility drugs, antibiotics, antacids, antihistamines.

Chemicals in food - preservatives, artificial sweetening agents, elementary idea of antioxidants.

Cleansing agents- soaps and detergents, cleansing action.

CHEMISTRY (Code No. 043)

QUESTION PAPER DESIGN

CLASS-XII

Time : 3 Hours   **Max. Marks : 70**

S. No.	Domains	Total Marks	%
1.	**Remembering and Understanding :** Exhibit memory of previously learned material by recalling facts, terms, basic concepts and answers. Demonstrate understanding of facts and ideas by organizing, comparing, translating, interpreting, giving descriptions and stating main ideas.	28	40
2.	**Applying :** Solve problems to new situations by applying acquired knowledge, facts, techniques and rules in a different way.	21	30
3.	**Analysing, Evaluating and Creating :** Examine and break information into parts by identifying motives or causes. Make inferences and find evidence to support generalizations. Present and defend opinions by making judgments about information, validity of ideas or quality of work based on a set of criteria. Compile information together in a different way by combining elements in a new pattern or proposing alternative solutions.	21	30

1. *No chapter wise weightage. Care to be taken to cover all the chapters.*
2. *Suitable internal variations may be made for generating various templates.*

Choice (s) :

There will be no overall choice in the question paper.

However, 33% internal choices will be given in all the sections.

YEARLY PLANNER

PLAN YOUR YEAR BETTER BY AIMING HIGH EVERY MONTH

JANUARY

FEBRUARY

MARCH

APRIL

MAY

JUNE

JULY

AUGUST

SEPTEMBER

OCTOBER

NOVEMBER

DECEMBER

Definitions | Set 1 |

Q. 1. What is a unit cell?

Ans. The smallest part of a crystal lattice which when repeated along different directions over and over again in three-dimensions, generates the entire lattice.

Q. 2. What is a crystal lattice?*

Ans. Crystal lattice or space lattice is a regular, three-dimensional arrangement of constituent particles of a crystal in space.

Q. 3. Give any two examples of amorphous solids.

Ans. Two amorphous solids are:

(i) glass, (ii) rubber.

Q. 4. Although ice is a molecular solid but it is not soft. Explain.

Ans. Ice is a molecular solid but the forces of attraction between the ice molecules are hydrogen bonding. These are strong intermolecular forces hence ice is generally hard in physical nature.

Q. 5. What is Curie temperature?

Ans. When a ferromagnetic substance becomes paramagnetic on heating above certain temperature, that temperature is called Curie temperature. Example Fe_3O_4 has 850 K as Curie temperature.

Q. 6. Define the following terms:*

(i) Primitive unit cells, (ii) Schottky defect, (iii) Ferromagnetism.

Ans. (i) **Primitive unit cells :** In this type of cells, the constituent particles, i.e., ions, atoms or molecules are present at the corners of the unit cell only.

(ii) **Schottky defect :** In this type of defects equal number of cations and anions are missing from the lattice sites. Due to this defect density of solid decreases.

(iii) **Ferromagnetism :** The property by virtue of which substances retain magnetism or become permanent magnets even if the magnetic field is removed is called ferromagnetism. Example : Ni, Co.

Q. 7. What is meant by the term 'coordination number'?

Ans. The number of nearest neighbours of any constituent particle present in the crystal lattice is called its coordination number.

Q. 1. Define strength of a solution.

Ans. Strength of a solution is mass in grams of solute dissolved per litre (dm^3) volume of the solution.

Q. 2. Define mole fraction of a substance in a solution.*

Ans. Mole fraction is the ratio of the number of moles of the solute to the total number of moles of the solute and solvent *i.e.*, of solution.

Q. 3. What is an ideal solution?

Ans. A solution which obeys Raoult's law exactly over a wide range of composition and temperature. For an ideal solution $DH_{mix} = 0$ and $DV_{mix} = 0$.

Q. 4. Define colligative properties.*

Ans. All the properties of a solution which depend on the number of solute particles (molecules or ions) in a known volume of solution irrespective of the nature of the solute are called colligative properties.

* are board exam questions from previous years

Q. 5. What is an antifreeze?

Ans. Antifreeze is a substance which lowers the freezing point of a solvent when added to it. It thus makes freezing difficult like ethylene glycol on being added in water decreases the freezing point of the mixture in the car radiators.

Q. 6. Define boiling point of a liquid.

Ans. The temperature at which the vapour pressure of a liquid becomes equal to the external atmospheric pressure is called the boiling point of that liquid.

Q. 7. Define osmotic pressure.*

Ans. The extra pressure applied on the solution side to just stop the flow of solvent via semipermeable membrane to the solution side is called osmotic pressure of the solution.

Q. 8. What is van't Hoff factor? Define it in terms of

    (i)   value of a colligative property,   (ii)   molar mass of solute.

Ans. The extent of association or dissociation of a solute is expressed with the help of van't Hoff factor (i), defined as:

    (i)

$$i = \frac{\text{Observed value of colligative property}}{\text{Expected value of colligative property}}$$

    (ii)   Value of colligative property depends upon the number of moles or molality of the solution and which in turn is inversely proportional to the molar mass of solute.

$$\text{Moles} = \frac{\text{Mass (g)}}{\text{Molar mass (g)}}$$

    Hence,

$$i = \frac{\text{Normal molar mass of solute}}{\text{Abnormal molar mass calculate from colligative property of its solution}}$$

Q. 9. Define the following terms:

    (i)   Mole fraction   (iii) Molarity

    (ii)   Molality   (iv) Mass percentage

Ans. (i)   **Mole fraction :** It is the ratio of the number of moles of a component (solute or solvent present) to the total number of moles of all components in the solution. Suppose a solution contains n_1 moles of A and n_2 moles of B.

        Then

        Mole fraction of A, $x_1 = \dfrac{n_1}{n_1 + n_2}$

        Mole fraction of A, $x_2 = \dfrac{n_2}{n_1 + n_2}$

        It should be noted that $x_1 + x_2 = 1$.

    (ii) **Molality:** It is defined as the number of g-moles of solute dissolved in 1000 g (1 kg) of the solvent. It is denoted by m. Its units are mole kg^{-1}.

    (iii) **Molarity:** It is defined as the number of gram-moles of solute dissolved per litre of the solution. It is denoted by M. Its units are mole L^{-1}.

$$M = \frac{\text{Weight in grams}}{\text{Molecular mass}} \times \frac{1000}{\text{Volume of solution (l)}}$$

    (iv) **Mass percentage:** In case of a solid dissolved in a liquid, the percentage by weight means the amount of solute in grams present in 100 g of the solution.

        $\therefore$ $\text{Weight percentage} = \dfrac{\text{Weight of solute}}{\text{Weight of solution}} \times 100$

        10% solution of sugar by weight means that 10 g of sugar is present in 100 g of the solution i.e., 10 g of sugar has been dissolved in 90 g of water. Percent by weight has the same meaning in case of a solution of a liquid in liquid.

Chapter 3. Electrochemistry

Q. 1. What is an electrochemical cell?

Ans. A device used to convert the chemical energy of a redox reaction into electrical energy is called an electrochemical cell, galvanic cell or voltaic cell.

Q. 2. Define discharge potential.

Ans. The minimum potential or charge required to bring about the discharge of an ion.

Q. 3. Define Ohm's law.*

Ans. Ohm's law states that, current (I) flowing through a conductor is directly proportional to the potential difference applied across the two ends of the conductor i.e., $V \propto I$

$$\therefore \quad \boxed{V = IR.}$$

Q. 4. Define cell constant.

Ans. Cell constant is the ratio of length over area of any particular cell. $G = l/a$.

Q. 5. Define over-voltage.

Ans. The additional voltage required to cause electrolysis of any particular ion is called over-voltage.

Chapter 4. Chemical Kinetics

Q. 1. Define the term order of a reaction for chemical reactions.*

Ans. The sum of the powers of concentration of the reactants as expressed in the rate law is termed as order of a reaction.

Chapter 5. Surface Chemistry

Q. 1. What are shape selective catalysts?

Ans. Shape selective catalyst: Zeolites are called shape selective catalyst as they have honeycomb structure of particular pore size and the catalytic action depends on the size of reactants and products.

Example : ZSM-5, alcohols are converted to gasoline using it.

Q. 2. Define reversible sol.*

Ans. A sol in which dispersion medium can be easily removed from dispersed phase and can be again added or mixed with it to regain back the sol, is known as reversible sol. For example the colloidal sol of starch in water.

Q. 3. Define peptization.*

Ans. The process of converting a precipitate into colloidal solution by shaking it with dispersion medium in the presence of small amount of suitable electrolyte, is called peptization.

Q. 4. Define 'gold number'.

Ans. Gold number is the minimum amount in milligrams of lyophilic sol that is needed to be added in 10 ml of standard red gold sol to prevent coagulation of it on adding 1 ml of 10% NaCl solution in it.

Chapter 6. General Principles and Processes of Isolation of Elements

Q. 1. Name the common ore of aluminium.

Ans. Bauxite $(Al_2O_3.xH_2O)$.

Q. 2. Name the methods used for refining of.

    (i) Nickel,

    (ii) Zirconium.

Ans. (i) Nickel : Mond's process.

    (ii) Zirconium : Van Arkel method.

Chapter 8. *d-* and *f*-Block Elements

Q. 1. What is the general electronic configuration of transition elements? *

Ans. Electronic configuration of transition elements:

$$(n - 1)\, d^{1-10}\, ns^2$$

Chapter 11. Alcohols, Phenols and Ethers

Q. 1. What is rectified spirit?

Ans. Ethyl alcohol at 95% concentration is called rectified spirit.

Chapter 12. Aldehydes, Ketones and Carboxylic Acids

Q. 1. What is transesterification?

Ans. When an ester is treated with an alcohol and the alkoxy part of the ester is replaced, then it is called transesterification. Example

$$CH_3 - \underset{\underset{O}{\|}}{C} - O - CH_3 - CH_3CH_2 - OH \longrightarrow CH_3 - \overset{\overset{O}{\|}}{C} - OCH_2CH_3 + CH_3OH$$

(old ester)　　　　　　　(excess alcohol)　　　　　　　(New ester)

Chapter 14. Biomolecules

Q. 1. Define mutarotation.

Ans. The spontaneous change in the degree of specific rotation of a solution of an optically active compound is called mutarotation. This happens in case of α-glucose solution.

Chapter 15. Polymers

Q. 1. Define the term polymerization. *

Ans. Polymerization is the process of forming high molecular mass (10^3–10^7 u) macromolecules called polymers which consist of repeating structural units derived from monomers. In a polymer, various monomer units are joined by strong covalent bonds.

Chapter 16. Chemistry in Everyday Life

Q. 1. Define tranquilizers.

Ans. Tranquilizers are drugs which work on the central nervous system (CNS) and thus helps in reducing anxiety and hypertension.

Q. 2. Define the term chemotherapy.

Ans. The use of chemicals for therapeutic effect is called chemotherapy. For example : the use of chemicals in the diagnosis, prevention and treatment of diseases.

Chapter 1. Solid State

1. Copper has the face centered cubic structure. The coordination number of each ion is:
   - (a) 4
   - (b) 12
   - (c) 14
   - (d) 8

2. In a crystal, the atoms are located at the position of:
   - (a) Maximum potential energy
   - (b) Minimum potential energy
   - (c) Zero potential energy
   - (d) Infinite potential energy

3. Designation of the patten as AB, AB, AB .... etc., of successive vertical layers of identical atoms gives the arrangement called as:
   - (a) Hexagonal close packing (hcp)
   - (b) Cubic close packing (ccp)
   - (c) Face centered cubic (fcc)
   - (d) Body centered cubic (bcc)

4. Cubic close packing arrangement is also known as:
   - (a) Hexagonal close packing
   - (b) Face centered cubic
   - (c) Body centered cubic
   - (d) None of these

5. In a rock salt structure each Cl^- ion is surrounded by:
   - (a) $4\,Na^+$ ion
   - (b) $6\,Na^+$ ions
   - (c) $8\,Na^+$ ions
   - (d) $12\,Na^+$ ions

6. CsCl has which type of lattice?
   - (a) sc
   - (b) fcc
   - (c) cubic structure
   - (d) hcp

7. Which of the following is an example of covalent crystal solid?
   - (a) Si
   - (b) Al
   - (c) Ar
   - (d) NaF

8. The soil NaCl is a bad conductor of electricity since:
   - (a) In solid NaCl there are no ions
   - (b) Solid NaCl is covalent
   - (c) In solid NaCl there is no movement of ions
   - (d) In solid NaCl these are no electrons

9. In a solid lattice the cation has left a lattice site and is located at an interstitial position, the lattice defect is:
   - (a) Interstitial defect
   - (b) Valency defect
   - (c) Frenkel defect
   - (d) Schottky defect

10. Piezoelectric crystals are used in:
    - (a) Radio
    - (b) T.V.
    - (c) Record player
    - (d) Refrigerator

11. Schottky defect in crystal is observed when:
    - (a) An ion leaves in normal site and occupies the interstitial site
    - (b) Equal number of cations and anions are missing from the lattice
    - (c) Unequal number of cations and anions are missing from the lattice
    - (d) Density of the crystal is increased

12. How many kinds of space lattice are possible in a cubic crystal?
    - (a) 23
    - (b) 7
    - (c) 30
    - (d) 14

13. A solid has a structure in which 'W' atoms are locates at the corners of a cubic lattice, 'O' atoms at the centre of edges and 'Na' atoms at the centre of the cube. The formula for the compound is:
    - (a) $NaWO_2$
    - (b) $NaWO_3$
    - (c) Na_2WO_3
    - (d) $NaWO_4$

14. In a compound, atmos of element Y forms ccp lattice and those of element X occupy $\frac{1}{2}$ rd of tetrahedral voids, the formula of the compound will be:

    (a) X_4Y_3 (b) X_2X_3 (c) X_2Y (d) X_3X_4

15. Which of the following is an example of paramagnetic solid?

    (a) $NaCl$ (b) KF (c) TiO_2 (d) CuO

16. A substance AxBy crystallizes in a face centered cubic (fcc) lattice in which atoms 'A' occupy each corner of the cube, atoms 'B' occupy the centres of each of the cube. Identify the correct composition of the substance AxBy:

    (a) AB_3 (c) A_3B

    (b) A_4B_3 (d) Composition cannot be specified

ANSWERS

1. (a)	3. (a)	5. (b)	7. (a)	9. (c)	11. (b)	13. (b)	15. (d)
2. (b)	4. (b)	6. (c)	8. (c)	10. (c)	12. (b)	14. (a)	16. (a)

Chapter 2. Solutions

1. The molal freezing point constant of water is $1 \cdot 86$ K kg mol^{-1}. Therefore, the freezing point of $0 \cdot 1$M NaCl solution in water is expected to be:

    (a) $-1 \cdot 86°C$ (b) $-0 \cdot 372°C$ (c) $-0 \cdot 186°C$ (d) $+0 \cdot 372°C$

2. Of the following terms used for denoting concentration of a solution, the one which does not gets affected by temperature is:

    (a) Molarity   (b) Molality   (c) Normality   (d) Formality

3. Out of the following solutions, the one having the highest boiling point will be:

    (a) $0 \cdot 1$ M $NaCl$ (c) $0 \cdot 1$ M KNO_3

    (b) $0 \cdot 1$ M $BaCl_2$ (d) $0 \cdot 1$ M $K_4\,[Fe(CN)_6]$

4. For a dissociated solute in solution the value of van't Hoff factor is:

    (a) Zero   (b) One   (c) Greater than one   (d) Less than one

5. An example of intensive property is:

    (a) Number of moles   (b) Mass   (c) Volume   (d) Density

6. The solubility of a gas varies directly with pressure of the gas, is based upon:

    (a) Raoult's law   (c) Nernst's distribution law

    (b) Henry's law   (d) None of these

7. The relative lowering of vapour pressure of a solvent by the addition of a solute is:

    (a) Proportional to the molarity of the solution   (c) Equal to the mole fraction of the solute

    (b) Proportional to the molality of the solution   (d) Equal to the mole fraction of the solvent

8. Which solution is isotonic to the blood?

    (a) $0 \cdot 75\%$ by weight of NaCl approximately   (c) $0 \cdot 90\%$ by weight of NaCl approximately

    (b) $0 \cdot 99\%$ by weight of NaCl approximately   (d) None of these

9. The osmotic pressure of equimolar solution of NaCl, $BaCl_2$ and glucose will be in the order of:

    (a) $NaCl > BaCl_2 > Glucose$ (c) $Glucose > NaCl > BaCl_2$

    (b) $BaCl_2 > NaCl > Glucose$ (d) $NaCl > Glucose > BaCl_2$

10. Which of the following is not a colligative property?

    (a) Depression in freezing point   (c) Osmotic pressure

    (b) Elevation in boiling point   (d) Modification of refractive index

11. The molecular weight of sodium chloride determined by measuring the osmotic pressure of its aqueous solution is:

(a) Double the theoretical value

(c) Half the theoretical value

(b) Same as the theoretical value

(d) Three times the theoretical value

12. **Determination of correct molecular mass from Raoult's law is applicable to:**
    (a) An electrolyte in solution
    (c) A non-electrolyte in conc. solution
    (b) A non-electrolyte in dilute solution
    (d) An electrolyte in a liquid solvent

13. **The number of moles of solute present in 1000 gm of the solvent is known as:**
    (a) Molarity
    (b) Molality
    (c) Normality
    (d) Mole fraction

14. **Which of the following 0·1 M aqueous solution will have the lowest freezing point?**
    (a) Potassium sulphate
    (c) Urea
    (b) Sodium chloride
    (d) Glucose

15. **Colligative properties of the solution depends on:**
    (a) Nature of solute
    (c) Number of particles present in the solution
    (b) Nature of solvent
    (d) Number of moles of solvent only

16. **Solution that obey's Raoult's law:**
    (a) Normal
    (b) Molar
    (c) Ideal
    (d) Saturated

17. **A liquid pair of benzene-toluene shows:**
    (a) Positive deviation from Raoult's law
    (c) Practically no deviation from Raoult's law
    (b) Negative deviation from Raoult's law
    (d) Irregular deviation from Raoult's law

18. **When 0·1 mole urea is dissolved in 9·9 mole water, then the vapour pressure is:**
    (a) Increased by 1%
    (c) Decreased by 1%
    (b) Increased by 10%
    (d) Decreased by 10%

19. **12 g of urea is dissolved in 1 litre of water and 68·4 g of sucrose is dissolved in 1 litre of water. The lowering of vapour pressure in the first case is:**
    (a) Equal to second
    (c) Less than second
    (b) Greater than second
    (d) Double that of second

20. **Molecular weight of non-volatile solute can be determined by:**
    (a) Victor-Mayer's method
    (c) Gay Lussac's law
    (b) Graham's law of diffusion
    (d) Raoult's law

ANSWERS

1. (c)	3. (d)	5. (d)	7. (c)	9. (b)	11. (a)	13. (b)	15. (d)	17. (c)	19. (a)
2. (b)	4. (c)	6. (d)	8. (c)	10. (d)	12. (b)	14. (a)	16. (c)	18. (c)	20. (d)

Chapter 3. Electrochemistry

1. **Electrochemical equivalent is the amount of substance which gets deposited from its solution on passing electrical charge equal to:**
    (a) 96,500 coulomb
    (b) 1 coulomb
    (c) 60 coulomb
    (d) 965 coulomb

2. **A current liberates 0·50 g of hydrogen in 2 hours. The weight of copper (at. wt. = 63·5) deposited at the same time by the same current through copper sulphate solution is:**
    (a) 63·5 g
    (b) 31·8 g
    (c) 15·9 g
    (d) 15·5 g

3. **The quantity of electricity required to deposit 1·15 g of sodium from molten NaCl (Na = 23, Cl = 35·5) is:**
    (a) 1 F
    (b) 0·5 F
    (c) 0·05 F
    (d) 1·5 F

4. **When zinc granule is dipped into copper sulphate solution, copper is precipitated because:**
    (a) Both, copper and zinc have a positive reduction potential
    (b) Reduction potential of copper is higher than that of zinc
    (c) Reduction potential of zinc is higher than that of copper
    (d) Both, zinc and copper have a negative reduction potential

5. **The unit of equivalent conductance is:**
   (a) $ohm^{-1} cm^2 equiv^{-1}$
   (b) $ohm^{-1} cm^2 gm^{-1}$
   (c) $ohm\ cm^2 equiv^{-1}$
   (d) $ohm^{-1} mole^{-1}$

6. **The number of Faradays required to reduce one mol of Cu^{+2} to metallic copper is:**
   (a) One
   (b) Two
   (c) Three
   (d) Four

7. **Conductivity of a solution is directly proportional to:**
   (a) Dilution
   (b) Number of ions
   (c) Current density
   (d) Volume of the solution

8. **Electrolysis involves oxidation and reduction respectively at:**
   (a) Anode and cathode
   (b) Cathode and anode
   (c) At both the electrode
   (d) None of these

9. **All galvanic cell do not contain:**
   (a) A cathode
   (b) An anode
   (c) Ions
   (d) A porous plate

10. **The reaction is spontaneous if the cell potential is:**
    (a) Positive
    (b) Negative
    (c) Zero
    (d) Infinite

11. **Which of the following cells can convert chemical energy of H_2 and O_2 directly into electrical energy?**
    (a) Mercury cell
    (b) Daniel cell
    (c) Fuel cell
    (d) Lead storage cell

12. **When lead storage battery discharges?**
    (a) SO_2 is evolved
    (b) $PbSO_4$ is consumed
    (c) Lead is formed
    (d) Sulphuric acid is consumed

13. **The electrode Pt, Hg (g) /HCl is reversible with respect to:**
    (a) Cl^- ions
    (b) HCl
    (c) H^+ ions
    (d) Both H^+ and Cl^- ions

14. **Saturated solution of KNO_3 is used to make salt bridge because:**
    (a) Velocity of K^+ is greater than that of NO_3^-
    (b) Velocity of NO_3^- is greater than that of K^+
    (c) Velocity of both K^+ and NO_3^- are nearly the same
    (d) KNO_3 is highly soluble in water

15. **Zn/Zn^{2+} ($a = 0.1M$) $||Fe^{2+}$ ($a = 0.1M$)/Fe. The e.m.f. of the above cell is 0.290V. Equilibrium constant for the cell reaction is:**
    (a) $10^{0.32/\ 0.0991}$
    (b) $10^{0.32/0.0295}$
    (c) $10^{0.26/0.0295}$
    (d) $e^{0.32/0.295}$

16. **The standard electrode potentials of four elements A, B, C and D are − 3.05, 1.66, − 0.40 and 0.80 volts respectively. The highest chemical activity will be shown by:**
    (a) A
    (b) B
    (c) C
    (d) D

17. **In a lead storage battery***
    (a) PbO_2 is reduced to $PbSO_4$ at the cathode.
    (b) Pb is oxidised to $PbSO_4$ at the anode.
    (c) Both electrodes are immersed in the same aqueous solution of H_2SO_4.
    (d) All the above are true.

18. **An electrochemical cell behaves like an electrolytic cell when:***
    (a) $E_{cell} = E_{external}$
    (b) $E_{cell} = 0$
    (c) $E_{external} > E_{cell}$
    (d) $E_{external} < E_{cell}$

19. **Which of the following is correct for spontaneity of a cell?***
    (a) $\Delta G = -ve\ E° = +ve$
    (b) $\Delta G = +ve\ E° = 0$
    (c) $\Delta G = -ve\ E° = 0$
    (d) $\Delta G = ve\ E° = -ve$

20. **Kohlrausch given the following realation for strong electrolytes:***
    $$\wedge = \wedge_0 - \Lambda \sqrt{C}$$

---

* are board exam questions from previous years

Which of the following equality holds?

(a) $\Lambda = \Lambda_0$ as $C \to \sqrt{\Lambda}$

(b) $\Lambda = \Lambda_0$ as $C \to \infty$

(c) $\Lambda = \Lambda_0$ as $C \to 0$

(d) $\Lambda = \Lambda_0$ as $C \to 1$

ANSWERS

1. (a)	3. (c)	5. (a)	7. (d)	9. (d)	11. (c)	13. (c)	15. (b)	17. (d)	19. (a)
2. (c)	4. (b)	6. (b)	8. (a)	10. (a)	12. (d)	14. (b)	16. (a)	18. (c)	20. (c)

Chapter 4. Chemical Kinetics

1. For a first order reaction the rate constant for decomposition of N_2O_5 is 6×10^{-4} sec^{-1}. The half-life period for the decomposition in seconds is:
   (a) 11·55
   (b) 115·5
   (c) 1155
   (d) 1·155

2. In a plot of $\log k$ vs. $1/T$, the slope is:
   (a) $- E_a/2\cdot303$
   (b) $E_a/2\cdot303 \, R$
   (c) $E_a/2\cdot303$
   (d) $- E_a/2\cdot303 \, R$

3. 75% of a first order reaction was completed in 32 minutes. When was 50% of the reaction completed?
   (a) 24 minutes
   (b) 16 minutes
   (c) 8 minutes
   (d) 4 minutes

4. The reaction between X and Y is first order with respect to X and second order with respect to Y. If the concentration of X is halved and the concentration of Y is doubled, the rate of the reaction will be:
   (a) Same as the initial value
   (b) Three times the initial value
   (c) Double the initial value
   (d) Half the initial value

5. The rate of a chemical reaction:
   (a) Increases as the reaction proceeds
   (b) Decrease as the reaction proceeds
   (c) May increase or decrease during the reaction
   (d) Remains constant as the reaction proceeds

6. The correct order indicating against the rate of reaction $A + B \xrightarrow{k}$ is:
   (a) $\dfrac{d[c]}{dt} = k\,[A]$
   (b) $-\dfrac{d[c]}{dt} = k\,[B]$
   (c) $\dfrac{-d[c]}{dt} = k\,[A]\,[B]$
   (d) $-\dfrac{d[A]}{dt} = k\,[A]$

7. The one which is unimolecular reaction is:
   (a) $2HI \longrightarrow H_2 + I_2$
   (b) $N_2O_5 \longrightarrow N_2O_4 + 1/2\,O_2$
   (c) $H_2 + Cl_2 \longrightarrow 2HCl$
   (d) $PCl_3 + Cl_2 \longrightarrow PCl_5$

8. If the concentration is expressed in moles per litre the unit of the rate constant for a first order reaction is:
   (a) mole litre^{-1} sec^{-1}
   (b) mole litre^{-1}
   (c) sec^{-1}
   (d) mole^{-1}

9. The rate of a chemical reaction is double for every 10°C rise in temperature because of:
   (a) Increase in the activation energy
   (b) Decrease in the activation energy
   (c) Increase in the number of molecular collisions
   (d) Increase in the number of activated molecules

10. The minimum energy required by reacting molecules to permit a reaction is:
    (a) Internal energy
    (b) Threshold energy
    (c) Activation energy
    (d) Free energy

11. A quantitative relationship between the temperature and rate constant of a reaction is given by:
    (a) Nernst equation
    (b) Arrhenius equation
    (c) van't Hoff equation
    (d) Henderson equation

12. For the first order reaction with rate constant k, which expression gives the half-life period?
    (a) $\dfrac{ln^2}{k}$
    (b) $\dfrac{1}{ka}$
    (c) $\dfrac{0.693}{k}$
    (d) $\dfrac{3}{2ka^2}$

13. The rate constant, the activation energy and the Arrhenius parameter of a chemical reaction at $25°C$ are $3.0 \times 10^{-4} s^{-1}$, 104.4 kJ mol^{-1} and $6.0 \times 10^{14} s^{-1}$ respectively. The value of the rate constant as $T \to \infty$ is:
    (a) $2.0 \times 10^{18} s^{-1}$
    (b) $6.0 \times 10^{14} s^{-1}$
    (c) Infinity
    (d) $3.6 \times 10^{30} s^{-1}$

14. The rate constant for the reaction $2N_2O_5 \to 4NO_2 + O_2$, is $3.0 \to 10^{-5} s-1$. If the rate is 2.40×10^{-5} mol L^{-1} s^{-1}, then the concentration of N_2O_5 (in mol L^{-1}) is:
    (a) 1.4
    (b) 1.2
    (c) 0.04
    (d) 0.8

15. For the reaction $2SO_2 + O_2 \rightleftharpoons 2SO_3$, the unit of equilibrium constant is:
    (a) L mol^{-1}
    (b) J mol^{-1}
    (c) mol L^{-1}
    (d) $[L\ mol^{-1}]^2$

16. The unit of rate constant depends upon the:*
    (a) molecularity of the reaction
    (b) activation energy of the reaction
    (c) order of the reaction
    (d) temperature of the reaction

17. In a chemical reaction $X \to Y$, it is found that the rate of reaction doubles when the concentration of X is increased four times. The order of the reaction with respect to X is:*
    (a) 1
    (b) 0
    (c) 2
    (d) 1/2

18. For a zero order reaction, the slope in the plot of [R] Vs. time is*
    (a) $-k/2.303$
    (b) $-k$
    (c) $+k/2.303$
    (d) $+k$
    (where [R] is the final concentration of reactant)

19. The slope in the plot of ln [R] Vs. time gives:*
    (a) $+k$
    (b) $+k/2.303$
    (c) $-k$
    (d) $-k/2.303$
    (where [R] is the final concentration of reactant.)

20. The half-life period for a zedro order reaction is equal to:*
    (a) $0.693/k$
    (b) $2k/[R_0]$
    (c) $2.303/k$
    (d) $[R]_0/2k$

ANSWERS

1. (c)	3. (b)	5. (b)	7. (b)	9. (d)	11. (b)	13. (c)	15. (a)	17. (d)	19. (c)
2. (d)	4. (c)	6. (c)	8. (c)	10. (c)	12. (c)	14. (d)	16. (c)	18. (b)	20. (d)

Chapter 5. Surface Chemistry

1. **Blue colour of water in sea is due to:**
    (a) Refraction of blue light by impurities in sea water
    (b) Scattering of light by water
    (c) Refraction of blue sky by water
    (d) None of these

2. **The coagulation power of an electrolyte for arsenious sulphide sol decreases in the order:**
    (a) $Na^+ > Al^{3+} > Ba^{2+}$
    (b) $PO_4^{3-} > SO_4^{2-} > Cl^-$
    (c) $Cl^- > SO_4^{2-} > PO_4^{3-}$
    (d) $Al^{3+} > Ba^{2+} > Na^+$

3. **Volume of a colloidal particle V_C as compared to the volume of a solute particle in a true solution, V_S could be:**
    (a) $\dfrac{V_C}{V_S} \approx 1$
    (b) $\dfrac{V_C}{V_S} \approx 1$
    (c) $\dfrac{V_C}{V_S} \approx 10^{-3}$
    (d) $\dfrac{V_C}{V_S} \approx 10^{3}$

4. **Lyophilic sols are:**
    (a) Reversible sols
    (b) They are prepared from inorganic compound
    (c) Coagulated by adding electrolytes
    (d) Self-stabilizing

5. **A plot of log x/m versus log P for the adsorption of a gas on a solid gives a straight line with slope equal to:**
    (a) n
    (b) $1/n$
    (c) log K
    (d) $-\log K$

6. On adding 1 mL of solution of 10% NaCl to 10 mL of gold sol in the presence of 0·25 g of starch the coagulation is just prevented, the gold number of starch is:
   (a) 0·25　　　　(b) 0·025　　　　(c) 250　　　　(d) 25

7. Hair cream is an example of:
   (a) Gel　　　　(b) Sol　　　　(c) Foam　　　　(d) Emulsion

8. Which of the following impurities present in colloidal solution cannot be removed by electrodialysis?
   (a) Sodium chloride
   (b) Potassium sulphate
   (c) Urea
   (d) Calcium chloride

9. The ion that is more effective for coagulation of As_2S_3 sol in:
   (a) Ba^{2+}
   (b) Na^+
   (c) Al^{3+}
   (d) SO_4^{2-}

10. The most adsorbed gas on activated charcoal is:
    (a) N_2
    (b) H_2
    (c) CO_2
    (d) CH_4

11. The charge of $Fe(OH)_3$ sol is due to:
    (a) Adsorption of hydroxyl ion
    (b) Adsorption of hydroxyl ion
    (c) Absorption of ferric acid
    (d) Adsorption of ferric acid

12. Which one of the following does not involve coagulation?
    (a) Formation of delta region
    (b) Peptization
    (c) Treatment of drinking water by potash alum
    (d) Clotting of blood by the use of ferric chloride

13. The dispersed phase and dispersion medium in soap lather are respectively:
    (a) Gas and liquid
    (b) Liquid and gas
    (c) Solid and gas
    (d) Solid and liquid

14. Milk is an example of:
    (a) W/O type of emulsion
    (b) O/W type of emulsion
    (c) W/W type of emulsion
    (d) O/O type of emulsion

15. The disease kala azar is cured by:
    (a) Colloidal antimony
    (b) Milk of magnesia
    (c) Argyrols
    (d) Colloidal gold

16. According to Freundlich adsorption isotherm, which of the following is correct?
    (a) $\dfrac{x}{m} \alpha P'$
    (b) $\dfrac{x}{m} \alpha P^{1/n}$
    (c) $\dfrac{x}{m} \alpha P^\circ$
    (d) All the above are correct for different ranges of pressure

17. Identify the positively charged sol.:
    (a) Haemoglobin (blood)
    (b) Clay
    (c) As_2S_3
    (d) Gold sols.

ANSWERS

1. (a)	**3.** (d)	**5.** (b)	**7.** (d)	**9.** (c)	**11.** (d)	**13.** (a)	**15.** (a)	**17.** (a)
2. (d)	**4.** (d)	**6.** (c)	**8.** (c)	**10.** (c)	**12.** (b)	**14.** (b)	**16.** (d)	

Chapter 6. General Principles and Processes of Isolation of Elements

1. The ore chromite is:
   (a) $FeCr_2O_4$
   (b) $CoCr_2O_3$
   (c) $CrFe_2O_4$
   (d) $FeCr_2O_3$

2. **When lime stone is heated, CO_2 is given off. The metallurgical operation is:**
   (a) Smelting (b) Reduction (c) Calcination (d) Roasting

3. **The process of zone refining is used in the purification of:**
   (a) Al (b) Ge (c) Cu (d) Ag

4. **Identify the alloy containing a non-metal as a constituent in it:**
   (a) Invar (b) Steel (c) Bell metal (d) Bronze

5. **Aluminium is extracted from alumina (Al_2O_3) by electrolysis of a molten mixture of:**
   (a) $Al_2O_3 + HF + NaAlF_4$
   (b) $Al_2O_3 + CaF_2 + NaHF_4$
   (c) $Al_2O_3 + Na_3AlF_6 + CaF_2$
   (d) $Al_2O_3 + KF + Na_3AlF_6$

6. **The ore magnetite is:**
   (a) Fe_3O_4
   (b) $ZnCO_3$
   (c) $CuCO_3.Cu(OH)_2$
   (d) FeS_2

7. **Which of the following is not a sulphide ore?**
   (a) Magnetite (b) Iron pyrites (c) Copper glance (d) Galena

8. **Duralumin is used in aircraft industry for its light weight and high strength. It is an alloy of:**
   (a) Al, Cu, Mg and Mn
   (b) Al, Zn, Fe and Sn
   (c) Al, Ti, Ce and Fe
   (d) Al, Fe, Zn and Sn

9. **Which of the following pair of metals is purified by Van-Arkel method?**
   (a) Ga and In (b) Zr and Ti (c) Ag and Au (d) Ni and Fe

10. **Which of the following element is present as the impurity to the maximum extent in the pig iron?**
    (a) Manganese (b) Carbon (c) Silicon (d) Phosphorus

11. **Which one of the following is an oxide ore?**
    (a) Malachite (b) Copper glance (c) Haematite (d) Zinc blende

12. **In the equation $4M + 8CN^- + 2H_2O + O_2 \longrightarrow 4\,[M(CN)_2]^- + 4OH^-$ the metal M is:**
    (a) Copper (b) Iron (c) Gold (d) Zinc

13. **For which ore of the metal, froth floatation process is used for concentration?**
    (a) Horn silver (b) Bauxite (c) Cinnabar (d) Haematite

14. **Which of the following metal is leached by cyanide process?**
    (a) Ag (b) Na (c) Al (d) Cu

15. **Which of the following ore is best concentrated by froth floatation process?**
    (a) Magnetite (b) Cassiterite (c) Galena (d) Malachite

16. **Which one contains both iron and copper?**
    (a) Cuprite (b) Chalcocite (c) Malachite (d) Copper pyrites

17. **In aluminothermic process, Al is used as:**
    (a) Reducing agent (b) Oxidising agent (c) Catalyst (d) Electrolyte

18. **The temperature of the slag zone in the metallurgy of iron using blast furnace is:**
    (a) 1500-1600° C (b) 400-700° C (c) 800-1000° C (d) 1200-1500° C

19. **Heating Cu_2O and Cu_2S will give:**
    (a) $Cu + SO_2$ (b) $Cu + SO_3$ (c) $CuO + CuS$ (d) Cu_2SO_3

20. **Copper matte contains:***
    (a) Cu_2S, Cu_2O and silica
    (b) Cu_2S, CuO and silica
    (c) Cu_2S, FeO and silica
    (d) Cu_2S, FeS and silica

ANSWERS

1. (a)	3. (d)	5. (c)	7. (a)	9. (b)	11. (c)	13. (c)	15. (c)	17. (a)	19. (a)
2. (c)	4. (b)	6. (a)	8. (a)	10. (b)	12. (c)	14. (a)	16. (d)	18. (c)	20. (d)

* are board exam questions from previous years

Chapter 7. *p*-Block Elements

1. The geometry of XeF_6 molecule and the hybridization of Xe atom in the molecule is:
   - (a) Distorted octahedral and sp^3d^3
   - (b) Square planar and sp^3d^2
   - (c) Pyramidal and sp^3
   - (d) Octahedral and sp^3d^3

2. Among the following halogens, the one which does not forms an oxyacid is:
   - (a) Fluorine
   - (b) Chlorine
   - (c) Bromine
   - (d) Iodine

3. The tendency of group 16 elements to form catenated compounds is greatest in case of:
   - (a) Oxygen
   - (b) Sulphur
   - (c) Selenium
   - (d) Tellurium

4. The minimum bond angle in hydrides of group 16 elements is in:
   - (a) H_2O
   - (b) H_2Te
   - (c) H_2Se
   - (d) H_2S

5. Which of the following has lowest reducing character?
   - (a) H_2O
   - (b) H_2S
   - (c) H_2Te
   - (d) H_2Se

6. Which of the following mainly exhibits (– 2) oxidation state?
   - (a) S
   - (b) O
   - (c) Se
   - (d) Te

7. Oxygen molecule is:
   - (a) Paramagnetic
   - (b) Diamagnetic
   - (c) Ferromagnetic
   - (d) Ferrimagnetic

8. The halogen with highest electron affinity:
   - (a) F
   - (b) Cl
   - (c) Br
   - (d) I

9. The halide ion easiest to oxidise is:
   - (a) F^-
   - (b) Cl^-
   - (c) Br^-
   - (d) I^-

10. The reaction, $3ClO^- (aq) \longrightarrow ClO_3^- (aq) + 2Cl^- (aq)$, is an example of:
    - (a) Oxidation reaction
    - (b) Reduction reaction
    - (c) Disproportionation reaction
    - (d) Decomposition reaction

11. The low bond energy is best explained by:
    - (a) The attainment of noble gas configuration
    - (b) The low electron affinity of F
    - (c) Repulsion by electron pairs on F
    - (d) The small size of F

12. The oxo-acid of halogen with maximum acidic character is:
    - (a) $HClO_4$
    - (b) $HClO_3$
    - (c) $HClO_2$
    - (d) HClO

13. Which of the following reaction will not occur spontaneously?
    - (a) $F_2 + 2Cl^- \longrightarrow 2F^- + Cl_2$
    - (b) $I_2 + 2Br^- \longrightarrow 2I^- + Br_2$
    - (c) $Br_2 + 2I^- \longrightarrow 2Br^- + I_2$
    - (d) $2I^- + Cl_2^- \longrightarrow 2Cl^- + I_2$

14. The high viscosity and high boiling point of HF is due to:
    - (a) Low dissociation energy of F_2 molecule
    - (b) Associated nature due to hydrogen bonding
    - (c) Ionic character of HF
    - (d) High electronegativity of fluorine

15. The most powerful oxidising agent is:
    - (a) Fluorine
    - (b) Chlorine
    - (c) Bromine
    - (d) Iodine

16. Shape of ClF_3 is:
    - (a) Trigonal planar
    - (b) Tetrahedral
    - (c) T-Shaped
    - (d) Distorted octahedral

17. Which of the following is not an interhalogen compound?
    - (a) ICl_4^-
    - (b) ClF_5
    - (c) IPO_4
    - (d) ClF_3

18. Which noble gas was discovered in chromosphere?
    - (a) He
    - (b) Ar
    - (c) Xe
    - (d) Rn

19. XeF_2 molecule is:
    (a) Trigonal planar
    (b) Square planar
    (c) Linear
    (d) Pyramidal

20. The noble gas used in the treatment of Cancer is:
    (a) Argon
    (b) Xenon
    (c) Radon
    (d) Helium

21. In XeF_2, Xenon involves the hybridisation:
    (a) sp
    (b) sp^2
    (c) sp^3d
    (d) sp^3

22. Which one of the following displaces bromine form an aqueous solution of bromine?
    (a) Cl_2
    (b) Cl^-
    (c) I_2
    (d) I_3^-

23. When SO_2 gas is passed through acidified $K_2Cr_2O_7$ solution, the colour of the solution changes to:
    (a) Red
    (b) Black
    (c) Orange
    (d) Green

24. Which of the following reagent does not give O_2 gas on reaction with Ozone?
    (a) $KMnO_4$
    (b) $SnCl_2/HCl$
    (c) $FeSO_4/H_2SO_4$
    (d) PbS

25. Aqua regia is a mixture of:
    (a) Conc. HNO_3 and conc. H_2SO_4
    (b) Conc. HCl and conc. H_2SO_4 in the ratio of 3: 1
    (c) Conc. HCl and conc. HNO_3 in the ratio of 3: 1
    (d) None of these

26. Tailing of mercury is due to the formation of:
    (a) Hg_2O
    (b) HgO
    (c) $Hg(OH)_2$
    (d) $HgCl_2$

27. Which one is called oleum?
    (a) Liq. NH_3
    (b) $H_2SO_4 + SO_3$
    (c) Conc. HNO_3
    (d) Dilute solution of H_2O_2

28. Which one absorbs U.V. radiation in stratosphere?
    (a) CO_2
    (b) N_2
    (c) O_3
    (d) H_2

ANSWERS

1. (a)	4. (b)	7. (a)	10. (c)	13. (b)	16. (c)	19. (c)	22. (a)	25. (c)	28. (c)
2. (a)	5. (a)	8. (b)	11. (c)	14. (b)	17. (c)	20. (c)	23. (d)	26. (a)	
3. (b)	6. (b)	9. (b)	12. (a)	15. (a)	18. (a)	21. (c)	24. (d)	27. (b)	

Chapter 8. *d*-and *f*-Block Elements

1. The general outer electronic configuration of transition elements is:
    (a) $(n-1) d^{1-10} ns^1$
    (b) $(n-1) d^{10} ns^2$
    (c) $(n-1) d^{1-10} ns^{1-2}$
    (d) $(n-1) d^5 ns^1$

2. Which one of the following does not show different oxidation states?
    (a) Iron
    (b) Copper
    (c) Zinc
    (d) Manganese

3. Which of the following is not a condition for complex salt formation?
    (a) Small size
    (b) Higher nuclear charge
    (c) Availability of vacant d-orbitals
    (d) Variable oxidation states

4. Which of the following metal is used in incandescent lamps?
    (a) Chromium
    (b) Tungsten
    (c) Zirconium
    (d) Molybdenum

5. The outer electronic configuration of chromium is:
    (a) $4s^1 3d^5$
    (b) $4s^2 3d^4$
    (c) $4s^0 3d^6$
    (d) $4s^2 3d^5$

6. Which ion gives coloured solution?
    (a) Cu^+
    (b) Zn^{2+}
    (c) Ag^+
    (d) Fe^{2+}

7. Paramagnetism is a property of:
    (a) Completely filled electronic sub-shells
    (b) Unpaired electrons
    (c) Non-transition elements
    (d) Melting point and boiling point of elements

8. **Which transition metal has the highest density?**
   (a) Os   (b) Zn   (c) Sc   (d) La

9. **Which transition metal shows highest oxidation state?**
   (a) Sc   (b) Ti   (c) Os   (d) Zn

10. **In KMnO4 oxidation number of Mn is:**
    (a) $+2$ (b) $+4$ (c) $+6$ (d) $+7$

11. **The most common oxidation state of lanthanoids is:**
    (a) $+4$ (b) $+3$ (c) $+6$ (d) $+2$

12. **Which element among the lanthanoids has the smallest atomic radius?**
    (a) Cerium   (b) Lutetium   (c) Europium   (d) Gadolinium

13. **Which of the following oxides of chromium is amphoteric in nature?**
    (a) CrO (b) Cr_2O_3 (c) CrO_3 (d) CrO_5

14. **Which compound of chromium is widely used in tanning of leather?**
    (a) $CrCl_3$ (c) CrO_2Cl_2
    (b) Cr_2O_3 (d) $K_2SO_4 \cdot Cr_2(SO_4)_3 \cdot 24H_2O$

15. **Which of the following element belongs to actinoid series?**
    (a) La   (b) Gd   (c) Lu   (d) Th

16. **Number of moles of $K_2Cr_2O_7$ reduced by one mole of Sn^{2+} ions is:**
    (a) 1/3   (b) 3   (c) 1/6   (d) 6

17. **The lanthanoid contraction is responsible for the fact that:**
    (a) Zr and Y have about the same radius
    (b) Zr and Nb have similar oxidation state
    (c) Zr and Hf have about the same radius
    (d) Zr and Zn have the same oxidation state

18. **Which lanthanoid is most commonly used?**
    (a) Lanthanum   (b) Nobelium   (c) Thorium   (d) Cerium

19. **Ammonium dichromate is use in some fireworks. The green coloured powder blown in air is:**
    (a) CrO_3 (b) Cr_2O_3 (c) Cr (d) $CrO(O_2)_2$

20. **Which of the following statement is not correct?**
    (a) $La(OH)_3$ is less basic than $Lu(OH)_3$
    (b) La is actually an element of transition series rather than lanthanoids
    (c) Atomic radii of Zr and Hf are same because of lanthanoid contraction
    (d) In lanthanoid series the ionic radius of Lu^{3+} is smallest

21. **What type of isomerism is shown by the pair $[Cr(H_2O)_6]\,Cl_3$ and $[Cr(H_2O)_5\,Cl]\,Cl_2\,H_2O?$**[*]
    (a) Ionization isomerism
    (b) Coordination isomerism
    (c) Solvate isomerism
    (d) Linkage isomerism

22. **The oxidation state of Ni in $[Ni(CO)_4]$ is:**[*]
    (a) 0   (b) 2   (c) 3   (d) 4

ANSWERS

| 1. (c) | 3. (d) | 5. (a) | 7. (b) | 9. (c) | 11. (b) | 13. (b) | 15. (d) | 17. (c) | 19. (b) | 21. (c) |
| 2. (c) | 4. (b) | 6. (d) | 8. (a) | 10. (d) | 12. (b) | 14. (d) | 16. (a) | 18. (a) | 20. (a) | 22. (a) |

Chapter 9. Coordination Compounds

1. **In the complexes $[Fe(CN)_6]^{3-}$ and $[Pt(en)\,(H_2O)_2(NO_2)\,(Cl)]^{2+}$ the respective oxidation numbers of central metal atoms are:**
   (a) $+3$ and $+4$ (b) $+6$ and $+4$ (c) $+6$ and $+3$ (d) $+3$ and $+3$

---

* are board exam questions from previous years

2. The complex ion $[Ni(CN)_4]^{2-}$ is:
   (a) Square planar and diamagnetic
   (b) Tetrahedral and paramagnetic
   (c) Square planar and paramagnetic
   (d) Tetrahedral and diamagnetic

3. Among the following coordination compounds, the one giving a white precipitate with $BaCl_2$ solution is:
   (a) $[Cr(H_2O)_5Br]SO_4$
   (b) $[Cr(H_2O)_5SCN]$
   (c) $[Co(NH_3)_5SO_4]Br$
   (d) $[Pt(NH_3)_6]Cl_4$

4. The hybridization of the iron atom in $[Fe(CN)_6]^{3-}$ complex is:
   (a) sp^3
   (b) d^2sp^3
   (c) sp^3d^2
   (d) dsp^2

5. Which of the following statement about primary and secondary valencies is true?
   (a) Both primary and secondary valency are ionisable
   (b) Both primary and secondary valencies are non-ionisable
   (c) Primary valencies are ionisable while secondary are non-ionisable
   (d) Primary valencies are non-ionisable while secondary are ionisable

6. What is the oxidation number of central atom in $Na[Hg(CN)_2]$?
   (a) $+4$
   (b) $+2$
   (c) 0
   (d) $+1$

7. What is the coordination number of central metal atom in $[Pt(NH_3)_2Cl_2]Cl$?
   (a) 6
   (b) 4
   (c) 3
   (d) 7

8. Which of the following is π-acid ligand?
   (a) NH_3
   (b) CO
   (c) F^-
   (d) Ethylene diamine

9. Which of these compound does not show paramagnetism?
   (a) $[Cu(NH_3)_4]Cl_2$
   (b) $[Ag(NH_3)_2]Cl$
   (c) NO
   (d) NO_2

10. The geometry of $Ni(CO)_4$ and $[Ni(CN)_4]^{2-}$ are:
    (a) Both square planar
    (b) Tetrahedral and square planar respectively
    (c) Both tetrahedral
    (d) Square planar and tetrahedral respectively

11. Which of the following compounds show optical isomerism?
    (a) $[Co(CN)_6]^{3-}$
    (b) $[Cr(C_2O_4)3]^{3-}$
    (c) $[ZnCl_4]^{2-}$
    (d) $[Cu(NH_3)_4]^{2+}$

12. The correct order of hybridization of the central atom in the following species NH_3, $[PtCl_4]^{2-}$, PCl_5 and BCl_3 is:
    (a) dsp^2, dsp^3, sp^2 and sp^3
    (b) sp^3, dsp^2, dsp^3, sp^2
    (c) $dsp^2, sp^2, sp^3\, dsp^3$
    (d) dsp^2, sp^3, sp^2, dsp^3

13. Which is not true about the coordination compound $[Co(en)_2Cl_2]Cl$?
    (a) Exhibits geometrical isomerism
    (b) Exhibits optical isomerism
    (c) Exhibits ionization isomerism
    (d) Is an octahedral complex

14. In $Fe(CO)_5$, the Fe–C bond possesses:
    (a) π-character only
    (b) Both σ and π-characters
    (c) Ionic character
    (d) σ–character only

15. The IUPAC name for the complex $[Co(NO_2)(NH_3)_5]Cl_2$ is:
    (a) Nitrito-N-pentaammine cobalt(III) chloride
    (b) Nitrito-N-pentaammine cobalt(II) chloride
    (c) Pentaammine nitrito-N-cobalt(II) chloride
    (d) Pentaammine nitrito-N-cobalt(III) chloride

16. How many ions are produced from the complex $[Co(NH_3)_5 Cl]Cl_2$ in solution?*
    (a) 4
    (b) 2
    (c) 3
    (d) 5

17. The pair $[Co(NH_3)_4 Cl_2]Br_2$ and $[Co(NH_3)_4Br_2]Cl_2$ will show.*
    (a) Linkage isomerism
    (b) Hydrate isomerism
    (c) Ionization isomerism
    (d) Coordinate isomerism

---

18. The coordination number of 'Co' in the complex $[Co(en)_3]^{3+}$ is:*
    (a) 3   (b) 6   (c) 4   (d) 5

19. The crystal field splitting energy for octahedral (Δ_0) and tetrahedral (Δ_t) complexes is related as:*
    (a) $\Delta_t = 2/9\ \Delta_0$ (b) $\Delta_t = 5/9\ \Delta_0$ (c) $\Delta_t = 4/9\ \Delta_0$ (d) $\Delta_t = 2\ \Delta_0$

20. Which of the following is the most stable complex?*
    (a) $[Fe(CO)_5]$
    (b) $[Fe(H_2O)_6]^{3+}$
    (c) $[Fe(C_2O_4)_3]^{3-}$
    (d) $[Fe(CN)_6]^{3-}$

21. Which of the following will give a white precipitate upon reacting with $AgNO_3$?*
    (a) $K_2[Pt(en)_2Cl_2]$
    (b) $[Co(NH_3)_3Cl_3]$
    (c) $[Cr(H_2O)_6]Cl_3$
    (d) $[Fe(H_2O)_3Cl_3]$

22. The formula of the complex triamminetri (nitrito-O) Cobalt (III) is:*
    (a) $[Co(ONO)_3(NH_3)_3]$
    (b) $[Co(NO_2)_3(NH_3)_3]$
    (c) $[Co(ONO_2)_3(NH_3)_3]$
    (d) $[Co(NO_2)(NH_3)_3]$

ANSWERS

1. (a)	3. (a)	5. (c)	7. (b)	9. (b)	11. (b)	13. (c)	15. (d)	17. (d)	19. (c)	21. (c)
2. (d)	4. (d)	6. (d)	8. (b)	10. (b)	12. (b)	14. (b)	16. (c)	18. (b)	20. (a)	22. (a)

Chapter 10. Haloalkanes and Haloarenes

1. Which of the following poisonous gas is formed when chloroform is exposed to light and air?
    (a) Mustard gas
    (b) Carbon monoxide
    (c) Phosgene
    (d) Chlorine

2. What is the IUPAC name of $CH_3{-}\underset{\underset{CH_3}{|}}{\overset{\overset{CH_3}{|}}{C}}{-}H_2Cl$?
    (a) 2-dimethylchloropropane
    (b) 1-chloro-2-dimethyl-pentane
    (c) 2, 2-dimethyl-chlorobutane
    (d) 1-chloro-2, 2-dimethyl propane

3. Halogenation of alkane gives:
    (a) Only required alkyl halide
    (b) Alkyl halide and unreacted halogen
    (c) A mixture of mono-, di-, tri- and tetra-halogen derivatives
    (d) Alkyl halide and unreacted alkane

4. Which of the following compound has been suggested as causing depletion of the ozone layer in the upper stratosphere?
    (a) CH_4 (b) CCl_2F_2 (c) CF_4 (d) CH_2Cl_2

5. Which of the following reagent cannot be used to prepare an alkyl chloride from an alcohol?
    (a) $HCl + ZnCl_2$ (b) $SOCl_2$ (c) $NaCl$ (d) PCl_5

6. Alkyl halides undergo:
    (a) Electrophilic substitution reactions
    (b) Electrophilic addition reactions
    (c) Nucleophilic substitution reactions
    (d) Nucleophilic addition reactions

7. Carbylamine test involves heating a mixture of:
    (a) Alcoholic KOH, methyl iodide, and sodium metal
    (b) Alcoholic KOH, methyl iodide, and primary amine
    (c) Alcoholic KOH, chloroform, and primary amine
    (d) Alcoholic KOH, methyl alcohol, and primary amine

8. **When chloroform is heated with aqueous NaOH, it gives:**
   - (a) Formic acid
   - (b) Sodium formate
   - (c) Acetic acid
   - (d) Sodium acetate

9. **Which alkyl halides react most readily by nucleophilic substitution?**
   - (a) CH_3CH_2Cl
   - (b) CH_3CH_2I
   - (c) CH_3CH_2Br
   - (d) CH_3CH_2F

10. **The action of sodium on alkyl halide to form an alkane is called:**
    - (a) Grignard reaction
    - (b) Wurtz coupling reaction
    - (c) Isocyanide reaction
    - (d) Halogenation reaction

11. **Conversion of ethyl bromide to ethylene is an example of:**
    - (a) Hydrohalogenation
    - (b) Intramolecular dehydrohalogenation
    - (c) Dehydration
    - (d) Hydration

12. **Which of the following compound is an organometallic compound?**
    - (a) CH_3COOAg
    - (b) CH_3MgI
    - (c) $MgCl_2$
    - (d) CH_3—O—Na

13. **The reaction,**

$$2C_2H_5Br + 2Na \xrightarrow{\text{dry ether}} C_2H_5{-}C_2H_5 + 2NaBr \text{ is an example of:}$$

   - (a) The Wurtz reaction
   - (b) Sandmeyer's reaction
   - (c) Aldol condensation
   - (d) Williamson's reaction

14. **Grignard's reagent is prepared by the action of magnesium metal on:**
    - (a) Alcohol
    - (b) Phenol
    - (c) Alkyl halide
    - (d) Benzene

15. **The major product of the following reaction is:**

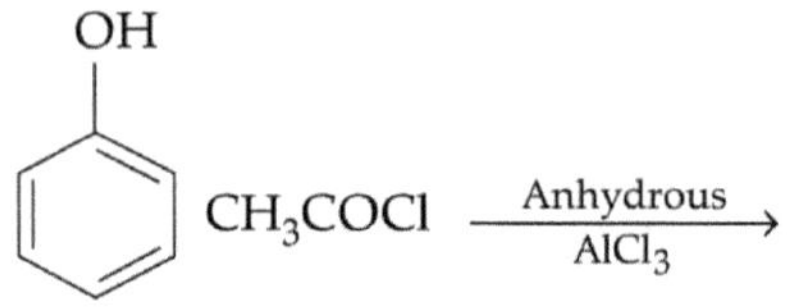

17. ***p - p'*-dichlorodiphenyl trichloroethane is used as:**
    - (a) 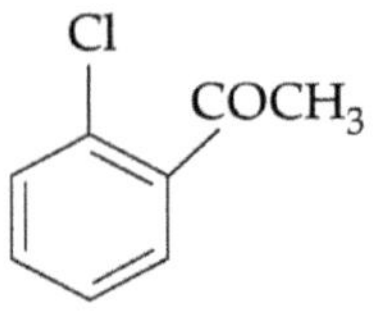 Insecticide
    - (b) 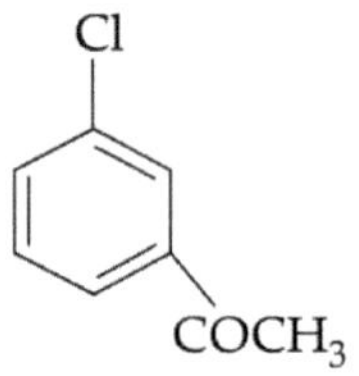 Anaesthetic
    - (c) 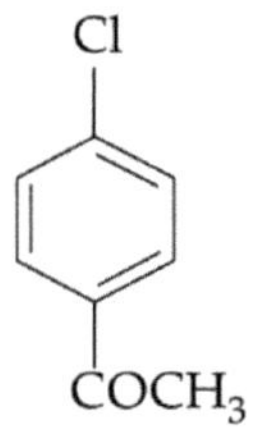 Antiseptic
    - (d) 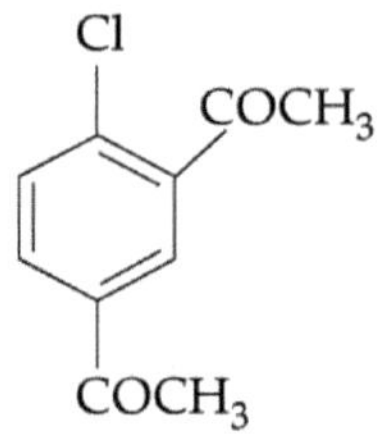 Refrigerant

16.

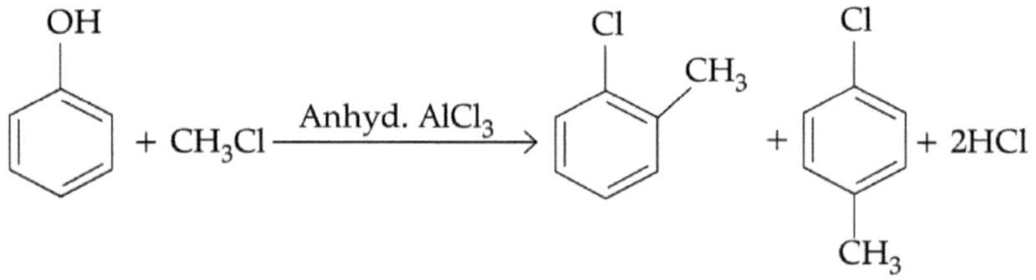

The above reaction is known as:
   - (a) Wurtz-Fittig reaction
   - (b) Friedel Craft's reaction
   - (c) Sandmeyer's reaction
   - (d) Swarts reaction

18. **The following compound is called:**

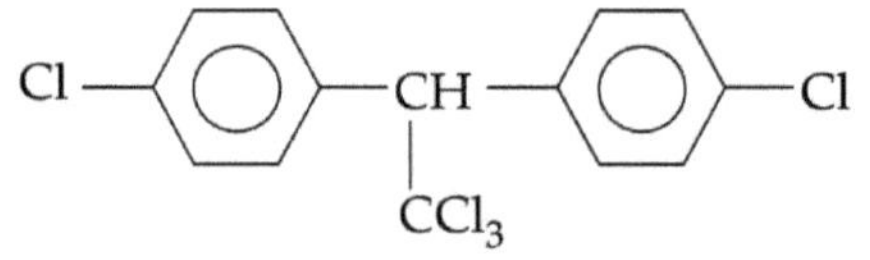

   - (a) Chloral
   - (b) DDT
   - (c) Lindane
   - (d) BHC

19. **DDT is prepared by the reaction of chlorobenzene with (in the presence of conc. H_2SO_4):**
    (a) Chloral
    (b) Chlorine
    (c) Chloroform
    (d) Carbon tetrachloride

20. **The conversion of an alkyl halide into an alcohol by aqueous NaOH is classified as***
    (a) a dehydrohalogenation reaction
    (b) a substitution reaction
    (c) an addition reaction
    (d) a dehydration reaction

ANSWERS

1. (c)	**3.** (c)	**5.** (c)	**7.** (c)	**9.** (b)	**11.** (b)	**13.** (a)	**15.** (c)	**17.** (a)	**19.** (a)
2. (d)	**4.** (b)	**6.** (c)	**8.** (b)	**10.** (b)	**12.** (b)	**14.** (c)	**16.** (d)	**18.** (b)	**20.** (b)

Chapter 11. Alcohols, Phenols and Ethers

1. **When acetaldehyde is treated with Grignard reagent, followed by hydrolysis the product formed is:**
   (a) Primary alcohol
   (b) Secondary alcohol
   (c) Carboxylic acid
   (d) Tertiary alcohol

2. **When oxalic acid is heated with glycerol we get:**
   (a) Formic acid
   (b) Acetic acid
   (c) Lactic acid
   (d) Tartaric acid

3. **Ethanol on heating with conc. H_2SO_4 at 445 K gives:**
   (a) Diethyl sulphate
   (b) Ethylene, C_2H_4
   (c) Diethyl ether, $(C_2H_5)_2O$
   (d) Ethyl hydrogensulphate, $C_2H_5HSO_4$

4. **Which of the following is most acidic?**
   (a) H_2O
   (b) CH_3OH
   (c) C_2H_5OH
   (d) $CH_3CH_2CH_2OH$

5. **Which of the following has highest boiling point?**
   (a) $CH_3CH_2CH_2OH$
   (b) $CH_3CH_2CH_2CH_2OH$
   (c) $(CH_3)_2CH-CH_2OH$
   (d) $CH_3-\underset{\underset{CH_3}{|}}{\overset{\overset{CH_3}{|}}{C}}-OH$

6. **$C_6H_5Cl \xrightarrow[\text{624K,300atm}]{\text{NaOH(aq)}}$ A. Here, A is:**
   (a) Phenol
   (b) Sodium phenoxide
   (c) Benzene
   (d) Cyclohexyl chloride

7. **Which one of the following will produce a primary alcohol by reacting with CH_3MgI?**
   (a) Acetone
   (b) Methyl cyanide
   (c) Ethylene oxide
   (d) Ethyl acetate

8. **In the sequence $HO-\langle C_6H_4\rangle-SO_3H \xrightarrow[H_2O]{Br_2} X$, X is:**
   (a) 2-Bromo-4-hydroxybenzene sulphonic acid
   (b) 3, 5-Dibromo-4-hydroxybenzene sulphonic acid
   (c) 2-Bromophenol
   (d) 2, 4, 6-Tribromophenol

9. **Phenol can be distinguished from ethyl alcohol by all reagents except:**
   (a) NaOH
   (b) $FeCl_3$
   (c) Br_2/H_2O
   (d) Na

---
* are board exam questions from previous years

10. **Alcohols can be obtained from all methods except:**
    (a) Hydroboration-oxidation
    (b) Oxymercuration-demercuration
    (c) Reduction of aldehyde/ketones with Zn-Hg/HCl
    (d) By fermentation of starch

11. **Chlorine reacts with ethanol to give:**
    (a) Diethyl chloride
    (b) Chloroform
    (c) Acetaldehyde
    (d) Chloral

12. **Which of the following alcohol is least soluble in water?**
    (a) N-Butyl alcohol
    (b) Iso-Butyl alcohol
    (c) Tert-Butyl alcohol
    (d) Sec-Butyl alcohol

13. **Glycerol on heating with potassium bisulphate yields:**
    (a) Acetone
    (b) Glyceraldehyde
    (c) Acrolein
    (d) Propanol

14. **The reaction of Lucas reagent is fastest with:**
    (a) $(CH_3)_3COH$
    (b) $(CH_3)_2CHOH$
    (c) $CH_3(CH_2)_2OH$
    (d) CH_3CH_2OH

15. **The ionization constant of phenol is higher than that of ethanol because:**
    (a) Phenoxide ion is a stronger base than ethoxide ion
    (b) Phenoxide ion is stabilized through delocalization
    (c) Phenoxide ion is less stable than ethoxide ion
    (d) Phenoxide ion is bulkier than ethoxide ion

16. **The correct order of boiling points for primary (1°), secondary (2°) and tertiary alcohol (3°) is:**
    (a) $1° > 2° > 3°$
    (b) $3° > 2° > 1°$
    (c) $2° > 1° > 3°$
    (d) $2° > 3° > 1°$

17. **Which of the following is the most suitable method for removing the traces of water from ethanol?**
    (a) Heating with Na metal
    (b) Passing dry HCl gas through it
    (c) Distilling Cl^-
    (d) Reacting with Mg

18. **Phenol is heated with $CHCl_3$ and alcoholic KOH when salicylaldehyde is produced. This reaction is known as:**
    (a) Rosenmund's reaction
    (b) Reimer-Tiemann reaction
    (c) Friedel-Crafts reaction
    (d) Sommelet reaction

19. **Lucas test is used for distinction of:**
    (a) Alcohols
    (b) Phenols
    (c) Alkyl halides
    (d) Aldehydes

20.

    The electrophile involved in the above reaction is:
    (a) Dichloromethyl cation ($\overset{+}{C}HCl_2$)
    (b) Dichlorocarbene (: CCl_2)
    (c) Trichloromethyl anion ($\overset{-}{C}Cl_3$)
    (d) Formylcation ($\overset{\oplus}{C}HO$)

21. **When phenol is treated with excess of bromine water, it gives:**
    (a) *m*-bromophenol
    (b) *o*-and *p*-bromophenol
    (c) 2, 4-dibromophenol
    (d) 2, 4, 6-tribromophenol

22. **Which of the following is simple ether?**
    (a) $C_2H_5OCH_3$
    (b) CH_3OCH_3
    (c) $C_6H_5OCH_3$
    (d) All are simple ethers.

ANSWERS

1. (b)	3. (b)	5. (d)	7. (c)	9. (d)	11. (d)	13. (c)	15. (b)	17. (d)	19. (a)	21. (d)
2. (a)	4. (a)	6. (b)	8. (b)	10. (c)	12. (a)	14. (a)	16. (d)	18. (d)	20. (b)	22. (b)

Chapter 12. Aldehydes, Ketones and Carboxylic Acids

1. **The compound which gives a positive haloform test and a positive Fehling solution test is:**
   (a) Acetone (b) Acetaldehyde (c) Formaldehyde (d) Diethyl ether

2. **Benzaldehyde, when heated with an alcoholic solution of potassium cyanide, forms:**
   (a) Benzyl alcohol
   (b) Benzoin
   (c) Hydrobenzamide
   (d) Benzoic acid

3. **Which of the following reagent can be used to prepare ketone from acid chloride?**
   (a) Grignard's reagent
   (b) $LiAlH_4$
   (c) Dimethyl cadmium
   (d) Cadmium chloride

4. **Which of the following reaction cannot be used for the reduction of**

$$\underset{R}{\overset{R}{>}}C = O \longrightarrow \underset{R}{\overset{R}{>}}CH_2$$

   (a) Clemmensen reaction
   (b) Wolff-Kishner reaction
   (c) Wurtz reaction
   (d) HI and red phosphorus

5. **Benzaldehyde can be prepared by the hydrolysis of:**
   (a) Benzyl chloride (b) Benzal chloride (c) Benzotrichloride (d) Benzo nitrite

6. **The reaction, $C_6H_5COCl + H_2 \xrightarrow[BaSO_4]{Pd} C_6H_5CHO + HCl$, is called:**
   (a) Rosenmund's reaction
   (b) Sandmeyer's reaction
   (c) HVZ reaction
   (d) Cannizzaro's reaction

7. **The end product 'C' in the following sequence of chemical reaction is:**

$$CH_3COOH \xrightarrow{CaCO_3} A \xrightarrow{Heat} B \xrightarrow{NH_2OH} C$$

   (a) Acetaldehyde oxime
   (b) Formaldehyde oxime
   (c) Methyl nitrate
   (d) Acetoxime

8. **Which of the following statements about benzaldehyde is/are true?**
   (a) Reduces Tollen's reagent
   (b) Undergoes aldol condensation
   (c) Undergoes Cannizzaro reaction
   (d) Does not form an addition compound with sodium hydrogen sulphite

9. **Which one of the following aldehyde gives Cannizzaro reaction when heated with strong alkali?**
   (a) Benzaldehyde (b) Acetaldehyde (c) Propionaldehyde (d) All of these

10. **In the Cannizzaro reaction given below,**

$$2Ph—CHO \xrightarrow{OH^-} Ph—CH_2OH + PhCO_2^-,$$

   the slowest step is:
   (a) The attack of —OH at the carbonyl group
   (b) The transfer of hydride ion to the carbonyl group
   (c) The abstraction of proton from the carboxylic acid
   (d) The deprotonation of Ph—CH_2OH.

11. **Acetaldehyde cannot show:**
    (a) Iodoform test (b) Lucas test (c) Benedict's test (d) Tollen's test

12. **Iodoform test is not given by:**
    (a) 2-Pentanone (b) 3-Pentanone (c) Ethanal (d) Ethanol

13. **The reaction in which sodium cyanide is used**
    (a) Perkin condensation
    (b) Reimer-Tiemann reaction
    (c) Benzoin condensation
    (d) Rosenmund's reduction

14. **Which one of the following reaction is a method for the conversion of a ketone into a hydrocarbon?**
    (a) Aldol condensation
    (b) Reimer-Tiemann reaction
    (c) Cannizzaro reaction
    (d) Wolff-Kishner reduction

15. **The IUPAC name of the compound having the formula, Cl_3CCH_2CHO is:**
    (a) 3, 3, 3-Trichloropropanal
    (b) 1, 1, 1-Trichloropropanal
    (c) 2, 2, 2-Trichloropropanal
    (d) Chloral

16. **When ethanal is treated with Fehling's solution, it gives precipitate of:**
    (a) Cu
    (b) CuO
    (c) Cu_2O
    (d) $Cu_2O + Cu_2O_3$

17. **A new carbon-carbon bond formation is possible in:**
    (a) Cannizzaro reaction
    (b) Friedel-Crafts reaction
    (c) Clemmensen reduction
    (d) Reimer-Tiemann reaction

18. **The reduction of benzoyl chloride with Pd and $BaSO_4$ produces:**
    (a) Benzoyl chloride
    (b) Benzaldehyde
    (c) Benzoic acid
    (d) None of these

19. **Which of the following cannot reduce Fehling's solution?**
    (a) Formic acid
    (b) Acetic acid
    (c) Formaldehyde
    (d) Acetaldehyde

20. **During reduction of aldehydes with hydrazine and potassium hydroxide, the first is formation of**
    (a) $R—C \equiv N$
    (b) $R—CO—NH_2$
    (c) $R—CH = NH$
    (d) $R—CH = N—NH_2$

21. **Reduction of $>C = O$ to $>CH_2$ can be carried out with:**
    (a) Catalytic reduction
    (b) Na/C_2H_5OH
    (c) Wolff-Kishner reduction
    (d) $LiAlH_4$

22. **Identify the compounds A and B in the following reaction sequence.**

$$(CH_3)_2C = O \xrightarrow[HCL]{NaCN} A \xrightarrow[Heat]{H_3O^+} B$$

    (a) $A = CH_3CO_2H$, $B = (CH_3CO)_2O$
    (b) $A = (CH_3)_2C(OH)CN$, $B = (CH_3)_2C(OH)CO_2H$
    (c) $A = CH_3CHO$, $B = CH_3CO_2H$
    (d) $A = (CH_3)_2C(OH)CN$, $B = (CH_3)_2C = O$

23. **Acetone on heating with conc. H_2SO_4 mainly gives:**
    (a) Mesitylene
    (b) Mesityl oxide
    (c) Toluene
    (d) Xylene

24. **The end product of the reaction is:**

$$HC \equiv CH \xrightarrow[20\% \ H_2SO_4]{1\% \ HgSO_4} A \xrightarrow{CH_3MgX} B \xrightarrow{[H_3O]}$$

    (a) Acetic acid
    (b) Isopropyl alcohol
    (c) Acetone
    (d) Ethanol

25. **Which one of the following undergoes reaction with 50% NaOH to give the corresponding alcohol and acid?**
    (a) Phenol
    (b) Benzoic acid
    (c) Butanal
    (d) Benzaldehyde

26. **Which of the following does not undergo Cannizzaro's reaction?**
    (a) Benzaldehyde
    (b) 2-methylpropanal
    (c) *p*-methoxybenzaldehyde
    (d) 2, 2-dimethyl propanal

27. **A carbonyl compound reacts with hydrogen cyanide to form cyanohydrin which on hydrolysis forms a racemic mixture of α-hydroxy acid. The carbonyl compound is:**
    (a) Formaldehyde
    (b) Acetaldehyde
    (c) Acetone
    (d) Diethyl ketone

28. **In the equation $CH_3COOH + Cl_2 \xrightarrow[-HCL]{Red \ P} A$, the compound A is:**
    (a) CH_3CH_2Cl
    (b) $ClCH_2COOH$
    (c) CH_3Cl
    (d) CH_3COCl

29. **When acetic acid is reacted with calcium hydroxide and the product is distilled dry, the compound formed is:**
    (a) Calcium acetate   (b) Acetone   (c) Acetaldehyde   (d) Acetic anhydride

30. **HVZ reaction is used to prepare:**
    (a) β-haloacid
    (b) α-haloacid
    (c) α, β-unsaturated acid
    (d) None of these

ANSWERS

1. (b)	4. (c)	7. (d)	10. (d)	13. (c)	16. (c)	19. (b)	22. (b)	25. (d)	28. (b)
2. (b)	5. (b)	8. (a)	11. (b)	14. (d)	17. (c)	20. (d)	23. (a)	26. (b)	29. (b)
3. (c)	6. (a)	9. (a)	12. (b)	15. (a)	18. (b)	21. (c)	24. (c)	27. (b)	30. (b)

Chapter 13. Amines

1. **The product formed when aniline is warmed with chloroform and caustic potash is:**
   (a) Phenyl chloride
   (b) Methyl isocyanide
   (c) Phenyl isocyanide
   (d) Nitro phenol

2. **The formula of acrylonitrile is:**
   (a) $CH_3CH = CHCN$
   (b) $CH_2 = CHCN$
   (c) $NC-CH = CH-CN$
   (d) $HC \equiv C-CN$

3. **Lower amines are soluble in water due to:**
   (a) Low molecular mass
   (b) Formation of complexes
   (c) Formation of hydrogen bonds with water
   (d) Affinity with water

4. **Which one of the following amines gives an alcohol with nitrous acid?**
   (a) CH_3NH_2 (b) $(CH_3)_2NH$ (c) $(CH_3)_3N$ (d) $C_6H_5NH_2$

5. **Reaction of $R-\overset{\overset{\displaystyle O}{\|}}{C}-NH_2$ with a mixture of Br_2 and KOH gives RNH_2 as main product. The intermediate involved in the reaction are:**
   (a) $R-\overset{\overset{\displaystyle O}{\|}}{C}-NHBr$ (b) $R-N = C = O$ (c) $R-NH-Br$ (d) $H-CO-NBr_2$

6. **Activation of benzene ring in aniline can be decreased by treating with:**
   (a) Dil. HCl
   (b) Ethyl alcohol
   (c) Acetic acid
   (d) Acetyl chloride

7. **Basic hydrolysis of alkyl cyanide produces:**
   (a) Carboxylic acid
   (b) Salt of ammonia
   (c) Salt of carboxylic acid
   (d) $NaNH_2$

8. **Which of the following does not reacts with Hinsberg reagent?**
   (a) Ethyl amine   (b) $(CH_3)_2NH$ (c) $(CH_3)_3N$ (d) Propane-2-amine

9. **Dehydration of an amide with phosphorus pentoxide yields:**
   (a) Ammonia   (b) Alkyl cyanide   (c) Alkyl isocyanide   (d) Alkyl amine

10. **Which of the following when heated with a mixture of ethanamine and alcoholic potash gives ethyl isocyanide?**
    (a) 2-chloropropane
    (b) 2, 2-dichloropropane
    (c) Trichloromethane
    (d) Tetrachloromethane

11. **Which of the following pairs of species will yield carbylamine?**
    (a) CH_3CH_2Br and KCN
    (b) CH_3CH_2Br and NH_3 (excess)
    (c) CH_3CH_2Br and AgCN
    (d) $CH_3CH_2\,NH_2$ and HCHO

12. **The main product of reaction of alcoholic silver nitrite and ethyl bromide is:**
    (a) Ethane
    (b) Ethylnitrite
    (c) Ethylisocyanide
    (d) Nitroethane

13. **Which of the following will not give primary amine?**
    (a) Dehydration of amides
    (b) Acidic hydrolysis of alkyl cyanides
    (c) Reduction of amides
    (d) Reduction of alkyl cyanides

14. **The reagents used in Hofmann's mustard oil reaction are:**
    (a) Mustard oil and 1° amine
    (b) CS_2 and aniline in $HgCl_2$
    (c) Nitrobenzene and CS_2
    (d) S and RNC

15. **The hybrid state of N in R_2NH is:**
    (a) sp^3
    (b) sp^2
    (c) sp
    (d) dsp^2

16. **Arrange the following—**

    (I) CH_3NH_2, (II) $(CH_3)_2NH$, (III) $C_6H_5NH_2$ and (IV) $(CH_3)_3N$

    in increasing order of basicity in aqueous medium:
    (a) II < I < IV < III
    (b) III < IV < I < II
    (c) I < II < III < IV
    (d) II < III < I < IV

17. **Identify the term C in the series:**

    $$CH_3CN \xrightarrow{Na/C_2H_5OH} A \xrightarrow{HNO_2} B \xrightarrow[573°K]{Cu} C$$

    (a) CH_3COOH
    (b) CH_3CH_2NHOH
    (c) CH_3CONH_2
    (d) CH_3CHO

18. **In the following reaction identify 'Y':**

    $$CH_3CN + 2H \longrightarrow X \xrightarrow[H_2O]{Boiling} Y$$

    (a) Acetone
    (b) Ethylamine
    (c) Acetaldehyde
    (d) Dimethyl amine

19. **Which is the end product in the following equation?**

    $$C_2H_5NH_2 \xrightarrow{PCl_2} A \xrightarrow{PCl_5} B \xrightarrow{NH_3} C$$

    (a) Ethylcyanide
    (b) Methylamine
    (c) Ethylamine
    (d) Acetamide

20. **CH_3CONH_2 on reaction with NaOH and Br_2 in alcoholic medium gives:***
    (a) $CH_3CH_2NH_2$
    (b) CH_3CH_2Br
    (c) CH_3NH_2
    (d) CH_3COONa

ANSWERS

1. (c)	3. (c)	5. (a)	7. (a)	9. (d)	11. (c)	13. (b)	15. (a)	17. (d)	19. (c)
2. (b)	4. (a)	6. (b)	8. (c)	10. (c)	12. (d)	14. (b)	16. (d)	18. (c)	20. (c)

Chapter 14. Biomolecules

1. **The deficiency of vitamin D causes:**
   (a) Rickets
   (b) Gout
   (c) Scurvy
   (d) Night blindness

2. **Which of the following is an example of aldohexose?**
   (a) Ribose
   (b) Fructose
   (c) Sucrose
   (d) Glucose

3. **The linkage which holds various amino acid units in primary structures of proteins is:**
   (a) Glycoside linkage
   (b) Peptide linkage
   (c) Ionic linkage
   (d) Hydrogen bond

4. **Maltose on hydrolysis gives:**
   (a) α-D-glucose
   (b) α and β-D-glucose
   (c) Glucose and fructose
   (d) Fructose only

5. **The amino acids are the end products of the digestion of:**
   (a) Lipids
   (b) Fats
   (c) Proteins
   (d) Enzymes

6. **α-helix refers to:**
   (a) Primary structure of proteins
   (b) Secondary structure of proteins
   (c) Tertiary structure of proteins
   (d) Quaternary structure of proteins

7. **Which of the following bases is not present in DNA?**
   (a) Adenine
   (b) Guanine
   (c) Uracil
   (d) Cytosine

8. **The relation between nucleotide triplets and the amino acids is called:**
   (a) Transcription
   (b) Duplication
   (c) Genetic code
   (d) Gene

9. **Nucleic acids are polymers of:**
   (a) Nucleotides
   (b) Nucleosides
   (c) Nuclei of heavy metals
   (d) Proteins

10. **The non-proteinous substances which certain enzymes require for their activity are called:**
    (a) Catalysts
    (b) Inhibitors
    (c) Co-enzymes
    (d) Epimers

11. **Which of the following α-amino acid is not optically active?**
    (a) Alanine
    (b) Glycine
    (c) Phenylanine
    (d) All are optically active

12. **Glucose on treatment with NH_2OH undergoes:**
    (a) Condensation
    (b) Reduction
    (c) Hydrolysis
    (d) Oxidation

13. **Niacin is vitamin:**
    (a) B_1
    (b) B_2
    (c) B_{12}
    (d) B_4

14. **Which of the following is a ketohexose?**
    (a) Fructose
    (b) Maltose
    (c) Glucose
    (d) Ribose

15. **The linkage that holds monosaccharide units together in a polysaccharide is called:**
    (a) Peptide linkage
    (b) Glycoside linkage
    (c) Ester linkage
    (d) Ionic linkage

16. **A nucleoside is made up of:**
    (a) A base and sugar
    (b) A base and phosphoric acid
    (c) A sugar and phosphoric acid
    (d) A sugar, a base and phosphoric acid

17. **The disease albinism is caused by the deficiency of enzyme:**
    (a) Trypsin
    (b) Tyrosinase
    (c) Phenylalanine hydroxylase
    (d) None of these

18. **Which of the following base is a purine?**
    (a) Thymine
    (b) Uracil
    (c) Cytosine
    (d) Adenine

19. **Which of the following is a pyrimidine base?**
    (a) Adenine
    (b) Gyanine
    (c) Uracil
    (d) None of these

20. **Which of the following is an example of globular protein?**
    (a) Myosin
    (b) Collagen
    (c) Keratin
    (d) Haemoglobin

21. **Which of the following is an example of fibrous protein?**
    (a) Insulin
    (b) Haemoglobin
    (c) Fibroin
    (d) Glycogen

22. **α-Amino acids behave as crystalline ionic solids and have high melting point due to the presence of:**
    (a) —NH_2 group
    (b) —COOH group
    (c) Both —NH_2 and —COOH group
    (d) None of these

23. **The main structural feature of proteins is:**
    (a) Ether linkage
    (b) Ester linkage
    (c) Peptide linkage
    (d) All the three

24. **Enzymes are:**
    (a) Fatty acids
    (b) Vitamins
    (c) Proteins
    (d) None of these

25. Enzymes belong to which class of compounds?
(a) Polysaccharides
(b) Polypeptides
(c) Polynitro heterocyclic compounds
(d) Hydrocarbons

26. An a-helix is a structural feature of:*
(a) Sucrose
(b) Polypeptides
(c) Nucleotides
(d) Starch

27. α–D(+) glucose and (β–D(+) glucose are.*
(a) Geometrical isomers
(b) Enantiomers
(c) Anomers
(d) Optical isomers

28. Which one is the complementary base of cytosine in one strand to that in other strand of DNA?*
(a) Adenine
(b) Guanine
(c) Thymine
(d) Uracil

29. Amino acids are:*
(a) acidic
(b) basic
(c) amphoteric
(d) neutral

30. The nucleic acid base having two possible binding sites is:
(a) Thymine
(b) Cytosine
(c) Guanine
(d) Adenine

ANSWERS

1. (a)	4. (a)	7. (c)	10. (c)	13. (d)	16. (a)	19. (c)	22. (b)	25. (b)	28. (b)
2. (d)	5. (c)	8. (c)	11. (d)	14. (a)	17. (b)	20. (d)	23. (c)	26. (b)	29. (c)
3. (b)	6. (b)	9. (a)	12. (a)	15. (b)	18. (d)	21. (c)	24. (c)	27. (c)	30. (a)

Chapter 15. Polymers

1. Natural rubber is a:
(a) Polyester
(b) Polyamide
(c) Polyisoprene
(d) Polysaccharide

2. The fibre obtained by the condensation of hexamethylene diamine and adipic acid is:
(a) Nylon-6 6
(b) Dacron
(c) Teflon
(d) Polyester

3. Polymers are:
(a) Micromolecules
(b) Macromolecules
(c) Sub-macromolecules
(d) None of these

4. Bakelite is:
(a) Addition polymer
(b) Elastomer
(c) Thermoplastic
(d) Thermosetting

5. The repeating units of PTFE are:
(a) $Cl_2CH{-}CH_3$
(b) $F_2C = CF_2$
(c) $F_3C{-}CF_3$
(d) $FClC = CF_2$

6. Which of the following is not a condensation polymer?
(a) Glyptal
(b) Nylon-6 6
(c) Dacron
(d) PTFE

7. Which of the following polymer is a copolymer?
(a) Polypropylene
(b) Nylon-6 6
(c) PVC
(d) Teflon

8. Which of the following types of polymer has the strongest inter particle forces?
(a) Elastomers
(b) Thermoplastics
(c) Fibers
(d) Thermosetting polymers

9. Synthetic polymer prepared by using ethylene glycol and terephthalic acid is known as:
(a) Teflon
(b) Terylene
(c) Nylon
(d) PVC

10. The fibre obtained by the condensation of hexamethylene diamine and adipic acid is:
(a) Nylon-6 6
(b) Dacron
(c) Teflon
(d) Polyester

11. **Which is not a macromolecule?**
    (a) DNA (b) Starch (c) Palmitate (d) Insulin

12. **Copolymer of acrylonitrile (40%) and vinyl chloride (60%) is called:**
    (a) Orlon (b) Dacron (c) Dynel (d) Perlon

13. **Copolymer of vinyl chloride (90%) and vinyl acetate (10%) is called:**
    (a) Saran (b) Teflon (c) Vinyon (d) All of these

14. **Polymers have:**
    (a) Absolute molecular weight
    (b) Average molecular weight
    (c) Low molecular weight
    (d) Absolute melting point

15. **Chemical name of melamine is:**
    (a) 2, 4-diamino-1, 3, 5-triazine
    (b) 2-amino-1, 3, 5-triazine
    (c) 2, 4, 6-triamino-1, 3, 5-triazine
    (d) 1, 3, 5-triamino-2, 4, 6-triazine

16. **Synthetic human hair wigs are made from a copolymer of vinyl chloride and acrylonitrile and is called:**
    (a) PVC (b) Polyacrylonitrile (c) Cellulose (d) Dynel

17. **Plexiglass (PMMA) is a polymer of:**
    (a) Acrylic acid
    (b) Methyl acrylate
    (c) Methyl methacrylate
    (d) None of these

18. **Which of the following is a step growth polymer?**
    (a) Bakelite (b) Polyethylene (c) Teflon (d) PVC

19. **Which of the follownig is a disaccharide?***
    (a) Glucose (b) Starch (c) Cellulose (d) Lactose

ANSWERS

1. (c)	3. (b)	5. (b)	7. (b)	9. (b)	11. (c)	13. (c)	15. (c)	17. (c)	19. (d)
2. (a)	4. (b)	6. (d)	8. (b)	10. (a)	12. (c)	14. (d)	16. (d)	18. (a)	

Chapter 16. Chemistry in Everyday Life

1. **An Antibiotic with a broad spectrum:**
   (a) Kills the antibodies
   (b) Act on a specific antigen
   (c) Act on different antigens
   (d) Act on both the antigen and antibodies

2. **Penicillin was first discovered by:**
   (a) Alexander Fleming
   (b) Tence and Salke
   (c) S. A. Waksna
   (d) Lewis Pasteur

3. **An example of psychedelic agent is:**
   (a) DNA (b) LSD (c) DDT (d) TNT

4. **Acetoxy benzoic acid in:**
   (a) Antiseptic (b) Aspirin (c) Antibiotic (d) Mordent dyes

5. **Antiseptic chloroxylenol is:**
   (a) 4-chloro-3, 5-dimethyl phenol
   (b) 3-chloro-4, 5 dimethyl phenol
   (c) 4-chloro-2, 5-dimethyl phenol
   (d) 5-chloro 3, 4-dimethyl phenol

6. **The bacteriostatic antibiotic among the following:**
   (a) Erythromycin (b) Penicillin (c) Aminoglycoside (d) Ofloxacin

7. **Which one of the following is employed as a tranquilizer?**
   (a) Equanil
   (b) Naproxen
   (c) Tetracycline
   (d) Chlorpheniramine

---

* are board exam questions from previous years

8. **Aspirin is also known as:**
   (a) Methyl salicylic acid
   (b) Acetyl salicylic acid
   (c) Acetyl salicylate
   (d) Methyl salicylate

9. **Which one of the following pair is the strongest pesticides?**
   (a) Chloroform and benzene hexachloride
   (b) D. D. T. and 666
   (c) 666 and ether
   (d) Isocyanides and alcohol

10. **The drug used as an antidepressant is:**
    (a) Luminel
    (b) Tofranil
    (c) Mescaline
    (d) Sulphadiazine

11. **Dettol is the mixture of:**
    (a) Chloroxylenol and Bithionel
    (b) Chloroxylenol and Terpineol
    (c) Phenol and Iodine
    (d) Terpineol and Bithionol

12. **Phenacetin is used as:**
    (a) Antipyretics
    (b) Antiseptic
    (c) Antimalarial
    (d) Analgesics

13. **Substance used for bringing down temperature in high fever are called:**
    (a) Pyretics
    (b) Antipyretics
    (c) Antibiotics
    (d) Antiseptic

14. **The correct structure of drug paracetamol is:**

(a) 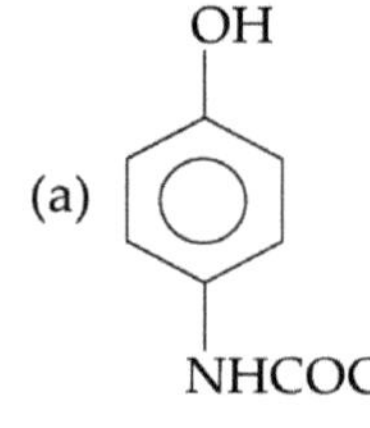

(b) 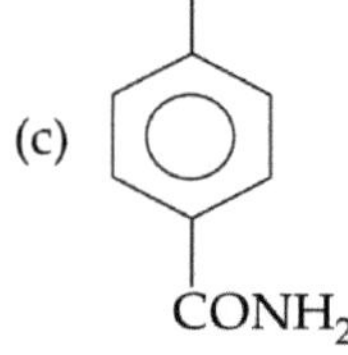

(c) 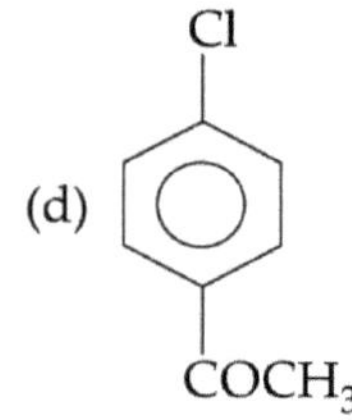

(d) *(structure with Cl and COCH$_3$)*

15. **Which is correct about Saccharin?**
    (a) It is *(structure of saccharin)*
    (b) It is 600 times sweeter than sugar
    (c) It is used as sweetening agent
    (d) All of these

16. **Bithional is an example of:**
    (a) Disinfectant
    (b) Antiseptic
    (c) Antibiotic
    (d) Analgesics

17. **Indigo is a or an:**
    (a) Organic dye
    (b) Organic polymer
    (c) Detergent
    (d) Pesticide

ANSWERS

1. (c)	3. (b)	5. (a)	7. (a)	9. (b)	11. (b)	13. (d)	15. (d)	17. (a)
2. (a)	4. (b)	6. (a)	8. (b)	10. (b)	12. (a)	14. (a)	16. (b)	

Chapter 9. Coordination Compounds

Q. 1. Write the IUPAC names of the following coordination compounds:*

  (i) $[Co(NH_3)_6]Cl_3$

  (ii) $[Co(NH_3)_5Cl]Cl_2$

  (iii) $K_3[Fe(CN)_6]$

  (iv) $K_3[Fe(C_2O_4)_3]$

  (v) $K_2[PdCl_4]$

  (vi) $[Pt(NH_3)_2Cl(NH_2CH_3)]Cl$

  (vii) $[Pt(NH_3)_2Cl(CH_3NH_2)]Cl$

Ans. (i)   Hexaamminecobalt (III) chloride

  (ii) Pentaamminechloridocobalt (III) chloride

  (iii) Potassium hexacyanoferrate (III)

  (iv) Potassium tioxalatoferrate (III)

  (v) Potassium tetrachloridopalladate (II)

  (vi) Diamminechlorido(methylamine) platinum (II) chloride

  (vii) Diamminechlorido (methaneamine) platinum (II) chloride

Q. 2. Using IUPAC norms write the formulae for the following:*

  (i)   Sodium dicyanidoaurate (I)

  (ii) Tetraamminechloridonitrito-N-platinum (IV) sulphate

Ans. (i)   Sodium dicyanoaurate (I)

       Na $[Au(CN)_2]$

  (ii) Tetraammine chloridonitrito-N-platinum (IV)

       $[Pt (NH_3)_4(Cl) (NO_2)]SO_4$

Q. 3. Using IUPAC norms write the formulae for the following:*

  (i)   Potassium trioxalatoaluminate (III).

  (ii) Dichloridobis (ethane-1, 2-diamine) cobalt (III)

Ans. (i) $K_3[Al(Ox)_3]$

  (ii) $[CO(3n)_2Cl_2]^+$

Q. 4. Using IUPAC norms write the formulae for the following:*

  (i)   Tris (ethane-1,2-diamine) chromium (III) chloride.

  (ii) Potassium tetrahydroxozincate (II).

Ans. (i) $[Cr(en)_3]Cl_3$

  (ii) $K_2[Zn(OH)_4$

Q. 5. Write the formulas for the following coordination compounds:

  (i)   Tetraamminediaquacobalt(III) chloride

  (ii) Potassium tetracyanonickelate(II)

  (iii) Tris(ethane-1, 2-diamine) chromium (III) chloride

  (iv) Amminebromidochloridonitrito-N-platinate(II)

  (v) Dichloridobis (ethane-1, 2-diamine) platinum (IV) nitrate

  (vi) Iron (III) hexacyanoferrate (II)

Ans. (i) $[Co(NH_3)_4(H_2O)_2]Cl_3$

  (ii) $K_2[Ni(CN)_4]$

  (iii) $[Cr(en)_3]Cl_3$

  (iv) $[Pt(NH)_3BrCl(NO_2)]$

  (v) $[PtCl_2(en)_2](NO_3)_2$

  (vi) $Fe_4[Fe(CN)_6]_3$

Q. 6. (i) Write down the IUPAC name of the following complex :

       $[Cr(NH_3)_2Cl_2 (en)]$ Cl (en = ethylenediamine)

  (ii) Write the formula for the given complex :*

       Penta amminenitrito-o-cobalt (III).

Ans. (i)   Diamminedichloridobis (ethane-1, 2-diamine) chromium (III) chloride.

  (ii) Formula : $[Co(NH_3)_5(ONO)]^{2+}$.

Q. 7. (i) Write down the IUPAC name of the following complex :

       $[Co(NH_3)_5Cl]^{2+}$.

  (ii) Write down the formula of the complex :*

       Potassium tetrachloridonickelate (II).

Ans. (i)   Pentaaminechlorido cobalt (III)

  (ii) $K_2[NiCl_4]$.

Q. 8. Using IUPAC norms write the formulas for the following :

  (i)   Tetrahydroxozincate (II)

  (ii) Potassium tetrachloridopalladate(II)

  (iii) Diamminedichlorido platinum(II)

  (iv) Potassium tetracyanonickelate(II)

  (v) Pentaamminenitrito-O-cobalt(III)

  (vi) Hexaamminecobalt(III) sulphate

  (vii) Potassium tri(oxalato) chromate(III)

  (viii) Hexaammineplatinum(IV)

  (ix) Tetrabromidocuprate(II)

  (x) Pentaamminenitrito-N-cobalt(III)

Ans. (i) $[Zn(OH)_4]^{2-}$

  (ii) $K_2[PdCl_4]$

  (iii) $[Pt(NH_3)_2Cl_2]$

(iv) $K_2[Ni(CN)_4]$

(v) $[CO(NH_3)_5(ONO)^{2+}]$

(vi) $[Co(NH_3)_6]_2 (SO_4)_3$

(vii) $K_3[Cr(C_2O_4)_3]$ or $K_3[Cr(Ox)_3]$

(viii) $[Pt(NH_3)_6]^{4+}$

(ix) $[Cu(Br)_4]^{2-}$

(x) $[Co(NH_3)_5 (NO_2)]^{2+}$.

Q. 9. Using IUPAC norms write the systematic names of the following:

(i) $[Co(NH_3)_6]Cl_3$

(ii) $[Pt(NH_3)_2Cl(NH_2CH_3)]Cl$

(iii) $[Ti(H_2O)_6]^{3+}$

(iv) $[Co(NH_3)_4Cl(NO_2)]Cl$

(v) $[Mn(H_2O)_6]^{2+}$

(vi) $[NiCl_4]^{2-}$

(vii) $[Ni(NH_3)_6]Cl_2$

(viii) $[Co(en)_3]^{3+}$

(ix) $[Ni(CO)_4]$

Ans. (i) Hexaamminecobalt(III) chloride

(ii) Diamminechlorido (methylamine) platinum (II) chloride

(iii) Hexaquatitanium (III) ion

(iv) Tetraamminichloridonitrito-N-Cobalt (III) chloride

(v) Hexaquamanganese(II) ion

(vi) Tetrachloridonickelate(II) ion

(vii) Hexaamminenickel(II) chloride

(viii) Tris(ethane-1, 2-diammine) cobalt (III) ion

(ix) Tetracarbonyl nickel

Chapter 10. Haloalkanes and Haloarenes

Q. 1. Write the IUPAC name of the compounds given below:*

(i)
$$\overset{CH_2CHO}{\underset{Br}{\bigcirc}}$$

(ii) $CH_2 = \underset{CH_3}{\overset{}{C}} - CH_2 - Br$

Ans. (i) 2-(2-bromophenyl) ethanol.

(ii) 3-Bromo-2-methylpro-1-ene.

Q. 2. (a) Name the following halides according to IUPAC system and classify them as alkyl, allyl, benzyl (primary, secondary, tertiary), vinyl or aryl halides:

(i) $(CH_3)_2CHCH(Cl)CH_3$

(ii) $CH_3CH_2CH(CH_3)CH(C_2H_5)Cl$

(iii) $CH_3CH_2C(CH_3)_2CH_2I$

(iv) $(CH_3)_3CCH_2CH(Br)C_6H_5$

(v) $CH_3CH(CH_3)CH(Br)CH_3$

(vi) $CH_3C(C_2H_5)_2CH_2Br$

(b) (i) $CH_3C(Cl)(C_2H_5)CH_2CH_3$

(ii) $CH_3CH = C(Cl)CH_2CH(CH_3)_2$

(iii) $CH_3CH = CHC(Br) (CH_3)_2$

(iv) $p\text{-}ClC_6H_4CH_2CH(CH_3)_2$

(v) $m\text{-}ClCH_2C_6H_4CH_2C(CH_3)_3$

(vi) $o\text{-}Br\text{-}C_6H_4CH(CH_3)CH_2CH_3$.

Ans. (a) (i) $\overset{4}{C}H_3 - \overset{3}{\underset{CH_3}{C}}H - \overset{2}{\underset{Cl}{C}}H - \overset{1}{C}H_3$

2-Chloro-3-methylbutane

(Secondary alkyl halide)

(ii) $\overset{6}{C}H_3 - \overset{5}{C}H_2 - \overset{4}{\underset{CH_3}{C}}H - \overset{3}{\underset{Cl}{C}}H - \overset{2}{C}H_2 - \overset{1}{C}H_3$

3-Chloro-4-methylhexane

(Secondary alkyl halide)

(iii) $\overset{4}{C}H_3 - \overset{3}{C}H_2 - \overset{2}{\underset{CH_3}{\overset{CH_3}{C}}} - \overset{1}{C}H_2 - I$

1-Iodo-2, 2-dimethylbutane

(Primary alkyl halide)

(iv) $\overset{4}{C}H_3 - \overset{3}{\underset{CH_3}{\overset{CH_3}{C}}} - \overset{2}{C}H_2 - \overset{1}{\underset{}{C}}H - \bigcirc$

1-Bromo-3, 3-dimethyl-1-phenylbutane

(secondary benzylic halide)

(v) $\overset{4}{C}H_3 - \overset{3}{\underset{CH_3}{C}}H - \overset{2}{\underset{Br}{C}}H - \overset{1}{C}H_3$

2-Bromo-3-methylbutane

(Secondary alkyl halide)

(vi) $CH_3 - \overset{2}{\underset{CH_2}{\overset{C_2H_5}{C}}} - \overset{1}{C}H_2 - Br$ with $\overset{3}{C}H_2 - \overset{4}{C}H_3$

1-Bromo-2-ethyl-2-methylbutane

(Primary alkyl halide)

(b) (i)

$$CH_3 - \overset{3}{C} - \overset{4}{CH_2} - \overset{5}{CH_3}$$

with Cl on C-3, and $\overset{2}{CH_2} - \overset{1}{CH_3}$ branch

3-Chloro-3-methylpentane
(Tertiary alkyl halide)

(ii)

$$\overset{1}{CH_3} - \overset{2}{CH} - \overset{3}{C} - \overset{4}{CH_2} - \overset{5}{CH} - \overset{6}{CH_3}$$

(Cl on C-2, CH_3 on C-3, CH_3 on C-5)

3-Chloro-5-methylhex-2-ene
(Vinyl halide)
[*Halide on the = bonded carbon vinylic position*]

(iii)

$$\overset{1}{CH_3} - \overset{2}{CH} = \overset{3}{CH} - \overset{4}{C} - \overset{5}{CH_3}$$

(Br and CH_3 on C-4)

4-Bromo-4-methylpent-2-ene
(allyl halide)
[*Halide next to = bonded carbon, allylic position*]

(iv)

$$\overset{1'}{CH_2} - \overset{2'}{CH} - \overset{3'}{CH_3}$$

with CH_3 on C-2', attached to benzene ring bearing Cl at position 1

1-Chloro-4-(2-methylpropyl) benzene
(Aryl halide)

(v)

$$\overset{1'}{CH_2} - \overset{2'}{C} - \overset{3'}{CH_3}$$

with CH_3, CH_3 substituents, attached to benzene ring bearing CH_2Cl

1-Chloromethyl-3-(2, 2-dimethylpropyl) benzene
(Primary benzyl halide) or (Benzylic halide)

(vi)

$$CH_3 - \overset{1'}{CH} - \overset{2'}{CH_2} - \overset{3'}{CH_3}$$

with benzene ring bearing Br at position 1

1-Bromo-2-(1-methylpropyl) benzene
(Aryl halide)

Q. 3. Give the IUPAC names of the following compounds:

(i) $CH_3CH(Cl)CH(Br)CH_3$

(ii) $CHF_2CBrClF$

(iii) $ClCH_2C \equiv CCH_2Br$

(iv) $(CCl_3)_3CCl$

(v) $CH_3C(p\text{-}ClC_6H_4)_2CH(Br)CH_3$

(vi) $(CH_3)_3CCH = CClC_6H_4I\text{-}p$

Ans. (i)

$$\overset{4}{CH_3} - \overset{3}{CH} - \overset{2}{CH} - \overset{1}{CH_3}$$

(Cl on C-3, Br on C-2)

2-Bromo-3-chlorobutane

(ii)

$$F - \overset{2}{CH} - \overset{1}{C} - F$$

(F on C-2, Cl and Br on C-1)

1-Bromo-1-chloro-1, 2, 2-trifluoroethane

(iii) $Cl - \overset{4}{CH_2} - \overset{3}{C} \equiv \overset{2}{C} - \overset{1}{CH_2} - Br$

1-Bromo-4-chlorobut-2-yne

(iv)

$$Cl - \overset{1}{C} - \overset{2}{C} - \overset{3}{C} - Cl$$

with CCl_3 group on C-2, and Cl substituents

1, 1, 1, 2, 3, 3, 3-heptachloro-2-(trichloromethyl) propane

(v)

A structure with $\overset{4}{CH_3}$, central $\overset{3}{C}$, two 4-chlorophenyl groups, $\overset{2}{CH_3} - Br$ and $\overset{1}{CH_3}$

2-Bromo-3, 3-bis (4-chlorophenyl) butane

(vi)

$$Cl - \overset{1}{C} = \overset{2}{CH} - \overset{3}{C} - CH_3$$

with CH_3 on C-3, and 4-iodophenyl group on C-1

1-chloro-1- (4-iodophenyl)-3, 3-dimethylbut-1-ene

Q. 4. Write IUPAC name of the following:

(i)

$$CH_2 - CH = CH - CH_2$$

with Br on each terminal CH_2

(ii) $I - CH_2 - CH - CH_2 - CH_2 - CH_2 - CH_2 - CH_3$

with benzene ring bearing Cl attached to C

(iii)

Cyclohexane bearing CH_2Cl

(iv)

Benzene ring bearing $CH_2 - CH_2 - Cl$

(v)

Benzene ring bearing CH_3 and I

Ans. (i)   1, 4-Dibromobut-2-ene.

(ii)   2-(2-chlorophenyl)-1-iodoheptane.

(iii)   Chloromethyl cyclohexane.

(iv)   (2-chloroethyl)-benzene.

(v)   1-iodo-2-methylbenzene.

Q. 5. Write the IUPAC name of the following compound:*

$$CH_3 - O - \overset{\overset{\displaystyle CH_3}{|}}{\underset{\underset{\displaystyle CH_3}{|}}{C}} - CH_3$$

Ans. $H_3C - O - \overset{\overset{\displaystyle CH_3}{|}}{\underset{\underset{\displaystyle CH_3}{|}}{C}} - CH_3$

2-Methoxy-2 methyl-propane

Q. 6. Write the structure of 1-Bromo-4-chlorobut-2-ene.*

Ans. $BrCH_2CH = CHCH_2Cl.$

Q. 7. Write the structure of 2, 4-dinitrochlorobenzene.*

Ans.

(2, 4-dinitrochlorobenzene)

Q. 8. Write the structure of 3-Bromo-2-methylprop-1-ene.*

Ans. $BrCH_2(CH_3)C = CH_2.$

Q. 9. Write the structures of the following organic halogen compounds.

(i)   2-Chloro-3-methylpentane

(ii)   *p*-Bromochlorobenzene

(iii)   1-Chloro-4-ethylcyclohexane

(iv)   2-(2-Chlorophenyl)-1-iodooctane

(v)   Perfluorobenzene

(vi)   4-tert-Butyl-3-iodoheptane

(vii)   1-Bromo-4-sec-butyl-2-methylbenzene

(viii) 1, 4-Dibromobut-2-ene.

Ans. (i) $\overset{1}{C}H_3 - \overset{\overset{\displaystyle Cl}{|}}{\overset{2}{C}H} - \overset{\overset{\displaystyle CH_3}{|}}{\overset{3}{C}H} - \overset{4}{C}H_2 - \overset{5}{C}H_3$

2-Chloro-3-methylpentane

(ii)

p-Bromochlorobenzene

1-Chloro-4-ethylcyclohexane

(iv) $I - \overset{1}{C}H_2 - \overset{2}{C}H - \overset{3}{C}H_2 - \overset{4}{C}H_2 - \overset{5}{C}H_2 - \overset{6}{C}H_2 - \overset{7}{C}H_2 - \overset{8}{C}H_3$

2-(2-Chlorophenyl)-1-iodooctane

(v)

Perfluoro benzene

(vi) $\overset{1}{C}H_3 - \overset{2}{C}H_2 - \overset{3}{C}H - \overset{4}{C}H - \overset{5}{C}H_2 - \overset{6}{C}H_2 - \overset{7}{C}H_3$

4-Tert-Butyl-3-iodoheptane

(vii) $CH_3 - CH - CH_2 - CH_3$

1-Bromo-4-sec-butyl-2-methylbenzene

(viii) $Br - \overset{1}{C}H_2 - \overset{2}{C}H = \overset{3}{C}H - \overset{4}{C}H_2 - Br$

1, 4-Dibromobut-2-ene

Q. 10. Write structures of the following compounds:*

(i)   2-Chloro-3-methylpentane

(ii)   1-Chloro-4-ethylcyclohexane

(iii)   4-tert. Butyl-3-iodoheptane

(iv)   1, 4-Dibromobut-2-ene

(v)   1-Bromo-4-sec. butyl-2-methylbenzene.

Ans. (i) $\overset{1}{C}H_3 - \overset{\overset{\displaystyle Cl}{|}}{\overset{2}{C}H} - \overset{\overset{\displaystyle CH_3}{|}}{\overset{3}{C}H} - \overset{4}{C}H - \overset{5}{C}H_3$

2–Chloro–3–methylpentane

(ii)

1-Chloro-4-ethylcyclohexane

(iii) $\overset{1}{C}H_3 - \overset{2}{C}H_2 - \overset{3}{C}H - \overset{4}{C}H - \overset{5}{C}H_2 - \overset{6}{C}H_2 - \overset{7}{C}H_3$

with substituents: I on C-3, and $CH_3 - \underset{CH_3}{\overset{|}{C}} - CH_3$ ($CH_3 - C - CH_3$ with CH_3) on C-4

4-tert-Butyl-3-iodoheptane

(iv) $Br - \overset{1}{C}H_2 - \overset{2}{C}H = \overset{3}{C}H - \overset{4}{C}H_2 - Br$

1, 4-Dibromobut-2-ene

(v) Br at C-1, CH_3 at C-2 on a benzene ring (positions 1–6)

(v) $CH_3 - CH - CH_2 - CH_3$

Q. 11. Write structures of different dihalogen derivatives of propane.

Ans. There are four different dihalogen derivatives of propane. The structures of these derivatives are shown below.

(i) $Br - \underset{Br}{\overset{|}{C}H} - CH_2 - CH_3$

1, 1-Dibromopropane

(ii) $CH_3 - \underset{Br}{\overset{Br}{\overset{|}{C}}} - CH_3$

2, 2-Dibromopropane

(iii) $Br - CH_2 - \underset{Br}{\overset{|}{C}H} - CH_3$

1, 3-Dibromopropane

(iv) $Br - CH_2 - CH_2 - CH_2 - Br$

1, 3-Dibromopropane

Chapter 11. Alcohols, Phenols and Ethers

Q. 1. Write the IUPAC names of the following compounds :*

(i) $CH_3 - \underset{CH_3}{\overset{CH_3}{\overset{|}{\underset{|}{C}}}} - CH_2 - CH_2 - OH$

(ii) $CH_3 - CH = CH - \underset{OH}{\overset{|}{C}H} - CH_2 - CH_3$

(iii) $\langle benzene\ ring \rangle - CH_2 - CH_2 - OH$

Ans. (i) 3, 3-Dimethylbutan-1-ol.

(ii) Hex-4-en-2ol

(iii) 2-Phenyl ethanol.

Q. 2. Write the IUPAC name of :*

(i) $CH_3 - \underset{CH_3}{\overset{OC_2H_5}{\overset{|}{\underset{|}{C}}}} - OH$

(ii) $C_2H_5 - O - \underset{CH_3}{\overset{|}{C}H} - C_2H_5$

Ans. (i) 2-Ethoxy-propan-2-ol

(ii) 2-Ethoxybutane.

Q. 3. Write the IUPAC name of the following compounds:*

(i) $CH_3 - \underset{CH_3}{\overset{|}{C}H} - CH_2 - OH$

(ii) $C_2H_5 - O - \underset{CH_3}{\overset{|}{C}H} - C_2H_5$

Ans. (i) 2-Methylpropan-1-ol

(ii) 2-Bromo-3-methylbut-2-en-1-ol.

Q. 4. Write IUPAC name of the following compounds:

(i) $CH_3 - \underset{CH_2}{\overset{|}{C}H} - \underset{OH}{\overset{|}{C}H} - \underset{C_2H_5}{\overset{|}{C}H} - \underset{OH}{\overset{|}{C}H} - CH_3$

(ii) cyclohexane with NO_2 and OCH_3 substituents

Ans. (i) 3-Ethyl-5-methylhexane-2, 4-diol

(ii) 1-Methoxy-3-nitrocyclohexane.

Q. 5. Write IUPAC names of the following compounds :

(i) $CH_3 - \underset{CH_3}{\overset{|}{C}H} - \underset{OH}{\overset{|}{C}H} - \underset{CH_3}{\overset{CH_3}{\overset{|}{\underset{|}{C}}}} - CH_3$

(ii) $H_3C - \underset{OH}{\overset{|}{C}H} - CH_2 - \underset{OH}{\overset{|}{C}H} - \underset{C_2H_5}{\overset{|}{C}H} - CH_2 - CH_3$

(iii) $CH_3 - \underset{OH}{\overset{|}{C}H} - \underset{OH}{\overset{|}{C}H} - CH_3$

(iv) $HO - CH_2 - \underset{OH}{\overset{|}{C}H} - CH_2 - OH$

(v) benzene ring with CH_3 and OH substituents

(vi)

CH_3 — (benzene ring, para) — OH

(vii)

CH_3, (benzene ring) — OH, CH_3

(viii)

CH_3, (benzene ring) — OH, CH_3

(ix) $CH_3 - O - CH_2 - \underset{\underset{CH_3}{|}}{CH} - CH_3$

(x) $C_6H_5 - O - C_2H_5$

(xi) $C_6H_5 - I - C_7H_{15}\ (n-)$

(xii) $CH_3 - CH_2 - O - \underset{\underset{CH_3}{|}}{CH} - CH_2 - CH_3$

Ans. (i) 2, 2, 4-Trimethylpentan-3-ol

(ii) 5-Ethylheptan-2, 4-diol

(iii) Butane-2, 3-diol

(iv) Propane-1, 2, 3-triol

(v) 2-Methylphenol

(vi) 4-Methylphenol

(vii) 2, 5-Dimethylphenol

(viii) 2, 6-Dimethylphenol

(ix) 1-methoxy-2 methyl propane

(x) Ethoxybenzene

(xi) 1-phenoxyheptane

(xii) 2-Ethoxybutane.

Q. 6. Give IUPAC names of the following ethers:

(i) $C_2H_5OCH_2 - \underset{\underset{CH_3}{|}}{CH} - CH_3$

(ii) $CH_3OCH_2CH_2Cl$

(iii) $O_2N - C_6H_4 - OCH_3(p)$

(iv) $CH_3CH_2CH_2OCH_3$

(v) H_3C CH_3 (cyclohexane) — OC_2H_5

(vi) (benzene ring) — OC_2H_5

Ans. (i) 1-Ethoxy-2-methylpropane

(ii) 2-Chloro-1-methoxyethane

(iii) 4-Nitroanisole

(iv) 1-Methoxypropane

(v) 4-Ethoxy-1-dimethyl cyclohexane

(vi) Ethoxybenzene.

Q. 7. Name the following compounds according to IUPAC system:

(i) $CH_3 - CH_2 - \underset{\underset{CH_2Cl}{|}}{CH} - \overset{\overset{CH_2OH}{|}}{OH} - \underset{\underset{CH_3}{|}}{CH} - CH_3$

(ii) $CH_3 - \underset{\underset{CH_3}{|}}{CH} - CH_2 - \underset{\underset{OH}{|}}{CH} - \overset{\overset{CH_2OH}{|}}{C} - CH_3$

(iii) (cyclohexane with OH and Br)

(iv) $H_2C = CH - \underset{\underset{OH}{|}}{CH} - CH_2 - CH_2 - CH_3$

(v) $CH_3 - \underset{\underset{CH_3}{|}}{C} = \underset{\underset{Br}{|}}{C} - CH_2OH$

Ans. (i) 3-Chloromethyl-2-isopropylpentan-1-ol

(ii) 2, 5-Dimetylhexane-1, 3-diol

(iii) 3-Bromocyclohexanol

(iv) Hex-1-en-3-ol

(v) 2-Bromo-3-methylbut-2-en-1-ol

Q. 8. Write the IUPAC name of the following :*

$CH_3 - \underset{\underset{C_2H_5}{|}}{\overset{\overset{CH_3}{|}}{C}} - \underset{\underset{OH}{|}}{CH} - CH_3$

Ans. The IUPAC name would be 3, 3-Dimethyl-pentan-2-ol.

Q. 9. Write the IUPAC name of the following compound:*

$H_3C - \underset{\underset{CH_3}{|}}{C} = \underset{\underset{Br}{|}}{C} - CH_2 - OH$

Ans. $H_3\overset{4}{C} - \underset{\underset{CH_3}{|}}{\overset{3}{C}} = \underset{\underset{Br}{|}}{\overset{2}{C}} - \overset{1}{C}H_2 - OH$

2-bromo-3-methyl-but-2-en-1-ol

Q. 10. Write the IUPAC name of the following compound.*

(benzene ring) — $CH = CH - CH_2 - H$

Ans. (benzene ring) — $CH = CH - CH_2 - H$

1-Phenylprop-1-en-3-ol

Q. 11. Write structures of the compounds whose IUPAC names are as follows:

(i) 2-Methylbutan-2-ol

(ii) 1-Phenylpropan-2-ol

(iii) 3, 5-Dimethylhexane-1, 3, 5-triol

(iv) 2, 3-Diethylphenol

(v) 1-Ethoxypropane

(vi) 2-Ethoxy-3-methylpentane

(vii) Cyclohexylmethanol

(viii) 3-Cyclohexylpentan-3-ol

(ix) Cyclopent-3-en-1-ol

(x) 3-Chloromethylpentan-1-ol.

Ans. (i)
$$CH_3 - \overset{OH}{\underset{CH_3}{C}} = CH_2 - CH_3$$

(ii) 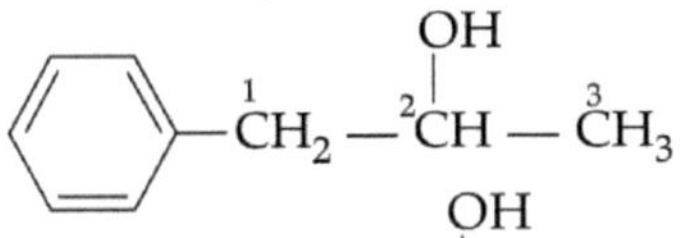 $C_6H_5 - CH_2 - \overset{OH}{CH} - CH_3$

or $C_6H_5 - CH_2 = \overset{OH}{CH} - CH_3$

(iii) $OH - CH_2 - CH_2 - \overset{OH}{\underset{CH_3}{C}} - CH_2 - \overset{OH}{\underset{CH_3}{C}} - CH_3$

(iv) 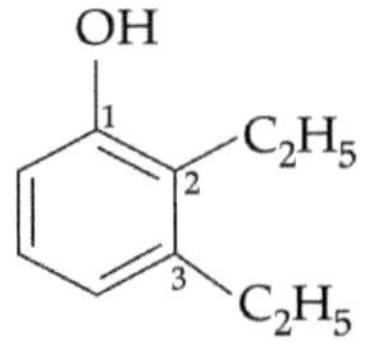 Phenol with C_2H_5 at position 2 and C_2H_5 at position 3.

(v) $CH_3 - CH_2 - O - CH_2 - CH_2 - CH_3$

(vi) $CH_3 - CH_2 - O - \overset{CH_3}{\underset{CH_3}{CH}} - CH - CH_2 - CH_3$

(vii) 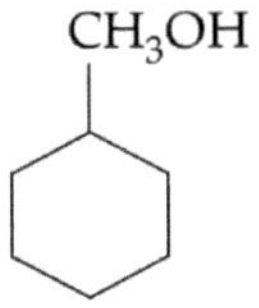 Cyclohexane with CH_3OH substituent.

(viii) $CH_3 - CH_2 - \overset{OH}{\underset{\text{cyclohexyl}}{C}} - CH_2 - CH_3$

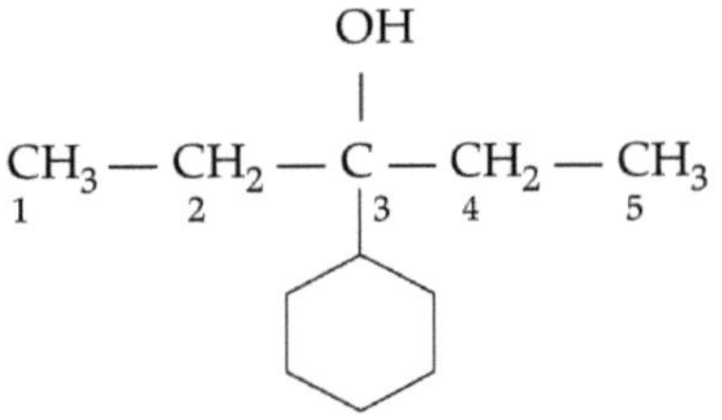

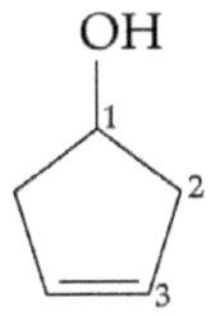

(ix) Cyclopentene with OH.

(x) $CH_3 - CH_2 - \overset{CH_2Cl}{CH} - CH_2 - CH_2 - OH$

Chapter 12. Aldehydes, Ketones and Carboxylic Acids

Q. 1. Write the IUPAC name of CH_3OCl.

Ans. Ethanoyl chloride.

Q. 2. Write IUPAC name of the compound

$$CH_3 - \overset{}{\underset{CH_3}{CH}} - CO - \overset{}{\underset{CH_3}{CH}} - CH_3 \,^*$$

Ans. 2, 4-Dimethylpentan-3-one.

Q. 3. Write IUPAC name of the following:*

(i) $CH_3 - C \equiv C - CH = CH - \overset{O}{\overset{\|}{C}} - OH$

(ii) 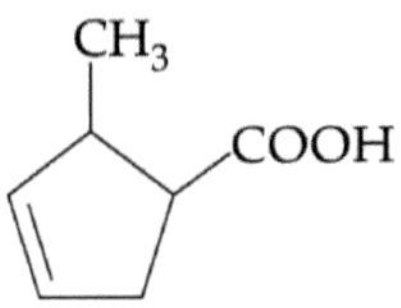 Cyclopentene with CH_3 and COOH substituents.

Ans. (i) Hex-2-en-4ynoic acid

(ii) 2-Methylcyclopenten-3-enecarboxylic acid

Q. 4. Write IUPAC names for the following:

(i) 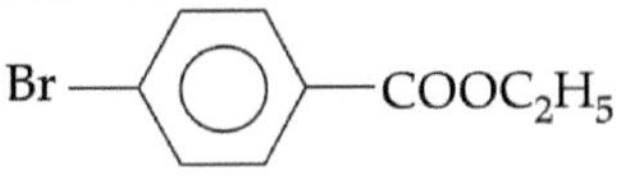 $Br - C_6H_4 - COOC_2H_5$

(ii) $CH_3 - CH_2 - \overset{NH_2}{CH} - \overset{O}{\underset{\|}{C}} - OCH_3$

Ans. (i) Ethyl-4-Bromobenzoate

(ii) Methyl 2-amine-butyrate/butanoate

Q. 5. Write the IUPAC names of the following:*

(i) $CH_3 - \overset{O}{\overset{\|}{C}} - CH_2 - \overset{O}{\overset{\|}{C}} - OCH_3$

(ii) 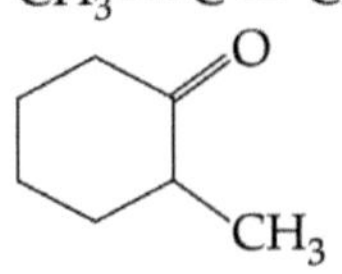 Cyclohexanone with CH_3 substituent.

(iii) $C_6H_5 - CH = CH - \overset{O}{\overset{\|}{C}} - H$

Ans. (i)   Pentane-2, 4-dione

    (ii)   2-Methylcyclohexanone

    (iii)   3-Phenylprop-2-enal.

Q. 6. Write IUPAC names of:

    (i) $CH_2 — COOH$
         |
         $CH_2 — COOH$

    (ii)

    (iii) $CH_3CH_2\ \overset{\displaystyle|}{\underset{\displaystyle CHO}{CH}} — COOH$

Ans. (i)   Butan-1, 4-dioic acid

    (ii)   4-Methylhexanoic acid

    (iii)   2-Formylbutanoic acid.

Q. 7. Name the following compounds according to IUPAC system of nomenclature:

    (i) $CH_3CH(CH_3)CH_2CH_2CHO$

    (ii) $CH_3CH_2COCH(C_2H_5)CH_2CH_2Cl$

    (iii) $CH_3CH = CHCHO$

    (iv) $CH_3COCH_2COCH_3$

    (v) $CH_3CH(CH_3)CH_2C(CH_3)_2COCH_3$

    (vi) $(CH_3)_3CCH_2COOH$

    (vii) $OHCC_6H_4CHO$.

Ans.

    (i)   4-methylpentanal

    (ii)   6-Chloro-4-ethylhexan-3-one

    (iii)   But-2-en-1-al

    (iv)   Pentane-2, 4-dione

    (v)   3, 3, 5-Trimethylhexan-2-one

    (vi)   3, 3-Dimethylbutanoic acid

    (vii)   Benzene-1, 4-dicarbaldehyde.

Q. 8. Write the IUPAC names of the following ketones and aldehydes. Wherever possible, also give common names.

    (i) $CH_3CO(CH_2)_4CH_3$

    (ii) $CH_3CH_2CHBrCH_2CH(CH_3)CHO$

    (iii) $CH_3(CH_2)_5CHO$

    (iv) $Ph—CH = CH — CHO$

    (v)

    (vi)   PhCOPh

Ans. (i) $CH_3CO(CH_2)_4CH_3$
         IUPAC Name : Heptan-2-one
         Common Name : Methyl-*n*-pentyl ketone.

    (ii) $CH_3CH_2CHBrCH_2CH(CH_3)CHO$
         IUPAC Name : 4-Bromo-2-methylhexanal
         Common Name : (γ-Bromo-α-methyl-caproaldehyde)

    (iii) $CH_3(CH_2)_5CHO$

         IUPAC Name : Heptanal

    (iv) $Ph – CH = CH – CHO$
         IUPAC Name : 3-phenylprop-2-enal
         Common name : Cinnamaldehyde.

    (v)
         IUPAC Name : Cyclopentanecarbaldehyde

    (vi)   PhCOPh
         IUPAC Name : Diphenylmethanone
         Common Name : Benzophenone.

Q. 9. Give the IUPAC names of the following compounds:

    (i) $PhCH_2CH_2COOH$

    (ii) $(CH_3)_2C = CHCOOH$

    (iii)

    (iv)

Ans. (i)   3-Phenylpropanoic acid

    (ii)   3-Methylbut-2-enoic acid

    (iii)   2-Methylcyclopentanecarboxylic acid

    (iv)   2, 4, 6-Trinitrobenzoic acid.

Q. 10. Draw the structures of the following compounds:

    (i)   3-methylbutanal

    (ii)   *p*-Nitropropiophenone

    (iii)   *p*-Methylbenzaldehyde

    (iv)   4-Methylpent-3-en-2-one

    (v)   4-Chloropentan-2-one

    (vi)   3-Bromo-4-phenylpentanoic acid

    (vii)   *p, p*'-Dihydroxybenzophenone

    (viii)   Hex-2-en-4-ynoic acid

Ans. (i) $H_3C — \overset{\displaystyle CH_3}{\overset{\displaystyle |}{C}} — CH — CH_2 — \overset{\displaystyle O}{\overset{\displaystyle ||}{C}} — H$
         3-Methylbutanal

    (ii) O_2N—(ring)—$\overset{\displaystyle O}{\overset{\displaystyle ||}{C}} — CH_2 — CH_3$
         p-Nitropropiophenone

    (iii) H_3C—(ring)—$\overset{\displaystyle O}{\overset{\displaystyle ||}{C}} — H$
         p-Methylbenzaldehyde

    (iv) $H_3C — \overset{\displaystyle O}{\overset{\displaystyle ||}{C}} — CH = \overset{\displaystyle CH_3}{\overset{\displaystyle |}{C}} — CH_3$
         4-Methylpent-3-en-2-one

(v) $H_3C - \overset{\overset{O}{\|}}{C} - CH = \overset{\overset{Cl}{|}}{C} - CH_3$
4-Chloropentan-2-one

(vi) $H_3C - \overset{\overset{C_6H_5}{|}}{CH} - \overset{\overset{Br}{|}}{CH} - CH_2 - \overset{\overset{O}{\|}}{C} - OH$
3-Bromo-4-phenylpentanoic acid

(vii) HO—⟨benzene⟩—$\overset{\overset{O}{\|}}{C}$—⟨benzene⟩—OH
p, p'-Dihydroxybenzophenone

(viii) $H_3C - C \equiv C - CH = CH - \overset{\overset{O}{\|}}{C} - OH$
Hex-2-en-4-ynoic acid

Chapter 13. Amines

Q. 1. Write IUPAC name of

$CH_3 - CH_2 - CH_2 - N{\overset{\displaystyle CH_3}{\underset{\displaystyle C_2H_5}{}}}$

Ans. N-ethyl-N-methyl propanamine.

Q. 2. Write IUPAC name of sulphanilic acid.

Ans. ⟨benzene ring with NH₂ and SO₃H⟩ , 4-Aminobenzenesulphonic acid

Sulphanilic acid.

Q. 3. Write IUPAC name of the following:

⟨benzene⟩—$\overset{+}{N}H(CH_3)_2 \overset{-}{O}C\overset{\overset{O}{\|}}{O}CH_3$

Ans. N, N-Dimethylaniliniumethanoate.

Q. 4. Give IUPAC names of the following compounds:*

(i) $CH_3 - CH_2 - CH_2 - N{\overset{\displaystyle CH_3}{\underset{\displaystyle C_2H_5}{}}}$

(ii) ⟨benzene ring with N(CH₃)₂ and NO₂⟩

Ans. (i) N-Ethyl-N-methyl propanamine
(ii) 4-Nitro, N, N-dimethylbenzamine.

Q. 5. Write IUPAC names of the following compounds and classify them into primary, secondary and tertiary amines.

(i) $(CH_3)_2CHNH_2$
(ii) $CH_3(CH_2)_2NH_2$
(iii) $CH_3NHCH(CH_3)_2$
(iv) $(CH_3)_3CNH_2$
(v) $C_6H_5NHCH_3$
(vi) $(CH_3CH_2)_2NCH_3$
(vii) *m*-$BrC_6H_4NH_2$

Ans. (i) Propan-2-amine   (1° amine)
(ii) Propan-1-amine   (1° amine)
(iii) N-methylpropan-2-amine   (2° amine)
(iv) 2-Methylpropan-2-amine   (1° amine)
(v) N-Methylbenzamine or N-methylaniline
                                        (2° amine)
(vi) N-Ethyl-N-methylethanamine   (3° amine)
(vii) 3-Bromobenzenamine or 3-bromoaniline
                                        (1° amine).

Q. 6. Write IUPAC name of the following compound:*
$CH_3NHCH(CH_3)_2$

Ans. N-methylpropan-2-amine.

Q. 7. Write IUPAC name of the following compound:*
$(CH_3)_2N–CH_2CH_3$

Ans. N, N-dimethylethanamine.

Q. 8. Write IUPAC name of the following compound:*
$(CH_3CH_2)_2NCH_3$

Ans. N-Ethyl-N-methylethanamine.

□□

Very Short Questions | Set 4 |

Q. 1. **What is the effect of presence of Schottky defect and Frenkel defect on the density of a crystal?**
Ans. In case of Schottky defect density decreases, in case of Frenkel defect the density remains same.

Q. 2. **What type of crystal defect is produced when NaCl is doped with $MgCl_2$?***
Ans. As each Mg^{2+} will replace two Na^+ in the crystal lattice hence cationic vacancy defect will be created.

Q. 3. **What is the coordination number of each type of ions in a rock salt type crystal structure?***
Ans. Rock salt has fcc structure. Hence each ion has 6 neighbouring opposite ions.

Q. 4. **What type of semiconductor is obtained when silicon is doped with arsenic?***
Ans. Arsenic has more valence electrons than silicon, hence n-type semiconductor is obtained.

Q. 5. **Which type of alignment in crystals makes them ferromagnetic?**
Ans. In ferromagnetic substances, magnetic dipoles (units) are parallel to one another, resulting in strong magnetic field attraction.

Q. 6. **What is meant by the term 'forbidden zone' in reference to band theory of solids?***
Ans. By 'forbidden zone' it means the large energy gap between conduction band and valence band in case of an insulator specially. These bands are formed by the combination of atomic orbitals to form molecular orbitals.

Q. 7. **Name the non-stoichiometric point defect responsible for the colour of alkali metal halides.***
Ans. Metal excess defect is responsible for the colour of alkali metal halides.

Q. 8. **Classify the following as amorphous or crystalline solids:**
Polyurethane, naphthalene, benzoic acid, teflon, potassium nitrate, cellophane, polyvinyl chloride, fibre glass, copper.
Ans. Amorphous solids : Polyurethane, teflon, cellophane, polyvinyl chloride, fibre glass.
Crystalline solids : Naphthalene, benzoic acid, potassium nitrate, copper.

Q. 9. **Classify the following solids in different categories based on the nature of intermolecular forces operating in them:**
Potassium sulphate, tin, benzene, urea, ammonia, water, zinc sulphide, graphite, rubidium, argon, silicon carbide.
Ans. Potassium sulphate → Ionic solid
Tin → Metallic solid
Benzene → Molecular (non-polar) solid
Urea → Polar molecular solid
Ammonia → Polar molecular solid
Water → Hydrogen bonded molecular solid
Zinc sulphide → Ionic solid
Graphite → Covalent or network solid
Rubidium → Metallic solid
Argon → Non-polar molecular solid
Silicon carbide → Covalent or network solid

Q. 10. **Solid A is a very hard electrical insulator in solid as well as in molten state and melts at extremely high temperature. What type of solid is it?**
Ans. The given properties are the properties of a covalent or network solid. Therefore, the given solid is a covalent or network solid.

* are board exam questions from previous years

Q. 11. **What type of solids are electrical conductors, malleable and ductile?**

Ans. Metallic solids are electrical conductors, malleable and ductile.

Q. 12. **Classify each of the following solids as ionic, metallic, molecular, network (covalent) or amorphous.**

    (i) Tetra phosphorus decaoxide (P_4O_{10})   (vii) Graphite

    (ii) Ammonium phosphate ($(NH_4)_3PO_4$)   (viii) Brass

    (iii) SiC   (ix) Rb

    (iv) I_2 (x) LiBr

    (v) P_4 (xi) Si

    (vi) Plastic

Ans. Ionic $\rightarrow$ (ii) Ammonium phosphate ($(NH_4)_3PO_4$, (x) LiBr.

    Metallic $\rightarrow$ (viii) Brass, (ix) Rb.

    Molecular $\rightarrow$ (i) Tetra phosphorus decaoxide (P_4O_{10}), (iv) I_2, (v) P_4.

    Covalent (network) $\rightarrow$ (iii) SiC, (vii) Graphite, (xi) Si.

    Amorphous $\rightarrow$ (vi) Plastic.

Q. 13. **Classify each of the following as being either a *p*-type or an *n*-type semiconductor:**

    (i) Ge doped with In,   (ii) B doped with Si.

Ans. (i) Ge (a group 14 element) is doped with In (a group 13 element). Therefore, a hole will be created and the semiconductor generated will be a *p*-type semiconductor.

    (ii) B (a group 13 element) is doped with Si (a group 14 element). So, there will be an extra electron and the semiconductor generated will be an *n*-type semiconductor.

Q. 14. **In a closed pack arrangement of N-spheres how many (i) tetrahedral and (ii) octahedral sites are present?**[*]

Ans. Number of octahedral voids = No. of atoms in the closed pack arrangement *i.e.*, (n)

    Number of tetrahedral voids = 2 × No. of atoms present in the closed pack arrangement *i.e.*, ($2 \times n$).

Q. 15. **Find out the number of atoms per unit cell in a face centered cubic structure having only single atom (like pure metals) at its lattice points.**[*]

Ans. Number of atoms per unit cell in a fcc structure is:

$$N = 8 \text{ (corners)} \times \frac{1}{8} + 6 \text{ (face centres)} \times \frac{1}{2} = 1 + 3 = 4.$$

Q. 16. **Analysis shows that FeO has a non-stoichiometric composition with formula $Fe_{0.95}O$. Give reason.**[*]

Ans. FeO crystal is difficult to prepare in stoichiometric composition and contains less amount of Fe metal compared to stoichiometric proportion. In this crystal some Fe^{2+} ions are missing and the loss of positive charge is made up by the presence of required number of Fe^{3+} ions.

Q. 17. **In order to arrange 50 lemons and a circular plate in an orderly manner. Which mode of packing should be used?**

Q. 18. **Name any substance which on addition of AgCl causes cationic vacancy in it.**[*]

Ans. $CdCl_2$ or $SrCl_2$ (Cations with higher valencies than Ag).

Q. 19. **Write a distinguishing feature of metallic solids.**

Ans. Metallic solids can conduct electricity in solid state.

Q. 20. **Which point defect in its crystal units increases the density of a solid?**

Ans. Interstitial defect.

Q. 21. **Name the type of point defect that occurs in a crystal of zinc sulphide?**

Ans. Frenkel defect (Zn^{2+} ions can occupy the interstitial sites).

Q. 22. **Give an example of molecular solid and ionic solid.**[*]

Ans. Molecular solid : Ice

    Ionic solid : $CaCl_2$

Q. 23. **What type of stoichiometric defect is shown by:**

    (i) ZnS   (ii) AgBr

Ans. (i)   ZnS shows Frenkel defect.

(ii) AgBr shows Frenkel defect as well as Schottky defect.

Q. 24. What is the coordination number of atoms:

(i)   in a cubic close-packed structure?

(ii) in a body-centred cubic structure?

Ans. The coordination number of atoms

(i)   in a cubic close-packed structure is 12.

(ii) in a body-centred cubic structure is 8.

Chapter 2. Solutions

Q. 1. How is solubility of gas in a liquid affected by pressure?

Ans. Solubility of gas increases with increase of pressure.

Q. 2. What are completely miscible liquids?

Ans. Liquids that mix with each other irrespective of the proportions they are mixed with it are called completely miscible liquids.

Q. 3. What are azeotropes? Give an example.

Ans. An azeotrope is a mixture of two or more liquids whose proportions cannot be altered by simple distillation because their composition is unchanged by distillation, azeotropes are also called constant boiling mixture.

Example : 95% ethanol and 5% water mixture has a boiling point 78.17°C. This is a minimum boiling azeotropic mixture.

Q. 4. State the situation in which reverse osmosis occurs.

Ans. If the external pressure applied is greater than the osmotic pressure of a solution then reverse osmosis takes place.

Q. 5. Suppose a solid solution is formed between two substances, one whose particles are very large and the other whose particles are very small. What type of solid solution is this likely to be?

Ans. The solution likely to be formed is interstitial solid solution.

Q. 6. What role does the molecular interaction plays in solution of alcohol and water?

Ans. Water and alcohol molecules interact very strongly with each other (due to hydrogen bonding) leading to complete miscibility.

Q. 7. What type of deviations are shown by the solution of carbon disulphide and acetone.

Ans. Positive deviation.

Q. 8. Two liquids X and Y boil at 110°C and 130°C respectively. Which one of the following has higher vapour pressure at 50°C?

Ans. Liquid X.

Q. 9. What is the value of van't Hoff factor (i) for a solution when the solute undergoes association?

Ans. $i < 1$.

Q. 10. Name the property in which number of moles of solute dissolved per kg of the solvent that is independent of temperature.

Ans. Molality (m).

Q. 11. Which solutions obeys Raoult's law over entire range of concentration?

Ans. Ideal solution.

Q. 12. What is the extent of dissociation or association or the ratio of the observed colligative property to the calculated colligative property known as?

Ans. Van't Hoff Factor (i).

Chapter 3. Electrochemistry

Q. 1. Give the cell notation of a galvanic cell.

Ans. B$Zn(s)|Zn^{2+}(aq)||Cu^{2+}(aq)|Cu(s)$.

Q. 2. How does fuel cell operate? Give one example.

Ans. In a fuel cell, chemical energy of a fuel is converted into electrical energy.

Example : $H_2 - O_2$ fuel cell.

Q. 3. What is a primary cell? Give an example.*

Ans. Cells which are not rechargeable are primary cells. The products cannot be converted into reactants.

Example : Dry cell or Leclanche cell.

Q. 4. Write the correct representation of the following cell:

$$Fe(s) + 2Ag^+(aq) \longrightarrow Fe^{2+}(aq) + 2Ag(s)$$

Ans. $Fe(s) | Fe^{2+}(aq) || Ag^+ (aq) | Ag(s)$

Q. 5. State Faraday's first law of electrolysis.

Ans. Faraday's First Law : Mass of any substance deposited is proportional to the quantity of electricity passing through the electrolyte

$$W = ZIt$$

Z = Electrochemical equivalent

I = Current; t = Time in sec.

Q. 6. What is a concentration cell?

Ans. A concentration cell is an electrolytic cell that is comprised of two half cells with the same electrodes, but differing in concentrations.

Example : $Zn|Zn^{2+} (C_1)|Anode || Zn^{2+} (C_2) + Zn | Cathode$.

Q. 7. Arrange the following metals in the order in which they displace each other from the solution of their salts. Al, Cu, Fe, Mg and Zn.

Ans. The following is the order in which the given metals displace each other from the solution of their salts based on reactivity series.

$$Mg > Al > Zn > Fe > Cu$$

Q. 8. Write the name of the cell which is generally used in transistors. Write the reactions taking place at the anode and the cathode of this cell.*

Ans. Dry cells are used in transistors.

At anode $\qquad\qquad\qquad Zn \longrightarrow Zn^{2+} + 2e^-$

At cathode $\qquad 2NH_4^+(aq.) + 2MnO_2(s) + 2e^- \longrightarrow 2MnO (OH) + 2NH_3$

Q. 9. What is the EMF of hydrogen electrode?

Ans. 0.0 V.

Q. 10. Which of the following cell (or battery) is used in automobiles and power inverters? Laclanche cell, mercury cell, lead storage battery.

Ans. Lead storage battery.

Q. 11. What is the unit of equivalent conductance?

Ans. $Ohm^{-1} cm^2 equiv^{-1}$.

Q. 12. Which of the cells can convert chemical energy of H_2 and O_2 directly into dectrial energy?

Ans. Fuel cell.

Q. 13. How much number of Faradays are required to reduce one mole of Cu^{+2} to metallic copper?

Ans. Two.

Q. 14. Name the cell used in hearing aids and watches.*

Ans. Mercury cell.

---

* are board exam questions from previous years

Q. 15. **How much charge in terms of Faraday is required to reduce one mol of MnO_4^- to Mn^{2+} ?***

Ans. $2 \times 96500 = 193,000$ F.

Chapter 4. Chemical Kinetics

Q. 1. **Does a zero order reaction has molecularity equal to zero?**

Ans. Molecularity of a reaction can never be zero.

Q. 2. **Give example of a reaction in which order and molecularity are equal.***

Ans. Decomposition of hydrogen iodide;

i.e., $2HI(g) \longrightarrow H_2(s) + I2(g)$; here order and molecularity are both 2.

Q. 3. **Give an example of pseudo first order reaction.***

Ans. Inversion of cane sugar:

$$C_{12}H_{22}O_{11} + H_2O \xrightarrow{H^+} C_6H_{12}O_6 + C_6H_{12}O_6$$

Cane sugar   (Excess)   Glucose   Fructose

Rate = $k[C_{12}H_{22}O_{11}]^1 [H_2O]^0$.

Q. 4. **For a reaction : $A + H_2O \longrightarrow B$,**

Rate $\propto [A]$

What is the (i) Molecularity, (ii) Order of the reaction?

Ans. (i)   It is a pseudo unimolecular reaction.

(ii)   Order is 1.

Q. 5. **Mention the factors that affect the rate of a chemical reaction.**

Ans. The factors that affect the rate of a reaction are as follows.

(i)   Concentration of reactants (pressure in case of gases).

(ii)   Temperature.

(iii) Presence of catalyst.

Q. 6. **A reaction is 50% complete in 2 hrs and 75% complete in 4 hrs. What is the order of the reaction?***

Ans. It is a first order reaction as in case of 1st order reaction half life period is independent of initial concentration,

i.e., $t_{1/2} = \dfrac{0.693}{k}$.

As 50% reaction is completed in 2 hrs and remaining half complete in 4 hrs. suggested that;

$$t_{75\%} = 2\, t_{50\%}$$

so first order reaction.

Q. 7. **What is the order of photochemical reactions?**

Ans. Zero order.

Q. 8. **For a reaction, $Cl_2(g) + 2NO(g) \longrightarrow 2NOCl(g)$, the rate law is expressed as; rate = $k[Cl_2][NO]^2$. What is the order of the reaction?***

Ans. Rate law; R = $k[Cl_2][NO]^2$

Hence order = $1 + 2 = 3$

Its a 3rd order reaction.

Q. 9. **Express the relation between half life period of a reactant and its initial concentration for a reaction of nth order.***

Ans. Half life period, $t_{1/2} = \dfrac{1}{[R]_0^{n-1}}$.

Q. 10. **For a reaction $R \longrightarrow P$, half-life ($t_{1/2}$) is observed to be independent of the initial concentration of reactants. What is the order of reaction?***

Ans. First order reaction.

Q. 11. **Which of the following order of reaction has unit of s^{-1}?**

Zero, first, second.

Ans. First order reaction.

Q. 12. **What is the expression for rate of reaction for the following reaction given below.**

$$A + B \xrightarrow{\ k\ } P$$

Ans. $\dfrac{-d[c]}{dt} = k\,[A]\,[B]$

Q. 13. **What is the equired energy for reacting molecules to permit a reaction?**

Ans. Activation energy.

Q. 14. **Write the slope value obtained in the plot of log $[R_0]/[R]$ Vs. time for a first order reaction.***

Ans. Slope $= k/2.303$.

Chapter 5. Surface Chemistry

Q. 1. **Why does physisorption decreases with rise in temperature?**

Ans. Physisorption is exothermic in nature (ΔH negative). According to Le-Chatelier's principle reverse reaction, *i.e.,* desorption is favoured with rise in temperature.

Q. 2. **What do you mean by activity of a catalyst?**

Ans. The capacity of a catalyst to enhance the speed of a reaction is called the activity of the catalyst.

Q. 3. **What happens when gelatin is added to gold sol?**

Ans. Gelatin is a lyophilic sol. Hence it forms a protective coating around gold sol which is otherwise lyophobic. Thus it increases the stability of gold sol.

Q. 4. **How will you obtain a colloidal solution of arsenious sulphide?**

Ans. It is obtained by passing H_2S gas through arsenious oxide solution.

$$As_2O_3 + 3H_2S \longrightarrow As_2S_3 + 3H_2O$$

Q. 5. **How does a catalyst work?**

Ans. It provides an alternate path involving lower activation energy for the reactants.

Q. 6. **What is ZSM-5? What is its formula?**

Ans. ZSM-5 is a zeolite sieve of molecular porosity 5. Its formula is $H_x[(AlO_2)_x.(SiO_2)_{96-x}].16H_2O$.

Q. 7. **Write the dispersed phase and dispersion medium of the following colloidal systems:**

(i) Smoke,   **(ii) Milk.**

Ans. Smoke : Carbon particles (dispersed phase), air (dispersed medium)

Milk : Liquid fats (dispersed phase) and Water (dispersion medium)

Q. 8. **$CO(g)$ and $H_2(g)$ react to give different products in the presence of different catalysts. Which ability of the catalyst is shown by these reactions?***

Ans. $CO(g)$ and $H_2(g)$ react in presence of different catalysts to give different products, this shows the action of a catalyst is highly selective in nature.

Q. 9. **What happens if dialysis is prolonged?**

Ans. If dialysis is prolonged in any colloidal solution then the solution will coagulate or precipitate out. Prolonged dialysis will remove all the electrolytes necessary for the stability of the colloidal solution along with the impurities, hence coagulation will take place.

Q. 10. **What is the effect of adding a catalyst on activation energy (E_a).***

Ans. Decreases.

Q. 11. **What type of colloid is formed when a liquid is dispersed in a solid?***

Ans. Gel.

Q. 12. What type of colloid is formed when a gas is dispersed in a liquid?*

Ans. Foam.

Q. 13. What is the range of particle size in colloidal solution in nm?

Ans. 1 – 1000 nm.

Q. 14. What is the nature of physiosorption reaction?

Ans. Exothermic.

Q. 15. Gelatin is what type of sol?

Ans. Lyophilic.

Chapter 6. General Principles and Processes of Isolation of Elements

Q. 1. How is wrought iron different from steel?

Ans. The only difference is the carbon content. Steel has 0.1 to 1.5% of carbon whereas wrought iron has only 0.2 to 0.5% carbon content in it. Also, steel is more hard in physical state than wrought iron.

Q. 2. Write the principles of Vapour phase refining.*

Ans. It is based on the principle that the metal is converted into its volatile compound and collected elsewhere. It is then decomposed to give pure metal.

Q. 3. Which type of ores are concentrated by froth floatation process?

Ans. Sulphide ores.

Q. 4. What is the process of reducing a metal oxide by heating it with core or some other reducing agents called?*

Ans. Pyrometallurgy.

Q. 5. What is the composition of invar steel?

Ans. 64% iron and 36% nickel.

Q. 6. Name the method used for refining of zirconium.

Ans. van Arkel method.

Q. 7. Name the process which is used for the extraction of a metal by heating the metal oxide with a suitable reducing agent.

Ans. Pyrometallurgy.

Q. 8. Name the method applied for the concentration of Bauxite ore in the extraction of Aluminium.*

Ans. Leaching.

Q. 9. Name the depressant which is used to separate PbS and ZnS containing ore in forth floatation process.

Ans. NaCN.

Q. 10. Name the method used for the refining of Zinc.

Ans. Electrolytic refining.

Q. 11. In the Mond's process the gas used for the refining of a metal is:*

Ans. CO.

Q. 12. Name the method of refining used to obtain semiconductor of very high purity.*

Ans. Zone refining.

Chapter 7. *p*-Block Elements

Q. 1. Chlorine water has both oxidizing as well as bleaching properties ? Explain.*

Ans. Chlorine reacts with water to release nascent oxygen which causes oxidation and bleaching.

As oxidising agent:

$$Cl_2 + H_2O \longrightarrow 2HCl + [O]$$
$$SO_2 + H_2O + [O] \longrightarrow H_2SO_4$$
$$\overline{Cl_2 + SO_2 + 2H_2O \longrightarrow 2HCl + H_2SO_4}$$

As bleaching agent.

Coloured substance + [O] $\longrightarrow$ colourless product.

Q. 2. Which aerosols deplete ozone?

Ans. Freons or chlorofluorocarbons (CFCs) are aerosols that accelerate the depletion of ozone. In the presence of ultraviolet radiations, molecules of CFCs break down to form chlorine free radicals that combine with ozone to form oxygen.

Q. 3. Explain why fluorine forms only one oxoacid, HOF?

Ans. Fluorine forms only one oxoacid *i.e.,* HOF because of its high electronegativity and small size. Also fluorine don't have any *d*-orbital.

Q. 4. Why are halogens coloured?

Ans. Almost all halogens are coloured. This is because halogens absorb radiations in the visible region. This results in the excitation of valence electrons to a higher energy region. Since the amount of energy required for excitation differs for each halogen, each halogen displays a different colour.

Q. 5. With what neutral molecule is ClO^- isoelectronic? Is that molecule a Lewis base?

Ans. ClO^- is isoelectronic to ClF. Also, both species contain 26 electrons in all as shown.

Total electrons $ClO^- = 17 + 8 + 1 = 26$. Also its iso electronic with OF_2.

In $ClF = 17 + 9 = 26$

ClF acts like a Lewis base as it accepts electrons from F to form ClF_3.

Q. 6. How are XeO3 and XeOF4 prepared?

Ans. (i) XeO_3 can be prepared in two ways as shown.
$$6XeF_4 + 12H_2O \longrightarrow 4Xe + 2XeO_3 + 24HF + 3O_2$$
$$XeF_6 + 3H_2O \longrightarrow XeO3 + 6HF$$

(ii) $XeOF_4$ can be prepared using XeF_6.
$$XeF_6 + H_2O \longrightarrow XeOF_4 + 2HF$$

Q. 7. Arrange the following in the order of property indicated for each set :

(i) F_2, Cl_2, Br_2, I_2 —increasing bond dissociation enthalpy.

(ii) HF, HCl, HBr, HI—increasing acid strength.

(iii) $NH_3, PH_3, AsH_3, SbH_3, BiH_3$—increasing base strength.

Ans. (i)   Bond dissociation energy usually decreases on moving down a group as the atomic size increases. However, the bond dissociation energy of F_2 is lower than that of Cl_2 and Br_2. This is due to the small atomic size of fluorine. Thus, the increasing order for bond dissociation energy among halogens is as follows:
$$I_2 < F_2 < Br_2 < Cl_2$$

(ii) HF < HCI < HBr < HI

The bond dissociation energy of H-X molecules where X = F, Cl, Br, I, decreases with an increase in the atomic size. Since H–I bond is the weakest, HI is the strongest acid.

(iii) $BiH_3 < SbH_3 < AsH_3 < PH_3 < NH_3$

On moving from nitrogen to bismuth, the size of the atom increases while the electron density on the atom decreases. Thus, the basic strength decreases.

Q. 8. Why are pentahalides more covalent than trihalides?

Ans. In pentahalides, the oxidation state is +5 and in trihalides, the oxidation state is +3. Since the metal ion with a high charge has more polarizing power, pentahalides are more covalent than trihalides.

Q. 9. List the important sources of sulphur.

Ans. Sulphur mainly exists in combined form in the earth's crust primarily as sulphates [Gypsum ($CaSO_4.2H_2O$), Epsom salt ($MgSO_4.7H_2O$), Baryte ($BaSO_4$)] and sulphides [(Galena (PbS), Zinc blends (ZnS), Copper pyrites ($CuFeS_2$)].

Q. 10. What happens when sulphur dioxide is passed through an aqueous solution of Fe(III) salt?

Ans. SO_2 acts as a reducing agent when passed through an aqueous solution containing Fe(III) salt. It reduces Fe(III) to Fe(II) *i.e.,* ferric ions to ferrous ions.

$$2Fe^{3+} + SO_2 + 2H_2O \longrightarrow 2Fe^{2+} + SO_4^{2-} + 4H^+$$

Q. 11. How is the presence of SO_2 detected?

Ans. SO_2 is a colourless and pungent smelling gas.

It can be detected with the help of potassium permanganate solution. When SO_2 is passed through an acidified potassium permanganate solution, it decolourises the solution as it reduces MnO_4^- ions to Mn^{2+} ions.

$$5SO_2 + 2MnO_4^- + 2H_2O \longrightarrow 5SO_4^{2-} + 4H^+ + 2Mn^{2+}$$

Q. 12. Name two poisonous gases which can be prepared from chlorine gas.

Ans. Two poisonous gases that can be prepared from chlorine gas are:

 (i)   Phosgene ($COCl_2$)   (ii) Mustard gas ($ClCH_2CH_2SCH_2CH_2Cl$)

Q. 13. Why is ICl more reactive than I_2?

Ans. ICl is more reactive than I_2 because I–Cl bond in I–Cl is weaker than I–I bond in I_2, because is more polarity.

Q. 14. Draw the structures of the following:*

 (i) H_2SO_3 (ii) $HClO_3$

Ans. (i) 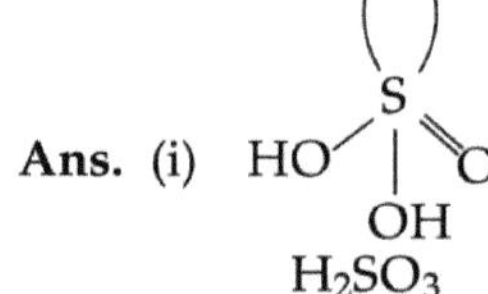   (ii) 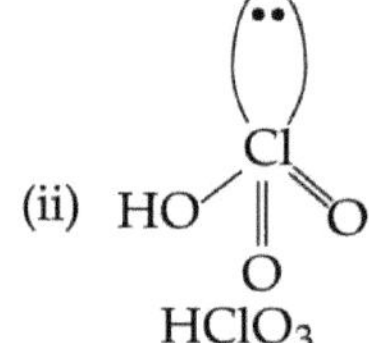

Q. 15. Draw the structures of the following:*

 (i) $H_2S_2O_8$ (ii) ClF_3

Ans. (i) 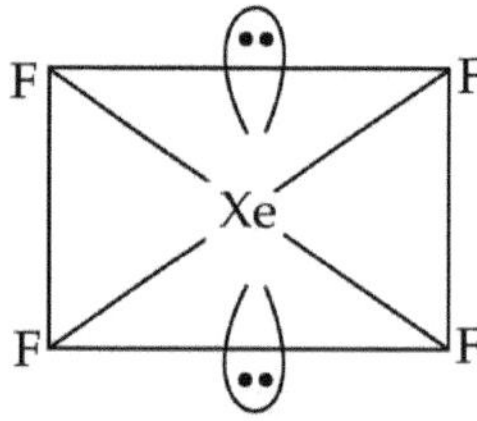   (ii) 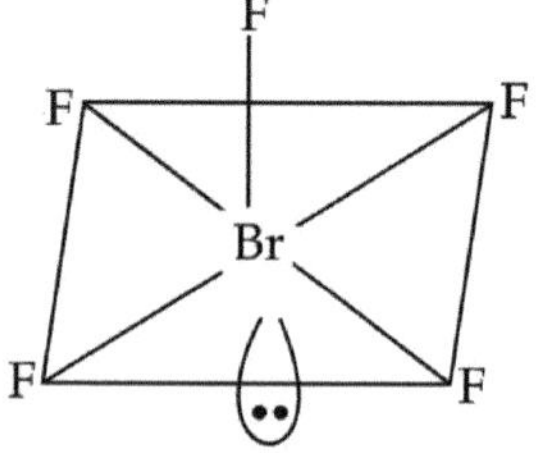

Q. 16. Write the formula of the compound of iodine which is obtained when conc. HNO_3 oxidises I_2.*

Ans. Iodic acid, HIO_3 is obtained on the oxidation of I_2 by HNO_3.

$$I_2 + 10HNO_3 \longrightarrow 2HIO_3 + 10NO_2 + 4H_2O$$
$$\text{Iodic acid}$$

Q. 17. Draw the structures of the following:

 (i) XeF_4 (ii) BrF_5

Ans. (i) XeF_4 (ii) BrF_5

Q. 18. Draw the structures of the following:*

 (i) $H_2S_2O_7$ (ii) FeF_6

Ans. (i) $H_2S_2O_7$ 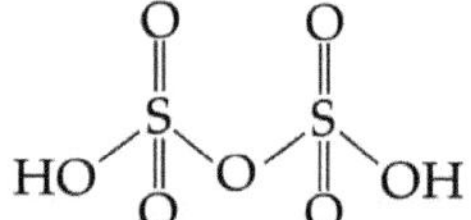   (ii) FeF_6 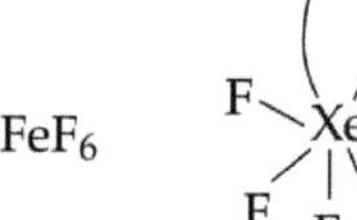

Q. 19. Draw the structures of the following:*

 (i) $H_4P_2O_7$ (ii) $XeOF_4$

Ans. (i) $H_4P_2O_7$

(ii) $XeOF_4$

Q. 20. (i) **How does CFC's and nitrogen dioxide deplete ozone?**

(ii) **Name major threats of ozone exposure.**

(iii) **Suggest ways to minimize ozone depletion.**

Ans. (i) CFC's are lighter than air and travel to upper part of the atmosphere without getting decomposed. There the CFC's like Cl_2CF_2 (freon) gets dissociated in presence of light (photochemical reaction) to generate free radicals, these radicals catalyse the process of conversion of ozone into oxygen.

$$CCl_2F_2 \longrightarrow + CClF_2$$
$$Cl + O_3 \longrightarrow ClO + O_2$$
$$ClO + [O] \longrightarrow Cl + O_2$$

Nitrogen dioxide on the other hand converts ozone into oxygen.

$$NO_2 + O_3 \longrightarrow NO + 2O_2$$

Thus these gases deplete ozone layer.

(ii) Depletion of ozone layer exposes human beings and animals to the harmful UV rays. These can cause skin cancer, eye problems even blindness, respiratory diseases etc.

(iii) Government should regulate such harmful emissions by putting a ban on products of CFC's where there is any alternative possible. Also the factories can have special chimneys which can selectively either block or convert the poisonous gases before emission.

Q. 21. **Why is BiH_3 the strongest reducing agent amongst all the hydrides of Group 15 elements?**

Ans. As we move down a group, the atomic size increases and the stability of the hydrides of group 15 elements decreases. Since the stability of hydrides decreases on moving from NH_3 to BiH_3, the reducing character of the hydrides increases on moving from NH_3 to BiH_3.

Q. 22. **What type of reaction is shown by the following reaction?**

$$3\ ClO^- (aq) \longrightarrow ClO^-_3 (aq) + 2Cl^{-1} (aq)$$

Ans. Disproportionation reaction.

Q. 23. **Out of F, Cl, Br and I which is the most powerful oxidising agent?**

Ans. F (Fluorine)

Q. 24. **What is the reason behind the high viscosity and high boiling point of HF?**

Ans. Hydrogen bonding.

Q. 25. **Which one of the element of Group 18 is used for the treatment of cancer?**

Ans. Radon.

Q. 26. **Which compound is formed in tailing of mercury?**

Ans. Hg_2O.

Chapter 8. *d*-and *f*-Block Elements

Q. 1. **Which metal of 1st transition series exhibits + 1 oxidation state in common and why?***

Ans. Element (Cu) copper exhibit + 1 oxidation state in common in the 1st transition series. It exists in the electronic configuration of Cu^+ ion as $4s^0 3d^{10}$, which is quite a stable configuration. Hence copper easily losses one electron to become Cu^+.

Q. 2. **What are the different oxidation states exhibited by the lanthanoids?**

Ans. + 3 oxidation state is most common in lanthanoids *i.e.,* Ln (III) compounds are predominant. However, +2 and +4 oxidation states can also be found in the solution or in solid compounds of some elements.

Q. 3. **Write the formula of an oxo-anion of Chromium (Cr) in which it shows the oxidation state equal to its group number.***

Ans. Chromium belongs to group number 6 and its oxidation state in $K_2Cr_2O_7$ is $+6$ *i.e.*,

$$K_2Cr_2O_7$$
$$1 \times 2 + 2x + (-2 \times 7) = 0$$
$$2 + 2x - 14 = 0$$
$$2x - 12 = 0$$
$$2x = 12$$
$$x = 6$$

Thus, the formula of the oxo-anion is $K_2Cr_2O_7$.

Q. 4. Name a metal of 1st transition series exhibits $+1$ oxidation state.

Ans. Copper.

Q. 5. Manganese belongs to group number 7 and what is its oxidation state in $KMnO_4$?

Ans. $+7$.

Q. 6. Which of the metal is used in incandescent lamps?

Ans. Tungsten.

Q. 7. Which compound of chromium is widely used is tanning of leather?

Ans. $K_2SO_4 \cdot Cr_2(SO_4)_3 \cdot 24 H_2O$.

Q. 8. Some green coloured powder blows in air when ammonium dichromate is used in fireworks. What is it?

Ans. Cr_2O_3.

Q. 9. Out of Cis $-$ [Pt (en)$_2$ Cl_2]$^{2+}$ and Trans $-$ [Pt(en)$_2$$Cl_2$]$^{2+}$, which one is optically active?*

Ans. Cis-[Pt(en)$_2$Cl$_2$]$^{2+}$.

Chapter 9. Coordination Compounds

Q. 1. How many ions are formed by the complex [Co(NH$_3$)$_6$]Cl$_3$ in aqueous solution?*

Ans. The complex dissociates as:

$$[Co(NH_3)_6]\, Cl_3 \xrightarrow{\text{aq.}} [Co(NH_3)_6]^{3+}\ (aq.) + 3Cl^-\ (aq.)$$

Hence 4 ions in solution.

Q. 2. Give name of a bidentate ligand with an example of complex formed by it.

Ans. Oxalato $\begin{bmatrix} O \\ \| \\ C - O \\ | \\ C - O \\ \| \\ O \end{bmatrix}^{2-}$; *e.g.*, K[Cr(H$_2$O)$_2$(C$_2O_4$)$_2$].

Q. 3. What is the oxidation number of cobalt in K [Co (CO)$_4$]?

Ans. -1.

Q. 4. What kind of isomerism is in the following compunds : [Co(NH$_3$)$_5$CN]Cl$_2$ and [Co(NH$_3$)$_5$NC] Cl$_2$.

Ans. Linkage isomerism.

Q. 5. What type of isomerism is exhibited by complex [Co(en)$_3$]$^{3+}$?*

Ans. Optical isomerism.

Q. 6. Write the coordination Bank number of Platinum in the complex [Pt(en)$_2$Cl$_2$].*

Ans. 6.

Q. 7. Name the entity in which di-or polydentate ligand uses its two or more donor sites to bind a single metal ion.

Ans. Chelate ligand.

Chapter 10. Haloalkanes and Haloarenes

Q. 1. What happens when benzal chloride is boiled with aqueous sodium hydroxide solution?

Ans. Benzalchloride, undergoes hydrolysis and forms benzaldehyde.

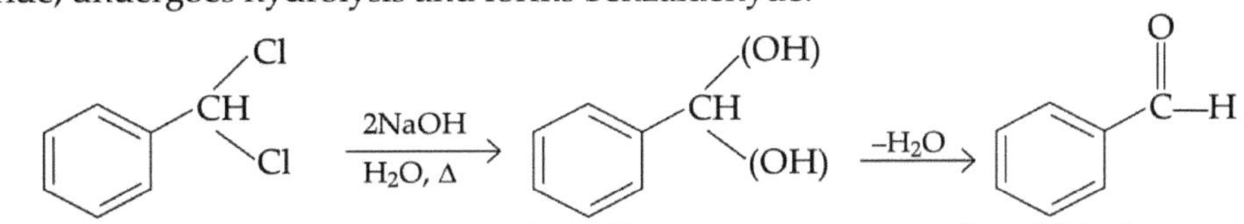

Benzyl chloride $\xrightarrow[\text{H}_2\text{O, }\Delta]{\text{2NaOH}}$ (unstable) $\xrightarrow{-\text{H}_2\text{O}}$ Benzaldehyde

Q. 2. Haloarenes are less reactive than haloalkanes and haloalkenes. Explain.

Ans. Haloarenes have resonance stabilized C–X bond having partial double bond character. Hence they are less reactive than haloalkanes. In case of haloalkanes *i.e.,* vinyl groups though C–C bonds have partial double bond character, but the extent of resonance in haloarenes is more than haloalkanes. Therefore, C–X bonds in haloarenes is more stable making them less reactive.

Q. 3. What is meant by chirality of a compound? Give an example.[*]

Ans. A compound with no point of symmetry and which is non-superimposable on its mirror image is called a chiral compound and the property is called chirality.

Example:

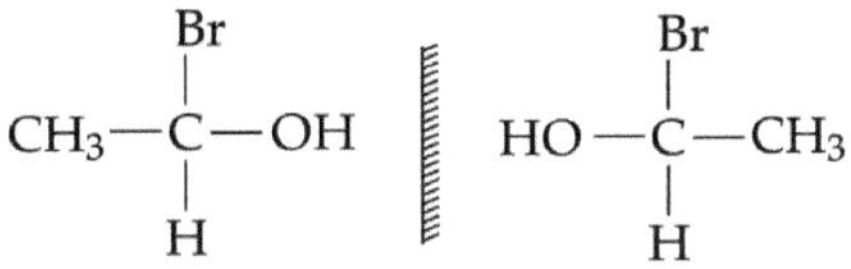

$$CH_3-\overset{\overset{\text{Br}}{|}}{\underset{\underset{\text{H}}{|}}{C}}-OH \qquad HO-\overset{\overset{\text{Br}}{|}}{\underset{\underset{\text{H}}{|}}{C}}-CH_3$$

Non-Superimposable mirror images

Q. 4. Out of chlorobenzene and benzyl chloride, which one gets easily hydrolysed by aqueous NaOH and why?[*]

Ans. Benzyl chloride would be easily hydrolysed compared to chlorobenzene. In the given reaction of condition hydrolysis proceeds by nucleophilic substitution mechanism and the benzylic carbonium ion formed after losing the leaving group (– Cl) is better stabilized (through resonating structures) hence reacts easily.

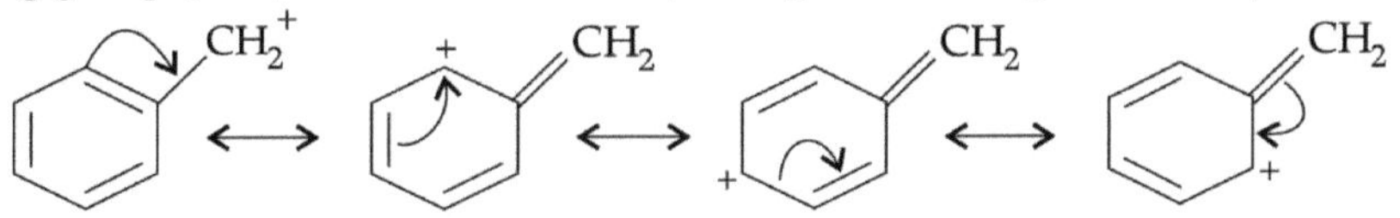

Q. 5. State what happens when benzene reacts with chlorine in the presence of ultraviolet light.

Ans. Benzene hexachloride.

Q. 6. Out of [structure] **and** [structure] **, which is an example of allylic halide?**[*]

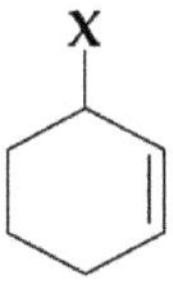

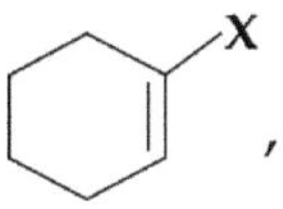

Ans. 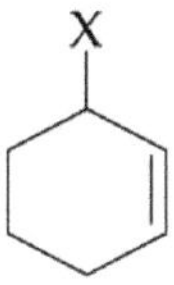 [structure]

Q. 7. Out of [structure with CHCl$_2$] **and** [structure with CH$_2$CH$_2$Cl] **, which is an example of benzylic halide?**

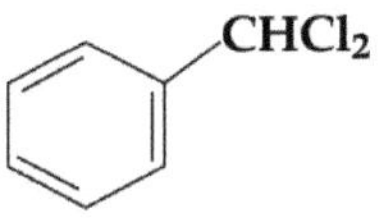

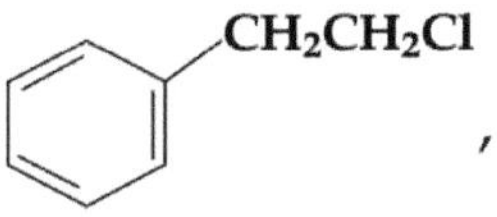

Ans. 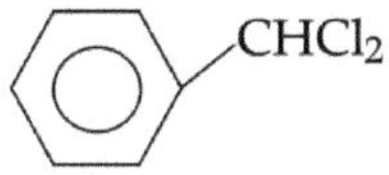 [structure with CHCl$_2$]

Q. 8. Which poisonous gas is formed when chloroform is exposed to light and air?

Ans. Phosgene.

* are board exam questions from previous years

Q. 9. Name the reaction involved in the following chemical equation?

$$2\,C_2H_5Br + 2Na \xrightarrow{\text{dry ether}} C_2H_5 - C_2H_5 + 2\,NaBr.$$

Ans. Wurtz reaction.

Q. 10. Out of 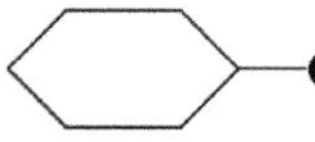 **$-Cl$ and** 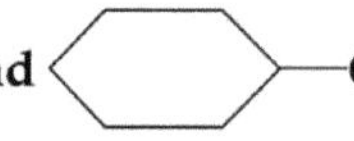 **$-CH_2-Cl$, which one is more reactive towards S_N1 reaction ?***

Ans. $C_6H_{11}Cl$.

Q. 11. Out of 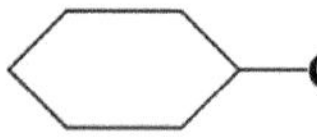 **$-CH_2-Cl$ and** 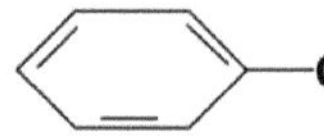 **$-CH_2-Cl$, which will react faster in S_N1 reaction with OH^-?***

Ans. 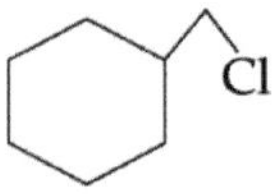

Q. 12. Out of $CH_3CH_2CH_2Cl$ and $CH_2 = CH - CH_2 - Cl$, which one is more reactive towards S_N1 reaction?*

Ans. $CH_2 = CH - CH_2Cl$.

Q. 13. Out of 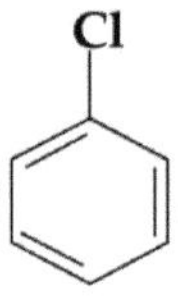

and 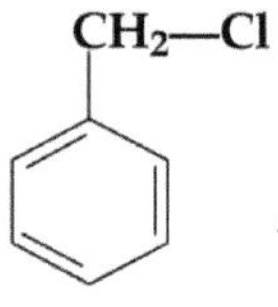

, which will undergo S_N1 reaction faster with OH^- ?*

Ans. $C_6H_5CH_2Cl$.

Q. 14. A hydrocarbon C_5H_{12} gives only one monochloride on photochemical chlorination. Identify the compound.*

Ans. The compound is 2, 2,-Dimethyl propane

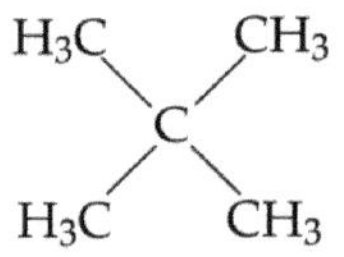

2,2-Dimethyl propane

Chapter 11. Alcohols, Phenols and Ethers

Q. 1. Explain the function of $ZnCl_2$ in Lucas test?

Ans. $ZnCl_2$ is an acid catalyst. In presence of HCl it forms H_2ZnCl_4 complex and protonates the alcohol readily, than simple HCl. Thus tertiary alcohols gives products or become turbid quickly.

Q. 2. Name the reagents used in the following reactions:*

(i) Bromination of phenol to 2, 4, 6-tribromophenol
(ii) Butan-2-one to Butan-2-ol
(iii) Butanol to Butanoic acid.

Ans. (i) Bromine water
(ii) Catalytic hydrogenation
(iii) Acidified $KMnO_4$ (potassium permanganate solution) *i.e.*, H_2 over Pt/Ni/Pd.

Q. 3. Name the product formed when oxylic acid is heated with glycerol.

Ans. Formic acid.

Q. 4. $C_6H_5Cl \xrightarrow[\text{624 K, 300 atm}]{\text{NaOH}}$ **A. What is A?**

Ans. Sodium phenoxide.

Q. 5. Phenol is heated with $CHCl_3$ and alcoholic KOH to give salicylaldehyde. Name the reaction.

Ans. Reimer - Tiemann reaction.

Q. 6. Glycerol on heating with potassium bisulphate yields a product X. Name it.

Ans. Acrolein.

* are board exam questions from previous years

Chapter 12. Aldehydes, Ketones and Carboxylic Acids

Q. 1. Explain the Friedel-Crafts reaction with an example.[*]

Ans. Replacement of hydrogen atom in a benzene ring or its derivative by an alkyl or acyl group using either, alkyl chloride or acyl chloride respectively, in presence of anhydrous $AlCl_3$ is called Friedel-Crafts reaction.

Example:

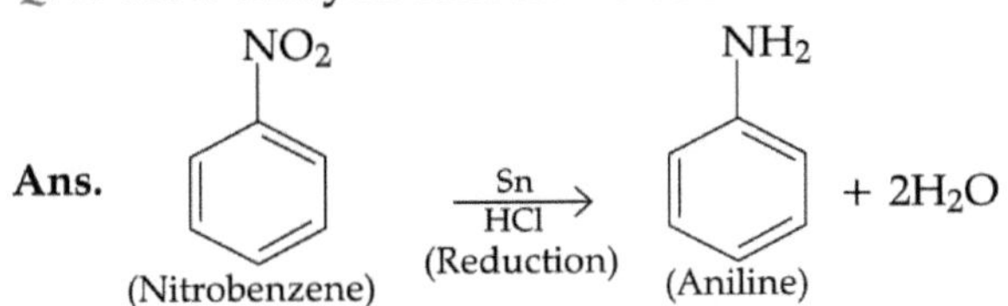

Q. 2. Arrange the following in the increasing order of their boiling points:
CH_3CHO, CH_3COOH, CH_3CH_2OH

Ans. $CH_3CHO < CH_3CH_2OH < CH_3COOH$

As carboxylic acids has the maximum extent of hydrogen bonding, so it has the maximum boiling point than alcohol of comparable molecular mass, followed by aldehyde.

Q. 3. (i) Why aldehydes are more soluble than ketone?
(ii) Name one use of aldehyde due to its solubility.

Ans. (i) Aldehydes can form hydrogen bond by involving the oxygen of carbonyl carbon and the hydrogen of 'CHO' group, hence they are quite soluble in water, even more than ketones.

(ii) Formalin, a 40% aqueous solution of formaldehyde in water is used as a germicide, antiseptic and also for biological preservation of specimen.

Q. 4. Write the reagents required for the following reactions.
$CH_2 = CH — CH_2OH \longrightarrow CH_2 = CH – CHO$

Ans. PCC.

Q. 5. Which of the following compound would undergo Cannizzaro reaction?
Propanone, 2, 2-Dimethyl-propanal, Butanal

Ans. Dimethyl propanal.

Q. 6. Out of acetaldehycle and benzaldehyde, which one will give Cannizzaro reaction?

Ans. Benzaldehyde.

Q. 7. Name the reagent that can be used to prepare ketone from acid chloride.

Ans. Dimethyl cadmium.

Q. 8. The reaction, $C_6H_5COCl + H_2 \xrightarrow[BaSO_4]{Pd} C_6H_5CHO + HCl$ is called as ....

Ans. Rosenmuind's reaction.

Chapter 13. Amines

Q. 1. How will you convert nitrobenzene to aniline?[*]

Ans.

$$NO_2 \xrightarrow[\text{(Reduction)}]{\frac{Sn}{HCl}} NH_2 + 2H_2O$$

(Nitrobenzene) (Aniline)

Q. 2. Arrange the following compounds in order of increasing solubility in water.[*]
$C_6H_5NH_2$, $(C_2H_5)_2NH$, $C_2H_5NH_2$.

Ans. $C_6H_5NH_2 < (C_2H_5)_2NH < C_2H_5NH_2$

$1°$ amines are more soluble because of more extensive hydrogen bonding in water. Aniline being an aryl amine, having a hydrophobic phenyl group is least soluble.

Q. 3. Classify the following amines as primary, secondary or tertiary:

(i) 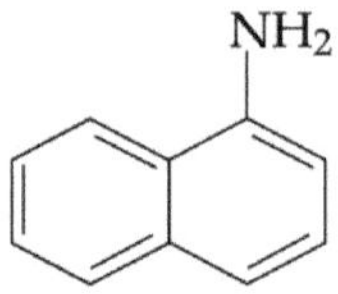 [naphthalene with NH_2]   (ii) 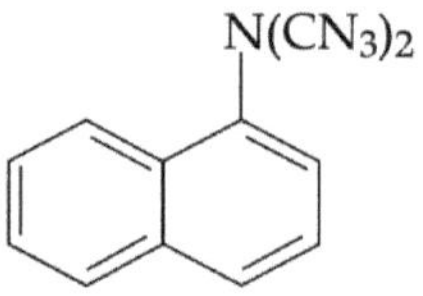 [naphthalene with $N(CN_3)_2$]   (iii) $(C_2H_5)_2CHNH_2$ (iv) $(C_2H_5)_2NH$

Ans. Primary : (i) and (iii)

Secondary : (iv)

Tertiary : (ii)

Q. 4. Name the complex nitrogeneous organic compounds which are produced by living plants and animals.

Ans. Enzymes.

Q. 5. Which catalyst is used for the commercial production of aniline?

Ans. Tin (Sn).

Q. 6. Which of the following compounds does not react with Hinsberg reagent?

$$\text{Ethylamine, } (CH_3)_2NH, (CH_3)_3N, (CH_3)_2 CH (NH_2)$$

Ans. $(CH_3)_3$ N.

Q. 7. Formulate acrylonitrile.

Ans. $CH_2 = CHCN$

Q. 8. What is the product formed when aniline is warmed with chloroform and caustic patash?

Ans. Phenyl isocyanide.

Q. 9. Write an isomer of C_3H_9N which gives foul smell of isocyanide when treated with chloroform and ethanolic NaOH.*

Ans. 1-Amino propane; $CH_3CH_2CH_2NH_2$.

Q. 10. Out of CH_3NH_2 and CH_3OH, which has higher boiling point?*

Ans. CH_3OH.

Q. 11. Write an isomer of C_3H_9N which does not react with Hinsberg reagent. *

Ans. $(CH_3)_3$ N, Trimethylamine;

Q. 12. Write the IUPAC name of $CH_3 - \underset{\underset{CH_3}{|}}{N} - \bigcirc$ **.***

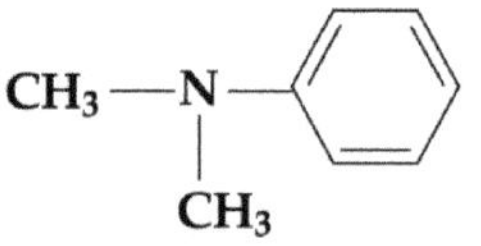

Ans. N, N-Dimethyl benzenamine.

Q. 13. Out of $(CH_3)_3N$ and $(CH_3)_2NH$, which one is more basic in aqueous solution?*

Ans. $(CH_3)_2NH$.

Chapter 14. Biomolecules

Q. 1. Name the vitamins whose deficiency causes the following diseases.

   (i)   Beri-beri and pain in joints.

   (ii) Scurvy.

Ans. (i)   Vitamin B_1,   (ii) Vitamin C.

Q. 2. Name one reducing and one non-reducing disaccharide.

Ans. Maltose (reducing)

Sucrose (Non-reducing).

Q. 3. What do you mean by 'invert sugar'?

Ans. An equimolar mixture of glucose (positive rotation) or dextrorotatory and of fructose (negative rotation) or laevorotatory is called invert sugar.

Q. 4. What is co-enzyme? Give an example.

Ans. The non-protein component of an enzyme which is loosely held by the enzyme is known as co-enzyme. This component is essential for the biological activity of the enzyme. Co-enzymes are generally derived from vitamins, they loosely attach themselves to enzymes. Vitamins like thiamine, niacin etc.

Q. 5. Name the type of bondings present in globular proteins.

Ans. Hydrogen bonding, disulphide linkages, dipolar interactions and some hydrophobic interactions.

Q. 6. Where does the water present in the egg go after boiling the egg?

Ans. When an egg is boiled, the proteins present inside the egg get denatured and coagulate. After boiling the egg, the water present in it is absorbed or adsorbed by the coagulated protein through H-bonding.

Q. 7. What products would be formed when a nucleotide from DNA containing thymine is hydrolyzed?

Ans. A nucleotide contains deoxyribose sugar + base + phosphoester linkage. Hence, when a nucleotide from the DNA containing thymine is hydrolyzed, thymine, 2-deoxy-D-ribose and phosphoric acid are obtained as products.

Q. 8. Classify the following into monosaccharides and disaccharides.
Ribose, 2-deoxyribose, maltose, galactose, fructose and lactose.

Ans. Monosaccharides : Ribose, 2-deoxyribose, galactose, fructose.

Disaccharides : Maltose, lactose.

Q. 9. What type of bonding helps in stabilizing the a-helical structure of proteins?

Ans. The H-bonds formed between the – NH group of one amino acid residue and the $\rangle C = O$ group of the adjacent (fourth) amino acid residue of the a-helix helps in stabilizing the helix.

Q. 10. The two strands in DNA are not identical but are complementary. Explain.

Ans. In the helical structure of DNA, the two strands are held together by hydrogen bonds between specific pairs of bases. Cytosine forms hydrogen bond with guanine, while adenine forms hydrogen bond with thymine. As a result, the two strands are complementary to each other.

Q. 11. What are the different types of RNA found in the cell?

Ans. (i) Messenger RNA (*m*-RNA)

(ii) Ribosomal RNA (*r*-RNA)

(iii) Transfer RNA (*t*-RNA)

Q. 12. Give one example of denatured protein.

Ans. Cheese.

Q. 13. Name the products of hydrolysis of sucrose.

Ans. Glucose + Fructose.

Q. 14. Which of the following is a pyrimidine base?
Adecine, Gyanine, Uracil.

Ans. Uracil.

Q. 15. What are the ultimate products of digestion of proteins?

Ans. α–Amino acids.

Q. 16. Name the base that is found in nucleotide of RNA only.

Ans. Uracil.

Q. 17. Which of the following amino acids is an essential amino acid?
Serine, Alanine, Lysine, Proline

Ans. Lysine.

Q. 18. Name the water insoluble component of starch.

Ans. Amylopectin.

Q. 19. Write the name of component of starch which is water soluble.*
Ans. Amylose.

Q. 20. Write the name of linkage joining two monosaccharides.*
Ans. Glycosidic linkage.

Q. 21. What type of protein is present in keratin?*
Ans. Fibrous protein.

Q. 22. What type of linkage is present in polysaccharides?*
Ans. Glycosidic linkages.

Chapter 15. Polymers

Q. 1. What does 6, 6 indicates in polymer nylon-6, 6?*
Ans. 6, 6 indicates the number of carbon atoms present in each of the monomer unit of the copolymer nylon 6, 6 that is hexamethylene diammine and adipic acid.

Q. 2. Draw structure of the monomers of the following polymers:*
    (i) Teflon,   (ii) Polyethene.
Ans. (i) Teflon $CF_2 = CF_2$ (tetrafluoroethene)
      (ii) Polyethene $CH_2 = CH_2$ (ethene)

Q. 3. Give an example of condensation polymer.*
Ans. Terylene made from ethylene glycol and terepthalic acid.

Q. 4. Write names of two synthetic polymers.
Ans. PVC (polyvinyl chloride) and Teflon.

Q. 5. Give one example of each:*
    (i)   Addition polymer   (ii) Condensation polymer   (iii) Co-polymer.
Ans. (i)   Teflon   (ii) Nylon-6, 6   (iii) Buna-S.

Q. 6. What are natural and synthetic polymers? Give two examples of each type.
Ans. Natural polymers are polymers that are found in nature. They are found in plants and animals. Examples include proteins, cellulose, starch, etc.

Synthetic polymers are polymers made by human beings. Examples include plastic, dacron (terylene), (polythene), synthetic fibres (nylon 6, 6), synthetic rubbers (Buna-S) etc.

Q. 7. Write the monomers used for obtaining the following polymers.
    (i)   Polyvinyl chloride,   (ii) Teflon,   (iii) Bakelite.
Ans. (i)   Vinyl chloride ($CH_2 = CHCl$)
     (ii) Tetrafluoroethylene ($CF_2 = CF_2$)
     (iii) Formaldehyde ($HCHO$) and Phenol (C_6H_5OH).

Q. 8. What is a biodegradable polymer? Give an example of a biodegradable aliphatic polyester.
Ans. A polymer that can be decomposed by bacteria is called a biodegradable polymer. Poly-β-hydroxybutyrate-CO-β-hydroxyvalerate (PHBV) is a biodegradable aliphatic polyester.

$$\left[O-CH-CH_2-\underset{\underset{O}{\|}}{C}-O-CH-CH_2-\underset{\underset{O}{\|}}{C} \right]_n$$
$$\underset{CH_3}{} \qquad \underset{CH_2CH_3}{}$$
PHBV

Q. 9. Classify the following as addition and condensation polymers. Terylene, Bakelite, Polyvinyl chloride, Polythene.
Ans. Addition polymers : Polyvinyl chloride, polythene

Condensation polymers : Terylene bakelite.

Q. 10. Explain the difference between Buna-N and Buna-S.
Ans. Buna—N is a copolymer of 1, 3-butadiene and acrylonitrile.

Buna—S is a copolymer of 1, 3-butadiene and styrene.

* are board exam questions from previous years

Q. 11. Write the structure of the monomers used for getting the following polymers:*

(i)   Dacron   (ii) Nylon-6

Ans. (i)   Monomers of Dacron:

$$HOH_2C - CH_2OH \text{ and } HOOC - \langle C_6H_4 \rangle - COOH$$

Ethylene glycol   Terephthalic acid

(ii) Monomers of Nylon-6:

Caprolactum

Q. 12. Name the form in which polymers of glucose is stored in animals.
Ans. Glycogen.

Q. 13. Identify the type of polymer:
$$- A - A - A - A - A -$$
Ans. Homopolymer.

Q. 14. Name one polyamide polymer.
Ans. Nylon 6,

Q. 15. Name the monomers of Nylon-2-Nylon-6.
Ans. Glycine and E-amino caproic acid.

Q. 16. What is the chemical name of melamine?
Ans. 2, 4, 6 triamino - 1, 3, 5 - triazine.

Q. 17. Name the polymer having repeating units of monomer, $F_2C = CF_2$.
Ans. PTFE.

Q. 18. Name the polymer which is used for making electrical switches and combs.
Ans. Bakelite.

Q. 19. Name the polymer which is used for making non-stick utensils.*
Ans. Teflon

Q. 20. Is $- CH_2 - CH = CH - CH_2 - CH_2 - CH -$
$$\underset{CN \quad n}{|}$$

a homopolymer or copolymer?*
Ans. Copolymer.

Chapter 16. Chemistry in Everyday Life

Q. 1. Give an example of a narcotic drug which is also used as an analgesic.*
Ans. Morphine is a narcotic drug which when prescribed in controlled doses acts as an analgesic and it reduces pain.

Q. 2. What structural property makes certain detergents non-biodegradable?
Ans. Heavy or mild branching in the hydrocarbon chains of the detergents make them non-biodegradable.

Q. 3. Role of fillers in soap. Explain.
Ans. Fillers are substances added to laundry soaps. They may be sodium silicate, carbonate or borax. These are added to give soap the additional physical characteristics like texture, consistency etc.

Q. 4. What are antagonistic drugs?

Ans. Those drugs which bind to the receptor site and thus inhibits the natural functioning of the receptor are called antagonistic drug.

Example: antacid cimetidine.

Q. 5. What are Barbiturates?

Ans. Barbiturates are derivative of barbituric acids and they are used as hypnotics and tranquilizers.

Q. 6. Name the macromolecules that are chosen as drug targets.

Ans. The macromolecules chosen as drug targets are carbohydrates, lipids, proteins and nucleic acids.

Q. 7. What are the main constituents of dettol?

Ans. The main constituents of dettol are chloroxylenol and a-terpineol in a suitable solvent like absolute alcohol.

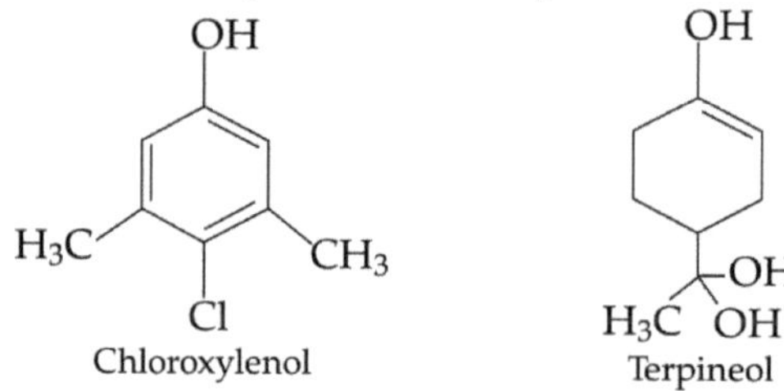

Chloroxylenol   Terpineol

Q. 8. What is tincture of iodine? What is its use?

Ans. Tincture of iodine is a 2-3 percent solution of iodine in alcohol and water. It is applied to wounds as a powerful antiseptic.

Q. 9. What are food preservatives?

Ans. Food preservatives are chemicals that prevent food from spoilage due to microbial growth like table salt, sugar, vegetable oil, sodium benzoate (C_6H_5COONa), and salts of propanoic acid are some examples of food preservatives.

Q. 10. What are artificial sweetening agents? Give two examples.

Ans. Artificial sweetening agents are chemicals that sweetens food. However, unlike natural sweeteners, they do not add calorie intake. They are safe for diabetic patients and weight management.

Some artificial sweeteners are aspartame, saccharin, sucrolose and alitame.

Q. 11. What problem arises in using alitame as artificial sweetener?

Ans. Alitame is a high potency sweetener. It is difficult to control the sweetness of food while using alitame as an artificial sweetener.

Q. 12. With reference to which classification has the statement, 'ranitidine is an antacid' been given?

Ans. The given statement refers to the classification of pharmacological effects of the drug. This is because any drug that is used to counteract the effects of excess acid in the stomach is called an antacid.

Q. 13. What type of drug is chloramphenicol?

Ans. Antibiotic.

Q. 14. What is the name of the alkaloid which is specifically used for treatment of malaria fever?

Ans. Quinine.

Q. 15. What type of detergents are used for dish washing?

Ans. Non-ionic detergents.

Q. 16. Which type of drug is brompheniramine (Dimetapp)?

Ans. Antihistamine.

Q. 17. Name one commonly used food preservative.*

Ans. Sodium benzoate.

Q. 18. Name one hynotic drug.

Ans. Valium.

Q. 19. Name a substance which can be used as an antiseptic as well as disinfectant.

Ans. Phenol.

Q. 20. Name a sweetening agent used in the preparation of sweets for a diabetic patient.

Ans. Saccharin, alitame, and aspartame.

Q. 21. Which are the substances applied on non-living objects to destroy microorganisms that are present on the objects?

Ans. Disinfectants.

Q. 22. Who discovered Penicillin?

Ans. A - Fleming.

Q. 23. What are the substances used to bring down the temperature in high fever?

Ans. Antipyretics.

Q. 24. Name a drug used in case of mental depression.

Ans. Barbituric acid derivatives like luminal, seconal or equanil are two such drugs used as antidepressant.

Q. 25. Give an example of a sulpha drug.*

Ans. Sulphanilamide is a sulpha drug.

$$NH_2-\langle\ \rangle-SO_2NH_2.$$

Q. 26. Which one of the following is an antidepressant drug ? Chloramphenicol, Luminal, Bithional.*

Ans. Luminal.

Q. 27. Which one of the following is a narcotic analgesic?*
Penicillin, Codeine, Ranitidine.

Ans. Codeine.

Q. 28. Name the compound which is added to soap to provide antiseptic properties.*

Ans. Bithional.

Q. 29. Name the sweetening agent used in the cooking of sweets for a diabetic patient.*

Ans. Sucralose.

Q. 30. Name an artificial sweetener whose use is limited to cold drinks.*

Ans. Aspartame.

Q. 1. Why are amorphous solids considered supercooled liquids?

Ans. Amorphous solids have the tendency to flow extremely slowly which is also a characteristics similar to liquids, that is why they are called supercooled liquids.

Q. 2. Why potassium chloride appears violet sometimes instead of pure white?*

Ans. Potassium chloride appears violet sometimes instead of pure white due to anionic vacancies which creates F-centre (colour centre) occupied by unpaired electrons.

Q. 3. Why Frenkel defect is not found in pure alkali halides?

Ans. In alkali halides cations are of comparable sizes as the anion and hence cannot occupy interstitial positions. Thus frenkel defect is not found in pure alkali halides.

Q. 4. Why glass is considered as a supercooled liquid?

Ans. Similar to liquids, glass has a tendency to flow, though very slowly. Therefore, glass is considered as a supercooled liquid. This is the reason why glass windows and doors are slightly thicker at the bottom than at the top.

Q. 5. Our country is facing shortage of electricity, especially during peak summers. The conventional sources of electricity is failing to meet the demands. The use of solar energy in that case seems like a possibility to quench the need of growing demand of electricity in future. As we know that photovoltaic cells can do the same. Answer the following:

(i) Why solar energy better than conventional energy?

(ii) Why solar power is not very popular in India?

Ans. (i) Traditional sources of energy like thermal and nuclear energy leads to emisson of harmful gases, smoke and radiations, which is not there in case of solar energy. Hence its better than conventional energy sources.

(ii) Solar power is still not very popular in India because of lack of awareness about how to use it in daily life by common people. Also government is not taking as much as required initiative to make solar power use common.

Q. 6. ZnO, zinc oxide on heating changes to yellow from white. Explain.

Ans. ZnO on heating looses an oxygen molecule and turns yellow in colour.

$$ZnO \rightarrow Zn^{2+} + \frac{1}{2} O_2 + 2e^-$$

These electrons moves to the interstitial sites and absorb radiation corresponding to certain visible range and emit yellow colour.

Q. 7. Why are solids rigid?

Ans. The intermolecular forces of attraction that are present in solids are very strong. The constituent particles of solids cannot move from their positions *i.e.,* they have fixed positions. However, they can oscillate about their mean positions. This is the reason why solids are rigid.

Q. 8. Why do solids have a definite volume?

Ans. The intermolecular forces of attraction that are present in solids are very strong. The constituent particles of solids have small intermolecular distances, they are rigid. Hence, solids have a definite volume.

Q. 9. Refractive index of a solid is observed to have the same value along all directions. Comment on the nature of this solid. Would it show cleavage property?

Ans. An isotropic solid has the same value of physical properties when measured along different directions. Therefore, the given solid, having the same value of refractive index along all directions is isotropic in nature. Hence, the solid is an amorphous solid. When an amorphous solid is cut with a sharp edged tool, it cuts into two pieces with irregular surfaces.

Chapter 2. Solutions

Q. 1. **Why does vapour pressure of a liquid decreases on mixing a non-volatile solute in it?**

Ans. The vapour pressure decreases as the non-volatile solute occupies some space in solution, and do not contribute to the vapour pressure.

Q. 2. **Which of the two, molarity or molality is a better way to express concentration and why?***

Ans. Molality is a better way to express concentration of a solution because it is independent on volume which otherwise changes with temperature. Molality involves weight of solvent which is always constant irrespective of temperature.

Q. 3. **Why is benzene insoluble in water but soluble in toluene?***

Ans. The principle of like dissolves like works for two substances to be soluble in each other. Both benzene and toluene are non-polar compounds whereas water is a polar compound. Hence benzene is soluble in toluene but insoluble in water.

Q. 4. **What happens when blood cells are placed in:**
    (i)   Pure water,
    (ii) sea water.

Ans. The blood cells will
    (i)   Swell in pure water, *i.e.*, endosmosis will take place.
    (ii) Shrink in sea water, *i.e.*, exosmosis will take place.

Q. 5. **Which will have a higher boiling point, 0.1 M NaCl or 0.1 M BaCl$_2$ solution in water?***

Ans. Both NaCl and BaCl$_2$ will dissociate in water as:
$$NaCl \rightarrow Na^+ (aq) + Cl^- (aq)$$
$$BaCl_2 \rightarrow Ba^{2+} (aq) + 2Cl^- (aq)$$
As BaCl$_2$ will provide more ions on per mole dissociation, hence BaCl$_2$ solution has higher boiling point.

Q. 6. **What changes we observe in the boiling points of a liquid:**
    (i)   at higher altitude.
    (ii) near or below sea level.

Ans. The boiling point of the liquid will:
    (i)   decrease in higher altitude due to lower atmospheric pressure.
    (ii) increase below sea level due to higher atmospheric pressure.

Q. 7. **When is the value of Van't Hoff factor more than one?***

Ans. Van't Hoff factor (*i*) is more than 1 in dissociations of the solute.

Q. 8. **Out of 1 M glucose and 2 M glucose which one has higher boiling point and why?***

Ans. 2 M glucose will have higher boiling point, as boiling of a solution of non-volatile solute increases with increase in concentration.

Q. 9. **Give reasons for the following:***
    (i)   Measurement of osmotic pressure method is preferred for the determination of molar masses of macromolecules such as proteins and polymers.
    (ii) Aquatic animals are more comfortable in cold water than in warm water.
    (iii) Elevation of boiling point of 1 M KCl solution is nearly double than that of 1 M sugar solution.

Ans. (i)   Molar masses of Macromolecules like polymers and proteins are measured through osmotic pressure method. The osmotic pressure method uses 'molarity' of solution (instead of molality) which has a large magnitude even for dilute solutions, given that polymers have poor solubility, osmotic pressure measurement is used for determination of their molar masses. Macromolecules such as proteins are not stable at high temperatures and because measurement of osmotic pressure is done at around room temperature, it is useful for determination of molar masses of proteins.

(ii) Solubility of gases in liquid decreases on increasing the temperature. Hence, the availability of dissolved oxygen in water is more at lower temperature hence, the aquatic animals feel more comfortable at lower temperatures than at the higher temperatures.

(iii) Elevation of boiling point is a colligative property and hence depends on the number of solute particles in the solution. Now, 1 M KCl would have twice the number of solute particles, as KCl dissociates into K^+ and Cl^-, compared to sugar solution (as sugar does not undergo any dissociation). So, elevation of boiling point is nearly double for 1 M KCl solution compared to 1 M sugar solution.

Q. 10. Why Scuba divers develop bends?*

Ans. Inside deep under water the concentration of dissolved gases is high. When the divers reach the surface, the pressure gradually decreases. Thus, the dissolved gases from their blood releases and forms bubbles of nitrogen in blood which blocks capillaries and creates medical condition called bends which is painful and dangerous.

Q. 11. Why is the vapour pressure of a solution of glucose in water lower than that of water?

Ans. Dissolved glucose occupies some surface area of solution, hence being a non-volatile solute it decreases the escaping tendency of surface molecules. Hence vapour pressure decreases.

Q. 12. Why do gases always tend to be less soluble in liquids as the temperature is raised?

Ans. The dissolution of a gas in a liquid is an exothermic process (heat is released)

$$\text{Gas + Solvent} \rightleftharpoons \text{Solution; } \Delta H = -ve$$

According to Le-Chatelier's principle, increase of temperature would shift the equilibrium in the backward direction. Thus, solubility of the gas in solution would decrease with the rise in temperature.

Q. 13. Based on solute-solvent interactions, arrange the following in order of increasing solubility in *n*-octane and explain. Cyclohexane, KCl, CH_3OH, CH_3CN.

Ans. *n*-octane is a non-polar solvent. Therefore, the solubility of a non-polar solute is more than that of a polar solute in the *n*-octane.

The order of increasing polarity is:

$$\text{Cyclohexane} < CH_3CN < CH_3OH < KCl$$

Therefore, the order of increasing solubility is:

$$KCl < CH_3OH < CH_3CN < \text{Cyclohexane}$$

Q. 14. A trainer nurse used distilled water and not saline water while giving injection to the patient. An immediate swelling was noticed in the area where the injection was given. What was the reason?

Ans. The swelling occurs because of osmosis inside the cell membrane. The hypotonic distilled water has less osmotic pressure than hypertonic blood. Hence immediate flow of injected fluid takes place inside the cell membrane. But in case of saline water, which is (0.91% of NaCl solution) its isotonic with blood RBC's, so no extra swelling would have occurred.

Q. 15. What are Reverse osmosis plants and why they are important?

Ans. Reverse osmosis is the process of applying extra pressure more than osmotic pressure to make solvent travel from more concentrated solution towards less concentrated solution. Like this we can extract water from saline sea water. Thus huge scale usable water can be generated. Hence its important.

Such plants are used for desalination of sea water, to recover fresh water from it.

Chapter 3. Electrochemistry

Q. 1. What is the sign of the DG for an electrolytic cell? Why?

Ans. Sign of ΔG is +*ve* for electrolytic cell because in electrolytic cell the reaction is non-spontaneous. The cell operates when electric charge is applied to carry forward the non-spontaneous redox reaction.

Q. 2. What is the effect of decreasing concentration on the molar conductivity of weak electrolyte?*

Ans. On decreasing concentration the molar conductivity of the weak electrolyte increases considerably as more and more dissociation of electrolyte takes place.

Q. 3. Rusting of iron is faster in saline water than in normal water. Explain.*

Ans. Saline water is a better conductor hence helps in the flow of ions and electrons involved in the process of rusting. Thus, this enhances the rate of corrosion.

Q. 4. Mention the source of drinking water for the astronauts in Appolo space flights.

Ans. The by-product of H_2-O_2 fuel cell, provided water for such spacecrafts.

Q. 5. What is the relationship between cell potential and equilibrium constant?*

Ans. At equilibrium, the value of cell potential is zero.

Q. 6. Draw a graph between Λ_m versus $\sqrt{C}$ for a weak electrolyte and explain why we cannot calculate Λ_m^0 by extrapolation.

Ans.

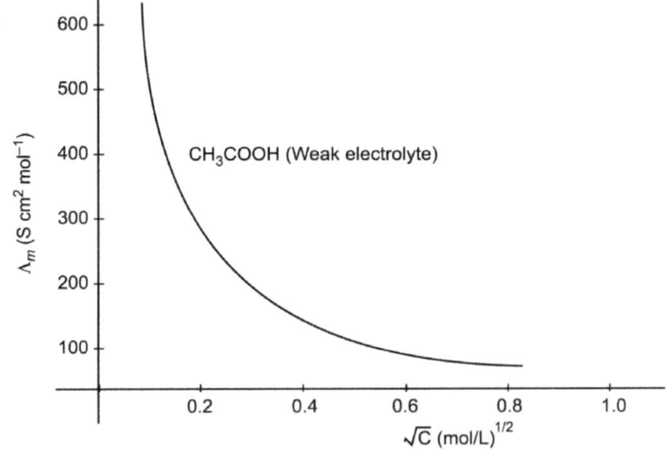

Λ_m^0 cannot be calculated by extrapolation as the plot becomes almost parallel to the Y-axis.

Q. 7. Why a porous plate of salt bridge not required in a lead storage cell?

Ans. In a lead storage cell, the oxidising agent PbO_2 and reducing agent Pb rods are solids. The product of cell reaction $PbSO_4$ is also solid, hence there is no possibility of oxidising and reducing agents migrating or mixing of ions of each. Thus salt bridge is not required.

Q. 8. Consult the table of standard electrode potentials and suggest three substances that can oxidise ferrous ions under suitable conditions.

Ans. Substances that are stronger oxidising agents than ferrous ions can oxidise ferrous ions.
$$Fe^{2+} \longrightarrow Fe^{3+} + e^-; \quad E° = -0.77\text{ V}$$

This implies that the substances having higher reduction potentials than $+0.77$ V can oxidise ferrous ions to ferric ions. Three substances that can do so are F_2, Cl_2 and O_2.

Q. 9. Why does the conductivity of a solution decrease with dilution?

Ans. The conductivity of a solution is the conductance of ion present in a unit volume of the solution. The number of ions (responsible for carrying current) decreases when the solution is diluted. As a result, the conductivity of a solution decreases with dilution.

Q. 10. Given the standard electrode potentials,
$$K^+/K = -2.93\text{ V,}$$
$$Ag^+/Ag = 0.80\text{ V,}$$
$$Hg^{2+}/Hg = 0.79\text{ V}$$
$$Mg^{2+}/Mg = -2.37\text{ V,}$$
$$Cr^{3+}/Cr = -0.74\text{ V}$$

Arrange these metals in their increasing order of reducing power.

Ans. The lower the reduction potential more the tendency to get oxidised, the higher is the reducing power. The given standard electrode potentials increase in the order of:
$$K^+/K < Mg^{2+}/Mg < Cr^{3+}/Cr < Hg^{2+}/Hg < Ag^+/Ag.$$

Hence, the reducing power of the given metals increases in the following order:
$$Ag < Hg < Cr < Mg < K$$

Q. 11. Why cadmium batteries are adviced to use over lead batteries although, they are more expensive than lead batteries?

Ans. Cadmium is not poisonous as lead. The vapours of lead storage battery which is commonly used in inverters. The sulphuric acid which act as electrolyte are very harmful to the human body. This can lead to serious health problems.

Q. 12. Explain why, fuel cell is preferred in space programme?

Ans. Fuel cell is used in space programme because;

    (i)   Can work continuously as long as fuel is supplied.

    (ii) These cells do not cause any pollution problems. Do not release any pollutant gases. The by-product is water which can be used for drinking.

    (iii) The efficiency of fuel cell is about 60 to 70%.

Chapter 4. Chemical Kinetics

Q. 1. If the concentration is expressed in mol L^{-1} units and time in seconds, what would be the unit of K*

    (i) for a zero order reaction,   **(ii) for a first order reaction?**

Ans. (i) For zero order reaction unit of K is mol L^{-1} sec^{-1}.

    (ii) For first order reaction unit of K is sec^{-1}.

Q. 2. Express the relation between the half life period of a reaction and its initial concentration if the reaction involved is of second order.*

Ans. For second order reaction:

$$t_{1/2} \propto \frac{1}{[R]_0} \text{ , where } [R]_0 \text{ is the initial concentration of the reactant.}$$

Q. 3. When is the rate of reaction equal to specific reaction rate?

Ans. When molar concentration of reactants becomes equal to 1.

$$\text{Rate} = k[A]^a [B]^b$$

if $[A] = [B] = 1$

Then, rate $= k$.

Q. 4. A reaction proceeds with a uniform rate throughout. What can we conclude?

Ans. When a reaction proceeds with a uniform rate it means it has no effect of concentration of reactants on the rate of reactions. Hence, it must be a zero order reaction.

Q. 5. Why molecularity of a reaction cannot be zero?

Ans. Molecularity is the number of given reactant molecules or atoms that are colliding in the elementary reaction. Hence a minimum of one reactant molecule, atom or iron is required to initiate a chemical reaction. Hence molecularity cannot be zero.

Q. 6. Give reason, why the rate of a reaction generally increases with rise in temperature.

Ans. Increase in temperature causes a total increase in the energy of the reacting species. Therefore, more and more reacting species are able to cross the activation energy required to form the product. Hence overall rate of reaction increases.

Q. 7. Why order of a reaction cannot be determined by looking at the balanced chemical reaction.

Ans. The sum of the stoichiometric coefficients of the reactants in a balanced chemical reaction displays the total number of moles involved in the reacting species but may or may not depict the correct order of the reaction. If the reaction is not an elementary reaction then only the slowest step reactants decides the order of reaction.

Q. 8. How is activation energy of a reaction affected

    (i) by using a catalyst?

    (ii) by increasing the temperature?*

Ans. In both the cases (i) by using a catalyst the activation energy decreases as catalyst provide a lower activation energy alternative path for the reaction to happen.

    (ii) On increasing temperature, more and more effective collisions take place as a result more species are able to cross the activation energy barrier required to form the product.

Q. 9. Account for the following:
   (i)   DG is positive for photochemical reactions.
   (ii) Photosensitizer are not just catalysts.
Ans. (i)   DG is positive because a part of the light energy used in or absorbed is converted to free energy.
   (ii) A photosensitizer initiates a photochemical reaction where a catalyst only changes the speed of the reaction.

Q. 10. What will be the effect of temperature on rate constant?
Ans. The rate constant of a reaction is nearly doubled with a $10°$ rise in temperature. However, the exact dependence of the rate of a chemical reaction on temperature is given by Arrhenius equation,

$$k = Ae^{-E_a/RT}$$

Where, A is the Arrhenius factor or the frequency factor
T is the temperature
R is the gas constant
E_a is the activation energy.

Chapter 5. Surface Chemistry

Q. 1. Why blisters generally appear when molten copper is allowed to cool in Bessemer converter?
Ans. Blisters appear on the surface of copper metal due to evolution of SO_2 gas. The bubbles of the gas get trapped when the molten mass solidifies and they appear as blisters.

Q. 2. Why are colloidal sol stable?*
Ans. The particles of colloidal sol carry the same charge and hence keep on repelling each other, thus does not get aggregated to form a bigger suspension size particle. Thus charge provides stability to colloids.

Q. 3. Gelatin is added in ice-creams. Give reason.
Ans. Ice-cream is an emulsion of milk and cream in water. Gelatin acts as an emulsifier hence it stabilizes the ice-cream.

Q. 4. Why silica gel is used as a dehumidifier?
Ans. Silica gel can easily adsorb moisture from air. Hence it is used as dehumidifier.

Q. 5. Why is $Fe(OH)_3$ colloid positively charged when prepared by adding $FeCl_3$ to hot water?
Ans. On adding hot water to $Fe(OH)_3$ colloid hydrated ferric oxide $Fe_2O_3.x\,H_2O$ is formed. It adsorbs Fe^{3+} ions from $FeCl_3$ on its surface. Hence a positively charged colloidal sol is formed.

$$Fe_2O_3.xH_2O + Fe^{3+} \longrightarrow [Fe_2O_3.xH_2O]\, Fe^{3+}$$

Q. 6. Why are substances like platinum and palladium often used for carrying out the electrolysis of aqueous solutions?
Ans. Metals like Pt and Pd are inert in nature and are not attacked by ions involved in the process of electrolysis.

Q. 7. Why are powdered substances more effective adsorbents than their crystalline forms?
Ans. Powdered substances are more effective adsorbents than their crystalline forms because when a substance is powdered, its surface area increases and physisorption is directly proportional to the surface area of the adsorbent.

Q. 8. Why is it essential to wash the precipitate with water before estimating it quantitatively?
Ans. When a substance gets precipitated, some ions that combine to form the precipitate gets adsorbed on the surface of the precipitate. Therefore, it becomes important to wash the precipitate before estimating it quantitatively in order to remove these adsorbed ions or other such impurities.

Q. 9. Give reason why a finely divided substance is more effective as an adsorbent.
Ans. Adsorption is a surface phenomenon. Therefore, adsorption is directly proportional to the surface area. A finely divided substance has a large surface area. Both physisorption and chemisorption increases with an increase in the surface area. Hence, a finely divided substance behaves as a good adsorbent.

Q. 10. Why bleeding stops on applying the ferric chloride? Name the phenomenon involved.
Ans. Bleeding stops on applying the ferric chloride because, $FeCl_3$ provides Fe^{3+} ions to neutralize negatively charged RBC's of colloidal blood which leads to coagulation. The phenomenon is called floculation.

Chapter 6. General Principles and Processes of Isolation of Elements

Q. 1. Steel is also called 'Stainless steel'. Why?

Ans. Steel in general is not reactive. It does not corrode by water and mild acids or alkalies. Stainless steel contains about 18% chromium, its a very useful variety of steel.

Q. 2. Why is zinc not extracted from zinc oxide through reduction using CO?

Ans. The standard Gibbs free energy of formation of ZnO from Zn is lower than that of CO_2 from CO. Therefore, CO cannot reduce ZnO to Zn. Hence, Zn is not extracted from ZnO through reduction using CO.

Q. 3. Name the common elements present in the anode mud in electrolytic refining of copper. Why are they so present?

Ans. In, electrolytic refining of copper, the common elements present in anode mud are selenium, tellurium, silver, gold, platinum, and antimony. These elements are very less reactive and are not affected during the purification process. Hence, they settle down below the anode as anode mud.

Q. 4. (i)   Which metal foils are used as wrappers for sweets, medicines, etc.?

     (ii) Why Aluminium vessels preferred over copper and Bronze vessels?

Ans. (i)   Aluminium foils are used because of high malleability and ductility.

     (ii) Aluminum vessels are not affected by either acids or alkalis, nor by other chemicals. Al forms a protective layer of oxide over it. On the other hand, copper and bronze vessels react easily forming poisonous chemical compounds. Hence, Aluminium vessels are preferred.

Chapter 7. *p*-Block Elements

Q. 1. PCl_5 is known but NCl_5 is not known. Explain.

Ans. Phosphorous has empty $3d$-orbitals in which the $3s$ electrons can get excited and thus expand its valency, but in case of nitrogen there is no such $2d$-orbital present. Hence nitrogen cannot extend its co-valency.

Q. 2. Molecular nitrogen is inert. Why?

Ans. Nitrogen molecule is diatomic, the bond dissociation energy for the triple bond in $N \equiv N$ is very high because of small size of N and strong overlapping of the bonding orbitals. Therefore, molecular nitrogen is very inert.

Q. 3. Why does solid PCl_5 behaves as an ionic compound.*

Ans. It exists as $[PCl_4]^+$ $[PCl_6]^-$ in solid state having tetrahedral and octahedral structures of ions respectively. Hence, it behaves as ionic compound in solid state.

Q. 4. PCl_3 fumes in moist air. Why?

Ans. PCl_3 gets hydrolysed in presence of moisture to give out fumes of HCl gas.

$$PCl_3 + 3H_2O \longrightarrow \underset{\text{acid}}{\underset{\text{Phosphorus}}{H3PO_3}} + \underset{\text{fumes in air}}{3HCl(g)}$$

Q. 5. Why does NO_2 dimerises?*

Ans. NO_2 is an odd electron molecule. By dimerisation NO_2 changes to N_2O_4 and thus becomes an even electron molecule which is more stable.

Q. 6. Sulphur vapours exhibit some paramagnetic behaviour. Explain.*

Ans. In vapour state sulphur exist as paramagnetic S_2 molecule and it has two unpaired electrons in H* orbitals, hence it exhibits paramagnetism.

Q. 7. H_2S is stronger acid than H_2O. Explain why?*

Ans. Bond dissociation enthalpy of H_2S is smaller than H_2O as H–S bond is weaker and longer than H—O bond. Hence H^+ is released easily in case of H_2S, making it a stronger acid.

Q. 8. Why SF_6 is kinetically inert compound?

Ans. In case of SF_6, six small fluorine atoms surrounds the S atom in such a way that it sterically hinders the attack of any reagent. Hence, its quite inert to chemical reactions and hydrolysis.

---

* are board exam questions from previous years

Q. 9. Give reasons:
    (i) $E°$ value for Mn^{3+}/Mn^{2+} couple is much more positive than that for Fe^{3+}/Fe^{2+}.
    (ii) Iron has higher enthalpy of atomization than that of copper.
    (iii) Sc^{3+} is colourless in aqueous solution whereas Ti^{3+} is coloured.

Ans. (i) Mn^{2+} has a d^5 configuration and the extra stability of half filled d-orbitals is compromised when another electron is taken out to give Mn^{3+}, on the contrary Fe^{3+} attains a half filled orbital configuration when Fe^{2+} gets oxidized to Fe^{3+}. Hence, the $E°$ value for Mn^{3+}/Mn^{2+} couple has more positive $E°$ value.

     (ii) Fe has a $3d^6 4s^2$ outer electronic configuration whereas Cu has $3d^{10} 4s^1$ configuration. Now, more the number of unpaired electrons in d-orbital, more favourable are interatomic attractions and thus higher atomization enthalpies. Hence, Fe having 4 unpaired d-electrons has more enthalpy of atomization than copper having no unpaired d-electron.

     (iii) Sc^{3+} has a $3d^0$ configuration whereas Ti^{3+} has a $3d^1$ configuration. As there are no electrons in d orbitals for Sc^{3+} ion, there is no transition of electrons by absorption of energy and hence no emission in visible range imparting colour to the Sc^{3+} ion.

Q. 10. H_3PO_3 is dibasic (diprotic) acid. Why?
Ans. From the structural formula of phosphorous acid it is clear that it has only two ionizable H-atoms from –OH bonds. Hence, it behaves as a dibasic acid.

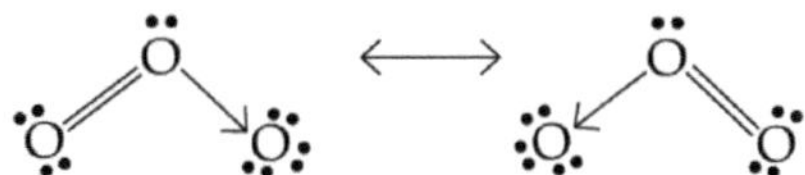

Q. 11. Why sulphur has more catenation tendency than oxygen?**
Ans. Oxygen atoms has smaller size and hence forms stronger $p\pi$-$p\pi$ bond whereas S–S bond is stronger than O—O single bond because of less repulsion of bond pair electrons, causing sulphur to have greater tendency for catenation than oxygen.

Q. 12. Why Bi(V) a stronger oxidising agent than Sb(V)?*
Ans. Bi (V) has stronger tendency to accept electrons and convert to Bi(III) as compared to Sb(V). This is because oxidation state V is more stable in case of Sb than Bi as a result of inert pair effect.

Q. 13. H_2S acts only as a reducing agent while SO_2 acts both as a reducing agent as well as oxidising agent. Why?
Ans. The oxidation number of S in SO_2 is +4. Hence, it can both increase and decrease its oxidation state from +4 to +6 or to – 2. But, in case of H_2S, oxidation number of S is – 2. Hence, it can only increase it but cannot decrease it further. So, H_2S sulphur can only loose electrons and act as a reducing agent while in SO_2 sulphur can both loose and gain electron and act both as oxidising and reducing agent.

Q. 14. The two O—O bond length of ozone molecule are equal. Assign reason.*
Ans. The ozone molecule is a hybrid structure of two resonance structure.

Hence both the O—O, bonds have partial double bond character and both have same bond length.

Q. 15. O_2 and F_2 both stabilise higher oxidation state of metals. But O_2 exceeds F_2 in doing so. Explain.*
Ans. Both O_2 and F_2 are non-metals and binds well with metals but O carry (– 2) charge while fluorine (– 1) charge, hence strength of ionic bond is more in case of oxides than fluorides. So O_2 stabilise higher oxidation state better. Also oxygen can form multiple bonds where as fluorine can not.

Q. 16. Bleaching by Cl_2 is permanent while by SO_2 is temporary. Why?*
Ans. Cl_2 oxidise the substance and thus bleach it while SO_2 reduce and bleach. The bleached substance when face air can again get oxidized by atmospheric oxygen hence bleaching action by SO_2 is temporary.

Q. 17. Why we can not explain xenon fluorides by valence bond approach?*
Ans. Valence bond theory treats bonds as local structures while VSEPR theory figure out molecular geometry. By valence bond theory for example XeF_2 should have trigonal bipyramidal structure while by VSEPR theory can

explain its linear structure Xe compounds (fluorides) specially have Xe as in central element which has a full 8 electrons outer shell, hence lone pairs play important role in geometry.

Q. 18. Justify:
    (i)   Bond angle of H_2S is lower than H_2O.
    (ii) Hydrogen sulphide cannot be dried by passing through conc. H_2SO_4.
    (iii) SO_2 is a more powerful reducing agent in alkaline medium than in acidic medium.

Ans. (i)   Both factors size and electronegativity of the central atom decides the bond angle. Oxygen is more electronegative than sulphur hence, electron density is more near 'O' atom in H_2O. This is added by the fact that 'O' is smaller in size than 'S' atoms, hence electrons are more closer to 'O' in H_2O than in case of 'S' in H_2S. As a result they face more bond pair-bond pair repulsion causing larger bond angle in H_2O than H_2S.

    (ii) Conc. H_2SO_4 reacts with hydrogen sulphide H_2S and thus cannot act as a dehydrating agent.

$$H_2SO_4 + H_2S \longrightarrow 2H_2O + SO_2 + S$$

    (iii) If we look at the reaction of SO2 in the alkaline medium its like.

$$SO_2 + 2OH^- \rightleftharpoons SO_4^{2-} + 2H^+ + 2e^-$$

This reaction is reversible in nature and in acidic medium the reverse reaction is favoured, while in basic medium forward reaction is more favoured.

Q. 19. Explain the following:
    (i)   Bond dissociation enthalpy of F_2 is low.
    (ii) Noble gases have low melting point.
    (iii) HF is weaker acid than HI.

Ans. (i)   Because of very small size of fluorine the F—F bond length is small, also the outermost shell has 8 electrons each in F of each F—F molecule. These cause both the fluorine atoms to repel each other hence F_2 has very low bond dissociation enthalpy.

    (ii) Noble gases have low melting points because of weak Van der Waals forces present between their atoms.

    (iii) H—F bond is stronger bond than H—I. Hence hydrogen is released easily and H—I stronger acid than iodine.

Q. 20. The HNH angle value is higher than HPH, HAsH and HSbH angles. Why? Explain on the basis of sp^3 hybridisation in NH_3 and only s-p bonding between hydrogen and other elements of the group.

Ans.

Hydride NH_3, PH_3, AsH_3, SbH_3

H–M–H angle 107°, 92°, 91°, 90°

The above trend in the H–M–H bond angle can be explained on the basis of the electronegativity of the central atom. Since, nitrogen is highly electronegative there is high electron density around nitrogen. This causes greater repulsion between the electron pairs around nitrogen, resulting in maximum bond angle. We know that electronegativity decreases on moving down a group. Consequently, the repulsive interactions between the electron pairs decrease, thereby decreasing the H—M—H bond angle.

Q. 21. Why halogens are strong oxidising agents?

Ans. The general electronic configuration of halogens is np^5, where $n = 2 - 6$. Thus, halogens need only one more electron to complete their octet and to attain the stable noble gas configuration. Also, halogens are highly electronegative with low bond dissociation energies and high negative electron gain enthalpies. Therefore, they have a high tendency to gain an electron. Hence, they act as strong oxidizing agents.

Q. 22. (i)   In your opinion, which is better way of disinfecting water in swimming pool. Why?
    (ii) Why chlorine water is used? Does it has bleaching action too?

Ans. (i)   Ozone is the better option for sanitizing swimming pool even though its more costilier than chlorine. Reasons being:

    (a) Ozone pools are much cleaner as ozone also break down grease, oil and other organic contaminants.
    (b) Easy maintenance.

(c) No skin and eye irritation or even respiratory problems in long run as in case of chlorinated swimming pools.

(ii) Chlorine has germicidal properties and it destroys harmful germs and bacteria in swimming pool water.

Q. 23. The N—O bond in NO_2^- is shorter than the N—O bond in NO_3^- ion. Explain.*

Ans. NO_2^- has resonance structure as:

[with each bond order about 1.5]

whereas NO_3^- has resonance structures as:

[with each bond order about 1.33]

Hence N—O bond is more stronger and shorter in NO_2^- than N—O bond in NO_3^-.

Chapter 8. *d*-and *f*-Block Elements

Q. 1. Why zinc, cadmium and mercury are not regarded as transition metals?*

Ans. Zn, Cd and Hg all have *d*-orbitals completely filled in both atomic and ionic state, hence cannot be considered as transition metals.

Q. 2. Explain why iron is a transition element but sodium is not?*

Ans. Iron atom Fe (26) and ions Fe^{+2}, Fe^{+3} both have incompletely filled d-orbitals while sodium atom Na (23) or ion does not have any incomplete d-orbitals to generate properties of transition metals.

Q. 3. Copper cannot liberate hydrogen from acids. Why?

Ans. Copper is less reactive than hydrogen as per the electrochemical series. Hence, it cannot reduce hydrogen and get oxidised itself. Therefore, neither hydrogen gas is released on adding Cu to acids.

Q. 4. Which is more stable $CuCl_2$ or Cu_2Cl_2 and why?

Ans. Cu^{2+} ion is always more stable than Cu^+ because of higher negative enthalpy of hydration (Δ_{hyd}, H°), because of smaller size. Hence $CuCl_2$ is more stable than Cu_2Cl_2 in aqueous medium.

Q. 5. The +3 oxidation state is common for all lanthanoids, but cerium shows +4 oxidation state in general. Why?

Ans. Ce has atomic number (Z = 58), has electronic configuration $[Xe]^{54}$ $4f^15d^16s^2$. The +3 state has configuration $[Xe]$ $4f^1$, so by loosing one more electron it attains noble gas configuration of $[Xe]^{54}$ hence Ce^{+4} state is quite stable.

Q. 6. Which metal in the first series of transition metals exhibits +1 oxidation state most frequently and why?

Ans. In the first transition series, Cu exhibits +1 oxidation state very frequently. It is because Cu(+ 1) has an electronic configuration of $[Ar]$ $3d^{10}$. The completely filled *d*-orbital makes it highly stable.

Q. 7. Which of the 3*d* series of the transition metals exhibits the largest number of oxidation states and why?

Ans. Mn (Z = 25) = $[Ar]$ $3d^54s^2$

Mn has the maximum number of unpaired electrons present in the *d*-subshell (5 electrons). Hence, Mn exhibits the largest number of oxidation states, ranging from +2 to +7.

Q. 8. Assign reason for the following:*

(i) Transition metals generally form coloured compounds.

(ii) Manganese exhibits highest oxidation state of +7 among 3d series.

Ans. (i) Transition metals generally have partially filled *d*-orbitals in ionic and compound state. Hence, they undergo *d–d* transition of electrons reflecting light within the visible range, thus appears coloured.

(ii) Manganese is the middle most element of the 3*d* transition series. It has $4s^23d^5$ configuration and because of possible participation of ns^2 and $(n-1)d^5$, all the electrons in bonding it can exhibit the highest oxidation state of + 7.

Q. 9. Size of zinc atom is slightly larger than copper. Why?

Ans. In case of transition metals the added electron in a period enters the $(n-1)$ d subshell not the last valence shell. Hence, it shields the nuclear charge and the sizes of atoms decreases. But, at the end of period as we move from Cu to Zn *i.e.,* $3d^9 - 3d^{10}$ configuration the step-wise increase of nuclear charge is almost cancelled by repulsive forces of $(4s^2\ 3d^{10})$ zinc atom. Hence a right increase in atomic size is observed. So Zn is larger in size than Cu atom.

Q. 10. **Why radius of Fe^{2+} less than Mn^{2+}?**

Ans. Fe^{2+} has electronic configuration $4s^0 3d^6$ and Mn^{2+} has $4s^0 3d^5$. The total nuclear charge pull in Fe atom (26) is more than Mn atom (25), and the weak shielding of 3d. Subshell can't alter the regular trend. Hence as expected Fe^{2+} will have stronger nuclear pull and smaller radius than Mn^{2+}.

Q. 11. **Which has a higher melting point Fe or Cu? Why?***

Ans. Fe has unpaired *d*-electrons $(4s^2\ 3d^2)$ in atomic state for *d–d* covalent metallic bond formation, while in Cu the *d*-electrons are paired $(4s^1 3d^{10})$, hence no additional *d–d* orbital overlap or intermetallic bonding.

Q. 12. **The second and third rows of transition elements resemble each other much more than they resemble the first row of transition elements. Why?**

Ans. As we move down in group the size of atom increases because of additional shell, but in case of 2nd and 3rd transition series their is not much change. This is because of poor shielding of *4d*-orbitals or lanthanoid contraction. Hence the 2nd and 3rd rows of transition elements resembles in size and other properties more than 1st row which does not encounter any lanthanoid contraction.

Q. 13. **It is very difficult to separate Zr of *4d* series from Hf of *5d* series. Why?**

Ans. Zr and Hf belongs to the same group and because of lanthanide contraction they have almost similar size (Zr : 160 pm; Hf : 159 pm). Hence having similar size, same valency electrons and other properties it becomes difficult to separate them from each other.

Q. 14. **(i) In moist air copper corrodes to produce a green layer on the surface. Explain.**
(ii) Why Cr_2O_3 is called an acid anhydride.
(iii) Identify A, B and C in the reaction:

$$CuSO_4.5H_2O \xrightarrow[100°C]{\Delta} [A] \xrightarrow{280°C} [B] \xrightarrow{800°C} [C] + 2SO_2 + O_2$$

Ans. (i)   A thin film of green colour basic copper carbonate is formed when copper corrodes in moist air.

$$2Cu + O_2 + H_2O + CO_2 \longrightarrow CuCO_3.Cu(OH)_2$$
Basic copper carbonate
(Green)

(ii)   If we dehydrate chromic acid,

     i.e., $H_2CrO_4 \xrightarrow{\Delta} CrO_3 + H_2O$, we get chromic oxide. Hence, it is called an acid anhydride.

(iii) $CuSO_4.5H_2O \xrightarrow{100°C} CuSO_4.H_2O \xrightarrow{300°C} CuSO_4 \times 2 \xrightarrow{800°C} 2CuO + 2SO_2 + O_2$
       Blue   Grey [A]   [B]   [C]

Q. 15. **Why is the highest oxidation state of a metal exhibited in its oxide or fluoride only?***

Ans. Both oxide and fluoride ions are most electronegative elements and have a very small size. Due to these properties, they are able to oxidize the metal to its highest oxidation state, specially in case of transition metals.

Chapter 9. Coordination Compounds

Q. 1. **Why are π-complexes known for transition metals only?***

Ans. Transition metals have half-filled or vacant *d*-orbitals so even after forming a dative bond with ligands they can donate back electrons from the filled *d*-orbitals to the empty π* orbitals of ligand to develop *pπ-dπ* bonding. Hence only transition metals form π-complexes.

Q. 2. **WWhy CO is a strong field ligand but not NH_3?***

Ans. CO can form back bonding with the central metal atom giving synergistic effect. Hence, the metal and CO bond is stronger as compared to single metal and NH_3 coordinate bond.

Q. 3. Aqueous copper sulphate solution (blue in colour) gives:

(i) A green precipitate with aqueous potassium fluoride.

(ii) A bright green solution with aqueous potassium chloride.

Explain these experimental results.

Ans. Aqueous $CuSO_4$ exists as $[Cu(H_2O)_4]SO_4$. It is blue in colour due to the presence of $[Cu(H_2O)_4]^{2+}$ ions. Its a labile complex entity.

(i) When KF is added:

$$[Cu(H_2O)_4]^{2+} + 4F^- \longrightarrow \underset{\text{(Green)}}{[Cu(F)_4]^{2-}} + 4H_2O,$$ because (H_2O) gets replaced by F^- ions.

(ii) When KCl is added:

$$[Cu(H_2O)_4]^{2+} + 4Cl^- \longrightarrow \underset{\text{(bright Green)}}{[CuCl_4]^{2-}} + 4H_2O,$$ here (H_2O) ligand is replaced by Cl^- ions.

Chapter 10. Haloalkanes and Haloarenes

Q. 1. Why do the alkyl halides show nucleophilic substitution reactions?

Ans. Alkyl halides are polar in nature, because of the polar C–X bond. Hence nucleophile attacks the electron-deficient carbon (alkyl) group in the bonds and substitution by the nucleophile takes place.

Q. 2. Out of Br^- and I^-, which one is a better nucleophile and why?

Ans. I^- is a better nucleophile than Br^-; I^- ion is bigger in size than Br^- ion and has less electronegativity. Therefore it can donate or release a pair of electron more easily and attack as a nucleophile.

Q. 3. Why vinyl chloride is less reactive than ethyl chloride?

Ans. The C—Cl bond in vinyl chloride is a resonance hybrid and has the less bond distance than single C—C bond. Hence in vinyl chloride C—Cl bond has double bond character and is less reactive than ethyl chloride.

Q. 4. Iodoform gives a precipitate with silver nitrate on heating while chloroform does not. Why?

Ans. In Iodoform the C—I bond is weaker than C—Cl bond of chloroform. Hence on heating with silver nitrate it gives a precipitate of silver iodide while chloroform does not.

Q. 5. Why is chloroform kept in coloured or dark bottles?*

Ans. Chloroform can react with oxygen present in air in the presence of light and can produce a poisonous gas called phosgene. Hence, it should always be kept inside dark coloured coated bottles to prevent exposure of sunlight. The bottles should also be filled till top and corked well to avoid entry of air.

$$2CHCl_3 + O_2 \xrightarrow{\text{Light}} \underset{\text{Phosgene}}{2COCl_2} + 2HCl$$

Q. 6. Out of $CH_3—\underset{\underset{CH_3}{|}}{CH}—CH_2—Cl$ and $CH_3—\underset{\underset{CH_3}{|}}{CH}—Cl$ which is more reactive towards S_N1 mechanism and why?*

Ans. In case of S_N1 mechanism, a carbocation is formed as an intermediate. As 3° > 2° > 1° hence $CH_3—CH_2—\underset{\underset{CH_3}{|}}{CH}—Cl$ is more reactive as it produces a 2° carbocation.

Q. 7. Which of the following compounds will react faster in the S_N1 reaction and why?*

(i)  or 

(ii) 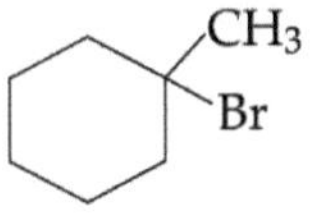 or 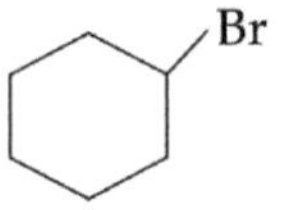

Ans. (i) S_N1 reaction is faster in case of carbocation 3° > 2° > 1°. Hence  will react faster as it will provide a 2° carbocation while 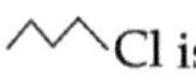 is 1° alkyl halide.

* are board exam questions from previous years

(ii) [structure: cyclohexane with CH₃ and Br] will react by S_N1 mechanism as is a 3° alkyl halide while [structure: cyclohexyl bromide] cyclohexyl bromide is a

2° alkyl halide.

Q. 8. **Which of the following compounds will undergo S_N1 reaction faster and why?**

[structure (A): cyclohexane with CH₂Cl]   [structure (B): benzene ring with CH₂Cl]

(A)   (B)

Ans. Compound (B) will undergo S_N1 reaction faster as the benzyl carbocation, intermediate formed is extra resonance stabilized.

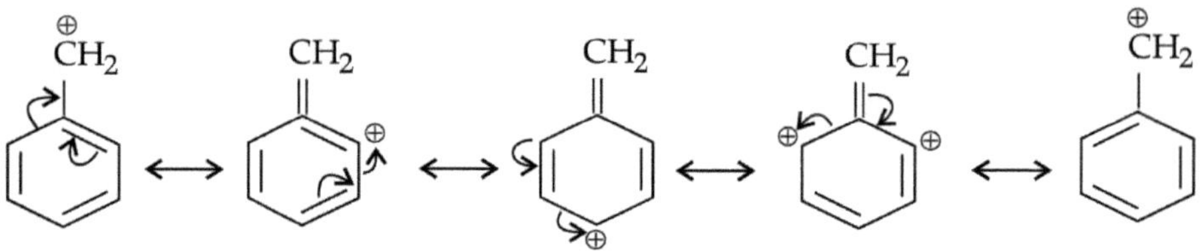

Which is not possible in case of compound (A).

Q. 9. **WWhich of the following pairs will undergo S_N2 reaction faster and why?**

(i) [structure: cyclohexane—CH₂Cl] or [structure: cyclohexane—Cl]

(ii) [structure: chain—I] or [structure: chain—Cl*]

Ans. (i) [structure: cyclohexane—CH₂Cl] will react faster in S_N2 mechanism as the order of reactivity is 1° > 2° > 3° and this is

a 1° alkyl halide while [structure: cyclohexane—Cl] —Cl is a 2° alkyl halide.

(ii) [structure: chain—I] will react faster than [structure: chain—Cl] as C — I bond is weaker than C — Cl and I– is a better leaving group.

Chapter 11. Alcohols, Phenols and Ethers

Q. 1. **Phenol has smaller dipole moment than methanol. Explain.***
Ans. The phenyl group (C_6H_5) in phenol is electron withdrawing. While (CH_3) group in methanol is electron releasing. Hence phenol has smaller dipole moment while methanol has higher dipole moment.

$$\overset{\delta+}{CH_3} >> \overset{\delta-}{OH}$$ [structure: benzene ring—OH]

Q. 2. **Sodium metal can not be used to dry alcohols. Why?**
Ans. Sodium reacts with alcohol to evolve H_2 gas. Hydrogen itself is an explosive gas. Hence sodium metal can't be used for drying alcohols.

Q. 3. **An alkoxide ion is a stronger base than hydroxide ion. Justify.**
Ans. R (alkyl) group is an electron releasing group, hence it increases electron density of alkoxide ion. On the other hand in hydroxide ion no such group is present, hence alkoxide ions can accept a H^+ ion more easily as compared to OH^- ion.

Q. 4. (i) Why boiling points of ethers are lower than those of alcohols of comparable molecular mass.*
(ii) Account for the solubility of ethoxyethane in water.

Ans. (i) Ethers have quite low boiling point compared to alcohols of comparable molecular mass because of presence of more polar O—H bonds compared to C—O bonds of ether. There is intermolecular hydrogen bonding present in alcohols which is absent in ethers.

(ii) Ethoxyethane is able to form intermolecular hydrogen bonding with water to same extent. These hydrogen bonds make it soluble in water to some degree.

Q. 5. Explain:

(i) Ethers are cleaned only by acids and not by bases.

(ii) Diethyl ether does not react with sodium.

Ans. (i) Ethers are lewis bases themselves. The bases cannot weaken the C—O—C bond in ethers, whereas acids can attack the 'O' atom as an electrophile causing clevage of C—O bond.

$$CH_3 - \overset{..}{\underset{..}{O}} - C_2H_5 \longrightarrow CH_3 - \overset{+}{O} - C_2H_5 \xrightarrow{Br^-} C_2H_5OH + CH_3Br$$

Protonated ether

(ii) Diethyl ether does not have the active hydrogen like alcohols. Hence can't react with sodium metal to release H_2 gas.

Q. 6. Alcohols are comparatively more soluble in water than hydrocarbons of comparable molecular masses. Explain this fact.

Ans. Alcohols form H-bonds with water due to the presence of –OH group. However, hydrocarbons cannot form H-bonds with water. Hence water and alcohol both are polar molecules with intermolecular hydrogen bonding. As "like dissolves like", thus alcohols are comparatively more soluble in water than hydrocarbons of comparable molecular masses.

Q. 7. While separating a mixture of *ortho* and *para* nitrophenols by steam distillation, name the isomer which will be steam volatile. Give reason.

Ans. Intramolecular H-bonding is present in *o*-nitrophenol. In *p*-nitrophenol, the molecules are strongly associated due to the presence of intermolecular hydrogen bonding. Hence, *o*-nitrophenol is steam volatile, and has less boiling point than *para* nitro phenol, which is strongly bonded with each other as a result of intermolecular H-bonding.

o-Nitrophenol

p-Nitrophenol

Q. 8. Give reason for the higher boiling point of ethanol in comparison to methoxymethane.

Ans. Ethanol undergoes intermolecular H-bonding due to the presence of –OH group, as shown below. Extra energy is required to break these hydrogen bonds whereas, methoxymethane does not undergo H-bonding, it has only weak dipole-dipole interactions present in it.

Hence, the boiling point of ethanol is higher than that of methoxymethane.

Q. 9. **Preparation of ethers by acid dehydration of secondary or tertiary alcohols is not a suitable method. Give reason.**

Ans. The formation of ethers by dehydration of alcohol is a bimolecular reaction (S_N2) involving the attack of an alcohol molecule on a protonated alcohol molecule. In this method, the alkyl group must be sterically unhindered. In case of secondary or tertiary alcohols, the alkyl group is having bulky substituents. As a result, elimination dominates substitution causing formation of alkenes rather than ethers.

Chapter 12. Aldehydes, Ketones and Carboxylic Acids

Q. 1. **What happens when ethanoyl chloride is treated with phenol?**

Ans. Phenol ethanoate is produced.

$$CH_3COCl + C_6H_5OH \longrightarrow CH_3COOC_6H_5$$

Q. 2. **Account for the following:**

    (i)   Why formaldehyde cannot be prepared by Rosenmund's reduction?

    (ii) Benzaldehyde is less reactive towards nucleophillic addition reaction than acetaldehyde. Why?

Ans. (i)   For Rosenmund's reaction, the acyl chloride required for the preparation of formaldehyde will be COCl, formyl chloride which is in itself an unstable compound. Hence the reaction is not very feasible.

    (ii) In benzaldehyde the phenyl group provides greater steric hindrance than methyl group ($-CH_3$) of acetaldehyde to the attacking nucleophile.

Chapter 13. Amines

Q. 1. **Why alkyl amine is more basic than ammonia?***

Ans. In alkyl amines, the presence of alkyl group or groups (R) make the nitrogen atom more electron rich by +I effect. As a result it is easier for N atom to donate the lone pair of electrons and act as a base, compared to ammonia.

Q. 2. **Aniline is a weaker base than cyclohexylamine. Explain.**

Ans. In aniline the lone pair of electrons of nitrogen atom are involved in resonance hence are less available for donation. There is no such effect in cyclohexylamine, hence it is a stronger base.

Q. 3. **What happens when nitroethane is boiled with HCl?**

Ans.
$$CH_3CH_2NO_2 + HCl(aq.) \xrightarrow{\Delta} CH_3COOH + NH_2OH$$

    Nitroethane   Ethanoic   Hydroxylamine

Q. 4. **Trimethylamine reacts with BF₃ while triphenylamine does not. Explain.**

Ans. Trimethylamine has three methyl groups with +I effect which increases the electron density on nitrogen and hence it acts as a lewis base and reacts with lewis acid BF_3. On the other hand in triphenyl amine, the presence of three phenyl groups with – I, effect decreases the electron density on nitrogen making it less basic.

Chapter 14. Biomolecules

Q. 1. **Why invert sugar is called inversion of sugar solution?**

Ans. As the sucrose solution, which is dextrotatory decomposes to glucose (dextro) and fructose (laevo) thus the total optical rotation of the solution becomes negative, *i.e.*, laevorotatory this is because the degree of rotation of fructose is more than the dextro-rotatory glucose, resulting in overall laevorotatory mixture.

Q. 2. **Why cellulose is not fit for human diet?***

---

* are board exam questions from previous years

Ans. Cellulose is a linear polymer of β-D-glucose. Human stomach does not produce enzyme cellulase to hydrolyse the β-glycosidic linkages of cellulose, hence it can't be digested.

Q. 3. Why vitamin C cannot be stored in our body?

Ans. Vitamin C can not be stored in our body because it is a water soluble vitamin. Hence, it is readily excreted via urine.

Q. 4. On heating glucose solution with Tollen's reagent we obtain a shining mirror on the surface of test tube. Why? State the chemical reaction to justify your answer.

Ans. Tollen's reagent is ammonical silver nitrate. It reduces on heating with glucose to produce metallic silver. This silver gets deposited on the walls of test tube, resulting in formation of shining mirror.

$$\underset{\text{Glucose}}{\overset{\displaystyle \text{CHO}}{\underset{\displaystyle \text{CH}_3\text{OH}}{|\;(\text{CHOH})_4\;|}}} + 2[\text{Ag(NH}_3)_2\text{OH}] \xrightarrow{\;\Delta\;} \underset{\text{Gluconic acid}}{\overset{\displaystyle \text{COOH}}{\underset{\displaystyle \text{CH}_2\text{OH}}{|\;(\text{CHOH})_4\;|}}} + \underset{\text{Silver mirror}}{2\text{Ag}\downarrow} + 4\text{NH}_3 + 2\text{H}_2\text{O}$$

(Tollen's reagent)

Q. 5. Glucose or sucrose are soluble in water but cyclohexane and benzene (simple six membered ring compounds) are insoluble in water. Explain.

Ans. A glucose molecule contains five –OH groups while a sucrose molecule contains eight –OH groups. Thus, glucose and sucrose undergo extensive H-bonding with water. Hence, these are water soluble carbohydrates. On the other hand cyclohexane and benzene do not contain any –OH groups. Hence, they cannot undergo H-bonding with water therefore are insoluble in water.

Q. 6. How do you explain the amphoteric behaviour of amino acids?

Ans. In aqueous solution, the carboxyl group of an amino acid can lose a proton and the amino group can accept a proton to give a dipolar ion known as zwitter ion.

$$\underset{\text{(Amino acid)}}{R - \underset{\underset{\displaystyle :\text{NH}_2}{|}}{\text{CH}} - \overset{\displaystyle \overset{\text{O}}{\|}}{\text{C}} - \text{O} - \text{H}} \rightleftharpoons \underset{\text{(Zwitter ion)}}{R - \underset{\underset{\displaystyle {}^{+}\text{NH}_3}{|}}{\text{CH}} - \overset{\displaystyle \overset{\text{O}}{\|}}{\text{C}} - \text{O}^{-}}$$

Therefore, in zwitter ionic form, the amino acid can act both as an acid and a base.

$$R - \underset{\underset{\displaystyle \text{NH}_2}{|}}{\text{CH}} - \overset{\displaystyle \overset{\text{O}}{\|}}{\text{C}} - \text{O}^{-} \underset{\text{OH}^{-}}{\overset{\text{H}^{+}}{\rightleftharpoons}} R - \underset{\underset{\displaystyle {}^{+}\text{NH}_3}{|}}{\text{CH}} - \overset{\displaystyle \overset{\text{O}}{\|}}{\text{C}} - \text{O}^{-} \underset{\text{OH}^{-}}{\overset{\text{H}^{+}}{\rightleftharpoons}} R - \underset{\underset{\displaystyle {}^{+}\text{NH}_3}{|}}{\text{CH}} - \overset{\displaystyle \overset{\text{O}}{\|}}{\text{C}} - \text{OH}$$

Thus, amino acids show amphoteric behaviour.

Chapter 15. Polymers

Q. 1. Why rubbers are called elastomers?

Ans. Rubbers have elastic properties. They can be stretched and will again regain their original shape on releasing. Hence rubbers are called elastomers.

Q. 2. Are polyacrylates and polyesters same? Justify your answer.

Ans. Polyacrylates are homopolymers. These are formed by addition polymerization. Polyesters on the other hand are co-polymers formed by ester linkage. These are condensation polymers.

Q. 3. Is $\left(\!\!-\text{NH} - \text{CHR} - \text{CO}\!\!\right)_n$, a homopolymer or a copolymer?

Ans. $\left(\!\!-\text{NH} - \text{CHR} - \text{CO}\!\!\right)_n$ is a homopolymer because it has a single monomer (repeating) unit,

NH_2 – CHR – COOH.

Chapter 16. Chemistry in Everyday Life

Q. 1. Why is bithional added to toilet soaps?*
Ans. On the toilet soaps bacterial decomposition of the organic matter of skin can take place. Hence to inhibit that antiseptic bithional is sometimes added to soaps.

Q. 2. Why is use of pencillin generally discouraged?
Ans. Pencillin is not a broad spectrum antibiotic and can have allergic reactions to many patients. Therefore its use is generally discouraged.

Q. 3. In what respect prontosil and salvarsan are similar? Discuss their resemblance with azo dye.
Ans. German bacteriologist Paul Ehrilch developed the first antimicrobial drug salvarsan or arsphenamine. This was used to treat syphillis. The chemical formula of this drug has — As = As — linkage. Prontosil an antibacterial agent has — N = N — bond present in its structure that resembles azo-dyes. In place of — As = As bond of salvasan, azodyes and prontosil has — N = N — structure. Also due to absence of arsenic atom in prontosil, it is much less toxic than salvarsan to human beings.

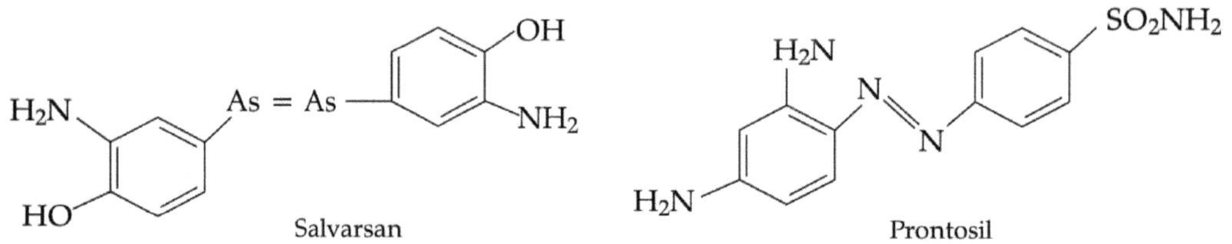

H_2N ... OH, $As = As$, NH_2, HO — **Salvarsan**

H_2N, H_2N, $N=N$, SO_2NH_2, H_2N — **Prontosil**

Q. 4. Which analgesics are called opiates?
Ans. Narcotic drugs derived from the opium plant family are called opiates. Example morphine, codeine.

Q. 5. Both antacids and antiallergic drugs are antihistamine but they cannot replace each other. Why?
Ans. Antacids work on different receptors than antiallergic drugs. Hence, they can not perform the role of each other.

Q. 6. Why is use of aspartame limited to cold foods and drinks?
Ans. Aspartame decomposes at higher baking or cooking temperature. This is the reason why its use is limited to cold foods and drinks.

Q. 7. How are synthetic detergents better than soap?
Ans. Soaps work in soft water. However, they are not effective in hard water. In contrast, synthetic detergents work both in soft water and hard water. Therefore, synthetic detergents are better than soaps.

Q. 8. Sleeping pills are recommended by doctors to the patients suffering from sleeplessness but it is not advisable to take its doses without consultation with the doctor, Why?
Ans. Most drugs when taken in doses higher than recommended may cause harmful side-effects and sometimes, may even lead to death. Hence, a doctor should always be consulted before taking any medicine.

Q. 9. Why do we require artificial sweetening agents?
Ans. A large number of people are suffering from diseases such as diabetes and obesity. These people can not take normal sugar *i.e.,* sucrose as it adds to the calorie intake. Therefore, artificial sweetening agents that do not add to the calorie intake of a person are required. Sucralose and aspartame, are the few examples of artificial sweeteners.

Q. 10. Why medicines should not be taken without consulting doctors?
Ans. A medicine can bind to more than one receptor site and thus may be toxic for some receptor sites. Further, in most cases, medicines cause harmful effects when taken in higher doses than recommended. As a result, medicines may be poisonous in such cases. Hence, medicines should not be taken without consulting doctors for knowing not only the correct medicine but also the correct potency or dose.

Chapter 1. Solid State

Q. 1. Give the significance of a 'lattice point'.

Ans. The significance of a lattice point is that each lattice point represents one constituent particle of a solid which may be an atom, a molecule (group of atom), or an ion.

Q. 2. Name the parameters that characterise a unit cell.

Ans. The six parameters that characterise a unit cell are as follows :

(a) Its dimensions along the three edges a, b, and c. These edges may or may not be equal.

(b) Angles between the edges. These are the angle α (between edges b and c), β (between edges a and c), and γ (between edges a and b).

Q. 3. What is the two-dimensional coordination number of a molecule in square close packed layer?

Ans. In square close-packed layer, a molecule is in contact with four of its neighbours. Therefore, the two-dimensional coordination number of a molecule in square close packed layer is 4.

Q. 4. Which of the following lattices has the highest packing efficiency (i) simple cubic, (ii) body-centred cubic and (iii) hexagonal close-packed lattice?

Ans. Hexagonal close-packed lattice has the highest packing efficiency of 74%. The packing efficiencies of simple cubic and body-centred cubic lattices are 52.4% and 68% respectively.

Q. 5. Explain with suitable examples of the following :

(i) *n*-type and *p*-type semiconductors.*

(ii) F-centres.

Ans. (i) *n*-type semiconductor: If a group-14 element like silicon crystal is doped with group-15 element such as P, As etc, then the fifth electron of the valence shell becomes delocalised and is thus free to contribute to electrical conduction. *n*-stands for negative and as electrons are responsible for semiconducting behaviour.

p-type semiconductor: It is obtained by doping silicon or group 14 elements with group 13 elements like Ga, which contain only three valence electrons. Due to missing of fourth valence electron, an electron hole or electron vacancy is created. As holes are conductors which are positive by charge hence are called *p*-type.

(ii) **F-centres:** The anionic sites occupied by unpaired electrons and are responsible for the colour of a crystal with metal excess defect are called F-centres. Example : $NaCl$, KCl etc.

Q. 6. What type of defect can arise when a solid is heated? Which physical property is affected by it and in what way?

Ans. When a solid is heated, vacancy defect can arise. A solid crystal is said to have vacancy defect when some of the lattice sites are vacant. Vacancy defect leads to a decrease in the density of the solid.

Q. 7. What are non-stoichiometric defects in crystals? Explain with example.

Ans. When the stoichiometry of a compound is not maintained because of a point defect then these are called non-stoichiometric defects. Example in vanadium oxide (VO_x), x can be between 0.6 to 1.3 or $Fe_{0.93}O$. These are again of two types: (a) metal excess, (b) metal deficiency defects.

Q. 8. A group 14 element is to be converted into *n*-type semiconductor by doping it with a suitable impurity. To which group should this impurity belong?

Ans. An *n*-type semiconductor conducts electricity because of the presence of extra electrons. Therefore, a group 14 element can be converted to *n*-type semiconductor by doping it with a group 15 element.

Q. 9. Define the term 'amorphous'. Give few examples of amorphous solids.

---

* are board exam questions from previous years

Ans. Amorphous solids are the solids whose constituent particles are of irregular shapes and have short range order. These solids are isotropic in nature and melt over a range of temperature. Therefore, amorphous solids are sometimes called pseudo-solids or super cooled liquids. Examples of amorphous solids include glass, rubber and plastic.

Q. 10. What makes a glass different from a solid such as quartz? Under what conditions could quartz be converted into glass?

Ans. The arrangement of the constituent particles makes glass different from quartz. In glass, the constituent particles have short range order, but in quartz, the constituent particles have both long range and short range order. Quartz can be converted into glass by heating and then cooling it rapidly.

Q. 11. (i) Based on the nature of intermolecular forces, classify the following solids:*

Silicon carbide, Argon

(ii) ZnO turns yellow on heating. Why?

(iii) What is meant by group 12-16 compounds? Give an example.

Ans. (i) Silicon carbide : covalent crystal.

Argon : Non polar molecular solid

(ii) When ZnO is heated, it loses oxygen as:

$$ZnO \xrightarrow{\text{Heat}} Zn^{2+} + \tfrac{1}{2}O_2 + 2e^-$$

Zn^{2+} are entrapped in the interstitial sites and electrons are entrapped in the neighbouring interstitial sites to maintain electrical neutrality. This results in metal excess defects and f-centres are created. Due to the presence of electrons in the interstitial voids and thus the colour is yellow.

(iii) When a compound is formed between group-12 and group-16 elements, then it is known as group 12-16 compound.

For *e.g.*, CO_2

C → Group-12 element

O → Group-16 element

Q. 12. (i) Based on the nature of intermolecular forces, classify the following solids:*
Benzene, Silver.

(ii) AgCl shows Frenkel defect while NaCl does not. Give reason.

(iii) What type of semiconductor is formed when Ge is doped with Al?

Ans. (i) Benzene : Non-polar molecular solid

Silver : Metallic solid.

(ii) Frenkel defect is not found in NaCl because Na^+ ions cannot get into the interstitial sites due to larger size. While, Ag^+ ion in AgCl has smaller size and easily fit into the interstitial sites.

(iii) When Ge is doped with Al, *p*-type semiconductor is formed.

Q. 13. (i) Based on the nature of intermolecular forces, classify the following solids:*
Sodium sulphate, Hydrogen

(ii) What happens when $CdCl_2$ is doped with AgCl?

(iii) Why do ferrimagnetic substances show better magnetism than antiferromagnetic substances?

Ans. (i) Sodium sulphate : Ionic solid.

Hydrogen : Non-polar molecular solid

(ii) When $CdCl_2$ is doped with AgCl, electrical conductivity of AgCl solid is increased.

(iii) In ferrimagnetic substances, magnetic moments of domains are aligned in parallel and antiparallel directions in unequal amount so that resulting magnetic moment is not zero. While in case of anti-ferromagnetic substances, due to equal number of opposite domains, net magnetic moment is zero. That's why ferrimagnetic substances show better magnetism than antiferromagnetic substances.

Q. 14. What is piezoelectricity and pyroelectricity?

Ans. A dielectric crystal which has a resultant dipole moment can produce electricity when external pressure is applied. Such a crystal is called piezo-electric crystal and the property is called piezo-electricity.

Example: Lead zirconate ($PbZrO_2$) (pressure electricity), quartz etc.

These are used in microphones, ultrasonic generators and sonar detectors.

Pyroelectricity: Some polar crystals upon heating produce small electric current. This phenomenon is called pyroelectricity. Example : Polyuinylidene Fluoride, lead zirconate titanate etc.

Chapter 2. Solutions

Q. 1. State the limitations of Henry's law.

Ans. Henry's law holds good when;
   (a) Pressure of gas is low and temperature is high.
   (b) The gas is reactive with the solvent.

Q. 2. Define the term solution. How many types of solutions are formed? Write briefly about each kind of solution with an example.

Ans. A solution is a homogeneous mixture of two or more than two chemically non-reacting substances whose composition can be varied within certain limits.

The solution which is made up of two components is referred as binary solution.

Types of solutions: Binary solutions. Various types of solutions depending upon the physical states of different components are listed below.

Types of Solution	Common Example
Gaseous Solutions	
Gas in gas	a mixture of oxygen and nitrogen gases
Liquid in gas	chloroform vapours mixed with nitrogen gas
Solid in gas	camphor vapours in nitrogen gas
Liquid Solutions	
Gas in liquid	oxygen dissolved in water
Liquid in liquid	ethanol dissolved in water
Solid in liquid	sucrose dissolved in water
Solid Solutions	
Gas in solid	solution of hydrogen in palladium
Liquid in solid	amalgam of mercury with sodium
Solid in solid	copper dissolved in gold

Q. 3. Suggest the most important type of intermolecular attractive interaction in the following pairs.
   (i) n-hexane and n-octane
   (ii) I_2 and CCl_4
   (iii) $NaClO_4$ and water
   (iv) Methanol and acetone
   (v)   Acetonitrile (CH_3CN) and acetone (C_3H_6O).

Ans. (i)   Van der Waal's forces of attraction. (London dispersion forces)
   (ii)   Van der Waal's forces of attraction. (London dispersion forces)
   (iii) Ion-dipole interaction.
   (iv) Dipole-dipole interaction. (As both are polar molecules)
   (v)   Dipole-dipole interaction. (Both are polar molecules)

Q. 4. What happens when:*
   (i)   a pressure greater than osmotic pressure is applied on the solution side separated from solvent by a semipermeable membrane?
   (ii) acetone is added to pure ethanol?

Ans. (i)   When a pressure greater than osmotic pressure is applied on the solution side, the solvent flows out to the solution through the semipermeable membrane. This is known as reverse osmosis.
   (ii) Mixture of ethanol and acetone shows a positive deviation from Raoult's law and the vapour pressure over the solution increases. The acetone molecules weaken the hydrogen bonding between molecules of ethanol hence making escape of ethanol molecules easy.

Chapter 3. Electrochemistry

Q. 1. How is equilibrium constant K related to only E°cell and not Ecell?

Ans. According to Nernst equation; $E_{cell} = E°_{cell} \dfrac{-2.303\,RT}{nF}$ or $\dfrac{[\text{Products}]^x}{[\text{Reactants}]^y}$

$$E°_{cell} = \dfrac{2.303\,RT}{nF} \log K_c$$

where,

$$K_c = \text{equilibrium const.} \dfrac{[\text{Products}]^x}{[\text{Reactants}]^y}$$

$$E_{cell} = 0, \text{ at equilibrium}$$

and at 298 K temperature.

$$E°_{cell} = \dfrac{0.0591}{nF} \log K_c.$$

Hence equilibrium constant (K_c) is related to $E°_{cell}$ and not E_{cell}.

Q. 2. Define galvanisation. Explain its benefits.

Ans. The process of coating iron with a thin layer of zinc on its surface to protect it from corrosion is called galvanisation. Galvanisation protects iron even when the zinc coating is scratched from certain sites on the surface. As zinc is more electropositive than iron, hence even if iron surface is exposed the nearby zinc gets oxidised but not iron. This is not possible in case of other metals like tin. Tin coating cannot protect iron in galvanisation.

Q. 3. (i) State the factors that influence the value of cell potential of the following cell.

$$Mg(s) \mid Mg^{2+} (aq) \mid\mid Ag^+ (aq) \mid Ag(s)$$

(ii) Write Nernst equation to calculate the cell potential of the above cell.*

Ans. (i) Cell potential depends upon the concentration of the electrolytes and temperature. Hence concentration of Mg^{2+} ions and Ag^+ ions will influence cell potential value.

(ii)
$$E_{cell} = E°_{cell} \dfrac{2.303\,RT}{nF} \log \dfrac{[Mg^{2+}(aq)]}{[Ag^+(aq)]^2}$$

$$n = 2$$
$$Mg + 2Ag^+(aq) \longrightarrow Mg^{2+}(aq) + 2Ag$$

So,
$$E_{cell} = E°_{cell} \dfrac{-2.303\,RT}{2F} \log \dfrac{[Mg^{2+}(aq)]}{[Ag^+(aq)]^2}$$

Q. 4. Suggest a way to determine the Λ^0_m value of water.

Ans. Applying Kohlrausch's law of independent migration of ions, the Λ^o_m value of water can be determined as follows:

$$\Lambda^o_{m(H_2O)} = \lambda^o_{H^+} + \lambda^o_{OH}$$

$$= (\lambda^o_{H^+} + \lambda^o_{Cl^-}) + (\lambda^o_{Na^+} + \lambda^o_{OH^+}) - (\lambda^o_{Na^+} + \lambda^o_{Cl^-})$$

$$\Lambda^o_{m(HCl)} + \Lambda^o_{m(NaCl)} - \Lambda^o_{m(NaCl)}$$

Hence, by knowing the Λ^o_m values of HCl, NaOH, and NaCl, the Λ^o_m value of water can be determined.

Q. 5. Depict the galvanic cell in which the reaction

$$Zn(s) + 2Ag^+ (aq) \rightarrow Zn^{2+} (aq) + 2Ag(s) \text{ takes place. Further show:}$$

(i) Which of the electrode is negatively charged?

(ii) The carriers of the current in the cell.

(iii) Individual reaction at each electrode.

Ans. The galvanic cell in which the given reaction takes place is depicted as:

$$Zn(s) \mid Zn^{2+}(aq) \mid\mid Ag^+(aq) \mid Ag(s)$$

(i) Zn electrode (anode) is negatively charged.

(ii) Ions are carriers of current in the cell and in the external circuit, current will flow from silver to zinc. Ions are Zn^{2+} and Ag^+.

(iii) The reaction taking place at the anode is given by,

$$Zn(s) \longrightarrow Zn^{2+}(aq) + 2e^-$$

The reaction taking place at the cathode is given by,

$$Ag^+(aq) + e^- \longrightarrow Ag(s)$$

Q. 6. **How much charge is required for the following reductions:**

(i) 1 mol of Al^{3+} to Al.

(ii) 1 mol of Cu^{2+} to Cu.

(iii) 1 mol of MnO_4^- to Mn^{2+}.

Ans. (i)

$$Al^{3+} + 3e^- \longrightarrow Al$$

$\therefore$ Required charge $= 3F$

$$= 3 \times 96487 \text{ C}$$
$$= 289{,}461 \text{ C}$$

(ii)

$$Cu^{2+} + 2e^- \longrightarrow Cu$$

$\therefore$ Required charge $= 2F$

$$= 2 \times 96487 \text{ C}$$
$$= 192{,}974 \text{ C}$$

(iii)

$$MnO_4^- \longrightarrow Mn^{2+}$$

i.e.,

$$Mn^{7+} + 5e^- \longrightarrow Mn^{2+}$$

$\therefore$ Required charge $= 5F$

$$= 5 \times 96487 \text{ C}$$
$$= 482{,}435 \text{ C.}$$

Q. 7. **Write the equation showing the relationship between molar conductance and concentration of a strong electrolyte.**[*]

Ans. Debye-Huckle-Onsager equation explains the same;

$$\boxed{\Lambda_c = \Lambda^\circ - A\sqrt{C}}$$

in which Λc is the molar conductance at concentration C and A is a constant.

Q. 8. **Write the name of the cell which is generally used in inverters. Write the reactions taking place at the anode and the cathode of this cell.**[*]

Ans. Lead storage battery is commonly used in inverters. Reactions taking place at anode.

$$Pb(s) \longrightarrow Pb^{2+}(aq) + 2e^-$$

$$Pb^{2+}_{(aq.)} + SO_4^{2-}{}_{(aq)} \longrightarrow PbSO_4(s)$$

The overall reaction at anode is

$$Pb(s) + SO_4^{2-}(aq) \longrightarrow PbSO_4(s) + 2e^-$$

Reactions taking place at cathode.

$$PbO_2(s) + 4H^+(aq) + SO_4^{2-} + 2e^- \longrightarrow PbSO_4(s) + 2H_2O(l)$$

Q. 9. (i) Write the principles of electrolytic refining.[*]

(ii) Why does copper obtained in the extraction from copper pyrites have a blistered appearance?

(iii) What is the role of depressants in the froth floatation process?

Ans. (i) **Electrolytic Refining:** This method is based on the principle of electrolysis. In this method impure metal is made to act as anode and a strip of same metal in pure form is used as cathode. Both anode and cathode are placed in a suitable electrolytic bath containing soluble salt of same metals.

(ii) In the extraction of copper from $CuFeS_2$, SO_2, N_2 and O_2 escape from the metal. As the metal solidifies, the dissolved gases escape producing blisters on the metal surface which provides blister appearance to copper.

(iii) Depressants are used to prevent certain types of particles from forming the froth with air bubbles. For example NaCN can be used as a depressant in the separation of ZnS and PbS.

Chapter 4. Chemical Kinetics

Q. 1. **From the two graphs/plot of rate of reaction vs. concentration of the reactant, determine the order of reaction.**

(i)

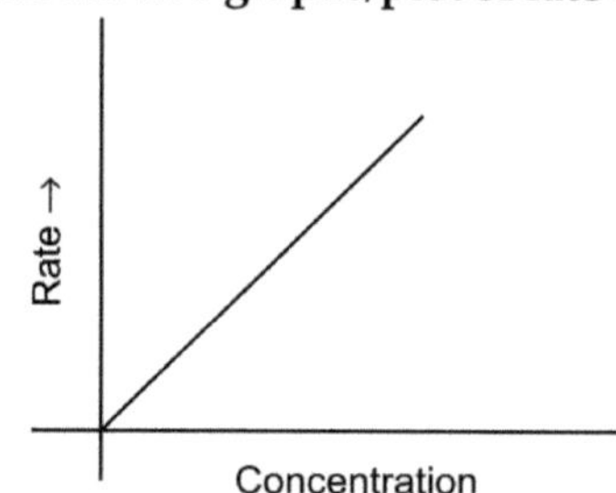

(ii)

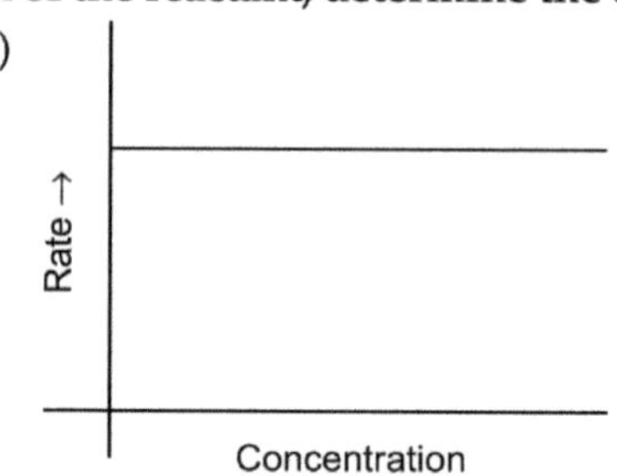

Ans. (i)   First order reaction.

(ii)   Zero order reaction.

Q. 2. (i)   Draw a schematic graph showing how the rate of reaction changes with change in concentration of reactant.

(ii)   Rate of a reaction is given by the equation:*

$$\text{Rate} = k[A]^2[B]^1$$

What are the units of rate and the rate constant for the reaction.

Ans. (i)

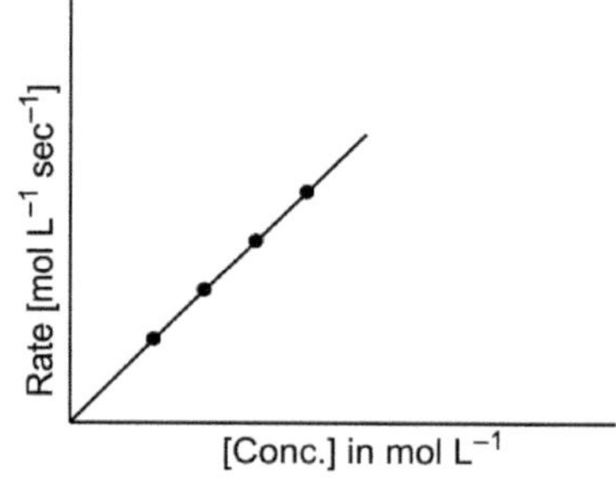

Graph between rate and concentration.

(ii)   Rate $= k[A]^2[B]^1$

$\text{mol L}^{-1}\,\text{s}^{-1} = k[\text{mol L}^{-1}]^2\,[\text{mol L}^{-1}]$

Hence unit of rate constant $k = \dfrac{\text{mol L}^{-1}\,\text{s}^{-1}}{[\text{mol L}^{-1}]^3}$

$= \text{L}^2\,\text{mol}^{-2}\,\text{s}^{-1}.$

Q. 3. **Sketch a potential energy diagram representing an exothermic reaction.**

Ans. E_a = Activation energy of forward reaction

H_R = Enthalpy of reactant

H_P = Enthalpy of product

ΔH = Enthalpy change during reaction

as $H_R - H_P = \Delta H$

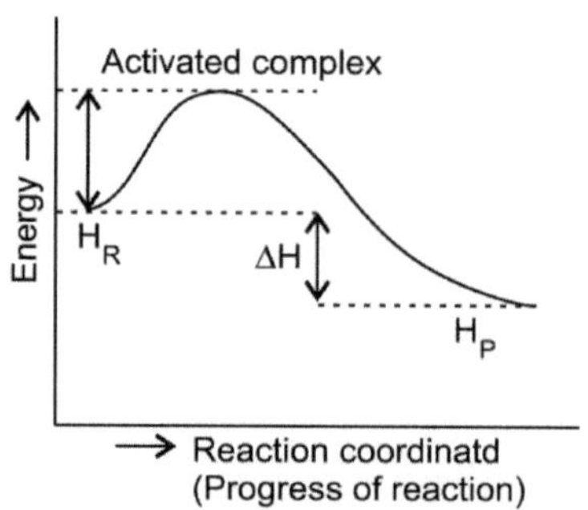

Hence release of heat will take place (exothermic) as reaction proceeds.

Q. 4. **From the rate expression for the following reactions, determine the order of reaction and the dimensions of the rate constants:**

(i) $3NO(g) \rightarrow N_2O\ (g)$ Rate $= k[NO]^2$

(ii) $H_2O_2\ (aq) + 3I^-\ (aq) + 2H^+ \rightarrow 2H_2O\ (I) + I_3^-$ Rate $= k[H_2O_2][I^-]$

(iii) $CH_3CHO(g) \rightarrow CH_4(g) + CO(g)$ Rate $= k[CH_3CHO]^{3/2}$

(iv) $C_2H_5Cl(g) \rightarrow C_2H_4(g) + HCl(g)$ Rate $= k[C_2H_5Cl]$

Ans. (i) Given rate $= k[NO]^2$

Therefore, order of the reaction $= 2$

$$\text{Dimension of } k = \frac{\text{Rate}}{[NO]^2}$$

$$= \frac{\text{mol } L^{-1} s^{-1}}{(\text{mol } L^{-1})^2}$$

$$= \frac{\text{mol } L^{-1} s^{-1}}{\text{mol}^2 L^{-2}}$$

$$= L\ mol^{-1} s^{-1}$$

(ii) Given rate $= k[H_2O_2]\ [I^-]$

Therefore, order of the reaction $= 2$

$$\text{Dimension of } k = \frac{\text{Rate}}{[H_2O_2]\ [I^-]}$$

$$= \frac{\text{mol } L^{-1} s^{-1}}{(\text{mol } L^{-1})\ (\text{mol } L^{-1})}$$

$$= L\ mol^{-1} s^{-1}$$

(iii) Given rate $= k[CH_3CHO]^{3/2}$

Therefore, order of reaction $= \dfrac{3}{2}$

$$\text{Dimension of } k = \frac{\text{Rate}}{[CH_3CHO]^{3/2}}$$

$$= \frac{\text{mol } L^{-1} s^{-1}}{(\text{mol } L^{-1})^{3/2}}$$

$$= \frac{\text{mol } L^{-1} s^{-1}}{\text{mol}^{3/2} L^{-3/2}}$$

$$= L^{1/2}\ mol^{-1/2} s^{-1}$$

(iv) Given rate $= k[C_2H_5Cl]$. Therefore, order of the reaction $= 1$

$$\text{Dimension of } k = \frac{\text{Rate}}{[C_2H_5Cl]}$$

$$= \frac{\text{mol } L^{-1} s^{-1}}{\text{mol } L^{-1}} = s^{-1}.$$

Q. 5. **A catalyst is a substance that enhances the rate of a reaction. Answer the following questions :**

(i) As a chemistry student explain what chemical process in heterogeneous catalysis of gases in catalytic converters.

(ii) Why is use of catalytic converters useful?

Ans. (i) The catalytic converters are placed near the exhausts of vehicle, and the gases like CO, NO and lead oxides etc., has to pass through it. The heterogeneous catalyst helps in first adsorbing the gases on its surface and then convert those to less polluting gases.

(ii) The catalytic converter oxidises CO to CO_2 and NO to NO_2 gas. The later gases are less harmful towards environment.

Chapter 5. Surface Chemistry

Q. 1. How artificial rain can be caused by throwing common salt on the clouds?

Ans. Clouds are colloidal dispersion of water droplets in air. On throwing salt over clouds the charge on the droplets gets neutralised causing coagulation. This results in formation of bigger droplets which falls down as rain.

Q. 2. What is the role of activated charcoal in gas masks used in coal mines?

Ans. Activated charcoal acts as an excellent adsorber of various poisonous gases specially carbon monoxide present in coal mines. Hence, gas masks prevent workers from inhaling poisonous gases.

Q. 3. Critical temperature of N_2, CO and CH_4 are 126, 134 and 190 K respectively. Arrange them in increasing order of adsorption on the surface of activated charcoal.

Ans. The minimum temperature above which a gas cannot be liquified is called critical temperature, irrespective of the magnitude of pressure. At the same time, higher is the critical temperature it will be much easier to liquify the gas as more will be the extent of adsorption. Hence, increasing order of adsorption is

$$N_2 < CO < CH_4$$

Q. 4. How is colloidion produced? What type of sol it is?*

Ans. Colloidion is produced by peptisation. Here a solution of cellulose nitrate is vigorously shaken in alcoholic medium in presence of electrolyte like sodium nitrate etc. It forms a lyophillic sol.

Q. 5. Explain what is observed when:*

    (i) Silver nitrate solution is added to potassium iodide solution.

    (ii) The size of the finest gold particles increases in a gold sol.

    (iii) Two oppositely charged sols are mixed in almost equal proportions.

Ans. (i) $AgNO_3$ (aq) + KI (aq) $\longrightarrow$ AgI(s) + KNO_3 (aq)

                (yellow)

    A yellow precipitate or coagulated silver iodide is formed.

    (ii) A colloidal sol of gold is formed and is called multimolecular colloid.

    (iii) Both the sols get coagulated.

Q. 6. Discuss the effect of pressure and temperature on the adsorption of gases on solids.

Ans. Effect of pressure: Adsorption is a reversible process and is accompanied by decrease in pressure. Therefore, adsorption increases with an increase in pressure.

Effect of temperature: Adsorption is an exothermic process. Thus, in accordance with Le-Chatelier's principle, the magnitude of adsorption decreases with an increase in temperature.

Q. 7. What is demulsification? Name two demulsifiers.

Ans. The process of decomposition of an emulsion into its constituent liquids is called demulsification and the chemicals which are used to separate emulsions are called demulsifiers. Examples of demulsifiers are surfactants, ethylene oxide, etc.

Q. 8. Give four examples of heterogeneous catalysis.

Ans. (i) Oxidation of sulphur dioxide to form sulphur trioxide. In this reaction, Pt acts as a catalyst.

$$2SO_2(g) \xrightarrow{Pt(s)} 2SO_3(g)$$

    (ii) Formation of ammonia by the combination of dinitrogen and dihydrogen in the presence of finely divided iron.

$$N_2(g) + 3H_2(g) \xrightarrow{Fe(s)} 2NH_3(g)$$

    This process is called the Haber's process.

    (iii) **Ostwald's process:** Oxidation of ammonia to nitric oxide in the presence of platinum.

$$4NH_3(g) + 5O_2(g) \xrightarrow{Pt(s)} 4NO(g) + 6H_2O(g)$$

    (iv) Hydrogenation of vegetable oils in the presence of Ni.

$$\text{Vegetable oil(l)} + H_2(g) \xrightarrow{Ni(s)} \text{Vegetable ghee(s)}$$

Q. 9. Give four uses of emulsions.

Ans. Four uses of emulsions:

(i) Cleansing action of soaps is based on the formation of emulsions.

(ii) Digestion of fats in intestine takes place by the process of emulsification.

(iii) Antiseptics and disinfectants when added to water form emulsions.

(iv) The process of emulsification is used to make medicines.

Q. 10. Write one differences in each of the following:[*]

(i) Multimolecular colloid and Associated colloid

(ii) Coagulation and Peptization

(iii) Homogeneous catalysis and Heterogeneous catalysis

Ans. (i) Multimolecular colloids are the colloids in which the dispersed phase consists of aggregates of atoms or molecules with molecular size less than 1 nm whereas, Associated colloids are the substances that are dissolved in a medium, behave as normal electrolytes at low concentration but as colloids at higher concentration.

(ii) Coagulation is the process of precipitation of a colloidal solution by the addition of excess of an electrolyte where as peptisation is the process responsible for the formation of stable dispersion of colloidal particles in dispersion medium.

(iii) Homogeneous catalysis is the one in which the phases of the reactants and the catalysts are the same whereas in Heterogeneous catalysis the phases of the reactants and the catalysts are not the same.

Q. 11. (i) Write the dispersed phase and dispersion medium of milk.[*]

(ii) Write one similarity between physisorption and chemisorption.

(iii) Write the chemical method by which $Fe(OH)_3$ sol is prepared from $FeCl_3$.

Ans. (i) Milk

Dispersed phase   — Liquid

Dispersion medium   — Liquid

(ii) Both physisorption and chemisorption depends on the surface area. Both increases with an increase in surface area.

(iii) $Fe(OH)_3$ sol is prepared from $FeCl_3$ by hydrolysis method.

$$FeCl_3 \longrightarrow Fe^{3+} + 3Cl^-$$
$$Fe(OH)_3 + Fe^{3+} \longrightarrow [Fe(OH)_3]Fe^{3+}$$
$$\text{(Colloidal solution)}$$

Q. 12. Write one differences in each of the following:[*]

(i) Lyophobic sol and Lyophilic sol.

(ii) Solution and Colloid

(iii) Homogeneous catalysis and Heterogeneous catalysis.

Ans. (i) Lyophobic colloidal sols are not hydrated and have weak affinity with the dispersion medium whereas lyophilic colloidal sols are heavily hydrated and have strong affinity with the dispersion medium.

(ii) Solution is a homogeneous mixture of solute and solvent whereas colloid is the heterogeneous mixture of dispersed phase and dispersion medium.

(iii) Homogeneous catalysis is the catalysis in which the reactants and the catalysts are in the same phase whereas in the heterogeneous catalysis the reactants and the catalysts are in the different phases.

Q. 13. Write one differences in each of the following:[*]

(i) Multimolecular colloid and Macromolecular colloid

(ii) Sol and Gel

(iii) O/W emulsion and W/O emulsion

Ans. (i) In a multimolecular colloids a large number of atoms or smaller molecules of a substance aggregates together to form species having size in the colloidal range. Example : Sulphur sol whereas in macro-molecular colloids the colloidal particles are large molecules having colloidal dimensions. Example : Starch.

(ii) In sol the dispersing phase is solid and dispersing medium is liquid; Example : paint, gold sol etc. whereas in Gel the dispersing phase is liquid and dispersing medium is solid; Example : Jelly, butter etc.

(iii) In O/W emulsion oil is the dispersed phase while water is the dispersion medium. Example : milk, vanishing cream etc. whereas in W/O emulsion water is the dispersed phase while oil is the dispersion medium. Example : Cold cream, butter etc.

Chapter 6. General Principles and Processes of Isolation of Elements

Q. 1. **Describe the role of NaCN in the extraction of gold from gold ore.**[*]

Ans. NaCN acts as the liquid solvent in the extraction of gold from its ore by hydrometallurgy. Gold reacts with NaCN and is leached out as $Na[Au(CN)_2]$, sodium dicyano aurate (III) from the ore.

Q. 2. (i) Which solution is used for the leaching of silver metal in the presence of air in the metallurgy of silver?

(ii) Out of C and CO which is a better reducing agent at a lower temperature range in the blast furnace to extra iron from the oxide ore.[*]

Ans. (i) Dilute solution of NaCN or KCN is used for leaching of silver metal in the presence of air (hydrometallurgy) in the metallurgy of silver.

(ii) Out of C and CO, CO is a better reducing agent at lower temperature range as from Ellingham's diagram. $\Delta G^{(CO \rightarrow CO2)} < \Delta G^{(Fe \rightarrow FeO)}$ at this temperature range. Hence CO will reduce FeO and itself will oxidised to CO_2.

Q. 3. (i) Name the method of refining to obtain silicon of high purity.

(ii) What is the role of SiO_2 in the extraction of copper?[*]

Ans. (i) Zone refining : Silicon of very high purity is obtained by this method.

(ii) SiO_2 helps in 'slag' formation. It acts as flux in the extraction of copper. It slags out iron oxide impurity as iron silicate.

$$FeO + SiO_2 \longrightarrow FeSiO_3$$

Q. 4. **Out of C and CO, which is a better reducing agent at 673 K?**

Ans. At 673 K, the value of $\Delta G(CO, CO_2)$ is less than that of $\Delta G(C, CO)$ from Ellingham's diagram. Therefore, CO can be oxidised more easily to CO_2 than C to CO. Hence, CO is a better reducing agent than C at 673 K.

Q. 5. **What is meant by the term 'chromatography'?**

Ans. The term chromatography is derived from Greek words 'chroma' meaning 'colour' and 'graphy' meaning 'to write'. Chromatographic techniques are based on the principle that different components are absorbed differently on an absorbent. There are several chromatographic techniques such as paper chromatography, column chromatography, gas chromatography etc.

Q. 6. **What criterion is followed for the selection of the stationary phase in chromatography?**

Ans. The stationary phase is selected in such a way that the components of the sample have different solubility's in the phase. Hence, different components have different rates of movement through the stationary phase and as a result, can be separated from each other.

That is high but selective adsorption. Also it should be catalytically inactive and should not react with the solvents used for elution or components of mixture to be separated.

Q. 7. **Describe a method for refining nickel.**

Ans. Nickel is refined by Mond's process. In this process, nickel is heated in the presence of carbon monoxide to form nickel tetracarbonyl, which is a volatile complex.

$$Ni + 4CO \xrightarrow{\text{330-350 K}} Ni(CO)_4$$
Nickel tetracarbonyl

Then, the obtained nickel tetracarbonyl is decomposed by subjecting it to a higher temperature (450 – 470 K) to obtain pure nickel metal.

$$Ni(CO)_4 \xrightarrow{\text{450-470 K}} Ni + 4CO$$
Nickel   Nickel
tetracarbonyl

Q. 8. **What is the role of cryolite in the metallurgy of aluminium?**

Ans. Cryolite (Na_3AlF_6) has two roles in the metallurgy of aluminium:

    (i)   To decrease the melting point of the mixture from 2323 K to 1140 K.

    (ii) To increase the electrical conductivity of Al_2O_3.

Q. 9. Which of the ores can be concentrated by magnetic separation method?

Ans. If the ore or the gangue can be attracted by the magnetic field, then the ore can be concentrated by the process of magnetic separation. Among the ores of iron such as haematite (Fe_2O_3), magnetite (Fe_3O_4), siderite ($FeCO_3$), and iron pyrites (FeS_2) can be separated by the process of magnetic separation.

Q. 10. Define the term:

    (i)   Liquation,   (ii) Distillation.

Ans. (i)   **Liquation:** When a metal is readily fusible and impurities are not like tin (Sn), lead (Pb) and bismuth (Bi) then liquation method for purification is used. The metal bars of the impure metals are heated on the hearth of a reverberatory furnace. The metal melts and flows down while the impurities remain behind in the hearth.

    (ii) **Distillation:** Volatile metals with non-volatile impurities and vice-versa are purified by distillation. Cd, Bi, Zn and Hg (mercury) metals are purified like this. The metals readily change into vapours leaving behind the impurities. The vapours are collected in receivers and upon cooling they provide pure metal.

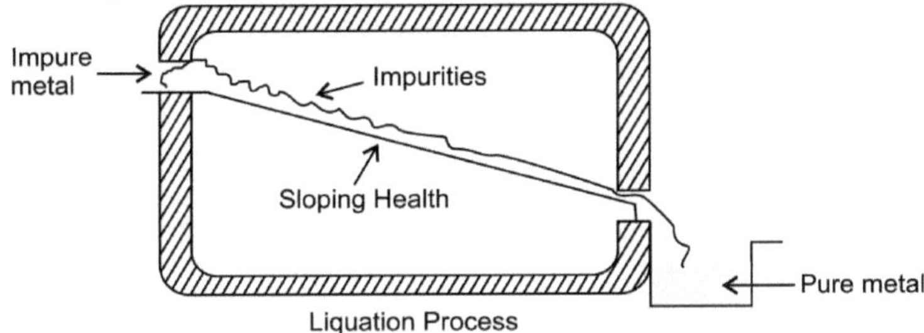

Liquation Process

Q. 11. Write the principle of the following:*

    (i)   Zone refining   (ii) Froth floatation process   (iii) Chromatography.

Ans. (i)   **Zone refining:**

        (a) This process is used for the metals which are required in very high purity like silicon, germanium, boron, gallium etc.

        (b) This method is based on the principle that : The impurities are more stable in the melt than in the solid state of the metal.

        (c) In this method, impure metal is casted into a thin bar.

    (ii) **Froth floatation process:**

        (a) This method is based on the principle that : Difference in the wetting properties of the ore and gangue particles with water and oil.

        (b) This method is used for the extraction of those metals in which the ore particles are preferentially wetted by oil and gangue by water.

        (c) This method has been used for the concentration of sulphide ores like PbS, ZnS, $CuFeS_2$ etc.

    (iii) **Chromatography:**

        (a) This is a modern method of purification based on the difference in the adsorbing capacities of the metal and its impurities on a suitable adsorbent.

        (b) This technique is based on the principle that different components of a mixture are differently adsorbed on an adsorbent.

Q. 12. (i)   Write the principle of method used for the refining of germanium.*

    (ii) Out of PbS and $PbCO_3$ (ores of lead), which one is concentrated by froth floatation process preferably?

    (iii) What is the significance of leaching in the extraction of aluminium?

Ans. (i)   Zone refining method is used for the refining of germanium and it is based on the principle that the impurities are more soluble in the melt than in the solid state of the metal.

    (ii) PbS, sulphide one has more tendency to stick to the oil which comes on the surface being lighter and easily skimmed off so PbS is concentrated by froth floatation method.

    (iii) Leaching of alumina is done to remove the impurities like SiO_2 by using NaOH solution and pure alumina is obtained.

---
* are board exam questions from previous years

Q. 13. (i) Write the principle of vapour phase refining.*

(ii) Write the role of dilute of NaCN in the extraction of silver.

(iii) What is the role of collectors in the froth floatation process? Give an example of a collector.

Ans. (i) This method is based on the principle that–'Certain metals are converted to their volatile compounds while the impurities are not affected during compound formation.'

(ii) NaCN is used to leach the silver ore in the presence of air. Pure silver is obtained by replacement in the process of extraction of silver.

$$Ag_2S + 4NaCN \longrightarrow 2Na[Ag(CN)_2] + Na_2S$$
Sodium dicyanoargentate

$$2Na[Ag(CN)_2] + Zn \longrightarrow 2Ag(s) + Na[Zn(CN_4)](aq.)$$
Sodium tetracyanozincate (II)

(iii) In the froth floatation process, collectors enhances the non-wettability of the mineral particles. Example of collectors are pine oil, eucalyptus oil, fatty acids etc.

Chapter 7. *p*-Block Elements

Q. 1. **Account for the following:***

(i) ICl is more reactive than I_2.

(ii) CN^- ion is known but CP^- ions is not known.

Ans. (i) Because of electronegativity difference between I – Cl, I and Cl the bond is more polar than I – I bond hence I – Cl is more reactive.

(ii) C and N atoms have similar sizes, hence can form multiple bonds like $C \equiv N^-$ but size of P is quite large than C and hence orbitals can't overlap effectively for multiple $p\pi$-$p\pi$ bond. So CP^- does not exist.

Q. 2. **Account for the following:***

(i) Which acid has lower pK_a value, $HClO_3$ and $HClO_4$?

(ii) Fluorine is the strongest oxidant among halogens.

Ans. (i) $HClO_4$ has lower pK_a value and is the thus a stronger acid than, $HClO_3$ because $HClO_4$ has an extra oxygen atom bond to chlorine which enhances the electron affinity of Cl and thus weakens the H—O bond further.

(ii) Fluorine is the most electronegative element among group 17 halogens and has the highest standard electrode potential, hence strongest oxidising agent.

Q. 3. **How will you prepare Chlorine from HCl?**

Ans. By heating manganese oxide MnO_2 with conc. HCl.

$$MnO_2 + 4HCl \xrightarrow{\Delta} MnCl_2 + H_2O + Cl_2$$

Q. 4. **Arrange the following in order of property indicated for each set :**

(i) $HOCl$, $HOClO$, $HOClO_2$, $HOClO_3$—Increasing acid strength

(ii) HF, HCl, HBr, HI—Increasing bond strength.

Ans. (i) $HOCl < HOClO < HOClO_2 < HOClO_3$

(ii) HI < HBr < HCl < HF.

Q. 5. **Account for the following:**

(i) $SnCl_4$ is more covalent than $SnCl_2$.

(ii) H_3PO_2 is stronger reducing agent than H_3PO_3.

Ans. (i) According to Fajan's rule if central metal has more positive oxidation number then it is more polarising. Hence $SnCl_4$ has +4 oxidation state, also because of inert pair effect Sn in +4 state can only share (*i.e.,* covalent bond) and can't donate 4 electrons.

(ii) Greater the number of P—H bond in oxoacid of phosphorus, more is the reducing character. H_3PO_2 contains 2, P—H bonds while H_3PO_3 has only one, P—H bond. So, former is more stronger reducing agent.

Q. 6. **Justify the placement of O, S, Se, Te and Po in the same group of the periodic table in terms of electronic configuration, oxidation state and hydride formation.**

Ans. The elements of group 16 are collectively called chalcogens.

(i) Elements of group 16 have six valence electrons each. The general electronic configuration of these elements is $ns^2\,np^4$, where n varies from 2 to 6.

(ii) **Oxidation state:** As these elements have six valence electrons ($ns^2\,np^4$), they should display an oxidation state of -2. Oxygen also exhibits the oxidation state of -1 (H_2O_2), 0 (O_2), and $+2$ (OF_2). However, the stability of the -2 oxidation state decreases on moving down a group due to a decrease in the electronegativity of the elements. The heavier elements of the group show an oxidation state of $+2$, $+4$, and $+6$ due to the availability of d-orbitals.

(iii) **Formation of hydrides:** These elements form hydrides of formula H_2E, where E = O, S, Se, Te, PO. Oxygen and sulphur also form hydrides of type H_2E_2. These hydrides are quite volatile in nature.

Q. 7. Why is dioxygen a gas but sulphur is a solid?

Ans. Oxygen is smaller in size as compared to sulphur. Due to its smaller size, it can effectively form $p\pi$-$p\pi$ bonds and form O_2 (O=O) molecule. Also, the intermolecular forces in oxygen are weak Vander Waals, which cause it to exist as gas. On the other hand, sulphur does not form M_2 molecule but exists as a puckered structure so this structure is held together by strong covalent bonds. Hence, it is a solid.

Q. 8. Knowing the electron gain enthalpy values for $O \rightarrow O^-$ and $O \rightarrow O2^-$ as -141 and 702 kJ mol^{-1} respectively, how can you account for the formation of a large number of oxides having O^{2-} species and not O^-?

[**Hint:** Consider lattice energy factor in the formation of compounds].

Ans. Stability of an ionic compound depends on its lattice energy. More the lattice energy of a compound, more stable it will be.

Lattice energy is directly proportional to the charge carried by an ion. When a metal combines with oxygen, the lattice energy of the oxide involving O^{2-} ion is much more than the oxide involving O^- ion. Hence, the oxide having O^{2-} ions are more stable than oxides having O^-. Hence, we can say that formation of O^{2-} is energetically more favourable than formation of O^-, because of more stable crystal lattice.

Q. 9. Describe the manufacture of H_2SO_4 by contact process?

Ans. Sulphuric acid is manufactured by the contact process. It involves the following steps:

Step (i): Sulphur or sulphide ores are burnt in air to form SO_2.

Step (ii): By a reaction with oxygen, SO_2 is converted into SO_3 in the presence of V_2O_5 as a catalyst.

$$2SO_2(g) + O_2(g) \xrightarrow{V_2O_5} 2SO_3(g)$$

Step (iii): SO_3 produced is absorbed on H_2SO_4 to give $H_2S_2O_7$ (oleum).

$$SO_3 + H_2SO_4 \longrightarrow H_2S_2O_7$$

This oleum is then diluted to obtain H_2SO_4 of the desired concentration.

In practice, the plant is operated at 2 bar (pressure) and 720 K (temperature). The sulphuric acid thus obtained is 96-98% pure.

Q. 10. How is SO_2 an air pollutant?

Ans. Sulphur dioxide causes harm to the environment in many ways:

(i) It combines with water vapour present in the atmosphere to form sulphuric acid. This causes acid rain. Acid rain damages soil, plants and buildings, especially those made of marble.

(ii) Even in very low concentrations, SO_2 causes irritation in the respiratory tract. It causes throat and eye irritation and can also affect the larynx to cause breathlessness.

(iii) It is extremely harmful to plants. Plants exposed to sulphur dioxide for a long time loose colour from their leaves. This condition is known as chlorosis. This happens because the formation of chlorophyll is affected by the presence of sulphur dioxide.

Q. 11. Why do noble gases have comparatively large atomic sizes?

Ans. Noble gases do not form molecules. In case of noble gases, the atomic radii corresponds to Van der Waals radii. On the other hand, the atomic radii of other elements correspond to their covalent radii. By definition, Van der Waals radii are larger than covalent radii. It is for this reason that noble gases are very large in size as compared to other atoms belonging to the same period.

Q. 12. Write the order of thermal stability of the hydrides of group 16 elements.

Ans. The thermal stability of hydrides decreases on moving down the group. This is due to a decrease in the bond dissociation enthalpy (H–E) of hydrides on moving down the group. Therefore,

$$H_2O > H_2S > H_2Se > H_2Te > H_2PO$$

$$
\left.
\begin{array}{l}
H_2O \\
H_2S \\
H_2Se \\
H_2Te \\
H_2Po
\end{array}
\right\} \text{Thermal stability decreases} \downarrow
$$

Q. 13. Mention three areas in which H_2SO_4 plays an important role.

Ans. Sulphuric acid is an important industrial chemical and is used for a lot of purposes. Some important uses of sulphuric acid are given below.

(i)   It is used in fertiliser industry. It is used to make various fertilisers such as ammonium sulphate and calcium super phosphate.

(ii) It is used in the manufacture of pigments, paints, detergents, chemicals like phosphoric acid nitric acid etc.

(iii) It is used in the manufacture of storage batteries.

Q. 14. Give two examples to show the anomalous behaviour of fluorine.

Ans. Anomalous behaviour of fluorine:

(a) It forms only one oxoacid and shows only –1, oxidation state as compared to other halogens that form a number of oxoacids and only SF_6 (hexafluoride) is stable.

(b) Ionisation enthalpy, electronegativity, and electrode potential of fluorine are much higher than expected.

Q. 15. Sea is the greatest source of some halogens. Comment.

Ans. Sea water contains chlorides, bromides, and iodides of Na, K, Mg and Ca. However, it primarily contains NaCl. The deposits of dried up sea beds contain sodium chloride and carnallite, $KCl.MgCl_2.6H_2O$. Marine life also contains iodine in their systems. For example, sea weeds contain upto 0.511% iodine as sodium iodide. Thus, sea is the greatest source of halogens.

Q. 16. Give the reason for bleaching action of Cl_2.

Ans. When chlorine reacts with water, it produces nascent oxygen. This nascent oxygen then combines with the coloured substances present in the organic matter to oxide and then into colourless substances.

$$Cl_2 + H_2O \longrightarrow 2HCl + [O]$$

Coloured substances + [O] → Oxidized colourless substance.

Q. 17. Complete the following reactions:*

(i) $NH_3 + 3Cl_2(\text{excess}) \rightarrow$

(ii) $XeF_6 + 2H_2O \rightarrow$

Ans.

$$NH_3 + 3Cl_2(\text{excess}) \longrightarrow NCl_3 + 3HCl$$
$$XeF_6 + 2H_2O \longrightarrow XeO_2F_2 + 4HF$$

Q. 18. Give reasons:*

(i)   Thermal stability decreases from H_2O to H_2Te.

(ii) Fluoride ion has higher hydration enthalpy than chloride ion.

Ans. (i)   As we move down in a group atomic radius increases as a result bond length increases. Larger the bond length lesser will be the bond dissociation enthalpy. So thermal stability decreases from O to Te.

(ii) Fluoride ion is the smallest ion in the group and it has high charge density and charge size ratio. That is why it has high hydration enthalpy.

Q. 19. (i)   What is the chemical formula of mustard gas or tear gas?

(ii) How can one prevent effect of tear gas?

(iii) What are the effects of mustard gas and tear gas on human being?

Ans. (i)   Mustard gas is a compound of ethylene, chlorine and sulphur formula $(ClCH_2—CH_2)_2S$. It is also called sulphur mustard. Tear gas is $C_{10}H_5ClN_2$, its a chloro compound.

(ii) One can wear a gas mask or a water wetted cloth on eyes to avoid the smoke from entering.

(iii) Mustard gas is poisonous gas, it causes severe skin rashes, blisters and even born down respiratory system hence high exposure can be fatal. Tear gas on the other side causes eye irritation, cough, vomiting and brings about tears.

Q. 20. On reaction with Cl_2, phosphorus forms two types of halides 'A' and 'B'. Halide 'A' is yellowish-white powder but halide 'B' is colourless oily liquid. Identify A and B and write the formulas of their hydrolysis products.

Ans. Yellowish white powder is PCl_5 (A) and the colourless oily liquid is PCl_3 (B). Hence halogen must be chlorine.

(a) $P_4(s) + 5Cl_2(g) \longrightarrow 4PCl_5(s)$

     (excess)   (yellowish white powder)

(b) $P_4(s) + 3Cl_2(g) \longrightarrow 4PCl_3(l)$

     (colourless oily liquid)

     (B)

The products of hydrolysis are:

$$PCl_3 + 3H_2O \longrightarrow H_3PO_4 + 3HCl$$
$$PCl_5 + 4H_2O \longrightarrow H_3PO_4 + 5HCl$$

Q. 21. Illustrate how copper metal can give different products on reaction with HNO_3.

Ans. Concentrated nitric acid is a strong oxidizing agent. It is used for oxidising most metals. The products of oxidation depend on the concentration of the acid, temperature and also on the material undergoing oxidation.

$$3Cu + 8HNO_{3(dilute)} \longrightarrow 3Cu(NO_3)_2 + 2NO + 4H_2O$$
$$Cu + 4HNO_{3(conc.)} \longrightarrow Cu(NO_3)_2 + 2NO_2 + 2H_2O$$

Q. 22. Among the hydrides of Group 15 elements, which have the*

    (i)   lowest boiling point?

    (ii) maximum basic character?

    (iii) highest bond angle?

    (iv) maximum reducing character?

Ans. Hydrides of group 15 element are : NH_3, PH_3, AsH_3, SbH_3, BiH_3

    (i)   Lowest boiling points of PH_3 (185.5 K)

    (ii) Maximum basic character is shown by NH_3

    (iii) Highest bond angle is for NH_3

    (iv) BiH_3, has the maximum reducing character.

Q. 23. Give reasons for the following:*

    (i)   Red phosphorus is less reactive than white phosphorus.

    (ii) Electron gain enthalpies of halogens are largely negative.

    (iii) N_2O_5 is more acidic than N_2O_3.

Ans. (i)   White phosphorous has a tetrahedral basic unit where four phoshorous atoms are arranged at the four corners of a tetrahedron.

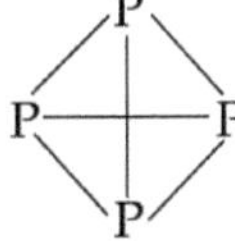

White phosphorous

This creates a very strained system which is unstable and very reactive. On the other hand red phosphorous has an enormous structure and is therefore a lot more stable and less reactive.

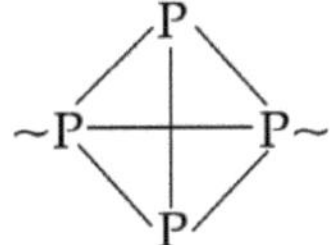

Red phosphorous

    (ii) Electron gain enthalpies of halogens are largely negative in their respective periods. This is due to the fact that the atoms of these elements have only one electron less than the stable noble gas ($ns^2 \, np^6$) configuration. Therefore they have maximum tendency to accept an additional electron.

    (iii) The oxidation state of N in N_2O_5 is +5 and that of N in N_2O_3 is +3 thus more number of oxygen atoms are attached with N in N_2O_5 as compared to N_2O_3. Thus the acidic strength of N_2O_5 is higher than N_2O_3.

Q. 24. Complete the following reactions:*

    (i) $NH_3 + 3Cl_2(excess) \rightarrow$

    (ii) $XeF_6 + 2H_2O \rightarrow$

Ans.
$$NH_3 + 3Cl_2(\text{excess}) \longrightarrow NCl_3 + 3HCl$$
$$XeF_6 + 2H_2O \longrightarrow XeO_2F_2 + 4HF$$

Q. 25. Give reasons:*
(i)   Thermal stability decreases from H_2O to H_2Te.
(ii) Fluoride ion has higher hydration enthalpy than chloride ion.
(iii) Nitrogen does not form pentahalide.

Ans. (i)   As we move down in a group atomic radius increases as a result bond length increases. Larger the bond length lesser will be the bond dissociation enthalpy. So thermal stability decreases from O to Te.
(ii) Fluoride ion is the smallest ion in the group and it has high charge density and charge size ratio. That is why it has high hydration enthalpy.
(iii) Nitrogen belongs to 2nd period and there is absence of 3d orbital so it can not extend its covalency beyond 3. Thus it does not forms pentahalides.

Q. 26. What happens when
(i) $(NH_4)_2Cr_2O_7$ is heated?
(ii) H_3PO_3 is heated?
Write the equations.

Ans.
$$(NH_4)_2Cr_2O_7(s) \longrightarrow Cr_2O_3(s) + N_2(g) + 4H_2O(g)$$
$$4H_3PO_3 \longrightarrow 3H_3PO_4 + PH_3$$

Chapter 8. *d*-and *f*-Block Elements

Q. 1. Account for the following:
(i)   ZnO yellow when hot and white when cold.
(ii) Cu_2O is red and Cu_2S is black but Cu^+ is colourless ion.

Ans. (i)   ZnO is white as Zn atom has $3d^{10}$ configuration and hence no unpaired electron for *d-d* transition, but on heating it develops lattice-defect or non-stoichiometric metal excess defect. As a result there are free electrons trapped in the interstitial sites which imparts colour on heating.
(ii) In case of Cu^+ ion, there is no d-d transition as the d-orbital is completely filled ($3d^{10}$). But in case of compounds Cu_2O and Cu_2S there is charge transfer from the S^{2-} or O^{2-} ion to some vacant d-orbital of Cu^+ ion which results in coloured compounds.

Q. 2. Describe the action of $KMnO_4$ in neutral and mildly alkaline medium over iodide and thiosulphate ions.

Ans. $KMnO_4$ is a very strong oxidising agent. It oxidises iodide to iodate and thiosulphate to sulphate ion.

Reactions:

(i)
$$2MnO_4^- + I^- + H_2O \longrightarrow 2MnO_2 + IO_3^- + 2OH^-$$
(neutral)

Iodine undergoes oxidation from -1 to $+5$ state.

(ii)
$$2MnO_4^- + 3S_2O_3^{2-} + H_2O \longrightarrow 2MnO_2 + 3SO_4^{2-} + 2OH^- + 3S$$

Sulphur ion disproportionate from $(+2)$ state in thiosulphate to $(+6)$ in sulphate and (0) state in elemental sulphur.

Q. 3. Which of the following cation are coloured in aqueous solutions and why?*
$$Sc^{3+}, V^{3+}, Ti^{4+}, Mn^{2+}.$$

Ans. The colour of the cations depends upon the electronic configuration of the ions. Those having partially or incomplete d-orbitals will impart colour as a result of d-d transition and others will be colourless.

Sc^{3+} (Z $=21$) $[Ar]^{18} 4s^0 3d^0$;   colourless
V^{3+} (Z $= 23$) $[Ar]^{18} 4s^0 3d^2$;   colourless
Ti^{4+} (Z $= 22$) $[Ar]^{18} 4s^0 3d^0$;   colourless
Mn^{2+} (Z $= 25$) $[Ar]^{18} 4s^0 3d^6$;   colourless

Q. 4. Answer the following questions:
(i)   Write an oxidising reaction of $K_2Cr_2O_7$ in acidic medium.
(ii) Write one reaction of $KMnO_4$ as a oxidant in basic medium.

Ans. (i) $K_2Cr_2O_7$ oxidises sulphite (SO_3) to sulphate (SO_4) in the presence of sulphuric acid.

$$K_2Cr_2O_7 + 3SO_2 + H_2SO_4 \longrightarrow K_2SO_4 + Cr_2(SO_4)_3 + H_2O$$

Sulphur dioxide — Acidic medium

(ii)
$$3CH_2{=}CH_2 + 4H_2O + 2KMnO_4 \xrightarrow{\text{Alkaline medium}} 3\ CH_2OH{-}CH_2OH + 2MnO_2 + 2KOH$$

Ethylene — Ethylene glycol

Q. 5. (i) What is meant by 'disproportionation' reaction? Give an example of such reaction in aqueous medium.

(ii) Complete the following equation:*

$$Cr_2O_7^{2-} + 8H^+ + 3NH_2^- \longrightarrow$$

Ans. (i) Disproportionation reaction involves oxidation and reduction of the same substance. The examples of such reaction are:

Aqueous NH_3 on reacting with calomel (Hg_2Cl_2) solid forms mercury aminochloride and mercury metal.

$$Hg_2Cl_2(s) + 2NH_3\ (aq) \longrightarrow Hg(l) + Hg(NH_2)Cl + NH_4Cl$$

(ii)
$$Cr_2O_7^{2-} + 8H^+ + 3NO_2^- \longrightarrow 3NO_3^- + 2Cr^{3+} + 4H_2O$$

Q. 6. Why are Mn^{2+} compounds more stable than Fe^{2+} towards oxidation to their +3 state?

Ans. Electronic configuration of Mn^{2+} is $[Ar]^{18}3d^5$.

Electronic configuration of Fe^{2+} is $[Ar]^{18}\ 3d^6$.

It is known that half-filled and fully-filled orbitals are more stable. Therefore, Mn in(+2) state has a stable d^5 configuration. This is the reason Mn^{2+} shows resistance to oxidation to Mn^{3+}. Fe^{2+} has $3d^6$ configuration and by losing one electron, it can achieve stable configuration of $3d^5$.

Hence, Fe^{2+} easily gets oxidized to Fe^{+3} oxidation state.

Q. 7. What may be the stable oxidation state of the transition element with the following d electron configurations in the ground state of their atoms : $3d^3$, $3d^5$, $3d^8$ and $3d^4$?

Ans. The number of oxidation states depends upon the sum of $s + d$ electrons.

Electronic configuration in ground state	Stable oxidation states
(i) $3d^3$ (Vanadium)	+ 3 and + 5
(ii) $3d^5$ (Chromium)	+ 3 and + 6
(iii) $3d^5$ (Manganese)	+ 2 , + 4, +6 and + 7
(iv) $3d^8$ (Cobalt)	+ 2
(v) $3d^4$	There is no $3d^4$ configuration in ground state.

Q. 8. Name the oxometal anions of the first series of the transition metals in which the metal exhibits the oxidation state equal to its group number.

Ans. (i) Vanadate, VO_3^-

Oxidation state of V is +5.

(ii) Chromate, $Cr_2O_7^{2-}$

Oxidation state of Cr + 6.

(iii) Permanganate, MnO_4^-

Oxidation state of Mn is + 7.

(iv) TiO_2

Oxidation state of Ti is +4.

Q. 9. In what way is the electronic configuration of the transition elements is different from that of the non-transition elements?

Ans. Transition metals have a partially filled d-orbital. Therefore, the electronic configuration of transition elements is $(n-1)d^{1-10}\ ns^{0-2}$. The non-transition elements either do not have a d-orbital or have a fully filled d-orbital. Therefore, the electronic configuration of non-transition elements is ns^{1-2} or ns^2np^6.

Q. 10. What are alloys? Name an important alloy which contains some of the lanthanoid metals. Mention its uses.

Ans. An alloy is a solid solution of two or more elements in a metallic matrix. It can either be a partial solid solution or a complete solid solution. Alloys are usually found to possess different physical properties than those of the component elements.

An important alloy of lanthanoids is Mischmetal. It contains lanthanoids (94-95%), iron (5%), and traces of S, C, Si, Ca and Al.

Uses:

(a) Mischmetal is used in cigarettes and gas lighters.

(b) It is used in flame throwing tanks.

(c) It is used in tracer bullets and shells.

Q. 11. What are inner transition elements? Decide which of the following atomic numbers are the atomic numbers of the inner transition elements : 29, 59, 74, 95, 102, 104.

Ans. Inner transition metals are those elements in which the last electron enters the f-orbital. The elements in which the 4f and 5f orbitals are progressively filled are called f-block elements. The lanthanoids from atomic number ($Z = 58$ to 71) and actinoids from atomic number ($Z = 90$ to 103). Among the given atomic numbers, the atomic numbers of the inner transition elements are 59, 95 and 102.

Q. 12. The chemistry of the actinoid elements is not so smooth as that of the lanthanoids. Justify this statement by giving some examples from the oxidation state of these elements.

Ans. Lanthanoids primarily show three oxidation states (+2, +3, +4). Among these oxidation states, +3 state is the most common. Lanthanoids display a limited number of oxidation states because the energy difference between 4f, 5d and 6s orbitals is quite large. On the other hand, the energy difference between 5f, 6d and 7s orbitals is comparable. Hence, actinoids display a large number of oxidation states. For example, uranium and plutonium display + 3, + 4, +5 and +6 oxidation states while neptunium displays +3, +4, +5 and +7. The most common oxidation state in case of actinoids is also +3.

Q. 13. Which is the last element in the series of the actinoids? Write the electronic configuration of this element. Comment on the possible oxidation state of this element.

Ans. The last element in the actinoid series is lawrencium, (Lr). Its atomic number is 103 and its electronic configuration is $[Rn]5f^{14}6d^{1}7s^{2}$. The most common oxidation state displayed by it is +3; because after losing 3 electrons it attains stable f^{14} configuration.

Q. 14. Use Hund's rule to derive the electronic configuration of Ce^{3+} ion and calculate its magnetic moment on the basis of 'spin-only' formula.

Ans. Ce : $1s^2\, 2s^2\, 2p^6\, 3s^2\, 3p^6\, 3d^{10}\, 4s^2\, 4p^6\, 4d^{10}\, 5s^2\, 5p^6\, 4f^1\, 5d^1\, 6s^2$

$[Xe]^{54}\, 4f^1\, 5d^1\, 6s^2$ for Ce^{3+} ion configuration is Ce^{3+}: $[Xe]^{54}\, 4f^1$ hence $n = 1$.

Magnetic moment can be calculated as:

$$\mu = \sqrt{n(n+2)}$$

Where,

$$n = \text{number of unpaired electrons.}$$

But for ion

$$\mu = \sqrt{1(1+2)} = \sqrt{3} = 1.73 \text{ PM.}$$

Q. 15. Name the members of the lanthanoid series which exhibit +4 oxidation state and those which exhibit +2 oxidation state. Try to correlate this type of behaviour with the electronic configurations of these elements.

Ans. The lanthanides that exhibit +2 and +4 states are shown in the given table. The atomic numbers of the elements are given in the parenthesis.

+2	+4
Nd (60	Ce (58)
Sm (62)	Pr (59)
Eu (63)	Nd (60)
Tm (69)	Tb (65)
Yb (70)	Dy (66)

Ce after forming Ce^{4+} attains a stable electronic configuration of $[Xe]$.

Tb after forming Tb^{4+} attains a stable electronic configuration of $[Xe]\, 4f^7$.

Eu after forming Eu^{2+} attains a stable electronic configuration of $[Xe]\, 4f^7$.

Yb after forming Yb^{2+} attains a stable electronic configuration of $[Xe]\, 4f^{14}$.

Q. 16. Write the electronic configurations of the elements with the atomic numbers 61, 91, 101 and 109.

Ans.

Atomic Number	Electronic configuration
61 (Pm)	$[Xe]^{54}\,4f^5\,5d^0\,6s^2$
91 (Pa)	$[Rn]^{86}\,5f^2\,6d^1\,7s^2$
101 (Md)	$[Rn]^{86}\,5f^{13}\,5d^0\,7s^2$
109 (Mt)	$[Rn]^{86}\,5f^{14}\,6d^7\,7s^2$

Q. 17. Silver atom has completely filled d orbitals $(4d^{10})$ in its ground state. How can you say that it is a transition element?

Ans. Ag has a completely filled $4d$ orbital $(4d^{10}5s^1)$ in its ground state. But silver displays two oxidation states ($+1$ and $+2$). In the $+2$ oxidation state, an electron is removed from the d-orbital and shows $4d^9$ configuration, having incompletely filled d-orbital.

Q. 18. In the series Sc (Z = 21) to Zn (Z = 30), the enthalpy of atomization of zinc is the lowest, *i.e.*, 126 kJ mol^{-1}. Why?

Ans. The extent of metallic bonding in an element decides the enthalpy of atomisation. The more extensive the metallic bonding of an element, the more will be its enthalpy of atomisation. In all transition metals (except Zn, electronic configuration : $3d^{10}\,4s^2$), there are some unpaired electrons that account for their stronger metallic bonding. Due to the absence of these unpaired electrons, no electrons are involved in metallic bonding in Zn and as a result, it has the least enthalpy of atomisation.

Q. 19. The E° (M^{2+}/M) value for copper is positive ($+\ 0.34$ V). What is possibly the reason for this?*

(Hint: consider its high $\Delta_a H°$ and low $\Delta_{hyd}H°$).

Ans. E° (M^{2+}/M) value of a metal depends on three factors, these are as follows:

1. Sublimation: The energy required for converting one mole of an atom from the solid state to the gaseous state or enthalpy of atomisation.
$$M_{(s)} \longrightarrow M_{(g)}\ \Delta_a H\ \text{(Sublimation energy) or Enthalpy of atomisation.}$$

2. Ionization: The energy required to take out electrons from one mole of atoms in the gaseous state.
$$M_{(g)} \longrightarrow M_{(g)}^{2+}\ \Delta_a H\ \text{(Ionisation energy)}$$

3. Hydration: The energy released when one mole of ions are hydrated.
$$M^{2+}{}_{(g)} \longrightarrow M^{2+}{}_{(g)}\ \Delta_a H\ \text{(Hydration energy)}$$

Copper has a high energy of atomisation and low hydration enthalpy. Hence, the E° (M^{2+}/M) value for copper is positive, as the $\Delta_i H$ required is not compensated by low hydration enthalpy $\Delta_{hyd}H$.

Q. 20. Which is stronger reducing agent Cr^{2+} or Fe^{2+} and why?**

Ans. The $E^o_{Cr^{3+}/Cr^{2+}}$ value is $-\,0.41$ and $E^o_{Fe^{3+}/Fe^{2+}}$ is $+\,0.77$ V. This means that Cr^{2+} can be easily oxidised to Cr^{3+}, but Fe^{2+} does not get oxidised to Fe^{3+} easily. Therefore, Cr^{2+} is a better reducing agent than Fe^{3+}. Reason being Cr^{2+} is at d^4 oxidation state and it easily converts to d^3, half t_{2g} oxidation state. Whereas Fe^{2+} is d^6 state with all paired electron in t_{2g} state and more stable than d^5 state hence difficult to convert.

Q. 21. Explain why Cu^+ ion is not stable in aqueous solutions?*

Ans. In an aqueous medium, Cu^{2+} is more stable than Cu^+. This is because although energy is required to remove one electron from Cu^+ to Cu^{2+}, high hydration energy of Cu^{2+} compensates for it. Therefore, Cu^+ ion in an aqueous solution is less stable and disproportionates to give Cu^{2+} and Cu.
$$2Cu^+{}_{(aq)} \longrightarrow Cu^{2+}{}_{(aq)} + Cu_{(s)}$$

Q. 22. Actinoid contraction is greater from element to element than lanthanoid contraction. Why?

Ans. In actinoids, $5f$ orbitals are filled. These $5f$ orbitals are more diffused and has a poorer shielding effect than $4f$ orbitals. Thus, the effective nuclear charge experiened by electrons in valence shells in case of actinoids is much more that experienced by lanthanoids. Hence, the size contraction in actinoids is greater as compared to that in lanthanoids.

Q. 23. Answer the following questions:
    (i)   Which chemical compound is used in 'Alcometer' or `breath analyser'?
    (ii) What is the chemistry of the above test?

Ans. (i)   The 'Alcometer' or 'breath analysers' are of various types. The one which uses chemical breath analyser has potassium dichromate ($K_2Cr_2O_7$) as the main chemical component.

(ii)   The alcometer has $K_2Cr_2O_7$ (orange colour) along with sulphuric acid in aqueous medium. On passing breadth for test, the alcohol to produce chromium sulphate and acetic acid. During this process the orange dichromate colour changes to green colour chromium ion. The degree of colour change is directly related to the level of alcohol in the expelled air. Which when compared with the unreacted mixture provides a reading showing the range of alcohol consumed by the faulter or the driver.

Q. 24. Answer the following questions:

(i)   What happens when potassium permanganate is heated?

(ii)   What is Baeyer's reagent? State its one use.

(iii) What are the other common uses of $KMnO_4$?

Ans. (i)   On heating it decomposes to potassium manganate and manganese oxides and it releases oxygen.

$$2KMnO_4 \xrightarrow[573K]{\Delta} K_2MnO_4 + MnO_2 + O_2$$

(ii)   Baeyer's reagent is dilute alkaline solution of potassium permanganate. It is used for test of unsaturation. On passing alkene (vapour or liquid) through Baeyer's solution the purple colour of the solution disappears.

(iii) Potassium permanganate is a very useful chemical in itself. Some of its uses are :

(a)   Treating drinking water as a disinfectant.

(b)   As an antiseptic for washing wounds.

(c)   As a bleaching agent for wool, silk, cotton fabric etc.

Chapter 9. Coordination Compounds

Q. 1. How many geometrical isomers are possible in the following coordination entities?

(i) $[Cr(C_2O_4)_3]^{3-}$;   (ii) $[Co(NH_3)_3Cl_3]$

Ans. (i)   For $[Cr(C_2O_4)_3]^{3-}$, no geometric isomer is possible as it is bidentate ligand with symmetry.

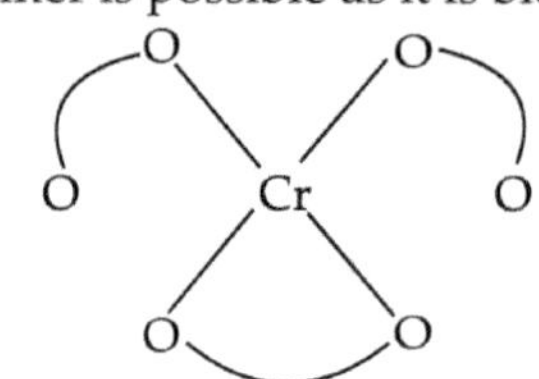

(ii) $[Co(NH_3)_3Cl_3]$

Two geometrical isomers are possible.

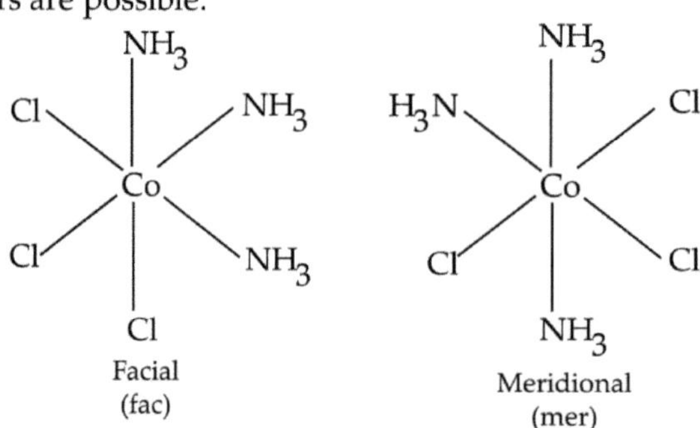

Q. 2. Write all the geometrical isomers of $[Pt(NH_3)(Br)(Cl)(Py)]$ and how many of these will exhibit optical isomers?

Ans. There are three geometrical isomers possible.

$[Pt(NH_3)(Br)(Cl)(Py)]$

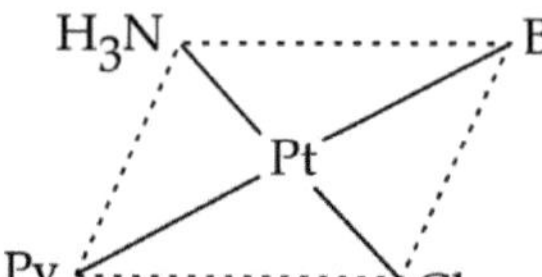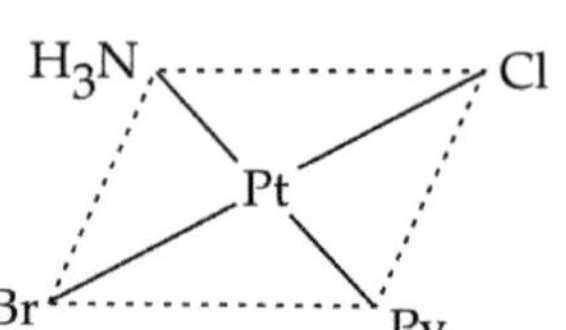

From the above isomers, none will exhibit optical isomers square planar complexes rarely show optical isomerisation.

Q. 3. What is the coordination entity formed when excess of aqueous KCN is added to an aqueous solution of copper sulphate? Why is it that no precipitate of copper sulphide is obtained when $H_2S(g)$ is passed through this solution?

Ans.
$$CuSO_{4(aq)} + 4KCN_{(aq)} \longrightarrow K_2[Cu(CN)_4]_{(aq)} + K_2SO_{4(aq)}$$

i.e.,
$$[Cu(H_2O)_4]^{2+} + 4CN^- \longrightarrow [Cu(CN)_4]^{2-} + 4H_2O$$

Thus, the coordination entity formed in the process is $K_2[Cu(CN)_4]$ potassium tetracyano cuprate(III) is a very stable complex, which does not ionize to give Cu^{2+} ions when added to water.

Hence, Cu^{2+} ions are not precipitated when $H_2S(g)$ is passed through the solution, as CuS is not formed.

Q. 4. $[Fe(CN)_6]^{4-}$ and $[Fe(H_2O)_6]^{2+}$ are of different colours in dilute solutions. Why?

Ans. The colour of a particular coordination compound depends on the magnitude of the crystal-field splitting energy, Δ. The CFSE in turn depends on the nature of the ligand. In case of $[Fe(CN)_6]^{4-}$ and $[Fe(H_2O)_6]^{2+}$, the colour differs because there is a difference in the CFSE, because in both cases the central metal has Fe^{2+}, *i.e.*, $4s^0$ $3d^6$ configuration. As CN^- is a strong field ligand having a higher CFSE value as compared to the CFSE value of water. Hence the absorption of energy for the intra *d-d* transition also differs. Hence, the transmitted colours are different.

Q. 5. Discuss the nature of bonding in metal carbonyls.

Ans. The metal-carbon bonds in metal carbonyls have both σ and n characters. A σ bond is formed when the carbonyl carbon donates a lone pair of electrons to the vacant orbital of the metal. A π bond is formed by the donation of a pair of electrons from the filled metal *d*-orbital into the vacant anti-bonding π^* orbital known as back bonding of the carbonyl group. The σ bond strengthens the π bond and vice-versa. Thus, a synergic effect is created due to this metal-ligand bonding. This synergic effect strengthens the bond between CO and the metal.

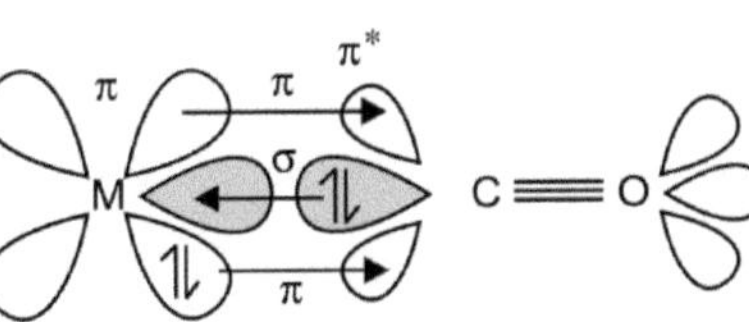
Synergic bonding in metal carbonyls

Q. 6. What is meant by the chelate effect? Give an example.

Ans. When a polydentate ligand attaches to the metal ion in a manner that forms a ring, then the metal-ligand association is found to be more stable. In other words, we can say that complexes containing chelate rings are more stable than complexes without rings. This is known as the chelate effect.

For example:

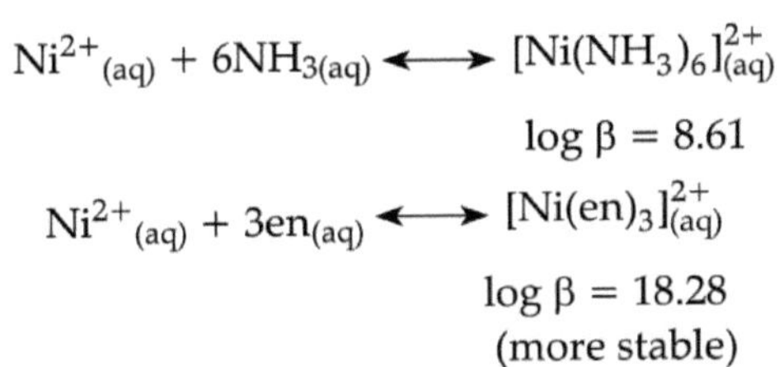

$$Ni^{2+}{}_{(aq)} + 6NH_{3(aq)} \longleftrightarrow [Ni(NH_3)_6]^{2+}_{(aq)}$$
$$\log \beta = 8.61$$

$$Ni^{2+}{}_{(aq)} + 3en_{(aq)} \longleftrightarrow [Ni(en)_3]^{2+}_{(aq)}$$
$$\log \beta = 18.28$$
$$\text{(more stable)}$$

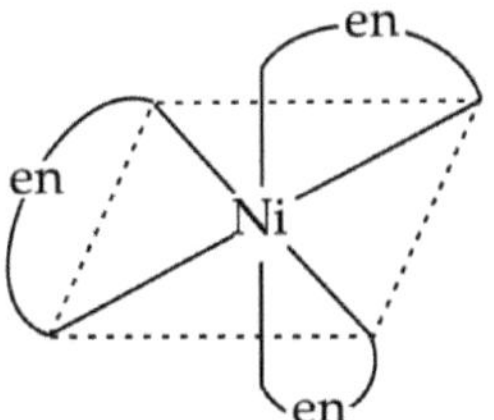

Q. 7. How many ions are produced from the complex $[Co(NH_3)_6]Cl_2$ in solution?

    (i) 6   (iii) 3

    (ii) 4   (iv) 2

Ans. (iii) The given complex can be written as $[Co(NH_3)_6]Cl_2$.

Thus, $[Co(NH_3)_6]^+$ along with two Cl^- ions are produced. *i.e.*,

$$[Co(NH_3)_6]Cl_2 \xrightarrow{aq} [Co(NH_3)_6]^{2+} + 2Cl^-$$

Hence 3 ions, one complex and 2 chloride ions are produced.

Q. 8. Amongst the following ions which one has the highest magnetic moment value?

    (i) $[Cr(H_2O)_6]^{3+}$ (iii) $[Zn(H_2O)_6]^{2+}$

    (ii) $[Fe(H_2O)_6]^{2+}$

Ans. (i) No. of unpaired electrons in $[Cr(H_2O)_6]^{3+} = 3$

Then,
$$\mu = \sqrt{n(n+2)}$$
$$= \sqrt{3(3+2)} = \sqrt{15}$$
$$\sim 4\ BM$$

(ii) No. of unpaired electrons in $[Fe(H_2O)_6]^{2+} = 4$

Then,
$$\mu = \sqrt{4(4+2)} = \sqrt{24}$$
$$\sim 5 \text{ BM}$$

(iii) No. of unpaired electrons in $[Zn(H_2O)_6]^{2+} = 0$

Hence, $[Fe(H_2O)_6]^{2+}$ has the highest magnetic moment value, because of 4 unpaired electrons.

Q. 9. Amongst the following, the most stable complex is

    (i) $[Fe(H_2O)_6]^{3+}$ (iii) $[Fe(C_2O_4)_3]^{3-}$

    (ii) $[Fe(NH_3)_6]^{3+}$ (iv) $[FeCl_6]^{3-}$

Ans. In all the complexes, Fe is in (+3) oxidation state and coordination number (CN) is 6. As the stability of a complex increases by chelation. Therefore, the most stable complex is $[Fe(C_2O_4)_3]^{3-}$.

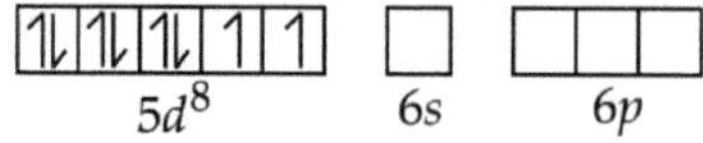

Then,

Q. 10. What will be the correct order for the wavelengths of absorption in the visible region for the following:
$[Ni(NO_2)_6]^{4-}$, $[Ni(NH_3)_6]^{2+}$, $[Ni(H_2O)_6]^{2+}$

Ans. The central metal ion in all the three complexes is the same with same oxidation number of (+2); Ni^{+2}. Therefore, absorption in the visible region depends on the ligands. The order in which the CFSE values of the ligands increases in the spectrochemical series is as follows:
$$H_2O < NH_3 < NO_2^{-}$$

Thus, the amount of crystal-field splitting oberved will be in the following order:
$$\Delta_{a(H_2O)} < \Delta_{a(NH_3)} < \Delta_{a(NO_2^{-})}$$

Hence, the wavelenghts of absorption in the visible region will be in the order:
$$[Ni(H_2O)_6]^{2+} > [Ni(NH_3)_6]^{2+} > [Ni(NO_2)_6]^{4-}$$

as wavelength λ is inversely proportional to the energy of the radiation.
$$E \propto \frac{1}{\lambda}.$$

Q. 11. Predict the number of unpaired electrons in the square planar $[Pt(CN)_4]^{2-}$ ion.

Ans. $[Pt(CN)_4]^{2-}$ in this complex, Pt is in the +2 state. In the Ni group hence it has $5d^8$ configuration in +2 state. It forms a square planar structure. This means that it undergoes dsp^2 hybridisation.

$$\boxed{\uparrow\downarrow}\,\boxed{\uparrow\downarrow}\,\boxed{\uparrow\downarrow}\,\boxed{\uparrow}\,\boxed{\uparrow} \quad \boxed{} \quad \boxed{}$$
$$\quad 5d^8 \qquad\qquad\quad 6s \qquad 6p$$

CN^{-} being a strong field ligand causes the pairing of unpaired electrons also that support the dsp^2 hybridisation. Hence, there are no unpaired electrons in $[Pt(CN)_4]^{2-}$.

Q. 12. When a co-ordination compound $CrCl_3.6H_2O$ is mixed with $AgNO_3$, 2 moles of AgCl are precipitated per mole of the compound. Write.*

    (i) Structural formula of the complex.

    (ii) IUPAC name of the complex.

Ans. (i) Structural formula of the complex must be $[Cr(H_2O)_5Cl]\ Cl_2.H_2O$, hence 2 moles of chlorine released per mole of compound to give 2 moles of precipitate of AgCl.

    (ii) Pentaaquachloridochromium (III) chloridemonohydro.

Q. 13. (i) Give the electronic configuration of the d-orbitals of Ti in $[Ti(H_2O)_6]^{3+}$ ion in the octahedral crystal field.

(ii) Why is this complex coloured? Explain on the basis of distribution of d-electron.

Ans. (i) Oxidation state of Ti is (+3) where Ti has $3d^1 4s^0$ configuration. On approach of octahedral crystal field it will split into $t_{2g}^1 e_g^0$ levels.

(ii) As the ground state t_{2g}^1 has 1 electron which easily gets extended to next e_g level, thus absorbing light in visible region. Therefore complex is coloured because of d-d transition.

Q. 14. Give shape and behaviour of the following complexes: *

 (i) $[Co(NH_3)_6]^{3+}$ (ii) $[Ni(CN)_4]^{2-}$

Ans. (i) Octahedral complex $[Co(NH_3)_6]^{3+}$.

Co, oxidation state (+3), $4s^0 3d^6$. NH_3 being strong field ligand causes pairing of $3d$-orbitals. Hence diamagnetic.

(ii) $[Ni(CN)_4]^{2-}$

Oxidation state of Ni is +2. Configuration $3d^8 4s^0$, CN being strong field ligand causes pairing for dsp^2 hybridisation.

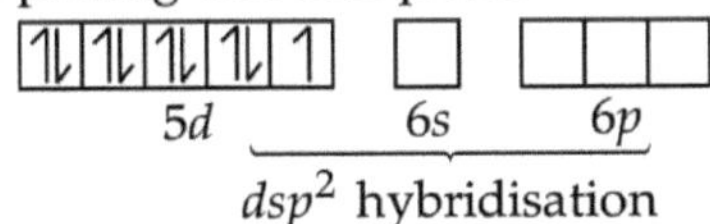

Leading to square planar, diamagnetic compound.

Q. 15. Write the structure and magnetic behaviour of the following complexes. *

 (i) $[Pt(NH_3)_2Cl(NO_2)]$ (ii) $[Co(NH_3)_4Cl_2]$ Cl.

Ans. (i) Pt has $5d^8 6s^0$ configuration.

As $(NH_3)_2$ is quite strong ligand pairing will take place.

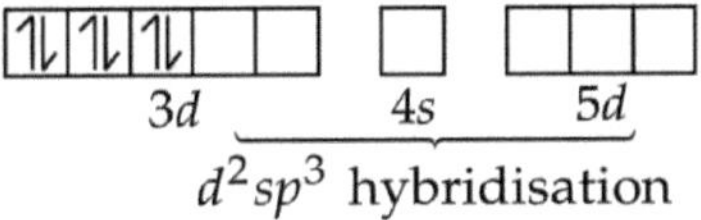

Hence square planar, diamagnetic inner orbital complex.

(ii) $[Co(NH_3)_4 Cl_2]$ Cl.

Co is in (+III) hence, $3d^6 4s^0$ configuration. There are 6 ligands inside coordination sphere, hence octahedral complex (NH_3) will cause pairing, hence diamagnetic, inner orbital complex.

$d^2 sp^3$ hybridisation

Q. 16. Give one examples each of: *

 (i) Coordination isomerism   (iii) Linkage isomerism

 (ii) Ionisation isomerism

Ans. (i) When the coordinate compound has both cationic complex and anionic complex then if the distribution of ligands differ, then coordination isomerism arises:

Ex. : $[Cr(NH_3)_6] [Cr(CN)_6]$ and $[Cr(NH_3)_4(CN)_2] [Cr(NH_3)_2 (CN)_4]$

(ii) Complexes which provides different ions in solution but have similar molecular composition like;

    $[Pt(NH_3)_4Cl_2]Br_2$ and $[Pt(NH_3)4Br_2]Cl_2$

       ↓   ↓

    Provides Br^- ion in   Provides Cl^- ions in

      solution   solution

(iii) When any ligand is an ambident ligand then linkage isomerism arises:

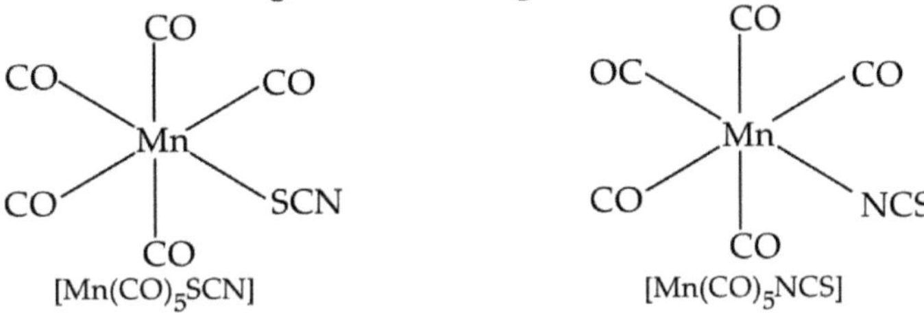

Q. 17. (i) What type of isomerism is shown by the complex $[Co(NH_3)_5(SCN)]^{2+}$?*

(ii) Why is $[NiCl_4]^{2-}$ paramagnetic while $[Ni(CN)_4]^{2-}$ is diamagnetic? (Atomic number of Ni = 28)

(iii) Why are low spin tetrahedral complexes rarely observed?

Ans. (i) Linkage isomerism.

(ii) $[NiCl_4]^{2-}$ $Ni^{21} = 1s^2 2s^2 2p^6 3s^2 3p^6 3d^8$

Cl^- is a weak field ligand.

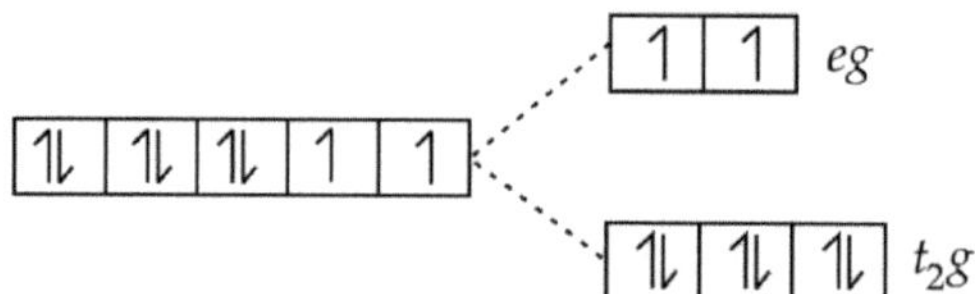

$2e^-$ are unpaired in $[NiCl_4]^{2-}$ which provides paramagnetism to the complex. $[Ni(CN)_4]^{2-}$

$Ni^{2+} = 1s^2 2s^2 2p^6 3s^2 3p^6 3d^8$

CN^- is a strong field ligand

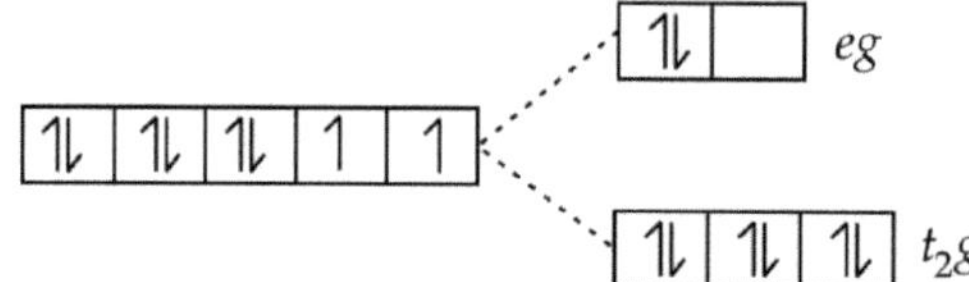

no electron is unpaired in $[Ni(CN)_4]^{2-}$ That's why the complex is diamagnetic.

(iii) In tetrahedral complex, CFSE is very low and it is difficult for the tetrahedral complexes to exceed the pairing energy. Usually electrons prefer to move to higher energy orbitals than to pair. Thus they usually forms high spin complex.

$$(CFSE)\ ted = \frac{4}{9}\ (CFSE)oh$$

Q. 18. (i) What type of isomerism is shown by the complex $[Co(NH_3)_6][Cr(CN)_6]$?*

(ii) Why a solution of $[Ni(H_2O)_6]^{2+}$ is green while a solution of $[Ni(CN)_4]^{2-}$ is colourless? (At. no. of Ni = 28)

(iii) Write the IUPAC name of the following complex:

$[Co(NH_3)_5(CO_3)]Cl$.

Ans. (i) Both shows coordination isomerism because both cationic and anionic entities and isomers differ in the distribution of ligands in the coordination entity of cationic and anionic part.

(ii) In $[Ni(H_2O)_6]^{2+}$ Ni is in +2 oxidation state with electronic configuration $3d^8$. In the presence of weak ligand H_2O the two unpaired electrons do not pair up and hence the complex has two unpaired electrons. Therefore it is coloured and shows d-d transitions which absorbs red light and emits green complimentary light.

In case of $[(Ni)(CN_4]^{2-}$ Ni also shows +2 oxidation state but CN ligand is strong ligand and two unpaired electrons undergo pairing, no d-d transititions and no colour so it is colourless.

(iii) Pentaamminecarbonatocobalt (III) chloride.

Q. 19. (i) What type of isomerism is shown by the complex $[Co(en)_3]Cl_3$?*

(ii) Write the hybridisation and magnetic character of $[Co(C_2O_4)_3]^{3-}$

(At. no. of Co = 27)

(iii) Write IUPAC name of the following complex $[Cr(NH_3)_3Cl_3]$.

Ans. (i) Since the given coordinate compound does not have a plane of symmetry and the ligand attached is bidentate ligand so it will show optical isomerism.

(ii) $[Co(C2O_4)_3]^{3-}$ Co is in +4 oxidation state electronic configuration $3d^6$ oxalate is a strong field ligand so pairing of electrons take place.

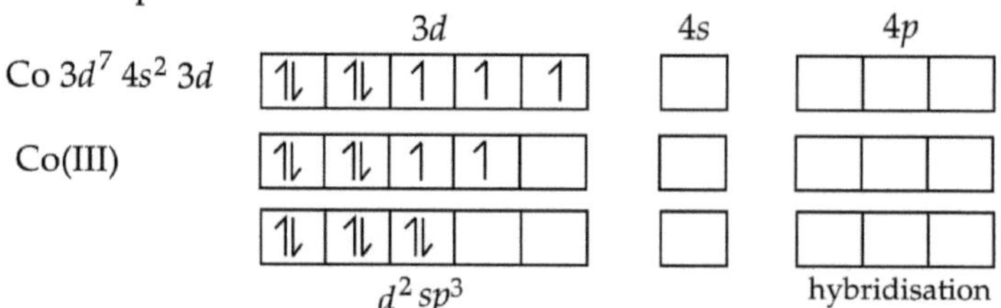

(iii) Triamminetrichloridochromium (III).

Q. 20. (i) Name the coordination compound use for chemotherapy purpose to reduce the cancereous tissue growth?

(ii) Is their any alternative to the common agent to avoid intense side effects.

Ans. (i) *cis*-platin, *i.e.*, *cis*-diamminedichloridoplatinum (II) complex is being used as a chelating chemotherapy agent.

(ii) Keeping the severe side effects of cis-platin in mind, its being replaced with dinuclear platinum complex.

Chapter 10. Haloalkanes and Haloarenes

Q. 1. What is the role of Lewis acids like $FeCl_3$ in the preparation of aryl halides in dark?

Ans. The Lewis acids help in generating the electrophile which in turn attacks the benzene ring for the formation of aryl halide.

Example : $Cl - Cl + FeCl_3 \longrightarrow FeCl_4{}^+ + Cl^+$

Q. 2. Why halogens when attached to benzene rings are deactivating but are ortho and para directing groups at the same time? Explain.

Ans. Halogen atoms when attached to benzene ring have two kinds of effects $(+R)$ and $(-I)$.

The $(+ R)$ effect causes halide ion to donate an electron pair to the benzene ring and participate in conjugation. Thus, it acts as a *ortho-para* directing group. But on the other hand as halides (X^-) are more electronegative than C of benzene ring they exhibit $-I$ effect, hence deactivating the overall ring towards electrophilic substitution reactions.

Q. 3. What is a racemic mixture? Give an example. [*]

Ans. A racemic mixture is a equimolar mixture of two optically active same compounds with different optical rotations represented as $(\pm)$. Such compounds are optically inactive mixtures as rotation due to dextro form is exactly cancelled by rotation due to laevo form.

Generally when we react an optically active compound for substitution reaction via S_N1 mechanism, we get a optically inactive racemic mixture as a product.

Example :

(100% optically active)
(+)

(50%)
(+)

(50%)
(–)

Q. 4. Which compound in the following pair will react via SN$_2$ reaction with –OH ion and why? [**]

(i) CH_3Br or CH_3I

(ii) $(CH)_3CCl$ or CH_3Cl

Ans. (i) Both CH_3Br and CH_3I will follow S_N2 mechanism as both are primary halides. The rate of reaction will be faster for CH_3I as (I^-) is a better leaving group.

(ii) CH_3Cl will follow S_N2 mechanism while S_N2 mechanism is difficult for $(CH_3)_3CCl$ as its a tertiary halide. The rate of reactivity for S_N2 mechanism is : $1° > 2° > 3°$ halides.

---

[*]   are board exam questions from previous years

[**]   are frequently asked board exam questions

Q. 5. What happens when:
    (i)   Methyl chloride is treated with alcoholic KCN.
    (ii) Ethyl chloride is treated with alcoholic KOH.
    (iii) Chloroform is heated with Ag powder.*

Ans. (i)   Methyl cyanide is formed CH_3CN as a result of nucleophilic substitution reaction.
    (ii) Ethene ($CH_2 = CH_2$) is formed as a, result of dehydrohalogenation reaction.
    (iii) Dehydrogenation of two moles of chloroform results in the formation of acetylene.

$$HCCl_3 + 6Ag + Cl_3CH \xrightarrow{\Delta} CH \equiv CH + 6AgCl$$
$$\text{Acetylene}$$

Q. 6. State the uses of the following compounds:
    (i)   Chloroform,   (iii) DDT.
    (ii) Iodoform,

Ans. (i)   It is used as an excellent organic solvent manufacture of freon-R-22.
    (ii) Iodoform is used as an antiseptic, particularly for dressing wounds. It releases iodine on coming in contact with the skin, which shows antiseptic properties.
    (iii) DDT or *p-p'*-dichlorodiphenyltrichloroethane was earlier used as an insecticide, also as an antimalarial usage.

Q. 7. What are ambident nucleophiles? Explain with an example.

Ans. Ambident nucleophiles are nucleophiles having two nucleophilic sites or ambident nucleophiles are the ones which can attack from two sites.

For example, nitrite ion is an ambident nucleophile.

$[\ddot{O} — \ddot{N} = O]$ or CN^{-1} as $[:\bar{C} \equiv N: \leftrightarrow :\ddot{N} \equiv C]$ can attack from both carbon or nitrogen site.

So, it can form alkyl cyanides or alkyl isocyanides.

Q. 8. The following compounds are given to you:*
    2-Bromopentane, 2-Bromo-2-methylbutane, 1-Bromopentane
    (i)   Write the compound which is most reactive towards S_N2 reaction.
    (ii) Write the compound which is optically active.
    (iii) Write the compound which is most reactive towards β-elimination reaction.

Ans. (i)   1-bromopentane > 2-bromopentane > 2-bromo-2-methylpentane (Reactivity towards, S_N2 reaction)
    (ii) 2-bromopentane
         $CH_3CH_2CH_2CHBrCH_3$

    (iii)
$$H_3C — CH_2 — CH_2 — \overset{\overset{\displaystyle Br}{|}}{\underset{\underset{\displaystyle CH_3}{|}}{C}} — CH_3$$
               2-bromo-2-methylpentane

    This compound is most reactive towards β-elimination.

Q. 9. Complete the following chemical equations:*
    (i) $F_2 + Cl^- \rightarrow$
    (ii) $2XeF_2 + 2H_2O \rightarrow$

Ans. (i) $F_2 + Cl^- \rightarrow 2F^- + Cl_2$
    (ii) $2XeF_2 + 2H_2O \rightarrow 2Xe + 4HF + O_2$

Q. 10. (i)   Give the chemical formula of Freon-12.
      (ii) Suggest some substitutes to Freon-12.

Ans. (i)   Chemical formula of Freon 12 is CF_2Cl_2.
    (ii) Apart from liquid ammonia, another recent substitute to Freon-12 is HCFC-123 *i.e.*, CF_3HCCl_2. The presence of hydrogen makes the compound less stable and it gets oxidised before reaching stratosphere. Thus it does not reacts with the ozone layer.

Q. 11. What happens when:[*]
    (i)   HCl is added to MnO_2?
    (ii) PCl_5 is heated?
    write the equations involved.

Ans. (i) $MnO_2 + 4HCl \rightarrow MnCl_2 + Cl_2 + 2H_2O$

     (ii) $PCl_5 \xrightarrow{\Delta} PCl_3 + Cl_2$

Chapter 11. Alcohols, Phenols and Ethers

Q. 1. Explain the following:
    (i)   *Ortho*-nitrophenol is more acidic than *ortho*-methoxyphenol.
    (ii) Ethers are less reactive chemically compared to alcohols.

Ans. (i) Acidity of nitrophenol is more than methoxy phenol because nitro group being electron withdrawing makes the –OH bond of phenol more polar and hence easier to release H^+. On the other hand methoxy group at ortho position makes the –OH bond less polar, satisfies the electron deficiency of oxygen of phenol group, hence makes release of H^+ difficult.

     (ii) Ethers (R–O–R) are less reactive as C–O–C bond is far less polar than R–C–OH bond of alcohols. Hence ethers, are quite less reactive and less involved in reactions compared to similar comparable (molecular mass) alcohols.

Q. 2. Account for the following:
    (i)   Phenol gives a light yellow precipitate with bromine water.
    (ii) Sec-Butyl alcohol gives positive iodoform test but *n*-Butyl alcohol does not.

Ans. (i) Phenol when reacts with bromine in aqueous medium forms 2, 4, 6-Tribromophenol derivative, which forms a yellow colour precipitate.

     (ii) Sec-Butyl alcohol, *i.e.*, $CH_3 — CH_2 — \overset{\overset{\displaystyle OH}{|}}{CH} — CH_3$ has a $(CH_3 — \overset{\overset{\displaystyle OH}{|}}{C} —)$ group present which results in the positive iodoform test.

$$CH_3CH_2 — \overset{\overset{\displaystyle OH}{|}}{CH} — CH_3 + NaOI \longrightarrow CH_3 — \overset{\overset{\displaystyle O}{||}}{C} — CH_3 — CH_2 — NaI + H_2O$$
$$\text{Butanone}$$

$$CH_3 — \overset{\overset{\displaystyle O}{||}}{C} — CH_2CH_3 + 3NaOI \longrightarrow CHI_3 + CH_3CH_2COONa + 2NaOH$$
$$\text{Butanone} \qquad \text{Yellow ppt.}$$
$$\text{of Iodoform}$$

     Whereas *n*-Butanol *i.e.*, $CH_3CH_2CH_2CH_2OH$ has no such group present. Hence, it does not gives any positive iodoform test.

Q. 3. Name the reagents used in the following reactions:
    (i)   Oxidation of a primary alcohol to carboxylic acid.
    (ii) Oxidation of a primary alcohol to aldehyde.
    (iii) Bromination of phenol to 2, 4, 6-tribromophenol.
    (iv) Benzyl alcohol to benzoic acid.
    (v) Dehydration of propan-2-ol to propene.
    (vi) Butan-2-one to butan-2-ol.

Ans. (i) Acidified potassium permanganate, $KMnO_4$.
     (ii) Pyridinium chlorochromate (PCC)
     (iii) Bromine water
     (iv) Acidified potassium permanganate, $KMnO_4$
     (v) 85% phosphoric acid or 60% H_2SO_4
     (vi) $NaBH_4$ or $LiAlH_4$.

Q. 4. Write the names of reagents and equations for the preparation of the following ethers by Williamson's synthesis:

(i) 1-Propoxypropane

(ii) Ethoxybenzene

(iii) 2-Methoxy-2-methylpropane

(iv) 1-Methoxyethane.

Ans. (i) $CH_3CH_2CHONa + CH_3CH_2CH_2Br \longrightarrow C_2H_5CH_2 - O - CH_2C_2H_5 + NaBr$

Sodium propoxide   1-Bromopropane   1-Propoxypropanes

(ii) 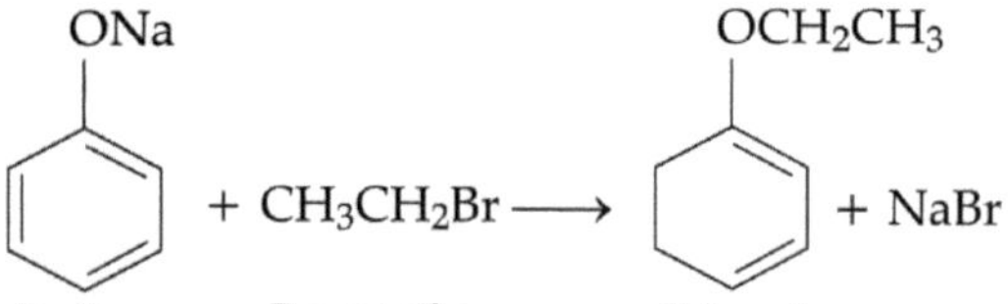 Sodium phenoxide (C_6H_5ONa) $+ CH_3CH_2Br \longrightarrow$ Ethoxybenzene ($C_6H_5OCH_2CH_3$) $+ NaBr$

Bromoethane

(iii)
$$CH_3 - \underset{\underset{CH_3}{|}}{\overset{\overset{CH_3}{|}}{C}} - ONa + CH_3 - Br \longrightarrow CH_3 - \underset{\underset{CH_3}{|}}{\overset{\overset{CH_3}{|}}{C}} - OCH_3 + NaBr$$

Sodium 2-methyl-2-propoxide   Bromomethane   2-methoxy-2-methylpropane

(iv) $CH_3CH_2 - ONa + CH_3 - Br \longrightarrow CH_3CH_2 - O - CH_3 + NaBr$

Sodium ethoxide   Bromomethane   1-Methoxyethane

Q. 5. Classify the following as primary, secondary and tertiary alcohols:

(i) $CH_3 - \underset{\underset{CH_3}{|}}{\overset{\overset{CH_3}{|}}{C}} - CH_2OH$

(ii) $H_2C = CH - CH_2OH$

(iii) $CH_3 - CH_2 - CH_2 - OH$

(iv) 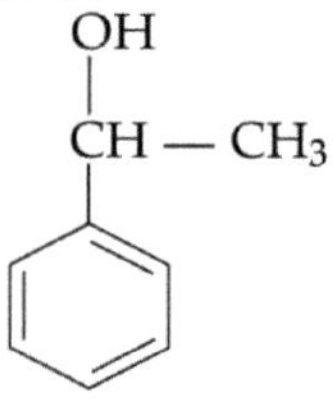 $C_6H_5 - \underset{\underset{OH}{|}}{CH} - CH_3$

(v) 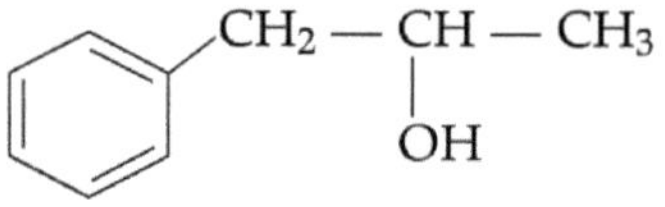 $C_6H_5 - CH_2 - \underset{\underset{OH}{|}}{CH} - CH_3$

(vi) 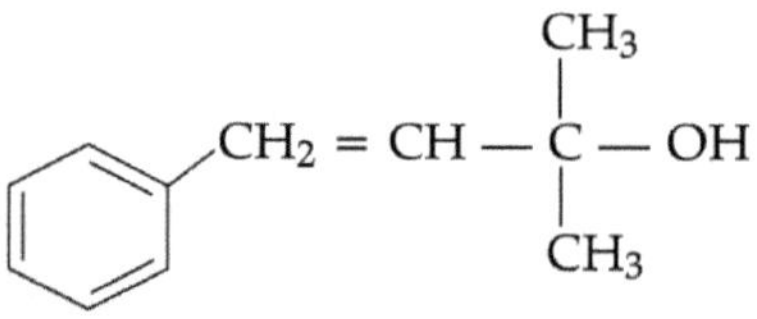 $C_6H_5 - CH_2 = CH - \underset{\underset{CH_3}{|}}{\overset{\overset{CH_3}{|}}{C}} - OH$

Ans. Primary alcohol → (i), (ii) and (iii)   Secondary alcohol → (iv) and (v)

Tertiary alcohol → (vi)

Q. 6. Show how the following alcohols are prepared by the reaction of a suitable Grignard reagent on methanal?

(i) $CH_3 - \underset{\underset{CH_3}{|}}{CH} - CH_2OH$

(ii) 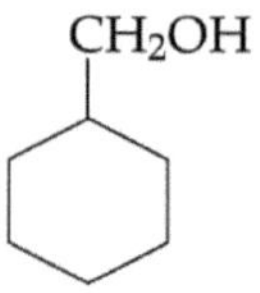 Cyclohexyl–CH_2OH

Ans. (i)
$$HCHO + CH_3 - \underset{\underset{CH_3}{|}}{CH} - MgBr \longrightarrow \left[CH_3 - \underset{\underset{CH_3}{|}}{CH} - \underset{\underset{OMgBr}{|}}{CH_2} \right]$$

$$\xrightarrow{H^+ \mid H_2O}$$

$$Mg(OH)Br + CH_3 - \underset{\underset{CH_3}{|}}{CH} - CH_2 - OH$$

(ii) **HCHO +** (Methanal) + Cyclohexylmagnesium bromide $\xrightarrow{}$ [CH$_2$—OMgBr] $\xrightarrow[\text{H}^+]{\text{H}_2\text{O}}$ CH$_2$OH (Cyclohexylmethanol) **+ Mg(OH)Br**

Q. 7. Predict the major product of acid catalysed dehydration of:

   (i) 1-methylcyclohexanol   (ii) butan-1-ol.

Ans. (i) 1-Methylcyclohexanol $\xrightarrow[\text{H}^+]{\text{Dehydration}}$ 1-Methylcyclohexene (Major product) $+ \text{H}_2\text{O} +$ 1-Methylenecyclohexane (Minor product)

   (ii) $\text{CH}_3\text{CH}_2\text{CH}_2\text{CH}_2\text{OH}$ (Butan-1-ol) $\xrightarrow[\text{H}^+]{\text{Dehydration}}$ $\text{CH}_3\text{CH} = \text{CHCH}_3 + \text{H}_2\text{O}$ (But-2-ene) (Major product)

As the reaction mechanism involves formation of carbocation, $\text{CH}_3 - \text{CH}_2 - \overset{+}{\underset{\text{H}}{\text{CH}}} - \text{CH}_2 \,(1°)$ which reorganises to more stable $(2°)$ carbocation, *i.e.*, $\text{CH}_3 - \overset{\oplus}{\text{CH}} - \text{CH}_2 - \text{CH}_3$ which results in the formation of But-2-ene.

Q. 8. Which of the following is an appropriate set of reactants for the preparation of 1-methoxy-4-nitrobenzene and why?

   (i) Br—C$_6$H$_4$—NO$_2$ $+ \text{CH}_3\text{ONa}$ (ii) ONa—C$_6$H$_4$—NO$_2$ $+ \text{CH}_3\text{Br}$

Ans. Set (ii) is an appropriate set of reactants for the preparation of 1-methoxy-4-nitrobenzene.

ONa—C$_6$H$_4$—NO$_2$ $+ \text{CH}_3\text{Br} \longrightarrow$ OCH$_3$—C$_6$H$_4$—NO$_2$ $+ \text{NaBr}$ (1-Methoxy-4-nitrobenzene)

In set (i), sodium methoxide (CH_3ONa) is a strong nucleophile as well as a strong base.

Hence, an elimination reaction predominates over a substitution reaction. Also its difficult to break C–Br bond in a sp^2 hybridised carbon atom.

Q. 9. (i) Arrange the following compounds in the increasing order of their acid strength:*

p-cresol, *p*-nitrophenol, phenol

   (ii) Write the mechanism (using curved arrow notation of the following reaction:

$$\text{CH}_2 = \text{CH}_2 \xrightarrow{\text{H}_3\text{O}^+} \text{CH}_3 - \text{CH}_2{}^+ + \text{H}_2\text{O}$$

Ans. (i)

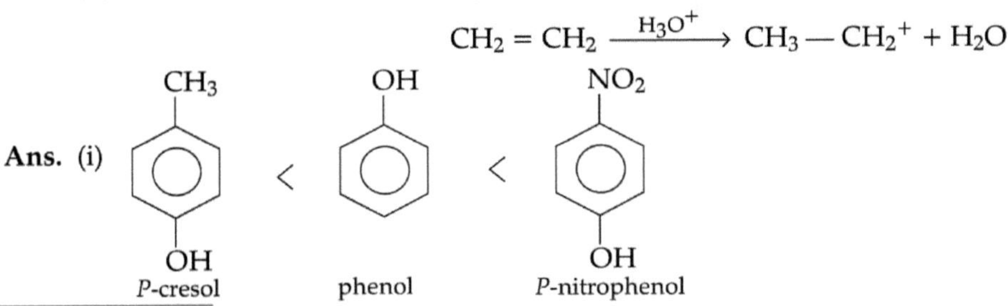

P-cresol $<$ phenol $<$ *P*-nitrophenol

(ii) $CH_2 = CH_2 \longrightarrow \overset{+}{C}H_2 - \bar{C}H_2 \xrightarrow{H^+/H_2O \text{ or } H_3O^+} \overset{+}{C}H_2 - CH_3 + H_2O$

Q. 10. **Write the structures of the products when Butan-2-ol reacts with the following:***

    (i) CrO_3 (ii) $SOCl_2$

Ans. (i) $CH_3 - CH_2 - \underset{\underset{\text{butane-2-ol}}{|}}{\overset{\overset{OH}{|}}{C}H} - CH_3 \xrightarrow{CrO_3} CH_3 - CH_2 - \underset{\underset{\text{2-chloro-butane}}{}}{\overset{\overset{O}{\parallel}}{C}} - CH_3$

    (ii) $H_3C - CH_2 - \underset{\underset{\text{butane-2-ol}}{|}}{\overset{\overset{OH}{|}}{C}H} - CH_3 \xrightarrow{SOCl_2} H_3C - CH_2 - \underset{\underset{\text{2-chloro-butane}}{}}{\overset{\overset{Cl}{|}}{C}H} - CH_2$

Q. 11. (i) Is aspirin derived from phenol? Write chemical formula of aspirin.

    (ii) How is aspirin used in medicines?

    (iii) Is phenol used in polymer industry? Name few.

    (iv) Name precautions taken before prescribing aspirin.

    (v) Name one azo-dye derived from phenol.

Ans. (i) Yes aspirin is derived from phenol. It is acetyl salicylic acid.

        (benzene ring with $OCOCH_3$ and $COOH$ substituents)

    (ii) Aspirin is used as an analgesic and an antipyretic.

    (iii) Synthesis of polymer bakelite (phenol formaldehyde resin).

    (iv) Aspirin should never be taken empty stomach since it can cause ulceration.

    (v) Phenolphthalein is an useful indicator and an azo-dye derived from phenol.

Chapter 12. Aldehydes, Ketones and Carboxylic Acids

Q. 1. **Arrange the following in decreasing order of acid catalysed esterification:**

(structures: 4-methylbenzoic acid derivative CH_3—ring—$COOH$ with CH_3 ; benzoic acid ring—$COOH$; 2,6-dimethylbenzoic acid ring—$COOH$ with two CH_3 groups)

Ans. As we know that in esterification, alcohol molecule attacks the carbonyl carbon protonated by acid. Presence of substitution in *ortho* position will cause steric hindrance to such attack in benzoic acid.

Hence increasing order of reactivity is,

2, 6-Dimethyl benzoic acid < 2, 4-Dimethylbenzoic acid < benzoic acid.

(structures: CH_3—ring—$COOH$ with CH_3 < 2,6-dimethyl ring—$COOH$ < ring—$COOH$)

Q. 2. **Out of $CH_3CH_2COCH_2CH_3$ and $CH_3CH_2CH_2COCH_3$ which gives positive iodoform test? Why?***

Ans. Iodoform test is given by compound containing a methyl ketone group *i.e.*, $CH_3CH_3CH_2COCH_3$ will give positive iodoform test.

Q. 3. **Give the formula of [A] and [B].**

$$CH_3 - \overset{\overset{O}{\parallel}}{C} - OH \xrightarrow{SOCl_2} [A] \xrightarrow{LiAlH_4} [B]$$

Ans.

$$CH_3 - \overset{\overset{\displaystyle O}{\|}}{C} - OH \xrightarrow{SOCl_2} CH_3 - \overset{\overset{\displaystyle O}{\|}}{C} - Cl \xrightarrow{LiAlH_4} CH_3CH_2OH$$

Q. 4. Arrange the following esters in decreasing order of alkaline hydrolysis. Justify your arrangement.

$$Cl \text{—⟨O⟩—} COOC_2H_5, \quad NO_2 \text{—⟨O⟩—} COOC_2H_5$$

$$CH_3 \text{—⟨O⟩—} COOC_2H_5, \quad \text{⟨O⟩—} COOC_2H_5$$

Ans. The rate of hydrolysis depends on the electron deficiency of the carbonyl carbon of the ester group. Hence presence of electron withdrawing groups increases the rate of reaction whereas electron donating group decreases the rate of hydrolysis. Hence the decreasing order of rate for the given esters is.

$$NO_2 \text{—⟨O⟩—} COOC_2H_5 \; > \; Cl \text{—⟨O⟩—} COOC_2H_5 \; > \; \text{⟨O⟩—} COOC_2H_5$$

$$> \; CH_3 \text{—⟨O⟩—} COOC_2H_5$$

Q. 5. Answer the following:
   (i)   What is Fehling's solution?
   (ii) To what oxidation state ethanal converts Fehling's solution.

Ans. (i)   Fehling's solution is alkaline solution of $CuSO_4$ along with some Rochelle salt.
   (ii) Ethanol converts Cu(II) of Fehling's solution to Cu(I) *i.e.*, + 1 state.

Q. 6. Account for the following:
   (i)   Acetaldehyde does not gives Cannizzaro's reaction, while formaldehyde does.
   (ii) Methanol is related to formalin and trioxane. Explain.*

Ans. (i)   Presence of an α-hydrogen atom in acetaldehyde makes it undergo aldol condensation whereas absence of α-hydrogen in formaldehyde, only allows it to undergo Cannizzaro's reaction in presence of a concentrated base like NaOH solution. It forms methyl alcohol and sodium formate in equimolar mixture.
   (ii) Methanol when mixed with 60% water, *i.e.*, a 40% aqueous solution of methanol is called formalin Trioxane is a stable cyclic trimer of formaldehyde. Formula $C_3H_6O_3$.

Q. 7. Arrange the following compounds in increasing order of their boiling points.
   CH_3CHO, CH_3CH_2OH, CH_3OCH_3, $CH_3CH_2CH_3$

Ans. The molecular masses of the given compounds are comparable CH_3CH_2OH undergoes extensive intermolecular H-bonding, resulting in the association of molecules. Therefore, it has the highest boiling point. CH_3CHO is more polar than CH_3OCH_3 and so CH_3CHO has stronger intermolecular dipole-dipole interaction than CH_3OCH_3. $CH_3CH_2CH_3$ has only weak Van der Waals force. Therefore, the increasing order of their boiling points is as:

$$CH_3CH_2CH_3 < CH_3OCH_3 < CH_3CHO < CH_3CH_2OH$$

Q. 8. Account for the following:*
   (i)   Aromatic carboxylic acids do not undergo Friedel-Crafts reaction.
   (ii) pK_a value of 4-nitrobenzoic acid is lower than that of benzoic acid.

Ans. (i)   Aromatic carboxylic acids do not undergo Friedel-Crafts reaction because the carboxyl group is deactivating for electrophilic substitution reaction, secondarily, the catalyst aluminium chloride gets bonded to the carboxyl group.
   (ii) pK_a value of 4-Nitrobenzoic acid is lower than benzoic acid, which means 4-Nitrobenzoic acid is more acidic than the benzoic acid. Being an electron withdrawing group, the $-NO_2$ group withdraws electrons towards itself resulting in ease of carboxylic proton release, hence increasing the acidity.

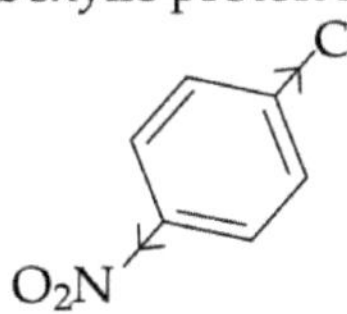

Q. 9. (i) Explain esterification reaction.

(ii) Name its reverse reaction.

Ans. (i) Esterification reaction is a reversible reaction where carboxylic acid reacts with an alcohol in presence of conc. H_2SO_4 and heat.

Example:

$$CH_3COOH + CH_3CH_2CH_2OH \xrightleftharpoons[\Delta]{Conc.H_2SO_4} CH_3COOCH_2CH_2CH_3 + H_2O$$

Ethanoic   Propanol   Propyl ethanoate

acid   (ester)

(ii) The reverse reaction is called hydrolysis of ester. Example

$$CH_3 - \overset{\overset{\displaystyle O}{\|}}{C} - O - CH_2CH_3 \xrightarrow[\Delta]{H_3O^+} CH_3COOH + CH_3CH_2OH$$

Ethylethanoate   Ethanoic   Ethanol

(ester)   acid

Chapter 13. Amines

Q. 1. Rearrange the following in decreasing order of basic strength. *

Aniline, *p*-nitroaniline, *p*-toluidine.

Ans. *p*-toluidine > aniline > *p*-nitroaniline.

In *p*-toluidine presence of CH_3 group in para-position of aniline makes it easier to donate electrons for nitrogen, whereas presence of electron withdrawing (– NO_2) group in *p*-nitroaniline makes it difficult for nitrogen atom of (– NH_2) group to donate electron as a result of – I effect.

Q. 2. Give reasons for the following:

(i) Acetylation of aniline reduces its activation effect.

(ii) CH_3NH_2 is more basic than $C_6H_5NH_2$

(iii) Although-NH_2 is o/p directing group, yet aniline on nitration gives a significant amount of *m*-nitroaniline.

Ans. (i)

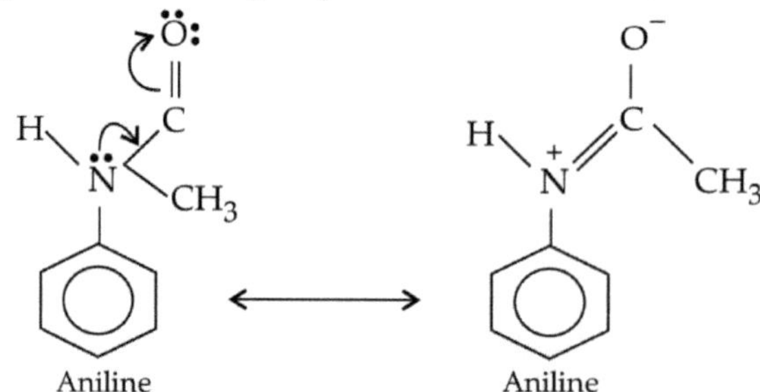

Aniline   Acetyl chloride   Acetanilide

In acetanilide, the oxygen atom of the group withdraws electrons from $\ddot{N}H_2$ group as shown below:

Aniline   Aniline

As a result, the electron pair on nitrogen gets displaced to the carboxyl group. Therefore the unshared pair of electron on nitrogen is less available for donation of the electron to aromatic ring.

(ii) In aniline, lone pair of e^- present on 'N' is in conjugation with the benzene ring and become less available for protonation because of resonance.

This conjugation of lone pair of e^- is not present in case of methyl amine and lone pair of e^- of 'N' are fully available for protonation. That's why the basicity order of aniline and methyl amine is:

(iii) $CH_3NH_2 > C_6H_5NH_2$

Aniline → (HNO₃, Conc. H₂SO₄, Δ) → o-nitro-aniline (2%) + m-nitro-aniline (47%) + p-nitro-aniline (51%)

The reason for the formation of large amount of m-nitroaniline is that under stongly acidic conditions, aniline gets protonated to anilinium ion ($-NH_3^+$ group). This is a deactivating group and is meta-directing, in nature.

Chapter 14. Biomolecules

Q. 1. **Name some industrial applications of enzymes along with their names.**

Ans. (i) Enzyme invertase is used in the manufacture of invert sugar solution from sucrose.

(ii) Renin, is used in manufacture of yeast.

(iii) Pepsin enzyme is used in processing of soy protein and gelatin.

Q. 2. **What are the expected products of hydrolysis of lactose?**

Ans. Lactose is a disaccharide composed of β-D-galactose and β-D-glucose. Thus, on hydrolysis, it gives β-D-galactose and β-D-glucose.

β-D-Galactose   β-D-Glucose

Lactose

$$C_{12}H_{22}O_{11} + H_2O \longrightarrow C_6H_{12}O_6 + C_6H_{12}O_6$$

Lactose   D-(+)-Glucose   D-(+)-Galactose

Q. 3. **When RNA is hydrolysed, there is no relationship among the quantities of different bases obtained. What does this fact suggest about the structure of RNA?**

Ans. A DNA molecule is double-stranded in which the pairing of bases occurs. Adenine always pairs with thymine, while cytosine always pairs with guanine. Therefore, on hydrolysis of DNA, the quantity of adenine produced is equal to that of thymine and similarly, the quantity of cytosine produced is equal to that of guanine. But when RNA is hydrolysed, there is no relationship among the quantities of the different bases obtained. RNA produces different bases cytosine, uracil, guanine and adenine. But as there is no ratio or relationship in the amount of these bases produced on hydrolysis, indicates that unlike DNA, RNA has single stranded structure.

Q. 4. **What are monosaccharides?**

Ans. Monosaccharides are carbohydrates that cannot be hydrolysed further to give simpler units of polyhydroxy aldehyde or ketone.

Monosaccharides are classified on the basis of number of carbon atoms and the functional group present in them. Monosaccharides containing an aldehyde group are known as aldoses and those containing a keto group are known as ketoses. Monosaccharides are further classified as trioses, tetroses, pentoses, hexoses, and heptoses according to the number of carbon atoms they contain. For example, a ketose containing 3 carbon atoms is called ketotriose and an aldose containing 3 carbon atoms is called aldotriose. There are about 20 monosaccharides found in nature.

Q. 5. What are reducing sugars?

Ans. Reducing sugars are carbohydrates that reduce Fehling's solution and Tollen's reagent. All monosaccharides and disaccharides, excluding sucrose, are reducing sugars. It is believed that monosaccharide in form of ketoses in alkaline medium convert into aldoses and reduces Fehling's solution and Tollen's reagent.

Q. 6. What is glycogen? How is it different from starch?

Ans. Glycogen is a carbohydrate (polysaccharide) found in animals, carbohydrates are stored as glycogen. It is insoluble in water.

Starch is a carbohydrate consisting of two components—amylose (15-20%) water soluble and amylopectin (80-85%), water insoluble.

However, glycogen consists of only one component whose structure is similar to amylopectin. Amylose is a linear polymer while glycogen and amylopectin are branched polymers of α-D-glucose. However glycogen is more highly branched compared to amylopectin.

Q. 7. What is the effect of denaturation on the structure of proteins?

Ans. As a result of denaturation, globules get unfolded and helixes get uncoiled. Secondary and tertiary structures of protein are destroyed, but the primary structure remains unaltered. As the secondary and tertiary structures of a protein are destroyed, the enzyme loses its activity and becomes inactive as a bio-catalyst.

Q. 8. Why vitamin A and vitamin C are essential to us? Give their important sources.

Ans. The deficiency of vitamin A leads to xerophthalmia (hardening of the cornea of the eye) and night blindness. The deficiency of vitamin C leads to scurvy (bleeding gums). The sources of vitamin A are fish liver oil, carrots, butter and milk. The sources of vitamin C are citrus fruits, amla and green leafy vegetables.

Chapter 15. Polymers

Q. 1. A copolymer can be a addition and condensation polymer both. Explain.

Ans. A copolymer is one in which the two different units join to become one monomer unit of the polymer. Hence, it can be either an addition or a condensation polymer.

Example : Buna-S is a copolymer and an addition polymer.

$$nCH_2 = CH — CH = CH_2 + n \overset{CH=CH_2}{\underset{\text{Styrene}}{\bigcirc}} \xrightarrow[\Delta]{Na} \left[nCH_2 — CH = CH — CH_2 — CH — CH_2 \right]_n$$

1,3 Butadiene   Styrene   Buna-S

Similarly terylene is a copolymer of ethylene glycol and terephthalic acid and it is a condensation polymer.

$$nOHCH_2CH_2OH + nHO — \underset{O}{\overset{O}{\underset{\|}{C}}} — \bigcirc — \underset{O}{\overset{O}{\underset{\|}{C}}} — OH \xrightarrow{-H_2O}$$

Ethylene glycol   Terephthalic acid

$$\left[O — CH_2 — CH_2 — O — \overset{O}{\overset{\|}{C}} — \bigcirc — \overset{O}{\overset{\|}{C}} \right]_n$$

Terylene (Dacron)

Q. 2. What does LDP and HDP signify? How are these prepared?

Ans. LDP represents low density polythene and HDP represents high density polythene.

Preparation: HDP is prepared by polymerisation of ethylene at about 340 K under 6 to 7 atm pressure in presence of catalyst triethyl aluminium and titanium tetrachloride (Zeigler-Natta catalyst).

The catalyst ensures that the polymer is formed in a regular linear chain manner and hence closely packed or staked giving a high density to the polyethene.

HDP is quite-inert chemically, tougher and has greater tensile strength.

LDP on the other hand is prepared by heating pure ethylene at about 400 K to 500 K under high pressure between 10,000-2,000 atm with some peroxide to initiate polymerisation.

This consist of highly branched molecules, because of branching it has empty space in between polymer chains and has low density. Its a poor conductor of electricity and is chemically inert.

Q. 3. Answer the following:

    (i) Polymer used in making disposable coffee cups.

    (ii) Percentage of sulphur present in vulcanisation of tyre rubber from natural rubber.

    (iii) Use of Novolac polymer.

    (iv) Polymer used in making handles of pressure cooker.

    (v) Name any two natural polyamides.

Ans. (i) Polystyrene.

    (ii) About 5 to 6%.

    (iii) Used in manufacture of paints.

    (iv) Bakelite or phenol formaldehyde resin.

    (v) Silk fibre and wool.

Q. 4. Explain the terms polymer and monomer.

Ans. The term 'poly' means many and 'mers' means units. Hence polymers are monomer units joined by strong covalent bonds. Polymers can be natural as well as synthetic. Polythene, rubber and nylon 6, 6 are examples of polymers. Monomers are simple, reactive molecules that combine with each other in large numbers through covalent bonds to give rise to polymers. For example, ethene, propene, styrene, vinyl chloride. Polymers are big macro molecules having high molecular mass (10_3-10^7 u).

Q. 5. What are the monomeric repeating units of Nylon-6 and Nylon-6, 6?

Ans. The monomeric repeating unit of nylon 6 is $\{ NH - (CH_2)_5 - CO \}$, which is derived from Caprolactum.

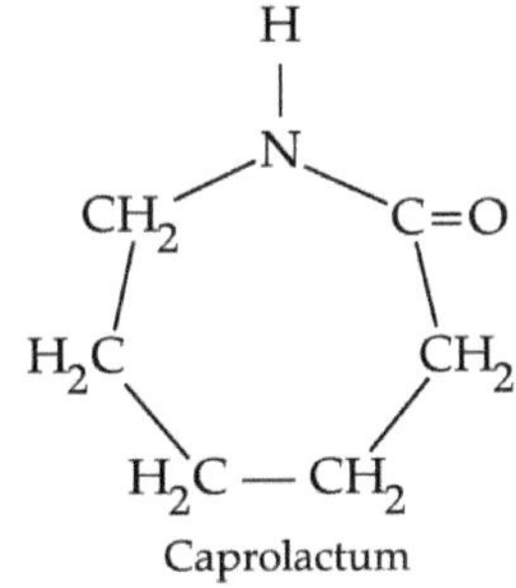

Caprolactum

The monomeric repeating unit of nylon 6, 6 is $\{ NH - (CH_2)_6 - NH - CO - (CH_2)_4 - CO \}$ which is derived from hexamethylene diamine and adipic acid.

Q. 6. How are polymers classified on the basis of structure?

Ans. Polymers are classified on the basis of structure as follows:

    (i) **Linear polymers:** The monomer units are linked to each other to form long straight chains. They can be depicted as:

    For *e.g.*, high density polythene (HDP), polyvinyl chloride, etc.

    (ii) **Branched chain polymers:** These polymers are basically linear chain polymers, which also have side chains of different lengths attached to them. These polymers are represented as:

    For *e.g.*, low density polythene (LDP), amylopectin, starch etc.

    (iii) **Cross-linked or network polymers:** These polymers have many cross-linking bonds that give rise to 3-dimensional network-like structure. These polymers contain bi-functional and tri-functional monomers and strong covalent bonds between various linear polymer chains. These are quite hard, rigid and brittle. Examples of such polymers include bakelite and melamine.

Q. 7. Write the names of monomers of the following polymers:

(i)
$$\left[\begin{array}{c}\overset{\displaystyle H}{|}\\N\end{array}-(CH_2)_6-\overset{\displaystyle H}{\underset{|}{N}}-\overset{\displaystyle O}{\overset{\|}{C}}-(CH_2)_4-\overset{\displaystyle O}{\overset{\|}{C}}\right]$$

(ii)
$$\left[\overset{\displaystyle O}{\overset{\|}{C}}-(CH_2)_3-\overset{\displaystyle H}{\underset{|}{N}}\right]_n$$

(iii) $\left[CF_2-CF_2\right]_n$

Ans. (i) Hexamethylenediamine $[H_2N-(CH_2)_6-NH_2]$ and adipic acid $[HOOC-(CH_2)_4-COOH]$ Polymer is nylon-6, 6.

(ii)

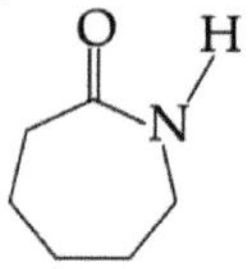

Polymer is nylon-6.

Caprolactum

(iii) Tetrafluoroethene $(CF_2 = CF_2)$. Polymer is Teflon.

Q. 8. Arrange the following polymers in increasing order of their intermolecular forces.
   (i)   Nylon-6, 6, Buna-S, Polythene.
   (ii) Nylon-6, Neoprene, Polyvinyl chloride.

Ans. Different types of polymers have different intermolecular forces of attraction. Elastomers or rubbers have the weakest while fibres have the strongest intermolecular forces of attraction. Plastics have intermediate intermolecular forces of attraction. Hence, the increasing order of the intermolecular forces of the given polymers is as follows :
   (i)   Buna–S < Polythene < Nylon-6, 6
   (ii) Neoprene < Polyvinyl chloride < Nylon-6.

Q. 9. Write the structures of the monomers used for getting the following polymers:*
   (i)   Nylon-6, 6
   (ii) Melamine-formaldehyde polymer
   (iii) Buna-S.

Ans. (i) Monomers of Nylon-6, 6
$$H_2N-(CH_2)_6-NH_2 \quad \text{and} \quad HOOC-(CH_2)_4-COOH$$
   Xexamethylenediamine   Adipic Acid

   (ii) Monomers of Melamine-formaldehyde polymer

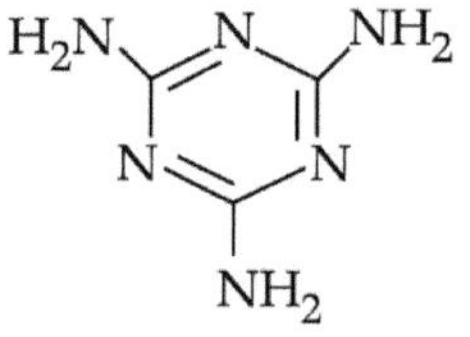

and   HCHO

   Melamine   Formaldehyde

   (iii) Buna-S (monomer)

$$CH2 = CH-CH = CH_2 \quad \text{and}$$

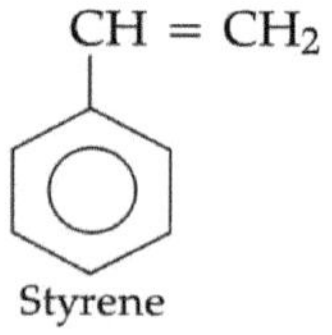

   1,3-butadiene   Styrene

Q. 10. Write the structures of the monomers used for getting the following polymers:*
   (i)   Polyvinyl chloride (PVC)   (ii) Buna-N

Ans. (i) Monomer of polyvinyl chloride (PVC)
$$\text{Vinyl chloride } CH_2 = CH-Cl$$

   (ii) Monomer of Buna-N
$$H_2C = CH-CH = CH_2 \quad \text{and} \quad CH_2 = CH-CN$$
   1, 3-butadiene   Acrylonitrile

Q. 11. Write the structures of the monomers used for getting the following polymers:*

    (i) Teflon

    (ii) Neoprene

Ans. (i) Monomer of Teflon:

$$F_2C = CF_2$$

Tetrafluoroethene

    (ii) Neoprene (monomer):

$$CH_2 = C - CH = CH_2$$
$$|$$
$$Cl$$

Chloroprene or

2-chlorobuta-1, 3-diene

Chapter 16. Chemistry in Everyday Life

Q. 1. Give one important use of each of the following:*

    (i) Streptomycin

    (ii) Paracetamol.

Ans. (i) Streptomycin is an antibiotic used specially to cure tuberculosis.

    (ii) Paracetamol is an antipyritic and analgesic, *i.e.,* it brings fever down and reduces pain due to injury.

Q. 2. Describe the following giving an example in each case:*

    (i) Edible colours

    (ii) Antifertility drugs

Ans. (i) **Edible colours:** These are artificial colours or sometimes natural dyes which are added in food items to impart attractive colours. Some examples are: carotene yellow obtained from carrots, orange is a synthetic dye.

    (ii) **Antifertility drugs:** These drugs are used to avoid unwanted pregnencies. Generally these are synthetic progesterone, Norethindrone is one such drug.

Q. 3. Describe the following with an example of each.*

    (i) Antimicrobials

    (ii) Analgesics

Ans. (i) **Antimicrobials:** Drugs which either inhibits or stops completely the growth of microbes such as fungi, bacteria, moulds etc., are all together called as antimicrobials.

    (ii) **Analgesics :** The category of drugs which can minimise the sensation of pain without affecting consciousness or any other bodily incoordination are called analgesics.

       Aspirin, paracetamol are some non-narcotic analgesics.

Q. 4. (i) Which of the following is a food preservative?

       Equanil, sodium benzoate, morphine.

    (ii) Which class of drugs is used in sleeping pills?

    (iii) Why use of sweetner aspartame is limited to cold drinks?

Ans. (i) Sodium benzoate is a food preservative.

    (ii) Sleeping pills are tranquilizers.

    (iii) Aspartame disintegrates or decompose at higher temperature and hence loses its sweetening capacity, so only used for cold drinks.

Q. 5. Explain the term target molecules or drug targets as used in medicinal chemistry.

Ans. In medicinal chemistry, drug targets refer to the key biomolecules involved in various metabolic pathways that results in specific diseases. Carbohydrates, proteins, lipids and nucleic acids are examples of drug targets.

    Drugs are chemical agents designed to inhibit these target molecules by binding with the active sites of the key molecules. These are designed to interact with specific targets so that these have the least chance to affect other molecules, hence minimising side effects.

Q. 6. Which forces are involved in holding the drugs to the active site of enzymes?

Ans. Any of these following forces can be involved in holding drugs to the active sites of enzymes.

(a) Hydrogen bonding

(b) Ionic bonding

(c) Dipole-dipole interaction

(d) Van der Waals force.

Q. 7. While antacids and antiallergic drugs interfere with the function of histamines, why they do not interfere with the functions of each other?

Ans. Specific drugs affect particular receptors. Antacids and anti-allergic drugs work on different receptors. This is the reason why antacids and anti-allergic drugs do not interfere with each other's function, but interfere with the functions of histamines. Like antacid cimetidine will control hyperacidity by preventing interaction of receptors and histamine of the stomach wall, but not with the histamine of nasal cavity or its receptors. They do not interfere as they work on different receptors.

Q. 8. Low level of noradrenaline is the cause of depression. What types of drugs are needed to cure this problem? Name two drugs.

Ans. Anti-depressant drugs are needed to counteract the effect of depression. These drugs inhibit enzymes catalysing the degradation of the neurotransmitter, noradrenaline. As a result, the important neurotransmitter is slowly metabolised and then it can activate its receptor for longer periods of time, thereby reducing depression.

Two anti-depressant drugs are:

(a) Iproniazid

(b) Phenelzine.

Q. 9. What is meant by the term 'board spectrum antibiotics'? Explain.

Ans. Antibiotics that are effective against a wide range of gram-positive and gram-negative bacteria are known as broad spectrum antibiotics. Chloramphenicol is a broad spectrum antibiotic.

$$O_2N - \langle \text{benzene ring} \rangle - CH - \overset{NHCOCHCl_2}{\underset{OH}{CH}} - CH_2OH$$

Chloramphenicol

It can be used for the treatment of typhoid, dysentery, acute fever, pneumonia, meningitis, and certain other forms of urinary infections. Two other broad spectrum antibiotics are vancomycin and ofloxacin. Ampicillin and amoxicillin–synthetically modified from penicillin are also broad spectrum antibiotics.

Q. 10. What are biodegradable and non-biodegradable detergents? Give one example of each.

Ans. Detergents that can be easily degraded by bacteria present in environment are called biodegradable detergents. Such detergents have straight hydrocarbon chains. For example: sodium lauryl sulphate. Detergents that are not easily degraded by bacteria are called non-biodegradable detergents. Such detergents have highly-branched hydrocarbon chains. For example:

sodium-4- (1, 3, 5, 7-tetra methyl octyl) benzene sulphonate. These slowly accumulate and add to land and water pollution.

Q. 11. If water contains dissolved calcium hydrogen carbonate, out of soaps and synthetic detergents which one will you use for cleaning clothes?

Ans. Synthetic detergents are preferred for cleaning clothes. When soaps are dissolved in water containing calcium ions, these ions form insoluble salts that are of no further use. However, when synthetic detergents are dissolved in water containing calcium ions, these ions form soluble salts that act as cleansing agents.

Q. 12. Label the hydrophilic and hydrophobic parts in the following compounds.

(i) $CH_3(CH_2)_{10}CH_2OSO_3^- \overset{+}{N}a$

(ii) $CH_3(CH_2)_{15} \overset{+}{N}(CH_3)_3Br^-$

(iii) $CH_3 (CH_2)_{16} COO(CH_2CH_2O)n\, CH_2CH_2OH$

Ans. (i) $\underbrace{CH_3(CH_2)_{10}CH_2}_{\text{hydrophobic part}} \quad \underbrace{OS_3^- \overset{+}{N}a}_{\text{hydrophilic part}}$

(ii) $\underset{\text{hydrophobic part}}{\underline{CH_3(CH_2)_{15}}}$ $\underset{\text{hydrophilic part}}{\underline{\overset{+}{N}(CH_3)_3Br^-}}$

(iii) $\underset{\text{hydrophobic part}}{\underline{CH_3(CH_2)_{16}}}$ $\underset{\text{hydrophilic part}}{\underline{COO(CH_2CH_2O)_nCH_2CH_2OH}}$

Q. 13. Define the following:*
    (i) Anionic detergents
    (ii) Limited spectrum antibiotics
    (iii) Antiseptics.

Ans. (i) **Anionic detergents:** These detergents contain anionic hydrophilic group. These are manufacture from long chain of alcohols. These long chain alcohols are treated with conc. H_2SO_4 to form alkyl hydrogen sulphates of high molecular mass and then are neutralised with alkali to form salts.

$$CH_3(CH_2)_{10}CH_2OH \xrightarrow{H_2SO_4} CH_3(CH_2)_{10}OSO_3H \xrightarrow[\text{(aq.)}]{NaOH} CH_3(CH_2)_{10}OSO_3^- Na^+$$

        Lauryl alcohol   Lauryl sulphonate   Sodium lauryl sulphonate

    (ii) **Limited Spectrum Antibiotics:** The antibiotics which are effective against single organism or disease are called limited spectrum antibiotics, example-streptomycin.

    (iii) **Antiseptics:** The chemical substances that are used to either kill or prevent the growth of micro-organisms are called antiseptics. These are not harmful to living tissues and can be safely applied on wounds, cuts, ulcers etc., example Soframycin.

Q. 14. Define the following:*
    (i) Narrow spectrum antibiotics
    (ii) Antacids

Ans. (i) **Narrow spectrum antibiotics:** The antibiotics which are effective mainly against gram-positive or gram-negative bacteria are called narrow spectrum antibiotics. Example : Penicillin.

    (ii) **Antacids:** The chemical substances which neutralizes excess acids in the gastric juices and gives relief from acid indigestion, acidity, heart burns and gastric ulcers are called antacids. Example sodiumhydrogencarbonate (baking soda) in water.

Q. 15. Define the following:*
    (i) Cationic detergents
    (ii) Broad spectrum antibiotics
    (iii) Tranquilizers

Ans. (i) **Cationic detergents:** These are the quaternary ammonium salts of amines with acetates, chlorides or bromides as anions. The cationic part possesses a long hydrocarbon chain with a positive charge on nitrogen atom. Example, cetyltrimethyl ammonium chloride.

$$\left[H_3C-(CH_2)_{15}-\overset{\overset{\displaystyle CH_3}{|}}{\underset{\underset{\displaystyle CH_3}{|}}{N}}-CH_3 \right]^+ Br^-$$

    (ii) **Broad spectrum antibiotics:** Antibiotics which kills or inhibit a wide range of gram-positive and gram-negative bacteria are called broad spectrum antibiotics. Example chloramphenicol.

    (iii) **Tranquilizers:** The chemical substances used for the treatment of stress, fatigue, mild and severe mental diseases are called tranquilizers. Example : phenelzine (Nardil).

❏❏

---

* are board exam questions from previous years

Chapter 1. Solid State

Q. 1. **An ionic solid conducts electricity in molten state but not in solid state. Explain.**

Ans. In ionic compounds, electricity is conducted by ions. In solid state, ions are held together by strong electrostatic forces and are not free to move about within the solid. Hence, ionic solids do not conduct electricity in solid state. However, in molten state or in solution form, the ions are free to move and can conduct electricity.

Q. 2. **Explain how much portion of an atom located at (i) corner and (ii) body-centre of a cubic unit cell is part of its neighbouring unit cell.**

Ans. (i) An atom located at the corner of a cubic unit cell is shared by eight adjacent unit cells.

Therefore, $\frac{1}{8}$th portion of the atom is shared by one unit cell.

(ii) An atom located at the body centre of a cubic unit cell is not shared by its neighbouring unit cell. Therefore, the atom belongs only to the unit cell in which it is present *i.e.*, its contribution to the unit cell is 1.

Q. 3. **Explain how vacancies are introduced in an ionic solid when a cation of higher valence is added as an impurity in it.**

Ans. When a cation of higher valence is added to an ionic solid as an impurity to it, the cation of higher valence replaces more than one cation of lower valence so as to keep the crystal electrically neutral. As a result, some sites become vacant. For example, when Sr^{2+} is added to NaCl, each Sr^{2+} ion replaces two Na^+ ions. However, one Sr^{2+} ion occupies the site of one Na^+ ion and the other site remains vacant. Hence, cationic vacancies are introduced.

Q. 4. **Ionic solids, which have anionic vacancies due to metal excess defect, develop colour. Explain with the help of a suitable example.**

Ans. The colour develops because of the presence of electrons in the anionic sites. These electrons absorb energy from the visible part of radiation and gets excited.

For example, when crystals of NaCl are heated in an atmosphere of sodium vapours, the sodium atoms get deposited on the surface of the crystal and the chloride ions from the crystal diffuse to the surface to form NaCl with the deposited Na atoms. During this process, the Na atoms on the surface lose electrons to form Na^+ ions and the released electrons diffuse into the crystal to occupy the vacant anionic sites called the F-centres. These electrons get excited by absorbing energy from the visible light and impart yellow colour to the crystals.

Q. 5. **Explain.**
(i) The basis of similarities and differences between metallic and ionic crystals.
(ii) Ionic solids are hard and brittle.

Ans. (i) The basis of similarities between metallic and ionic crystals is that both these crystal types are held by the electrostatic force of attraction. In metallic crystals, the electrostatic force acts between the positive ions and the electrons. In ionic crystals, it acts between the oppositely-charged ions. Hence both have high melting points.

The basis of differences between metallic and ionic crystals is that in metallic crystals, the electrons are free to move and so, metallic crystals can conduct electricity. However, in ionic crystals, the ions are not free to move. As a result, they cannot conduct electricity. However, in molten state or in aqueous solution, they do conduct electricity.

(ii) The constituent particles of ionic crystals are ions. These ions are held together in three-dimensional arrangements by the electrostatic force of attraction. Since the electrostatic force of attraction is very strong, the charged ions are held in fixed positions. This is the reason why ionic crystals are hard and brittle.

Q. 6. **Explain the following terms with suitable examples:**
(i) Schottky defect   (ii) Frenkel defect   (iii) Interstitials

Ans. (i) **Schottky defect :** Schottky defect is basically a vacancy defect shown by ionic solids. In this defect, an equal number of cations and anions are missing to maintain electrical neutrality. It decreases the density of a substance. Significant number of Schottky defects is present in ionic solids. For example, in NaCl, there are approximately 10^6 Schottky pairs per cm^3 at room temperature. Ionic substances containing similarised cations and anions show this type of defect. For example : NaCl, KCl, CsCl, AgBr, etc.

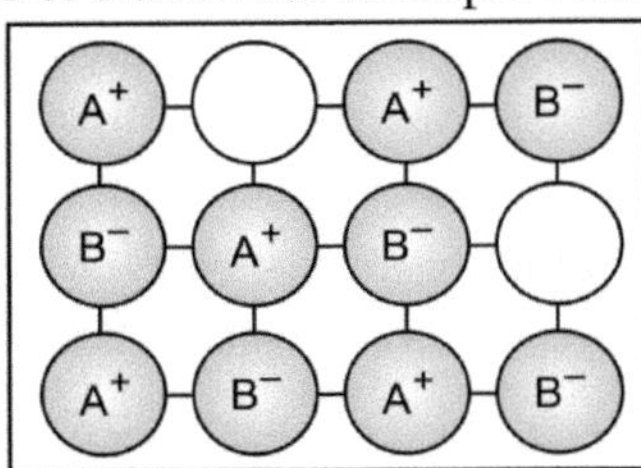

(ii) **Frenkel defect :** Ionic solids containing large differences in the sizes of ions show this type of defect. When the smaller ion (usually cation) is dislocated from its normal site to an interstitial site, Frenkel defect is created. It creates a vacancy defect as well as an interstitial defect. Frenkel defect is also known as dislocation defect. Ionic solids such as AgCl, AgBr, AgI and ZnS shows this type of defect.

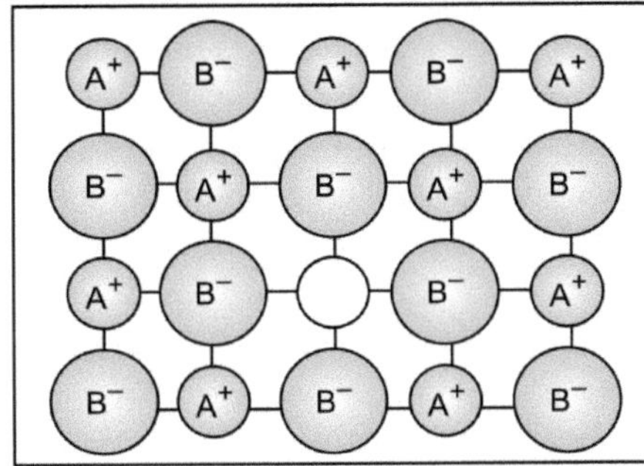

(iii) **Interstitials :** Interstitial defect is shown by non-ionic solids. This type of defect is created when some constituent particles (atoms or molecules) occupy an interstitial site of the crystal. The density of a substance increases because of this defect.

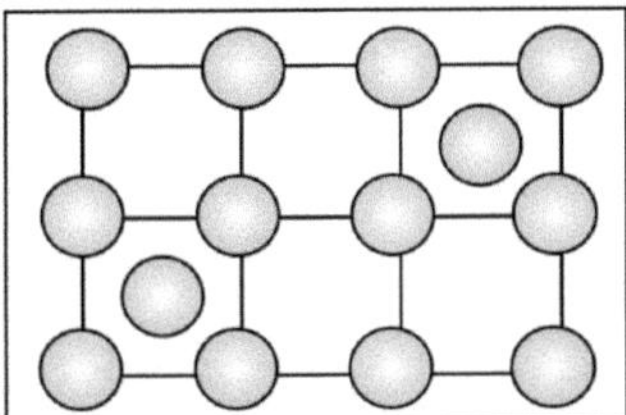

Q. 7. **Non-stoichiometric cuprous oxide, Cu_2O can be prepare in laboratory. In this oxide, copper to oxygen ratio is slightly less than 2 : 1. Can you account for the fact that this substance is a *p*-type semiconductor?**

Ans. In the cuprous oxide (Cu_2O) prepared in the laboratory, copper to oxygen ratio is slightly less than 2 : 1. This means that the number of Cu^+ ions is slightly less than twice the number of O^{2-} ions. This is because some Cu^+ ions have been replaced by Cu^{2+} ions. Every Cu^{2+} ion replaces two Cu^+ ions thereby creating holes. As a result, the substance conducts electricity with the help of these positive holes. Hence, the substance is a *p*-type semiconductor.

Q. 8. **Explain the following:**
    (i) The electrical conductivity of a metal decreases with rise in temperature while that of a semi-conductor increases.
    (ii) Zinc oxide exhibits enhanced electrical conductivity on heating.

Ans. (i) In case of metals as their packing is described by electron-sea-model, the positive kernels start vibrating on increasing the temperature and offers resistance to the smooth flow of electrons. This results in total decrease in conductivity of a metal with increasing temperature.

    (ii) On heating ZnO undergo decomposition as :

$$ZnO \xrightarrow{\Delta} Zn^{2+} + \frac{1}{2}O_2 + e^-$$

The Zn^{2+} ions and the electrons get trapped in the interstitial sites known as metal excess defect because of which these contribute in electrical conductivity. So conductivity increases.

Q. 9. Explain the following with suitable examples:

    (i) Ferromagnetism   (iv) Antiferromagnetism

    (ii) Paramagnetism   (v) 12-16 and 13-15 group compounds.

    (iii) Ferrimagnetism

Ans. (i) **Ferromagnetism :** The substances that are strongly attracted by a magnetic field are called ferromagnetic substances. Ferromagnetic substances can be permanently magnetised even in the absence of a magnetic field. Some examples of ferromagnetic substances are iron, cobalt, nickel, gadolinium, and CrO_2.

In solid state, the metal ions of ferromagnetic substances are grouped together into small regions called domains and each domain acts as a tiny magnet. In an unmagnetised piece of a ferromagnetic substance, the domains are randomly-oriented and so, their magnetic moments get cancelled. However, when the substance is placed in a magnetic field, all the domains get oriented in the direction of the magnetic field. As a result, a strong magnetic effect is produced. This ordering of domains persists even after the removal of the magnetic field. Thus, the ferromagnetic substance becomes a permanent magnet.

Schematic alignment of magnetic moments in ferromagnetic substances

(ii) Paramagnetism : The substances that are attracted by a magnetic field are called paramagnetic substances. Some examples of paramagnetic substances are O_2, Cu^{2+}, Fe^{3+}, and Cr^{3+}.

Paramagnetic substances get magnetised in a magnetic field in the same direction, but lose magnetism when the magnetic field is removed. To undergo paramagnetism, a substance must have one or more unpaired electrons. This is because the unpaired electrons are attracted by a magnetic field, thereby causing paramagnetism.

(iii) Ferrimagnetism : The substances in which the magnetic moments of the domains are aligned in parallel and anti-parallel directions, in unequal numbers are said to have ferrimagnetism. Examples include Fe_3O_4 (magnetite), ferrites such as $MgFe_2O_4$ and $ZnFe_2O_4$.

Ferrimagnetic substances are weakly attracted by a magnetic field as compared to ferromagnetic substances. On heating, these substances become paramagnetic.

Schematic alignment of magnetic moments in ferrimagnetic substances

(iv) Antiferromagnetism : Antiferromagnetic substances have domain structures similar to ferromagnetic substances, but are oppositely-oriented. The oppositely-oriented domains cancel out each other's magnetic moments.

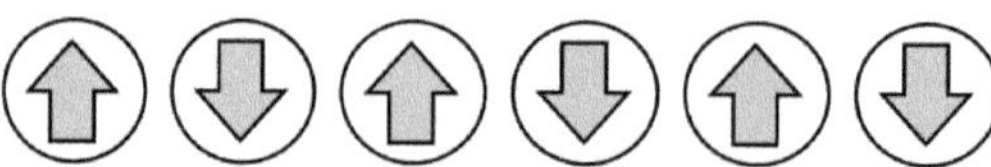

Schematic alignment of magnetic moments in antiferromagnetic substances

(v) 12-16 and 13-15 group compounds : The 12-16 group compounds are prepared by combining group 12 and group 16 elements and the 13-15 group compounds are prepared by combining group 13 and group15 elements. These compounds are prepared to stimulate average valence of four as in Ge or Si., Indium (III) antimonide (InSb) aluminium phosphide (AlP) and gallium arsenide (GaAs) are typical compounds of groups 13-15. GaAs semiconductors have a very fast response time and have revolutionised the designing of semiconductor devices. Examples of group 12-16 compounds include zinc sulphide (ZnS), cadmium sulphide (CdS), cadmium selenide (CdSe), and mercury (II) telluride (HgTe). The bonds in these compounds are not perfectly covalent. The ionic character of the bonds depends on the electronegativities of the two elements.

Q. 10. What type of substances would make better permanent magnets, ferromagnetic or ferrimagnetic. Justify your answer.

Ans. Ferromagnetic substances would make better permanent magnets.

In solid state, the metal ions of ferromagnetic substances are grouped together into small regions. These regions are called domains and each domain acts as a tiny magnet. In an unmagnetised piece of a ferromagnetic substance, the domains are randomly oriented. As a result, the magnetic moments of the domains get cancelled. However, when the substance is placed in a magnetic field, all the domains get oriented in the direction of the magnetic field and a strong magnetic effect is produced.

The ordering of the domains persists even after the removal of the magnetic field. Thus, the ferromagnetic substance becomes a permanent magnet.

Q. 11. How can you determine the atomic mass of an unknown metal if you know its density and the dimension of its unit cell? Explain.

Ans. By knowing the density of an unknown metal and the dimension of its unit cell, the atomic mass of the metal can be determined.

Let 'a' be the edge length of a unit cell of a crystal, 'd' be the density of the metal, m be the atomic mass of the metal and 'z' be the number of atoms in the unit cell.

Now,
$$\text{Density of the unit cell} = \frac{\text{Mass of the unit cell}}{\text{Volume of the unit cell}}$$

$$\Rightarrow \qquad d = \frac{Zm}{a^3} \qquad \text{...(i)}$$

$$\text{Since mass of the unit cell} = \text{Number of atoms in the unit cell} \times \text{Atomic mass}$$
$$\text{Volume of the unit cell} = (\text{Edge length of the cubic unit cell})^3$$

From equation (i), we have
$$m = \frac{da^3}{Z} \qquad \text{...(ii)}$$

Now,
$$\text{Mass of the metal } (m) = \frac{\text{Alomic mass (M)}}{\text{Avogadro's number } (N_A)}$$

$$M = \frac{da^3 N_A}{Z} \qquad \text{...(iii)}$$

Therefore, if the edge lengths are different (say, a, b and c), then equation (ii) becomes
$$m = \frac{d(abc)N_A}{Z} \qquad \text{...(iv)}$$

From equations (iii) and (iv), we can determine the atomic mass of the unknown metal.

Chapter 2. Solutions

Q. 1. On mixing accetone and chloroform, negative deviation from Raoult's law takes place. Explain.*

Ans. On mixing chloroform with acetone, new hydrogen bonds are formed between the two molecules, due to which the escaping tendency of both the molecules becomes less.

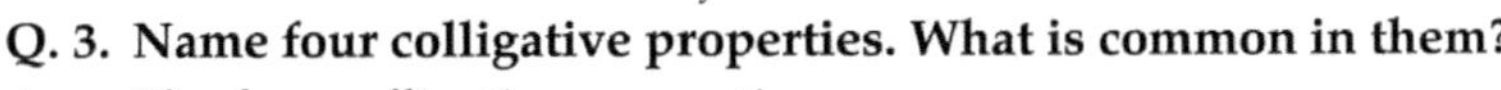

Hence, the total vapour pressure decreases. Formation of stronger bonds causes evolution of heat and slight decrease in volume occurs. ΔH and ΔV both are negative.

Q. 2. An aqueous solution of sodium chloride freezes below 273 K. Explain the lowering in freezing point of water with the help of suitable diagram.*

Ans. NaCl being a non-volatile solute lowers the vapour pressure of the solution. Hence lowering of freezing point takes place.

$$T_f = \text{Freezing point of solution}$$
$$T_f^o = \text{Freezing point of solvent}$$
$$\Delta T_f = \text{Depression in freezing point}$$

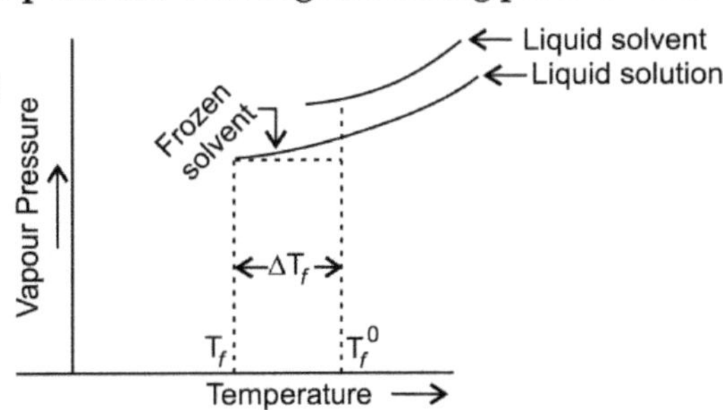

Q. 3. Name four colligative properties. What is common in them?

Ans. The four colligative properties are:

(i) Relative lowering of vapour pressure, $\dfrac{p^o - p}{p^o} = x_2$

    (ii) Elevation of boiling point, $\Delta T_b = K_b m$

    (iii) Depression in freezing point, $\Delta T_f = K_f m$

    (iv) Osmotic pressure, $\pi = CRT$

All these properties depends upon the amount of solute dissolved not on its type and each colligative property is inversely proportional to the molar mass of the solute (M).

Q. 4. Explain with the help of a diagram, solution showing non-ideal positive deviation from Raoult's law.

Ans. In a solution (binary) when compound A mix with B if the forces of attraction between A and B molecules is less than pure compounds (A–A) and (B–B) forces of attraction then positive deviation from Raoult's law takes place. Therefore, the vapour pressure of solution at any mole fraction is more than that of pure solvents.

Example : Chloroform and methanol, ethanol and acetone.

Always, $P_s > P_1^0 x_1 + P_2^0 x_2$

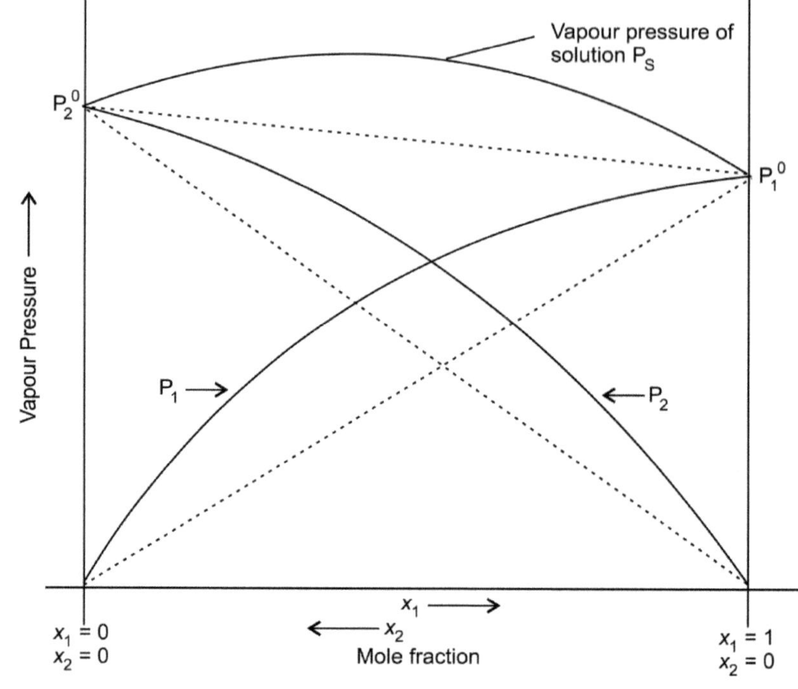

Q. 5. (i) Conc. H_2SO_4 has density of 1.9 g/ml and 99% by weight. Calculate the molarity of H_2SO_4.

    (ii) The bottle of liquid ammonia is cooled before opening the seal. Why ?

    (iii) Mention a large scale use of the phenomenon of reverse osmosis.

Ans. (i) Given,

$$d = 1.9 \text{ g/ml}, \ W_B = 99.0 \text{ g}, \ M_B = \text{g/mol}$$

$$\text{Volume} = \frac{\text{Mass}}{\text{Density}} = \frac{100}{1.9} = 52.63 \text{ ml/cm}^3$$

$$\text{Molarity} = \frac{W_B}{M_B} \times \frac{1000}{\text{Volume of solution}} = \frac{99.0 \times 1000}{98 \times 52.63} = 19.19 \text{ M.}$$

    (ii) Ammonia gas is cooled and compressed to liquid under high pressure. So while opening the bottle it needs to be cooled down otherwise it will escape as gas as outside pressure decrease.

    (iii) Desalination of sea water.

Q. 6. (i) What is de-icing agent ? How does it work?

    (ii) Differentiate between osmosis and diffusion.

    (iii) A 500 g toothpaste sample has 0.18 g fluoride concentration. What is its concentration in ppm?

Ans. (i) Salt is used as de-icing agent. It lowers the freezing point of water, thus presents further icing and melts the ice which block the roads.

(ii)

Osmosis	Diffusion
1. It involves the movement of solvent molecules from low concentrated solution to high solution to high concentrated solution via semi-permeable membrane.	It involves the movement of solute and solvent molvent molecules both from high concentration to low concentration solution.
2. Semi-permeable membrane is required for osmosis.	No membrane is required diffusion.
3. It occurs in solutions.	It occurs in liquids and gases both.

(iii)
$$ppm = \text{parts per million}$$
$$= \frac{0.18}{500} \times 10^6 = 360$$

Q. 7. (i) Gas (A) is more soluble in water than gas (B) at the same temperature. Which one of these gases will have the higher value of k_H (Henry's law constant) and why?

(ii) In non-ideal solutions, what type of deviations shows the formation of maximum boiling azeotropes?

Ans. (i) Gas (A) is more soluble than gas (B), hence gas (B) has higher value of k_H (Henry's law constant). As k_H is inversely proportional to mole fraction of gas.

$$p = k_H.x$$
$$x \propto \frac{1}{k_H}$$

(ii) A large negative deviation from Raoult's law forms maximum boiling azeotrope at a specific composition.

Q. 8. Why is freezing point depression of 0.1 M sodium chloride is nearly twice of that of 0.1 M glucose solution.[*]

Ans. Sodium chloride is a strong electrolyte and hence dissociates to give Na^+ and Cl^- ions. Thus total number of particles increases. Since NaCl give almost double the number of particles than glucose in solution. So ΔT_f is nearly double than glucose.

Q. 9. State Henry's law. Mention some of its important applications.

Ans. Henry's law states that the solubility of a gas in a liquid is directly proportional to the pressure of the gas. Further mole fraction of the gas in a solution is proportional to the partial pressure of the gas.

$\therefore$ Partial pressure of the gas in solution $= k_H \times$ Mole fraction of gas in solution

or
$$p = k_H \times x,$$

where k_H is Henry's law constant.

(i) To increase the solubility of CO_2 in soft drinks and soda water, the bottle is sealed under high pressure.

(ii) At high altitudes, the partial pressure of oxygen is less than that at the ground level because the atmospheric pressure is less. Low blood oxygen causes anoxia.

(iii) To avoid bends (painful effects during the decompression of scuba divers), oxygen diluted with less soluble helium gas is used by the sea divers.

Q. 10. What is meant by positive and negative deviations from Raoult's law and how is the sign of $\Delta_{sol}H$ related to positive and negative deviations from Raoult's law?

Ans. According to Raoult's law, the partial vapour pressure of each volatile component in any solution is directly proportional to its mole fraction. The solutions which obey Raoult's law over the entire range of concentration are known as ideal solutions. The solutions that do not obey Raoult's law (non-ideal solutions) have vapour pressures either higher or lower than that predicted by Raoult's law. If the vapour pressure is higher, then the solution is said to exhibit positive deviation, and if it is lower, then the solution is said to exhibit negative deviation from Raoult's law.

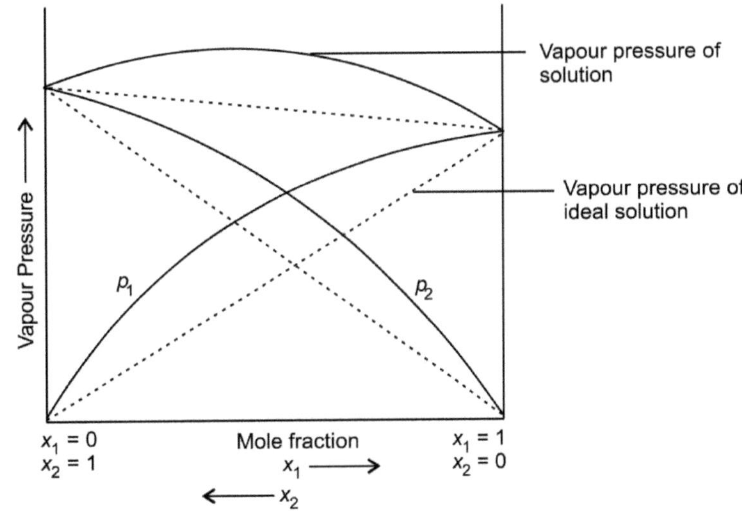

Vapour pressure of a two-component solution showing positive deviation from Raoult's law

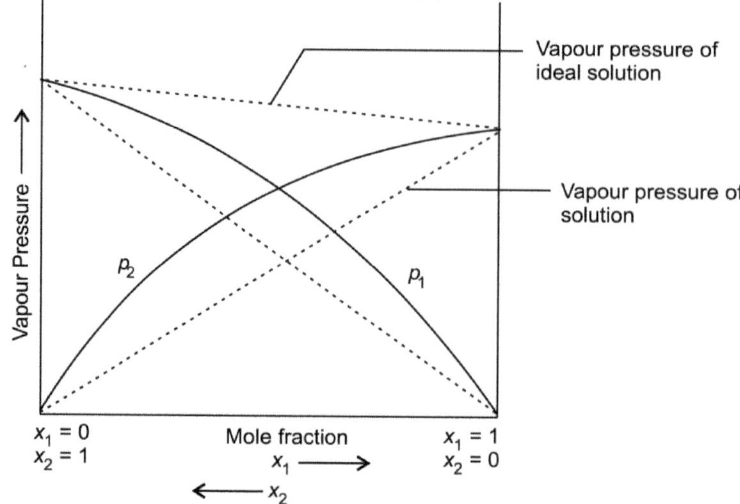

Vapour pressure of a two-component solution showing negative deviation from Raoult's law

In the case of an ideal solution, the enthalpy of the mixing of the pure components for forming the solution is zero.

$$\Delta_{sol}H = 0$$

In the case of solutions showing positive deviations, absorption of heat takes place.

$$\therefore \qquad \Delta_{sol}H = \text{Positive}$$

In the case of solutions showing negative deviations, evolution of heat takes place.

$$\therefore \qquad \Delta_{sol}H = \text{Negative}$$

Q. 11. Amongst the following compounds, identify which are insoluble, partially soluble and highly soluble in water ?

   (i)   phenol   (iii) formic acid   (v)   chloroform

   (ii) toluene   (iv) ethylene glycol   (vi) pentanol

Ans. (i)   Phenol (C_6H_5OH) has the polar group $-OH$ and non-polar group $-C_6H_5$. Thus, phenol is partially soluble in water.

     (ii) Toluene ($C_6H_5-CH_3$) has no polar groups. Thus, toluene is insoluble in water.

     (iii) Formic acid (HCOOH) has the polar group $-$ OH and can form H-bond with water. Thus, formic acid is highly soluble in water.

     (iv) Ethylene glycol $\left(\text{HO}\diagdown\diagup^{\text{OH}}\right)$ has polar $-OH$ group and can form H-bond. Thus, it is highly soluble in water.

     (v) Chloroform is insoluble in water.

     (vi) Pentanol is partially soluble as $-OH$ group is polar but the large (C_5H_{11}) group is non-polar.

Q. 12. The depression in freezing point of water observed for the same amount of acetic acid, trichloroacetic acid and trifluoroacetic acid increases in the order given above. Explain briefly.

Ans.

$$\begin{array}{ccc}
\overset{\displaystyle H}{\underset{\displaystyle H}{H - C - COOH}} & \overset{\displaystyle Cl}{\underset{\displaystyle Cl}{Cl - C - COOH}} & \overset{\displaystyle F}{\underset{\displaystyle F}{F - C - COOH}} \\
\text{Acetic acid} & \text{Trichloro acetic acid} & \text{Trifluoroacetic acid}
\end{array}$$

Among H, Cl and F, H is least electronegative while F is most electronegative. Then, F can withdraw electrons towards itself more than Cl and H. Thus, trifluoroacetic acid can easily lose H^+ ions *i.e.*, trifluoroacetic acid ionizes to the largest extent. Now, the more ions produced, the greater is the depression of the freezing point. Hence, the depression in the freezing point increases in the order :

$$\text{Acetic acid} < \text{Trichloroacetic acid} < \text{Trifluoroacetic acid}$$

Q. 13. Vapour pressure of pure acetone and chloroform at 328 K are 632.8 mm Hg and 741.8 mm Hg respectively. Assuming that they form ideal solution over the entire range of composition, plot p_{total}, $p_{chloroform}$ and $p_{acetone}$ as a function of $x_{acetone}$, the experimental data observed for different compositions of mixtures is:

$100 \times x_{acetone}$	0	11.8	23.4	36.0	50.8	58.2	64.5	72.1
$p_{acetone}$/mm Hg	0	54.9	110.1	202.4	322.7	405.7	454.1	521.1
$p_{chloroform}$/ mm Hg	632.8	548.1	469.4	359.7	257.7	193.6	161.2	120.7

Plot this data also on the same graph paper. Indicate whether it has positive deviation or negative deviation from the ideal solution.

Ans.

$x_{acetone}$	0.0	0.118	0.234	0.360	0.508	0.582	0.645	0.721
$p_{acetone}$/mm Hg	0	54.9	110.1	202.4	322.7	405.7	454.1	521.1
$p_{chloroform}$/ mm Hg	632.8	548.1	469.4	359.7	257.7	193.6	161.2	120.7
p_{total}	632.8	603.0	579.5	562.1	580.4	599.5	615.3	641.8

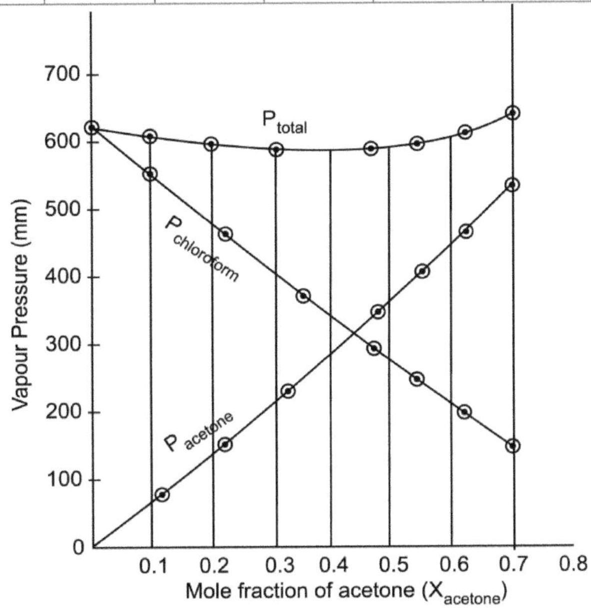

As the plot for p_{total} dips downwards, the solution shows **negative** deviation from the ideal behaviour.

Chapter 3. Electrochemistry

Q. 1. State the use of the following cells:

   (i)   Lead storage cell (battery)   (iii) Fuel cell.

  (ii)   Nickel-cadmium cell   (iv) Dry cell.

Ans. (i)   Automobiles and invertors uses this cell. It is a secondary cell and can be recharged.

  (ii)   Emergency lighting, flash lights.

 (iii) Used in space shuttles.

 (iv) Used in transistors and clocks. Its a primary cell and non-rechargeable.

Q. 2. Why we cannot recharge Leclanche cell?

Ans. Lechlanche (dry) cell contain Zn container (anode), carbon rod as (cathode), ammonium chloride, manganese dioxide and $ZnCl_2$ parts. During cell operation, Zn gets oxidised to Zn^{2+} (aq) ion. If a reverse potential in excess (more than 1.5 V) is applied in place of reduction of Zn^{2+} (aq) ion back to Zn, the ammonium ion is reduced.

Q. 3. Explain what happens when an opposing external voltage is applied on a galvanic cell when it is (i) smaller than (ii) equal to (iii) greater than cell potential.

Ans. (i)   Cell performs normally. Electrons flow from anode to cathode and conventional current in the opposite way.

  (ii)   No current flow. The external voltage balances cell potential, hence equilibrium is reached.

 (iii) The cell now act as a electrolytic cell, zinc act as cathode and copper acts as anode. Flow of charge from copper to zinc and conventional current flow from zinc to copper electrode.

Q. 4. (i)   In a cell reaction, the equilibrium constant K is less than one. Is E° for the cell positive or negative ?

  (ii)   What will be the value of K if $E^{\circ}_{cell} = 0$?

Ans. (i) For a cell if, $E° = \dfrac{0.0591}{n} \log K$ (at 298 K)

Let the value of K is less than one *i.e.,* 0.01

$$E° = \dfrac{0.0591}{n} \log 0.01 = \dfrac{0.0591}{n} \log (10^{-2}) \qquad [\log 10 = 1]$$

$$= \dfrac{(-2) \times 0.0591}{n} = -\,ve.$$

Hence E° value of cell will be negative.

(ii) $E° = 0$, hence $0 = \dfrac{0.0591}{n} \log K$.

i.e., $\log K = 0$ *i.e.,* $K = $ antilog $(0) = 1$.

Q. 5. How would you determine the standard electrode potential of the system $Mg^{2+} | Mg$?

Ans. The standard electrode potential of Mg^{2+} | Mg can be measured with respect to the standard hydrogen electrode, represented by Pt(s), $H_2(g)$ (1 atm) | $H^+(aq)$ (1 M).

A cell, consisting of Mg | $MgSO_3$ (aq. 1 M) as the anode and the standard hydrogen electrode as the cathode, is set up

$$Mg \,|\, Mg^{2+} \text{ (aq. 1 M)} \,||\, H^- \text{ (aq. 1M)} \,|\, H_2 \text{ (g 1 bar), Pt(s)}.$$

Then, the emf of the cell is measured and this measured emf is the standard electrode potential of the magnesium electrode (– 2.36 V).

$$E^- = E_R^- - E_L^-$$

Here, E_R^0 for the standard hydrogen electrode is zero.

$$\therefore \qquad E^- = 0 - E_L^-$$

$$= E_L^- \text{ which, comes out to be} -2.36 \text{ V}.$$

Q. 6. Can you store copper sulphate solutions in a zinc pot?

Ans. Zinc is more reactive than copper. Therefore, zinc can displace copper from its salt solution. If copper sulphate solution is stored in a zinc pot, then zinc will displace copper from the copper sulphate solution.

$$Zn + CuSO_4 \longrightarrow ZnSO_4 + Cu$$

Hence, copper sulphate solution cannot be stored in a zinc pot.

Q. 7. Predict the products of electrolysis in each of the following:

(i) An aqueous solution of $AgNO_3$ with platinum electrodes.

(ii) An aqueous solution of $CuCl_2$ with platinum electrodes.

Ans. (i) **At cathode :** The following reduction reactions compete to take place at the cathode.

$$Ag^+(aq) + e^- \longrightarrow Ag(s); \quad E° = 0.80 \text{ V}$$

$$H^+(aq) + e^- \longrightarrow \dfrac{1}{2} H_2(g); \ E° = 0.00 \text{ V}$$

The reaction with a higher value of E° takes place at the cathode. Therefore, deposition of silver will take place at the cathode.

At anode : Since Pt electrodes are inert, the anode is not attacked by NO_3^- ions. Therefore, OH^- or NO_3^- ions can be oxidized at the anode. But OH^- ions having a lower discharge potential and get preference and decompose to liberate O_2.

$$OH^- \longrightarrow OH + e^-$$

$$4OH^- \longrightarrow 2H_2O + O_2$$

(ii) **At cathode :** The following reduction reactions compete to take place at the cathode.

$$Cu^{2+}(aq) + 2e^- \longrightarrow Cu(s) ; \quad E° = 0.34 \text{ V}$$

$$H^+(aq) + e^- \longrightarrow \dfrac{1}{2} H_2(g); \ E° = 0.00 \text{ V}$$

The reaction with a higher value of E° takes place at the cathode. Therefore, deposition of copper will take place at the cathode.

At anode : The following oxidation reactions are possible at the anode.

At the anode, the reaction with a lower value of,

$$Cl^-(aq) \longrightarrow \dfrac{1}{2} Cl_2(g) + e^{-1}; \qquad E° = 1.36 \text{ V}$$

$$2H_2O(s) \longrightarrow O_2(g) + 4H^+(aq) + 4e^- \; ; E° = + 1.23 \text{ V}$$

E° is preferred. But due to the over potential of oxygen, Cl^- gets oxidized at the anode to produce Cl_2 gas.

Q. 8. Write the chemistry of recharging the lead storage battery, high lighting all the materials that are involved during recharging.

Ans. A lead storage battery consists of anode of lead, a grid of lead packed with lead dioxide (PbO_2) as cathode and 38% solution of sulphuric acid as electrolyte. During discharging the following reactions takes place :

Anode : $$Pb(s) + SO_4^{2-} (aq) \longrightarrow PbSO_4 (s) + 2e^-$$

Cathode : $$PbO_2 (s) + SO_4^{2-} (aq) + 4H^+ (aq) + 2e^- \longrightarrow PbSO_4 (s) + 2H_2O (l)$$

Overall reaction :
$$Pb(s) + PbO_2(s) + 2H_2SO_4 (aq) \longrightarrow 2PbSO_4(s) + 2H_2O(l)$$

While recharging the battery the reverse reaction takes place, *i.e.*, $PbSO_4$ deposited on the electrodes is converted back into Pb and PbO_2 and H_2SO_4 is generated.

i.e., $$PbSO_4 (s) + 2e^- \longrightarrow Pb(s) + SO_4^{2-} (aq) \hspace{3cm} \text{(Cathode)}$$
$$PbSO_4 (s) + 2H_2O \longrightarrow PbO_2 (s) + SO_4^{2-} (aq) + 4H^+ (aq) 2e^- \hspace{1cm} \text{(Anode)}$$

Overall recharging reaction :
$$2PbSO_4 (s) + 2H_2O (l) \longrightarrow Pb(s) + PbO_2(s) + 4H^+(aq) + 2SO_4^{2-} (aq)$$

Q. 9. Explain how rusting of iron is envisaged as setting up of an electrochemical cell.

Ans. In the process of corrosion, due to the presence of air and moisture, oxidation takes place at a particular spot of an object made of iron. That spot behaves as the anode. The reaction at the anode is given by,
$$Fe(s) \longrightarrow Fe^{2+} (aq) + 2e^-$$

Electrons released at the anodic spot move through the metallic object and go to another spot of the object. There, in the presence of H^+ ions, the electrons reduce oxygen. This spot behaves as the cathode. These H^+ ions come either from H_2CO_3, which are formed due to the dissolution of carbon dioxide from air into water or from the dissolution of other acidic oxides from the atmosphere in water.

The reaction corresponding at the cathode is given by
$$O_2(g) + 4H^+ (aq) + 4e^- \longrightarrow 2H_2O(l)$$

Reaction of anode is:
$$2Fe (s) \longrightarrow 2Fe^{2+} (aq) + 4e^-$$

The electrons released move along the body of the metal of another spot which behaves like cathode. As shown in figure.

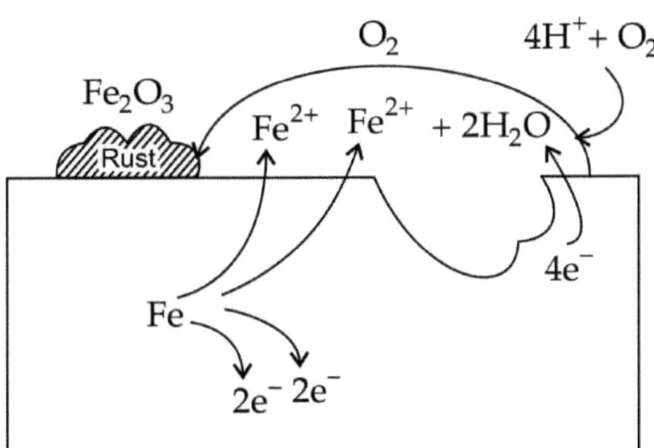

Rusting of Iron

The overall reaction is:
$$2Fe(s) + O_2(g) + 4H^+ (aq) \longrightarrow 2Fe^{2+} (aq) + 2H_2O(l)$$

Also, ferrous ions are further oxidized by atmospheric oxygen to ferric ions. These ferric ions combine with moisture, present in the surroundings, to form hydrated ferric oxide (Fe_2O_3, xH_2O) *i.e.*, rust.

Hence, the rusting of iron is envisaged as the setting up of an electrochemical cell.

Chapter 4. Chemical Kinetics

Q. 1. Thermodynamic feasibility of the reaction alone cannot decide the rate of the reaction. Account for the following statement with example.

Ans. By thermodynamically feasible reaction we mean that the enthalpy of the reaction *i.e.,* ΔH_r is negative. But kinetics of the reaction is also responsible for a reaction to occur. The activation energy of the reaction also plays an important role. The proper orientation of the molecules, so that when they collide, they reach sufficient activation energy to form the product.

$$\text{Reactants} \longrightarrow \text{Activated complex} \longrightarrow \text{Products}$$

The rate of reactions, *i.e.,* speed of reactions (kinesis) is another factor. Example : Conversion of diamond to graphite is thermodynamically feasible, but in reality because of slow rate of reaction.

Chapter 5. Surface Chemistry

Q. 1. **Give reasons for the origin of charge on colloidal particles.**[*]

Ans. The dispersed particles carry either positive or negative charge on the surface. As a whole the solution is neutral. The origin of charge is because of:

(i) **Frictional electrification :** Rubbing of colloidal particles against each other make them electrically charged because of frictional electrification.

(ii) **Preferential adsorption of ions from solution :** Colloidal particles become electrically charged by preferential adsorption of ions from solution. They generally adsorb the common ion.

For example if AgCl sol is prepared by shacking AgCl ppt with dilute $AgNO_3$ solution then we get a positive sol.

$$AgCl + Ag^+ \longrightarrow AgCl/Ag^+$$

and at the same time if it is prepared by shaking AgCl with dilute HCl solution, we get a negative sol.

$$AgCl + Cl^- \longrightarrow AgCl/Cl^-$$

i.e., preferential adsorption of common ion.

Q. 2. **Account for the following :**[*]

(i) Delta formation occurs at the meeting of sea water and silver water.

(ii) Leather gets hardened after tanning.

(iii) Milk curdle's when it gets soured.

Ans. (i) River water is full of colloidal particles. When it falls into sea water, the higher concentration of electrolytes present in sea water coagulates the colloidal impurities and hence sedimentation in the form of deltas occurs at the meeting of sea water and river water.

(ii) Animal skin is colloidal in nature (inner skin), and has positively charged particles. During tanning the skin is dipped into tannin, an acidic chemical compound that is negatively charged. Hence coagulation takes place and leather gets hardened.

(iii) When milk turns sour, lactic acid is produced in milk this coagulates milk which is an emulsion, into curd.

Q. 3. **Explain the following:**

(i) Enzymes are different from ordinary chemical catalyst.

(ii) Role of co-enzymes in a reaction.

(iii) Specificity of enzyme action.

Ans. (i) Enzymes are bio-catalyst and can act only under mild conditions of temperature and pH, while catalysts work under high temperature and extreme pH conditions too.

(ii) A co-enzyme acts as a catalyst for the activation of enzymes. It is usually a non-protein moiety or metal ion.

(iii) The active site of an enzyme is shaped so that only a specific substrate can fit into it, just like a key and lock pair. Hence, they are highly specific in their action.

Q. 4. **How are the following sols prepared by chemical methods:**[*]

(i) Gold sol, (ii) Silver sol, (iii) Platinum sol, (iv) Sulphur sol, (v) Arsenious sulphide sol?

Ans. (i) Gold sol can be prepared by reducing gold(III) chloride with formaldehyde solution.

$$2AuCl_3 + 3HCHO + 3H_2O \longrightarrow \underset{\text{Gold sol}}{2Au} + 3HCOOH + 6HCl$$

(ii) Silver sol can be prepared by treating $AgNO_3$ (ammonical silver nitrate) with organic reducing agents.

$$AgNO_3 + \text{Tannic acid} \longrightarrow \text{Silver ppt.}$$

(iii) Same as gold sol, platinum sol can be prepared using formaldehyde.

$$\underset{\text{Platinum (II) chloride}}{PtCl_2} + HCHO + H_2O \longrightarrow \underset{\text{Platinum sol}}{Pt} + HCOOH + 2HCl$$

(iv) When SO_2 gas is bubbled through a solution of H_2S, sulphur sol is formed;

$$SO_2 + 2H_2S \longrightarrow 3S + 2H_2O$$
$$\text{Sulphur sol}$$

(v) When equal volume of aqueous arsenious oxide solution and hydrogen sulphide are mixed we get arsenious sulphide sol.

$$As_2O_3 + 3H_2S \longrightarrow As_2S_2 + 3H_2O$$
$$\text{Arsenious}$$
$$\text{sulphide sol}$$

Q. 5. Why is it necessary to remove CO when ammonia is obtained by Haber's process ?*

Ans. It is important to remove CO in the synthesis of ammonia as CO adversely affects the activity of the iron catalyst, used in Haber's process. CO acts as deactivating agent for Fe and promoter molybdenum is used in Haber's process (catalyst).

Q. 6. Why is the ester hydrolysis slow in the beginning and becomes faster after sometime?

Ans. Ester hydrolysis can be represented as :

$$\text{Ester + Water} \longrightarrow \text{Acid + Alcohol}$$

The acid produced in the reaction acts as a catalyst and makes the reaction faster. Substances that act as catalysts in the same reaction in which they are obtained as products are known as autocatalysts.

Q. 7. What is the role of desorption in the process of catalysis?

Ans. The role of desorption in the process of catalysis is to make the surface of the solid catalyst free for the fresh adsorption of the reactants on the surface. Hence adsorption can only be possible further if desorption follows it.

Q. 8. What modification can you suggest in the Hardy-Schulze law?

Ans. Hardy-Schulze law states that "the greater the valence of the flocculating ion added, the greater is its power to cause precipitation."

This law takes into consideration only the charge carried by an ion, not its size. The smaller the size of an ion, the more will be its polarising power. Thus, Hardy-Schulze law can be modified in terms of the polarising power of the flocculating ion. Thus, the modified Hardy-Schulze law can be stated as "the greater the polarising power of the flocculating ion added, the greater is its power to cause precipitation."

Q. 9. What are the factors which influence the adsorption of a gas on a solid?

Ans. There are various factors that affect the rate of adsorption of a gas on a solid surface.

(i) **Nature of the gas :** Easily liquefiable gases such as NH_3, HCl etc., are adsorbed to a great extent in comparison to gases such as H_2, O_2 etc. This is because Van der Waal's forces are stronger in easily liquefiable gases.

(ii) **Surface area of the solid :** The greater the surface area of the adsorbent, the greater is the adsorption of a gas on the solid surface.

(iii) **Effect of pressure :** Adsorption is a reversible process and is accompanied by a decrease in pressure. Therefore, adsorption increases with an increase in pressure.

(iv) **Effect of temperature :** Adsorption is an exothermic process. Thus, in accordance with Le-Chatelier's principle, the magnitude of adsorption decreases with an increase in temperature.

Q. 10. What do you understand by activation of adsorbent ? How is it achieved?

Ans. By activating an adsorbent, we tend to increase the adsorbing power of the adsorbent. Some ways to activate an adsorbent are :

(i) By increasing the surface area of the adsorbent. This can be done by breaking it into smaller pieces or powdering it.

(ii) Some specific treatments can also lead to the activation of the adsorbent. For example, wood charcoal is activated by heating it between 650 K and 1330 K in vacuum or air. It expels all the gases absorbed or adsorbed and thus, creates a space for adsorption of gases.

Q. 11. What role does adsorption play in heterogeneous catalysis?

Ans. Heterogeneous catalysis : A catalytic process in which the catalyst and the reactants are present in different phases is known as a heterogeneous catalysis. This heterogeneous catalytic action can be explained in terms of the adsorption theory. The mechanism of catalysis involves the following steps :

(i) Adsorption of reactant molecules on the catalyst surface.

(ii) Occurrence of a chemical reaction through the formation of an intermediate.

(iii) De-sorption of products from the catalyst surface.

(iv) Diffusion of products away from the catalyst surface.

In this process, the reactants are usually present in the gaseous state and the catalyst is present in the solid state. Gaseous molecules are then adsorbed on the surface of the catalyst. As the concentration of reactants on the surface of the catalyst increases, the rate of reaction also increases. In such reactions, the products have very less affinity for the catalyst and are quickly desorbed, thereby making the surface free for other reactants.

Q. 12. Why is adsorption always exothermic?

Ans. Adsorption is always exothermic. This statement can be explained in two ways.

(i) Adsorption leads to a decrease in the residual forces on the surface of the adsorbent. This causes a decrease in the surface energy of the adsorbent. Therefore, adsorption is always exothermic.

(ii) ΔH of adsorption is always negative. When a gas is adsorbed on a solid surface, its movement is restricted leading to a decrease in the entropy of the gas *i.e.*, ΔS is negative. Now for a process to be spontaneous, ΔG should be negative.

$$\therefore \qquad \Delta G = \Delta H - T\Delta S$$

Since ΔS is negative, ΔH has to be negative to make ΔG negative. Hence, adsorption is always exothermic.

Q. 13. How are the colloidal solutions classified on the basis of physical states of the dispersed phase and dispersion medium?

Ans. One criterion for classifying colloids is the physical state of the dispersed phase and dispersion medium. Depending upon the type of the dispersed phase and dispersion medium (solid, liquid and gas), there can be eight types of colloidal systems.

Dispersed phase	Dispersion medium	Type of colloid	Example
Solid	Solid	Solid Sol	Gemstone
Solid	Liquid	Sol	Paint
Solid	Gas	Aersol	Smoke
Liquid	Solid	Gel	Cheese
Liquid	Liquid	Emulsion	Milk
Liquid	Gas	Aerosol	Fog
Gas	Solid	Solid foam	Pumica stone
Gas	Liquid	Foam	Froth

Q. 14. How are colloids classified on the basis of:

(i) Physical states of components

(ii) Nature of dispersion medium

(iii) Interaction between dispersed phase and dispersion medium ?

Ans. Colloids can be classified on various basis:

(i) On the basis of the physical state of the components (by components we mean the dispersed phase and dispersion medium). Depending on whether the components are solids, liquids, and gases, we can have eight types of colloids.

(ii) On the basis of the dispersion medium, sols can be divided as :

Dispersion medium	Name of sol
Water	Aquasol or hydrosol
Alcohol	Alcosol
Benzene	Benzosol
Gases	Aerosol

(iii) On the basis of the nature of the interaction between the dispersed phase and dispersion medium, the colloids can be classified as lyophilic (solvent attracting) and lyophobic (solvent repelling).

Q. 15. What are emulsions? What are their different types ? Give example of each type.

Ans. The colloidal solution in which both the dispersed phase and dispersion medium are liquids is called an emulsion. There are two types of emulsions:

(i) Oil in water type: Here, oil is the dispersed phase while water is the dispersion medium. For example : milk, vanishing cream etc.

(ii) Water in oil type: Here, water is the dispersed phase while oil is the dispersion medium. For example : cold cream, butter etc.

Q. 16. Describe some features of catalysis by zeolites.

Ans. Zeolites are alumino-silicates that are micro-porous in nature. Zeolites have a honeycomb-like structure, which makes them shape-selective catalysts. They have an extended 3D-network of silicates in which some silicon atoms are replaced by aluminium atoms, giving them an Al–O–Si framework. The reactions taking place in zeolites are very sensitive to the pores and cavity size of the zeolites. Zeolites are commonly used in the petrochemical industry.

Q. 17. What is shape selective catalysis?

Ans. A catalytic reaction which depends upon the pore structure of the catalyst and on the size of the reactant and the product molecules is called shape selective catalysis. For example, catalysis by zeolites is a shape-selective catalysis. The pore size present in the zeolites ranges from 260-740 pm. Thus, molecules having a pore size more than this cannot enter the zeolite and undergo the reaction.

Q. 18. What are micelles? Give an example of a micelles system.

Ans. Micelle formation is done by substances such as soaps and detergents when dissolved in water. The molecules of such substances contain a hydrophobic and a hydrophilic part. When present in water, these substances arrange themselves in spherical structures in such a manner that their hydrophobic parts are present towards the centre, while the hydrophilic parts are pointing towards the outside (as shown in the given figure). This is known as micelle formation.

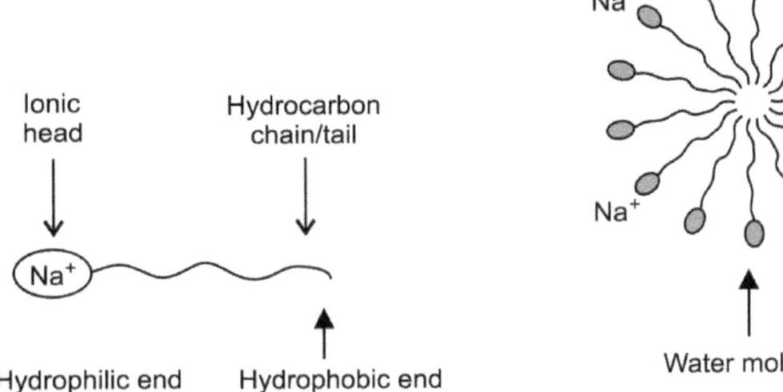

Q. 19. Explain the terms with suitable examples:

(i) Alcosol, (ii) Aerosol, (iii) Hydrosol.

Ans. **(i) Alcosol :** A colloidal solution having alcohol as the dispersion medium and a solid substance as the dispersed phase is called an alcosol.

For example: Colloidal sol of cellulose nitrate in ethyl alcohol is an alcosol.

(ii) Aerosol : A colloidal solution having a gas as the dispersion medium and a solid as the dispersed phase is called an aerosol.

For example: Fog.

(iii) Hydrosol : A colloidal solution having water as the dispersion medium and a solid as the dispersed phase is called a hydrosol.

For example: Starch sol or gold sol.

Q. 20. What happens when:*

(i) a freshly prepared precipitate of $Fe(OH)_3$ is shaken with a small amount of $FeCl_3$ solution?

(ii) persistent dialysis of a colloidal solution is carried out?

(iii) an emulsion is centrifuged?

Ans. **(i)** When $FeCl_3$ is added to a freshly prepared precipitate of $Fe(OH)_3$, a positively charged sol of hydrated ferric oxide is formed due to adsorption of Fe^{3+} ions.

(ii) When persistent dialysis of colloidal solution is carried out, traces of electrolytes present in the sol removed almost completely leaving the colloids unstable and finally coagulaion takes place.

(iii) Emulsions are centrifuged to separate them into constituent liquids.

Chapter 6. General Principles and Processes of Isolation of Elements

Q. 1. State the limitations of Ellingham diagram.

Ans. Limitations of Ellingham diagram.

    (i)   The plots simply indicates whether a reaction is possible or not. Does not tells anything about the kinetics of the reaction or rate of reaction.

    (ii) It is assumed that the reactants and products are in equilibrium *i.e.,*

$$\Delta G^\circ = - RT \ln k.$$

    Which may not be the case at every temperature region in actual practice.

    (iii) At high temperature many metals have a tendency to react with carbon to form carbides.

Q. 2. State two uses of each of these metals:

    (i)   Aluminium, (ii) Iron, (iii) Copper.

Ans. Uses of each:

    (i)   **Aluminium :** (a) Manufacture of aircraft structures because of light weight. Alloy duralumin (Al 95%, Mg 0.5%, Mn and Cu $\approx$ 4%).

       (b) Can be beaten into then foils and used for packing food stuffs and medicines.

    (ii) **Iron :** (a) In form of stainless steel in shaving blades, medical or surgical purpose, household utensils etc.

       (b) As electromagnets in generator, ocean cables etc.

    (iii) **Copper :** (a) Used in electrical appliances and wires because of good conductivity.

       (b) For making alloys like brass, bronze, german silver etc.

Q. 3. Account for the following:

    (i)   Compound A and B passed through column of Al_2O_3 by using alcohol as eluant. Compound A is eluted first and compound B remained adsorbed.

    (ii) Carbon and hydrogen even being good reducing agents are not used to reduce metallic oxides at high temperature.

    (iii) Partial roasting of sulphide ores is done in metallurgy of copper.

Ans. (i)   Compound A is eluted first, this shows that compound B is far more strongly adsorbed in the column of Al_2O_3 than compound A.

    (ii) Carbon and hydrogen are not very effective in high temperatures as they themselves react with the pure metals to form metal carbides and hydrides.This does not happen in low temperature.

    (iii) Partial roasting of sulphide ores convert the copper sulphide into oxide. The oxide form then reduces the remaining sulphide ore to metallic sulphur. This is called 'auto-reduction'.

$$2CuS + 3O_2 \longrightarrow 2CuO + 2SO_2\uparrow$$
$$2CuO + CuS \longrightarrow 3Cu + SO_2\uparrow$$

Auto-reduction

Q. 4. Copper can be extracted by hydrometallurgy but not zinc. Explain.

Ans. The reduction potentials of zinc and iron are lower than that of copper. In hydrometallurgy, zinc and iron can be used to displace copper from their solution.

$$Fe(s) + Cu^{2+}\,(aq) \longrightarrow Fe^{2+}(aq) + Cu(s)$$

But to displace zinc, more reactive metals *i.e.,* metals having lower reduction potentials than zinc such as Mg, Ca, K, etc., are required. But all these metals react with water with the evolution of H_2 gas.

$$2K(s) + 2H_2O(l) \longrightarrow 2KOH(aq) + H_2(g)$$

As a result, these metals cannot be used in hydrometallurgy to extract zinc.

Hence, copper can be extracted by hydrometallurgy but not zinc.

Q. 5. What is the role of depressants in froth floatation process?*

Ans. In the froth floatation process, the role of the depressants is to separate two sulphide ores by selectively preventing one ore from forming froth. For example, to separate two sulphide ores (ZnS and PbS), NaCN is used as a depressant which selectively allows PbS to come with froth, but prevents ZnS from coming to froth. This happens because NaCN reacts with ZnS to form $Na_2[Zn(CN)_4]$.

$$4NaCN + ZnS \longrightarrow Na_2[Zn(CN)_4] + Na_2S$$

Q. 6. Why is the extraction of copper from pyrites more difficult than that from its oxide ore through reduction?

Ans. The Gibbs free energy of formation $(\Delta_f G)$ of Cu_2S (Pyrite ore) is less than that of H_2S and CS_2. Therefore, H_2 and C cannot reduce Cu_2S to Cu.

On the other hand, the Gibbs free energy of formation of Cu_2O is greater than that of CO * lower than CO_2. Hence, C can reduce Cu_2O to Cu.

$$C(s) + Cu_2O(s) \longrightarrow 2Cu(s) + CO(g)$$

Hence, the extraction of copper from its pyrite ore is difficult than from its oxide ore through reduction.

Q. 7. State the role of silica in the metallurgy of copper. *

Ans. During the roasting of pyrite ore, a mixture of FeO and Cu_2O is obtained.

$$2CuFeS_2 + O_2 \xrightarrow{\Delta} Cu_2S + 2FeS + SO_2$$

$$2Cu_2S + 3O_2 \xrightarrow{\Delta} 2Cu_2O + 2SO_2$$

$$2FeS + 3O_2 \xrightarrow{\Delta} 2FeO + 2SO_2$$

The role of silica in the metallurgy of copper is to remove the iron oxide obtained during the process of roasting as 'slag'. If the sulphide ore of copper contains iron, then silica (SiO_2) is added as flux before roasting. Then, FeO combines with silica to form iron silicate, $FeSiO_3$ (slag).

$$FeO + SiO_2 \xrightarrow{\Delta} FeSiO_3$$

$$\text{(Slag)}$$

Q. 8. Why copper matte is put in silica lined converter?

Ans. Copper matte contains Cu_2S and FeS. Copper matte is put in a silica-lined converter to remove the remaining FeO and FeS present in the matte as slag ($FeSiO_3$). Also, some silica is added to the silica-lined converter. Then, a hot air blast is blown. As a result, the remaining FeS and FeO are converted to iron silicate ($FeSiO_3$) and Cu_2S is converted into metallic copper.

$$2FeS + 3O_2 \longrightarrow 2FeO + 2SO_2$$

$$FeO + SiO_2 \longrightarrow FeSiO_3$$

$$2Cu_2S + 3O_2 \longrightarrow 2Cu_2O + 2SO_2$$

$$2Cu_2O + Cu_2S \longrightarrow 6Cu + SO_2$$

Q. 9. How is leaching carried out in case of low grade copper ores?

Ans. In case of low grade copper ores, leaching is carried out using acid or bacteria in the presence of air. In this process, copper goes into the solution as Cu^{2+} ions, by getting oxidised.

$$Cu(s) + 2H^+(aq) + \frac{1}{2}O_2(g) \longrightarrow Cu^{2+}(aq) + 2H_2O(l)$$

The resulting solution is treated with scrap iron or H_2 to get metallic copper.

$$Cu^{2+}(aq) + H_2(g) \longrightarrow Cu(s) + 2H^+(aq)$$

$$Cu^{2+}(aq) + Fe(aq) \longrightarrow Cu(s) + Fe^{2+}(aq)$$

Q. 10. The value of $\Delta_f G^-$ for formation of Cr_2O_3 is – 540 kJ mol^{-1} and that of Al_2O_3 is – 827 kJ mol^{-1}. Is the reduction of Cr_2O_3 possible with Al?

Ans. The value of $\Delta_f G^-$ for formation of Cr_2O_3 from Cr (– 540 kJ mol^{-1}) is higher than that of Al_2O_3 from Al (– 827 kJ mol^{-1}). Therefore, Al can reduce Cr_2O_3 to Cr. Hence, the reduction of Cr_2O_3 with Al is possible. Alternatively,

$$2Al + \frac{3}{2}O_2 \longrightarrow Al_2O_3 \qquad \Delta_f G^- = -827 \text{ kJ mol}^{-1} \qquad \text{...(i)}$$

$$2Cr + \frac{3}{2}O_2 \longrightarrow Cr_2O_3 \qquad \Delta_f G^- = -540 \text{ kJ mol}^{-1} \qquad \text{...(ii)}$$

Subtracting equation (ii) from (i), we have

$$2Al + Cr_2O_3 \longrightarrow Al_2O_3 + 2Cr \qquad \Delta_f G^- = -827 - (-540)$$
$$= -287 \text{ kJ mol}^{-1}$$

As $\Delta_f G^-$ for the reduction reaction of Cr_2O_3 by Al is negative, this reaction is possible.

Q. 11. What is the role of graphite rod in the electrometallurgy of aluminium?

Ans. In the electrometallurgy of aluminium, a fused mixture of purified alumina (Al_2O_3), cryolite (Na_3AlF_6) and fluorspar (CaF_2) is electrolysed. In this electrolysis, graphite is used as the anode and graphite-lined iron is used as the cathode. During the electrolysis, Al is liberated at the cathode, while CO and CO_2 are liberated at the anode, according to the following equation.

Cathode: $\qquad Al^{3+}_{(melt)} + 3e^- \longrightarrow Al(l)$

Anode: $\qquad C(s) + O^{2-}_{(melt)} \longrightarrow CO(g) + 2e^-$

$$C(s) + 2O^{2-}_{(melt)} \longrightarrow CO_2(g) + 4e^-$$

If a metal is used instead of graphite as the anode, then O_2 will be liberated. This will not only oxidise the metal of the electrode, but also convert some of the Al liberated at the cathode back into Al_2O_3. Hence, graphite is used for preventing the formation of O_2 at the anode. Moreover, graphite is cheaper than other metals.

---

* are board exam questions from previous years

Q. 12. Predict conditions under which Al might be expected to reduce MgO.

Ans. Above 1350°C, the standard Gibbs free energy of formation of Al_2O_3 from Al is less than that of MgO from Mg. Therefore, above 1350°C, Al can reduce MgO.

Hence, if we look at Ellingham diagram. The point of intersection of Al and Mg oxides graphs each is where the ΔG° becomes zero for reduction of MgO by Al metal.

Hence reduction of MgO by Al can occur below this temperature only.

Also Al metal can reduce MgO to Mg above this temperature

$$3MgO + 2Al \xrightarrow{\ >1665\ } Al_2O_3 + 3Mg$$

Q. 13. The reaction,

$$Cr_2O_3 + 2Al \longrightarrow Al_2O_3 + 2Cr \qquad\qquad (\Delta G^{\circ} = -421\ kJ)$$

is thermodynamically feasible as is apparent from the Gibbs energy value.
Why does it not take place at room temperature?

Ans. The change in Gibbs energy is related to the equilibrium constant, K as

$$\Delta G = -RT \ln K$$

At room temperature, all reactants and products of the given reaction are in the solid state. As a result, equilibrium does not exist between the reactants and the products. Hence, the reaction does not take place at room temperature. However, at a higher temperature, chromium melts and the reaction takes place. We also know that according to the equation,

$$\Delta G = \Delta H - T\Delta S.$$

Increasing the temperature increases the value of $T\Delta S$, making the value of ΔG more and more negative. Therefore, the reaction becomes more and more feasible as the temperature is increased.

Q. 14. Write the chemical reactions involved in the process of extraction of gold. Explain the role of dilute NaCN and Zn in this process.*

Ans. Extraction of gold and silver involves leaching the metal with dilute solution of NaCN or KCN in the presence of air (for O_2) from which the metal is obtained later by replacement method (using Zinc). The reactions involved are :

$$4Au(s) + 8CN^-(aq) + 2H_2O(aq) + O_2(g) \longrightarrow 4[Au(CN)_2]^-\ (aq) + 4OH^-(aq)$$
$$2[Au(CN)_2]^-\ (aq) + Zn(s) \longrightarrow 2Au(s) + [Zn(CN)_4]^{2-}\ (aq)$$

Chapter 7. *p*-Block Elements

Q. 1. What inspired N. Bartlett for carrying out reaction between Xe and PtF_6?

Ans. Neil Bartlett initially carried out a reaction between oxygen and PtF_6. This resulted in the formation of a red compound, $O_2^+ [PtF_6]^-$.

Later, he realized that the first ionization energy of oxygen (1175 kJ/mol) and Xe (1170 kJ/mol) is almost the same. Thus, he tried to prepare a compound with Xe and PtF_6. He was successful and a red-coloured compound, Xe* $[PtF_6]^-$ was formed.

Q. 2. How are Xenon fluorides XeF_2, XeF_4 and XeF_6 obtained?

Ans. XeF_2, XeF_4, and XeF_6 are obtained by a direct reaction between Xe and F_2. The condition under which the reaction is carried out determines the product.

$$\underset{\text{(Excess)}}{Xe(g)} \quad + \quad F_2(g) \xrightarrow{\ 673\ K,\ 1\ bar\ } XeF_2(s)$$

$$\underset{\text{(1 : 5 ratio)}}{Xe(g)} \quad + \quad 2F_2(g) \xrightarrow{\ 873\ K,\ 7\ bar\ } XeF_4(s)$$

$$\underset{\text{(1 : 20 ratio)}}{Xe(g)} \quad + \quad 3F_2(g) \xrightarrow{\ 573\ K,\ 60\text{–}70\ bar\ } XeF_6(s)$$

Q. 3. Why is H_2O a liquid and H_2S a gas?

Ans. H_2O has oxygen as the central atom. Oxygen has smaller size and higher electronegativity as compared to sulphur. Therefore, there is extensive intermolecular hydrogen bonding in H_2O, which is absent in H_2S. Molecules of H_2S are held together only by weak Van der waals forces of attraction.

Hence, H_2O exists as a liquid while H_2S is a gas at room temperature.

Q. 4. Why does O_3 act as a powerful oxidising agent?[*]

Ans. Ozone is not a very stable compound under normal conditions and decomposes readily on heating to give a stable molecule of oxygen and nascent oxygen. Nascent oxygen, being a free radical, is very reactive and takes part in oxidation reactions.

$$O_3 \xrightarrow{\Delta} O_2 \quad + \quad [O]$$

$$\text{Ozone} \qquad \text{Oxygen} \qquad \text{Nascent oxygen}$$

Therefore, ozone acts as a powerful oxidising agent.

Q. 5. How is O_3 estimated quantitatively?

Ans. Quantitatively, ozone can be estimated with the help of potassium iodide. When ozone is made to react with potassium iodide solution buffered with a borate buffer (pH 9.2), iodine is liberated. This liberated iodine can be titrated against a standard solution of sodium thiosulphate using starch as an indicator. The reactions involved in the process are given below.

$$2I^- + H_2O + O_3 \longrightarrow 2OH^- + I_2 + O_2 \text{ (iodide gets oxidised to iodine)}$$

$$\text{Iodide} \qquad\qquad \text{Ozone} \qquad\qquad \text{Iodine}$$

$$I_2 + 2Na_2S_2O_3 \longrightarrow Na_2S_4O_6 + 2NaI$$

$$\text{Sodium} \qquad\qquad \text{Sodium}$$

$$\text{thiosulphate} \qquad \text{tetrathionate}$$

$$\text{(with starch)}$$

Q. 6. Comment on the nature of two S–O bonds formed in SO_2 molecule. Are the two S–O bonds in this molecule equal ?

Ans. The electronic configuration of S is $1s^2\, 2s^2\, 2p^6\, 3s^2\, 3p^4$.

During the formation of SO_2, one electron from $3p$ orbital goes to the $3d$ orbital and S undergoes sp^2 hybridization. Two of these orbitals form sigma bonds with two oxygen atoms and the third contains a lone pair. p-orbital and d-orbital contain an unpaired electron each. One of these electrons forms $p\pi$- $p\pi$ bond with one oxygen atom and the other forms $p\pi$- $d\pi$ bond with the other molecule. This is the reason SO_2 has a bent structure. Also, it is a resonance hybrid of structures I and II.

Both S–O bonds are equal in length (143 pm) and have a multiple bond character.

Q. 7. Write the conditions to maximize the yield of H_2SO_4 by Contact process.

Ans. Manufacture of sulphuric acid by Contact process involves three steps.

(i)   Burning of ores to form SO_2

(ii) Conversion of SO_2 to SO_3 by the reaction of the former with O_2

(V_2O_5 is used in this process as a catalyst.)

(iii) Absorption of SO_3 in H_2SO_4 to give oleum ($H_2S_2O_7$).

The key step in this process is the second step. In this step, two moles of gaseous reactants combine to give one mole of gaseous product. Also, this reaction is exothermic. Thus, in accordance with Le Chatelier's principle, to obtain the maximum amount of SO_3 gas, temperature should be low and pressure should be high.

Q. 8. Why is $K_{a_2} << K_{a_1}$ for H_2SO_4 in water?

Ans.

$$H_2SO_4(aq) + H_2O\,(l) \longrightarrow H_3O^+\,(aq) + HSO_4^-\,(aq); \, K_{a_1} > 10$$

$$H_2SO_4^-(aq) + H_2O\,(l) \longrightarrow H_3O^+\,(aq) + SO_4^-\,(aq); \, K_{a_2} > 1.2 \times 10^{-2}$$

It can be noticed that $K_{a_1} >> K_{a_2}$

This is because a neutral H_2SO_4 has a much higher tendency to lose a proton than the negatively charged HSO_4^-. Thus, the former is a much stronger acid than the latter.

Q. 9. Considering the parameters such as bond dissociation enthalpy, electron gain enthalpy and hydration enthalpy, compare the oxidising power of F_2 and Cl_2.

Ans. Fluorine is a much stronger oxidizing agent than chlorine. The oxidizing power depends on three factors.

(i)   Bond dissociation energy

(ii) Electron gain enthalpy

(iii) Hydration enthalpy

The electron gain enthalpy of chlorine is more negative than that of fluorine. However, the bond dissociation energy of fluorine is (158 kJ/mol) much lesser than that of chlorine (348.5 kJ/mol). Also, because of its small size, the hydration energy of fluorine is much higher than that of chlorine. Therefore, the latter two factors more than compensate for the less negative electron gain enthalpy of fluorine. Thus, fluorine is a much stronger oxidizing agent than chlorine.

Q. 10. Why is helium used in diving apparatus?

Ans. Air contains a large amount of nitrogen and the solubility of gases in liquids increases with increase in pressure. When sea divers dive deep into the sea, large amount of nitrogen dissolves in their blood. When they come back to the surface, solubility of nitrogen decreases and it separates from the blood and forms small air bubbles. This leads to a dangerous medical condition called bends. Therefore, air in oxygen cylinders used for diving is diluted with helium gas. This is done as He is sparingly less soluble in blood.

Q. 11. What are the oxidation states of phosphorus in the following:

(i) H_3PO_3,   (iii) Ca_3P_2,   (v) POF_3,

(ii) PCl_3,   (iv) Na_3PO_4,   (vi) H_3PO_2.

Ans. Let the oxidation state of P be x

(i) H_3PO_3

$$3 + x + 3(-2) = 0$$
$$3 + x - 6 = 0$$
$$x - 3 = 0$$
$$x = +3$$

(ii) PCl_3

$$x + 3(-1) = 0$$
$$x - 3 = 0$$
$$x = +3$$

(iii) Ca_3P_2

$$3(+2) + 2(x) = 0$$
$$6 + 2x = 0$$
$$2x = -6$$
$$x = -3$$

(iv) Na_3PO_4

$$3(+1) + x + 4(-2) = 0$$
$$3 + x - 8 = 0$$
$$x - 5 = 0$$
$$x = +5$$

(v) POF_3

$$x + (-2) + 3(-1) = 0$$
$$x - 5 = 0$$
$$x = +5.$$

(vi) H_3PO_2 (Phosphinic acid) :

$$x + (-2)2 + (+1)3 = 0$$
$$x - 4 + 3 = 0$$
$$x = +1$$

Chapter 8. *d*- and *f*-Block Elements

Q. 1. Explain the following:

(i)   Europium (II) more stable than cerium (II).*

(ii) Transition elements from interstitial compounds.

(iii) Actinoids shows irregularity in their electronic configuration.*

Ans. (i)   Electronic configuration Eu^{2+} is [Xe] $4f^7 5d^0$ while Ca^{2+} is [Xe] $4f^2 5d^0$. Hence Eu(II) has stable configuration as d-orbital is half filled whereas Ce^{2+} configuration has no such extra stability.

(ii) In transition metals small size atoms like carbon, boron, nitrogen etc., occupy the interstices or holes present in the metal lattice. *e.g.*, TiC, $VH_{0.6}$ Fe_3H. These compounds are more maleable, high melting point, chemically inert.

(iii) Actinoids have $5f$ and $6d$ subshells having similar energies. Hence electrons can move within the subshells causing irregular stability trend. Also in between $5f^0$, $5f^7$ and $5f^{14}$, configuration are extra stable which again alters the trend.

Q. 2. **Gas (A) and gas (B) both turn $K_2Cr_2O_7$ green in acidic medium. Gas (A) also turns lead acetate paper black. On passing gas (A) into aqueous solution of gas (B), yellowish white turbidity is observed. Identify gas (A) and gas (B) and write the chemical reaction involved.**

Ans. As we know that sulphide salts on treating with HCl (dil.) releases H_2S gas which turns lead acetate paper black, hence gas (A) is H_2S. On passing H_2S in gas (B) we get a yellowish turbidity, that is because of unsoluble sulphur. Hence gas (B) must be SO_2, as both turns acidified $K_2Cr_2O_7$ paper green.

Reactions :

$$H_2S + (CH_3COO)_2Pb \longrightarrow PbS\downarrow + 2CH_3COOH$$
$$\text{(gas A)} \quad \text{(lead acetate)} \quad \text{(Black)}$$

$$2H_2S + SO_2 \longrightarrow 2H_2O + 3S$$
$$\text{gas A} \quad\quad \text{gas B} \quad\quad\quad\quad \text{Sulphur causes}$$
$$\text{yellow turbidity}$$

$$K_2Cr_2O_7 + 4H_2SO_4 + 3H_2S \longrightarrow K_2SO_4 + Cr_2(SO_4) + 3S + 7H_2O$$
$$\text{Orange} \quad\quad\quad\quad\quad\quad\quad \text{Green}$$

Here S^{2-} is oxidised to S by potassium dichromate.

$$K_2Cr_2O_7 + H_2SO_4 + 3SO_2 \longrightarrow K_2SO_4 + Cr_2(SO_4)_3 + H_2O$$
$$\text{Orange} \quad\quad\quad\quad\quad\quad \text{Green}$$

Here SO_2 where S^{4+} sulphur is oxidised to SO_4^{3-} *i.e.*, S^{6-}.

Q. 3. (i) Explain why a green potassium manganate turns purple and a brown solid is precipitated when CO_2 gas is bubbled into the solution.

(ii) On adding acidic potassium dichromate solution to test tube containing acetaldehyde and another having potassium iodide we get smell of vinegar from one test tube and violet vapours appear in another test tube. Explain.

Ans. (i) In aqueous medium CO_2 gas releases H^+ ions and turns if acidic.

$$CO_2 + H_2O \rightleftharpoons H_2CO_3 \rightleftharpoons H^+ + HCO_3^-$$
$$\text{carbonic acid}$$

In acidic medium green potassium manganate disproportionate as purple permanganate ion and brown solid manganese oxide.

$$3Mn^{+6}O_4^{2-} + 4H^+ \longrightarrow 2Mn^{+7}O_4^- + Mn^{+4}O_2 + 2H_2O$$
$$\text{Green} \quad\quad\quad\quad\quad \text{Purple} \quad\quad \text{Brown}$$
$$\text{solution} \quad\quad\quad\quad \text{solution} \quad\quad \text{solid}$$

(ii) Vinegar smell will arise from test tube having acetaldehyde as it converts to acetic acid by $K_2Cr_2O_7$ and H_2SO_4.

$$3CH_3CHO + K_2Cr_2O_7 + 4H_2SO_4 \longrightarrow 3CH_3COOH + K_2SO_4 + Cr_2(SO_4)_3 + 4H_2O$$

Similarly we observe violet vapours of I_2 as potassium iodide is oxidised by acidic $K_2Cr_2O_7$.

$$K_2Cr_2O_7 + 7H_2SO_4 + 6KI \longrightarrow 4K_2SO_4 + Cr_2(SO_4)_3 + 7H_2O + 3I_2$$
$$\text{Violet}$$
$$\text{vapours}$$

Q. 4. **Write down the electronic configuration of :**

(i) Cr^{3+} (iii) Cu^+ (v) Co^{2+} (vii) Mn^{2+}

(ii) Pm^{3+} (iv) Ce^{4+} (vi) Lu^{2+} (viii) Th^{4+}

Ans. (i) Cr (24)—$[Ar]^{18}3d^44s^1$

$Cr^{3+} : 1s^22s^22p^63s^23p^63d^3$

Or, $[Ar]^{18}\,3d^3$

(ii) Pm(61) — $[Xe]^{54}4f^53d^06s^2$

$Pm^{3+} : 1s^22s^22p^63s^23p^63d^{10}4s^24p^64d^{10}5s^25p^64f^4$

Or, $[Xe]^{54}\,4f^4$

(iii) $Cu(29)$—$[Ar]^{18}4s^13d^{10}$

$Cu^+ : 1s^22s^22p^63s^23p^63d^{10}$

Or, $[Ar]^{18}3d^{10}$

(iv) $Ce(58)$—$[Xe]^{54}4f^15d^16s^2$

$Ce^{4+} : 1s^22s^22p^63s^23p^63d^{10}4s^24p^64d^{10}5s^25p^6$

Or, $[Xe]^{54}$

(v) $Co(27)$—$[Ar]^{18}4s^23d^7$

$Co^{2+} : 1s^22s^22p^63s^23p^63d^7$

Or, $[Ar]^{18}\,3d^7$

(vi) $Lu(71)$—$[Xe]^{54}4f^{14}5d^16s^2$

$Lu^{2+} : 1s^2\,2s^2\,2s^2\,2p^6\,3s^2\,3p^6\,3d^{10}\,4s^2\,4p^6\,4d^{10}\,5s^2\,5p^6\,4f^{14}\,5d^1$

Or, $[Xe]^{54}\,4f^{14}5d^1$

(vii) $Mn(25)$—$[Ar]^{18}\,4s^23d^5$

$Mn^{2+} : 1s^2\,2s^2\,2p^6\,3s^2\,3p^6\,3d^5$

Or, $[Ar]^{18}\,3d^5$

(viii) $Th(90)$—$[Rn]^{86}\,6d^27s^2$

$Th^{4+} : 1s^2\,2s^2\,2p^6\,3s^2\,3p^6\,3d^{10}\,4s^2\,4p^6\,4d^{10}\,4f^{14}\,5s^2\,5p^6\,5d^{10}\,6s^2$

Or, $[Rn]^{86}$

Q. 5. **Explain briefly how + 2 state becomes more and more stable in the first half of the first row transition elements with increasing atomic number ?**

Ans. We know that, except Sc, all others metals display + 2 oxidation state. Also, on moving from Sc to Mn, the atomic number increases from 21 to 25. This means the number of electrons in the $3d$-orbital also increases from 1 to 5.

$$Sc\,(+\,2) = d^1$$
$$Ti\,(+\,2) = d^2$$
$$V\,(+2) = d^3$$
$$Cr\,(+2) = d^4$$
$$Mn\,(+2) = d^5$$

$+2$ oxidation state is attained by the loss of the two $4s$ electrons by these metals. Since the number of d electrons in ($+2$) state also increases from Ti (+ 2) to Mn (+ 2), the number of unpaired electrons decreases. Mn (+2) has d^5 electrons (that is half-filled d-shell, which is highly stable), hence stability of (+ 2) oxidation state increases.

Q. 6. **To what extent do the electronic configurations decide the stability of oxidation states in the first series of the transition elements ? Illustrate your answer with examples.**

Ans. The half filled and fully filled d-orbitals are found to be more stable, hence the electronic configurations having such configuration are more stable.

e.g., Like Mn^{2+} is stable as it has half filled $3d$ orbital. Similarly Cr has + 1 stable oxidation state as Cr^{+1} has half filled orbital.

The (+3) state of Sc is stable as by loosing all electrons it attains stable noble gas configuration.

Q. 7. **What are the characteristics of the transition elements and why are they called transition elements ? Which of the d-block elements may not be regarded as the transition elements ?**

Ans. Transition elements are those elements in which the atoms or ions (in stable oxidation state) contain partially filled d-orbital. These elements lie in the d-block and show a transition of properties between s-block and p-block. Therefore, these are called transition elements.

Main characteristics of transition elements are :

(i)   Most are metals.

(ii) Show variable oxidation state. Elements such as Zn, Cd and Hg cannot be classified as transition elements because these have completely filled d-subshell.

(iii) Acts as good catalyst.

(iv) Metal ions are generally coloured and forms complexes.

Q. 8. **What are interstitial compounds ? Why are such compounds well known for transition metals ?**

Ans. Transition metals are large in size and contain lots of interstitial sites. Transition elements forms interstitial compounds in which small size atoms, such as B, C, N occupies the holes in the crystal lattices. The resulting compounds are called interstitial compounds, example, TiC, $VH_{0.56}$ and are common in transition metals.

Q. 9. For M^{2+}/M and M^{3+}/M^{2+} systems, the $E°$ values for some metals are as follows:

$Cr^{2+}/Cr - 0.9$ V
$Cr^{3+}/Cr^{2+} - 0.4$ V
$Mn^{2+}/Mn - 1.2$ V
$Mn^{3+}/Mn^{2+} + 1.5$ V
$Fe^{2+}/Fe - 0.4$ V
$Fe^{3+}/Fe^{2+} + 0.8$ V

Use this data to comment upon:

(i) The stability of Fe^{3+} in acid solution as compared to that Cr^{3+} or Mn^{3+}.

(ii) The ease with which iron can be oxidised as compared to a similar process for either chromium or manganese metal.

Ans. (i) The $E°$ value for Fe^{3+}/Fe^{2+} is higher than that for Cr^{3+}/Cr^{2+} and lower than that for Mn^{3+}/Mn^{2+}. So, the reduction of Fe^{3+} to Fe^{2+} is easier than the reduction of Mn^{3+} to Mn^{2+}, but not as easy as the reduction of Cr^{3+} to Cr^{2+}. Hence, Fe^{3+} is more stable than Mn^{3+}, but less stable than Cr^{3+}. These metal ions can be arranged in the increasing order of their stability as : $Mn^{3+} < Fe^{3+} < Cr^{3+}$.

(ii) The reduction potentials for the given pairs increase in the following order.
$$Mn^{2+}/Mn < Cr^{2+}/Cr < Fe^{2+}/Fe$$

So, the oxidation of Fe to Fe^{2+} is not as easy as the oxidation of Cr to Cr^{2+} and the oxidation of Mn to Mn^{2+}. Thus, these metals can be arranged in the increasing order of their ability to get oxidised as : Fe < Cr < Mn.

Q. 10. Predict which of the following will be coloured in aqueous solution ? Ti^{3+}, V^{3+}, Cu^+, Sc^{3+}, Mn^{2+}, Fe^{3+} and Co^{2+}. Give reason for each.

Ans. Only the ions that have electrons in d-orbital will be coloured. The ions in which d-orbitals is empty will be colourless.

Element	Atomic Number	Ionic State	Electronic configuration in ionic state	
Ti	22	Ti^{3+}	[Ar] $3d^1$	
V	23	V^{3+}	[Ar] $3d^2$	
Cu	29	Cu^+	[Ar] $3d^{10}$	(Colourless)
Sc	21	Sc^{3+}	[Ar] $3d^0$	(Colourless)
Mn	25	Mn^{2+}	[Ar] $3d^5$	
Fe	26	Fe^{3+}	[Ar] $3d^5$	
Co	27	Co^{2+}	[Ar] $3d^7$	

From the above table, it can be easily observed that only Sc^{3+} has an empty d-orbital. All other ions, except Sc^{3+} and Cu^+ ions have filled d-orbital and will be coloured in aqueous solution because of d-d transition.

Q. 11. Give examples and suggest reason for the following features of the transition metal chemistry:*

(i) The lowest oxide of transition metal is basic, the highest is amphoteric or acidic.

(ii) A transition metal exhibits highest oxidation state in oxides and fluorides.

(iii) The highest oxidation state is exhibited in oxoanions of a metal.

Ans. (i) In case of a lower oxide of a transition metal the metal atom has a low oxidation state. This means that all the valence electrons of the metal atom are not involved in bonding. As a result, it can donate electrons and behave as a base.

In the case of a higher oxide of a transition metal, the metal atom has a high oxidation state. This means that the valence electrons are involved in bonding and so, they are unavailable. There is also a high effective nuclear charge.

As a result, it can accept electrons and behave as an acid.

For example, $\overset{II}{Mn}O$ is basic and $\overset{VIII}{Mn_2O_7}$ is acidic.

(ii) Oxygen and fluorine acts as strong oxidising agents because of their high electronegativities and small sizes. Hence, they bring out the highest oxidation states from the transition metals. In other words, a transition metal exhibits higher oxidation state in oxides and fluorides. For example, in OsF_6 and V_2O_5, the oxidation states of Os and V are $+6$ and $+5$ respectively.

(iii) Oxygen is a strong oxidising agent due to its high electronegativity, small size and can form multiple bonds. So, oxo-anions of a metal have the highest oxidation state. For example, in MnO_4^-, the oxidation state of Mn is $+7$.

Q. 12. **Indicate the steps in the preparation of:**

   (i) $K_2Cr_2O_7$ from chromite ore.*

   (ii) $KMnO_4$ from pyrolusite ore.*

Ans. (i)   Potassium dichromate $(K_2Cr_2O_7)$ is prepared from chromite ore $(FeCr_2O_4)$ in the following steps.

Step 1. Preparation of sodium chromate : Chromite ore is fused with sodium hydroxide or sodium carbonate.

$$4FeCr_2O_4 + 16NaOH + 7O_2 \xrightarrow{\text{Fuse}} 8Na_2CrO_4 + 2Fe_2O_3 + 8H_2O$$
$$\text{Sodium chromate}$$

Step 2. Conversion of sodium chromate into sodium dichromate. Sodium chromate is yellow in colour.

$$2Na_2CrO_4 + \text{conc. } H_2SO_4 \longrightarrow Na_2Cr_2O_7 + Na_2SO_4 + H_2O$$
$$\text{Orange}$$

Step 3. Conversion of sodium dichromate to potassium dichromate, because sodium dichromate is more soluble and less stable than potassium dichromate.

$$Na_2Cr_2O_7 + 2KCl \longrightarrow K_2Cr_2O_7 + 2NaCl$$
$$\text{(Orange)}$$
$$\text{Potassium}$$
$$\text{dichromate}$$

Potassium chloride being less soluble than sodium chloride is obtained in the form of orange coloured crystals and can be removed by filtration.

The dichromate ion $(Cr_2O_7^{2-})$ exists in equilibrium with chromate (CrO_4^{2-}) ion at pH 4.

However, by changing the pH, they can be interconverted.

$$2CrO_4^{2-} \xrightarrow[\text{Alkali}]{\text{Acid}} 2HCrO_4^- \xrightarrow[\text{Alkali}]{\text{Acid}} Cr_2O_7^{2-}$$

Chromate	Hydrogen	Dichromate
(Yellow)	chromate	(Orange)

(ii)   Potassium permanganate $(KMnO_4)$ can be prepared from pyrolusite (MnO_2). The ore is fused with KOH in the presence of either atmospheric oxygen or an oxidising agent, such as KNO_3 or $KClO_4$, to give K_2MnO_4 potassium manganate.

$$2MnO_2 + 4KOH + O_2 \xrightarrow{\text{Heat}} 2K_2MnO_4 + 2H_2O$$
$$\text{(Green)}$$

The green mass can be extracted with water and then oxidized either electrolytically or by passing chlorine or ozone into the solution. Electrolytic oxidation

$$K_2MnO_4 \longrightarrow 2K^+ + MnO_4^{2-}$$
$$H_2O \longrightarrow H^+ + OH^-$$

At anode, manganate ions are oxidized to permanganate ions.

$$MnO_4^{2-} \longrightarrow MnO_4^- + e^-$$
$$\text{Green} \qquad \text{Purple}$$

Oxidation by chlorine

$$2K_2MnO_4 + Cl_2 \longrightarrow 2KMnO_4 + 2KCl$$
$$2MnO_4^{2-} + Cl_2 \longrightarrow 2MnO_4^- + 2Cl^-$$

Oxidation by ozone

$$2K_2MnO_4 + O_3 + H_2O \longrightarrow 2KMnO_4 + 2KOH + O_2$$
$$2MnO_4^{2-} + O_3 + H_2O \longrightarrow 2MnO_4^- + 2OH^- + O_2$$

Q. 13. **Write down the number of $3d$ electrons in each of the following ions:**

   Ti^{2+}, V^{2+}, Cr^{3+}, Mn^{2+}, Fe^{2+}, Fe^{3+}, CO^{2+}, Ni^{2+} and Cu^{2+}.

Indicate how would you expect the five $3d$ orbitals to be occupied for these hydrated ions (octahedral).

Ans.

Metal ion	Number of d-electrons	Filling of d-orbitals
Ti^{2+}	2	$4s^0 3d^2$
V^{2+}	3	$4s^0 3d^3$
Cr^{3+}	3	$4s^0 3d^3$
Mn^{2+}	5	$4s^0 3d^5$
Fe^{2+}	6	$4s^0 3d^6$
Fe^{3+}	5	$4s^0 3d^5$
CO^{2+}	7	$4s^0 3d^7$
Ni^{2+}	8	$4s^0 3d^8$
Cu^{2+}	9	$4s^0 3d^0$

Q. 14. How would you account for the irregular variation of ionization enthalpies (first and second) in the first series of the transition elements?

Ans. Ionization enthalpies are found to increase in the given series due to a continuous filling of the inner d-orbitals. The irregular variations of ionization enthalpies can be attributed to the extra stability of configurations such as d^0, d^5, d^{10}. Since these half filled and fully filled orbitals are exceptionally stable, their ionization enthalpies are very high.

In case of first ionization energy, Cr has low ionization energy. This is because after losing one electron, it attains the stable configuration ($3d^5$). On the other hand, Zn has exceptionally high first ionization energy as an electron has to be removed from stable and fully-filled orbitals ($3d^{10}4s^2$).

Second ionization energies are higher than the first since it becomes difficult to remove an electron when an electron has already been taken out. Also, elements like Cr and Cu have exceptionally high second ionization energies as after losing the first electron, they have attained the stable configuration ($Cr^+ : 3d^5$ and $Cu^+ : 3d^{10}$). Hence irregular trends in ionization enthalpies are observed.

Q. 15. Following ions are given:*
$$Cr^{2+}, Cu^{2+}, Cu+, Fe^{2+}, Fe^{3+}, Mn^{3+}$$

Identify the ion which is
(i) a strong reducing agent.   (iii) a strong oxiding agent.
(ii) unstable in aqueous solution.
Give suitable reason in each.

Ans. (i) Cr^{2+} is a strong reducing agent as it is very easily oxidized to more stable Cr^{3+} (d^3) where it attains^{2+} a stable half-filled t_{2g} configuration.

(ii) Cu^+ is unstable in aqueous solution because it disproportionates in water to form Cu^{2+} and Cu.

(iii) Mn^{3+} is a strong oxidising agent because it gets reduced to Mn^{2+} (d^5) in the process and attains an extra stable half-filled d orbital configuration.

Chapter 9. Coordination Compounds

Q. 1. Specify the oxidation numbers of the metals in the following coordination entities:
(i) $[Co(H_2O)(CN)(en)_2]^{2+}$ (iii) $[PtCl_4]^{2-}$ (v) $[Cr(NH_3)_3Cl_3]$
(ii) $[CoBr_2(en)_2]^+$ (iv) $K_3[Fe(CN)_6]$

Ans. (i) $[Co(H_2O)(CN)(en)_2]^{2+}$

Let the oxidation number of Co be x.
The charge on the complex is $+ 2$.

$[Co\ (H_2O)\ (CN)\ (en)_2]^{2+}$
$\downarrow\quad\ \downarrow\quad\ \ \downarrow\quad\ \ \downarrow$
$x\ +\ 0\ +\ (-1) + 2(0) = +2$
$$x - 1 = +2$$
$$x = +3$$

(ii) $[Co\ (Br)_2\quad (en)_2]^+$
$\ \downarrow\quad\ \downarrow\qquad\ \downarrow$
$x\ +\ 2\,(-1) +\ 2(0) = +1$

$$x - 2 = + 1$$
$$x = + 3$$

(iii) $[Pt(Cl)_4]^{2-}$

Let the oxidation number of Pt be x.

The charge on the complex is -2.

$$[Pt \quad (Cl)_4]^{2-}$$

$x + 4(-1) = -2x$
$$= + 2$$

(iv) $K_3[Fe(CN)_6]$

i.e., $[Fe \quad (CN)_6]^{3-}$

$$x + 6(-1) = -3$$

$$x - 6 = -3$$
$$x = 6 - 3$$
$$x = + 3$$

(v) $[Cr(NH_3)_3Cl_3]$

$$x + 3(0) + 3(-1) = 0$$

$$x - 3 = 0$$
$$x = + 3$$

Q. 2. Draw the structures of optical isomers of:

   (i) $[Cr(C_2O_4)_3]^{3-}$ (ii) $[PtCl_2(en)_2]^{2+}$ (iii) $[Cr(NH_3)_2Cl_2(en)]^+$

Ans. (i) $[Cr(C_2O_4)_3]^{3-}$

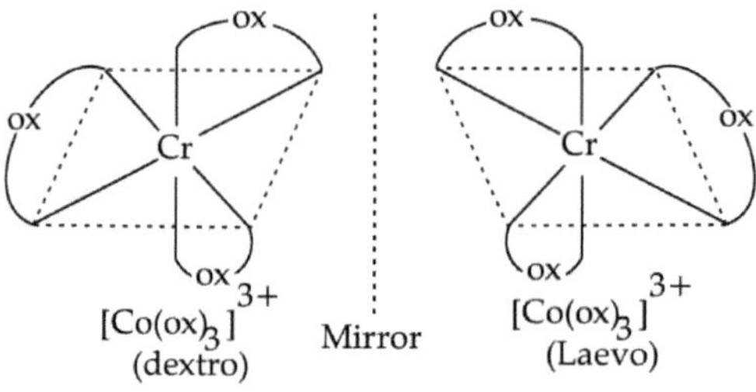

(ii) $[PtCl_2(en)_2]^{2+}$

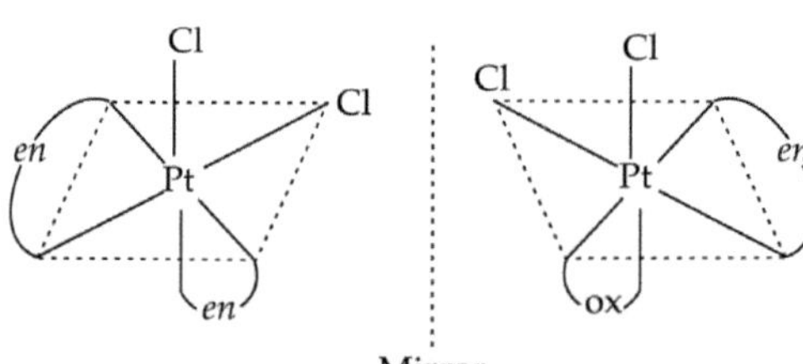

(iii) $[Cr(NH_3)_2Cl_2(en)]^+$

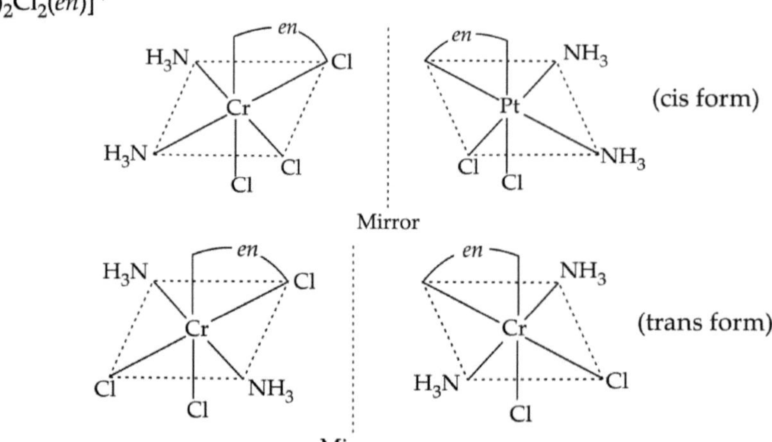

Q. 3. Draw all the isomers (geometrical and optical) of:

(i) $[CoCl_2(en)_2]^+$ (ii) $[Co(NH_3)Cl(en)_2]^{2+}$ (iii) $[Co(NH_3)_2Cl_2(en)]^+$

Ans. (i) $[CoCl_2(en)_2]^+$

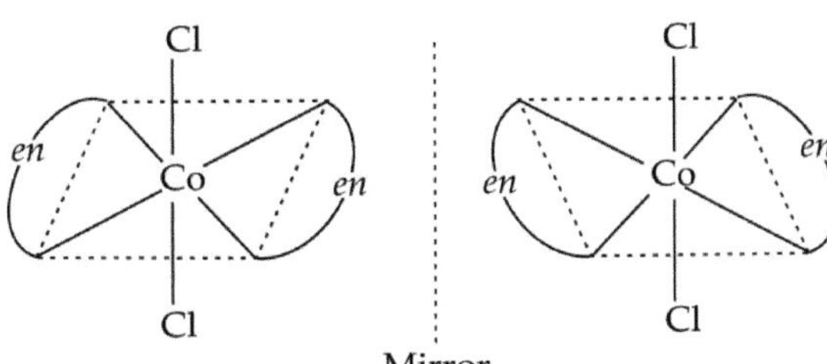

Trans $[CoCl_2 (en)_2]^+$ isomer-optically inactive
(Superimosable mirror images)

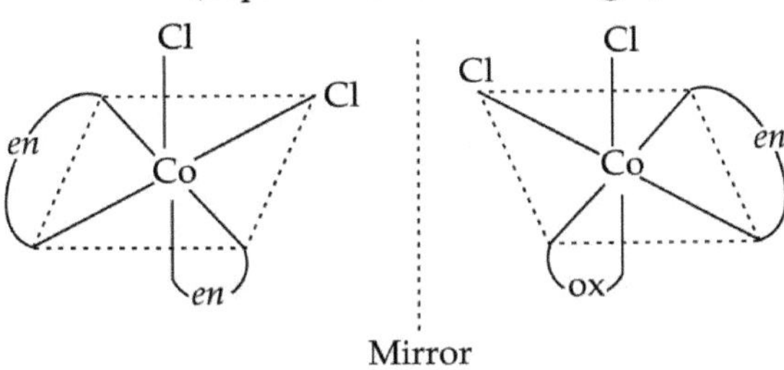

Cis $[CoCl_2 (en)_2]^+$ isomer-optically active
(Non-superimosable mirror images)

In total, three isomers are possible.

(ii) $[Co(NH_3)Cl(en)_2]^{2+}$

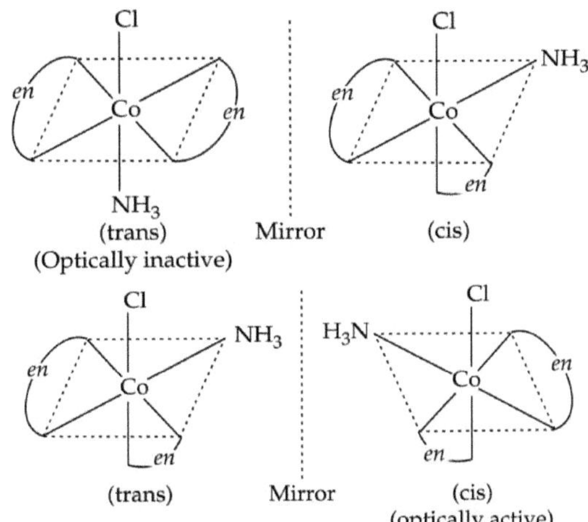

trans-isomers are optically inactive.

cis-isomers are optically active.

(iii) $[Co(NH_3)_2Cl_2(en)]^+$

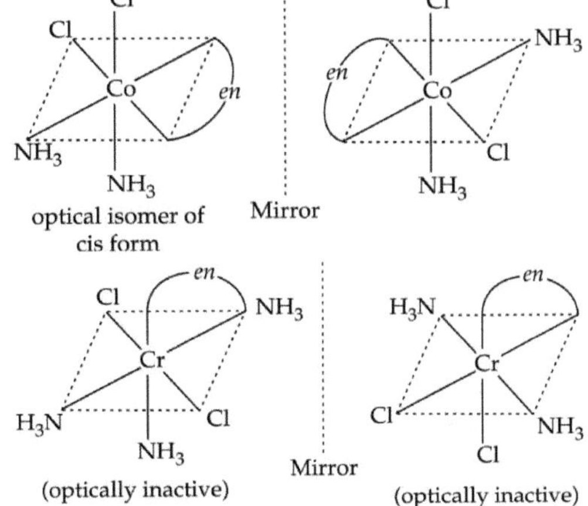

Q. 4. What is spectrochemical series? Explain the difference between a weak field ligand and a strong field ligand.

Ans. A spectrochemical series is the arrangement of common ligands in the increasing order of their crystal-field splitting energy (CFSE) values. The ligands present on the R.H.S. of the series are strong field ligands while that on the L.H.S. are weak field ligands. Also, strong field ligands cause higher splitting in the d-orbitals than weak field ligands. *i.e.*, the Δ_0 or Δt is high for strong field ligands.

$$I^- < Br^- < S^{2-} < SCN^- < Cl^- < N_3 < F^- < OH^- < C_2O_4^{2-} \sim H_2O < NCS^- \sim H^- CN^- < NH_3 < en \sim SO_3^{2-}$$
$$< NO_2^- < phen < CO$$

Q. 5. What is crystal field splitting energy? How does the magnitude of Δ_0 decides the actual configuration of d-orbitals in a coordination entity?

Ans. The degenerate d-orbitals (in a spherical field environment) split into two levels *i.e.*, e_g and t_{2g} in the presence of ligands. The splitting of the degenerate levels due to the presence of ligands is called the crystal-field splitting while the energy difference between the two levels [(e_g (high) and t_{2g} (low)] is called the crystal-field splitting energy. It is denoted by Δ_0 for a octahedral complexes.

After the orbitals have split, the filling of the electrons takes place. According to Hund's rule 1 electron is been filled in the three t_{2g} orbitals, the filling of the fourth electron takes place in two ways. It can enter the e_g orbital (giving rise to $t_{2g}{}^3 e_g{}^1$ like electronic configuration) or the pairing of the electrons can take place in the t_{2g} orbitals (giving rise to $t_{2g}{}^4 e_g{}^0$ like electronic configuration). If the Δ_0 value of a ligand is less than the pairing energy (P) ($\Delta_0 < p$) then the electrons enter the e_g orbital. On the other hand, if the Δ_0 value of a ligand is more than the pairing energy (P) ($\Delta_0 > p$) then the electrons enter the t_{2g} orbital. Thus, the value of Δ_0 decides the configuration and magnetic matrix of the complex.

Q. 6. $[Cr(NH_3)_6]^{3+}$ is a paramagnetic while $[Ni(CN)_4]^{2-}$ is diamagnetic. Explain why?

Ans. Cr is in the +3 oxidation state *i.e.*, d^3 configuration. Also, NH_3 is a weak field ligand that does not cause the pairing of the electrons in the $3d$ orbital. Cr^{3+}:

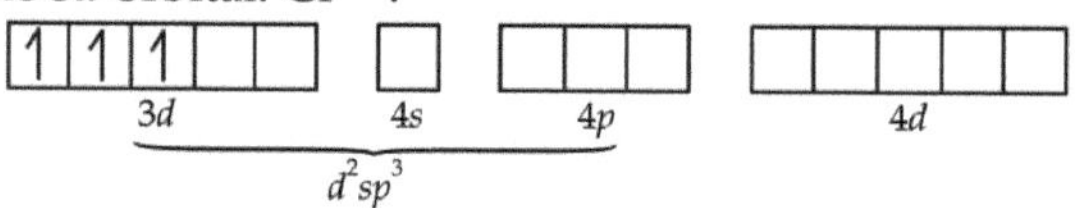

Therefore, it undergoes d^2sp^3 hybridization and the electrons in the $3d$ orbitals remain unpaired. Hence, it is paramagnetic in nature because of 3 unpaired electrons.

In $[Ni(CN)_4]^{2-}$, Ni exists in the +2 oxidation state *i.e.*, d^8 configuration. Ni^{2+}:

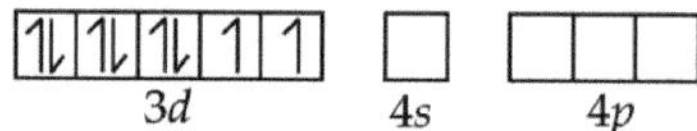

CN^- is a strong field ligand. It causes the pairing of the $3d$-orbital electrons. Then, Ni^{2+} undergoes dsp^2 hybridization, square planar geometry and diamagnetic as no unpaired electron.

Q. 7. Give the oxidation state, d-orbital occupation and coordination number of the central metal ion in the following complexes:

(i) $K_3[Co(C_2O_4)_3]$ (ii) *cis*-$[Cr(en)_2Cl_2]Cl$ (iii) $(NH_4)_2[CoF_4]$ (iv) $[Mn(H_2O)_6SO_4]$

Ans. (i) $K_3[Co(C_2O_4)_3]$

The central metal ion is Co.

Its coordination number is 6. The oxidation state can be given as:
$$x - 6 = -3$$
$$= +3$$

The d-orbital occupation for Co^{3+} is $t_{2g}{}^6 e_g{}^0$.

(ii) *cis*-$[Cr(en)_2Cl_2]Cl$

The central metal ion is Cr.

The coordination number is 6. The oxidation state can be given as:
$$x + 2(0) + 2(-1) = +1$$
$$x - 2 = +1 = +3$$

The d-orbital occupation for Cr^{3+} is $t_{2g}{}^3$.

(iii) $(NH_4)_2[CoF_4]$

The central metal ion is Co.

The coordination number is 4.

The oxidation state can be given as:

$$x - 4 = -2x$$
$$= +2$$

The d-orbital occupation for Co^{2+} $3d^7$ after splitting (e_g^4, t_{2g}^3).

(iv) $[Mn(H_2O)_6SO_4]$.

The central metal ion is Mn.

The coordination number is 6. The oxidation state can be given as:

$$x + 0 = +2 = +2$$

The d-orbital occupation for Mn is $t_{2g}^3 e_g^2$.

Q. 8. Discuss briefly giving an example in each case the role of coordination compounds in:

(i) Biological system   (iii) Analytical chemistry

(ii) Medicinal chemistry   (iv) Extraction or metallurgy of metals

Ans. (i) Role of coordination compounds in biological systems : Photosynthesis is made possible by the presence of the chlorophyll pigment. This pigment is a coordination compound of magnesium. In the human biological system, several coordination compounds play important roles. For example, the oxygen-carrier of blood, *i.e.*, haemoglobin, is a coordination compound of iron. Enzymes sometimes use chelation to perform biological catalytic reactions.

(ii) Role of coordination compounds in medicinal chemistry : Certain coordination compounds of platinum (for example, *cis*-platin) are used for inhibiting the growth of tumours. Specially the cis isomer. Now a days it is replaced by dinuclear platinum complex because of certain side effects.

(iii) Role of coordination compounds in analytical chemistry : During salt analysis, a number of basic radicals are detected with the help of the colour changes they exhibit with different reagents. These colour changes are a result of the coordination compounds or complexes that the basic radicals form with different ligands. *e.g.*, Cu^{2+} ion detection where deep blue and chocolate colour ppt. are produced where both are complex compounds.

(iv) Role of coordination compounds in extraction of metallurgy of metals : The process of extraction of some of the metals from their ores involves the formation of complexes. For example, in aqueous solution, gold combines with cyanide ions to form $[Au(CN)_2]$. From this solution, gold is later extracted by the addition of zinc metal. Also silver ore can be extracted using same method.

Q. 9. Give evidence that $[Co(NH_3)_5Cl]SO_4$ and $[Co(NH_3)_5SO_4]Cl$ are ionization isomers.

Ans. When ionization isomers are dissolved in water, they ionize to give different ions. These ions when they react differently with different reagents to give confirmatory products. According to their property with testing on adding few drops of $BaCl_2$ solution to $[Co(NH_3)_5Cl] SO_4$ we get white ppt. while its ionisation isomer does not show any change.

Similarly on adding few drops of $AgNO_3$ solution to $[Co(NH_3)_5SO_4] Cl$ we get white ppt. of AgCl while its ionisation isomer does not provide any such ppt.

$$[CO(NH_3)_5Cl] SO_4 + Ba^{2+} \longrightarrow BaSO_4 \downarrow$$
$$\text{White precipitate}$$

$$[CO(NH_3)_5Cl] SO_4 + Ag^+ \longrightarrow \text{No reaction}$$
$$[CO(NH_3)_5Cl] SO_4 + Ba^+ \longrightarrow \text{No reaction}$$
$$[CO(NH_3)_5SO_4] Cl + Ag^+ \longrightarrow AgCl \downarrow$$
$$\text{White precipitate}$$

Q. 10. Explain on the basis of valence bond theory that $[Ni(CN)_4]^{2-}$ ion with square planar structure is diamagnetic and the $[NiCl_4]^{2-}$ ion with tetrahedral geometry is paramagnetic.

Ans. Ni is the +2 oxidation state *i.e.*, in d^8 configuration.

d^8 configuration :

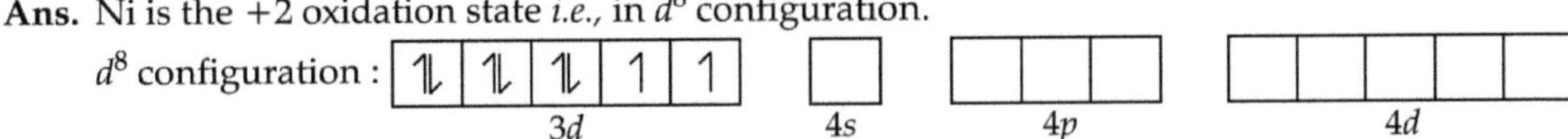

There are 4 CN^- ions. Thus, it can either have a tetrahedral geometry or square planar geometry. Since CN^- ion is a strong ligand, it causes the pairing of unpaired $3d$ electrons.

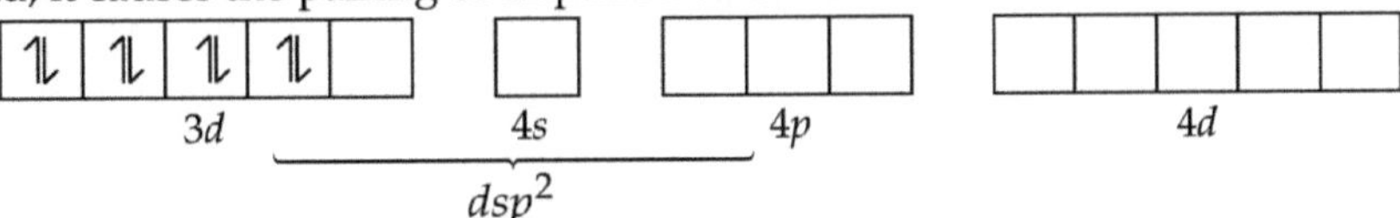

It now undergoes dsp^2 hybridization resulting in square planar geometry. Since all electrons are paired, it is diamagnetic. In case of $[NiCl_4]^{2-}$, Cl^- ion is a weak field ligand. Therefore, it does not lead to the pairing of unpaired $3d$ electrons. Therefore, it undergoes sp^3 hybridization, having tetrahedral geometry.

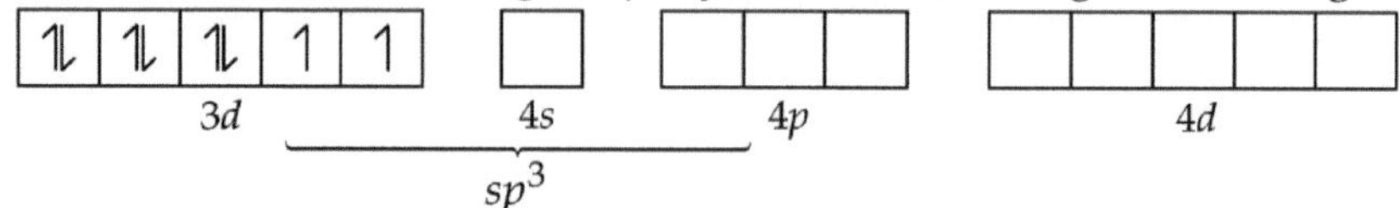

Since there are 2 unpaired electrons in this case, it is paramagnetic in nature.

Q. 11. $[NiCl_4]^{2-}$ is paramagnetic while $[Ni(CO)_4]$ is diamagnetic though both are tetrahedral. Why ?

Ans. Though both $[NiCl_4]^{2-}$ and $[Ni(CO)_4]$ are tetrahedral, their magnetic characters are different. This is due to a difference in the nature of ligands. Cl^- is a weak field ligand and it does not cause the pairing of unpaired $3d$ electrons. Hence, $[NiCl_4]^{2-}$ is paramagnetic.

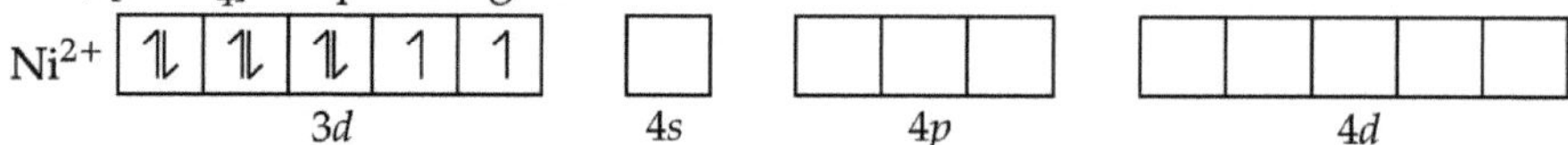

In $Ni(CO)_4$, Ni is in the zero oxidation state *i.e.*, it has a configuration of $3d^8 4s^2$.

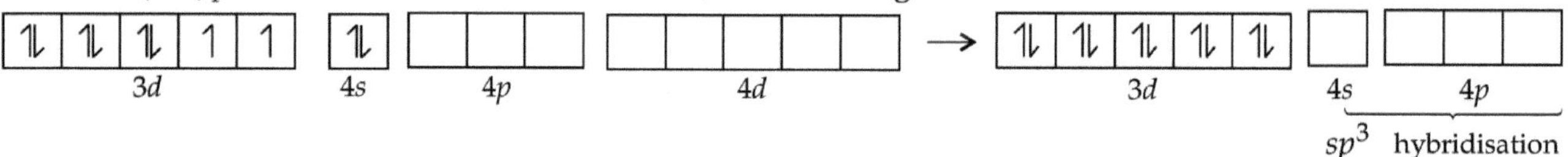

But CO is a strong field ligand. Therefore, it causes the pairing of unpaired $3d$ electrons. Also, it causes the $4s$ electrons to shift to the $3d$-orbital, thereby giving rise to sp^3 hybridization. Since no unpaired electrons are present in this case, $[Ni(CO)_4]$ is diamagnetic.

Q. 12. $[Fe(H_2O)_6]^{3+}$ is strongly paramagnetic whereas $[Fe(CN)_6]^{3-}$ is weakly paramagnetic. Explain.

Ans. In both $[Fe(H_2O)_6]^{3+}$ and $[Fe(CN)_6]^{3-}$, Fe exists in the $+3$ oxidation state *i.e.*, in d^5 configuration.

Since CN^- is a strong field ligand, it causes the pairing of unpaired electrons. Therefore, there is only one unpaired electron left in the d-orbital.

Therefore,

$$\mu = \sqrt{n(n+2)}$$

$$= \sqrt{1(1+2)}$$

$$= \sqrt{3}$$

$$= 1.732 \text{ BM}$$

On the other hand, H_2O is a weak field ligand. Therefore, it cannot cause the pairing of electrons. This means that the number of unpaired electrons is 5.

Therefore,

$$\mu = \sqrt{n(n+2)}$$

$$= \sqrt{5(5-2)}$$

$$= \sqrt{35}$$

$$= 5.916 \text{ BM}$$

Hence, $[Fe(H_2O)_6]^{3+}$ is strongly paramagnetic, while $[Fe(CN)_6]^{3-}$ is weakly paramagnetic.

Q. 13. The hexaquo manganese(II) ion contains five unpaired electrons, while the hexacyano ion contains only one unpaired electron. Explain using Crystal Field Theory.

Ans. $[Mn(H_2O)_6]^{2+}$ $[Mn(CN)_6]^{4-}$

Mn is in the $+2$ oxidation state.   Mn is in the $+2$ oxidation state.

The electronic configuration is d^5.   The electronic configuration is d^5.

In both the cases a strong field ligand. Therefore, the arrangement of the electrons in hexacyano manganese is octahedral in this complex all electrons are paired *i.e.*, $[Mn(CN)_6]^{4-}$

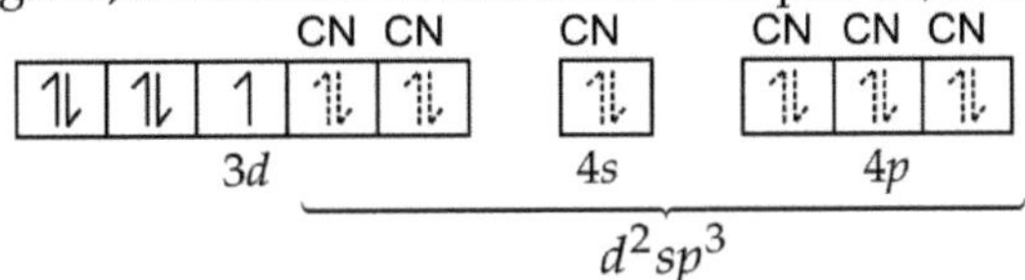

Leaving only single unpaired electron as H_2O is a weak field ligand so no pairing takes place thus it $[Mn(H_2O)_6]^{2+}$ is white in colour. Hence, hexaquo manganese (II) ion has five unpaired electrons, while hexacyano ion has only one unpaired electron.

Q. 14. (i) For the complex $[Fe(CN)_6]^{3-}$, write the hybridisation type, magnetic character and spin nature of the complex. (At. no : Fe = 26).*

(ii) Draw one of the geometrical isomers of the complex $[Pt\ (en)_2Cl_2]^{2+}$, which is optically active.

Ans. (i) $[Fe(CN)_6]^{3-}$ in this complex Fe has (+ 3) oxidation state, *i.e.*, $4s^0 3d^5$ outer configuration.

$$Fe^{3+}\quad \boxed{\uparrow|\uparrow|\uparrow|\uparrow|\uparrow}\ \ \boxed{\ }\ \ \boxed{\ |\ |\ }$$
$$3d^5 \qquad 4s^0 \qquad 4p$$

As CN^- is a strong field ligand, it will make the electrons of $3d$ pair *i.e.*, leading to d^2sp^3 octahedral hybridisation.

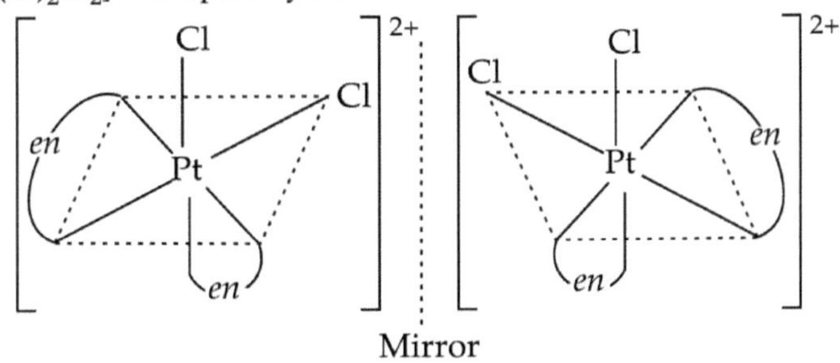

Hence, the complex is inner orbital complex having octahedral geometry.

Because of presence of one unpaired electron in $3d$-orbital it has mild paramagnetism. Total electron spin moment as : $\mu = \sqrt{n(n+2)} = \sqrt{3} = 1.732$. Its a low spin complex.

(ii) The *cis* isomer of $[Pt(en)_2Cl_2]^{2+}$ is optically active.

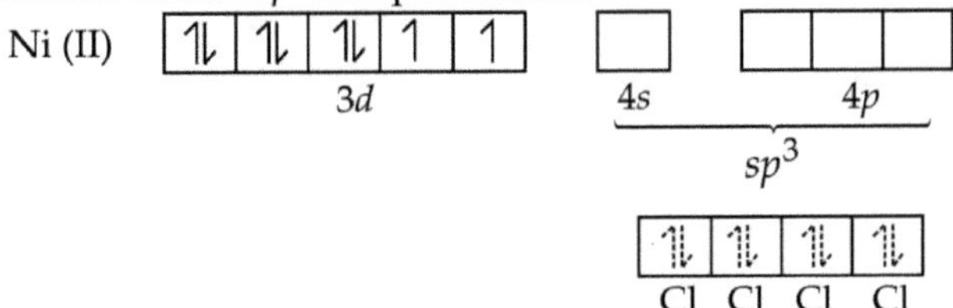

Non superimposable mirror images.

Q. 15. For the complex $[NiCl_4]^{2-}$, write.

(i) The IUPAC name and the hybridization state of metal atom.

(ii) The shape of the complex (At. no. of Ni = 28).*

Ans. (i) $[NiCl_4]^{2-}$

tetrachloridonickelate (II) ion.

(ii) Ni has + 2 state so $4s^0 3d^3$ configuration Cl being a weak field ligand causes pairing of the d-electrons, hence an outer orbital sp^3 complex formed.

$$Ni\ (II)\quad \boxed{\uparrow\downarrow|\uparrow\downarrow|\uparrow\downarrow|\uparrow|\uparrow}\ \ \boxed{\ }\ \ \boxed{\ |\ |\ }$$
$$3d \qquad\qquad 4s \qquad 4p$$
$$sp^3$$
$$\boxed{\uparrow\downarrow|\uparrow\downarrow|\uparrow\downarrow|\uparrow\downarrow}$$
$$Cl\ \ Cl\ \ Cl\ \ Cl$$

(iii) Shape of complex is tetrahedral.

$$Cl$$
$$|$$
$$Cl\!-\!\!\!\overset{}{\underset{|}{Ni}}\!\!\!-\!Cl$$
$$Cl$$

Q. 16. (i) Predict the number of unpaired electron in $[MnBr_4]^{2-}$.

(ii) Draw structures of geometrical isomers of $[Co(NH_3)_4Cl_2]^-$

Ans. (i) $[MnBr_4]^{2-}$, Mn has $(+2)$ oxidation state hence $4s^0 3d^5$ configuration. Br^- is a weak field ligand, five unpaired electrons. So, highly paramagnetic.

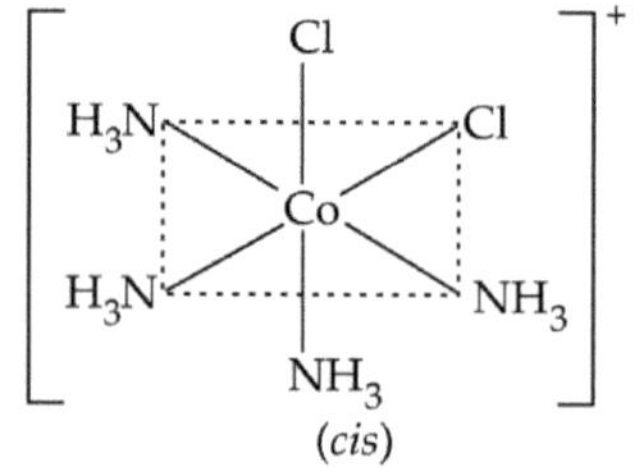

So highly paramagnetic.

(ii) $[Co(NH_3)_4Cl_2]^+$.

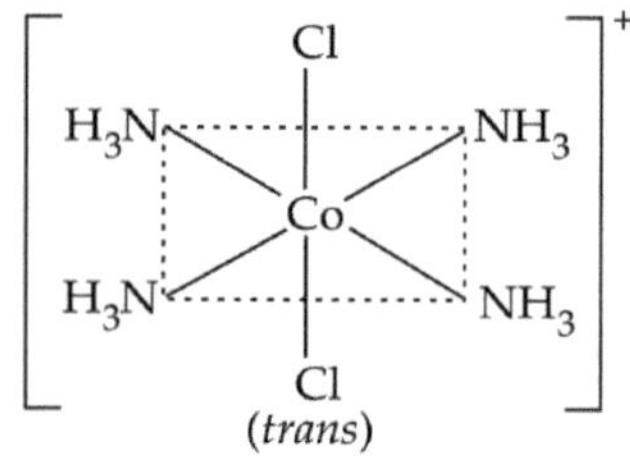

Q. 17. (i)   List the drawbacks of Valence Bond Theory.

(ii)   Write IUPAC name of the following compounds.

(a) $[Ag(NH_3)_2]$ Cl and (b) $K[Ag(CN)_2]$.

Ans. (i)   Valence Bond Theory has three drawbacks.

(a)   It cannot explain why certain complexes of a single oxidation state are low spin and some are high spin complex.

(b)   It cannot predict the correct magnetic behaviour of complexes. Example according to VBT all Ni (II), four ligand complexes should be diamagnetic square planar. But that is not so, in some cases it is paramagnetic as one electron get excited to $4p$ orbital.

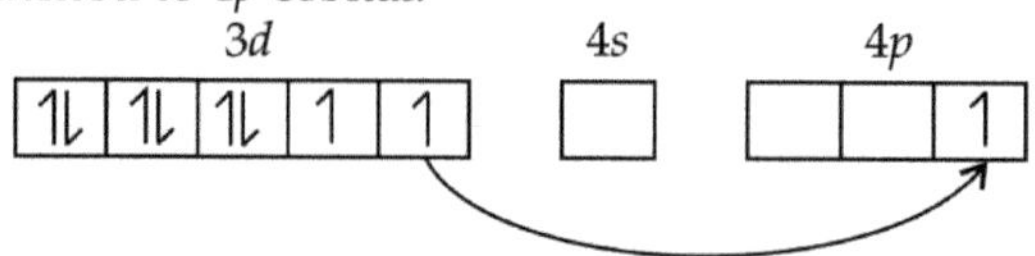

(c)   It cannot explain colour of the complexes. Hence cannot explain absorption spectra of coordination compounds.

(ii)   (a)   Diammine silver (I) chloride.

(b)   Potassium dicyanoargentate (I).

Q. 18. (i)   Write the formula of the following coordination compound:*

Iron (III) hexacyanoferrate (II)

(ii)   What type of isomerism is exhibited by the complex $[Co(NH_3)_5Cl]SO_4$?

(iii)   Write the hybridisation and number of unpaired electrons in the complex $[CoF_6]^{3-}$. (Atomic No. of Co = 27).

Ans. (i)   Molecular formula of Iron(III) hexacyanoferrate(II) is $Fe_4[Fe(CN)_6]_3$.

(ii) $[Co(NH_3)_5Cl]SO_4$ will show Ionisation isomerism and the possible isomers are $[Co(NH_3)_5Cl]SO_4$ and $[Co(NH_3)_5SO_4]Cl$

(iii)   Electronic configuration of Co^{3+} ion is,

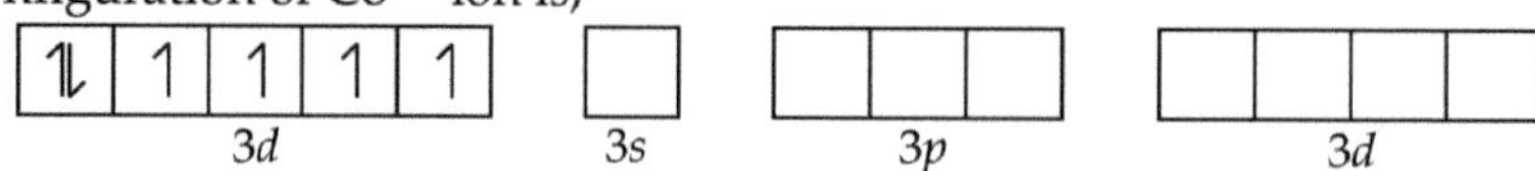

Electronic configuration of sp^3d^3 hybridized (as F^- is a weak field ligand) orbitals of Co^{3+}, with six pairs of electrons from six F^- ions :

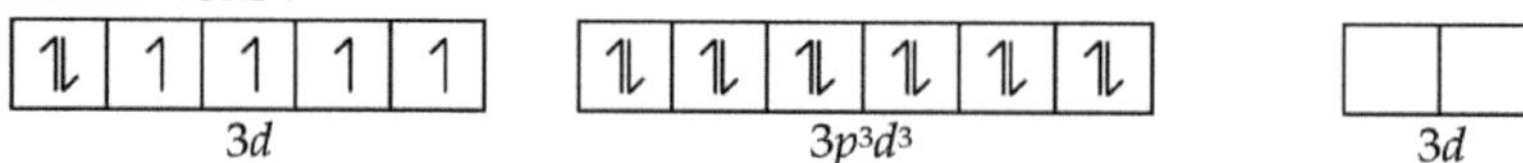

There are 4 unpaired electrons in $[CoF_6]^3$.

Chapter 10. Haloalkanes and Haloarenes

Q. 1. Identify 'A' and 'B' in the following reactions:

(i) $C_2H_5Br \xrightarrow{\text{alc. KOH}} [A] \xrightarrow{Br_2} [B]$

(ii) $CH_3—CH = CH_2 \xrightarrow{\text{HBr}} [A] \xrightarrow{\text{Alc. KOH}} [B]$

Ans. (i) $C_2H_5Br \xrightarrow[\text{KOH}]{\text{alc.}} CH_2 = CH_2 \xrightarrow{\text{Br}_2} \underset{[B]}{CH_2 - CH_2}$ (with Br on each carbon)
$\underset{[A]}{}$

(ii) $CH_3–CH = CH_2 \xrightarrow{\text{HBr}} \underset{[A]}{CH_3 - \underset{\underset{Br}{|}}{CH} - CH_3} \xrightarrow[\text{KOH}]{\text{Alc.}} \underset{[B]}{CH_3 - CH = CH_2}$

Q. 2. (i) Chlorobenzene is extremely less reactive towards nucleophillic substitution reactions. Give three reasons to justify the above statement.

(ii) What happens when chlorobenzene is subjected to strong hydrolysis?*

Ans. (i) **Reasons :** (a) Partial double bond character of the C– Cl bond in aryl halide or chlorobenzene.

(b) The sp^2 hybridized carbon of C–Cl bond in chlorobenzene, holds the electron pair tightly because to break the C–Cl bond.

(c) If ever C – Cl bond breaks, then the phenyl cation formed as a result of that will not be stabilized by resonance, hence S_N1 mechanism is also ruled out.

(ii) Phenol is formed as a result of vigorous (high temperature and pressure) hydrolysis of chlorobenzene.

$$\text{(Chlorobenzene)} + NaOH\ (aq.) \xrightarrow[\text{300 atm}]{\text{673 K}} \text{(Phenol)}$$

Chlorobenzene   Phenol

Q. 3. Which compound in each of the following pair will react faster in S_N2 reaction with OH^- ?*

(i) CH_3Br or CH_3I (ii) $(CH_3)_3CCl$ or CH_3Cl.

Ans. (i) In the S_N2 mechanism, the reactivity of halides for the same alkyl group increases in the order. As bigger the halide (X^-) ion size, better it acts as a leaving group.

$$R—F << R—Cl < R — Br < R — I$$

Therefore, CH_3I will react faster than CH_3Br in S_N2 reactions with OH^-.

(ii) $$H_3C — \underset{\underset{CH_3}{|}}{\overset{\overset{CH_3}{|}}{C}} — Cl \ < \ CH_3 — Cl$$

In S_N^2 mechanism, the lesser the steric hindrance, the faster the attack of the neucleophile.

In case of $(CH_3)_3CCl$, the attack of the nucleophile at the carbon atom is hindered because of the presence of bulky substituents on that carbon atom bearing the leaving group. But, no bulky substituents on the carbon atom bearing the leaving group in CH_3Cl. Hence, CH_3Cl reacts faster than $(CH_3)_3CCl$ in S_N2 reaction with OH^-.

Q. 4. Give the uses of freon 12, DDT, carbon tetrachloride and iodoform.

Ans. Uses of Freon-12:

Freon-12 (dichlorodifluoromethane, CF_2Cl_2) is commonly known as CFC. It is used as a refrigerant in refrigerators and air conditioners. It is also used in aerosol spray propellants such as body sprays, hair sprays, etc. However, it damages the ozone layer. Hence, its manufacture was banned in the United States and many other countries in 1994.

Uses of DDT:

DDT (*p, p*-dichlorodiphenyltrichloroethane) is one of the best known insecticides. It is very effective against mosquitoes and lice. But due to its harmful effects, it was banned in the United States in 1973.

Uses of carbontetrachloride (CCl_4):

(a) It is used for manufacturing refrigerants and as fire extinguisher by the name pyrene.

(b) It is used as feedstock in the synthesis of chlorofluorocarbons and other chemicals.

(c) It is used as a solvent in the manufacture of pharmaceutical products. It is a very good solvent for oils, fats and resins.

(d) Until the mid 1960's, carbon tetrachloride was widely used as a cleaning fluid, a degreasing agent in industries, a spot reamer in homes and as a fire extinguisher.

Uses of iodoform (CHI_3):

Iodoform was used earlier as an antiseptic, now a days it has been replaced by other better substituents containing iodine-due to its un-pleasant smell. The antiseptic property of iodoform is only due to the liberation of free iodine when it comes in contact with the skin.

Q. 5. Out of $C_6H_5CH_2Cl$ and $C_6H_5CHClC_6H_5$, which is more easily hydrolysed by aqueous KOH?

Ans.

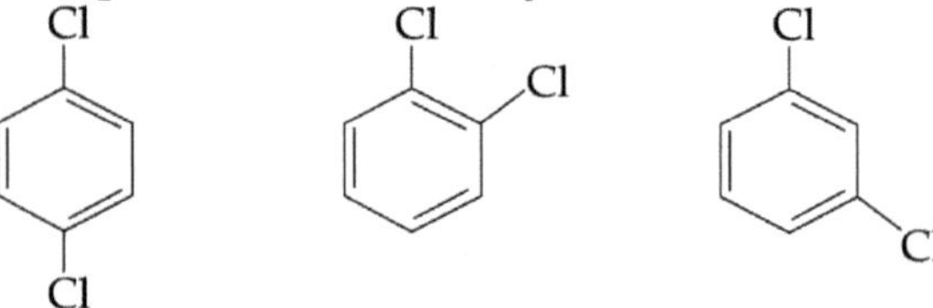

$$C_6H_5 - CH_2 - Cl \xrightarrow[-Cl^-]{} C_6H_5 - \overset{+}{C}H_2$$

Benzyl chloride (1°)   1° Carbocation

$$C_6H_5 - \overset{\overset{Cl}{|}}{C}H - C_6H_5 \xrightarrow[-Cl^-]{} C_6H_5 - \overset{+}{C}H - C_6H_5$$

Chlorodiphenylmethane   2° Carbocation

Hydrolysis by aqueous KOH proceeds through the formation of carbocation *i.e.*, S_N2 mechanism primarily, hence more stable the carbocation the compound is easily hydrolyzed by aqueous KOH. $C_6H_5CH_2Cl$ forms 1°-carbocation, while $C_6H_5CHClC_6H_5$ forms 2°-carbocation, which is more stable than 1°-carbocation. Hence, $C_6H_5CHClC_6H_5$ is hydrolyzed more easily than $C_6H_5CH_2Cl$ by aqueous KOH.

Q. 6. *p*-Dichlorobenzene has higher m.p. and lower solubility than those of *o*- and *m*-isomers. Discuss.

Ans.

p-Dichlorobenzene   *o*-Dichlorobenzene   *m*-Dichlorobenzene

All these three are the position isomers of dichlorobenzene.

p-Dichlorobenzene is more symmetrical than *o*- and *m*-isomers. Hence, if fits more closely in the crystal lattice. Therefore, more energy is required to break the crystal lattice of *p*-dichlorobenzene. As a result, *p*-dichlorobenzene has a higher melting point and solubility than *o*- and *m*-isomers.

Q. 7. The treatment of alkyl chlorides with aqueous KOH leads to the formation of alcohols but in the presence of alcoholic KOH, alkenes are major products. Explain.*

Ans. In an aqueous solution which is a polar medium it completely ionizes KOH to give OH^- ions. OH^- ion is a strong nucleophile, which causes the alkyl chloride to undergo a substitution reaction to form alcohol.

$$R - Cl + KOH_{(aq)} \longrightarrow R - OH + KCl$$

Alkyl chloride   Alcohol

On the other hand in an alcoholic solution of KOH alkoxide (RO^-) ion, is a strong base than OH^- ion. Thus, it can abstract a hydrogen from the β-carbon of the alkyl chloride and form an alkene by eliminating a molecule of HCl.

$$R - \underset{\beta}{C}H_2 - \underset{\alpha}{C}H_2 - Cl + KOH(alc) \longrightarrow R - CH = CH_2 + KCl + H_2O$$

Alkyl chloride   Alkene

As, OH^- ion is highly solvated in an aqueous solution and as a result, the basic character of OH^- ion decreases. Hence, it cannot abstract a hydrogen from the β-carbon.

Q. 8. Why is sulphuric acid not used during the reaction of alcohols with KI?

Ans. In the presence of sulphuric acid (H_2SO_4), KI is oxidised to I_2, because H_2SO_4 is an oxidizing agent, it oxidizes HI (produced in the reaction to I_2).

$$2KI + H_2SO_4 \longrightarrow 2KHSO_4 + 2HI$$
$$2HI + H_2SO_4 \longrightarrow I_2 + SO_2 + H_2O$$

As a result, the reaction between alcohol and HI to produce alkyl iodide cannot occur. Therefore, sulphuric acid is not used during the reaction of alcohols with KI. To solve the problem non-oxidixing acid such as H_3PO_4 is used, which provides HI for the reaction but does not oxidise it to I_2.

---

* are board exam questions from previous years

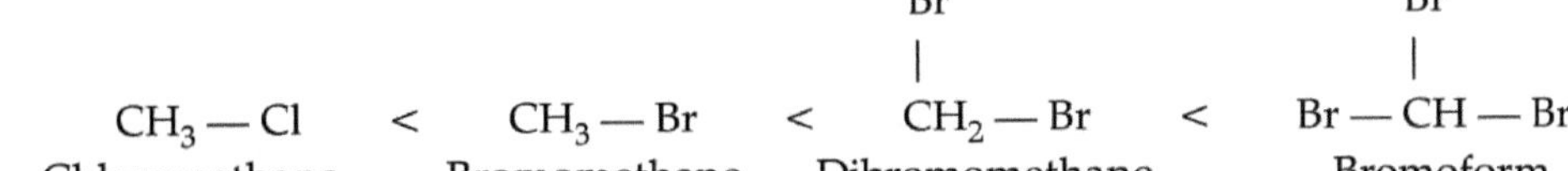

$$KI + H_3PO_4 \longrightarrow KH_2PO_4 + HI$$
$$\text{Potassium dihydrogen Phosphate}$$

Q. 9. Arrange each set of compounds in order of their increasing boiling points.

   (i)   Bromomethane, Bromoform, Chloromethane, Dibromomethane.

   (ii) 1-Chloropropane, Isopropyl chloride, 1-Chlorobutane.

Ans. (i)

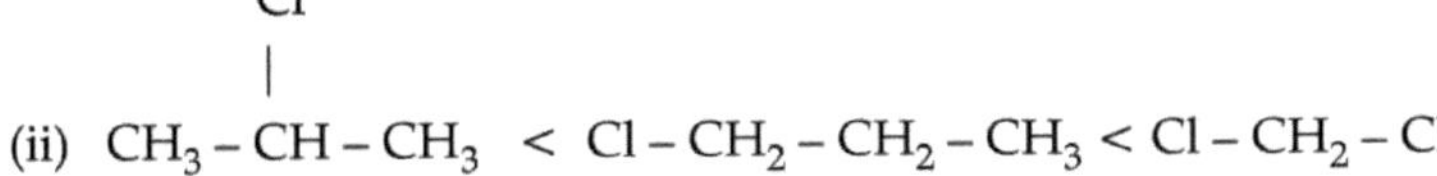

$$\underset{\text{Chloromethane}}{CH_3-Cl} < \underset{\text{Bromomethane}}{CH_3-Br} < \underset{\text{Dibromomethane}}{\overset{\overset{\displaystyle Br}{|}}{CH_2}-Br} < \underset{\text{Bromoform}}{Br-\overset{\overset{\displaystyle Br}{|}}{CH}-Br}$$

For alkyl halides containing the same alkyl group, the boiling point increases with an increase in the atomic mass of the halogen atom and number of substituent halogens.

Since the atomic mass of Br is greater than that of Cl, the boiling point of bromomethane is higher than that of chloromethane.

   (ii)

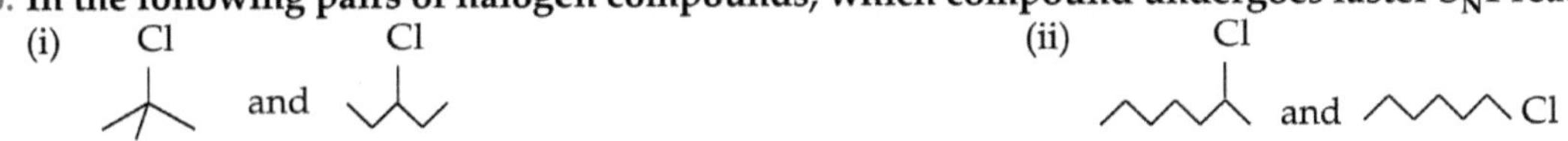

$$\underset{\text{Isopropyl chloride}}{CH_3-\overset{\overset{\displaystyle Cl}{|}}{CH}-CH_3} < \underset{\text{1-chloropropane}}{Cl-CH_2-CH_2-CH_3} < \underset{\text{1-Chlorobutane}}{Cl-CH_2-CH_2-CH_2-CH_3}$$

For alkyl halides containing the same halide, the boiling point increases with an increase in the size of the alkyl group.

Also, the boiling point decreases with an increase in branching in the chain.

Thus, the compounds can be arranged in the increasing order of their boiling points as :

$$\text{Isopropyl chloride} < \text{1-Chloropropane} < \text{1-Chlorobutane}$$

Q. 10. In the following pairs of halogen compounds, which compound undergoes faster S_N1 reaction?[**]

(i) and   (ii) and

Ans. The reactivity in case of S_N1 mechanism depends on the stability of the intermediate carbocation is

(i)

   2-Chloro-2-methylpropane (3°)   3-chloropentane (2°)
         (I)   (II)

S_N1 reaction proceeds via the formation of carbocation. The alkyl halide (I) is 3° while (II) is 2°. Since 3° carbocation is more stable than 2° carbocation. (I) *i.e.,* 2-chloro-2-methylpropane, undergoes faster S_N1 reaction than (II) *i.e.,* 3-chloropentane.

(ii)

   2-Chloroheptane (2°)   1-Chlorohexane (1°)
       (I)   (II)

The alkyl halide (I) is 2° while (II) is 1°, 2° carbocation is more stable than 1° carbocation. Therefore, (I) 2-chloroheptane, undergoes faster S_N1 reaction than (II), 1-chlorohexane.

Q. 11. Which one of the following has the highest dipole moment?

   (i) CH_2Cl_2 (ii) $CHCl_3$ (iii) CCl_4

Ans. (i)   (ii)   (iii)

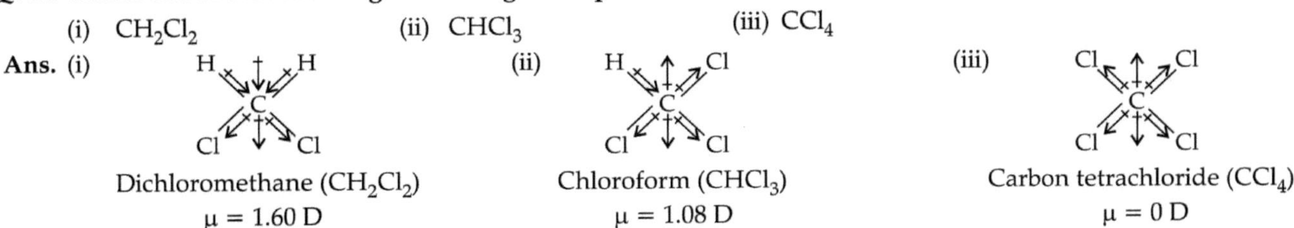

   Dichloromethane (CH_2Cl_2)   Chloroform ($CHCl_3$)   Carbon tetrachloride (CCl_4)
      $\mu = 1.60 \, D$ $\mu = 1.08 \, D$ $\mu = 0 \, D$

CCl_4 is a symmetrical molecule. Therefore, the dipole moments of all four C—Cl bonds cancel each other. Hence, its resultant dipole moment is zero.

While in $CHCl_3$, the resultant of dipole moments of two C—Cl bonds is opposed by the resultant of dipole moments of one C—H bond and one C—Cl bond. Since the resultant of one C—H bond and one C—Cl bond dipole moments is smaller than two C—Cl bonds, the molecule as a whole still have dipole moment. Hence, $CHCl_3$ has a small dipole moment of 1.08 D.

On the other hand, in case of CH_2Cl_2, the resultant of the dipole moments of two C—Cl bonds is strengthened by the resultant of the dipole moments of two C—H bonds. As a whole, CH_2Cl_2 has a higher dipole moment of 1.60 D than $CHCl_3$ *i.e.*, CH_2Cl_2 has the highest dipole moment.

So, the compounds can be arranged in the increasing order of their dipole moments as :

$$CCl_4 < CHCl_3 < CH_2Cl_2$$

Q. 12. **A hydrocarbon C_5H_{10} does not react with chlorine in dark but gives a single monochloro compound C_5H_9Cl in bright sunlight. Identify the hydrocarbon.**

Ans. A hydrocarbon with the molecular formula, C_5H_{10} belongs to the group with a general molecular formula C_nH_{2n}. Hence either it can be alkene or a cycloalkane. Since hydrocarbon does not react with chlorine in the dark, so its not an alkene. Thus, it must be a cycloalkane.

As the hydrocarbon gives a single monochloro compound, C_5H_9Cl by reacting with chlorine in bright sunlight, the hydrocarbon must contain H-atoms that are all equivalent. Thus the compound is cyclopentane.

Cyclopentane (C_5H_{10})

The reactions involved in the question are :

Q. 13. **Write the isomers of the compound having formula C_4H_9Br.**

Ans. There are four isomers of the compound having the formula C_4H_9Br. These isomers are given below:

(a)
$$\overset{4}{C}H_3 - \overset{3}{C}H_2 - \overset{2}{C}H_2 - \overset{1}{C}H_2 - Br$$
1-Bromobutane

(b)
$$\overset{4}{C}H_3 - \overset{3}{C}H_2 - \overset{2}{\underset{\overset{|}{Br}}{C}H} - \overset{1}{C}H_3$$
2-Bromobutane

(c)
$$\overset{3}{C}H_3 - \overset{2}{\underset{\overset{|}{CH_3}}{C}H} - \overset{1}{C}H_2 - Br$$
1-Bromo-2-methylpropane

(d)
$$\overset{3}{C}H_3 - \overset{2}{\underset{\overset{|}{CH_3}}{\underset{\overset{\;}{}}{C}}} - \overset{1}{C}H_3$$
with Br and CH₃ substituents on C-2
2-Bromo-2-methylpropane

Q. 14. **Write the equations for the preparation of 1-iodobutane from**

   (i)   1-butanol   (ii)   1-chlorobutane   (iii)   but-1-ene.

Ans. (i) $CH_3 - CH_2 - CH_2 - CH_2 - OH + HI \xrightarrow{ZnCl_2} CH_3 - CH_2 - CH_2 - CH_2 - I + H_2O$

                1-Butanol   1-Iodobutane

(ii) $CH_3 - CH_2 - CH_2 - CH_2 - Cl + NaI \xrightarrow[\substack{(Finkelstein \\ reaction)}]{dry\ acetone} NaCl + CH_3 - CH_2 - CH_2 - CH_2 - I$

            1-chlorobutane   1-Iodobutane

(iii)   (a) $CH_3 - CH_2 - CH = CH_2 + HBr \xrightarrow[\text{addition)}]{\text{Peroxide (Anti-Markovnikov's}}$

     But-1-ene

$NaBr + CH_3 - CH_2 - CH_2 - CH_2 - I \xleftarrow[\substack{\text{(b)}\\\text{Finkelstein}\\\text{reaction}}]{\text{NaI/dry acetone}} CH_3 - CH_2 - CH_2 - CH_2 - Br$

  1-Iodobutane   1-Bromobutane

Q. 15. (i) Identify the chiral molecule in the following pair:*

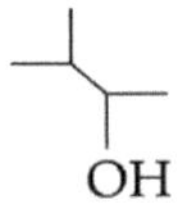

                OH   and   OH
                (a)   (b)

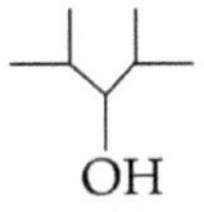

  (ii) Write the structure of the product when chlorobenzene is treated with methyl chloride in the present of sodium metal and dry ether.

  (iii) Write the structure of the alkene formed by dehydrohalogenation of 1-bromo-1-methylcyclohexane with alcoholic KOH.

Ans. (i) The molecule (a) is chiral molecule.

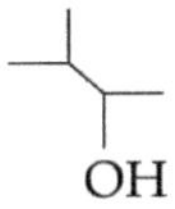

                OH

  (ii) Chlorobenzene reacts with methyl chloride in presence of sodium metal and dry ether to give toluene. This reaction is known as Wurtz-Fittig reaction.

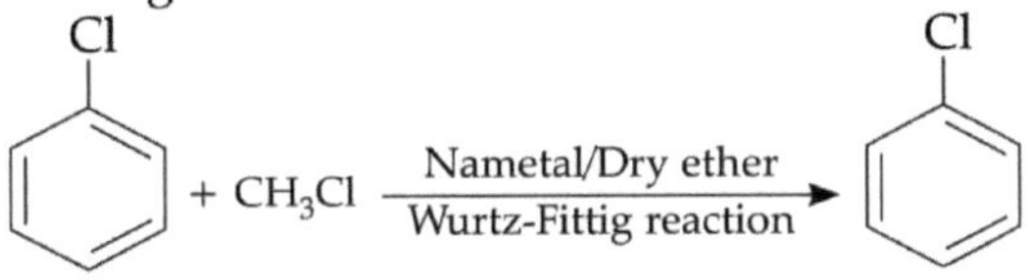

                Cl   Cl

            $+ CH_3Cl \xrightarrow[\text{Wurtz-Fittig reaction}]{\text{Nametal/Dry ether}}$

         Chlorobenzene   Toluene

  (iii) In the 1-bromo-1-methylcyclohexane, all β-hydrogen atoms are equivalent. Thus dehydro-halogenation takes place, in the reaction of this compound with KOH.

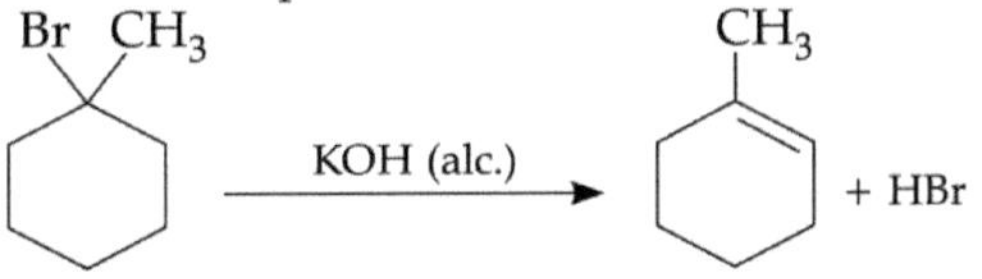

        Br CH_3 CH_3

             $\xrightarrow{\text{KOH (alc.)}}$ $+ HBr$

Chapter 11. Alcohols, Phenols and Ethers

Q. 1. State the products of the following reactions:*

  (i) $CH_3 — CH_2 — CH_2 — O — CH_3 + HBr \longrightarrow$

  (ii) 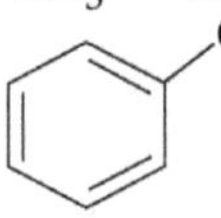 (structure with OCH_3) $+ HBr \longrightarrow$

  (iii) $(CH_3)_3C — O — C_2H_5 + HI \longrightarrow$

Ans. (i) $CH_3 — CH_2 — CH_2 — O — CH_3 + HBr \longrightarrow CH_3{-}CH_2{-}CH_2{-}OH + CH_3Br$
                                           Propan-1-ol

  (ii) 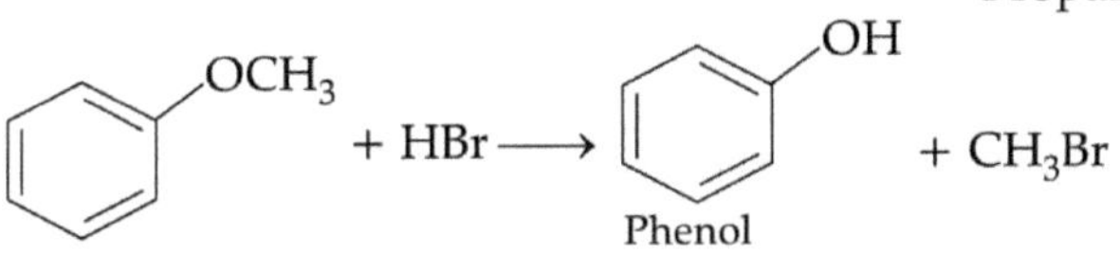 (structure with OCH_3) $+ HBr \longrightarrow$ (structure with OH) $+ CH_3Br$
                              Phenol

  (iii) $(CH_3)_3C — O — C_2H_5 + HI \longrightarrow$ $CH_3 — \underset{\underset{CH_3}{|}}{\overset{\overset{CH_3}{|}}{C}} — I$ $+ C_2H_5OH$

                                     2-Iodo-2-methyl propane

Q. 2. What happens when :

(i)   Diethyl ether is heated with HI at 373 K.

(ii) Sodium salicylate is heated with soda lime.

(iii) Ethanol is heated with conc. H_2SO_4 at 443 K.

Ans. (i) $C_2H_5O-OC_2H_5 + HI \xrightarrow{373\ K} C_2H_5-OH +\ \ C_2H_5I$

$\qquad\qquad\qquad\qquad\qquad\qquad\qquad$ Ethanol $\qquad$ Ethyl iodide

Ethanol and ethyl iodide is formed. In case when HI is in excess then the remaining ethanol will also get converted to ethyl iodide.

$$C_2H_5-OH + HI \longrightarrow C_2H_5-I + H_2O$$

(ii) [structure: sodium salicylate] $+ \underbrace{CaO + NaOH}_{\text{Soda lime}} \xrightarrow{\Delta}$ [Phenol] $+ Na_2CO_3$

(iii) $CH_3CH_2OH \xrightarrow[443\ K]{\text{conc. } H_2SO_4} CH_2 = CH_2 + H_2O$

$\qquad\qquad\qquad\qquad\qquad\qquad$ Ethene

Dehydration of alcohol results in the formation of ethene.

Q. 3. Explain why propanol has higher boiling point than that of the hydrocarbon, butane?

Ans. Propanol undergoes intermolecular H-bonding because of the presence of – OH group whereas Butane does not have any hydrogen bonding.

$$----\overset{\delta+}{H}-\overset{\delta-}{O}-----\overset{\delta+}{H}-\overset{\delta-}{O}-----\overset{\delta+}{H}-\overset{\delta-}{O}-----$$
$$\quad\quad\quad | \qquad\qquad\qquad | \qquad\qquad\qquad |$$
$$\quad\quad\ C_3H_7 \qquad\qquad\ C_3H_7 \qquad\qquad\ C_3H_7$$

Therefore, extra energy is required to break hydrogen bonds. For this reason, propanol has a higher boiling point than hydrocarbon butane, even if both have comparable molecular mass.

Q. 4. Show how will you synthesise:

(i)   1-phenylethanol from a suitable alkene.

(ii) Cyclohexylmethanol using an alkyl halide by an S_N2 reaction.

(iii) Pental-1-ol using a suitable alkyl halide.

Ans. (i)   By acid-catalyzed hydration of ethylbenzene (styrene), 1-phenylethanol can be synthesized.

[structure: Phenylethene] $+ H_2O \underset{}{\overset{H^+}{\rightleftharpoons}}$ [structure: 1-phenylethanol]

$\qquad$ Phenylethene $\qquad\qquad\qquad\qquad\qquad$ 1-phenylethanol

(ii) When chloromethylcyclohexane is treated with potassium hydroxide, cyclohexylmethanol is obtained.

[structure: CH_2Cl cyclohexane] $+ KOH\ (aq) \longrightarrow$ [structure: CH_2OH cyclohexane] $+ KCl$

$\qquad$ Chloromethylcyclohexane $\qquad\qquad$ Cyclohexylmethanol

(iii) When 1-chloropentane is treated with NaOH, pentan-1-ol is produced.

$$CH_3CH_2CH_2CH_2CH_2Cl + NaOH \longrightarrow CH_3CH_2CH_2CH_2CH_2OH + NaCl$$

$\quad$ 1-Chloropentane $\qquad\qquad$ (aq.) $\qquad\qquad\qquad$ Pentan-1-ol

Q. 5. Explain why is *ortho*-nitrophenol more acidic than *ortho*-methoxyphenol?

Ans.

[structure: o-Nitrophenol] $\qquad$ [structure: o-Methoxyphenol]

$\qquad$ o-Nitrophenol $\qquad\qquad\qquad$ o-Methoxyphenol

The nitro-group is an electron-withdrawing group hence this group in the *ortho*-position decreases the electron density in the OH bond. Therefore, it is easier to lose a proton. Also, the o-nitrophenoxide ion formed after the loss of protons is stabilized by resonance. Hence, *ortho*-nitrophenol is a stronger acid.

On the other hand, methoxy group is an electron-releasing group. Hence, it increases the electron density in the O–H bond so, the proton cannot be given out easily.

For this reason, *ortho*-nitrophenol is more acidic than *ortho*-methoxyphenol.

Q. 6. Explain how does the – OH group attached to a carbon of benzene ring activate it towards electrophilic substitution ?

Ans. The – OH group is an electron-donating group *i.e.*, shows (+ R) effect. Thus, it increases the electron density in the benzene ring as shown in the given resonance structure of phenol.

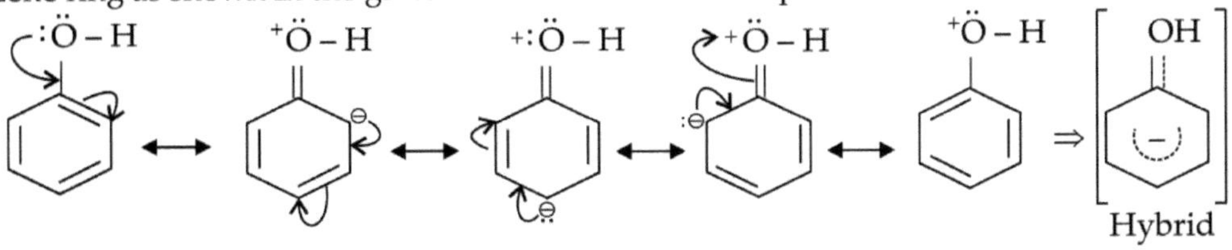

Hence, the benzene ring is activated towards electrophilic substitution.

Q. 7. Explain the fact that in aryl alkyl ethers

    (i)   The alkoxy group activates the benzene ring towards electrophilic substitution.

    (ii) It directs the incoming substituents to *ortho* and *para* positions in benzene ring.

Ans. (i)

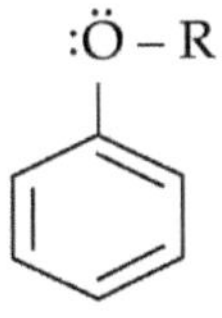

Aryl alkyl ether

In aryl alkyl ethers, due to the +R effect of the alkoxy group, the electron density in the benzene ring increases in the *ortho* and *para* position as shown in the following resonance structure.

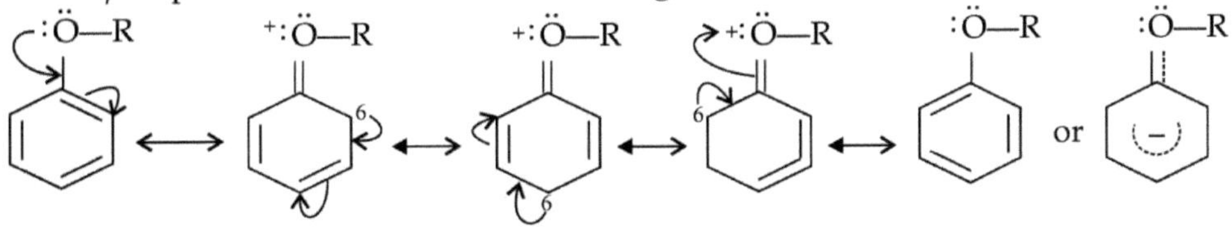

Thus, benzene is activated towards electrophilic substitution by the alkoxy group.

    (ii) It can also be observed from the resonance structures that the electron density increases more at the *ortho* and *para* positions than at the *meta* position. As a result, the incoming substituents are directed to the *ortho* and *para* positions in the benzene ring and we get mixture of isomeric products.

Q. 8. Predict the products of the following reactions :

    (i) 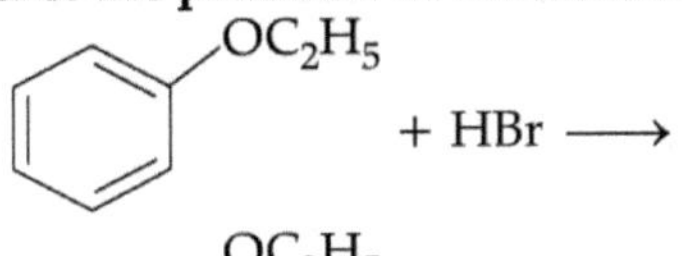 OC_2H_5 + HBr ⟶

    (ii) 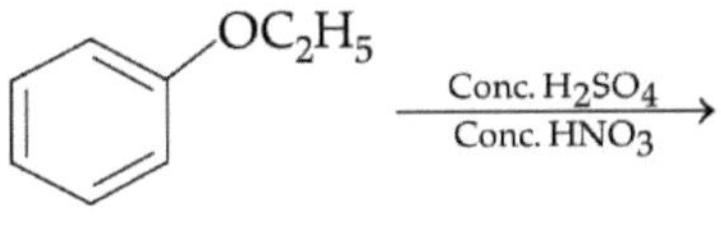 OC_2H_5 $\xrightarrow{\text{Conc. } H_2SO_4 \text{, Conc. } HNO_3}$

Ans. (i) 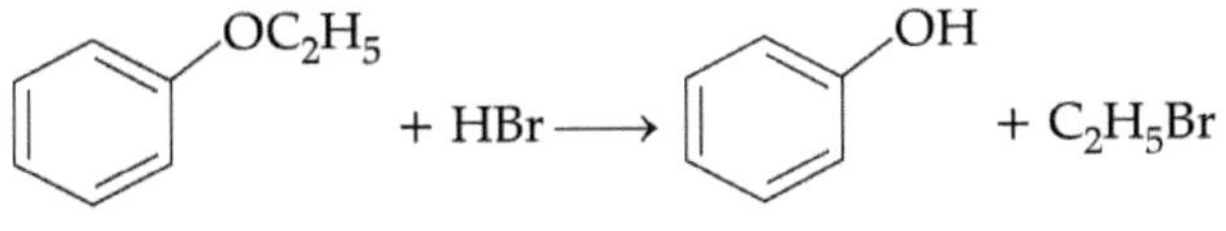 OC_2H_5 + HBr ⟶ OH + C_2H_5Br

    Ethoxybenzene   Phenol   Bromoethane

    (ii) 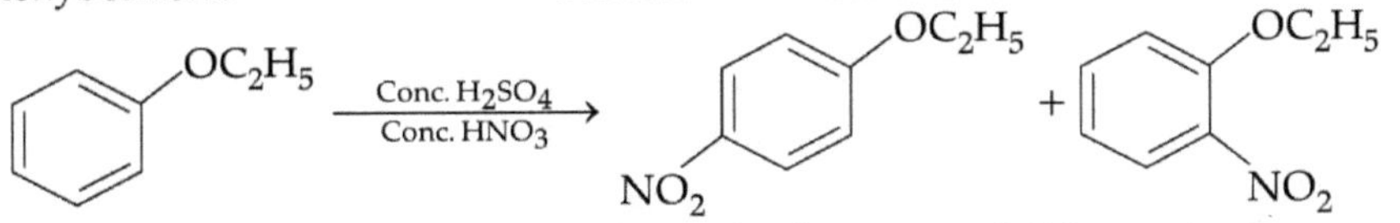 OC_2H_5 $\xrightarrow{\text{Conc. } H_2SO_4 \text{, Conc. } HNO_3}$ OC_2H_5 (NO_2) + OC_2H_5 (NO_2)

    Ethoxybenzene   4-Ethoxynitrobenzene   2-Ethoxynitrobenzene

                              (Major)   (Minor)

Ethoxy group is an activating group, hence 'o' and 'p' directing.

Q. 9. An alcohol of unknown structure gave a positive Lucas test in about five minutes. On heating the alcohol with conc. H_2SO_4, it gives an alkene, formula C_4H_8. Ozonolysis of the same alkene gives a single product C_2H_4O. Predict the structure of the alcohol.

Ans. A positive Lucas test in five minutes indicates the secondary nature of the alcohol.

The alkene produced as a result of dehydration by conc. H_2SO_4 is C_4H_8, which on ozonolysis provides single product. Hence, the double bond of alkene must be at symmetrical position.

So, alkene must be But-2-ene.

$$CH_3 - CH = CH - CH_3 \xrightarrow[H_2O]{O_3} CH_3 - CHO + CH_3CHO$$
$$\text{But-2-ene}$$

So the alcohol must be Butan-2-ol.

$$\begin{array}{c} OH \\ | \\ CH_3 - CH - CH_2 - CH_3 \\ \text{Butan-2-ol} \end{array} \textit{ i.e., a secondary alcohol.}$$

Chapter 12. Aldehydes, Ketones and Carboxylic Acids

Q. 1. Account for the following:

(i) Aldehydes are more volatile than alcohols.

(ii) Carboxylic acids do not give the characteristic reactions of carbonyl group.

(iii) Treatment of benzaldehyde with HCN produces a racemic mixture which cannot be separated even by fractional distillation.*

Ans. (i) In aldehydes the intermolecular forces of attraction are dipole-dipole interactions, which are far weaker than the hydrogen bondings present in the alcohols. Hence aldehydes are more volatile than alcohols.

(ii) The carboxylic group in carboxylic acids is a resonance hybrid of the given structures:

Hence, the carbonyl carbon of the resonance hybrid, of structure (I), (II) and (III) is less electrophilic than the carbonyl carbon of aldehydes and ketones. Therefore, it does not give some characteristic reactions like 2-4 DNP, oxime test *etc.*, like carbonyl compounds.

(iii) On treating benzaldehyde with HCN, nucleophilic addition take place and tetrahedral intermediate is formed.

The carbon in this intermediate is a chiral carbon and is sp^3 hybridised.

H^+ get added to this, resulting in the formation of an equimolar mixture of two enantiomers.

Q. 2. Account for the following:*

(i) Benzoic acid does not undergo Friedel-Craft's reaction.

(ii) pK_a value of chloroacetic acid is lower than pK_a of acetic acid.

(iii) Acetyl chloride is a better acetylating agent than acetic acid.

Ans. (i) – COOH group of benzoic acid is highly deactivating towards electrophilic attack on benzene ring, as it withdraws the electron density towards itself. Hence Friedel-Craft's reaction, involving an electrophilic attack of alkyl or acyl group in presence of $AlCl_3$ (anhydrous) does not happen.

(ii) Higher the acidic strength, lower is the pK_a value

$$pK_a = - \log K_a$$

As chloroacetic acid has electron withdrawing Cl group present at the α-carbon atom, it is a stronger acid and hence releases H^+ easily compared to acetic acid.

$$CH_3COOH > CClCH_2COOH$$
$$\quad pK_a \qquad\qquad pK_a$$

Therefore acetic acid is weaker acid and have higher pK_a value than chloroacetic acid.

(iii) Acetylation occurs as a result of attack of CH_3CO^+ group. As acetyl of chloride readily dissociate to provide the electrophile because of polar (C – Cl) bond, compared to acetic acid. Its a stronger acetylating agent.

$$CH_3 - \overset{\overset{O}{\|}}{C} - Cl \rightleftharpoons CH_3 - \overset{\overset{O}{\|}}{C} + Cl^-$$
$$+$$
(acetyl carbocation)

$$CH_3 - \overset{\overset{O}{\|}}{C} - OH \rightleftharpoons CH_3 - \overset{\overset{O}{\|}}{C} + O^- \quad +H^+$$
(acetate ion)

Q. 3. Answer the following:

(i)   What is glacial acetic acid?

(ii) Name a reagent to convert carboxylic acids directly to alcohols.

(iii) What are fatty acids?

Ans. (i)   100% pure acetic acid is called glacial acetic acid. It has an ice like appearance while dry, hence the name coined glacial.

(ii) Lithium aluminium hydride.

(iii) Higher molecular mass carboxylic acids are called fatty acids. These are generally obtained by saponification of oils and fats.

Q. 4. Account for the following:

(i) p-Nitrobenzoic acid has higher K_a than benzoic acid.*

(ii) Carboxylic acids have higher boiling points than alcohols.

(iii) Acetone is soluble in water but benzophenone is not.

Ans. (i)   Nitro group is an electron withdrawing group. Hence, its presence in *para* position makes the release of H^+ ion from benzoic acid easier than unsubstituted benzoic acid. Hence p-Nitrobenzoic acid is more acidic and have higher K_a value.

(ii) The extent of hydrogen bonding in carboxylic acids is far more than alcohols. The OH bond of –(COOH) group is far more polarized than OH bond of alcohols; because of presence of electron withdrawing carbonyl group. Additional H–bonds are also formed by the negatively charged oxygen atom of carbonyl carbon with a positively charged hydrogen of some adjacent molecule.

$$R-C \overset{\overset{\delta-}{O} - - - \overset{\delta+}{H} - O}{\underset{\underset{\delta-}{O} - \overset{\delta+}{H} - - - O}{}} C-R$$

(iii) Acetone can undergo some degree of hydrogen bonding with water molecules by the presence of polar carbonyl $\left(\overset{\overset{O}{\|}}{C}\right)$ group. In case of benzophenone the carbonyl group is sterically hindered by two big phenyl group $(C_6H_5COC_6H_5)$, hence the carbonyl oxygen is masked and cannot participate in hydrogen bonding with water.

Q. 5. An organic compound A $(C_7H_6Cl_2)$ on treatment with NaOH solution gives another compound B (C_7H_6O). B on oxidation gives an acid C$(C_7H_6O_2)$ which on treatment with a mixture of conc. HNO_3 and H_2SO_4 gives compound D $(C_7H_5NO_4)$. B on treatment with conc. NaOH gives a compound E (C_7H_8O) and C_6H_5COONa. Deduce the structures of [A], [B], [C], [D] and [E].*

Ans. [A] seems like an organic compound of benzene from formula $C_7H_6Cl_2$.

[B] on oxidation gives [C], hence [B] must be (benzene ring with CHO) and [C] must be (benzene ring with COOH).

Therefore [A] will be

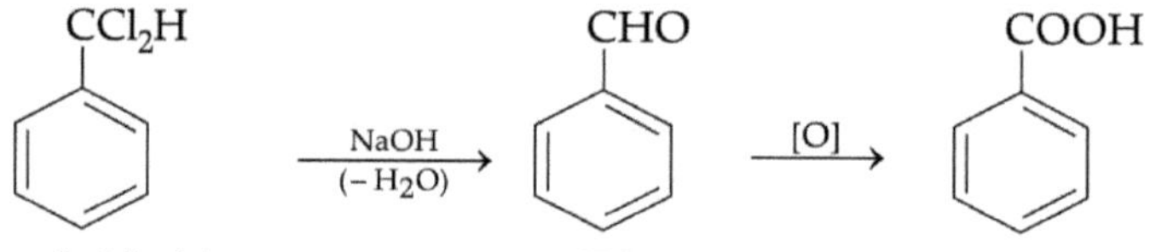

$$
\text{Benzal chloride (} CCl_2H\text{)} \xrightarrow[(-H_2O)]{NaOH} \text{[B] Benzaldehyde (CHO)} \xrightarrow{[O]} \text{Benzoic acid [C] (COOH)}
$$

$$
\text{[C] (COOH)} \xrightarrow[\text{Conc. } H_2SO_4]{\text{Conc. } HNO_3} \textit{m}\text{-Nitrobenzoic acid [D] (COOH, } NO_2\text{)}
$$

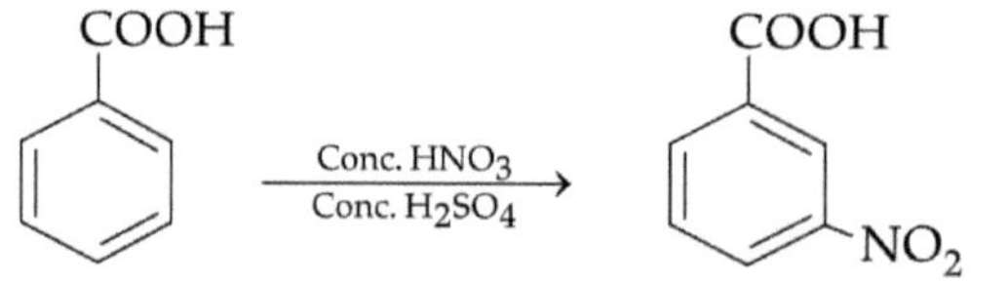

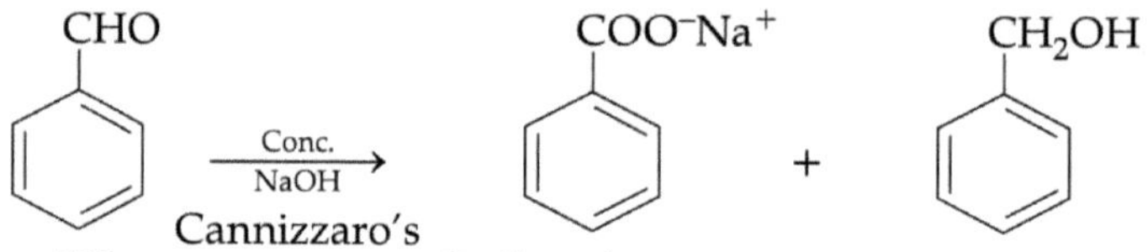

$$
\text{[B] (CHO)} \xrightarrow[\text{NaOH}]{\text{Conc.}} \text{Cannizzaro's Reaction} \longrightarrow \text{Sodium benzoate (} COO^-Na^+\text{)} + \text{Benzyl alcohol [E] (} CH_2OH\text{)}
$$

Q. 6. Predict the products of the following reactions:

(i) 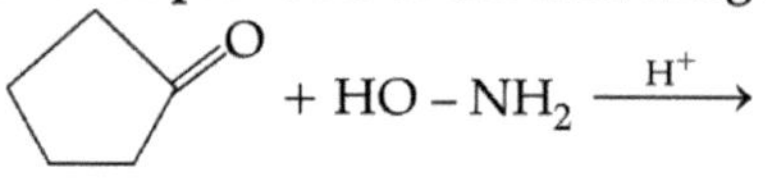 Cyclopentanone $+ HO-NH_2 \xrightarrow{H^+}$

(ii) 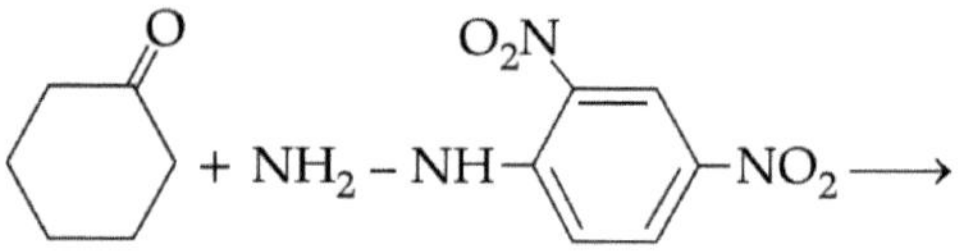 Cyclohexanone $+ NH_2-NH-$(2,4-dinitrophenyl, O_2N, NO_2) $\longrightarrow$

(iii)
$$
R-CH=CH-CHO + NH_2 - \overset{\overset{\displaystyle O}{\|}}{C} - NH - NH_2 \xrightarrow{H^-}
$$

(iv) 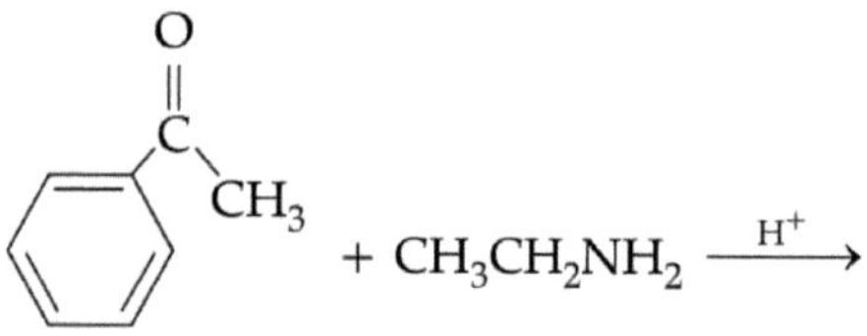 Acetophenone ($\overset{\overset{\displaystyle O}{\|}}{C}-CH_3$) $+ CH_3CH_2NH_2 \xrightarrow{H^+}$

Ans. (i)

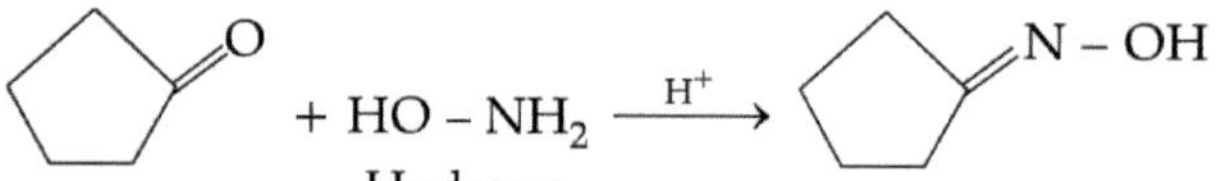

$$
\text{Cyclohexanone} + \underset{\substack{\text{Hydroxy} \\ \text{amine}}}{HO-NH_2} \xrightarrow{H^+} \text{Cyclopentanoxime (} N-OH\text{)}
$$

(ii)

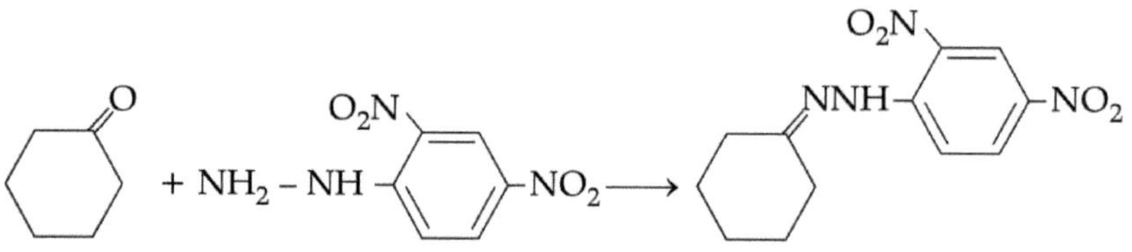

$$
\underset{\text{Cyclohexanone}}{\text{(cyclohexanone)}} + \underset{\substack{\text{2, 4-Dinitrophenyl} \\ \text{hydrazine}}}{NH_2-NH-(O_2N, NO_2)} \longrightarrow \underset{\substack{\text{2, 4-Dinitrophenylhydrazine} \\ \text{cyclohexanone}}}{=NNH-(O_2N, NO_2)}
$$

(iii)

$$
R-CH=CH-CHO + NH_2 - \overset{\overset{\displaystyle O}{\|}}{C} - NH - NH_2 \xrightarrow{H^+} R-CH=CH-CH=N-NH-\overset{\overset{\displaystyle O}{\|}}{C}-NH_2
$$

(iv)

$$\text{Acetophenone} \quad \underset{\text{(Acetophenone)}}{\overset{O}{\underset{CH_3}{\|}}} + CH_3CH_2NH_2 \xrightarrow{H^+} \underset{H_3C}{\overset{}{}}C = N - CH_2CH_3$$

Q. 7. (A), (B) and (C) are three non-cyclic functional isomers of a carbonyl compound with molecular formula C_4H_8O. Isomers (A) and (C) give positive Tollens' test whereas isomer (B) does not give Tollens' test but gives positive Iodoform test. Isomers (A) and (B) on reduction with Zn (Hg)/conc. HCl give the same product (D).**

(i) Write the structures of (A), (B), (C) and (D).

(ii) Out of (A), (B) and (C) isomers, which one is least reactive towards addition of HCN?

Ans. (i) Compound A and C give positive Tollen's test which indicates that they are aldehydes. Compound C gives Iodoform test which means it contains a carbonyl group with a methyl group attached to the carbonyl carbon so, with formula C_4H_8O the structure of compound would be $CH_3COCH_2CH_3$ (Butanone). Now upon reduction with Zn(Hg)/conc. HCl, the corresponding alkanes are obained, so reduction of B gives Butane (D), so the isomer A have to be a linear chain aldehyde (Butanal), giving Butane (compound D) on reduction. So, the last isomer possible is compound C, 2-Methyl propanaldehyde. As shown below:

$$H_3C\diagup\diagdown CH_3 \xrightarrow{\text{NaOH, }I_2} CH_3CH_2COONa \xrightarrow[\text{Clemmenson reduction}]{\text{Zn(Hg)/Conc. HCl}} H_3C\diagup\diagdown CH_3$$

$$H_3C\diagdown\diagup\underset{O}{\overset{H}{\diagup}} \xleftarrow{\text{Zn(Hg) HCl}} H_3C\diagdown\underset{CH_3}{\overset{O}{\diagup}}-H$$

(ii) Out of the three isomers A, B and C compound B (Butanone) would be least reactive towards addition of HCl as the carbonyl carbon is sterically hindered and most reactive would be compound A (Butanal) towards addition of HCN.

Chapter 13. Amines

Q. 1. Account for the following:

(i) Tertiary amines does not undergo acylation reaction.

(ii) *o*-Toluidine is less basic than aniline.

Ans. (i) Tertiary amines can't undergo acylation as they dont have any replaceable hydrogen atom. Tertiary amines thus are non-reactive towards acylation.

(ii) *o*-Toluidine is less basic than aniline because of *ortho* effect. The *ortho* position substitution makes it difficult for $-NH_2$ group to donate electron inspite of the electron donating tendency of (CH_3) methyl group as a substituent.

Q. 2. Justify the following:

(i) Observed order of basicity in amines.**

$Et_2NH > Et_3N > EtNH_2$ in aqueous solution whereas $Et_3N > Et_2NH > EtNH_2$ in gas phase.

(ii) $[CH_3NH_3]^+ OH^-$ is stronger base than $[NH_4{}^+]^+OH^-$.

Ans. (i) In gas phase, the inductive effect of ethyl groups are only responsible for increasing the basic strength of amines, as there is no solvation effect present. Hence order is

$$\underset{\text{3° (maximum)}}{Et_3N} > \underset{2°}{Et_2NH} > \underset{1°}{EtNH_2}$$

But in case of aqueous medium the solvation effect plays a role. The 1° amine is solvated to the maximum extent because of formation of hydrogen bonds. Hence, it is most stable based on H-bonding the basicity of amines follows order 1° > 2° > 3°.

The third factor steric effect also hinders the basicity of 3° amines as H^+/electrophile finds it difficult to approach the lone pair of electrons in presence of three bulky groups. In case of ethylamines as +I effect is stronger than methyl group (methylamines) hence overall order of basicity in aqueous medium is thus,

$$\underset{2° \quad 3° \quad 1°}{Et_2NH > Et_3N > EtNH_2}$$

(ii) Presence of electron donating group increases the basicity of $[CH_3NH_3]^+OH^-$ ion compared to $[NH_4]^+OH^-$ salt.

Q. 3. Arrange the following in increasing order of their basic strength:

(i) $C_2H_5NH_2$, $C_6H_5NH_2$, NH_3, $C_6H_5CH_2NH_2$ and $(C_2H_5)_2NH$.

(ii) $C_2H_5NH_2$, $(C_2H_5)_2NH$, $(C_2H_5)_3N$, $C_6H_5NH_2$.

(iii) CH_3NH_2, $(CH_3)_2NH$, $(CH_3)_3N$, $C_6H_5NH_2$, $C_6H_5CH_2NH_2$.

Ans. (i) Considering the inductive effect of alkyl groups. Basicity of amines depends upon : (a) inductive effect of alkyl or aryl group and (b) steric hindrance of the alkyl or aryl group towards the electrophile. Amines can be arranged in the increasing order of their basic strengths as:

$$C_6H_5NH_2 < NH_3 < C_2H_5NH_2 < (C_2H_5)_2NH$$

Due to the – I effect of C_6H_5 group, the electron density on the N-atom in $C_6H_5CH_2NH_2$ is lower than that on the N-atom in $C_2H_5NH_2$, but more than that in NH_3. Therefore, the given compounds can be arranged in the order of their basic strengths as :

$$C_6H_5NH_2 \quad < NH_3 \quad < C_6H_5CH_2NH_2 < C_2H_5NH_2 < (C_2H_5)_2NH$$
$$(1°)\ \text{aniline} \quad \text{ammonia} \qquad\qquad 1° \qquad\qquad 1° \qquad\qquad 2°$$

(ii) Considering the inductive and the steric hindrance of the alkyl groups, $C_6H_5NH_2$, $(C_2H_5)_2NH$ and their basic strengths is as follows:

$$C_6H_5NH_2 < C_2H_5NH_2 < (C_2H_5)_3N < (C_2H_5)_2NH$$

Ethyl group has a prominent +I effect, which balances steric hindrance.

(iii) Considering the inductive effect and the steric hindrance of alkyl groups, CH_3NH_2, $(CH_3)_2NH$, and $(CH_3)_3N$ can be arranged in the increasing order of their basic strength as:

$(CH_3)_3N < CH_3NH_2 < (CH_3)_2NH$ *i.e.*, $3° < 1° < 2°$, as steric hindrance is more prominent than +I effect of methyl group.

In $C_6H_5NH_2$, N is directly attached to the benzene ring. Thus, the lone pair of electrons on the N-atom is delocalized over the benzene ring. In $C_6H_5CH_2NH_2$, N is not directly attached to the benzene ring. Thus, its lone pair is not delocalized over the benzene ring. Therefore, the electrons on the N atom are more easily available for protonation in $C_6H_5CH_2NH_2$ than in $C_6H_5NH_2$ *i.e.*, $C_6H_5CH_2NH_2$ is more basic than $C_6H_5NH_2$. Due to the – I effect of C_6H_5 group, the electron density on the N-atom in $C_6H_5CH_2NH_2$ is lower than on the N-atom in $(CH_3)_3N$. Therefore, $(CH_3)_3N$ is more basic than $C_6H_5CH_2NH_2$. Thus, the given compounds can be arranged in the increasing order of their basic strengths as follows:

$$C_6H_5NH_2 < C_6H_5CH_2NH_2 < (CH_3)_3N < CH_3NH_2 < (CH_3)_2NH$$
$$\qquad\qquad\qquad\qquad\qquad\qquad 3° \qquad\quad 1° \qquad\quad 2°$$

Q. 4. Arrange the following:

(i) In decreasing order of the pK_b values:
$C_2H_5NH_2$, $C_6H_5NHCH_3$, $(C_2H_5)_2NH$ and $C_6H_5NH_2$.

(ii) In increasing order of basic strength:
$C_6H_5NH_2$, $C_6H_5N(CH_3)_2$, $(C_2H_5)NH$ and CH_3NH_2.

(iii) In increasing order of basic strength:
   (a) Aniline, *p*-nitroaniline and *p*-toluidine
   (b) $C_6H_5NH_2$, $C_6H_5NHCH_3$, $C_6H_5CH_2NH_2$.

(iv) In decreasing order of basic strength in gas phase:
$C_2H_5NH_2$, $(C_2H_5)_2NH$, $(C_2H_5)_3N$ and NH_3.

(v) In increasing order of boiling point:
C_2H_5OH, $(CH_3)_2NH$, $C_2H_5NH_2$.

(vi) In increasing order of solubility in water:*
$C_6H_5NH_2$, $(C_2H_5)_2NH$, $C_2H_5NH_2$.

Ans. (i) Higher pK_b value, lower is the basic strength. In $C_2H_5NH_2$, only one $-C_2H_5$ group is present while in $(C_2H_5)_2NH$, two $-C_2H_5$ groups are present. Thus, the +I effect is more in $(C_2H_5)_2NH$ than in $C_2H_5NH_2$. Therefore, the electron density over the N-atom is more in $(C_2H_5)_2NH$ than in $C_2H_5NH_2$. Hence, $(C_2H_5)_2NH$ is more basic than $C_2H_5NH_2$.

$C_6H_5NHCH_3$ is more basic than $C_6H_5NH_2$ and less basic than $(C_2H_5)_2NH$ and $C_2H_5NH_2$ due to the delocalization of the lone pair in the former two. Hence, the order of increasing basicity of the given compounds are as follows:

$$C_6H_5NH_2 < C_6H_5NHCH_3 < C_2H_5NH_2 < (C_2H_5)_2NH$$
Therefore decreasing pK_b values are:
$$C_6H_5NH_2 > C_6H_5NHCH_3 > C_2H_5NH_2 > (C_2H_5)_2NH$$

(ii) $C_6H_5N(CH_3)_2$ is more basic than $C_6H_5NH_2$ due to presence of $+I$ effect of two $-CH_3$ groups in $C_6H_5N(CH_3)_2$. Further, CH_3NH_2 contains one $-CH_3$ group while $(C_2H_5)_2NH$ contains two $-C_2H_5$ groups. Thus, $(C_2H_5)_2NH$ is more basic than $C_2H_5NH_2$.

Now, $C_6H_5N(CH_3)_2$ is less basic than CH_3NH_2 because of the $-I$ effect of $-C_6H_5$ group.

Hence, the decreasing order of the basic strengths of the given compounds is as follows:
$$(C_2H_5)_2NH > CH_3NH_2 > C_6H_5N(CH_3)_2 > C_6H_5NH_2$$

(iii) (a)

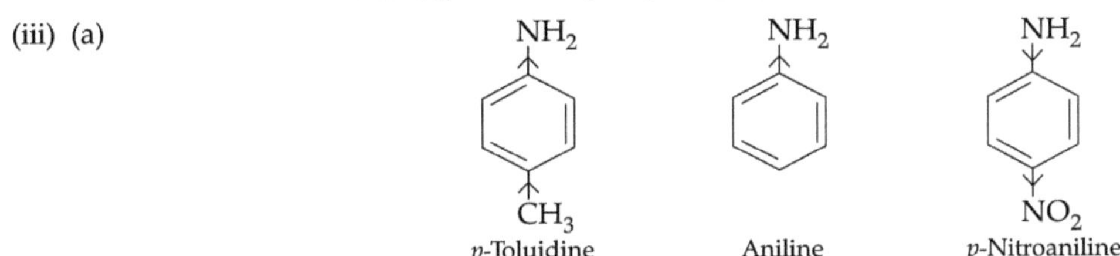

In p-toluidine, the presence of electron-donating $-CH_3$ group increases the electron density on the N-atom. Thus, p-toluidine is more basic than aniline.

On the other hand, the presence of electron withdrawing $-NO_2$ group decreases the electron density over the N-atom in p-nitroaniline. Thus, p-nitroaniline is less basic than aniline. Hence, the increasing order of the basic strengths of the given compounds is as follows:
$$p\text{-Nitroaniline} < \text{Aniline} < p\text{-Toluidine}.$$

(b) $C_6H_5NHCH_3$ is more basic than $C_6H_5NH_2$ due to the presence of electron-donating $-CH_3$ group in $C_6H_5NHCH_3$. Again, in $C_6H_5NHCH_3$, $-C_6H_5$ group is directly attached to the N-atom. However, it is not so in $C_6H_5CH_2NH_2$. Thus, in $C_6H_5NHCH_3$, the $-I$ effect of $-C_6H_5$ group decreases the electron density over the N-atom. Therefore, $C_6H_5CH_2NH_2$ is more basic than $C_6H_5NHCH_3$. Hence, the increasing order of the basic strengths of the given compounds is as follows:
$$C_6H_5NH_2 < C_6H_5NHCH_3 < C_6H_5CH_2NH_2$$

(iv) In the gas phase, there is a no solvation effect. Hence, the basic strength only depends upon the $+I$ effect. Also, greater the number of alkyl groups, the higher is the $+I$ effect. Hence decreasing basic strength follows order:
$$(C_2H_5)_3N > (C_2H_5)_2NH > C_2H_5NH_2 > NH_3$$

(v) The boiling point of compounds depend on the extent of H-bonding present in that compound. The more extensive the H-bonding in the compound, the higher is the boiling point. $(CH_3)_2NH$ contains only one H-atom whereas $C_2H_5NH_2$ contains two H-atoms.

Hence, the boiling point of $C_2H_5NH_2$ is higher than that of $(CH_3)_2NH$. Further, O is more electronegative than N. Thus, C_2H_5OH form stronger H-bonds than $C_2H_5NH_2$. As a result, the boiling point of C_2H_5OH is higher than that of $C_2H_5NH_2$ and $(CH_3)_2NH$. Therefore, compounds can be arranged in the increasing order of their boiling points as follows:
$$(CH_3)_2NH < C_2H_5NH_2 < C_2H_5OH$$

(vi) The more extensive the H-bonding, the higher is the solubility. $C_2H_5NH_2$ contains two H-atoms whereas $(C_2H_5)_2NH$ contains only one H-atom. Thus, $C_2H_5NH_2$ undergoes more extensive H-bonding than $(C_2H_5)_2NH$. Aniline has a bulky hydrophobic part. Hence less solubility of $C_6H_5NH_2$ than $C_2H_5NH_2$ and $(C_2H_5)_2NH$.

Hence, the increasing order of their solubility in water is as follows:
$$C_6H_5NH_2 < (C_2H_5)_2NH < C_2H_5NH_2$$

Q. 5. Give plausible explanation for each of the following:
(i) Why amines are less acidic than alcohols of comparable molecular masses?
(ii) Why do primary amines have higher boiling point than tertiary amines?
(iii) Why are aliphatic amines stronger bases than aromatic amines.*

Ans. (i) Amines undergo protonation to give amide ion as
$$R - NH_2 \longrightarrow R - \overline{N}H + H^+$$
$$\text{Amide ion}$$

Similarly, alcohol loses a proton to give alkoxide ion as conjugate base.

$$R-OH \longrightarrow R-\bar{O}+H^+$$

$$\text{Alcohol} \qquad \text{Alkoxide} \atop \text{ion}$$

In an amide ion, the negative charge is on the N-atom whereas in alkoxide ion, the negative charge is on the O-atom. Since O is more electronegative than N, O can accommodate the negative charge more easily than N. As a result, the amide ion is less stable than the alkoxide ion. Hence, amines are less acidic than alcohols of comparable molecular masses.

(ii) In a molecule of tertiary amine, there are no H-atoms whereas in primary amines, two hydrogen atoms are present. Due to the presence of H-atoms, primary amines undergo extensive intermolecular H-bonding.

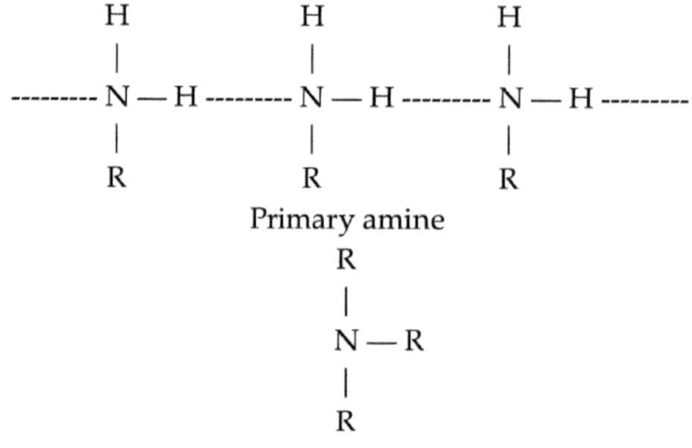

As a result, extra energy is required to separate the molecules of primary amines. Hence, primary amines have higher boiling points than tertiary amines.

(iii) Due to the –I effect of the benzene ring, the electrons on the N-atom are involved in resonance and are available as base. Therefore, the electrons on the N-atom in aromatic amines cannot be donated easily. This explains why aliphatic amines are stronger bases than aromatic amines.

Chapter 14. Biomolecules

Q. 1. Give two functions of protein in living organisms. State the differences between polypeptide and protein.

Ans. (i) Proteins are the main constituents of protoplasm of animal and plant body cells and tissues. They are the building blocks.

(ii) Enzymes, hormones and antibodies are various types of proteins. They act as biocatalyst, regulate metabolic activities and fight against toxic germs as antibodies.

When a large number of peptide bonds are present we call it a polypeptide chain. Only those polypeptides which have molecular mass more than 10,000 u are called proteins.

Q. 2. Describe the mechanism of enzyme activity.

Ans. (i) Enzymes are very specific in their actions. They bind to the active site of the substrate and form enzyme substrate complex (E + S = ES).

(ii) The complex ES, promotes the chemical reaction generally by bringing down the activation energy required for the reaction to occur.

Once the products are formed the enzyme returns back to its original shape.

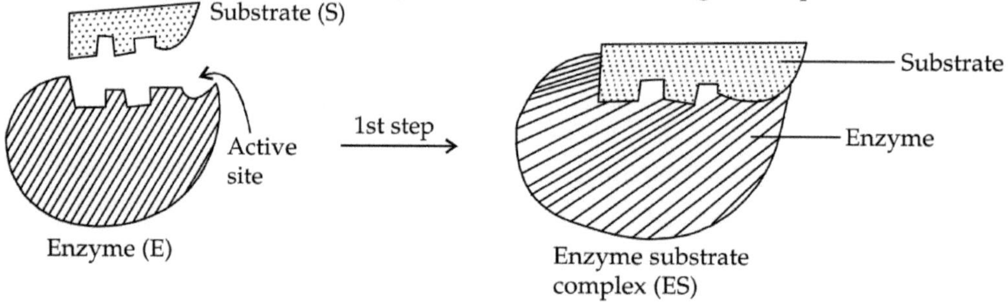

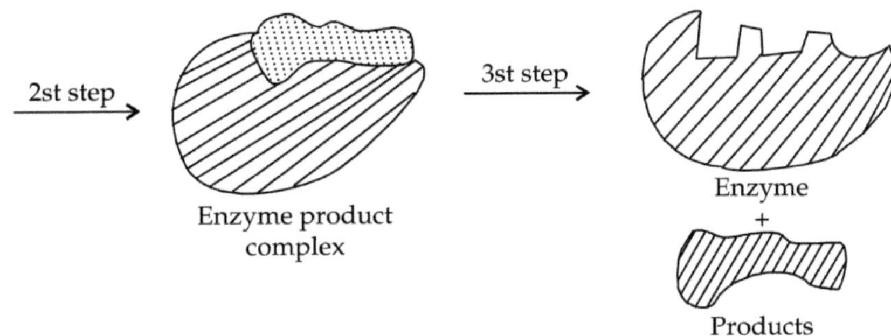

Also enzymes work best under optimal pH and temperature. They are required in very small quantity.

Q. 3. Answer the following:*
    (i)   Where does protein synthesis occurs?
    (ii) How do 64 codons code for only 20 α-amino acids?
    (iii) Which bases of codon are most important for coding?

Ans. (i)   Proteins are synthesized inside the cell cytoplasm.
    (ii) Codons are each three letter words or triplets. More than one codon can code for same amino acids hence 20 α-amino acids.
    (iii) Every first two bases of codon are most important for coding.

Q. 4. Explain the following:*
    (i)   Pyranose ring of glucose.
    (ii) Full form of DNA and RNA.
    (iii) Chemical name and source of vitamin C.

Ans. (i)   Pyranose ring is a six membered heterocyclic ring with an oxygen atom. It is the base structure for both α and β-D-glucose.

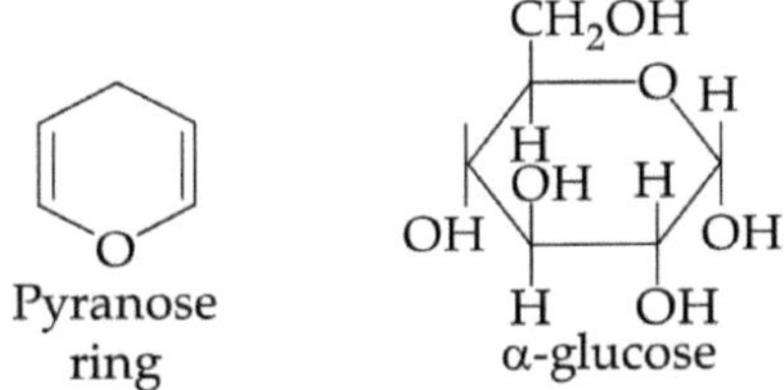

    (ii) DNA : Deoxyribose nucleic acid
          RNA : Ribose nucleic acid.
    (iii) Chemical name of vitamin C is ascorbic acid and its sources are citrus fruits, oranges, grapes amla etc.

Q. 5. Give reasons for the following:*
    (i)   Glucose does not give 2-4 DNP or Schiff's reagent test.
    (ii) Amino acids have high melting point and are water soluble.
    (iii) α and β-glucose are called anomers.

Ans. (i)   2-4-DNP and Schiff's reagent test are very specific tests for aldehydic (–CHO) group. As the majority concentration of glucose solution has the molecules in pyranose ring form, the (–CHO) group is not free. Hence glucose don't give the above tests.
    (ii) Amino acids are highly polar compounds with (COOH) and (–NH₂) both group present. The dipole-dipole interactions make their melting point high. Also they can very well form H-bonds with water, so they are water soluble too.
    (iii) α and β D-glucose have difference in the relative positions of (–OH) group at [C1]. Hence, they are anomers or diastereomers (stereoisomers).

Q. 6. The melting points and solubility of amino acids in water is generally higher than that of the corresponding halo-acids. Explain.

Ans. Both acidic (carboxyl) as well as basic (amino) groups are present in the same molecule of amino acids. In aqueous solutions, the carboxyl group can lose a proton and the amino group can accept a proton, thus giving rise to a dipolar ion known as a zwitter ion.

$$R-CH-\overset{\overset{\displaystyle O}{\|}}{C}-O-H \rightleftharpoons R-CH-\overset{\overset{\displaystyle O}{\|}}{C}-O^-$$
$$\overset{|}{NH_2} \qquad\qquad\qquad \overset{|}{{}^+NH_3}$$

(Zwitter ion)

Due to this dipolar salt like behaviour, they have strong electrostatic interactions within them and with water. But halo-acids do not exhibit such dipolar behaviour. For this reason, the melting points and the solubility of amino acids in water is higher than those of the corresponding halo-acids.

Q. 7. What do you understand by the term glycosidic linkage?

Ans. Glycosidic linkage is the etheral linkage formed between two monosaccharide units through an oxygen atom by the loss of water molecule.

For example, in a sucrose molecule, two monosaccharide units, α-glucose and β-fructose, are joined together by a glycosidic linkage.

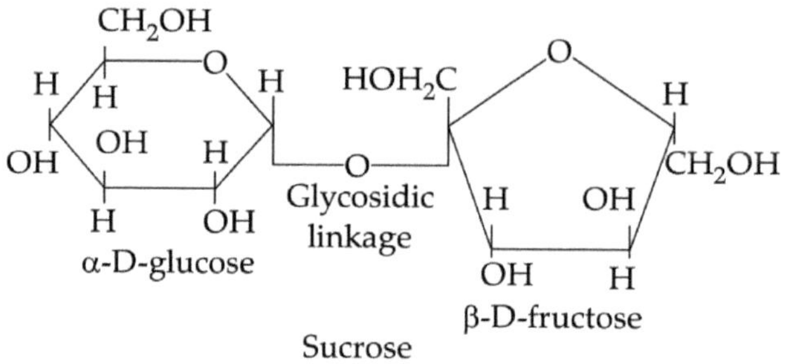

Sucrose

Q. 8. Enumerate the reactions of D-glucose which cannot be explained by its open chain structure.

Ans. (i)   Aldehydes give 2, 4-DNP test, Schiff's test and react with $NaHSO_4$ to form the hydrogen sulphite addition product. However, glucose does not undergo these reactions.

(ii) The penta-acetate of glucose does not react with hydroxylamine. This indicates that a free –CHO group is absent in glucose.

(iii) Glucose exists in two crystalline forms α and β. Both these forms undergo mutarotation in aqueous solution. This behaviour cannot be explained by the open chain structure of glucose.

Q. 9. What are essential and non-essential amino acids? Give two examples of each type.

Ans. There are 20 commonly occurring amino acids in nature which forms the basic units of proteins in body. Essential amino acids are required by the human body, but they cannot be synthesized in the body. They must be taken through food. For example: valine and leucine.

Non-essential amino acids are also required by the human body, but they can be synthesized within the body itself. For example: glycine and proline.

Q. 10. What are enzymes?

Ans. Enzymes are proteins that catalyse biological reactions. They are very specific in nature and catalyse only a particular reaction for a particular substrate. Enzymes are usually named after the particular substrate or class of substrate and some times after the particular reaction. They function best at normal temperature (about 300 K) and neutral pH (7).

For example, the enzyme used to catalyse the hydrolysis of maltose into glucose is named as maltase.

$$C_{12}H_{22}O_{11} \xrightarrow{\text{Maltase}} 2C_6H_{12}O_6$$
$$\text{Maltose} \qquad\qquad \text{Glucose}$$

Again, the enzymes used to catalyse the oxidation of one substrate with the simultaneous reduction of another substrate are named as oxidoreductase enzymes.

The name of an enzyme ends with '– ase'. Sometimes presence of non-protein component called co-factor effects the action of enzymes. Example: Fe^{2+}, Co^{2+} ions etc.

Q. 11. How are vitamins classified? Name the vitamin responsible for the coagulation of blood.

Ans. Vitamins are classified on the basis of their solubility in water or fat and they are classified into two groups:

(a) **Fat-soluble vitamins:** Vitamins that are soluble in fat and oils, but not in water, belong to this group. For example: Vitamin A, D, E and K.

(b) **Water-soluble vitamins:** Vitamins that are soluble in water belong to this group. For example: B group vitamins (B_1, B_2, B_6, B_{12} etc.) vitamin C, etc. But biotin and vitamin H is neither soluble in water nor in fat. Vitamin K is responsible for the coagulation of blood.

Q. 12. What are nucleic acids? Mention their two important functions.

Ans. Nucleic acids are biomolecules found in the nuclei of all living cells, as one of the constituents of chromosomes. There are mainly two types of nucleic acids deoxyribonucleic acid (DNA) and ribonucleic acid (RNA). Nucleic acids are also known as polynucleotides as they are long-chain polymers of nucleotides.

Two main functions of nucleic acids are:

(a) DNA is responsible for the transmission of inherent characters from one generation to the next. This process of transmission is called heredity. It has a unique property of replication.

(b) Nucleic acids (both DNA and RNA) are responsible for protein synthesis in a cell. Even though the proteins are actually synthesised by the various RNA molecules in a cell, the message for the synthesis of a particular protein is present in DNA.

Q. 13. Define the following with an example of each: *

    (i) Polysaccharides   (ii) Denatured protein   (iii) Essential amino acids

Ans. (i) Polysaccharides: Polysaccharides are food storage materials and most commonly found carbohydrates in nature. These are the compound which are formed of large number of monosaccharide units joined together by glycosidic linkages. Example. Starch is the main storage polysaccharide of plants.

(ii) Denatured protein: Proteins have an unique three dimensional structure in their native form. If the native form of protein is subjected to any physical change (such as temperature change) or any chemical change (such as change in pH), the hydrogen bonds are disturbed. Due to this globule unfold and helix get uncoiled and protein loses its biological activity. This is called denaturation of protein. During denaturation $2°$ and $3°$ structures of proteins are destroyed but $1°$ structure remains intact. Coagulation of egg white is an example of denaturation of protein.

(iii) Essential amino acids: The amino acids which are not synthesized in our body and have to be obtained through diet are known as essential amino acids. Example: Tryptophan.

Q. 14. (i) Write the product when D-glucose reacts with conc. HNO_3. *

    (ii) Amino acids show amphoteric behaviour. Why?

    (iii) Write one difference between α-helix and β-pleated structures of proteins.

Ans. (i) D-glucose gets oxidised to give saccharic acid, a dicarboxylic acid on reacting with nitric acid.

$$\begin{array}{ccc}
\text{CHO} & & \text{COOH} \\
| & & | \\
(\text{CHOH})_4 & \xrightarrow{\text{Conc. } HNO_3} & (\text{CHOH})_4 \\
| & & | \\
\text{CH}_2\text{OH} & & \text{COOH} \\
\text{Glucose} & & \text{Saccharic acid}
\end{array}$$

(ii) Amino acids show amphoteric behaviour due to the presence of both acidic (carboxylic group) and basic (amino group) in the same molecule. So, in basic medium the carboxyl group can lose a proton and in acidic medium amino group can accept a proton.

(iii) In α-helix structure the polypeptide chain forms all possible hydrogen bonds by twisting into a right handed screw (helix) with the — NH group of each amino acid residue hydrogen bonded to the — C = O of an adjacent turn of the helix (intra molecular bonding), whereas in β-structure all peptide chains are stretched out to nearly maximum extension and then laid side by side which are held together by intermolecular hydrogen bonds (intermolecular bonding).

Chapter 15. Polymers

Q. 1. Answer the following:

    (i) How is PAN prepared?

    (ii) What does SBR stands for?

    (iii) What are monomers of glyptal?

Ans. (i) PAN is polyacrylonitrile it is an addition polymer prepared by polymerisation of acrylonitrile.

$$n CH_2 = CHCN \xrightarrow[\text{Catalyst}]{\text{Peroxide}} \left[CH_2 - \underset{\underset{CN}{|}}{CH} \right]_n$$. It is used for making synthetic wool.

PAN

(ii) Styrene Butadiene rubber.

(iii) Monomers of glyptal are

Glycol   and   Phthalic acid

$$n HO - CH_2 - CH_2 - OH$$

Q. 2. Account for the following:
  (i)   Sulphur is added during vulcanisation of rubber.
  (ii) Melamine is used for making plastic crockery.
  (iii) Nylon-6 is used for making fabrics and ropes.

Ans. (i)   Sulphur forms cross links between the polymer chains of natural rubber thus increasing its tensile strength, elasticity and resistance towards abrasion.

  (ii) Melamine is a highly cross linked thermosetting polymer. Hence cups, plates and other crockery items made from it will be durable and will not break easily.

  (iii) Nylon-6 is a fibre category of polymer. Its intermolecular forces of attraction are very strong and polymer chains have close packing and hence strong enough for making ropes and fabrics of high durability.

Q. 3. Define thermoplastics and thermosetting polymers with two examples of each.

Ans. (i)   Thermoplastic polymers are linear (slightly branched) long chain polymers hold by weak Van der Waal's forces. These can be repeatedly softened and hardened on heating. So their shapes can be modified again and again. Examples include polythene, polystyrene, polyvinyls etc. Used for making toys, buckets, cabinets etc.

  (ii) Thermosetting polymers are cross-linked or heavily branched polymers which get hardened during the molding process. These plastics cannot be softened again on heating, as the polymer chains cross links and becomes infusible. Example of thermosetting polymers include bakelite, urea-formaldehyde resins. Used for making electrical boards.

Q. 4. How does the presence of double bonds in rubber molecules influence their structure and reactivity?

Ans. Natural rubber is a linear cis-polyisoprene in which the double bonds are present between C_2 and C_3 of the isoprene units. Isoprene is 2-methyl-1, 3-butadiene, found in rubber latex, *i.e.*, a colloidal dispersion of rubber in water.

Natural rubber

Weak Van der Waal's forces hold the cis-chains together resulting in a coiled structure. Hence can be stretched like spring and it shows elasticity.

Q. 5. Discuss the main purpose of vulcanization of rubber.

Ans. Natural rubber though useful has some problems associated with its use. Vulcanisation modifies its properties and makes it more useful.

  (i)   By vulcanisation the elasticity of natural rubber increases and it can be now used over a wide range of temperature.

  (ii) It makes rubber more resistant to chemicals and organic acids.

  (iii) Also it improves its capacity to wear and tear.

  (iv) It makes rubber more flexible and protects from air and oxygen.

Vulcanisation of natural rubber is done to improve upon all these properties. In this process, a mixture of raw rubber with sulphur and appropriate additive is heated at a temperature range between 373 K and 415 K.

Q. 6. Write the names and structures of the monomers of the following polymers:
  (i) Buna-S   (ii) Buna-N   (iii) Neoprene   (iv) Dacron

Ans.

	Polymer	Monomer	Structure of monomer
(i)	Buna-S	1, 3-butadiene	$CH_2 = CH – CH – CH_2$
		Styrene	$C_6H_5CH = CH_2$
(ii)	Buna-N	1, 3-butadiene	$CH_2 = CH – CH = CH_2$
		Acrylonitrile	$CH_2 = CH – CN$
(iii)	Neoprene	Chloroprene	$CH_2 = \overset{\overset{\displaystyle Cl}{\displaystyle |}}{C} — CH = CH_2$
(iv)	Dacron	Ethylene glycol	$HOH_2C – CHO_2H$
		Terephthalic acid	$COOH\!-\!\langle\bigcirc\rangle\!-\!COOH$

Q. 7. Identify the monomer in the following polymeric structures.

(i)
$$\left[C-(CH_2)_8-\overset{\overset{\displaystyle O}{\displaystyle \|}}{C}-NH-(CH_2)_6-NH \right]_n$$
with the first C carrying $\overset{\displaystyle O}{\displaystyle \|}$.

(ii)
$$\left[HN\!-\!\langle triazine \rangle\!-\!NH-CH_2 \right]_n$$

Ans. (i) The monomers of the given polymeric structure are decanedioic acid $[HOOC – (CH_2)_8 – COOH]$ and hexamethylene diamine $[H_2N(CH_2)_6NH_2]$.

(ii) The monomers of the given polymeric structure are:

$$H_2N\!-\!\langle triazine \rangle\!-\!NH_2 \quad \text{with } NH_2$$

and   HCHO
        Formaldehyde

2, 4, 6-triamino –1, 3, 5-triazine

Q. 8. How is dacron obtained from ethylene glycol and terephthalic acid?

Ans. The condensation polymerization of ethylene glycol and terephthalic acid leads to the formation of dacron.

$$n\,HOH_2C — CH_2OH + n\,HOOC\!-\!\langle\bigcirc\rangle\!- COOH$$

Ethylene glycol   Terephthalic acid

$$\left[OCH_2 — CH_2 — \overset{\overset{\displaystyle O}{\displaystyle \|}}{C}\!-\!\langle\bigcirc\rangle\!- C \right]_n$$

Dacron

Chapter 16. Chemistry in Everyday Life

Q. 1. Mention the use of following drugs:*

    (i) Ranitidine   (ii) Tincture of Iodine   (iii) Equanil.

Ans. Uses of the following:

    (i) **Ranitidine:** Used as an antacid.

    (ii) **Tincture of Iodine:** A very effective antiseptic solution.

    (iii) **Equanil:** A drug to control depression and hypertension.

Q. 2. Explain the following terms giving one example each:*

    (i) Antacids   (ii) Disinfectants   (iii) Enzymes.

Ans. (i) **Antacids :** These are drugs given to patients suffering from excess production of acids, inside the stomach. Bases like sodium hydrogen carbonate, magnesium hydroxide helps in neutralising the excess acids. Sometimes antihistamines like cimetidine (Tagamet) helps decrease acidity and these have less side effects as compared to basic antacids.

(ii) **Disinfectants :** These are solutions which are applied on inanimate objects such as floors, drainage system, wash basins etc., but not on living tissues. For example a 1% solution of phenol in water is a disinfectant.

(iii) **Enzymes :** Enzymes are bio-catalysts. Chemically these are proteins and these helps in enhancing the rate of a reaction. Example enzyme maltase catalyze the hydrolysis of maltose to glucose.

Q. 3. Explain the role of allosteric site in enzyme inhibition.

Ans. The enzyme (E), substrate (S) complex formation is the main step in the action of enzyme. The role of drug is to hinder the formation of (E + S) complex. Sometimes the drug binds itself to a different site in enzyme, known as allosteric site. This causes a change in the shape of the active site of the enzyme and hence the substrate is not able to bind with the active site of the enzyme properly. This type of inhibition in enzyme action is called allosteric inhibition.

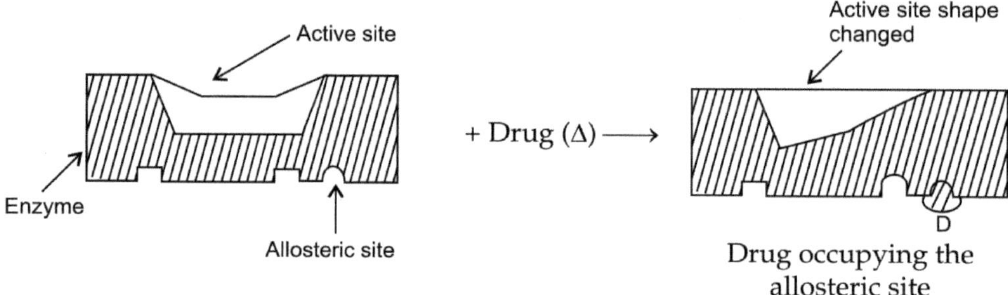

Drug occupying the allosteric site

Q. 4. Why do we need to classify drugs in different ways?

Ans. The classification of drugs and the reasons for classification are as follows:

(i) **On the basis of pharmacological effect:** This classification provides doctors the whole range of drugs available for the treatment of a particular type of problem. For example analgesics have pain killing effect, while antiseptics resist growth of micro-organisms.

(ii) **On the basis of drug action:** This classification is based on the action of a drug on a particular biochemical process. Thus, this classification is important. Like antihistamines which can block production of histamine in various ways.

(iii) **On the basis of chemical structure:** This classification provides the range of drugs sharing common structural features and often having similar pharmacological activity. Like all sulphanamides have similar pharmacological activity.

(iv) **On the basis of molecular targets:** This classification provides medicinal chemists the drugs having the same mechanism of action on targets. Drug targets are biomolecules like lipids, proteins, nucleic acids etc. This classification helps the medicinal chemists in understanding the drug action.

Q. 5. Why are cimetidine and ranitidine better antacids than sodium hydrogen carbonate, magnesium hydroxide or aluminium hydroxide?

Ans. Antacids such as sodium hydrogen carbonate, magnesium hydroxide, and aluminium hydroxide work by neutralising the excess hydrochloric acid present in the stomach, their excessive intake can make stomach alkaline and hence can trigger production of even more acid.

Cimetidine and ranitidine are better antacids and they control the root cause of acidity. These drugs prevent the interaction of histamine with the receptors present in the stomach walls. Consequently, there is a decrease in the amount of acid released by the stomach. This is why cimetidine and ranitidine are better antacids than sodium hydrogen carbonate, magnesium hydroxide and aluminium hydroxide.

Q. 6. Why soaps do not work in hard water?

Ans. Soaps are sodium or potassium salts of long-chain fatty acids. Hard water contains calcium and magnesium ions. When soaps are dissolved in hard water, these ions displace sodium or potassium from their salts and form insoluble calcium or magnesium salts of fatty acids. These insoluble salts separate as scum and thus are useless as cleansing agents. Most of the soap gets lost as scum.

$$2C_{17}H_{35}COONa + MgCl_2 \longrightarrow 2NaCl + (C_{17}H_{35}COO)_2Mg$$

Soap   Insoluble

Magnesium stearate

(soap)

Q. 7. Explain the cleansing action of soaps.

Ans. Soap molecules form micelles around an oil droplet (dirt) or grease in such a way that the hydrocarbon chain (hydrophobic) parts of the stearate ions attach themselves to the oil droplet and the anionic (hydrophilic) parts project outside the oil droplet. Due to the polar nature of the hydrophilic parts, the stearate ions (along with the dirt) are pulled into water while rinsing and thereby removing the dirt from the cloth. Rubbing the cloth helps in removing the grease or dirt further. The micelles surface carry same charge, hence the repulsion covering each dirt molecule micelle prevents them from coagulation.

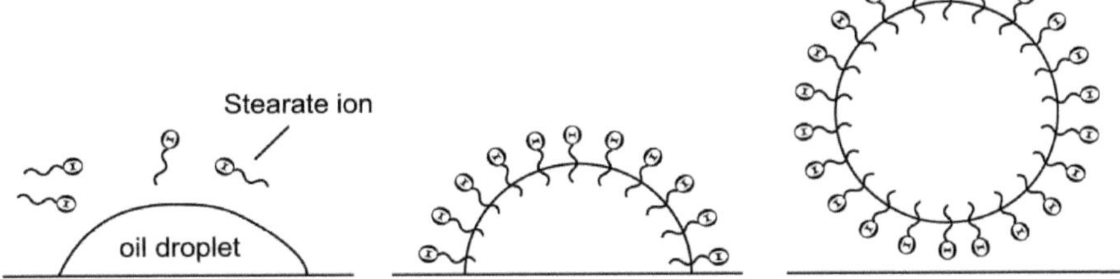

Q. 8. Following type of non-ionic detergents are present in liquid detergents, emulsifying agents and wetting agents. Label the hydrophilic and hydrophobic parts in the molecule.
Identify the functional group (s) present in the molecule.

$$C_9H_{19} - \!\!\bigcirc\!\! - O\,[CH_2CH_2O]_x CH_2CH_2OH$$

$$(x = 5 \text{ to } 10)$$

Ans. $C_9H_{19} - \!\!\bigcirc\!\! - O\,[CH_2CH_2O]_x CH_2CH_2OH$

  Hydrophobic part   Hydrophilic part

Functional groups present in the molecule are:
(a) Ether ($-O-$).
(b) Primary alcoholic group (OH).

Q. 9. (i) Why is bithional added to soap?*
  (ii) What is tincture of iodine? Write its one use.
  (iii) Among the following, which one acts as a food preservative?
    Aspartame, Aspirin, Sodium Benzoate, Paracetamol.

Ans. (i) Bithional is added to soaps to impart antiseptic properties to soap.
  (ii) Tincture of iodine is 2-3 percent mixture of iodine in alcohol water mixture. It is used as an antiseptic.
  (iii) Sodium benzoate is used as a food preservative.

Long Answers - II | Set 8 |

Q. 1. Solids have various defects. The basic two types of defects are point defects and line defects. Answer the following questions based on that:

    (i) How many types of defects are found in ionic solids?

    (ii) If we heat a solid particle, can it generate any defect?

Ans. (i) Two types of point defects in ionic solids are Schottky defect and Frenkel defect.

    (ii) On heating a solid particle, sometimes decomposition of the molecule constituting it can takes place, which on further heating can generate vacancy defect.

Q. 2. As we know diamond and graphite are two allotropes of carbon, they vary in their physical properties a lot. Based on this knowledge answer the following questions.

    (i) Diamond is transparent and has beauty of brilliance, but graphite is opaque and dark. Why?

    (ii) Diamond does not conduct electricity on the other hand graphite is an excellent conductor. Explain.

    (iii) Why the shine of diamond to diamond varies?

Ans. (i) In diamond carbon is sp^3 hybridised on the otherhand graphite has a layer structure with sp^2 hybridised carbon. So, the tetrahedral structure chain gives diamond a compact structure with fine cuts, which reflects light and makes the diamond shine. Diamonds reflects the light which falls on them they don't have any shine of their own.

    (ii) In diamond all the valency electrons (4) are involved in bonding while in graphite, three valency electrons are involved and one is delocalised in the layer structure to conduct electricity.

    (iii) Diamonds have high refractive index (2.42). These further can cut into various ways to add extra reflection (internal reflection). Sometimes presence of impurities also imparts different colours.

Q. 3. (a) An element has atomic mass 93 g mol^{-1} and density 11.5 g cm^{-3}. If the edge length of its unit cell is 300 pm, identify the type of unit cell.*

    (b) Write any two differences between amorphous solids and crystalline solids.

Ans. (a) Given :

$$\text{Atomic mass} = 93 \text{ g mol}^{-1}$$
$$\text{Density} = 11.5 \text{ g cm}^{-3}$$
$$\text{Edge length} = 300 \text{ pm}$$

We know that

$$\rho = \frac{Z \times m}{a^3 \times Na}$$

$$11.5 = \frac{Z \times 93}{[(300 \times 10^{-10})^3 \times 6.022 \times 10^{23}]}$$

$$Z = 2$$

∴ The unit cell is Body centered structure (BCC) since Z = 2.

    (b) Difference between crystalline and amorphous solids :

	Crystalline Solids	Amorphous Solids
1.	The internal arrangement of particles is irregular.	The internal arrangement of particles in regular.
2.	They have sharp melting point.	They do not have sharp metting point.

Q. 4. (a) Calculate the number of unit cells in 8.1 g of aluminium if it crystallizes in a f.c.c. structure. (Atomic mass of Al = 27 g mol^{-1})*

(b) Give reasons:

    (i) In stoichiometric defects, NaCl exhibits Schottky defect and not Frenkel defect.

    (ii) Silicon on doping with phosphorous forms *n*-type semiconductor.

    (iii) Ferrimagnetic substances show better magnetism than antiferromagnetic substances.

Ans. (a) Given : Aluminium crystallises in f.c.c. structure.

Atomic mass of Al $= 27$ g mol^{-1}

We know that :

$$n = \frac{\text{Given mass}}{\text{Molar mass} \times \text{Avogadro's number}}$$

$$= \frac{8.1}{27 \times 6.022 \times 10^{23}}$$

Number of atoms in one unit cell $= 4$ (fcc)

$$\text{Number of unit cells} = \frac{8.1}{27 \times 6.022 \times 10^{23} / 4}$$

$$= 4.5 \times 10^{22}$$

Thus 8.1 g of aluminium has 4.5×10^{22} unit cells.

(b) (i) In stoichiometric defects NaCl exhibits Schottky defect due to the comparable size of Na$^+$ (cation) and Cl$^-$ (anion). So it can't occupy the interstitial sites and does not shows Frenkel defect.

    (ii) Phosphorous has 5 valence e^-, when it is doped with silicon which has 4 valence electrons it leaves one electron. This extra electron helps in conducting current and results in the formation of *n*-type semiconductor.

    (iii) Ferrimagnetic substances shows better magnetism than antiferromagnetic substances because in ferrimagnetic substances domains or magnetic moments are aligned in opposite directions in unequal numbers whereas in the antiferromagnetic substances domains are aligned in opposite direction in equal numbers so they cancel the magnetic moments completely and thus the net magnetism is zero.

Chapter 2. Solutions

Q. 1. (i) Define the term osmosis and osmotic pressure. Is the osmotic pressure of a solution a colligative property? Explain.

    (ii) Calculate the boiling point of a solution prepared by adding 15.00 g of NaCl to 250.0 g of water. (K_b for water $= 0.512$ K kg/mol, molar mass NaCl $= 58.44$ g/ml)*

Ans. (i) The net spontaneous flow of solvent molecules from a less concentrated solution to a more concentration solution via a semi-permeable membrane is called osmosis.

The exact pressure required to stop this flow of solvent molecules is called the osmotic pressure.

Yes, osmotic pressure is a colligative property because, $\pi = CRT$.

Where C is the molar concentration. Since osmotic pressure depends upon the molar concentration of the solution (solute in solvent) and not upon the nature of solute, therefore it is a colligative property.

    (ii) $W_2 = 15.00$ g, $M_2 = 58.44$ g/mol, $W_1 = 250$ g*

$K_b = 0.512$ K kg/mol, $\Delta T_b =$?

$$NaCl \longrightarrow Na^+ + Cl^-$$

Hence,

$$i = 2$$

$$\Delta T_b = i \times K_b \times \frac{W_2}{M_2} \times \frac{1}{W_1}$$

$$= \frac{2 \times 0.512 \text{ K kg mol}^{-1} \times 15.00 \times 10^{-3} \text{ kg} \times 1}{58.44 \times 10^{-3} \text{ kg mol}^{-1} \times 250 \times 10^{-3} \text{ kg}}$$

$$= 1.051 \text{ K}$$

$$T_b = (273 + 1.051)$$

$$= 274.051 \text{ K}$$

Q. 2. (i) A 10% solution (by mass) of sucrose in water has a freezing point of 269.15 K. Calculate the freezing point of 10% glucose in water if the freezing point of pure water is 273.15 K.*

Given:

(Molar mass of sucrose = 342 g mol^{-1})

(Molar mass of glucose = 180 g mol^{-1})

(ii) Define the following terms:

(i) Molality (m)

(ii) Abnormal molar mass

Ans. (i) T_o (freezing point of water) = 273.15 K

T_s (freezing point of sucrose solution) = 269.15 K

Weight of sucrose in solution = 10 g

Weight of glucose in solution = 10 g

Molar mass of sucrose = 342 g mol^{-1}

Molar mass of glucose = 180 g mol^{-1}

Depression in freezing point

$$\Delta T_f = \frac{K_f \times W_B \times 1000}{W_A \times 1000}$$

$$K_f = \frac{\Delta T_f \times W_A \times M_B}{W_B \times 1000}$$

In case of sucrose solution

$$K_f = \frac{(273.15 - 269.15) \times 90 \times 342}{10 \times 1000} \qquad \text{...(i)}$$

In case of glucose solution

$$K_f = \frac{(273.15 - x) \times 90 \times 180}{10 \times 1000} \qquad \text{...(ii)}$$

$\because$ K_f is constant

thus equation (i) = equation (ii)

$$\frac{(273.15 - 269.15)}{10 \times 1000} = \frac{273.15 - x \times 90 \times 180}{10 \times 1000}$$

$$4 \times 342 = (273.15 - x) \times 180$$

$$(273.15 - x) = \frac{40 \times 342}{180} = 7.6$$

$$x = 265.55 \text{ K}$$

So, freezing point of glucose solution = 265.55 K.

(ii) (a) Molality: It is the number of moles of the solute dissolved per 1000 g of the solvent. It is denoted by m.

$$\text{Molality} = \frac{\text{Moles of solute}}{\text{Mass of solvent (in gram)}} \times 1000$$

(b) Abnormal molar mass: Those solute that dissociate or associate in solution, show abnormal molar mass in solution. for example, Molar mass of ethanoic acid is greater than normal molar mass.

$$2CH_3COOH \rightleftharpoons (CH_3COOH)_2$$

Ethanoic acid

Molar mass of KCl in solution is reduced than normal molar mass.

$$KCl \rightleftharpoons K^+ + Cl^-$$

Q. 3. (i) 30 g of urea (M = 60 g mol^{-1}) is dissolved in 846 g of water. Calculate the vapour pressure of water for this solution if vapour pressure of pure water at 298 K is 23.8 mm Hg.*

(ii) Write two differences between ideal solutions and non-ideal solutions.

Ans. (i) $W_B = 30$ g $\quad\quad\quad\quad$ $M_B = 60$ g mol^{-1}
$W_A = 846$ g $\quad\quad\quad\quad$ $M_A = 18$ g mol^{-1}
$P° = 23.8$ mmHg
$P_s = x$

Relative lowering of vapour pressure

$$\frac{P° - P_S}{P°} = \frac{W_B \times M_A}{M_B \times W_A}$$

$$\frac{23.8 - x}{23.8} = \frac{30 \times 18}{60 \times 846}$$

$$23.8 - x = 0.253$$

$$x = 23.8 - 0.253 = 23.547$$

So, vapour pressure of water for this solution = 23.547 mmHg

(ii)

		Ideal Solutions	Non-ideal Solutions
1.		The int eract ions between the components are similar to those in the pure components.	The interactions between the components are similar to those in the pure components.
2.		There is no enthalpy change on mixing $\Delta H_{mix} = 0.$	There is enthalpy change on mixing $\Delta H_{mix} \neq 0.$

Chapter 3. Electrochemistry

Q. 1. (i) Explain why electrolysis of aqueous solution of NaCl gives H_2 at cathode and Cl_2 at anode. Write overall reaction. [$E°_{Na+/Na} = -2.17$ V; $E°_{H+ +O2/H_2O} = -0.83$ V]
$$[E°_{Cl_2/Cl^-} = -1.36 \text{ V}; E°_{H+ + O_2/H_2O} = 1.23 \text{ V}]$$

(ii) Calculate the emf of the cell.*
$$\text{Zn/Zn}^{2+} (0.1 \text{ M}) \,\|\, \text{Cd}^{2+} (0.01 \text{ M}) \,|\, \text{Cd at 298 K.}$$

Given; [$E°_{Zn^{2+}|Zn} = 0.76$ V and $E°_{Cd^{2+}/Cd} = -0.40$ V]

Ans. (i) The electrode reactions are:
$$\text{NaCl (aq)} \longrightarrow \text{Na}^+ \text{(aq)} + \text{Cl}^- \text{(aq)}$$
$$\text{H}_2\text{O (l)} \longrightarrow \text{H}^+ \text{(aq)} + \text{OH}^- \text{(aq)}$$

So we have cation H^+ and Na^+ competing for cathode and we have anions Cl^- and OH^- competing at anode.

Reaction at cathode: (Reduction)
$$2\text{H}^+ \text{(aq)} + 2e^- \longrightarrow \text{H}_2 \text{ (g)}$$

because reduction potential of $E°_{H+/H_2}$ is more than $E°_{Na+/Na}$

Reaction at anode: (Oxidation)

Though oxidation potential (opposite of reduction potential) of $O_2 (E°_{2O2-/O_2})$ is more than oxidation potential of $(E°_{2Cl^-/Cl_2})$ Cl_2, the former requires an extra voltage or over voltage to discharge. Hence Cl_2 gas is liberated at anode.
$$2\text{Cl}^- \text{(aq)} - 2e^- \longrightarrow \text{Cl}_2 \text{ (g)}$$

Overall reaction:
$$2\text{NaCl (aq)} + 2\text{H}_2\text{O (aq)} \xrightarrow{\text{Electrolysis}} \text{H}_2\text{(g)} + \text{Cl}_2\text{(g)} + 2\text{Na}^+ \text{(aq)} + 2\text{OH}^- \text{(aq)}$$

(ii) The half cell reaction for the cell
$$\text{Zn}|\text{Zn}^{2+} (0.01 \text{ M}) \,\|\, \text{Cd}^{2+} (0.01 \text{ M}) \,|\, \text{Cd}$$

Anode: $\quad\quad\quad\quad\quad\quad$ $\text{Zn (s)} \longrightarrow \text{Zn}^{2+} \text{(aq)} + 2e^-$
Cathode: $\quad\quad$ $\text{Cd}^{2+} \text{(aq)} + 2e^- \longrightarrow \text{Cd(s)}$
Total equation:
$$\text{Zn(s)} + \text{Cd}^{2+} \text{(aq)} \longrightarrow \text{Zn}^{2+} \text{(aq)} + \text{Cd(s)}$$

Using Nernst equation.

$$E_{cell} = E°_{cell} - \frac{0.0591}{n} \log \frac{[Zn^{2+}]^1}{[Cd^{2+}]^1}$$

$n = 2$ from the equation. [Temp. = 298 K]

$$E_{cell} = \left[E°_{Cd^{2+}/Cd} - E°_{Zn^{2+}/Zn}\right] - \frac{0.0591}{2} \log \frac{0.1}{0.01}$$

$$= [-0.40 \text{ V} - (-0.76 \text{ V})] - \frac{0.0591}{2} \log \frac{10^{-1}}{10^{-2}}$$

$$= 0.36 \text{ V} - \frac{0.0591}{2} \log 10$$

$$= 0.36 \text{ V} - 0.0295 = 0.3305 \text{ V}.$$

Q. 2. (i) State the products of electrolysis obtained on the cathode and anode in the following:

(a) Dil. solution of H_2SO_4 with Pt electrodes.

(b) Aq. solution of $AgNO_3$ with Ag electrodes.

(ii) Write the cell formation and calculate the standard cell potential of the galvanic cell for the following reaction:

$$Fe^{2+} \text{ (aq)} + Ag^+ \text{ (aq)} \longrightarrow Fe^{3+} \text{ (aq)} + Ag(s)$$

Also, calculate $\Delta_r G°$ for the above reaction.

Given : $[E°_{Ag^+/Ag} = +0.80 \text{ V}, E°_{Fe^{3+}/Fe^{2+}} = 0.77 \text{ V}]$ 1 F = 96500 C mol^{-1}

Ans. (i) (a) Dilute solution of H_2SO_4 with Pt electrode have ions, H^+, SO_4^{2-} and OH^- in it as Pt is an inert electrode.

At cathode (Reduction) : $2H^+ \text{ (aq)} + 2e^- \longrightarrow H_2(g)$

At anode (Oxidation) : $2OH^- \text{ (aq)} \longrightarrow O_2(g) + 2H^+ \text{ (aq)} + 4e^-$

SO_4^{2-} will remain in solution as it has a higher discharge potential than OH^-.

So, H_2 gas is evolved at cathode and O_2 gas is evolved at anode.

(b) Aqueous solution of $AgNO_3$ with Ag electrode.

Ions present are : Ag^+, H^+, OH^-, NO_3^- and Ag atom.

At cathode (Reduction) : $Ag^+ \text{ (aq)} + e^- \longrightarrow Ag(s)$

At anode (Oxidation) : $Ag(s) \longrightarrow Ag^+ \text{ (aq)} + e^-$

As Ag has highest discharge potential compared to all other ions hence it gets dissolved as Ag^+ (aq) ion. Hence at cathode we get solid Ag deposit and at anode the silver electrode dissolves.

(ii) $Pt, Fe^{2+} \mid Fe^{3+} \text{ (aq)} \parallel Ag^+ \text{ (aq)} \mid Ag \text{ (s)}$

$$E°_{cell} = E°_{Ag^+/Ag} - E°_{Fe^{3+}/Fe^{2+}}$$
$$= +0.80 \text{ V} - (+0.77 \text{ V}) = 0.03 \text{ V}$$
$$\Delta G° = -nFE°_{cell} \quad n = 1$$
$$\Delta G° = -1 \times 96500 \text{ C mol}^{-1} \times 0.03 \text{ V}$$
$$= -2895 \text{ J mol}^{-1} = -2.895 \text{ kJ/mol}^{-1}.$$

Q. 3. (i) Give reasons for the following:

(a) Rusting of iron is quicker in saline water than in ordinary water.

(b) Aluminium metal cannot be produced by electrolysis of aqueous solution of aluminium salt.

(ii) Resistance of a conductivity cell filled with 0.1 M KCl solution is 100 ohm. If the resistance of the same cell when filled with 0.02 M KCl solution is 520 ohm, calculate the conductivity and molar conductivity of 0.02 M KCl solution. Conductivity of 0.1 M KCl solution is 1.29 S m^{-1}.*

Ans. (i) (a) Saline water is a good source of ions, specially H^+ ions. Hence the rusting process is faster.

(b) Aluminium is a reactive metal and its reactivity is more than hydrogen. Hence in place of Al being discharged it reacts with H_2O.

(ii) Cell constant (G*) = κ × R

(Conductivity) (Resistance)

For 0.1 M KCl solution.

$$G^* = 1.29 \text{ S m}^{-1} \times 100 \text{ ohm} = 129 \text{ m}^{-1}$$

$$= 1.29 \text{ cm}^{-1}$$

$$\kappa = \rho\frac{l}{A} = \frac{1}{R} \times \frac{l}{A} = \frac{1}{R} \times G$$

i.e., for 0.02 M KCl solution.

$$\kappa = \frac{1}{520} \times 129 \text{cm}^{-1} = 2.48 \times 10^{-1} \text{S cm}^{-1}$$

Molar conductivity,

$$\Lambda_m = \frac{1000 \text{ K}}{\text{M (Concertration)}}$$

$$\therefore \qquad \Lambda_m = -\frac{1000 \times 2.48 \times 10^{-1} \text{S cm}^{-1}}{0.02 \text{ mol cm}^{-3}}$$

$$= 12400 \text{ S cm}^2 \text{ mol}^{-1}.$$

Q. 4. (i) What type of cell is a lead-storage battery? Write the anode and the cathode reactions and the overall cell reaction occurring in a lead storage battery.

(ii) A copper-silver cell is set up. The copper ion concentration in it is 0.10 M. The concentration of silver ion is not known. The cell potential measured is 0.422 V. Determine the concentration of Ag ion in the cell.**

[Given : $E°_{Ag+/Ag} = + 0.80$ V, $E°_{Cu+/Cu} = + 0.34$ V]

Ans. (i) Lead storage battery is a secondary cell, which can be recharged by passing current.

Reactions :

At Cathode : $PbO_2 + SO_4^{2-} + 4H^+ + 2e^- \longrightarrow PbSO_4 + 2H_2O$

At Anode : $\qquad\qquad Pb + SO_4^{2-} \longrightarrow PbSO_4 + 2e^-$

Overall reaction :

$$Pb + PbO_2 + 2H_2SO_4 \longrightarrow 2PbSO_4 + 2H_2O$$

(ii) The cell reaction :

$$Cu \text{ (s)} + 2Ag^+ \text{ (s)} \longrightarrow Cu^{2+} \text{ (aq)} + 2Ag \text{ (s)}$$

Thus $n = 2$, Cu is oxidised and Ag is reduced.

Let the concentration of silver ions be C moles/L.

Using Nernst equation :

$$E_{cell} = [E°_{Ag+/Ag} - E°_{Cu2+/Cu}] \frac{0.0591}{2} \log \frac{[Cu^{2+}]}{[Ag^+]^2}$$

or

$$E_{cell} = (+ 0.80 \text{ V} - 0.34 \text{ V}) - \frac{0.0591}{2} \log \frac{0.1}{C^2}$$

or $\qquad\qquad E_{cell} = 0.46 - 0.02955 [\log 0.1 - 2 \log C]$

As $\qquad\qquad E_{cell} = 0.422$ V (given)

Hence, $\qquad 0.422 = 0.46 - 0.02955 (-1 - 2 \log C)$

$\Rightarrow \qquad -0.038 = + 0.02955 (1 + 2 \log C)$

$\Rightarrow \qquad 1 + 2 \log C = \dfrac{-0.038}{0.02955}$

or $\qquad 2 \log C = -1.286 - 1 = -2.286$

or $\qquad \log C = -\dfrac{2.286}{2} = -1.143$

$$C = \text{Antilog} (-1.143) = \text{Antilog} \left(\bar{2}.857\right)$$

$$= 7.194 \times 10^{-2} = 0.07194 \text{ moles/L.}$$

Q. 5. Define conductivity and molar conductivity for the solution of an electrolyte. Discuss their variation with concentration.

Ans. Conductivity of a solution is defined as the conductance of a solution of 1 cm in length and area of cross-section 1 sq. cm. The inverse of resistivity is called conductivity or specific conductance. It is represented by the symbol κ. If ρ is resistivity, then we can write :

$$\kappa = \frac{1}{\rho}, \text{ units ohm}^{-1}\,\text{cm}^{-1} \text{ or } \Omega^{-1}\,\text{cm}^{-1} \text{ or S cm}^{-1}$$

Conductivity always decreases with a decrease in concentration, both for weak and strong electrolytes. This is because the number of ions per unit volume that carry the current in a solution decreases with a decrease in concentration.

Molar conductivity: Molar conductivity of a solution at a given concentration is the conductance of volume V of a solution containing 1 mole of the electrolyte kept between two electrodes with the area of cross-section A and distance of unit length.

$$\Lambda_m = \kappa\frac{A}{l} \text{ Also, } \Lambda_m = \frac{\kappa \times 1000}{C} \text{ where C = concentration}$$

Now, $l = 1$ and A = V (volume containing 1 mole of the electrolyte).

$$\therefore \qquad \Lambda_m = \kappa V$$

Molar conductivity increases with a decrease in concentration. This is because the total volume V of the solution containing one mole of the electrolyte increases on dilution.

The variation of Λ_m with $\sqrt{c}$ for strong and weak electrolytes is shown in the following plot:

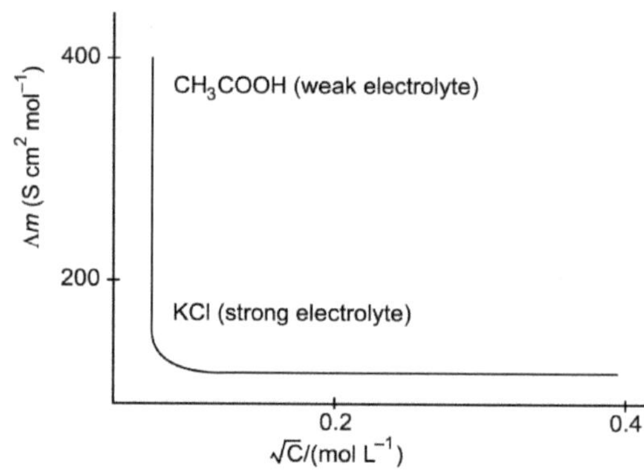

Q. 6. Using the standard electrode potentials given in Table, predict if the reaction between the following is feasible:

(i) Fe^{3+} (aq) and I^- (aq)

(ii) Ag^+ (aq) and Cu(s)

(iii) Fe^{3+} (aq) and Br^- (aq)

(iv) Ag(s) and Fe^{3+} (aq)

(v) Br_2 (aq) and Fe^{2+} (aq).

Ans. (i)

$$Fe^{3+}(aq) + e^- \longrightarrow Fe^{2+}(aq)\,] \times 2; \qquad E^\circ = +0.77\text{ V }[E_R] \qquad \text{(Reduction electrode)}$$
$$2I^-(aq) \longrightarrow I_2(s) + 2e^-; \qquad E^\circ = -0.54\text{ V }[E_L] \qquad \text{(Oxidation electrode)}$$
$$2Fe^{3+}(aq) + 2I^-(aq) \rightarrow 2Fe^{2+}(aq) + I_2(s); \qquad E^\circ = +0.23\text{ V}$$

E_{cell} is positive the reaction is feasible.

(ii)

$$Ag^+(aq) + e^- \longrightarrow Ag(s)] \times 2; \qquad E^\circ = +0.80\text{ V }[E_R] \qquad \text{(Reduction electrode)}$$
$$Cu(s) \longrightarrow Cu^{2+}(aq) + 2e^-; \qquad E^\circ = -0.34\text{ V }[E_L] \qquad \text{(Oxidation electrode)}$$
$$2Ag^+(aq) + Cu(s) \longrightarrow 2Ag(s) + Cu^{2+}(aq)\,; \qquad E^\circ = +0.46\text{ V}$$

E° for the overall reaction is positive, the reaction between Ag^+ (aq) and Cu(s) is feasible.

(iii)

$$Fe^{3+}(aq) + e^- \longrightarrow Fe^{2+}(aq)\,] \times 2; \qquad E^\circ = +0.77\text{ V }[E_R] \qquad \text{(Reduction electrode)}$$
$$2Br^-(aq) \longrightarrow Br_2(s) + 2e^-; \qquad E^\circ = -1.09\text{ V }[E_L] \qquad \text{(Oxidation electrode)}$$
$$2Fe^{3+}(aq) + 2Br^-(aq) \rightarrow 2Fe^{2+}(aq) \text{ and } Br_2(l); \qquad E^\circ = -0.32\text{ V}$$

Since E° for the overall reaction is negative, the reaction between Fe^{3+}(aq.) and Br_2 (aq) is not feasible.

(iv)

$$Fe^{3+}(aq) + e^- \longrightarrow Fe^{2+}(aq); \qquad E^\circ = +0.77\text{ V }[E_L] \qquad \text{(Reduction electrode)}$$
$$Ag(s) \longrightarrow Ag^+(aq) + e^-]; \qquad E^\circ = -0.80\text{ V }[E_R] \qquad \text{(Oxidation electrode)}$$
$$Ag + Fe^{3+} \longrightarrow Ag^+ + Fe^{2+}; \qquad E^\circ = -0.03\text{ V}$$

Since the emf of the cell is –ve, hence reaction between Ag(s) and Fe^{3+} (aq) is not feasible.

(v)

$$Fe^{2+}(aq) \longrightarrow Fe^{3+}(aq) + e^-\,] \times 2; \qquad E^\circ = +1.09\text{ V }[E_L] \qquad \text{(Reduction electrode)}$$
$$Br_2(aq) + 2e^- \longrightarrow 2Br^-(aq)\,; \qquad E^\circ = +1.09\text{ V }[E_R] \qquad \text{(Oxidation electrode)}$$
$$2Br_2(aq) + 2Fe^{2+}(aq) \longrightarrow 2Br^-(aq) + 2Fe^{3+}(aq); \quad E^\circ = +0.32\text{ V}$$

E° for the overall reaction is positive, the reaction between Br_2 and Fe^{2+}(aq) is feasible.

Q. 7. (i) Write the cell reaction and calculate the e.m.f. of the following cell at 298 K:*

$Sn(s)|Sn^{2+}$ (0.004)M $||$ H^+ (0.020 M) $|$ $H_2(g)$ (1 bar)$|Pt(s)$

(Given : $E°_{Sn^{2+}/Sn} = -0.14$ V)

(ii) Give reasons:

(a) On the basis of E° values O_2 gas should be liberated at anode but it is Cl_2 gas which is liberated in the electrolysis of aqueous NaCl.

(b) Conductivity of CH_3COOH decreases on dilution.

Ans. (i) The half cell reactions can be written as:

$$Sn^{2+} + 2e^- \rightarrow Sn$$

$$E_{el} = -0.14 + \frac{0.0591}{2}(\log[Sn^{2+}])$$

$$= -0.11 \times (\log 0.004) \text{ V}$$

$$= 0.26 \text{ V} \qquad \qquad ...(i)$$

$$2H^+ + 2e^- \rightarrow H_2$$

$$E_{el} = 0.0 + 0.0591(\log[H^+])$$

$$= 0.0591 \times (-1.7)$$

$$= -0.10 \text{ V} \qquad \qquad ...(ii)$$

Considering,

$2H^+(aq) + Sn(s) \rightarrow Sn^{2+}(aq) + H_2(g)$, as the cell reaction

So, E_{cell} will be,

$$E_{cell} = 0.26 \text{ V} - (-0.10) \text{ V}$$

$$= 0.36 \text{ V}$$

(ii) (a) During the electrolysis of aqueous NaCl, there are two possible reactions at anode.

$$Cl^-(aq) \rightarrow \tfrac{1}{2}Cl_2(g) + e^- \quad E_{cell} = 1.36 \text{ V}$$

$$2H_2O(l) \rightarrow O_2(g) + 4H^+(aq) + 4e^- \quad E_{cell} = 1.23 \text{ V}$$

The reaction at anode with lower value of E_{cell} is preferred and therefore, water should get oxidised to give O_2 but on account of over potential of oxygen, Cl^- gets oxidised preferably, liberating Cl_2 gas.

(b) Conductivity of CH_3COOH decreases on dilution because the number of ions per unit volume that carry the current in a solution decreases on dilution.

Q. 8. (i) For the reaction*

$$2AgCl(s) + H_2(g) \text{ (1 atm)} \rightarrow 2Ag(s) + 2H^+ \text{ (0.1 M)} + 2Cl^- \text{ (0.1 M)}$$

$$\Delta G° = -43600 \text{ J at } 25°C$$

Calculate the e.m.f. of the cell. $\qquad \qquad [\log 10^{-n} = -n]$

(ii) Define fuel cell and write its two advantages.

Ans. (i) $E°_{cell}$ can be obtained from the formula,

$$\Delta G° = -nFE°_{cell}$$

$$E°_{cell} = \frac{\Delta G°}{nf}$$

$$= \frac{-43600 \text{ J}}{1 \times 96487 \text{ C mol}^{-1}}$$

$$= -0.45 \text{ V}$$

Now, let us consider the given reaction equation,

$$2AgCl(s) + H_2(g) \text{ (1 atm)} \rightarrow 2Ag(s) + 2H^+ \text{ (0.1 M)} + 2Cl^- \text{ (0.1 M)}$$

or $\qquad AgCl(s) + \tfrac{1}{2}H_2(g) \text{ (1 atm)} \rightarrow Ag(s) + H^+ \text{ (0.1 M)} + Cl^- \text{ (0.1 M)}$

According to Nernst equation:

$$E_{cell} = E°_{cell} \frac{-2.303 \text{ RT}}{nF} \log \frac{[\text{Product}]}{[\text{Reactant}]}$$

$$E_{cell} = E°_{cell} - \frac{2.303\ RT}{nF} \log \frac{[H^+][Cl][Ag]}{[AgCl][H_2]^{1/2}}$$

As the activity of solid and H_2 gas at 1 atm is taken unity, the equation becomes,

$$E_{cell} = E°_{cell} - \frac{2.303\ RT}{nF} \log ([H^+][Cl^-]) \qquad \qquad ...(i)$$

Now, putting the values in equation (i) above,

$$\begin{aligned}
E_{cell} &= -0.45 - (0.059) \log (0.1 \times 0.1) \\
&= -0.51 \log (10^{-2}) \\
&= -0.51 \times (-2) \\
&= 1.02\ V
\end{aligned}$$

So, EMF of the given cell is 1.02 V.

(ii) Galvanic cells that are designed to convert the energy of combustion of fuels like hydrogen, methane, methanol etc. directly into electrical energy are called fuel cells.

Advantages of fuel cells are:

(i) Fuel cells produce electricity with an efficiency of about 70% compared to thermal plants whose efficiency is about 40%.

(ii) Fuel cells are pollution free.

Q. 9. (a) The electrical resistance of a column of 0.05 M KOH solution of length 50 cm and area of cross-section 0.625 cm^2 is 5×10^3 ohm. Calculate its resistivity, conductivity and molar conductivity.*

(b) Predict the products of electrolysis of an aqueous solution of $CuCl_2$ with platinum electrodes.

(Given : $E°Cu^{2+}/Cu = 0.34\ V$, $E°\ (½\ Cl_2/Cl^-) = +1.36\ V$

$$E°H+/H_2\ (g),\ Pt = 0.00V,\ E°(½\ O_2/H_2O) = +1.23\ V)$$

Ans. (a) Resistivity, $\rho = \dfrac{RA}{l}$ where, R is the electrical resistance; l is the length and A is the area of cross-section of the column.

$$\rho = \frac{RA}{l}$$

Substituting the given values:

$$\begin{aligned}
\rho &= \frac{RA}{l} \\
&= \frac{(5 \times 10^3\ ohm \times 0.625\ cm^2)}{50\ cm} \\
&= 62.5\ ohm\ cm
\end{aligned}$$

The inverse of resistivity is called conductivity. hence,

$$\begin{aligned}
\kappa &= \frac{1}{\rho} \\
&= \frac{1}{62.5\ ohm^{-1}cm^{-1}} \\
&= 0.016\ S\ cm^{-1}
\end{aligned}$$

Now, the molar conductivity is given by:

$$\Lambda_m = \frac{\kappa}{c}$$

Substituting the values:

$$\begin{aligned}
\Lambda_m &= \frac{0.016 \times 1000}{0.05} \\
&= 320\ S\ cm^2 mol^{-1}
\end{aligned}$$

(b) Reactions which will occur in the solution are :

$$\begin{aligned}
CuCl_2(s) &\rightleftharpoons Cu^{2+} + 2Cl^- \\
H_2O &\rightleftharpoons H^+ + OH^-
\end{aligned}$$

Reaction at cathode:
$$Cu^{2+} + 2e^- \rightarrow Cu(s)$$

Reaction at anode:
$$2Cl^- \rightarrow Cl^2 + 2e^-$$

Hence, Cu will deposit at cathode and Cl_2 gas will be liberated at anode.

Q. 10. (a) Calculate e.m.f. of the following cell:*

$Zn(s)/Zn^{2+}$ (0.1 M) || (0.01 M) $Ag^+/Ag(s)$

Given : $E^\circ Zn^{2+}/Zn = -0.76$ V, $E^\circ Ag^+/Ag = +0.80$V   [Given : long 10 = 1]

(b) X and Y are two electrolytes. On dilution molar conductivity of 'X' increases 2.5 times while that Y increases 25 times. Which of the two is a weak electrolyte and why?

Ans. (a) The half-cell reactions can be written as :

$Zn^{2+} + 2e^- \rightarrow Zn$ $E_{el} = -0.76 + (0.0591/2)$ (log $[Zn^{2+}]$)

Substituting the concentration value and calculating:

$$\begin{aligned}
E_{el} &= -0.76 + (0.0591/2) \text{ (log 0.1)} \\
&= -0.76 - 0.0295 \\
&= -0.789 \text{ V} \qquad \qquad ...(i)
\end{aligned}$$

$$Ag^+ + e^- \rightarrow Ag;$$
$$E_{el} = 0.8 \text{ V} + 0.0591 \text{ (log } [Ag^+])$$

Substituting the concentration value and calculating:

$$\begin{aligned}
E_{el} &= 0.8 + 0.0591 \text{ (log 0.01)} \\
&= 0.8 - 0.1182 \\
&= 0.6818 \qquad \qquad ...(ii)
\end{aligned}$$

Here, Ag^+ will reduce and Zn will oxidise—

$2Ag^+$ (aq) + Zn(s) $\rightarrow Zn^{2+}$ (aq) + 2Ag(s) will be the cell reaction

So, E_{cell} will be: $E_{cell} = 0.6818 - (-0.789)$ V
$$= 1.471 \text{ V}$$

(b) Y is weak electrolyte. On dilution weak electrolytes undergo complete dissociation and thus, there is a steep increase in molar conductivity observed. Whereas, in case of strong electrolytes, as they are already dissociated completely, dilution does not affect the conductivity very much. So, in this case X is a strong electrolyte.

Chapter 4. Chemical Kinetics

Q. 1. (i) Explain the following terms:

(a) Rate of a reaction.

(b) Activation energy of a reaction.

(ii) The decomposition of phosphine PH_3, proceeds according to the following equation:

$$4PH_3 \text{ (g)} \longrightarrow P_4\text{(g)} + 6H_2\text{(g)}$$

Its found that the reaction follows the following rate equation.

$$\text{Rate} = k[PH_3]$$

The half life period of PH_3 is 37.9 s at 120°C.

(a) How much time is required for 3/4th of the PH_3 to decompose?

(b) What fraction of the original sample of PH_3 remains behind after 1 minute?*

Ans. (i) (a) Rate of a reaction is the change in concentration of a reactant or product in per unit time.

i.e., $$R = \frac{-\Delta[A]}{\Delta t} = \frac{[C]}{\Delta t}$$

where R = Rate, [A] = concentration of reactant and [C] = concentration of product.

(b) The minimum extra energy absorbed by the reactant molecules so that their energy becomes same as the threshold energy to cross the barrier and form the product is called activation energy. It is denoted by E_a.

(ii) (a) As we can see from the rate equation that its a first order reaction.

Initial concentration, let be $= a$

Then concentration after time, $t = \dfrac{3}{4} a = x$

$\therefore \qquad t = \dfrac{2.303}{k} \log \dfrac{a}{a-x}$ also $t_{1/2} = \dfrac{0.693}{k}$

$$= \dfrac{2.303}{\dfrac{0.693}{37.9}} \log \dfrac{a}{a - \dfrac{3}{4}a}$$

$\Rightarrow \qquad k = \dfrac{0.693}{37.9} = 0.0183 \text{ s}^{-1}$

$$= \dfrac{2.303 \times 37.9}{0.693} \log 4. \qquad\qquad [\log 4 = 0.6021]$$

$$= \dfrac{2.303 \times 37.9}{0.693} \times 0.6021 = 75.83 \text{ sec.}$$

(ii) $\qquad k = \dfrac{2.303}{t} \log \dfrac{[A_0]}{[A]}$

$$t = 60 \text{ s}$$

$$\log \dfrac{[A_0]}{[A]} = \dfrac{k \times 60}{2.303}$$

$$\log \dfrac{[A_0]}{[A]} = \dfrac{0.0183 \times 60}{2.303}$$

$$\log \dfrac{[A_0]}{[A]} = 0.4762$$

Thus $\qquad \dfrac{[A_0]}{[A]} = 2.99.$

Q. 2. (a) A first order reaction is 25% complete in 40 minutes. Calculate the value of rate constant. In what time will the reaction be 80% completed? *

(b) Define order of reaction. Write the condition under which a bimolecular reaction follows first order kinetics.

Ans. (a) For a first order reaction–

$$k = \left(\dfrac{2.303}{t}\right) \log \left(\dfrac{a}{a} - x\right)$$

When $\qquad x = \left(\dfrac{25}{100}\right) a = 0.25\,a$

$$t = 40 \text{ minutes (given)}$$

Therefore, $\qquad k = \left(\dfrac{2.303}{40}\right) \log \left(\dfrac{a}{a} - 0.25a\right)$

$$k = \left(\dfrac{2.303}{40}\right) \log \left(\dfrac{1}{0.75}\right)$$

$$= 0.00719 \text{ min}^{-1}$$

Hence the value of the rate constant is 0.00719 min^{-1}

Now, we need to find time for rest 75% reaction $t =$?, when $x = 0.75\,a$

From above, $k = 0.00719$ min^{-1}

Therefore, $\qquad t = \left(\dfrac{2.303}{0.00719}\right) \log \left(\dfrac{a}{a} - 0.75a\right)$

$$= \left(\frac{2.303}{0.00719}\right) \log \left(\frac{1}{0.25}\right)$$

$$= 192.84$$

The time at which the reaction will be 75% complete is 192.84 min.

(b) Order of reaction for elementary reaction is the sum of the powers to which the reactant concentrations are raised in the rate law equation. It relates the rate of a chemical reaction with the concentrations of the reacting substances.

When concentration of one of the reactant is in excess and practically unchanged during the reaction for example when solvent used for reaction is one of the reactants, then the reaction follows first order kinetics as it depends on the concentration of only one reactant in practical sense.

Q. 3. (a) A first order reaction is 50% complete in 30 minutes at 300 K and in 10 minutes at 320 K. Calculate activation energy (Ea) for the reaction.*

$(R = 8.314 \text{ JK}^{-1} \text{ mol}^{-1})$

(b) Write the two conditions for collisions to be effective collisions.

(c) How order of reaction and molecularity differ towards a complex reaction?

[Given : log 2 = 0.3010, log 3 = 0.4771, log 4 = 0.6021, log 5 = 0.6991]

Ans. (a) The problem can be solved by using half-life equation–

by using half life equation, we get

$$K = \frac{0.693}{t_{1/2}}$$

$$K = \frac{0.693}{30 \text{ min}} = 0.0231 \text{ at } 300 \text{ K}$$

$$K = \frac{0.693}{10 \text{ min}} = 0.0693 \text{ at } 320 \text{ K}$$

From the Arrhenius equation

$$\log \frac{k_2}{k_1} = \frac{E_a}{2.303R} \left[\frac{T_2 - T_1}{T_1 T_2} \right]$$

$$E_a = \frac{2.303 \times R \times T_1 \times T_2}{T_2 - T_1} \log \frac{k_2}{k_1}$$

$$= \frac{2.303 \times 8.314 \text{ JK}^{-1} \text{ mol}^{-1} \times 300 \times 320\text{K}}{320\text{K} - 300\text{K}}$$

$$\left(\log \frac{0.06935}{0.2315} \right) = 43.848 \text{ kJ mol}^{-1}$$

(b) Two conditions for collisions to be effective collisions are -

(i) Collisions must be sufficiently energetic to break chemical bonds; the threshold energy is known as the activation energy.

(ii) The reacting particle must be properly oriented during collision, so as to confirm maximum interaction between the reacting particles for successful reaction.

(c) (i) Order of reaction is an experimental quantity. It can be zero and even in fraction but molecularity cannot be zero or a non integer.

(ii) Order is applicable to elementary as well as complex reaction where as molecularity is applicable only for elementary reactions.

(iii) For complex reaction, order is given by the slowest step and molecularity of the slowest step is same as the order of overall reaction.

Chapter 5. Surface Chemistry

Q. 1. Answer the following questions:
   (i)   What is zeta potential? Explain.
   (ii) Why colloidal solutions have different solutions?
   (iii) Medicines are more effective in colloidal states. Why?
   (iv) What is added to gasoline to decrease knocking?

Ans. (i)   As colloidal particles adsorb a specific charge on their surface, to acquire either negative or positive charge, they attract further oppositely charged ions from the dispersed medium which forms a second layer of mobile opposite charge which surrounds the first fix layer. Such a double layer of opposite charges is called Helmholtz-double layer, as shown in figure.

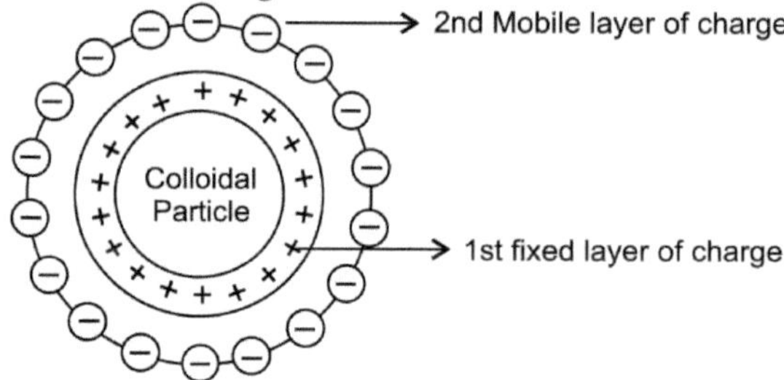

The mobile layer differences into the bulk of the liquid. The potential difference between the fixed layer and the mobile diffused layer is called electrokinetic potential or zeta potential.

   (ii) Colour of a colloidal solution depends upon the size and shape of dispersed phase and nature of dispersion medium. Hence different colloidal solutions transmit different light of spectrum depending upon the variations and hence have different colours.

   (iii) Mostly drugs are solid as emulsions and digestive enzymes easily acts upon these colloidal solutions to carry out their metabolic functions.

   (iv) Tetraethyl lead (TEL).

Q. 2. What is an adsorption isotherm? Describe Freundlich adsorption isotherm.

Ans. The plot between the extent of adsorption $\left(\dfrac{x}{m}\right)$ against the pressure of gas (P) at constant temperature (T) is called the adsorption isotherm.

Freundlich adsorption isotherm : Freundlich adsorption isotherm gives an empirical relationship between the quantity of gas adsorbed by the unit mass of solid adsorbent and pressure at a specific temperature.

Case I. At low pressure : The plot is straight and sloping, indicating that the pressure is directly proportional to

$$\dfrac{x}{m}, i.e., \dfrac{x}{m} \propto P$$

$$\dfrac{x}{m} = kP \ (k \text{ is a constant})$$

Case II. At high pressure : When pressure exceeds the saturated pressure, $\dfrac{x}{m}$ becomes independent of P values.

$$\dfrac{x}{m} \propto P^{\circ}$$

$$\dfrac{x}{m} = kP^{\circ}$$

$$\Rightarrow \qquad \dfrac{x}{m} = k$$

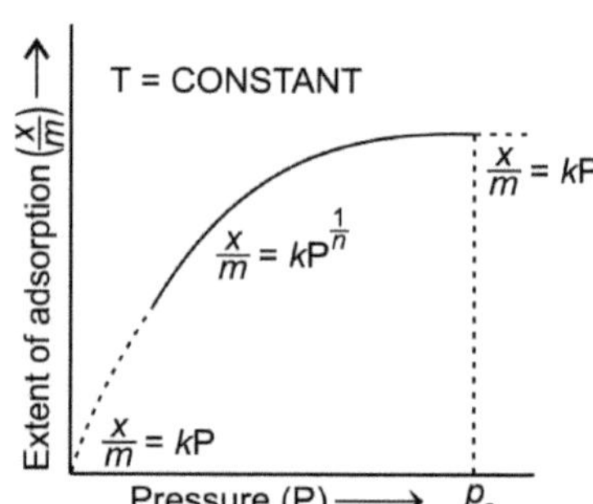

Case III. At intermediate pressure : At intermediate pressure, $\dfrac{x}{m}$ depends on P raised to the powers between 0 and 1. This relationship is known as the Freundlich adsorption isotherm.

$$\dfrac{x}{m} \propto P^{\frac{1}{n}}$$

$$\frac{x}{m} = kP^{\frac{1}{n}}, n > 1$$

Now, taking log:

$$\log \frac{x}{m} = \log k + \frac{1}{n} \log P$$

On plotting the graph between $\log \left(\dfrac{x}{m} \right)$ and log P, a straight line is obtained with the slope equal to $\dfrac{1}{n}$ and the

intercept equal to log k.

Q. 3. What are lyophilic and lyophobic sols? Give one example of each type. Why are hydrophobic sols easily coagulated?

Ans. (i) Lyophilic sols : Colloidal sols that are formed by mixing substances such as gum, gelatin, starch, etc., with a suitable liquid (dispersion medium) are called lyophilic sols. These sols are reversible in nature *i.e.*, if two constituents of the sol are separated by any means (such as evaporation), then the sol can be prepared again by simply mixing the dispersion medium with the dispersion phase and shaking the mixture.

(ii) Lyophobic sols : When substances such as metals and their sulphides etc., are mixed with the dispersion medium, they do not form colloidal sols. Their colloidal sols can be prepared only by special methods. Such sols are called lyophobic sols. These sols are irreversible in nature. For example : Sols of metals, sols of Au and Ag.

Now, the stability of hydrophilic sols depends on two things the presence of a charge and the solvation of colloidal particles. On the other hand, the stability of hydrophobic sols is only because of the presence of a charge. Therefore, the latter are much less stable than the former. If the charge of hydrophobic sols is removed (by addition of electrolytes), then the particles present in them come closer and form aggregates, leading to precipitation or coagulation.

Q. 4. What is the difference between multimolecular and macromolecular colloids? Give one example of each. How are associated colloids different from these two types of colloids?

Ans. (i) In multi-molecular colloids: The colloidal particles are an aggregate of atoms or small molecules with a diameter of less than 1 nm. The molecules in the aggregate are held together by Van der Waal's forces of attraction. Examples of such colloids include gold sol and sulphur sol.

(ii) In macro-molecular colloids: The colloidal particles are large molecules having colloidal dimensions. These particles have a high molecular mass. When these particles are dissolved in a liquid, sol is obtained. For example : Starch, nylon, cellulose, etc.

(iii) Certain substances tend to behave like normal electrolytes at lower concentrations. However, at higher concentrations, these substances behave as colloidal solutions due to the formation of aggregated particles. Such colloids are called aggregated colloids.

Q. 5. What are enzymes? Write in brief the mechanism of enzyme catalysis.

Ans. Enzymes are basically protein molecules of high molecular masses. These form colloidal solutions when dissolved in water. These are complex, nitrogeneous organic compounds produced by living plants and animals. Enzymes are also called 'biochemical catalysts'.

$$E + S \rightleftharpoons [E - S] \rightarrow E + P$$

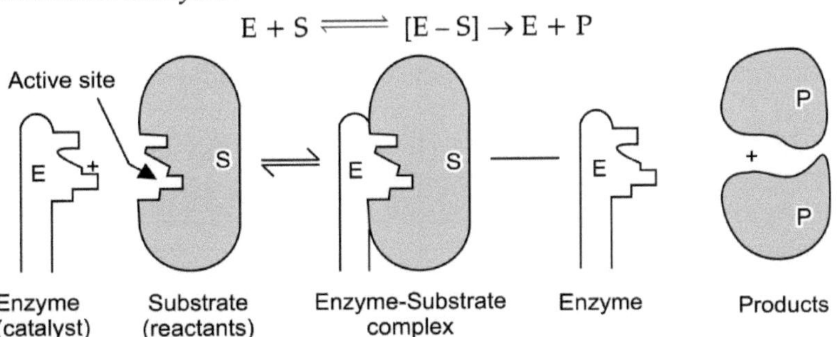

Mechanism of enzyme catalysis: On the surface of the enzymes, various cavities are present with characteristic shapes. These cavities possess active groups such as $-NH_2$, $-COOH$, etc. The reactant molecules having a complementary shape fit into the cavities just like a key fits into a lock. This leads to the formation of an activated complex. This complex then decomposes to give the product.

Hence,

Step 1: $$E + S \rightarrow ES^+$$

(Activated complex)

Step 2: $$ES^+ \rightarrow E + P$$

Q. 6. Explain what is observed:

    (i)   When a beam of light is passed through a colloidal sol.

    (ii) An electrolyte, NaCl is added to hydrated ferric oxide sol.

    (iii) Electric current is passed through a colloidal sol?

Ans. (i)   When a beam of light is passed through a colloidal solution, then scattering of light is observed. This is known as the Tyndall effect. This scattering of light illuminates the path of the beam in the colloidal solution.

    (ii) When NaCl is added to ferric oxide sol, it dissociates to give Na^+ and Cl^- ions. Particles of ferric oxide sol are positively charged. Thus, they get coagulated in the presence of negatively charged Cl^- ions as opposite charges neutralises the colloid particles.

    (iii) The colloidal particles are charged and carry either a positive or negative charge. The dispersion medium carries an equal and opposite charge. This makes the whole system neutral. Under the influence of an electric current, the colloidal particles move towards the oppositely charged electrode. When they come in contact with the electrode, they lose their charge and coagulate. This process is called electrophoresis.

Q. 7. Action of soap is due to emulsification and micelle formation. Comment.

Ans. The cleansing action of soap is due to emulsification and micelle formation. Soaps are basically sodium and potassium salts of long chain fatty acids, $R\text{–}COO^-Na^+$. The end of the molecule to which the sodium is attached is polar in nature, while the alkyl-end is non-polar. Thus, a soap molecule contains a hydrophilic (polar) and a hydrophobic (non-polar) part.

When soap is added to water containing dirt, the soap molecules surround the dirt particles in such a manner that their hydrophobic part gets attached to the dirt molecule and the hydrophilic part point away from the dirt molecule. This is known as micelle formation. Thus, we can say that the polar group dissolves in water while the non-polar group dissolves in the dirt particle. Now, as these micelles are negatively charged, they do not coagulate and a stable emulsion is formed.

Q. 8. What do you mean by activity and selectivity of catalysts?

Ans. **(i)** **Activity of a catalyst:** The activity of a catalyst is its ability to increase the rate of a particular reaction. Chemisorption is the main factor in deciding the activity of a catalyst. The adsorption of reactants on the catalyst surface should be neither too strong nor too weak. It should just be strong enough to make the catalyst active.

    (ii) **Selectivity of the catalyst:** The ability of the catalyst to direct a reaction to yield a particular product is referred to as the selectivity of the catalyst. For example, by using different catalysts, we can get different products for the reaction between H_2 and CO;

      (i) $CO(g) + 3H_2(g) \xrightarrow{\ Ni\ } CH_4(g) + H_2O(g)$

      (ii) $CO(g) + 2H_2(g) \xrightarrow{\ Cu/ZnO\text{-}CrO_3\ } CH_3OH(g)$

      (iii) $CO(g) + H_2(g) \xrightarrow{\ Cu\ } HCHO(g)$

Q. 9. Explain the following terms:

    (i) Electrophoresis   (ii) Coagulation   (iii) Dialysis   (iv) Tyndall effect

Ans. **(i)** **Electrophoresis:** The movement of colloidal particles under the influence of an applied electric field is known as electrophoresis. Positively charged particles move to the cathode, while negatively charged particles move towards the anode. As the particles reach oppositely charged electrodes, they become neutral and get coagulated.

    (ii) **Coagulation:** The process of settling down of colloidal particles *i.e.,* conversion of a colloid into a precipitate is called coagulation.

    (iii) **Dialysis:** The process of removing a dissolved substance from a colloidal solution by the means of diffusion through a membrane is known as dialysis. This process is based on the principle that ions and small molecules can pass through animal membranes unlike colloidal particles.

    (iv) **Tyndall effect:** When a beam of light is allowed to pass through a colloidal solution, it becomes visible like a column of light. This is known as the Tyndall effect. This phenomenon takes place as particles of colloidal dimensions scatter light in all directions.

Chapter 6. General Principles and Processes of Isolation of Elements

Q. 1. Answer the following:
   (i) Difference between electrolyte reduction and reduction with carbon. Explain.
   (ii) Why roasting of cinnabar (HgS) produce mercury and not mercury oxide.
   (iii) Gold extraction with NaCN involves both oxidation and reduction. Explain.

Ans. (i) In electrolytic reduction: The reduction of metal occurs at cathode by gain of electrons by passing current while in carbon reduction its done by heating the metal oxide with coke.

$$\text{NaCl (Molten)} \xrightarrow{\text{Electrolysis}} \text{Na}^+ + \text{Cl}^- \text{ (Electrolytic red.)}$$

e.g.,

$$\text{Na}^+ + e^- \longrightarrow \text{Na}$$

Coke Reduction:
$$\text{ZnO} + \text{C} \xrightarrow{\text{Heat}} \text{Z} + \text{CO}$$

(ii) Hg is a less reactive metal. $\Delta G°$ of formation of HgO is positive hence, it is unstable as compared to other oxides. So on heating with air the HgO formed, decomposes simultaneously to give metallic Hg.

$$2\text{HgS} + 3\text{O}_2 \xrightarrow{\Delta} 2\text{HgO} + 2\text{SO}_2$$

$$2\text{HgO} \xrightarrow{\Delta} 2\text{Hg} + \text{O}_2$$

(iii) The hydrometallurgy step is a redox reaction by itself.
$$4\text{Au} + 8\text{NaCN} + \text{O}_2 + \text{H}_2\text{O} \longrightarrow 4\text{Na [Au(CN)}_2] + 4\text{NaOH}$$

Here gold is oxidised,
$$\text{Au} \longrightarrow \text{Au}^+ \text{ ions}$$
and O_2 is reduced,
$$\text{O}_2 \longrightarrow \text{OH}^- \text{ ions}$$

Q. 2. Explain: (i) Zone refining, (ii) Column chromatography.

Ans. (i) Zone refining: This method is based on the principle that impurities are more soluble in the molten state of metal (the melt) than in the solid state. In the process of zone refining, a circular mobile heater is fixed at one end of a rod of impure metal. As the heater moves, the molten zone of the rod also moves with it. As a result, pure metal crystallises out of the melt and the impurities pass onto the adjacent molten zone. This process is repeated several times, which leads to the segregation of impurities at one end of the rod. Then, the end with the impurities is cut off. Silicon, boron, gallium, indium etc., can be purified by this process.

(ii) Column chromatography : Column chromatography is a technique used to separate different components of a mixture. It is a very useful technique used for the purification of elements available in minute quantities. It is also used to remove the impurities that are not very different in chemical properties from the element to be purified.

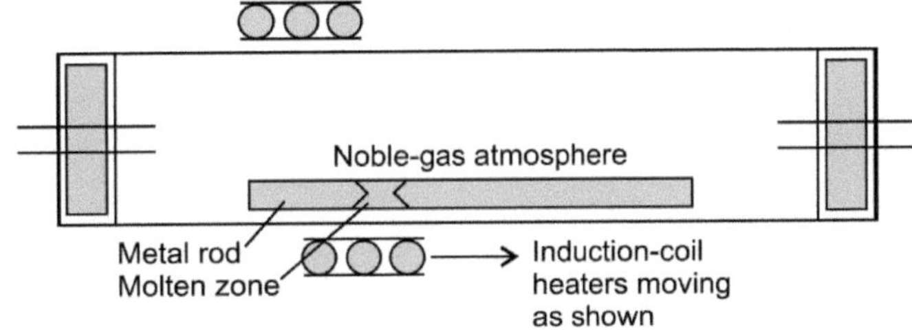

Chromatography is based on the principle that different components of a mixture are differently adsorbed on an adsorbent. In chromatography, there are two phases- mobile phase and stationary phase. The stationary phase is immobile and immiscible. Alumina (Al_2O_3) column is usually used as the stationary phase in column chromatography. The mobile phase may be a gas, liquid or supercritical fluid in which the sample extract is dissolved. Then, the mobile phase is forced to move through the stationary phase. The component that is more strongly adsorbed on the column takes a longer time to travel through it than the component that is weakly adsorbed. The adsorbed components are then removed (eluted) using a suitable solvent (eluant).

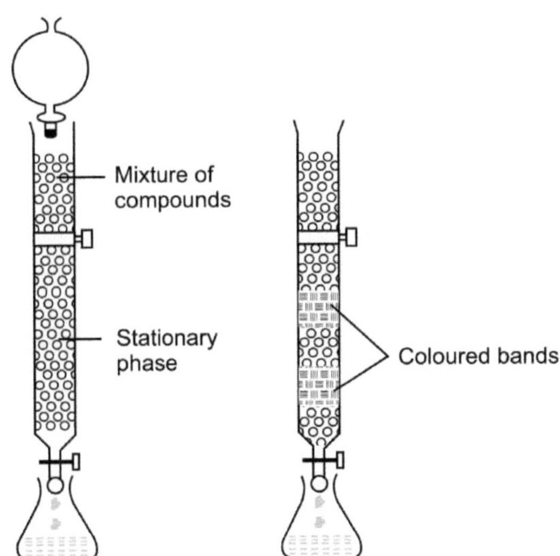

Q. 3. Write down the different reactions taking place in different zones in the blast furnace during extraction of iron.

Ans. During extraction of iron from haematite ore by smelting (reduction by carbon), charge *i.e.,* 8 parts calcinated ore + 4 parts coke and a part lime stone (flux) is added from the top of the furnace. The hot air is blown from the bottom of the blast furnace as shown in given fig. Throughout the length of the furnace various temperature zones are produced where various reactions takes place. The molten iron is collected from a tapping hole near the bottom, just below the slag layer. The various zones and the reactions are as follows:

(i) Zone of combustion; (2100-1500 K): At the bottom of the furnace where blast of hot air flowing inside through furnace causes combustion of coke into carbon dioxide. Its a highly exothermic reaction.

(a) $$C(s) + O_2(g) \longrightarrow CO_2(s); \Delta H = -393.5 \text{ kJ.}$$
Coke   Air

This reaction supplies heat for all the other reactions.

(ii) Zone of heat absorbtion (1500-1200 K): As CO_2 gas rises up, it combines with more coke to form carbon monoxide. This reaction is endothermic hence brings down the temperature of the middle zone of furnace.

(b) $$C(s) + CO_2(g) \longrightarrow 2CO(g) ; \Delta H = +173 \text{ kJ}$$

(iii) Zone of slag formation (1100 K-1200 K): In the middle of the blast furnace only, lime stone decomposes to form CaO and CO_2. The CaO combines with impurity silica (SiO_2) to form slag, calcium silicate:

(c) $$CaCO_3(s) \xrightarrow{1123 \text{ K}} CaO(s) + CO_2(g)$$

(d) $$CaO(s) + SiO_2(s) \xrightarrow{1123 \text{ K}} CaSiO_3(s)$$
Slag

(iv) Zone of reduction (500 K - 900 K): In the upper part of the blast furnace, the reduction reactions takes place.

(e) $$3Fe_2O_3(s) + CO(g) \xrightarrow{573K - 673K} 2Fe_3O_4(s) + CO_2(g)$$

(f) $$FeO.Fe_2O_3 + CO(g) \xrightarrow{873 \text{ K}} 3FeO(s) + CO_2(g)$$

(g) $$Fe_2O_3(s) + CO(g) \xrightarrow{800 \text{ K}} 2FeO(s) + CO_2(g)$$

(h) $$FeO(s) + CO(g) \xrightarrow{1173 \text{ K}} Fe(s) + CO_2(g)$$

(i) $$Fe_2O_3(s) + 3C(s) \xrightarrow{1150 \text{ K}} 2Fe(l) + 3CO(g)$$
Direct   Molten
reduction   iron

(v) Zone of fusion (500-200 K) : This is the lower part of the furnace where iron melts and dissolves small amount of C, S, P, Si and Mn etc. The slag also melts here and get collected over the molten iron which is heavier.

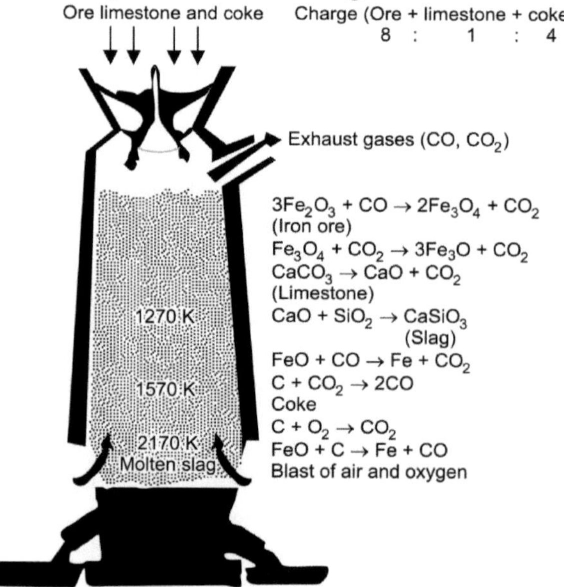

Q. 4. How can you separate alumina from silica in bauxite ore associated with silica? Give equations, if any.

Ans. To separate alumina from silica in bauxite ore associated with silica, first the powdered ore is digested with a concentrated NaOH solution at 473 – 523 K and 35 – 36 bar pressure. This results in the leaching out of alumina (Al_2O_3) as sodium aluminate and silica (SiO_2) as sodium silicate leaving the impurities behind.

$$Al_2O_3(s) + 2NaOH(aq) + 3H_2O(l) \longrightarrow 2Na[Al(OH)_4](aq)$$

Alumina   Sodium aluminate

$$SiO_2 + 2\,NaOH(aq) \longrightarrow Na_2SiO_3(aq) \quad + \quad H_2O(l)$$

Silica   Sodium silicate

Then, CO_2 gas is passed through the resulting solution to neutralise the aluminate in the solution, which results in the precipitation of hydrated alumina. To induce precipitation, the solution is seeded with freshly prepared samples of hydrated alumina.

$$2Na[Al(OH)_4](aq) + CO_2(g) \longrightarrow Al_2O_3.xH_2O(s) \quad + \quad 2NaHCO_3(aq)$$

Sodium aluminate   Hydrated alumina   Sodium hydrogen carbonate

During this process, sodium silicate remains in the solution. The obtained hydrated alumina is filtered, dried and heated to get back pure alumina.

$$Al_2O_3.xH_2O(s) \xrightarrow{\;\;1470\ K\;\;} Al_2O_3(s) + xH_2O(g)$$

Hydrated alumina   Alumina

Q. 5. Out of C and CO, which is a better reducing agent for ZnO?

Ans. Reduction of ZnO to Zn is usually carried out at 1673 K. From the above figure, it can be observed that above 1073 K, the Gibbs free energy of formation of CO from C and above 1273 K, the Gibbs free energy of formation of CO_2 from C is lesser than the Gibbs free energy of formation of ZnO. Therefore, C can easily reduce ZnO to Zn.

On the other hand, the Gibbs free energy of formation of CO_2 from CO is always higher than the Gibbs free energy of formation of ZnO. Therefore, CO cannot reduce ZnO. Hence, C is a better reducing agent than CO for reducing ZnO.

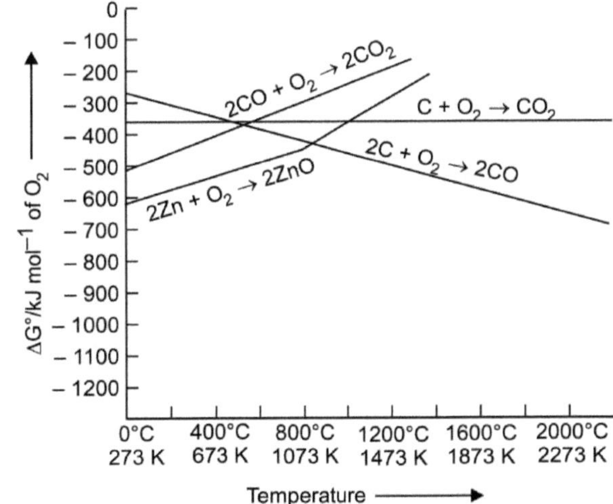

Q. 6. The choice of a reducing agent in a particular case depends on thermodynamic factor. How far do you agree with this statement? Support your opinion with two examples.

Ans. The below figure is a plot of Gibbs energy ($\Delta G°$) Vs. T for formation of some oxides. It can be observed from the above graph that a metal can reduce the oxide of other metals, if the standard free energy of formation ($\Delta_f G°$) of the oxide of the former is more negative than the latter. For example, since $\Delta_f G°_{(Al_2,\ Al_2O_3)}$ is more negative than $\Delta_f G°_{(Cu,\ Cu_2O)}$, Al can reduce Cu_2O to Cu, but Cu cannot reduce Al_2O_3. Similarly, Mg can reduce ZnO to Zn, but Zn cannot reduce MgO because $\Delta_f G°_{(Mg,\ MgO)}$ is more negative than $\Delta_f G°_{(Zn,\ ZnO)}$. Hence a metal oxide placed lower in the Ellingham diagram cannot be reduced by the metal involved in the formation of the oxide placed higher in the diagram.

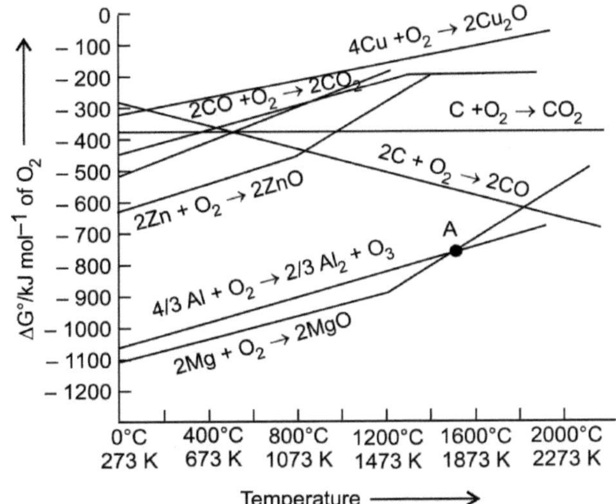

Q. 7. **Name the processes from which chlorine is obtained as a by-product. What will happen if an aqueous solution of NaCl is subjected to electrolysis?**

Ans. In the electrolysis of molten NaCl, Cl_2 is obtained at the anode as a by-product. This is called Dow's process.

At cathode:
$$NaCl_{(melt)} \longrightarrow Na^+_{(melt)} + Cl^-_{(melt)}$$

At anode:
$$Na^+_{(melt)} + e^- \longrightarrow Na(s)$$
$$Cl^-_{(melt)} \longrightarrow Cl(g) + e^-$$
$$2Cl(g) \longrightarrow Cl_2(g)$$

The overall reaction is as follows:

$$NaCl_{(melt)} \xrightarrow{\text{Electrolysis}} Na(s) + \frac{1}{2} Cl_2(g)$$

If an aqueous solution of NaCl is electrolysed, Cl_2 will be obtained at the anode but at the cathode, H_2 will be obtained (instead of Na). This is because the standard reduction potential of Na. ($E° = -2.71$ V) is more negative than that of H_2O ($E° = -0.83$ V). Hence, H_2O will get preference to get reduced at the cathode and as a result, H_2 is evolved.

$$NaCl(aq) \longrightarrow Na^+(aq) + Cl^-(aq)$$

At cathode:
$$2H_2O(l) + e^- \longrightarrow H_2(g) + 2OH^-(aq)$$

At anode:
$$Cl^-_{(melt)} \longrightarrow Cl_2(g) + e^-$$
$$2Cl(g) \longrightarrow Cl_2(g)$$

Q. 8. **Outline the principles of refining of metals by the following methods:**

    (i)   Electrolytic refining   (ii) Vapour phase refining

Ans. **(i)** **Electrolytic refining:** Electrolytic refining is the process of refining impure metals by using electricity. In this process, impure metal is made the anode and a strip of pure metal is made the cathode. A solution of a soluble salt of the same metal is taken as the electrolyte. When an electric current is passed, metal ions from the electrolyte are deposited at the cathode as pure metal and the impure metal from the anode dissolves into the electrolyte in the form of ions. The impurities present in the impure metal gets collected below the anode.

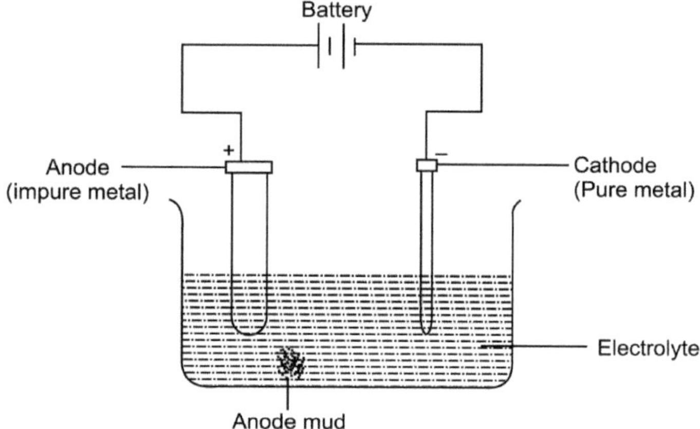

This is known as anode mud.

Anode:
$$M \longrightarrow M^{n+} + ne^-$$

Cathode:
$$M^{n-} + ne^- \longrightarrow M$$

(ii) **Vapour phase refining:** Vapour phase refining is the process of refining metal by converting it into its volatile compound and then, decomposing it to obtain a pure metal. To carry out this process,

(i)   The metal should form a volatile compound with an available reagent.

(ii) The volatile compound should be easily decomposable so that the metal can be easily recovered.

Nickel, zirconium and titanium are refined using this method.

Example:

$$Ti + 2I_2 \xrightarrow{500 \text{ K}} TiI_4$$
$$\text{(Impure metal)}$$

$$TiI_4 \xrightarrow{1700 \text{ K}} Ti + 2I_2$$
$$\text{(Pure metal)}$$

Q. 9. **What is the significance of leaching in the extraction of aluminium?**

Ans. In the extraction of aluminium, the significance of leaching is to concentrate pure alumina (Al_2O_3) from bauxite ore.

Bauxite usually contains silica, iron oxide and titanium oxide as impurities. In the process of leaching, alumina is concentrated by digesting the powdered ore with a concentrated solution of NaOH at 473-523 K. Alumina

(Al_2O_3) dissolves as sodium meta-aluminate and silica (SiO_2) dissolves as sodium silicate leaving the impurities behind.

$$Al_2O_3(s) + 2NaOH(aq) + 3H_2O(l) \xrightarrow[\text{35–36 bar}]{\text{473–523 K}} 2Na[Al(OH)_4](aq)$$

Alumina   Sodium aluminate

$$SiO_2(l) + 2NaOH(aq) \xrightarrow[\text{35–36 bar}]{\text{473–523 K}} NaSiO_3(aq) + H_2O(l)$$

Silica   Sodium silicate

The impurities are then filtered and the solution is neutralised by passing CO_2 gas. In this process, hydrated Al_2O_3 gets precipitated and sodium silicate remains in the solution. Precipitation is induced by seeding the solution with freshly prepared samples of hydrated Al_2O_3.

$$2Na[Al(OH)_4](aq) + CO_2(g) \longrightarrow Al_2O_3.xH_2O(s) + 2NaHCO_3(aq)$$

Hydrated alumina

Hydrated alumina thus obtained is filtered, dried and heated to give back pure alumina (Al_2O_3).

$$Al_2O_3.xH_2O(s) \xrightarrow{1470} Al_2O_3(s) + xH_2O(g)$$

Q. 10. Write chemical reactions taking place in the extraction of zinc from zinc blende.

Ans. The different steps involved in the extraction of zinc from zinc blende (ZnS) are given below:

  (i) **Concentration of ore:** First, the gangue from zinc blende is removed by the froth floatation method.

 (ii) **Conversion to oxide (Roasting):** Sulphide ore is converted into oxide by the process of roasting. In this process, ZnS is heated in a regular supply of air in a furnace at a temperature, which is below the melting point of Zn.

$$2ZnS + 3O_2 \longrightarrow 2ZnO + 2SO_2$$

(iii) **Extraction of zinc from zinc oxide (Reduction):** Zinc is extracted from zinc oxide by the process of reduction. The reduction of zinc oxide is carried out by mixing it with powdered coke and then, heating it at 673 K.

$$ZnO + C \xrightarrow{\text{coke, 673 K}} Zn + CO$$

(iv) **Electrolytic Refining:** Zinc can be refined by the process of electrolytic refining. In this process, impure zinc is made the anode while a pure copper strip is made the cathode. The electrolyte used is an acidified solution of zinc sulphate $(ZnSO_4)$. Electrolysis results in the transfer of zinc in pure form, from the anode to the cathode.

Anode: $Zn \longrightarrow Zn^{2+} + 2e^-$

Cathode: $Zn^{2+} + 2e^- \longrightarrow Zn$

Chapter 7. *p*-Block Elements

Q. 1. (i) Account for the following:

    (a) Fluorine forms only one oxoacid HOF.   (b) HClO is a stronger acid than HBrO.

 (ii) Draw the structures of:

    (a) ClF_3 (b) XeF_6

Ans. (i) (a) Due to small size, high electronegativity and absence of *d*-orbitals fluorine forms only one oxo-acid.

      (b) HBrO is less acidic than HClO because chlorine is more electronegative than bromine. More electronegative halogen attracts the electron cloud towards itself and makes the O—H bond more polar for easy release of H^+ ion.

(ii) (a) 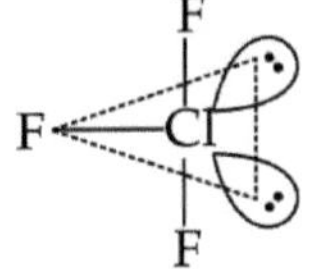   T-shape

(b) 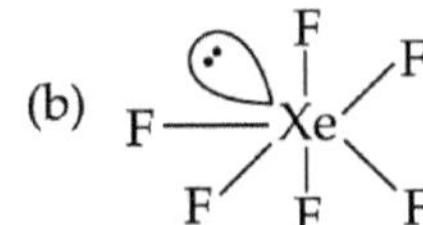   Distorted Octahedral

Q. 2. (i)   Complete the following chemical reactions:

      (a) $XeF_4 + H_2O \longrightarrow$

  (ii)   Explain the following:

      (a)   Halogens are strong oxidizing agents.

  (iii)   Draw structure of $H_2S_2O_8$.

Ans. (i) $6XeF_4 + 12H_2O \longrightarrow 2XeO_3 + 4Xe + 24HF + 3O_2$

  (ii)   Halogens readily accept electron hence they are good oxidising agents.

  (iii) $H_2S_2O_8$ (Peroxodisulphuric acid)

Q. 3. (i)   Draw the structures of the following:

      (a) $HClO_3$ (b) $H_2S_2O_7$

  (ii)   Explain the following observations:

      (a)   In the structure of HNO_3, the N—O bond (121 pm) is shorter than the N—OH bond.

      (b)   Sulphur has greater tendency for catenation than oxygen.

      (c)   The negative value of electron gain enthalpy of fluorine is less than that of chlorine.

Ans. (i)   (a) $HClO_3$ (b) $H_2S_2O_7$ (Oleum)

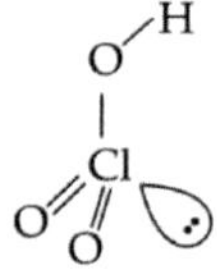 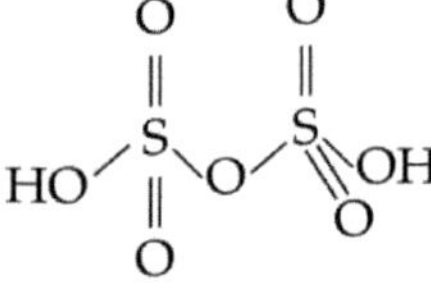

  (ii)   (a)   In the structure of HNO_3, the double bond character of N—O bond shortens the bond length, whereas N—OH bond has no such double bond character.

      (b)   The S—S bond is much more strong than O—O bond so sulphur has more tendency of catenation.

      (c)   Due to small size of fluorine, strong repulsion of electrons is there which causes negative electron gain enthalpy.

Chapter 8. *d-* and *f-*Block Elements

Q. 1. (i)   Give reason for the following:

      (a) Mn^{3+} is a good oxidising agent.   (c)   Transition elements acts as good catalyst.

      (b)   Cadmium salts are white.

  (ii)   Explain chromyl chloride test, write the reaction involved.

Ans. (i)   (a) Mn^{3+} has $3d^4 4s^0$ electronic configuration, which energy changes to $4s^0 3d^5$ by accepting an electron and acting as a good oxidising agent. It has a very high $E°Mn^{3+}/Mn^{2+}$ value about 1.57 V.

      (b)   Cd salts are white as Cd^{2+} ion has $3d^{10} 4s^0$ configuration with all electrons paired, hence no d-d transition so no colour.

      (c)   As transition elements have variable oxidation states hence they can easily tend and take electrons. Thus can bind with compounds, provides surface area, decrease the activation energy of the reactant compounds and again unbind after formation of products.

  (ii)   **Chromyl Chloride Test:** The test is for chloride ions in qualitative analysis. The chromyl chloride vapours when passed through aqueous solution of sodium hydroxide it turns yellow. On adding few drops of lead acetate along with acetic acid a yellow precipitate of lead chromate is formed.

      This chromyl chloride is formed on treating the chloride salt with potassium dichromate and conc. H_2SO_4 and heating.

$$K_2Cr_2O_7 + 2H_2SO_4 \longrightarrow 2KHSO_4 + 2CrO_3 + H_2O$$

$$CaCl_2 + H_2SO_4 \longrightarrow CaSO_4 + 2HCl$$

$$CrO_3 + 2HCl \longrightarrow CrO_2Cl_2 + H_2O$$

$$\text{Chromyl chloride}$$

$$K_2Cr_2O_7 + 2CaCl_2 + 4H_2SO_4 \longrightarrow 2CrO_2Cl_2 + 2CaSO_4 + 3H_2O + 2KHSO_4$$

Q. 2. On the basis of lanthanoid contraction, explain the following:

(i) Nature of bonding in Ca_2O_3 and Cu_2O_3.

(ii) Trends in the stability of oxo salts of lanthanoids from La to Lu.

(iii) Stability of the complexes of lanthanoids.

(iv) The atomic radius of the $4d$ and $5d$ series elements are quite similar.

(v) Acidic character of lanthanoid oxides increases from left to right.

Ans. (i) La (57) is present in d-block and 3rd group of periodic table, while Lu(+1) is the last element of lanthanoid series. Hence La is more metallic than Lu. Also there is steady decrease in size along a period because of lanthanoid contraction. As a result La_2O_3 is more ionic in nature than Lu_2O_3, which is covalent.

(ii) As one proceeds from La (57) to Lu (71) the size of the elements decreases, as a result oxo-salts becomes more and more covalent. As ionic oxo salts are more stable, hence stability of the oxo-salts decreases.

(iii) Smaller the size of central metal, more strong is the complex bond formation, hence ligands binds better. So stability of complexes of lanthanoids increases on moving left to right in period.

(iv) The atomic radius of the $4d$ and $5d$ series elements are quite similar because of lanthanoid contraction.

(v) As we move in lanthanoid series the size decreases and that too the metallic character of oxides. M_2O_3 generally dissolves in water to give $M(OH)_3$. As size of M, decreases the M–OH, bonds become more covalent leading to increase in acidic nature of M–O–H bond as H^+ can be easily released. Hence acidic character of lanthanoid oxides increases from left to right.

Q. 3. What is lanthanoid contraction? What are the consequences of lanthanoid contraction?*

Ans. The steady decrease in atomic size with increase in atomic number among the lanthanoids on moving from left to right in a series is called lanthanoid contraction. This happens because of the increase in nuclear attraction because the addition of proton is more pronounced than the increase in the interelectronic repulsions due to the addition of electrons. The $4f$ electrons have poor shielding effect. Therefore, the effective nuclear charge experienced by the outer electrons increases. This results in a steady decrease in the size of lanthanoids with the increase in the atomic number.

Consequences of lanthanoid contraction:

(i) There is similarity in the properties of second and third transition series.

(ii) Separation of lanthanoids is very difficult due to lanthanide contraction ion-exchange method is employed for that.

(iii) It is due to lanthanide contraction that covalent character increases in lanthanide hydroxides. Basic strength decreases from $La(OH)_3$ to $Lu(OH)_3$; where $La(OH)_3$ is most basic and $Lu(OH)_3$ is least basic.

Q. 4. Explain giving reasons:

(i) Transition metals and many of their compounds show paramagnetic behaviour.

(ii) The enthalpies of atomisation of the transition metals are high.

(iii) The transition metals generally form coloured compounds.**

(iv) Transition metals and their many compounds act as good catalyst.*

Ans. (i) Transition metals show paramagnetic behaviour due to the presence of unpaired electrons in the d-orbitals. Each electron having a magnetic moment associated with its spin angular momentum. However, in the first transition series, the orbital angular momentum is quenched. Therefore, the resulting paramagnetism is only because of the unpaired electron.

(ii) Transition elements have large number of d-shell valence electrons. Therefore, they form very strong metallic bonds. As a result, the enthalpy of atomisation of transition metals is high.

(iii) Most of the complexes of transition metals are coloured. This is because of the absorption of radiation from visible light region to promote an electron from one of the d-orbitals to another that is d-d transition. In the presence of ligands, the d-orbitals split up into two sets of orbitals having different energies. Therefore, the transition of electrons can take place from one set to another. The energy required for these transitions is quite small and falls in the visible region of radiation. Hence reflected radiation is visible in the form of coloured solutions.

(iv) The catalytic activity of the transition elements can be explained by two basic facts:

(a) Because of their ability to show variable oxidation states and form complexes, transition metals form unstable intermediate compounds. Thus, they provide a new path with lower activation energy, E_a, for the reaction to proceed.

(b) Transition metals also provide a suitable surface for the reactions to occur, *i.e.*, act as a solid adsorption medium.

Q. 5. (i) How is the variability in oxidation states of transition metals different from that of the non-transition metals? Illustrate with examples.

(ii) Describe the preparation of potassium dichromate from iron chromite ore. What is the effect of increasing pH on a solution of potassium dichromate?*

Ans. (i) The transition metal shows huge variety of oxidation states of the participation of ns and $(n-1)$ d orbital electrons. Whereas the non-transition elements have limited number of oxidation state as only s and ns orbital electrons can participate in bonding. Also the oxidation states can vary by unity like V^{II}, V^{III}, V^{IV} etc. While in case of p-block it varies by 2 electrons. Like Ga + 1, +3.

(ii) Potassium dichromate is prepared from chromite ore ($FeCr_2O_4$) in the following steps.

Step 1. Preparation of sodium chromate

$$4FeCr_2O_4 + 16NaOH + 7O_2 \longrightarrow 8Na_2CrO_4 + 2Fe_2O_3 + 8H_2O$$

Step 2. Conversion of sodium chromate into sodium dichromate.

$$2Na_2CrO_4 + conc.\ H_2SO_4 \longrightarrow Na_2Cr_2O_7 + Na_2SO_4 + H_2O$$

Step 3. Conversion of sodium dichromate to potassium dichromate.

$$Na_2Cr_2O_7 + 2KCl \longrightarrow K_2Cr_2O_7 + 2NaCl$$

Potassium chloride being less soluble than sodium chloride is obtained in the form of orange coloured crystals and can be removed by filtration.

The dichromate ion ($Cr_2O_7^{2-}$) exists in equilibrium with chromate (CrO_4^{2-}) ion at pH 4.

However, by changing the pH, they can be interconverted. Thus on increasing pH the colour of solution changes from orange to yellow by conversion of dichromate to chromate.

$$2CrO_4^{2-} \underset{Base}{\rightleftharpoons} 2HCrO_4^- \underset{Acid}{\rightleftharpoons} Cr_2O_7^{2-}$$

Chromate   Hydrogen   Dichromate

(Yellow)   chromate   (Orange)

Q. 6. Compare the stability of +2 oxidation state for the elements of the first transition series.

Ans.

Sc			+3				
Ti	+1	+2	+3	+4			
V	+1	+2	+3	+4	+5		
Cr	+1	+2	+3	+4	+5	+6	
Mn	+1	+2	+3	+4	+5	+6	+7
Fe	+1	+2	+3	+4	+5	+6	

Co	+1	+2	+3	+4	+5
Ni	+1	+2	+3	+4	
Cu	+1	+2	+3		
Zn		+2			

From the above table, it is evident that the maximum number of oxidation states is shown by Mn, varying from +2 to +7. The number of oxidation states increases on moving from Sc to Mn. On moving from Mn to Zn, the number of oxidation states decreases due to a decrease in the number of available unpaired electrons. The relative stability of the +2 oxidation state increases on moving from top to bottom. This is because on moving from top to bottom, it becomes more and more difficult to remove the third electron from the d-orbital.

Q. 7. Compare the chemistry of actinoids with that of the lanthanoids with special reference to:

(i) Electronic configuration   **(iii)** Atomic and ionic sizes

(ii) Oxidation state   **(iv)** Chemical reactivity

Ans. (i) **Electronic configuration:** The general electronic configuration for lanthanoids is $[Xe]^{54}\, 4f^{\,0\text{-}14}\, 5d^{0\text{-}1}\, 6s^2$ and that for actinoids is $[Rn]^{86}\, 5f^{1\text{-}14}\, 6d^{0\text{-}1}\, 7s^2$. Unlike $4f$ orbitals, $5f$ orbitals are not deeply buried and participate in bonding to a greater extent.

(ii) **Oxidation states:** The principal oxidation state of lanthanoids is $(+3)$. However, sometimes we also encounter oxidation states of $+2$ and $+4$. This is because of extra stability of fully-filled and half-filled orbitals. Actinoids exhibit a greater range of oxidation states $+4$, $+5$, $+6$ and $+7$ too. This is because the $5f$, $6d$ and $7s$ levels are of comparable energies. Again $(+3)$ is the most common oxidation state for actinoids. Actinoids like lanthanoids have more compounds in $+3$ state than in $+4$ state.

(iii) **Atomic and Ionic sizes:** Similar to lanthanoids, actinoids also exhibit actinoid contraction (overall decrease in atomic and ionic radii). The contraction is greater due to the poor shielding effect of $5f$ orbitals.

(iv) **Chemical reactivity:** In the lanthanide series, the earlier members of the series are more reactive. They have reactivity that is comparable to Ca. With an increase in the atomic number, the lanthanides start behaving similar to Al, Actinoids, are highly reactive metals, especially when they are finely divided. On adding boiling water, they give a mixture of oxide and hydride. Actinoids combine with most of the non-metals at moderate temperatures. Alkalies have no action on these actinoids. In case of acids, they are slightly affected by nitric acid (because of the formation of a protective oxide layer). They react with HCl to form respective chlorides.

Q. 8. How would you account for the following:

(i) Of the d^4 species, Cr^{2+} is strongly reducing while manganese (III) is strongly oxidising.

(ii) Cobalt (II) is stable in aqueous solution but in the presence of complexing reagents it is easily oxidised.

(iii) The d^1 configuration is very unstable in ions.

Ans. (i) Cr^{2+} is strongly reducing in nature because of d^4 configuration as a reducing agent, it gets oxidised to Cr^{3+} (electronic configuration, d^3) configuration. This d^3 configuration can be written as $t_{2g}^{\,3}$ configuration, which is half-filled and is more stable configuration. In the case of Mn^{3+} (d^4), it acts as an oxidizing agent and gets reduced to Mn^{2+} (d^5). This has an exactly half-filled d-orbital and is highly stable.

(ii) Co (II) is stable in aqueous solutions. However, in the presence of strong field complexing reagents, it is oxidized to Co (III). Although the 3rd ionization energy for Co is high, but the large value of crystal field stabilisation energy (CFSE) released in the presence of strong field ligands overcomes this ionisation energy.

(iii) The ions in d^4 configuration easily loses one more electron to get into stable d^0 configuration. Also, the hydration of lattice energy is more than sufficient to remove the only electron present in the d-orbital of these ions. Therefore, they act as reducing agents.

Q. 9. Compare the general characteristics of the first series of the transition metals with those of the second and third series metals in the respective vertical columns. Give special emphasis on the following points:

(i) Electronic configurations

(ii) Oxidation states

(iii) Ionisation enthalpies

Ans. (i) In the 1st, 2nd and 3rd transition series, the $3d$, $4d$ and $5d$ orbitals are respectively filled.

We know that elements in the same vertical column generally have similar electronic configurations.

In the first transition series, two elements show unusual electronic configurations :

$Cr\ (24) = 3d^5 4s^1$ (Because of extra stability of half filled and fully filled orbitals)

$Cu\ (29) = 3d^{10}\, 4s^1$

Similarly, there are exceptions in the second transition series. These are :

$Mo(42) = 4d^5 5s^1$	$Ru(44) = 4d^7 5s^1$	$Pd(46) = 4d^{10} 5s^0$
$Te(43) = 4d^6 5s^1$	$Rh(45) = 4d^8 5s^1$	$Ag(47) = 4d^{10} 5s^1$

There are some exceptions in the third transition series as well. These are :

$W(74) = 5d^4 6s^2$	$Pt(78) = 5d^9 6s^1$	$Au(79) = 5d^{10} 6s^1$

As a result of these exceptions, it happens many times that the electronic configurations of the elements present in the same group are dissimilar.

(ii) In each of the three transition series the number of oxidation states shown by the elements is the maximum in the middle and the minimum at the extreme ends.

However, $+2$ and $+3$ oxidation states are quite stable for all elements present in the first transition series. All metals present in the first transition series form stable compounds in the $+2$ and $+3$ oxidation states. The stability of the $+2$ and $+3$ oxidation states decreases in the second and the third transition series, where in higher oxidation states are more common.

For example, chromate ion $(CrO_4)^{2-}$ is strong oxidant while molybdate $(MoO_4)^{2-}$ and tungstate $(WO_4)^{2-}$ are stable.

For example: WCl_6, ReF_7, RuO_4, etc., are stable but no such compound of 1st transition series exists.

(iii) In each of the three transition series, the first ionisation enthalpy increases from left to right. The first ionisation enthalpies of the third transition series are higher than those of the first and second transition series. This occurs due to the poor shielding effect of $4f$ electrons in the third transition series. The removal of one electron alters the relative energies of $4s$ and $3d$ orbitals. Hence, their is marginal and irregular increase in ionisation enthalpies.

Q. 10. Comment on the statement that elements of the first transition series possess many properties different from those of heavier transition elements.

Ans. The properties of the elements of the first transition series differ from those of the heavier transition elements in many ways.

(i) The atomic sizes of the elements of the first transition series are smaller than those of the heavier elements (elements of 2nd and 3rd transition series) because of more number of electron shells.

However, the atomic sizes of the elements in the third transition series are quite the same as those of the corresponding members in the second transition series because of lanthanoid contraction.

(ii) $+2$ and $+3$ oxidation states are more common for elements in the first transition series, while higher oxidation states are more common for the $4d$ and $5d$ elements.

(iii) The ionisation enthalpies of the elements in the first $3d$ series are lower than those of the corresponding elements in the second and third transition series.

(iv) Because of the occurrence of stronger metallic bonding (M-M bonding), or inter atomic bonding the m.p. and b.p. of $4d$ and $5d$ transition series are higher.

(v) The elements of the first transition series form low-spin or high-spin complexes depending upon the strength of the ligand field, but the heavier transition elements form only low-spin complexes, irrespective of the strength of the ligand field.

Q. 11. What can be inferred from the magnetic moment values of the following complex species?

$K_4[Mn(CN)_6]$ and magnetic moment (BM) $= 2.2$

$[Fe(H_2O)_6]^{2+}$ and magnetic moment (BM) $= 5.3$

$K_2[MnCl_4]$ and magnetic moment (BM) $= 5.9$

Ans. μ is given as $\mu = \sqrt{n(n+2)}$ moment

For value $n = 1$, $\mu = \sqrt{1(1+2)} = \sqrt{3} = 1.732$

For value $n = 2$, $\mu = \sqrt{2(2+2)} = \sqrt{8} = 2.83$

For value $n = 3$, $\mu = \sqrt{3(3-2)} = \sqrt{15} = 3.87$

For value $n = 4$, $\mu = \sqrt{4(4+2)} = \sqrt{24} = 4.899$

For value $n = 5$, $\mu = \sqrt{5(5+2)} = \sqrt{35} = 5.92$

(i) $K_4[Mn(CN)_6]$

For in transition metals, the magnetic moment is calculated from the spin-only formula. Therefore,

$$\sqrt{n(n+2)} = 2.2$$

We can see from the above calculation that the given value is nearer to $n = 1$. Also, in this complex, Mn is in the $+2$ oxidation state. This means that Mn has 5 electrons in the d-orbital, but presence of only 1 unpaired electron suggests that CN^- is a strong field ligand that causes the pairing of electrons.

(ii) $[Fe(H_2O)_6]^{2+}$

$$\sqrt{n(n+2)} = 5.3$$

We can see from the above calculation that the given value is closest to $n = 4$. Also, in this complex, Fe is in the $+2$ oxidation state. This means that Fe has 6 electrons in the d-orbital, $3d^6 4s^0$, hence electron pairing has not taken place.

Hence, we can say that H_2O is a weak field ligand.

(iii) $K_2[MnCl_4]$

$$\sqrt{n(n+2)} = 5.9$$

We can see from the above calculation that the given value is closest to $n = 5$. Also, in this complex, Mn is in the $+ 2$ oxidation state. This means that Mn has 5 electrons in the d-orbital, $3d^5 4s^0$, hence pairing of electron has not occurred.

Hence, we can say that Cl^- is a weak field ligand.

Q. 12. (i) Account for the following:*

    (a) Transition metals show variable oxidation states.

    (b) Zn, Cd and Hg are soft metals.

    (c) E° value for the Mn^{3+}/Mn^{2+} couple is highly positive ($+ 1.57$ V) as compared to Cr^{3+}/Cr^{2+}.

(ii) Write one similarity and one difference between the chemistry of lanthanoid and actinoid elements.

Ans. (i) (a) Transition metal ions shows variable oxidation states due to the participation of $(n-1)$ d electrons in addition to outer ns-electrons because the energies of ns and $(n-1)d$ subshells are almost equal. As a result of which the electrons of $(n-1)d$ and ns subshell both takes part in bond formation.

    (b) Zn, Cd and Hg are soft metals because of their completely filled $3d$, $4s$ and $5d$ orbitals respectively due to completely filled d-orbitals these metals are reluctant to form Zn – Zn, Cd – Cd and Hg – Hg bonds are comparatively soft metals.

    (c) Highly positive value of E° for Mn^{3+}/Mn^{2+} shows that $Mn^{2+}(d^5)$ is particularly stable. While low value of E° for Cr^{3+}/Cr^{2+} shows that $Cr^{2+}(d^4)$ is less stable than $Cr^{3+}(d^3)$.

(ii) Similarity: In lanthanoids and actinoids both the added e^- enters the antipenultimate shell $4f$ and $5f$ respectively.

Difference: Lanthanoids show a common oxidation state of $+ 3$ while actinoids show different oxidation states other than $+ 3$.

Q. 13. (i) Following are the transition metal ions of $3d$ series:*

$$Ti^{3+}, V^{2+}, Mn^{3+}, Cr^{3+}$$

(Atomic numbers : Ti = 22, V = 23, Mn = 25, Cr = 24)

Answer the following:

    (a) Which ion is most stable in an aqueous solution and why?

    (b) Which ion is a strong oxidising agent and why?

    (c) Which ion is colourless and why?

(ii) Complete the following equation :

    (a) $2MnO_4^- + 16H^+ + 5S^{2-} \rightarrow$ (b) $KMnO_4 \xrightarrow{\text{heat}}$

Ans. (i)

$$Ti^{4+} = 1s^2 2s^2 2p^6 3s^2 3p^6$$
$$V^{2+} = 1s^2 2s^2 2p^6 3s^2 3p^6 3d^3$$
$$Mn^{3+} = 1s^2 2s^2 2p^6 3s^2 3p^6 3d^4$$
$$Cr^{3+} = 1s^2 2s^2 2p^6 3s^2 3d^3$$

    (a) Ti^{4+} is most stable in an aqueous solution because of fully filled valence shell ($3s^2 3p^6$) configuration (noble gas configuration).

    (b) Mn^{3+} is the strong agent as it oxidises other species it will reduce itself by taking an e^- and will stabilise its configuration ($3d^5$).

    (c) Ti^{4+} is colourless due to absence of unpaired electrons ($3s^2 3p^6$)

(ii) (a) $2MnO_4^- + 16H^+ + 5S^{2-} \longrightarrow 2Mn^{2+} + 5S + 8H_2O$

    (b) $2KMnO_4 \xrightarrow{\text{heat}} K_2MnO_4 + MnO_2 + O_2$

Q. 14. Account for the following :*

    (i) Transition metals form large number of complex compounds.

    (ii) The lowest oxide of transition metal is basic whereas the highest oxide is amphoteric or acidic.

    (iii) E° value for the Mn^{3+}/Mn^{2+} couple is highly positive ($+ 1.57$ V) as compare to Cr^{3+}/Cr^{2+}.

Ans. (i) Transition metals forms large number of complexes due to:

    (a) Small size of atoms and ions of transition metals.

---

* are board exam questions from previous years

(b) High nuclear charge.

(c) Presence of incompletely filled d-orbitals.

(ii) As the oxidation state increases the size of ion goes on decreasing thus the covalent character increases as a result of this amphoteric and acidic strength increases. While in case of lower oxides of transition metals ionic size increases and thus basic character increases.

(iii) Because Mn^{2+} has $3d^5$ as a stable oxidation state which is half filled and stable. Mn has very high third ionization energy for change from d^5 to d^4 but in case of Cr^{3+} $3d^3$ is more stable due to t_{2g}^3 (crystal field splitting theory) that is why Mn^{3+}/Mn^{2+} is highly positive as compared to Cr^{3+}/Cr^{2+}.

Q. 15. (i)   (a) How is the variability in oxidation states of transition metals different from that of the p-block elements?*

     (b) Out of Cu^+ and Cu^{2+}, which ion is unstable in aqueous solution and why?

     (c) Orange colour of $Cr_2O_7^{2-}$ ion changes to yellow when treated with an alkali. Why?

  (ii) Chemistry of actinoids is complicated as compared to lanthanoids. Give two reasons.

Ans. (i)   (a) In p block elements the difference in oxidation state is 2 and in transition elements the difference is 1.

     (b) Cu^+ is unstable in aq. solution because it undergoes disproportion reaction and has low hydration enthalpy.

     (c) In alkaline medium dichromate ions $Cr_2O_7^{2-}$ changes to chromate ion CrO_4^{2-}, which is yellow in colour due to which the colour changes when treated with an alkali.

  (ii) Chemistry of actinoids is complicated as compared to lanthanoids due to following reasons :

     (a) They show multiple oxidation states namely $+5$, $+6$ and $+7$ oxidation states respectively which permits the formation of higher oxidation states through the removal of the periphery electrons.

     (b) They are radioactive and have a strong propensity to form complex reactions because of its unstable isotopes, some actinides are formed naturally by radioactive decay.

Chapter 9. Coordination Compounds

Q. 1. **Explain the bonding in coordination compounds in terms of Werner's postulates.**

Ans. Werner's postulates explains the bonding in coordination compounds as follows:

(i) In a coordinate compound a metal exhibits two types of valency namely, primary and secondary valency. Primary valency is satisfied by negative ions while secondary valency is satisfied by both negative and neutral ions.

Primary valency corresponds to the oxidation number of the metal ion, whereas the secondary valency refers to the coordination number of the metal ion and is satisfied by ligands.

(ii) A metal ion has a definite number of secondary valency around the central atom. Also, this valency project in a specific direction in the space assigned to the definite geometry of the coordination compound.

(iii) Primary valency is usually ionisable, while secondary valency is non-ionisable.

(iv) The negative ligands satisfies both primary and secondary valency.

Q. 2. **$FeSO_4$ solution mixed with $(NH_4)_2SO_4$ solution in 1 : 1 molar ratio gives the test of Fe^{2+} ion but $CuSO_4$ solution mixed with aqueous ammonia in 1 : 4 molar ratio does not gives the test of Cu^{2+} ion. Explain why?**

Ans.
$$(NH_4)_2SO_4 + FeSO_4 + 6H_2O \longrightarrow FeSO_4(NH_4)_2 SO_4.6H_2O$$
$$\text{Mohr's salt}$$

$$CuSO_4 + 4NH_3 + 5H_2O \longrightarrow [Cu(NH_3)_4]SO_4.5H_2O$$
$$\text{Tetraamminocopper (II) sulphate}$$

Both the compounds *i.e.,* $FeSO_4.(NH_4)_2SO_4.6H_2O$ and $[Cu(NH_3)_4]SO_4.5H_2O$ fall under the category of addition compounds. But Mohr's salt is an example of a double salt, while the latter is a coordination compound.

A double salt is an addition compound that is stable in the solid state but it dissociates up into its constituent ions in the dissolved state. Hence will give test of each individual constituent ion. For *e.g.,* $FeSO_4.(NH_4)_2SO_4.6H_2O$ breaks into Fe^{2+}, NH_4^+ and SO_4^{2-} ions. Hence, it gives a positive test for Fe^{2+} ions. A coordination compound is an addition compound which retains its identity in the solid as well as in the dissolved state. However, the individual properties of the constituents are lost. In $[Cu(NH_3)_4]SO_4.5H_2O$ does not show the test for Cu^{2+} because Cu^{2+} ion is present inside the complex entity, $[Cu(NH_3)_4]^{2+}$.

Q. 3. Explain with two examples each of the following: coordination entity, ligand, coordination number, coordination polyhedron, homoleptic and heteroleptic complexes.

Ans. **(i) Coordination entity:** A coordination entity is a complex species enclosed in square bracket. In a coordination entity, the central atom or ion is surrounded by a suitable number of neutral molecules or (ligands). For example :

$$[Ni(NH_3)_6]^{2+},\ [Fe(CN)_6]^{4+} = \text{Cationic complex}$$
$$[Fe(CN)_6]^{3-},\ [PtCl_4]^{2-},\ [Ag(CN)_2]^- = \text{Anionic complex}$$
$$[Ni(CO)_4],\ [Co(NH_3)_3Cl_3] = \text{Neutral complex}$$

(ii) Ligands: The neutral molecules are negatively charged or even positively charged ions sometimes that surround the metal atom in a coordination entity or complex are known as ligands. For example, NO_3^-, NO_2^+, $\ddot{N}H_3$, $H_2\ddot{O}$, Cl^-, OH. Ligands are Lewis bases and possess at least one unshared pair of valence electrons. They are also called dentates and forms coordination or dative bonds with the central metal atom.

(iii) Coordination number: The total number of ligands (either neutral molecules or negative ions) that get attached to the central metal atom in the coordination sphere is called the coordination number of the central metal atom. It is also the total number of coordination bonds.

For example:

(a) In the complex, $K_2[PtCl_6]$, there are six chloride ions attached to Pt in the coordinate sphere. Therefore, the coordination number of Pt is 6.

(b) Similarly, in the complex $[Co(NH_3)_3Cl]$ the coordination number of the central atom (Co) is 6.

(iv) Coordination polyhedron: Coordination polyhedrons about the central atom can be defined as the spatial arrangement of the ligands that are directly attached to the central metal ion in the coordination sphere. For example :

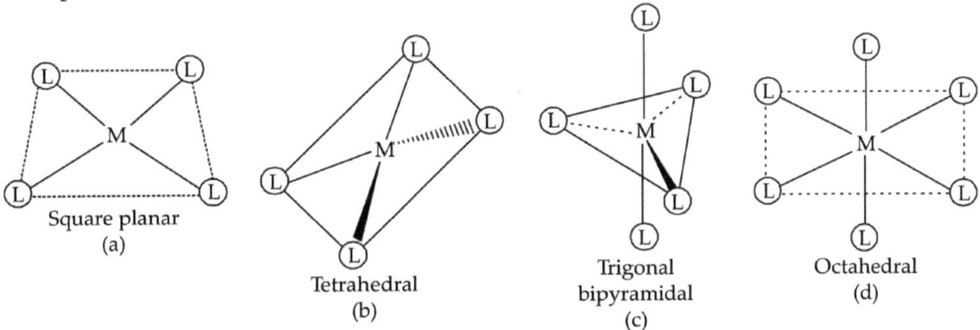

(v) Homoleptic complexes: These are those complexes in which the metal ion is bound to only one kind of a donor group. For *e.g.,* : $[Co(NH_3)_6]^{3+}$, $[PtCl_4]^{2-}$ etc.

(vi) Heteroleptic complexes: Heteroleptic complexes are those complexes where the central metal ion is bound to more than one type of a donor group.

For *e.g.,* : $[Co(NH_3)_4Cl_2]^+$, $[Co(NH_3)_5Cl]^{2+}$.

Q. 4. What is meant by unidentate, bidentate and ambidentate ligands? Give two examples for each.

Ans. A ligand may contain one or more unshared pairs of electrons which are called the donor group of ligands. Now, depending on the number of these donor group or atoms ligands can be classified, this is also called denticity of ligands. Example :

(i) Unidentate ligands: Ligands with only one donor atom are unidentate ligands. For *e.g.,* $\ddot{N}H_3$ (ammine), Cl^- (chloride), ONO^- (nitrito), $H_2\ddot{O}$ (aqua) etc.

(ii) Bidentate ligands: Ligands that have two donor atom are called bidentate ligands.

For *e.g.,*

(a) Ethane-1, 2-diamine $H_2\ddot{N}$——CH_2

$\qquad\qquad\qquad\quad H_2\ddot{N}$——$CH_2$

(b) Oxalate ion $(C_2O_4^{2-})$ or $\begin{matrix} COO^- \\ | \\ COO^- \end{matrix}$

(c) Carbonate ion 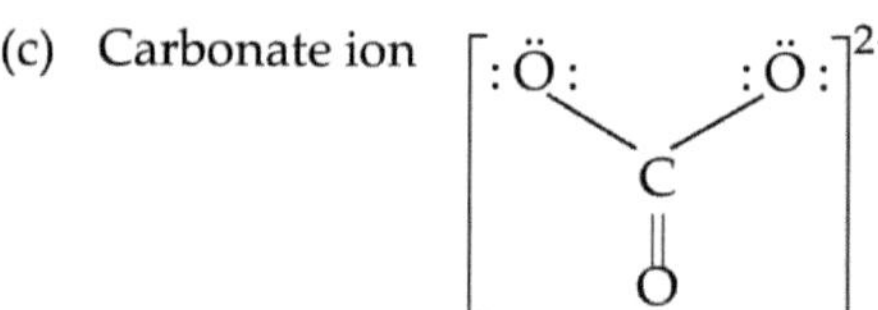

They form two coordinate bonds with the central metal.

(iii) Ambidentate ligands : Ligands that can attach themselves to the central metal atom through two different atoms in the same molecule are called ambidentate ligands. For example,

(a) $M—N \longrightarrow$ Nitro group

(The donor atom is N)

$M—N—N=O \longrightarrow$ Nitrito group

(The donor atom is oxygen)

(b) $M–SCN \rightarrow$ Thiocyanate

(The donor atom is S)

$M–NCS \rightarrow$ Isothiocyanate

(The donor atom is N)

Q. 5. List various types of isomerism possible for coordination compounds, giving an example of each.

Ans.

Isomerism in coordination compounds

- Stereoisomerism
  - Geometrical isomerism
  - Optical isomerism
- Structural isomerism
  - Solvate isomerism
  - Linkage isomerism
  - Coordination isomerism
  - Ionization isomerism

(i) Geometric isomerism : This type of isomerism is common in heteroleptic complexes. It arises due to a different possible geometric arrangements of the ligands. For example :

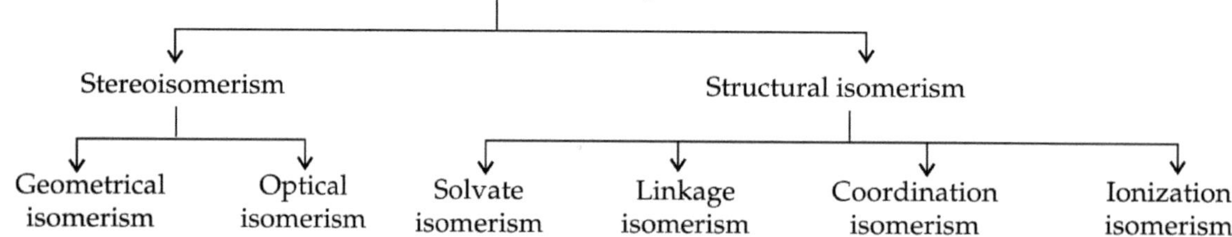

cis-isomer　　　*trans*-isomer　　　*cis* form (Violet)　　　*trans* form (Green)

(ii) Optical isomerism : This type of isomerism arises in chiral molecules. Isomers are mirror images of each other and are non-superimposable.

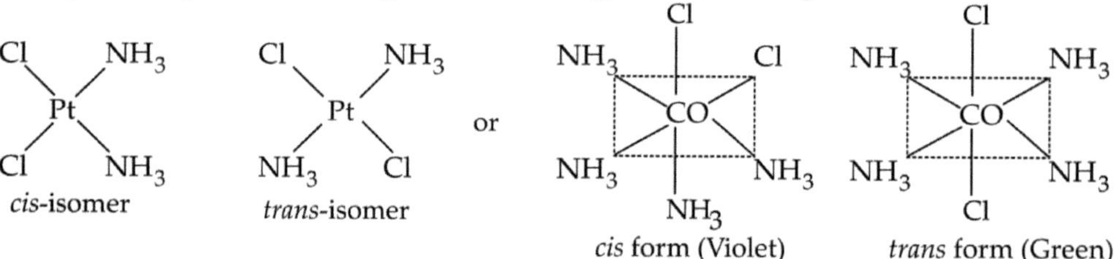

$[Co(en)_3]^{3+}$ (dextro)　　Mirror　　$[Co(en)_3]^{3+}$ (laevo)

(iii) Linkage isomerism : This type of isomerism is found in complexes that contain ambidentate ligands. For example :

$[Co(NH_3)_5 (NO_2)]Cl_2$ and $[Co(NH_3)_5 (ONO)]Cl_2$ as NO_2 group can bind from $– NO_2$ nitro or $– (NO – O)$ nitrito site.

(iv) Coordination isomerism : This type of isomerism arises when the ligands are interchanged between complex cationic and anionic entities of different metal ions present in the complexes, *e.g.* :

$[Co(NH_3)_6] [Cr(CN)_6]$ and $[Cr(NH_3)_6] [Co(CN)_6]$, here the ligands are exchanged.

(v) Ionization isomerism: This type of isomerism arises when a counter ion replaces a ligand within the coordination sphere. Thus, complexes that have the same composition, but furnish different ions when dissolved in water are called ionization isomers. For *e.g.,* $[Co(NH_3)_5Cl]SCN.Cl$ and $[Co(NH_3)_55CN]\,Cl_2$, the thiocyanate ligand and chlorido exchange the positions.

(vi) Solvate isomerism: (Hydrate isomerism) Solvate isomers differ by whether or not the solvent molecule is directly bonded to the metal ion or merely present as a free solvent molecule in the crystal lattice, *i.e.,* whether H_2O molecule is in coordination sphere or ionisation sphere.

$$[Cr(H_2O)_6]Cl_3 \qquad [Cr(H_2O)_5Cl]Cl_2.H_2O \qquad [Cr(H_2O)_5Cl_2]Cl.2H_2O$$
Violet   Blue-green   Dark green

Q. 6. **Discuss the nature of bonding in the following coordination entities on the basis of valence bond theory.**

   (i) $[Fe(CN)_6]^{4-}$ (ii) $[FeF_6]^{3-}$ (iii) $[Co(C_2O_4)_3]^{3-}$ (iv) $[CoF_6]^{3-}$

Ans. (i) $[Fe(CN)_6]^{4-}$

In the above coordination complex, iron exists in the $+2$ oxidation state.

Fe^{2+} : Electronic configuration is $3d^6$ orbitals of Fe^{2+} ion.

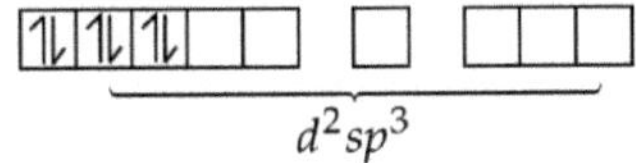

As CN^- is a strong field ligand, it causes the pairing of the unpaired $3d$ electrons.

Since there are six ligands around the central metal ion, the most feasible hybridisation is d^2sp^3.

6 electron pairs from CN^- ions occupy the six hybrid d^2sp^3 orbitals.

Then,

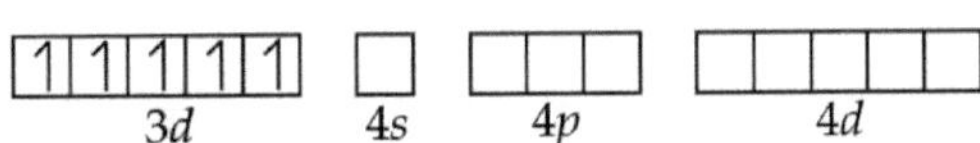
6 pairs of electrons
from 6 CN$^-$ ions

Hence, the geometry of the complex is octahedral and complex is diamagnetic inner orbital complex.

(ii) $[FeF_6]^{3-}$

In this complex, the oxidation state of Fe is $+3$.

Orbitals of Fe^{+3} ion:

There are $6F^-$ ions. Thus, it will undergo d^2sp^3 or sp^3d^2 hybridization as F^- is a weak field ligand and it does not cause the pairing of the electrons in the $3d$ orbital. Hence, hybridisation is sp^3d^2.

sp^3d^2 hybridized orbitals of Fe are:

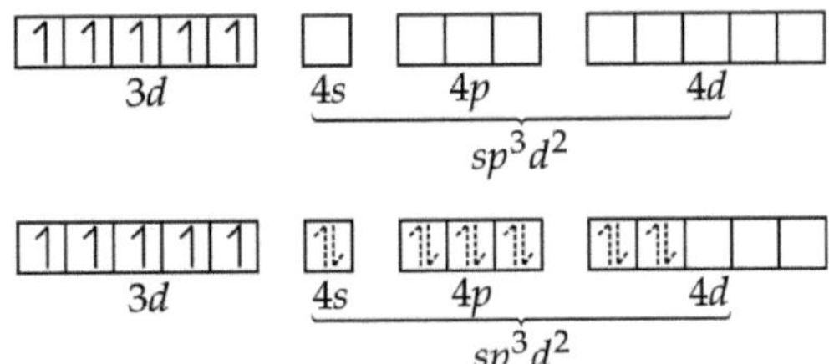
6 electron pairs from F$^-$ions

Hence, the geometry of the complex is found to be octahedral, strongly paramagnetic and outer orbital complex.

(iii) $[Co(C_2O_4)_3]^{3-}$

Cobalt exists in the $+3$ oxidation state in the given complex.

Orbitals of Co^{3+} ion : $4s^0 3d^6$ configuration.

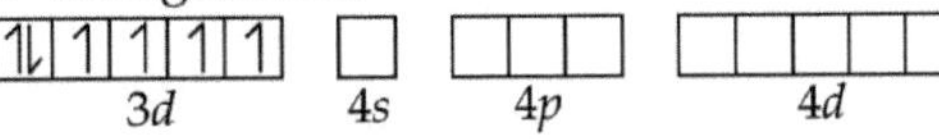

Oxalate is a weak field ligand so, it cannot cause the pairing of the $3d$ orbital electrons. As there are 6 ligands, hybridisation has to be either sp^3d^2 hybridisation of Co^{3+}.

$$sp^3d^2$$

The 6 electron pairs from 3 oxalate ions (oxalate anion is a bidentate ligand) occupy these sp^3d^2 orbitals.

6 electron pairs from
3 oxalate ions

Hence, the geometry of the complex is found to be octahedral, outer orbital, paramagnetic.

(iv) $[CoF_6]^{3-}$

Cobalt exists in the +3 oxidation state.

Orbitals of Co^{3+} ion:

$3d \qquad 4s \qquad 4p \qquad 4d$

Again, fluoride is a weak field ligand. It cannot cause the pairing of the $3d$ electrons.

As a result, the Co^{3+} ion will undergo sp^3d^2 hybridisation. sp^3d^2 hybridised orbitals of Co^{3+} ion are:

$$sp^3d^2$$

$3d \qquad 4s \qquad 4p \qquad 4d$

$$sp^3d^2$$

6 electron pairs from F^- ions

Hence, the geometry of the complex is octahedral and paramagnetic and outer orbital complex.

Q. 7. **Write down the IUPAC name for each of the following complexes and indicate the oxidation state, electronic configuration and coordination number. Also give stereochemistry and magnetic moment of the complex:**

(i) $K[Cr(H_2O)_2(C_2O_4)_2].3H_2O$
(ii) $[Co(NH_3)_5Cl]Cl_2$
(iii) $CrCl_3(py)_3$
(iv) $Cs[FeCl_4]$
(v) $K_4[Mn(CN)_6]$

Ans. (i) Potassium diaquadioxalatochromate (III) trihydrate.

Oxidation state of chromium = 3

Electronic configuration : $3d^3(t_{2g}^2, e_g^6)$

Coordination number = 6

Shape : Octahedral

Stereochemistry:

trans

cis

trans is optically inactive

cis is optically active

Magnetic moment,

$$\mu = \sqrt{n(n+2)}$$

$$= \sqrt{3(3+2)}$$

$$= \sqrt{15} = 3.87 \text{ cm}$$

$$\sim 4BM$$

(ii) $[Co(NH_3)_5Cl]Cl_2$

IUPAC name : Pentaamminechloridocobalt(III) chloride

Oxidation state of CO = + 3
Coordination number = 6
Shape: Octahedral.
Electronic configuration: $d^6 : (t_{2g}^6, e_g^0)$
Stereochemistry:

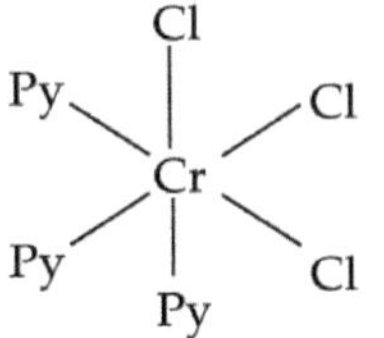

2 isomers

Magnetic Moment = 0 as $n = 0$ *i.e.,* no unpaired electron.

(iii) $CrCl_3(py)_3$

IUPAC name: Trichloridotripyridinechromium (III)

Oxidation state of chromium = + 3

Electronic configuration for $d^3 = t_{2g}^3$

Coordination number = 6

Shape: Octahedral.

Stereochemistry:

Facial isomer   Meriodional isomer

Both isomers are optically active. Therefore, a total of 4 isomers exist.

Magnetic moment,
$$\mu = \sqrt{n(n+2)}$$
$$= \sqrt{3(3+2)}$$
$$= \sqrt{15} = 3.87 \text{ BM}$$
$$\sim 4 \text{BM}$$

(iv) $Cs[FeCl_4]$

IUPAC Name: Caesium tetrachloroferrate (III)

Oxidation state of Fe = + 3

Electronic configuration of $d^6 = e^2, t_{2g}^3$.

Coordination number = 4

Shape: Tetrahedral

Stereochemistry: Optically inactive

Magnetic moment,
$$\mu = \sqrt{n(n+2)}$$
$$= \sqrt{5(5-2)}$$
$$= \sqrt{35} \sim 6 \text{ BM}$$

(v) $K_4[Mn(CN)_6]$

Potassium hexacyanomanganate(II)

Oxidation state of manganese = + 2

Electronic configuration: $d^{5+} : (t_{2g}^5, e_g^0)$

Coordination number = 6

Shape: Octahedral.

Stereochemistry: Optically inactive

Magnetic moment,
$$\mu = \sqrt{n(n+2)}$$
$$= \sqrt{1(1+2)}$$
$$= \sqrt{3}$$
$$= 1.732 \text{ BM}$$

Q. 8. What is meant by stability of a coordination compound in solution? State the factors which govern the stability of complexes.

Ans. The stability of a complex in a solution refers to the degree of association between the two species involved in a state of equilibrium. Stability can be expressed quantitatively in terms of stability constant (K) or formation constant (k_f).

$$M + L \rightleftharpoons ML \, ; k_1 = \frac{[ML]}{[M][L]}$$

Similarly, $ML + L \rightleftharpoons [ML_2]; k_2 = \dfrac{[ML_2]}{[ML][L]}$ like that.

$$M + 3L \leftrightarrow ML_3$$

Stability constant β, $\dfrac{[ML]}{[M][L]^3}$.

For this reaction, the greater the value of the stability constant, the greater is the proportion of ML_3 in the solution. Also β is $= K_1 \times K_2 \times K_3$ where K_1, K_2 and K_3 are stability constant of individual steps in the formation of final complex.

Stability can be of two types :

(a) **Thermodynamic stability**: The extent to which the complex will be formed or will be transformed into another species at the point of equilibrium is determined by thermodynamic stability.

(b) **Kinetic stability:** This helps in determining the speed with which the transformation will occur to attain the state of equilibrium.

Factors that affect the stability of a complex are:

(a) **Charge on the central metal ion:** The greater the charge on the central metal ion, the greater is the stability of the complex.

(b) **Basic nature of the ligand:** A more basic ligand forms a more stable complex. Because ligands donate electron pairs, hence more basic ligands more ease with which it can donate its lone pair to central metal. Thus F^-, CN^- and NH_3^- acts as good ligands, whereas H_2O is a weak ligand.

(c) **Presence of chelate rings:** Chelation increases the stability of complexes. This is called chelation effect and is found to be maximum in five and six membered rings.

e.g., $[Ni(en)_3]^{2+}$ is for more stable than $[Ni(NH_3)_6]^{2+}$.

Q. 9. Indicate the types of isomerism exhibited by the following complexes and draw the structures for these isomers:

(i) $K[Cr(H_2O)_2(C_2O_4)_2]$ (ii) $[Co(en)_3]Cl_3$

(iii) $[Co(NH_3)_5(NO_2)](NO_3)_2$ (iv) $[Pt(NH_3)(H_2O)Cl_2]^*$

Ans. (i)   Both geometrical (*cis-*, *trans-*) isomers for $K[Cr(H_2O)_2(C_2O_4)_2]$ can exist. Also, optical isomers for *cis-*isomer exist, CN$= 6$ or oxalato is a bidentate ligand.

OH₂ — O–Cr–O — OH₂ (*trans*) and OH₂ — O–Cr–OH₂ — O (*cis*)

Trans-isomer is optically inactive. On the other hand, *cis*-isomer is optically active.

(ii) Two optical isomers for $[CO(en)_3]Cl_3$ exists, CN = 6. octahedral complex.

Two optical isomers are possible for this structure.

or

(iii) $[CO(NH_3)_5 (NO_2)] (NO_3)_2$ a pair of optical isomers :

It can also show linkage isomerism, as NO_2 is an ambidentate ligand.

$[CO(NH_3)_5 (NO_2)] (NO_3)_2$ and $[CO(NH_3)_5 (ONO)] (NO_3)_2$

It can also show ionization isomerism, by exchange of ligands from outersphere to complex sphere.

$[Co(NH_3)_5 (NO_2)] (NO_3)_2$

$[CO(NH_3)_5(NO_3)] (NO_3)(NO_2)$

(iv) Geometrical (*cis-*, *trans-*) isomers of $[Pt(NH_3)(H_2O)Cl_2]$, can exist.

cis   *trans*   (square planar geometry).

Q. 10. Explain the following:

  (i) Different colours observed for the same metal ligand pair for tetrahedral and octahedral complexes.

  (ii) Lead poisoning can be cured by use of EDTA.

  (iii) Oxalic acid is used to remove rust strains.

  (iv) Tetrahedral complexes does not show geometrical isomerism.

  (v) Low spin octahedral complexes for Ni are not known.*

Ans. (i) According to crystal field theory (CFT) the splitting energy by approach of an octahedral field is almost 45% more than that of tetrahedral field for the same ligand. Hence, the energy absorbed in the form of visible light during *d-d* transition for Δ_0 (octahedral complex) will be more than Δ_t (tetrahedral complex), hence different colours are observed.

(ii) During lead poisoning the calcium-EDTA chelate complex mixes with blood and the calcium of the complex is exchanged with lead forming lead-EDTA chelate. The new complex being more soluble in water is eliminated through urine, thus curing severe lead poisoning.

(iii) Rust is hydrated iron (III) oxide. On mixing with oxalic acid, iron forms a soluble oxalate complex and thus stains of rust are removed $[Fe(C_2O_4)_3]^{3-}$ soluble complex.

(iv) In tetrahedral complexes like $[Ni(CO)_4]$ all the four positions occupied by the ligands are symmetrical and there is free rotation along each bond. Hence no restriction and no *cis-trans* isomerism.

(v) In octahedral complex we need six orbitals of $(d^2sp^3)/(sp^3d^2)$ orbitals to accommodate ligands. For low spin we need d-electrons to be paired also. As electronic configuration of Ni is generally. $4s^0\, 3d^8$ only one orbitals of $3d$ subshell can remain free for hybridisation even after pairing of other d-electrons. Hence low spin, octahedral complex of Ni is not known.

Q. 11. Using valence bond theory, explain the following for the complexes given below:

$[Mn(CN)_6]^{3-}$, $[Co(NH_3)_6]^{3+}$, $[FeCl_6]^{4-}$.

(i)   Type of hybridisation

(ii) Geometry

(iii) Magnetic behaviour

(iv) Inner or outer orbital complex

(v) Spin only magnetic moment value.

Ans. $[Mn(CN)_6]^{3-}$ oxidation state of Mn is (+ 3)

$[Co(NH_3)_6]^{3+}$ oxidation state of Co is (+ 3)

$[FeCl_6]^{4-}$ oxidation state of Fe is (+ 2)

In $[Mn(CN)_6]^{3-}$ CN is strong field ligand.

$[Co(NH_3)_6]^{3+}$ NH_3 is weak field ligand.

$[FeCl_6]^{4-}$ Cl^- is a weak field ligand.

Now $[Mn(CN)_6]^{3-}$; $Mn^{3+}(3d^4)$.

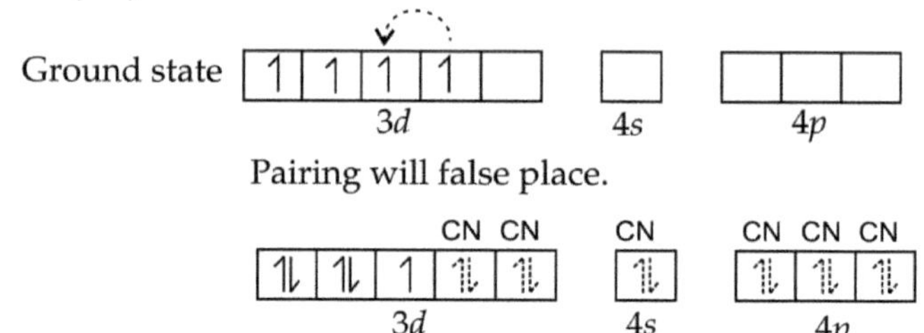

Pairing will false place.

(i)   Hybridisation d^2sp^3

(ii) Octahedral geometry

(iii) Paramagnetic

(iv) Inner orbital complex

(v) $\mu = \sqrt{n(n+2)} = \sqrt{2(2+2)}$

$ = \sqrt{8} = 2.87$ BM

For $[Co(NH_3)_6]^{3+}$ $Co^{3+}(4s^0\,3d^6)$

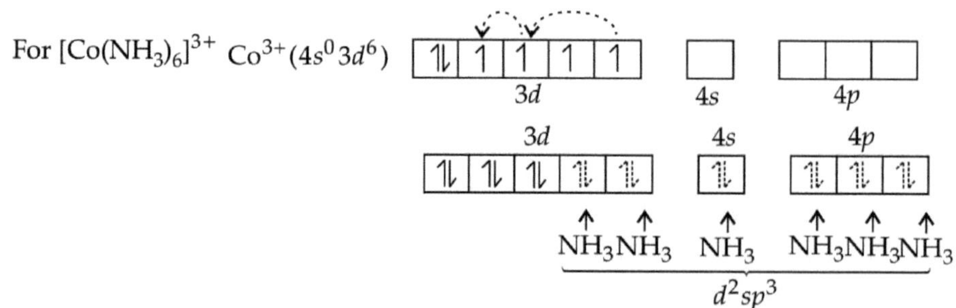

(i)   Hybridisation d^2sp^3

(ii) Octahedral

(iii) Diamagnetic

(iv) Inner orbital complex

(v) $\mu = \sqrt{0(0+2)} = 0$

For $[FeCl_6]^{4-}$, $Fe(4s^0 3d^6)$

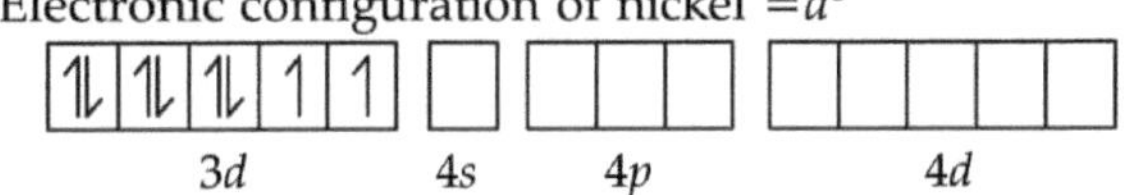

(i)   Hybridisation sp^3d^2.

(ii) Octahedral

(iii) Paramagnetic

(iv) Outer orbital complex

(v) $\mu = \sqrt{n(n+2)} = \sqrt{4(4+2)}$

$= \sqrt{24} - 4.9$ BM

Q. 12. Explain $[CO(NH_3)_6]^{3+}$ is an inner orbital complex whereas $[Ni(NH_3)_6]^{2+}$ is an outer orbital complex.

Ans.

$[Co(NH_3)_6]^{3+}$	$[Ni(NH_3)_6]^{2+}$
Oxidation state of cobalt $= +3$	Oxidation state of Ni $= +2$
Electronic configuration of cobalt $= d^6$	Electronic configuration of nickel $= d^8$
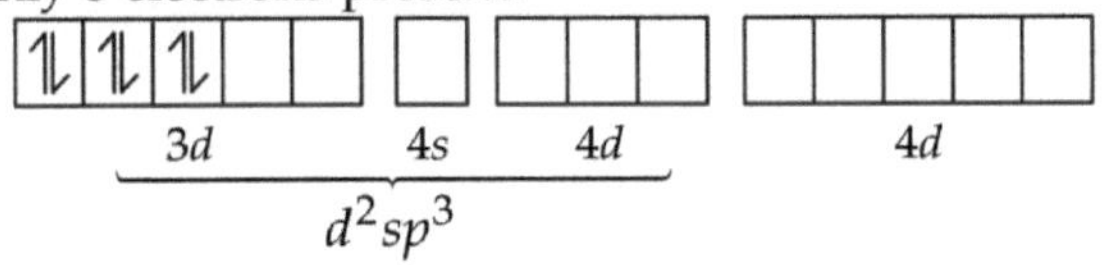	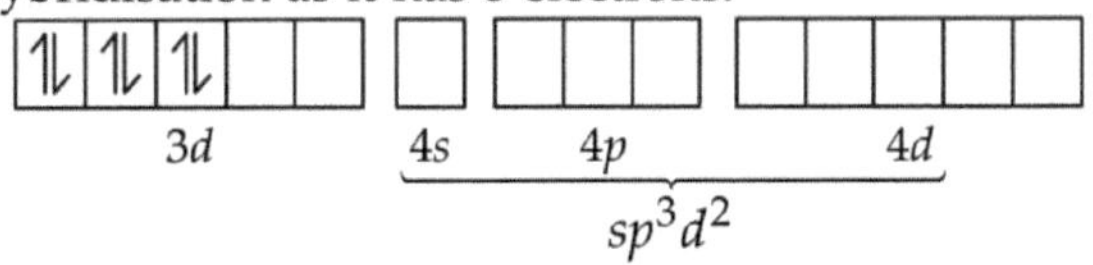
NH_3 being a strong field ligand causes the pairing. Therefore, Ni can undergo d^2sp^3 hybridisation as only 6 electrons present.	Even if NH_3 causes the pairing, then only one $3d$ orbital is empty. Thus, it cannot undergo d^2sp^3 hybridisation. Therefore, it undergoes d^2sp^3 hybridisation. Therefore, it undergoes sp^3d^2 hybridisation as it has 8 electrons.
Hence, it is an inner orbital complex. Its diamagnetic in nature.	Hence, it forms an outer orbital complex. Its paramagnetic in nature.

Chapter 10. Haloalkanes and Haloarenes

Q. 1. Predict all the alkenes that would be formed by dehydrohalogenation of the following halides with sodium ethoxide in ethanol and identify the major alkene:

(i)   1-Bromo-1-methylcyclohexane

(ii) 2-Chloro-2-methylbutane

(iii) 2,2,3-Trimethyl-3-bromopentane.

Ans. (i)

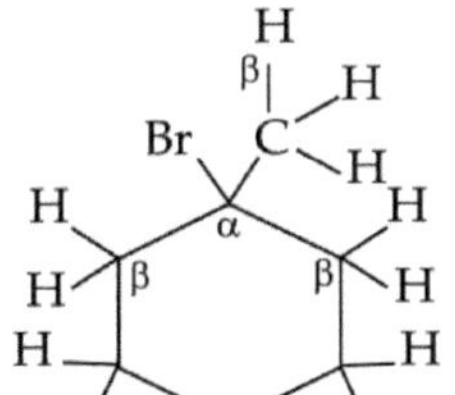

1-Bromo-1-methylcyclohexane

In the given compound we have two types of equivalent β-hydrogen atoms. Thus, dehydrohalogenation of this compound gives two alkenes.

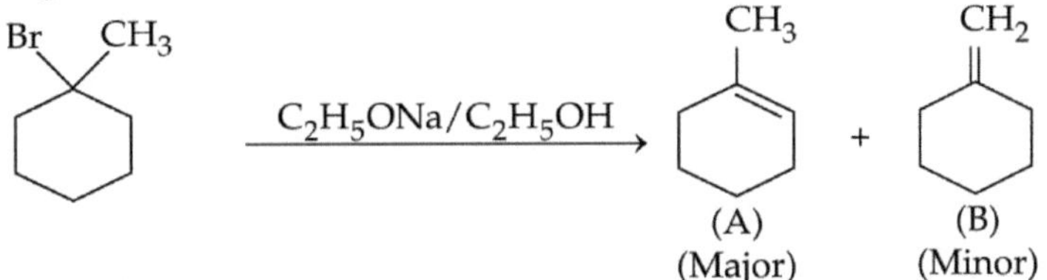

Since alkene (A) is more substituted, hence as per the Saytzeff's rule, it will be the major product.

(ii)
$$\overset{\beta}{\underset{a}{C}H_3} - \overset{\overset{Cl}{|}}{\underset{\underset{\underset{\beta}{CH_3}}{|}}{\overset{\alpha}{C}}} - \overset{\beta}{\underset{b}{C}H_2} - CH_3$$

In the given compound, there are two different sets of equivalent β-hydrogen atoms labelled as *a* and *b*. Thus, dehydrohalogenation of the compound yields two alkenes.

$$CH_3 - \overset{\overset{Cl}{|}}{\underset{\underset{CH_3}{|}}{C}} - CH_2 - CH_3 \xrightarrow[-HCl]{C_2H_5ONa/C_2H_5OH} CH_3 - \overset{}{\underset{\underset{CH_3}{|}}{C}} = CH - CH_3 + CH_2 = \overset{}{\underset{\underset{CH_3}{|}}{C}} - CH_2 - CH_3$$

2-Methylbut-2-ene (A)   2-Methylbut-1-ene (B)

[Major]   [Minor]

According to Saytzeff's rule during dehydrohalogenation reactions, the alkene having a greater number of alkyl groups attached to a double bonded carbon atom is preferably produced. Hence, alkene (A) *i.e.*, 2-methylbut-2-ene is the major product in this reaction.

(iii)
$$CH_3 - \overset{\overset{CH_3}{|}}{\underset{\underset{CH_3}{|}}{C}} - \overset{\overset{Br}{|}}{\underset{\underset{\underset{\beta}{CH_3}}{|}}{\overset{\alpha}{C}}} - \overset{\beta}{\underset{\alpha 2}{C}H_2} - CH_3$$

2, 2, 3-Trimethyl-3-bromopentane

In the given compound, there are two different sets of equivalent β-hydrogen atoms labelled as *a* and *b*. Thus, dehydrohalogenation of the compound yields two alkenes.

$$CH_3 - \overset{\overset{CH_3}{|}}{\underset{\underset{CH_3}{|}}{C}} - \overset{\overset{Br}{|}}{\underset{\underset{CH_3}{|}}{C}} - CH_2 - CH_3 \xrightarrow[-HBr]{C_2H_5ONa/C_2H_5OH} CH_3 - \overset{\overset{CH_3}{|}}{\underset{\underset{CH_3}{|}}{C}} - C = CH - CH_3$$

3, 4, 4-Trimethylpent-2-ene (A) (Major)

+

$$CH_3 - \overset{\overset{CH_3}{|}}{\underset{\underset{CH_3}{|}}{C}} - \overset{\overset{CH_2}{||}}{C} - CH_2 - CH_3 \text{ (Minor)}$$

2-Ethyl-3, 3-dimethylbut-1-ene (B)

According to Saytzeff's rule, in dehydrohalogenation reactions, the alkene having a greater number of alkyl group attached to the double bonded carbon atom is preferably formed. Thus, alkene (A) *i.e.*, 3, 4, 4-trimethylpent-2-ene is the major product in this reaction.

Q. 2. Explain why:*

   (i)   The dipole moment of chlorobenzene is lower than that of cyclohexyl chloride?

  (ii)   Alkyl halides, though polar are immiscible with water?

 (iii)   Grignard reagents should be prepared under anhydrous conditions?

Ans. (i)

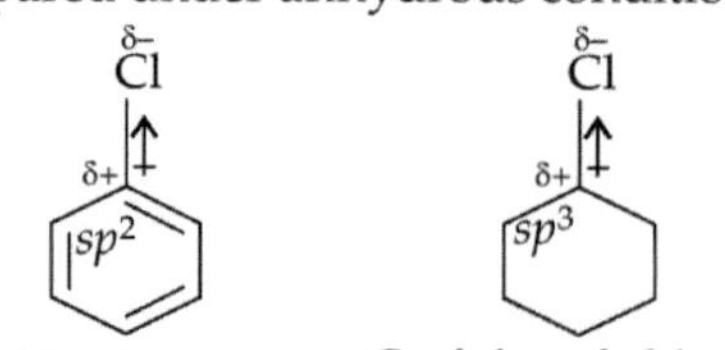

Chlorobenzene   Cyclohexyl chloride

In chlorobenzene, (Cl carbon is) sp^2 hybridised carbon atom. In cyclohexyl chloride, C–Cl bond C-atom is a sp^3 hybridised carbon atom. Since sp^2 hybridised carbon has more s-character than sp^3 hybridised carbon atom, hence, sp^2 is more electronegative than sp^3. Therefore, the density of electrons of C–Cl bond near the Cl-atom is less in chlorobenzene than in cyclohexyl chloride.

Moreover, the –R effect of the benzene ring of chlorobenzene decreases the electron density of the C–Cl bond near the Cl-atom. As a result, the polarity of the C–Cl bond in chlorobenzene decreases. Hence, the dipole moment of chlorobenzene is lower than that of cyclohexyl chloride.

(ii) Water as a solvent has strong intermolecular H-bonding, which cannot be broken by R–X bonds, as the alkyl halides are polar but the polarity is far less than H-bonding in water.

Hence, alkyl halides (though polar) are immiscible with water.

(iii) Grignard reagents are very reactive. In the presence of moisture, they readily decompose to form alkanes.

$$\overset{\delta-\ \ \delta+\ \ \ \delta-}{R\,Mg\,X} + H_2O \longrightarrow \underset{\text{Alkane}}{R-H} + Mg(OH)X$$
$$\underset{\underset{\text{reagent}}{\text{Grignard}}}{}$$

Therefore, Grignard reagents should be prepared under anhydrous conditions.

Q. 3. Arrange the compounds of each set in order of reactivity towards S_N2 displacement :[*]
  (i)   2-Bromo-2-methylbutane, 1-Bromopentane, 2-Bromopentane
  (ii) 1-Bromo-3-methylbutane, 2-Bromo-2-methylbutane, 3-Bromo-2-methylbutane
  (iii) 1-Bromobutane, 1-Bromo-2, 2-dimethylpropane, 1-Bromo-2-methylbutane, 1-Bromo-3-methylbutane.

Ans. (i) $CH_3CH_2CH_2CH_2CH_2 - Br$ $CH_3CH_2CH_2\overset{\overset{\displaystyle Br}{|}}{C}HCH_3$ $CH_3CH_2\overset{\overset{\displaystyle Br}{|}}{\underset{\underset{\displaystyle CH_3}{|}}{C}}CH_3$

        1-Bromopentane (1°)   2-Bromopentane (2°)   2-Bromo-2-methylbutane (3°)

The S_N2 reaction involves the approaching of the nucleophile to the carbon atom to which the leaving group is attached. The carbon atom if, sterically hindered, then the reactivity towards S_N2 displacement decreases, Due to the presence of substituents, hindrance to the approaching nucleophile decides the rate of reaction.

Hence, the increasing order of reactivity towards S_N2 displacement is :

2-Bromo-2-methylbutane < 2-Bromopentane < 1-Bromopentane

(ii) $CH_3 - \overset{\overset{\displaystyle CH_3}{|}}{C}H - CH_2 - CH_2 - Br$ $CH_3 - CH_2 - \overset{\overset{\displaystyle Br}{|}}{\underset{\underset{\displaystyle CH_3}{|}}{C}} - CH_3$ $CH_3 - \overset{\overset{\displaystyle Br}{|}}{C}H - \overset{\overset{\displaystyle}{}}{\underset{\underset{\displaystyle CH_3}{|}}{C}}H - CH_3$

  1-Bromo-3-methylbutane   2-Bromo-2-methylbutane   2-Bromo-3-methylbutane
         (1°)   (3°)   (2°)

Since steric hindrance in alkyl halides increases in the order of 1° < 2° < 3°, the increasing order of reactivity towards S_N2 displacement is 3° < 2° < 1°.

Hence, the given set of compounds can be arranged in the increasing order of their reactivity towards S_N2 displacement as :

2-Bromo-2-methylbutane < 2-Bromo-3-methylbutane < 1-Bromo-3-methylbutane

(iii) $CH_3 - CH_2 - CH_2 - CH_2 - Br$ $CH_3 - \overset{\overset{\displaystyle CH_3}{|}}{C}H - CH_2 - CH_2 - Br$

     1-Bromobutane   1-Bromo-3-methylbutane

$CH_3 - CH_2 - \overset{\overset{\displaystyle CH_3}{|}}{C}H - CH_2 - Br$ $CH_3 - \overset{\overset{\displaystyle CH_3}{|}}{\underset{\underset{\displaystyle CH_3}{|}}{C}} - CH_2 - Br$

  1-Bromo-2-methylbutane   1-Bromo-2, 2-dimethylpropane

The steric hindrance of the nucleophile in the S_N2 mechanism increases with the decrease in the distance of the substituents from the atom containing the leaving group. Also, the steric hindrance increases with an increase in the number of substituents.

Hence, the increasing order of reactivity of the given compounds towards S_N2 displacement is :

1-Bromo-2, 2-dimethylpropane < 1-Bromo-2-methylbutane < 1-Bromo-3-methylbutane < 1-Bromobutane

Q. 4. Primary alkyl halide C_4H_9Br (a) reacted with alcoholic KOH to give compound (b). Compound (b) is reacted with HBr to give (c) which is an isomer of (a). When (a) is reacted with sodium metal it gives compound (d), C_8H_{18} which is different from the compound formed when n-butyl bromide is reacted with sodium. Give the structural formula of (a) and write the equations for all the reactions.

Ans. There are two primary alkyl halides possible from the formula, C_4H_9Br. They are *n*-butyl bromide and isobutyl bromide.

$$CH_3 - CH_2 - CH_2 - CH_2 - Br \qquad\qquad CH_3 - \underset{\underset{CH_3}{|}}{CH} - CH_2 - Br$$

     n-Butyl bromide   Isobutyl bromide

Therefore, compound (a) is either *n*-butyl bromide or isobutyl bromide.

Now, compound (a) reacts with Na metal to give compound (b) of molecular formula, C_8H_{18}, which is different from the compound formed when *n*-butyl bromide reacts with Na metal. Hence, compound (a) must be isobutyl bromide.

$$\underset{\text{\scriptsize \textit{n}-Butyl bromide}}{2CH_3CH_2CH_2CH_2Br} \xrightarrow[\text{(Wurtz reaction)}]{\text{2Na/dry ether}} \underset{\text{\scriptsize \textit{n}-Octane}}{CH_3CH_2CH_2CH_2CH_2CH_2CH_2CH_3} + 2NaBr$$

$$CH_3 - \underset{\underset{CH_3}{|}}{CH} - CH_2 - Br \xrightarrow[\text{(Wurtz reaction)}]{\text{2Na/dry ether}} CH_3 - \underset{\underset{CH_3}{|}}{CH} - CH_2 - CH_2 - \underset{\underset{CH_3}{|}}{CH} - CH_3 + 2NaBr$$

   Isobutyl bromide   2, 5 Dimethylhexane

        (a)   (d)

Thus, compound (d) is 2, 5-dimethylhexane, and (a) is the correct isomer. Compound (a) reacts with alcoholic KOH to give compound (b). So, compound (b) is 2-methylpropene, formed as a result of dehydrohalogenation.

$$CH_3 - \underset{\underset{CH_3}{|}}{CH} - CH_2 - Br \xrightarrow[\text{(Dehydrohalogenation)}]{\text{KOH(alc)/}\Delta} CH_3 - \underset{\underset{CH_3}{|}}{C} = CH_2 + HBr$$

    Isobutyl chloride   2-Methylpropene

         (a)   (b)

Also, compound (b) reacts with HBr to give compound (c) which is an isomer of (a). Hence, compound (c) is 2-bromo-2-methylpropane.

$$CH_3 - \underset{\underset{CH_3}{|}}{C} = CH_2 \xrightarrow[\text{(Markovnikov addition)}]{\text{HBr}} CH_3 - \underset{\underset{CH_3}{|}}{\overset{\overset{Br}{|}}{C}}H - CH_3$$

    2-Methylpropene   2-Bromo-2-methylpropane

        (b)   (c)

                                           (an isomer of (a))

Q. 5. What happens when:

  (i)   *n*-butyl chloride is treated with alcoholic KOH.

  (ii) Bromobenzene is treated with Mg in the presence of dry ether.

  (iii) Chlorobenzene is subjected to hydrolysis.

  (iv) Ethyl chloride is treated with aqueous KOH.

  (v) Methyl bromide is treated with sodium in the presence of dry ether.

  (vi) Methyl chloride is treated with KCN.

Ans. (i)   When *n*-butyl chloride is treated with alcoholic KOH, but-1-ene is produced. This reaction is a dehydrohalogenation reaction.

$$\underset{\text{\scriptsize \textit{n}-Butyl chloride}}{CH_3 - CH_2 - CH_2 - CH_2 - Cl} \xrightarrow[\text{(Dehydrohalogenation)}]{\text{KOH(alc)/}\Delta} \underset{\text{\scriptsize But-1-ene}}{CH_3 - CH_2 - CH = CH_2} + KCl + H_2O$$

(ii) When bromobenzene is treated with Mg in the presence of dry ether, phenylmagnesium bromide a Grignard's reagent is formed.

$$\underset{\text{Bromobenzene}}{\text{Br}-C_6H_5} + Mg \xrightarrow{\text{Dry ether}} \underset{\text{Phenylmagnesium bromide}}{MgBr-C_6H_5}$$

(iii) Chlorobenzene does not undergo hydrolysis under normal conditions. It only undergoes hydrolysis when heated in an aqueous sodium hydroxide solution at a temperature of 623 K and a pressure of 300 atm to form phenol.

$$\underset{\text{Bromobenzene}}{Cl-C_6H_5} \xrightarrow[\text{(ii) } H^+]{\text{(i) NaOH, 623 K, 300 atm}} \underset{\text{Phenol}}{OH-C_6H_5}$$

(iv) When ethyl chloride is treated with aqueous KOH, it undergoes hydrolysis to form ethanol.

$$\underset{\text{Ethyl chloride}}{CH_3 - CH_2 - Cl} \xrightarrow[\text{(Hydrolysis)}]{KOH_{(aq.)}} \underset{\text{Ethanol}}{CH_3 - CH_2 - OH} + KCl$$

(v) When methyl bromide is treated with sodium in the presence of dry ether, ethane is formed. This reaction is known as the Wurtz reaction.

$$\underset{\text{Methyl bromide}}{2CH_3 - Br} + 2Na \xrightarrow[\text{(Wurtz reaction)}]{\text{Dry ether}} \underset{\text{Ethane}}{CH_3 - CH_3} + 2NaBr$$

(vi) When methyl chloride is treated with KCN, it undergoes a substitution reaction to give methyl cyanide.

$$\underset{\text{Methylchloride}}{CH_3 - Cl} + KCN \xrightarrow{\text{Nucleophilic substitution}} \underset{\text{Methylcyanide}}{CH_3 - C \equiv N} + KCl$$

Q. 6. Among the isomeric alkanes of molecular formula C_5H_{12}, identify the one that on photochemical chlorination yields

(i) A single monochloride   (iii) Four isomeric monochlorides.

(ii) Three isomeric monochlorides

Ans. (i) To have a single monochloride, there should be only one type of H-atom in the isomer of the alkane of the molecular formula C_5H_{12}. Thus, replacement of any one of the H-atom leads to the formation of the same product. Hence the isomer is neopentane.

$$\underset{\text{Neopentane}}{CH_3 - \overset{\overset{\displaystyle CH_3}{|}}{\underset{\underset{\displaystyle CH_3}{|}}{C}} - CH_3} ;\ CH_3 - \overset{\overset{\displaystyle CH_3}{|}}{\underset{\underset{\displaystyle CH_3}{|}}{C}} - CH_3 + Cl_2 \xrightarrow{h\nu}\ \underset{\text{1-Chloro-2,2-dimethyl propane}}{CH_3 - \overset{\overset{\displaystyle CH_3}{|}}{\underset{\underset{\displaystyle CH_3}{|}}{C}} - CH_2Cl + HCl}$$

(ii) To have three isomeric monochlorides, the isomer of the alkane of the molecular formula C_5H_{12} should contain three equivalent H-atoms.

In the straight chain isomer, *n*-pentane. It can be observed that there are three equivalent H-atoms, as *a*, *b* and *c* in *n*-pentane.

$$\overset{c}{C}H_3 - \overset{b}{C}H_2 - \overset{a}{C}H_2 - \overset{b}{C}H_2 - \overset{c}{C}H_3$$

n-Pentane

Thus formation of 1-chloropentane and 3-chloropentane, 2-chloropentane will solve the problem.

It can be observed that H-atoms labelled as *a*, *b*, *c* and *d* in 2-methylbutane, *i.e.*, branched chain isomer has 4 equivalent H-atoms. It will produce; 2-chloropentane, 2-chloro-2-methyl butane. 2-chloro-3-methyl butane and 1-chloro-3-methyl butane as the four isomeric monochlorides.

Q. 7. **Which alkyl halide from the following pairs would you expect to react more rapidly by an S_N2 mechanism? Explain your answer.**

(i) $CH_3 — CH_2 — CH_2 — CH_2 — Br$ or $CH_3 — CH_2 — \underset{\underset{Br}{|}}{CH} — CH_3$

(ii) $CH_3 — CH_2 — \underset{\underset{Br}{|}}{CH} — CH_3$ or $H_3C — \underset{\underset{CH_3}{|}}{\overset{\overset{CH_3}{|}}{C}} — Br$

(iii) $CH_3 — \underset{\underset{CH_3}{|}}{CH} — CH_2 — Br$ or $CH_3 — CH_2 — \underset{\underset{CH_3}{|}}{CH} — CH_2 — Br$

Ans. In S_N^2 mechanism, the reactivity of compound decreases with increasing steric hinderance.

(i) $CH_3 — CH_2 — CH_2 — CH_2 — Br$ $CH_3 — CH_2 — \underset{\underset{Br}{|}}{CH} — CH_3$

1-Bromobutane (1°)   2-Bromobutane (2°)

2-bromobutane is a 2° alkylhalide whereas 1-bromobutane is a 1° alkyl halide. The approaching of nucleophile is more hindered in 2-bromobutane than in 1-bromobutane. Hence, 1-bromobutane reacts more rapidly than 2-bromobutane by S_N2 mechanism.

(ii) $CH_3 — CH_2 — \underset{\underset{Br}{|}}{CH} — CH_3$ $CH_3 — \underset{\underset{Br}{|}}{\overset{\overset{CH_3}{|}}{C}} — Br$

2-Bromobutane (2°)   2-Bromo-2-methylpropane (3°)

2-Bromobutane is 2° alkylhalide whereas 2-bromo-2-methylpropane is 3° alkyl halide. Therefore, 2-bromobutane reacts more rapidly than 2-bromo-2-methylpropane by the S_N2 mechanism.

(iii) $CH_3 — \underset{\underset{CH_3}{|}}{CH} — CH_2 — CH_2 — Br$ $CH_3 — CH_2 — \underset{\underset{CH_3}{|}}{CH} — CH_2 — Br$

1-Bromo-3-methylbutane (1°)   1-Bromo-2-methylbutane (1°)

Both the alkyl halides are primary. However, the substituent $–CH_3$ is at a greater distance to the carbon atom linked to Br in 1-bromo-3-methylbutane (C_3-position) than in 1-bromo-2-methylbutane (C_2-position). Hence, the nucleophile is less hindered in case of the former than in case of the latter. So, 1-Bromo-3-methylbutane faces less steric hindrance and reacts faster in the S_N2 mechanism.

Q. 8. **Identify A, B, C, D, E, R and R^1 in the following:**

$$\text{Cyclohexyl} — Br + Mg \xrightarrow{\text{Dryether}} A \xrightarrow{H_2O} B$$

$$R – Br + Mg \xrightarrow{\text{Dryether}} C \xrightarrow{D_2O} CH_3\underset{\underset{D}{|}}{CH}CH_3$$

$$\underset{\underset{CH_3\ CH_3}{|}}{\overset{\overset{CH_3\ CH_3}{|}}{CH_3 + + CH_3}} \xleftarrow{\text{Na/ether}} R^1 – X \xrightarrow{Mg} D \xrightarrow{H_2O} E$$

Ans.

$$\text{Cyclohexyl} — Br + Mg \xrightarrow{\text{Dryether}} \text{Cyclohexyl} — MgBr \xrightarrow{H_2O} \text{Cyclohexane} + Mg(OH)Br$$

Bromocyclohexane   Cyclohexylmagnesium bromide (A) [Grignard reagent]   Cyclohexane (B)

must be RMgBr as reflected from structure of compound : $CH_3 - CH - CH_3$
|
D

CH_3CHCH_3
|
MgBr

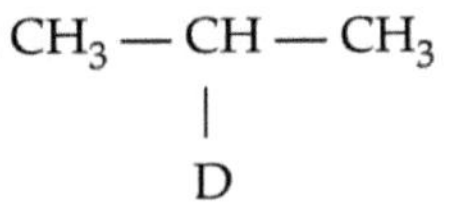

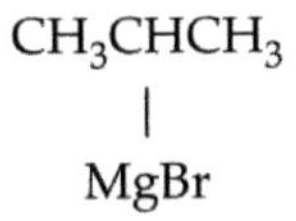

Isopropylmagnesium bromide

Therefore, the compound R — Br is

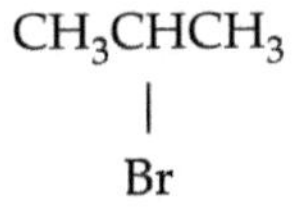

CH_3CHCH_3
|
Br

2-Bromopropane

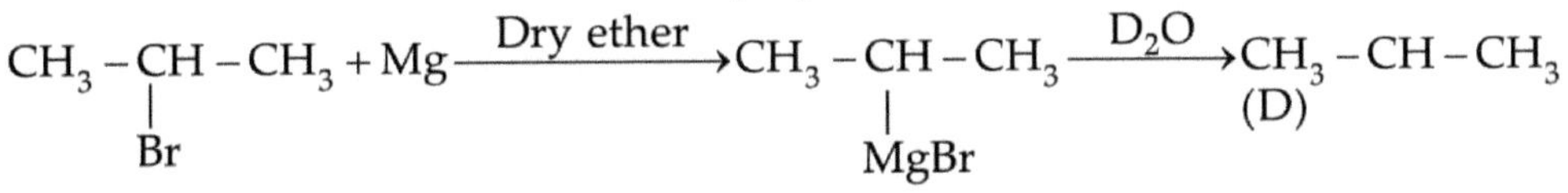

$$CH_3 - CH - CH_3 + Mg \xrightarrow{\text{Dry ether}} CH_3 - CH - CH_3 \xrightarrow{D_2O} CH_3 - CH - CH_3$$

with the Br below the first, MgBr below the second, and (D) beside the third, and (C) below.

When an alkyl halide is treated with Na in the presence of ether, a hydrocarbon containing double the number of carbon atoms as present in the original halide is obtained as the product. This is known as Wurtz reaction. Therefore, the halide, $R^1 - X$, is

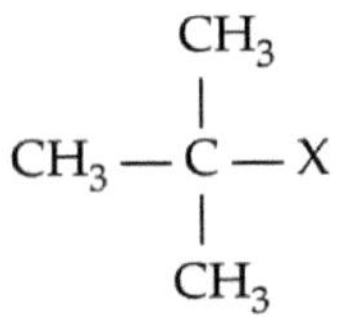

CH_3
|
$CH_3 - C - X$
|
CH_3

tert-Butylhalide

Therefore, compound D is

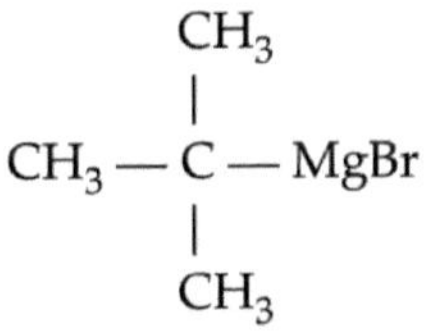

CH_3
|
$CH_3 - C - MgBr$
|
CH_3

tert-Butylmagnesiumbromide

And, compound E is

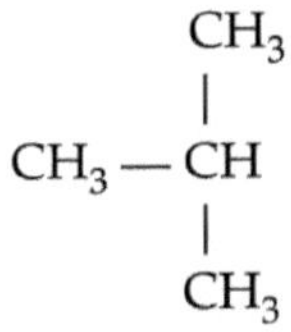

CH_3
|
$CH_3 - CH$
|
CH_3

2-Methylpropane

$$\underset{\substack{| \quad | \\ CH_3 \; CH_3}}{CH_3 - \overset{\substack{CH_3 \; CH_3 \\ | \quad |}}{C - C} - CH_3} \xleftarrow[\substack{\text{(Wurtz} \\ \text{reaction)}}]{\text{Na/ether}} \underset{CH_3}{\overset{CH_3}{CH_3 - C - X}} \xrightarrow{\text{Mg}} \underset{CH_3}{\overset{CH_3}{CH_3 - C - MgBr}} \text{(Grignard reagent)}$$

2, 2, 3, 3-tetramethylbutane

(D)

$\downarrow H_2O$

CH_3
|
$CH_3 - CH$ $+ Mg(OH)X$
|
CH_3

2-Methyl propane

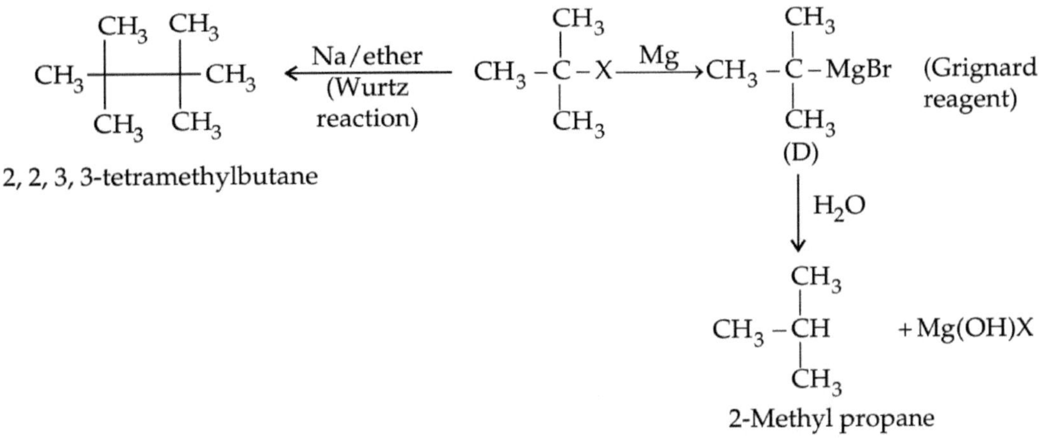

Chapter 11. Alcohols, Phenols and Ethers

Q. 1. (i) Draw the structures of all isomeric alcohols of molecular formula $C_5H_{12}O$ and give their IUPAC names.

(ii) Classify the isomers of alcohols in above (part i) as primary, secondary and tertiary alcohols.

Ans. (i) The structures of all isomeric alcohols of molecular formula, $C_5H_{12}O$ are shown below :

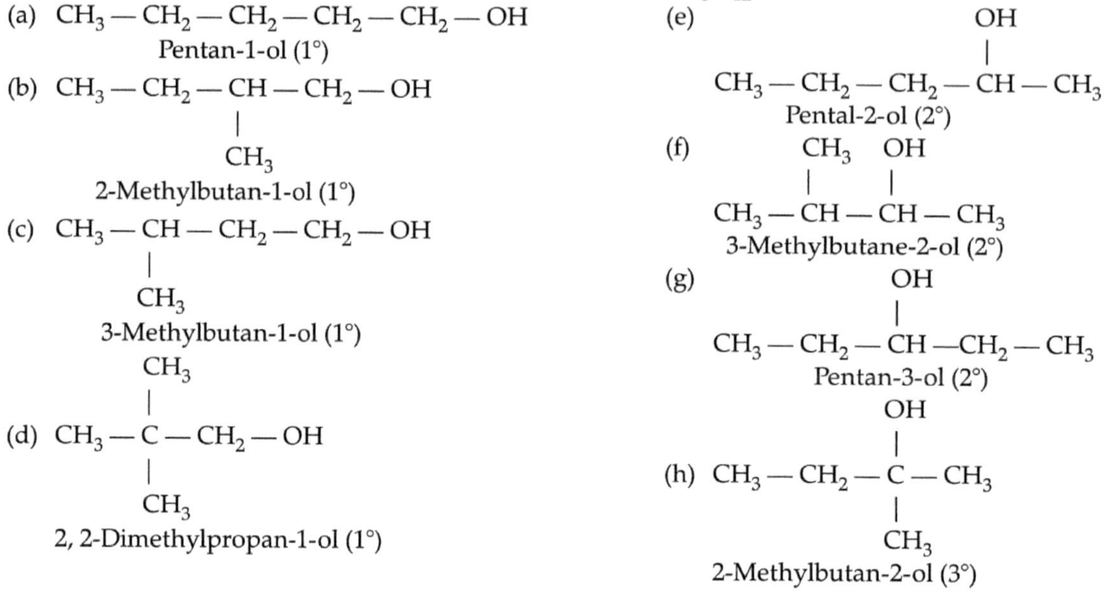

(a) $CH_3 — CH_2 — CH_2 — CH_2 — CH_2 — OH$
Pentan-1-ol (1°)

(b) $CH_3 — CH_2 — CH — CH_2 — OH$
$\quad\quad\quad\quad\quad | $
$\quad\quad\quad\quad\quad CH_3$
2-Methylbutan-1-ol (1°)

(c) $CH_3 — CH — CH_2 — CH_2 — OH$
$\quad\quad\quad | $
$\quad\quad\quad CH_3$
3-Methylbutan-1-ol (1°)

(d) $CH_3 — C — CH_2 — OH$
$\quad\quad\quad\ |$
$\quad\quad\quad CH_3$
2, 2-Dimethylpropan-1-ol (1°)

(e) $CH_3 — CH_2 — CH_2 — CH — CH_3$, with OH on the CH
Pental-2-ol (2°)

(f) $CH_3 — CH — CH — CH_3$, with CH_3 and OH substituents
3-Methylbutane-2-ol (2°)

(g) $CH_3 — CH_2 — CH —CH_2 — CH_3$, with OH on the central CH
Pentan-3-ol (2°)

(h) $CH_3 — CH_2 — C — CH_3$, with OH and CH_3 substituents
2-Methylbutan-2-ol (3°)

(ii) **Primary alcohol** : Pentan-1-ol; 2-Methylbutan-1-ol; 3-Methylbutan-1-ol; 2, 2-Dimethylpropan-1-ol

Secondary alcohol : Pentan-2-ol; 3-Methylbutan-2-ol; Pental-3-ol

Tertiary alcohol : 2-methylbutan-2-ol.

Total 8 isomeric forms.

Q. 2. Give two reactions that show the acidic nature of phenol. Compare acidity of phenol with that of ethanol.

Ans. The acidic nature of phenol can be represented by the following two reactions :

(i) Phenol reacts with sodium to give sodium phenoxide, liberating H_2 gas like in general reactions of acids with metal.

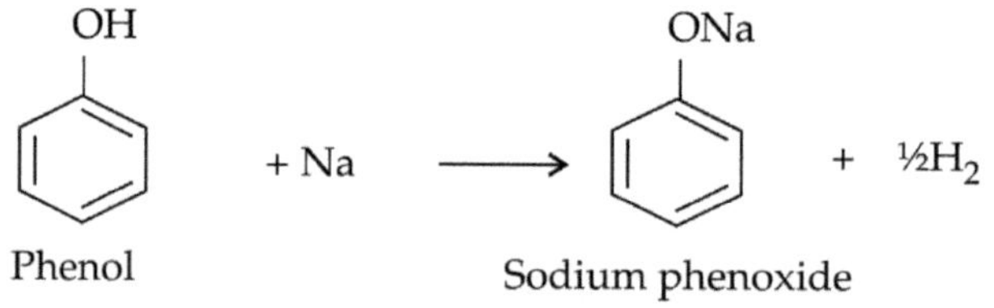

Phenol $+ Na \longrightarrow$ Sodium phenoxide $+\ \frac{1}{2}H_2$

(ii) Phenol reacts with sodium hydroxide to give sodium phenoxide and water as by-products. This is same as acid base reaction.

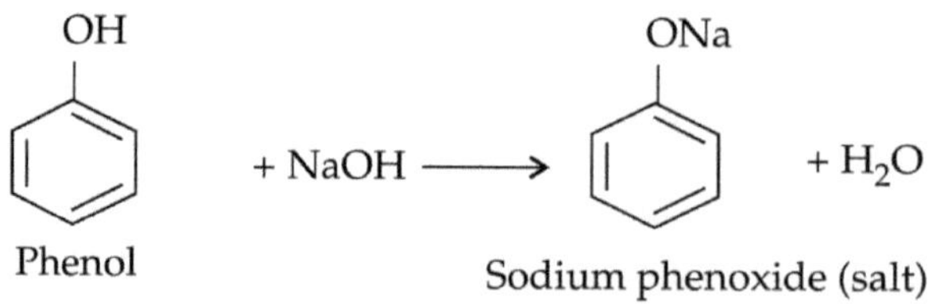

Phenol $+ NaOH \longrightarrow$ Sodium phenoxide (salt) $+ H_2O$

The acidity of phenol is more than that of ethanol. This is because after losing a proton, the phenoxide ion undergoes resonance and gets stabilised whereas ethoxide ion does not.

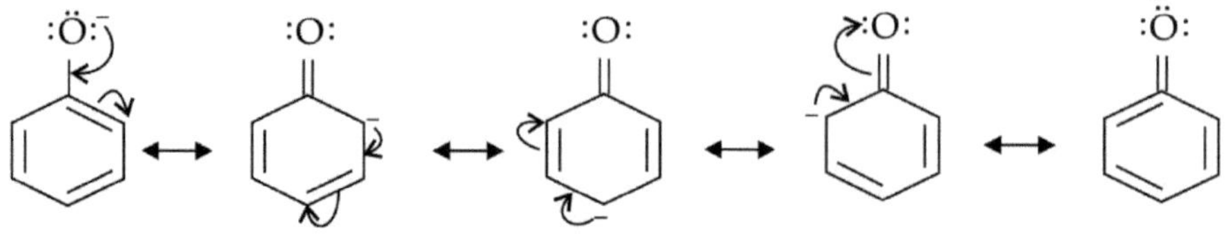

Q. 3. Give equations of the following reactions:

    (i)   Oxidation of propan-1-ol with alkaline $KMnO_4$ solution.

    (ii)   Bromine in CS_2 with phenol.

    (iii) Dilute HNO_3 with phenol.

    (iv) Treating phenol with chloroform in presence of aqueous NaOH.

Ans. (i)

$$CH_3CH_2CH_2OH \xrightarrow{\text{alk. } KMnO_4} CH_3CH_2COOH$$

Propan–1–ol   Propanoic acid

(ii)

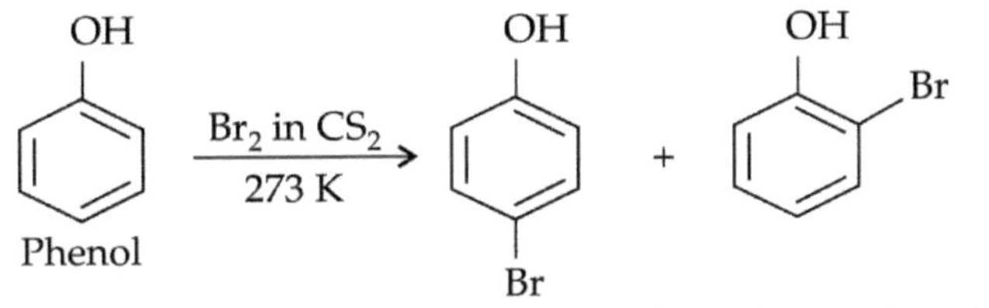

Phenol $\xrightarrow[\text{273 K}]{Br_2 \text{ in } CS_2}$ p-bromophenol (Major) + o-Bromophenol (Minor)

(iii)

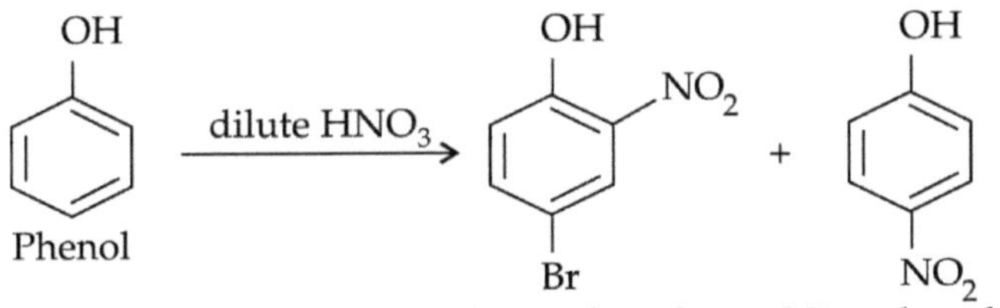

Phenol $\xrightarrow{\text{dilute } HNO_3}$ o-Nitrophenol + p-Nitrophenol

(iv)

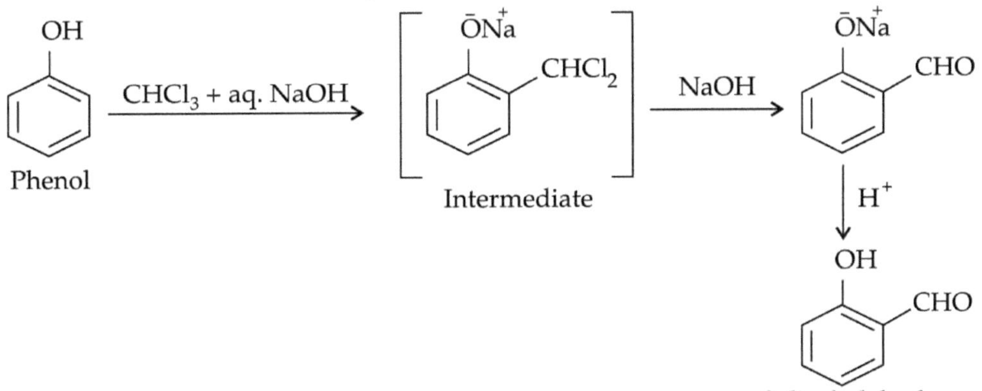

Phenol $\xrightarrow{CHCl_3 + \text{aq. NaOH}}$ [Intermediate] $\xrightarrow{NaOH}$ → $\xrightarrow{H^+}$ Salicyladehyde

Q. 4. Illustrate with examples the limitations of Williamson synthesis for the preparation of certain types of ethers.

Ans. The reaction of Williamson synthesis involves S_N2 attack of an alkoxide ion on a primary alkyl halide, which involves a pentavalent transition state.

$$(CH_3)_3C-\ddot{\overset{-}{O}}\overset{+}{Na} + CH_3-Cl \longrightarrow CH_3-\ddot{O}-C(CH_3)_3 + NaCl$$

But if secondary or tertiary alkyl halides are taken in place of primary alkyl halides, then elimination would compete over substitution. As a result, alkenes would be produced. As alkoxides are nucleophiles as well as strong bases, they react with alkyl halides, which results in an elimination reaction. Another short coming of Williamson synthesis is that it gives good yields for symmetrical ethers having secondary or tertiary alkyl groups. Same for aryl alkyl ethers, aryl halide can't be used.

$$(CH_3)_3C-Cl + Na\ddot{\overset{..}{O}}-CH_3 \longrightarrow (CH_3)_2C=CH_2 = CH_2 + CH_3OH + NaCl$$

Tertiary alkyl halide   Alkene

Q. 5. Show how would you synthesise the following alcohols from appropriate alkenes?

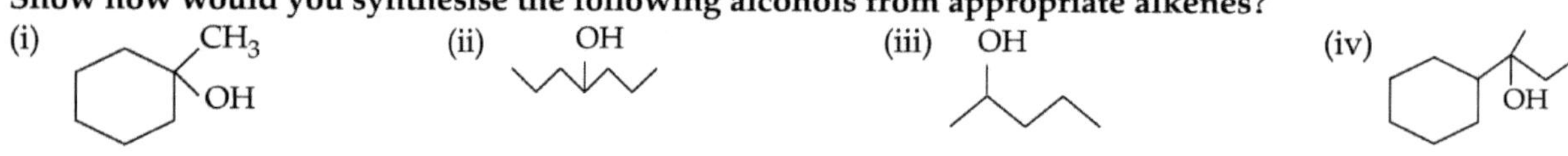

Ans. The given alcohols can be synthesised by acid-catalysed hydration of appropriate alkenes. The addition will follow Markovnikov's rule.

(i)

1-Methylcyclohexene   1-Methylcyclo-hexan-1-ol

or

Methylenecyclohexane

(ii)

4-Methylhept-3-ene   4-Methylheptan-4-ol

(iii)

Pent-1-ene   Pentan-2-ol

Acid-catalysed hydration of pent-2-ene also produces pentan-2-ol but along with pentan-3-ol.

Pent-2-ene   Pentan-2-ol   Pentan-3-ol

Thus, the first reaction is preferred over the second one to get pentan-2-ol.

(iv)

2-Cyclohexylbut-2-ene   2-Cyclohexylbuta-2-ol

Q. 6. *Ortho* and *para* nitrophenols are more acidic than phenol. Draw the resonance structures of the corresponding phenoxide ions.

Ans.

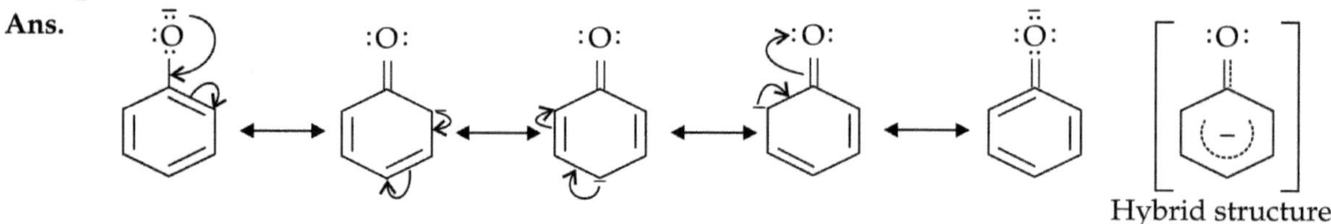

Hybrid structure

Resonance structure of the phenoxide ion.

Resonance structures of *p*-nitrophenoxide ion.

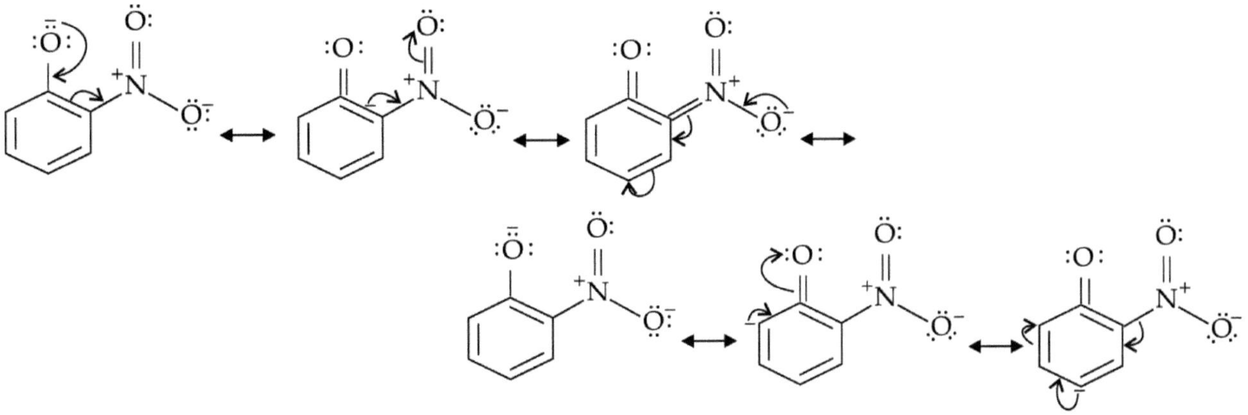

Resonance structures of *m*-nitrophenoxide ion.

It can be observed that the presence of nitro groups increases the stability of phenoxide ion.

Q. 7. (i) Write the product(s) in the following reactions:*

(a) 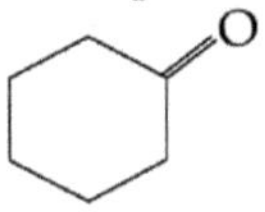 (cyclohexanone) $+ HCN \longrightarrow$?

(b) 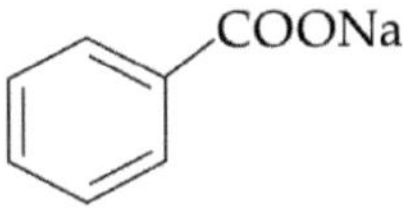 (sodium benzoate, COONa) $+ NaOH \xrightarrow[\Delta]{CaO}$?

(c) $CH_3 - CH = CH - CN \xrightarrow[(b)H_2O]{(a)\ DIBAL\text{-}H}$?

(ii) Give simple chemical tests to distinguish between the following pairs of compounds:

(a) Butanal and Butan-2-one

(b) Benzoic acid and Phenol

Ans. (i) (a) 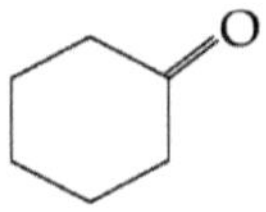 (cyclohexanone) $+ HCN \longrightarrow$ (cyclohexane ring with OH and CN)

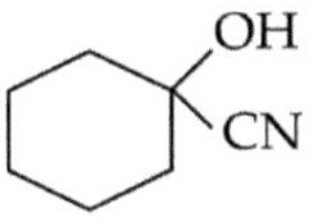

(b) 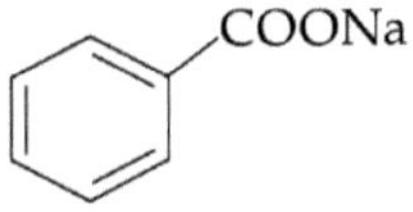 (COONa) $+ NaOH \xrightarrow[\Delta]{CaO}$ (benzene) $+ Na_2 CO_3$

Benzene

(c) $CH_3 - CH = CH - CN \xrightarrow[(b)\ H_2O]{(a)\ DIBAL\text{-}H} CH_3 - CH = CH - CHO$

(ii) (a) Butanal and Butan-2-one

(i) $CH_3CH_2CH_2CHO + 2[Ag(NH_3)_2]^+\ 3OH^- \rightarrow CH_3CH_2CH_2COO^- + 2Ag + 2H_2O + 4NH_3$

        Butanal   Tollen's reagent

This reaction is known as silver mirror test

(ii)

$$CH_3-CH_2-\overset{\overset{\textstyle O}{\|}}{C}-CH_3 + 2[Ag(NH_3)_2]^+ + 3OH^-$$

    Butan-2-one $\downarrow$ Tollen's reagent

        No reaction

Thus, Butanal gives silver mirror test with Tollen's reagent whereas Butan-2-one does not.

(b) Benzoic acid and phenol

Q. 8. (i) Write the reactions involved in the following:*

(a) Etard reaction.   (b) Stephen reduction.

(ii) How will you convert the following in not more than two steps:

(a) Benzoic acid to Benzaldehyde.   (b) Acetophenone to Benzoic acid.

(c) Ethanoic acide to 2Hydroxyethanoic acid.

1. $C_6H_5COOH + NaHCO_3 \longrightarrow C_6H_5COONa + H_2O + CO_2$
   Benzoic acid　Sodium bicarbonate　Sodium benzoate

2. $C_6H_5OH + NaHCO_3 \longrightarrow$ No reaction
   Phenol　Sodium bicarbonate

Thus Benzoic acid gives sodium benzoate on reaction with sodium bicarbonate whereas phenol gives no reaction with sodium bicarbonate.

Ans. (i) (a) **Etard Reaction:** The oxidation of toluene to benzaldehyde with chromyl chloride (CrO_2Cl_2) dissolved in CCl_4 or CS_2.

Tolyene $\xrightarrow[CCl_4]{2CrO_2Cl_2}$ Brown complex $\xrightarrow{H_2O}$ Benzaldehyde

(b) **Stephen Reaction:** The partial reduction of alkyl or aryl cyanides to the corresponding aldehydes with a suspension of anhydrous $SnCl_2$ in ether saturated with HCl at room temperature followed by hydrolysis.

$$SnCl_2 + 2HCl \longrightarrow SnCl_4 + 2[H]$$

$$CH_3C \equiv N + 2[H] + 2HCl \longrightarrow CH_3CH \equiv NHHCl \xrightarrow[Boil]{H_2O} CH_3CHO + NH_4Cl$$

Acetaldoxime hydrochloride　　Acetaldehyde

$$C_6H_5 - C \equiv N + 2[H] + 2HCl \longrightarrow C_6H_5CH = NH.HCl \xrightarrow[Boil]{H_2O} C_6H_5CHO + NH_4Cl$$

Benzaldoxime hydrochloride　　Benzaldehyde

(ii) (a) Benzoic acid to Benzaldehyde

Benzoic acid $\xrightarrow{Soda\ lime}$ Benzene $\xrightarrow[Anhy.\ AlCl_3]{CO.HCl}$ Benzaldehyde

(b) Acetophenone to Benzoic acid

Acetophenone $\xrightarrow{Zn/Hg-HCl}$ Ethyl Benzene $\xrightarrow{[O]}$ Benzoic acid

(c) Ethanoic acid to 2-hydroxyethanoic acid

$$CH_3COOH \xrightarrow{P,\ Cl_2} \underset{Cl}{CH_2COOH} \xrightarrow{aq.\ KOH} \underset{OH}{CH_2-COOH}$$
Acetic acid or Ethanoic acid

2-Hydroxyethanoic acid

Q. 9. (i) Write the products in the following reactions:*

(a) 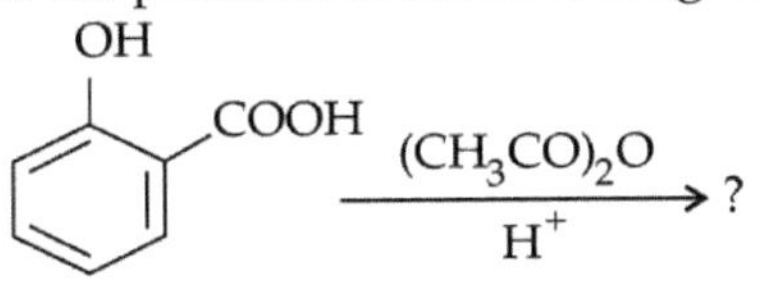 [structure: benzene ring with OH and COOH groups] $\xrightarrow[\text{H}^+]{(CH_3CO)_2O}$?

(b) $CH_3 - \underset{\underset{CH_3}{|}}{CH} - O - CH_2 - CH_3 \xrightarrow{HI} ? + ?$

(c) $CH_3 - CH = CH - CH_2 - OH \xrightarrow{PCC} ?$

(ii) Give simple chemical tests to distinguish between the following pairs of compounds:

(a) Ethanol and Phenol

(b) Propanol and 2-methylpropan-2-ol

Ans. (i) (a) 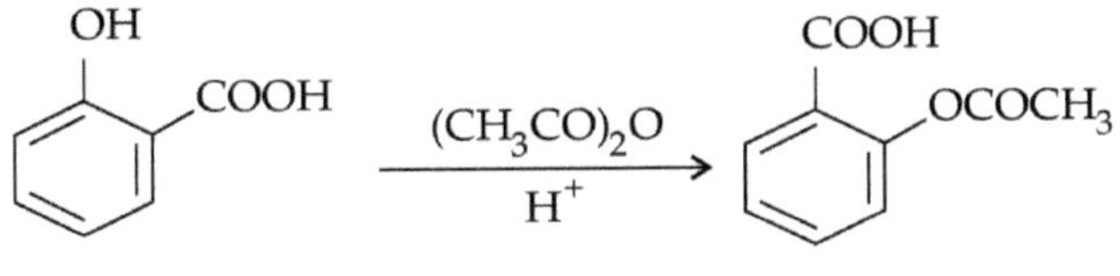 [structure: benzene ring with OH and COOH] $\xrightarrow[\text{H}^+]{(CH_3CO)_2O}$ [structure: benzene ring with COOH and OCOCH$_3$]

(b) $CH_3 - \underset{\underset{CH_3}{|}}{CH} - O - CH_2 - CH_3 \xrightarrow{HI} (CH_3)_2CHOH + CH_3CH_2I$

(c) $CH_3 - CH = CH - CH_2 - OH \xrightarrow{PCC} CH_3CH = CHCHO$

(ii) (a) **Ethanol and phenol :** When neutral ferric chloride is added to both the compounds phenol gives violet coloured complex whereas ethanol does not gives this complex when treated with ferric chloride solution.

(b) **Propanol and 2-methyl propan-2-ol:** When both the solutions were treated with anhydrous $ZnCl_2$ and conc. HCl (Luca's test) the 2-methylpropan-2-ol gives the turbidity immediately whereas propanol does not gives the turbidity immediately.

Q. 10. (i) Write the formula of reagents used in the following reactions:*

(a) Bromination of phenol to 2, 4, 6-tribromophenol

(b) Hydroboration of propene and then oxidation to propanol.

(ii) Arrange the following compound groups in the increasing order of their property indicated:

(a) *p*-nitrophenol, ethanol, phenol (acidic character)

(b) Propanol, propane, Propanal (boiling point)

(iii) Write the mechanism (using curved arrow notation) of the following reaction:

$$CH_3 - CH_2 - \overset{+}{O}H_2 \xrightarrow{CH_3CH_2OH}$$

$$CH_3 - CH_2 - \underset{\underset{H}{|}}{\overset{+}{O}} - CH_2 - CH_3 + H_2O$$

Ans. (i) (a) Aq Br_2

(b) B_2H_6 and then H_2O_2 and OH^-

(ii) (a) Ethanol < Phenol < *p*-Nitrophenol.

(b) Propane < Propanal < Propanol

(iii) $CH_3 - CH_2 - \overset{+}{O}H_2 \xrightarrow{CH_3CH_2OH} CH_3 - CH_2 - \underset{\underset{H}{|}}{\overset{+}{O}} - CH_2 - CH_3 + H_2O$

Mechanism for this above reaction is:

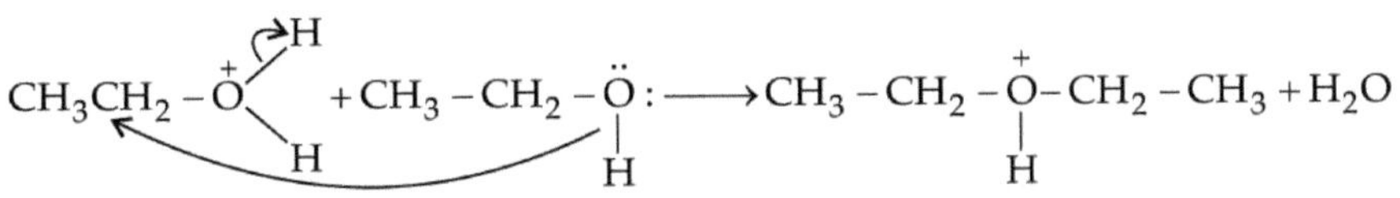

$$CH_3CH_2 - \overset{+}{O} \overset{\curvearrowright H}{\underset{H}{}} + CH_3 - CH_2 - \ddot{\underset{\underset{H}{|}}{O}} : \longrightarrow CH_3 - CH_2 - \underset{\underset{H}{|}}{\overset{+}{O}} - CH_2 - CH_3 + H_2O$$

Chapter 12. Aldehydes, Ketones and Carboxylic Acids

Q. 1. An acid [A] $C_8H_7O_2Br$ on bromination in the presence of $FeBr_3$ gives two isomers [B] and [C] of the formula $C_8H_6O_2Br_2$. Vigorous oxidation of [A], [B] and [C] gives acids [D], [E] and [F] respectively. The acid [D] $C_7H_5O_2Br$ is the strongest acid among all the isomers whereas [E] and [F] each has molecular formula of $C_7H_4O_2Br_2$. Give structure of [A] to [F] with justification.

Ans. (i) From the formula $C_8H_7O_2Br$ seems like a carboxylic acid. Formation of two isomers [B] and [C] of formula $C_8H_6O_2Br_2$ must have given an *ortho* and *para* isomer.

Compound [A] can be any of these I, II or III structure.

(ii) As vigorous oxidation of [A] alongwith acid [B] and [C] produces strongest acid [D] from structure [A] hence compound [A] must be structure [I].

[D] is strongest acid because of *ortho*-effect whereas presence of Br molecule at the meta position weakens the acidic strength.

Q. 2. An organic compound [A] having molecular formula C_3H_6O, gives iodoform reaction and forms a compound [B]. [B] on heating with Ag powder, gives compound [C]. [C] reacts with dil. H_2SO_4 and mercuric sulphate to obtain compound [D]. Compound [D] undergoes Aldol condensation. Write down the names and structures of all the compounds starting from [A] to [D] with the help of chemical equations.

Ans. Compound [A] gives iodoform reaction hence it must have a (CH_3CO-) group. $CH_3-\overset{\overset{\textstyle O}{\|}}{C}-CH_3$, must be [A]. Hence the reactions are:

$$CH_3-\overset{\overset{\textstyle C}{\|}}{C}-CH_3 + I_2 + NaOH \xrightarrow{\Delta} \underset{\text{Iodoform}}{CHI_3} + CH_3COONa + H_2O + NaI \xrightarrow[\Delta]{\text{Ag powder}}$$

[A]   [B]

$$CH \equiv CH \xrightarrow[H_2SO_4,\ H_2O]{HgSO_4} CH_3CHO$$

Ethyne [C] (Oxymercuration Ethanol [D]
demercuration)

Aldol condensation of [D] *i.e.*, ethanol occurs.

$$2CH_3CHO \xrightarrow[NaOH]{dil.} CH_3-\underset{\underset{\textstyle OH}{|}}{CH}-CH_2-CHO \xrightarrow[-H_2O]{\Delta} CH_3CH = CH - CHO$$

(3-hydroxy butanal)   But-2-enal

Q. 3. What is meant by the following terms?

Give an example of the reaction in each case.

(i)   Cyanohydrin   (ii)   Acetal

(iii) Semicarbazone   (iv) Aldol

(v) Hemiacetal   (vi) Oxime

(vii) Ketal   (viii) Imine

(ix) 2, 4-DNP-derivative   (x)   Schiff's base

Ans. (i)   Cyanohydrin: Cyanohydrins are organic compounds having hydroxyl (– OH) and cyano (CN) groups on the same carbon atom.

$$\underset{R \quad R'}{\overset{N}{\underset{\parallel}{\underset{C}{\diagdown}}}\diagup OH}$$

Aldehydes and ketones react with hydrogen cyanide (HCN) in the presence of excess sodium cyanide (NaCN) as a catalyst to give cyanohydrin. These reactions are known as cyanohydrin reactions.

$$\underset{\text{Ketone}}{RR'C = O} + HCN \xrightarrow{\text{NaCN}} \underset{\text{Cyanohydrin}}{RR'C(OH)CN}$$

Cyanohydrins are useful synthetic intermediates.

(ii) Acetal : Acetals are gem-dialkoxy alkanes in which two alkoxy groups are present on the terminal carbon atom.

$$R - \overset{\overset{\displaystyle H}{|}}{\underset{\underset{\displaystyle OR''}{|}}{C}} - OR'$$

General structure of an acetal

When aldehydes are treated with two equivalents of a monohydric alcohol in the presence of dry HCl gas, hemiacetals are produced that further reacts with one more molecule of alcohol to yield acetal.

$$\underset{\text{Aldehyde}}{RCHO} \underset{}{\overset{R'OH, \text{ dry HCl gas}}{\rightleftharpoons}} \left[\underset{\text{Hemiacetal}}{R - CH \overset{OH'}{\underset{OH'}{\diagup}}} \right] \underset{H^+}{\overset{R'' - OR}{\rightleftharpoons}} \underset{\text{Acetal}}{R - CH \overset{OR'}{\underset{OR'}{\diagup}}} + H_2O$$

(iii) Semicarbazone : Semicarbazones are derivatives of aldehydes and ketones produced by the condensation reaction between a ketone or aldehyde and semicarbazide.

$$C \!\!=\!\! O + H_2 \vdots N - NH - \overset{O}{\overset{\parallel}{C}} - NH_2 \rightleftharpoons \left[C \overset{OH}{\underset{N - NH - \overset{O}{\overset{\parallel}{C}} - NH_2}{\diagup}} \right] \longrightarrow$$

Semicarbazide

$$H_2O + {>}C = N - NH - \overset{O}{\overset{\parallel}{C}} - NH_2$$

Semicarbazide

Semicarbazones are useful for identification and characterization of aldehydes and ketones.

(iv) Aldol: A β-hydroxy aldehyde or ketone is known as an aldol. It is produced by the condensation reaction of two molecules of the same or one molecule each of two different aldehydes or ketones in the presence of a base, atleast one of which either aldehyde should have an α-hydrogen atom.

$$\underset{\text{Propanal}}{2CH_3CH_2 - CHO} \overset{\text{dil. NaOH}}{\rightleftharpoons} CH_3 - CH_2 - \underset{\underset{\displaystyle OH}{|}}{CH} - CH_2 - CH_2 - CHO$$

4-Hydroxyhexanal (Aldol)

(v) Hemiacetal: Hemiacetals are α-alkoxyalcohols or gem-alkoxyalcohols.

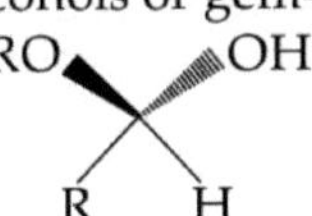

$$\underset{R \quad H}{\overset{RO \diagdown \quad \diagup OH}{\diagup \diagdown}}$$

General structure of a hemiacetal:

Aldehyde reacts with one molecule of a monohydric alcohol in the presence of HCl gas.

$$RCHO \overset{R'OH, \text{ Dry HCl gas}}{\rightleftharpoons} \left[R - CH \overset{OR'}{\underset{OH}{\diagup}} \right]$$

Hemiacetal

(vi) Oxime: Oximes are a class of organic compounds derived from aldehydes and ketones. If R′ is H, then it is known as aldoxime and if R′ is an organic side chain, then it is known as ketoxime.

Aldoxime $\qquad$ Ketoxime

On treatment with hydroxylamine in a weakly acidic medium, aldehydes or ketones form oximes.

$$C = O + H_2NOH \longrightarrow C = N - OH + H_2O$$

Hydroxylamine

(vii) Ketal: Ketals are gem-dialkoxyalkanes in which two alkoxy groups are present on the same carbon atom within the chain. The other two bonds of the carbon atom are connected to two alkyl groups.

$$R - \underset{OR''}{\overset{R'}{\underset{|}{\overset{|}{C}}}} - OR''$$

General structure of an ketal

Ketones react with ethylene glycol in the presence of dry HCl gas to give a cyclic product known as ethylene glycol ketals.

$$\underset{R'}{\overset{R}{>}}C = O + \underset{CH_2OH}{\overset{CH_2OH}{|}} \underset{\text{dil.HCl}}{\overset{\text{HCl gas}}{\rightleftharpoons}} \underset{R'}{\overset{R}{>}}C\underset{O-CH_2}{\overset{O-CH_2}{<}} + H_2O$$

Ketone $\qquad$ Ethylene glycol $\qquad$ Ethylene glycol ketal

(viii) Imine: Imines are chemical compounds containing a carbon nitrogen double bond.

General structure of an imine

Imines are produced when aldehydes and ketones react with ammonia and its derivatives.

$$C = O + H_2N - Z \rightleftharpoons \left[C \overset{OH}{\underset{NHZ}{<}} \right] \longrightarrow C = N - Z + H_2O$$

(ix) 2, 4-DNP-derivative: 2, 4-dinitrophenylhydrazones are 2, 4-DNP-derivatives, which are produced when aldehydes or ketones react with 2, 4-dinitrophenylhydrazine in a weakly acidic medium.

$$C = O + H_2 - NNH - \underset{NO_2}{\underset{|}{\bigcirc}} - NO_2 \longrightarrow H_2O + C = NH - \underset{NO_2}{\underset{|}{\bigcirc}} - NO_2$$

2, 4-Dinitrophenylhydrazone

The 2, 4-DNP derivatives are generally orange-red or yellow insoluble solids.

Hence are used to identify and characterise tests for aldehydes and ketones, 2, 4-DNP derivatives are used.

(x) Schiff's base: Schiff's base (or azomethine) is a chemical compound containing a carbon-nitrogen double bond with the nitrogen atom connected to an aryl or alkyl group but not hydrogen. They have the general formula $R_1R_2C = NR_3$. Hence, it is a substituted imine.

General structure of Schiff's base

Aldehydes and ketones on treatment with primary aliphatic or aromatic amines in the presence of trace of an acid yields a Schiff's base.

$$R - CH = O + H_2 - N - R' \xrightarrow{\text{Trace of } H^+} R - CH = N - R' + H_2O$$

Aldehyde 1° amine $\qquad$ Schiff's base

Q. 4. **Predict the products formed when cyclohexanecarbaldehyde reacts with the following reagents:**

(i) PhMgBr and then H_3O^+

(ii) Tollen's reagent

(iii) Semicarbazide and weak acid

(iv) Excess ethanol and acid

(v) Zinc amalgam and dilute hydrochloric acid.

Ans. (i)

Cyclohexane-carbaldehyde $\xrightarrow[\text{Dry ether}]{\text{Ph – MgBr}}$ (intermediate with $OMgBr$ group, $\underset{Ph}{\overset{H}{C}}$) $\xrightarrow[\text{Hydrolysis}]{H_3O^+}$ Cyclohexylphenylcarbinol/ cyclohyxylphenyl methanol (with OH group, $\underset{Ph}{\overset{H}{C}}$)

(ii)

Cyclohexane-carbaldehyde ($CH=O$) $+ 2\,[Ag(NH_3)_2]^+ + 3OH^- \longrightarrow$ Cyclohexane-carboxylate ion ($\overset{O}{\overset{\|}{C}} = O-$) $+ 2Ag \downarrow + 4NH_3 + 2H_2O \longrightarrow$ Silver mirror

Tollen's reagent

(iii)

Cyclohexane-carbaldehyde (CHO) $+ H_2NNH - \overset{O}{\overset{\|}{C}} - NH_2 \xrightarrow[\text{weak acid}]{\text{pH 3.5}} H_2O +$ Cyclohexanecarbaldehyde semicarbazone ($CH=NNH - \overset{O}{\overset{\|}{C}} - NH_2$)

Semicarbazide

(iv)

Cyclohexane-carbaldehyde (CHO) $+ \begin{array}{c} H\,OC_2H_5 \\ H\,OC_2H_5 \end{array}$ Ethanol (Excess) $\xrightarrow{\text{Dry HCl gas}}$ Cyclohexanecarbaldehyde diethyl acetal ($\underset{H}{\overset{OC_2H_5}{C}}-OC_2H_5$) $+ H_2O$

(v)

Cyclohexane-carbaldehyde (CHO) $\xrightarrow[\substack{\text{Clemmensen} \\ \text{reduction}}]{\text{Zn/Hg – HCl}}$ Methylcyclohexane (CH_3)

Q. 5. **Which of the following compounds would undergo aldol condensation, which Cannizzaro reaction and which neither? Write the structures of the expected products of aldol condensation and Cannizzaro reaction.**

(i) Methanal   (iv) Benzophenone   (vii) Phenylacetaldehyde

(ii) 2-Methylpentanal   (v) Cyclohexanone   (viii) Butan-1-ol

(iii) Benzaldehyde   (vi) 1-Phenylpropanone   (ix) 2, 2-Dimethylbutanal

Ans. Aldehydes and ketones having at least one α-hydrogen atom undergo aldol condensation. The compounds (ii) 2-methylpentanal, (v) cyclohexanone, (vi) 1-phenylpropanone, and (vii) phenylacetaldehyde contains one or more α-hydrogen atoms. Therefore, these undergo aldol condensation.

Aldehydes having no α-hydrogen atoms undergoes Cannizzaro reactions. The compounds (i) Methanal, (iii) Benzaldehyde, and (ix) 2, 2-dimethylbutanal do not have any α-hydrogen atom. Therefore, these undergo Cannizzaro reactions

Compound (iv) Benzophenone is ketone having no α-hydrogen atom and compound (viii) Butan-1-ol is an alcohol. Hence, these compounds do not undergo either aldol condensation or Cannizzaro reaction.

Aldol condensation :

(ii) $2CH_3CH_2CH_2 - \underset{\underset{CH_3}{|}}{CH} - CHO \xrightarrow{\text{dil.NaOH}} CH_3CH_2CH_2 - \underset{\underset{CH_3}{|}}{CH} - \underset{\underset{OH}{|}}{CH} - \underset{\underset{CHO}{|}}{\overset{\overset{CH_3}{|}}{CH}} - CH_2CH_2CH_3$

2-Methylpentanal   3-Hydroxy-2, 4-dimethyl-1-2-propylheptanal

(v) 2 Cyclohexanone ($=O$) $\xrightarrow{\text{dil. NaOH}}$ 2-(1'-Hydroxy-1'-cyclohexyl)-cyclohexan-1-one

(vi) 2 [1-Phenylpropanone] $C(=O)-CH_2CH_3$ (α) $\xrightarrow{\text{dil. NaOH}}$ 3-Hydroxy-2-methyl-1, 3-diphenylpentan-1-one

(vii) 2 [Phenylacetaldehyde] $-CH_2CHO$ $\xrightarrow{\text{dil. NaOH}}$ 3-Hydroxy-2, 4-diphenylbutanal

Cannizzaro reaction:

(i) $2\,{}^{H}_{H}{>}C = O + \text{Conc. NaOH} \longrightarrow H - \underset{H}{\overset{H}{C}} - OH + {}^{H}_{H}{>}C - ONa$

Methanal   Methanal   Sodium methanoate

(iii) 2 [Benzaldehyde] $-CHO + \text{Conc. NaOH} \rightarrow$ [Benzyl alcohol] $-CH_2 - OH +$ [Sodium benzoate] $-C(=O)-ONa$

(ix) $CH_3CH_2 - \underset{CH_3}{\overset{CH_3}{C}} - CHO \xrightarrow{\text{Conc. NaOH}} CH_3CH_2 - \underset{CH_3}{\overset{CH_3}{C}} - CH_2 - OH + CH_3CH_2 - \underset{CH_3}{\overset{CH_3}{C}} - \underset{O}{\overset{}{C}} - ONa$

2, 2-Dimethylbutanal   2, 2-Dimethylbutan-1-ol   Sodium 2, 2-dimethylbutanonate

Q. 6. Write structural formulas and names of four possible aldol condensation products from propanal and butanal. In each case, indicate which aldehyde acts as nucleophile and which as electrophile.

Ans. (i) Taking two molecules of propanal, one which acts as a nucleophile and the other as an electrophile.

$$CH_3CH_2CHO + CH_3CH_2CHO \xrightarrow{\text{dil. NaOH}} CH_3CH_2 - \underset{}{\overset{OH}{CH}} - \underset{}{\overset{OH}{CH}} - CHO$$

Propanal   3-Hydroxy-2-methylpentanal

(ii) Taking two molecules of butanal, one which acts as a nucleophile and the other as an electrophile.

$$CH_3CH_2CH_2CHO + CH_3CH_2CH_2CHO \xrightarrow{\text{dil. NaOH}} CH_3CH_2CH_2 - \underset{}{\overset{OH}{CH}} - \underset{}{\overset{CH_2CH_3}{CH}} - CHO$$

Butanal   2-Ethyl-3-hydroxyhexanal

(iii) Taking one molecule each of propanal and butanal in which propanal acts as a nucleophile and butanal acts as an electrophile.

$$CH_3CH_2CH_2CHO + CH_3CH_2CHO \longrightarrow CH_3CH_2CH_2 - \underset{}{\overset{OH}{CH}} - \underset{}{\overset{CH_3}{CH}} - CHO$$

Butanal   Propanal   3-Hydroxy-2-methyl hexanal
(Electrophile)   (Nucleophile)   6 5 4   3   2   1

(iv) Taking one molecule each of propanal and butanal in which propanal acts as an electrophile and butanal acts as a nucleophile.

$$CH_3CH_2CHO + CH_3CH_2CH_2CHO \longrightarrow CH_3CH_2 - \underset{}{\overset{OH}{CH}} - \underset{}{\overset{CH_2CH_3}{CH}}CHO$$

Propanal   Butanal   2-Ethyl-3-hydroxypentanal
(Electrophile)   (Nucleophile)

Q. 7. Arrange the following compounds in increasing order of their property as indicated:
   (i) Acetaldehyde, Acetone, Di-*tert*-butyl ketone, Methyl *tert*-butyl ketone (reactivity towards HCN)
   (ii) $CH_3CH_2CH(Br)COOH$, $CH_3CH(Br)CH_2COOH$, $(CH_3)_2CHCOOH$, $CH_3CH_2CH_2COOH$ (acid strength)
   (iii) Benzoic acid, 4-Nitrobenzoic acid, 3, 4-Dinitrobenzoic acid, 4-methoxybenzoic acid (acid strength).

Ans. When HCN reacts with a compound, the attacking species is a nucleophile (CN⁻). In the given compounds, the + I effect increases as shown below. It can be observed that steric hindrance also increases in the same.

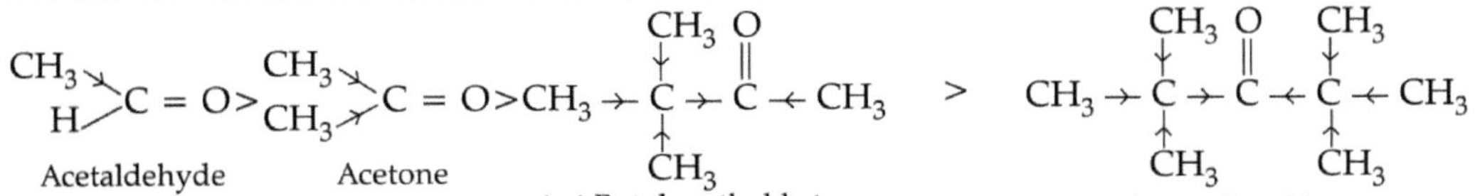

$$CH_3{-}\underset{H}{\overset{}{C}}=O > CH_3{-}\underset{CH_3}{\overset{}{C}}=O > CH_3{-}C{-}\overset{O}{\overset{\|}{C}}{-}CH_3 \quad > \quad CH_3{-}\overset{CH_3}{\overset{|}{C}}{-}\overset{O}{\overset{\|}{C}}{-}\overset{CH_3}{\overset{|}{C}}{-}CH_3$$

Acetaldehyde   Acetone   *tert*-Butyl methyl ketone   Di-*tert*-butyl ketone

Hence, the given compounds can be arranged according to their increasing reactivities towards HCN as :

Di-*tert*-butyl ketone < Methyl *tert*-butyl ketone < Acetone < acetaldehyde

(ii) After losing a proton, carboxylic acids gain a negative charge as shown:

$$R-COOH \longrightarrow R-COO^- + H^+$$

Now, any group that will help stabilise the negative charge will increase the stability of the carbonyl ion and as a result, will increase the strength of the acid. Thus, groups having + I effect will decrease the strength of the acids and groups having – I effect will increase the strength of the acids. In the given compounds $-CH_3$ group has + I effect and Br^- group has –I effect. Thus, acids containing Br^- are stronger.

Further (+ I) and (– I) effect both are stronger as nearer they are to the functional group. Hence, $(CH_3)_2CHCOOH$ is a weaker acid than $CH_3CH_2CH_2COOH$.

The–I effect grows weaker as distance increases. Hence, $CH_3CH(Br)CH_2COOH$ is a weaker acid than $CH_3CH_2CH(Br)COOH$.

Hence, the strengths of the given acids increase as:

$(CH_3)_2CHCOOH < CH_3CH_2CH_2COOH < CH_3CH(Br)CH_2COOH < CH_3CH_2CH(Br)COOH$

(iii) As we have seen in the previous case, electron-donating groups decrease the strengths of acids, while electron-withdrawing groups increase the strengths of acids. As methoxy group is an electron-donating group, 4-methoxybenzoic acid is a weaker acid of all the given acids. Nitro group is an electron-withdrawing group and will increase the strengths of acids. As 3, 4-dinitrobenzoic acid contains two nitro groups, is a slightly stronger acid than 4-nitrobenzoic acid. Hence, the strengths of the given acids increases as:

4-Methoxybenzoic acid < Benzoic acid < 4-Nitrobenzoic acid < 3, 4-Dinitrobenzoic acid.

Q. 8. How will you prepare the following compounds from benzene? You may use any inorganic reagent and any organic reagent having not more than one carbon atom.

(i) Methyl benzoate   (iii) *p*-Nitrobenzoic acid   (v) *p*-Nitrobenzaldehyde.

(ii) *m*-Nitrobenzoic acid   (iv) Phenylacetic acid

Ans. (i)

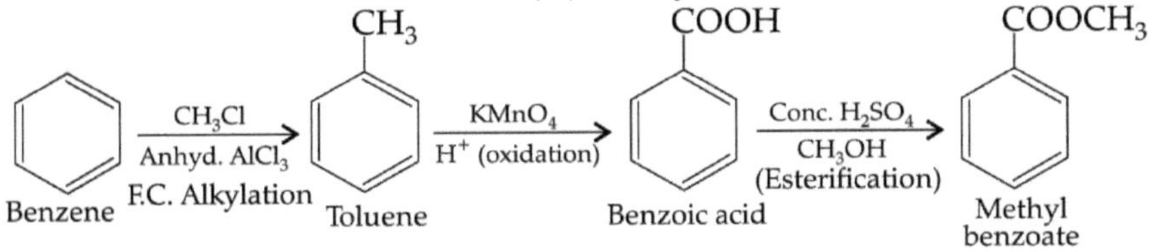

Benzene $\xrightarrow[\text{F.C. Alkylation}]{\underset{\text{Anhyd. AlCl}_3}{CH_3Cl}}$ Toluene (CH_3) $\xrightarrow[\text{H}^+ \text{ (oxidation)}]{KMnO_4}$ Benzoic acid (COOH) $\xrightarrow[\substack{CH_3OH \\ \text{(Esterification)}}]{\text{Conc. H}_2SO_4}$ Methyl benzoate ($COOCH_3$)

(ii)

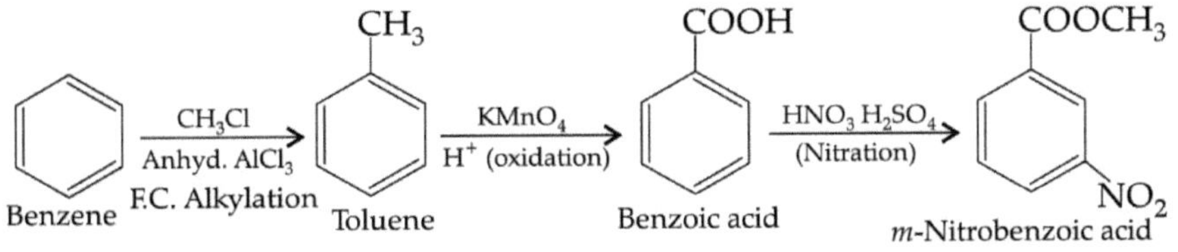

Benzene $\xrightarrow[\text{F.C. Alkylation}]{\underset{\text{Anhyd. AlCl}_3}{CH_3Cl}}$ Toluene (CH_3) $\xrightarrow[\text{H}^+ \text{ (oxidation)}]{KMnO_4}$ Benzoic acid (COOH) $\xrightarrow[\text{(Nitration)}]{HNO_3\ H_2SO_4}$ *m*-Nitrobenzoic acid ($COOCH_3$, NO_2)

(iii)

Benzene $\xrightarrow[\substack{\text{(Friedel-Craft's} \\ \text{alkylation)}}]{\underset{\text{Anhyd. AlCl}_3}{CH_3Cl}}$ Toluene (CH_3) $\xrightarrow[\text{(Nitration)}]{HNO_3\ H_2SO_4}$ (CH_3, NO_2 Major) + (CH_3, NO_2) (Minor) *o*-and *p*-nitrotoluene

$\xrightarrow[]{\Delta\ KMnO_4 - KOH}$ (COOH, NO_2) $\xleftarrow{H_3O^+}$ (COOH, NO_2) (*p*-Nitrobenzoic acid)

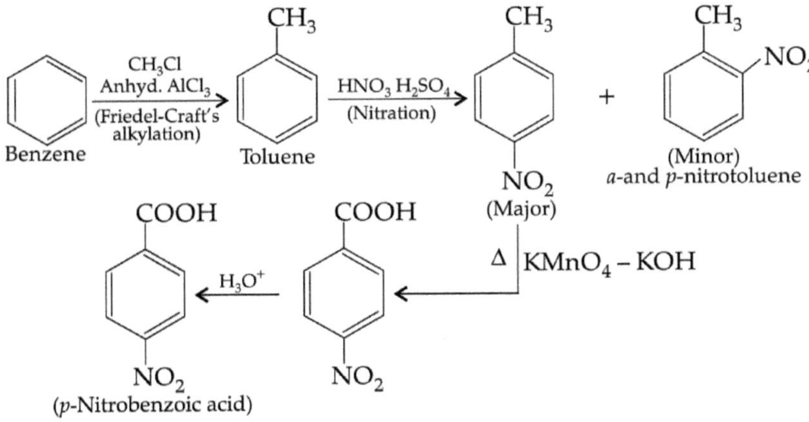

(iv) Benzene $\xrightarrow[\text{Anhyd. AlCl}_3]{\text{CH}_3\text{Cl/}}$ Toluene (CH$_3$) $\xrightarrow[\text{Br}_2 \text{ H}, \Delta \text{ and } hv]{\text{NBS, } hv \text{ or}}$ Benzyl bromide (CH$_2$Br) $\xrightarrow{\text{Alc. KCN, } \Delta}$ Benzyl Cyanide (CH$_2$CN) $\xrightarrow{\text{H}^+/\text{H}_2\text{O}}$ Phenylacetic acid (CH$_2$COOH)

(v) Benzene $\xrightarrow[\text{Anhyd. AlCl}_3]{\text{CH}_3\text{Cl/}}$ Toluene (CH$_3$) $\xrightarrow{\text{HNO}_3 \text{ H}_2\text{SO}_4}$ (CH$_3$, NO$_2$) $\xrightarrow[\substack{\text{CrO}_2\text{Cl}_2 \\ \text{[Partial oxidation} \\ \text{by Etards} \\ \text{reaction]}}]{\text{CS}_2}$ (CHO, NO$_2$) $\xleftarrow{\text{H}_3\text{O}^+}$ (CH(OCrOHCl$_2$)$_2$, NO$_2$)

p-Nitrobenzaldehyde

Q. 9. Complete each synthesis by giving missing starting material, reagent or products.

(i) (C$_6$H$_5$–CH$_2$CH$_3$) $\xrightarrow[\text{KOH, heat}]{\text{KMnO}_4}$

(ii) (C$_6$H$_4$(COOH)$_2$) $\xrightarrow[\text{heat}]{\text{SOCl}_2}$

(iii) $\text{C}_6\text{H}_5\text{CHO} \xrightarrow{\text{H}_2\text{NCONHNH}_2}$

(iv) (Benzene) $\longrightarrow$ (Benzophenone)

(v) (4-oxocyclohexanecarbaldehyde) $\xrightarrow{[\text{Ag(NH}_3)_2]^+}$

(vi) (C$_6$H$_4$(CHO)(COOH)) $\xrightarrow{\text{NaCN/HCl}}$

(vii) $\begin{array}{c} \text{C}_6\text{H}_5\text{CHO} \\ + \\ \text{CH}_3\text{CH}_2\text{CHO} \end{array} \xrightarrow{\text{dil. NaOH}}$

(viii) $\text{CH}_3\text{COCH}_2\text{COOC}_2\text{H}_5 \xrightarrow[\text{(ii) H}^+]{\text{(i) NaBH}_4}$

(ix) (cyclohexanol) $\text{–OH} \xrightarrow{\text{CrO}_3}$

(x) (=CH$_2$ cyclohexane) $\longrightarrow$ (–CHO cyclohexane)

(xi) $\xrightarrow[\text{(ii) Zn-H}_2\text{O}]{\text{(i) O}_3} 2$ (cyclohexanone =O)

Ans. (i) (C$_6$H$_5$–CH$_2$CH$_3$) Ethylbenzene $\xrightarrow[\text{KOH, heat}]{\text{KMnO}_4}$ (C$_6$H$_5$–COOK) Potassium benzoate $+ \text{CO}_2 + 3\text{H}_2\text{O}$

(ii) (C$_6$H$_4$(COOH)$_2$) Phthalic acid $\xrightarrow[\text{Heat}]{\text{SOCl}_2}$ (C$_6$H$_4$(COCl)$_2$) Potassium benzoate $+ 2\text{SO}_2 + 3\text{HCl}$

(iii) $\underset{\text{Benzaldehyde}}{\text{C}_6\text{H}_5\text{CHO}} + \underset{\text{Semicarbazide}}{\text{H}_2\text{NCONHNH}_2} \longrightarrow \underset{\text{Benzaldehyde semicarbazone}}{\text{C}_6\text{H}_5\text{CH} = \text{NNHC} - \text{NH}_2} + \text{H}_2\text{O}$

(iv) (Benzene) $+$ (Benzoyl chloride, COCl$_2$) $\xrightarrow[\text{F.C. acylation}]{\text{Anhyd. AlCl}_3}$ (Benzophenone) $+ \text{HCl}$

(v) (4-Oxocyclohexanecarbaldehyde, CHO) $\xrightarrow{[\text{Ag(NH}_3)_2]^+}$ (4-Oxocyclohexanecarboxylate, COO$^-$) $+ 4\text{NH}_3 + 2\text{Ag}\downarrow$ Silver mirror

(vi)

2-Formylbenzoic acid → 2-(1-Hydroxycyanomethyl benzoic acid)

$$\text{(with NaCN/HCl)} \quad + NaCl$$

(vii) C_6H_5CHO
Benzaldehyde
+
CH_3CH_2CHO
Propanal
$\xrightarrow[\Delta]{\text{dil. NaOH}}$ $C_6H_5\overset{3}{C}H = \overset{2}{C} - \overset{1}{C}HO$ with CH_3

[Cross aldol condensation]   2-methyl-3-phenyl-pro-2-enal

(viii) $CH_3COCH_2COOC_2H_5 \xrightarrow[\text{(ii) } H^+]{\text{(i) NaBH}_4} CH_3CH(OH)CH_2COOC_2H_5$
Ethyl 3-oxobutanoate   Ethyl 3-hydroxybutanoate
* $NaBH_4$ reduces only the keto group.

(ix) Cyclohexanol $-OH \xrightarrow{CrOO_3H_2SO_4}$ Cyclohexanone $=O$

(x) Methylenecyclohexane $-CH_2 \xrightarrow{BH_3} [-CH_2]B]_3 \xrightarrow{H_2O_2/OH^-}$ Cyclohexanecarbaldehyde $-CHO \xrightarrow{PCC}$ Cyclohexylmethanol $-CH_2OH$

(xi) Cyclohexylidenecyclohexane $\xrightarrow[\text{(ii) Zn -H}_2\text{O}]{\text{(i) O}_3}$ 2 Cyclohexanone $=O$
(Ozonolysis)

Q. 10. Give plausible explanation for each of the following:

(i) Cyclohexanone forms cyanohydrin in good yields but 2, 2, 6 trimethylcyclohexanone does not.

(ii) There are two $-NH_2$ groups in semicarbazide. However, only one is involved in the formation of semicarbazones.

(iii) During the preparation of esters from a carboxylic acid and an alcohol in the presence of an acid catalyst, the water or the ester should be removed as soon as it is formed.

Ans. (i) Cyclohexanone forms cyanohydrins according to the following equation.

Cyclohexanone $\xrightarrow{HCN}$ Cyanohydrin (OH, CN) $\xrightarrow{HCN}$

In this case, the nucleophile CN^- can easily attack without any steric hindrance. However, in the case of 2, 2, 6 – trimethylcyclohexanone, methyl groups at α-positions offers steric hindrance and as a result, CN^- cannot attack effectively. Also the $+ I$ effect of three methyl groups reduces the positive charge in the carbonyl carbon making it less reactive towards nucleophilic attack.

2, 2, 6-Trimethylcyclohexanone

For this reason, it does not forms a cyanohydrin.

(ii) Semicarbazide undergoes resonance involving only one of the two $-NH_2$ groups, which is attached directly to the carbonyl-carbon atom.

Therefore, the electron density on $-NH_2$ group involved in the resonance also decreases. As a result, it cannot act as a nucleophile. Since the other $-NH_2$ group is not involved in resonance it can act as a nucleophile and can attack carbonyl-carbon atoms of aldehydes and ketones to produce semicarbazones.

(iii) Ester along with water is formed reversibly from a carboxylic acid and an alcohol in presence of an acid.

$$RCOOH \quad + \quad R'OH \quad \xrightleftharpoons{H^+} \quad RCOOR' \quad + \quad H_2O$$

Carboxylic acid · · · · · Alcohol · · · · · Ester · · · · · Water

If either water or ester is not removed as soon as it formed, then they react to give back the reactants as the reaction is reversible. Therefore, to shift the equilibrium in the forward direction *i.e.*, to produce more ester, either of the two should be removed.

Q. 11. Although phenoxide ion has more number of resonating structures than carboxylate ion, carboxylic acid is a stronger acid than phenol. Why?

Ans. Resonance structures of phenoxide ion are:

$$I \quad\quad II \quad\quad III \quad\quad IV \quad\quad V$$

It can be observed from the resonance structures of phenoxide ion that in II, III and IV, less electronegative carbon atoms carry negative charge. Therefore, these three structures contribute negligibly towards the resonance stability of the phenoxide ion.

Hence, these structures can be eliminated. Only structures I and V carry a negative charge on the more electronegative oxygen atom. On the other hand, resonance structures of carboxylate ion are :

$$I' \quad\quad\quad II'$$

In carboxylate ion, resonating structures I′ and II′ contain a charge carried by a more electronegative oxygen atom. So the charge is always on oxygen. Also, resonating structures I′ and II′, the negative charge is delocalised over two oxygen atoms. But in resonating structures I and V of the phenoxide ion, the negative charge is localised on the same oxygen atom. Therefore, the resonating structures of carboxylate ion contributes more towards its stability than those of phenoxide ion. As a result, carboxylate ion is more resonance-stabilised than phenoxide ion. Hence, carboxylic acid is a stronger acid than phenol.

Q. 12. Arrange the following compounds in increasing order of their reactivity in nucleophilic addition reactions.

(i) Ethanal, Propanal, Propanone, Butanone.

(ii) Benzaldehyde, *p*-Tolualdehyde, *p*-Nitrobenzaldehyde, Acetophenone.

Hint : Consider steric effect and electronic effect.

Ans. Steric hindrance at the carbonyl carbon and presence of more electron-donating groups *i.e.*, (+ I) effect, lowers down the reactivity towards a nucleophilic reaction.

Ethanal · · · · · Propanal · · · · · Propanaone · · · · · Butanone

The +I effect of the alkyl group increases in the order:

$$Ethanal < Propanal < Propanone < Butanone$$

Because the electron density at the carbonyl carbon increases with the increase in the + I effect. Thus the affinity of attack by a nucleophile decrease. Hence, the increasing order of the reactivities of the given carbonyl compounds in nucleophilic addition reactions is :

$$Butanone < Propanone < Propanal < Ethanal$$

(ii) Presence of electron with drawing group (–I) effect, increases the reactivity for nucleophilic reactions.

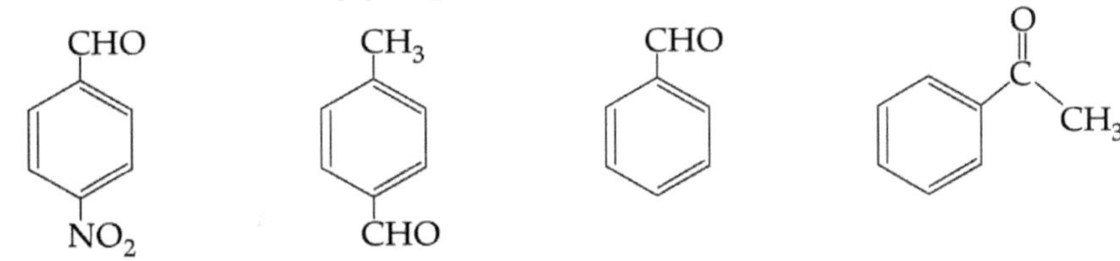

p-Nitrobenzaldehyde   *p*-Tolualdehyde   Benzaldehyde   Acetophenone

The + I effect is more in ketone than in aldehyde. Therefore acetophenone is the least reactive. Among aldehydes, the + I effect is the highest in *p*-tolualdehyde because of the presence of the electron-donating – CH_3 group and the lowest in *p*-nitrobenzaldehyde because of the presence of the electron-withdrawing – NO_2 group. Hence, the increasing order of the reactivities of the given compounds is:

Acetophenone < *p*-tolualdehyde < Benzaldehyde < *p*-Nitrobenzaldehyde.

Q. 13. Which acid of each pair shown here would you expect to be stronger? Why?

(i) CH_3CO_2H or CH_2FCO_2H

(ii) CH_2FCO_2H or CH_2ClCO_2H

(iii) $CH_2FCH_2CH_2CO_2H$ or $CH_3CHFCH_2CO_2H$

(iv) F_3C—⟨ ⟩—COOH or H_3C—⟨ ⟩—COOH

Ans. (i) Presence of electron withdrawing group (– I) effect, increases the acidic strength of carboxylic acids. They make the –OH bond more polar and hence release of H^+ ion easier.

$$CH_3 \rightarrow C \rightarrow O \rightarrow H \qquad\qquad F \leftarrow CH_2 \leftarrow C \leftarrow O \leftarrow H$$

Whereas the + I effect of –CH_3 group increases the electron density on the O–H bond. Therefore, release of proton becomes difficult. Hence, CH_2FCO_2H is a stronger acid than CH_3CO_2H.

(ii) $F \leftarrow CH_2 \leftarrow C \leftarrow C \leftarrow H \qquad Cl \leftarrow CH_2 \leftarrow C \leftarrow O \leftarrow H$

F has stronger – I effect than Cl. Therefore, CH_2FCO_2H can release proton more easily than CH_2ClCO_2H. Hence, CH_2FCO_2H is stronger acid than CH_2ClCO_2H.

(iii) $F \leftarrow CH_2 \leftarrow CH_2 \leftarrow CH_2 \leftarrow C \leftarrow O \leftarrow H \qquad F \leftarrow CH \leftarrow CH_2 \leftarrow C \leftarrow O \leftarrow H$ (with CH_3)

Inductive effect decreases with increase in distance. Hence, the –I effect of F in $CH_3CHFCH_2CO_2H$ is more than it is in $CH_2FCH_2CH_2CO_2H$. Hence, $CH_3CHFCH_2CO_2H$ is stronger acid than $CH_2FCH_2CH_2CO_2H$.

(iv) $F\leftarrow C$ (with F up, F down) $\leftarrow$⟨ ⟩$\leftarrow C \leftarrow O \leftarrow H$ $H_3C \rightarrow$⟨ ⟩$\rightarrow C \rightarrow O - H$

       (A)   (B)

Due to the –I effect of F, it is easier to release proton in the case of compound (A). However, in the case of compound (B), release of proton is difficult due to the +I effect of –CH_3 group. Hence, $F_3C – Ph – COOH$ is stronger acid than $CH_3 – Ph – COOH$.

Q. 14. An organic compound [A] which has characteristic odour, on treatment with NaOH forms two compound [B] and [C]. Compound [B] has molecular formula C_7H_8O which on oxidation with CrO_3 gives a back compound [A]. Compound [C] is the sodium salt of the acid. [C] when heated with soda-lime yields an aromatic hydrocarbon [D]. Deduce the structures of [A], [B], [C] and [D].*

Ans. Compound [A] must be an aldehyde that gets self oxidised reduced to an alcohol [B] and carboxylic acid salt of sodium [C]. As the alcohol has molecular formula C_7H_8O, which on oxidation with CrO_3 gives back compound [A]. Hence compound [A] must be benzaldehyde.

CHO

or C_7H_6O ; Also benzaldehyde has a characteristic bitter almond odour.

(i) $2C_6H_5CHO + NaOH \longrightarrow C_6H_5COONa + C_6H_5CH_2OH$
    [A]   (conc.)   Sodium benzoate   Benzyl alcohol
                                    [C]   [B]

This above reaction is also called Cannizzaro's reaction.

(ii) $C_6H_5CH_2OH + [O] \xrightarrow{CrO_3} C_6H_5CHO + H_2O$
     Benzyl alcohol   Benzaldehyde
        [B]   [A]

(iii) $C_6H_5COONa + NaOH \xrightarrow{CaO/\Delta} C_6H_6 + Na_2CO_3$
     [C]   Decarboxylation   Benzene [D]
         Sodium benzoate   reaction by soda lime

Q. 15. An organic compound contains 69.77% carbon, 11.63% hydrogen and rest oxygen. The molecular mass of the compound is 86. It does not reduces Tollen's reagent but forms an addition compound with sodium hydrogensulphite and gives positive iodoform test. On vigorous oxidation it gives ethanoic and propanoic acid. Write the possible structure of the compound.

Ans. Step I: Percentage of carbon $= 69.77\%$

               Percentage of hydrogen $= 11.63\%$

               Percentage of oxygen $= \{100 - (69.77 + 11.63)\}\%$

                                    $= 18.6\%$

Thus, the ratio of the number of carbon, hydrogen and oxygen atoms in the organic compound can be given as :

$$C:H:O = \frac{69.77}{12} : \frac{11.63}{1} : \frac{18.6}{16}$$

$$= 5.81 : 11.63 : 1.16$$

$$= 5 : 10 : 1$$

Therefore, the empirical formula for the compound is $C_5H_{10}O$. Now, the empirical formula mass of the compound can be given as :

$$5 \times 12 + 10 \times 1 + 1 \times 16 = 86$$

Molecular mass of the compound $= 86$.

Therefore, the molecular formula of the compound is given by $C_5H_{10}O$.

Step II : Since the given compound does not reduce Tollen's reagent, it is not an aldehyde. Again, the compound forms sodium hydrogen sulphate addition product and gives a positive iodoform test. Since, the compound is not an aldehyde, it must be a methyl ketone.

The given compound also gives a mixture of ethanoic acid and propanoic acid.

Hence, the given compound is pentan-2-ol.

$$\overset{\displaystyle O}{\overset{\displaystyle \|}{CH_3 - C - CH_2 - CH_2 - CH_3}}$$
Pentan-2-ol

The given reactions can be explained by the following equations :

$$\overset{\displaystyle OH}{\overset{\displaystyle |}{CH_3 - C - CH_2CH_2CH_3}}$$
$$\overset{|}{SO_3Na^+}$$
(Addition Product)

$NaHSO_3$

$$\overset{\displaystyle O}{\overset{\displaystyle \|}{CH_3 - C - CH_2 - CH_2 - CH_3}}$$
Pentan-2-ol

$\xrightarrow{NaOI}$ $CH_3CH_2CH_2COONa + CHI_3$
[O]   Sodium butanoate   Iodoform (Yellow ppt.)

$CH_2COOH + CH_3CH_3COOH$
Ethanoic acid   Propanoic acid

Q. 16. (i) Give reasons:*

(a) H_3PO_3 undergoes disproportionation reaction but H_3PO_4 does not.

(b) When Cl_2 reacts with excess of F_2, ClF_3 is formed and not FCl_3.

(c) Dioxygen is a gas while Sulphur is a solid at room temperature.

(ii) Draw the structures of the following:

(a) XeF_4

(b) $HClO_3$

Ans. (i) (a) In H_3PO_3, orthophosphorus acid oxidation state of Phosphorus is + 3 and it contains one P-H bond in addition to P = O and P – OH bonds. These type of oxoacids tend to undergo disproportionation to give orthophosphoric acid (P has + 5 state) and phosphine (P has + 3 state). Whereas in H_3PO_4 (orthophosphoric acid) Phosphorus is in + 5 state hence no disproportionation takes place in H_3PO_4.

(b) When Cl_2 reacts with excess of F_2, ClF_3 is formed and not FCl_3 because Fluorine can't expand its valency and can show only – 1 oxidation state, whereas Cl can expand its valency due to the availability of d-orbitals.

(c) Dioxygen is a gas while sulphur is a solid at room temperature this is because sulphur have S_8 molecules and these are packed to give different crystal structure, whereas dioxygen is a diatomic molecule (O_2) and it does not have enough intermolecular attraction and thus exits in gaseous form.

(ii)

(i) XeF_4 is square planar in structure	(ii) $HClO_3$ or chloric acid

Q. 17. (i) When concentrated sulphuric acid was added to an unknown salt present in a test tube a brown gas (A) was evolved. This gas intensified when copper turnings were added to this test tube. On cooling, the gas (A) changed into a colourless solid (B).*

(a) Identify (A) and (B).

(b) Write the structures of (A) and (B).

(c) Why does gas (A) change to solid on cooling?

(ii) Arrange the following in the decreasing order of their reducing character:

$$HF, HCl, HBr, HI$$

(iii) Complete the following reaction:

$$XeF_4 + SbF_5 \rightarrow$$

Ans. (i) (a) The brown gas A is NO_2 or nitrogen dioxide. On cooling it dimerises to N_2O_4 and solidifies as a colourless solid.

$$2NO_2 \underset{\text{Heat}}{\overset{\text{Cool}}{\rightleftharpoons}} N_2O_4$$

(b)

(c) Compound A, that is, NO_2 contains odd number of valence electrons. It behaves as a typical odd molecule. On dimerisation, it is converted to stabel N_2O_4 molecule with even number of electrons (thus colourless) and have better intermolecular forces to get solidified. Thus it changes to solid on cooling.

(ii) Decreasing order of reducing character:

$$HI > HBr > HCl > HF$$

(iii) $XeF_4 + SbF_5 \rightarrow [XeF_3]^+ + [SbF_6]^-$

Q. 18. (a) An organic compound (A) having molecular formula C4H8O gives orange red precipitate with 2, 4-DNP reagent. It does not reduce Tollens' reagent but gives yellow precipitate of iodoform on heating with NaOH and I_2. Compound (A) on reduction with $NaBH_4$ gives compound (B) which undergoes dehydration reaction on heating with conc. H_2SO_4 to form compound (C). Compound (C) Ozonolysis gives two molecules of ethanal.*

Identify (A), (B) and (C) and write their structures. Write the reactions of compound (A) with (i) $NaOH/I_2$ and (ii) $NaBH_4$.

(b) Give reasons:

(i) Oxidation of propanal is easier than propanone.

(ii) a-hydrogen of aldehydes and ketones is acidic in nature.

Ans. (a) C_4H_8O (A) gives precipitate with 2, 4-DNP, it indicates that compound A contains a carbonyl group. It does not reduce Tollen's reagent so it is a ketone compound. It gives Iodoform test as it contains a methyl ketone group ($-COCH_3$). Let us assume tentative structure of A as X—$COCH_3$. Now, A gives compound B on $NaBH_4$ reduction, so the structure of compound B becomes X-CHOH-CH_3. Compound B further is subjected to dehydration which means the new compound C will contain a double bond. Compound C gives two molecules of ethanal on Ozonolysis, this tells us that compound C is symmetrical and the double bond divides the molecule in two equal parts.

Collecting all the above given information, the reaction sequence can be formulated as:

$$\text{Butanone (A)} \xrightarrow[\text{Reduction}]{NaBH_4} \text{Butan-2-ol (B)} \xrightarrow{\text{Conc. } H_2SO_4} \text{But-2-ene (C)} \xrightarrow{\text{Ozonolysis}} 2CH_3CHO \text{ (Ethanal, D)}$$

(i) $$\text{Butanone (A)} \xrightarrow{NaOH/I_2} \text{Sodium propanoate} + CHI_3 \text{ (Iodomethane)}$$

(ii) $$\text{Butanone (A)} \xrightarrow[\text{Reduction}]{NaBH_4} \text{Butan-2-ol}$$

(b) (i) Oxidation of aldehyde is easier than ketones as in propanal there is one oxidisable –H present attached to the carbonyl carbon whereas propanone being ketone does not have the oxidisable –H atom. Also, as the carbonyl carbon contains two alkyl groups attached to it in ketone, it becomes less reactive responsible for less reactivity of propanone compared to propanal.

Molecular formula ($_3H_6C$)

$$CH_3 - \overset{O}{\underset{||}{C}} - CH_3 \text{ (Propanone)} \qquad CH_3 - CH_2\overset{O}{\underset{||}{C}} -\textcircled{H} \text{ (Propanal, Oxidisable Hydrogen atom)}$$

(ii) In aldehydes and ketone, α-hydrogen is the hydrogen atom attached to the alpha (α) carbon atom, which in turn is attached to the carbonyl carbon. After removal of α-hydrogen atom, conjugated base so obtained is resonance stabilised. Hence, it becomes easy to lose the α-hydrogen atoms in basic medium and thus aldehydes and ketones are acidic in nature. The phenomenon is shown below :

Q. 19. (a) Draw structures of the following derivatives.*

(i) Cyanohydrin of cyclobutanone

(ii) Hemiacetal of ethanal

(b) Write the major product (s) in the following :

(i) $CH_3 - CH = CH - CH_2CN \xrightarrow[\text{(ii) } H_3O^+]{\text{(i) DIBAL – H}}$

(ii) $CH_3 - CH_2 = OH \xrightarrow{CrO_3}$

(c) How can you distinguish between propanal and propanone?

Ans. (a) (i) Cyanohydrin of cyclobutanone

$$\text{Cyclobutanone} \xrightarrow{\text{HCN}} \text{Cyclobulane cyanohydrin}$$

(ii) H emiacetal of Ethanal

$$\text{Ethanal} \underset{H^+}{\overset{ROH}{\rightleftharpoons}} \text{Hemiacetal of ethanal}$$

(b) (i) $\text{H}_3\text{C}\text{—CN}$ (Pent-3-enenitrile) $\xrightarrow[\text{(ii) H}_3\text{O}^+]{\text{(i) DIBAL – H}}$ $\text{H}_3\text{C}\text{—CHO}$ (Hemiacetal of ethanal)

(ii) $\text{H}_3\text{C}\text{—OH}$ (Ethanol) $\xrightarrow[\text{Oxidation}]{\text{CrO}_3}$ $\text{H}_3\text{C}\text{—CHO}$ (Ethanal)

(c) Propanal and propanone can be distinguished by Iodoform reaction. When both are treated with NaOH and I_2, propanone (Acetone) gives a yellow precipitate of Iodoform whereas propanal does not react in these conditions.

$$\underset{\text{Acetone}}{CH_3 - \overset{O}{\overset{\|}{C}} - CH_3} + 3I_2 + 4NaOH \longrightarrow \underset{\text{Iodoform}}{CHI_3} + CH_3COONa + 3NaI + 3H_2O$$

$$\text{Propanal} + I_2 + NaOH \longrightarrow \text{No reaction}$$

Q. 20. (a) Write the product formed when benzaldehyde reacts with the following reagents:*

(i) CH_3CHO in presence of dilute NaOH   (iii) Conc. NaOH

(ii) $H_2N – NH$— (phenyl ring)

(b) Distinguish between following:

(i) $CH_3 – CH = CH – CH_3$ and $CH_3 – CH_2 – CO – CH = CH_2$

(iii) Benzaldehyde and Benzoic acid.

Ans. (a) (i) Cinnamaldehyde is formed when benzaldehyde reacts with acetaldehyde in presence of dil NaOH by aldol condensation.

$$\underset{\substack{\text{Benzaldehyde}\\(\text{no }\alpha\text{-hydrogen})}}{C_6H_5CHO} + CH_3CHO \xrightarrow{\text{dil. NaOH}} \underset{\substack{\text{Aldol}\\\text{Aldol condensation}}}{C_6H_5CHCH_2CHO} \xrightarrow{\text{H+, Heat – H}_2\text{O}} \underset{\text{Cinnamaldehyde}}{C_6H_5CH = CHCH}$$

(ii) Benzaldehyde reacts with phenylhydrazine to give phenylhydrazone.

$$\underset{\text{Phenylhydrazine}}{} + \underset{\text{Benzaldehyde}}{} \longrightarrow \underset{\text{Phenylhydrazone}}{}$$

(iii) Benzaldehyde do not have α-hydrogen so on heating with concentrated KOH solution a mixture of alcohol and salt is formed this is Cannizzaro's reaction.

$$\underset{\text{Benzaldehyde}}{\text{CHO}} + \text{Conc.KOH} \longrightarrow \underset{\text{Potassium benzoate}}{\text{COOK}} + \underset{\text{Benzyl alcohol}}{\text{CH}_2\text{OH}}$$

(b) (i) Among the two compounds given, $CH_3CH = CH–CO–CH_3$, has a terminal $–CH_3$ group attached to carbonyl carbon $(–CO – CH_3)$ is present which will undergo Iodoform reaction to give yellow coloured precipitate of triiodomethane:

$$CH_3CH = CH - CO - CH_3 + 4NaOH + 3I_2 \rightarrow CH_3CH = CH - COO - Na^+ + 3NaI + 3H_2O + CHI_3$$
(Yellow solid)

Whereas the other compound, $CH_3 - CH_2 - CO - CH = CH_2$ will not give any such reaction.

(ii) Benzaldehyde when treated with ammoniacal silver nitrate gets oxidized and reduces Ag^+ ions to Ag (elemental) hence, a deposition of silver is obtained which is known as silver mirror, whereas benzoic acid does not undergo this reaction hence can be distinguished with the help of Silver mirror test from benzaldehyde:

Benzaldehyde   metallic silver is deposited in a thin mirror coating

Q. 21. (a) Write the final products in the following:*

(i) $\underset{CH_3}{\overset{CH_3}{>}}C = O \xrightarrow[\text{Conc. HCl}]{Zn/Hg}$

(ii) $\text{C}_6\text{H}_5 - COONa \xrightarrow[\Delta]{NaOH/CaO}$

(iii) $CH_2 = CH - CH_2 - CN \xrightarrow[\text{(b) } H_3O^+]{\text{(a) OH/CaO}}$

(b) Arrange the following in the increasing order of their reactivity towards nucleophilic addition reaction:

$$CH_3COCH_3, \ HCHO, \ CH_3CHO, \ C_6H_5-COCH_3$$

(c) Draw the structure of 2, 4 DNP derivative of acetaldehyde.

Ans. (a) (i) Clemmenson reduction:

$$CH_3 - CO - CH_3 \xrightarrow[\text{Conc.HCl}]{Zn/Hg} CH_3 - CH_2 - CH_3 + H_2O$$
Acetone   Propane

(ii) Sodium benzoate $\xrightarrow[\Delta]{NaOH + CaO}$ benzene $+ \ Na_2CO_3 + H_2O$

(iii) $\underset{\text{But-3-enenitrete}}{H_2C\diagup\diagdown CN} \xrightarrow[\text{(ii) } H_3O^+]{\text{(i) DIBAL – H}} \underset{\text{But-3-enal}}{H_2C\diagup\diagdown CHO}$

(b) Reactivity in increasing order is:

$$C_6H_5COCH_3 < CH_3COCH_3 < CH_3CHO < HCHO$$

(c) (2, 4-dinitrophenyl) hydrazine   (1E)-acetaldehyde (2-methyl-4-nitrophenyl) hydrazone

Chapter 13. Amines

Q. 1. Account for the following:

(i) Aniline dissolves in hydrochloric acid.

(ii) Sulphanilic acid is insoluble in water but soluble in aqueous base and aqueous mineral acids.

(iii) Silver chloride dissolves in methyl amine solution.

Ans. (i) Aniline being a base dissolves in acid. The lone pair of aniline nitrogen ($- NH_2$) forms a bond with H^+ of hydrochloric acid to give water soluble anilinium ion $C_6H_5^+NH_3$.

(ii) Sulphanilic acid forms zwitter ion and hence not soluble in water and organic solvents. But, it is soluble in base [NaOH] by forming soluble sulphonate ion

$$NH_3 \text{—}\langle\text{benzene ring}\rangle\text{—} SO_3Na^+.$$

$$\overset{+}{N}H_3\text{—}\langle\text{ring}\rangle\text{—}SO_3H \rightleftharpoons \overset{+}{N}H_3\text{—}\langle\text{ring}\rangle\text{—}SO_3^-$$
(Insoluble Dipolar zwitter ion)

Similarly, it is soluble in mineral acids by forming soluble cations like;

$$\langle\text{ring}\rangle\text{—}NH_3^+,\ SO_3^- + HCl \longrightarrow \langle\text{ring}\rangle\text{—}NH_3^+Cl^-,\ SO_3^-H$$

(iii) Methylamine can act as a base or a ligand. With silver chloride it acts as a ligand. A silver methyl amine complex is formed.

$$AgCl + 2CH_3NH_2 \longrightarrow [Ag(CH_3NH_2)_2]^+ Cl^-$$
Soluble complex

Q. 2. Answer the following questions:

(i) An aromatic compound `A' on treatment with aqueous ammonia and heating forms compound `B' which on heating with Br_2 and KOH forms a compound `C' of molecular formula $C_6H_7N$. Write the structures and IUPAC names of compound `A', `B' and `C'.

(ii) Arrange the following in increasing order of their boiling point:
$$C_2H_5NH_2,\ C_2H_5OH \text{ and } (CH_3)_3N.$$

(iii) Give a chemical test to distinguish between the following:
$$(CH_3)_2NH \text{ and } (CH_3)_3N.$$

Ans. (i) $[A] + aq.NH_3 \xrightarrow{\Delta} [B] \xrightarrow{Br_2,KOH} C_6H_7N\ [C]$

Compound `C' of molecular formula C_6H_7N is formed as a result of Hoffmann bromamide degradation, hence [C] must be an amine and compound [B] must be an amide. Amine with molecular formula C_6H_7N is aniline. Hence, compound [C] is

$$NH_2\text{—}\langle\text{ring}\rangle$$
Aniline

Therefore compound [B] must be benzamide *i.e.,*

$$CONH_2\text{—}\langle\text{ring}\rangle$$

As compound [A] on heating with aqueous ammonia gives compound [B], so [A] must be benzoic acid, *i.e.,*

$$COOH\text{—}\langle\text{ring}\rangle$$

$$\underset{[A]}{COOH\text{—}\langle\text{ring}\rangle} + NH_3 \xrightarrow{\Delta} \underset{[B]}{CONH_2\text{—}\langle\text{ring}\rangle} \xrightarrow{Br_2 +4KOH} \underset{\substack{[C]\\ \text{Aniline}}}{NH_2\text{—}\langle\text{ring}\rangle} + K_2CO_3 + KBr + 2H_2O$$

(ii) $(CH_3)_3N < C_2H_5NH_2 < C_2H_5OH$

Alcohol has the highest boiling point because the extent of H-bonding is maximum as oxygen is more electronegative than nitrogen of amines. Tertiary amines have the lowest boiling point because of absence of hydrogen bonding as it has no hydrogen bonded to nitrogen atom in the tertiary amines.

(iii) $(CH_3)_2NH$ and $(CH_3)_3N$ can be distinguished by use of Hinsberg's reagent *i.e.,* benzene sulphonyl chloride. $(CH_3)_2NH$ being a 2° amine forms N, N-Dimethylbenzene sulphonamide ion which is insoluble in aqueous ROH. While $(CH_3)_3N$ is a 3° amine and it does not reacts with Hinsberg's reagent.

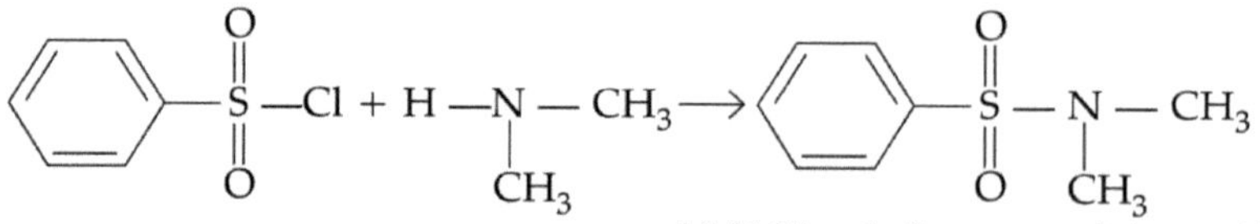

N, N-Dimethylbenzene sulphonamide

Q. 3. **An organic compound `A' having molecular formula  soluble in mineral acid, but insoluble in water. It produces a foul smelling substance on treatment with chloroform in presence of potassium hydroxide. On treating `A' with Hinsberg's reagent it gives compound `D'. Compound `D' is soluble in alkali compound `A' gives compound `E' on reaction with $NaNO_2$ and HCl. `E' on the other hand reacts with phenol in basic medium to give an orange dye `F'. Identify compounds `A' to `F'.**

Ans. Compound [A] must be basic in nature as it is soluble in acid. Since, it produces a foul smell on treatment with $CHCl_3$ and KOH, [A] must be a primary amine, primary amine with molecular formula C_6H_7N, must be aniline. Hence the reactions are as follows:

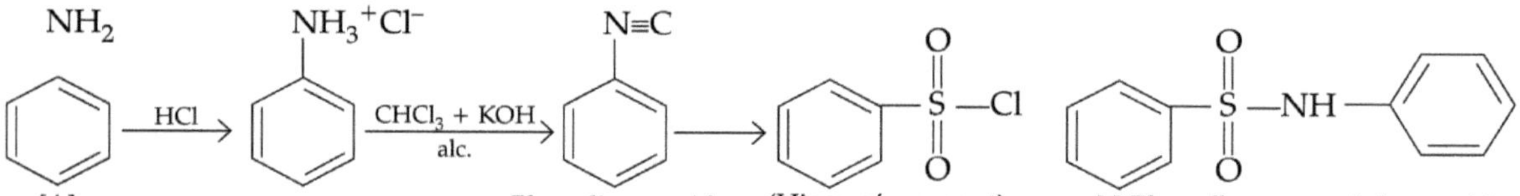

[A] Aniline $\xrightarrow{HCl}$ $NH_3^+Cl^-$ $\xrightarrow[\text{alc.}]{CHCl_3 + KOH}$ Phenylisocyanide (foul smell) $\longrightarrow$ (Hinserg's reagent) N-Phenylbenzenesulphonamide (Soluble in alkali base) [D]

Diazotisation reaction:

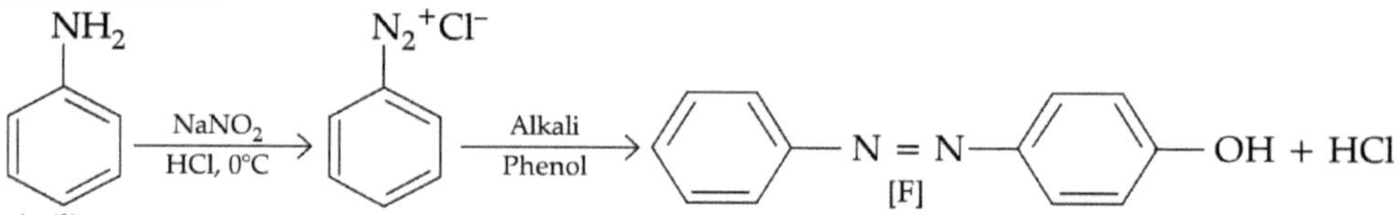

Aniline $\xrightarrow[HCl, 0°C]{NaNO_2}$ [E] (Benzenediazonium chloride) $\xrightarrow[\text{Phenol}]{\text{Alkali}}$ [F] *p*-hydroxyazo benzene (Orange dye) $N = N$ — OH + HCl

Q. 4. **Answer the following questions:**

(i) How will you prepare 2-aminoethanoic acid from ethanal?

(ii) Why acylation of amines is carried out in presence of a base?

(iii) What happens when primary amine linked with a tertiary carbon is oxidised with $KMnO_4$?

(iv) How is monohalogenated product of aniline obtained?

(v) Why CH_3CONH_2 is a weaker base than $CH_3CH_2NH_2$?

Ans. (i) $CH_3CHO \xrightarrow[H^+]{KMnO_4} CH_3COOH \xrightarrow[Cl_2]{Red\ P} CH_2{-}COOH$ (with Cl) $\xrightarrow{NH_3\ (aq.)} CH_2{-}COOH$ (with NH_2), 2-Aminoethanoic acid

(ii) During acylation of amines by using acetyl chloride, the acid produced as a byproduct can react with remaining amine to form a salt of amine and thus stopping the reaction from completion. Hence addition of base, absorbs the acid by product and allows the entire amine to react.

$$RNH_2 + R'COCl \xrightarrow{Base} RNHCOR' + HCl$$
Amide

(iii) $R_3C - NH_2 \xrightarrow[[O]]{KMnO_4} R_3C - NO_2,$ we get a very good yield of nitro compound.

(iv) To obtain mono-halo product the highly activated aniline ring has to be protected by acetylation followed by halogenation. The required monohalo compound can be obtained by hydrolysis of the acetanilide halo compound.

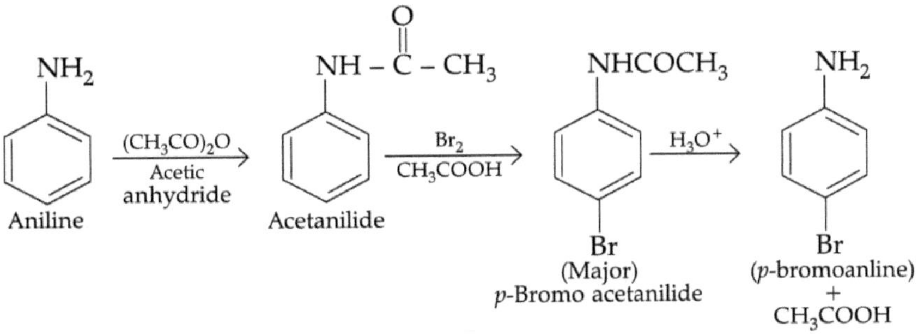

(v) In CH_3CONH_2, the lone pair of electrons of nitrogen atom are involved in resonance with $-\overset{O}{\overset{\|}{C}}-$ group, hence less available for donation as a base. Whereas in case of $CH_3CH_2NH_2$, the lone pair of electrons of nitrogen are readily available to act as a base. Also the $+$ I effect of the ethyl group addup to it.

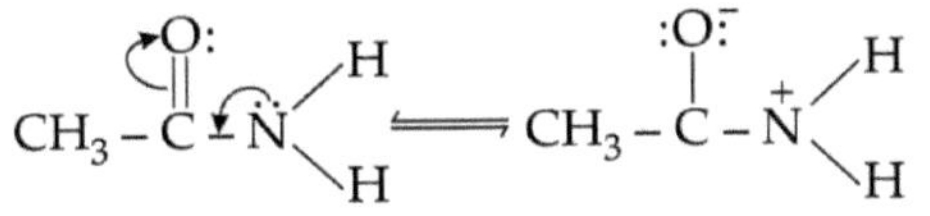

$$CH_3 - \overset{O:}{\overset{\|}{C}} - \overset{..}{N} \overset{H}{\underset{H}{<}} \rightleftharpoons CH_3 - \overset{:O^-}{\overset{\|}{C}} - \overset{+}{N} \overset{H}{\underset{H}{<}}$$

Q. 5. A compound [A] has molecular formula as C_3H_7NO. It gives the following reactions:
   (i)   Hydrolysis of [A] gives an amine [B] and carboxylic acid [C].
   (ii) Amine [B] with Hinsberg's reagent forms water insoluble product. Identify [A], [B] and [C]. Justify your answer.
   (iii) Acid [C] on treatment with Tollen's reagent gives a positive silver mirror test.

Ans. Compound [A] C_3H_7NO, must be an amide because it gives carboxylic acid and an amine on hydrolysis.

$$C_3H_7NO \xrightarrow{H_3O^+} \underset{[C]}{acid} + \underset{[B]}{amine}$$

Amine [B] must be a secondary amine as it produces an insoluble compound on treatment with Hinsberg's reagent, *i.e.*, benzene sulphonyl chloride. Also as only formic acid gives a positive silver mirror test, hence acid [C] must be HCOOH. Keeping in mind the above facts, the only structure of compound [A] that supports the above is:

(i) $H - \overset{O}{\overset{\|}{C}} - \underset{[A]}{N} \overset{CH_3}{\underset{CH_3}{<}} \xrightarrow[\text{Hydrolysis}]{H_3O^+} \underset{\substack{\text{Formic acid}\\ [C]}}{H - \overset{O}{\overset{\|}{C}} - OH} + \underset{\substack{\text{N, N-Dimethylamine}\\ [B]}}{H - N \overset{CH_3}{\underset{CH_3}{<}}}$

N, N-Dimethylformamide

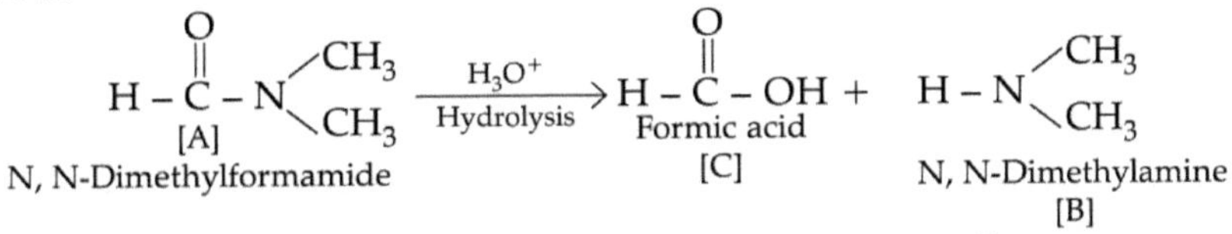

(ii) $\underset{\text{Secondary amine}}{H - N \overset{CH_3}{\underset{CH_3}{<}}} + \underset{\substack{\text{Benzene sulphonyl}\\ \text{chloride}}}{\left[\text{Ph} - \overset{O}{\underset{O}{\overset{\|}{\underset{\|}{S}}}} - Cl \right]} \longrightarrow \underset{\substack{\text{N, N-Dimethyl benzene}\\ \text{sulphonamide}\\ \text{(Insoluble in water)}}}{\left[\text{Ph} - \overset{O}{\underset{O}{\overset{\|}{\underset{\|}{S}}}} - N \overset{CH_3}{\underset{CH_3}{<}} \right]}$

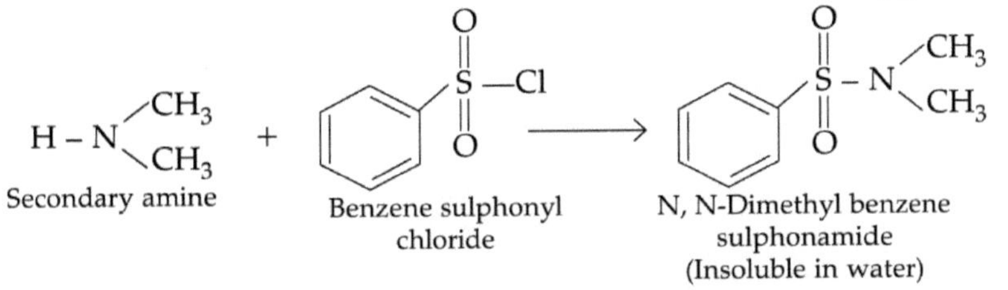

(iii) $\underset{[C]}{HCOOH} + 2[Ag(NH_3)_2]^+ + 2OH^- \longrightarrow \underset{\text{Silver mirror}}{2Ag \downarrow} + CO_2 + 2H_2O + 4NH^3$

Q. 6. Arrange the following nitrogenous bases in order of increasing basic strength:
    Pyrrole, pyridine, aniline. Explain.

Ans. Structures of the above bases are:

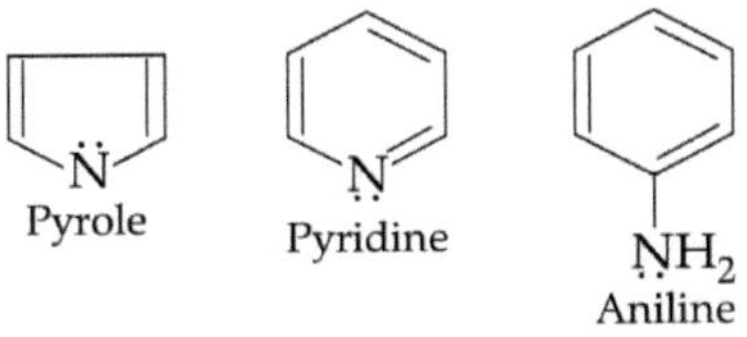

Pyrole   Pyridine   Aniline

As we can see from the structure, in pyrrole the lone pair of electrons of nitrogen is involved in aromatisation over five membered ring, while in aniline it is involved in simple delocalisation of an already aromatic benzene ring. In other words the pyrrole lone pairs of nitrogen are not available for acting as base. Hence it is weaker base than aniline.

In pyridine the lone pairs are in sp^2 nitrogen hence difficult to orient for the delocalisation with the π-electron could. While in aniline the sp^3 nitrogen lone pairs can align themself to delocalise with the aromatic π-electron cloud. Hence pyridine lone pairs are more available to act as a base.

Hence the order of basicity is.

Pyrole < Aniline < Pyridine

Q. 7. Answer the following questions:

   (i)   Write IUPAC names and structures of all the isomers of the amines corresponding to the formula $C_4H_{11}N$.

   (ii) What type of isomerism is exhibited by different pairs of amines?

Ans. (i)   The structures and the IUPAC names of different isomeric amines corresponding to the molecular formula, $C_4H_{11}N$ are given below:

(a) $CH_3 - CH_2 - CH_2 - CH_2 - NH_2$
Butanamine (1°)

(b) $CH_3 - CH_2 - \overset{\overset{\displaystyle NH_2}{|}}{CH} - CH_3$
Butan-2-amine (1°)

(c) $CH_3 - CH_2 - \overset{\overset{\displaystyle CH_3}{|}}{CH} - NH_2$
2-Methylpropanamine (1°)

(d) $CH_3 - \overset{\overset{\displaystyle CH_3}{|}}{\underset{\underset{\displaystyle CH_3}{|}}{C}} - NH_2$
2-Methylpropan-2-amine (1°)

(e) $CH_3 - CH_2 - CH_2 - NH - CH_3$
N-Methylpropanamine (2°)

(f) $CH_3 - CH_2 - NH - CH_2CH_3$
N-Ethylethanamine (2°)

(g) $CH_3 - \overset{\overset{\displaystyle CH_3}{|}}{CH} - NH - CH_3$
N-Methylpropan-2-amine (2°)

(h) $CH_3 - CH_2 - \overset{\overset{\displaystyle CH_3}{|}}{N} - CH_3$
N, N-Dimethylethanamine (3°)

   (ii) The pairs (a) and (b) and (e) and (g) exhibit *position isomerism.*
The pairs (a) and (c); (a) and (d); (b) and (c); (b) and (d) exhibit *chain isomerism.*
The pairs (e) and (f) and (f) and (g) exhibit *metamerism.*
All primary amines exhibit functional isomerism with secondary and tertiary amines and *vice-versa.*

Q. 8. Write structures of different isomers corresponding to the molecular formula, C_3H_9N.

Write IUPAC names of the isomers which will liberate nitrogen gas on treatment with nitrous acid.

Ans. The structures of different isomers corresponding to the molecular formula, C_3H_9N are given below:

(a) $CH_3 - CH_2 - CH_2 - NH_2$
Propan-1-amine (1°)

(b) $CH_3 - \overset{\overset{\displaystyle NH_2}{|}}{CH} - CH_3$
Propan-2-amine (1°)

(c) $CH_3 - NH - C_2H_5$
N-Methylethanamine (2°)

(d) $CH_3 - \overset{\overset{\displaystyle CH_3}{|}}{N} - CH_3$
N, N-Dimethylmethanamine (3°)

Only 1° amines, (a) propan-1-amine and (b) Propan-2-amine will liberate nitrogen gas on treatment with nitrous acid.

$$CH_3CH_2CH_2NH_2 + HNO_2 \longrightarrow CH_3CH_2CH_2OH + N_2 + HCl$$
Propan-1-amine   Propan-1-ol

$$CH_3 - \underset{\underset{\displaystyle NH_2}{|}}{CH} - CH_3 - HNO_2 \longrightarrow CH_3 - \underset{\underset{\displaystyle OH}{|}}{CH} - CH_3 - N_2 + HCl$$
Propan-2-amine   Propan-2-ol

Q. 9. Account for the following:

   (i) pK_b of aniline is more than that of methylamine.[**]

   (ii) Ethylamine is soluble in water whereas aniline is not.[*]

   (iii) Methylamine in water reacts with ferric chloride to precipitate hydrated ferric oxide.[*]

   (iv) Although amino group is *o, p*-directing in aromatic electrophilic substitution reactions, aniline on nitration gives a substantial amount of *m*-nitroaniline.

(v) Aniline does not undergo Friedel-Craft's reaction.*

(vi) Diazonium salts of aromatic amines are more stable than those of aliphatic amines.

(vii) Gabriel phthalimide synthesis is preferred for synthesizing primary amines.

Ans. (i) **pK_b of aniline is more than that of methylamine:** Higher the pK_b value lower is the basic strength.

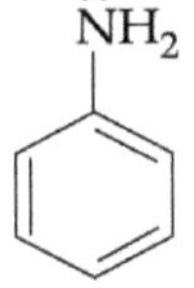

$$CH_3 - \ddot{N}H_2$$
Methylamine

Aniline

In Aniline due to resonance, the electrons on the N-atom are delocalised over the benzene ring. Therefore, the electrons on the N-atom are less available to donate.

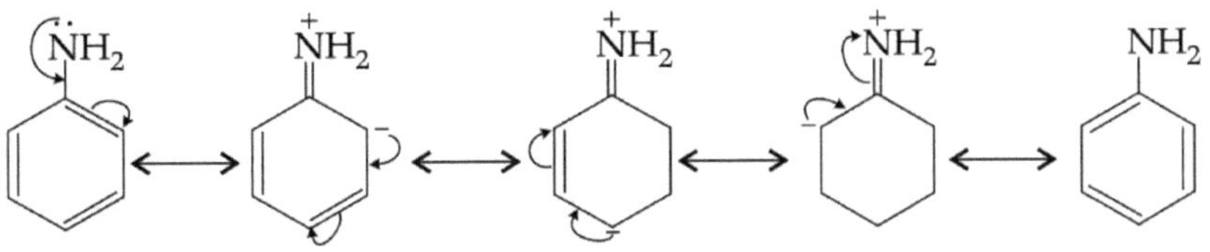

On the other hand, in case of methylamine (due to the +I effect of methyl group), the electron density on the N-atom is increased. As a result, aniline is less basic than methylamine. Thus, pK_b of aniline is more than that of methylamine.

(ii) **Ethylamine is soluble in water whereas aniline is not:** Ethylamine when added to water forms intermolecular H-bonds with water. Hence, it is soluble in water.

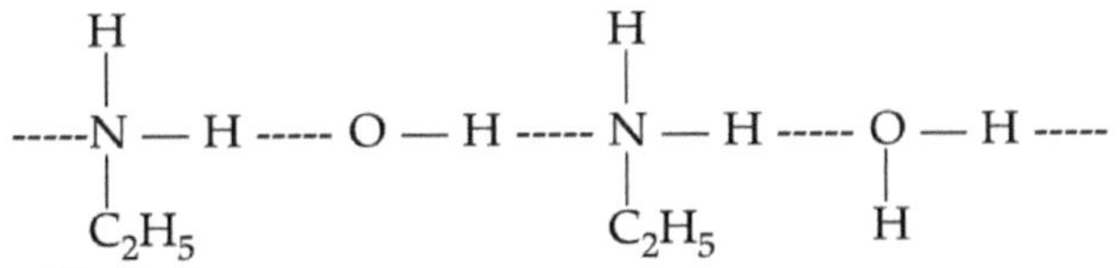

Ethylamine

But aniline does not undergo H-bonding with water to a very large extent due to the presence of a bulky hydrophobic $-C_6H_5$ group. Hence, aniline is insoluble in water.

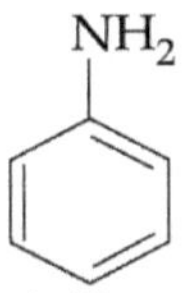

Aniline

(iii) **Methylamine in water reacts with ferric chloride to precipitate hydrated ferric oxide:** Methylamine is more basic than water. Therefore, in water, methylamine produces OH^- ions by accepting H^+ ions from water.

$$CH_3 - NH_2 + H - OH \longrightarrow CH_3 - \overset{+}{N}H_3 + OH^-$$

Then, OH^- ion reacts with Fe^{3+} ion, from dissociated $FeCl_3$ to form a precipitate of hydrated ferric oxide.

$$3Fe^{3+} + 6OH^- \longrightarrow Fe_2O_3.3H_2O$$
Hydrated ferric oxide

(iv) **Although amino group is *o, p*-directing in aromatic electrophilic substitution reactions, aniline on nitration gives a substantial amount of *m*-nitroaniline:** Nitration is carried out in an acidic medium. In an acidic medium, aniline is protonated to give anilinium ion (which is *meta*-directing).

Aniline   Anilinium ion

m-Nitroaniline (47%)

For this reason, aniline on nitration gives a substantial amount of *m*-nitroaniline.

(v) **Aniline does not undergo Friedel-Craft's reaction:** A Friedel-Craft's reaction is carried out in the presence of $AlCl_3$ but $AlCl_3$ is a Lewis acid while aniline is a strong base. Thus, aniline reacts with $AlCl_3$ to form a salt (as shown in the following equation).

$$\underset{\text{Aniline}}{C_6H_5NH_2} + AlCl_3 \longrightarrow \underset{\text{Salt}}{C_6H_5\overset{+}{N}H_2\, AlClH_3^{-}} + AlCl_3$$

Due to the positive charge on the N-atom, electrophilic substitution in the benzene ring is deactivated. Hence, aniline does not undergo the Friedel-Craft's reaction.

(vi) **Diazonium salts of aromatic amines are more stable than those of aliphatic amines:** The diazonium ion undergoes resonance as shown below:

$$\overset{+}{N}\equiv\overset{\cdot\cdot}{N}: \quad\longleftrightarrow\quad \overset{+}{N}=\overset{\cdot\cdot}{\overset{-}{N}}: \quad\longleftrightarrow\quad \overset{+}{N}=\overset{-}{N}: \quad\longleftrightarrow\quad \overset{+}{N}=\overset{-}{N}:$$

This resonance accounts for the stability of the diazonium ion. Hence, diazonium salts of aromatic amines are more stable than those of aliphatic amines.

(vii) **Gabriel phthalimide synthesis is preferred for synthesising primary amines:** Gabriel phthalimide synthesis follows the addition of alkyl halide R – X to form N-alkyl derivative.

The derivative further undergoes hydrolysis to form only a primary amine. Also aromatic 1° amines cannot be made by this method. Only 1° aliphatic amines can be prepared.

Q. 10. Describe a method for the identification of primary, secondary and tertiary amines. Also write chemical equations of the reactions involved.

Ans. Primary, secondary and tertiary amines can be identified and distinguished by Hinsberg's test. In this test, the amines are allowed to react with Hinsberg's reagent, benzenesulphonyl chloride ($C_6H_5SO_2Cl$). The three types of amines react differently with Hinsberg's reagent. Therefore, they can be easily identified using Hinsberg's reagent.

(i) Primary amines react with benzenesulphonyl chloride to form N-alkylbenzenesulphonyl amide which is soluble in alkali.

$$C_6H_5\underset{\overset{\|}{O}}{\overset{\overset{O}{\|}}{S}}-Cl + H-\underset{H}{\underset{|}{N}}-C_3H_7 \longrightarrow C_6H_5\underset{\overset{\|}{O}}{\overset{\overset{O}{\|}}{S}}-N-C_3H_7 + HCl$$

(Hinsberg's reagent) Propanamine   N-Propylbenzenesulphonamide
Benzenesulphonyl
chloride

Due to the presence of a strong electron-withdrawing sulphonyl group in the sulphonamide, the H-atom attached to nitrogen can be easily released as proton. So, it is acidic and dissolves in alkali.

(ii) Secondary amines react with Hinsberg's reagent to give a sulphonamide which is insoluble in alkali.

$$C_6H_5\underset{\overset{\|}{O}}{\overset{\overset{O}{\|}}{S}}-Cl + H-\underset{CH_3}{\underset{|}{N}}-CH_3 \longrightarrow C_6H_5\underset{\overset{\|}{O}}{\overset{\overset{O}{\|}}{S}}-N-C_3H_7 + HCl$$

Benzenesulphonyl   N, N-Dimethylamine   N-Propylbenzenesulphonamide
chloride

There is no H-atom attached to the N-atom in the sulphonamide. Therefore, it is not acidic and insoluble in alkali.

(iii) On the other hand, tertiary amines do not react with Hinsberg's reagent at all.

Q. 11. An aromatic compound `A' on treatment with aqueous ammonia and heating forms compound `B' which on heating with Br_2 and KOH forms a compound `C' of molecular formula C_6H_7N. Write the structures and IUPAC names of compounds A, B and C.

Ans. It is given that compound `C' having the molecular formula, $C_6H_7N$ is formed by heating compound `B' with Br_2 and KOH. This is a Hoffmann bromamide degradation reaction. Therefore, compound `B' is an amide and compound `C' is an amine. The only amine having the molecular formula, C_6H_7N is aniline, $(C_6H_5NH_2)$.

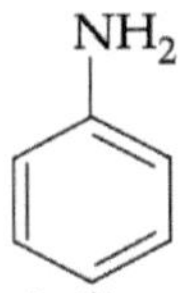

Therefore, compound `B' (from which `C' is formed) must be benzamide, $(C_6H_5CONH_2)$.

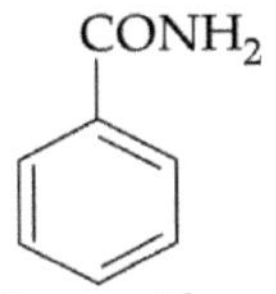

Aniline

Benzamide

Further, benzamide is formed by heating compound `A' with aqueous ammonia.

Therefore, compound `A' must be benzoic acid.

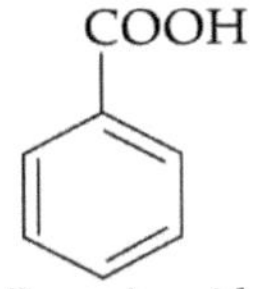

Benzoic acid

The given reactions can be explained with the help of the following sentences:

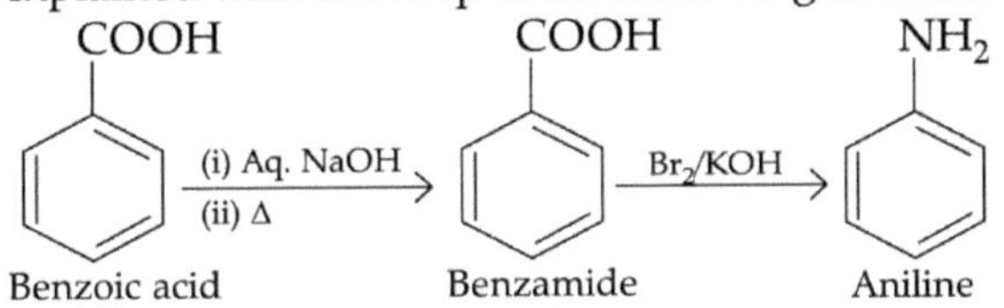

Benzoic acid (A) $\xrightarrow[\text{(ii) } \Delta]{\text{(i) Aq. NaOH}}$ Benzamide (B) $\xrightarrow{Br_2/KOH}$ Aniline (C)

Q. 12. Why aromatic primary amines can not be prepared by Gabriel phthalimide synthesis?

Ans. Gabriel phthalimide synthesis is used for the preparation of aliphatic primary amines. It involves nucleophilic substitution (S_N2) of alkyl halides by the anion formed by the phthalimide.

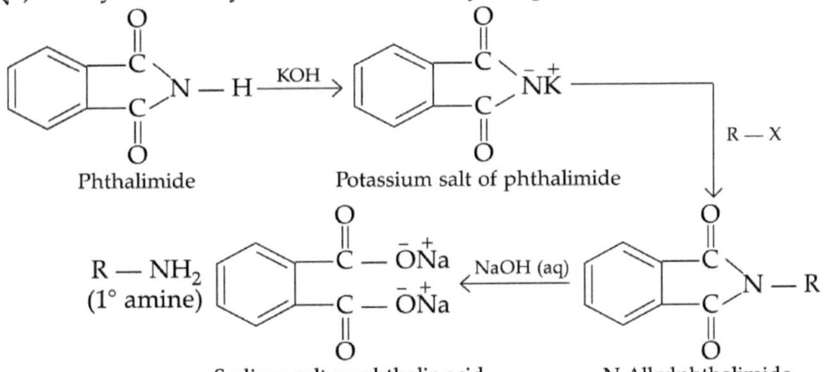

Phthalimide $\xrightarrow{KOH}$ Potassium salt of phthalimide $\xrightarrow{R-X}$ N-Alkylphthalimide $\xrightarrow{NaOH \text{ (aq)}}$ Sodium salt or phthalic acid + $R-NH_2$ ($1°$ amine)

But aryl halides do not undergo nucleophilic substitution with the anion formed by the phthalimide.

Potassium salt of phthalimide $\xrightarrow{Ar-X}$ No reaction

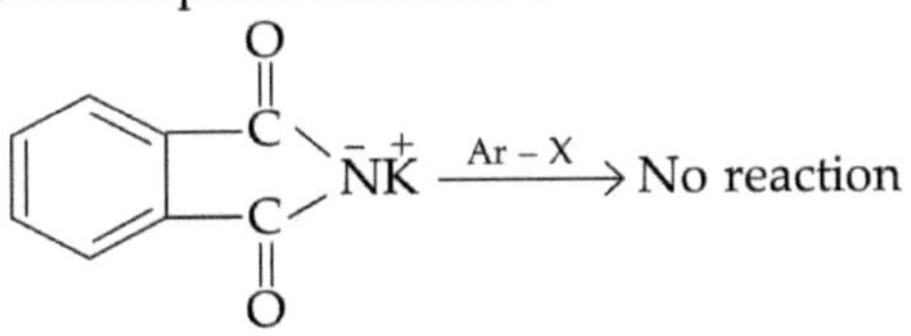

Hence, aromatic primary amines cannot be prepared by this process.

Q. 13. (i) Write the reactions involved in the following:*

    (a) Hofmann bromamide degradation reaction

    (b) Diazotisation

    (c) Gabriel phthalimide synthesis

(ii) Give reasons:

    (a) $(CH_3)_2NH$ is more basic than $(CH_3)_3N$ in an aqueous solution.

    (b) Aromatic diazonium salts are more stable than aliphatic diazonium salts.

---

* are board exam questions from previous years

Ans. (i) (a) Hoffmann bromamide degradation reaction: Acetamide can be considered for example. In this reaction Acetamide (CH_3CONH_2) undergoes Hofmann degradation in presence of Bromine and NaOH to give Methanamine.

$$CH_3CONH_2 + Br_2 + 4NaOH \rightarrow CH_3NH_2 + Na_2CO_3 + 2NaBr + 2H_2O$$

(b) Diazotisation: The conversion of primary aromatic amines into diazonium salts is known as diazotization.

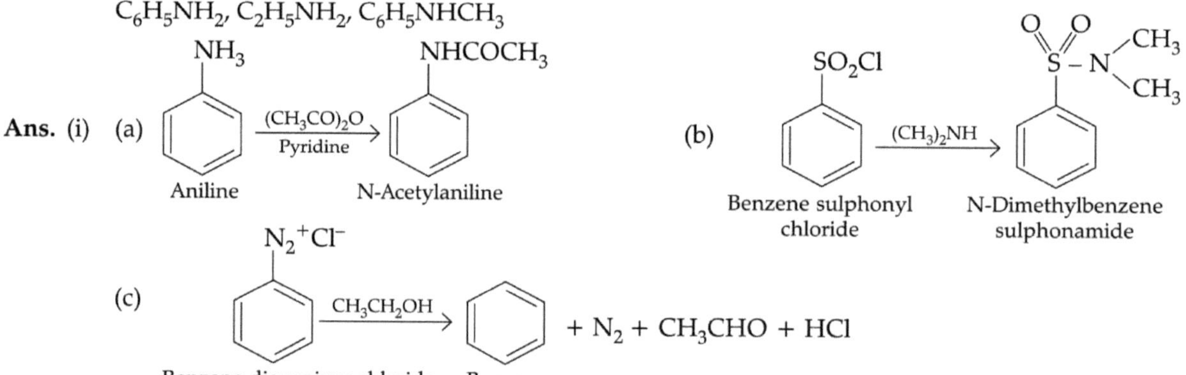

Aniline

Benzene diazonium chloride

$$+ NaNO_2 + 2HCl \xrightarrow{273\text{-}278\ K} + NaCl + 2H_2O$$

(c) Gabriel phthalimide synthesis: This reaction is used for the preparation of primary amines. Phthalimide on treatment with ethanolic potassium hydroxide forms potassium salt of phthalimide which on heating with alkyl halide followed by alkaline hydrolysis produces the corresponding primary amine.

Phthalimide $\xrightarrow{KOH}$ N-Alkylophthalimide $\xrightarrow{RX}$ NaOH (aq) $\xrightarrow{}$ + RNH_2 Primary amine

(ii) (a) $(CH_3)_2NH$ is more basic than $(CH_3)_3N$ in aqueous solutions because, in $(CH_3)_3N$ the line pair of electrons on nitrogen atom is responsible for its basicity are quite hindered by the three methyl groups, hence are less available. Due to which it is less basic as compared to $(CH_3)_2NH$.

(b) Aromatic diazonium salts are more stable than aliphatic diazonium salts because the positive charge on nitrogen atom is stablized by the resonance with attached phenyl group.

Q. 14. (i) Write the structures of the main products of the following reactions:*

(a) $\xrightarrow[\text{Pyridine}]{(CH_3CO)_2O}$

(b) $-SO_2Cl \xrightarrow{(CH_3)_2NH}$

(c) $\xrightarrow{CH_3CH_2OH}$

(ii) Give a simple chemical test to distinguish between Aniline and N, N-dimethylaniline.

(iii) Arrange the following in the increasing order of their pK_b values:

$C_6H_5NH_2, C_2H_5NH_2, C_6H_5NHCH_3$

Ans. (i) (a) $\xrightarrow[\text{Pyridine}]{(CH_3CO)_2O}$

Aniline → N-Acetylaniline

(b) $\xrightarrow{(CH_3)_2NH}$

Benzene sulphonyl chloride → N-Dimethylbenzene sulphonamide

(c) $\xrightarrow{CH_3CH_2OH}$ + N_2 + CH_3CHO + HCl

Benzene diazonium chloride Benzene

(ii) Aniline can be distinguished from N, N-dimethyl aniline by diazo coupling reaction. Aniline would react with benzene diazonium chloride to give a yellow dye, whereas N, N-dimethyl aniline won't undergo this reaction.

$\xrightarrow{H^+}$ $-N=N-$ $-NH_2 + Cl^- + H_2O$

Benzene diazonium chloride

p-Aminoazobenzene (yellow dye)

$$N_2{}^+Cl^-$$

Benzene diazonium chloride

$+$

N, N-dimethylaniline

$\longrightarrow$ No Reaction

(iii) Increasing order of pK_b values is :

$$C_2H_5NH_2 < C_6H_5NH_2 < C_6H_5NH_2CH_3$$

Chapter 14. Biomolecules

Q. 1. Write the various reactions of glucose to answer the following and justify your answer based on its structure.

(i) Glucose forms mono glucoxime.

(iii) It forms pentaacetate, but not hexacetate.

(ii) Glucose contains 6-carbon chain.

(iv) Glucose pentaacetate does not reacts with NH_2OH.

(v) Does not gives positive Schiff's test or $NaHSO_3$ addition product in spite of having an aldehyde group.

Ans. (i) Because of the presence of a single carbonyl group glucose forms glucoxime.

$$\underset{\text{Glucose}}{\overset{\displaystyle CHO}{\underset{\displaystyle CH_2OH}{|\;(CHOH)_4\;|}}} + \underset{\text{Hydroxylamine}}{NH_2OH} \xrightarrow{\;-H_2O\;} \underset{\text{Glucoxime}}{\overset{\displaystyle C=NOH}{\underset{\displaystyle CH_2OH}{\overset{\displaystyle H}{|}\;(CHOH)_4\;|}}}$$

(ii) Glucose on reduction with HI in presence of red P at about 373 K produces *n*-hexane. This reaction confirms the presence of 6-carbon chain in glucose.

$$\underset{\text{Glucose}}{C_6H_{12}O_6} \xrightarrow[\text{373 K}]{\text{HI/ Red P}} \underset{\text{n-Hexane}}{CH_3CH_2CH_2CH_2CH_2-CH_3}$$

(iii) In glucose all the hydroxy (– OH) *i.e.*, 5 groups react with acetic anhydride to form a pentaacetate except the aldehydic group. This product indicates presence of 5, hydroxyl group in normal structure of D-glucose.

$$\xrightarrow[\;-\,5\;CH_3COOH\;]{+\,5\;(CH_3CO)_2O}$$

Glucose

α-D-glucose pentaacetate

(iv) The aldehydic group is absent in the α-D-glucose pentaacetate or β-D-glucose pentaacetate. It is involved in the cyclic bond between first and the 5th carbon of the chain. Hence glucose pentaacetate does not give any reaction with NH_2OH.

(v) The open chain form of glucose is responsible for the positive tests of aldehyde given by glucose. But in case of Schiff's reagent and $NaHSO_3$ which are weak reagents, the reactions are reversible and the equilibrium cannot be shifted to get more and more open chain form, which is smaller in amount in the mixture of α and β cyclic glucose forms.

Q. 2. Answer the following:

(i) How do you explain the presence of five (OH) groups in glucose molecule?

(ii) Name the linkage connecting monosaccharide units in polysaccharides.

(iii) Amino acids are classified as α, β, γ and δ based on the relative position of amino group with respect to the carboxyl group. What type of amino acids are involved in protein chains?

(iv) What happens to the sugar in milk during curdling of it?

(v) Define the term D and L configuration used for amino acids.

Ans. (i) Acetylation of glucose with acetic anhydride in presence of pyridine and slight conc. H_2SO_4, converts glucose into glucose pentaacetate indicating presence of 5 hydroxyl groups.

(ii) Ether linkages called glycosidic linkages connect two molecules of monosaccharides.

(iii) α-amino acids are involved in protein chain.

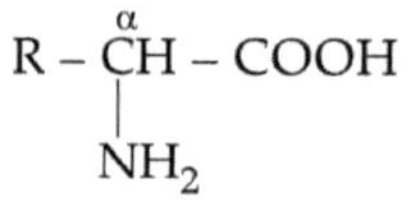

$$R - \overset{\alpha}{\underset{\underset{NH_2}{|}}{C}H} - COOH$$

(iv) During curdling of milk sugar lactose gets converted to lactic acid.

(v) D and L are symbols of two different configurations.

Example :

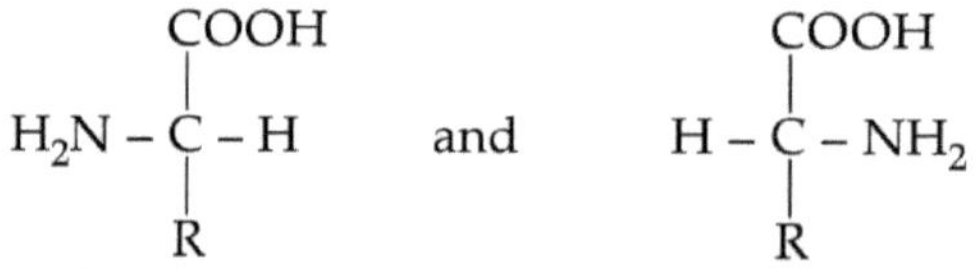

$$\underset{\text{(Left) L-Amino acid}}{H_2N - \underset{\underset{R}{|}}{\overset{\overset{COOH}{|}}{C}} - H} \qquad \text{and} \qquad \underset{\text{(Right) D-Amino acid}}{H - \underset{\underset{R}{|}}{\overset{\overset{COOH}{|}}{C}} - NH_2}$$

The oxidation of the $(-NH_2)$ group on the α-carbon decides the D and L configuration. Left orientation is referred as L and right one as D configuration respectively.

Q. 3. What is the basic structural difference between starch and cellulose?

Ans. Starch consists of two components-amylose and amylopectin. Amylose is a long linear chain of 200-1000 units of α-D-(+)-glucose units joined by C_1-C_4 glycosidic linkage (α-link).

α-Link Amylose

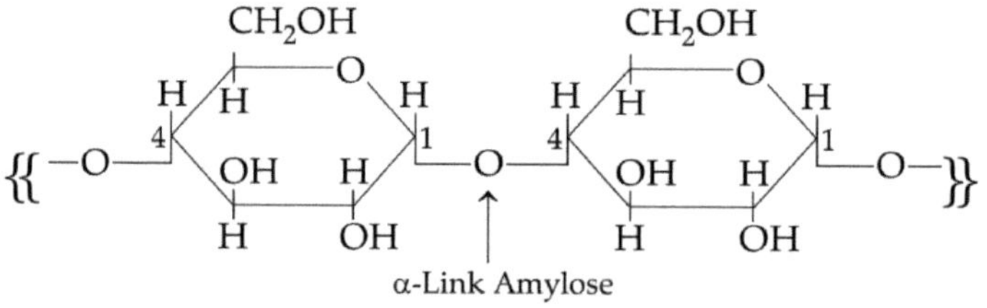

Amylopectin is a branched-chain polymer of α-D-glucose units, in which the chain is formed by C_1-C_4 glycosidic linkage and the branching occurs by C_1-C_6 glycosidic linkage.

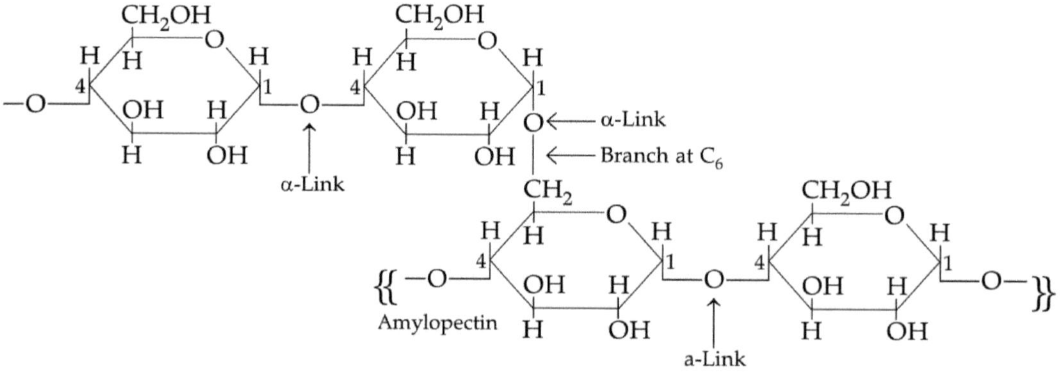

Amylopectin

On the other hand, cellulose is a straight-chain polysaccharide of β-D-glucose units joined by C_1-C_4 glycosidic linkage (β-link).

Cellulose

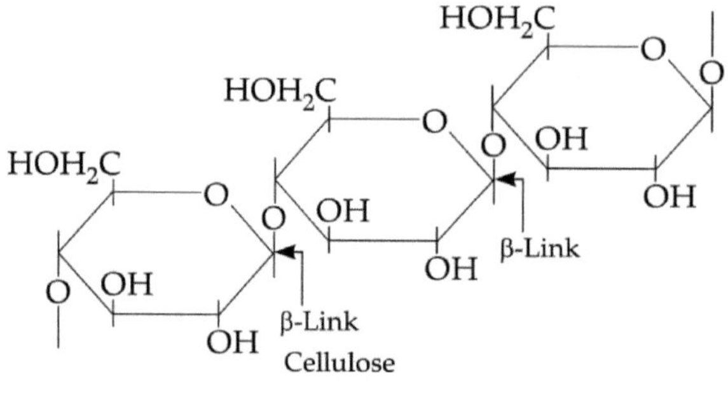

Q. 4. Define the following as related to proteins

(i) Peptide linkage, (ii) Primary structure, (iii) Denaturation.

Ans. (i) Peptide linkage: The amide linkage formed between –COOH group of one molecule of an amino acid and –NH$_2$ group of another molecule of the amino acid by the elimination of a water molecule is called a peptide linkage. These are the basic linkages present in proteins.

(a) $H_2N - CH - COOH + H_2N - CH - COOH \xrightarrow{-H_2O} H_2N - CH - [CO - NH] - CH - COOH$

      CH(CH$_3$)$_2$ CH$_3$ CH(CH$_3$)$_2$ CH$_3$

      Valine   Alanine   Valylananine (Val-Ala)

(b) $H_2N - CH_2 - \overset{O}{\overset{\|}{C}} - OH + NH_2 - CH - COOH \xrightarrow{-H_2O} H_2N - CH_2 - \overset{O}{\overset{\|}{C}} - N - \overset{CH_3}{\underset{|}{CH}} - COOH$

      Glycine   Alanine   H   Peptide linkage

                    CH$_3$

                      Glycylalanine (Gly-Ala)

(ii) Primary structure: The primary structure of protein refers to the specific sequence in which various amino acids are present in it. The sequence in which amino acids arranged is different in each protein. A change in the sequence creates a different protein.

(iii) Denaturation: In a biological system, a protein is found to have a unique 3-dimensional structure and a unique biological activity. In such a situation, the protein is called native protein. However, when the native protein is subjected to physical changes such as change in temperature or chemical changes such as change in pH, its H-bonds are disturbed. This disturbance unfolds the globules and uncoils the helix. As a result, the protein loses its biological activity. This loss of biological activity by the protein is called denaturation. During denaturation, the secondary (2°) and the tertiary (3°) structures of the protein gets destroyed, but the primary structure remains unaltered.

One of the examples of denaturation of proteins is the curdling of milk due to change in pH.

Q. 5. What are the common types of secondary structure of proteins?

Ans. There are two common types of secondary structure of proteins:

(i) α-helix structure   (ii) β-pleated sheet structure.

(a) **α-Helix structure:** In this structure, the –NH group of an amino acid residue forms H-bond with the group of the adjacent turn of the right-handed screw (α-helix). The most common way of twisting of a polypeptide chain. Generally proteins having larger alkyl (R) group in amino acid chain forms this structure.

(b) **β-pleated sheet structure:** This structure is called so because it looks like the pleated folds of drapery. In this structure, all the peptide chains are stretched out to nearly the maximum extension and then laid side by side. These peptide chains are held together by intermolecular hydrogen bonds. Generally proteins with smaller (R) groups in amino acids forms such structures.

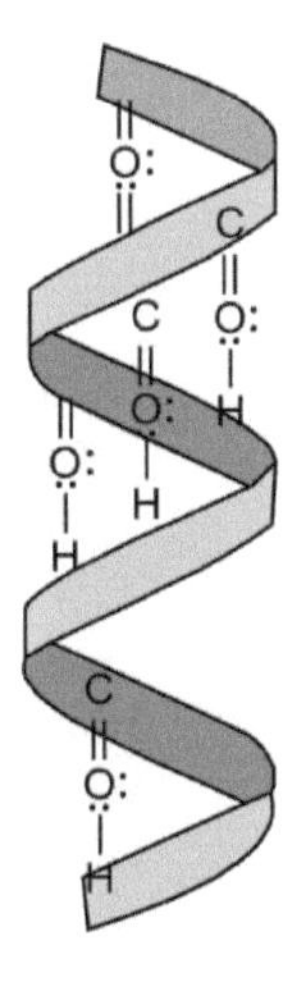

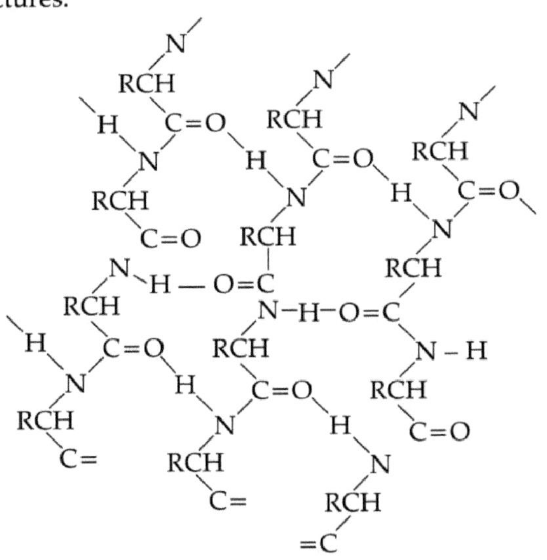

Chapter 15. Polymers

Q. 1. (i)   Write the names of monomers of the following polymers:

(a) 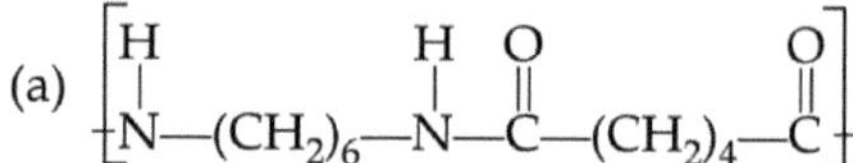   (b) 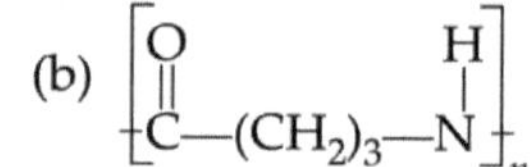   (c) $+CF_2 - CF_2\}_n$

(ii) Arrange the following polymers in increasing order of their intermolecular forces.

(a) Nylon 6, 6, Buna-S, Polythene.

(b) Nylon 6, Neoprene, Polyvinyl chloride.

Ans. (i) (a) Hexamethylenediamine $[H_2N - (CH_2)_6 - NH_2]$ and adipic acid $[HOOC - (CH_2)_4 - COOH]$ Polymer is nylon-6, 6.

(b) 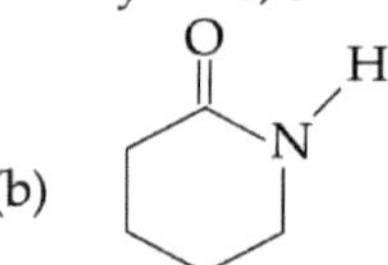

Caprolactum   Polymer is nylon 6.

(c) Tetrafluoroethene $(CF_2 = CF_2)$. Polymer is Teflon.

(ii) Different types of polymers have different intermolecular forces of attraction. Elastomers or rubbers have the weakest while fibres have the strongest intermolecular forces of attraction. Plastics have intermediate intermolecular forces of attraction. Hence, the increasing order of the intermolecular forces of the given polymers is as follows:

(a) Buna—S < Polythene < Nylon 6, 6   (b) Neoprene < Polyvinyl chloride < Nylon 6.

Q. 2. Answer the following questions:

(i) What are polymers?

(ii) How are polymers classified on the basis of structure?

Ans. (i) Polymers are high molecular mass macromolecules, which consist of repeating structural units derived from monomers. They have a high molecular mass $(10^3 - 10^7$ u$)$. In a polymer, various monomer units are joined by strong covalent bonds. These polymers can be natural as well as synthetic. Polythene, rubber and nylon 6, 6 are examples of polymers.

(ii) Polymers are classified on the basis of structure as follows:

(a) **Linear polymers:** The monomer units are linked to each other to form long straight chains. They can be depicted as:

For *e.g.*, high density polythene (HDP), polyvinyl chloride, etc.

(b) **Branched chain polymers:** These polymers are basically linear chain polymers, which also have side chains of different lengths attached to them. These polymers are represented as:

For *e.g.*, low density polythene (LDP), amylopectin, starch etc.

(c) **Cross-linked or Network polymers:** These polymers have many cross-linking bonds that give rise to 3-dimensional network-like structure. These polymers contain bi-functional and tri-functional monomers and strong covalent bonds between various linear polymer chains. These are quite hard, rigid and brittle. Examples of such polymers include bakelite and melamine.

Q. 3. Answer the following questions:

(i) What does LDP and HDP signify? How are these prepared?

(ii) A copolymer can be a addition and condensation polymer both. Explain.

Ans. (i) LDP represents low density polythene and HDP represents high density polythene.

Preparation: HDP is prepared by polymerisation of ethylene at about 340 K under 6 to 7 atm pressure in presence of catalyst triethyl aluminium and titanium tetrachloride (Zeigler-Natta catalyst).

The catalyst ensures that the polymer is formed in a regular linear chain manner and hence closely packed or staked giving a high density to the polyethene.

HDP is quite-inert chemically, tougher and has greater tensile strength.

LDP on the other hand is prepared by heating pure ethylene at about 400 K to 500 K under high pressure between 1,000-2,000 atm with some peroxide to initiate polymerisation.

This consist of highly branched molecules, because of branching it has empty space in between polymer chains and has low density. Its a poor conductor of electricity and is chemically inert.

(ii) A copolymer is one in which we have two different units joining to become one monomer unit of the polymer. Hence it can be either an addition or a condensation polymer.

Example: Buna-S is a copolymer and an addition polymer.

$$nCH_2 = CH - CH = CH_2 + n \underset{\text{Styrene}}{\overset{CH=CH_2}{\bigcirc}} \xrightarrow[\Delta]{Na} \left[CH_2 - CH = CH - CH_2 - CH - CH_2 \right]_{\text{Buna-S}}$$

1, 3 Butadine

Similarly terylene is a copolymer of ethylene glycol and terephthalic acid and its a condensation polymer.

$$n OHCH_2CH_2OH + nHO - \underset{O}{\overset{}{C}} - \bigcirc - \underset{O}{\overset{}{C}} - OH \xrightarrow{-H_2O} \left[O - CH_2 - CH_2 - O - \overset{O}{\overset{\|}{C}} - \bigcirc - \overset{O}{\overset{\|}{C}} \right]$$

Ethylene glycol   Terephthalic acid   Terylene (Dacron)

Chapter 16. Chemistry in Everyday Life

Q. 1. Explain the following terms with suitable examples:

   (i) Cationic detergents   (ii) Anionic detergents   (iii) Non-ionic detergents.

Ans. (i) **Cationic detergents:** Cationic detergents are quaternary ammonium salts of amines with acetates, chlorides, or bromides. These are called cationic detergents because the cationic part of these detergents contains a long hydrocarbon chain and a positive charge on the N atom.

     For example: Cetyltrimethylammonium bromide

$$\left[CH_3(CH_2)_{15} - \overset{\overset{\displaystyle CH_3}{|}}{\underset{\underset{\displaystyle CH_3}{|}}{N}} - CH_3 \right]^+ Br^-$$

Cetyltrimethylammonium bromide

   These detergents have germicidal properties.

(ii) **Anionic detergents:** Anionic detergents are those detergents in which the anionic part of the detergent is involved in the cleansing action.

   Anionic detergents are of two types:

   (a) **Sodium alkyl sulphates:** These detergents are sodium salts of long chain alcohols. They are prepared by first treating these alcohols with concentrated sulphuric acid and then with sodium hydroxide. Examples of these detergents include sodium lauryl sulphate

     $[CH_3(CH_2)_{10}CH_2OSO_3^-Na^+]$ and sodium stearyl sulphate $(C_{17}H_{35}CH_2OSO_3^-Na^+)$.

   (b) **Sodium alkylbenzenesulphonates:** These detergents are sodium salts of long chain alkylbenzenesulphonic acids. Alkyl benzenes are first treated with concentrated sulphuric acid and then with sodium hydroxide. Sodium 4-(1-dodecyl) benzenesulphonate (SDS) is an example of anionic detergents.

(iii) **Non-ionic detergents:** Molecules of these detergents do not contain any ions. These detergents are esters of alcohols having high molecular mass. They are obtained by reacting polyethylene glycol and stearic acid.

$$CH_3(CH_2)_{16}COOH + HO(CH_2CH_2CH_2O)_nCH_2CH_2OH] \xrightarrow{-H_2O} CH_3(CH_2)_{16}CO(CH_2CH_2O)_nCH_2CH_2OH]$$

Stearic acid   Polyethyleneglycol

Named Reactions or Laws | Set 9 |

Chapter 2. Solutions

Q. 1. State Henry's law.[*]

Ans. According to this law, "The mass of a gas dissolved in a given volume of liquid at constant temperature is directly proportional to the pressure of the gas present in equilibrium with the liquid."

Hence, it relates pressure of the gas with mole fraction of it in a liquid solution.

$$P_{gas} = K_H \times x$$

$$K_H = \text{Henry's law constant}$$

Chapter 3. Electrochemistry

Q. 1. State Kohlrausch's law of independent migration of ions. Explain its one application.

Ans. Kohlrausch's law of independent migration of ions states that limiting molar conductivity of an electrolyte can be represented as the sum of individual contributions of the anion and cation of the electrolyte.

Thus limiting molar conductivity of sodium chloride solution can be calculated as:

$$\Lambda^0_{m(NaCl)} = \lambda^0_{Na^+} + \lambda^0_{Cl^-}$$

where $\lambda^0_{Na^+}$ and $\lambda^0_{Cl^-}$ are limiting molar conductivities of Na^+ and Cl^- ions respectively.

Chapter 10. Haloalkanes and Haloarenes

Q. 1. Write a short note on:

    (i)   Finkelstein reaction   (ii)   Saytzeff's rule   (iii)   Balz-Scheimann's reaction.

Ans. (i)   **Finkelstein reaction :** This reaction is used to prepare iodoalkanes from the corresponding chloroalkanes or bromoalkanes by heating the alkyl halide with NaI or KI dissolved in acetone. The by product NaCl or NaBr are less soluble in acetone and are easily precipitated, thus maintaining the forward direction of the reaction.

       Ex.: $CH_3CH_2Cl + NaI \xrightarrow{\text{Acetone}} CH_3-CH_2-I + NaCl$

(ii)   **Saytzeff's rule :** According to this rule if we have two different alkyl halides then the one which can produce more substituted alkene will react fast. Similarly if we have an alkyl halide in which dehydrohalogenation can produce two or more different alkenes, then the major product will be the most substituted alkene.

       Ex.:

$$CH_3-CH_2-\underset{\underset{Br}{|}}{CH}-CH_3 \xrightarrow[\text{Dehydrohalogenation}]{\text{alc. KOH}} \underset{\text{(Major)}}{CH_3-CH=CH-CH_3} + \underset{\text{(Minor)}}{CH_3-CH_2-CH=CH_2}$$

(iii) **Balz-Scheimann's reaction :** Preparation of fluorobenzene from benzene diazonium chloride can be done by this named reaction by treating it with hydrofluoroboric acid (HBF$_4$) followed by heating.

$$\underset{\text{(benzene diazonium chloride)}}{\overset{+}{N}=N\overset{-}{Cl}} + HBF_4 \xrightarrow{-HCl} \left[\overset{+}{N}=N\overset{-}{BF_4} \right] \xrightarrow{\Delta} \underset{\text{Fluorobenzene}}{F} + N_2 + BF_3$$

Q. 2. Give example of each of the following reactions:

    (i)   Friedel-Crafts alkylation   (iv) Swart's reaction

    (ii) Gattermann reaction   (v) Sandmeyer's reaction

    (iii) Wurtz-Fittig reaction

Ans. (i) Friedel-crafts-alkylation:

$$
\text{Chlorobenzene} + CH_3Cl \xrightarrow[\text{AlCl}_3]{\text{Anhyd.}} \text{1-chloro-2-methylbenzene (Minor)} + \text{1-chloro-4-methylbenzene (Major)}
$$

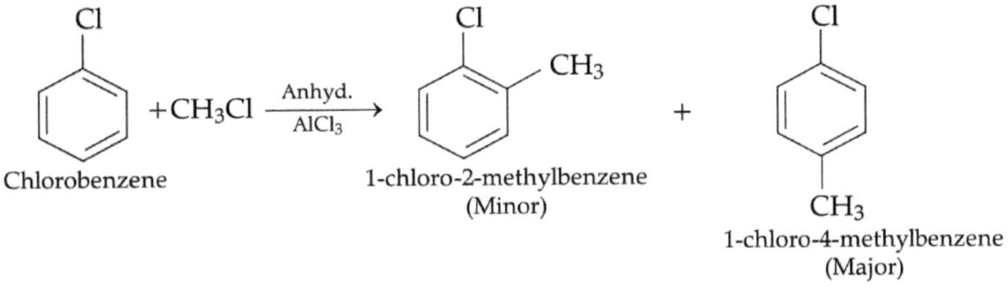

The *para* isomer is the major product of alkylation reaction because of steric hindrance faced by the *ortho* position.

    (ii) **Gattermann Reaction:** A modified form of Sandmeyer's reaction.

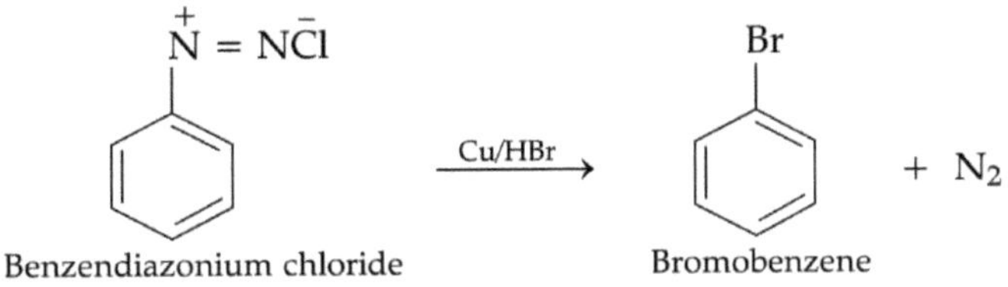

$$
\overset{+}{N} = \overset{-}{N}Cl \text{ (Benzendiazonium chloride)} \xrightarrow{\text{Cu/HBr}} Br \text{ (Bromobenzene)} + N_2
$$

    (iii) **Wurtz-Fittig reaction:**

$$
C_2H_5I + 2Na + \text{(Iodobenzene)} \xrightarrow{\text{Dry ether}} \text{(ethylbenzene, } C_2H_5) + 2\,NaI
$$

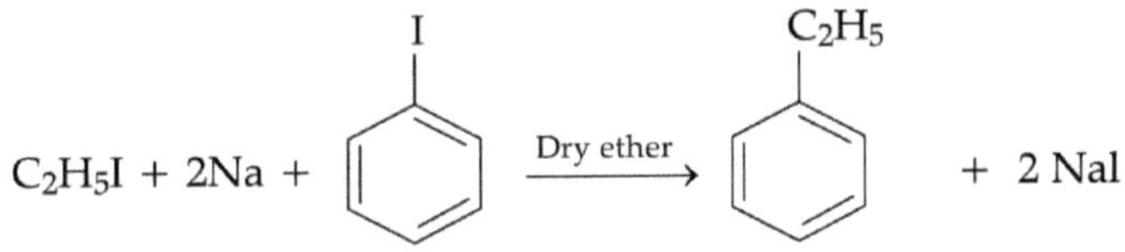

    (iv) **Swart's reaction:** For the preparation of fluoroalkanes.

$$
2CH_3CH_2Cl + \underset{\substack{\text{Mercurous}\\\text{fluoride}}}{Hg_2F_2} \longrightarrow 2\underset{\text{Fluoroethane}}{CH_3CH_2F} + Hg_2Cl_2
$$

       SbF_3, AgF or CoF_2, other metallic fluorides can also be used.

    (v) **Sandmeyer's reaction:**

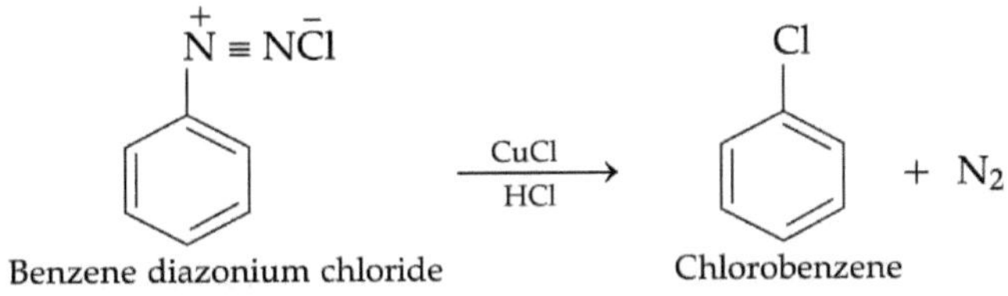

$$
\overset{+}{N} \equiv \overset{-}{N}Cl \text{ (Benzene diazonium chloride)} \xrightarrow[\text{HCl}]{\text{CuCl}} Cl \text{ (Chlorobenzene)} + N_2
$$

Chapter 11. Alcohols, Phenols and Ethers

Q. 1. Write reaction for secondary alcohol when passed through copper at 573 K.[*]

Ans.

$$
\underset{\substack{CH_3\\CH_3}}{}\!\!>\!CHOH \xrightarrow{\text{Cu/573 K}} \underset{\substack{CH_3\\CH_3}}{}\!\!>\!C=O + H_2
$$

               2° Alcohol   Ketone

Q. 2. Write chemical reaction for the preparation of phenol from chlorobenzene.

Ans. Chlorobenzene is fused with NaOH (at 623 K and 340 atm pressure) to produce sodium phenoxide, which gives phenol on acidification.

Chlorobenzene $+ 2NaOH \xrightarrow[340\ atm]{623\ K}$ Sodium phenoxide $\xrightarrow{HCl}$ Phenol

Q. 3. Explain the following with an example:

  (i) Kolbe's reaction

  (ii) Reimer-Tiemann reaction

  (iii) Williamson ether synthesis

  (iv) Fries rearrangement

Ans. (i) **Kolbe's reaction:** When phenol is treated with sodium hydroxide, sodium phenoxide is produced. This sodium phenoxide when treated with carbon dioxide, followed by acidification, undergoes electrophilic substitution to give ortho-hydroxybenzoic (salicylic acid) acid as the main product. This reaction is known as Kolbe's reaction.

Phenol $\xrightarrow{NaOH}$ Sodium phenoxide $\xrightarrow[(ii)\ H^+]{(i)\ CO_2}$ Ortho-hydroxybenzoic acid (Salicylic acid)

(ii) **Reimer-Tiemann reaction:** When phenol is treated with chloroform ($CHCl_3$) in the presence of sodium hydroxide, a –CHO group is introduced at the ortho position of the benzene ring.

Phenol $\xrightarrow{CHCl_3\ +\ aq.\ NaOH}$ Intermediate

This reaction is known as the Reimer-Tiemann reaction.

The intermediate is hydrolysed in the presence of alkalis to produce salicylaldehyde.

Intermediate $\xrightarrow{NaOH}$ $\xrightarrow{H^+}$ Salicylaldehyde

(iii) **Williamson ether synthesis:** Williamson ether synthesis is a laboratory method to prepare symmetrical and unsymmetrical ethers by allowing alkyl halides to react with sodium alkoxides.

$$R-X + R'-\ddot{O}Na \longrightarrow R-\ddot{O}-R' + NaX$$

Alkylhalide   Sodium alkoxide   Ether

This reaction involves S_N2 attack of the alkoxide ion on the alkyl halide. Better results are obtained in case of primary alkyl halides.

$$CH_3-CH(CH_3)-\ddot{O}Na + CH_3-Br \longrightarrow CH_3-\ddot{O}-CH(CH_3)-CH_3 + NaBr$$

If the alkyl halide is secondary or tertiary, then elimination competes over substitution.

(iv) **Fries rearrangement:** This is an important reaction which results in the formation of ketone from rearrangement of ester phenyl acetate when heated with anhydrous $AlCl_3$, the acyl group moves to *ortho* and *para* positions in the benzene ring.

Phenyl acetate $\xrightarrow[AlCl_3,\ D]{Anhydrous}$ *o*-hydroxyacetophenone $+$ *p*-hydroxyacetophenone

Q. 4. What is meant hydroboration-oxidation reaction ? Illustrate it with an example.

Ans. The addition of borane to an alkene followed by oxidation is known as the hydroboration-oxidation reaction. For example, propan-1-ol is produced by the hydroboration-oxidation reaction of propene. In this reaction, propene reacts with diborane $(BH_3)_2$ to form trialkyl borane as an addition product. This addition product is oxidised to alcohol by hydrogen peroxide in the presence of aqueous sodium hydroxide. As a result of hydroboration oxidation we get alcohols as addition product following Anti-Markovnikov's rule.

$$CH_3 — CH = CH_2 + (H + BH_2)_2 \xrightarrow{\text{THF}} CH_3 — \underset{\underset{H}{|}}{CH} — \underset{\underset{BH_2}{|}}{CH_2}$$

$$\xrightarrow{CH_3-CH=CH_2}$$

$$(CH_3 — CH_2 — CH_2)_3\, B \xleftarrow{CH_3-CH=CH_2} (CH_3 — CH_2 — CH_2)_2\, BH$$

$$\underset{H_2O \mid 3H_2O_2,\ OH}{\Big\downarrow}$$

$$\underset{\text{Propan-1-ol}}{3CH_3 — CH_2 — CH_2 — OH} + \underset{\text{Boric acid}}{B(OH)_3}$$

Q. 5. Write the reactions of Williamson synthesis of 2-ethoxy-3-methylpentane starting from ethanol and 3-methylpentan-2-ol.

Ans. In Williamson synthesis alkyl halide reacts with sodium salt of an alcohol. In this reaction, alkyl halides should be primary having the least steric hindrance, to avoid formation of an alkene. Hence, an alkyl halide is obtained from ethanol and alkoxide ion from 3-methylpentan-2-ol.

$$\underset{\text{Ethanol}}{C_2H_5OH} \xrightarrow{\text{HBr}} \underset{\text{Bromoethane}}{C_2H_5Br} + H_2O$$

$$\underset{\underset{\text{3-Methylpentan-2-ol}}{}}{CH_3 — CH_2 — \underset{\underset{CH_3}{|}}{CH} — \underset{\underset{OH}{|}}{CH} — CH_3} \xrightarrow{\text{Na}} \underset{\underset{\text{Sodium 3-Methylepentan-2-oxide}}{}}{CH_3 — CH_2 — \underset{\underset{CH_3}{|}}{CH} — \underset{\underset{CH_3}{|}}{CH} — ONa} + \tfrac{1}{2}H_2$$

$$CH_3 — CH_2 — \underset{\underset{CH_3}{|}}{CH} — \underset{\underset{CH_3}{|}}{CH} — ONa + C_2H_5Br \longrightarrow \underset{\underset{\text{2-Ethoxy-3-Methylpentane}}{}}{CH_3 — CH_2 — \underset{\underset{CH_3}{|}}{CH} — \underset{\underset{CH_3}{|}}{CH} — OC_2H_5} + NaBr$$

Chapter 12. Aldehydes, Ketones and Carboxylic Acids

Q. 1. Write chemical equation to illustrate Hell-Volhard-Zelinsky reaction.[*]

Ans. It is a reaction of a carboxylic acid (aliphatic) having one or more a-hydrogen atoms with halogen Cl_2 or Br_2 to produce a substituted halogen derivative.

$$\underset{\text{Propionic acid}}{CH_3CH_2COOH} \xrightarrow{Br_2,\ P} \underset{\alpha\text{-Bromopropionic acid}}{CH_3CHBrCOOH} + HBr$$

Q. 2. Describe the following reactions :

(i) Acetylation (FC)

(ii) Aldol condensation

Ans. (i) **Friedel-Crafts acylation or acetylation:** The treatment of a benzene ring or its substituent with acyl chloride (RCOCl) in presence of anhydrous aluminium chloride to replace one hydrogen of benzene ring with acyl group resulting in formation of a ketone is called Friedel-Crafts acylation or acetylation.

$$\underset{\text{Phenyl acetate}}{\text{(benzene with } CH_3)} + CH_3COCl \xrightarrow[\text{AlCl}_3]{\text{Anhydrous}} \underset{\text{2-Methyl acetophenone}}{\text{(benzene with } CH_3 \text{ and } C{-}CH_3)}$$

(ii) **Aldol condensation:** The reaction of an aldehyde or ketone having atleast one α-hydrogen atom in presence of dilute base like NaOH, to produce an adduct called aldol. On heating the aldol further gives an α, β-unsaturated aldehyde or ketone, this reaction is called aldol condensation.

---

[*] are board exam questions from previous years

$$CH_3 - CH_2 - CHO + CH_3CH_2CHO \xrightarrow[\text{NaOH}]{\text{dil.}} CH_3CH_2 - \overset{\displaystyle OH}{\underset{\underset{\underset{CH_3}{|}}{\underset{H}{|}}}{C}} - CH - CHO \xrightarrow[\Delta]{-H_2O}$$

(Aldol)

$$CH_3CH_2 - \underset{\underset{H}{|}}{C} = \underset{\underset{CH_3}{|}}{C} - CHO$$

α,β-unsaturated aldehyde

Q. 3. Describe the following:

    (i) Acetylation   (iii) Cross aldol condensation

    (ii) Cannizzaro reaction   (iv) Decarboxylation.

Ans. (i) Acetylation: The introduction of an acetyl functional group in place of active hydrogen in alcohols, amino acids or even other organic compounds is known as acetylation. It is usually carried out in the presence of a base such as pyridine, dimethylaniline, etc. Acetyl chloride and acetic anhydride are commonly used as acetylating agents.

For example, acetylation of ethanol produces ethyl acetate.

$$CH_3 - CH_2 - OH + CH_3COCl \xrightarrow{\text{Pyridine}} CH_3COOC_2H_5 + HCl$$
      Ethanol   Acetyl Chloride   Ethy lacetate

  (ii) **Cannizzaro reaction:** The self oxidation-reduction (disproportionation) reaction of aldehydes having no α-hydrogen atom on treatment with concentrated alkalis is known as the Cannizzaro reaction. In this reaction, two molecules of aldehydes participate where one is reduced to alcohol and the other is oxidised to carboxylic acid.

For example, when ethanol is treated with concentrated potassium hydroxide, ethanol and potassium ethanoate are produced.

$$2 \overset{\displaystyle O}{\underset{\underset{CH_3 \quad H}{\diagup \diagdown}}{\overset{\|}{C}}} + \text{Conc. KOH} \longrightarrow CH_3 - CH_2 - OH + CH_3COOK$$

      Ethanal   Ethanol   Potassium ethanoate

(iii) **Cross aldol condensation:** When aldol condensation is carried out between two different aldehydes, or two different ketones, or an aldehyde and a ketone, then the reaction is called a cross-aldol condensation. If both the reactants contain α-hydrogen, four compounds are obtain as products. Atleast one of the reactants should have an α-hydrogen.

For example, ethanal and propanal reacts to give four products.

$$CH_3CHO + CH_3CH_2CHO$$
     Ethanol   Propanal

$$\Delta \downarrow \text{NaOH}$$

$$CH_3 - CH = CH - CHO + CH_3CH_2 - CH = \underset{\underset{CH_3}{|}}{C} - CHO$$
   But-2-enal   2-methylpent-2-enal

| (From two molecules of ethanal)   (From two molecules of propanal) |

(Self-aldol products)

$$CH_3 - \underset{\underset{CH_3}{|}}{C} = C - CHO + CH_3CH_2 - CH = CHCHO$$
 2-methylbut-2-enal   Pent-2-enal

(From one molecule of ethanal and one molecule of propanal)

(Cross-aldol products)

(iv) **Decarboxylation:** Decarboxylation refers to the reaction in which carboxylic acids lose carbon dioxide to form hydrocarbons when their sodium salts are heated with soda-lime.

$$CH_3 - COONa \xrightarrow[\Delta]{\text{Soda-lime (mixture of NaOH and CaO in 3 : 1 ratio)}}$$

Sodium ethanoate

$$CH_4 + NaCO_3$$
Methane

Decarbonylation also takes place when aqueous solutions of alkali metal salts of carbonylic acids are electrolysed. This electrolytic process is known as Kolbe's electrolysis.

Chapter 13. Amines

Q. 1. Write chemical equations to represent:[*]
    (i) Gattermann reaction
    (ii) Mendius reaction.

Ans. (i) **Gattermann reaction:** In this reaction, benzene diazonium chloride is treated with copper powder and halogen acid (HCl or HBr) to give haloarene as the product.

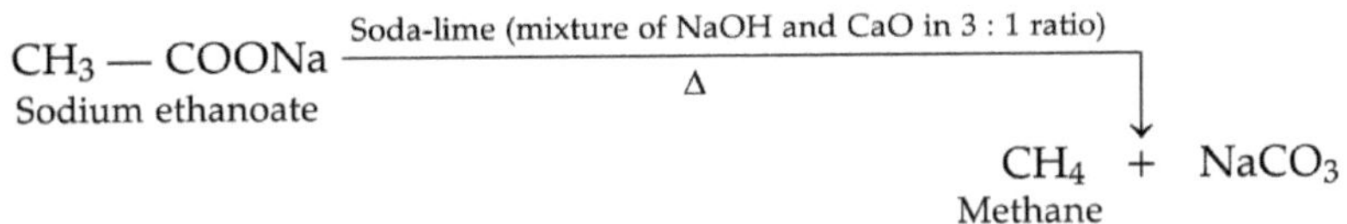

(ii) **Mendius reaction:** In this reaction an alkyl or aryl cyanide is reduced with sodium mercury amalgam in presence of ethyl alcohol to produce primary amines.

$$CH_3C \equiv N + 4[H] \xrightarrow[C_2H_5OH]{Na—Hg} CH_3CH_2NH_2$$
  Methyl cyanide   Ethylamine

Q. 2. Write short notes on the following:
    (i) Carbylamine reaction
    (ii) Diazotisation
    (iii) Hoffmann's bromamide reaction
    (iv) Coupling reaction
    (v) Ammonolysis
    (vi) Acetylation
    (vii) Gabriel phthalmide synthesis

Ans. (i) **Carbylamine reaction:** Also called as isocyanide reaction which is used as a test for the identification of primary amines. When aliphatic and aromatic primary amines are heated with chloroform and ethanolic potassium hydroxide, carbylamines (or isocyanides) are formed. These carbylamines have very unpleasant odours. Secondary and tertiary amines do not respond to this test.

$$R - NH_2 + CHCl_3 + 3KOH \text{ (alc.)} \xrightarrow{\Delta} R - NC + 3KCl + 3H_2O$$
  Primary   Chloroform   Potassium   Carbylamine
  amine   hydroxide

For example,

$$CH_3 - NH_2 + CHCl_3 + 3KOH \text{ (alc.)} \xrightarrow{\Delta} CH_3 - NC + 3KCl + 3H_2O$$
  Methanamine   Methyl carbylamine
                                       or methyl isocyanide

(ii) **Diazotisation:** Aromatic primary amines react with nitrous acid (prepared in situ from $NaNO_2$ and a mineral acid such as HCl) at low temperature (273-278 K) to form diazonium salts. This conversion of aromatic primary amines into diazonium salts is known as diazotisation. For example, on treatment with $NaNO_2$ and HCl at 273-278 K, aniline produces benzene diazonium chloride, with NaCl and H_2O as by-products.

(iii) **Hofmann bromamide reaction:** When an amide is treated with bromine in an aqueous or ethanolic solution of sodium hydroxide, a primary amine with one carbon atom less than the original amide is produced. This degradation reaction is known as Hoffmann bromamide reaction. This reaction involves the migration of an alkyl or aryl group from the carbonyl carbon atom of the amide to the nitrogen atom. Carboxylic group leaves as metal carbonate by-product.

$$\underset{\text{Amide}}{R - \overset{\overset{\displaystyle O}{\|}}{C} - NH_2} + Br_2 + 4NaOH \longrightarrow \underset{\substack{\text{Primary} \\ \text{amine}}}{R - NH_2} + \underset{\substack{\text{Sodium} \\ \text{carbonate}}}{Na_2CO_3} + 2NaBr + 2H_2O$$

For example,

$$\underset{\text{Benzamide}}{C_6H_5 - \overset{\overset{\displaystyle O}{\|}}{C} - NH_2} + Br_2 + 4NaOH \longrightarrow \underset{\text{Aniline}}{C_6H_5 - NH_2} + Na_2CO_3 + 2NaBr + 2H_2O$$

(iv) Coupling reaction: The reaction of joining two aromatic rings through the $- N = N -$ bond is known as coupling reaction. Arene diazonium salts such as benzene diazonium salts react with phenol or aromatic amines to form coloured azo compounds, *i.e.,* dyes.

Benzene diazonium chloride + Phenol $\xrightarrow{OH^-}$ *p*-Hydroxyazobenzene (Orange dye) $+ Cl^- + 2H_2O$

Benzene diazonium chloride + Aniline $\xrightarrow{OH^-}$ *p*-Aminozobenzene (Yellow dye) $+ Cl^- + 2H_2O$

It can be observed that, the para-positions of phenol and aniline are coupled with the diazonium salt. This reaction proceeds through electrophilic substitution.

(v) Ammonolysis: When an alkyl or benzyl halide is allowed to react with an ethanolic solution of ammonia, it undergoes nucleophilic substitution reaction in which the halogen atom is replaced by an amino ($- NH_2$) group. This process of cleavage of the carbon-halogen bond is known as ammonolysis.

$$\underset{\substack{\text{Ammonia} \\ \text{(Nucleophile)}}}{NH_3 \text{ (alc.)}} + \underset{\text{Alkyl halide}}{R - X} \longrightarrow \underset{\substack{\text{Substituted} \\ \text{ammonium salt}}}{R - \overset{+}{N}H_3\overset{-}{X}}$$

When this substituted ammonium salt is treated with a strong base such as sodium hydroxide, amine is obtained.

$$R - \overset{+}{N}H_3\overset{-}{X} + NaOH \longrightarrow \underset{\text{Amine}}{R - NH_2} + H_2O + NaX$$

Though primary amine is produced as the major product, this process produces a mixture of primary, secondary and tertiary amines and also a quaternary ammonium salt as shown.

$$\underset{(1°)}{RNH_2} \xrightarrow{RX} \underset{(2°)}{R_2NH} \xrightarrow{RX} \underset{(3°)}{R_3N} \xrightarrow{RX} \underset{\substack{\text{Quaternary} \\ \text{ammonium salt}}}{R_4\overset{+}{N}\overset{-}{X}}$$

(vi) Acetylation: Acetylation (or ethanoylation) is the process of introducing an acetyl group into a molecule.

$$\underset{\text{Acetyl group}}{\overset{\overset{\displaystyle O}{\|}}{C} \diagdown R}$$

Aliphatic and aromatic primary and secondary amines undergo acetylation reaction by nucleophilic substitution when treated with acid chlorides, anhydrides or esters. This reaction involves the replacement of the hydrogen atom of $- NH_2$ or $- NH$ group by the acetyl group, which in turn leads to the production of amides. To shift the equilibrium to the right hand side, the HCl formed during the reaction is removed as soon as it is formed. This reaction is carried out in the presence of a base (such as pyridine) which is stronger than the amine.

When amines react with benzoyl chloride, the reaction is also known as benzoylation. For example,

(vii) **Gabriel phthalimide synthesis:** Gabriel phthalimide synthesis is a very useful method for the preparation of aliphatic primary amines. It involves the treatment of phthalimide with ethanolic potassium hydroxide to form potassium salt of phthalimide. This salt is further heated with alkyl halide, followed by alkaline hydrolysis to yield the corresponding primary amine.

Q. 1. **Hexagonal close-packing and Cubic close-packing.**

Ans. 2-D hexagonal close-packing contains two types of triangular voids (a and b) as shown in figure 1. Let us call this 2-D structure as layer A. Now, particles are kept in the voids present in layer A (it can be easily observed from figures 2 and 3 that only one of the voids will be occupied in the process, *i.e.,* either *a* or *b*)

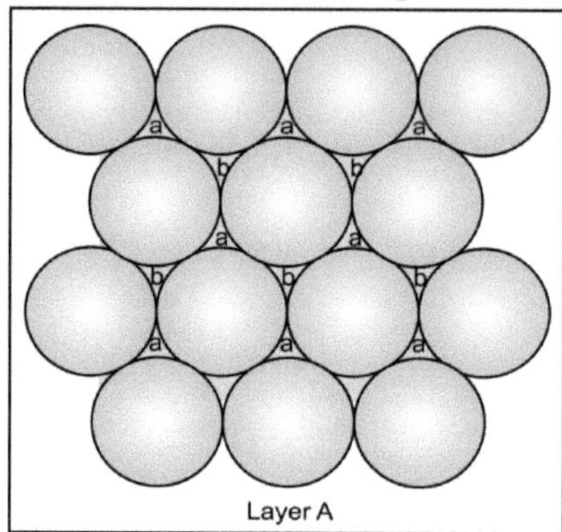

Fig. 1

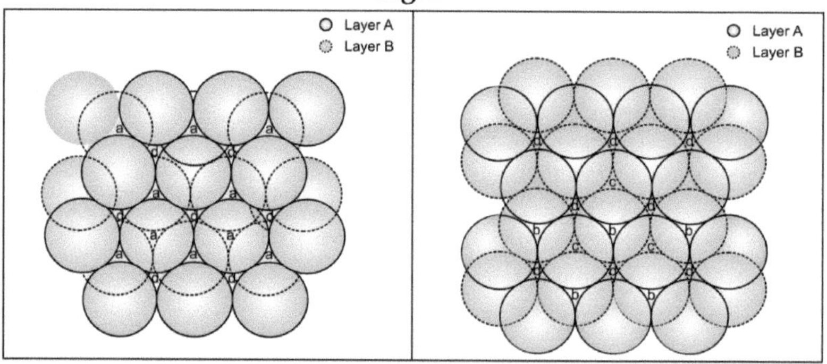

Fig. 2   **Fig. 3**

Now, the next layer can be placed over layer B in 2 ways.

Case 1 : When the third layer (layer C) is placed over the second one (layer B) in such a manner that the spheres of layer C occupy the tetrahedral voids c. In this case we get hexagonal close-packing. This is shown in figure. 4. surrounded by 4 sphere. The spheres present in layer C are present directly above the spheres of layer A. Hence, we can say that the layers in hexagonal close-packing are arranged in an ABAB..... pattern.

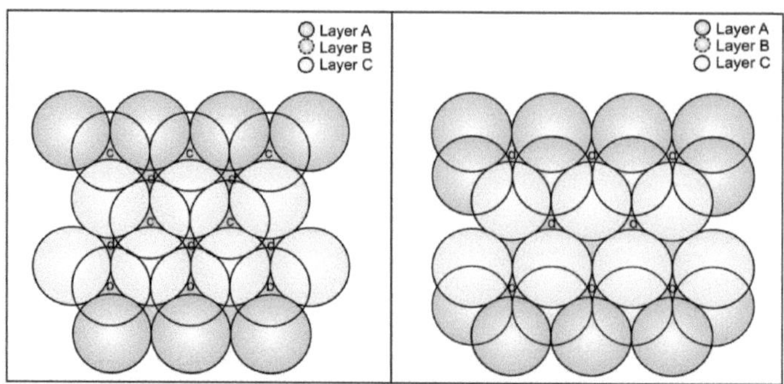

Fig. 4.1   **Fig. 4.2**

Case 2 : When the third layer (layer C) is placed over layer B in such a manner that the spheres of layer C occupy the octahedral voids d.

In this case we get cubic close-packing. (Figure 5.1, 5.2). It can be observed from the figures 5 that the arrangement of particles in layer C is completely different from that in layers A or B. When the fourth-layer is kept over the third layer, the arrangement of particles in this layer is similar to that in layer A. Hence, we can say that the layers in cubic close packing are arranged in an ABCABC..... pattern.

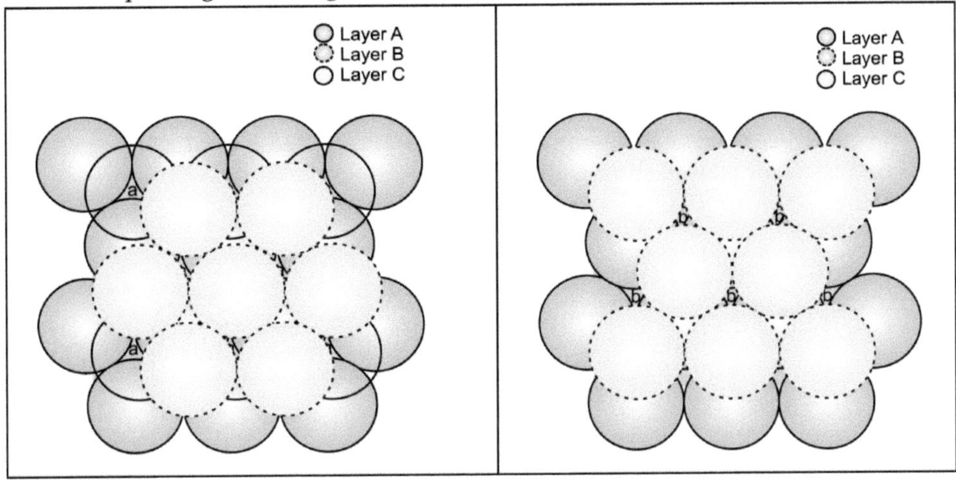

Fig. 5.1   **Fig. 5.2**

The side views of *hcp* and *ccp* are given in figures 6.1 and 6.2 respectively.

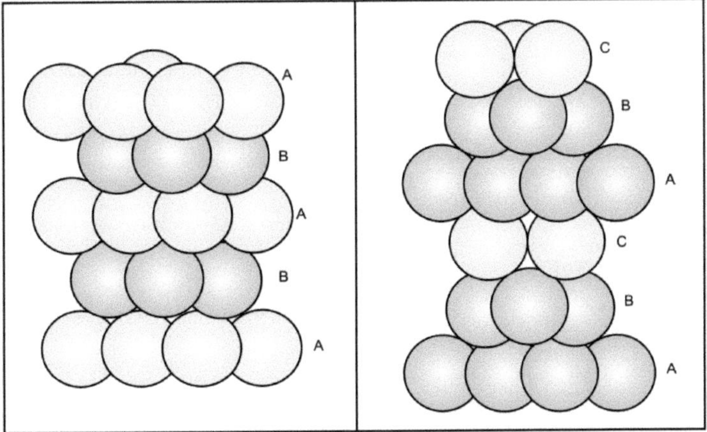

Fig. 6.1   **Fig. 6.2**

Chapter 5. Surface Chemistry

Q. 1. **Explain the process of removal of carbon and dust particles from smoke. With the help of a diagram.**

Ans.

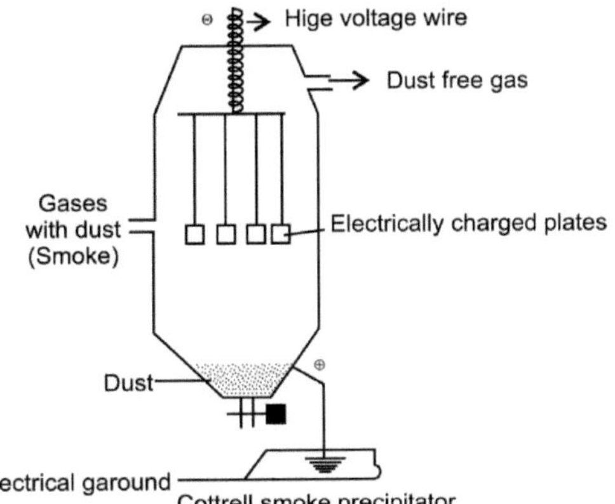

Smoke contains electrically charged particles basically unburnt carbon and dust. When it is passed through cottrell smoke precipitator, which contains electrically charged plates, the charged particles of smoke gets attracted to the plates and get deposited there. The smoke coming out of the chimney will now be free from carbon particles and dust and hence will not cause pollution.

Chapter 6. General Principles and Processes of Isolation of Elements

Q. 1. How is ammonia manufactured industrially? Give the diagram for the process.

Ans. Ammonia is prepared on a large-scale by the Haber's process.

$$N_2(g) + 3H_2(g) \longrightarrow 2NH_3(g) \quad \Delta_f H° = -46.1 \text{ kJ/mol}$$

The optimum conditions for manufacturing ammonia are:

(i)   Pressure (around 200×10^5 Pa).

(ii) Temperature (4700 K).

(iii) Catalyst such as iron oxide with, small amounts of Al_2O_3 and K_2O.

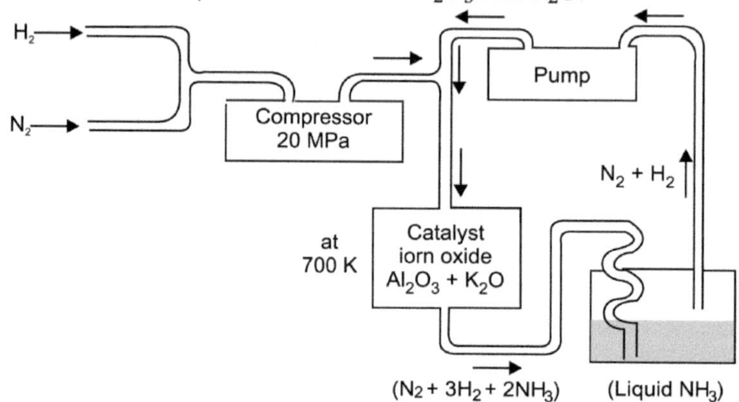

Chapter 7. *p*-Block Elements

Q. 1. Draw the structure of SF_4 and XeF_4.[*]

Ans. Lewis dot structures:

$$SF_4 \rightarrow \text{F:S:F (with F above and F below)}$$

4 bond pair, 1 lone pair

$$XeF_4 \rightarrow \text{F:Xe:F (with F below)}$$

4 bond pair, 1 lone pair

Q. 2. Draw shape of sulphuric acid.[*]

Ans.

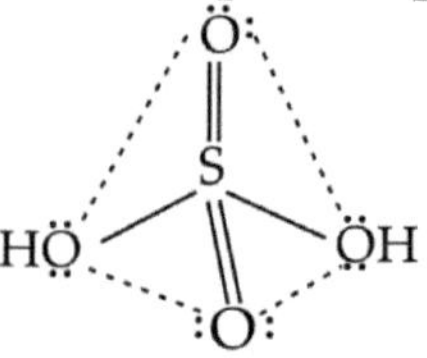

Tetrahedral structure of sulphuric acid (H_2SO_4)

Q. 3. Draw the shape of XeF_4.[*]

Ans.

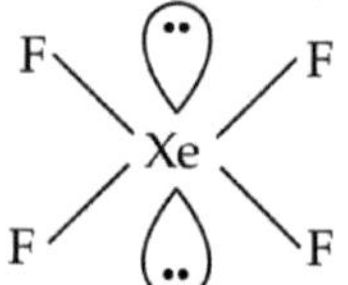

Square planar

Q. 4. Draw the structure of BrF_3.[*]

Ans.

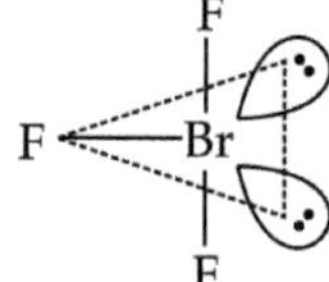

T-shaped molecule

Q. 5. **Draw structure of XeF$_2$ molecule.***

Ans.

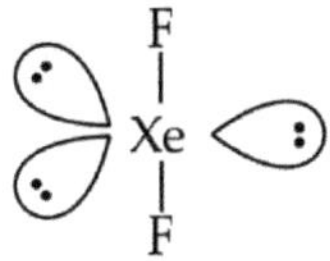

(Linear)

Q. 6. **Draw the structure of:***

    (i)   BrF$_5$ (ii) H$_2$S$_2$O$_7$.

Ans. (i)

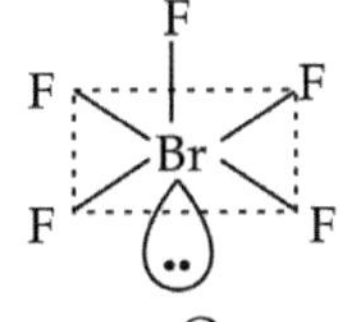

Square pyramidal

    (ii)

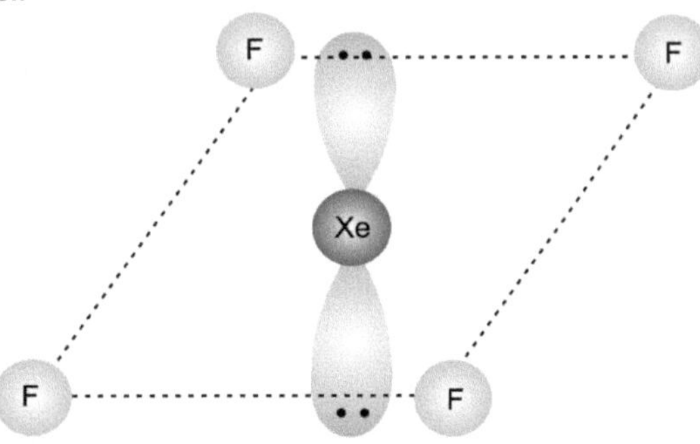

Q. 7. **Give the formula and describe the structure of a noble gas species which is isostructural with:**

    (i)   ICl$_4^-$ (ii) IBr$_2^-$ (iii) BrO$_3^-$

Ans. (i) XeF$_4$ is isoelectronic with ICl$_4^-$ and has square planar geometry.

       ICl$_4^-$ has $(7 + 4 \times 7 + 1 = 36)$

       electrons same as XeF$_4$.

       $(8 + 4 \times 7 = 36)$ electrons..

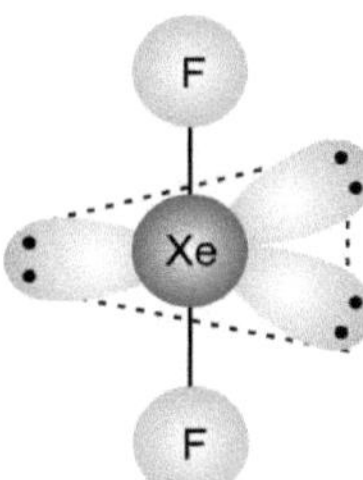

    (ii) XeF$_2$ is isoelectronic to IBr$_2^-$ and has a linear structure.

        In IBr$_2^-$ ion the central I atom has 8 valency electrons $(7 + 1)$ and Br$_2$ has $7 \times 2 = 14$. *i.e.*, $8 + 14 = 22$ electrons

        XeF$_2$ has $(8 + 7 \times 2 = 22)$ electron

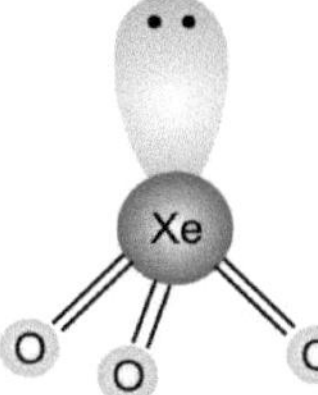

    (iii) XeO$_3$ is isostructural to BrO$_3^-$ and has a pyramidal molecular structure.

        BrO$_3^-$ has $(7 + 1 + 3 \times 6 = 26)$ electrons

        and XeO$_3$ has $(8 + 3 \times 6 = 26)$ electrons.

Chapter 9. Coordination Compounds

Q. 1. Draw the structure of $[PtCl_3(C_2H_4)]$. *

Ans. The complex compound name is Zeise's salt. Its an organometallic compound.

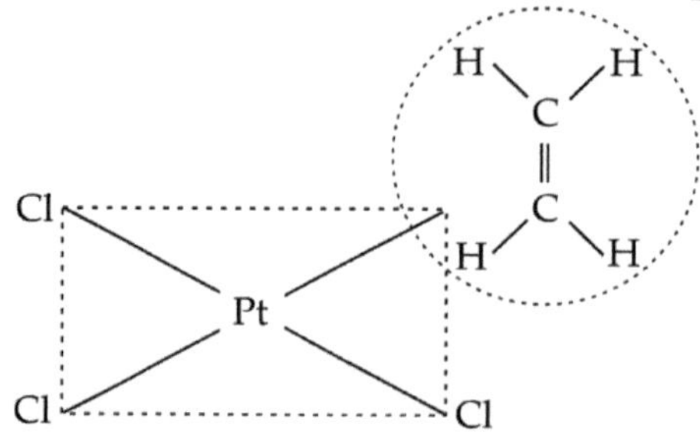

π-bond between the metal atom (Pt) and the $\!>\!C = C\!<$ bond of ethene.

Q. 2. Draw the structures of isomers of $[Pt(NH_3)_2Cl_2]$. *

Ans. The coordination compound has cis and trans geometric isomers.

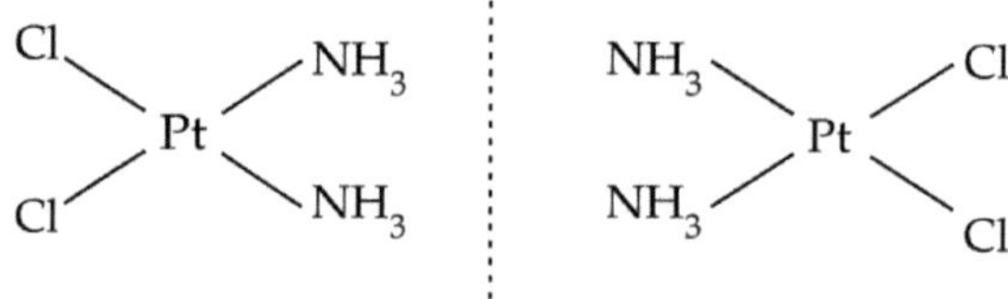

cis-form (*cis*-platin), (yellow), aquare planar

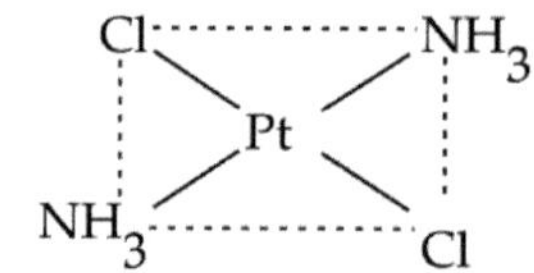

trans-isomer, square planar

Q. 3. Draw structures of geometric isomers of $[Fe(NH_3)_2(CN)_4]$.

Ans.

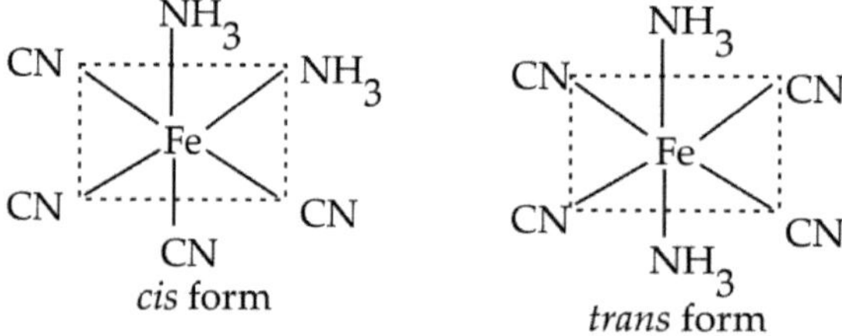

Q. 4. Draw figure to show the splitting of d-orbitals in an octahedral crystal field.

Ans.

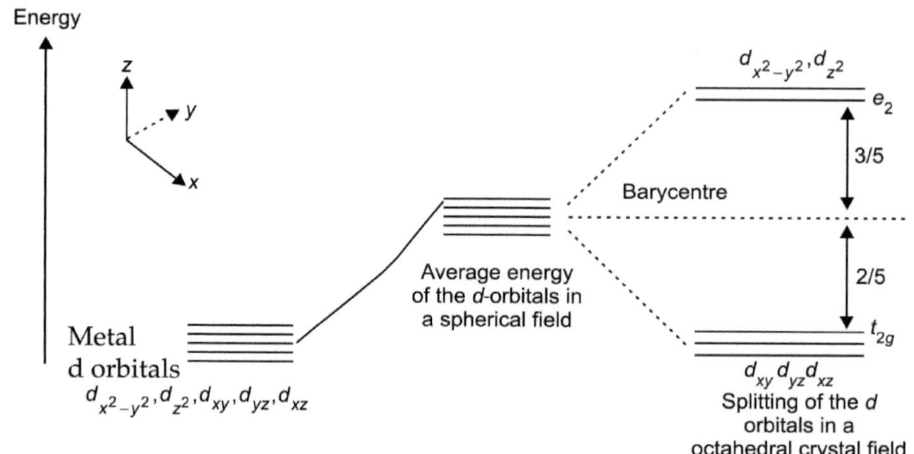

The splitting of the d-orbitals in an octahedral field takes place in such a way that $d_{x^2-y^2}$ d_{z^2} experiences a rise in energy and forms the e_g level, while d_{xy}, d_{yz} and d_{zx} experience a fall in energy and forms the t_{2g} level. This is because ligands approach direct through coordinates, hence orbitals which are oriented over-coordinates face stronger repulsion *i.e.*, $d_{x^2-y^2}$ and d_{z^2} repelled more than d_{xy}, d_{yz} and d_{zx}.

Chapter 10. Haloalkanes and Haloarenes

Q. 1. **Write the structure of the compound 1-Bromo-4-sec-butyl-2-methyl benzene?**

Ans.

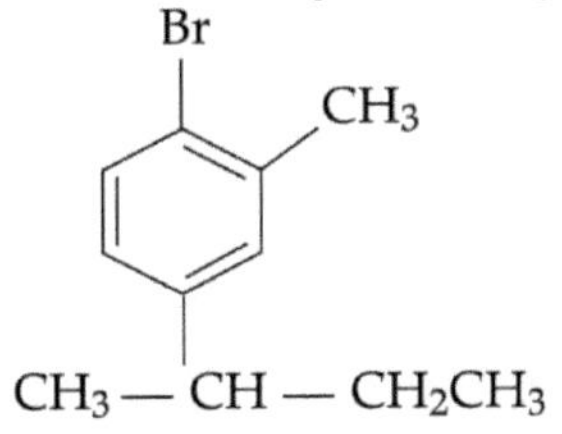

Chapter 11. Alcohols, Phenols and Ethers

Q. 1. **Draw the structure of the following:***

(i) 2-methylpropan-2-ol   (ii) 1, 2-Dimethoxy ethane

Ans. (i) $CH_3 - \underset{\underset{CH_3}{|}}{\overset{\overset{CH_3}{|}}{C}} - OH$

(ii) $CH_3 - O - CH_2 - CH_2 - O - CH_3$

Q. 2. **Give the structures of the following A, B and C in the given reactions:***

$$CH_3Br \xrightarrow{KCN} A \xrightarrow{LiAlH_4} B \xrightarrow[273K]{HNO_2} C$$

Ans. $CH_3Br \xrightarrow{KCN} \underset{\text{Methyl cyanide}}{CH_3CN} \xrightarrow{LAH} \underset{\text{Ethylamine}}{CH_3CH_2NH_2} \xrightarrow[273K]{HNO_2} \underset{\text{Ethanol}}{CH_3CH_2OH}$

Q. 3. **Write the structures of the main products in the following reactions:***

(i) $\xrightarrow{NaBH_4}$

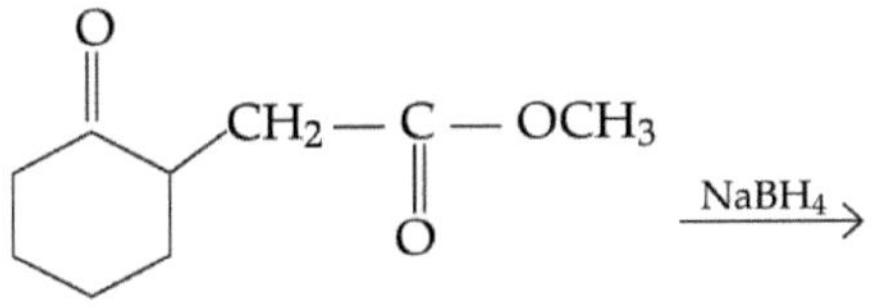

(ii) $CH=CH_2$ $+ H_2O \xrightarrow{H^+}$

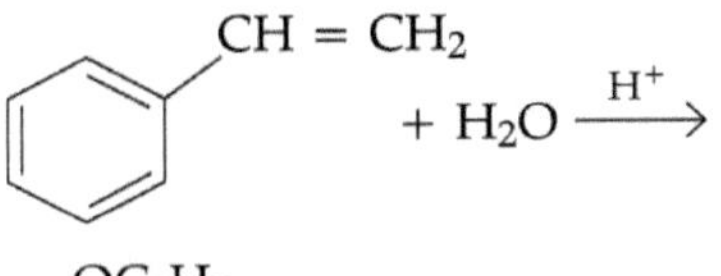

(iii) OC_2H_5 $+ HI \longrightarrow$

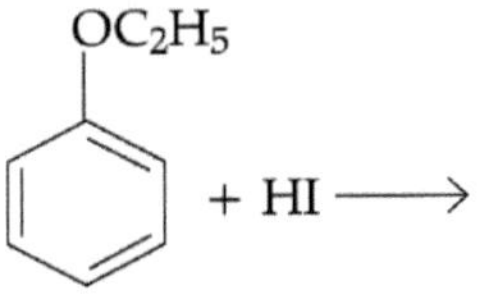

Ans. (i) Sodium borohydride doesn't reduce esters, so product would be,

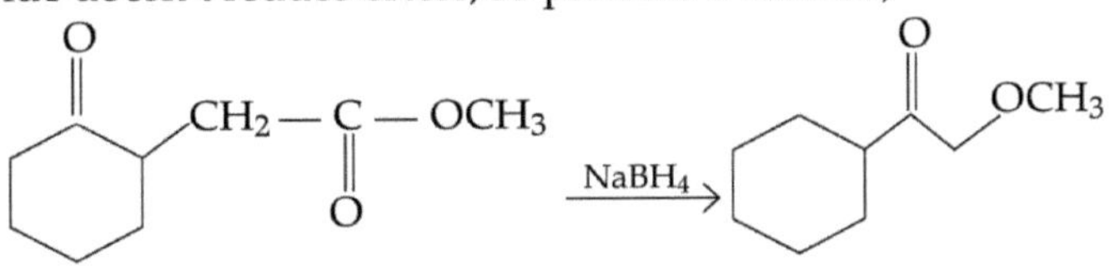

(ii)

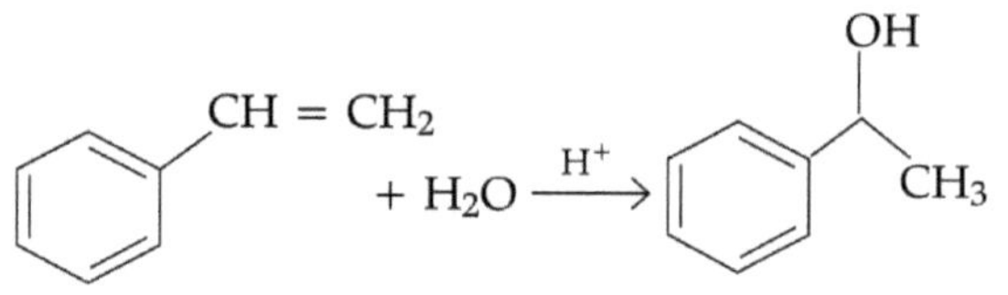

$$\underset{\text{(styrene)}}{C_6H_5-CH=CH_2} + H_2O \xrightarrow{H^+} C_6H_5-\underset{\underset{\displaystyle CH_3}{|}}{\overset{\overset{\displaystyle OH}{|}}{CH}}$$

(iii)

$$\underset{\text{Phenyl ethyl ether}}{C_6H_5-OC_2H_5} + HI \longrightarrow \underset{\text{Phenol}}{C_6H_5-OH} + \underset{\text{Ethyl iodide}}{C_2H_5}$$

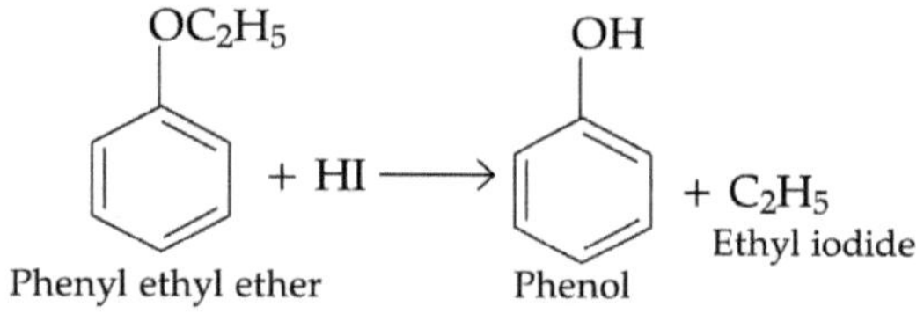

Chapter 12. Aldehydes, Ketones and Carboxylic Acids

Q. 1. Write the structure of 3-oxopentanal?*

Ans.

$$CH_3-CH_2-\overset{\overset{\displaystyle O}{\|}}{C}-CH_2-CHO$$

Q. 2. Draw the structure of 3-methyl-pentanol.*

Ans.

$$CH_3-CH_2-\underset{\underset{\displaystyle CH_3}{|}}{CH}-CH_2-CHO$$

Q. 3. Give the structures of :

    (i) Methylvinyl ketone

    (ii) Crotonaldehyde.

Ans. (i) $CH_2 = CHCOCH_3$

    (ii) $CH_3 - CH = CH - CHO$

Q. 4. Write the structure of A and B in the following reactions:

    (i) $CH_3COCl \xrightarrow{H_2,\ Pd-BaSO_4} A \xrightarrow{H_2N-OH} B$ *

    (ii) $CH_3MgBr \xrightarrow[2.H_3O^+]{1.CO_2} A \xrightarrow{PCl_5} B$

Ans. (i) $CH_3COCl \xrightarrow[\text{Rosenmund reduction}]{H_2,\ Pd-BaSO_4} \underset{(A)}{CH_3CHO} \xrightarrow{H_2N-OH} \underset{(B)}{CH_3-\overset{\overset{\displaystyle H}{|}}{C}=NOH}$

    (ii) $CH_3MgBr \xrightarrow[2.H_3O^+]{1.CO_2} \underset{(A)}{CH_3COOH} \xrightarrow{PCl_5} \underset{(B)}{CH_3COCl}$

Q. 5. Write the structures of the following compounds.

    (i)   α-Methoxypropionaldehyde

    (ii) 3-Hydroxybutanal

    (iii) 2-Hydroxycyclopentane carbaldehyde

    (iv) 4-Oxopentanal

    (v) Di-sec-butyl ketone

    (vi) 4-Fluoroacetophenone.

Ans. (i) $H_3C-\underset{\underset{\displaystyle OCH_3}{|}}{CH}-\overset{\overset{\displaystyle O}{\|}}{C}-H$

    (ii) $H_3C-\underset{\underset{\displaystyle OH}{|}}{CH}-CH_2-\overset{\overset{\displaystyle O}{\|}}{C}-H$

    (iii) 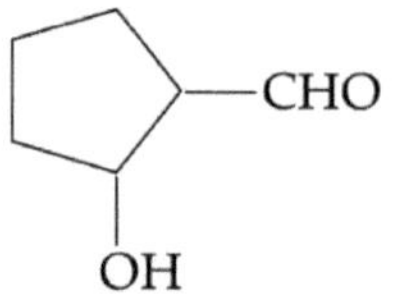 2-hydroxycyclopentane carbaldehyde (cyclopentane ring with —CHO and —OH substituents)

(iv) 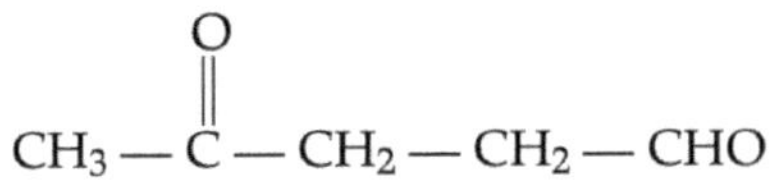 $CH_3 - \overset{\displaystyle O}{\overset{\|}{C}} - CH_2 - CH_2 - CHO$

(v) 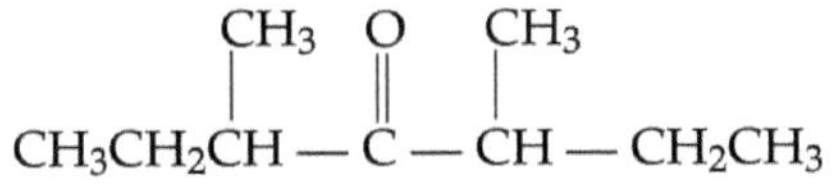 $CH_3CH_2\overset{\displaystyle CH_3}{\overset{|}{CH}} - \overset{\displaystyle O}{\overset{\|}{C}} - \overset{\displaystyle CH_3}{\overset{|}{CH}} - CH_2CH_3$

(vi) 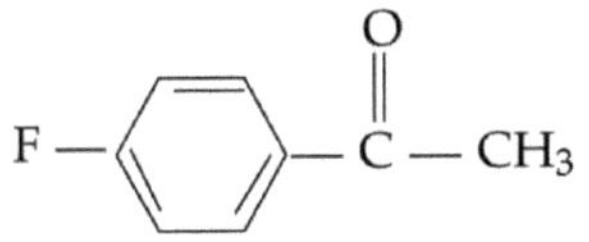 $F - \langle \text{benzene} \rangle - \overset{\displaystyle O}{\overset{\|}{C}} - CH_3$

Q. 6. Draw structures of the following derivatives:

(i) The 2, 4-dinitrophenylhydrazone of benzaldehyde

(ii) Cyclopropanone oxime

(iii) Acetaldehyde dimethylacetal

(iv) The semicarbazone of cyclobutanone

(v) The ethylene ketal of hexan-3-one

(vi) The methyl hemiacetal of formaldehyde.

Ans. (i) 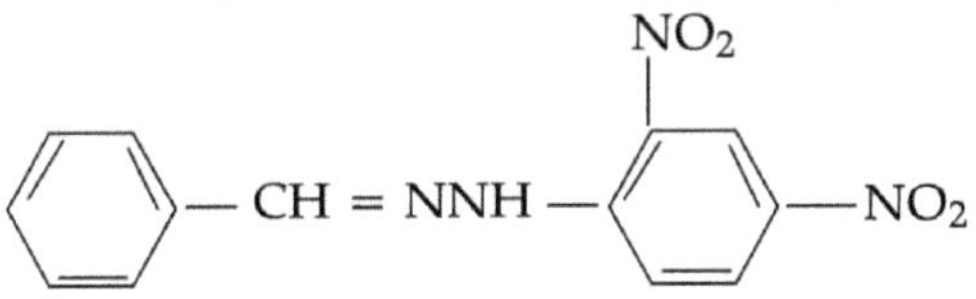 $\langle \rangle - CH = NNH - \langle \rangle - NO_2$ (with NO_2 on ring)

(ii) 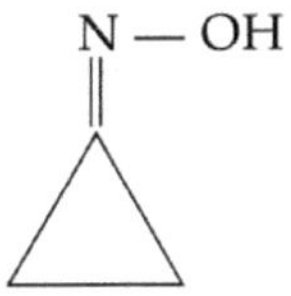 (cyclopropane with $N - OH$)

(iii) 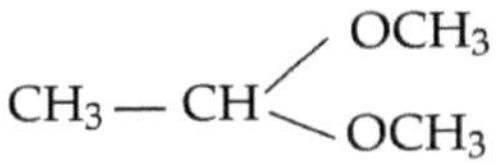 $CH_3 - CH\underset{OCH_3}{\overset{OCH_3}{\diagdown}}$

(iv) 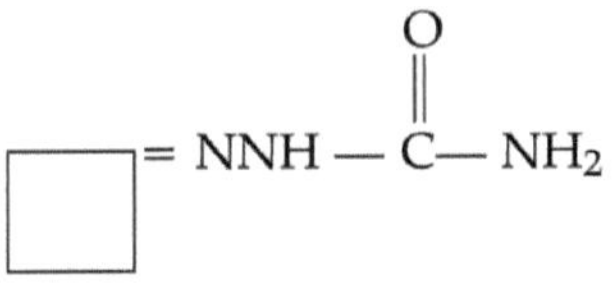 (cyclobutane) $= NNH - \overset{\displaystyle O}{\overset{\|}{C}} - NH_2$

(v) 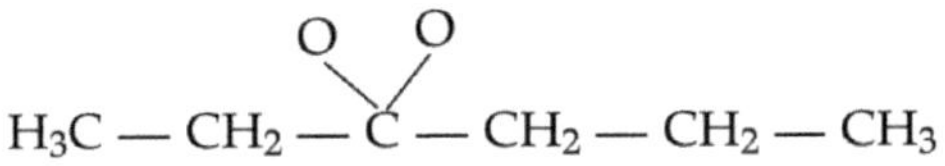 $H_3C - CH_2 - \overset{\overset{\displaystyle O \quad O}{\diagup\diagdown}}{C} - CH_2 - CH_2 - CH_3$

(vi) 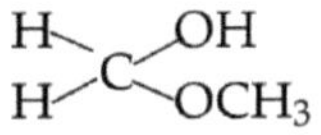 $\overset{H}{\underset{H}{\diagdown}}C\overset{OH}{\underset{OCH_3}{\diagup}}$

Q. 7. Write the structures of products of the following reactions :

(i) 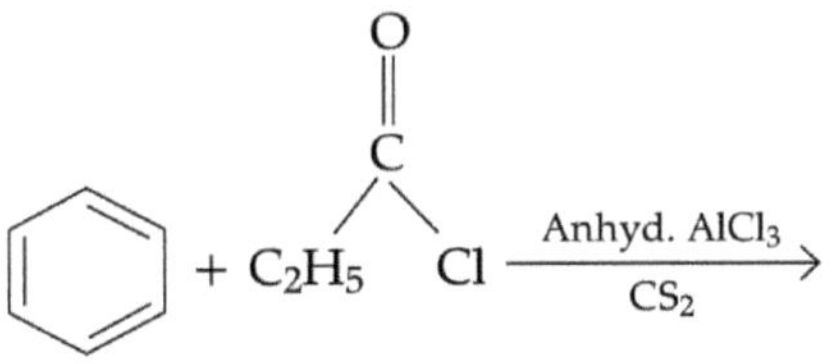 $\langle \text{benzene} \rangle + C_2H_5 \quad \overset{\displaystyle O}{\overset{\|}{C}} \quad Cl \xrightarrow[\text{CS}_2]{\text{Anhyd. AlCl}_3}$

(ii) $(C_6H_5CH_2)_2Cd + 2CH_3COCl \longrightarrow$

(iii) $H_3C - C \equiv C - H \xrightarrow{Hg^{2+},\ H_2SO_4}$

(iv) 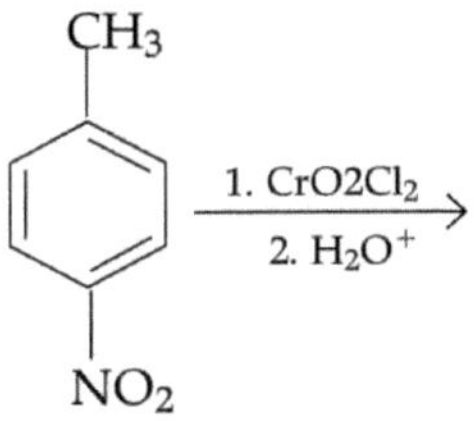 $\langle \text{toluene with } CH_3 \text{ and } NO_2 \rangle \xrightarrow[\text{2. H}_2O^+]{\text{1. CrO2Cl}_2}$

Ans. (i) 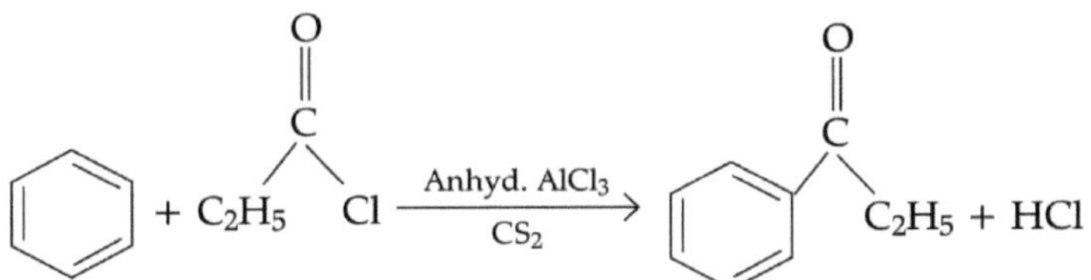 $\langle \text{Benzene} \rangle + C_2H_5 \quad \overset{\displaystyle O}{\overset{\|}{C}} \quad Cl \xrightarrow[\text{CS}_2]{\text{Anhyd. AlCl}_3} \langle \rangle \overset{\displaystyle O}{\overset{\|}{C}} C_2H_5 + HCl$

Propiophenone (or)
ethylphenyl ketone

(ii) 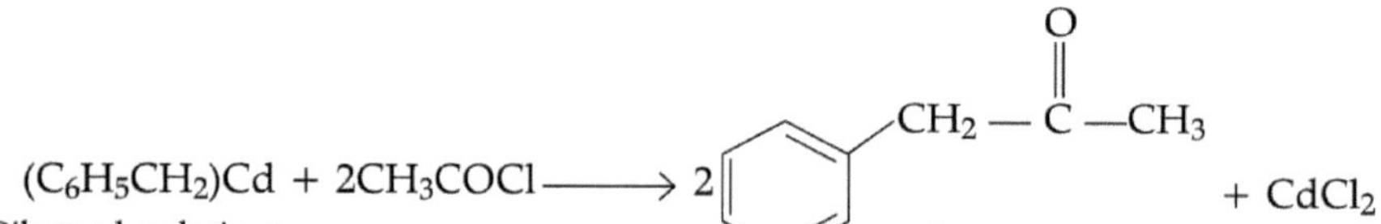 $(C_6H_5CH_2)Cd + 2CH_3COCl \longrightarrow$ 2 [benzene ring]$CH_2 - \overset{\overset{\displaystyle O}{\|}}{C} - CH_3$ $+ CdCl_2$

Dibenzyl cadmium

1-Phenylpropanone

or

Benzylmethyl ketone

(iii) $H_3C - C \equiv C - H \xrightarrow{Hg^{2+},\ dil.\ H_2SO_4}$ $\left[H_3C - \overset{\overset{\displaystyle OH}{|}}{C} = CH_2 \right]$ $\xrightarrow[\text{tautomerism)}]{\substack{\text{Tautomerises} \\ \text{(ketenol}}}$ $H_3C - \overset{\overset{\displaystyle O}{\|}}{C} = CH_3$

Propyne

(Enol)

Propanone/Acetone

(iv) 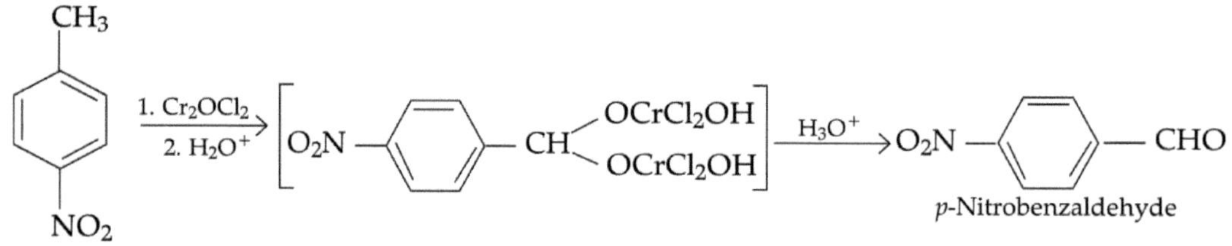 [p-Nitro toluene structure with CH_3 top, NO_2 bottom] $\xrightarrow[\text{2. } H_2O^+]{\text{1. } Cr_2OCl_2}$ $\left[O_2N - \text{[benzene ring]} - CH \overset{OCrCl_2OH}{\underset{OCrCl_2OH}{<}} \right]$ $\xrightarrow{H_3O^+}$ $O_2N - \text{[benzene ring]} - CHO$

CH₃ / NO₂
p-Nitro toluene

p-Nitrobenzaldehyde

Chapter 13. Amines

Q. 1. Write the structure of 2-amino toluene?

Ans. 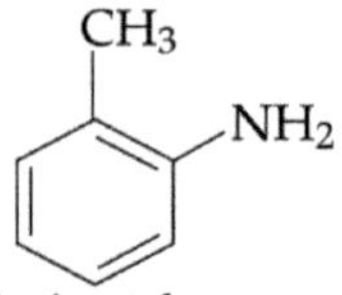 [benzene ring with CH_3 and NH_2 substituents]

2-Amino toluene

Chapter 14. Biomolecules

Q. 1. Draw the zwitter ion form of amino acetic acid.*

Ans. 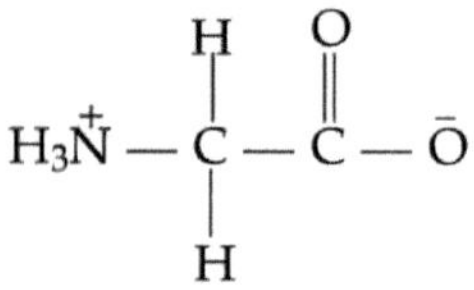 $H_3\overset{+}{N} - \overset{\overset{\displaystyle H}{|}}{\underset{\underset{\displaystyle H}{|}}{C}} - \overset{\overset{\displaystyle O}{\|}}{C} - \bar{O}$

Zwitter ion of amino acetic acid

❑❑

Differentiate Between or Derivations

|Set 11|

Q. 1. Differentiate between Isotropic and Anisotropic solids.

Ans.

	Isotropic	Anisotropic
1.	Physical properties have same value irrespective of the direction, side or angle of measurement than that property of solid is called isotropy.	Physical properties such as refractive index, resistance, etc., gives different values on measuring from different directions in the same crystal this property is called anisotropy.
2.	Short range order. Example: Amorphous solids.	Long range order. Example: Crystalline solids.

Q. 2. Distinguish between Schottky and Frenkel defect.

Ans.

	Schottky defect	Frenkel defect
1.	Ions are missing from the normal sites in crystal lattice.	Ions do not leave the lattice but occupy positions eleswhere in it.
2.	The density of the crystal decreases.	Density of crystal remains unaffected.
3.	No change in the dielectric constant values.	The value of dielectric constant increases.
4.	Generally, solids with high coordination number exhibits such defects. Example: NaCl, KCl, CsCl, KBr	Solids with low coordination number exhibits such defects. Example: AgCl, AgBr, Agl
5.	Cations and Anions have similar size.	Anions are larger than cations. Hence cations can occupy interstitial sites.

Q. 3. Distinguish between:
  (i)   Hexagonal and Monoclinic unit cells
  (ii) Face-centred and End-centred unit cells.

Ans. (i) **Hexagonal unit cell:** For a hexagonal unit cell,

$$a = b \neq c$$

and

$$\alpha = \beta = 90°$$

$$\gamma = 120°$$

Monoclinic unit cell: For a monoclinic cell,

$$a \neq b \neq c$$

and

$$a = \gamma = 90°$$

$$\beta \neq 90°$$

  (ii) **Face-centered unit cell:** In a face-centred unit cell, the constituent particles are present at the corners and one at the centre of each face.

  End-centered unit cell: An end-centred unit cell contains particles at the corners and one at the centre of any two opposite faces.

Q. 4. How will you distinguish between the following pairs of terms:
  (i)   Crystal lattice and Unit cell.
  (ii) Tetrahedral void and Octahedral void.

Ans. (i) The diagrammatic representation of the constituent particles (atoms, ions or molecules) present in a crystal in a regular three-dimensional arrangement is called crystal lattice.

A unit cell is the smallest three-dimensional portion of a crystal lattice. When repeated again and again in different directions, it generates the entire crystal lattice.

(ii) A void surrounded by 4 spheres is called a tetrahedral void and a void surrounded by 6 spheres is called an octahedral void. Figure 1 represents a tetrahedral void and Figure 2 represents an octahedral void.

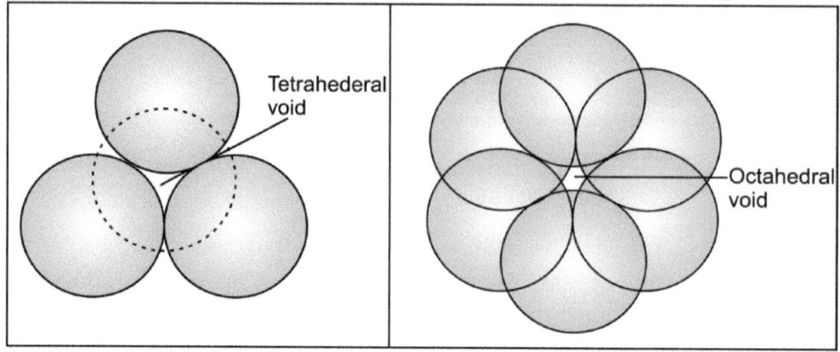

Q. 5. **In terms of band theory, what is the difference**

    (i) between a conductor and an insulator.

    (ii) between a conductor and a semiconductor.

Ans. (i) The valence band of a conductor is partially-filled or it overlaps with a higher energy, unoccupied conduction band.

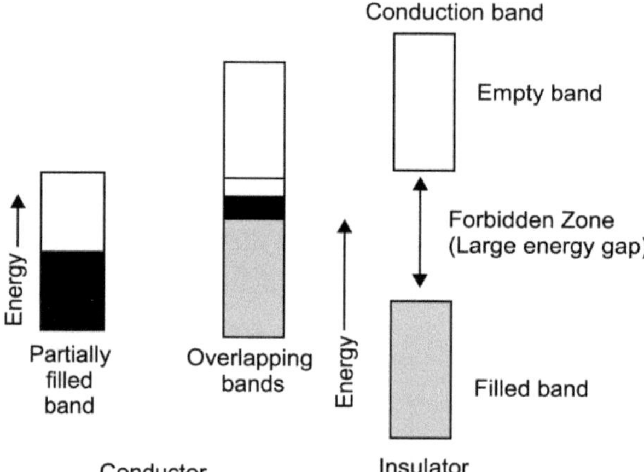

On the other hand, in the case of an insulator, the valence band is fully- filled and there is a large gap between the valence band and the conduction band.

(ii) In the case of a conductor, the valence band is partially-filled or it overlaps with a higher energy, unoccupied conduction band. So, the electrons can flow easily under an applied electric field.

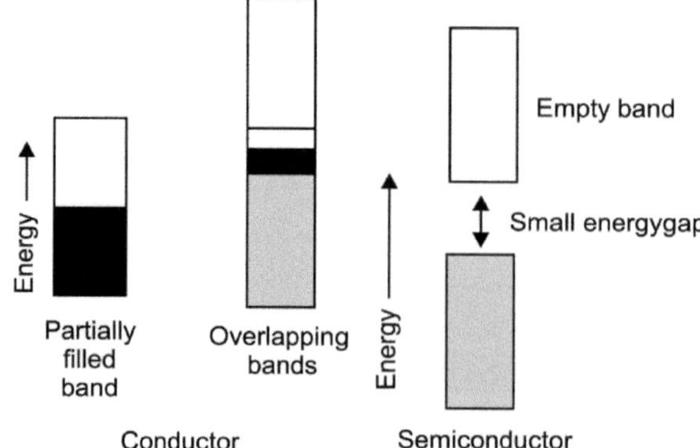

On the other hand, the valence band of a semiconductor is filled and there is a small gap between the valence band and the next higher conduction band. Therefore, some electrons can jump from the valence band to the conduction band and conducts electricity under an applied electric field.

Chapter 3. Electrochemistry

Q. 1. Distinguish between metallic conductors and electrolyte as conductors.

Ans.

	Metallic conductors	Electrolytic conductors
1.	Flow of electrons is responsible for conduction.	Flow of charged species *i.e.,* ions is responsible for conductions.
2.	No chemical change takes place.	Chemical change occurs.
3.	Increase in temperature decreases conduction.	Increase in temperature further promotes the degree of conduction.

Chapter 4. Chemical Kinetics

Q. 1. Distinguish between order and molecularity of a reaction.

Ans.

	Order	Molecularity
1.	It is the sum of the power of the reacting species involved in rate law equation.	It is the number of reacting species involved in the elementary single step reaction.
2.	Order of reaction is determined experimentally.	It is derived from mechanism of the reaction.
3.	It depends upon the pressure and temperature.	It is independent of pressure and temperature.
4.	Order of a reaction can be zero of even fractional in some cases.	Molecularity of a reaction cannot be zero and is always a whole number.
5.	Order of a complex reaction is determined from its slowest step.	Multiple steps have their own molecularity in a complex reaction. There is no overall molecularity.

Chapter 5. Surface Chemistry

Q. 1. State two differences between dialysis and osmosis.

Ans.

	Osmosis	Dialysis
1.	Osmosis is movement is solvent particles through a semi-permeable membrane from less concentrated solution to higher concentrated solution.	In dialysis the movement of solvent as well as small ions of solute electrolyte can also pass through the semi-permeable membrane. Only colloidal size particles do not pass through it.
2.	Osmosis is used in desalination of sea water.	Dialysis is used for purification of sols. It is also used in case of purification of blood in human kidney failure.

Q. 2. State differences between micelles and colloidal solutions.*

Ans.

	Micelles	Colloidal Solutions
1.	Aggregate of high molecular particles like soaps and detergents. Contains about 100 or more molecules.	Heterogeneous mixtures of dispersed phase scattered over-dispersed medium.
2.	These are also called associated colloids.	These are either multimolecular or macro-molecular colloid.
3.	Does not behave as a colloidal solution below a certain concentration (CMC).	Remains colloidal solution even on dilution.
4.	High conductivity as charged species are present. Example: Solutions of soaps and detergents.	General low in conductivity. Example: Solution of starch in water, proteins in water, Ag sol.

Q. 3. Distinguish between the terms adsorption and absorption.

Ans.

	Absorption	Adsorption
1.	When a species gets distributed uniformly throughout the body or bulk of another substance, its called absorption.	When a species get concentrated mainly on the surface of another substance, but not inside the body or bulk its called adsorption.
2.	Its a bulk phenomenon which occurs throughout the material. Example: Absorption of ink by a cotton swab.	Its a surface phenomenon which occurs only on the surface. Example: Adsorption of gases on the surface of metals. Example: Adsorption of gases on the surface of metals.

Q. 4. What is the difference between physisorption and chemisorption?

Ans.

	Physisorption	Chemisorption
1.	In this type of adsorption, the adsorbate is attached to the surface of the adsorbent with weak Van der Waals forces of attraction.	In this type of adsorption, strong chemical bonds are formed between the adsorbate and the surface of the adsorbent.
2.	No new compound is formed in the process.	New compounds are formed at the surface of the adsorbent.
3.	It is generally found to be reversible in nature.	It is usually irreversible in nature.
4.	Enthalpy of adsorption is low as weak Van der Waals forces of attraction are involved. The values lie in the range of 20-40 kJ mol^{-1}.	Enthaply of adsorption is high as chemical bonds are formed. The values lie in the range of 40-400 kJ mol^{-1}.
5.	It is favoured by low temperature conditions.	It is favoured by high temperature conditions.
6.	It is an example of multi-layer adsorption.	It is an example of mono-layer adsorption.

Chapter 6. General Principles and Processes of Isolation of Elements

Q. 1. Giving examples, differentiate between 'roasting' and 'calcination'.

Ans.

	Roasting	Calcination
1.	Roasting in the process of conventing sulphide ores to oxides by heating the ores in a regular supply of air at a temperature below the melting point of the metal.	On the other hand, calcination is the process of converting hydroxide and carbonate ores to oxides by heating the ores either in the absence or in a limited supply of air at a temperature below the melting points of the metal.
2.	For example, sulphide ores of Zn, Pb and Cu are converted to their respective oxides by process. $2ZnS + 3O_2 \xrightarrow{\Delta} 2ZnO + 2SO_2$ zinc blende $2PbS + 3O_2 \xrightarrow{\Delta} 2PbO + 2SO_2$ Galena $2Cu_2S + 3O_2 \xrightarrow{\Delta} 2Cu_2O + 2SO_2$ Copper glance	For example, hydroxide of Fe, carbonates of Zn, Ca, Mg are converted to their respective oxides by this process. $Fe_2O_3.3H_2O \xrightarrow{\Delta} Fe_2O_3 + 3H_2O$ Limonite $ZnCO_3(s) \xrightarrow{\Delta} ZnO(s) + CO_2(g)$ Calamine $CaMg(CO_3)_2 \xrightarrow{\Delta} CaO(s) + MgO(s) + 2CO$ Dolomite

Q. 2. How is 'cast iron' different from 'pig iron'?

Ans. The iron obtained from blast furnaces is known as pig iron. It contains around 4% carbon and many impurities such as S, P, Si, Mn in smaller amounts.

Cast iron is obtained by melting pig iron and coke using a hot air blast. It contains a lower amount of carbon (3%) than pig iron. Unlike pig iron, cast iron is extremely hard and brittle.

Q. 3. Differentiate between "minerals" and "ores".

Ans.

	Minerals	Ores
1.	Minerals are naturally occurring chemical substances containing metals. They are found in the Earth's crust and are obtained by mining.	Ores are rocks and minerals viable to be used as a source of metal. For example, there are many minerals containing zinc, but zinc connot be extracted profitably (conveniently and economically) from all these minerals.
2.	All minerals are not ores.	All ores are minerals.

Chapter 8. *d*-and *f*-Block Elements

Q. 1. Differentiate between lanthanides and actinides.

Ans.

	Lanthanides	Actinides
1.	Shown variable oxidation states but (+3) is most common.	Shown (+3) state but other variable states are more common too like, + 4, +5, +6, +7.
2.	Except promethium (Pm) all are radioactive.	All are radioactive.
3.	Does not from oxocation.	From oxocations like PuO_2^{2+}.
4.	Have lesser tendency of complex formation.	Have greater tendency of complex formation.

Chapter 9. Coordination Compounds

Q. 1. Differentiate between bidentate ligand and ambident ligands.

Ans. A bidentate ligand is one in which a single molecule has two donor sites or atoms at the same time. Hence, it can bind with two coordinate bonds with a metal, whereas an ambident ligand has two donor sites or atoms but only one can bind with metal at same time. So, ambident ligands can form only one coordinate bond at a time. Example CN^-, where C and N any one atom can bind as cyano or isocyano with the metal.

Chapter 10. Haloalkanes and Haloarenes

Q. 1. Distinguish between the following compounds:

    (i) Benzyl chloride and chlorobenzene

    (ii) Chloroform and carbontetrachloride

    (iii) Chloroethane and bromoethane.

Ans. (i) On adding NaOH solution followed by few days of $AgNO_3$ solution, benzyl chloride gives white ppt. of AgCl whereas chlorobenzene will show no such change.

$$CH_2Cl\text{-}C_6H_5 + NaOH \xrightarrow{\Delta} CH_2OH\text{-}C_6H_5 + NaCl \xrightarrow{AgNO_3} AgCl\downarrow + NaNO_3 + CH_2OH\text{-}C_6H_5$$

(white ppt)

    (ii) Chloroform ($CHCl_3$) will give positive carbylamine test, *i.e.*, on heating both the solutions with aniline and alcoholic KOH, chloroform will give out pungent smelling isocyanide gas while carbontetrachloride will not.

$$CHCl_3 + C_6H_5NH_2 + 3KOH \text{ (Alc.)} \xrightarrow{\Delta} C_6H_5N{\equiv}C + 3KCl + 3H_2O$$

Phenyl isocyanide (Pungent smell)

$$CCl_4 + \underset{}{\text{(benzene with } NH_2\text{)}} + KOH \text{ (Alc.)} \xrightarrow{\Delta} \text{No reaction}$$

(iii) On adding aqueous KOH solution to both the test tubes followed by dil. HNO_3 and $AgNO_3$ solution we will get a white ppt. for chloroethane while light yellow ppt. for bromoethane.

$$\underset{\text{Chloroethane}}{CH_3CH_2C} \xrightarrow{\text{aq. KOH}} CH_3CH_2OH + KCl \xrightarrow[\text{dil. } HNO_3]{AgNO_3} AgCl^- + KNO_3 \quad \text{white ppt.}$$

$$\underset{\text{Chloroethane}}{CH_3CH_2Br} \xrightarrow{\text{aq. KOH}} CH_3CH_2OH + KBr \xrightarrow[\text{dil. } HNO_3]{AgNO_3} AgBr\downarrow \quad \text{Light yellow ppt.}$$

Q. 2. Distinguish between the following pairs:

(i) Ethylchloride and vinyl chloride

(ii) Benzylbromide and bromobenzene.

Ans. (i) CH_3CH_2Cl and $CH_2 = CH—Cl$.

The vinyl group will give partial double bond character to the C—Cl bond in vinyl chloride hence, it will not undergo nucleophilic substitution reactions easily unlike CH_3CH_2Cl.

Hence, we will add aq. KOH to both the solutions or samples followed by dil. HNO_3 and $AgNO_3$ solution in excess. Ethyl chloride will give white ppt. of $AgCl^-$ but vinyl chloride will not.

$$C_2H_5Cl + KOH \text{ (aq.)} \xrightarrow{\Delta} C_2H_5OH + KCl \xrightarrow[\text{dil. } HNO_3]{AgNO_3} AgCl\downarrow + KNO_3 \quad \text{White ppt.}$$

$$CH_2 = CHCl + KOH\text{(aq.)} \xrightarrow{\Delta} \text{No reaction}$$

(ii)

$$\text{(benzene with } CH_2Br\text{)} \quad \text{and} \quad \text{(benzene with } Br\text{)}$$

Same test as above. Benzyl bromide being a primary alkyl halide will give nucleophilic substitution product with benzyl alcohol and KBr with aq. KOH.

$$\text{(benzene with } CH_2Br\text{)} + KOH \text{ (aq.)} \xrightarrow{\Delta} \text{(benzene with } CH_2OH\text{)} + KBr \xrightarrow[\text{dil. } HNO_3]{AgNO_3} AgBr\downarrow + KNO_3$$

No light yellow ppt. will be formed in case of bromobenzene.

$$\text{(benzene with } Br\text{)} + KOH \text{ (aq.)} \xrightarrow{\Delta} \text{No reaction.}$$

Chapter 11. Alcohols, Phenols and Ethers

Q. 1. State a test to distinguish between methanol and ethanol.

Ans. Iodoform test: Ethanol has $CH_3 — \underset{\underset{H}{|}}{\overset{\overset{OH}{|}}{C}} — H$ group hence, it will give the positive test of yellow ppt. while methanol will not give the test.

Q. 2. Distinguish between the following:

(i) Phenol and ethanol   (ii) Isopropyl alcohol and ethanol.

Ans. (i) Ethyl alcohol is neutral towards litmus while phenol will give positive test. It will turn blue litmus solution red.

Or

Ferric Chloride Test: Take both the solutions in two different test tubes and add few drops of freshly prepared, neutral ferric chloride solution. Test tube containing phenol will show a violet colouration while there will be no change in case of ethanol.

$$2C_6H_5OH + FeCl_3 \longrightarrow (C_6H_5O)_3\,Fe + 3HCl$$

Phenol $\qquad\qquad$ (Violet)

$$C_2H_5OH + FeCl_3 \longrightarrow \text{No colouration}$$

(Ethanol)

(ii) Isopropyl alcohol and ethanol.

$$\left[CH_3 - \underset{\underset{OH}{|}}{CH} - CH_3 \right] \qquad (C_2H_5OH)$$

Isopropyl alcohol is a $2°$ alcohol, hence will give a turbidity on standing for few minute in Lucas test, *i.e.*, on adding anhydrous $ZnCl_2$ and conc. HCl. Ethanol as a $1°$ alcohol will only provide turbidity on heating.

Q. 3. Write chemical tests to distinguish between:
   (i)   Phenol and cyclohexanol
   (ii) Propan-2-ol and benzyl alcohol.

Ans. (i)   Phenol will give yellowish white ppt. on treating with bromine water whereas cyclohexanol will not.

(ii) Propan-2-ol ($CH_3 - \underset{\underset{OH}{|}}{CH} - CH_3$) will give positive iodoform test, *i.e.*, will give yellow ppt. on treating it

with NaOI but benzyl alcohol (benzene ring with CH_2OH group) will not give positive test.

Chapter 12. Aldehydes, Ketones and Carboxylic Acids

Q. 1. Give a chemical test to distinguish between benzaldehyde and benzoic acid.*

Ans. Benzaldehyde has a bitter almond odour and also it gives positive tollen's test of silver mirror test. Also on adding sodium bicarbonate, benzoic acid will produce brisk effervescence of CO_2 gas while benzaldehyde will not react.

(benzene ring with COOH) $+ NaHCO_3 \longrightarrow$ (benzene ring with COONa) $+ H_2O + CO_2 \uparrow$

Q. 2. Give the chemical tests to distinguish between the following pairs of compounds:
   (i)   Acetone and Acetic acid $\qquad\qquad$ (iii) Phenol and propanoic acid.
   (ii) Formic acid and benzoic acid

Ans. (i)   Acetic acid will give effervescence of $CO_2 \uparrow$ gas on adding $NaHCO_3$ solution to it, whereas acetone will not give this test.

$$CH_3COOH + NaHCO_3 \longrightarrow CH_3COONa + H_2O + CO_2 \uparrow$$
$$CH_3 - CO - CH_3 + NaHCO_3 \longrightarrow \text{No reaction}$$

(ii) Formic acid has both an aldehyde $\left[- \underset{\underset{H}{|}}{C} = O \right]$ as well as a carbonyl group. Hence, it gives some reactions of aldehydes which benzoic acid will not give.

Fehling's solution test will be positive for formic acid.

$$HCOOH + 2Cu^{2+} + 4OH^- \longrightarrow Cu_2O \downarrow + CO_2 \uparrow + 3H_2O$$

$\qquad\qquad$ Fehling's solution $\qquad$ Cuprous oxide

$\qquad\qquad\qquad\qquad\qquad$ (Red ppt.)

There will be no such red ppt. formation with benzoic acid.

(iii) Phenol will give a violet colouration with neutral $FeCl_3$ solution but propanoic acid will not.

$$3C_6H_5OH + FeCl_3 \longrightarrow (C_6H_5O)_3Fe + 3HCl$$

Phenol   (Violet colour)

$$3CH_3CH_2COOH + FeCl_3 \longrightarrow (CH_3CH_2COO)_3Fe + 3HCl$$

Propanoic acid   (Buff coloured)

Or

Sodium bicarbonate test ($NaHCO_3$). Propanoic acid will generate $CO_2 \uparrow$ gas but phenol will not decompose sodium bicarbonate.

Q. 3. Distinguish between:

(i) $C_6H_5COCH_3$ and C_6H_5CHO (ii) CH_3COOH and $HCOOH$.

Ans. (i) $C_6H_5COCH_3$ *i.e.*, acetophenone will give positive iodoform test because of presence of ($COCH_3$) group while C_6H_5CHO *i.e.*, benzaldehyde will not.

(Structure: benzene ring with $COCH_3$) $+ NaOH + I_2 \longrightarrow$ (benzene ring with $COONa$) $+ CHI_3 \downarrow$

[Yellow ppt. of iodoform]

(Structure: benzene ring with CHO) $+ NaOH + I_2 \longrightarrow$ No reaction

(ii) CH_3COOH acetic acid, does not reduces Tollen's reagent, while $HCOOH$, formic acid reduce Tollen's reagent and gives positive silver mirror test. The presence of ($-CHO$) group in formic acid, is responsible for this test.

$$HCOOH + 2[Ag(NH_3)_2]^+ + 2OH^- \longrightarrow CO_2 + 2H_2O + 2Ag^- + 4NH_3$$

(basic medium)

Q. 4. Give simple chemical tests to distinguish between the following pairs of compounds:

(i) Propanal and Propanone   (iii) Phenol and Benzoic acid

(ii) Acetophenone and Benzophenone   (iv) Benzoic acid and Ethyl benzoate.

Ans. (i) Propanal and propanone can be distinguished by any of the following tests:

(a) **Tollen's test:** Propanal is an aldehyde. So, it reduces Tollen's reagent whereas, propanone being a ketone does not reduces Tollen's reagent, hence only propanal gives positive silver mirror test.

$$CH_3H_2CHO + 2[Ag(NH_3)_2]^+ + 3OH^- \longrightarrow CH_3CH_2COO^- + Ag \downarrow + 4NH_3 + 2H_2O$$

Propanal   Tollen's reagent   Propanoate ion   Silver mirror

(b) **Fehling's test:** Aldehydes respond to Fehling's test, but ketones do not.

Propanal being an aldehyde reduces Fehling's solution to a red-brown precipitate of Cu_2O, but propanone being a ketone does not.

$$CH_3CH_2CHO + 2Cu^{2+} + 5OH^- \longrightarrow CH_3CH_2COO^- + Cu_2O \downarrow + 3H_2O$$

Propanal   Propanoate ion   Cuprous oxide (Red-brown ppt.)

(c) **Iodoform test:** Aldehydes and ketones having at least one methyl group linked to the carbonyl carbon atom responds to iodoform test. They are oxidised by sodium hypoiodite (NaOI) to give iodoforms. Propanone being a methyl ketone responds to this test, but propanal does not.

$$CH_3COCH_3 + 3NaOI \longrightarrow CH_3COONa + CHI_3 + 2NaOH$$

Propanone   Sodium   Sodium acetate   Iodoform

hypoiodite   (Yellow ppt.)

(ii) Acetophenone and Benzophenone can be distinguished using the iodoform test.

(a) **Iodoform test:** Methyl ketones are oxidised by sodium hypoiodite to give yellow ppt. of iodoform. Acetophenone being a methyl ketone responds to this test but benzophenone does not.

$$C_6H_5COCH_3 + 3NaOI \longrightarrow C_6H_5COONa + CHI_3 + 2NaOH$$

Acetophenone   Sodium   Sodium   Iodoform

hypoidite   benzoate   (Yellow ppt.)

$$C_6H_5COC_6H_5 + NaOI \longrightarrow \text{No yellow ppt. of } CHI_3$$
Benzophenone

(iii) Phenol and benzoic acid can be distinguished by ferric chloride test.

(a) **Ferric chloride test:** Phenol reacts with neutral $FeCl_3$ to form an iron-phenol complex giving violet colouration.

$$6C_6H_5OH + FeCl_3 \longrightarrow [Fe(OC_6H_5)_6]^{3-} + 3H^+ + 3Cl^-$$
Phenol $\qquad\qquad$ Iron-phenol complex
(Violet colour)

But benzoic acid reacts with neutral $FeCl_3$ to give a buff coloured ppt. of ferric benzoate.

$$3C_6H_5COOH + FeCl_3 \longrightarrow (C_6H_5COO)_3Fe + 3HCl$$
Benzoic acid $\qquad\qquad$ Ferric benzoate
(Buff coloured ppt.)

(b) **By sodium bicarbonate test:** Benzoic acid gives $CO_2 \uparrow$ gas while phenol does not react with sodium bi-carbonate.

(iv) Benzoic acid and ethyl benzoate can be distinguished by sodium bicarbonate test.

(a) Acids react with $NaHCO_3$ to produce brisk effervescence due to the evolution of CO_2 gas.
Benzoic acid being an acid responds to this test, but ethylbenzoate does not.

$$C_6H_5COOH + NaHCO_3 \longrightarrow C_6H_5COONa + CO_2 \uparrow + H_2O$$
Benzoic acid $\qquad\qquad$ Sodium benzoate

$$C_6H_5COOC_2H_5 + NaHCO_3 \longrightarrow \text{No effervescence as no evolution of } CO_2 \text{ gas takes place.}$$

(b) **Litmus test:** Benzoic acid will turn blue litmus solution red, but ethyl benzoate will not show any colour change.

Q. 5. Give simple chemical tests to distinguish between the following pairs of compounds :

(i) Pentan-2-one and Pentan-3-one $\qquad\qquad$ (iii) Ethanal and Propanal.

(ii) Benzaldehyde and Acetophenone

Ans. (i) Pentan-2-one and pentan-3-one can be distinguished by iodoform test.

(a) **Iodoform test:** Pentan-2-one is a methyl ketone. Thus, it responds to this test. But pentan-3-one not being a methyl ketone does not respond to this test.

$$CH_3CH_2CH_2 - \overset{\overset{\textstyle O}{\|}}{C} - CH_3 + 3NaOI \longrightarrow CH_3CH_2CH_2COONa + CHI_3 \downarrow + 2NaOH$$
Pentan-2-one $\qquad$ Sodium $\qquad$ Sodium butanoate $\qquad$ Iodoform
hypoiodite $\qquad\qquad\qquad$ (Yellow ppt.)

$$CH_3CH_2 - \overset{\overset{\textstyle O}{\|}}{C} - CH_2CH_3 + NaOI \longrightarrow \text{No yellow ppt. of iodoform}$$
Pentan-2-one $\qquad$ Sodium
hypoiodite

(ii) Benzaldehyde and acetophenone can be distinguished by the following tests.

(a) **Tollen's Test:** Benzaldehyde being an aldehyde reduces Tollen's reagent to give silver mirror formation but acetophenone being a ketone does not.

$$C_6H_5CHO + 2[Ag(NH_3)_2]^+ + 3OH^- \longrightarrow C_6H_5COO^- + Ag \downarrow + 4NH_3 + 2H_2O$$
Benzaldehyde $\qquad$ Tollen's reagent $\qquad\qquad$ Benzoate ion $\qquad$ Silver mirror

(b) **Iodoform test:** Acetophenone being a methyl ketone undergoes oxidation by sodium hypoiodite (NaOI) to give a yellow ppt. of iodoform. But benzaldehyde does not responds to this test.

$$C_6H_5COCH_3 + 3NaOI \longrightarrow C_6H_5COONa + CHI_3 + 2NaOH$$
Acetophenone $\qquad\qquad$ Sodium benzoate $\qquad$ Iodoform
(Yellow ppt.)

(iii) Ethanal and propanal can be distinguished by iodoform test.

Iodoform test: Aldehydes and ketones having at least one methyl group linked to the carbonyl carbon atom responds to the iodoform test. Ethanal having one methyl group linked to the carbonyl carbon atom responds to this test. But propanal does not have a methyl group linked to the carbonyl carbon atom and thus, it does not responds to this test.

$$CH_3CHO + 3NaOI \longrightarrow HCOONa + CHI_3 + 2NaOH$$

Ethanal $\quad$ Sodium $\quad$ Iodoform

methanoate $\quad$ (Yellow ppt.)

Chapter 13. Amines

Q. 1. Give a chemical test to distinguish between aniline and N-methylaniline?*

Ans. Aniline, $C_6H_5NH_2$ is a primary amine and N-methylaniline, $C_6H_5NH(CH_3)$ is a secondary amine. Hence aniline will give positive carbylamine test while N-methylaniline will not.

$$NH_2 \text{ (Aniline)} + CHCl_3 + 3KOH \text{ (alc.)} \xrightarrow{\Delta} NC \text{ (Benzene isocyanide, Foul smelling gas)} + 3KCl + 3H_2O$$

Q. 2. Give one chemical test to distinguish between the following pairs of compounds:

   (i)   Methylamine and dimethylamine   (iv) Aniline and benzylamine

   (ii) Secondary and tertiary amines   (v) Aniline and N-methylaniline.

   (iii) Ethylamine and aniline

Ans. (i) Methylamine being a 1° amine, can be distinguished by the carbylamine test from dimethylamine

     Carbylamine test: Aliphatic and aromatic primary amines on heating with chloroform and ethanolic potassium hydroxide forms foul-smelling isocyanides or carbylamines. Methylamine gives a positive carbylamine test, but dimethylamine does not.

$$CH_3-NH_2 + CHCl_3 + 3KOH \xrightarrow{\Delta} CH_3-NC + 3KCl + 3H_2O$$

Methylamine (1°) $\qquad\qquad$ Methylisocyanide (Foul smell)

$$(CH_3)_2NH + CHCl_3 + 3KOH \xrightarrow{\Delta} \text{No reaction}$$

   (ii) Secondary and tertiary amines can be distinguished by allowing them to react with Hinsberg's reagent (benzenesulphonyl chloride, $C_6H_5SO_2Cl$).

     Secondary amines react with Hinsberg's reagent to form a product that is insoluble in an alkali. For example, N, N-diethylamine reacts with Hinsberg's reagent to form N, N-diethyl-benzenesulphonamide, which is insoluble in an alkali. Tertiary amines, however, do not react with Hinsberg's reagent.

Benzenesulphonyl chloride + H—C(C_2H_5)(C_2H_5)—N $\longrightarrow$ N, N-Diethylbenzene-sulphonamide + HCl

   (iii) Ethylamine and aniline can be distinguished using the azo-dye test. A dye is obtained when aromatic amines react with HNO_2 ($NaNO_2$ + dil. HCl) at 0-5°C to from benzene diazonium chloride followed by a reaction with the alkaline solution of 2-naphthol. The dye is usually yellow, red or orange in colour. Aliphatic amines give a brisk effervescence due under similar conditions.

$$C_6H_5-NH_2 + HONO \xrightarrow{273\text{-}278\ K} C_6H_5-\overset{+}{N} \equiv N\,Cl^- + 2H_2O$$

Benzene diazonium chloride

$$C_6H_5-\overset{+}{N} \equiv N\,Cl^- + \text{2-Naphthol (OH)} \xrightarrow[\text{pH 9-10}]{\text{dil. NaOH}} C_6H_5-\overset{+}{N} \equiv N-\text{naphthol} + HCl$$

Benzene diazonium chloride $\qquad$ 2-Naphthol $\qquad$ 1-Phenylazo-2-naphthol (Orange dye)

$$CH_3CH_2-NH_2 + HONO \xrightarrow{0-5°C} C_2H_5OH + N_2 \uparrow + H_2O$$

(iv) Aniline and benzylamine can be distinguished by their reactions with the help of nitrous acid, which is prepared in situ from a mineral acid and sodium nitrite. Benzylamine reacts with nitrous acid to form unstable diazonium salt, which in turn gives alcohol with the evolution of nitrogen gas.

$$\underset{\text{Benzylamine}}{C_6H_5CH_2-NH_2} + HNO_2 \xrightarrow{NaNO_2 + HCl} \underset{\text{(Unstable)}}{[C_6H_5CH_2-\overset{+}{N_2}Cl^-]}$$

$$\downarrow H_2O$$

$$\underset{\text{Benzyl alcohol}}{N_2 \uparrow + C_6H_5CH_2OH + HCl}$$

On the other hand, aniline reacts with HNO_2 at low temperature to form stable diazonium salt. Thus, nitrogen gas is not evolved. Also it gives azo-dye test.

$$C_6H_5NH_2 \xrightarrow[\text{273-278 K}]{NaHO_2 + HCl} C_6H_5\overset{+}{N_2}Cl^- + NaCl + 2H_2O$$

(v) Aniline and N-methylaniline can be distinguished using the carbylamine test. Primary amines, on heating with chloroform and ethanolic potassium hydroxide, forms foul smelling isocyanides or carbylamines. Aniline, being a aromatic primary amine, gives positive carbylamine test. However, N-methylaniline, being a secondary amine does not.

$$\underset{\text{Benzylamine (1°)}}{C_6H_5-NH_2} + CHCl_3 + 3KOH \xrightarrow{\Delta} \underset{\substack{\text{(Benzylisocyanide)}\\\text{(Foul smell)}}}{C_6H_5-NC} + 3 KCl + 3H_2O$$

$$\underset{\text{N-Methylaniline}}{C_6H_5NHCH_3} + CHCl_3 + 3KOH \xrightarrow{\Delta} \text{No reaction}$$

Chapter 14. Biomolecules

Q. 1. State two main differences between globular proteins and fibrous proteins.[*]

Ans.

	Globular proteins	Fibrous proteins
1.	Water soluble.	Water insoluble.
2.	Very sensitive to small change in pH or temperature.	Not so sensitive to small change in pH or temperature.
3.	Haemoglobin is an example.	Keratin of hair is an example.

Q. 2. Write three points of differences between enzymes and catalysts.

Ans.

	Enzymes	Catalysts
1.	Biocatalyst which help in bio-chemical reaction and are highly specific by nature. Follow lock and key mechanism.	Chemicals which alter the rate of reaction without undergoing any change in themselves. Not specific in action.
2.	Work best at optimum temperature and pH, *i.e.*, pH $\approx$ 7 and body temperature $\approx$ 37°C.	Generally work better at, high temperature and pressure.
3.	These are very effective in their catalytic action. Can enhance the rate of reaction upto 10^{20} times.	These are generally not so highly effective as enzymes.

Q. 3. Write the important structural and functional differences between DNA and RNA.

Ans. The structural differences between DNA and RNA are as follows:

	DNA	RNA
1.	The sugar moiety in DNA molecules is β-D-2 deoxyribose.	The sugar moiety in RNA molecules is β-D-ribose.
2.	DNA contains thymine (T). It does not contain uracil (C) and has cytosine.	RNA contains uracil (C). It does not contain thymine (T).
3.	The helical structure of DNA is double-stranded and it has large molecules.	The helical structure of RNA is single-stranded and has smaller structure.

The functional differences between DNA and RNA are as follows:

	DNA	RNA
1.	DNA is the chemical basis of heredity. Also has unique property of replication.	RNA is not responsible for heredity. It does not replicates.
2.	DNA molecules do not synthesise proteins, but transfer coded message for the synthesis of proteins in the cells.	Proteins are synthesised by RNA molecules in the cells.

Q. 4. What is the difference between a nucleoside and a nucleotide?*

Ans. A nucleoside is formed by the attachment of a base to C–1 position of ribose or deoxyribose sugar.

Nucleoside = Sugar + Base

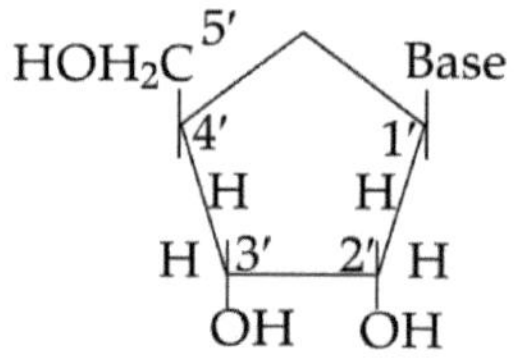

Structure of a nucleoside

On the other hand, all the three basic components of nucleic acids (*i.e.*, pentose sugar, phosphoric acid, and base) are present in a nucleotide. Nucelotide = Sugar + Base + Phosphoric acid.

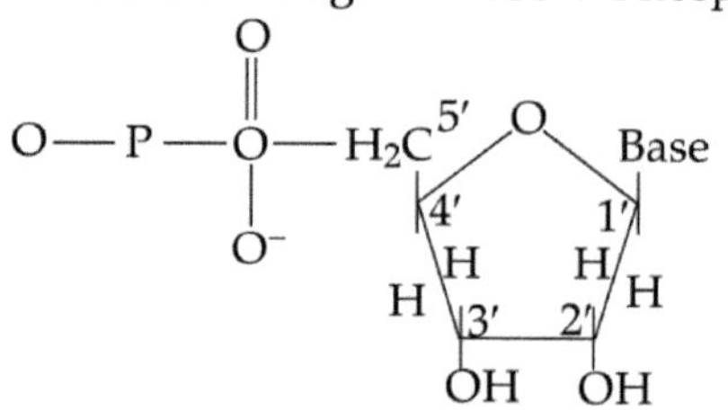

Structure of a nucleotide

Chapter 15. Polymers

Q. 1. Differentiate between condensation polymerisation and addition polymerisation.

Ans.

	Addition polymers	Condensation polymers
1.	The monomer unit has atlaest one double or triple bond present.	The monomer units have active functional group present.
2.	If follows either free radical addition polymerisation or ionic mechanism.	These follow simple chemical reactions with no reaction intermediate in mechanism.
3.	The mechanism is chain growth in nature.	These follow step growth mechanism.
4.	Polymers are exact multiples of monomers.	A small molecule like H_2O, NH_3 or HCl are lost during the polymerisation process in condensation polymers.

---

* are board exam questions from previous years

Q. 2. Differentiate between elastomers and fibers.*

Ans.

	Elastomers	Fibers
1.	Polymers having weakest intermolecular forces, Van der Wall's forces.	These have strong intermolecular forces such as hydrogen bonding holding the polymer chains.
2.	These have elastic properties, can be stretched by applying force and can regain their shape once released.	These are thread like and can be woven into fabrics. These have high tensile strength
3.	They have a range of melting point.	They have sharp melting point.
4.	Example: Natural rubber, Neoprene.	Example: Nylon-6, 6, terylene.

Q. 3. Differentiate between polyesters and polyacrylates.

Ans.

	Polyesters	Polyacrylates
1.	Polymers made from the condensation of a dicarboxylic acid and a diol.	Polymers are made from the monomer acrylic acid with other compounds. $CH_2 = CH - C - OH$ Acrylic acid
2.	They contain an ester functional group in their main chain.	There is no ester group bonding.
3.	Example: Terylene used in dress fabrics, curtains etc.	Example: Acrylonitrile, used in marking plastics etc.

Q. 4. Distinguish between the terms homopolymer and copolymer and give an example of each.*

Ans.

Homopolymer	Copolymer
The polymers that are formed by the polymerisation of a single monomer are known as homopolymers. In other words, the repeating units of homopolymers are derived only from one monomer. For example, polystyrene is a homopolymer of styrene only.	The polymers whose repeating units are derived from two types of monomers are known as copolymers. From example, Nylon 6, 6 where monomers are hexamethylene diamine and adipic acid.

Q. 5. How can you differentiate between addition and condensation polymerisation?

Ans. Addition polymerisation is the process of repeated addition of monomers, possessing atleast one double or triple bond to form polymers. For example, polythene is formed by addition polymerisation of ethene. Also polystyrene, PVC and teflon are some more examples of addition polymers.

$$nCH_2 = CH_2 \longrightarrow (CH_2 - CH_2)_n$$

Ethene   Polyethene

Condensation polymerisation is the process of formation of polymers by repeated condensation reactions between two different bi-functional or tri-functional monomers. A small molecule such as water or hydrochloric acid is eliminated in each condensation. For example, nylon 6, 6 is formed by condensation polymerisation of hexamethylenediamine and adipic acid.

$$nH_2N(CH_2)_6NH_2 \quad + \quad nHOOC(CH_2)_4COOH \longrightarrow$$

Hexamethylene diamine   Adipic acid

$$(NH(CH_2)_6NHCO(CH_2)_4CO)_n \quad + \quad nH_2O$$

Nylon 6, 6

Some more examples are : Nylon 6, Bakelite etc.

Chapter 16. Chemistry in Everyday Life

Q. 1. How do antiseptics differ from disinfectants? Give one example of each.

Ans.

	Antiseptics	Disinfectants
1.	Antiseptics can kill or resist the growth of micro-organisms which are affecting living cells or tissues.	Disinfectants can kill the growth of micro-organisms on non-living substances.
2.	Antiseptics can be applied to cuts or wounds safely.	Disinfectants are toxic for living tissues or cells and connot be applied on cuts or wounds.
3.	Example of antiseptics are dettol, 0.2% aqueous phenol.	Example of disinfectants are Cl_2 water, 1% aqueous phenol, etc.

❑❑

Chapter 7. *p*-Block Elements

Q. 1. Complete the following reactions:*

   (i) $I^-(aq) + H_2O(l) + O_2(g) \longrightarrow$

   (ii) $Cl_2 + Ba(OH)_2 \longrightarrow$

Ans. (i) $2I^-(aq) + H_2O(l) + O_2(s) \longrightarrow I_2(g) + O_2(s) + 2OH^-(aq)$

   (ii) $6Cl_2 + 6Ba(OH)_2 \longrightarrow Ba(ClO_3)_2 + 5BaCl_2 + 6H_2O$

                  Barium chlorate

Q. 2. Write balanced chemical equation:

   (i) NaCl is heated with sulphuric acid in presence of MnO_2

   (ii) Iodine is treated with conc. HNO_3.

Ans. (i) $2NaCl + MnO_2 + 3H_2SO_4 \longrightarrow 2NaHSO_4 + MnSO_4 + Cl_2 + 2H_2O$

   (ii) $I_2 + 10HNO_3 \longrightarrow 2HIO_3 + 4H_2O$.

Q. 3. Complete the following reactions:

   (i) $NaOH(aq) + Cl_2(g) \longrightarrow$

     (hot and conc.)

   (ii) $XeF_6(s) + H_2O(l) \longrightarrow$

Ans. (i) $NaOH(aq) + Cl_2(s) \longrightarrow 5NaCl + NaClO_3 + 3H_2O$

     (conc.)

   (ii) $XeF_6(s) + 3H_2O(l) \longrightarrow XeO_3 + 6HF$

Q. 4. Complete the following equations:*

   (i) $CaF_2 + H_2SO_4 \longrightarrow$

   (ii) $Ca + H_2SO_4 (conc.) \longrightarrow$

   (iii) $Ag + PCl_5 \longrightarrow$

Ans. (i) $CaF_2 + H_2SO_4 \longrightarrow CaSO_4 + 2HF$

   (ii) $Cu + 2H_2SO_4 (conc.) \longrightarrow CuSO_4 + SO_2 + 2H_2O$

   (iii) $2Ag + PCl_5 \longrightarrow 2AgCl + PCl_3$

Q. 5. Write the reactions of F_2 and Cl_2 with water.

Ans. (i) $Cl_2 + H_2O \longrightarrow HCl + HOCl$

               Hydrochloric Hypochlorous

                  acid   acid

   (ii) $2F_2(g) + 2H_2O(l) \longrightarrow O_2(g) + 4HF(aq)$

Q. 6. How can you prepare Cl_2 from HCl and HCl from Cl_2? Write reactions only.

Ans. (i) Cl_2 can be prepared from HCl by Deacon's process.

$$4HCl + O_2 \xrightarrow{CuCl_2} 2Cl_2 + 2H_2O$$

   or by using oxidising agents like $KMnO_4$, MnO, $K_2Cr_2O_7$

   e.g., $\qquad 4HCl + MnO_2 \longrightarrow MnCl_2 + Cl_2 + 2H_2O$

   (ii) HCl can be prepared from Cl2 on treating it with water.

$$4HCl + MnO_2 \longrightarrow MnCl_2 + Cl_2 + 2H_2O$$

$$Cl_2 + H_2O \longrightarrow HCl + HOCl$$

               Hydrochloric Hypochlorous

                  acid   acid

Q. 7. Write balanced equation:

Chlorine gas is passed into a solution of NaI in water.

Ans.
$$Cl_2 + NaI \longrightarrow 2NaCl + I_2$$

Q. 8. Write a balanced equation for the hydrolytic reaction of PCl_5 in heavy water.

Ans.
$$PCl_5 + D_2O \longrightarrow POCl_3 + 2DCl$$
$$POCl_3 + 3D_2O \longrightarrow D_3PO_4 + 3DCl$$

Therefore, the net reaction can be written as
$$PCl_5 + 4D_2O \longrightarrow D_3PO_4 + 5DCl$$

Q. 9. Complete the following reactions:

(i) $C_2H_4 + 3O_2 \longrightarrow$

(ii) $4Al + 3O_2 \longrightarrow$

Ans.   (i) $C_2H_4 + 3O_2 \xrightarrow{\Delta} 2CO_2 + 2H_2O$

  Ethene   Oxygen   Carbon dioxide   Water

(ii) $4Al + 3O_2 \xrightarrow{\Delta} 2Al_2O_3$

  Aluminium   Oxygen   Alumina

Q. 10. Complete and balance the following chemical equations:*

(i) $Fe^{2+} + MnO_4 + H^+ \longrightarrow$

(ii) $MnO_4^- + H_2O + I^- \longrightarrow$

Ans.   (i) $5Fe^{2+} + MnO_4^- + 8H^+ \longrightarrow Mn^{2+} + 4H_2O + 5Fe^{3+}$

(ii) $MnO_4^- + H_2O + I^- \longrightarrow 2MnO_2 + 2OH^- + IO_3^-$

Q. 11. Complete the following reactions:

(i) $Cl_2 + H_2O \longrightarrow$

(ii) $XeF_6 + 3H_2O \longrightarrow$

Ans.   (i) $Cl_2 + H_2O \longrightarrow 2HCl + [O]$

(ii) $XeF_6 + 3H_2O \longrightarrow XeO_3 + 6HF$

Q. 12. What happen when:

(i)   conc. H_2SO_4 is added to Cu?

(ii) SO_3 is passed through water?

Ans. Write the equations.

(i) $Cu + 2H_2SO_4 \longrightarrow CuSO_4 + SO_2 + 2H_2O$

(ii) $SO_3 + H_2O \longrightarrow H_2SO_4$

Q. 13. Write balanced chemical equation for the following:

(i) $Ca_3P_2 + H_2O \longrightarrow$

(ii) $P_4 + KOH + H_2O \longrightarrow$

Ans.   (i) $Ca_3P_2 + 6H_2O \longrightarrow 3Ca(OH)_2 + 2PH_3$

  Phosphine

(ii) $P_4 + 3KOH + 3H_2O \longrightarrow PH_3 + 3KH_2PO_2$

Q. 14. Give the disproportionation reaction of H_3PO_3.

Ans. On heating, orthophosphorus acid (H_3PO_3) disproportionates to give orthophosphoric acid (H_3PO_4) and phosphine (PH_3). The oxidation states of P in various species involved in the reaction are mentioned below.

$$4\overset{3+}{H_3PO_3} \longrightarrow 3\overset{5+}{H_3PO_4} + \overset{-3}{PH_3}$$

Chapter 8. *d*-and *f*-Block Elements

Q. 1. Complete the following:**

(i) $Na_2CrO_4 + H_2SO_4 \longrightarrow$

---

*   are board exam questions from previous years
**   are frequently asked board exam questions

(ii) $MnO_2 + KOH + O_2 \longrightarrow$

(iii) $HgCl_2 + SnCl_2 \longrightarrow$

Ans. (i) $2 Na_2CrO_4 + H_2SO_4 \text{ (conc.)} \longrightarrow Na_2Cr_2O_7 + Na_2SO_4 + H_2O$

(ii) $2MnO_2 + 4KOH + O_2 \longrightarrow 2K_2MnO_4 + 2H_2O$

(iii) $HgCl_2 + SnCl_2 \longrightarrow Hg_2Cl_2 + SnCl_4$

Q. 2. Answer the following questions:*

(i) Draw the structure of dichromate ion.

(ii) Mn^{3+} is a good oxidising agent. Explain.

(iii) Potassium permanganate is thermally unstable at 513K. Explain.

Ans. (i)

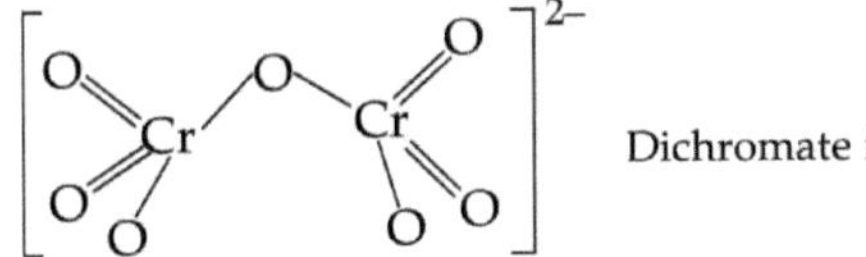

Dichromate ion

(ii) Mn^{3+} is a good oxidising agent, it easily accepts electron to become Mn^{2+} having electronic configuration $4s^0 3d^5$, which is quite stable as half filled than Mn^{3+} ($4s^0 3d^4$). Also $E^0 Mn^{3+}/Mn^{2+}$ is quite high (+ 1.57 V).

(iii) At 513K potassium permanganate undergoes decomposition and disproportionates into two lower oxidation states. The products being more stable at this temperature.

$$\overset{+7}{4KMnO_4} \xrightarrow[513\,K]{\Delta} \overset{+6}{K_2MnO_4} + \overset{+6}{K_2MnO_4} + 4O_2$$

Q. 3. Complete the following reactions:*

(i) $Cr_2O_7^{2-} \text{ (aq.)} + H_2S \text{ (g)} + H^+ \text{ (aq)} \longrightarrow$

(ii) $Cu^{2+} \text{ (aq.)} + I^- \text{ (aq)} \longrightarrow$

(iii) $MnO_4^- + S_2O_3^{2-} + H_2O \longrightarrow$

(iv) $KMnO_4 \xrightarrow{\Delta}$

(v) $MnO_4^- + I^- + H_2O \longrightarrow$

Ans. (i) $Cr_2O_7^{2-} \text{ (aq)} + 3H_2S(g) + 8H^+ \text{ (aq.)} \longrightarrow 2Cr^{3+} \text{ (aq.)} + 7H_2O \text{ (}l\text{)} + 3S(s)$

(ii) $2Cu^{2+} \text{ (aq.)} + 4I^- \text{ (aq.)} \longrightarrow Cu_2I_2 \text{ (s)} + I_2 \text{ (s)}$

(iii) $2MnO_4^- + 2S_2O_3^{2-} + H_2O \longrightarrow 2OH^- + 2MnO_2 + 3S + 3SO_4^{2-}$

(iv) $2KMnO_4 \xrightarrow[513\,K]{\Delta} K_2MnO_4 + MnO_2 + O_2$

(v) $2MnO_4^- \text{ (aq)} + I^- \text{ (aq)} + H_2O \text{ (}l\text{)} \longrightarrow 2MnO_2 \text{ (s)} + 2OH^- \text{ (aq.)} + IO_3^- \text{ (aq.)}$

Q. 4. Describe the oxidising action of potassium dichromate and write the ionic equations for its reaction with:

(i) iodide, (ii) iron (II) solution, (iii) H_2S.

Ans. $K_2Cr_2O_7$ acts as a very strong oxidising agent in the acidic medium.

$$K_2Cr_2O_7 + 4H_2SO_4 \longrightarrow K_2SO_4 + Cr_2(SO_4)_3 + 4H_2O + 3[O]$$

$K_2Cr_2O_7$ takes up electrons to get reduced and acts as an oxidising agent. The reaction of $K_2Cr_2O_7$ with other iodide, iron (II) solution and H_2S are given below.

(i) $K_2Cr_2O_7$ oxidizes iodide to iodine.

$$Cr_2O_7^{2-} + 14H^+ + 6e^- \longrightarrow 2Cr^{3+} + 7H_2O$$
$$\underline{\qquad\qquad 2I^- \longrightarrow I_2 + 2e^-] \times 3 \qquad\qquad}$$
$$Cr_2O_7^{2-} + 6I^- + 14H^+ \longrightarrow 2Cr^{3+} + 3I_2 + 7H_2O$$

(ii) $K_2Cr_2O_7$ oxidizes iron (II) solution to iron (III) solution *i.e.*, ferrous ions to ferric ions.

$$Cr_2O_7^{2-} + 14H^+ + 6e^- \longrightarrow 2Cr^{3+} + 7H_2O$$
$$\underline{\qquad\qquad Fe^+ \longrightarrow Fe^{3+} + e^-] \times 6 \qquad\qquad}$$
$$Cr_2O_7^{2-} + 14H^+ + 6Fe^{2+} \longrightarrow 2Cr^{3+} + 6Fe^{3+} + 7H_2O$$

(iii) $K_2Cr_2O_7$ oxidizes H_2S to sulphur.

$$Cr_2O_7^{2-} + 14H^+ + 6e^- \longrightarrow 2Cr^{3+} + 7H_2O$$
$$\underline{\qquad\qquad H_2S \longrightarrow S + 2H^+ + e^-] \times 3 \qquad\qquad}$$
$$Cr_2O_7^{2-} + 3H_2S + 8H^+ \longrightarrow 2Cr^{3+} + 3S + 7H_2O$$

Q. 5. **Describe the preparation of potassium permanganate. How does the acidified permanganate solution react with (i) iron (II) ions, (ii) SO₂, (iii) oxalic acid? Write the ionic equations for the reactions.****

Ans. Potassium permanganate can be prepared from pyrolusite ore (MnO_2). The ore is fused with KOH in the presence of either atmospheric oxygen or an oxidising agent, such as KNO_3 or $KClO_4$ to give K_2MnO_4.

$$2MnO_2 + 4KOH + O_2 \xrightarrow{\text{Heat}} 2K_2MnO_4 \qquad + 2H_2O$$

(Green)
Potassium manganate

The green mass can be extracted with water and then oxidized either electrolytically or by passing chlorine or ozone into the solution. Electrolytic oxidation.

$$K_2MnO_4 \longrightarrow 2K^+ + MnO_4^{2-}$$
$$H_2O \longrightarrow H^+ + OH^-$$

An anode manganate ions are oxidized to permanganate ions.

$$MnO_4^{2-} \longrightarrow MnO_4^- + e^-$$

Green   Purple

Oxidation by chlorine (chemical oxidation)

$$2K_2MnO_4 + Cl_2 \longrightarrow 2KMnO_4 + 2KCl$$
$$2MnO_4^{2-} + Cl_2 \longrightarrow 2MnO_4^- + 2Cl^-$$

Oxidation by ozone (chemical oxidation)

$$2K_2MnO_4 + O_3 + H_2O \longrightarrow 2KMnO_4 + 2KOH + O_2$$
$$2MnO_4^{2-} + O_3 + H_2O \longrightarrow 2MnO_4^- + 2OH- + O_2$$

(i) Acidified $KMnO_4$ solution oxidizes Fe (II) ions to Fe (III) ions *i.e.*, ferrous ions to ferric ions.

$$MnO_4^- + 8H^+ + 5e^- \longrightarrow Mn^{2+} + 4H_2O$$
$$Fe^{2+} \longrightarrow Fe^{3+} + e^-] \times 5$$
$$\overline{MnO_4^- + 5Fe^{2+} + 8H^+ \longrightarrow Mn^{2+} + 5Fe^{3+} + 4H_2O}$$

(ii) Acidified potassium permanganate oxidizes SO_2 to sulphuric acid.

$$2KMnO_4 + 3H_2SO_4 \longrightarrow K_2SO_4 + 2MnSO_4 + 3H_2O + 5\,[O]$$
$$SO_2 + H_2O + [O] \longrightarrow H_2SO_4\,] \times 5$$
$$\overline{2MnO_4^- + 5SO_2 + 2H_2O \longrightarrow 5SO_4^{2-} + 2Mn^+ + 4H^+}$$

(iii) Acidified potassium permanganate oxidizes oxalic acid to carbon dioxide.

$$MnO_4 + 8H^+ + 5e^- \longrightarrow Mn^{2+} + 4H_2O] \times 2$$
$$C_2O_4^{2-} \longrightarrow 2CO_2 + 2e^-\,] \times 5$$
$$\overline{2MnO_4^- + 5C_2O_4^{2-} + 16H^+ \longrightarrow 2Mn^{2+} + 10CO_2 + 8H_2O}$$

Q. 6. **Complete the following reactions:***

(i) $Cr_2O_7^{2-} + Sn^{2+} + H^+ \longrightarrow$

(ii) $MnO_4^- + Fe^{2+} + H^+ \longrightarrow$

Ans. (i) $Cr_2O_7^{2-} + 3Sn^{2+} + 14H^+ \longrightarrow 2Cr^{3+} + 3Sn^{4+} + 7H_2O$

(ii) $2MnO_4^- + 10Fe^{2+} + 16H^+ \longrightarrow 2Mn^{2+} + 10Fe^{3+} + 8H_2O$

Chapter 9. Coordination Compounds

Q. 1. **Answer the following questions:**

(i) Draw the geometrical isomers of complex $[Pt(NH_3)_2Cl_2]$.

(ii) On the basis of crystal field theory, write the electronic configuration of d^4 ion if $\Delta_0 < p$

(iii) Write the hybridization and the magnetic behaviour of the complex $[Ni(CO)_4]$. At no. of N = 28).*

Ans. Geometrical isomers of complex $[Pt(NH_3)_2Cl_2]$ are:

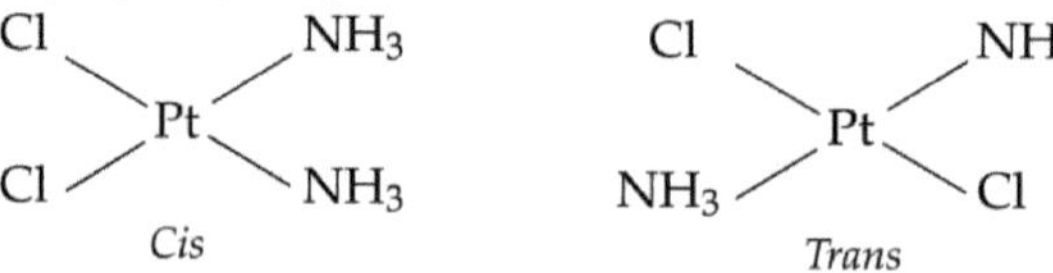

(ii) For $ns^0 (n-1)d^4$ configuration if *i.e.*, the crystal field splitting energy is less than pairing energy, shows that the ligand must be a weak field ligand. Hence the 4th electron will go to *eg* level rather than pairing in t_{2g} level. So configuration will be $t_{2g}^3 e_g^1$.

(iii) [Ni(CO)$_4$] here Ni has oxidation number 0, *i.e.*, $3d^8 4s^2$ state. Also CO is a strong field ligand.

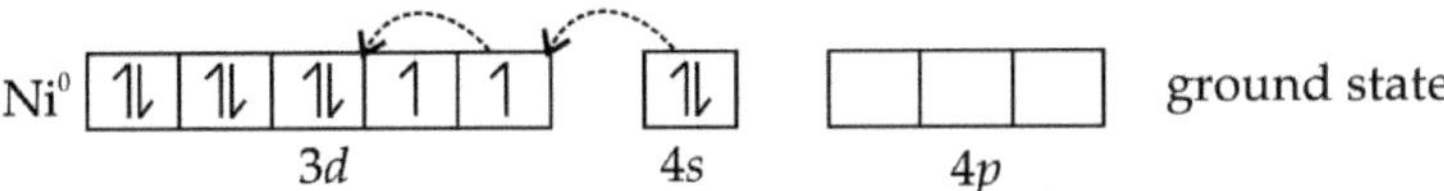

Either for sp^3 or dsp^2 hybridization for 4 ligands the s-orbital should be empty. The ligand CO forces the electrons to pair and the $4s$ electrons are transformed to $3d$-orbitals.

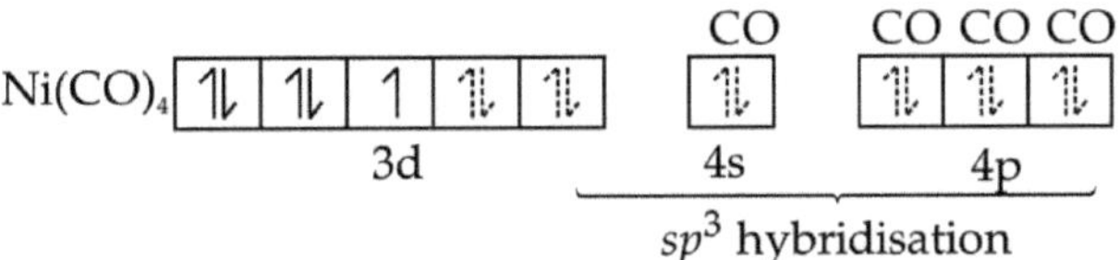

Inner orbital complex, diamagnetic and tetrahedral shape.

Chapter 10. Haloalkanes and Haloarenes

Q. 1. Complete the following equations:

(i) [cyclohexanol structure with OH] $+ SOCl_2 \longrightarrow$

(ii) HO–[benzene ring]–CH$_2$OH $+ HCl \longrightarrow$*

Ans. (i) [cyclohexanol with OH] $+ SOCl_2 \longrightarrow$ [cyclohexyl chloride with Cl] $+ SO_2 + HCl$

(ii) HO–[benzene ring]–CH$_2$OH $+ HCl \longrightarrow$ HO–[benzene ring]–CH$_2$Cl $+ H_2O$

Q. 2. Write the structural formula of the organic compounds A, B, C and D in the following sequence of reactions.

$$CH_3 - \underset{\underset{Br}{|}}{CH} - CH_2 - CH_3 \xrightarrow[KOH]{alc.} A \xrightarrow{Br_2} B \xrightarrow{Alc. KOH} C \xrightarrow[Hg^{2+}/H^+]{H_2O} D$$

Ans. $CH_3 - \underset{\underset{Br}{|}}{CH} - CH_2 - CH_3 \xrightarrow[KOH]{alc.} CH_3 - CH = CH - CH_3 \xrightarrow{Br_2}$ $CH_3 - \underset{\underset{Br}{|}}{CH} - \underset{\underset{Br}{|}}{CH} - CH_3 \xrightarrow{alc. KOH}$

[A] But-2-ene

[B] 2, 3-Dibromobutane

$$CH_3 - C \equiv C - CH_3 \xrightarrow[Hg^{2+}/H^+]{H_2O} CH_3 - CH_2 - \underset{}{C} - CH_3$$

[C] But-2-yne reaction

(Oxymercuration)

[D] Butan-2-one

Q. 3. (i) Complete the following reactions :

(a) $CH_3CH = CH_2 + HBr \xrightarrow{Peroxide}$

(b) 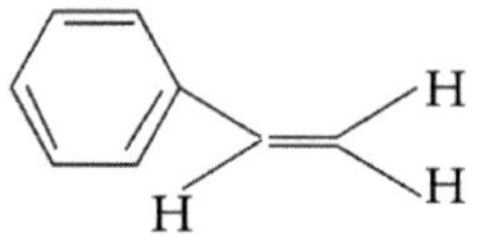 (phenyl)CH=CH$_2$ (styrene) + HBr $\longrightarrow$

(c) 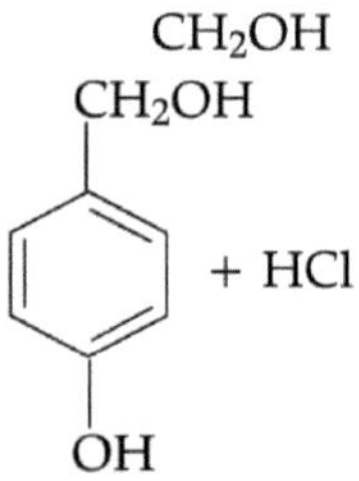 p-hydroxybenzyl alcohol (CH$_2$OH, OH) + HCl $\longrightarrow$

(ii) (a) Why does ammonolysis of alkyl halides does not yield pure amines?*

(b) Why do haloalkanes dissolve in organic solvents.

Ans. (i) (a) $CH_3CH = CH_2 + HBr \xrightarrow[\text{Anti-Markovnikov Rule}]{\text{Peroxide}} CH_3 - CH_2 - CH_2Br$

(b) 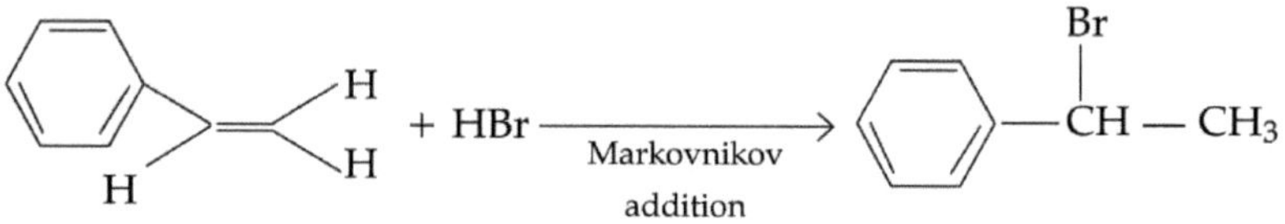 (phenyl)CH=CH$_2$ + HBr $\xrightarrow[\text{addition}]{\text{Markovnikov}}$ (phenyl)$-\underset{\underset{Br}{|}}{C}H - CH_3$

(c) p-hydroxybenzyl alcohol (CH$_2$OH, OH) + HCl $\longrightarrow$ p-hydroxybenzyl chloride (CH$_2$Cl, OH) + H$_2$O

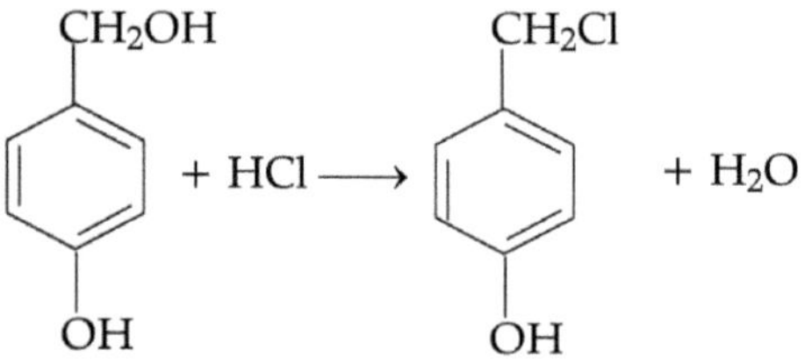

(ii) (a) When alkyl halides reacts with ammonia, then they don't stop at secondary or tertiary alkyl halides. They undergo exhaustive ammoniation thus resulting in the formation of a mixture of primary, secondary, tertiary and even quaternary amines (salts). Therefore pure amines can not be obtained from ammonolysis of alkyl halides.

Example.

$$CH_3CH_2Br + NH_3 \longrightarrow CH_3CH_2NH_2 + HBr \xrightarrow{NH_3} CH_3CH_2NHCH_2CH_3 + HBr \xrightarrow{NH_3} (C_2H_5)_3N$$

$$(1°) \qquad\qquad (2°) \qquad\qquad (3°)$$

(b) Haloalkanes being less polar are covalent in nature. Hence, they dissolve in organic solvents easily rather than water.

Q. 4. **Write the structure of the major organic product in each of the following reactions:**

(i) $CH_3CH_2CH_2Cl + NaI \xrightarrow[\text{Heat}]{\text{Acetone}}$

(ii) $(CH_3)_3CBr + KOH \xrightarrow[\text{Heat}]{\text{Ethanol}}$

(iii) $CH_3CH(Br)CH_2CH_3 + NaOH \xrightarrow{\text{Water}}$

(iv) $CH_3CH_2Br + KCN \xrightarrow{\text{aq. Ethanol}}$

(v) $C_6H_5ONa + C_2H_5Cl \longrightarrow$

(vi) $CH_3CH_2CH_2OH + SOCl_2 \longrightarrow$

(vii) $CH_3CH_2CH = CH_2 + HBr \xrightarrow{\text{Peroxide}}$

(viii) $CH_3CH = C(CH_3)_2 + HBr \longrightarrow$

Ans. (i) $\underset{\text{1-Chloropropane}}{CH_3\,CH_2CH_2Cl} + NaI \xrightarrow[\text{(Finkelstein reaction) Heat}]{\text{Acetone}} \underset{\text{1-Iodopropane}}{CH_3\,CH_2CH_2I} + NaCl$

(ii) $\underset{\text{2-Bromo-2-methylpropane}}{(CH_3)_3CBr} + KOH \xrightarrow[\text{(Dehydrohalogenation)}]{\underset{\text{Heat}}{\text{Ethanol}}} \underset{\underset{\underset{\text{(2-Methylpropene)}}{CH_3}}{|}}{CH_3 - C} = CH_2 + KBr + H_2O$

(iii) $\underset{\text{2-Bromobutane}}{CH_3CH(Br)CH_2CH_3} + NaOH \xrightarrow[\text{Hydrolysis}]{\text{Water}} \underset{\text{Butan-2-ol}}{CH_3CH(OH)CH_2CH_3} + NaBr$

(iv) CH_3CH_2Br + KCN $\xrightarrow[\text{(Nucleophilic substitution)}]{\text{aq. Ethanol}}$ CH_3CH_2CN + KBr

Bromobutane   (Propanenitrile)
Cyanoethane

(v) C_6H_5ONa + C_2H_5Cl $\xrightarrow{\text{(Williamson synthesis)}}$ $C_6H_5 — O — C_2H_5$ + NaCl

Sodium phenoxide   Chloroethane   Phenetole

(vi) $CH_3CH_2CH_2OH$ + $SOCl_2$ $\xrightarrow{\text{Pyridine}}$ $CH_3CH_2CH_2Cl$ + $SO_2\uparrow$ + HCl $\uparrow$

1-Propanol   1-Chloropropane   (gaseous by products)

(vii) $CH_3CH_2CH = CH_2$ + HBr $\xrightarrow[\substack{\text{(Anti-Markovnikov's}\\ \text{addition)}}]{\text{Peroxide}}$ $CH_3CH_2CH_2CH_2 — Br$

2-Methylbut-2-ene   1-Bromobutane

(viii) $CH_3CH = C(CH_3)_2$ + HBr $\xrightarrow{\text{(Markovnikov's addition)}}$ $CH_3 — CH — \overset{\displaystyle Br}{\underset{\displaystyle CH_3}{\overset{|}{\underset{|}{C}}}} — CH_3$

2-Methylbut-2-ene

2-Bromo-2-methylbutane

Q. 5. Draw the structures of major monohalo products in each of the following reactions:

(i) 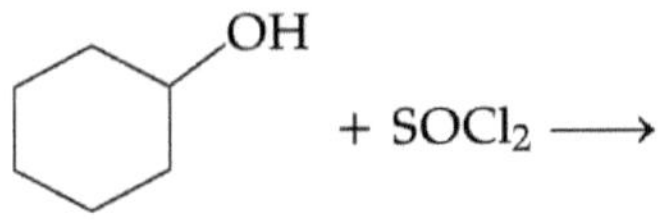   [cyclohexanol with OH] + $SOCl_2 \longrightarrow$

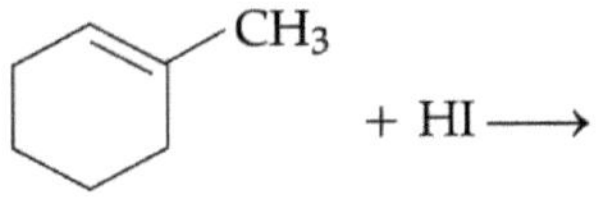

(ii)* 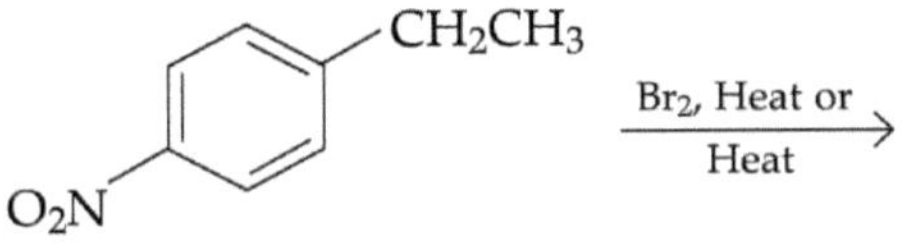   [4-ethyl, O₂N benzene] $\xrightarrow[\text{Heat}]{\text{Br}_2, \text{Heat or}}$

(iii) HO— [benzene with CH₂OH] + HCl $\xrightarrow{\text{Heat}}$

(iv)*   [methylcyclohexene with CH₃] + HI $\longrightarrow$

(v) CH_3CH_2Br + NaI $\longrightarrow$

(vi) 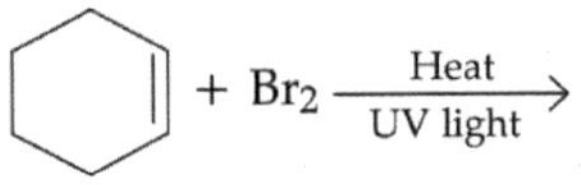   [cyclohexene] + Br_2 $\xrightarrow[\text{UV light}]{\text{Heat}}$

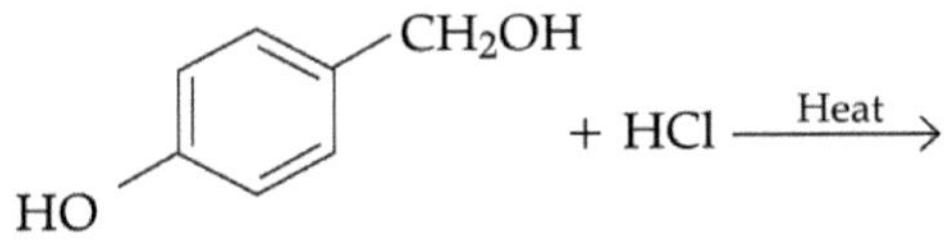

Ans. (i) 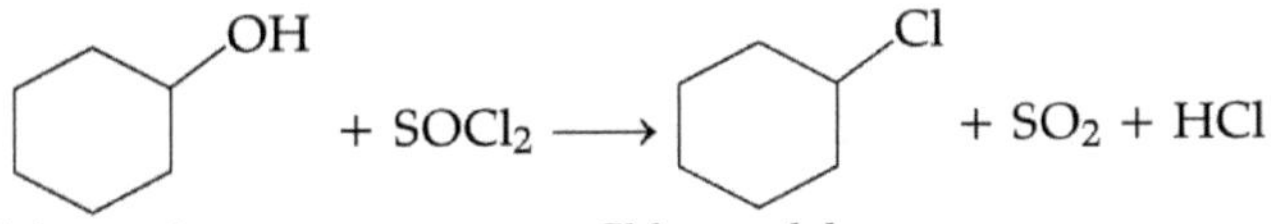   [cyclohexanol with OH] + $SOCl_2 \longrightarrow$ [cyclohexane with Cl] + SO_2 + HCl

Chclohexanol   Chlorocyclohexane

(ii) 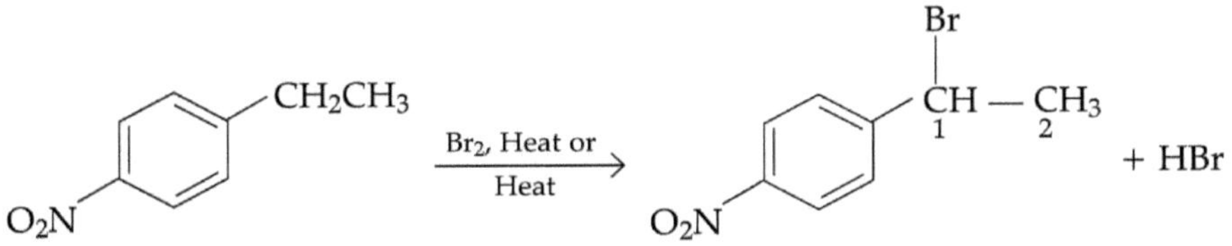 O₂N— [benzene with CH₂CH₃] $\xrightarrow[\text{Heat}]{\text{Br}_2, \text{Heat or}}$ O₂N— [benzene with $\overset{\displaystyle Br}{\overset{|}{CH}} — CH_3$] + HBr

4-Ethylnitrobenzene   4-(1-Bromoethyl) nitrobenzene
(Allylic substitution)

(iii) 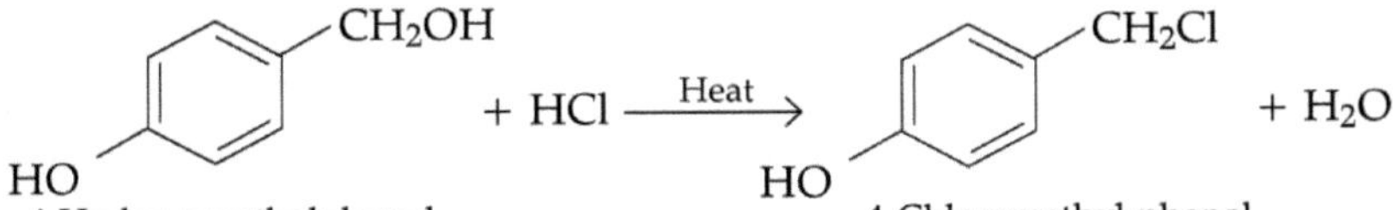 HO— [benzene with CH₂OH] + HCl $\xrightarrow{\text{Heat}}$ HO— [benzene with CH₂Cl] + H_2O

4-Hydroxymethylphenol   4-Chloromethyl phenol

(iv) 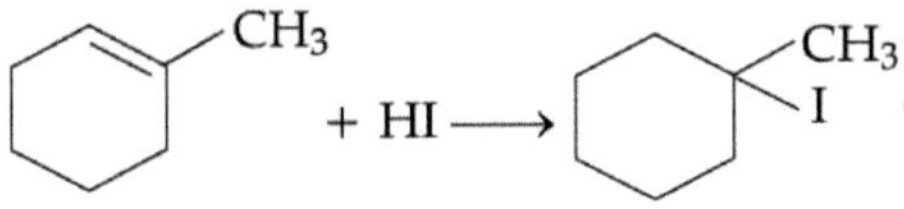   [methylcyclohexene with CH₃] + HI $\longrightarrow$ [cyclohexane with CH₃ and I]   (Markovnikov's rule is followed)

(v) CH_3CH_2Br + NaI $\xrightarrow[\text{Acetone}]{\text{Heat}}$ CH_3CH_2I + NaBr (Finkelstein reaction)

Bromoethane   Iodoethane

---

*   are board exam questions from previous years

(vi) Cyclohexane $+ Br_2 \xrightarrow[\text{UV light}]{\text{Heat}}$ 3-Bromocyclohexene $+ HBr$ (Allylic halogenation)

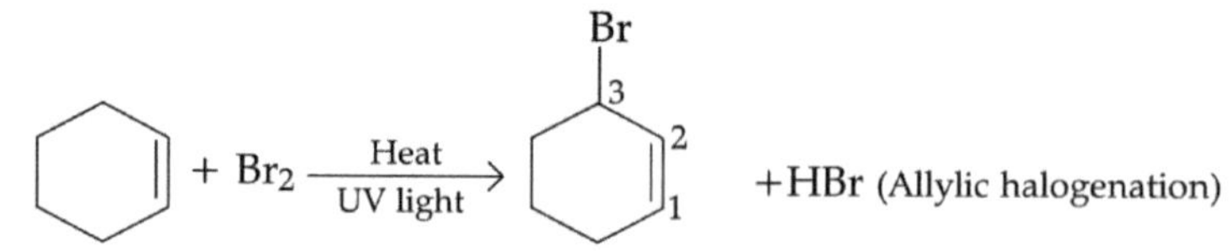

Q. 6. Complete the following equations:*

(i) 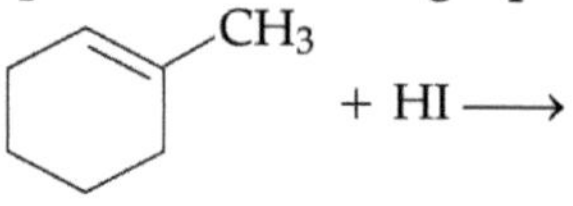 [1-methylcyclohexene] $+ HI \longrightarrow$

(ii) $CH_3CH_2CH = CH_2 + HBr$

Ans. (i) 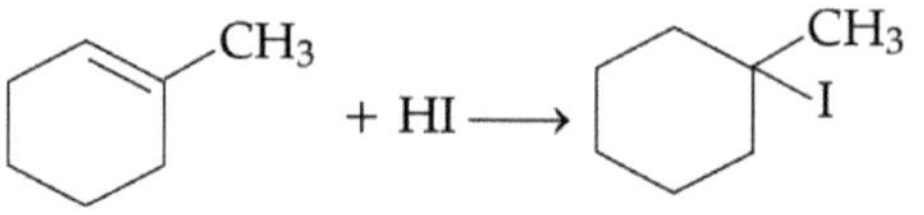 [1-methylcyclohexene] $+ HI \longrightarrow$ [1-iodo-1-methylcyclohexane]

(ii) $CH_3CH_2CH = CH_2 + HBr \longrightarrow CH_3CH_2 - \underset{\underset{Br}{|}}{CH} - CH_3$

Q. 7. Write the reaction involved in the following reactions:

(i) Clemmensen reduction

(ii) Cannizzaro reaction.

Ans. (i) Clemmensen reduction:

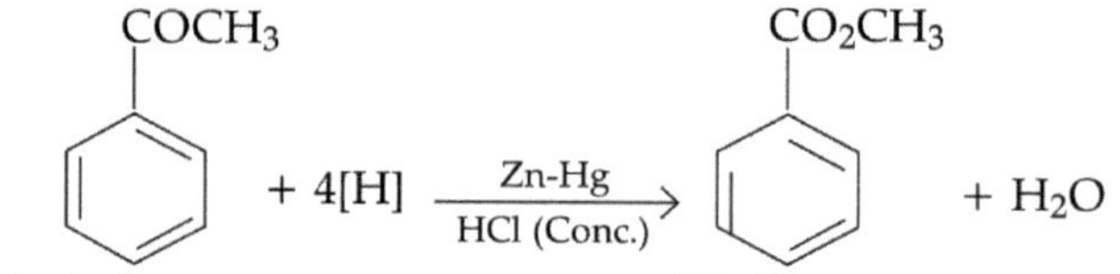

Acetophenone ($C_6H_5COCH_3$) $+ 4[H] \xrightarrow[\text{HCl (Conc.)}]{\text{Zn-Hg}}$ Ethylbenzene ($C_6H_5CO_2CH_3$) $+ H_2O$

(ii) Cannizzaro reaction.

$$2C_6H_5CHO \xrightarrow{\text{Conc. KOH}} C_6H_5CH_2OH + C_6H_5COO^-Na^+$$

Benzaldehyde   Benzylalcohol   Sodium benzoate

Chapter 11. Alcohols, Phenols and Ethers

Q. 1. Identify A to D in the following word problem:

$$[A] \xleftarrow[H_2O_2/OH^-]{BH_3,THF} CH \equiv CCH_3 \xrightarrow[H_2SO_4]{HgSO_4} [C] \xrightarrow[H_3O^+]{CH_3MgBr} [D]$$

$$\downarrow$$

$$[B]$$

Ans.

$CH_3CH_2CHO \xleftarrow[H_2O_2/OH^-]{BH_3,THF} CH \equiv CCH_3 \xrightarrow[H_2SO_4]{HgSO_4} CH_2 - \underset{[C]}{\overset{\overset{O}{\|}}{C}} - CH_3 \xrightarrow[CH_3MgBr/H_3O^+]{\text{Grignard's reagent}}$

[A] (Hydroboration oxidation)   (Oxymercuration demercuration)   Propanone

Propanone

Grignard's reagent CH_3MgBr/H_3O^+ $\longrightarrow CH_3CH_2 - \underset{\underset{OH}{|}}{CH} - CH_3$

Butan-2-ol

[B]

$CH_3 - \underset{\underset{CH_3}{|}}{\overset{\overset{OH}{|}}{C}} - CH_3$

[D]

2-Methyl-propan-2-ol

Q. 2. How will you convert the following:*

(i) Phenol to anisole

(ii) Propan-2-ol to 2-methyl propan-2-ol

(iii) Aniline to phenol.*

Ans. (i)

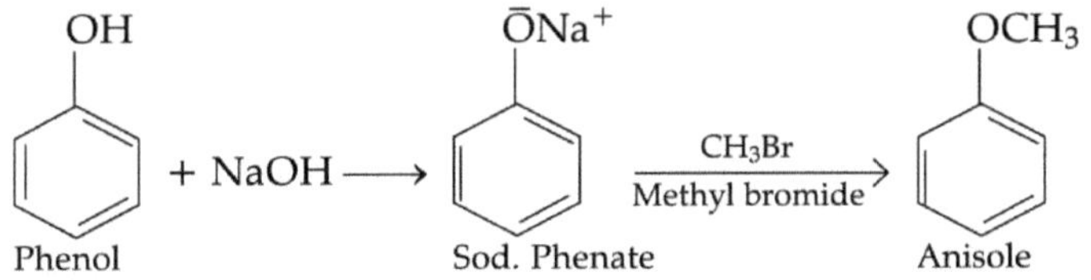

Phenol + NaOH $\longrightarrow$ Sod. Phenate $\xrightarrow[\text{Methyl bromide}]{CH_3Br}$ Anisole

(ii)

$$CH_3 - \underset{\underset{OH}{|}}{CH} - CH_3 \xrightarrow[H_3O^+]{K_2Cr_2O_7} CH_3 - \underset{\underset{O}{\|}}{C} - CH_3 \xrightarrow[\text{Grignard's reagent}]{CH_3 - MgBr} \left[CH_3 - \underset{\underset{CH_3}{|}}{\overset{\overset{OMgBr}{|}}{C}} - CH_3 \right] \xrightarrow[\text{hydrolysis}]{H_3O^+}$$

Propan-2-ol   [O]   Propanone   Adduct

$$CH_3 - \underset{\underset{CH_3}{|}}{\overset{\overset{OH}{|}}{C}} - CH_3 + Mg(OH)Br$$

2-Methylpropan-2-ol

(iii)

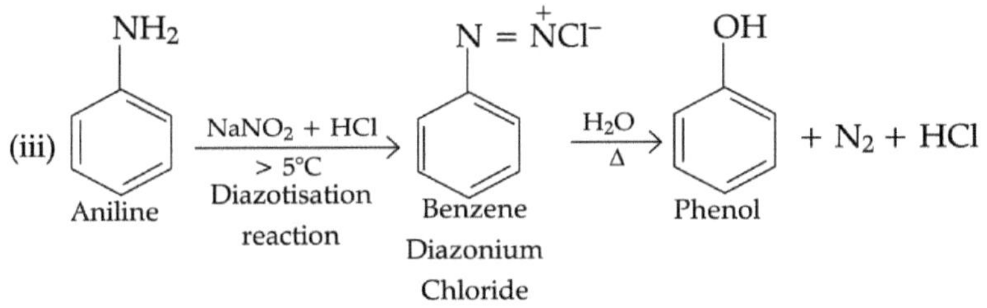

Aniline $\xrightarrow[\substack{> 5°C \\ \text{Diazotisation} \\ \text{reaction}}]{NaNO_2 + HCl}$ Benzene Diazonium Chloride $\xrightarrow[\Delta]{H_2O}$ Phenol $+ N_2 + HCl$

Q. 3. Write the main products in each of the reactions:*

(i) $CH_3 - \underset{\underset{CH_3}{|}}{\overset{\overset{CH_3}{|}}{C}} - O - CH_3 + HI \longrightarrow$

(ii) $CH_3 - CH = CH_2 \xrightarrow[\text{(ii) } 3H_2O_2/OH^-]{\text{(i) } B_2H_6}$

(iii) $C_6H_5 - OH \xrightarrow[\text{(i) } CO_2,H^+]{\text{(i) aq. NaOH}}$

Ans. (i) $CH_3 - \underset{\underset{CH_3}{|}}{\overset{\overset{CH_3}{|}}{C}} - O - CH_3 + HI \longrightarrow CH_3 - \underset{\underset{CH_3}{|}}{\overset{\overset{CH_3}{|}}{C}} - I + CH_3OH$

(ii) $CH_3 - CH = CH_2 \xrightarrow[\text{(ii) } 3H_2O_2/OH^-]{\text{(i) } B_2H_6} 3CH_3 CH_2 - CH_2 - OH$

Propene   (Anti-Markovnikov addition)   (Propanol)

(iii) $C_6H_5 - OH$ Phenol $\xrightarrow[\substack{\text{(i) } CO_2,H^+ \\ \text{(Kolbe's reaction)}}]{\text{(i) aq. NaOH}}$

2-Hydroxybenzoic acid (ortho-hydroxybenzoic acid with OH and COOH)

$+$

4-Hydroxybenzoic acid (para-hydroxybenzoic acid with OH and COOH)

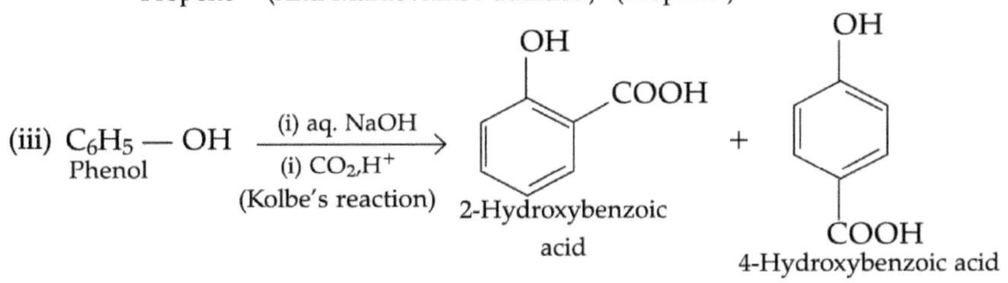

Q. 4. Predict the product of the following reaction.

$$C_6H_5 - CH_2 - \underset{\underset{OH}{|}}{CH} - CH \overset{CH_3}{\underset{CH_3}{<}} \xrightarrow[H_2SO_4, \Delta]{\text{Conc.}}$$

Ans.

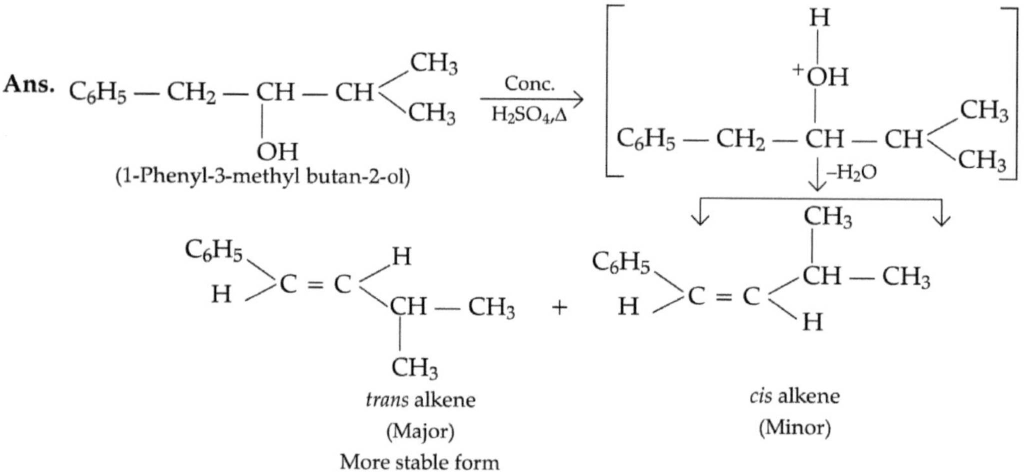

$$C_6H_5-CH_2-CH-CH\big<{}^{CH_3}_{CH_3}$$ (with OH below) (1-Phenyl-3-methyl butan-2-ol) $\xrightarrow[\text{H}_2\text{SO}_4,\Delta]{\text{Conc.}}$

$$\left[C_6H_5-CH_2-CH-CH\big<{}^{CH_3}_{CH_3} \;({}^{+}OH,\,H \text{ above}) \right] \xrightarrow{-H_2O}$$

trans alkene (Major) — More stable form

$$\big<{}^{C_6H_5}_{H}C=C\big<{}^{H}_{CH-CH_3}$$ (with CH₃ below) **trans** alkene (Major) More stable form

$$+ \quad \big<{}^{C_6H_5}_{H}C=C\big<{}^{CH-CH_3}_{H}$$ **cis** alkene (Minor)

Q. 5. Write the intermediate steps in the following reaction.

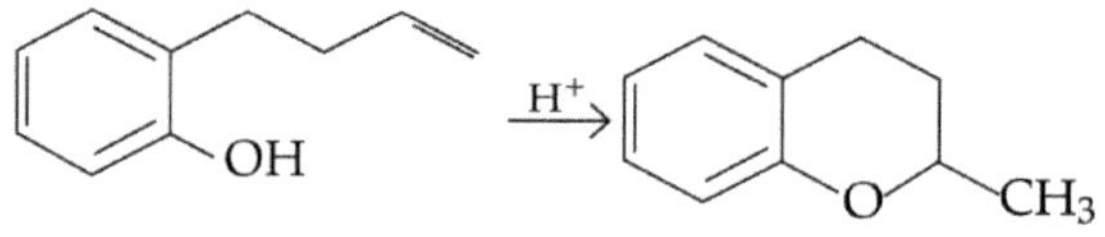

The addition of H+ occurs in accordance to Markovnikov's rule to give a more stable carbocation (A).

Ans. The addition of H+ occurs in accordance to Markovnikov's rule to give a more stable carbocation (A).

Nucleophilic attack of OH group

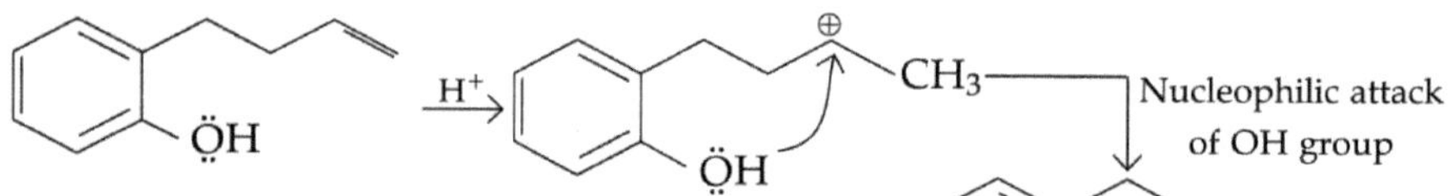

But the intermolecular nucleophilic attack occurs to form another product (B). It looses proton to give the final cyclic product.

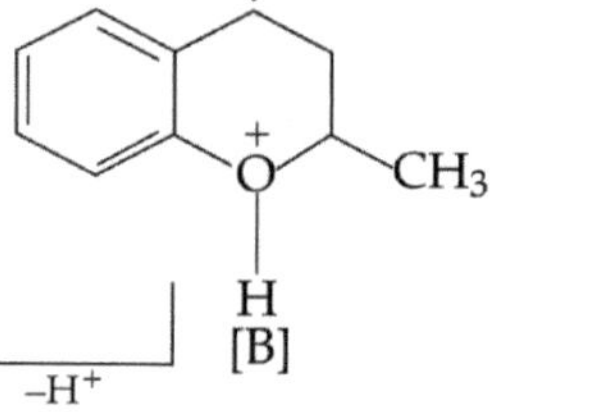

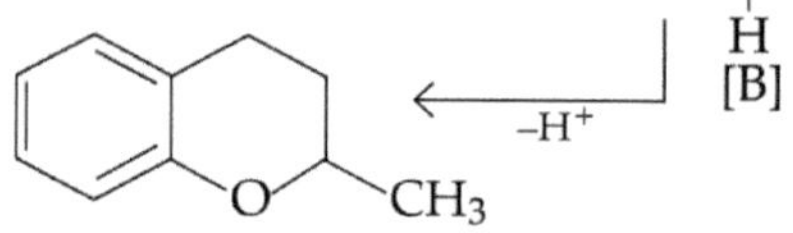

[B]

Q. 6. Give structures of [A], [B] and [C] in the following:

$$[A]\xrightarrow[250°C]{Al_2O_3}[B]\xrightarrow[\text{(ii) AgOH}]{\text{(i) HI}}[C]\xrightarrow[250°C]{Al_2O_3}[B]\xrightarrow[\text{(ii) H}_2\text{O}_2/\text{OH}]{\text{(i) B}_2\text{H}_6}[A]$$

Given: [A] and [C] are isomers. [B] has molecular formula C_5H_{10} and can be obtained by reacting. CH_3CH_2MgBr with $(CH_3)_2CO$.

Ans.
$$CH_3-\underset{CH_3}{\overset{O}{C}} + CH_3CH_2MgBr \xrightarrow{H_3O^+} CH_3-\underset{\underset{[C]}{CH_3}}{\overset{OH}{C}}-CH_2-CH_3 \xrightarrow{-H_2O} CH_3-\underset{\underset{[C_5H_{10}]}{CH_3}}{C}=CH-CH_3$$

As [B] can be produced by dehydration of [C] by Al_2O_3 at 250°C. Hence, [C] must be a tertiary alcohol. Also [C] is isomeric to [A]. Hence [C] is

$$CH_3-\underset{CH_3}{\overset{OH}{C}}-CH_2-CH_3 \quad \text{and [A] is} \quad CH_3-\underset{CH_3}{CH}-\overset{OH}{CH}-CH_3$$

Sequence of reactions,

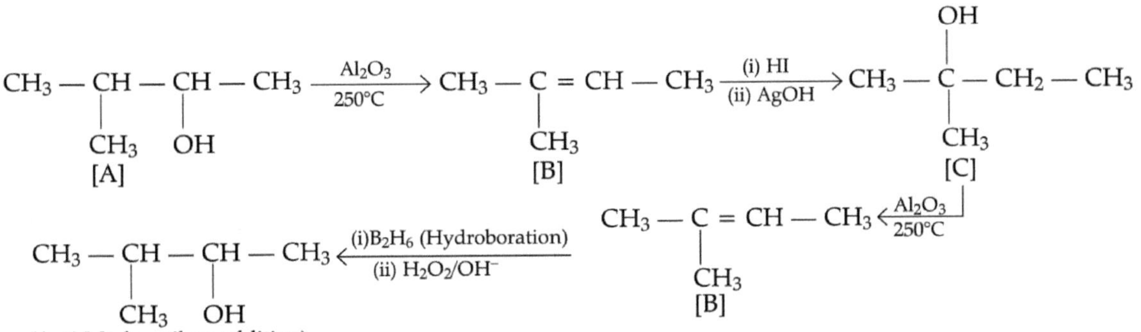

$$CH_3-\underset{\underset{CH_3}{|}}{CH}-\underset{\underset{OH}{|}}{CH}-CH_3 \xrightarrow[250°C]{Al_2O_3} CH_3-\underset{\underset{CH_3}{|}}{C}=CH-CH_3 \xrightarrow[\text{(ii) AgOH}]{\text{(i) HI}} CH_3-\underset{\underset{CH_3}{|}}{\overset{\overset{OH}{|}}{C}}-CH_2-CH_3$$

$$\text{[A]} \qquad\qquad \text{[B]} \qquad\qquad \text{[C]}$$

$$CH_3-\underset{\underset{CH_3}{|}}{C}=CH-CH_3 \xleftarrow[250°C]{Al_2O_3}$$

$$\text{[B]}$$

$$CH_3-\underset{\underset{CH_3}{|}}{CH}-\underset{\underset{OH}{|}}{CH}-CH_3 \xleftarrow[\text{(ii) } H_2O_2/OH^-]{\text{(i)}B_2H_6 \text{ (Hydroboration)}}$$

(Anti-Markovnikov addition)

Q. 7. Give the structures and IUPAC names of monohydric phenols of molecular formula, C_7H_8O.

Ans

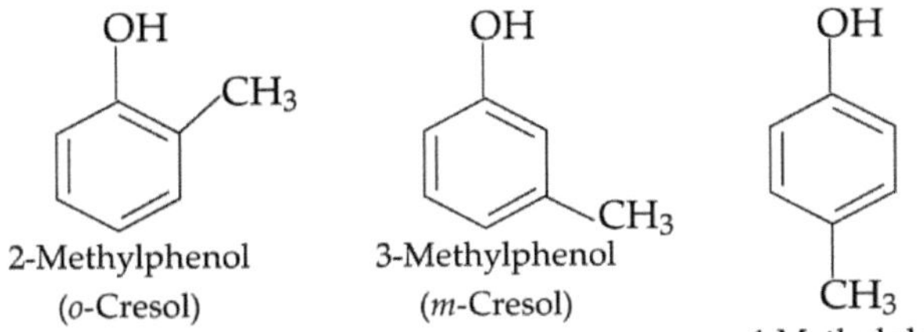

2-Methylphenol
(*o*-Cresol)

3-Methylphenol
(*m*-Cresol)

4-Methylphenol
(*p*-Cresol)

Q. 8. Give the reactions for the preparation of phenol from cumene.

Ans. To prepare phenol, cumene is first oxidized in the presence of air of cumene hydroperoxide.

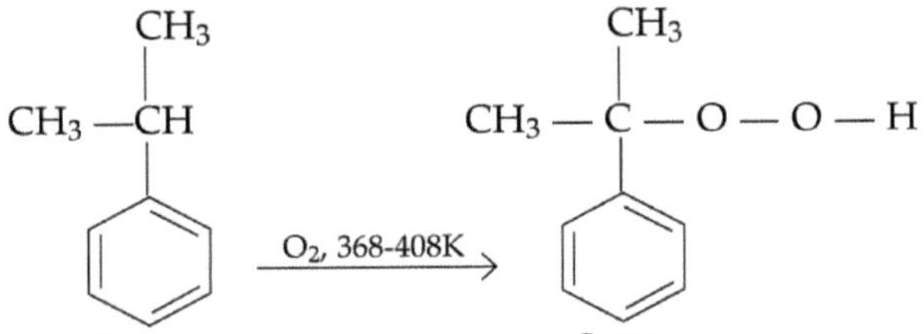

$$\xrightarrow{O_2,\ 368\text{-}408K}$$

Cumene
(Isopropylbenzene)

Cumene
(Hydroperoxide)

Then, cumene hydroxide is treated with dilute acid to prepare phenol and acetone as by products.

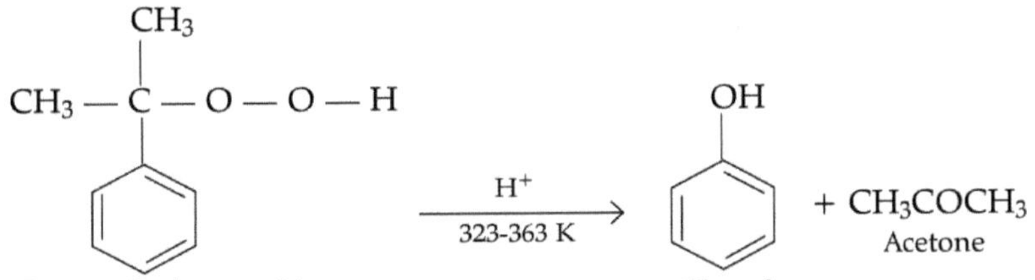

$$\xrightarrow[323\text{-}363\ K]{H^+}$$

$$+ CH_3COCH_3$$

Cumene hydroperoxide

Phenol

Acetone

Q. 9. You are given benzene, conc. H_2SO_4 and NaOH. Write the equations for the preparation of phenol using these reagents.

Ans.

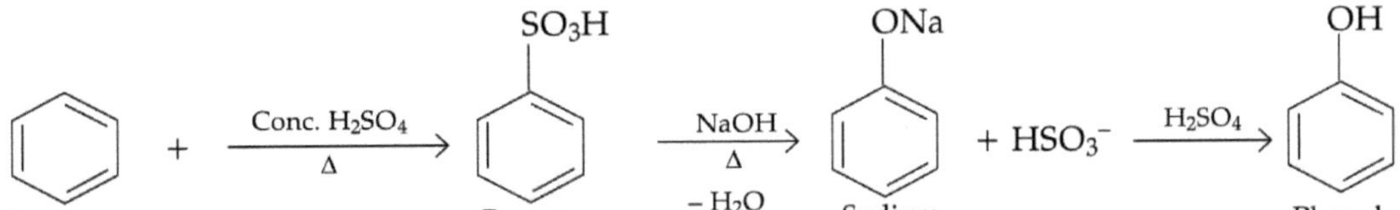

$$\xrightarrow[\Delta]{\text{Conc. } H_2SO_4} \xrightarrow[-H_2O]{\text{NaOH}}{\Delta} + HSO_3^- \xrightarrow{H_2SO_4}$$

Benzene

Benzene
sulphonic acid

Sodium
phenoxide

Phenol

Q. 10. Write the equation of the reaction of hydrogen iodide with :

    (i) 1-propoxypropane   (ii) Methoxybenzene   (iii) Benzyl ethyl ether.

Ans. (i) $C_2H_5CH_2-O-CH_2C_2H_5 + HI \xrightarrow{373\ K} CH_3CH_2CH-OH + CH_3CH_2CH_2-I$

      1-Propoxypropane   Propan-1-ol   1-Iodopropane

(ii)

$$\text{Methoxybenzene} + HI \longrightarrow \text{Phenol} + CH_3-I \text{ (Iodomethane)}$$

(iii)

$$\text{Benzyl ethyl ether} + HI \longrightarrow \text{Benzyl iodide} + C_2H_5-OH \text{ (Ethanol)}$$

Q. 11. Write equations of the following reactions:

(i) Friedel-Craft's reaction—alkylation of anisole.

(ii) Nitration of anisole.

(iii) Bromination of anisole in ethanoic acid medium.

(iv) Friedel-Craft's acetylation of anisole.

Ans. (i) Anisole $+ CH_3Cl \xrightarrow[CS_2]{\text{Anhyd. AlCl}_3}$ 4-Methoxytoluene (Major) $+$ 2-Methoxytoluene (Major)

(ii) Anisole $\xrightarrow[\text{HNO}_3]{\text{H}_2\text{SO}_4}$ 2-Nitroanisole (Minor) $+$ 4-Nitroanisole (Major)

(iii) Anisole $\xrightarrow[\text{Ethanoic acid}]{\text{Br}_2 \text{ in}}$ p-Bromoanisole (Major) $+$ o-Bromoanisole (Minor)

(iv) Anisole $+ CH_3COCl$ (Ethanoyl chloride) $\xrightarrow{\text{Anhyd. AlCl}_3}$ 2-Methoxy-acetophenone (Minor) $+$ 4-Methoxy-acetophenone (Major)

Q. 12. Write structures of the products of the following reactions:

(i) $CH_3-CH=CH_2 \xrightarrow{\text{H}_2\text{O/H}^+}$

(ii) [cyclohexanone with substituent] $CH_2 - C - OCH_3 \xrightarrow{NaBH_4}$

(iii) $CH_3 - CH_2 - \underset{\underset{CH_3}{|}}{CH} - CHO \xrightarrow{NaBH_4}$

Ans. (i) $CH_3 - CH = CH_2 \xrightarrow{H_2O/H^+} CH_3 - \underset{\underset{OH}{|}}{CH} - CH_3$ (Markovnikov addition)

(propan-2-ol)

(ii) [structure: Methyl (2-Oxocyclohexyl) Ethanoate] $\xrightarrow{NaBH_4}$ [structure: Methyl (2-Hydroxycyclohexyl) Ethanoate]

Methyl (2-Oxocyclohexyl) Ethanoate

Methyl (2-Hydroxycyclohexyl) Ethanoate

$NaBH_4$ only reduces ketonic group and leaves the ester group as it is.

(iii) $CH_3 - CH_2 = CH - \underset{\underset{CH_3}{|}}{} CHO \xrightarrow{NaBH_4} CH_3 - CH_2 - \underset{\underset{CH_3}{|}}{CH} - CH_2OH$

2-Methylbutanal

2-Methylbutan-1-ol

Q. 13. Give structures of the products you would expect when each of the following alcohol reacts with (i) HCl-ZnCl$_2$ (ii) HBr, (iii) SOCl$_2$.

(a) Butan-1-ol

(b) 2-Methylbutan-2-ol.

Ans. (i) (a) $CH_3 - CH_2 = CH_2 - CH_2 - OH \xrightarrow{HCl + ZnCl_2}$ No reaction at room temperature

Butan-1-ol

Primary alcohols do not react appreciably with Lucas' reagent (HCl-ZnCl$_2$) at room temperature.

$CH_3 - CH_2 - CH_2 - OH \xrightarrow[\text{(Lucas reagent)}]{ZnCl_2 - HCl} CH_3 - CH_2 - CH_2 - CH_2 - Cl$

Butan-1-ol

1-Chloro-butane

(b) $CH_3 - CH_2 - \underset{\underset{CH_3}{|}}{\overset{\overset{OH}{|}}{C}} - CH_3 \xrightarrow{HCl + ZnCl_2} CH_3 - CH_2 - \underset{\underset{CH_3}{|}}{\overset{\overset{Cl}{|}}{C}} - CH_3 + H_2O$

2-Methylbutan-2-ol (3°)

2-Chloro-2-Methylbutane (White turbidity)

Tertiary alcohols react immediately with Lucas' reagent.

(ii) (a) $CH_3CH_2CH_2CH_2OH + HBr \xrightarrow[-H_2O]{} CH_3 CH_2CH_2CH_2Br$

Butan-1-ol

1-Bromobutane

(b) $CH_3 - CH_2 - \underset{\underset{CH_3}{|}}{\overset{\overset{OH}{|}}{C}} - CH_3 + HBr \longrightarrow CH_3 - CH_2 - \underset{\underset{CH_3}{|}}{\overset{\overset{Br}{|}}{C}} - CH_3 + H_2O$

2-Methylbutan-2-ol (3°)

2-Bromo-2-Methylbutane

(iii) (a) $CH_3CH_2CH_2CH_2OH + SOCl_2 \longrightarrow CH_3CH_2CH_2CH_2Cl + SO_2 + HCl$

Butan-1-ol

1-Chlorobutane

(b) $CH_3 - CH_2 - \underset{\underset{CH_3}{|}}{\overset{\overset{OH}{|}}{C}} - CH_3 + SOCl \longrightarrow CH_3 - CH_2 - \underset{\underset{CH_3}{|}}{\overset{\overset{Cl}{|}}{C}} - CH_3 + SO_2 + HCl$

2-Methylbutan-2-ol (3°)

2-Chloro-2-Methylbutane

Q. 14. Complete the following reactions:*

(i) 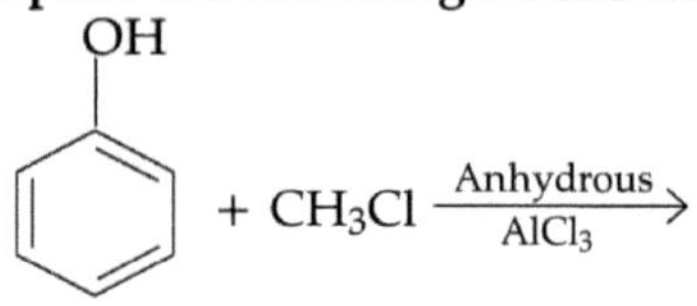 [phenol structure, OH] $+ CH_3Cl \xrightarrow[\text{AlCl}_3]{\text{Anhydrous}}$

(ii) 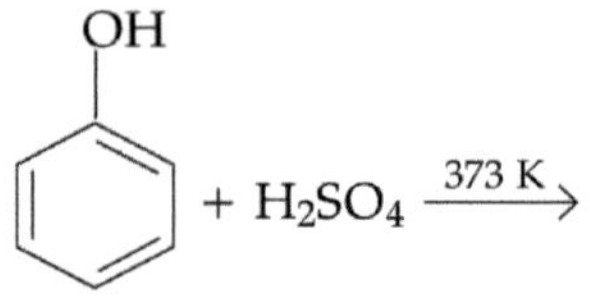 [phenol structure, OH] $+ H_2SO_4 \xrightarrow{373 \text{ K}}$

Ans. (i) 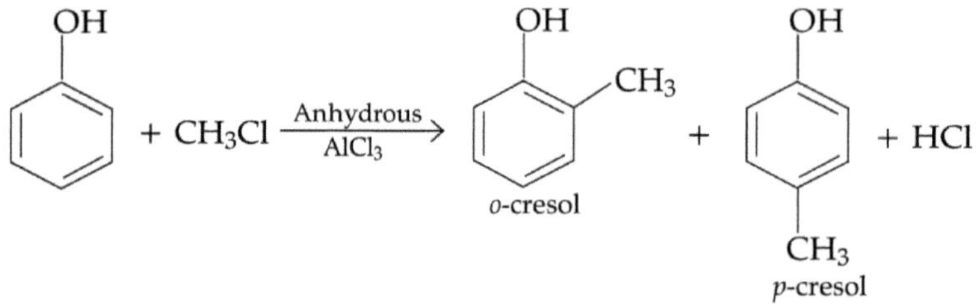 [phenol, OH] $+ CH_3Cl \xrightarrow[\text{AlCl}_3]{\text{Anhydrous}}$ [o-cresol: OH, CH$_3$] *o*-cresol $+$ [p-cresol: OH, CH$_3$] *p*-cresol $+ HCl$

(ii) 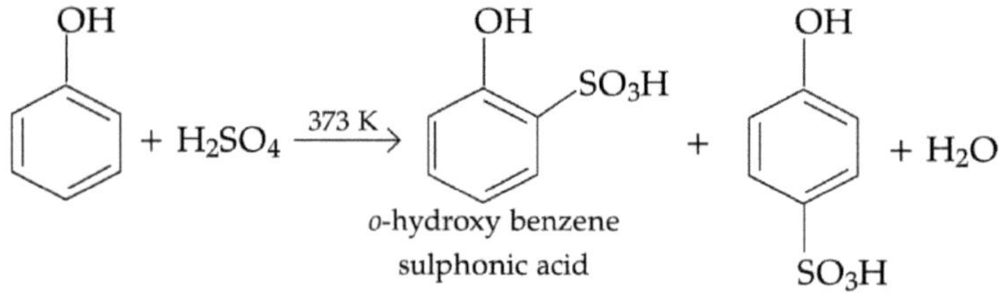 [phenol, OH] $+ H_2SO_4 \xrightarrow{373 \text{ K}}$ [o-hydroxy benzene sulphonic acid: OH, SO$_3$H] *o*-hydroxy benzene sulphonic acid $+$ [OH, SO$_3$H] $+ H_2O$

Q. 15. Complete the following reactions:*

(i) $C_6H_5ONa + C_6H_5Cl \longrightarrow$

(ii) 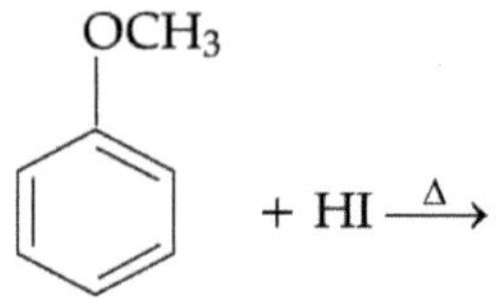 [anisole, OCH$_3$] $+ HI \xrightarrow{\Delta}$

Ans. (i) $C_6H_5ONa + C_6H_5Cl \longrightarrow C_6H_5OC_6H_5 + NaCl$

(ii) 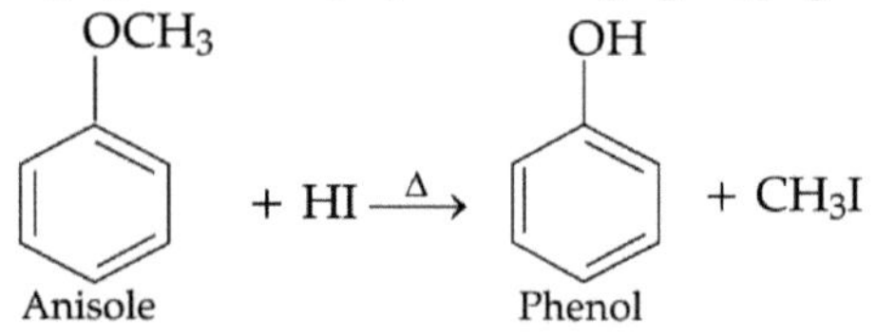 [Anisole, OCH$_3$] $+ HI \xrightarrow{\Delta}$ [Phenol, OH] $+ CH_3I$

Anisole   Phenol

Chapter 12. Aldehydes, Ketones and Carboxylic Acids

Q. 1. Predict the product of the following reactions:*

(i) $CH_3 - \underset{\underset{CH_3}{|}}{C} = O \xrightarrow{H_2N - NH_2}$

(ii) $C_6H_5 - CH_3 \xrightarrow[\text{(b) } H^+]{\text{(a) KMnO}_4\text{/KOH}}$

(iii) 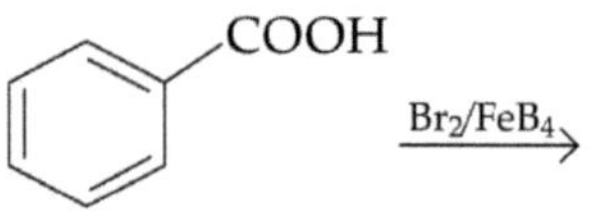 [benzene ring with COOH] $\xrightarrow{Br_2/FeB_4}$

Ans. (i) $CH_3 - \underset{\underset{CH_3}{|}}{C} = O \xrightarrow{H_2N - NH_2} CH_3 - \underset{\underset{CH_3}{|}}{C} = N - NH_2 + H_2O$

(ii) $C_6H_5 - CH_3 \xrightarrow[\text{(b) } H^+]{\text{(a) KMnO}_4/\text{KOH}} C_6H_5 - COOH + 2MnO_2 + 2KOH$

(iii) 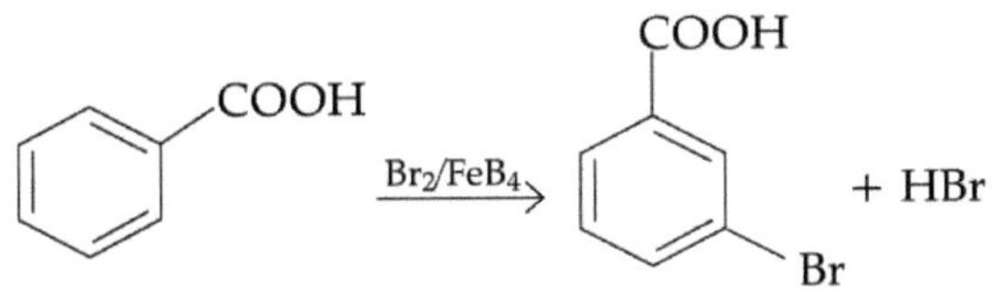 [benzene ring with COOH] $\xrightarrow{\text{Br}_2/\text{FeB}_4}$ [benzene ring with COOH and Br] $+ HBr$

Q. 2. Write the products of the following reactions:

(i) $CH_3 - COOH \xrightarrow{\text{Br}_2/\text{P}} ?$

(ii) $CH_3 - CHO \xrightarrow{\text{LiAlH}_4} ?$

(iii) $CH_3 - \underset{\underset{O}{\|}}{C} - CH_3 \xrightarrow[\text{Conc. HCl}]{\text{Zn} - \text{Hg}} ?$

Ans. (i) $CH_3 - COOH \xrightarrow{\text{Br}_2/\text{P}} \underset{\overset{|}{Br}}{CH_2} - COOH$

(ii) $CH_3 - CHO \xrightarrow{\text{LiAlH}_4} CH_3CH_2OH$

(iii) $CH_3 - \underset{\underset{O}{\|}}{C} - CH_3 \xrightarrow[\text{Conc. HCl}]{\text{Zn} - \text{Hg}} CH_3CH_2CH_3 + H_2O$

Q. 3. What happens when:

(i) Acetic acid reacts with $SOCl_2$

(ii) Calcium acetate is dry distilled.

Ans. (i) $CH_3COOH + SOCl_2 \xrightarrow[\text{Base}]{\text{Pyridine}} \underset{\text{Acetlyl chloride}}{CH_3COCl} + SO_2\uparrow + HCl$

(ii) Calcium acetate $\xrightarrow[\text{Distillation}]{\text{Dry}} \underset{\text{Acetone}}{CH_3 - \overset{\overset{O}{\|}}{C} - CH_3} + CaCO_3$

Q. 4. An aldehyde 'A' ($C_{11}H_8O$) which does not undergo self aldol condensation, gives one mole benzaldehyde and 2 moles of a compound 'B' on ozonolysis. Compound 'B' on oxidation with silver ions gives oxalic acid. Identifying the compound 'A' and 'B'.

Ans. As [A] is an aldehyde, but does not undergo aldol condensation, hence it does not have any α-hydrogen present. It undergoes ozonolysis hence it must be unsaturated compound. Also as it provides one mole benzaldehyde and 2 moles of compound [B], so it must have two compounds [B] on, points of unsaturation oxidation gives oxalic acid *i.e.*, (COOH–COOH), hence compound [B] must be (CHO–COOH), one end from ozonolysis of alkene, other from alkyne. The reactions are:

(CHO–COOH) Formyl methanoic acid $\xrightarrow[\text{[O]}]{\text{Ag}^+}$ (COOH–COOH) Oxalic acid

Hence compound (A) must be

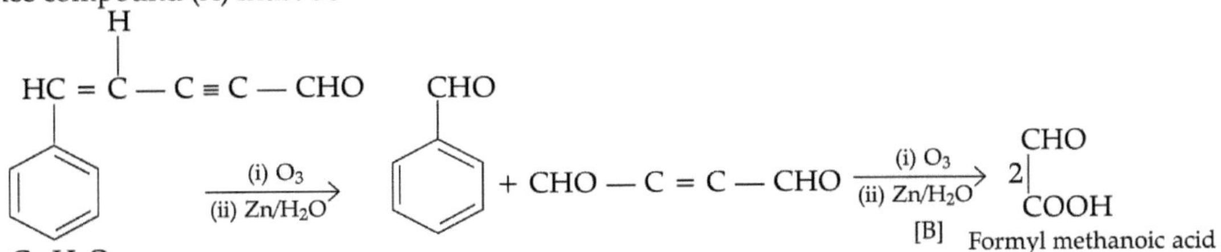

$HC = \overset{\overset{H}{|}}{C} - C \equiv C - CHO$ [benzene ring] $C_{11}H_8O$ [A]

$\xrightarrow[\text{(ii) Zn/H}_2\text{O}]{\text{(i) O}_3}$ [benzene ring with CHO] $+ CHO - C = C - CHO \xrightarrow[\text{(ii) Zn/H}_2\text{O}]{\text{(i) O}_3} 2 (CHO–COOH)$ [B] Formyl methanoic acid

Q. 5. Write product of the following reactions:*

(i) 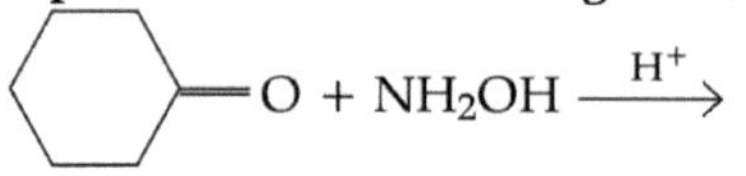 (cyclohexanone) $=O + NH_2OH \xrightarrow{H^+}$

(ii) 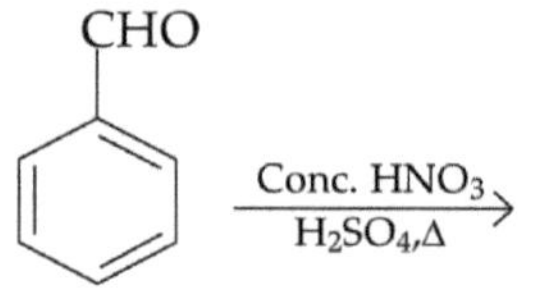 (benzaldehyde, CHO) $\xrightarrow[H_2SO_4, \Delta]{Conc. HNO_3}$

Ans. (i) 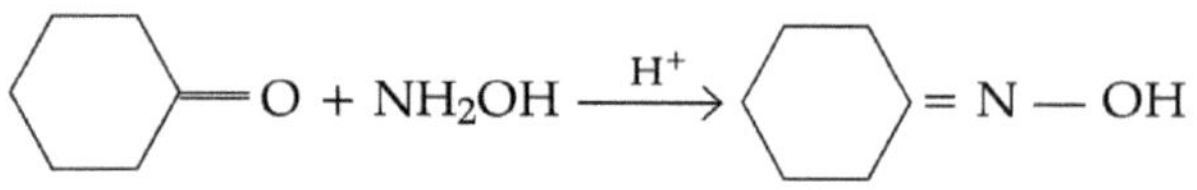 (cyclohexanone) $=O + NH_2OH \xrightarrow{H^+}$ (cyclohexanone oxime) $= N - OH$

(ii) 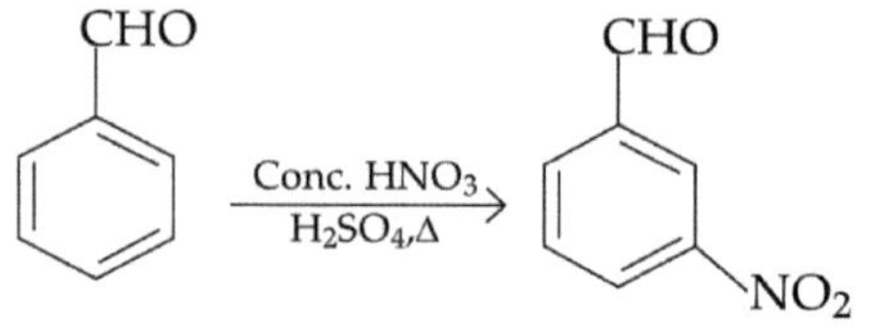 (benzaldehyde, CHO) $\xrightarrow[H_2SO_4, \Delta]{Conc. HNO_3}$ (m-nitrobenzaldehyde, CHO ... NO_2)

Q. 6.

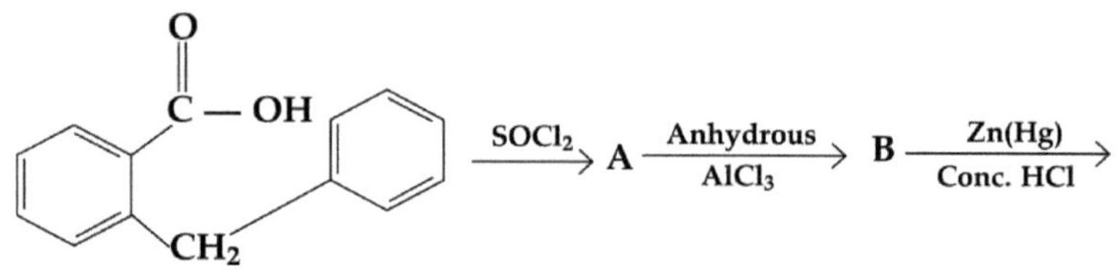

(2-benzyl benzoic acid, $\overset{O}{\overset{\|}{C}} - OH$, CH_2) $\xrightarrow{SOCl_2} A \xrightarrow[AlCl_3]{Anhydrous} B \xrightarrow[Conc. HCl]{Zn(Hg)} C$ **Write structures of A, B and C.**

Ans.

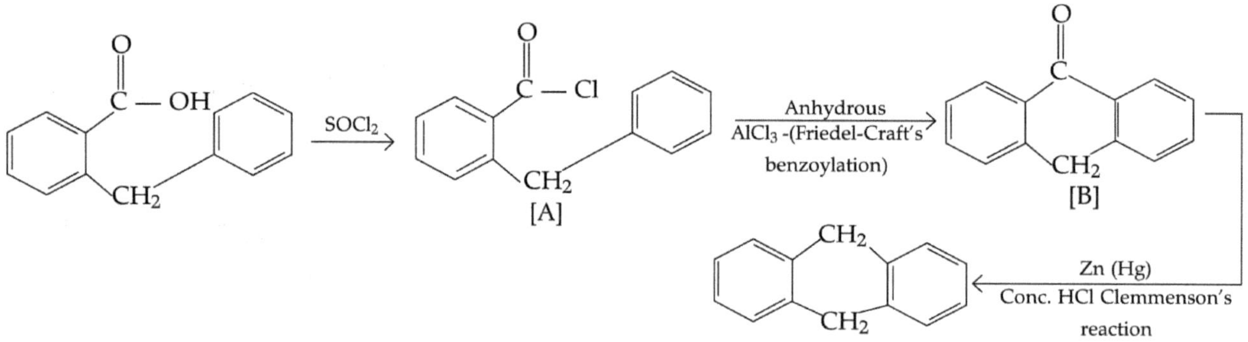

(acid, $\overset{O}{\overset{\|}{C}} - OH$, CH_2) $\xrightarrow{SOCl_2}$ (acid chloride [A], $\overset{O}{\overset{\|}{C}} - Cl$, CH_2) $\xrightarrow[\text{benzoylation)}]{\substack{\text{Anhydrous} \\ AlCl_3 \text{-(Friedel-Craft's}}}$ (ketone [B], CH_2)

[B] $\xrightarrow[\substack{\text{Conc. HCl Clemmenson's} \\ \text{reaction}}]{Zn (Hg)}$ (reduced product, CH_2, CH_2)

Q. 7. Write the reactions involved in the following:

(i) Hell-Volhard Zelinsky reaction   (ii) Decarboxylation reaction.

Ans. (i) Hell-Volhard Zelinsky reaction

$$CH_3COOH \xrightarrow[- HCl]{+ Cl_2, Red P} CH_2Cl.COOH \xrightarrow[- HCl]{+ Cl_2, Red P} CHCl_2.COOH \xrightarrow[- HCl]{+ Cl_2, Red P} CCl_3.COOH$$

Acetic acid   Monochloro acetic acid   Dichloro acetic acid   Trichloro acetic acid

(ii) Decarboxylation reaction.

$$CH_3COONa \xrightarrow[\Delta]{NaOH \text{ and } CaO} CH_4 + Na_2CO_3$$

Sodium acetate   Methane

Q. 8. Write the structures of compound A, B and C in each of the following sentences:

(i) $C_6H_5Br \xrightarrow{Mg/dry\ ether} A \xrightarrow[(b)\ H_3O^+]{(a)\ CO_{2(g)}} B \xrightarrow{PCl_5} C$

(ii) $CH_3CN \xrightarrow[(b)\ H_3O^+]{(a)\ SnCl_2/HCl} A \xrightarrow{dil.\ NaOH} B \xrightarrow{\Delta} C$

Ans. (i) $C_6H_5Br \xrightarrow[dry\ ether]{Mg/} \underset{(A)}{C_6H_5MgBr} \xrightarrow[(b)\ H_3O^+]{(a)\ CO_{2(g)}} \underset{(B)}{C_6H_5COOH} \xrightarrow{PCl_5} \underset{(C)}{C_6H_5COCl}$

(ii) $CH_3CN \xrightarrow[(b)\ H_3O^+]{(a)\ SnCl_2/HCl} \underset{(A)}{CH_3CHO} \xrightarrow{dil.\ NaOH} \underset{(B)}{CH_3CH(OH)CH_2CHO} \xrightarrow{\Delta} \underset{(C)}{CH_3CH = CHCHO}$

Chapter 13. Amines

Q. 1. State the reaction taking place when bromine water is added to the aqueous solution of aniline.*

Ans.

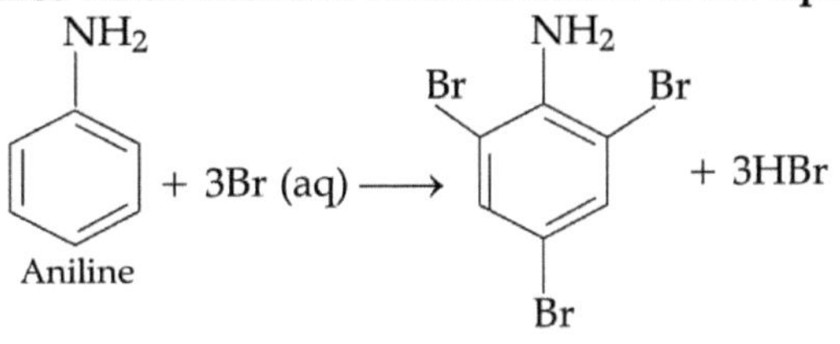

$$\text{Aniline} + 3Br\ (aq) \longrightarrow \text{2,4,6-tribromoaniline} + 3HBr$$

Q. 2. Complete and name the following reactions:*

(i) $RNH_2 + CHCl_3 + 3KOH \longrightarrow$

(ii) $RCONH_2 + Br_2 + 4NaOH \longrightarrow$

Ans. (i) $RNH_2 + CHCl_3 + 3\ KOH \longrightarrow R-NC + 3KCl + 3H_2O$

(Isocyanide reaction)

(ii) $RCONH_2 + Br_2 + 4NaOH \longrightarrow RNH_2 + Na_2CO_3 + 2NaBr + 2H_2O$

(Hofmann Bromamide degradation reaction)

Q. 3. Identify A and B in the following processes:*

(i) $CH_3CH_2Cl \xrightarrow{\text{NaCN}} A \xrightarrow[\text{Ni/H}_2]{\text{[H]}} B$

(ii) $C_6H_5NH_2 \xrightarrow[\text{HCl}]{\text{NaNO}_2/} A \xrightarrow[\text{OH}^-]{C_6H_5NH_2} B$

Ans. (i) A is CH_3CH_2CN and B is $CH_3CH_2CH_2NH_2$

    Ethylcyanide   Propylamine

(ii) A is $C_6H_5N_2+Cl^-$ and B is $C_6H_5N = NC_6H_4NH_2$

    Benzene diazonium   (*para* substitution)
       chloride

$$\text{C}_6\text{H}_5 - N = N - \text{C}_6\text{H}_4 - NH_2$$

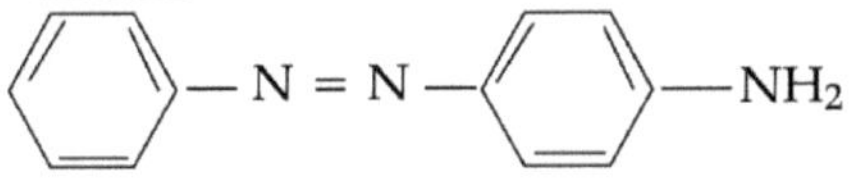

Q. 4. Identify substance A and B in the following reactions:

(i) $C_6H_5NH_2 \xrightarrow{CH_3COCl} A \xrightarrow{HNO_3/H_2SO_4} B$

(ii) $C_6H_5NH_2 \xrightarrow{H_2SO_4} A \xrightarrow[-H_2O]{\Delta} B$

Ans. (i)

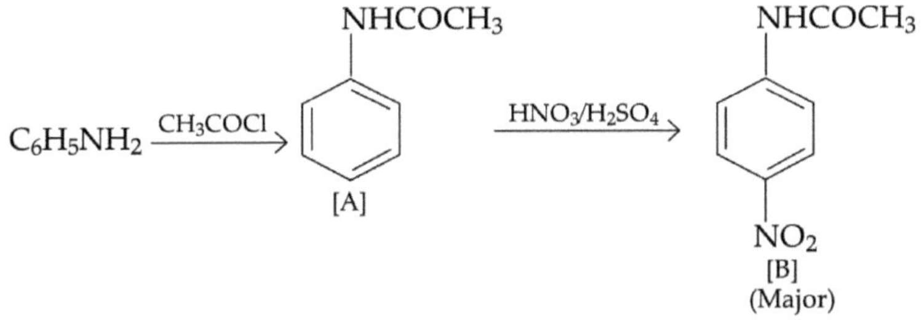

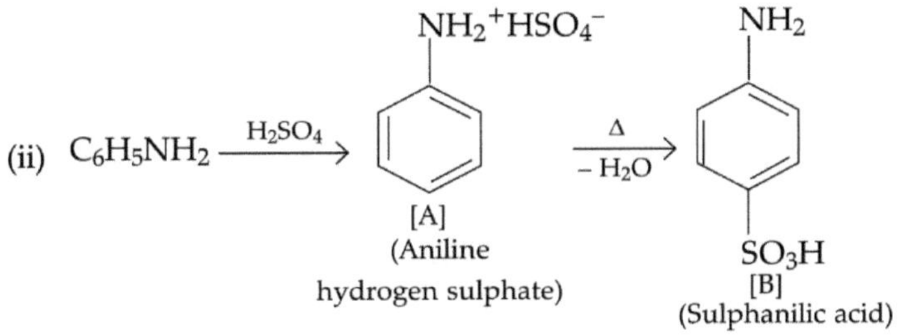

$$C_6H_5NH_2 \xrightarrow{CH_3COCl} \underset{[A]}{\text{(acetanilide, NHCOCH}_3) } \xrightarrow{HNO_3/H_2SO_4} \underset{\substack{[B]\\(Major)}}{\text{(p-nitroacetanilide, NHCOCH}_3,\ NO_2)}$$

(ii)

$$C_6H_5NH_2 \xrightarrow{H_2SO_4} \underset{\substack{[A]\\(\text{Aniline}\\ \text{hydrogen sulphate})}}{(NH_2{}^+HSO_4{}^-)} \xrightarrow[-H_2O]{\Delta} \underset{\substack{[B]\\(\text{Sulphanilic acid})}}{(NH_2,\ SO_3H)}$$

Q. 5. Complete the following reactions:*

(i) $C_6H_5N_2Cl \xrightarrow{H_3PO_2/H_2O}$

(ii) $C_6H_5NH_2 \xrightarrow{Br_2/H_2O}$

Ans. (i) $C_6H_5N_2Cl \xrightarrow{H_3PO_2/H_2O} C_6H_6$ (Benzene) $+ H_3PO_3$ (Phosphorous acid) $+ N_2 + HCl$

(ii) 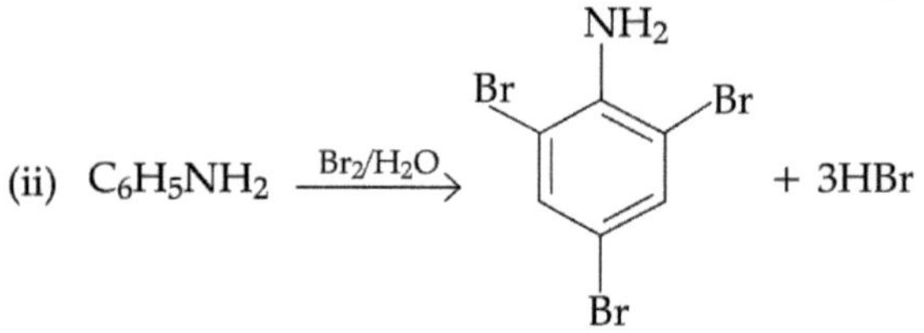 $C_6H_5NH_2 \xrightarrow{Br_2/H_2O}$ 2,4,6-tribromoaniline ($C_6H_2Br_3NH_2$) $+ 3HBr$

Q. 6. Write the structures of A, B and C in the following:

(i) $C_6H_5CO-NH_2 \xrightarrow[KOH]{Br_2/aq} A \xrightarrow[0-5°C]{NaNO_2 + HCl} B \xrightarrow{KI} C$

(ii) $CH_3-Cl \xrightarrow{KCN} A \xrightarrow{LiAlH_4} B \xrightarrow[alc.\ KOH]{CHCl_3^+} C^*$

Ans. (i) 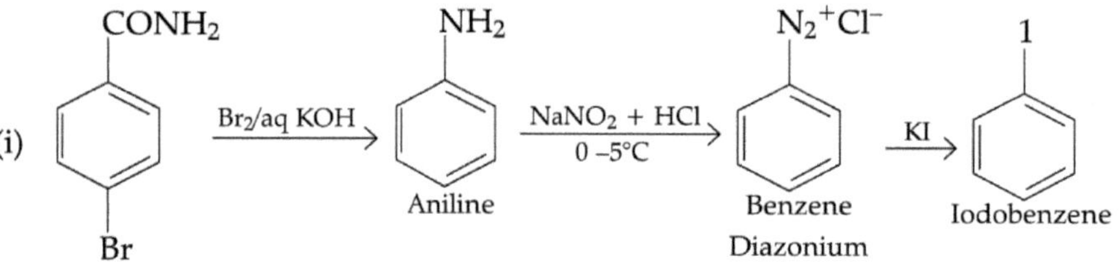 (CONH₂ with Br) $\xrightarrow{Br_2/aq\ KOH}$ Aniline (NH₂) $\xrightarrow[0-5°C]{NaNO_2+HCl}$ Benzene Diazonium chloride ($N_2^+Cl^-$) $\xrightarrow{KI}$ Iodobenzene

(Hofmann Bromamide degradation)

(ii) $CH_3-Cl \xrightarrow{KCN} CH_3-CN \xrightarrow{LiAlH_4} CH_3-CH_2-NH_2 \xrightarrow[alc.\ KOH]{CHCl_3} CH_3-CH_2-N\equiv C$ (Ethylisocyanide)

Q. 7. Fill in the blanks with reagents/organic compounds:

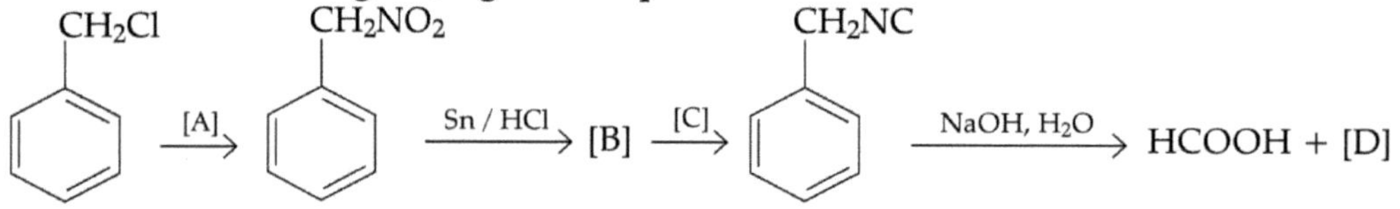

CH_2Cl (benzene) $\xrightarrow{[A]}$ CH_2NO_2 (benzene) $\xrightarrow{Sn/HCl}$ [B] $\xrightarrow{[C]}$ CH_2NC (benzene) $\xrightarrow{NaOH, H_2O}$ $HCOOH + [D]$

Ans. 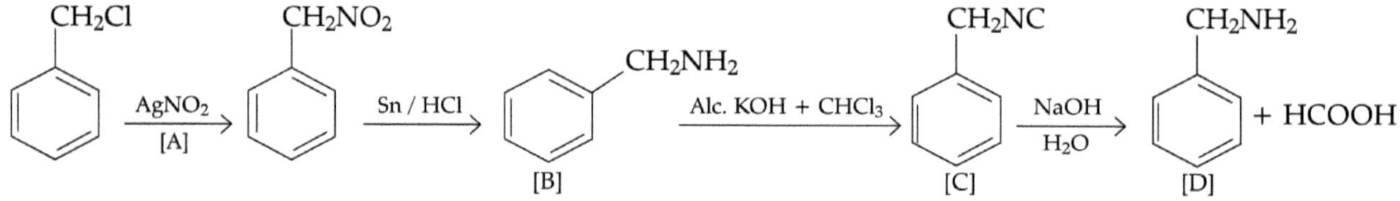 CH_2Cl (benzene) $\xrightarrow[[A]]{AgNO_2}$ CH_2NO_2 (benzene) $\xrightarrow{Sn/HCl}$ CH_2NH_2 (benzene) [B] $\xrightarrow{Alc.\ KOH + CHCl_3}$ CH_2NC (benzene) [C] $\xrightarrow[H_2O]{NaOH}$ CH_2NH_2 (benzene) [D] $+ HCOOH$

Q. 8. Identify the missing links in the following sequence of reactions.

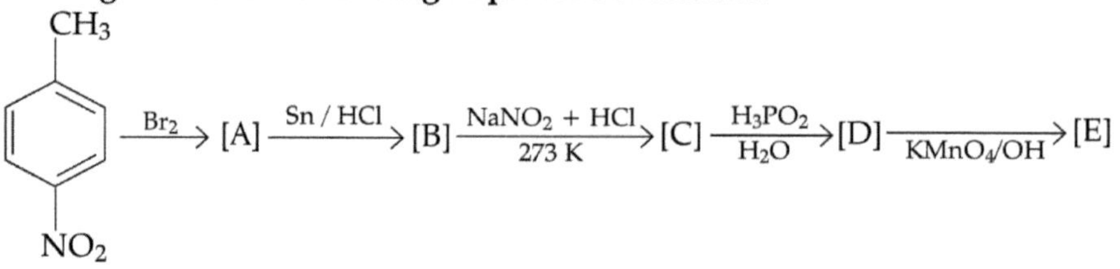

(toluene with NO₂, CH₃) $\xrightarrow{Br_2}$ [A] $\xrightarrow{Sn/HCl}$ [B] $\xrightarrow[273\ K]{NaNO_2 + HCl}$ [C] $\xrightarrow[H_2O]{H_3PO_2}$ [D] $\xrightarrow{KMnO_4/OH}$ [E]

Ans. 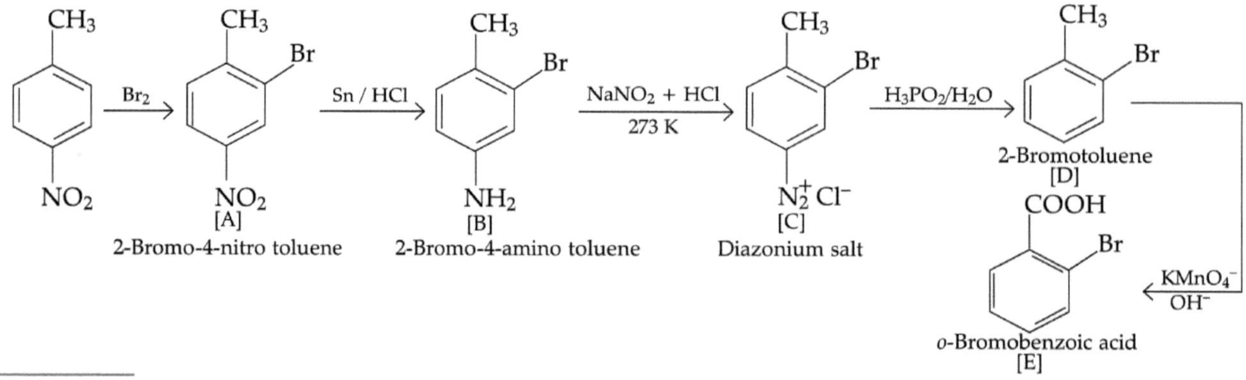 (CH₃, NO₂ toluene) $\xrightarrow{Br_2}$ 2-Bromo-4-nitro toluene [A] (CH₃, Br, NO₂) $\xrightarrow{Sn/HCl}$ 2-Bromo-4-amino toluene [B] (CH₃, Br, NH₂) $\xrightarrow[273\ K]{NaNO_2 + HCl}$ Diazonium salt [C] (CH₃, Br, $N_2^+Cl^-$) $\xrightarrow{H_3PO_2/H_2O}$ 2-Bromotoluene [D] (CH₃, Br) $\xrightarrow[OH^-]{KMnO_4^-}$ o-Bromobenzoic acid [E] (COOH, Br)

Q. 9. Complete the following reactions:

(i) [structure: benzene ring with CH_2CONH_2 and $COOCH_3$ substituents] $\xrightarrow[\text{2. H}_2\text{O}]{\text{1. Br}_2/\text{KOH}}$

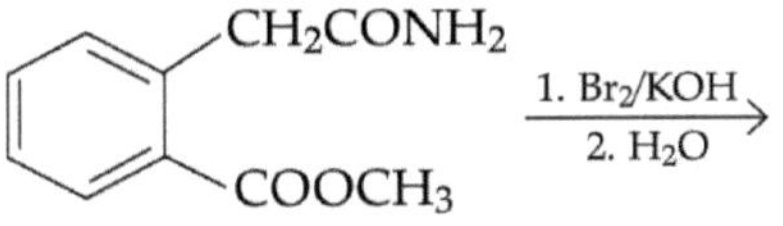

(ii) [structure: C₆H₅–NH–CO–C₆H₅ (benzanilide)] $\xrightarrow[\text{Conc. H}_2\text{SO}_4]{\text{Conc. HNO}_3}$

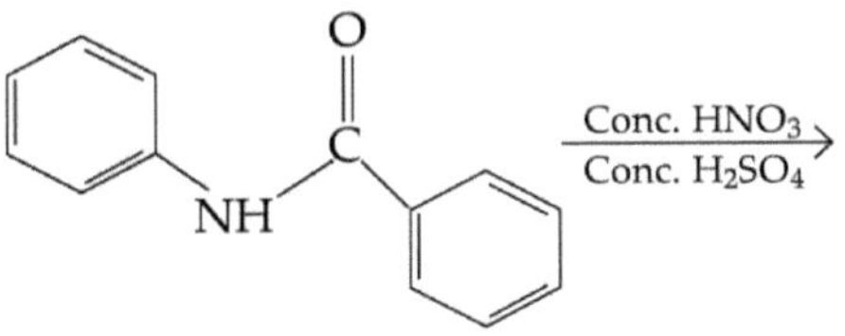

Ans. (i) [structure: benzene ring with CH_2CONH_2 and $COOCH_3$] $\xrightarrow[\text{2. }\Delta]{\text{1. Br}_2/\text{KOH}}$ [structure: benzene ring with CH_2NH_2 and $COOCH_3$]

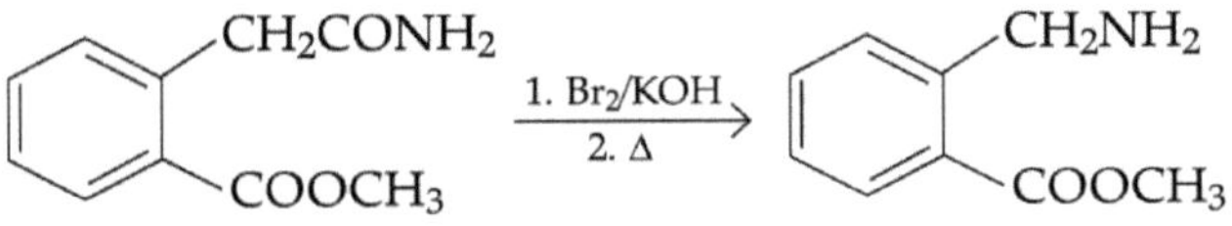

(ii) [structure: benzanilide] $\xrightarrow[\text{Conc. H}_2\text{SO}_4]{\text{Conc. HNO}_3}$ [structure: p-nitro benzanilide with NO_2 group]

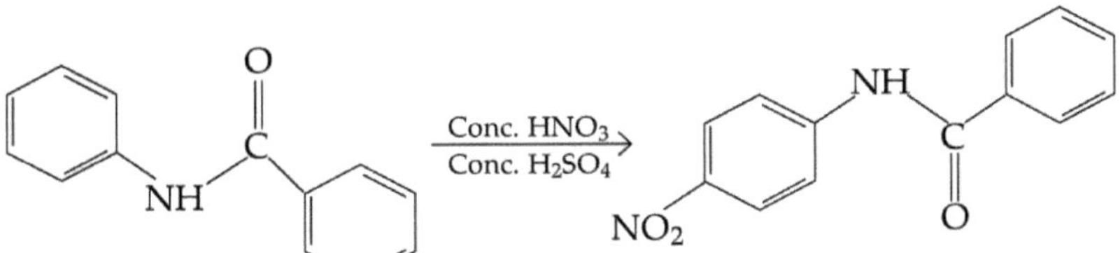

Q. 10. Identify product A, B and C in the series:

$$CH_3CN \xrightarrow{\text{Na/ethanol}} A \xrightarrow{\text{HNO}_2} B \xrightarrow{\text{Cu/573K}} C$$

Ans. $CH_3CN \xrightarrow[\text{Reduction}]{\text{Na/ethanol}} \underset{\substack{\text{Ethylamine}\\ \text{[A]}}}{CH_3CH_2NH_2} \xrightarrow[\text{Nitrous acid}]{\text{HNO}_2} \underset{\substack{\text{Ethanol}\\ \text{[B]}}}{CH_3CH_2OH} \xrightarrow{\text{Cu/573K}} \underset{\substack{\text{Ethanol}\\ \text{[C]}}}{CH_3CHO}$

Q. 11. Complete the following acid-base reactions and name the products:

(i) $CH_3CH_2CH_2NH_2 + HCl \longrightarrow$ **(ii)** $(C_2H_5)_3N + HCl \longrightarrow$

Ans. (i) $\underset{\text{n-Propylamine}}{CH_3CH_2CH_2NH_2} + HCl \longrightarrow \underset{\text{n-Propylammoniumchloride}}{CH_3CH_2CH_2\overset{+}{N}\overset{-}{H_3}\overset{-}{Cl}}$

(ii) $\underset{\text{Triethylamine}}{(C_2H_5)_3N} + HCl \longrightarrow \underset{\text{Triethylammoniumchloride}}{(C_2H_5)\overset{+}{N}\overset{-}{H_3}\overset{-}{Cl}}$

Q. 12. Write reactions of the final alkylation product of aniline with excess of methyl iodide in the presence of sodium carbonate solution.

Ans. Aniline reacts with methyl iodide to produce N, N-dimethylaniline.

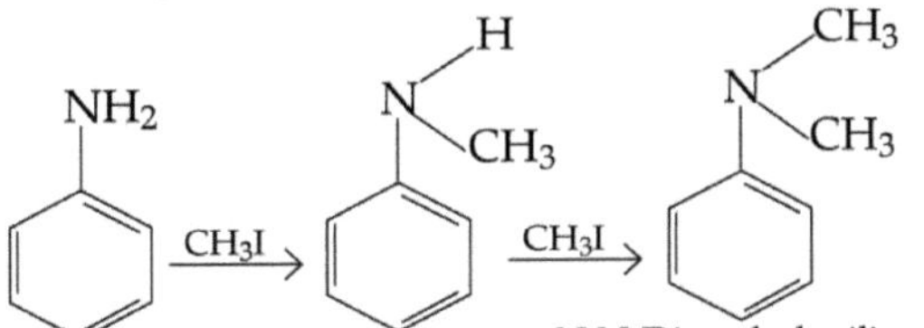

[reaction scheme: Aniline (NH_2) $\xrightarrow{CH_3I}$ N-methylaniline (N–H, N–CH₃) $\xrightarrow{CH_3I}$ N,N-Dimethylaniline (N–CH₃, N–CH₃)]

With excess methyl iodide, in the presence of Na_2CO_3 solution, N, N-dimethylaniline produces N, N, N-trimethylanilinium carbonate.

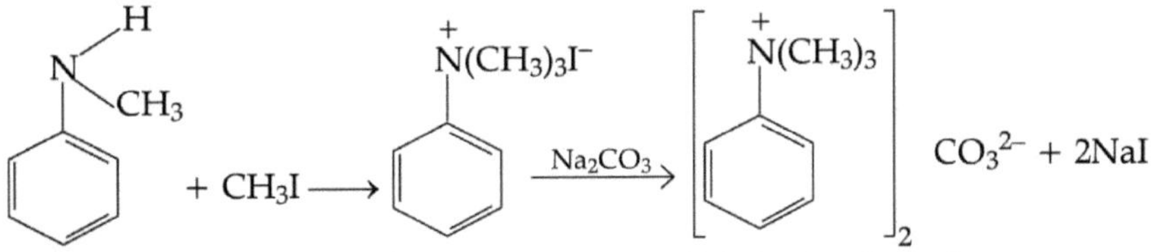

[reaction scheme: N,N-Dimethylaniline $+ CH_3I \longrightarrow$ N,N,N-Trimethylanilinium iodide ($\overset{+}{N}(CH_3)_3I^-$) $\xrightarrow{Na_2CO_3}$ $\left[\overset{+}{N}(CH_3)_3\text{-phenyl}\right]_2 CO_3^{2-} + 2NaI$ (N,N,N-Trimethylanilinium carbonate)]

Q. 13. Write chemical reaction of aniline with benzoyl chloride and write the name of the product obtained.

Ans.

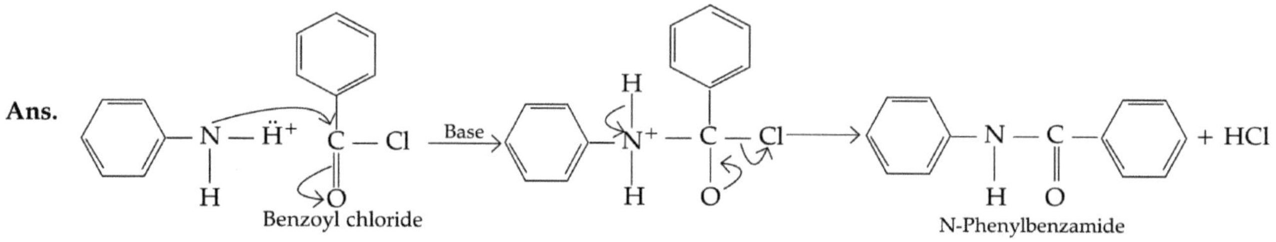

[Reaction scheme: aniline + benzoyl chloride $\xrightarrow{\text{Base}}$ intermediate $\longrightarrow$ N-Phenylbenzamide + HCl]

Benzoyl chloride

N-Phenylbenzamide
(Benzanilide)

Q. 14. Give the structures of A, B and C in the following reactions:

(i) $CH_3CH_2I \xrightarrow{NaCN} A \xrightarrow[\text{Partial hydrolysis}]{OH^-} B \xrightarrow{NaOH, Br_2} C$

(ii) $C_6H_5N_2Cl \xrightarrow{CuCN} A \xrightarrow{H_2O/H^+} B \xrightarrow[\Delta]{NH_3} C^*$

(iii) $CH_3CH_2Br \xrightarrow{KCN} A \xrightarrow{LiAlH_4} B \xrightarrow[0°C]{HNO_2} C$

(iv) $C_6H_5NO_2 \xrightarrow{Fe/HCl} A \xrightarrow[273K]{NaNO_2 + HCl} B \xrightarrow[\Delta]{H_2O/H^+} C$

(v) $CH_3COOH \xrightarrow[\Delta]{NH_3} A \xrightarrow{NaOBr} B \xrightarrow{NaNO_2/HCl} C^*$

(vi) $C_6H_5NO_2 \xrightarrow{Fe/HCl} A \xrightarrow[273K]{HNO_2} B \xrightarrow{C_6H_5OH} C$

Ans. (i) $CH_3CH_2I \xrightarrow{NaCN} CH_3CH_2CN \xrightarrow[\text{Partial hydrolysis}]{OH^-} CH_3-CH_2-\overset{O}{\overset{\|}{C}}-NH_2 \xrightarrow[\text{Degradation}]{\text{NaOH, Br}_2 \atop \text{Hofmann Bromamide}}$

Ethyliodide — Propane nitrile / Ethylcyanide (A) — Propanamide (B)

$CH_3-CH_2-NH_2$
Ethanamine

(ii) $C_6H_5\overset{+}{N_2}\overset{-}{Cl} \xrightarrow{CuCN} C_6H_5CN \xrightarrow{H_2O/H^+} C_6H_5COOH \xrightarrow[\Delta]{NH_3} C_6H_5CONH_2$

Benzene diazonium chloride — Cyanobenzene (A) — Benzoic acid (B) — Benzamide (C)

(iii) $CH_3CH_2Br \xrightarrow{KCN} CH_3CH_2CN \xrightarrow{LiAlH_4} CH_3CH_2CH_2NH_2 \xrightarrow[0°C]{HNO_2} CH_3CH_2CH_2OH$

Ethyl bromide — Ethylcyanide — Propan-1-amine (B) — Propan-1-ol (C)

(iv) $C_6H_5NO_2 \xrightarrow{Fe/HCl} C_6H_5NH_2 \xrightarrow[273K]{NaNO_2 + HCl} C_6H_5-\overset{+}{N_2}\overset{-}{Cl} \xrightarrow[\Delta]{H_2O/H^+} C_6H_5OH$

Nitrobenzene — Aniline (A) — Benzene diazonium chloride (B) — Phenol (C)

(v) $CH_3COOH \xrightarrow[\Delta]{NH_3} CH_3CONH_2 \xrightarrow{NaOBr} CH_3NH_2 \xrightarrow{NaNO_2/HCl} CH_3OH$

Acetic acid — Ethanamide (A) — Methanamine (B) — Methanol (C)

(vi) $C_6H_5NO_2 \xrightarrow{Fe/HCl} C_6H_5NH_2 \xrightarrow[273K]{HNO_2} C_6H_5-\overset{+}{N_2}\overset{-}{Cl} \xrightarrow{C_6H_5OH}$

[structure: $\langle C_6H_4 \rangle -N=N- \langle C_6H_4 \rangle -OH$]

Nitrobenzene — Aniline (A) — Benzene diazonium chloride (B) — p-Hydroxyazobenzene (C)

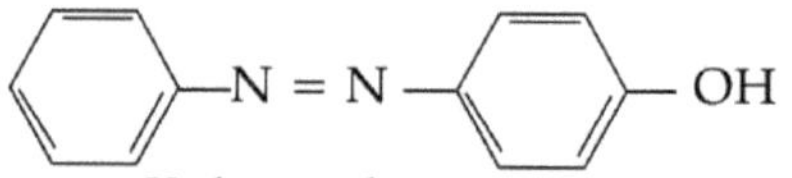

Q. 15. Complete the following reactions:

(i) $C_6H_5NH_2 + CHCl_3 + alc. KOH \longrightarrow$

(ii) $C_6H_5N_2Cl + H_3PO_2 + H_2O \longrightarrow$

(iii) $C_6H_5NH_2 + H_2SO_4 \text{ (conc.)} \longrightarrow$

---

* are board exam questions from previous years

(iv) $C_6H_5N_2Cl + C_2H_5OH \longrightarrow$

(v) $C_6H_5NH_2 + Br_2(aq.) \longrightarrow$

(vi) $C_6H_5NH_2 + (CH_3CO)_2O \longrightarrow$

(vii) $C_6H_5N_2Cl \xrightarrow[\text{(ii) NaNO2 / Cu, } \Delta]{\text{(i) HBF}_4}$

Ans. (i) $C_6H_5NH_2 + CHCl_3 + \text{alc. KOH} \xrightarrow{\text{Carbylamine reaction}} 3H_2O + 3KCl + C_6H_5 - NC$

Aniline / Phenyl isocyanide

(ii) $C_6H_5\overset{+}{N_2}\overset{-}{Cl} + H_3PO_2 + H_2O \longrightarrow C_6H_6 + N_2 + H_3PO_3 + HCl$

Benzene diazonium chloride / Benzene

(iii) $C_6H_5NH_2 + H_2SO_4 \text{ (conc.)} \longrightarrow C_6H_5\overset{+}{N}H_3HSO_4 \xrightarrow{\Delta}$

Aniline / Anilinium hydrogen sulphate / Sulphanilic acid (NO_2 ... SO_3H)

(iv) $C_6H_5N_2{}^+Cl^- + C_2H_5OH \longrightarrow C_6H_6 + CH_3CHO + N_2 + HCl$

Benzenediazonium chloride / Ethanol / Benzene / Ethanol

(v) $C_6H_5NH_2 + Br_2(aq.) \longrightarrow$ (2,4,6-tribromoaniline) $+ 3HBr$

Aniline

(vi) $C_6H_5NH_2 + (CH_3CO)_2O \longrightarrow C_6H_5 - \underset{|}{N} - \underset{\|}{C} - CH_3 + CH_3COOH$

Aniline / Acetic anhydride / (H, O) N-Phenylethanamide / acetic acid

(vii) $C_6H_5\overset{+}{N_2}\overset{-}{Cl} \xrightarrow[\text{(ii) NaNO2 / Cu, } \Delta]{\text{(i) HBF}_4} C_6H_5NO_2 + N_2 + NaBF_4$

Benzenediazonium chloride / Nitrobenzene

Q. 16. Write the reactions of (i) Aromatic (ii) Aliphatic primary amines with nitrous acid.

Ans. (i) Aromatic amines react with nitrous acid (prepared in situ from $NaNO_2$ and a mineral acid such as HCl) at 273-278 K to form stable aromatic diazonium salts *i.e.,* NaCl and H_2O.

(Aniline) $NH_2 + HNO_2 \xrightarrow[273–278(0–5°C)]{NaNO_2 + HCl}$ (Benzene diazonium chloride) $N_2{}^+\bar{C}l + NaCl + 2H_2O$

Aniline / Nitrous acid / Benzene diazonium chloride

(ii) Aliphatic primary amines react with nitrous acid (prepared in situ from $NaNO_2$ and a mineral acid such as HCl) to form unstable aliphatic diazonium salts, which further produce alcohol and HCl with the evolution of N_2 gas.

$R - NH_2 + HNO_2 \xrightarrow{NaNO_2 + HCl} [R - \overset{+}{N_2}\bar{C}l] \xrightarrow{H_2O} N_2 \uparrow + HCl + ROH$

Aliphatic primary amine / Nitrous acid / Aliphatic diazonium salt (unstable) / Alcohol

Q. 17. **Write the structures of compounds A, B and C in the following sentences:** *

(i) $CH_3COOH \xrightarrow{NH_3/\Delta} A \xrightarrow{Br_2/KOH(aq)} B \xrightarrow{CHCl_3 + alc.\ KOH} C$

(ii) $C_6H_5N_2^+ BF_4^- \xrightarrow[\Delta]{NaNO_2\,/\,Cu} A \xrightarrow{Fe/HCl} B \xrightarrow{CH_3COCl/pyridine} C$

Ans. (i) $CH_3COOH \xrightarrow[\Delta]{NH_3} \underset{(A)}{CH_3CONH_2} \xrightarrow{Br_2/KOH(aq)} \underset{(B)}{CH_3NH_2} \xrightarrow{CHCl_3 + alc.\ KOH} \underset{(C)}{CH_3NH}$

    (A) $CH_3CONH_2 \longrightarrow$ Acetamide

    (B) $CH_3NH_2 \longrightarrow$ Methylamine

    (C) $CH_3NC \longrightarrow$ Methylisocyanide

(ii)

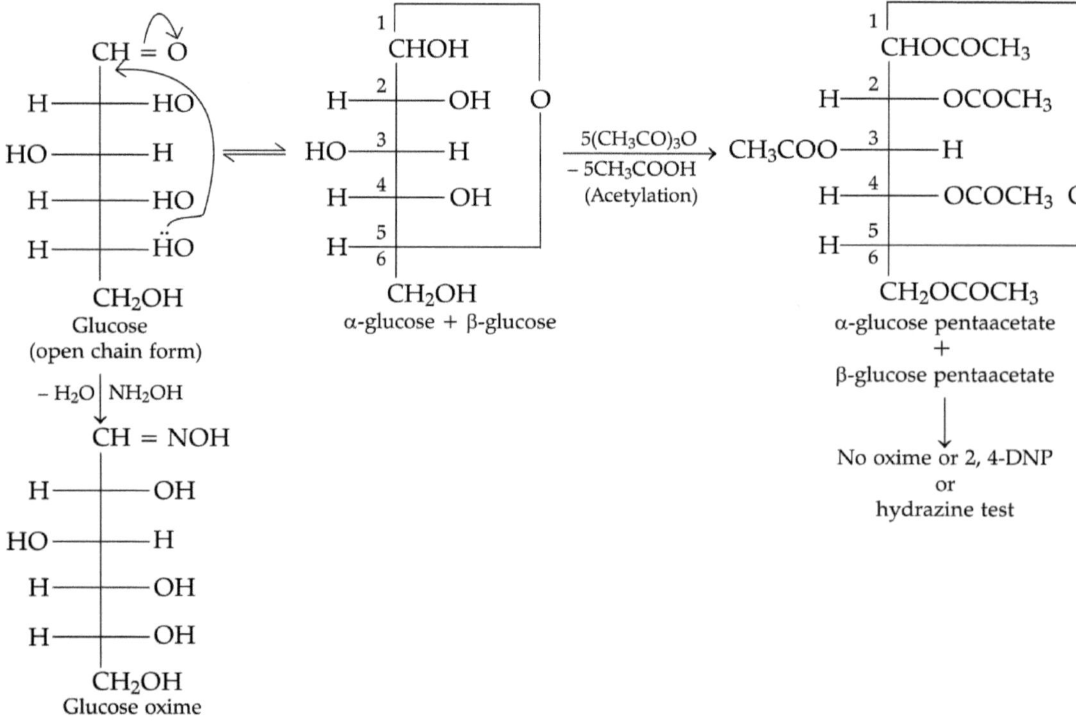

    (A) Nitrobenzene—$C_6H_5NO_2$

    (B) Aniline—$C_6H_5NH_2$

    (C) Acetanilide—$C_6H_5NHCOCH_3$

Chapter 14. Biomolecules

Q. 1. **How do you explain the absence of aldehyde group in the penta-acetate of D-glucose?**

Ans. The penta-acetate of D-glucose does not gives typical reaction of aldehydes. This is because penta-acetate does not form an open chain structure, as the C-1 position does not have free OH group for hydrolysis to form open chain structure.

Open chain form of glucose is responsible for the positive aldehyde tests like 2, 4-DNP, hydroxylamine etc.

Q. 2. What are the hydrolysis products of (i) sucrose and (ii) lactose?

Ans. Both sucrose and lactose are disaccharides.

(i) On hydrolysis, sucrose gives one molecule of a-D glucose and one molecule of β-D-fructose.

$$C_{12}H_{22}O_{11} + H_2O \xrightarrow[H^+]{Invertase} C_6H_{12}O_6 \quad + \quad C_6H_{12}O_6$$

Sucrose   D(+) Glucose   D(−) Fructose

(ii) The hydrolysis of lactose gives β-D galactose and β-D-glucose.

$$C_{12}H_{22}O_{11} + H_2O \xrightarrow[H^+]{Lactase} C_6H_{12}O_6 \quad + \quad C_6H_{12}O_6$$

Lactose   D-(+) Glucose   D-(+)-Galactose

Q. 3. What happens when D-glucose is treated with the following reagents?

(i) HI, (ii) Bromine water, (iii) HNO_3.

Ans. (i) When D-glucose is heated with HI for a long time, n-hexane is formed as a result of reduction reaction.

$$\begin{array}{c} CHO \\ | \\ (CHOH)_4 \\ | \\ CH_2OH \end{array} \xrightarrow[\Delta]{HI} CH_3 - CH_2 - CH_2 - CH_2 - CH_2 - CH_3$$

D-Glucose   n-Hexane

(ii) When D-glucose is treated with Br_2 water, D-gluconic acid is produced, as a result of oxidation of – CHO group to – COOH group.

$$\begin{array}{c} CHO \\ | \\ (CHOH)_4 \\ | \\ CH_2OH \end{array} \xrightarrow{Br_2\ water} \begin{array}{c} COOH \\ | \\ (CHOH)_4 \\ | \\ CH_2OH \end{array}$$

D-Glucose   D-Gluconic acid

(iii) On being treated with HNO_3, D-glucose gets oxidised to give saccharic acid, as a result of oxidation of both —CHO and 1° alcohol group –CH_2OH to —COOH.

$$\begin{array}{c} CHO \\ | \\ (CHOH)_4 \\ | \\ CH_2OH \end{array} \xrightarrow{HNO_3} \begin{array}{c} COOH \\ | \\ (CHOH)_4 \\ | \\ COOH \end{array}$$

D-Glucose   Saccharic acid

Chapter 15. Polymers

Q. 1. Write chemical reactions to prepare*

(i) Nylon-6   (ii) Nylon-6, 6.

Ans. (i) Nylon-6:

Cyclohexanone $\xrightarrow[- H_2O]{NH_2OH}$ Cyclohexanone oxime $\xrightarrow{H_2SO_4}$ Caprolactum of (Monomer of polymer) $\xrightarrow[\Delta-500]{H_2O}$ $\{NH - (CH_2)_5 - C\}_n$ (Nylon-6) $\xleftarrow{\Delta}$ $NH_2 - (CH_2)_5 - COOH$ (Amino caproic acid)

(ii) Nylon-6, 6:

$$H_2N - (CH_2)_6 - NH_2 + HOOC(CH_2)_4COOH \xrightarrow{n(H_2O)} \{NH(CH_2)_6NH - \overset{O}{\overset{||}{C}} - (CH_2)_4 - \overset{O}{\overset{||}{C}}\}_n$$

Hexamethylene diamine   Adipic acid   Nylon-6, 6

Q. 2. Write the name and structure of one of the common initiators used in free radical addition polymerisation.

Ans. One common initiator used in free radical addition polymerisation is benzoyl peroxide. Its structure is given below.

$$C_6H_5 - \overset{O}{\overset{||}{C}} - O - \overset{O}{\overset{||}{C}} - C_6H_5$$

Chapter 16. Chemistry in Everyday Life

Q. 1. Write the chemical equation for preparing sodium soap from glyceryl oleate and glyceryl palmitate. Structural formulae of these compounds are given below.

   (i) $(C_{15}H_{35}COO)_3C_3H_5$–Glyceryl palmitate

   (ii) $(C_{17}H_{32}COO)_3C_3H_5$–Glyceryl oleate

Ans. (i)

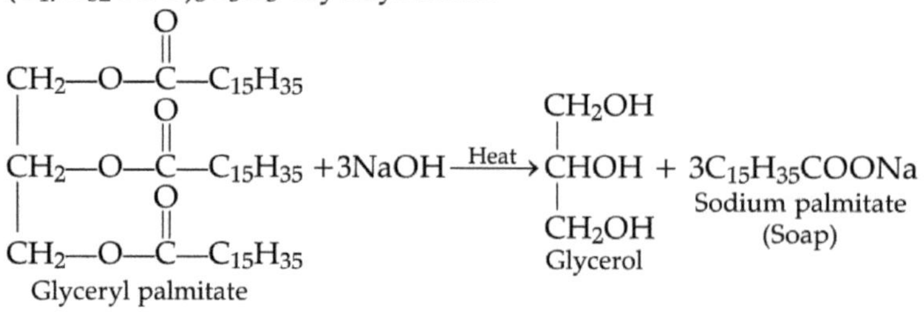

$$\underset{\text{Glyceryl palmitate}}{\begin{array}{l} CH_2\!-\!O\!-\!\overset{\displaystyle O}{\overset{\|}{C}}\!-\!C_{15}H_{35} \\[2pt] \;\;| \\[2pt] CH_2\!-\!O\!-\!\overset{\displaystyle O}{\overset{\|}{C}}\!-\!C_{15}H_{35} \\[2pt] \;\;| \\[2pt] CH_2\!-\!O\!-\!\overset{\displaystyle O}{\overset{\|}{C}}\!-\!C_{15}H_{35} \end{array}} + 3NaOH \xrightarrow{\text{Heat}} \underset{\text{Glycerol}}{\begin{array}{l} CH_2OH \\ | \\ CHOH \\ | \\ CH_2OH \end{array}} + \underset{\substack{\text{Sodium palmitate}\\ \text{(Soap)}}}{3C_{15}H_{35}COONa}$$

(ii)

$$\underset{\text{Glyceryl oleate}}{\begin{array}{l} CH_2\!-\!O\!-\!\overset{\displaystyle O}{\overset{\|}{C}}\!-\!C_{17}H_{32} \\[2pt] \;\;| \\[2pt] CH_2\!-\!O\!-\!\overset{\displaystyle O}{\overset{\|}{C}}\!-\!C_{17}H_{32} \\[2pt] \;\;| \\[2pt] CH_2\!-\!O\!-\!\overset{\displaystyle O}{\overset{\|}{C}}\!-\!C_{17}H_{32} \end{array}} + 3NaOH \xrightarrow{\text{Heat}} \underset{\text{Glycerol}}{\begin{array}{l} CH_2OH \\ | \\ CHOH \\ | \\ CH_2OH \end{array}} + \underset{\substack{\text{Sodium oleate}\\ \text{(Soap)}}}{3C_{17}H_{32}COONa}$$

❑❑

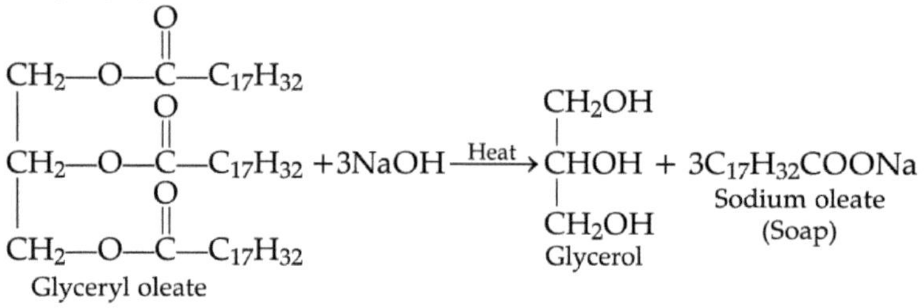

Mechanism |Set **13**|

Chapter 10. Haloalkanes and Haloarenes

Q. 1. Write the mechanism of the following reaction:[*]

$$CH_3CH_2OH \xrightarrow{\text{HBr}} CH_3CH_2Br + H_2O$$

Ans. As CH_3CH_2OH is a primary alcohol, it follows S_{Ni} mechanism, and inversion of configuration takes place.

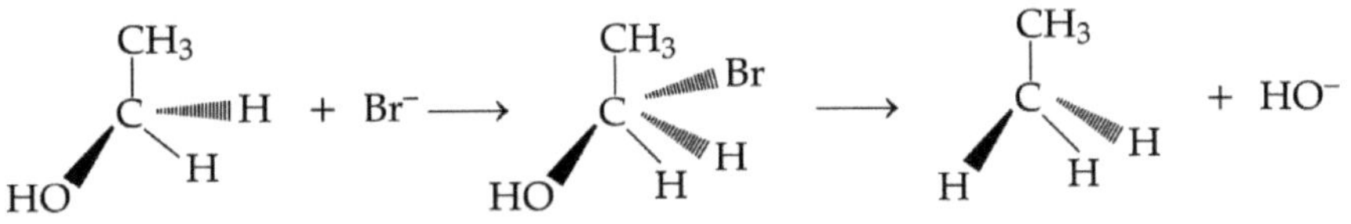

Q. 2. Write the mechanism of the following reaction:

$$n\text{BuBr} + KCN \xrightarrow{\text{ErOH–H}_2\text{O}} n\text{BuCN}$$

Ans. The given reaction is:

$$n\text{BuBr} + KCN \xrightarrow{\text{ErOH–H}_2\text{O}} n\text{BuCN}$$

The given reaction is an S_N2 reaction. In this reaction, CN^- acts as the nucleophile and attacks the carbon atom to which Br^- is attached. CN^- ion is an ambident nucleophile and can attack through both C and N. In this case, it attacks through the C-atom, predominantly as reaction takes place in a polar solvent. Here KCN readily ionizes to provide K^+ and CN^- ions. The C–C bond is more stable than C–N bond, hence C atom becomes the nucleophilic site.

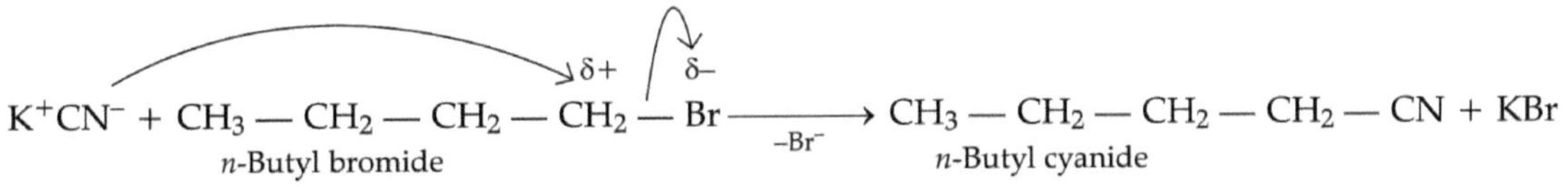

$$K^+CN^- + CH_3 - CH_2 - CH_2 - CH_2 - Br \xrightarrow[-Br^-]{} CH_3 - CH_2 - CH_2 - CH_2 - CN + KBr$$

n-Butyl bromide $\qquad\qquad\qquad$ n-Butyl cyanide

Chapter 11. Alcohols, Phenols and Ethers

Q. 1. Write the mechanism of hydration of ethene to yield ethanol.

Ans. Ethene does not react with simple water. But in presence of H_2SO_4, the acid provides proton for the initial electrophilic attack.

Step 1: Protonation of ethene to form carbocation by electrophilic attack of H_3O^+:

$$H_2O + H^+ \longrightarrow H_3O^+$$

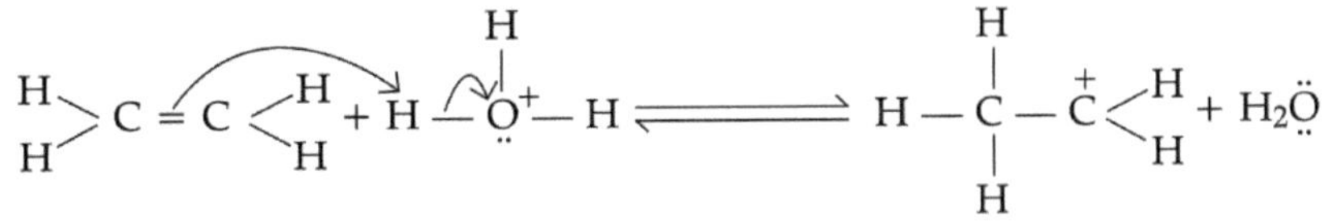

Step 2: Nucleophilic attack of water on carbocation:

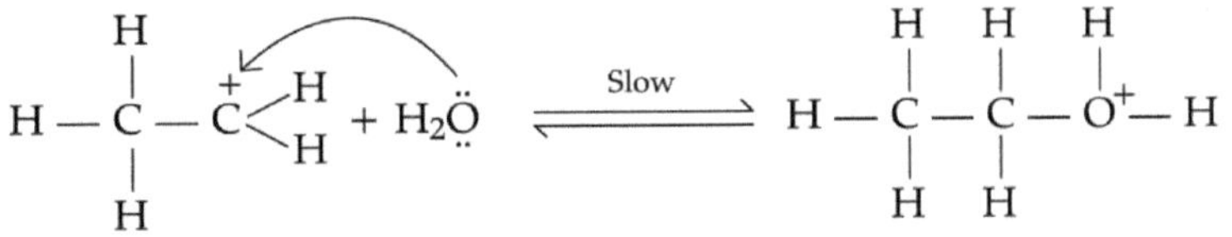

Step 3: Deprotonation to form ethanol:

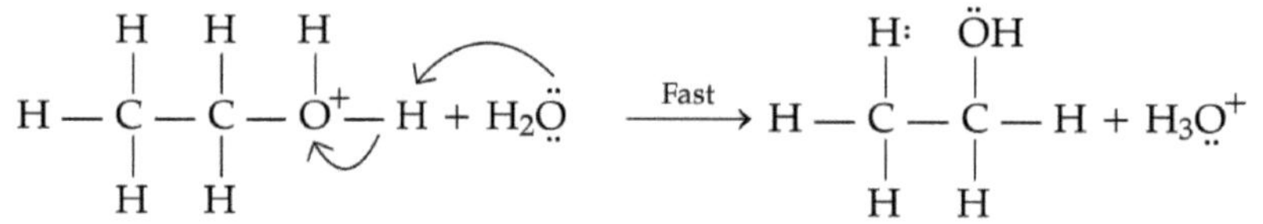

$$CH_3CH_2-\overset{+}{O}H_2 + H_2O \xrightarrow{\text{Fast}} CH_3CH_2-OH + H_3O^+$$

Q. 2. **Write the mechanism of acid-catalysed dehydration of ethanol to yield ethene.**

Ans. The mechanism of acid dehydration of ethanol to yield ethene involves the following three steps:

Step 1 : Protonation of ethanol to form ethyl oxonium ion:

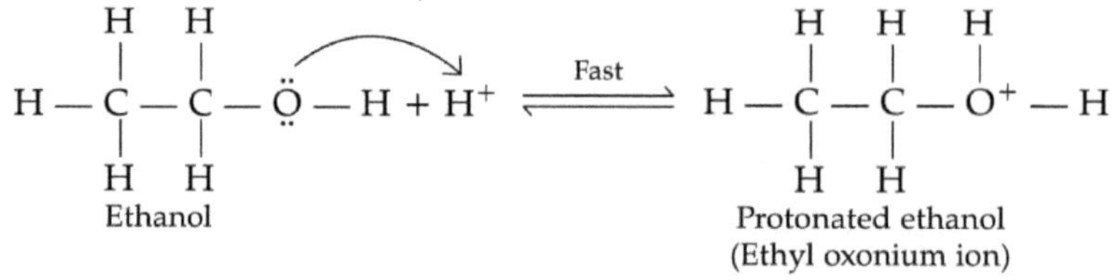

$$CH_3CH_2-\overset{..}{O}-H + H^+ \xrightleftharpoons{\text{Fast}} CH_3CH_2-\overset{+}{O}-H$$

Ethanol   Protonated ethanol (Ethyl oxonium ion)

Step 2 : Formation of carbocation (rate determining step):

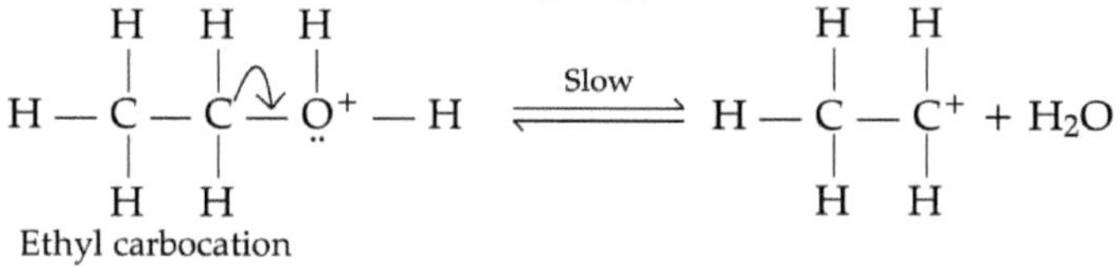

$$CH_3CH_2-\overset{+}{O}-H \xrightleftharpoons{\text{Slow}} CH_3CH_2^+ + H_2O$$

Ethyl carbocation

Step 3 : Elimination of a proton to form ethene:

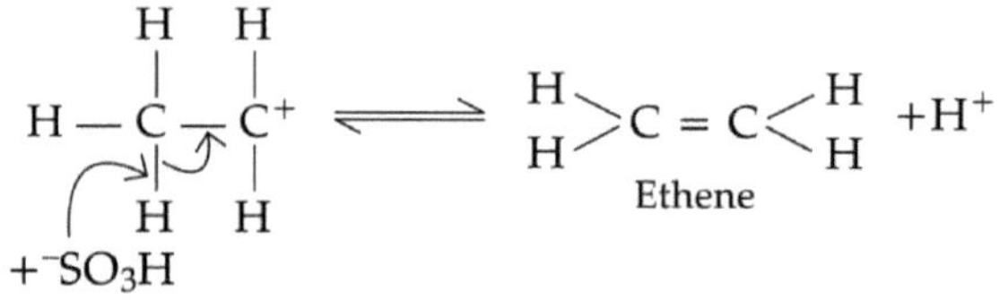

$$CH_3-CH_2^+ \ (+^-SO_3H) \rightleftharpoons \ H_2C=CH_2 + H^+$$

Ethene

The acid consumed in step 1 is released in step 3. After the formation of ethene, it is removed to shift the equilibrium in a forward direction.

Primary alcohol is dehydrated slowly as compared to secondary and tertiary alcohol because of stability of tert. carbocation.

Q. 3. **How is 1-propoxypropane synthesised from propan-1-ol ? Write mechanism of this reaction.** *

Ans. 1-propoxypropane can be synthesised from propan-1-ol by dehydration or by Williamson's synthesis. If propan-1-ol undergoes dehydration in the presence of protic acids (such as H_2SO_4, H_3PO_4) to give 1-propoxypropane.

$$2CH_3CH_2CH_2-OH \xrightarrow{H^+} CH_3CH_2OH-O-CH_2CH_2CH_3$$

Propane-1-ol   1-Propoxypropane

The mechanism of this reaction involves the following three steps:

Step 1: Protonation

$$CH_3CH_2CH_2-\overset{..}{O}-H^+ \xrightarrow[H^+]{\text{Conc. } H_2SO_4} CH_3CH_2CH_2-\overset{H}{\underset{..}{O}}-H$$

Propane-1-ol   Protonated alcohol

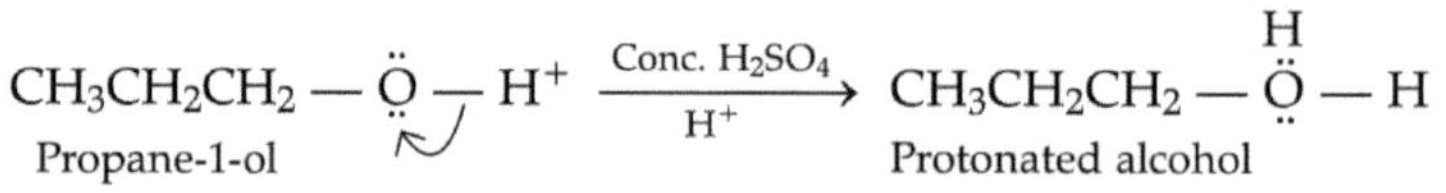

Step 2: Nucleophilic attach on protonated alcohol by another alcohol molecule.

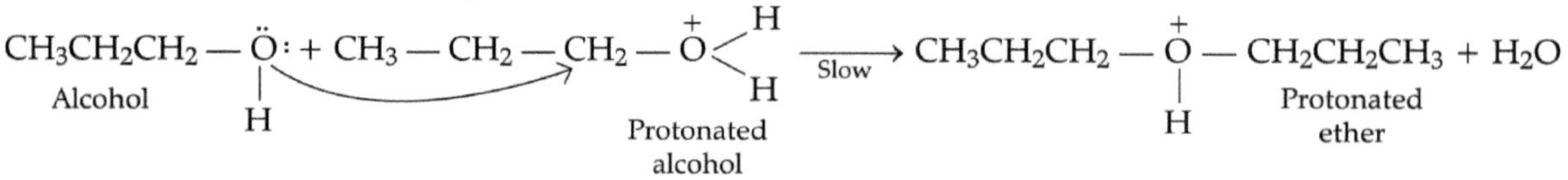

$$CH_3CH_2CH_2-\overset{..}{O}: + CH_3-CH_2-CH_2-\overset{+}{O}\overset{H}{\underset{H}{<}} \xrightarrow{\text{Slow}} CH_3CH_2CH_2-\overset{+}{\underset{H}{O}}-CH_2CH_2CH_3 + H_2O$$

Alcohol   Protonated alcohol   Protonated ether

Step 3: Deprotonation

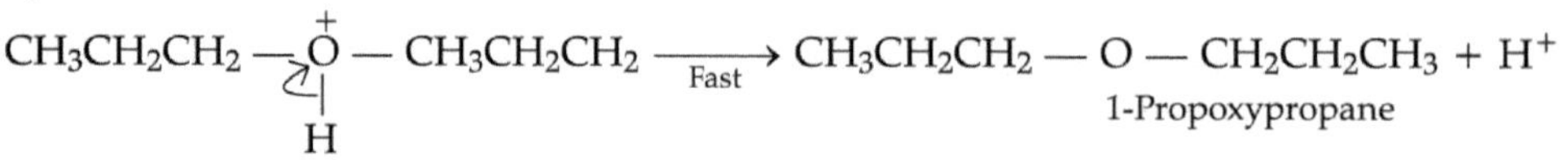

$$CH_3CH_2CH_2-\overset{+}{\underset{H}{O}}-CH_3CH_2CH_2 \xrightarrow{\text{Fast}} CH_3CH_2CH_2-O-CH_2CH_2CH_3 + H^+$$

1-Propoxypropane

Q. 4. **Write the mechanism of the reaction of HI with methoxymethane.**

Ans. The mechanism of the reaction of HI with methoxymethane involves the following steps:

Step 1: Protonation of methoxymethane:

$$CH_3 - \ddot{O} - CH_3 + H - I \rightleftharpoons CH_3 - \overset{+}{\underset{\displaystyle H}{\ddot{O}}} - CH_3 + I^-$$

Step 2: Nucleophilic attack of I^-, this in case of primary and secondary alkyl halides follows S_N2 mechanism.

$$I^- + CH_3 - \overset{+}{\underset{\displaystyle H}{\ddot{O}}} - CH_3 \longrightarrow \left[I {-}{-}{-} CH_3 {-}{-}{-} \overset{+}{\ddot{O}} {-}{-}{-} CH_3 \right]^- \longrightarrow \underset{\text{Iodomethane}}{CH_3 - I} + \underset{\text{Methanol}}{CH_3 - OH}$$

Step 3: When HI is in excess and the reaction is carried out at a high temperature, the methanol formed in the second step reacts with another HI molecule and gets converted to methyl iodide.

$$CH_3 - \ddot{O} - H + H - I \rightleftharpoons CH_3 - \overset{+}{\underset{\displaystyle H}{O}} - H + I^-$$

$$I^- + CH_3 - \overset{+}{O}H_2 \longrightarrow CH_3 - I + H_2O$$

Q. 5. **When 3-methylbutan-2-ol is treated with HBr, the following reaction takes place:**

$$\underset{\underset{\displaystyle CH_3 \quad OH}{|\qquad |}}{CH_3 - CH - CH - CH_3} \xrightarrow{HBr} \underset{\underset{\displaystyle CH_3}{|}}{CH_3 - \overset{\overset{\displaystyle Br}{|}}{C} - CH_2 - CH_3}$$

Give a mechanism for this reaction.

[Hint: The secondary carbocation formed in step II rearranges to a more stable tertiary carbocation by a hydride ion shift from 3rd carbon atom.]

Ans. The mechanism of the given reaction involves the following steps:

Step 1: Protonation.

$$\underset{\underset{\displaystyle \text{3-Methylbutan-2-ol}}{\underset{\displaystyle CH_3 \quad OH}{|\qquad |}}}{CH_3 - CH - CH - CH_3} \xrightarrow{H^+} \underset{\underset{\displaystyle \text{Protonated alcohol}}{\underset{\displaystyle CH_3 \quad \overset{+}{O}H_2}{|\qquad |}}}{CH_3 - CH - CH - CH_3}$$

Step 2: Formation of $2°$ carbocation by the elimination of a water molecule.

$$\underset{\underset{\displaystyle +}{\underset{\displaystyle CH_3 \quad OH_2}{|\qquad |}}}{CH_3 - CH - CH - CH_3} \xrightarrow{H_2O} \underset{\underset{\displaystyle \text{2° Carbocation}}{\underset{\displaystyle CH_3}{|}}}{CH_3 - CH - \overset{+}{C}H - CH_3}$$

Step 3: Re-arrangement by the hydride-ion shift for formation of more stable $3°$ carbocation.

$$\underset{\underset{\displaystyle \text{(Less stable)}}{\underset{\displaystyle CH_3}{|}}}{CH_3 - \overset{\overset{\displaystyle H}{|}}{C} - \overset{+}{C}H - CH_3} \xrightarrow{1,\,2\text{-hydride shift}} \underset{\underset{\displaystyle \text{(More stable)}}{\underset{\displaystyle \text{3° Carbocation}}{\underset{\displaystyle CH_3}{|}}}}{CH_3 - \overset{+}{C} - CH_2 - CH_3}$$

Step 4: Nucleophilic attack.

$$\underset{\underset{\displaystyle CH_3}{|}}{CH_3 - \overset{+}{C} - CH_2 - CH_3} + Br^- \longrightarrow \underset{\underset{\displaystyle \text{3-Bromo-2-methylbutane}}{\underset{\displaystyle CH_3}{|}}}{CH_3 - \overset{\overset{\displaystyle Br}{|}}{C} - CH_2 - CH_3}$$

Chapter 12. Aldehydes, Ketones and Carboxylic Acids

Q. 1. **Write the mechanism of esterification reaction.**

Ans. Esterification of carboxylic acids with alcohols is a kind of nucleophilic acyl substitution. It is done in acidic medium (conc. H_2SO_4). The acid protonates the carbonyl oxygen and thus activates the nucleophilic attack of alcohol molecule.

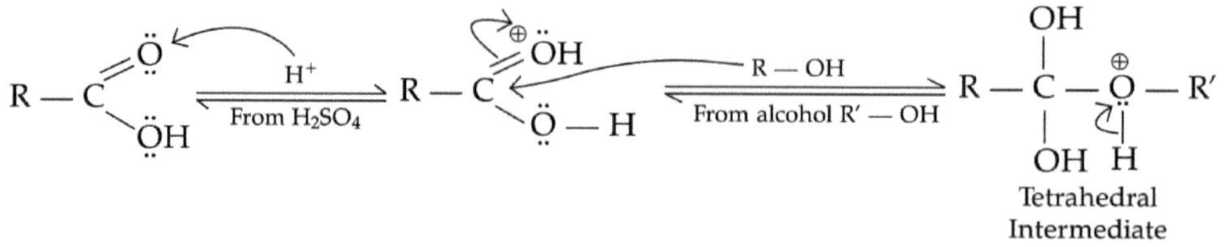

The tetrahedral intermediate gets a proton transferred leading to formation of a $(\overset{+}{O}H_2)$ group, which acts as a good leaving group, and is eliminated.

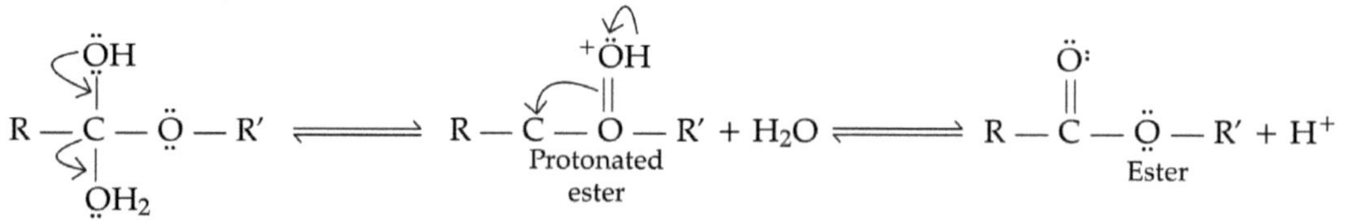

All these steps are reversible. The water molecule released as a by product, has its oxygen coming from carboxylic acid and not from alcohol.

Chapter 10. Haloalkanes and Haloarenes

Q. 1. Convert the following:

(i) Methyl chloride into ethyl chloride.

(ii) Ethyl chloride to propanoic acid.

(iii) Diphenyl from chlorobenzene.

Ans. (i) $CH_3Cl \xrightarrow{KCN} CH_3CN \xrightarrow[\text{Catalyst}]{H_2NH} CH_3CH_2NH_2 \xrightarrow{HNO_2}$

Methyl chloride   (Ethylamine)

$$CH_3CH_2OH \xrightarrow{PCl_5} CH_3CH_2Cl$$

(ii) $CH_3CH_2Cl \xrightarrow{KCN} CH_3CH_2CN \xrightarrow[\Delta]{H^+/H_2O} CH_3CH_2COOH$

Ethyl chloride   Propanoic acid

(iii) Chlorobenzene $+ 2Na \xrightarrow[\text{Ether}]{\text{Dry}}$ Diphenyl $+ 2NaCl$

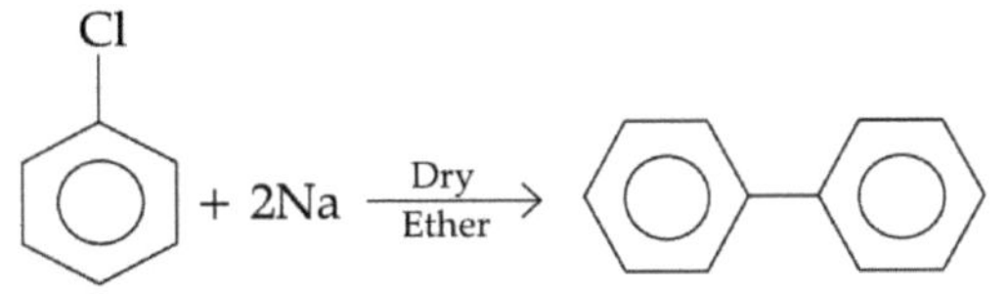

Chlorobenzene   Diphenyl

Fittig's reaction

Q. 2. How will you bring about the following conversions?

(i) Ethanol to but-1-yne

(ii) Ethane to bromoethane

(iii) Propene to 1-nitropropane

(iv) Toluene to benzyl alcohol

(v) Propene to propyne

(vi) Ethanol to ethyl fluoride

(vii) Bromomethane to propanone

(viii) But-1-ene to but-2-ene

(ix) 1-Chlorobutane to n-octane

(x) Benzene to biphenyl.

Ans. (i)
$$CH_3CH_2OH \xrightarrow{SOCl_2,\ \text{Pyridine}} CH_3CH_2Cl + SO_2 + HCl$$

Ethanol   Chloroethane

$$HC \equiv CH + NaNH_2 \xrightarrow{\text{Liq.NH}_3} HC \equiv \overset{+}{C}\overset{-}{N}a$$

Ethyne   Chloroethane

$$CH_3CH_2 - Cl \ + \ CH \equiv \overset{-}{C}\overset{+}{N}a \longrightarrow CH_3CH_2C \equiv CH + NaCl$$

Chloroethane   Sodium   But-1-yne

acetylide

(ii) $CH_3 - CH_3 \xrightarrow[\text{or }\Delta]{Br_2/\text{UV light}} CH_3 - CH_2Br + HBr$

Ethane   Bromoethane

(iii) $CH_3 - CH = CH_2 + HBr \xrightarrow[\text{Anti-Markovnikov}]{\text{Peroxide}} CH_3 - CH_2 - CH_2Br \xrightarrow{AgNO_2}$

Propene   1-Bromopropane

$$AgBr + CH_3 - CH_2 - CH_2NO_2$$

1-Nitropropane

(iv) Toluene $\xrightarrow[\text{or Heat}]{Cl_2/\text{UV light}}$ Benzyl chloride $\xrightarrow[- NaCl]{\text{NaOH (alc.)}}$ Benzyl alcohol

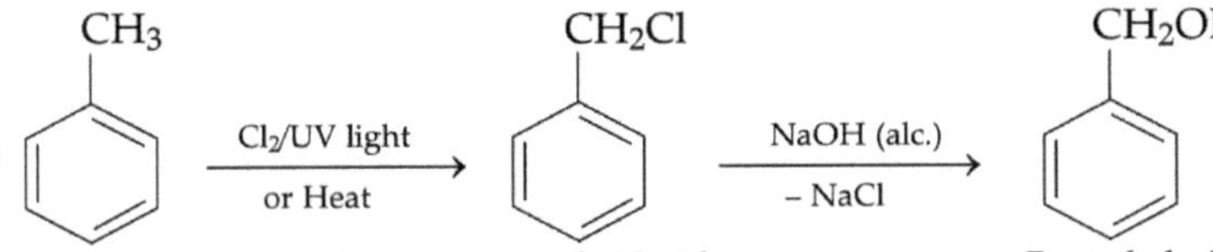

    CH_3 CH_2Cl CH_2OH

Toluene   (Allylic   Benzyl chloride   Benzyl alcohol

Substitution)

(v) $CH_3 — CH = CH_2 \xrightarrow{Br_2/CCl_4} CH_3 — CH — CH_2 \xrightarrow[\text{(Dehydrohalogenation)}]{\text{Alcoholic KOH}} CH_3 — C \equiv CH$

Propene   Propyne

$\underset{\text{Br} \quad \text{Br}}{|\quad\quad|}$

1, 2-Dibromopropane

(vi) $CH_3 — CH_2 — OH \xrightarrow[\text{Pyridine}]{SOCl_2} CH_3 — CH_2 — Cl + SO_2 \uparrow + HCl \uparrow \xrightarrow{\text{AgF or Hg}_2F_2} CH_3 — CH_3 — F$

Ethanol   Chloroethane   Gaseous   Ethyl fluoride
by products

(vii) $CH_3 — Br \xrightarrow{\text{KCN (alc.)}} CH_3 — CN \xrightarrow{CH_3 — MgBr} CH_3 — C \equiv NMgBr \xrightarrow[\text{Hydrolysis}]{H_3O^+} CH_3 — C = O$

Bromomethane   Acetonitrile $|$ $|$

                                      CH_3 CH_3

                                                Propanone

(viii) $CH_3 — CH_2CH = CH_2 \xrightarrow[\text{addition)}]{\substack{\text{HBr} \\ \text{(Markovnikov}}} CH_3 — CH_2\overset{\overset{\displaystyle Br}{|}}{C}HCH_3 \xrightarrow[- \text{HBr}]{\text{KOH (alc.), } \Delta} CH_3CH = CHCH_3$

But-1-ene   2-Bromobutane   But-2-ene
(Major)

(ix) $2CH_3CH_2CH_2CH_2 — Cl + 2Na \xrightarrow[- 2NaCl]{\text{Dry ether}} CH_3CH_2CH_2CH_2CH_2CH_2CH_2CH_3$

1-Chlorobutane   (Wurtz reaction)   *n*-Octane

(x) Benzene $\xrightarrow[\text{Dark or Br}_2/\text{FeBr}_3]{Br_2/Fe}$ Bromobenzene $\xrightarrow[\text{Dry ether}]{Na}$ Diphenyl $+ 2NaBr$

Benzene   Bromobenzene   (Fitting reaction)   Diphenyl

Q. 3. How the following conversions can be carried out?

   (i)   Propene to propan-1-ol

   (ii)   1-Bromopropane to 2-bromopropane

   (iii)   Toluene to benzyl alcohol

   (iv)   Benzene to 4-bromonitrobenzene

   (v)   Benzyl alcohol to 2-phenyl ethanoic acid

   (vi)   Ethanol to propanenitrile

   (vii)   Aniline to chlorobenzene

   (viii) 2-Chlorobutane to 3, 4-dimethylhexane

   (ix)   2-Methyl-1-propene to 2-chloro-2-methylpropane

   (x)   Ethyl chloride to propanoic acid

   (xi)   But-1-ene to n-butyliodide

   (xii)   2-Chloropropane to 1-propanol

   (xiii) Isopropyl alcohol to iodoform

   (xiv) Chlorobenzene to *p*-nitrophenol

   (xv)   2-Bromopropane to 1-bromopropane

   (xvi) Chloroethane to butane

   (xvii) Benzene to diphenyl

   (xviii) *tert*-Butyl bromide to isobutyl bromide

   (xix) Aniline to phenylisocyanide.

Ans. (i) $CH_3 — CH = CH_2 \xrightarrow[\substack{\text{(Anti-Markovnikov} \\ \text{addition)}}]{\text{HBr/Peroxide}} CH_3 — CH_2 — CH_2 — Br \xrightarrow[\substack{\text{(Nucleophilic} \\ \text{substitution)}}]{\text{Aq. KOH} / \Delta} CH_3 — CH_2 — CH_2 — OH$

Propene   1-Bromopropane   Propan-1-ol

(ii) $CH_3 — CH_2 — CH_2 — Br \xrightarrow[\substack{\text{(Dehydrohalo-} \\ \text{genation)}}]{\text{KOH (alc.)} / \Delta} CH_3 — CH = CH_2 \xrightarrow[\text{HBr}]{\substack{\text{Markovnikov} \\ \text{addition}}} CH_3 — \overset{\overset{\displaystyle Br}{|}}{C}H = CH_3$

1-Bromopropane   Propene   2-Bromopropane

(iii) Toluene $\xrightarrow[\text{or heat}]{\text{Cl}_2/\text{UV light}}$ [allylic halogenation] Benzyl chloride (CH$_2$Cl) $\xrightarrow[\text{(Nucleophilic substitution)}]{\text{Aq. KOH / }\Delta}$ Benzyl alcohol (CH$_2$OH)

(iv) Benzene $\xrightarrow[\text{Dark}]{\text{Br}_2/\text{FeBr}_3}$ Bromobenzene (Br) $\xrightarrow[\text{(Nitration)}]{\text{HNO}_3/\text{H}_2\text{SO}_4}$ 4-Bromonitrobenzene (Major) (Br, NO$_2$)

(v) Benzyl alcohol (CH$_2$OH) $\xrightarrow[-\text{ POCl}_3 - \text{HCl}]{\text{PCl}_5}$ (CH$_2$Cl) $\xrightarrow[-\text{ KCl}]{\text{KCN, Aq. Ethanol}}$ Benzyl cyanide (CH$_2$CN) $\xrightarrow[\text{(Hydrolysis)}]{\text{H}^+/\text{H}_2\text{O}}$ 2-Phenyl ethanoic acid ($\overset{2}{\text{C}}\text{H}_2\overset{1}{\text{C}}\text{OOH}$)

(vi) $\underset{\text{Ethanol}}{\text{CH}_3 - \text{CH}_2 - \text{OH}} \xrightarrow{\text{Red P/Br}_2} \underset{\text{Bromoethane}}{\text{CH}_3 - \text{CH}_2 - \text{Br}} \xrightarrow{\text{KCN, aq. ethanol}} \underset{\text{Propanenitrile}}{\text{CH}_3 - \text{CH}_2 - \text{C} \equiv \text{N}^-}$

(vii) Aniline (NH$_2$) $\xrightarrow[- \text{NaCl}, - 2\text{H}_2\text{O}]{\substack{\text{NaNO}_2 + 2\text{HCl}, \\ \text{273-278 K}}}$ (Diazotisation) Benzenediazonium chloride ($\overset{+}{\text{N}}_2\overset{-}{\text{Cl}}$) $\xrightarrow[\text{CuCl/HCl}]{\text{Cu}_2\text{Cl}_2}$ Chlorobenzene (Cl) $+ \text{N}_2$

(viii) $2\,\underset{\text{2-Chlorobutane}}{\text{CH}_3 - \overset{\overset{\text{Cl}}{|}}{\text{CH}} - \text{CH}_2 - \text{CH}_3} \xrightarrow[\text{(Wurtz's reaction)}]{2\text{Na/Dry ether}} \underset{\text{3, 4-Dimethylhexane}}{\text{CH}_3 - \text{CH}_2 - \overset{\overset{\text{CH}_3}{|}}{\text{CH}} - \overset{\overset{\text{CH}_3}{|}}{\text{CH}} - \text{CH}_2 - \text{CH}_3} + 2\text{NaCl}$

(ix) $2\,\underset{\text{2-Methyl-1propene}}{\text{CH}_3 - \overset{\overset{\text{CH}_3}{|}}{\text{C}} = \text{CH}_2} \xrightarrow[\text{(Markovnikov addition)}]{\text{HCl}} \underset{\text{2-Chloro-2-methylpropane}}{\text{CH}_3 - \overset{\overset{\text{CH}_3}{|}}{\underset{\underset{\text{Cl}}{|}}{\text{C}}} - \text{CH}_3}$

(x) $\underset{\text{Ethylchloride}}{\text{CH}_3 - \text{CH}_2 - \text{Cl}} \xrightarrow[\substack{\text{(Nucleophilic} \\ \text{substitution)}}]{\text{KCN, aq. ethanol}} \underset{\text{Propanenitrile}}{\text{CH}_3 - \text{CH}_2 - \text{CN}} + \text{KCl} \xrightarrow[\text{Hydrolysis}]{\text{H}^+/\text{H}_2\text{O}} \underset{\text{Propanoic acid}}{\text{CH}_3 - \text{CH}_2 - \text{COOH}}$

(xi) $\underset{\text{But-1-ene}}{\text{CH}_3 - \text{CH}_2 - \text{CH} = \text{CH}_2} \xrightarrow[\substack{\text{(Anti-Markovnikov} \\ \text{addition)}}]{\text{HBr/Peroxide}} \underset{\text{1-Bromobutane}}{\text{CH}_3 - \text{CH}_2 - \text{CH}_2 - \text{CH}_2 - \text{Br}} \xrightarrow[\substack{\text{Finkelstein} \\ \text{reaction}}]{\text{NaI, dry acetone}}$

$\underset{\text{$n$-Butyliodide}}{\text{CH}_3 - \text{CH}_2 - \text{CH}_2 - \text{CH}_2 - \text{I}}$

(xii) $\underset{\text{2-Chloropropane}}{\text{CH}_3 - \text{CH} - \text{CH}_3} \xrightarrow[\text{(Dehydrohalogenation)}]{\text{KOH (alc.)/}\Delta} \underset{\text{Propene}}{\text{CH}_3 - \text{CH} = \text{CH}_2} + \text{HCl} \xrightarrow[\text{(Anti-Markovnikov addition)}]{\text{HBr/Peroxide}}$

$\underset{\text{1-Bromopropane}}{\text{CH}_3 - \text{CH}_2 - \text{CH}_2 - \text{Br}} \xrightarrow[\text{(Nucleophilic substitution)}]{\text{Aq. KOH /}\Delta} \underset{\text{1-Propanol}}{\text{CH}_3 - \text{CH}_2 - \text{CH}_2 - \text{OH}}$

(xiii) $\underset{\text{Isopropyl alcohol}}{\text{CH}_3 - \overset{\overset{\text{OH}}{|}}{\text{CH}} - \text{CH}_3} \xrightarrow[\substack{\text{(Oxidation) or} \\ \text{K}_2\text{Cr}_2\text{O}_7/\text{H}^+}]{\text{CrO}_3} \underset{\text{Propanone}}{\text{CH}_3 - \overset{\overset{\text{O}}{||}}{\text{C}} - \text{CH}_3} \xrightarrow[\substack{\text{I}_2/\text{Na}_2\text{CO}_3 \text{ or} \\ \text{(Iodoform reaction)}}]{\text{NaOI}} \text{CH}_3 - \overset{\overset{\text{O}}{||}}{\text{C}} - \text{ONa} + \underset{\text{Iodoform}}{\text{CHI}_3}$

(xiv) Chlorobenzene $\xrightarrow[\text{(Nitration)}]{\text{HNO}_3/\text{H}_2\text{SO}_4}$ *p*-Chloronitrobenzene (Major product) + *m*-Chloronitrobenzene + *o*-Chloronitrobenzene

p-Chloronitrobenzene $\xrightarrow[\text{(ii) dil. HCl}]{\text{(i) NaOH, 433 K}}$ *p*-Nitrophenol

Or

Chlorobenzene $\xrightarrow[\substack{623 \text{ K/300 atn} \\ \text{(Dow's process)}}]{\text{NaOH}}$ Phenol $\xrightarrow[\text{(Nitration)}]{\text{HNO}_3/\text{H}_2\text{SO}_4}$ *p*-Nitrophenol

(xv) $CH_3 - \underset{\underset{\text{Br}}{|}}{CH} - CH_3$ (2-Bromopropane) $\xrightarrow[\text{Dehydrohalogenation}]{\text{KOH (alc.)/ }\Delta}$ $CH_3 - CH = CH_2$ (Propene) $+ HBr \xrightarrow[\substack{\text{(Anti-Markovnikov} \\ \text{addition)}}]{\text{HBr/Peroxide}}$ $CH_3 - CH_2 - CH_2 - Br$ (1-Bromopropane)

(xvi) $CH_3 - CH_2 - Cl$ (Chloroethane) $\xrightarrow[\text{(Wurtz reaction)}]{2\text{Na/Dry ether}}$ $CH_3 - CH_2 - CH_2 - CH_3$ (Butane) $+ 2NaCl$

(xvii) Benzene $\xrightarrow{\text{Br}_2/\text{FEBr}_3}$ Bromobenzene $\xrightarrow[\text{(Fittig reaction)}]{2\text{Na/Dry ether}}$ Biphenyl $+ 2NaBr$

(xviii) $CH_3 - \underset{\underset{\text{Br}}{|}}{\overset{\overset{\text{Br}}{|}}{C}} - CH_3$ (*tert*-Butyl bromide) $\xrightarrow[\text{(Dehydrohalogenation)}]{\text{KOH (alc.)/ }\Delta}$ $CH_3 - \underset{\underset{\text{CH}_3}{|}}{C} = CH_2$ (2-Methylpropene) $\xrightarrow[\text{(Anti-Markovnikov addition)}]{\text{HBr/Peroxide}}$ $CH_3 - \underset{\underset{\text{CH}_3}{|}}{CH} - CH_2 - Br$ (Isobutyl bromide)

(xix) Aniline $\xrightarrow[\text{(Carbylamine reaction)}]{\text{CHCl}_3,\ 3\text{KOH},\ \Delta}$ Phenylisocyanide $+ 3KCl + 3H_2O$

Chapter 11. Alcohols, Phenols and Ethers

Q. 1. **How are the following conversions carried out,**[*]
    (i)   Propene to propan-2-ol
    (ii) Ethyl magnesium chloride to propane-1-ol
    (iii) Acetone to tertiary butyl alcohol.

Ans. (i) $CH_3 — CH = CH_2 + H_2O \xrightarrow{H^+} CH_3 — \overset{\overset{\displaystyle OH}{|}}{CH} — CH_3$

Propane-2-ol

(ii) $C_2H_5MgCl + HCHO \xrightarrow[\text{Ether}]{\text{Dry}} \left[C_2H_5 — \overset{\overset{\displaystyle OH}{|}}{\underset{\underset{\displaystyle H}{|}}{C}} — \overset{+}{O}MgCl \right] \xrightarrow{H_3O^+} C_2H_5 — CH_2OH + MgCl(OH)$

Propane-1-ol

(iii) $CH_3 — \overset{\overset{\displaystyle O}{||}}{C} — CH_3 + CH_3 — Mg — Br \rightarrow \left[CH_3 — \overset{\overset{\displaystyle OMgBr}{|}}{\underset{\underset{\displaystyle CH_3}{|}}{C}} — CH_3 \right] \xrightarrow{H_3O^+} CH_3 — \overset{\overset{\displaystyle OH}{|}}{\underset{\underset{\displaystyle CH_3}{|}}{C}} — CH_3 + Mg(OH)Br$

tert-butyl alcohol

Q. 2. How will you convert

(i) Phenol to salicyclic acid

(ii) Chlorobenzene to phenol*

(iii) Phenol to toluene.

Ans. (i) (Phenol with OH) $\xrightarrow[\text{NaOH (Under pressure)}]{CO_2}$ (OCOONa) $\xrightleftharpoons{\text{Rearrangement}}$ (OH, COONa) $\xrightarrow{\text{HCl, NaCl}}$ (OH, COOH) Salicylic acid

(ii) (Cl) $+ NaOH \xrightarrow[\substack{\text{300 atm or} \\ \text{Super heated} \\ \text{(steam)}}]{\text{623 K}}$ (ONa$^+$) $+ NaCl + H_2O \xrightarrow{HCl}$ (OH) Phenol (Dow's process)

(iii) Phenol (OH) $\xrightarrow[\Delta]{\text{Zn dust}}$ Benzene $+ ZnO \xrightarrow[CH_3Cl]{\text{Anhydrous AlCl}_3}$ Toluene (CH$_3$)

Q. 3. Convert the following:

(i) Benzene to resorcinol

(ii) Dimethyl ether to Diethyl ether

(iii) Ethanol to Acetylene.

Ans. (i) Benzene $\xrightarrow[\Delta]{H_2SO_4}$ Benzenedisulphonic acid (SO$_3$H, SO$_3$H) $\xrightarrow[\text{Fuse}]{2NaOH}$ Disodium resorcinol (ONa, ONa) $\xrightarrow{H_3O^+}$ Resorcinol (OH, OH)

(ii) $CH_3 — O — CH_3 + HI \longrightarrow CH_3I \xrightarrow[\text{No (Dry ether)}]{\text{Wurtz reaction}} CH_3CH_3 + NaI \xrightarrow[hv]{Cl_2}$

Dimethyl ether · Ethane

$CH_3CH_2Cl \xrightarrow{Ag_2O} CH_3CH_2 — O — CH_3CH_2$

Chloroethane · Diethyl ether

Or

$CH_3CH_2Cl \xrightarrow[\text{KOH}]{\text{aq.}} CH_3CH_2OH \xrightarrow[H_2SO_4]{<413 K} CH_3CH_2 — OCH_2 — CH_3$

Chloroethane · Diethyl ether

(iii) $CH_3CH_2OH \xrightarrow[H_2SO_4]{\text{Conc.}} CH_2 = CH_2 \xrightarrow{Br_2} \underset{\underset{\displaystyle Br}{|}}{CH_2} — \underset{\underset{\displaystyle Br}{|}}{CH_2} \xrightarrow[\text{KOH}]{\text{alc.}} CH \equiv CH + 2KBr$

Acetylene

Q. 4. How are the following conversions carried out?
(i)   Propene → Propan-2-ol
(ii) Benzyl chloride → Benzyl alcohol
(iii) Ethyl magnesium chloride → Propan-1-ol
(iv) Methyl magnesium bromide → 2-Methylpropan-2-ol.

Ans. (i) If propene is allowed to react with water in the presence of an acid as a catalyst, then propan-2-ol is obtained also called acid hydration.

$$CH_3 - CH_2 = CH_2 + H_2O \underset{}{\overset{H^+}{\rightleftharpoons}} CH_3 - \underset{\underset{OH}{|}}{CH} - CH_3$$

Propene   Propan-2-ol

(ii) If benzyl chloride is treated with NaOH (followed by acidification) then benzyl alcohol is produced.

$$\underset{\text{Benzyl chloride}}{C_6H_5CH_2Cl} + NaOH \xrightarrow[-HCl]{} C_6H_5CH_2ONa \xrightarrow{H^+} \underset{\text{Benzyl alcohol}}{C_6H_5CH_2OH}$$

(iii) When ethyl magnesium chloride is treated with methanal, an adduct is the product which gives propan-1-ol on hydrolysis.

$$\underset{H}{\overset{H}{>}}C = O + C_2H_5 - MgCl \longrightarrow \begin{bmatrix} CH_2 - \bar{O}MgCl \\ | \\ C_2H_5 \end{bmatrix} \xrightarrow{H_2O/H^+} Mg(OH)Cl + \underset{\text{Propan-1-ol}}{C_3H_7 - OH}$$

Adduct

$$\textbf{Or}\quad CH_2 - OH,\ CH_2 - CH_2 - CH_3$$

(iv) When methyl magnesium bromide is treated with propane, an adduct is the product which gives 2-methylpropane-2-ol on hydrolysis.

$$\underset{H_3C}{\overset{H_3C}{>}}C = O + CH_3 - MgBr \longrightarrow \begin{bmatrix} CH_3 \\ | \\ CH_3 - C - \bar{O}\overset{+}{M}gBr \\ | \\ CH_3 \end{bmatrix} \xrightarrow{H_2O/H^+} Mg(OH)Br + CH_3 - \underset{\underset{CH_3}{|}}{\overset{\overset{OH}{|}}{C}} - CH_3$$

Propane   Adduct   (2-Methylpropan-2-ol)

Chapter 12. Aldehydes, Ketones and Carboxylic Acids

Q. 1. Convert propanone to propene.[*]

Ans.
$$CH_3 - \overset{\overset{O}{||}}{C} - CH_3 \xrightarrow[[H]]{LiAlH_4} CH_3 - \overset{\overset{OH}{|}}{CH} - CH_3 \xrightarrow[H_2SO_4,\ \Delta]{Conc.} CH_3 - CH = CH_2$$

(Propanone)   (Reduction)   (Dehydration)   (Propene)

Q. 2. How is toluene converted to benzaldehyde?

Ans.
$$\underset{\text{(Toluene)}}{C_6H_5CH_3} \xrightarrow[CS_2\ (ii)\ H_2O]{(i)\ CrO_2Cl_2} \underset{\text{(Benzaldehyde)}}{C_6H_5CHO}$$

Q. 3. How will you convert ethylcyanide to ethanoic acid?

Ans.
$$CH_3CH_2C \equiv N \xrightarrow[\text{[Partial]}]{H_2O/H^+} CH_3CH_2CONH_2 \xrightarrow[\substack{\text{[Hofmann Bromanide} \\ \text{degradation]}}]{Br_2/KOH}$$

$$\underset{\text{(Ethanoic acid)}}{CH_3COOH} \xleftarrow[\text{[Oxidation]}]{KMnO_4} CH_3CH_2OH \xleftarrow{HNO_2} CH_3CH_2NH_2$$

Q. 4. How are the following conversions carried out?*

(i) Butan-1-ol to butanoic acid.

(ii) Acetic acid to ethylamine.

Ans. (i) $CH_3CH_2CH_2CH_2OH \xrightarrow[H_2SO_4]{KMnO_4} CH_3-CH_2-CH_2-COOH$

(ii) $\underset{\text{Acetic acid}}{CH_3COOH} \xrightarrow{LiAlH_4} CH_3CH_2OH \xrightarrow[Br_2]{\text{Red P}} CH_3CH_2Br \xrightarrow{\text{Alc. } NH_3} \underset{\text{Ethylamine}}{CH_3CH_2NH_2}$

Q. 5. Write the steps involved in the following conversions:*

(i) Acetophenone to 2-phenyl butan-2-ol

(ii) Propene to acetophenone.

Ans. (i)

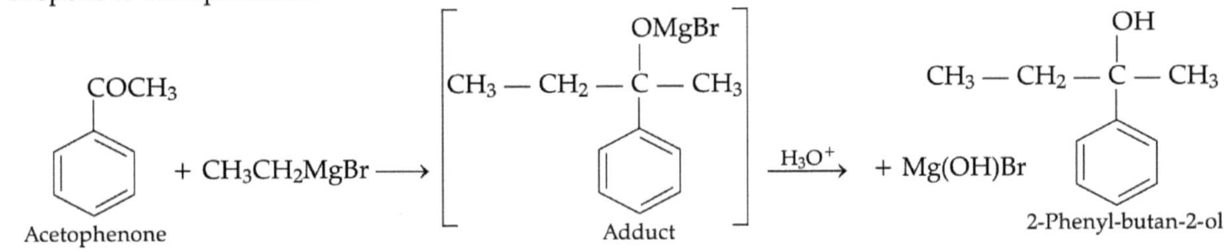

COCH3
+ CH3CH2MgBr
Acetophenone
OMgBr
CH3 — CH2 — C — CH3
Adduct
H3O+
+ Mg(OH)Br
OH
CH3 — CH2 — C — CH3
2-Phenyl-butan-2-ol

(ii)

CH3CH = CH2
Propene
(i) O3
(ii) H2/Zn
(Ozonolysis)
CH3CHO + HCHO
PhMgBr
OMgBr
CH3 — C — Ph
H
Adduct
H3O+
Δ
OH
CH3 — C — Ph
H
[O]
Cr2O3
O
CH3 — C — Ph
Acetophenone
or
C — CH3

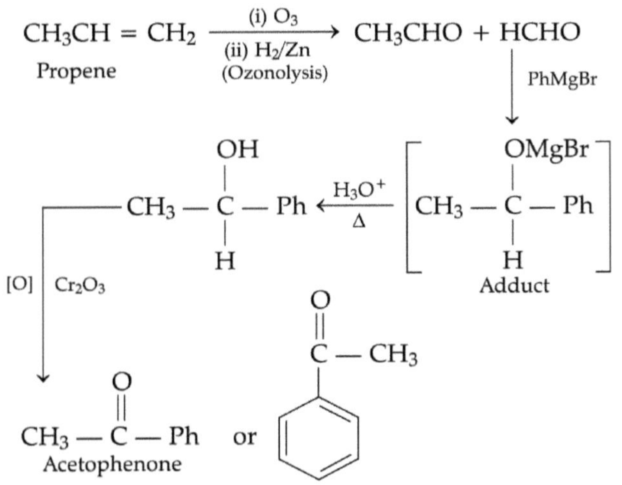

Q. 6. Convert Butan-1-ol to pent-2-enoic acid?

Ans. $\underset{\text{Butanol}}{CH_3CH_2CH_2CH_2OH} \xrightarrow[\text{(ii) Mg}]{\text{(i) } P/Br_2} CH_3CH_2CH_2CH_2MgBr \xrightarrow{CO_2}$

$CH_3CH_2CH_2CH_3COOH$

$\downarrow$ [H, V, Z Rxn] (i) P/Br_2

$\underset{\text{Pent-2-enoic acid}}{CH_3CH_2CH = CHCOOH} \xleftarrow[KOH]{\text{alc.}} CH_3CH_2CH_2-\underset{Br}{\underset{|}{CH}}-COOH$

Q. 7. How will you convert ethanal into the following compounds?

(i) Butane-1, 3-diol, (ii) But-2-enal, (iii) But-2-enoic acid.

Ans. (i) On treatment with dilute alkali, ethanal produces 3-hydroxybutanal gives butane-1, 3-diol on reduction.

$$\underset{\text{Ethanal}}{2CH_3CHO} \xrightarrow[\text{[Aldol condensation]}]{\text{dil. NaOH}} \underset{\text{(3-Hydroxybutanal aldol)}}{CH_3-\overset{OH}{\overset{|}{CH}}-CH_2-CHO} \xrightarrow[\text{(Reduction)}]{NaBH_4} \underset{\text{Butane-1, 3-diol}}{CH_3-\overset{OH}{\overset{|}{CH}}-CH_2-CH_2-OH}$$

(ii) On treatment with dilute alkali, ethanal gives 3-hydroxybutanal which on heating produces but-2-enal.

$$\underset{\text{Ethanal}}{2CH_3CHO} \xrightarrow[\text{[Aldol condensation]}]{\text{dil. NaOH}} \underset{\text{(3-Hydroxybutanal)}}{CH_3-\overset{OH}{\overset{|}{CH}}-CH_2-CHO} \xrightarrow[-H_2O]{\Delta} \underset{\text{But-2-enal}}{CH_3-CH = CH-CHO}$$

* are board exam questions from previous years

(iii) When treated with Tollen's reagent, But-2-enal produced in the above reaction produces but-2-enoic acid.

$$CH_3 — CH = CH — CHO \xrightarrow[\text{Tollen's reagent}]{[Ag(NH_3)_2]+ OH^-} CH_3 — CH = CHCOOH$$

But-2-enal → But-2-enoic acid

Q. 8. Show how each of the following compounds can be converted to benzoic acid.

(i) Ethylbenzene
(ii) Acetophenone
(iii) Bromobenzene
(iv) Phenylethene (Styrene)

Ans. (i) Ethylbenzene $\xrightarrow[\Delta]{KMnO_4 – KOH}$ (COOK) $\xrightarrow{H_3O^+}$ Benzoic acid (COOH)

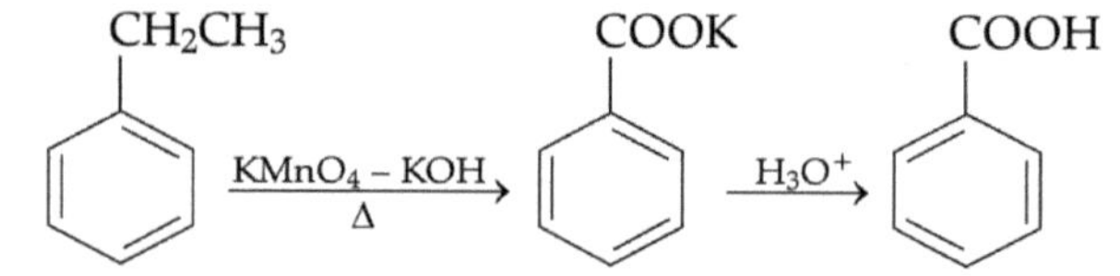

(ii) Acetophenone $\xrightarrow[\Delta]{KMnO_4 – KOH}$ (COOK) $\xrightarrow{H_3O^+}$ Benzoic acid (COOH)

(iii) Bromobenzene $\xrightarrow[\text{Ether}]{Mg}$ (MgBr) $\xrightarrow[\text{dry ice}]{O = C = O}$ (C–OMgBr) $\xrightarrow{H_3O^+}$ Benzoic acid (COOH) + Mg(OH)Br

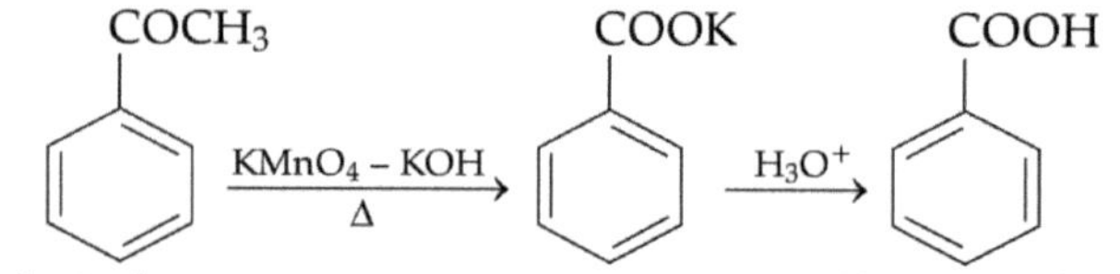

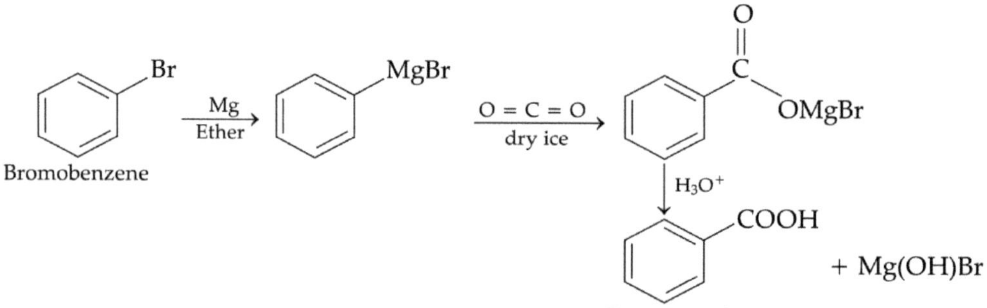

(iv) Phenylethene (CH = CH$_2$) $\xrightarrow[\Delta]{KMnO_4 – KOH}$ (COOK) + HCOOK $\xrightarrow{H_3O^+}$ Benzoic acid (COOH)

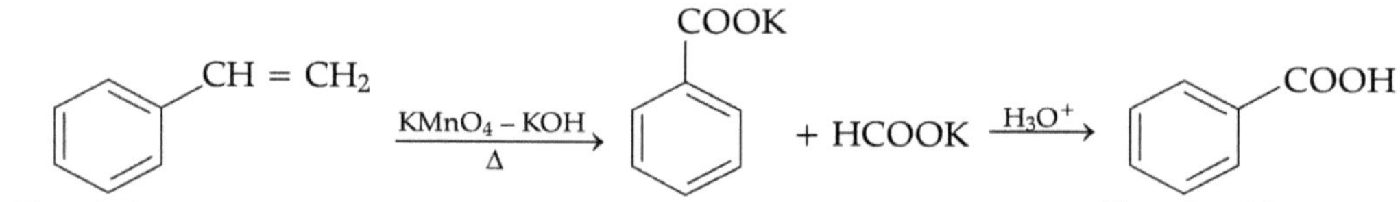

Q. 9. How will you bring about the following conversions?*

(i)   Benzoic acid to Benzaldehyde
(ii) Benzene to *m*-Nitroacetophenone.
(iii) Ethanol to 3-hydroxybutanal.

Ans. (i) Benzoic acid (COOH) $\xrightarrow{SOCl_2}$ Benzoyl chloride (COCl) + SO$_2$ + HCl $\xrightarrow[\text{H}_2]{\substack{\text{Pd, BaSO}_4 \\ \text{(Rosenmund's reaction)}}}$ Benzaldehyde (CHO)

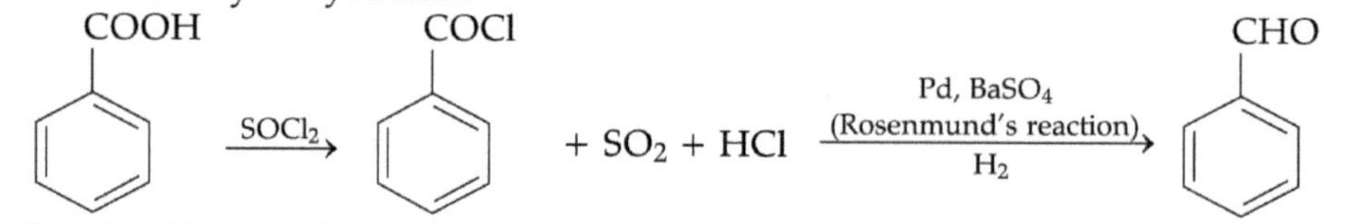

(ii) Benzene + CH$_3$COCl $\xrightarrow[\substack{\text{(Friedel crafts}\\\text{Arylation)}}]{\substack{\text{Anhydrous}\\ \text{AlCl}_3}}$ Acetophenone (C(=O)—CH$_3$) $\xrightarrow[\text{Nitration}]{\text{Conc. HNO}_3 + \text{Conc. H}_2\text{SO}_4}$ (*m*-Nitroacetophenone) (COCH$_3$, NO$_2$)

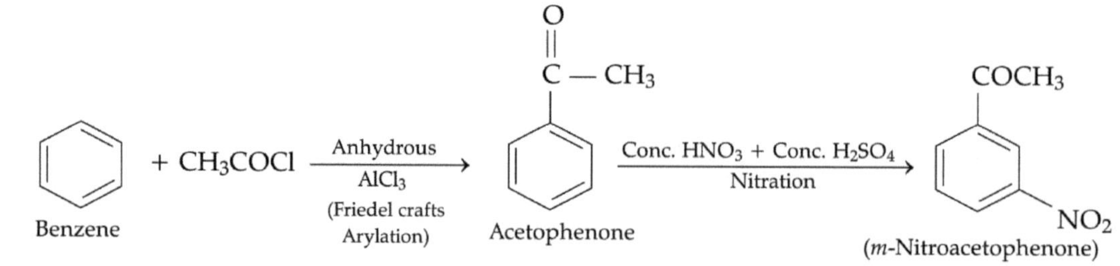

(iii) $CH_3CH_2OH \xrightarrow[\substack{573\ K\\ \text{(Oxidation)}}]{Cu} CH_3CHO \xrightarrow{\text{dil. NaOH}} CH_3 — \underset{\underset{OH}{|}}{CH} — CH_2 — CHO$

Ethanol → 3-Hydroxybutanal (aldol)

Q. 10. How will you bring about the following conversions in not more than two steps?

   (i)   Propanone to Propene

   (ii) Benzoic acid to Benzaldehyde*

   (iii) Ethanol to 3-Hydroxybutanal*

   (iv) Benzene to *m*-Nitroacetophenone

   (v) Benzaldehyde to Benzophenone.

Ans. (i) Propanone $\xrightarrow[\text{or LAH}]{\text{NaBH}_4}$ $CH_3-CH(CH_3)-CH_3$ $\xrightarrow[\Delta]{\text{Conc. H}_2\text{SO}_4}$ $CH_3-CH=CH_2$ (Propene)

(ii) Benzoic acid (COOH) $\xrightarrow{\text{SOCl}_2}$ (COCl) $\xrightarrow[\text{Pd. BaSO}_4]{\text{H}_2}$ Benzaldehyde (CHO) — (Rosenmund's Benzaldehyde Reduction)

(iii) CH_3-CH_2-OH (Ethanol) $\xrightarrow[\text{[O]}]{\text{CrO}_3}$ CH_3CHO $\xrightarrow[\substack{\text{(Aldol}\\\text{condensation)}}]{\text{dil. NaOH}}$ $CH_3-CH(OH)CH_2CHO$ (3-Hydroxybutanal)

(iv) Benzene $\xrightarrow[\substack{\text{(Friedel-Craft's}\\\text{alkylation}}]{\substack{\text{CH}_3\text{COCl,}\\\text{Anhyd. AlCl}_3}}$ (acetophenone, COCH$_3$) $\xrightarrow{\text{HNO}_3/\text{H}_2\text{SO}_4}$ *m*-Nitroacetophenone (COCH$_3$, NO$_2$)

(v) Benzaldehyde (CHO) $\xrightarrow[\text{(Oxidation)}]{\text{HNO}_3}$ (COOH) $\xrightarrow{\text{SOCl}_2}$ (COCl$_2$) + benzene $\xrightarrow[\text{Anhyd. AlCl}_3]{\text{(Friedel-Crafts acylation)}}$ Benzophenone

Q. 11. How will you bring about the following conversions in not more than two steps?

   (i)   Bromobenzene to 1-Phenylethanol

   (ii) Benzaldehyde to 3-Phenylpropan-1-ol

   (iii) Benzaldehyde to α-Hydroxyphenylacetic acid

   (iv) Benzoic acid to *m*-Nitrobenzyl alcohol.*

Ans. (i) Bromobenzene (Br) $\xrightarrow{\text{Mg/dry ether}}$ (MgBr) $\xrightarrow[\text{(ii) H}_2\text{O}]{\text{(i) CH}_3\text{CHO}}$ $H_3C-CH(OH)$ (1-Phenylethanol)

(ii) Benzaldehyde (CHO) $+ CH_3CHO$ $\xrightarrow[\substack{\text{(ii) }\Delta\\\text{(Aldol}\\\text{condensation)}}]{\text{(i) NaOH}}$ $CH=CHCHO$ $\xrightarrow[\substack{\text{(Catalytic}\\\text{hydrogenation)}}]{\text{Ni/H}_2}$ $CH_2CH_2CH_2OH$ (3-Phenylpropan-1-ol)

(iii) Benzaldehyde $\xrightarrow{\text{NaCN/HCl}}$ $C_6H_5 - \overset{\underset{|}{OH}}{CH} - CN$ (Benzaldehyde cyanohydrin) $\xrightarrow{\text{H}^+/\text{H}_2\text{O}}$ $C_6H_5 - \overset{\underset{|}{OH}}{CH} - COOH$ (α-Hydroxyphenylacetic acid)

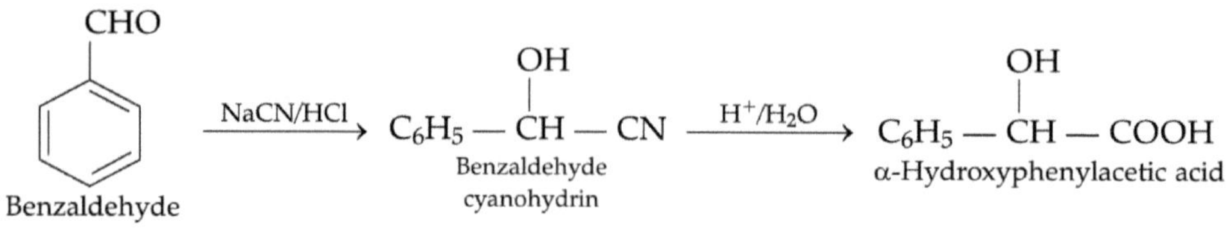

(iv) Benzoic acid (COOH) $\xrightarrow[\text{+ Conc. H}_2\text{SO}_4]{\text{Conc. HNO}_3}$ (COOH, NO$_2$) $\xrightarrow{\text{NaBH}_4}$ (CH$_2$OH, NO$_2$) (*m*-Nitrobenzyl alcohol)

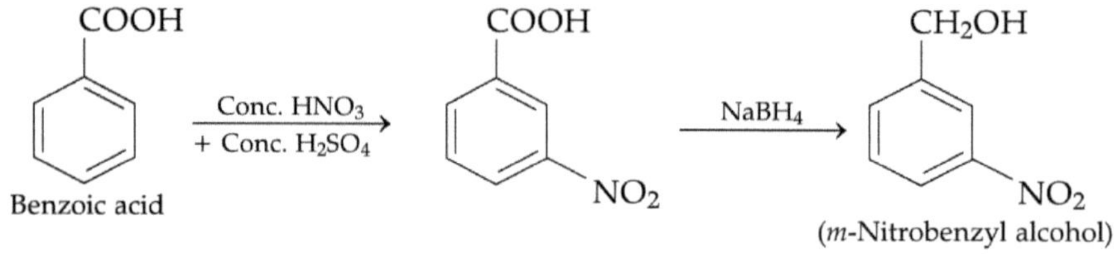

Q. 12. How do you convert the following?*

(i) Ethanal to Propanone
(ii) Toluene to Benzoic acid

Ans. (i) Conversion of ethanal to Propanone:

$$H_3C - CHO \xrightarrow[\text{Grignard reaction}]{\text{(i) CH}_3\text{MgBr, (ii) H}_2\text{O}} H_3C - \overset{OH}{\underset{CH_3}{C}} \xrightarrow[\text{Oxidation}]{\text{CrO}_3} H_3C \overset{O}{\underset{CH_3}{=}}$$

Ethanal → Propan-2-ol → Propanone

(ii) Conversion of toluene to benzoic acid:

Toluene (CH$_3$) $\xrightarrow[\text{Heat}]{\text{KMnO}_4 - \text{KOH}}$ (COOK) $\xrightarrow{\text{H}_3\text{O}^+}$ (COOH) Benzoic acid

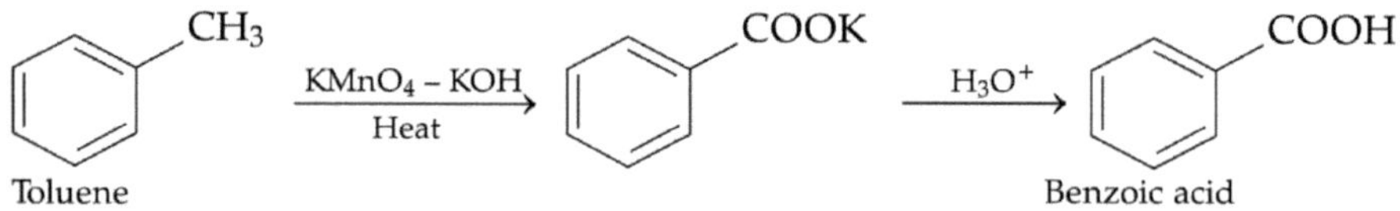

Q. 13. Do the following conversions in not more than two steps:

(i) Benzoic acid to Benzaldehyde
(iii) Propanone to Propane
(ii) Ethyl benzene to Benzoic acid

Ans. (i) $C_6H_5COOH \xrightarrow{\text{SOCl}_2} C_6H_5COCl \xrightarrow[\text{BaSO}_4]{\text{H}_2/\text{Pd}} C_6H_5CHO$
Benzoic acid → Benzaldehyde

(ii) $C_6H_5C_2H_5 \xrightarrow[\Delta]{\text{KMnO}_4\text{-KOH}} C_6H_5COOK \xrightarrow{\text{H}_3\text{O}^+} C_6H_5COOH$
Ethylbenzene → Benzoic acid

(iii) $CH_3COCH_3 \xrightarrow{\text{NaBH}_4} CH_3CH(OH)CH_3 \xrightarrow[\text{dehydration}]{\text{Conc. H}_2\text{SO}_4} CH_3CH = CH_2$
Propanone → Propane

Chapter 13. Amines

Q. 1. How will you convert:

(i) Nitrobenzene into acetanilide
(ii) Acetanilide into paranitroaniline.

Ans. (i) Nitrobenzene (NO$_2$) $\xrightarrow{\text{Sn/HCl}}$ Aniline (NH$_2$) $\xrightarrow{\text{CH}_3\text{COCl}}$ Acetanilide (NHCOCH$_3$)

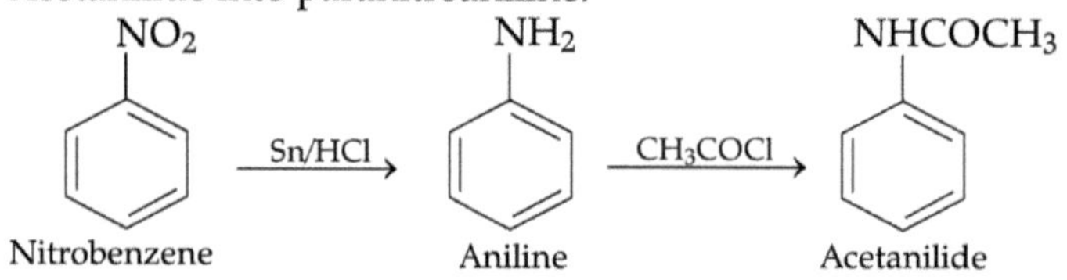

(ii) Acetanilide (NHCOCH$_3$) $\xrightarrow[\text{Nitration}]{\text{NHO}_3 + \text{H}_2\text{SO}_4}$ *p*-nitroacetanilide (major product) (NHCOCH$_3$, NO$_2$) $\xrightarrow{\text{H}_3\text{O}^+}$ *p*-nitroaniline (NH$_2$, NO$_2$)

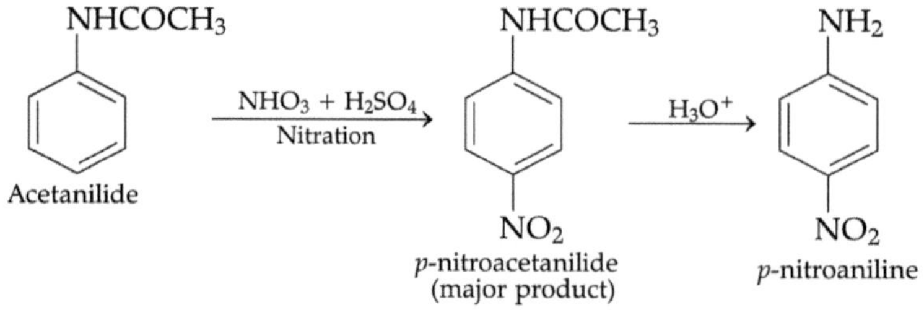

Q. 2. **How will you convert an alkyl halide to quaternary ammonium salt?**[*]

Ans. Alkyl halides react with ammonia to undergo substitution reaction and a small molecule of hydrogen halide is removed in each step. Thus ammoniation can result in the formation of quarternary salt if excess of alkyl halide is taken.

Example:

$$R - Cl \xrightarrow[-HCl]{NH_3} R - NH_2 \xrightarrow[-HCl]{R-Cl} R_2NH \xrightarrow[-HCl]{R-Cl} R_3N \xrightarrow[-HCl]{R-Cl} [R_4N^+]Cl^-$$

1° amine   2° amine   3° amine   Quarternary ammonium chloride salt

Q. 3. **How will you convert:**

  (i)   Aniline to benzonitrile

  (ii) Aniline to benzoic acid.

Ans. (i)

Aniline $\xrightarrow[HCl, <5°C]{NaNO_2}$ Benzene diazonium chloride ($N_2^+Cl^-$) $\xrightarrow[\Delta]{CuCN}$ Benzonitrile (CN)

(ii)

Aniline $\xrightarrow[NaNO_2 + HCl]{Diazotisation}$ Benzene diazonium chloride ($N_2^+Cl^-$) $\xrightarrow[HCN]{Cu\ Powder}$ Benzonitrile (CN) $\xrightarrow[\Delta]{H_3O^+}$ Benzoic acid (COOH)

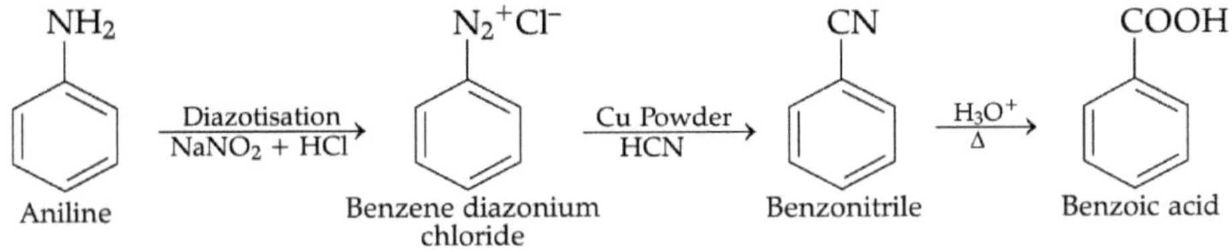

Q. 4. **How the following conversions can be brought about:**

  (i)   *m*-Nitroaniline to *m*-chloroaniline

  (ii) *p*-chloroaniline to *p*-chlorobenzyl amine

  (iii) Hexanenitrile to aminopentane.

Ans. (i)

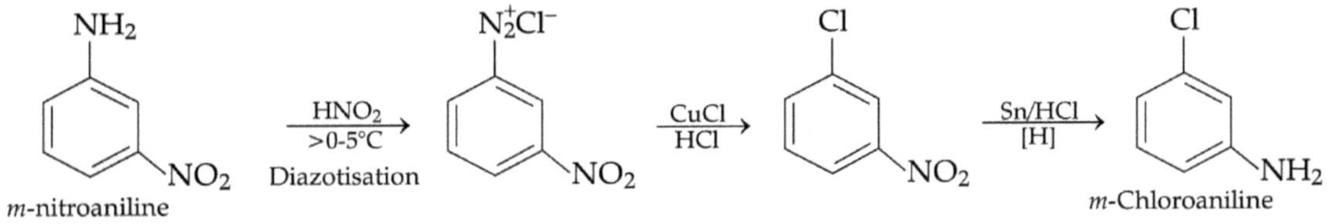

m-nitroaniline (NH_2, NO_2) $\xrightarrow[>0-5°C]{HNO_2}$ Diazotisation ($N_2^+Cl^-$, NO_2) $\xrightarrow[HCl]{CuCl}$ (Cl, NO_2) $\xrightarrow[[H]]{Sn/HCl}$ *m*-Chloroaniline (Cl, NH_2)

(ii)

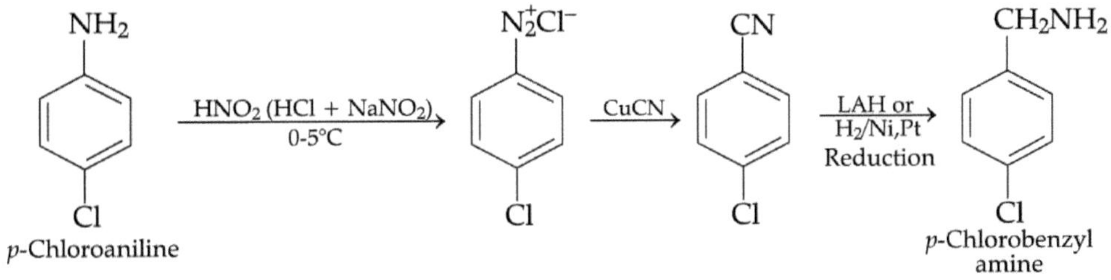

p-Chloroaniline (NH_2, Cl) $\xrightarrow[0-5°C]{HNO_2\ (HCl + NaNO_2)}$ ($N_2^+Cl^-$, Cl) $\xrightarrow{CuCN}$ (CN, Cl) $\xrightarrow[\substack{H_2/Ni,Pt \\ Reduction}]{LAH\ or}$ *p*-Chlorobenzyl amine (CH_2NH_2, Cl)

(iii) $CH_3CH_2CH_2CH_2CH_2CN$ $\xrightarrow[\text{Partial hydrolysis}]{H^+, \Delta}$ $CH_3CH_2CH_2CH_2 - CH_2 - CONH_2$

    Hexanenitrile   Hexanamide

                                    Hofmann's degradation $\downarrow$ Br_2,KOH

$$CH_3CH_2CH_2CH_2CH_2NH_2$$

                              1-Aminopentane

Q. 5. **How will you convert:**

  (i)   Benzene into aniline.

  (ii) Benzene into N, N-dimethylaniline.

  (iii) $Cl - (CH_2)_4 - Cl$ into hexane-1, 6-diamine.

Ans. (i)

Benzene $\xrightarrow[\text{(Nitration)}]{\text{HNO}_3/\text{H}_2\text{SO}_4}$ Nitrobenzene (NO_2) $\xrightarrow[\substack{\text{Ethanol} \\ \text{or} \\ \text{Sn/HCl}}]{\text{H}_2/\text{Pd}}$ Aniline (NH_2)

(ii) Benzene $\xrightarrow[\text{(Nitration)}]{\text{HNO}_3/\text{H}_2\text{SO}_4}$ (NO_2) $\xrightarrow[\text{Ethanol}]{\text{H}_2/\text{Pd}}$ Aniline (NH_2) $\xrightarrow[\substack{(2\text{ mol}) \\ \text{HCl}}]{\text{CH}_3\text{Cl}}$ N-methylaniline $\xrightarrow[-\text{HCl}]{\text{CH}_3\text{Cl}}$ N, N-Dimethylaniline

(iii) $\text{Cl}—(\text{CH}_2)_4—\text{Cl} \xrightarrow[\text{or alc KCN}]{\text{Ethanolic NaCN}} \text{N}\equiv\text{C}—(\text{CH}_2)_4—\text{C}\equiv\text{N}$

1, 4-Dichlorobutane

$\downarrow \text{H}_2/\text{Ni or Na(Hg)/C}_2\text{H}_5\text{OH}$

$$\text{H}_2\text{N}—\text{CH}_2—(\text{CH}_2)_4—\text{CH}_2—\text{NH}_2$$

Hexane 1, 6-diamine

Q. 6. Convert:

(i) 3-Methylaniline into 3-nitrotoluene

(ii) Aniline into 1, 3, 5-tribromobenzene.

Ans. (i) 3-Methylaniline (NH_2, CH_3) $+ \text{NaNO}_2 + 2\text{HCl} \xrightarrow[\text{(Diazotisation)}]{273\text{-}278\text{ K}}$ ($N_2^+Cl^-$, CH_3) $+ \text{NaCl} + 2\text{H}_2\text{O} \xrightarrow{\text{HBF}_4}$ ($N_2^+BF_4^-$, CH_3)

$\downarrow \text{NaNO}_2 \mid \text{Cu, }\Delta$

$\text{NaBF}_4 + \text{N}_2 +$ 3-Nitrotoluene (NO_2, CH_3)

(ii) Aniline (NH_2) $\xrightarrow[-3\text{ HBr}]{\text{Br}_2/\text{H}_2\text{O}}$ 2,4,6-tribromoaniline (NH_2, Br, Br, Br) $\xrightarrow{\text{NaNO}_2/\text{HCl}}$ ($N_2^+\bar{Cl}$, Br, Br, Br) $\xrightarrow[\text{H}_3\text{PO}_2]{\text{H}_2\text{O}}$ 1, 3, 5-Tribromobenzene (Br, Br, Br)

Q. 7. How will you convert:

(i) Ethanoic acid into methanamine

(ii) Hexanenitrile into 1-aminopentane

(iii) Methanol to ethanoic acid

(iv) Ethanamine into methanamine

(v) Ethanoic acid into propanoic acid

(vi) Methanamine into ethanamine

(vii) Nitromethane into dimethylamine

(viii) Propanoic acid into ethanoic acid.

Ans. (i) $\text{CH}_3\text{COOH} \xrightarrow{\text{SOCl}_2} \text{CH}_3\text{COCl} \xrightarrow{\text{NH}_3\text{ (excess)}} \text{CH}_3\text{CONH}_2 \xrightarrow[\substack{\text{Hofmann} \\ \text{Bromamide} \\ \text{degradation}}]{\text{Br}_2/\text{NaOH}} \text{CH}_3\text{NH}_2$

Ethanoic acid — Methanamine

(ii) $\text{C}_5\text{H}_{11}\text{CN} \xrightarrow[\substack{\text{Partial} \\ \text{hydrolysis}}]{\text{NH}_3\text{ (excess)}} \text{C}_5\text{H}_{11}—\text{CONH}_2 \longrightarrow \text{C}_5\text{H}_{11}—\text{NH}_2$

Hexanenitrile — Amide — 1-aminopentane

(iii) $\text{CH}_3\text{OH} \xrightarrow{\text{PCl}_5} \text{CH}_3\text{Cl} \xrightarrow{\text{Ethanolic NaCN}} \text{CH}_3\text{CN} \xrightarrow[\text{Hydrolysis}]{\text{H}^+/\text{H}_2\text{O}} \text{CH}_3\text{COOH}$

Methanol — Ethanoic acid

(iv) $CH_3 — CH_2 — NH_2 \xrightarrow[\text{(HONO)}]{\text{NaNO}_2/\text{HCl}} CH_3 — CH_2 — OH \xrightarrow{\text{KMnO}_4/\text{H}^+} CH_3COOH \xrightarrow[\Delta]{\text{NH}_3 \text{ (excess)}} CH_3CONH_2$

Ethanamine

$\downarrow$ Br$_2$ /NaOH

$CH_3 — NH_2$
Methanamine

(v) $CH_3COOH \xrightarrow[\text{(ii) H}_3\text{O}^+]{\text{(i) LiAlH}_4 \text{/ether}} CH_3CH_2OH \xrightarrow{\text{PCl}_5} CH_3CH_2Cl \xrightarrow{\text{Ethanolic NaCN}} CH_3CH_2CN$

Ethanoic acid

Hydrolysis, Δ | H$^+$/H$_2$O $\downarrow$

CH_3CH_2COOH
Propanoic acid

(vi) $CH_3 — NH_2 \xrightarrow{\text{NaNO}_2/\text{HCl}} CH_3OH \xrightarrow{\text{PCl}_5} CH_3Cl \xrightarrow{\text{Ethanolic NaCN}} CH_3CN \xrightarrow[\text{Na(Hg)/C}_2\text{H}_5\text{OH}]{\text{H}_2 /\text{Ni}} CH_3CH_2NH_2$

Methanamine

Ethanamine

(vii) $CH_3 — NO \xrightarrow{\text{Sn/HCl}} CH_3 — NH_2 \xrightarrow[\text{(Carbylamine reaction)}]{\text{CHCl}_3 /\text{KOH}/\Delta} CH_3 — NC \xrightarrow[[H]]{\substack{\text{Na/C}_2\text{H}_5\text{OH} \\ \text{Reduction}}} CH_3 — N — NH_3$

Nitromethane

Dimethylamine (2° amine)

(viii) $CH_3CH_2COOH \xrightarrow[\Delta]{\text{NH}_3 \text{ (excess)}} CH_3CH_2CONH_2 \xrightarrow[\substack{\text{(Hofmann bromamide} \\ \text{reaction)}}]{\text{Br}_2 /\text{KOH}} CH_3CH_2NH_2$

Propanoic acid

$\downarrow$ NaNO$_2$/HCl

$CH_3COOH \xleftarrow{\text{KMnO}_4/\text{H}^+} CH_3CH_2OH \xleftarrow{\text{H}_2\text{O}} [CH_3CH_2\overset{+}{N}_2\overset{-}{Cl}]$
Ethanoic acid $\qquad$ Alcohol

Q. 8. Accomplish the following conversions:

(i) Nitrobenzene to benzoic acid

(ii) Benzene to *m*-bromophenol

(iii) Benzoic acid to aniline

(iv) Aniline to 2, 4, 6-tribromofluorobenzene

(v) Benzyl chloride to 2-phenylethanamine

(vi) Chlorobenzene to *p*-chloroaniline

(vii) Aniline to *p*-bromoaniline

(viii) Benzamide to toluene

(ix) Aniline to benzyl alcohol.

Ans. (i)

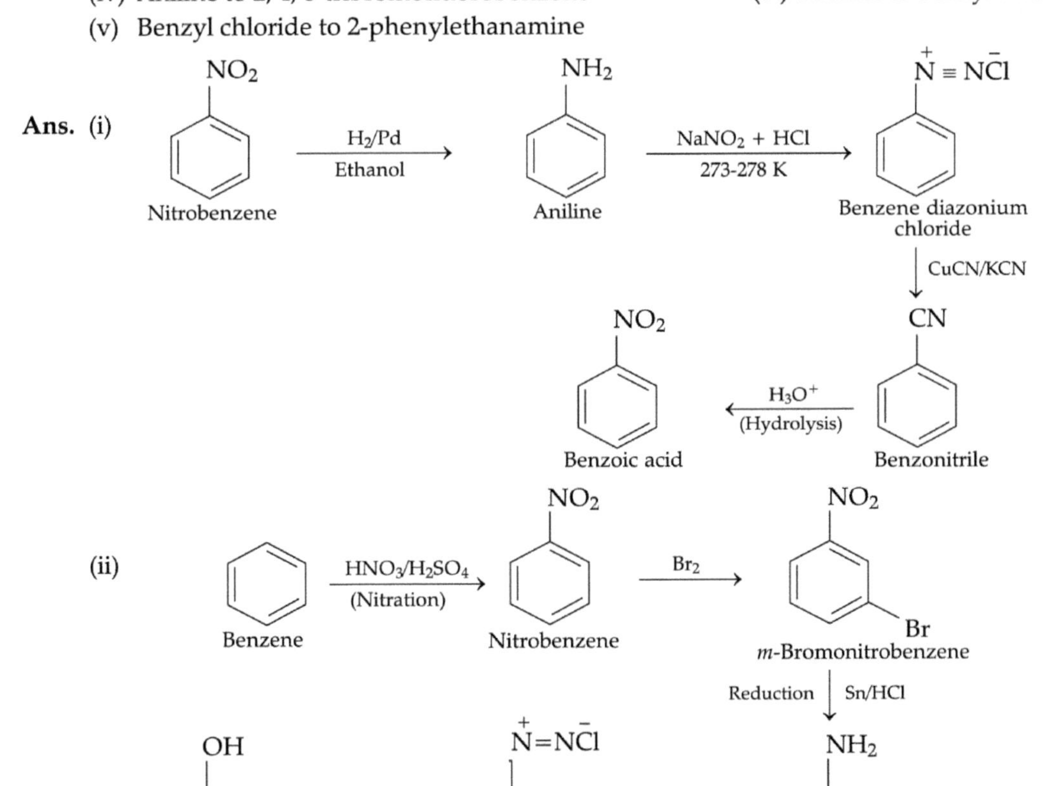

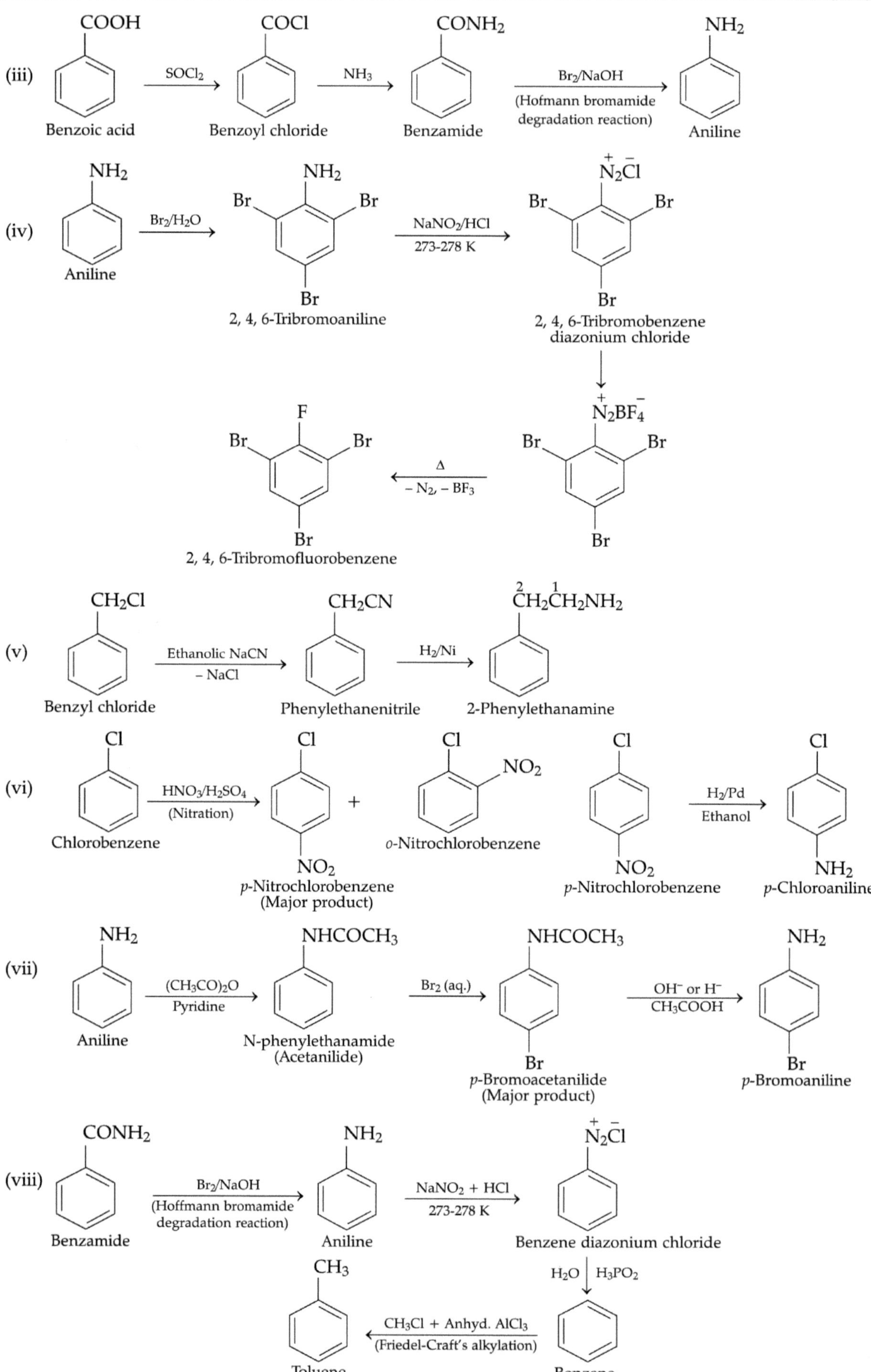
(iii)
COOH
Benzoic acid
SOCl2
COCl
Benzoyl chloride
NH3
CONH2
Benzamide
Br2/NaOH
(Hofmann bromamide degradation reaction)
NH2
Aniline

(iv)
NH2
Aniline
Br2/H2O
NH2
Br   Br
Br
2, 4, 6-Tribromoaniline
NaNO2/HCl
273-278 K
N2Cl
Br   Br
Br
2, 4, 6-Tribromobenzene diazonium chloride
N2BF4
Br   Br
Br
F
Br   Br
Br
2, 4, 6-Tribromofluorobenzene
Δ
– N2, – BF3

(v)
CH2Cl
Benzyl chloride
Ethanolic NaCN
– NaCl
CH2CN
Phenylethanenitrile
H2/Ni
CH2CH2NH2
2-Phenylethanamine

(vi)
Cl
Chlorobenzene
HNO3/H2SO4
(Nitration)
Cl
NO2
p-Nitrochlorobenzene
(Major product)
+
Cl
NO2
o-Nitrochlorobenzene
Cl
NO2
p-Nitrochlorobenzene
H2/Pd
Ethanol
Cl
NH2
p-Chloroaniline

(vii)
NH2
Aniline
(CH3CO)2O
Pyridine
NHCOCH3
N-phenylethanamide
(Acetanilide)
Br2 (aq.)
NHCOCH3
Br
p-Bromoacetanilide
(Major product)
OH– or H–
CH3COOH
NH2
Br
p-Bromoaniline

(viii)
CONH2
Benzamide
Br2/NaOH
(Hoffmann bromamide degradation reaction)
NH2
Aniline
NaNO2 + HCl
273-278 K
N2Cl
Benzene diazonium chloride
H2O   H3PO2
Benzene
CH3Cl + Anhyd. AlCl3
(Friedel-Craft's alkylation)
CH3
Toluene

(ix)

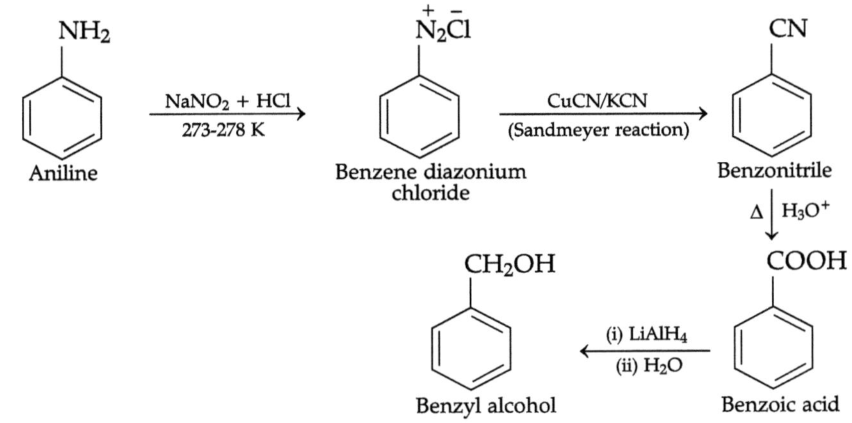

$$\underset{\text{Aniline}}{\text{C}_6\text{H}_5\text{NH}_2} \xrightarrow[\text{273-278 K}]{\text{NaNO}_2 + \text{HCl}} \underset{\substack{\text{Benzene diazonium} \\ \text{chloride}}}{\text{C}_6\text{H}_5\overset{+}{\text{N}}_2\overset{-}{\text{Cl}}} \xrightarrow[\text{(Sandmeyer reaction)}]{\text{CuCN/KCN}} \underset{\text{Benzonitrile}}{\text{C}_6\text{H}_5\text{CN}}$$

$$\Delta \mid \text{H}_3\text{O}^+$$

$$\underset{\text{Benzyl alcohol}}{\text{C}_6\text{H}_5\text{CH}_2\text{OH}} \xleftarrow[\text{(ii) H}_2\text{O}]{\text{(i) LiAlH}_4} \underset{\text{Benzoic acid}}{\text{C}_6\text{H}_5\text{COOH}}$$

OR

$$\underset{\text{Aniline}}{\text{C}_6\text{H}_5\text{NH}_2} \xrightarrow[\text{273-278 K}]{\text{NaNO}_2 + \text{HCl}} \underset{\substack{\text{Benzene diazonium} \\ \text{chloride}}}{\text{C}_6\text{H}_5\overset{+}{\text{N}}_2\overset{-}{\text{Cl}}} \xrightarrow[\text{(Sandmeyer reaction)}]{\text{CuCN/KCN}} \underset{\text{Benzonitrile}}{\text{C}_6\text{H}_5\text{CN}}$$

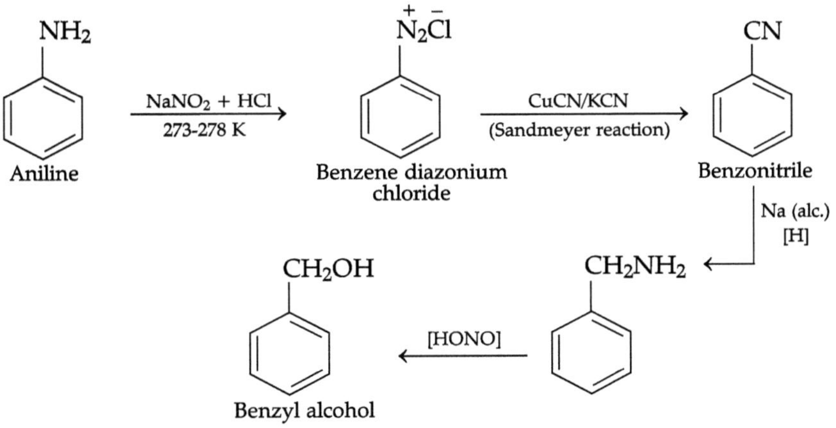

$$\text{Na (alc.)} \mid [\text{H}]$$

$$\underset{\text{Benzyl alcohol}}{\text{C}_6\text{H}_5\text{CH}_2\text{OH}} \xleftarrow{[\text{HONO}]} \text{C}_6\text{H}_5\text{CH}_2\text{NH}_2$$

Chapter 1. Soild State

Q. 1. A well-known mineral of fluorite is calcium fluoride in which one unit cell of this mineral contains $4Ca^{2+}$ ions and $8F^-$ ions and the Ca^{2+} ions are arranged in a fcc lattice. The F^- ions fill all the tetrahedral voids in the face centered cubic lattice of Ca^{2+} ions. The edge of the unit cell is 5.46×10^{-8} cm in length. The density of the solid is 3.18 g cm^{-3}. (molar mass of calcium fluoride is 78.08 g mol^{-3})

(1) Determine the total number of atoms present per unit cell in a fcc crystal structure.

(2) Define tetrahedral voids.

(3) In the calcium fluoride structure, what would be the coordination number of calcium and fluoride ions?

(4) What is the relation of edge length and the radius of the atom in a fcc unit cell?

(5) From the above information, calculate the Avogadro's number.

Ans. (1) Total number of atoms per unit cell in a fcc crystal structure is four.

(2) The void created by the four spheres in contact is called a tetrahedral void.

(3) Coordination number of calcium is 8 and fluoride is 4.

(4) Edge length of the face centred unit cell,

$$a = 2\sqrt{2}\,.r$$

$$a = \sqrt{2}\,.d$$

Here, r and d represents radius and distance respectively.

(5) Calculation for the Avogadro's number

For fcc lattice,

$$Z = 4$$

Given,
$$M = 78.08 \text{g mol}^{-1}$$
$$a = 5.46 \times 10^{-8} \text{ cm}$$
$$d = 3.18 \text{g cm}^{-1}$$

$$d = \frac{ZM}{a^3.N_A}$$

$$3.18 \text{g cm}^{-1} = \frac{4 \times 78.08 \text{g mol}^{-1}}{(5.46 \times 10^{-8})^3.N_A}$$

$$N_A = \frac{4 \times 78.08 \text{g mol}^{-1}}{(5.46 \times 10^{-8})^3.3.18 \text{g cm}^{-1}}$$

$$= 6.033 \times 10^{23} \text{ mol}^{-1}$$

Q. 2. Radha suggested that the conductivity of the semiconductors can be increased by heating. Her friend Mira advised her to dope the semiconductor with either group 13 or group 15 elements to increase the conductivity.

(1) Define semiconductor.

(2) Explain the cause of increase in conductivity by doping.

(3) Which type of semiconductor is formed if it is doped with group 13 or group 15 elements?

(4) What are intrinsic semiconductors?

(5) What is F-centres?

Ans. (1) The solids having the conductivity in the range of 10^{-6} to 10^4 ohm^{-1} are known as semiconductors.

(2) Doping is generally used in semiconductor crystals either to increase the number of electrons (with donor or n-type semiconductor) or to increase the number of voids or holes, missing electrons from the

interatomic bonds in the crystal, (with acceptor or *p*-type conductor). When these kind of doping takes place in semiconductors and voltage is applied, these electrons will conduct electricity.

(3) *p*-type semiconductor is formed if it is doped with group 13 and *n*-type semiconductor is formed if it is doped with group 15 elements.

(4) Intrinsic semiconductors are those substances whose conductivity can be increased with rise in temperature since more electrons can jump to the conduction band because the gap between the valence band and conduction band is small. For example: Silicon and Germanium etc.

(5) When some of the anions, in a crystal, are absent they leave holes which are occupied by the electrons. These vacant anion sites occupied by electrons are called F-centres. They are responsible for the colour of the compounds because of the electronic transitions.

Q. 3. **An element crystallizes in body centred cubic structure. If the edge length of the cell is 1.469 $\times$ 10^{-10} m and the density is19.3g cm^3.**

(1) Determine the atomic mass of the element.

(2) What is the percentage of filled space in body centred cubic unit cell?

(3) Calculate the radius of an atom of this element.

(4) Determine the number of lattice points present in one unit cell of body centred cubic structure.

(5) What is the percentage of free space in the given body centred cubic unit cell?

Ans. (1) For bcc lattice,

$$Z = 2$$
$$M = ?$$
$$\text{edge length } (a) = 1.469 \times 10^{-10} \text{ m}$$
$$= 1.469 \times 10^{-8} \text{ cm}$$
$$d = 19.3 \text{ g/cm}^3$$
$$d = \frac{ZM}{a^3 . N_A}$$
$$M = \frac{d \times a^3 \times N_A}{Z}$$
$$M = \frac{19.3 \times (1.469 \times 10^{-8}) \times 6.023 \times 10^{23}}{2}$$
$$M = \frac{368.49 \times 10^{-1}}{2}$$
$$= \frac{368.49}{20}$$
$$= 18.424 \text{ g/cm}^3$$

(2) Percentage of filled space in body centred cubic unit cell is 68%.

(3)
$$\text{radius (r)} = \frac{\sqrt{3}}{4} \times a$$
$$= \frac{1.732 \times 1.469 \times 10^{-10} \text{m}}{4}$$
$$= \frac{2.54 \times 10^{-10} \text{m}}{4}$$
$$= 0.6360 \times 10^{-10} \text{ m}$$

(4) There are 9 lattice points in one unit cell of body centred cubic structure.

(5) Percentage of free space in body centred cubic unit cell is 100 − 68 = 32%.

Q. 4. **A compound is formed by two elements X and Y. Atoms of element Y (present as anions) make ccp and atoms of element X (present as cation) occupy all the octahedral voids.**

(1) What will be the formula of the given compound?

(2) Define coordination number.

(3) What do you understand by term voids?

(4) If the number of sphere in close packing structure is n, then what will be the number of octahedral voids?

(5) Define octahedral voids.

Ans. (1) Element Y makes ccp lattice. In this lattice number of atom Y will be equal to the number of octahedral voids present in it. These voids are occupied by atom X, thus number of atoms of X and Y will be in equal ratio *i.e.*, 1:1. Therefore, the formula of the given compound is XY.

(2) Number of nearest neighbours (atoms or ions) of any atom or ion is known as its coordination number In ionic crystals the number of oppositely charged ions surrounding a particular ion is called coordination number.

(3) Voids in solid state mean the unoccupied space between the constituent particles in a closed packed structure.

(4) If the number of sphere in close packing structure is n, then the number of octahedral voids will be n.

(5) The void created by the six spheres in contact is called an octahedral void.

Q. 5. Examine the given figure of a portion of a defective crystal given below and answer the following questions.

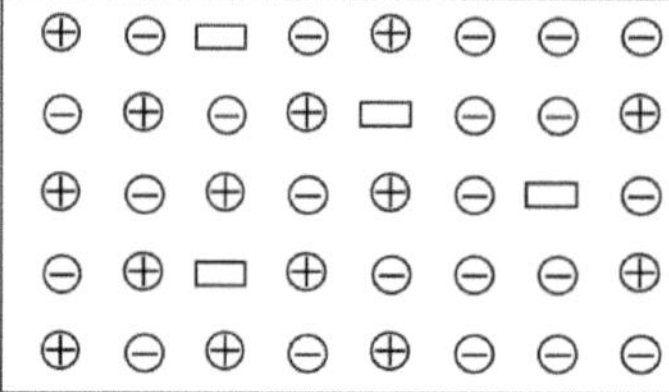

(1) What is meant by 'point defects' in crystals?

(2) What are these type of vacancy defects called?

(3) How is the density of a crystal affected by these defects?

(4) Give the name of an ionic compound showing this type of defect in crystalline state.

(5) How the stoichiometry of the compound is affected?

Ans. (1) When the atoms or ions are misplaced or missing from the crystal, the defects are called point defects.

(2) These type of vacancy defects are termed as Schottky defect.

(3) Density of the crystal decreases in the Schottky defect.

(4) NaCl shows Schottky defect.

(5) Stoichiometry of the compound remains the same it is not affected by these defects.

Q. 6. An element X having atomic mass 60 g/mol with the density of 6.23 g/cm³. The edge length of its cubic unit cell is 400 pm.

(1) Predict the type of cubic cell.

(2) Find out the radius of atom of this element.

(3) What is the filled space in this cubic cell?

(4) What is the percentage of free space in this cubic unit cell?

(5) How the density of the element is related to the Avogadro number?

Ans. (1)

$$\text{Atomic mass of X} = 60 \text{ g/mol}$$
$$\text{density of element} = 6.23 \text{ g/cm}^3$$
$$\text{edge length } (a) = 400 \text{ pm}$$
$$= 400 \times 10^{-10} \text{ cm}$$

$$d = \frac{ZM}{a^3 . N_A}$$

$$Z = \frac{d \times a^3 \times N_A}{M}$$

$$Z = \frac{6.23 \times (400 \times 10^{-10})^3 \times 6.023 \times 10^{23}}{60}$$

$$= 4$$

The number of unit cell is 4, it should have face centred cubic lattice.

(2) For face centered cubic lattice

$$\text{radius } (r) = \frac{a}{2\sqrt{2}}$$

$$= \frac{400}{2 \times 1.414}$$

$$= 141.44 \text{ pm}$$

$$= 141.44 \times 10^{-10} \text{ cm}$$

(3) Percentage of filled space in face centred cubic unit cell is 74%.

(4) Percentage of free space in face centred cubic unit cell is $100 - 74 = 26\%$.

(5) The density of the molecule has an inverse relationship with the Avogadro number.

Q. 7. X – Ray diffraction is a method used for the determination of shape or geometry of a molecule. Using this method, it was observed that the atoms in a crystal of gold are packed in the form of layers such that starting from any layer, every fourth layer is found to be exactly same. The density of the gold is found to be 19.4 gcm^{-3} and its atomic mass is 197 a.m.u.

(1) What is the coordination number of gold atom in the crystal?

(2) Find out the fraction occupied by the gold atoms in the crystal.

(3) What will be the length of the edge of unit cell?

(4) By assuming the gold atom to be spherical, determine its radius.

(5) What is XRD?

Ans. (1) From the given information, the arrangement of layers is ABC ABC... type that is the given crystal has a cubic closed packing arrangement. Hence, the coordination number is 12.

(2) In cubic closed packing, the occupied fraction is 0.74.

(3) For CCP, *i.e.*, fcc $Z = 4$

To determine the length of the edge of the unit cell, use the given formula to get,

$$\rho = \frac{Z \times M}{a^3 \times N_0 \times 10^{-3}} \qquad \text{or} \qquad a^3 = \frac{Z \times M}{\rho^3 \times N_0 \times 10^{-3}}$$

$$a^3 = \frac{4 \times 197}{19.4 \times 6.02 \times 10^{23} \times 10^{-30}}$$

$$= 6.747 \times 10^7 = 67.47 \times 10^6$$

$$a = (67.47 \times 10^6)^{1/3}$$

$$= 4.07 \times 10^2 \text{ pm}$$

$$a = 407 \text{ pm}$$

(4) For fcc radius of the gold atom can be calculated as:

$$r = \frac{a}{2\sqrt{2}} = 0.3535a$$

$$= 0.3535 \times 407 \text{ pm}$$

$$= 143.9 \text{ pm}$$

(5) X – Ray diffraction (XRD) is a method used for the determination of shape or geometry of a molecule and can be used to predict the crystal structure and molecular formula of crystalline compounds.

Q. 8. Not a single crystal is found to be perfect at room temperature. Defect present in the crystal is either a stoichiometric or a non-stoichiometric. The formula of the ionic compound is different from the ideal formula due to non-stoichiometric defect. These effects change the properties of the crystal. In some cases, these defects are introduced to have the crystal of desired properties. Doping of group 13 and 15 element is the most common.

(1) Give an example of *p*–type semiconductor.

(2) Which type of defect does not affect the density of the crystal?

(3) NaCl was doped with 10^{-3} mol% $SrCl_2$, calculate the concentration of cationic-vacancies.

(4) What type of semiconductor will be obtained when silicon is doped with arsenic?

(5) Why semiconductors conduct electricity?

Ans. (1) Germanium is the element which belongs to group 14 while aluminium belongs to group 13. Hence, germanium doped with aluminium will create a *p*–type semiconductor.

(2) Frenkel defect does not affect the density of the crystal because the cations are missing from the lattice sites and occupy the interstitial sites.

(3) Doping of NaCl with 10^{-3} mol% $SrCl_2$ means that 100 moles of NaCl are doped with 10^{-3} mol of $SrCl_2$.

$$1 \text{ mole of NaCl is doped with } SrCl_2 = \frac{10^{-3}}{100} \text{ mole} = 10^{-5} \text{ mole}$$

Concentration of cationic vacancies can be calculated as follows:

(4) n–type semiconductor will be obtained when silicon is doped with arsenic.

(5) Due to the presence of impurities and defects, semiconductors are electrically conductive in nature.

Chapter 2. Solutions

Q. 1. When a non-volatile solute is added to a solvent, the freezing point of thus formed solution is always lower than that of pure solvent. This difference in freezing points is known as depression in freezing point. If ΔT_f^o is the freezing point temperature of pure solvent and T_f is the freezing point temperature of the solution when non-volatile solute is dissolved in it, then depression in freezing point (ΔT_f) is given by,

$$\Delta T_f = T_f^o - T_f$$

For the dilute solutions, $\Delta T_f = K_f m$

[where, m = molal concentration of the solution]

  (a) Why the freezing point of solution is always lower than the of pure solvent?

  (b) Write the formula relating depression in freezing point with molar mass of solute.

  (c) Define the proportionality constant (K_f).

  (d) Write the unit of K_f.

  (e) Calculate the depression in freezing point of 5% glicose in water.

     [$K_f = 13.962$]

Ans. (a) The freezing point of the solution is always lower than that of pure solvent as the vapour pressure of the solvent decreases in the pressence of non-volatile solute.

  (b) Depression in freezing point $(DT_f) = K_f \times m$

$$= \frac{W_f \times W_{solute} \times 1000}{W_{solvent} \times M_{solute}}$$

$$M_{solute} = \frac{K_f \times W_{solute} \times 1000}{\Delta T_f \times W_{solvent}}$$

  (c) Molal freezing point depression constant (K_f) or cryoscopic constant is defined as the depression in freezing point for 1 molal solution *i.e.*, a solution containing 1g mole of solute dissolved in 1000g of solvent.

  (d) The unit of K, is K kg mol^{-1}.

  (e) $W_{solute} = 5g$, $M_{solute} = 180$ gmol^{-1} $W_{solvent} = 95$ g

$$\text{Molality of glucose solution} = \frac{5}{180} \times \frac{1000}{95} = 02924$$

$$\Delta T_f = K_f \times m$$

$$\Delta T_f = \frac{2.15}{0.154} \times 02924 = 4.08$$

Q. 2. A person suffering from high blood pressure is advised to take minimum quantity of common salt. Explain.

Ans. Our body fluids contains Na^+ and Cl^- ions. Hence, if a person with high blood pressure takes more salt the concentration of these ions will further increase leading to high osmotic pressure of blood.

Q. 3. How much molecular mass of NaCl is obtained experimentally using colligative properties?

Ans. NaCl dissociates as, $NaCl \longrightarrow Na^+ + Cl^-$

Hence, Molecular mass/2 ($n = 2$) so $58.5/2 = 29.25$ g/mol.

Q. 4. Why do aquatic species feel more comfortable in the lakes in winter than in summer?

Ans. Aquatic species survive on dissolved oxygen for breathing. As solubility of gases decreases with increase in temperature, hence oxygen amount in summers is lesser than winters in lake. Therefore, the aquatic species feel more comfortable in winters.

Q. 5. Why water cannot be separated from ethyl alcohol completely by fractional distillation?

Ans. Ethyl alcohol and water (95.4% ethyl alcohol and 4.6% water) forms a constant boiling mixture *i.e.*, azeotrope with boiling point at 351.1 K. Hence water cannot be separated by fractional distillation.

Q. 6. The solutions which obey Raout's law over the entire range of concentration are known as ideal solution. However, there are many solutions which do not obey Raoult's law, such solutions are called non-ideal solutions. They show deviation from Raoult's law *i.e.*, ideal behaviour which may be positive or negative. Solution of ethanol and acetone, chloroform and acetone etc., fall into this category.

   (a) State Raoult's law.

   (b) Write characteristics of ideal solutions.

   (c) What type of deviation from Raoult's law is shown by a mixture of ethanol and acetone and why?

   (d) What type of deviation from Raoult's law is shown by a solution of chloroform and acetone and why?

   (e) Give two examples of solutions which are nearly ideal in behaviour.

Ans. (a) It states that for a solution of volatile liquids, the partial vapour pressure of each component is directly proportional to its mole fraction.

   (b) For an ideal solution

      (i) Raoult's low is obeyed *i.e.*, $P_A = P_A^o X_A$ and $P_B = P\,P_B^o X_B$.

      (ii) The enthalpy of mixing of pure component to form the solution is zero, *i.e.*, $\Delta_{mix} H = 0$.

      (iii) The volume of mixing is zero, *i.e.* $\Delta_{mix} V = 0$.

   (c) A solution of ethanol and acetone shows position deviation from Raoult's law. In pure ethanol, molecules are hydrogen boned. On adding acetone to ethanol, its molecules get in between the ethanol molecules and break some of the H-bonds between them.

      Due to weakening of interactions, the escaping tendency of molecules for each component increases. Consequently, the vapour pressure increases resulting in positive deviation from Raoult's law.

   (d) A solution of chloroform and acetone shown negative deviation from Raoult's low. This is because chloroform molecule is able to form H-bond with acetone molecule as shown below.

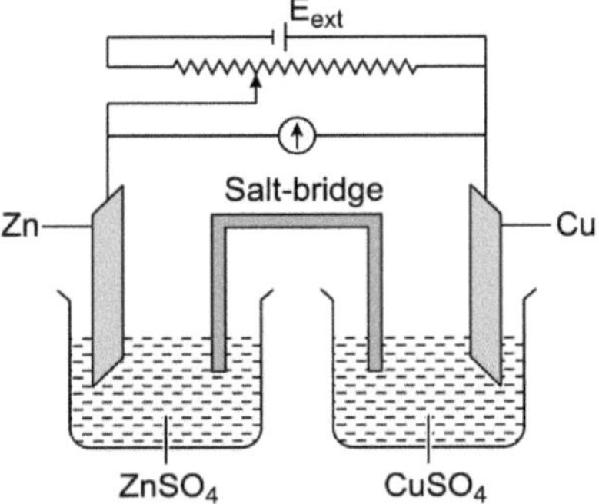

      It decreases the escaping tendency of molecules for each component from the surface of solution and consequently the vapour pressure decreases resulting in negative deviation from Raoult's law.

   (e) Solution of *n*-hexane and *n*-heptane

      Solution of benzene and toluene.

Q. 7. Why great care has to be taken in intravenous injection to have a comparable concentration of the solution to be injected to blood plasma?

Ans. Our blood cells (RBCs) have semipermeable membrane. Hence, if in case the intravenous injection liquid has concentration more (hypertonic) or less (hypotonic) than blood plasma then in either case it will be fatal. Hypertonic injection will cause RBCs to shrink (crenation) while hypotonic will cause them to swell (hemolysis) as a result of osmosis. Thus, medicine to be injected should have isotonic concentration as blood plasma.

Chapter 3. Electrochemistry

Q. 1. The electrochemical cell given alongside converts the chemical energy released during the redox reaction to electrical energy.

$$Zn(s) + Cu^{2+} (aq) \longrightarrow Zn^{2+} (aq) + Cu (s)$$

It gives an electrical potential of 1.1 V when concentration of Zn^{2+} and Cu^{2+} ions is units. State the direction of flow of current and also specify whether zinc and copper are deposited or dissolved at their respective electrodes when:

(a) An external opposite potential of less than 1.1 V is applied.

(b) An external potential of 1.1 is applied.

(c) An external potential of greater than 1.1 V is applied.

(d) What would happed if no salt bridge were used in an electrochemical cell (like Zn–Cu cell)?

(e) How can the reduction potential of an electrode be increased?

Ans. (a) Reaction continues to take place.

Electrons flow Zn electrode to copper electrode, hence current flows Cu to Zn.

Zn dissolves and copper deposits at their respective electrodes.

(b) The reaction stops and no current flows.

A state of equilibrium is achieved and no change is observed at zinc and copper electrodes.

(c) Reaction takes place in opposite direction.

Electrons flow from copper electrode to zine electrode and hence current flows from Zn to Cu. Zinc deposits and copper dissolves at their respective electrodes. The cell functions as an electrolytic cell.

(d) The metal ions (Zn^{2+}) formed by the loss of electrons will accumulate in one electrode and the negative ions $\left(SO_4^{2-}\right)$ will accumulate in the other. Thus, the solutions will develop changes and the current willl

stop flowing. Moreover, the inner circuit will not be comopleted.

(e) $M^{n+} + ne^- \rightarrow M$, $E_{M^{n+}/M} = E^{o}_{M^{n+}/M} - \dfrac{RT}{nF} \ln \dfrac{1}{[M^{n+}]} = E^{o}_{M^{n+}/M} + \dfrac{RT}{nF} \ln [M^{n+}]$

Thus, electrode potential can be increased by increasing the metal ion concentration.

Q. 2. The process of chemical decomposition of the electrolyte by passing electricity through its molten or dissolved state is called electrolysis. The products of electrolysis depend on the nature of material being electrolysed, types of the electrodes, different oxidising and reducing species present in the electrolytic cell, kinetic barrier and overvoltage. During the electrolysis of aqueous solution of sodium chloride the probable reactions at the electrodes are:

At cathode:

$$Na^+ (aq) + e^- \longrightarrow Na (s) \qquad\qquad E^{o}_{red} = 2.71 \text{ V}$$

$$H^+ (aq) + e^- \longrightarrow 1/2\ H_2 (g) \qquad\qquad E^{o}_{red} = 0.00 \text{ V}$$

$$H_2O (l) + e^- \longrightarrow 1/2\ H_2 (g) + OH^- \qquad\qquad E^{o}_{red} = 1.23 \text{ V}$$

At anode:

$$Cl^- (aq) \longrightarrow 1/2\ Cl_2 (g) + e^- \qquad\qquad E^{o}_{red} = 1.36 \text{ V}$$

$$2H_2O (l) \longrightarrow O_2 (g) + 4H^+ (aq) + 4e^- \qquad\qquad E^{o}_{red} = 1.23 \text{ V}$$

(a) On the basis of standard reduction potential values, which reaction is feasible at the cathode and why?

(b) Which gas is liberated at the anode and why?

(c) Give net reaction for the above process.

(d) State Faraday's first law of electrolysis.

(e) What is the change in free energy for electrolytic cell?

Ans. (a) The reaction $H^+ (aq) + e^- \longrightarrow 1/2\ H_2 (g)$ is feasible the cathode as it has higher standard reduction potential than other reaction.

(b) Cl_2 is liberated at the anode on account of over potential of oxygen.

(c) $NaCl (aq) + H_2O (l) \longrightarrow Na + (aq) + OH^- (aq) + \dfrac{1}{2} H_2 (g) + \dfrac{1}{2} Cl_2 (g)$

(d) It states that the amount of chemical reaction which occurs at any electrode during electrolysis by a current is proportional to the quantity of electricity passed through the electrolyte (solution or melt).

(e) Changes in free energy, ΔG is positive for an electrolytic cell because electrical energy is supplied to carry out the reaction which is non-spontaneous.

Chapter 4. Chemical Kinetics

Q. 1. The change in concentration of a reactant or product in unit time is called rate of reaction. The reaction, $2NO(g) + O_2(g) \longrightarrow 2NO_2(g)$, was studied by the initial rate method. The following kinetic data was obtained.

Experiment	Initial [NO]/mol L^{-1}	Initial [O$_2$]/mol L^{-1}	Initial rate of formation of No$_2$/mol L^{-1} s^{-1}
1.	0.30	0.30	0.096
2.	0.60	0.30	0.384
3.	0.30	0.60	0.192
4.	0.60	0.60	0.768

  (a) What do you understand by rate law?

  (b) What is the order of the reaction with respect to NO and O_2?

  (c) Determine the rate law for the reaction.

  (d) Calculate the rate constant for the reaction.

  (e) Find out the rate of formation of NO_2 when [NO] is 0.1 and [O$_2$] is 0.2 mol L^{-1}.

Ans. (a) Rate law is an experimentally determined expression which relates the rate of reaction with concentration of the reactants.

  (b) Suppose the order of reaction w.r.t. NO is x and w.r.t. O_2, it is y, then,

$$\text{Rate} = k\,[NO]^x\,[O2]^y$$
$$0.096 = k\,(0.03)^x\,(0.30)^y \qquad \ldots (i)$$
$$0.384 = k\,(0.60)^x\,(0.30)^y \qquad \ldots (ii)$$
$$0.192 = k\,(0.30)^x\,(0.60)^y \qquad \ldots (iii)$$
$$0.768 = {}^k\,(0.60)^x\,(0.60)^y \qquad \ldots (iv)$$

Dividing equation *(ii)* by *(i)*, we get

$$\frac{0.384}{0.096} = \frac{k\,(0.60)^x(0.30)^y}{k\,(0.30)^x(0.30)^y}$$

$$4 = 2^x \text{ or } 22 = 2^x \text{ or } x = 2$$

Dividing *(iv)* by *(ii)*, we get

$$\frac{0.768}{0.384} = \frac{k\,(0.60)^x(0.60)^y}{k\,(0.60)^x(0.30)^y}$$

$$2 = 2^y \text{ or } y = 1$$

Hence, order or reaction w.r.t NO = 2

order of reaction w.r.t O_2 = 1

  (c) Rate = $k\,[NO]^2\,[O_2]^1$

  (d) Rate = $k\,[NO]^2\,[O_2]^1$

$$0.096 = k\,(0.30)^2\,(0.30)^{-1}$$

$$k = \frac{0.096}{0.09 \times 0.30} = 3.55\ \text{mol}^{-2}\,\text{L}^2\,\text{s}^{-1}$$

  (e) Rate = $k\,[NO]^2\,[O_2]$

Rate = $11.85\,(0.1)^2\,(0.2)$ or rate = $2.37 \times 10^{-2}\ \text{mol}^{-2}\,\text{L}^1\,\text{s}^{-1}$

Chapter 5. Surface Chemistry

Q. 1. There are two terms used in surface chemistry are adsorption and absorption. Different factors affect the rate of adsorption. Greater the surface area of the adsorbent, greater is adsorption. Adsorption is an exothermic process. Adsorption is of two types (*i.e.*, physical adsorption and chemical adsorption). To explain the mechanism of adsorption Freundlich gave an adsorption isotherm equation by

$$\frac{x}{m} = k.p^{1/n}$$

where, x is the amount of the gas adsorbed by m gram of the adsorbent at equilibrium pressure P and K and *n* are constants.

(a) Are adsorption and absorption same?

(b) What is the change in rate of adsorption with time when a gas adsorbs on a surface of charcoal?

(c) In above example what will be the effect of increasing temperature on adsorption.

(d) Which one of the adsorption is an axample of reversibe process, physical adsorption or chemical adsorption?

(e) Choose the correct graph for Freundlich adsorption isotherm:

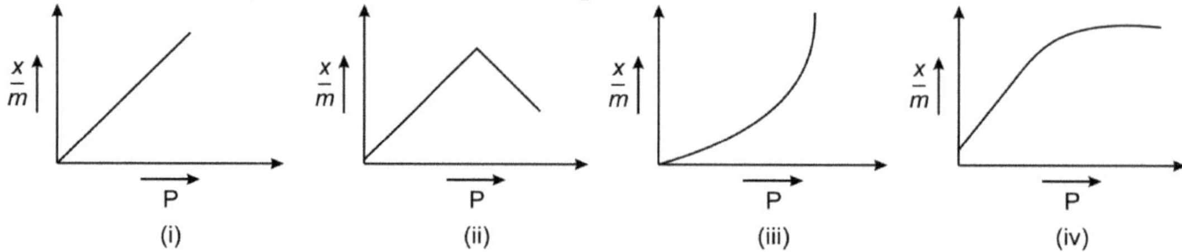

(i)   (ii)   (iii)   (iv)

Ans. (a) No, adsorption is surface phenomena and absorption is bulk phenomena.

(b) The rate of adsorption decreases with time due to decrease in surface area.

(c) According to Le-Chatelieor principle, adsorption decreases with increase in temperature.

(d) Due to Van der Waal's force physical adsorption is reversible process whereas in chemical adsorption a strong chemical bond formed between adsorbent and adsorbate.

(e) (iv)

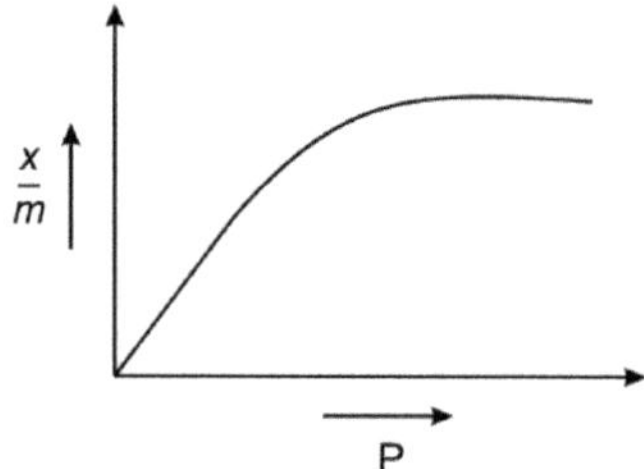

Q. 2. A substance which accelerate the rate of a chemical reaction and itself remains chemically and quantitatively unchanged after the reaction, is known as catalyst and this process is known as catalysis. There are two types of catalysis *i.e.* homogenous catalysis and heterogeneous catalysis. Most important type of catalysis is enzyme catalysis. Number of reactions that occur in the body of living organisms are catalysed by enzymes. Mechanisms of enzyme-catalysed reactions completes in two steps:

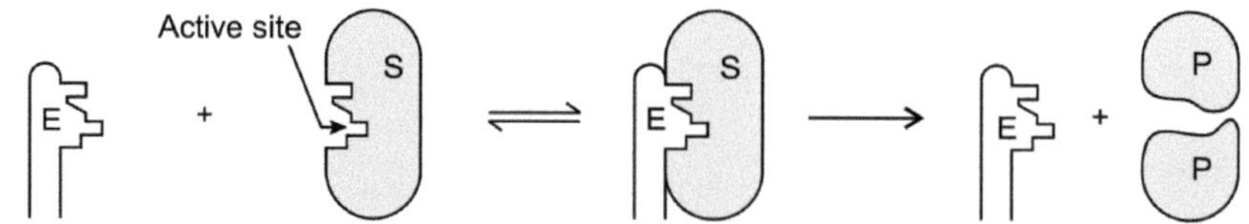

(a) What is the homogeneous catalysis?

(b) Write a chemical reaction which involves hemogeneous catalysis.

(c) Name two industrial processes in which heterogeneous catalysts are used.

(d) What is the role of desorption in the process of catalysis?

(e) Write any two characteristics of enzyme catalysis.

Ans. (a) The phenomenon in which the reactants and the catalyst are present in the same phase is known as homogeneous catalysis.

(b) The chemical reaction which involves homogeneous catalysis is as follows:

$$2SO_2\ (g) + O_2\ (g) \xrightarrow{\ NO(g)\ } 2SO_3\ (g)$$

(c) Contact process and Ostwald's process.

(d) Due to desorption, the products of the reaction get detached from the catalyst's surface thereby making the surface available again for more reactions.

(e) (i) They are highly specific in nature.

(ii) They are highly efficient.

Q. 3. Account for the followings:

(i) Sun looks red at the time of sunset.

(ii) Milk of magnesia used for stomach disorders.

(iii) Alum added to purify muddy water.

Ans. (i) Sun rays have to travel longer distance while travelling the horizon during sunset. Hence, the rays get scattered more and while passing through blanket of dust in the atmosphere only red part reaches our eye.

(ii) Milk of magnesia is $Mg(OH)_2$ colloidal emulsion in water. It is basic in nature and helps in decreasing acidity.

(iii) Impurities in water are mud particles in colloidal state. Alum *i.e.*, K_2SO_4. $Al_2(SO_4)_3$.$24H_2O$, provides ions in solution, which in turn neutralises the charge on colloids and coagulates the mud particles which then separate out as suspension.

Q. 4. **Colloidal particles always carry an electric charge which may be either positive or negative. For example, when $AgNO_3$ solution is added to KI solution, a negatively charged colloidal sol is obtained. The presence of equal and similar charges on collodial particles provide stability to the colloidal sol and if, somehow, charge is removed, coagulation of sol occurs. Lyophobic sols are readily coagulated as compare to lyophilic sols.** *

(i) What is the reason for the charge on sol particles?

(ii) Why the presence of equal and similar charges on colloidal particles provide stability?

(iii) Why a negatively charged sol is obtained on adding $AgNO_3$ solution to KI solution?

(iv) Name one method by which coagulation of lyophobic sol can be carried out.

(v) Out of KI or K_2SO_4, which electrolyte is better in the coagulation of positive sol?*

Ans. (i) Preferential adsorption of either positive or negative ions on surface of sol particles is reason of the charge on them.

(ii) Due to the presence of similar and equal charges, the colloidal particles repel one another and are thus unable to combine together to form larger particles and coagulate. Hence, presence of equal and similar charge on colloidal particles provide stability to colloidal solution.

(iii) When $AgNO_3$ solution is added to KI solution then negatively charged sol is formed due to the adsorption of iodide ions from KI which is disperse medium onto the precipitated AgI particles.

(iv) The coagulation of the lyophobic sols can be carried out by electrophoresis.

(v) K_2SO_4 would be better in coagulation of positive sol due to higher flocculating power of SO_4^{2-} .

Chapter 6. General Principles and Processes of Isolation of Elements

Q. 1. Gold dissolves in aqua regia, but silver remains insoluble. Explain.

Ans. Aqua regia is chemically conc. HCl (3 parts) and conc. HNO_3 (1 part) mixture. It dissolves gold in form of soluble chloroacetic acid.

$$3HCl + HNO_3 \xrightarrow{\Delta} NOCl + 2H_2O + 2[Cl]$$

Nitrosyl chloride   (Nascent)

$$Au + 3[Cl] \longrightarrow AuCl_3$$
$$AuCl_3 + Cl \longrightarrow H^+[AuCl_4]^-$$

Gold   Nascent   Chloroauric acid

Whereas Ag, silver forms an insoluble white ppt. of AgCl.

$$Ag + [Cl] \longrightarrow AgCl\downarrow$$

Nascent   Water insoluble silver chloride

Q. 2. A sulphide ore (A) on roasting leaves residue (B) which on reacting with HCl forms a water soluble compound (C). Addition of KI to the solution of (C), a solution (D) is formed. A brown precipitate (E) is formed when ammonia is passed into an alkaline solution of (D). Identify (A) to (E).

Ans. For testing ammonia we use Nessler's reagent which is (K_2HgI_4) to give a brown ppt. Hence the sulphide ore must be of Hg, mercury.

$$2HgS + 3O_2 \xrightarrow{\text{Roasting}} 2HgO + 2SO_2$$

[A] → [B]

$$HgO + 2HCl \longrightarrow HgCl_2 + H_2O$$

[B] → [C]

$$HgCl2 + 4KI \longrightarrow K_2HgI_4 + 2\,KCl$$

[C] → [D] Nessler's reagent

$$2K_2HgI_4 + NH_3 + 3KOH \longrightarrow H_2N - Hg - O - Hg - I + 7KI + 2H_2O$$

(D) → Iodide of Millon's base (Brown ppt.)

Q. 3. **Removal of unwanted materials (*e.g.* sand, clays, etc.) from the one is known as concentration, dressing or benefaction. If involves several steps and selection of these steps depends upon the differences in physical properties of the compound of the metal present and that of the gangue. It also depends upon the type of the metal and the environmental factors. Froth flotation is one of the important method used for the concentration of ores.**

(a) Write the principle behind froth flotation process.

(b) What is the role of collectors and froth stabilisers in this method?

(c) Which of the following oren can be concentrated by this and why?

Fe_2O_3, ZnS, Al_2O_3

(d) What are depressants and give their significance in froth flotation method?

(e) Name any other method used for the concentration of ores.

Ans. (a) Froth flotation is based upon the preferential wetting properties with the frothening agent and water.

(b) Collectors enhance non-wettability of mineral particles *e.g.* pine oils, fatty acids, xanthates, etc.

Froth stabilisers stabilise the froth. *e.g.* cresols, aniline, etc.

(c) Froth flotation method is used to concentrate only sulphide ores, because of their preferential wettability by pine oil. Thus, ZnS being a sulphide ore will be concentrated by this method.

(d) The substances which selectively prevent certain type of particles from forming the froth with bubbles are called depressants. In froth flotation method, depressants prevents the formation of froth.

It is used to separate two sulphide ores by preventing the formation of froth of one sulphide ore and allowing the other to form the froth.

(e) Hydraulic washing or magnetic separation.

Chapter 7. *p*-Block Elements

Q. 1. **A greenish yellow gas 'X' is paired through water to form a saturated solution. The aqueous solution on treatment with silver nitrate solution gives white precipitate. The saturated aqueous solution also dissolves magnesium ribbon with evolution of colourless gas 'Y'. Identify gases 'X' and 'Y'.**

Ans. The greenish yellow gas 'X' must be chlorine. As chlorine dissolves in water to produce hypochlorous and hydrochloric acid which provides Cl^- ions. These ions reacts with silver nitrate solution to give white ppt. of AgCl, silver chloride.

The solution being acidic dissolves magnesium ribbon to form magnesium chloride with release of hydrogen gas 'Y'.

Chemical reactions are:

$$Cl_2 + H_2O \longrightarrow HCl + HClO$$
$$(X)$$

$$AgNO_3 + HCl \longrightarrow AgCl^- + HNO_3$$
$$\text{White ppt.}$$

$$Mg + 2HCl \longrightarrow MgCl_2 + H_2 \uparrow$$
$$(Y)$$

Q. 2. **An aqueous solution of gas 'A' gave the following reactions:**

(i) It decolourises acidified $KMnO_4$ solution.

(ii) On heating with H_2O_2 followed by cooling, then on adding an aqueous solution of $BaCl_2$ gives a white precipitate insoluble in dilute HCl.

(iii) On passing H_2S gas through the solution, white turbidity is obtained. Identify the gas and give equations for steps (i), (ii) and (iii).

Ans. (i) Acidified potassium permanganate solution is decolourised by SO_2 gas. Hence aqueous solution of gas 'A' must be SO_2 (aq).

$$2KMnO_4 + 5SO_2 + 2H_2O \longrightarrow K_2SO_4 + 2MnSO_4 + 2H_2SO_4$$
$$\text{(Purple)} \qquad\qquad \text{(Colourless)}$$

(ii) On heating with H_2O_2, SO_2 gas gets converted to sulphuric acid (oxidised).

$$H_2O_2 + \overset{4}{S}O_2 \xrightarrow{\Delta} H_2\overset{4}{S}O_4$$

The white precipitate insoluble in dilute HCl, on adding $BaCl_2$ is of $BaSO_4$.

$$H_2SO_4 + BaCl_2 \longrightarrow BaSO_4 + 2HCl$$

(iii) H_2S gas produces white turbidity because of formation of elemental sulphur.

$$2H_2S + SO_2 \longrightarrow 3S + 2H_2O$$
$$\text{(Turbidity)}$$

Q. 3. **A translucent white waxy solid 'A' on heating in an inert atmosphere is converted to solid 'B'. Solid 'A' on reaction with dilute KOH liberates a poisonous gas 'C' having a rotten fish smell. With excess chlorine, (A) forms (D) which on hydrolysis gives to compound (E). Identify compounds (A) to (E).** *

Ans. The white waxy solid is white phosphorus (A) on heating in inert atmosphere it converts to its allotropic form (B) red phoshorus.

(i)
$$P_4 \xrightarrow[\text{Inert}]{CO_2} P_4$$
$$\text{(A, white)} \qquad \text{(B, red)}$$

With excess of chlorine, (A) forms phosphorus pentachloride.

$$\text{(ii)} \quad P_4 + 10Cl_2 \longrightarrow 4PCl_5$$
$$\text{(D)}$$

Solid (A) on reacting with dilute KOH forms poisonous gas phosphine, PH_3(C).

(iii)
$$P_4 + 3KOH + 3H_2O \longrightarrow PH_3 + K_2H_2PO_2$$
$$\text{(C)} \quad \text{Potassium hypophosphite}$$

(iv) Compound (D), PCl_5 on hydrolysis provides phosphoric acid H_3PO_4 (E).

$$PCl_5 + 4H_2O \longrightarrow H_3PO_4 + 5HCl$$
$$\text{(E)}$$

Q. 4. **All the elements of group of 15 form volatile trihydrides of the formula MH_3. The lighter elements also from hydrides of the formula M_2H_4. Nitrogen forms hydride of the formula NH_3 as well. The most important trihaliades, *viz.*, ammonia, NH_3 is prepared by the Haber process. The reaction is reversible, exothermic. The characteristics of hydrides depend upon the electronegativity and size of the central elements.**

(a) What is the oxidation number of nitrogen in hydrazoic acid?

(b) Write the condition of temperature and pressure for better yeild of ammonia in Born-Haber process.

(c) In which of the following lowest bond angle is found? Hydrides are given below:

$$NH_3, PH_3, SbH_3, AsH_3.$$

(d) Which one is strongest reducing agent among trihydrides of group 15 elements.

(e) Write the boiling point order of trihydrides of group 16 elements.

Ans. (a) $\left(-\dfrac{1}{3}\right)$.

(b) Low temperature and high pressure.

(c) SbH_3.

(d) BiH_3.

(e) $NH_3 > PH_3 < AsH_3 < SbH_3 < BiH_3$.

Q. 5. **The halogens have the smallest atomic radii in their respective periods. The atomic radius of fluorine is extremely small. All halogens exhibit –1 oxidation state. They are strong oxidising agents and have maximum**

---

negative electron gain enthalpy. Among halogens, fluorine shows anomalous behaviour in many properties. For example electronegativity and ionisation enthalpy are higher for fluorine than expected whereas bond dissociation enthalpy, m.p. and b.p. and electron gain enthalpy are quite lower than expected. Halogens react with hydrogen to give hydrogen halides (HX) and combine amongst themselves to form a number of compounds of the type XX′, XX′$_3$, XX′$_5$ and XX′$_7$ called inter-halogens.*

(i)   Why halogens have maximum negative electron gain enthalpy?

(ii) Why fluorine shows anomalous behaviour as compared to other halogens?

(iii) Arrange the hydrogen halides (HF to HI) in the decreasing order of their reducing character.

(iv) Why fluorine is a stronger oxidizing agent than chlorine?

(v)   What are the sizes of X and X′ in the interhalogen compounds?

Ans. (i)   The outer electronic configuration of halogens is ns^2 np^5, hence it completes its octet and gets stabilised by accepting one electron. So, halogens have maximum electron gain enthalpy.

(ii) Fluorine is the first element in halogen group, its atomic number is 9 and electronic configuration is [He]2s^2 2p^5. The anomalous behaviour of fluorine is due to its small size, highest electronegativity, low F-F bond dissociation enthalpy, and non-availability of d-orbitals in valence shell.

(iii) HF < HCl < HBr < HI

(iv) Fluorine has high electronagativity low heat of dissociation, high heat a hyaration and low electron affinity than chlorine which makes attraction of electrons towards fluorine more easy than chlorine, hence it is a better oxidising agent compared to oxygen.

(v)   X is halogen of larger size and X′ is halogen of smaller size.

Chapter 8. *d*-and *f*-Block Elements

Q. 1. In modern periodic table, *d*-block elements are called transition metals since their properties are intermediate between those of s and *p*-block elements having their general electronic configuration $(n - 1)d^{1-10} ns^{1-2}$. In transition elements the valence electron are present in outermost shell as well as *d*-orbital of the penultimate shell. The oxidation elements differ from each other by unity and they show oxidation state +1 to +7. In the first series of transition elements Cu exhibits +1 oxidation state most frequently.

(a)   Which *d*-block elements are not normally considered as transition elements?

(b)   In which orbital last e^- is filled in transition element?

(c)   Why oxidation states of transition element differ from each other by unity?

(d)   Which transition elements show high oxidation state and how much?

(e)   Why transition elements have high melting and boiling point?

Ans. (a)   Zn, Cd, Hg (due to d^{10} configuration).

(b)   *d*-orbital.

(c)   Due to incomplete filling of d-orbital, oxidation states vary.

(d)   Mn, + 7.

(e)   The high melting and boiling point in due to greater number of electrons from $(n - 1)d$ in addition to the ns electrons in the interatomic bonding.

Chapter 9. Coordination Compounds

Q. 1. Isomerism is a phenomena in which compounds have the same molecular formula but different physical and chemical properties on account of different structures. The two major types of isomerism are structural and stereoisomerism. The structural isomerism is further divided into four types: Linkage, coordination, ionisation and solvate isomerism. While, the stereoisomerism is divided into two types: Geometrical and optical isomerism.

(a)   What is meant by the term ionisation isomerism?

(b)   What type of coordination compounds show linkage isomerism?

(c)   Give one example of coordination isomerism.

(d)   [Co (NH$_3$)$_5$ SO$_4$] Br and [Co (NH$_3$)$_5$ Br] SO$_4$ represents which type of isomerism?

(e)   What type of complexes shows geometrical isomerism?

Ans. (a) Ionisation isomerism arises when compounds give different ions in the solution, although they have same composition.

(b) Linkage isomerism is shown by the coordination compounds containing ambidendate ligands.

(c) $[Pt (NH_3)_4] [PtCl_4]$ show coordination isomerism.

(d) $[Co (NH_3)_5 SO_4] Br$ and $[Co (NH_3)_5 Be] SO_4$ shows ionisation isomerism.

(e) Heteroleptic complexes with coordination numbers 4 and 6 shows geometrical isomerism.

Q. 2. **The crystal field theory assumes that the interaction between the metal ion and ligand is purely electrostatic. When ligands approach central metal atom/ion the five degenarate d-orbitals of the central metal atom become differential. In a complex, the central metal atom or ion is surrounded by various atoms or groups of atoms called ligands.**

(a) What is the type of bond in metal complex according to crystal field theory?

(b) What is the number of ligands in $Cu_2 [Fe (CN)_6]$.

(c) Which one is lower energy set between t_{2g} and e_g, after splitting of five degenerate orbital or metal atom/ion on complexation in tetrahedral complex?

(d) Define crystal field splitting.

(e) What do you mean by weak field ligands?

Ans. (a) Ionic bond or electrostatic bond.

(b) Number of ligands $= 6$.

(c) Lower energy set $= e_g$.

(d) The splitting of degenerate levels due to the presence of ligands in a definite geometry is termed as crystal field splitting.

(e) If energy separation for octahedral crystal field is less than energy required for electron pairing energy in single orbital, then fourth electron enters e_g orbital giving $t_{2g}^3 e_g^1$. So, ligands whose $\Delta_0 < P$ are weak field ligands.

Q. 3. (i) Account for the following:

(a) $K_4[Fe(CN)_6]$ is not toxic whereas KCN is highly toxic.

(b) $[AuCl_4]$ is square planar while $[GaCl_4]^-$ is tetrahedral.

(ii) IUPAC name of $Na_3[Co(NO_2)_6]$.

(iii) Why ferrocene is an organometallic compound?

Ans. (i) (a) In $K_4[Fe(CN)_6]$ the CN^- ions are inside the coordinate sphere, hence non-ionisable. Therefore its not going to show the poisonous effect of KCN itself.

(b) $[AuCl_4]$ is Au in $(+ III)$ state *i.e.*, $6s^0 5d^8$. Cl is a weak field ligand, but in this case of Au we consider valence bond theory their pairing takes place and Au (III) configuration look like.

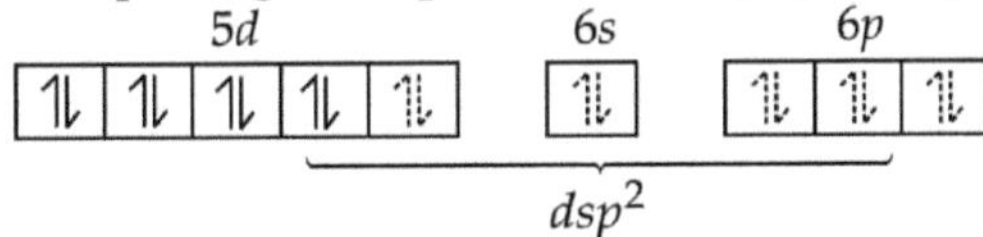

Hence inner orbital, square planar complex. In case of $[GaCl_4]^-$ $4s^0 4p^0 3d^{10}$, hence d-orbital $(n-1)$ completely filled, not a d-block element, it expands its valency for ligand to next $4p$ orbital.

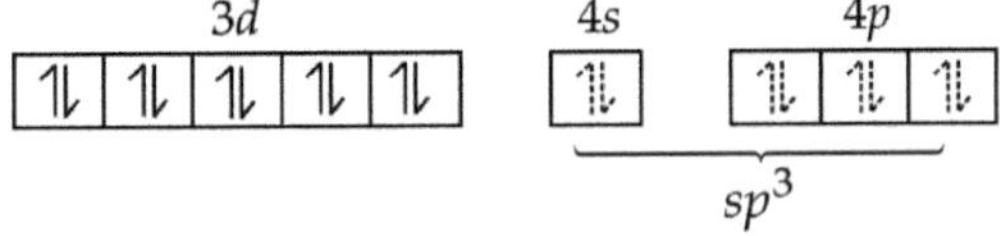

Hence tetrahedral geometry.

(ii) Sodium hexanitrocobaltate (III).

(iii) Ferrocene $Fe(C_5H_5)_2$: It is π-bonded complex formed by passing chromium gas into benzene solution.

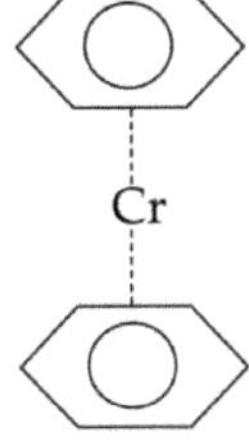

Chapter 10. Haloalkanes and Haloarenes

Q. 1. Compound 'A' with molecular formula C_4H_9Br is optically active reacts with aqueous KOH to give compound 'B'. Compound 'B' reacts with $SOCl_2$ in pyridine to give compound 'C'. Compound with alcoholic KOH to give compound 'D' (major).

(a) Draw the structure of compound along with its IUPAC name.

(b) Draw the enantiomer of compound 'C' with its R and S configuration.

(c) 'D' is the major compound and what is the structure of major product?

(d) What is the structure of compound?

(e) Why minor product is formed in less amount?

Ans. (a) Compound A is C_4H_9Br having structural formula.

$$IUPAC\ name: \quad CH_3 - CH_2 - \underset{\underset{\displaystyle Br}{|}}{CH} - CH_3$$

2-Bromobutane

(b)

$$\underset{\text{R-configuration}}{\overset{\displaystyle Cl}{H_3C \diagdown \diagup CH_2CH_3}} \qquad \underset{\text{S-configuration}}{\overset{\displaystyle Cl}{H_3CH_2C \diagdown \diagup CH_3}}$$

(c) D is the major compound having molecular formula C_4H_8 and structural formula is:

$$H_3C - HC = HC - CH_2$$

2-Butene or But-2-ene

(d) Minor compound is C_4H_8 having structure as:

$$H_3C - H_2C - CH = CH_2$$

1-Butene

(e) Minor compound is formed in less amount because dehydrohalogenation occurs where the stable carbocation is formed at intermediate which is formed in D compound rather than in minor compound.

Q. 2. An aromatic compound 'I' ($C_8H_8Br_2$) on treatment with aqueous KOH gives 'II' (C_8H_9BrO). On heating 'I' with alcoholic KOH 'III' (C_8H_7Br) is formed. The compound (III) on reacting with Br_2 or CCl_4 forms (IV). The compound (IV) reacts with fused KOH to give compound (V). Identify all the compounds that are involved.

Ans.

$$\underset{\displaystyle (I)}{\overset{\displaystyle CH_3}{\underset{\displaystyle |}{\overset{\displaystyle |}{CH - Br}}}}$$

($C_8H_8Br_2$) must be compound (I). As from the given information.

Compound (I) reacts with aq. KOH to give (II) (C_8H_9BrO), hence it must be undergoing nucleophilic substitution reaction. But only one (Br) group is substituted. Hence only one alkyl halide (1°, 2° or 3°) and another (Br) must be an aryl halide group.

Also heating (I) with alcoholic KOH provides (III) (C_8H_7Br) confirming the aryl halide theory. The compound (III) must be an alkene as it undergoes addition reaction to form compound (IV).

$$CH_3 - CH - Br \xrightarrow[\text{KOH}]{\text{aqueous}} CH_3 - CH - OH \xrightarrow{\text{alcoholic KOH}} CH = CH_2$$

(I) — Br (II) — Br (III) — Br $Br_2 \mid CCl_4$

(V) $CH = CH_2$, Br $\xleftarrow[\text{(fusion)}]{\text{KOH}}$ (IV) $Br - CH - CH_2 - Br$, Br

Hence compound (III) and (IV) are similar.

Bromine mentioned is in para position to offer least or no steric hindrance to the above reactions.

Q. 3. A sweet smelling organic compound 'X' is slowly oxidised by air in the presence of light to a highly poisonous gas. On warming with Ag powder, it forms a gaseous substance 'Y', which can also be obtained by the action of CaC$_2$ (calcium carbide) on water. Identify 'X' and 'Y'. Write the chemical equations involved.

Ans. 'X' must be chloroform (CHCl$_3$) as it produces phosgene, a highly poisonous gas on being exposed to air and light.

$$2CHCl_3 + O_2 \xrightarrow{\text{Light}} 2COCl_2 + 2HCl$$
$$\text{[A]} \qquad\qquad\qquad \text{Phosgene}$$

Chloroform on heating with Ag powder undergoes dehydrogenation and produces acetylene *i.e.*, 'Y'.

$$CHCl_3 + 6Ag + Cl_3CH \xrightarrow{\Delta} CH \equiv 6AgCl$$
$$\text{Acetylene}$$
$$\text{[Y]}$$

Acetylene can also be obtained by treating calcium carbide with water.

$$CaC_2 + 2H_2O \longrightarrow CH \equiv CH + Ca(OH)_2$$
$$\text{Acetylene}$$

Chapter 11. Alcohols, Phenols and Ethers

Q. 1. In phenol OH-group directly attached to *sp*^{2} hybridised carbon of benzene ring acts as a electron with drawing group and is responsible for the acidic nature of phenol. Due to this, the lone pair of electrons of O—H are involved in resonance with C-atoms of benzene ring. As a result of resonance, the oxygen atom acquires a partial positive charge. This weakens the O—H bond and thus facilitates the release a proton.

  (a) Show the delocalisation of electrons in phenols.

  (b) Which one is stronger acid, phenol or alcohol?

  (c) Give one reaction showing the acidic nature of phenol.

  (d) Arrange the following compounds in the increasing order of acidic strength.

    o-nitrophenol, *o*-cresol, phenol.

  (e) Write the name and give the structure of intermediate formed after the loss of H$^+$ ion from phenol.

Ans. (a) Delocalisation of electrons (resonance) in phenols.

  (b) Phenol is stronger acid than alcohol because phenoxide ion formed after a loss of H$^+$ ion is resonance stabilised which is not possible in case of alkoxide ion.

(c)

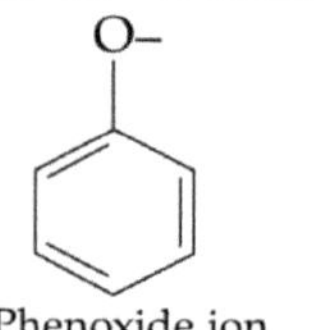

This reaction indicates the acidic nature of phenols.

(d) Electron withdrawing groups increases the acidic character, while electron donating groups decreases the acidic character of phenols.

Thus, the increasing order of acidic strength is,

o-cresol $<$ phenol $<$ o-nitrophenol

(e) Phenoxide ion is formed when phenol loses H^+ ion and its structure is,

Phenoxide ion

Chapter 12. Aldehydes, Ketones and Carboxylic Acids

Q. 1. Aldehydes and ketones containing atleast one α-H atom undergo a reaction in the presence of dilute alkali as catalyst to from β-hydroxy ketones. β-hydroxy aldehydes are called aldols while hydroxyketones are collectively called ketols. When different aldehydes or ketones combine then mixture of four products are formed, then reaction is called cross-aldol condensation.

(a) Write the equation involved in aldol condensation using simplest aldehyde.

(b) What happens, when aldols readily lose water?

(c) Write the name and formulae of three carbonyl compounds that do not undergo aldol condensation.

(d) Write all the possible products formed when acetaldehyde reacts with propanal.

(e) Write the products formed in the following reaction,

$$\text{C}_6\text{H}_5-\text{CHO} + \text{C}_6\text{H}_5-\overset{\overset{\text{O}}{\|}}{\text{C}}-\text{CH}_3 \xrightarrow[293\ K]{OH^-}$$

Ans. (a)

$$2CH_3CHO \underset{\text{Ethanol}}{\overset{\text{Dil. NaOH}}{\rightleftharpoons}} CH_3-\underset{\underset{\text{3-hydroxy butanal}}{\overset{|}{OH}}}{CH}-CH_2CHO \xrightarrow[-H_2O]{\Delta} \underset{\text{But-2-enal}}{CH_3CH = CH - CHO}$$

(b) Aldols readily loss water to give α-β unsaturated carbonyl compounds.

(c) Formaldehyde (HCHO), benzaldehyde (C_6H_5CHO) and benzophenone ($C_6H_5COC_6H_5$) do not undergo aldol condensation as they do not contain α-H atoms.

(d) CH_3CHO

$$\underset{CH_3CH_2CHO}{\overset{+}{}} \xrightarrow{NaOH} \underset{\text{But-2-enal}}{CH_3CH = CHCHO} + CH_3CH_2CH = \underset{\underset{\underset{\text{2-methypent-2-enal}}{CH_3}}{|}}{CH} - CHO$$

Self-aldol products

$$+ CH_3 - CH = \underset{\underset{\text{2-methylbut-2-enal}}{CH_3}}{\overset{|}{C}} - CHO + \underset{\text{Pent-2-enal}}{CH_3CH_2 - CH = CHCHO}$$

Cross-aldol products

(e)

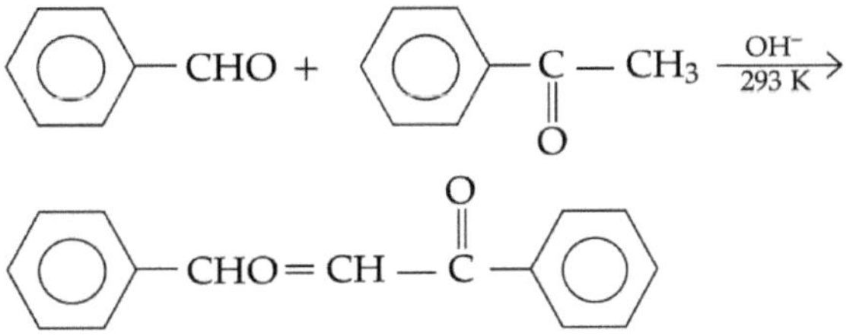

$$\text{C}_6\text{H}_5\text{—CHO} + \text{C}_6\text{H}_5\text{—}\overset{\displaystyle O}{\underset{\displaystyle \|}{\text{C}}}\text{—CH}_3 \xrightarrow[293\ K]{OH^-}$$

$$\text{C}_6\text{H}_5\text{—CHO}=\text{CH}-\overset{\displaystyle O}{\underset{\displaystyle \|}{\text{C}}}\text{—C}_6\text{H}_5$$

Q. 2. An organic compound [A]. Molecular formula $C_4H_8Cl_2$ is hydrolysed to a compound [B] C_4H_8O, which forms an oxime with NH_2OH and gives a negative Tollen's test. What are the structures of A and B? Write balanced chemical equations for the reactions involved.

Ans. **Step I:** Molecular formula of [A] $C_4H_8Cl_2$, hence it must be a substituted alkane.

Step II: It gives C_4H_8O [B] on hydrolysis and [B] does not gives a positive Tollen's test. Hence [B] must be a ketone.

Hence compound [A] must be a gem dihalide $CH_3 - \overset{\displaystyle Cl}{\underset{\displaystyle Cl}{CH_2}} - CH_3$ reactions are:

(2, 2-Dichlorobutane)

$$CH_3 - \overset{\displaystyle Cl}{\underset{\displaystyle \underset{\displaystyle [A]}{Cl}}{C}} - CH_2 - CH_3 \xrightarrow{H_3O^+} CH_3 - \overset{\displaystyle O}{\underset{\displaystyle \underset{\displaystyle [B]}{\|}}{C}} - CH_2CH_3 \xrightarrow{NH_2OH} CH_3 - \overset{\displaystyle NOH}{\underset{\displaystyle \|}{C}} - CH_2 - CH_3$$

$\quad\quad\quad\quad\quad\quad\quad\quad\quad\quad\quad\quad$ Butanone $\quad\quad\quad\quad\quad\quad\quad$ Butane oxime

Q. 3. An organic compound with the molecular formula $C_9H_{10}O$ forms 2, 4-DNP derivative, reduces Tollen's reagent and undergoes Cannizzaro reaction. On vigorous oxidation, it gives 1, 2-benzenedicarboxylic acid. Identify the compound.

Ans. (i) It is given that the compound (with molecular formula $C_9H_{10}O$) forms 2, 4-DNP derivative and reduces Tollen's reagent. Therefore, the given compound must be an aldehyde.

(ii) The compound undergoes Cannizzaro reaction.

(iii) Also oxidation gives 1, 2-benzenedicarboxylic acid. Therefore, the – CHO group is directly attached to a benzene ring and this benzaldehyde is ortho-substituted. Therefore compound must be 2-Ethylbenzaldehyde.

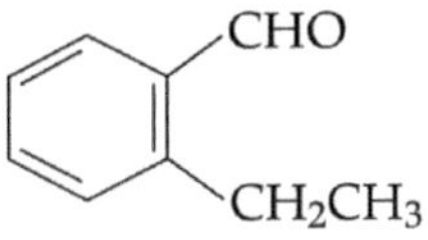

2-Ethylbenzaldehyde

The given reactions can be explained by the following equations.

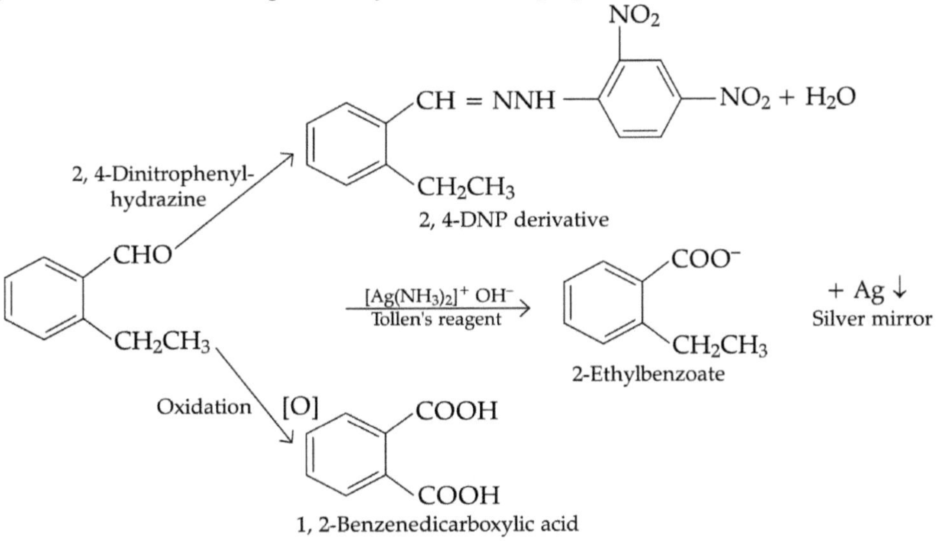

Note: The reaction can be written as three separate reactions also.

Q. 4. **An organic compound [A] (molecular formula $C_8H_{16}O_2$) was hydrolysed with dilute sulphuric acid to give a carboxylic acid [B] and an alcohol [C]. Oxidation of [C] with chromic acid produced [B]. [C] on dehydration gives but-1-ene. Write equations for the reactions involved.***

Ans. (i)   Since compound [A] with molecular formula $C_8H_{16}O_2$ gives a carboxylic acid [B] and an alcohol [C] on hydrolysis with dilute sulphuric acid. Thus, compound [A] must be an ester.

(ii)   Further, alcohol [C] gives an acid B on oxidation with chromic acid. Thus, B and C must contain equal number of carbon atoms.

(iii)   Since compound [A] contains a total of 8 carbon atoms, each of [B] and [C] contain 4 carbon atoms.

(iv)   Also on dehydration, alcohol [C] gives but-1-ene. Therefore, [C] is of straight chain butan-1-ol and [C] gives [B] on oxidation. Hence [B] is butanoic acid.

Hence, the ester with molecular formula $C_8H_{16}O_2$ is butylbutanoate.

$$CH_3CH_2CH_2 - \overset{\overset{\displaystyle O}{\|}}{C} - OCH_2CH_2CH_2CH_3$$
Butylbutanoate

All the given reactions can be explained by the following equations.

1. $$CH_3CH_2CH_2 - \overset{\overset{\displaystyle O}{\|}}{C} - OCH_2CH_2CH_2CH_3 \xrightarrow{\text{dil. } H_2SO_4} CH_3CH_2CH_2 - \overset{\overset{\displaystyle O}{\|}}{C} - OH + CH_3CH_2CH_2CH_2OH$$

Butylbutanoate   Butanoic acid   Butanoic-1-ol
[A]   [B]   [C]

2. $CH_3CH_2CH_2\ CH_2 - OH$

  $\xrightarrow{\text{CrO}_3/\text{CH}_3\text{COOH}}$ Oxidation $\longrightarrow$ $CH_3CH_2CH_2 - \overset{\overset{\displaystyle O}{\|}}{C} - OH$ Butanoic acid [B]

  $\xrightarrow[-H_2O]{\text{Dehydration}}$ $CH_3CH_2CH = CH_2$ But-1-ene

Chapter 13. Amines

Q. 1. **Amines may be regarded as derivatives of ammonia in which one, two or three H atoms have been replaced by alkyl or aryl group. It is also designated as 1°, 2°, 3° amina according as one, two or three H atom in ammonia molecule have been substituted by alkyl, aryl group. Aliphatic 1° amines are named as alkanamines while 2° and 3° amines are named as nitrogen substituted 1° amine. The simplest aromatic aromatic amine is aniline and its name is benzamine. Amines shows basic nature. The order of basicity in solution phase of amine is $2° > 1° > 3° > NH_3$. The mixture of 1°, 2° and 3° amines are separated by Hinsberg's method.**

(a)   What is the hybridisation of N atom in alkyl amine and aromatic amine?

(b)   Why aromatic amines shows sp^2 hybridisation?

(c)   What is chemical structure of aniline?

(d)   Why basicity order in gas is different that solution?

(e)   Which compound is used in Hinsberg's method in separation of 1°, 2° and 3° amines?

Ans. (a) sp^3, sp^2.

(b)   Because lone pair e^- of N atom participates in resonance.

(c) $C_6H_5-NH_2$

(d)   In gas phase, solvent effect is missing.

(e)   Benzylsulphonyl chloride $(C_6H_5SO_2Cl)$.

Chapter 14. Biomolecules

Q. 1. Write the structure of alanine (an amino acid) at pH = 2 and at pH = 10. [*]

Ans. Structure of alanine at neutral pH = 7 is $NH_2 - \overset{\overset{\displaystyle CH_3}{|}}{CH} - COOH$.

(Alanine)

At pH = 2 *i.e.*, acidic medium the basic group will accept a proton to form a cation (I).

$$NH_2 - \overset{\overset{\displaystyle CH_3}{|}}{CH} - COOH \xrightarrow{\;H^+\;} \overset{+}{N}H_3 - \overset{\overset{\displaystyle CH_3}{|}}{CH} - COOH$$
$$(I)$$

At pH = 10, *i.e.*, in basic medium the amino acid will loose the H^+ group to form an anion (II).

$$NH_2 - \overset{\overset{\displaystyle CH_3}{|}}{CH} - COOH \xrightarrow{\;OH^-\;} NH_2 - \overset{\overset{\displaystyle CH_3}{|}}{CH} - COO^-$$
$$(II)$$

Q. 2. Ketones does not give positive Tollen's test. Then why fructose, being a ketohexose acts as a reducing sugar? Explain.

Ans. Tollen's reagent is ammonical silver nitrate solution. Hence as we place fructose into a basic medium it changes to enolic form.

$$
\begin{array}{ccc}
CH_2OH & HC-OH & CHO \\
| & | & | \\
C=O & C-OH & H-C-OH \\
| & | & | \\
(CHOH)_3 & (CH-OH)_3 & (CHOH)_3 \\
| & | & | \\
CH_2OH & CH_2OH & CH_2OH \\
(Fructose) & (Enol\ form) & (Glucose)
\end{array}
$$

$\xrightarrow[{-H_2O}]{OH^-}$ $\qquad$ $\xrightarrow[{H_2O}]{OH^-}$

This enolic form interconverts to glucose and is in equilibrium with it. Hence, the glucose form is responsible for the positive Tollen's test.

Chapter 15. Polymers

Q. 1. Should the handle and bristles of the tooth brush be made from same material? Explain why?

Ans. Bristles are made from soft fibers like nylon which must not hurt the gums while the tooth brush body is made of hard strong durable plastic.

Q. 2. Why styrene undergoes anionic polymerisation easily?

Ans. For anionic polymerisation presence of electron withdrawing group like nitrile, phenyl, vinyl groups are favourable. The polymerisation is initiated by nucleophilic addition to the unsaturated site of the monomer.

$$n\ \underset{\text{Styrene}}{\underset{\bigcirc}{CH=CH_2}} \xrightarrow[\text{Anionic initiator}]{Bu^-Li^+} n\ \left[CH_2-\underset{\bigcirc}{CH} \right]$$

Chapter 16. Chemistry in Everyday Life

Q. 1. Soaps containing sodium salts are formed by heating far with aqueous sodium hydroxide solution. This reaction is known as saponification. Soaps do not work in hard water. Synthetic detergents are cleansing agents which have all the properties of soaps, but which actually do not contain any soap. These can be used both in soft and hard water. These are mainly classified as anionic degergents, cationic detergents and non-

---

ionic detergents. **Anionic detergents are sodium salts of sulphonated long chain alcohols or hydrocarbons. Main problem that appears in the use of detergents is that, water gets polluted.**

(a) What are the products of saponification?
(b) What do soape not work in hard water?
(c) Give an example of anionic detergents.
(d) What is the drawback of synthetic detergents?
(e) What types of detergents are degradable by bacteria?

Ans. (a) $C_{17}H_{35}COONa$ (Sodium stearate)
+

$$\begin{array}{l} CH_2-OH \\ \quad | \\ CH-OH \qquad \text{(Glycerol) or (Glycerine)} \\ \quad | \\ CH_2-OH \end{array}$$

(b) Hard water contains calcium and magnesium ions. These ions from insoluble calcium and magnesium salts respectively.

(c) $CH_3\,(CH_2)_{10}\,CH_2\,OSO_3^-\,Na^+$ (Sodium laurylsulphate)

or

$CH_3\,(CH_2)_{11}$ —⟨benzene ring⟩— $SO_3^-\,Na^+$ (Sodium dodecylbenzenesulphonate)

(d) Highly branched detergents cannot degrade by bacteria hence their water gets polluted.
(e) Less or no branched detergents can be degraded by bacteria.

Q. 2. (i) Aspirin is a pain relieving antipyretic drug but can also be used to prevent heart attacks. Explain.
(ii) Why aspirin should not be taken empty stomach?

Ans. (i) Aspirin although a very effective medicine as an antipyretic has additional effects. It is an anti-blood coagulant. It is acetyl salicylic acid (2-acetoxybenzoic acid) and can thus prevent heart attacks.

(ii) Aspirin if taken empty stomach it may undergo hydrolysis to form salicylic acid. This acid may lead to stomach ulcers which are very painful.

$$\text{Aspirin} + H_2O \longrightarrow \text{Salicylic acid} + CH_3COOH \ (\text{Acetic acid})$$

Assertion and Reason Based Questions | Set 16 |

Chapter 1. Solid State

1. **Assertion:** Quartz glass is crystalline soild and quartz is an amorphous soild.
   Reason: Quartz glass has no long range order.

2. **Assertion:** Graphite is a good conductor of electricity however diamond belongs to the category of insulators.
   Reason: Graphite is soft in nature on the other hand diamond is very hard and brittle.

3. **Assertion:** In crystalline solids, the value of resistance is diffierent in different directions.
   Reason: Crystalline soilds are isotropic in nature.

4. **Assertion:** Glass panes fixed to windows or panes of old buildings are found to be slightly thicker at the bottom.
   Reason: Amorphous soilds have a tendency to flow.

5. **Assertion:** Face-centred cubic cell has four atoms per unit cell.
   Reason: In *fcc* unit, there are right atoms at the corner and six atoms at face centers.

6. **Assertion:** The total number of atoms present in a simple cubic unit cell is one.
   Reason: Simple cubic unit cell has atoms at its corners, each of which is shared between eight adjacent unit cells.

7. **Assertion:** CsCl has body centred cubic arrangement.
   Reason: CsCl has one Cs^+ ion and eight Cl^- ions in its unit cell.

8. **Assertion:** In crystal lattice, the size of the tetrahedral hole is large than an octahedral hole.
   Reason: The cations occupy less space than anions in crystal packing.

9. **Assertion:** The packing efficiency is maximum for the *fcc* structure.
   Reason: The coordination number is 12 in *fcc* structure.

10. **Assertion:** On heating ferromagnetic of ferrimagnetic substances, they become paramagnetic.
   Reason: The electrons change their spin on heating.

ANSWERS

1. **(d)** The structure of quartz is crystalline and that of quartz glass is amorphous. The two structures are almost identical yet in case of amorphous quartz glass, there is no long range order.
2. **(b)** Diamond is bad conductor of electricity because cell valence electrons of corbon are invalved in bonding. In graphite however three out of four velence electrons are involved in bonding and the fourth electron remain free between adjacent layers which makes it a good conductor. Graphite is soft because parallel layers are held together weak Vander Waal's force. However, diamond is hard due to compact three-dimen sional network of bonding.
3. **(c)** Crystalline solids are anisotropic in nature that is, some of their physical properties like electrical resistance show different values along different directons due to different arrangement of particles in different directions.

4. **(a)** Solids have a tendency to flow, though very slowly. Glass is sometimes called a supercooled liquid because it does not form a crystalline structure, but instead forms an amorphous soild that allows molecules in the material to continue to move.

5. **(a)** The face-centred cubic structure has atoms located at each of the corners and the centres of all the cubic faces. Each of the corner atoms is the corner of another cube so the corner atoms are shared among eight-unit cells.

6. **(a)** The total number of atoms present in a simple cubic unit cell is one. Simple cubic unit cell has atoms at its corners, each of which is shared between eight adjacent unit cells.

7. **(c)** CsCl has one Cs^+ ion and one Cl^- ion in its unit cell. The excess Zn^{2+} ions move to interstitial sites and the electrons to neighboring interstitial sites.

8. **(d)** Tetrahedral holes are smaller in size than octahedral holes. Cations usually occupy less space than anions.

9. **(b)** Both *ccp* and *hcp* are highly efficient lattice; in terms of packing. The packing efficiency of both types of close packed structure is 74%, *i.e.* 74% of the space in *hcp* and *ccp* is filled. The hcp and ccp structure are equally efficient; in terms of packing. The packing efficiency of simple cubic lattice is 52.4% and the packing effiency of body centred cabic lattice (*bcc*) is 68%.

10. **(a)** All magnetically ordered solids (ferromagnetic, ferrimagnetic and anti-frerromagneti solids) transform to the paramagnetic state at high temperature due to the randomisation of spins.

Chapter 2. Solutions

1. **Assertion:** In solution, amalgam of mercury with sodium is an example of solid solutions.
   Reason: Mercury is solvent and sodium is solute in the solution.

2. **Assertion:** One molar aqueous solution is more concentrated than that of 1 molal aqueous solution.
   Reason: Molarity is a function of temperature as volume depends on temperature in the solution.

3. **Assertion:** Molarity of a solution in liquid state changes with temperature.
   Reason: The volume of a solution changes with change in temperature.

4. **Assertion:** Pressure have any effect on solubility of solids in liquids.
   Reason: Solids and liquids are not incompressible.

5. **Assertion:** The concentration of pollutants in water or atmosphere is often expressed in terms of ppm.
   Reason: Concentration in parts per million can be expressed as mass to mass, volume to volume and mass to volume.

6. **Assertion:** Azeotropic mixtures are not formed only by non-ideal solutions and they may have boiling points either greater than both the components or less than both the components.
   Reason: The composition of the vapour phase is not same as that of the liquid phase of an azeotropic mixture.

7. **Assertion:** At equilibrium, vapour phase will not be always rich in component which is more volatile.
   Reason: The composition of vapour phase in equilibrium with the solution is not determined by the partial pressures of the components.

8. **Assertion (A):** Elevation in boiling point is a colligative property.*
   Reason (R): Elevation in boiling point is directly proportional to molarity.

9. **Assertion (A):** 0.1 M solution of KCl has greater osmotic pressure than 0.1 M solution of glucose at same temperature.
   Reason (R): In solution, KCl dissociates to produce more number of particles.

10. **Assertion (A):** An ideal solution obeys Henry's law.
    Reason (R): In an ideal solution, solute-solute as well as solvent solvent interactions are similar to solute-solvent interaction.

11. **Assertion:** 1 M solution of KCl has greater osmotic pressure than 1 M solution of glucose at the same temperature.
    Reason: In solution KCl dissociates to produce more number of particles in the solution.

12. **Assertion:** When a solution is separated from the pure solvent by a semi-permeable membrane, the solvent molecules pass through it from pure solvent side to the solution side.

    Reason: Diffusion of solvent occurs from a region of high concentration solution to a region of low concentration solution.

13. **Assertion:** A solution of phenol and aniline will show negative deviations from Raoult's law.

    Reason: In case of negative deviations from Raoult's law, A - B forces are stronger than A - A and B - B forces.

14. **Assertion:** The solutions which show large positive Deviations from Raoult's law form maximum boiling azeotropes.

    Reason: 95% aqueous solution of ethanol is maximum boiling azeotrope solution.

15. **Assertion:** Molecular mass of KCl calculated on the basis of colligative properties will be lower than the normal molecular mass.

    Reason: Experimentally determined molar mass is always lower than the true value.

ANSWERS

1. **(c)** Amalgam of mercury with sodium is an example of liquid in solid type solid solution. Here mercury (liquid metal) acts as solute and sodium as solvent.

2. **(b)** 1 molar solution has 1mole of solute per litre of solution or per 1000 cm^3 of solution.

    Now, density of water = 1 g/cc

    $\therefore$ 1000 cm^3 = 1000 g

    Hence, 1 mole is present in less than 1000 g of solvent.

    $\because$ 1000 g of solution = solute and solvent

    Whereas 1 molal solution has 1 mole of solute in 1000 g of solvent.

3. **(a)** Molarity is the number of moles of solute dissolved per litre of solution. molarity changes as temperature changes.

4. **(d)** Liquids and solids exhibit practically no change of solubility with changes in pressure. Gases as might be expected, increase in solubility with an increase in pressure.

5. **(d)** When a solute is present in trace quantities it is convenient to express concentration in ppm.

6. **(c)** An azeotrope or a constant boiling point mixture is a mixture of two or more liquids whose proportions cannot be altered or changed by simple distillation. This happens because when an azeotrope is boiled.

7. **(d)** A substance with higher vapour pressure vaporizes more readily than a substance with a lower vapour pressure. In case of a volatile solute this has a high vapour pressure and hence produces vapour. While in the case of a non-volatile solute due to its lower vapour pressure it does not produce vapour. The vapor pressure of a substance is the pressure at which its gas phase is in equilibrium with its condensed phases

8. **(c)** Assertion (A) is correct, but Reason (R) is wrong statement.

9. **(a)** Both Assertion (A) and Reason (R) are correct statements and reason (R) is the correct explanation of the Assertion (A).

10. **(d)** Assertion (A) is wrong, but Reason (R) is correct statement.

11. **(a)** Osmotic pressure is a colligative property and depends upon the number of solute particles in solution NaCl dissociate into two ions while glucose being covalent does not. So the number of particles in 1 mole NaCl will be twice as much is in glucose.

12. **(d)** With the semipermeable membrane in place, and if one compartment contains the pure solvent, this can never happen; no matter how much liquid flows through the membrane, the solvent in the right side will always be more concentrated than that in the left side.

13. **(b)** In case of negative deviations from Raoult's law, the intermolecular attractive forces between A-A and B-B are weaker than those between A-B and leads to decrease in vapour pressure resulting in negative deviations. An example of this type is a mixture of phenol and aniline.

14. **(a)** The solutions which show a large positive deviation from Raoult's law form minimum boiling azeotrope, and 95% ethanol solution is minimum boiling azeotrope.

15. **(c)** KCl undergoes dissociation in solution, hence observed molar mass will be lower. Experimentally determined molar mass can be higher or lower depending upon whether solute undergoes dissociation or association.

Chapter 3. Electrochemistry

1. **Assertion:** In cell Current stops flowing when $E_{cell} = 0$.

   Reason: Equilibrium of the cell reaction is attained.

2. **Assertion:** The rusting of iron, tarnishing of silver, development of green coating on copper and bronze are some of the examples of corrosion.

   Reason: It causes enormous damage to buildings, bridges, ships and to all objects made of metals especially that of iron.

3. **Assertion:** Molar conductivity increases with decrease in concentration of solution.

   Reason: Conductivity always decreases with decrease in concentration of solution.

4. **Assertion:** Zinc can be used while copper cannot be used in the recovery of Ag from the complex $[Ag(CN)_2]^-$.

   Reason: Zinc is a powerful reducing agent than copper.

5. **Assertion:** The resistivity for a substance is its resistance when it is one meter long and its area of cross section is one square meter.

   Reason: The SI units of resistivity is ohm metre (Ωm).

6. **Assertion:** On increasing dilution, the specific conductance keep on increasing.

   Reason: On increasing dilution, degree of ionisation of weak electrolyte increases and molality of ions also increases.

7. **Assertion:** The conductivity of electrolytic solutions increases with increase of temperature.

   Reason: Electronic conductance decreases with increase of temperature.

8. **Assertion:** During electrolysis of $CuSO_4$(aq) using copper electrodes, copper is dissolved at anode and deposited at cathode.

   Reason: Oxidation takes place at anode and reduction at cathode.

9. **Assertion:** Zinc metal can be used while copper cannot be used in the recovery of Ag from the complex $[Ag(CN)_2]^-$.

   Reason: Zinc is not a powerful reducing agent than copper.

10. **Assertion:** To obtain maximum work from a galvanic cell charge has to be passed reversibly.

    Reason: The reversible work done by a galvanic cell is equal to decrease in its Gibbs energy.

11. **Assertion (A):** Conductivity of an electrolyte increases with decrease in concentration.*

    Reason (R): Number of ions per unit volume decreases on dilution.

ANSWERS

1. **(a)** Eventually the electric field is large enough to stop any electrons moving from the positive terminal to the negative terminal.

2. **(a)** Rust is hydrated ferric oxide, $Fe_2O_3 \, H_2O$.

3. **(a)** $\lambda_m = \kappa V$

   With decrease in concentration, total volume V of the solution containing one mole of electrolyte also increases and decrease in κ (conductivity) on dilution of a solution is more than compensated by increase in its volume, hence molar conductivity (λ_m) increases with decrease conductivity.

4. **(a)** Zinc can easily substitute silver from $[Ag(CN)_2]^-$ while copper cannot do that.

5. **(b)** We know, $R \propto \dfrac{\ell}{A}$ or $R = \rho\left(\dfrac{\ell}{A}\right)$ where proportionality A constant ρ is called resistivity. If $\ell = 1m$ and $A = 1m^2$

   then $R = \rho$ i.e. Resistance = Resistivity.

6. **(d)** The specific conductivity decreases while equivalent and molar conductivities increase with dilution.

7. **(b)** Conductivity of electrolytic solutions depends upon the ions produced in solution which increases with increase of temperature, (ionization increases).

8. **(c)** By the reaction

   At cathode : $Cu^{2+}(aq) + 2e^- \rightarrow Cu(s)$ (reduction)

   At anode : $Cu(s) \rightarrow Cu^2(aq) + 2e^-$ (oxidation)

9. **(b)** Zinc is used instead of copper for the said purpose because zinc reacts with faster rate and it also more economical than Cu.

10. **(b)** Electrical work done in one second is equal to electrical potential multiplied by total charge passed and is related to Gibbs energy of the reaction as follows:

$$\Delta_r G = -nFE_{cell}$$

11. **(d)** Assertion (A) is wrong, but Reason (R) is correct statement.

Chapter 4. Chemical Kinetics

1. **Assertion:** The rate of reaction is the rate of change of concentration of a reactant or a product.

   Reason: Rate of reaction remains constant during the complete reaction.

2. **Assertion:** The rate of reaction is always negative.

   Reason: Minus sign used in expressing the rate shows that concentration of reactant is decreasing.

3. **Assertion:** The rate of the reaction is the rate of change of concentration of a reactant or a product.

   Reason: Rate of reaction remains constant during the course of reaction.

4. **Assertion:** The kinetics of the reaction,

   $mA + nB + pC \rightarrow m'X + n'Y + p'Z$, obey the rate expression as

   $$\frac{dX}{dt} = k[A]^m[B]^n$$

   Reason: The rate of the reaction does not depend upon the concentration of C.

5. **Assertion:** Complex reaction takes place in different steps and the slowest step determines the rate of reaction.

   Reason: Order and molecularity of a reaction are always equal.

6. **Assertion:** It is not always convenient to determine the instantaneous rate.

   Reason: Instantaneous rate is measured by the determination of slope of the tangent at point $^*t$ *in concentration versus time plot.

7. **Assertion:** Order of the following reaction, $2NO(g) + 2H_2(g) \rightarrow 2H_2O(g) + N_2(g)$ is 3 .

   Reason: Order of the reaction with respect to given reactant is the power of the reactant's concentration in the rate equation.

8. **Assertion:** The reaction,

   $H_2 + Br_2 \rightarrow 2HBr$, has a molecularity of two.

   Reason: Order of reaction is 3/2.

9. **Assertion:** In Arrhenius equation, frequency factor, A = PZ.

   Reason: With increasing E_a the rate constant increases too.

10. **Assertion:** The multi molecular reactions are quite rare in comparison with bimolecular reactions.

    Reason: At normal pressure, triple collisions are much less frequent than double ones.

ANSWERS

1. **(c)** Rate of reaction does not remain constant during the complete reaction because rate depends upon the concentration of reactants which decreases with time.

2. **(c)** The rate of reaction is never negative. Minus sign used in expressing the rate only shows that the concentration of the reactant is decreasing.

3. **(c)** Rate of reaction does not remain constant during the complete reaction because rate depends upon the concentration of reactants which decreases with time.

4. **(a)** Rate expression

$$\frac{dX}{dt} = k[A]^m[B]^n,$$ shows that the total order of reaction is $m + n + 0 = m + n$. As the rate of reaction

is independent of concentration of C, *i.e.*, the order with respect to C is zero. This is the reason that C does not figure in the rate expression.

5. **(c)** Order and molecularity are different for a complex reaction.

6. **(a)** It is not always convenient to determine the instantaneous rate, as it is measured by determining the slope of the tangent at point 't' in concentration Vs time plot. This generally makes it difficult to determine the rate law and hence, the order of the reaction.

7. **(a)** Order of the following reaction $2NO(g) + 2H_2(g) \rightarrow 2H_2O(g) + N_2(g)$ is 3

As we know that order of the reaction with respect to given reactant is the power of the reactants concentration in the rate equation.

8. **(b)** The molecularity is two and order is 3/2.

9. **(c)** With increasing E_a, the rate constant decreases.

10. **(a)** The multi molecular reactions are quite rare in comparison with bimolecular reactions because at normal pressure, triple collisions are much less frequent than double ones.

Chapter 5. Surface Chemistry

1. **Assertion:** Solids in finely divided state act as good adsorbents.

   Reason: Adsorption is a surface phenomenon.

2. **Assertion:** The relation $\frac{x}{m} = k \cdot p^{1/n}$ is known as Freundlich adsorption isotherm, where x is the mass of gas

   adsorbed by 'm' grams of adsorbate, 'p' is the equilibrium pressure, k and n are constants for given system and temperature.

   Reason: When several substances have same value of $1/n$ the lines by which their adsorption isotherms can be represented will meet at a point.

3. **Assertion:** For adsorption, ΔG is negative.

   Reason: Adsorption is an exothermic process accompanied by decrease in randomness.

4. **Assertion:** A reaction can become fast by itself unless a catalyst is added.

   Reason: A catalyst always increases the rate of reaction.

5. **Assertion:** Hydrolysis of ester is an example of auto-catalytic reaction.

   Reason: A catalyst speeds up the process without participating in the mechanism.

6. **Assertion:** Alcohols are dehydrated to hydrocarbon in the presence of acidic zeolite.

   Reason: Zeolites are non-porous catalyst.

7. **Assertion:** Detergents with low CMC are more economical to use.

   Reason: Cleansing action of detergents involves the formation of micelles. These are formed when the concentration of detergents becomes equal to CMC.

8. **Assertion:** The value of colligative properties are of small order for colloids as compared to true solution.

   Reason: Number of particles in colloidal solution is comparatively smaller than true solutions.

9. **Assertion:** The values of colligative properties are of smaller order as compared to values shown by true solutions at same concentrations.

   Reason: Colloidal particles show Brownian movement.

10. **Assertion (A):** Hydrolysis of an ester follows first order kinetics.*

    Reason (R): Concentration of water remains nearly constant during the course of the reaction.

ANSWERS

1. **(b)** Solids in finely divided state have large surface area.

2. **(c)** Assertion is true, reason is false. When several lines have the same value of $1/n$ then the lines by which their adsorption isotherms can be represented will be parallel and will not meet at a point.

3. **(a)** We know that, $\Delta G = \Delta H - T\Delta S$

   Since, adsorption is exothermic, so $\Delta H = + ve$ further, it occurs with decrease in randomness, so $\Delta S = (-)ve$
   $\Delta G = - ve - T(- ve) = - ve + T$

   So, at low temperature $\Delta G = -ve$.

4. **(c)** A reaction may become faster by its own (autocatalysis). Further, a catalyst may increase or decrease the rate of reaction.

5. **(c)** A catalyst participates in the mechanism of the reaction and is regenerated after the reaction.

6. **(c)** Zeolites are porous catalyst.

7. **(a)** Detergents with low CMC are more economical to use.

8. **(a)** Colligative properties depend upon number of particles.

9. **(b)** Colloidal particles being bigger aggregates, the number of particles in a colloidal solution is comparatively small as compared to a true solution.

10. **(a)** Both Assertion (A) and Reason (R) are correct statements, and Reason (R) is the correct explanation of the Assertion (A).

Chapter 6. General Principles and Processes of Isolation of Elements

1. **Assertion:** Minerals are naturally occurring chemical substances in the earth's crust obtainable by mining.
   Reason: Minerals are also known as ores.

2. **Assertion:** Roasting is a process in which the ore is heated strongly in presence of air.
   Reason: Concentration of sulphide ore is done by calcination.

3. **Assertion:** Levigation is used for the separation of oxide ores from impurities.
   Reason: Ore particles are removed by washing in a current of water.

4. **Assertion:** Reduction of a metal oxide is easier if the metal formed is in liquid state at the temperature of reduction.
   Reason: The entropy is lower if the metal is in liquid state.

5. **Assertion:** Leaching is a process of concentration.
   Reason: Leaching involves treatment of the ore with a suitable reagent so as to make it soluble while impurities remains insoluble.

6. **Assertion:** Nitrate ores are very rare.
   Reason: Bond dissociation energy of N_2 is very high.

7. **Assertion:** Reduction of the metal oxide usually involves heating it with some other substance acting as a reducing agent.
   Reason: The reducing agent combines with the oxygen of the metal oxide.

8. **Assertion:** Cu is leached out using acid or bacteria.
   Reason: The solution containing Cu^{2+} is treated with scrap iron or H_2.

9. **Assertion:** In froth floatation method, collectors such as pine oil or xanthates are added to the suspension of powdered ore.
   Reason: Collectors stabilise the froth.

10. **Assertion:** Iron pyrite is not useful in the extraction of Fe.
    Reason: SO_2 polluting gas is produced during extraction.

ANSWERS

1. **(c)** Only those minerals which are viable to be used as sources of metal are known as ores.

2. **(c)** Roasting is a process in which the ore is heated in presence of air. Sulphide ores are concentrated mainly by froth floatation process.

3. **(c)** Oxide ores being heavier than the earthy or rocky Gangue particles, settle down while lighter impurities are washed away.

4. **(c)** The entropy is higher if the metal is in liquid state.

5. **(a)** Leaching is a process of concentration. It is a process where ore is soluble and impurities are insoluble.

6. **(a)** Nitrate ores are very rare. Bond dissociation energy of nitrogen is very high.

7. **(b)** Reduction of the metal oxide usually involves heating it with some other substance acting as reducing agent (C or CO or even another metal). The reducing agent (*e.g.* carbon) combines with the oxygen of the metal oxide.

$$M_xO_y + yC \rightarrow xM + yCO$$

8. **(b)** Copper is extracted by hydrometallurgy from low grade ores. It is leached out using acid or bacteria. The solution containing Cu^{2+} is treated with scrap iron.

9. **(c)** Collectors enhance non-wettability of the mineral particles.

10. **(a)** For iron, generally the oxide ores which are abundant and do not produce polluting gases (like SO_2 is produced in case of iron pyrites).

Chapter 7. *p*-Block Elements

1. **Assertion:** Catenation tendency is weaker in nitrogen.
   Reason: Nitrogen exists as diatomic gas.

2. **Assertion:** N_2 is said to be less reactive than P_4.
   Reason: Electron gain enthalpy of N is higher than that of P.

3. **Assertion:** When iron is exposed to HNO_3, it becomes passive.
   Reason: A layer of ferric nitrate is formed on the surface of iron due to interaction with HNO_3.

4. **Assertion:** White phosphorus is more reactive than red phosphorus.
   Reason: It readily catches fire in air to give dense white fumes of P_4O_{10}.

5. **Assertion:** S shows paramagnetic nature, when present in vapour state.
   Reason: S exists as S_2 in vapour state.

6. **Assertion:** Ozone layer in the upper region of atmosphere protects earth from UV radiations of sun.
   Reason: Ozone is a powerful oxidising agent as compared to oxygen.

7. **Assertion:** Ozone layer serves as the protective layer from UV radiations.
   Reason: Ozone is more oxidizing in nature than oxygen.

8. **Assertion:** Acidic character of group 16 hydrides increases from H_2O to H_2Te.
   Reason: Thermal stability of hydrides decreases down the group.

9. **Assertion:** Super oxides of alkali metals are paramagnetic.
   Reason: Superoxide contain the ion of O_2^- which has one unpaired electron

10. **Assertion:** Halogens are not found in free state in nature.
    Reason: Halogens are highly reactive compounds.

11. **Assertion:** PbI_4 is not a stable compound.
    Reason: Iodide stabilizes higher oxidation state.

12. **Assertion:** Interhalogen compounds are more reactive than halogens (except fluorine).
    Reason: They all undergo hydrolysis giving halide ion derived from the smaller halogen and anion derived from larger halogen.

13. **Assertion:** Valency of noble gas is 0.

    Reason: Noble gases possess complete octet.

14. **Assertion (A):** F_2 is a strong oxidising agent.*

    Reason (R): Electron gain enthalpy of fluorine is less negative.

15. **Assertion (A):** F_2 has lower bond dissociation enthalpy than Cl_2.*

    Reason (R): Fluorine is more electronegative than chlorine.

16. **Assertion (A):** F_2 has low reactivity.*

    Reason (R): F-F bond has low $\Delta_{bond} H°$

ANSWERS

1. **(b)** Single N—N bond is weaker because of high inter-electronic repulsions of the non-bonding electrons owing to the small bond length.

2. **(c)** Dinitrogen is formed by sharing three electron pairs between two nitrogen atoms. Both atoms are joined by triple bond (N≡N). The nitrogen atom is very small in size, therefore the bond length is also quite small (109.8 pm) and as a result the bond dissociation energy is quite high (946 Kj / mol) .This reason leads N_2 to be very less reactive.

3. **(c)** The concentrated acid forms a metal-oxide layer that protects the bulk of the metal from further oxidation. The formation of this protective layer is called passivation.

4. **(b)** White phosphorus is less stable and more reactive than red phosphorus because of angular strain in the P4 molecule where the angles are only 60°.

5. **(a)** In vapour state S exists as S_2 and it behaves like O_2. It has 2 unpaired electrons in antibonding *pi* orbitals. Presence of these unpaired electrons make S paramagnetic.

6. **(b)** Ozone layer filters the radiation coming from sun, hence serves as the protective layer.

7. **(b)** Ozone layer in the atmosphere reflects the UV radiation and protects biosphere from the exposure to UV radiations. Ozone is not a very stable compound under normal conditions and decomposes readily on heating to give a molecule of oxygen and nascent oxygen. Nascent oxygen, being a free radical, is very reactive. Therefore, ozone acts as a powerful oxidising agent.

8. **(b)** The acidic character increases down the group and thermal stability of hydrides decreases down the group due to decrease in bond (H—E) dissociation enthalpy down the group.

9. **(a)** Superoxide of alkali metals are paramagnetic due to the presence of unpaired electron.

10. **(a)** It is fact that halogens are highly reactive as they have seven electrons in their outermost orbit and they want to stabilize by acquiring an electron. Therefore, they do not occur in free state.

11. **(c)** PbI_4 is not a stable compound because Pb shows (II) oxidation state more frequently than Pb (IV) due to inert pair effect. Iodide cannot stabilize higher oxidation states.

12. **(b)** Interhalogen compounds are more reactive than halogens because X—X′ bond in interhalogens is weaker than X—X bond in halogen (except F—F bond).

13. **(a)** Noble gases possess the electronic configuration $ns^2 np^6$ and has 8 electrons in their outer shell, hence there valency is 0.

14. **(c)** Assertion (A) is correct, but Reason (R) is wrong statement.

15. **(b)** Both Assertion (A) and Reason (R) are correct statements, but Reason (R) is the not the correct explanation of the Assertion (A).

16. **(a)** Both Assertion (A) and Reason (R) are correct statements, and Reason (R) is the correct explanation of the Assertion (A).

Chapter 8. *d*-and *f*-Block Elements

1. **Assertion:** Cu^{2+} iodide is not known.

    Reason: Cu^{2+} oxidises I^- to iodine.

2. **Assertion:** Cu cannot liberate hydrogen from acids.

   Reason: Because it has positive electrode potential.

3. **Assertion:** The highest oxidation state of osmium is +8.

   Reason: Osmium is a 5d-block element.

4. **Assertion:** The lowest oxide of transition metal is basic, the highest is amphoteric/acidic.

   Reason: The lower oxide of transition metal is basic because the metal atom has low oxidation state whereas higher once are acidic due to high oxidation state.

   [**Hint:** *Oxides in lower oxidation states are ionic hence basic.*]

5. **Assertion:** A transition metal exhibits highest oxidation state in oxides and fluorides.

   Reason: Because oxygen and fluorine are highly electronegative elements, small in size and strongest oxidising agents.

6. **Assertion:** The highest oxidation state is exhibited in oxo-anions of a metal.

   Reason: This is again due to the combination of the metal with oxygen, which is highly electronegative and oxidising agent.

7. **Assertion:** Transition metals and many of their compounds show paramagnetic behaviour.

   Reason: Transition metals show paramagnetic behaviour. Paramagnetism arises due to the presence of unpaired electrons with each electron having a magnetic moment associated with its spin angular momentum and orbital angular momentum.

8. **Assertion:** Transition metals and their many compounds act as good catalyst.

   Reason: It is due to variable magnetic property.

9. **Assertion:** The enthalpies of atomisation of the elements in the first transition series are lower than those of the corresponding elements in the second and third transition series.

   Reason: +2 and +3 oxidation states are more common for elements in the first transition series, while higher oxidation states are more common for the heavier elements.

10. **Assertion:** Generally, transition elements and their salts are coloured due to the presence of unpaired electrons in metal ions.

    Reason: $KMnO_4$ and $Ce(SO_4)_2$ are coloured.

11. **Assertion (A):** Transition metals have low melting points.*

    Reason (R): The involvement of greater number of $(n-1)d$ and ns electrons in the interatomic metallic bonding.

12. **Assertion (A):** Transition metals have high melting point.*

    Reason (R): Transition metals have completely filled d-orbitals.

13. **Assertion (A):** Low spin tetrahedral complexes are rarely observed.*

    Reason (R): Crystal field splitting energy is less than pairing energy for tetrahedral complexes.

ANSWERS

1. **(a)** Cu^{2+} oxidises iodide to iodine hence cupric iodide is converted to cuprous iodide.

2. **(a)** Copper (Cu) does not liberate hydrogen from acids due it of the presence of positive electrode potential.

3. **(b)** The highest oxidation state of osmium (Os) is + 8. It is due to its ability to expand their octet by using its all 8 electrons.

4. **(a)** The lower oxide of transition metal is basic because the metal atom has low oxidation state whereas higher once are acidic due to high oxidation state. For example: MnO is basic whereas Mn_2O_7 is acidic. Oxides in lower oxidation states are ionic hence basic. Oxides in higher oxidation state are covalent hence acidic.

5. **(a)** A transition metal exhibits higher oxidation states in oxides and fluorides because oxygen and fluorine are highly electronegative elements, small in size and strongest oxidising agents. For example; Osmium shows an oxidation states of +6 in OsF_6 and vanadium shows an oxidation state of +5 in V_2O_5.

6. **(a)** Oxo metal anions have highest oxidation state, example Cr in $Cr_2O_7^{2-}$ has an oxidation state of +6 whereas Mn in MnO_4^- has an oxidation state of +7. This is again due to the combination of the metal with oxygen, which is highly electronegative and oxidising agent.

7. **(a)** Transition metals show paramagnetic behaviour. Paramagnetism arises due to the presence of unpaired electrons with each electron having a magnetic moment associated with its spin angular momentum and orbital angular momentum. However, in the first transition series, the orbital angular momentum is quenched. Therefore, the resulting para-magnetism is only because of the unpaired electron.

8. **(c)** It is due to variable oxidation states. They have large surface and can form intermediate with reactants which readily change into products.

9. **(b)** The enthalpies of atomisation of the elements in the first transition series are lower than those of the corresponding elements in the second and third transition series. +2 and +3 oxidation states are more common for elements in the first transition series, while higher oxidation states are more common for the heavier elements.

10. **(a)** $KMnO_4$ and $Ce(SO_4)_2$ are coloured due to charge transfer.

11. **(d)** Assertion (A) is wrong, but Reason (R) is correct statement.

12. **(c)** Assertion (A) is correct, but Reason (R) is wrong statement.

13. **(a)** Both Assertion (A) and Reason (R) are correct statements, and Reason (R) is the correct explanation of the Assertion (A).

Chapter 9. Coordination Compounds

1. **Assertion:** Tetrahedral complexes does not show geometrical isomerism.

   Reason: Unidentate ligands attached to the central metal ion are same.

2. **Assertion:** $[Fe(CN)_6]^{3-}$ is weakly paramagnetic while $[Fe(CN)_6]^{4-}$ is diamagnetic.

   Reason: $[Fe(CN)_6]^{3-}$ has +3 oxidation state while $[Fe(CN)_6]^{4-}$ has +2 oxidation state.

3. **Assertion:** $[Pt(NH_3)_3Cl]$ will not show geometrical isomerism.

   Reason: $[Pt(NH_3)_3Cl]$ does not exhibit *cis* and *trans* isomers.

4. **Assertion:** Cl^-, H_2O, NH_3 are the examples of unidentate ligands.

   Reason: Unidentate ligands bind to central metal ion through a single donor atom.

5. **Assertion:** $N(CH_2CH_2NH_2)_3$ and EDTA are examples of polydentate ligands.

   Reason: Ligands which can ligate through two different atoms are called polydentate ligand.

6. **Assertion:** Complexes of MX_6 and MX_5L type (X and L are unidentate) do not show geometrical isomerism.

   Reason: Geometrical isomerism is not shown by complexes of coordination number 6.

7. **Assertion:** $[Ti(H_2O)_6]^{3+}$ is coloured while $[Sc(H_2O)_6)]^{3+}$ is colourless.

   Reason: d-d Transition is not possible in $[Sc(H_2O)_6)]^{3+}$

8. **Assertion:** $K_3[Al(C_2O_4)_3]$ is less stable than $K_2[Ni(EDTA)]$

   Reason: Al is a non-transition element while Ni is a transition element.

9. **Assertion:** $[Fe(H_2O)_6]^{2+}$ is sp^3d^2 hybridised and paramagnetic complex ion.

   Reason: $[Fe(H_2O)_6]^{2+}$ has four unpaired electrons as H_2O is a weak field ligand.

10. **Assertion:** $[Cr(H_2O)_6]Cl_2$ and $[Fe(H_2O)_6]Cl_2$ are reducing in nature.

    Reason: Unpaired electrons are present in their d-orbitals.

11. **Assertion:** Secondary valency of an ion is non ionizable.

    Reason: Secondary valency is also known as coordination number of the metal ion.

12. **Assertion:** When $[Ti(H_2O)_6]Cl_3$ is heated, it becomes colourless.

    Reason: Water is removed after heating.

13. **Assertion:** Inner orbital complexes behave as low spin complexes.

    Reason: Inner d orbitals are used in hybridization by low spin complexes.

14. **Assertion:** $\beta 4$ for the $[Cu(NH_3)_4]^{2+}$ ion is 2.1×10^{13}, hence its instability constant is 4.76×10^{-14}.

    Reason: Instability constant or dissociation constant is reciprocal of the formation constant.

ANSWERS

1. **(a)** Tetrahedral complexes do not show geometrical isomerism because the relative position of the unidentate ligands attached to the central metal atom are the same wrt each other.

2. **(b)** $[Fe(CN)_6]^{3-}$ possesses, unpaired electron to show paramagnetic nature while $[Fe(CN)_6]^{4-}$ possesses no unpaired electron and thus shows diamagnetic nature.

3. **(a)** In the given compound three groups are NH_3, therefore *cis* and *trans* isomerism is not possible.

4. **(a)** Cl^-, H_2O, NH_3 attaches with central metal ion through one donor atom hence these are unidentate ligands.

5. **(c)** Ligands which can ligate through two different atoms is called ambidentate ligand. In polydentate ligands several donor atoms are present in single ligand.

6. **(a)** Correctly explained.

7. **(a)** $[Sc(H_2O)_6)]^{3+}$ has no unpaired electron in its if-subshell and thus d-d transition is not possible whereas $[Ti\,(H_2O)_6]^{3+}$ has one unpaired electron in its if d sub shell which gives rise to d-d transition to impart colour.

8. **(b)** Greater stability of $K_2[Ni(EDTA)]$ is due to greater number of chelate (rings) formed by EDTA as compared to $C_2O_4^{2-}$

9. **(a)** Due to presence of unpaired electrons, it is paramagnetic in nature.

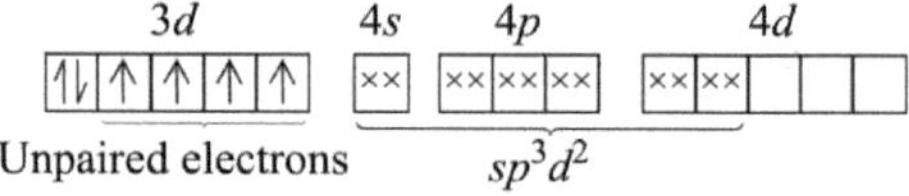

10. **(b)** The compounds are reducing in nature because Cr and Fe both are in their lower oxidation states and can be oxidised further, due to which they act as reducing agent.

11. **(b)** Both statements are correct, but they explain about the properties of secondary valency.

12. **(a)** In the absence of ligand, crystal field splitting does not occur and hence the substance is colourless.

13. **(a)** Because inner d-orbital is involved in hybridisation, pairing of electrons occur and hence due to less or no unpaired electrons the complexes are low spin complexes.

14. **(a)** Correctly explained.

Chapter 10. Haloalkanes and Haloarenes

1. **Assertion:** Hydrogen iodide readily reacts with alkenes to form alkyl halides.

   Reason: Aqueous hydrohalogen acids are used to prepare alkyl halides from alkenes.

2. **Assertion:** $CHCl_3$ is stored in dark bottles.

   Reason: $CHCl_3$ is oxidised in dark.

3. **Assertion:** CCl_4 is a fire extinguisher.

   Reason: CCl_4 is insoluble in water.

4. **Assertion:** $CH_2=CH-CH_2-X$ is an example of allyl halides.

   Reason: These are the compounds in which the halogen atom is bonded to an sp^2 hybridised carbon atom.

5. **Assertion:** Optically active 2-iodobutane on treatment with NaI in acetone undergoes racemisation.

   Reason: Repeated Walden inversions on the reactant and its product eventually gives a racemic mixture.

6. **Assertion:** $CH_3CH=CHCH_3$ is obtained as the result of dehydrohalogenation of $CH_3-CH(Br)-CH_2CH_3$ when it reacts with alco. KOH.

   Reason: Elimination reaction occurs according to Markovnikov's rule.

7. **Assertion:** Alkylbenzene is not prepared by Friedel-Crafts alkylation of benzene.

   Reason: Alkyl halides are less reactive than aryl halides.

8. **Assertion:** Aryl halides cannot be prepared by replacement of hydroxyl group of phenol by halogen atom.

   Reason: Phenols react with halogen acids violently.

9. **Assertion:** Presence of nitro group on chlorobenzene makes replacement of –Cl easier when attacked by –OH.

   Reason: Nitro group strengthens the C–Cl bond in chlorobenzene.

10. **Assertion:** Halogens are *ortho* and *para*-directing atoms.

    Reason: Electrophilic substitution reactions in haloarenes occur slowly and require more drastic conditions as compared to those in benzene.

11. **Assertion:** Electron withdrawing groups in aryl halides increase the reactivity towards nucleophilic substitution.

    Reason: 2, 4-Dinitrochlorobenzene is less reactive than chlorobenzene.

12. **Assertion:** Exposure of ultraviolet rays to human causes the skin cancer, disorder and disrupt the immune system.

    Reason: Carbon tetrachloride is released into air it rises to atmosphere and depicts the ozone layer.

13. **Assertion (A):** $(CH_3)_3 C—O—CH_3$ gives $(CH_3)_3 C—I$ and CH_3OH on treatment with HI.*

    Reason (R): The reaction occurs by S_N1 mechanism.

ANSWERS

1. **(c)** Dry gaseous hydrohalogen acids are better electrophiles. In aqueous solution, H_2O. acting as nucleophile may produce alcohol.

2. **(c)** $CHCl_3$ is stored in dark bottles to avoid reaction in the presence of light. $CHCl_3$ in the presence of light gets oxidised by air.

3. **(b)** CCl_4 is carbon tetrachloride and is used in fire extinguisher. because it is a heavy non-combustible liquid. CCl_4 is insoluble in water due to absence of hydrogen atom that can form hydrogen bonding with water.

4. **(c)** Allyl halides are the compounds in which the halogen atom is bonded to an sp^3 hybridised carbon atom next to carbon-carbon double bond.

5. **(a)** Correctly explained.

6. **(c)** Elimination reaction takes place in accordance with Saytzeff's rule.

7. **(c)** Assertion is correct. Aryl halides are more stable and less reactive due to resonance where the lone pair of electrons are in conjugation with a *pi* bond.

8. **(c)** Aryl halides cannot be prepared by replacing hydroxyl group of phenols because the carbon oxygen bond in phenols has a partial double bond character and is difficult to break being stronger than a single bond.

9. **(c)** Nitro group is an electron withdrawing group which leads to weakening of C—Cl bond, hence making it easier to replace the –Cl group.

10. **(b)** Halogen atom because of its -I effect has some tendency to withdraw electrons from the benzene ring, as a result, the ring gets somewhat deactivated as compared to benzene.

11. **(c)** Halobenzene becomes reactive to nucleophilic substitution reactions when electorn withdrawing groups (nitro, cyano) are present at *ortho* and *para* position.

12. **(b)** UV rays alters the DNA of the body. CCl_4 attacks the ozone layer and depletes it.

13. **(a)** Both Assertion (A) and Reason (R) are correct statements, and Reason (R) is the correct explanation of the Assertion (A).

Chapter 11. Alcohols, Phenols and Ethers

1. **Assertion:** The bond angle in alcohols is slightly less than the tetrahedral angle.

   Reason: In alcohols, the oxygen of —OH group is attached to sp^3 hybridised carbon atom.

2. **Assertion:** In Lucas test, 3° alcohols react immediately.

   Reason: An equimolar mixture of anhyd.$ZnCl_2$ and conc. HCl is called Lucas reagent.

3. **Assertion:** The water solubility of the alcohols follow the order: *tert*-butyl alcohol > *sec*-butyl alcohol > *n*-butyl alcohol.

   Reason: Alcohols form H-bonding with water to show soluble nature.

---

4. **Assertion:** *Tert*-butyl alcohol undergoes acid catalysed dehydration readily than propanol.

   Reason: 3°Alcohols do not give Victor-Meyer's test.

5. **Assertion:** Reimer-Tiemann reaction of phenol with CCl_4 in NaOH at 340 K gives salicylic acid as the major product.

   Reason: The reaction occurs through intermediate formation of dichlorocarbene.

6. **Assertion:** Ethanol is a weaker acid than phenol.

   Reason: Sodium ethoxide may be prepared by the reaction of ethanol with aqueous NaOH.

7. **Assertion:** Phenol is more reactive than benzene towards electrophilic substitution reaction.

   Reason: In the case of phenol, the intermediate carbocation is more resonance stabilised.

8. **Assertion:** Phenol cannot be converted into ester by direct reaction with carboxylic acid.

   Reason: Electron withdrawing groups increase the acidity of phenols.

9. **Assertion:** Phenol undergo Kolbe reaction, ethanol does not.

   Reason: Phenoxide ion is more basic than ethoxide ion.

10. **Assertion:** Phenol is less acidic than *p*-nitrophenol.

    Reason: Phenolate ion is more stable than *p*-nitrophenolate ion.

11. **Assertion:** Ethyl phenyl ether on reaction with HBr forms phenol and ethyl bromide.

    Reason: Cleavage of C–O bond takes place on ethyl-oxygen bond due to the more stable phenyl-oxygen bond.

12. **Assertion:** Etherates are coordination complexes of ethers with Lewis acids.

    Reason: Ethers are easily cleaved by mineral acids such as HCl and H_2SO_4 at 373 K.

13. **Assertion:** *tert*-Butyl methyl ether is not prepared by the reaction of *tert*-butyl bromide with sodium methoxide.

    Reason: Sodium methoxide is a strong nucleophile.

14. **Assertion:** $(CH_3)_3$–CONa and CH_3CH_2Br react to form $(CH_3)_3C$—O—CH_2CH_3

    Reason: Good yields of ethers are obtained when *tert*-alkyl halides are treated with alkoxides.

15. **Assertion (A):** The C—O—C bond angle in ethers is slightly less than tetrahedral angle.

    Reason (R): Due to the repulsive interaction between the two alkyl groups in ethers.

16. **Assertion (A):** Ortho and para-nitrophenols can be separated by steam distillation.*

    Reason (R): Ortho isomer associates through intermolecular hydrogen bonding while Para isomer associates through intramolecular hydrogen bonding.

ANSWERS

1. **(b)** The bond angle $\overset{\text{:O:}}{\underset{}{C}}$ H in alcohols is slightly less than the tetrahedral angle (109°-28'). It is due to the repulsion between the unshared electron pairs of oxygen.

2. **(b)** In Lucas test, tertiary alcohols react immediately because of the formation of the more stable tertiary carbocations.

3. **(b)** The tendency to show H-bonding decreases with increasing hydrophobic character of carbon chain. The hydrophobic character of carbon chain increases with the length of carbon chain.

4. **(b)** Alcohols which form the more stable carbocations undergo dehydration more readily. Since *tert*-butyl alcohol forms more stable *tert*-butyl cation, therefore, it undergoes dehydration more readily than propanol.

5. **(c)** Nucleophilic attack of phenolate ion through the *ortho*-carbon atom occurs on CCl_4 (a neutral electrophile) to form an intermediate which on hydrolysis gives salicylic acid (ArSE reaction).

6. **(c)** Phenol is stronger acid than ethanol as phenoxide ion is stabilised by resonance whereas no such stabilisation occurs in ethoxide ion. Sodium ethoxide can be prepared by reaction of ethanol with sodium.

7. **(a)** Due to +M-effect of —OH, its intermediate carbocation is more stable than the one in benzene.

8. **(b)** Phenols cannot be convened into esters by direct reaction with carboxylic acids since phenols are less nucleophilic than alcohols

---

9. (b) On using *tert*-butyl bromide and sodium ethoxide as reactants, the major product would be 2-methylpropene and ethanol (elimination reaction).

$$CH_3 - \underset{\underset{CH_3}{|}}{\overset{\overset{CH_3}{|}}{C}} - Br - CH_3ONa \longrightarrow CH_3 - \underset{\underset{CH_3}{|}}{C} = CH_2$$

10. (c) *p*-Nitrophenolate ion is more stable than phenolate ion.

11. (c) Alkyl aryl ethers are cleaved at the alkyl-oxygen bond due to the more stable aryl-oxygen bond. The reaction yields phenol and alkyl halide

$$\underset{\text{(phenyl)}}{C_6H_5}-O-R + H-X \longrightarrow \underset{\text{(phenyl)}}{C_6H_5}-OH + R-X$$

Ethers with two different alkyl groups are also cleaved in the same manner.

$$R - O - R' + HX \rightarrow R - X + R' - OH$$

12. (c) Ethers being Lewis bases form etherates with Lewis acids. Ethers are not easily cleaved by H_2SO_4.

13. (b) Sodium methoxide is a strong base and a strong nucleophile. Thus, elimination predominates substitution.

14. (c) $(CH_3)_3CONa$ and CH_3CH_2Br react to form $(CH_3)_3C-O-CH_2CH_3$. Good yields of ether are obtained when primary alkyl halides are treated with alkoxides derived from any alcohol, 1°, 2°, or 3°.

15. (d) Assertion (A) is wrong, but Reason (R) is correct statement.

16. (c) Assertion (A) is correct, but Reason (R) is wrong.

Chapter 12. Aldehydes, Ketones and Carboxylic Acids

1. **Assertion:** A bright silver mirror is produced during the warming of an aldehyde with freshly prepared ammoniacal silver nitrate solution.

   Reason: A bright silver mirror is produced due to the formation of silver metal.

2. **Assertion:** In aromatic aldehydes and ketones electrophilic substitution reaction takes place at *m* position.

   Reason: Due to presence of carbonyl group, the ring becomes activate towards electrophilic substitution.

3. **Assertion:** Acetophenone and benzophenone can be distinguished by iodoform test.

   Reason: Acetophenone and benzophenone both are carbonyl compounds.

4. **Assertion:** Aldol condensation can be catalysed both by acids and bases.

   Reason: β-Hydroxy aldehydes or ketones readily undergo acid catalysed dehydration

5. **Assertion:** 2, 2-Dimethylpropanal undergoes Cannizzaro reaction with concentrated NaOH.

   Reason: Cannizzaro reaction is a disproportionation reaction.

6. **Assertion:** Characteristic carbonyl reactions are not given by carboxylic acids.

   Reason: Carboxylic acids exist as cyclic dimers in solid, liquid and even in vapour state.

7. **Assertion:** Most carboxylic acids exist as dimers in the vapour phase or in aprotic solvents.

   Reason: Higher carboxylic acids are practically insoluble in water due to the increased hydrophobic interaction of hydrocarbon part.

8. **Assertion:** KMnO4 solution is decolourised by both, oxalic acid and formic acid.

   Reason: hese compounds can be oxidised to CO_2 and H_2O easily.

9. **Assertion:** $(CH_3)_3CCOOH$ does not give HVZ reaction.

   Reason: $(CH_3)_3CCOOH$ does not have α hydrogen atom.

10. **Assertion:** IUPAC name of $CH_3CH_2CH_2COOH$ is butanoic acid.

Reason: In the IUPAC system, aliphatic carboxylic acids are named by replacing the ending-*e* in the name of the corresponding alkane with -*oic* acid.

11. **Assertion:** Phenols are less acidic than carboxylic acids.

    Reason: Phenoxide ion is more stable than carboxylate ion.

12. **Assertion:** Direct attachment of groups such as phenyl or vinyl to the carboxylic acid, increases the acidity of the carboxylic acid.

    Reason: Resonance effect always increases the acidity of carboxylic acids.

13. **Assertion:** The planar benzene ring in the aromatic acids can fit more closely in the crystal lattice than zigzag structure of aliphatic acids.

    Reason: The melting points and boiling points of aliphatic acids are usually higher than those of aromatic acids of comparable molecular masses.

14. **Assertion (A):** Benzoic acid does not undergo Friedal-Crafts reaction.*

    Reason (R): The carboxyl group is activating and undergo electrophilic substitution reaction.*

15. **Assertion (A):** Benzaldehyde is less reactive than ethanal towards nucleophilic addition reactions.

    Reason (R): Ethanal is more sterically hindered.

ANSWERS

1. **(a)** On warming an aldehyde with freshly prepared ammoniacal silver nitrate solution (Tollen's reagent), a bright silver mirror is produced due to the formation of silver metal. The aldehydes are oxidised to corresponding carboxylate anion. The reaction occurs in alkaline medium.

2. **(c)** Carbonyl group is deactivating group.

3. **(b)** Acetophenone and benzophenone can be distinguished by iodoform test. Both are carbonyl compounds.

4. **(b)** Both carbanions (formed in presence of base) and enol form (formed in presence of an acid) act as nucleophiles and hence add on the Carbonyl group of aldehydes and ketones to give aldols.

5. **(b)** Aldehydes which do not contain α-hydrogen undergo Cannizzaro reaction.

$$H_3C - \overset{\overset{\displaystyle CH_3}{|}}{\underset{\underset{\displaystyle CH_3}{|}}{C^\alpha}} - CHO$$

2, 2-dimethylpropanal (no α-hydrogen

6. **(b)** As carboxylic acids are resonance stabilized they do not contain true carbonyl group as is present in carbonyl compounds.

7. **(b)** Carboxylic acids exist as dimers due to intermolecular hydrogen bonding which is not broken completely even in the vapour phase or in aprotic solvents.

8. **(a)** Both formic acid and oxalic acid behave as reducing agent and decolourise acidified $KMnO_4$ solution.

    $2KMnO_4 + 3H_2SO_4 \rightarrow K_2SO_4 + 2MnSO_4 + 3H_2O + 5(O)$

    $RCOOH + [O] \rightarrow CO_2 + H_2O$

9. **(b)** Carboxylic acids do not undergo Friedel—Crafts reaction because the —COOH group is deactivating and the catalyst aluminium chloride (Lewis acid) gets bonded to the carboxyl group.

10. **(a)** Correctly explained.

11. **(c)** Carboxylate ion is more stable than phenoxide ion due to two equivalent resonating structures in which negative charge is at the O-atom. In phenoxide ion, negative charge is at the less-electronegative carbon atom. Therefore, corresponding acid of the carboxylate ion, *i.e.*, carboxylic acid is more acidic than phenol.

12. **(c)** This is due to greater electronegativity of sp^2 hybridised carbon to which carboxyl carbon is attached.

13. **(c)** Carboxylate ion is more stable than phenoxide ion due to two equivalent resonating structures in which negative charge is at the O-atom. In phenoxide ion, negative charge is at the less-electronegative carbon atom. Therefore, corresponding acid of the carboxylate ion, *i.e.*, carboxylic acid is more acidic than phenol.

14. **(c)** Assertion (A) is correct, but Reason (R) is wrong statement.

15. **(c)** Assertion (A) is correct, but Reason (R) is wrong statement.

Chapter 13. Amines

1. **Assertion:** The angle of C—N—C in the trimethylamine is 108°.

   Reason: There is unshared pair of electrons in the trimethylamine which makes the angle less than 109.5°.

2. **Assertion:** In ammonolysis of alkyl halides, primary amine is obtained as a major product by taking large excess of NH_3.

   Reason: The process of cleavage of the C—X bond by ammonia molecule is known as ammonolysis.

3. **Assertion:** During reduction of nitrobenzene, Fe + HCl is preferred as the reagent.

   Reason: During oxidation of nitroalkanes into alkanamines the preferred reagent is Fe + HCl.

4. **Assertion:** Substituted ammonium ion formed from the amine is stable.

   Reason: There is dispersal of the positive charge on ammonium ion by the +I effect of the alkyl group.

5. **Assertion:** The order of basic strength in case of methyl substituted and ethyl substituted amines in aqueous state is different.

   Reason: Methyl group has stronger inductive effect than ethyl group.

6. **Assertion:** It is impossible to prepare aromatic primary amines through Gabriel phthalimide synthesis process.

   Reason: Aryl halides does not show electrophilic substitution with anion formed by phthalimide.

7. **Assertion:** In acylation reaction of amines equilibrium shifts to the right hand side in the presence of pyridine.

   Reason: In the presence of strong base, HCl is removed and reaction shifts toward the right hand side.

8. **Assertion:** The diazotisation reaction must be carried in ice cold solution (0–4 °C).

   Reason: At higher temperature, benzenediazonium chloride reacts with water to give phenol.

9. **Assertion:** Alkylation and acetylation does not occur in aniline.

   Reason: In the presence of $AlCl_3$ nitrogen of aniline adopts positive charge.

10. **Assertion:** Consider the given reaction,

$$CH_3NH_2 \rightarrow H_2CNHCH_2CH_2OH$$
b-amino alcohol

   Reason: β-amino alcohol is less reactive than the starting amines.

11. **Assertion:** In strongly acidic solution, aniline becomes less reactive towards electrophilic reagents.

   Reason: Due to protonation of amino group the lone pair of electrons on nitrogen is not available for donation to benzene ring by resonance.

12. **Assertion:** Salts of benzene diazonium are water soluble.

   Reason: Because of the covalent nature of such salts these are water soluble.

13. **Assertion:** *p*-fluoro anilinium ion is more acidic than anilinium ion.

   Reason: Electron density in the N—H bond of *p*-fluoroanilinium ion decreases and release of a proton from *p*-fluoroanilinium ion is much easier than from anilinium ion.

14. **Assertion:** Anilinium hydrogen sulphate, on heating forms a mixture of *ortho-* and *para-* aminobenzene sulphonic acids

   Reason: *p*-Aminobenzene sulphonic acid exists as zwitter ion.

ANSWERS

1. **(a)** Correctly explained.

2. **(b)** Ammonolysis has the disadvantage of yielding a mixture of primary, secondary and tertiary amines and also a quaternary ammonium salt. Hence by taking large excess of NH_3 primary amine is obtained as major product.

3. **(c)** Reduction of nitro compounds with Fe scrap and HCl is preferred because $FeCl_2$ formed gets hydrolysed to release HCl during the reaction. Thus, only a small amount of HCl is required to initiate the reaction.

4. **(a)** The substituted ammonium ion formed from the amine gets stabilised due to dispersal of positive charge by the $+I$-effect of alkyl group.

5. **(c)** In aqueous phase, the substituted ammonium cations get stabilised not only by electron releasing effect of alkyl group but also by solvation with water molecules.

   In case of $-CH_3$ group, there is no steric hindrance to H-bonding, but in case of bigger groups there is steric hindrance and hence the order changes.

6. **(c)** Aromatic primary amines cannot be prepared by the Gabriel phthalimide synthesis because aryl halides do not undergo nucleophilic substitution reaction with the anion formed by phthalimide.

7. **(a)** In acylation reaction of amines, equilibrium shifts to the right side in the presence of pyridine because it is a stronger base than amine which removes HCl so formed in the reaction.

8. **(a)** Correctly explained.

9. **(a)** Aniline does not undergo Friedel Crafts reaction (alkylation and acetylation) due to salt formation with $AlCl_3$, (the Lewis acid) which is used as a catalyst. Due to this nitrogen of aniline acquires positive charge and hence, act as a strong deactivating group for further reaction.

10. **(b)** β amino alcohol is less reactive than the starting amines because it stabilised by intramolecular hydrogen bonding which lowers nucleophilicity of—OH group.

11. **(a)** Correctly explained.

12. **(c)** Benzene diazonium salts are soluble in water because they are ionic in nature.

13. **(a)** Due to $-I$ effect of F-atom, it withdraws electrons from N^+H_3 group. As a result, electron density in the N—H bond of *p*-fluoroanilinium ion decreases and hence release of a proton from *p*-fluoroanilinium ion is much more easier than from anilinium ion. Thus, *p*-fluoroanilinium ion is more acidic than anilinium ion.

$$F-\underset{}{\bigcirc}-\overset{\overset{H}{|}}{\underset{\underset{H}{|}}{N^{\oplus}}}-H$$

14. **(b)** Amine group is *ortho* and *para-* directing, hence it directs the SO_3 electrophile to *ortho-* and *para* positions.

Chapter 14. Biomolecules

1. **Assertion:** D (+) – glucose is dextrorotatory in nature.

   Reason: 'D' represents its dextrorotatory nature.

2. **Assertion:** Deoxyribose, $C_5H_{10}O_4$ is not a carbohydrate.

   Reason: Carbohydrates are hydrates of carbon so compounds which follow $C_x(H_2O)_y$ formula are carbohydrates.

3. **Assertion:** All naturally occurring α-amino acids except glycine are optically active.

   Reason: Most naturally occurring amino acids have L-configuration.

4. **Assertion:** When the native protein is subjected to physical changes such as change in temperature or chemical changes such as change in pH, its H-bonds are disturbed. This disturbance unfolds the globules and uncoils the helix. As a result, the protein loses its biological activity. This loss of biological activity by the protein is called denaturation.

   Reason: One of the examples of denaturation of proteins is the coagulation of egg white when an egg is boiled.

5. **Assertion:** Fibrous protein is a fibre-liked structure formed by the polypeptide chain. These proteins are held together by strong hydrogen and disulphide bonds.

   Reason: It is usually soluble in water.

6. **Assertion:** The polypeptide chain in globular protein is folded around itself, giving rise to a spherical structure.

   Reason: Some enzymes are globular proteins.

7. **Assertion:** There are two common types of secondary structure of proteins:

   α-helix structure

   β-pleated sheet structure

   Reason: In α- Helix structure, the $-NH$ group of an amino acid residue forms H-bond with the $>C=O$ group of the adjacent turn of the right handed screw (α-helix).

8. **Assertion:** In presence of enzyme, substrate molecule can be attacked by the reagent effectively.

   Reason: Active sites of enzymes hold the substrate molecule in a suitable position.

9. **Assertion:** Vitamin D can be stored in our body.

   Reason: Vitamin D is fat soluble vitamin.

10. **Assertion:** DNA is responsible for the transmission of inherent characters from one generation to the next. This process of transmission is called heredity.

    Reason: Nucleic acids (both DNA and RNA) are responsible for protein synthesis in a cell.

11. **Assertion:** There is difference between a nucleoside and a nucleotide.

    Reason: A nucleoside is formed by the attachment of a base to position of sugar and on the other hand, all the three basic components of nucleic acids (*i.e.*, pentose sugar, phosphoric acid and base) are present in a nucleotide.

12. **Assertion:** The helical structure of DNA is double-stranded.

    Reason: The helical structure of RNA is single-stranded.

ANSWERS

1. **(c)** D corresponds to the position of –OH group on the right side on the farthest asymmetric C-atom.

2. **(b)** Deoxyribose, $C_5H_{10}O_4$ is a carbohydrate and is the sugar moiety of DNA. Carbohydrates are optically active polyhydroxy aldehyde or polyhydroxy ketone or substances which give these on hydrolysis.

3. **(b)** All amino acids except glycine contain at least one chiral carbon.

4. **(a)** In a biological system, a protein is found to have a unique three-dimensional structure and a unique biological activity. In such a situation, the protein is called native protein. However, when the native protein is subjected to physical changes such as change in temperature or chemical changes such as change in pH, its H-bonds are disturbed. This disturbance unfolds the globules and uncoils the helix. As a result, the protein loses its biological activity. This loss of biological activity by the protein is called denaturation. During denaturation, the secondary and the tertiary structures of the protein get destroyed, but the primary structure remains unaltered. One of the examples of denaturation of proteins is the coagulation of egg white when an egg is boiled.

5. **(c)** Fibrous protein is usually insoluble in water.

6. **(c)** All enzymes are globular proteins.

7. **(a)** Reason is correct explanation of assertion.

8. **(a)** In presence of enzyme, substrate molecule can be attacked by the reagent effectively because active sites of enzymes hold the substrate molecule in a suitable position.

9. **(a)** Vitamin D can be stored in our body because it is fat soluble vitamin.

10. **(b)** Nucleic acids (both DNA and RNA) are responsible for protein synthesis in a cell. Even though the proteins are synthesised by the various RNA molecules in a cell, the message for the synthesis of a particular protein is present in DNA.

11. **(a)** A nucleoside is formed by the attachment of a base to position of sugar.

    Nucleoside = Sugar + Base

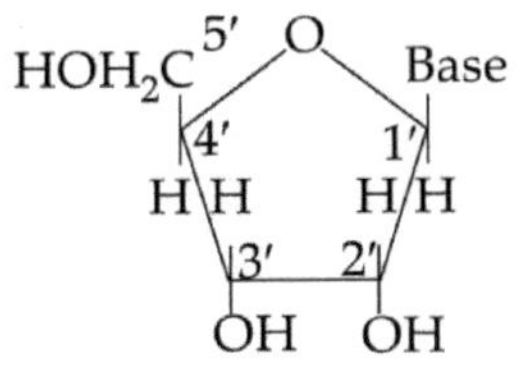

$$HOH_2C\overset{5'}{-}\underset{\underset{OH}{|}}{\overset{4'}{C}}\cdots\underset{\underset{OH}{|}}{\overset{1'}{C}}\text{—Base}$$

Structure of a nucleotide nucleoside

On the other hand, all the three basic components of nucleic acids (*i.e.*, pentose sugar, phosphoric acid and base) are present in a nucleotide.

Nucleotide = Sugar + Base + Phosphoric acid

Structure of a nucleotide

12. **(b)** Double helix is the description of the structure of a DNA molecule. A DNA molecule consists of two strands that wind around each other like a twisted ladder. RNA is a single-stranded molecule in many of its biological roles and consists of a much shorter chain of nucleotides.

Chapter 15. Polymers

1. **Assertion:** Teflon has high thermal stability and chemical inertness.
   Reason: Teflon is a thermoplastic.

2. **Assertion:** Bakelite is a thermosetting polymer.
   Reason: Bakelite can be melted again and again without any change.

3. **Assertion:** Buna-S is a copolymer.
   Reason: Buna-S is formed by condensation reaction between two different monomers.

4. **Assertion:** Polyamides are best used as fibres because of high tensile strength.
   Reason: Strong intermolecular forces (like hydrogen bonding within polyamides) lead to close packing of chains and increase the crystalline character, hence, provide high tensile strength to polymers.

5. **Assertion:** In vulcanisation of rubber, sulphur cross-links are introduced.
   Reason: Vulcanisation is a free radical initiated chain reaction.

6. **Assertion:** The physical properties of natural rubber can be improved by vulcanisation.
   Reason: Neoprene is the monomer of natural rubber.

7. **Assertion:** Rayon is a semi-synthetic polymer and is taken as a better choice than cotton fabric.
   Reason: Mechanical and aesthetic properties of cellulose can be improved by acetylation.

8. **Assertion:** Network polymers are thermosetting.
   Reason: Network polymers have high molecular mass.

9. **Assertion:** Polytetrafluoroethylene is used in making non-stick cookware.
   Reason: Fluorine has highest electronegativity.

10. **Assertion:** Bakelite is formed when novolac is heated with formaldehyde which is a thermosetting polymer.
    Reason: Bakelite is infusible solid mass.

11. **Assertion:** PHBV is a biodegradable polymer.
    Reason: PHBV is an aliphatic polyester.

12. **Assertion:** Most of the synthetic polymers are not biodegradable.
    Reason: Polymerisation process induce toxic character in organic molecule.

ANSWERS

1. **(b)** Due to the presence of strong C-F bonds, teflon has high thermal stability and chemical inertness.
2. **(c)** Bakelite can be heated only once.
3. **(c)** Buna-S is formed by addition reaction between two different monomers, 1,3-butadiene and styrene.

4. **(b)** Polyamides like nylons are best used fibres. They have high tensile strength due to presence of strong inter molecular hydrogen bond.

5. **(b)** Vulcanisation is a process of treating natural rubber with sulphur or some compounds of sulphur under heat to modify its properties. This cross-linking gives mechanical strength to the rubber.

6. **(c)** Isoprene (2-methyl-1,3-butadiene) is the monomer of natural rubber.

7. **(b)** Rayon is semi-synthetic polymer and is a better choice than cotton because properties of cellulose are improved by acetylation while processing.

8. **(a)** Extensive cross-linking during polymerisation leads to the formation of three-dimensional network which is hard, infusible and insoluble.

9. **(a)** Teflon is used in making non-stick cookware as it is chemically inert and thermally stable.

10. **(b)** Bakelite is formed when novolac is heated with formaldehyde which is a thermosetting polymer.

11. **(a)** Poly(3-hydroxybutyrate-co-3-hydroxyvalerate), is a polyhydroxyalkanoate-type polymer. It is biodegradable, non-toxic, plastic produced naturally by bacteria and a good alternative for many non-biodegradable synthetic polymers.

12. **(c)** Most of the synthetic polymers are not degraded by enzymatic hydrolytic and environmental oxidation. Polymerisation does not induce toxic characters.

Chapter 16. Chemistry in Everyday Life

1. **Assertion:** Sulpha drug contains sulphonamide group.
   Reason: Salvarsan is a sulpha drug.

2. **Assertion:** Equanil is a tranquilizer.
   Reason: Equanil is used to cure depression and hypertension.

3. **Assertion:** Competitive inhibitors compete with natural substrate for their attachment on the active sites of enzymes.
   Reason: In competitive inhibition, inhibitor binds to the allosteric site of the enzyme.

4. **Assertion:** Antiseptics are applied to living tissues.
   Reason: Iodine is a powerful antiseptic.

5. **Assertion:** Enzymes have active sites that hold substrate molecule for a chemical reaction.
   Reason: Drugs compete with natural substrate by attaching covalently to the active site of enzyme.

6. **Assertion:** Antibiotics are used as drugs to treat infections.
   Reason: These are less toxic for humans and animals.

7. **Assertion:** Similarity exist in the structures of salvarsan and azo dyes.
   Reason: Linkage between As—As in arsphenamine and linkage between N—N in azo dyes are similar.

8. **Assertion:** Penicillin-G is not an antihistamine.
   Reason: Penicillin-G is effective against gram positive as well as gram negative bacteria.

9. **Assertion:** Chemicals added to foods for increasing their shelf life are called preservatives.
   Reason: Natural sweeteners like sucrose and artificial sweeteners like saccharin are commonly used as food preservatives.

10. **Assertion:** Use of aspartame is limited to cold foods and soft drinks.
    Reason: Aspartame is roughly 100 times as sweet as cane sugar.

11. **Assertion:** Artificial sweeteners are added to the food to control the intake of calories.
    Reason: Most of the artificial sweeteners are inert and do not metabolise in the body.

12. **Assertion:** Low level of noradrenaline causes depression.
    Reason: Equanil is used in controlling depression.

13. **Assertion:** Shaving soaps contain glycerol.
    Reason: It prevents rapid drying.

14. **Assertion:** Detergents with straight chain of hydrocarbons are preferred over branched chain.

    Reason: Detergents with branched chain hydrocarbon part are expensive.

15. **Assertion:** Synthetic detergents do not contain soap.

    Reason: They have all the properties of soap.

16. **Assertion:** Transparent soaps are made by dissolving soaps in ethanol.

    Reason: Ethanol makes things invisible.

17. **Assertion:** Clothes washed with soap using hard water do not absorb dyes evenly.

    Reason: Hard water contains calcium and magnesium ions.

ANSWERS

1. **(c)** Salvarsan is not a sulpha drug.

2. **(a)** Tranquilizers are chemicals which are used to cure mental diseases.

3. **(c)** Drugs can compete with the natural substrate for their attachment on the active sites of enzymes, such drugs are known as competitive inhibitors. Some drugs do not bind to the enzyme active site. These bind to a different site of enzyme, called allosteric site. This binding of inhibitor at allosteric site changes the shape of the active site in such a way that substrate cannot recognise it.

4. **(b)** Antiseptics are those chemicals which kill or prevent the growth of micro organism. Antiseptics do not harm the living tissues and can be applied on cuts and wounds. They help to reduce odour resulting from the bacterial decomposition in the mouth and on the body.

5. **(c)** Enzyme hold the substrate for a chemical reaction. Active sites of enzymes hold the substrate molecule in a suitable position, so that it can be attacked by the reagent effectively. Substrates then bind to the active site of the enzyme through a variety of interactions such as ionic bond, hydrogen bonding, van der Waals' interaction.

6. **(a)** Antibiotics are used as drugs to treat infection because of their low toxicity for human and animals.

7. **(c)** Similarity in the structures of salvarsan (arsphenamine) and azo dyes exist in the similar double bonds between As-atoms in former and N-atoms in latter.

8. **(c)** Penicillin-G is a narrow spectrum antibiotic.

9. **(c)** Sweeteners are added to impart sweetness to the food. Sodium benzoate, tables salt, vegetable oils etc. are some commonly used preservatives.

10. **(b)** Aspartame is unstable at cooking temperature hence its use is limited to cold foods and soft drinks.

11. **(b)** Both are true but R does not explain A.

12. **(b)** If the level of noradrenaline is low then the signal sending activity becomes low and person suffers from depression.

13. **(a)** Shaving soap contains glycerol as it prevents rapid drying.

14. **(c)** Detergents with branched chain hydrocarbon part are non-biodegradable as bacteria cannot degrade them easily.

15. **(a)** Synthetic detergents do not contain soap because they have all the properties of soap.

16. **(c)** Ethanol does not make things invisible.

17. **(b)** Calcium and magnesium ions form insoluble calcium and magnesium soaps which adheres on to the fiber of the cloth as gummy mass. So that dye does not get absorbed evenly.

□□

Chapter 1. Solid State

1. **Read the passage given below and answer the following questions:**

   Point defects play an important part in determining the physical properties of most crystalline substances, most notably those controlling the transport of matter and the properties that stem from it. Even a crystal of high purity under conditions of no irradiation contains point defects in thermal equilibrium. Some lattice sites are vacant, and some atoms are displaced from their normal lattice sites into interstitial positions or onto "wrong" lattice sites. For stochiometric compounds of high purity, the concentrations of these point defects are very low, even at temperatures up to the melting point. A meaningful model, then, is to consider the crystal as a solvent containing a very dilute solution of simple, individual vacancies and interstitials. Long-range interactions among the defects and with impurity atoms, and short-range interactions that produce pairs or other clusters can be introduced in a first order approximation.

   (Reference: Crawford, J.H. & Slifkin, L.M. (2013). Point Defects in Solids: General and Ionic Crystals, Chapter 1, Volume 1, 1-2.)

   The following questions are multiple choice questions. Choose the most appropriate answer:

   (i)   Which one of the given below statements is wrong about Frenkel defect:

       (a)   It is a combination of vacancy and interstitial defects.

       (b)   Cations leave their actual lattice sites and occupy the interstitial space in the solid.

       (c)   Density remains the same.

       (d)   Density of the crystal increases.

   (ii) Which one of the following is an 'interstitial void'?

       (a)   Octahedral void   (c)   None of the above

       (b)   Tetrahedral void   (d)   Both (a) and (b)

   (iii) This type of defect arises due to absence of equal number of cations and anions from lattice sites in the crystalline solid of the type A^+B^- and it lowers the density of the crystal.

       (a)   Vacancy defect   (c)   Interstitial defect

       (b)   Schottky defect   (d)   Frenkel defect

   (iv) Which one of the following cannot be called as a 'non-stoichiometric defect'?

       (a)   Metal excess defect due to anion vacancies.

       (b)   Metal excess defect due to presence of extra cations.

       (c)   Metal deficiency due to absence of cations.

       (d)   Combination of vacancy and interstitial defects.

   OR

   What will be the number of octahedral voids in terms of the number 'N' where N is number of closed packed particles

       (a)   2N   (b) N   (c)   1/2N   (d)   3N

Ans. (i)   (d)   Density of the crystal increases.

    (ii) (d)   Both (a) and (b)

    (iii) (b)   Schottky defect

    (iv) (d)   Combination of vacancy and interstitial defects.

OR

    (b)   N

2. **Read the passage given below and answer the following questions:**

   Ionic solids band melts are compounds in which the interactions are dominated by electrostatic effects. However, the polarisation of the ions also plays an important role in many respects as has been clarified in recent years thanks to the development of realistic polarisable interaction potentials. After detailing these models, we illustrate the importance of polarisation effects on a series of examples concerning the structural properties, such as the stabilisation of particular crystal structures or the formation of highly-coordinated multivalent ions in the melts, as well as the dynamic properties such as the diffusion of ionic species. The effects on the structure of molten salt interfaces (with vacuum and electrified metal) is also described. Although most of the results described here concern inorganic compounds (molten fluorides and chlorides, ionic oxides...), the particular case of the room-temperature ionic liquids, a special class of molten salts in which at least one species is organic, will also be briefly discussed to indicate how the ideas gained from the study of 'simple' molten salts are being transferred to these more complex systems.

(Reference: Salanne, M., & Madden, P. A. (2011). Polarisation effects in ionic solids and melts, Molecular Physics, 109(19), 2299-2315.)

In these questions, a statement of assertion followed by a statement of reason is given. Choose the correct answer out of the following choices.

(a) Assertion and reason both are correct statements and reason is correct explanation for assertion.

(b) Assertion and reason both are correct statements but reason is not correct explanation for assertion.

(c) Assertion is correct statement but reason is wrong statement.

(d) Assertion is wrong statement but reason is correct statement.

(i) **Assertion:** Diamond is a precious stone.

    Reason: Carbon atoms are tetrahedrally arranged in diamond.

(ii) **Assertion:** The total number of atoms present in a simple cubic unit cell is one.

    Reason: Simple cubic unit cell has atoms at its corners, each of which is shared between eight adjacent unit cells.

(iii) **Assertion:** Graphite is a good conductor of electricity however diamond belongs to the category of insulators.

    Reason: Graphite is soft in nature on the other hand diamond is very hard and brittle.

(iv) **Assertion:** Total number of octahedral voids present in unit cell of cubic close packing including the one that is present at the body center, is four.

    Reason: Besides the body center there is one octahedral void present at the center of each of the six faces of the unit cell and each of which is shared between two adjacent unit cells.

OR

    Assertion: The packing efficiency is maximum for the fcc structure.

    Reason: The coordination number is 12 in fcc structures.

Ans. (i) (a) Assertion and reason both are correct statements and reason is correct explanation for assertion.

    (ii) (a) Assertion and reason both are correct statements and reason is correct explanation for assertion.

    (iii) (b) Assertion and reason both are correct statements but reason is not correct explanation for assertion.

    (iv) (c) Assertion is correct statement but reason is wrong statement.

OR

    (d) Assertion is wrong statement but reason is correct statement.

Chapter 2. Solutions

1. **Read the passage given below and answer the following questions:**

In general, the vapor-pressure change due to the addition of a solute to a solvent mixture does not follow Raoult's law. We have demonstrated thermodynamically that if one adds to a binary solvent mixture solute and solvents in such a way that the vapor-phase composition remains constant, then the decrease of total pressure follows Raoult's law; a supplementary term which vanishes for very dilute solute concentration is introduced as a consequence of the non-ideality of the ternary solution. Precise vapor-pressure measurements of dilute solutions of electrolytes and non-electrolytes in a 40.000 wt. % watertetrahydrofuran mixture is used in order to illustrate the applicability of Raoult's law under the above conditions. These may be regarded as a particular case of what has been called endostatic conditions, i.e., addition of a solute under constant solvent activity ratio.

(Reference: Tzias, P., Treiner, C. & Chemla, M. (1977). Applicability of Raoult's law in non-ideal mixed solvents. J Solution Chem 6, 393–402.)

The following questions are multiple choice questions. Choose the most appropriate answer:

(i) In comparison to a 0.01 M solution of glucose, the depression in freezing point of a 0.01 M $MgCl_2$ solution is __________.

    (a) the same

    (b) about twice

    (c) about three times

    (d) about six times

(ii) According to Raoult's law

    (a) The vapour-pressure exerted by a volatile component of a solution is directly proportional to its mole fraction in the solution.

    (b) The vapour-pressure exerted by a non-volatile component of a solution is directly proportional to its mole fraction in the solution.

    (c) The vapour-pressure exerted by a volatile component of a solution is inversely proportional to its mole fraction in the solution.

    (d) The vapour-pressure exerted by a volatile component of a solution is directly proportional to its volume in the solution.

(iii) Which of the following is incorrect for an ideal solution?

    (a) $\Delta H_{mix} = 0$

    (b) $\Delta V_{mix} = 0$

    (c) $\Delta P = P_{obs} - P_{calculated} = 0$

    (d) $\Delta G_{mix} = 0$

(iv) Which of the following condition is not satisfied by an ideal solution?

    (a) $\Delta H_{mixing} = 0$

    (b) $\Delta V_{mixing} = 0$

    (c) Raoult's Law is obeyed

    (d) Formation of an azeotropic mixture

OR

The boiling point of an azeotropic mixture of water and ethanol is less than that of water and ethanol. The mixture shows

    (a) No deviation from Raoult's Law.

    (b) Positive deviation from Raoult's Law.

    (c) Negative deviation from Raoult's Law.

    (d) That the solution is unsaturated.

Ans. (i) (c) About three times

    (ii) (a) The vapour-pressure exerted by a volatile component of a solution is directly proportional to its mole fraction in the solution.

    (iii) (d) $\Delta G_{mix} = 0$

    (iv) (d) Formation of an azeotropic mixture.

OR

    (b) Positive deviation from Raoult's Law.

2. **Read the passage given below and answer the following questions:**

The vapor pressure of a solvent decrease when a nonvolatile component is dissolved in the liquid phase. The depression of the vapor pressure of the solution (at constant temperature) results in a rise of the boiling point of the solution (at constant pressure). The degree of the boiling point rise (BPR), being a colligative property, depends on the concentration of the dissolved particles and on the nature of the solvent. In dilute solutions it is observed to be relatively independent of the nature of the solute. BPR measurements of dilute solutions have been used for many years to obtain the molecular weight of the solute.

(Reference: Meranda, D. & Furter, W. F. (1977). Elevation of the boiling point of water by salts at saturation: data and correlation. Journal of Chemical & Engineering Data, 22(3), 315-317.)

In these questions, a statement of assertion followed by a statement of reason is given. Choose the correct answer out of the following choices.

(a) Assertion and reason both are correct statements and reason is correct explanation for assertion.

(b) Assertion and reason both are correct statements but reason is not correct explanation for assertion.

(c) Assertion is correct statement but reason is wrong statement.

(d) Assertion is wrong statement but reason is correct statement.

(i) **Assertion:** At boiling point, vapour pressure of a liquid is equal to the atmospheric pressure.

    Reason: Vapour pressure of a liquid decreases with a liquid.

(ii) **Assertion:** Blood cells collapse when suspended in saline water, having more concentration compared to fluid inside the blood cells.

    Reason: Solvent molecules always flow from higher concentration to lower concentration.

    (iii) **Assertion:** When NaCl is added to water a depression in freezing point is observed.

       Reason: The lowering of the vapour pressure of a solution causes depression in the freezing point compared to the pure solvent.

    (iv) **Assertion:** Colligative property is used to determine the molecular mass of particle.

       Reason: Colligative properties depend upon number of solute particles in solution irrespective of their nature.

OR

    Assertion: Colloidal solution show colligative properties.

    Reason: Colloidal particles are large in size.

Ans. (i)   (c)   Assertion is correct statement but reason is wrong statement.

    (ii)   (c)   Assertion is correct statement but reason is wrong statement.

    (iii) (a)   Assertion and reason both are correct statements and reason is correct explanation for assertion.

    (iv) (b)   Assertion and reason both are correct statements but reason is not correct explanation for assertion.

OR

    (b)   Assertion and reason both are correct statements but reason is not correct explanation for assertion.

Chapter 3. Electrochemistry

1. **Read the passage given below and answer the following questions:**

The calculation of cell potential for emf requires only the addition of the emf values for each half reaction, while the same cell potential calculation using standard potentials requires the usage of the following convention:

$$E°cell = E°cathode - E°anode$$

Each half-cell reaction has a specific standard potential reported as the potential of the reduction reaction vs. the normal hydrogen electrode (NHE). In an electrochemical cell, there is a half-cell corresponding to the working electrode (WE), where the reactions under study take place, and a reference half-cell. Experimentally the cell potential is measured as the difference between the potentials of the WE half-cell and the reference electrode/reference half-cell. The archetypal reference electrode is the NHE, also known as the standard hydrogen electrode (SHE) and is defined, by convention, as 0.000 V for any temperature.

(Reference: Ciobanu, M., Wilburn, J.P., Krim, M.L., Clieffel, D.E. "Fundamentals". In Handbook of Electrochemistry, Edited by Cynthia G. Zoski, 3-28, Netherlands: Elsevier, 2007.)

The following questions are multiple choice questions. Choose the most appropriate answer:

(i)   EMF of a cell depends on

    (a)   Nature of electrolyte

    (b)   Concentration of electrolyte in two half cells

    (c)   Temperature

    (d)   All of the above

(ii)   Electrical conductance __________ with increasing temperature.

    (a)   Decreases   (c)   Remains unaffected

    (b)   Increases   (d)   Nullifies

(iii) A salt bridge maintains the _________ between solutions of both the half cells.

    (a)   Electricity   (c)   Resistivity

    (b)   Electrical neutrality   (d)   Connectivity

(iv) Predict the value of EMF of a cell in which the chemical reactions achieve equilibrium.

    (a)   –1   (b)   0.5   (c)   +1   (d)   Zero

OR

Reduction of 1 mol of Zn^{2+} to give 1 mol of Zn would require:

    (a)   96500 C   (b)   193000 C   (c)   4875 C   (d)   48750 C

Ans. (i)   (d)   All of the above

    (ii)   (b)   Increases

    (iii) (b)   Electrical neutrality

(iv) (d) Zero

OR

(b) 193000 C

2. **Read the passage given below and answer the following questions:**

It is well known that the theory of Arrhenius is unable to explain the way in which the conductivity of a "strong" electrolyte changes with changing concentration. An alternative theory advanced by several writers supposes strong electrolytes in dilute aqueous solution to be completely dissociated, and attributes the diminution in equivalent conductivity with increase in concentration entirely to the electrical forces which exist between the ions. This theory has attracted attention especially since its recent mathematical development by Debye.

The objects of the present paper are to show that the postulation of complete dissociation is in complete harmony with the experimental data for very dilute aqueous solutions of uni-univalent electrolytes; and to advance an empirical relationship which expresses the conductivity of such a solution in terms of the concentration, the mobilities of the ions present and a universal constant.

(Reference: Davies, C. W. (1925). The Conductivity of Electrolytes. The Journal of Physical Chemistry, 29(4), 473-481.)

In these questions, a statement of assertion followed by a statement of reason is given. Choose the correct answer out of the following choices.

(a) Assertion and reason both are correct statements and reason is correct explanation for assertion.

(b) Assertion and reason both are correct statements but reason is not correct explanation for assertion.

(c) Assertion is correct statement but reason is wrong statement.

(d) Assertion is wrong statement but reason is correct statement.

(i) **Assertion:** Equivalent conductance of an electrolyte solution increases with dilution.

Reason: Degree of ionisation of the electrolyte decreases with dilution.

(ii) **Assertion:** Fused sodium chloride conducts electricity.

Reason: Fused sodium chloride contains sodium and chloride ions.

(iii) **Assertion:** Gaseous hydrogen chloride is a very poor conductor of electricity but a solution of hydrogen chloride gas in water is a good conductor of electricity.

Reason: Molecule of hydrogen chloride remains unionized in water.

(iv) **Assertion:** Electrolytic conduction differs from metallic conduction.

Reason: The resistance of electrolytes decreases with increasing temperature.

OR

Assertion: Conductivity of a strong electrolyte change considerably on dilution.

Reason: Strong electrolyte ionize completely at all dilutions and the number of ions does not increase on dilution.

Ans. (i) (c) Assertion is correct statement but reason is wrong statement.

(ii) (a) Assertion and reason both are correct statements and reason is correct explanation for assertion.

(iii) (c) Assertion is correct statement but reason is wrong statement.

(iv) (b) Assertion and reason both are correct statements but reason is not correct explanation for assertion.

OR

(d) Assertion is wrong statement but reason is correct statement.

Chapter 4. Chemical Kinetics

1. **Read the passage given below and answer the following questions:**

All chemical reactions proceed through one or more transition-state intermediates whose content of free energy is greater than that of either the reactants or the products. For the simple reaction R (reactants) $\rightleftharpoons$ P (products), we can write $R \underset{}{\overset{K^{\pm}}{\rightleftharpoons}} S \overset{v}{\longrightarrow} P$, where S is the reaction intermediate with the highest free energy; $K^{\pm}$ is the equilibrium constant for the reaction $R \rightleftharpoons S$, the conversion of the reactant to the high-energy intermediate S; and v is the rate constant for conversion of S into the product P. The energetic relation between the initial reactants and the products of a reaction can usually be depicted as shown in given figure. The free energy of activation $\Delta G^{\pm}$ is equal to the difference in free energy between the transition-state intermediate S and the reactant R. Because $\Delta G^{\pm}$ generally has a very large positive value, only a small fraction of the reactant molecules will at any one time have acquired this free energy, and the overall rate of the reaction will be limited by the rate of formation of S.

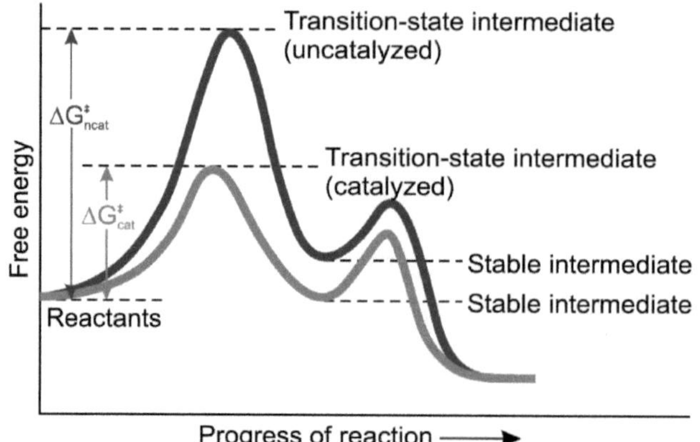

The following questions are multiple choice questions. Choose the most appropriate answer:

(i) A catalyst:

    (a) Accelerates the rate of reaction by bringing down the activation energy.

    (b) Does not participate in reaction mechanism.

    (c) Makes the reaction feasible by making ΔG more negative.

    (d) Makes equilibrium constant more favourable for forward reaction.

(ii) For a chemical reaction $X \rightarrow Y$, it is found that the rate of reaction doubles when the concentration of A is increased four times. Predict the order of the reaction -

    (a) Two   (b) One   (c) Half   (d) Zero

(iii) Which one of the following given graphs depicts an endothermic reaction with high activation energy for the forward reaction—

(a)

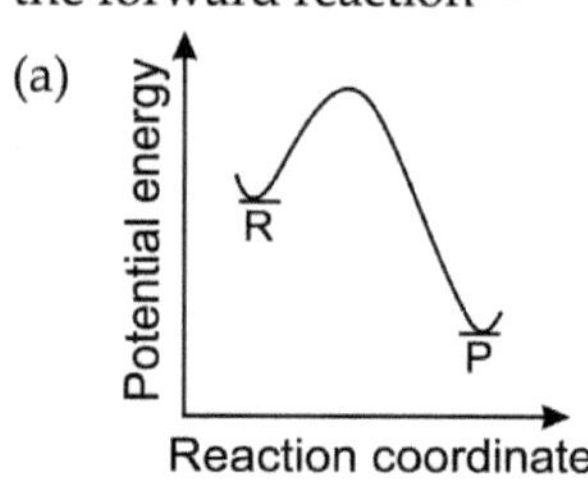

(c)

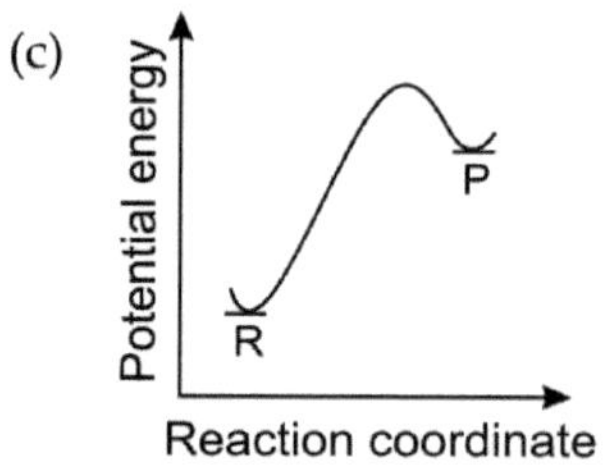

(b)

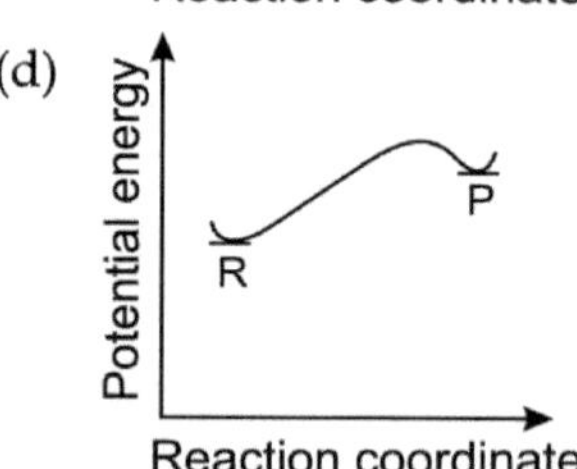

(d)

(iv) In the hydrolysis of an organic chloride in presence of large excess of water, $RCl + H_2O \rightarrow ROH + HCl$

    (a) Molecularity and order of reaction both are 2.

    (b) Molecularity is 2 but order of reaction is 1.

    (c) Molecularity is 1 but order of reaction is 2.

    (d) Molecularity is 1 and order of reaction is also 1.

OR

Which of these changes with time for a first-order reaction?

    A. Rate of reaction; B. Rate constant; C. Half-life

    (a) A only   (c) A and B only

    (b) C only   (d) B and C only

Ans. (i) (a) Accelerates the rate of reaction by bringing down the activation energy.

     (ii) (c) Half

(iii) (c)

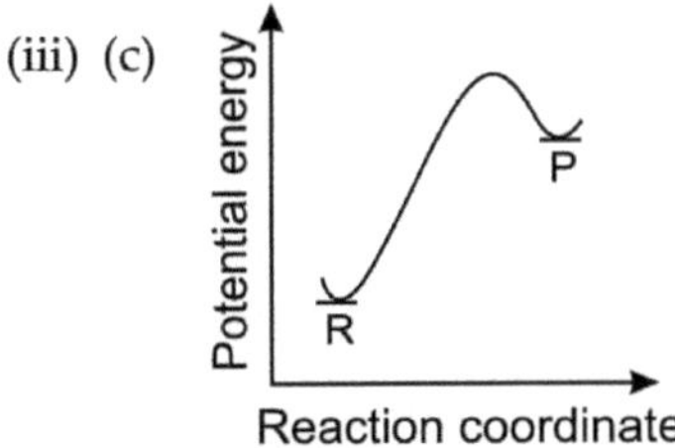

(iv) (b) Molecularity is 2 but order of reaction is 1

OR

(a) A only

2. **Read the passage given below and answer the following questions.**

Zero-order systems provide an interesting opportunity for students to think about the underlying mechanism behind the physical phenomena being modelled. The work reported here is part of a larger study that seeks to characterise how students integrate chemistry and mathematics in the context of chemical kinetics. Thirty-six general chemistry students, five physical chemistry students, and three chemical engineering students were asked to think aloud as they responded to an interview prompt about the half-life of a catalyst-driven zero-order reaction. Our findings revealed that students often described zero-order in mathematical terms (*i.e.,* the zero-order rate law, integrated rate law, and graphical representation), but lacked a clear understanding of the particulate nature of zero-order systems.

(Reference: Bain, K., Rodriguez, J. G., Towns, M. H. (2018). Zero-Order Chemical Kinetics as a Context to Investigate Student Understanding of Catalysts and Half-Life. Journal of Chemical Education, 95 (5), 716-725).

In these questions, a statement of assertion followed by a statement of reason is given. Choose the correct answer out of the following choices.

(a) Assertion and reason both are correct statements and reason is correct explanation for assertion.

(b) Assertion and reason both are correct statements but reason is not correct explanation for assertion.

(c) Assertion is correct statement but reason is wrong statement.

(d) Assertion is wrong statement but reason is correct statement.

(i) **Assertion:** The decomposition of gaseous ammonia on a hot platinum surface is a zero-order reaction at high pressure.

   Reason: Platinum metal acts as a catalyst and at high pressure the metal surface gets saturated with ammonia gas and hence concentration of ammonia is not a limiting factor in the reaction.

(ii) **Assertion:** Zero order reaction means that the rate of reaction is proportional to zero power of the reaction concentration.

   Reason: There are no reactants in zero order reaction.

(iii) **Assertion:** Rate constant of a zero-order reaction can be calculated from concentration Vs time graph.

   Reason: In case of zero order reaction, slope of the concentration Vs time graph is equal to the reaction constant.

(iv) **Assertion:** Activated complex is high in energy.

   Reason: Activation energy can be found out by calculating energy difference between product and reactant energies.

OR

   Assertion: A catalyst can be recovered from the reaction mixture and used again in the next reaction.

   Reason: A catalyst is a substance which increases the rate of a reaction without itself undergoing any permanent change.

Ans. (i) (a) Assertion and reason both are correct statements and reason is correct explanation for assertion.

   (ii) (c) Assertion is correct statement but reason is wrong statement.

   Explanation: Zero order reaction means that the rate of reaction is proportional to zero power of the reaction concentration because usually the reactant is in abundance and its concentration does not limit the reaction.

   (iii) (b) Assertion and reason both are correct statements but reason is not correct explanation for assertion.

   Explanation: In case of zero order reaction, slope of the concentration Vs time graph is equal to negative of the reaction constant.

(iv) (c)   Assertion is correct statement but reason is wrong statement.

Explanation: Activation energy can be found out by calculating energy difference between energies of reactant and the activated complex.

OR

(a)   Assertion and reason both are correct statements and reason is correct explanation for assertion.

Chapter 5. Surface Chemistry

1. **Read the passage given below and answer the following questions:**

Colloidal particles carry charges on their surface, which lead to the stabilisation of the suspension. Hence in coagulation process, the suspended particles are removed by combining small particles into large particles. By adding some chemicals, the surface property of such colloidal particles can be changed or dissolved material can be precipitated so as to facilitate the separation of solids by gravity or filtration. There are certain types of mechanisms to destabilize natural water in coagulation which are double layer compression, adsorption and charge neutralisation, entrapment of particles in precipitate and absorption, sweep coagulation and bridging between particles.

The sufficient amount of counter ions presents on the diffuse layer in a colloidal dispersion, resulting in an electrical double layer. It is used to balance the electrical charge on the particle. During the compression of electrical double layer of water suspension, colloidal particles are more bonded together due to the effect of van der Waals attraction forces and Brownian motion. Besides, colloidal particles can be destabilised via adsorption and charge neutralisation mechanism using hydrolysed metal salt or cationic polymers as positively charged coagulants.

(Reference: Zahrim, A.Y., Azreen, Jie, S.S., Yoiying, C. Felijia, J.Hasmilah, H., Gloriana, C., & Khairunis, I. "Nanoparticles Enhanced Coagulation of Biologically Digested Leachate". In Nanotechnology in Water and Wastewater Treatment: Theory and Applications, Elsevier, 2019, 205-241)

The following questions are multiple choice questions. Choose the most appropriate answer:

(i)   Which of the following colloids are solvent hating?

(a)   Lyophilic

(b)   Lyophobic

(c)   Hydrophilic

(d)   None of these

(ii)   The movement of colloidal particles towards the oppositely charged electrodes on passing electric current is known as:

(a)   Tyndall effect

(b)   Cataphoresis

(c)   Brownian movement

(d)   None of these

(iii) If the dispersed phase is a liquid and the dispersion medium is solid, the colloid is known as:

(a)   Foam   (b)   Sol   (c)   Emulsion   (d)   Gel

(iv) Lyophillic colloids are stable due to:

(a)   Charge on the particles.

(b)   Large size of the particles.

(c)   Small size of the particles.

(d)   Layer of dispersion of medium on the particles.

OR

An emulsifier is a substance which:

(a)   Stabilises the emulsion.

(b)   Homogenises the emulsion.

(c)   Coagulates the emulsion.

(d)   Accelerates the dispersion of liquid in liquid.

Ans. (i)   (b)   Lyophobic

(ii) (b)   Cataphoresis

(iii) (d)   Gel

(iv) (d)   Layer of dispersion of medium on the particles.

OR

(a)   Stabilises the emulsion.

2. **Read the passage given below and answer the following questions:**

   The present investigate was intended for adsorption of heavy metals *i.e.* Pb, Cu, Cr, Zn, Ni and Cd onto activated charcoal prepared from neem leaf powder (AC-NLP) using batch and column studies. Batch adsorption was performed using different variables like adsorbent dose, temperature and contact duration. Thermodynamic analysis of batch treatment concluded that adsorption is thermodynamically feasible and endothermic. This adsorption followed the Pseudo second-order kinetic model derived from correlation coefficient values of chemical kinetic studies.

   Though several methods such as adsorption, coagulation, membrane, oxidation, biological, chemical precipitation, flotation, ion exchange, and electrochemical deposition with their merits and demerits, but adsorption process is widely utilized for removal of contaminations including metals from raw water. Activated charcoal is used as an adsorbent due to its remarkably high porosity, enhanced pore size and higher adsorption capacities. However due to high cost, it operation is someway inadequate.

   (Reference: Patel, H. (2020). Batch and continuous fixed bed adsorption of heavy metals removal using activated charcoal from neem (Azadirachta indica) leaf powder. Scientific Reports, 10, 16895.)

   In these questions, a statement of assertion followed by a statement of reason is given. Choose the correct answer out of the following choices.

   (a) Assertion and reason both are correct statements and reason is correct explanation for assertion.

   (b) Assertion and reason both are correct statements but reason is not correct explanation for assertion.

   (c) Assertion is correct statement but reason is wrong statement.

   (d) Assertion is wrong statement but reason is correct statement.

   (i) **Assertion:** Physisorption is a non-specific phenomenon.

   Reason: A given surface of an adsorbent does not show any preference for a particular gas as the van der Waal's forces are universal.

   (ii) **Assertion:** Chemisorption involves a high energy of activation.

   Reason: A physical adsorption may convert into chemisorption upon increasing temperature.

   OR

   Assertion: Enthalpy of physiosorption in usually in the range of 80-240 kJ/mol compared to 20-40 kJ/mol in case of chemisorption.

   Reason: Chemisorption involves formation of either covalent or ionic bonds.

   (iii) **Assertion:** Activated charcoal is used to adsorb various metal catalysts for organic reactions.

   Reason: Activated charcoal does not have adsorption capacities.

   (iv) **Assertion:** Silica and aluminium gels are used to control humidity.

   Reason: Humidity cannot be controlled by using adsorbents.

Ans. (i) (a) Assertion and reason both are correct statements and reason is correct explanation for assertion.

   (ii) (b) Assertion and reason both are correct statements but reason is not correct explanation for assertion.

   OR

   (d) Assertion is wrong statement but reason is correct statement.

   (iii) (c) Assertion is correct statement but reason is wrong statement.

   (iv) (c) Assertion is correct statement but reason is wrong statement.

Chapter 6. General Principles and Processes of Isolation of Elements

1. **Read the passage given below and answer the following questions:**

   The reason for the chemical stability of copper, silver and gold is similar; it is due to the high reduction potential of the ions of these metals. Because these valuable metals have high reduction potentials, they have similar processing. The conventional processing that is presently used to extract metal ion from ore involves toxic and aggressive chemical reagents in water, followed by application of electrical energy to electrodes in aqueous solution of complex copper silver or gold ions, which decomposes the metal ion complexes leading to the deposition of the desired metal. The conventional processing is expensive and environmentally invasive, but is tolerated because of the value of these metals .These metals are often found in the same ore. Typically, gold is the least abundant; silver is more abundant and copper is the most abundant naturally occurring species. The conventional processing is used to produce copper on a large scale, which leads to the accumulation of a substantial amount of toxic materials, which time to time is dumped into the environment (soil and ground water) due to accidents, such as flooding from violent weather. A new approach for extracting copper from copper concentrates (20–30% Cu) is presented here.

(Reference: Elsentriecy, H.H., Jalbout, A.F., Gervasio, D.F. (2015). Clean and efficient extraction of copper ions and deposition as metal. Resource-Efficient Technologies, 1(1), 28-33)

The following questions are multiple choice questions. Choose the most appropriate answer.

(i) Extraction of gold and silver involves leaching the metal with CN ion. The required metal is finally recovered by

   (a) Displacement of metal by some other reactive metal from the complex ion formed.

   (b) Roasting of metal complex.

   (c) Calcination followed by roasting.

   (d) Thermal decomposition of metal complex.

(ii) The copper ore is heated in a reverberatory furnace after mixing with silica. In the furnace, iron oxide 'slags of' and copper is produced in the form of copper matte. Which equation correctly represents formation of slag?

   (a) $Cu_2S + FeS \rightarrow FeSiO_3$ (c) $FeS + SiO_2 \rightarrow FeSSiO_2$

   (b) $FeO + FeS \rightarrow FeSO_3$ (d) $FeO + SiO_2 \rightarrow FeSiO_3$

(iii) The metal commonly used as reducing agent in gold and silver metallurgy is

   (a) Cu   (b) CN   (c) Zn   (d) Mn

(iv) The method used for extraction of copper from its low-grade ore using acid or bacteria is

   (a) Oxidation-Reduction   (c) Zone Refining

   (b) Hydrometallurgy   (d) Liquation

OR

It is difficult to obtain reactive metals by electrolytic reduction of their molten salts because

   (a) reactive metals have large negative values of the electrode potential.

   (b) reactive metals have large positive values of the electrode potential.

   (c) reactive metals do not form molten salts.

   (d) metal ions are discharged at positive electrodes.

Ans. (i) (a) Displacement of metal by some other reactive metal from the complex ion formed.

   (ii) (d) $FeO + SiO_2 \rightarrow FeSiO_3$

   (iii) (c) Zn

   (iv) (b) Hydrometallurgy

OR

(iv) (a) reactive metals have large negative values of the electrode potential.

2. **Read the passage given below and answer the following questions.**

Thus, the extraction of the metals can be meant as a separation of metals from its source, which is usually in the form of the ore. The process of extracting metal from the ore is usually done with some separation techniques, such as pyrometallurgy, hydrometallurgy, and precipitation. The making process of precipitation affects some of the properties of the basic material such as iron oxide phase formed, impurities and agglomeration. Therefore, a lot of research on synthesis of iron oxide to produce its pure mineral. The precipitation technique is the most widespread attention because of its simple, easy and cheap process. In this work, we introduce the co– precipitation method to extract the pure hematite from local iron ore.

$$Fe_2O_3 + 6HCl \rightarrow 2FeCl_3 + 3H_2O \underline{\hspace{2cm}}$$

(Reference: Muhammad, M., Fatmaliana, A., Jalil, Z. (2019). Study of hematite mineral (Fe₂O₃) extracted from natural iron ore prepared by co-precipitation method. IOP Conf. Ser.: Earth Environ. Sci. 348.)

In these questions, a statement of assertion followed by a statement of reason is given. Choose the correct answer out of the following choices.

(a) Assertion and reason both are correct statements and reason is correct explanation for assertion.

(b) Assertion and reason both are correct statements but reason is not correct explanation for assertion.

(c) Assertion is correct statement but reason is wrong statement.

(d) Assertion is wrong statement but reason is correct statement.

(i) **Assertion:** Volatile matter escapes during calcination leaving behind the metal oxide.

Reason: Calcination is a process of converting metal ore into oxide by heating.

(ii) **Assertion:** Burning of coke supplies all the heat required in a blast furnace.

Reason: In a blast furnace reduction of iron oxides takes place at different ranges.

(iii) **Assertion:** Cast iron is hard and brittle.

Reason: Cast iron is the purest form of iron.

(iv) **Assertion:** At temperatures above 1073 K (approx.), coke will reduce FeO and will itself be oxidised to CO.

Reason: At temperatures above 1073 K, the C, CO line comes below the Fe, FeO line in Ellingham Diagram.

OR

Assertion: Ellingham Diagram cannot indicate whether a reaction is possible or not.

Reason: Ellingham Diagram is based on thermodynamic approach.

Ans. (i) (a) Assertion and reason both are correct statements and reason is correct explanation for assertion.

(ii) (b) Assertion and reason both are correct statements but reason is not correct explanation for assertion.

Explanation: Burning of coke supplies all the heat required in a blast furnace as coke burns in lower portion of furnace to give up to 2200 K temperature.

(iii) (c) Assertion is correct statement but reason is wrong statement.

Explanation: The iron obtained from blast furnace with about 3% carbon content is known as cast iron. It is impure, hard, and brittle.

(iv) (a) Assertion and reason both are correct statements and reason is correct explanation for assertion.

OR

(d) Assertion is wrong statement but reason is correct statement.

Explanation: Ellingham Diagram indicates whether a reaction is possible or not by indicating the tendency of reduction with a reducing agent. This is so because Ellingham Diagram is based on thermodynamic approach.

Chapter 7. *p*-Block Elements

1. **Read the passage given below and answer the following questions:**

Chemistry of xenon represents the field with the largest number of synthesized Noble gas (Ng) compounds. Xenon(II) fluoride is the only Ng compound that is commercially available and has a wider practical application both in the laboratory use and in the industry. Its main use is in its ability of fluorination of various organic compounds and as an etching reagent for surfaces of various metals, oxides, nitrides, etc. Since the first reported case of a compound with a XeF_2 ligand coordinated to a metal center, i.e., $[Ag(XeF_2)_2](AsF_6)$, a large number of other examples have been synthesized. A variety of compounds exist, where different numbers of XeF_2 molecules are bound to various metal centers yielding $[M(XeF_2)x]\ n^+$ cationic part. The oxidation states of the metals are M(I), M(II), or M(III). The most important aspects that influence the formation of XeF_2 coordination compounds are charge and the size of the cation, the type of the anion that compensates the positive charge of the cationic part, solubility of the salt, and the concentration of the XeF_2 ligand.

(Reference: Mazej, Z. (2020). Noble-Gas Chemistry More than Half a Century after the First Report of the Noble-Gas Compound. Molecules, 25, 3014.)

The following questions are multiple choice questions. Choose the most appropriate answer:

(i) During preparation of XeF_4 from Xenon and Fluorine, these two elements are reacted in which of the following given ratios?

    (a) Xenon (1) Fluorine (Excess)　　(c) Xenon (1) Fluorine (20)

    (b) Xenon (1) Fluorine (5)　　(d) Xenon (1) Fluorine (4)

(ii) XeF_2 is hydrolysed to give:

    (a) Xe and O_2　　(c) Xe, HF and O_2

    (b) Xe, F_2 and O_2　　(d) Xe and F_2

(iii) XeF_2 and XeF_4 have

    (a) Linear and square planar structures respectively.

    (b) Square planar and linear structures respectively.

    (c)   Square planar structure.

    (d)   Linear structure.

(iv) Complete the following reaction –

    $XeF_6 + KF \rightarrow$

    (a) $K + XeF_7$ (c) $KXeF_6$

    (b) $[XeF_3]^+ [KF_6]^-$ (d) $K^+[XeF_7]^-$

OR

Helium is used for filling meteorological balloons and:

    (a)   In gas cooled-nuclear reactor   (c)   Both (a) and (b)

    (b)   As a cryogenic agent   (d)   None of these

Ans. (i)   (b)   Xenon (1) Fluorine (5)

    (ii) (c) Xe, HF and O_2

    (iii) (a)   Linear and square planar structures respectively:

    (iv) (d) $K^+[XeF_7]^-$

OR

    (c)   Both (a) and (b)

2. **Read the passage given below and answer the following questions:**

Current investigations, for example, on antimony(III) and arsenic(III) halogen compounds, have indicated quite similar structural principles as in Te(IV) analogues. In the series of the binary halides of selenium and tellurium, the crystal structure determinations of tellurium tetrafluoride and of tellurium tetrachloride on twinned crystals were the key to understanding the various and partly contradictory spectroscopic and other macroscopic properties, as well as the synthetic potential of the compounds. The chapter discusses the characteristic structural and bonding features of the halogen compounds of the chalcogen(IV) systems, in which the role of the inert pair determines much of the stereochemistry and reactive properties of the whole class of compounds. SCl_4, as the only stable tetrahalide of sulfur besides SF_4, is known to be easily prepared at temperatures below –34°C from the elements or from the reversible reaction of equimolar amounts of SC_{12} and chlorine.

(Reference: Krebs, B., & Ahlers, F. (1990). Developments in chalcogen-halide chemistry. Advances in Inorganic Chemistry, 35, 235-317.)

In these questions, a statement of assertion followed by a statement of reason is given. Choose the correct answer out of the following choices.

(a) Assertion and reason both are correct statements and reason is correct explanation for assertion.

(b) Assertion and reason both are correct statements but reason is not correct explanation for assertion.

(c) Assertion is correct statement but reason is wrong statement.

(d) Assertion is wrong statement but reason is correct statement.

(i)   **Assertion:** S shows paramagnetic nature, when present in vapour state.

    Reason: S exists as S_2 in vapour state.

(ii) **Assertion:** Ozone layer in the upper region of atmosphere protects earth from UV radiations of sun.

    Reason: Ozone is a powerful oxidising agent as compared to oxygen.

(iii) **Assertion:** Ozone layer serves as the protective layer from UV radiations.

    Reason: Ozone is more oxidizing in nature than oxygen.

(iv) **Assertion:** Acidic character of group 16 hydrides increases from H_2O to H_2Te.

    Reason: Thermal stability of hydrides increases down the group.

OR

Assertion: Super oxides of alkali metals are paramagnetic.

Reason: Superoxide contain the ion of O^{2-} which has one unpaired electron.

Ans. (i)   (b)   Assertion and reason both are correct statements but reason is not correct explanation for assertion.

    (ii) (b)   Assertion and reason both are correct statements but reason is not correct explanation for assertion.

    (iii) (a)   Assertion and reason both are correct statements and reason is correct explanation for assertion.

    (iv) (d)   Assertion is wrong statement but reason is correct statement.

OR

    (a)   Assertion and reason both are correct statements and reason is correct explanation for assertion.

Chapter 8. *d*-and *f*-Block Elements

1. **Read the passage given below and answer the following questions.**

   Incorporation of metallic or intermetallic phases into the SiOC matrix is greatly desired in the field of energy and catalysis especially for transition metals. With partially filled *d* orbitals, transition metal oxides can be used as catalyst support(s) in harsh environments where traditional oxide-based ceramics fail due to their physical and chemical stabilities. CeO_2/SiOC nanocomposites were studied as a thermocatalyst support for CO_2 thermochemical decomposition. Ni-containing porous SiOC ceramics exhibited the highest conversion efficiency from CO_2 to CH_4 with selectivity up to ~77% and good stability. Moreover, transition metals act more than a catalysis support .Ni has shown to induce the formation of β-SiC, cristobalite silica, and graphitic carbon. Active metal nanoparticles (M = Fe, Co, Pt, Cu, Ag, and Au) promoted the growth of multiwalled carbon nanotubes and SiC nanowires. New combinations of transition metals and PDCs should be investigated in order to enable advancement in catalytic, magnetic, hydrogen storage, and battery applications.

   (References: Yang, N., Lu, K. (2021). Effects of transition metals on the evolution of polymer-derived SiOC ceramics. Carbon. 171, 88-95).

   The following questions are multiple choice questions. Choose the most appropriate answer.

   (i)   In case of the transition elements:

       (a)   group similarities are more than horizontal similarities among the metals.

       (b)   no similarity is found horizontally.

       (c)   horizontal similarities are more than group similarities among the metals.

       (d)   no similarity is found down the group.

   (ii) Most of the transition metals are hard and less volatile, *except*:

       (a)   Mercury   (c)   Zinc and Cadmium

       (b)   Zinc   (d)   Mercury, Zinc and Cadmium

   (iii) Common oxidation states for Nickel and Zinc are:

       (a)   +2 and +2   (b)   +3 and +2   (c)   +4 and +2   (d)   +2 and +4

   (iv) Out of Mo (VI) and Cr (VI), group 6 transition metals, which one is more stable?

       (a)   Mo (VI)   (c)   both are equally stable

       (b)   Cr (VI)   (d)   both are unstable

   OR

   Catalytic activity of transition metals and their complexes can be attributed to:

       (a)   ability to adopt multiple oxidation states.   (c)   ability to form alloys.

       (b)   ability to show various colours.   (d)   ability to react rapidly.

   Ans. (i)   (c)   horizontal similarities are more than group similarities among the metals.

       (ii) (d)   Mercury, Zinc and Cadmium

       (iii) (a)   +2 and +2

       (iv) (b)   Cr (VI)

   OR

       (a)   ability to adopt multiple oxidation states.

2. **Read the passage given below and answer the following questions:**

   The d-block metals are central within the periodic table and are at the core of numerous branches of inorganic chemistry, including materials chemistry, applied biological and analytical sciences, and catalysis. The term 'transition metal' is still much used but this strictly excludes the group 10 metals (Zn, Cd, and Hg) since IUPAC defines a transition metal as an 'element whose atom has an incomplete *d* sub-shell, or which can give rise to cations with an incomplete *d* sub-shell'. The traditional picture of the d-block is often triads or three rows of metallic elements. The fourth row (Ac, Rf–Cn) is often ignored by those of us who teach inorganic chemistry courses, largely because of the paucity of data and chemistry of the elements from rutherfordium (Rf, Z = 104) onwards. And, of course, categorization of group 3 (Sc, Y, La and Ac) is ambiguous because of the insertion of the f-block elements after lanthanum and actinium. The latter metals are therefore typically grouped with the f-block, rather than the d-block elements. Definitions aside, there is no question that the d-block elements at the centre of the periodic table play a central role in the field of inorganic chemistry.

(Reference: Housecroft, C.E., Thomas, C.M. & Mi Hee, L. (2019). The central role of the d-block metals in the periodic table. Dalton Trans., 48, 9405-9407.).

In these questions, a statement of assertion followed by a statement of reason is given. Choose the correct answer out of the following choices.

(a) Assertion and reason both are correct statements and reason is correct explanation for assertion.

(b) Assertion and reason both are correct statements but reason is not correct explanation for assertion.

(c) Assertion is correct statement but reason is wrong statement.

(d) Assertion is wrong statement but reason is correct statement.

(i) **Assertion:** The atomic radii of second and third row transition elements is almost same.

Reason: The elements of second and third row transition elements resemble much.

(ii) **Assertion:** Transition metals have high melting points compared to alkali or alkaline earth metals.

Reason: Greater number of electrons are involved in interatomic metallic bonding from (n-1)d orbitals in addition to ns electrons.

(iii) **Assertion:** Transition metals and many of their compounds show paramagnetic behaviour.

Reason: More is the number of unpaired electrons; more is the paramagnetic character and more is the magnetic moment.

OR

Assertion: Transition metals are good catalysts.

Reason: Transition metals have fixed oxidation states.

(iv) **Assertion:** Transition metals, ions or their aqueous solutions are usually coloured.

Reason: Unpaired electrons in *d*-orbitals undergo transition within the *d*-sub-shell (*d-d* transition) for which small amount of energy is required from the visible region. Thus, one colour is absorbed and the complementary colour is emitted

Ans. (i) (b) Assertion and reason both are correct statements but reason is not correct explanation for assertion.

(ii) (a) Assertion and reason both are correct statements and reason is correct explanation for assertion.

(iii) (b) Assertion and reason both are correct statements but reason is not correct explanation for assertion.

OR

(c) Assertion is correct statement but reason is wrong statement.

(iv) (a) Assertion and reason both are correct statements and reason is correct explanation for assertion.

Chapter 9. Coordination Compounds

1. **Read the passage given below and answer the following questions.**

Transition-metal–carbonyl complexes are common organometallic reagents that feature metal–CO bonds. These complexes have proven to be powerful catalysts for various applications. By contrast, silicon–carbonyl complexes, organosilicon reagents poised to be eco-friendly alternatives for transition-metal carbonyls, have remained largely elusive. They have mostly been explored theoretically and/or through low-temperature matrix isolation studies, but their instability had typically precluded isolation under ambient conditions. Here we present the synthesis, isolation and full characterisation of stable silyl-substituted silicon–carbonyl complexes, along with bonding analysis. Initial reactivity investigations showed examples of CO liberation, which could be induced either thermally or photochemically, as well as substitution and functionalisation of the CO moiety. Importantly, the complexes exhibit strong Si–CO bonding, with CO→Si σ-donation and Si→CO π-backbonding, which is reminiscent of transition-metal carbonyls. This similarity between the abundant semi-metal silicon and rare transition metals may provide new opportunities for the development of silicon-based catalysis.

(References: Reiter, D., Holzner, R., Porzelt, A., Frisch, P., Inoue, S. (2020). Silylated silicon–carbonyl complexes as mimics of ubiquitous transition-metal carbonyls. Nat. Chem. 12, 1131–1135).

The following questions are multiple choice questions. Choose the most appropriate answer.

(i) Coordination compounds containing only carbonyl group as ligands are known as

(a) heteroleptic carbonyls

(b) homoleptic carbonyls

(c) tetra carbonyls

(d) homomeric carbonyls

(ii) Shape of Tetracarbonylnickel (0) is

    (a) square planar   (c) tetrahedral

    (b) trigonal pyramidal   (d) trigonal bipyramidal

(iii) Synergic bonding interaction in carbonyl complexes occurs due to formation of:

    (a) σ bond between metal and carbonyl carbon

    (b) π bond between metal and carbonyl carbon

    (c) both σ and π bond between metal and carbonyl carbon

    (d) a double bond

(iv) The colour in the coordination compound is better explained by

    (a) secondary valence theory   (c) crystal field theory

    (b) coordination theory   (d) valence bond theory

OR

In the complexes $[Fe(C_2O_4)_3]^{3-}$ and $[Co(en)_3]^{3+}$ the coordination numbers of Fe and Co are respectively

    (a) 3 and 6   (c) 3 and 3

    (b) 6 and 3   (d) 6 and 6

Ans. (i)   (b)   homoleptic carbonyls

    (ii)   (c)   tetrahedral

    (iii) (c)   both σ and π bond between metal and carbonyl carbon

    (iv) (c)   crystal field theory

OR

    (d) 6 and 6

2. **Read the passage given below and answer the following questions:**

Four new mononuclear complexes, [MnIV(L1)2] (1), [CoII(HL1)2] (2), [NiII(HL1)2] (3), and [NiII(HL2)2] (4), with ligands H2L1 (2-hydroxyethylimino)methylnaphthol) and H2L2 (3-hydroxy propylimino) methylnaphthol) have been synthesized, characterized, and their catecholase activities have been studied. Single-crystal X-ray diffraction study shows that 1 crystallizes in P43212 space group and adopts an octahedral geometry in meridional fashion, whereas 4 with a square planar geometry crystallises in P21/n space group. The catecholase activity has been investigated in acetonitrile by UV-Vis spectrophotometric technique. The kinetic study revealed that 1 has a moderate catecholase activity (k cat = $812\ h^{-1}$), whereas 2–4 are inactive. Electronic structure of 1 and 4 has been established by theoretical calculation. Structures of both complexes have been optimized by DFT. Experimental electronic spectra of the complexes have been corroborated by TD-DFT analysis.

(Reference: Sagar, S., Parween, A., Mandal, T.K., Lewis, W. & Naskar, S. (2020). Mn(IV), Co(II) and Ni(II) complexes of the Schiff bases of 2-hydroxy-naphthaldehyde with amino alcohols: synthesis, characterisation and electrochemical study; DFT study and Catecholase activity of Mn(IV) complex. Journal of Coordination Chemistry, 2020, published online https:// doi.org/10.1080/00958972.2020.1832657.)

In these questions, a statement of assertion followed by a statement of reason is given. Choose the correct answer out of the following choices.

(a) Assertion and reason both are correct statements and reason is correct explanation for assertion.

(b) Assertion and reason both are correct statements but reason is not correct explanation for assertion.

(c) Assertion is correct statement but reason is wrong statement.

(d) Assertion is wrong statement but reason is correct statement.

(i) **Assertion:** Toxic metal ions are removed by chelating ligands.

    Reason: Chelated complexes are less stable.

(ii) **Assertion:** Linkage isomerism arises in coordination compounds containing ambidentate ligands.

    Reason: Ambidentate ligands has two different donor atoms.

(iii) **Assertion:** $[Cr(H_2O)_6]Cl_2$ and $[Fe(H_2O)_5]Cl_2$ are reducing in nature.

    Reason: Unpaired electrons are present in their d-orbitals.

OR

Assertion: $[NiCl_4]^{2-}$ is paramagnetic while $[Ni(CO)_4]$ is diamagnetic though both are tetrahedral.

Reason: In $[Ni(CO)_4]$ no unpaired electron is present and hence it is diamagnetic. In $[NiCl_4]^{2-}$, there are two unpaired electrons and is paramagnetic.

(iv) **Assertion:** The primary valency of metal ion is always satisfied by a negative ion according to Werner's theory.

Reason: Primary valencies are non-ionisable.

Ans. (i) (c) Assertion is correct statement but reason is wrong statement.

(ii) (a) Assertion and reason both are correct statements and reason is correct explanation for assertion.

(iii) (b) Assertion and reason both are correct statements but reason is not correct explanation for assertion.

OR

(a) Assertion and reason both are correct statements and reason is correct explanation for assertion.

(iv) (c) Assertion is correct statement but reason is wrong statement.

Chapter 10. Haloalkanes and Haloarenes

1. **Read the passage given below and answer the following questions:**

Experimental kinetic data on reactions of the chlorine atom with halogenated derivatives of methane and ethane (37 reactions) have been analysed by the intersecting-parabolas method. The following five factors have an effect on the activation energy of these reactions: the enthalpy of reaction, triplet repulsion, the electronegativities of the reaction center atoms, the dipole–dipole and multidipole interactions between the reaction center and polar groups, and the effect of π electrons in the vicinity of the reaction center. The increments characterising the contribution from each factor to the activation energy of the reaction have been calculated. The contribution from the polar interaction, $\Delta E\mu$, to the activation energy depends on the dipole moment of the polar group and obeys the following empirical equation: $\ln (\Delta E\mu/\Sigma\mu) = -0.74 + 0.87 (\Delta E\mu/\Sigma\mu) - 0.084 (\Delta E\mu/\Sigma\mu)^2$.

(Reference: Denisov, E.T., Denisova, T.G. (2017). Reactivity of haloalkanes in their reactions with the chlorine atom. Kinetics and Catalysis, 58, 219–226.)

The following questions are multiple choice questions. Choose the most appropriate answer:

(i) Nucleophilic reactions are the most useful classes of organic reactions of alkyl halides in which halogens are bonded to __________ hybridised carbon.

(a) sp^2 (b) sp^3 (c) sp   (d) pp

(ii) The spatial arrangement of four groups (valences) around a central carbon atom is tetrahedral and if all the substituents attached to that carbon are different, and then such a carbon is called __________ .

(a) Achiral   (b) Chiral   (c) Asymmetric   (d) Symmetric

(iii) In alkyl halides, due to greater polarity as well as higher molecular mass, as compared to the parent hydrocarbon, the intermolecular __________ and __________ of attraction are stronger in the halogen derivatives.

(a) Dipole-dipole and van der Waals forces   (c) Van der Waals and hydrogen bond forces

(b) Hydrogen bond and dipole-dipole forces   (d) Dipole-dipole and London forces

(iv) Alkyl halides are prepared from alcohols, which are easily accessible. The hydroxyl group of an alcohol is replaced by halogen on reactions with certain compounds. Which one of the below compounds is inappropriate as a reagent?

(a) Concentrated halogen acid   (c) Thionyl chloride

(b) Sodium dihalide   (d) Phosphorus halides

OR

Which of the following is not an Electrophilic substitution reaction of haloarenes?

(a) Sulphonation   (c) Halogenation

(b) Nitration   (d) Wurtz-Fittig reaction

Ans. (i) (b) sp^3

(ii) (b) Chiral

(iii) (a) Dipole-dipole and van der Waals forces

(iv) (b) Sodium dihalide

OR

(d) Wurtz-Fittig reaction

2. **Read the passage given below and answer the following questions:**

Roughly 120 years ago, Grignard invented his eponymous reaction that converts alkyl halides into nucleophilic organomagnesium reagents that engage electrophilic C=O bonds.1 This reaction forms one of the foundational reactions of organic synthesis and although the precise mechanism of carbonyl addition is not fully understood, it is generally regarded (and taught to undergraduates) as a two-electron (anionic) process. Grignard reagents and related species are routinely used to generate some of the most useful functional groups such as ketones (via addition to activated ester or amide derivatives), alcohols (via addition to aldehydes), and amines (via addition to imines) as depicted in the given Figure 1.

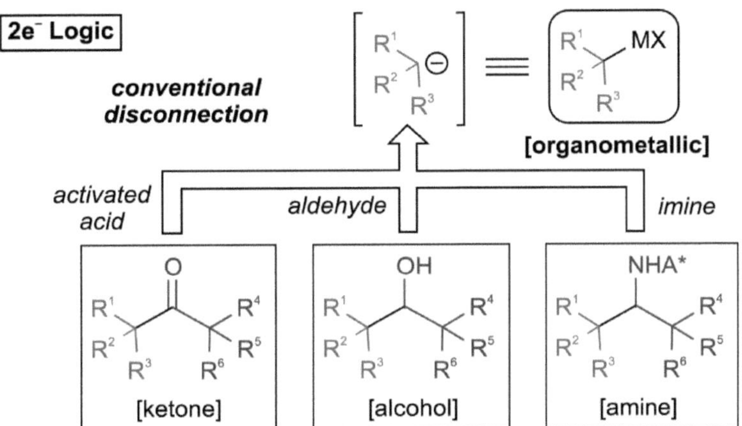

(Reference: Ni, S., Padial, N. M., Kingston, C., Vantourout, J. C., Schmitt, D. C., Edwards, J. T., Kruszyk, M. M., Merchant, R. R., Mykhailiuk, P. K., Sanchez, B. B., Yang, S., Perry, M. A., Gallego, G. M., Mousseau, J. J., Collins, M. R., Cherney, R. J., Lebed, P. S., Chen, J. S., Qin, T., & Baran, P. S. (2019). A Radical Approach to Anionic Chemistry: Synthesis of Ketones, Alcohols, and Amines. Journal of the American Chemical Society, 141(16), 6726–6739.)

In these questions, a statement of assertion followed by a statement of reason is given. Choose the correct answer out of the following choices.

(a) Assertion and reason both are correct statements and reason is correct explanation for assertion.

(b) Assertion and reason both are correct statements but reason is not correct explanation for assertion.

(c) Assertion is correct statement but reason is wrong statement.

(d) Assertion is wrong statement but reason is correct statement.

(i) **Assertion:** Hydrogen iodide readily reacts with alkenes to form alkyl halides.

   Reason: Aqueous hydrohalogen acids are used to prepare alkyl halides from alkenes.

(ii) **Assertion:** $CHCl_3$ is stored in dark bottles

   Reason: $CHCl_3$ is oxidised in dark

(iii) **Assertion:** CCl_4 is a fire extinguisher.

   Reason: CCl_4 is insoluble in water.

(iv) **Assertion:** $CH_2 = CH—CH_2— X$ is an example of allyl halides.

   Reason: These are the compounds in which the halogen atom is bonded to a sp2 hybridised carbon atom.

OR

Assertion: Optically active 2-iodobutane on treatment with NaI in acetone undergoes racemisation.

Reason: Repeated Walden inversions on the reactant and its product eventually gives a racemic mixture.

Ans. (i) **(b)** Assertion and reason both are correct statements but reason is not correct explanation for assertion.

(ii) **(a)** Assertion and reason both are correct statements and reason is correct explanation for assertion.

(iii) **(b)** Assertion and reason both are correct statements but reason is not correct explanation for assertion.

(iv) **(d)** Assertion is wrong statement but reason is correct statement.

OR

(b) Assertion and reason both are correct statements but reason is not correct explanation for assertion.

Chapter 11. Alcohols, Phenols and Ethers

1. **Read the passage given below and answer the following questions:**

   An efficient, aerobic catalytic system for the transformation of alcohols into carbonyl compounds under mild conditions, copper-based catalyst has been discovered. This copper-based catalytic system utilises oxygen or air as the ultimate, stoichiometric oxidant, producing water as the only by product.

$$R_2\underset{H_1}{\overset{R_1}{\diagup}}OH \xrightarrow[\substack{5\%DBADH_2:O_2 \\ Toluene:\ 70°to\ 90°C}]{\substack{5\%CuCl:5\%\ Phen \\ 2\ equiv,\ K_2CO_3;}} \underset{R_2\ 2}{\overset{R_1}{\diagup}}=O$$

   A wide range of primary, secondary, allylic, and benzylic alcohols can be smoothly oxidised to the corresponding aldehydes or ketones in good to excellent yields. Air can be conveniently used instead of oxygen without affecting the efficiency of the process. However, the use air requires slightly longer reaction times.

   This process is not only economically viable and applicable to large-scale reactions, but it is also environmentally friendly.

   (Reference:Ohkuma, T., Ooka, H., Ikariya, T., & Noyori, R. (1995). Preferential hydrogenation of aldehydes and ketones. Journal of the American Chemical Society, 117(41), 10417-10418.)

   The following questions are multiple choice questions. Choose the most appropriate answer:

   (i) The copper based catalyst mention in the study above can be used to convert:

      (a) propanol to propanonic acid   (c) propanone to propan-2-ol

      (b) propanone to propanoic acid   (d) propan-2-ol to propanone

   (ii) The carbonyl compound formed when ethanol gets oxidised using this copper-based catalyst can also be obtained by ozonolysis of:

      (a) But-l-ene   (c) Ethene

      (b) But-2-ene   (d) Pent-l-ene

   OR

   Which of the following is a secondary allylic alcohol?

      (a) But-3-en-2-ol   (c) Prop-2-enol

      (b) But-2-en-2-ol   (d) Butan-2-ol

   (iii) Benzyl alcohol on treatment with this copper-based catalyst gives a compound 'A' which on reaction with KOH gives compounds 'B' and 'C'. Compound 'B' on oxidation with $KMnO_4$-KOH gives compound 'C'. Compounds 'A', 'B' and 'C' respectively are:

      (a) Benzaldehyde, Benzyl alcohol, potassium salt of Benzoic acid

      (b) Benzaldehyde, potassium salt of Benzoic acid, Benzyl alcohol

      (c) Benzaldehyde, Benzoic acid, Benzyl alcohol

      (d) Benzoic acid, Benzyl alcohol, Benzaldehyde

   (iv) An organic compound 'X' with molecular formula C_3H_8O on reaction with this copper based catalyst gives compound 'Y' which reduces Tollen's reagent. 'X' on reaction with sodium metal gives 'Z'. What is the product of reaction of 'Z' with 2-chloro-2-methylpropane?

      (a) $CH_3CH_2CH_2OC(CH_3)_3$ (c) $CH_2 = C(CH_3)_2$

      (b) $CH_3CH_2OC(CH_3)_3$ (d) $CH_3CH_2CH = C(CH_3)_2$

Ans. (i) (d) Propan-2-ol to propanone

    (ii) (b) But-2-ene

OR

    (a) But-3-en-2-ol

    (iii) (b) Benzaldehyde, potassium salt of Benzoic acid, Benzyl alcohol

    (iv) (c) $CH_2 = C(CH_3)_2$

2. **Read the passage given below and answer the following questions:**

   In 2005, the ACS Green Chemistry Institute (GCI) and the global pharmaceutical corporations developed the ACS GCI Pharmaceutical Roundtable to encourage the development of green chemistry and green engineering in the pharmaceutical industry. The Roundtable has established a list of key research areas including the direct nucleophilic reactions of alcohols. The substitution of activated alcohols is a frequently used approach for the preparation of active pharmaceutical ingredients. Alcohols are transformed into the reactive halides or sulfonate esters, thereby allowing their reaction with nucleophiles. Although the direct nucleophilic substitution of an alcohol should be an attractive process, as one of the byproducts from the reaction yields water, hydroxide is a poor leaving group that hinders the reaction. Recently, the direct substitution of allylic, benzylic, and tertiary alcohols has been achieved through an SN1 reaction with catalytic amounts of Brönsted or Lewis acids. In this review, the approaches leading to a greener process are examined in detail, and the advances achieved to date in this important transformation are presented.

(Reference: Emer, E. J., Sinisi, R., Capdevila, M.G., Petruzziello, G., Vincentiis, F.D., Cozzi, P.G. (2011). Direct Nucleophilic SN1-Type Reactions of Alcohols. European Journal of Organic Chemistry, 2011(4), 647-666.)

In these questions, a statement of assertion followed by a statement of reason is given. Choose the correct answer out of the following choices.

(a) Assertion and reason both are correct statements and reason is correct explanation for assertion.

(b) Assertion and reason both are correct statements but reason is not correct explanation for assertion.

(c) Assertion is correct statement but reason is wrong statement.

(d) Assertion is wrong statement but reason is correct statement.

(i) **Assertion:** Alcohols are soluble in water.

   Reason: Alcohol molecules can form hydrogen bonds with water molecules.

(ii) **Assertion:** Presence of –OH group deactivates the aromatic ring towards electrophilic aromatic substitution.

   Reason: The –OH group creates a resonance effect in aromatic ring.

(iii) **Assertion:** Aliphatic alcohols can be converted into alkyl bromides using phosphorus tribromide.

   Reason: The –OH group of an aliphatic alcohol can undergo direct SN1 reaction under acidic conditions.

(iv) **Assertion:** Alkenes can be obtained by treating aliphatic alcohols with conc. H_2SO_4.

   Reason: Alcohols undergo dehydration upon treatment with basic reagents.

OR

   Assertion: The C–O–H bond angle in aliphatic alcohols is slightly less than the tetrahedral angle.

   Reason: The unshared pair of electrons on oxygen atom repel each other.

Ans. (i) (a) Assertion and reason both are correct statements and reason is correct explanation for assertion.

   (ii) (d) Assertion is wrong statement but reason is correct statement.

   (iii) (a) Assertion and reason both are correct statements and reason is correct explanation for assertion.

   (iv) (c) Assertion is correct statement but reason is wrong statement.

OR

   (a) Assertion and reason both are correct statements and reason is correct explanation for assertion.

Chapter 12. Aldehydes, Ketones and Carboxylic Acids

1. **Read the passage given below and answer the following questions:**

   Ketones play a prominent role in organic chemistry. The ketone moiety is extremely common in natural products and pharmaceuticals and in dyes, fragrancies and flavors. It is also a versatile reaction center in organic synthesis. Many frequently used reactions, including the Mannich reaction, Wittig reaction, Grignard reaction, Passerini reaction, Baeyer–Villiger oxidation, and Wolff–Kishner–Huang reduction describe a wide array of transformations of ketones. The development of a practical route to ketones from feedstock chemicals has long been a subject of interest. Carboxylic acids and organohalides are commercially abundant and structurally diverse, bench-stable feedstock chemicals commonly used in organic synthesis. When producing ketones from carboxylic acids and organohalides, the stoichiometric approach requires preparation of necessary intermediates such as amides or aldehydes and Grignard reagents.

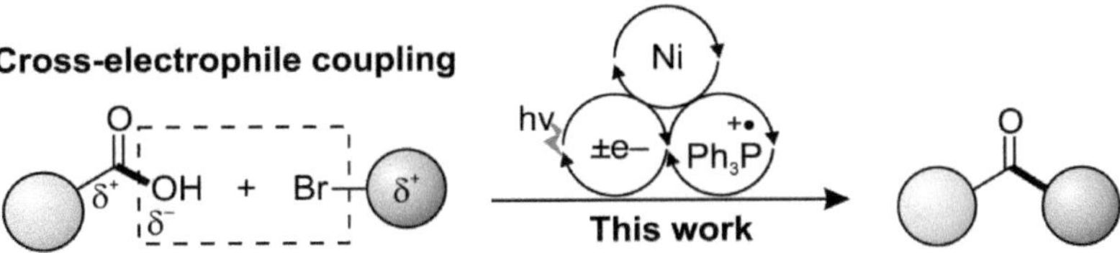

(Reference: Ruzi, R., Liu, K., Zhu, C., Xie, J. (2020). Upgrading ketone synthesis direct from carboxylic acids and organohalides. Nature Communications, 11, 3312.)

The following questions are multiple choice questions. Choose the most appropriate answer:

(i) Which of the following has most acidic hydrogen?

    (a) 3-Hexanone   (c) 2, 5-Hexanedione

    (b) 2, 4-Hexanedione   (d) 2, 3-Hexanedione

(ii) Which of the following acids does not exhibit optical isomerism?

    (a) Lactic acid   (c) Maleic acid

    (b) Tartaric acid   (d) α-amino acids

(iii) Benzaldehyde and acetone can be best distinguished using

    (a) Hydrazine   (c) Sodium hydroxide solution

    (b) Tollen's reagent   (d) 2, 4-DNP

(iv) Which of the following reactions will not result in the formation of carbon-carbon bond?

    (a) Reimer-Tieman reaction   (c) Wurtz reaction

    (b) Friedel Crafts acylation   (d) Cannizzaro reaction

OR

The correct order of decreasing acid strength of trichloroacetic acid (A), trifluoroacetic acid (B), acetic acid (C) and formic acid (D) is

    (a) A > B > C > D   (c) B > A > D > C

    (b) A > C > B > D   (d) B > D > C > A

Ans. (i) (b) 2, 4-Hexanedione

    (ii) (c) Maleic acid

    (iii) (b) Tollen's reagent

    (iv) (d) Cannizzaro reaction

OR

    (c) B > A > D > C

2. **Read the passage given below and answer the following questions:**

Ethers have been synthesised by the different protocols such as Williamson ether synthesis, the Mitsunobu reaction, bimolecular dehydration, the Ullmann method, a transition metal-free coupling reaction between aliphatic alcohols and unsymmetric diaryliodonium salts, room temperature ionic liquid promoted synthesis, Cu(II) catalyzed synthesis, microwave assisted synthesis, and synthesis under solvent free micellar conditions. A good number of homogeneous Brönsted acids and Lewis acid based transition metals have also been reported as catalysts in the etherification of alcohols. The above-mentioned pathway has exhibited some drawbacks including their deactivation through decomposition caused by the water formed during the course of the reaction.

The Williamson Ether Synthesis–A Typical Example:

(*Reference: Mandal, S., Mandal, S., Ghosh, S., Sar, P., Ghosh, A., Saha, R. & Saha, B. (2016). A Review on the Advancement of Ether Synthesis from Organic Solvent to Water. RSC Advances, 6. 69605-69614.*)

In these questions, a statement of assertion followed by a statement of reason is given. Choose the correct answer out of the following choices.

(a) Assertion and reason both are correct statements and reason is correct explanation for assertion.

(b) Assertion and reason both are correct statements but reason is not correct explanation for assertion.

(c) Assertion is correct statement but reason is wrong statement.

(d) Assertion is wrong statement but reason is correct statement.

(i) **Assertion:** Williamson ether synthesis the alkoxide (RO⁻) is used in addition to the alcohol (ROH) in the reaction.

   Reason: The conjugate base is always a better nucleophile.

(ii) **Assertion:** Rate of reaction of alkyl halides with alcohol, in presence of a strong base, follows the order –1° RX > 2° RX > 3° RX, where RX is alkyl halide.

   Reason: It is a type of unimolecular substitution reaction (SN_1).

(iii) **Assertion:** Boiling points of alcohols and ethers are high.

   Reason: They can form intermolecular hydrogen-bonding.

(iv) **Assertion:** Acid catalysed dehydration of butan-1-ol gives but-1-ene as the major product.

   Reason: In acid catalysed dehydration process a molecule of water is liberated according to Saytzeff's rule and formation of more substituted alkene takes place.

OR

   Assertion: Di-tert-butyl ether can be prepared by Williamson's ether synthesis.

   Reason: Tertiary alkyl halides prefer to undergo elimination rather than substitution.

Ans. (i) (a) Assertion and reason both are correct statements and reason is correct explanation for assertion.

   (ii) (c) Assertion is correct statement but reason is wrong statement.

   (iii) (a) Assertion and reason both are correct statements and reason is correct explanation for assertion.

   (iv) (d) Assertion is wrong statement but reason is correct statement.

OR

   (d) Assertion is wrong statement but reason is correct statement.

Chapter 13. Amines

1. **Read the passage given below and answer the following questions:**

   Although the literature contains numerous references to the boiling points of individual *n*-alkyl primary amines, no systematic study of the boiling points the series of *n*-alkyl primary amines has ever been reported. The increased interest in these amines, together with their recent commercial availability, indicates the need for such a study. The purpose of this paper is to report the boiling points at various pressures of the members of the series of saturated n-alkyl primary amines containing from six to eighteen carbon atoms, inclusive.

   In general the amines used were prepared by conversion of the corresponding acids to nitriles and hydrogenation of the nitriles to amines. The nitriles were purified by fractional distillation, with the exception of stearonitrile which was purified by crystallisation. After hydrogenation the amines were fractionally distilled in order to separate them from any unchanged nitriles or secondary amines.

   (Reference: Ralston, A. W., Selby, W. M., Pool, W. O. & Potts, R. H. (1940). Boiling Points of n-Alkyl Primary Amines. Industrial & Engineering Chemistry, 32 (8), 1093-1094.)

   The following questions are multiple choice questions. Choose the most appropriate answer:

   (i) The order of basicity of amines in gaseous state is:

   (a) $1° > 2° > 3° > NH_3$

   (b) $3° > 2° > NH_3 > 1°$

   (c) $3° > 2° > 1° > NH_3$

   (d) $NH_3 > 1° > 2° > 3°$

   (ii) The amine that does not react with acetyl chloride is

   (a) CH_3NH_2

   (b) $(CH_3)_2NH$

   (c) $(CH_3)_3N$

   (d) $C_2H_5NH_2$

   (iii) Nitrosoamines ($R_2N-N = O$) are insoluble in water. On heating with conc. H_2SO_4, they give secondary amines. The reaction is called:

   (a) Liebermann nitroso reaction

   (b) Etard reaction

   (c) Fries reaction

   (d) Perkin reaction

OR

   Which of the following amine has highest boiling point?

   (a) Butyl amine

   (b) Diethylamine

   (c) Triethylamine

   (d) Dipropylamine

    (iv) Which of the following is true characteristic feature of pure aniline?

        (a) Colourless solid   (c) Colourless liquid

        (b) Brown coloured solid   (d) Brown coloured liquid

Ans. (i) (c) $3° > 2° > 1° > NH_3$

     (ii) (c) $(CH_3)_3N$

    (iii) (a) Liebermann nitroso reaction

OR

        (d) Dipropylamine

    (iv) (c) Colourless liquid

2. Read the passage given below and answer the following questions:

Aromatic amines are a class of organic compounds in which an amino ($-NH_2$) group is directly attached to aromatic carbon. These are used for the synthesis of many compounds like azo dyes, Schiff's bases, zeolites, polyimides, polyamides, stationary phase for HPLC, epoxy resins, and plastics. These compounds also act as a catalyst for the cross-linking of polyester, a stabiliser for phenolic resins, coagulants, and antiknock additives for gasoline and diesel fuel. Due to their biological activities, amines are also named as alkaloids in phytochemistry.

$$N_2H_2 + R-O-\text{(aryl)}-NO_2 \xrightarrow[\text{reflux, 18h}]{\text{Ethanol, Pd/C(5\%)}} R-O-\text{(aryl)}-NO_2$$

$$R = (1)\text{-phenyl-} \quad (2) \quad (3)$$

In the present study, new aromatic amines were synthesised and biological potential was evaluated along with one previously reported compound.

(Reference: Ismail, H., Mirza, B., Haq, I., Shabbir, M., Akhter, Z., & Basharat, A. (2015). Synthesis, Characterisation, and Pharmacological Evaluation of Selected Aromatic Amines. Journal of Chemistry, 2015, Article ID 465286, 9 pages, https://doi.org/10.1155/2015/465286)

In these questions, a statement of assertion followed by a statement of reason is given. Choose the correct answer out of the following choices.

(a) Assertion and reason both are correct statements and reason is correct explanation for assertion.

(b) Assertion and reason both are correct statements but reason is not correct explanation for assertion.

(c) Assertion is correct statement but reason is wrong statement.

(d) Assertion is wrong statement but reason is correct statement.

(i) **Assertion:** Amines are regarded as derivatives of ammonia.

    Reason: One, two or all three hydrogen atoms of ammonia molecule are replaced by alkyl or aryl group in amines.

(ii) **Assertion:** Ethylamine can be prepared by oxidation of nitroethane.

    Reason: Nitroalkanes provide aminoalkanes upon reduction with metals like tin, zinc or nickel in acidic medium.

(iii) **Assertion:** Diazonium salts can conduct electricity in aqueous solution.

    Reason: Diazonium salts have the general formula $ArN_2{}^+X^-$, where X^- may be an anion like Cl^-, Br^-.

OR

Assertion: Bromine and potassium hydroxide are the reagents used in Hofmann's bromamide reaction.

Reason: Hofmann's bromamide reaction or degradation is the most convenient method for preparing primary amine containing one carbon atom less than the starting amide.

(iv) **Assertion:** Acetamide can be converted to ethyl amine using lithium aluminium hydride as reducing agent.

Reason: Amide group is dehydrohalogenated to amino group in presence of lithium aluminium hydride as reducing agent.

Ans. (i)   (a)   Assertion and reason both are correct statements and reason is correct explanation for assertion.

(ii)   (d)   Assertion is wrong statement but reason is correct statement.

(iii)   (a)   Assertion and reason both are correct statements and reason is correct explanation for assertion.

OR

(b)   Assertion and reason both are correct statements but reason is not correct explanation for assertion.

(iv)   (c)   Assertion is correct statement but reason is wrong statement.

Chapter 14. Biomolecules

1. **Read the passage given below and answer the following questions:**

The interactions between DNA/RNA strands are controlled by orthogonal base pairing of adenine (A) to thymine (T) and cytosine (C) to guanine (G) and are essential for fundamental cellular activities and practical molecular therapeutic and diagnostic purposes, such as gene replication, gene regulation and diagnostics as well as anti-sense oligonucleotide drugs. Furthermore, recent years have also witnessed the emerging field of DNA nanotechnology, which uses DNA to build complex designed molecular nanostructures and molecular machines by taking advantage of its programmability and predictable interactions, allowing for unprecedented precise control of structure and dynamic behaviour at the nanoscale. The properties of DNA strand interactions, such as the thermodynamics and kinetics of duplex formation, determine the assembly efficiency and stability of the DNA structures that affect cellular functions, anti-sense drug efficiency, and the performance of designed molecular machines.

(Reference: Hong, F., Schreck, J. S., Šulc, P. (2020). Understanding DNA interactions in crowded environments with a coarse-grained model, Nucleic Acids Research, Online publication, gkaa854)

The following questions are multiple choice questions. Choose the most appropriate answer:

(i) Which one of the following is not a pyrimidine derivative?

   (a) Uracil   (b) Thymine   (c) Cytosine   (d) Guanine

OR

Which one of the following statements is incorrect about RNA?

   (a) RNA has a single helix structure   (c) It is not responsible for protein synthesis

   (b) Sugar unit is ribose   (d) It contains Uracil

(ii) A chemical or physical change that alters the sequence of bases in DNA molecule is also known as:

   (a) Mutation   (c) Translation

   (b) Replication   (d) Denaturation

(iii) Thymine combines with:

   (a) Only ribose sugar   (c) Only deoxyribose sugar

   (b) Both deoxyribose and ribose sugars   (d) None of these

(iv) Double helix completes a spiral at every __________ nucleotides in DNA

   (a) Five   (b) Twenty   (c) Ten   (d) Fifteen

Ans. (i) (d) Guanine

OR

(c) It is not responsible for protein synthesis

(ii) (a) Mutation

(iii) (c) Only deoxyribose sugar

(iv) (c) Ten

2. **Read the passage given below and answer the following questions:**

Carbohydrates are the main source of energy that is ingested by the human body (Caffall et al., 2009) Brain mainly utilizes the glucose. Red blood cells also use glucose only. Fiber in the diet is not digested by human body due to lack of cellulase enzyme. Glucose is the major energy source in the body. Glycogen is the storage form of glucose and glycogen is stored in skeletal muscles and liver. If glucose intake exceeds than it is utilised in the body it is converted into fat. Riboses are utilised in formation of deoxyribonucleic acid (Houetal. 2009). Carbohydrates are polyhydroxy alcohol with potentially active carbonyl group which may be aldehyde or keto group. Carbohydrates can be classified on the basis of carbon atom present in the carbohydrates. Carbohydrates are classified into four types monosaccharides, disaccharides, oligosaccharides, polysaccharides. Monosaccharides cannot be hydrolyzed further into simpler form. Disaccharides give two monosaccharides on hydrolysis. Polysaccharides may be homopolysaccharides and heteropolysaccharides.

(Reference: Asif, M., Akram, M., Saeed, T., Khan, I., Naveed, A., Riaz Ur Rehman, M., Ali Shah, S. Khalil, N & Ghazala, S. (2011). Carbohydrates. Journal of Biochemistry and Bioinformatics, 1(1), 01-05.)

In these questions, a statement of assertion followed by a statement of reason is given. Choose the correct answer out of the following choices.

(a) Assertion and reason both are correct statements and reason is correct explanation for assertion.

(b) Assertion and reason both are correct statements but reason is not correct explanation for assertion.

(c) Assertion is correct statement but reason is wrong statement.

(d) Assertion is wrong statement but reason is correct statement.

(i) **Assertion:** Carbohydrates are more suitable for the production of energy in the body than proteins and fats.

　Reason: Carbohydrates can be stored in the tissues as glycogen for use in the production of energy, whenever necessary.

(ii) **Assertion:** Sucrose (cane sugar) is a disaccharide.

　Reason: One molecule of sucrose on hydrolysis gives one molecule of glucose and one molecule of fructose.

(iii) **Assertion:** Glucose gives a bright orange precipitate with 2,4-dinitrophenydlhylrazine (2,4-DNP) test.

　Reason: Glucose does not contain any free aldehydic group in its cyclic form.

(iv) **Assertion:** Sucrose is a disaccharide and it is also a reducing sugar.

　Reason: Carbohydrates are classified on the basis of their behaviour on hydrolysis and also as reducing or non-reducing sugar.

OR

Assertion: Deoxyribose, $C_5H_{10}O_5$ is not a carbohydrate molecule.

Reason: Carbohydrates are hydrates of carbon compounds that may or may not follow $Cx(H_2O)y$ formula.

Ans. (i)　(b)　Assertion and reason both are correct statements but reason is not correct explanation for assertion.

　(ii)　(a)　Assertion and reason both are correct statements and reason is correct explanation for assertion.

　(iii)　(d)　Assertion is wrong statement but reason is correct statement.

　(iv)　(a)　Assertion and reason both are correct statements and reason is correct explanation for assertion.

OR

　(d)　Assertion is wrong statement but reason is correct statement.

Chapter 15. Polymers

1. **Read the passage given below and answer the following questions.**

Most conventional polymers derived from petroleum resources are resistant to degradation. To facilitate their biodegradation, additives are added. One method to degrade polyolefins consists in the introduction of antioxidants into the polymer chains. Antioxidants will react under UV, inducing degradation by photo-oxidation. Nevertheless, the biodegradability of such systems is still controversial. We prefer to consider them as oxo-degradable polymers. Polyolefins are resistant to hydrolysis, to oxidation and to biodegradation due to photo initiators and stabilisers. They can be made oxo-degradable by use of pro-oxidant additives. These additives are based on metal combinations, such as Mn^{2+}/Mn^{3+}. The polyolefin will then degrade by a free radical chain reaction. Hydroperoxides are first produced and then thermolysed or pyrolysed to give chain scission, yielding low molecular mass oxidation products with hydrophilic properties favourable to microorganisms.

(Reference: Vroman, I., Tighzert, L. (2009). Biodegradable Polymers. Materials, 2, 307-344)

The following questions are multiple choice questions. Choose the most appropriate answer.

(i)   Biodegradable polymers usually contain functional groups similar to the functional groups present in:
    (a)   crosslinked polymers   (c)   heteropolymers
    (b)   biopolymers   (d)   copolymers

(ii) Which one out of the given below options is an important class of biodegradable polymers?
    (a)   Aliphatic polyesters   (c)   Synthetic rubbers
    (b)   Aromatic polyesters   (d)   Thermosetting polymers

(iii) Rubber latex is a colloidal dispersion of rubber in _________ .
    (a)   butadiene   (b)   acid   (c)   water   (d)   isoprene

(iv) Teflon coatings undergo decomposition at temperatures above
    (a)   300 °C   (b)   300 K   (c)   400 °C   (d)   400 K

OR

Which one of the below given options is a biodegradable polyamide copolymer?
    (a)   Glyptal   (c)   Nylon-2-Nylon-6
    (b)   PVC   (d)   PHBV

Ans. (i)   (b)   biopolymers
    (ii)   (a)   Aliphatic polyesters
    (iii) (c)   water
    (iv) (a)   300 °C

OR

    (c)   Nylon-2-Nylon-6

2. Read the passage given below and answer the following questions.

Rubber is one of commercially used polymeric matrix mainly due to good energy absorbing properties. It can undergo much more elastic deformations under stress than other materials and still return to its original shape without permanent deformation after the stress is released. This unique property gives rubber an extensive variety of applications. Previous researchers have studied a lot of different types of rubbers which include Natural Rubber (NR), Polybutadiene Rubber (BR), Styrene-Butadiene Rubber (SBR), Isobutylene Isoprene Rubber (IIR) and poly (Styrene-Butadiene-Styrene, SBS) rubber primary due to their domestic applicability. For example, natural rubber is widely used in production of tyres, gloves and condoms. It finds all these applications because it is a biomaterial and it has superior mechanical properties.

(Reference: Mente, P., Motaung, T.E., Hlangothi, S.P. (2016). Natural Rubber and Reclaimed Rubber Composites – A Systematic Review. Polym. Sci., 1-18).

In these questions, a statement of assertion followed by a statement of reason is given. Choose the correct answer out of the following choices.

(a)   Assertion and reason both are correct statements and reason is correct explanation for assertion.

(b)   Assertion and reason both are correct statements but reason is not correct explanation for assertion.

(c)   Assertion is correct statement but reason is wrong statement.

(d)   Assertion is wrong statement but reason is correct statement.

(i)   **Assertion:** Natural rubber is often subjected to chemical modifications.

    Reason: Natural rubber has low thermal resistance and low organic solvent resistance.

(ii) **Assertion:** Rubber can be stretched like a spring and exhibits elastic properties.

    Reason: The cis-polyisoprene has a cross linked structure.

(iii) **Assertion:** Vulcanised rubber is stiff as it contains sulphur.

    Reason: In the manufacture of tyre rubber, 5% of sulphur is used.

(iv) **Assertion:** Neoprene is used for manufacturing hoses and gaskets.

    Reason: Polychloroprene is formed by free radical isomerisation of 1,3-butadiene.

OR

    Assertion: Synthetic rubber is non-stretchable.

    Reason: Synthetic rubber is any vulcanisable rubber like polymer.

Ans. (i)   (a)   Assertion and reason both are correct statements and reason is correct explanation for assertion.
    (ii)   (c)   Assertion is correct statement but reason is wrong statement.

Explanation: Rubber can be stretched like a spring and exhibits elastic properties because the cis-polyisoprene molecule consists of various chains held together by weak van der Waals interactions and it has coiled structure.

(iii) (b) Assertion and reason both are correct statements but reason is not correct explanation for assertion.

Explanation: Vulcanised rubber is stiff as it contains sulphur. Sulphur forms cross links at the reactive sites of double in rubber molecules and thus the rubber gets stiffened.

(iv) (c) Assertion is correct statement but reason is wrong statement.

Explanation: Neoprene is used for manufacturing hoses and gaskets because it has superior resistance to vegetable and mineral oils. Neoprene or polychloroprene is formed by free radical isomerisation of 2-chloro-1,3-butadiene.

OR

(d) Assertion is wrong statement but reason is correct statement.

Explanation: Synthetic rubber is any vulcanisable rubber like polymer, which is capable of getting stretched to twice its length.

Chapter 16. Chemistry in Everyday Life

1. **Read the passage given below and answer the following questions.**

A detergent is any compound that can be used as a cleaning agent. Although soap is a detergent, this term is generally used to refer to synthetic substitutes of soap. The soap, called anionic surfactant, of general formula RCO-ONa, is a salt of carboxylic acid of long chain containing 10–18 carbon atoms, wherein one hydrogen has been replaced by a cation. The long chain of hydrocarbon of the carboxylic acid salts is non-polar and capable of interacting with non-polar species as fats and other impurities. The group ionised carboxylic acid, being polar, is able to interact with water molecules. This characteristic explains the interaction of soap with water and fats (Penteado et al., 2006, Cai and Hakkinen, 2014).

(References: Kogawa, A.C., Cernic, B.G., Domingos do Couto, L.G., Nunes Salgado, H.R. (2017). Synthetic detergents: 100 years of history. Saudi Pharmaceutical Journal, 25(6), 934-938).

The following questions are multiple choice questions. Choose the most appropriate answer.

(i) Which one of the following is not a fatty acid used in making soap?

   (a) Oleic acid   (c) Palmitic acid

   (b) Aspartic acid   (d) Stearic acid

(ii) Manufacturing of toilet soap needs removal of excess

   (a) alkali   (b) fat   (c) perfume   (d) disinfectant

(iii) Detergents can form foam with

   (a) soft water   (c) ice-cold water

   (b) hard water   (d) All of these

(iv) Quarternary ammonium salts of amines with acetates, chlorides or bromide anions are better known as

   (a) non-ionic detergents   (c) cationic detergents

   (b) anionic detergents   (d) quarternary detergents

OR

The major obstacle in bacterial degradation of detergents is

(a) linear and long hydrocarbon chain in the detergent structure.

(b) soluble hydrocarbon chain in the detergent structure.

(c) foam causing tendency of the detergent.

(d) highly branched hydrocarbon chain in the detergent structure.

Ans. (i) (b) Aspartic acid

   (ii) (a) alkali

   (iii) (d) All of these

   (iv) (c) cationic detergents

OR

(d) highly branched hydrocarbon chain in the detergent structure.

2. **Read the passage given below and answer the following questions.**

A common mechanism of action of antidepressant drugs has not been found. This stems partly from the failure to recognise the underlying cause(s) of depression and elaborate the biological substrate of the illness. The multi-factorial nature of depression also suggests that it has more than a single cause. Furthermore, antidepressants tend to be broad spectrum drugs effective in anxiety states as well as depression, suggesting that many neuroreceptors are involved. Given the complex inter-relationship of neuronal systems, it is unlikely that changes in one would account for all of the manifestations of depression and anxiety. Until better models of depression are devised, establishing the mode of action of antidepressants will be difficult. The current focus has been on alterations to simple neuronal models based around serotonin and nor-adrenaline. Clearly, these models are not sufficient to completely explain the clinical effects of antidepressants. More complex models, taking into account other transmitters or indeed adaptive changes at the level of the gene, may be necessary.

(References: Norman, T.R. (1999). The new antidepressants - mechanisms of action. Aust. Prescr., 22, 106-8).

In these questions, a statement of assertion followed by a statement of reason is given. Choose the correct answer out of the following choices.

(a) Assertion and reason both are correct statements and reason is correct explanation for assertion.

(b) Assertion and reason both are correct statements but reason is not correct explanation for assertion.

(c) Assertion is correct statement but reason is wrong statement.

(d) Assertion is wrong statement but reason is correct statement.

(i) **Assertion:** A person suffering from depression needs an antidepressant drug that inhibits the enzymes catalysing degradation of nor-adrenaline.

Reason: Nor-adrenaline neurotransmitter plays a role in mood changes.

(ii) **Assertion:** Equanil is used to control depression sometimes.

Reason: Equanil is a tranquiliser.

(iii) **Assertion:** Morphine does not belong to opiate category.

Reason: Drugs obtained from opium poppy are also referred to as opiates.

(iv) **Assertion:** Aspirin is never used in prevention of heart attacks.

Reason: Aspirin has anti-blood clotting action along with analgesic properties.

OR

Assertion: Narcotic analgesics are used for the relief of postoperative pain and terminal cancer pain.

Reason: A narcotic analgesic may turn out to be poisonous if administered in high doses.

Ans. (i) (a) Assertion and reason both are correct statements and reason is correct explanation for assertion.

(ii) (b) Assertion and reason both are correct statements but reason is not correct explanation for assertion.

Explanation: Some mild tranquilisers, such as Equanil, are sometimes used to control depression.

(iii) (d) Assertion is wrong statement but reason is correct statement.

Explanation: Morphine is obtained from opium poppy and hence belongs to opiate category.

(iv) (d) Assertion is wrong statement but reason is correct statement.

Explanation: Aspirin is used in prevention of heart attacks because it has anti-blood clotting action.

OR

(b) Assertion and reason both are correct statements but reason is not correct explanation for assertion.

Explanation: Narcotic analgesics are generally used for acute pain conditions.

Numericals |Set **18**|

Q. 1. If three elements A, B and C crystallise in a cubic solid with A atoms at the corners, B atoms at the cube centres and C atoms at the face of the cube, then give the formula of the compound.

Ans. A atoms are at the corners, hence

$$\text{Atom A per unit cell, } 8 \times \frac{1}{8} = 1$$

$$\text{Atom B at body centre, } 1 \times 1 = 1$$

$$\text{Atom C at the face, } 6 \times \frac{1}{2} = 3$$

Hence, the formula of the compound is ABC_3.

Q. 2. Gold (atomic radius = 0.144 nm) crystallises in a fcc unit. What is the length of the side of the unit cell?

Ans. For fcc structure

$$\text{Edge length } (a) = 2\sqrt{2}r$$

$$= 2 \times 1.4142 \times 0.144 \text{ nm}$$

$$= 0.407 \text{ nm}$$

Hence edge length is 0.407 nm.

Q. 3. An element crystallises in a b.c.c. lattice with cell edge of 500 pm. The density of the element is 7.5 g/cm^3. How many atoms are present in 300 g of element?*

Ans. BCC lattice, $Z = 2$

$a = 500$ pm $= 500 \times 10^{-10}$ cm

Density $(r) = 7.5$ g cm^{-3}

M = Molar mass of element.

$$\rho = \frac{Z \times M}{N_A \times a^3}$$

$$\therefore \quad M = \frac{\rho \times a^3 \times N_A}{Z}$$

$$M = \frac{7.5 \text{ g cm}^{-3} \times (500 \times 10^{-10} \text{ cm})^3 \times 6.022 \times 10^{23}}{2}$$

$$M = 468.75 \times 10^{-24} \times 6.022 \times 10^{23} \text{ g}$$

Now $\qquad$ 300 g of element has $= \dfrac{6.022 \times 10^{23} \times 300 \text{ g}}{M}$

$$\Rightarrow \quad \frac{6.022 \times 10^{23} \times 300}{468.75 \times 10^{-24} \times 6.022 \times 10^{23}} = 6.4 \times 10^{23} \text{ atoms.}$$

Q. 4. An element with density 2.8 g/cm^3 forms fcc unit cell, with edge length 4×10^{-8} cm. Calculate the molar mass of the element. ($N_A = 6.022 \times 10^{23}$ mol^{-1}).*

Ans. fcc lattice (unit cell) means, $Z = 4$

$$a = 4 \times 10^{-8} \text{ cm}$$

$$\text{Density } (\rho) = 2.8 \text{ g/cm}^3$$

Applying the formula :

$$\rho = \frac{Z \times M}{N_A \times a^3}$$

or

$$M = \frac{\rho \times N_A \times a^3}{Z} = 2.8 \text{ g cm}^{-3} \times (6.022 \times 10^{23}) \times \frac{(4 \times 10^{-8} \text{ cm})^3}{4}$$

$$= \frac{2.8 \text{ g cm}^{-3} \times 6.022 \times 10^{23} \text{ mol}^{-1} \times 64 \times 10^{-24} \text{ cm}^3}{4}$$

$$= 269.79 \times 10^{-1} = 26.979 \text{ g/mol.}$$

Q. 5. **Iron has a body centered cubic structure (bcc) unit cell with a cell dimension of 286.65 pm. The density of iron is 7.874 g cm^{-3}. Use the information to calculate Avogadro's number. (Atomic mass of Fe = 55.845 u).**[*]

Ans. BCC unit cell implies; Z = 2

$$\text{Cell edge length (a)} = 286.65 \text{ pm}$$
$$= 286.65 \times 10^{-10} \text{ cm}$$
$$\text{Density (r)} = 7.874 \text{ g cm}^{-3}$$
$$M_{(mass)} = 55.845 \text{ g/mol}$$
$$N_A = ?$$

Applying the formula:

$$\rho = \frac{Z \times M}{N_A \times a^3}$$

$$\Rightarrow \quad N_A = \frac{Z \times M}{\rho \times a^3} = \frac{2 \times 55.845 \text{ g mol}^{-1}}{7.874 \text{ g cm}^{-3} \times (286.65 \times 10^{-10} \text{ cm})^3}$$

$$= \frac{14.187 \text{ mol}^{-1}}{(2.86 \times 10^{-8} \text{cm})^3} = \frac{14.187 \times 10^{24}}{23.394}$$

$$= 6.06 \times 10^{23} \text{ atoms.}$$

Q. 6. **A compound forms hexagonal close-packed structure. What is the total number of voids in 0.5 mol of it ? How many of these are tetrahedral voids?**

Ans. Number of close-packed particles = 0.5 × 6.022 × 10^{23} = 3.011 × 10^{23} (1 mol = 6.022 × 10^{23})

Therefore, number of octahedral voids = 3.011 × 10^{23} (As octahedral voids = No. of particles)

And, number of tetrahedral voids = 2 × 3.011 × 10^{23} = 6.022 × 10^{23} (Tetrahedral voids =2 × no. of particle in unit cell)

Therefore, total number of voids = 3.011 × 10^{23} + 6.022 × 10^{23} = 9.033 × 10^{23}.

Q. 7. **Silver crystallises in fcc lattice. If edge length of the cell is 4.07 × 10^{-8} cm and density is 10.5 g cm^{-3}, calculate the atomic mass of silver.**

Ans. It is given that the edge length, $a = 4.077 \times 10^{-8}$ cm

$$\text{Density, } d = 10.5 \text{ g cm}^{-3}$$

As the lattice is fcc type, the number of atoms per unit cell, Z = 4

We also know that, $N_A = 6.022 \times 10^{23}$ mol^{-1}. Using the relation:

$$d = \frac{ZM}{a^3 N_A}$$

$$\Rightarrow \quad M = \frac{da^3 N_A}{Z}$$

$$= \frac{10.5 \text{ g cm}^{-3}(4.077 \times 10^{-8}\text{cm})^3 \times 6.022 \times 10^{23} \text{ mol}^{-1}}{4}$$

$$= 107.13 \text{ g mol}^{-1}$$

Therefore, atomic mass of silver = 107.13 u.

Q. 8. A cubic solid is made of two elements P and Q. Atoms of Q are at the corners of the cube and P at the body-centre. What is the formula of the compound? What are the coordination numbers of P and Q?

Ans. It is given that the atoms of Q are present at the corners of the cube.

Therefore, number of atoms of Q in one unit cell $= 8 \times \dfrac{1}{8} = 1$

It is also given that the atoms of P are present at the body-centre.

Therefore, number of atoms of P in one unit cell $= 1$

This means that the ratio of the number of P atoms to the number of Q atoms, P : Q 1 : 1 Hence, the formula of the compound is PQ.

The coordination number of both P and Q is 8.

Q. 9. Copper crystallises into a fcc lattice with edge length 3.61×10^{-8} cm. Show that the calculated density is in agreement with its measured value of 8.92 g cm^{-1}.

Ans.   Edge length, $a = 3.61 \times 10^{-8}$ cm

As the lattice is fcc type, the number of atoms per unit cell, $Z = 4$

Atomic mass, $M = 63.5$ g mol^{-1}.

We also know that, $N_A = 6.022 \times 10^{23}$ mol^{-1}

Applying the relation :

$$d = \frac{ZM}{a^3 N_A}$$

$$= \frac{4 \times 63.5 \text{ g mol}^{-1}}{(3.61 \times 10^{-8} \text{ cm})^3 \times 6.022 \times 10^{23} \text{mol}^{-1}}$$

$$= 8.97 \text{ g cm}^{-3}$$

The measured value of density is given as 8.92 g cm^{-3}. Hence, the calculated density 8.97 g cm^{-3} is in agreement with its measured value.

Q. 10. Niobium crystallises in body centered cubic structure. If the density is 8.55 g/cm^3. Calculate atomic radius of Nb, given that its atomic mass is 93 g/mol.*

Ans. Let us calculate the edge length of unit cell (a).

b.c.c. structure means $Z = 2$

Atomic mass of Nb $= 93$ g/mol

$$\text{Mass of unit cell} = \frac{Z \times M}{N_0} = \frac{(2 \times 93 \text{ g/mol})}{(6.022 \times 10^{23} \text{g/mol})}$$

$$= 30.89 \times 10^{-23} \text{ g}$$

Density of unit cell (d) $= 8.55$ g/cm^3

$$\text{Volume of unit cell} = a^3 = \frac{\text{Mass of unit cell}}{\text{Density of unit cell}}$$

$$= \frac{30.89 \times 10^{-23} \text{g}}{8.55 \text{ g/cm}^3} = 36.13 \times 10^{-24} \text{cm}^3$$

$$\text{Edge length } (a) = \sqrt[3]{V} = (36.13 \times 10^{-24} \text{cm}^3)^{1/3}$$

$$= 3.31 \times 10^{-8} \text{ cm}$$

(Use log table for calculation of 1/3 root)

Now, calculate atomic radius of Nb(r).

In a b.c.c. structure.

$$\text{Body diagonal} = \sqrt{3}a = 4r$$

$$\therefore \qquad r = \frac{\sqrt{3}a}{4} = \frac{\sqrt{3}}{4} \times 3.31 \times 10^{-8}$$

$$= 1.43 \times 10^{-8} \text{ cm} = 143 \text{ pm}.$$

Q. 11. An element crystallises into a cubic structure in a way that one atom is on each corner of the cube and two atoms on one of its diagonals. If the volume of the unit cell is 24×10^{-24} cm^3 and the density of the element is 7.2 g/cm^3, calculate the number of atoms present in 200 g of the element.

Ans.

$$\text{Volume of unit cell} = 24 \times 10^{-24} \text{ cm}^3$$

$$\text{Density of element} = 7.2 \text{ g/cm}^3$$

$\therefore$
$$\text{Mass of unit cell} = 7.2 \text{ g/cm}^3 \times 24 \times 10^{-24} \text{ cm}^3$$

$$= 172.8 \times 10^{-24} \text{ g}$$

$$\text{Number of atoms per unit cell} = \frac{1}{8} \times 8 + 2 \text{ corners diagonal}$$

$$= 1 + 2 = 3.$$

Unit cells present in 200 g of element is,

$$\frac{200 \text{ g}}{172.8 \times 10^{-24}} = 1.157 \times 10^{24}$$

No. of atoms present in 200 g of element is,

$$1.157 \times 3 = 3.4722 \times 10^{24} \text{ atoms.}$$

Q. 12. N An element crystallises in fcc structure. 200 g of this element has 4.12×10^{24} atoms. The density of A is 7.2 g/cm^3. Calculate the edge lengths of the unit cell.*

Ans. $Z = 4$ (fcc), $r = 7.2$ g/cm^3, a = edge ?

200 g of element contains 4.12×10^{24} atoms.

$$6.022 \times 10^{23} \text{ atoms have mass} = \frac{200}{4.12 \times 10^{24}} \times 6.023 \times 10^{23}$$

$$= 29.23 \text{ g}$$

$$\text{Density } (\rho) = \frac{Z \times M}{a^3 \times N_A}$$

$$a^3 = \frac{Z \times M}{\rho \times N_A} = \frac{4 \times 29.33}{7.2 \times 6.023 \times 10^{23}}$$

$$a^3 = 27.05 \times 10^{-24} \text{ cm}^3$$

or
$$a = 2.97 \times 10^{-8} \text{ cm}$$

$$= 2.97 \text{ Å.}$$

Q. 13. The nearest neighbouring silver atoms in a silver crystal piece are 2.87×10^{-10} m apart. What is the density of silver if it crystallises as face centred cubic structure. [Atomic mass: Ag = 1080 g/mol].

Ans. In a fcc structure nearest neighbour is the corner atom and face centered atom.

Hence ½ of body diagonal is the distance between two nearest neighbours (x).

$$x = \frac{1}{2}(\text{face diagonal}) = \frac{1}{2}(\sqrt{2}a)$$

Given,
$$x = 2.87 \times 10^{-10} \text{ m} = \frac{1}{2}(\sqrt{2}a)$$

$Z = 4, m = 108$

So,
$$2.87 \times 10^{-10} \text{ m} = \frac{1}{2}(\sqrt{2}a)$$

or
$$a = 2.87 \times 10^{-10} \times \sqrt{2}$$

$$= 2.87 \times 1.414 \times 10^{-10} \text{ m}$$

$$= 4.05 \times 10^{-10} \text{ m} = 4.05 \times 10^{-8} \text{ cm}$$

$$\text{Volume} = a^3 = (4.05 \times 10^{-8} \text{ cm})^3$$

$$\text{Density } (\rho) = \frac{Z \times M}{a^3 \times N_A} = \frac{4 \times 108 \text{ g}}{(4.05)^3 \times 10^{-24} \times 6.022 \times 10^{23}}$$

$$\text{Density of silver} = \frac{108}{1.008 \times 10} = \frac{108}{10.08} = 10.7 \text{ g/cm}^3.$$

Hence, density of silver = 10.7 g/cm^3.

Q. 14. A compound is formed by two elements M and N. The element N forms ccp and atoms of M occupy 1/3rd of tetrahedral voids. What is the formula of the compound?

Ans. The ccp lattice is formed by the atoms of the element N.

Here, the number of tetrahedral voids generated is equal to twice the number of atoms of the element N, *i.e.,* tetrahedral voids = 2n.

According to the question, the atoms of element M occupy 1/3rd of the tetrahedral voids.

$$2n \times \frac{1}{3} = \frac{2}{3} n$$

Therefore, the number of atoms of M is equal to 2/3rd of the number of atoms of N = $\frac{2}{3} : 1$

Therefore, ratio of the number of atoms of M to that of N is M : N = 2 : 3

Thus, the formula of the compound is M$_2$N$_3$.

Q. 15. An element with molar mass 2.7 $\times$ 10^{-2} kg mol^{-1} forms a cubic unit cell with edge length 405 pm. If its density is 2.7 $\times$ 10^3 kg m^{-3}, what is the nature of the cubic unit cell?

Ans. It is given that density of the element, $\quad d = 2.7 \times 10^3 \text{ kg m}^{-3}$

$$\text{Molar mass, M} = 2.7 \times 10^{-2} \text{ kg mol}^{-1}$$

$$\text{Edge length, } a = 405 \text{ pm} = 405 \times 10^{-12} \text{ m} = 4.05 \times 10^{-10} \text{ m}$$

It is known that, Avogadro's number, N$_A$ = 6.022 $\times$ 10^{23} mol^{-1}

Applying the relation,

$$d = \frac{Z.M}{a^3.N_A}$$

$$Z = \frac{d.a^3 N_A}{M}$$

$$= \frac{2.7 \times 10^3 \text{ kg m}^{-3} \times (4.05 \times 10^{-10} \text{ m})^3 \times 6.022 \times 10^{23} \text{mol}^{-1}}{2.7 \times 10^{-2} \text{ kg mol}^{-1}}$$

$$= 4.004$$

$$= 4$$

This implies that four atoms of the element are present per unit cell. Hence, the unit cell is face centered cubic (fcc) or cubic close packed (ccp).

Q. 16. Analysis shows that nickel oxide has the formula Ni$_{0.98}$O$_{1.00}$. What fractions of nickel exist as Ni^{2+} and Ni^{3+} ions?

Ans. The formula of nickel oxide is Ni$_{0.98}$O$_{1.00}$.

Therefore, the ratio of the number of Ni atoms to the number of O atoms,

$$\text{Ni : O} = 0.98 : 1.00 = 98 : 100$$

Now, $\qquad$ Total charge on 100 O^{2-} ions = 100 $\times$ (–2)

$$= -200$$

Let the number of Ni^{2+} ions be x.

So, the number of Ni^{3+} ions is 98 – x.

Now, $\qquad$ total charge on Ni^{2+} ions = x(+2) = +2x

and, $\qquad$ total charge on Ni^{3+} ions = (98 – x)(+3) = 294 – 3x

Since, the compound is neutral, we can write:

$$2x + (294 - 3x) + (-200) = 0$$

$$-x + 94 = 0$$

$$x = 94$$

Therefore, $\qquad$ number of Ni^{2+} ions = 94

and, number of Ni^{3+} ions $= 98 - 94 = 4$

Hence, fraction of nickel that exists as $Ni^{2+} = \dfrac{94}{98} = 0.959$

and, fraction of nickel that exists as

$$Ni^{3+} = \dfrac{4}{98}$$

$$= 0.041$$

Q. 17. An element 'X' (At. mass $= 40$ g mol^{-1}) having f.c.c. structure, has unit cell edge length of 400 pm. Calculate the density of 'X' and the number of unit cells in 4 g of 'X'. ($N_A = 6.022 \times 10^{23}$ mol^{-1}).*

Ans. Given: Atomic mass of element (M) $= 40$ g mol^{-1}

Length of unit cell (a) $= 400$ pm $= 4 \times 10^{-8}$ cm; Z $= 4$ (fcc).

Now density is given by formula,

$$\text{Density } (d) = (Z \times M)/N_A \times V$$

Volume of the unit cell, $V = a^3 = (4 \times 10^{-8})^3$ cm $= 64 \times 10^{-24}$

Putting the values

$$\text{Density } (d) = \dfrac{(4 \times 40)}{[(6.022 \times 10^{23}) \times 64 \times 10^{-24}]}$$

$$= 160/38.5 = 4.1 \text{ g cm}^{-3}.$$

Q. 18. Calculate the number of unit cells in 8.1 g of aluminium if it crystallises in a facecentered cubic (f.c.c.) structure. (Atomic mass of Al $= 27$ g mol^{-1}).*

Ans. 1 mol of Al $= 27$ g mol^{-1} $= 6.022 \times 10^{23}$ atoms

$$\text{No. of atoms present in 8.1 g of Al} = \dfrac{6.02 \times 10^{23}}{27} \times 8.1$$

$$= 1.8069 \times 10^{23}$$

An fcc unit cell contains 4 atoms

$$\text{No. of unit cells present} = \dfrac{1.8069 \times 10^{23}}{4}$$

$$= 0.4517 \times 10^{23}.$$

Q. 19. The length of body diagonal for CsCl which crystallises into a cubic structure with Cl^- ions at the corners and Cs^+ ions at the centre of the unit cell is 7Å and the radius of the Cs^+ ion is 1.69 Å, what is the radius of Cl^- ions?

Ans.

$$\text{Length of the body diagonal} = 2\left(r_{Cl^-} + r_{Cs^+}\right)$$

$$\left(r_{Cl^-} + r_{Cs^+}\right) = 7\overset{\circ}{A}.$$

$$r_{Cs^+} = 1.69,$$

$$\therefore \quad 2(r_{Cl^-} + 1.69) = 7 \overset{\circ}{A}$$

$$2r_{Cl^-} = 7 - 3.38$$

$$\Rightarrow \quad r_{Cl^-} = \dfrac{7 - 3.38}{2} = \dfrac{3.62}{2} = 1.81 \text{ Å}$$

Q. 20. The composition of a sample of Wustite is $Fe_{0.93}O_{1.00}$. What percentage of iron is present in the form of Fe(III)?*

Ans. $Fe_{0.93}O_{1.00}$ shows some Fe^{2+} ions are replaced by Fe^{3+} ions.

Let us assume ions of $Fe^{2+} = x$

ions of $Fe^{3+} = y$

For 93 Fe atoms (ions) there are 100 oxygen atoms (ions).

Total charge on Fe, should be equal to total charge of oxygen (O). So that the sample of Wustite is neutral. Hence,

$$(+2) \times x + (+3)y = (-2) \times 100 = 200$$

Now
$$x + y = 93$$

So
$$y = 93 - x.$$

Substituting value of y, we get

$$2x + 3 \times (93 - x) = 200$$
$$2x + 279 - 3x = 200$$
$$\Rightarrow \qquad x = 79$$
$$\therefore \qquad y = 93 - 79 = 14$$

Formula is, $Fe^{2+}_{0.79}\ Fe^{3+}_{0.14}\ O^{2-}_{1.00}$

$$\text{Total molar mass} = 0.93 \times 56 + 1 \times 16 = 68.08 \text{ g}$$
$$Fe^{3+} = 0.14 \times 56 = 7.84 \text{ g}$$
$$\text{Percentage of Fe(III)} = \frac{7.84 \times 100}{68.08} = 11.5\%.$$

Chapter 2. Solutions

Q. 1. **The boiling point of a solution of urea in water is 101.11°C. Calculate the freezing point of the solution. [K_f and K_b for water are 1.86 K/m and 0.52 K/m respectively]**

Ans. Boiling point of water = 100°C.

$\Delta T_b = 101.11°C - 100°C = 1.11°C$

$\Delta T_b = K_b \times m \text{ (molality)}$

$$\therefore \qquad m = \frac{\Delta T_b}{K_b} = \frac{1.11}{0.52} = 2.13$$

$$\Delta T_f = K_f \times m = 1.86 \text{ K mol}^{-1} \times 2.13 \text{ mol} = 3.962 \text{ K}$$
$$\text{Freezing point of solution} = \text{Freezing point of water} - \Delta T_f$$
$$= (273 - 3.962) \text{ K} = 269.04 \text{ K}.$$

Q. 2. **A 6.90 M solution of KOH in water contains 30% by mass of KOH. Calculate the density of the KOH solution. (Molar mass of KOH = 56 g/mol).** *

Ans. 6.90 M = 6.9 moles of KOH in 1000 ml solution.

i.e., 6.9 × 56 g = 386.4 of KOH in 1000 ml solution.

30% of mass of KOH means, 30 g of KOH in 100 g of solution.

Hence, $\qquad$ 386.4 g of KOH in $\dfrac{100}{30} \times 386.4$ g = 1288 g of solution.

$$\text{Density} = \frac{\text{Mass}}{\text{Volume}} = \frac{1288 \text{ g}}{1000 \text{ ml}} = 1.288 = \text{g/ml of solution.}$$

Q. 3. **Calculate relative lowering of vapour pressure for the below mentioned solution.**

   (i)   0.8 vapour pressure of pure liquid at 25°C is 100 mm Hg and mole fraction of solvent is.

   (ii) 0.8 vapour pressure of water at 293 K is 17.51 mm Hg and lowering of vapour pressure of sugar solution is 0.0614 mm of Hg.

Ans. Relative lowering of vapour pressure is

$$\frac{P° - P_s}{P°} = x^2 \text{ (mole fraction of solute)}$$

P^0 = Vapour pressure of pure solvent.

P_S = Vapour pressure of solution

(i)   Mole fraction of solvent = 0.8

     Hence of solute $(x^2) = 1 - 0.8 = 0.2$

$$\therefore \qquad \frac{P^\circ - P_s}{P^\circ} = 0.2$$

(ii) $P^0 = 17.51$ mm, Hg, $P^0 - P_s = 0.0614$ mm Hg.

$$\therefore \qquad \frac{P^\circ - P_s}{P^\circ} = \frac{0.0614}{17.51} = 0.00350.$$

Q. 4. Calculate the mass percentage of benzene (C_6H_6) and carbon tetrachloride (CCl_4). If 22 g of benzene is dissolved in 122 g of carbon tetrachloride.

Ans.   Mass percentage of C_6H_6

$$= \frac{\text{Mass of } C_6H_6}{\text{Total mass of the solution}} \times 100\%$$

$$= \frac{\text{Mass of } C_6H_6}{\text{Mass of } C_6H_6 + \text{Mass of } CCl_4} \times 100\%$$

$$= \frac{22}{22+122} \times 100\%$$

$$= 15.28\%$$

$$\text{Mass percentage of } CCl_4 = \frac{\text{Mass of } CCl_4}{\text{Total mass of the solution}} \times 100\%$$

$$= \frac{\text{Mass of } CCl_4}{\text{Mass of } C_6H_6 + \text{Mass of } CCl_4} \times 100\%$$

$$= \frac{122}{22+122} \times 100\%$$

$$= 84.72\%.$$

Alternatively,   Mass percentage of $CCl_4 = (100 - 15.28)\% = 84.72\%$.

Q. 5. Calculate the mole fraction of benzene in solution containing 30% by mass in carbon tetrachloride.

Ans. Let the total mass of the solution be 100 g and the mass of benzene be 30 g.

$$\therefore \qquad \text{Mass of carbon tetrachloride} = (100 - 30)g = 70 \text{ g}$$

$$\text{Molar mass of benzene } (C_6H_6) = (6 \times 12 + 6 \times 1) \text{ g mol}^{-1} = 78 \text{ g mol}^{-1}$$

$$\therefore \qquad \text{Number of moles of } C_6H_6 \text{ mol} = \frac{30}{78} \text{ mol} = 0.3846 \text{ mol}$$

$$\text{Molar mass of carbon tetrachloride } (CCl_4) = 1 \times 12 + 4 \times 35.5 = 154 \text{ g mol}^{-1}$$

$$\therefore \qquad \text{Number of moles of } CCl_4 = \frac{70}{154} \text{ mol} = 0.4545 \text{ mol}$$

Thus, the mole fraction of C_6H_6 is given as :

$$\frac{\text{Number of moles of } C_6H_6}{\text{Number of moles of } C_6H_6 + \text{Number of moles of } CCl_4} = \frac{0.3846}{0.3846 + 0.4545}$$

$$= 0.458.$$

Q. 6. Boiling point of water at 750 mm Hg is 99.63°C. How much sucrose is to be added to 500 g of water such that it boils at 100°C. Molal elevation constant for water is 0.52 K kg mol^{-1}.

Ans. Here, elevation of boiling point

$$\Delta T_b = (100 + 273) - (99.63 + 273) = 0.37 \text{ K}$$

Mass of water, $w_1 = 500$ g

Molar mass of sucrose ($C_{12}H_{22}O_{11}$),

$$\therefore \qquad M_2 = 11 \times 12 + 22 \times 1 + 11 \times 16 = 342 \text{ g mol}^{-1}$$

Molal elevation constant,

$$K_b = 0.52 \text{ K kg mol}^{-1}$$

We know that

$$\Delta T_b = \frac{K_b \times 1000 \times w_2}{M_2 \times w_1}$$

$$\Rightarrow \quad w_2 = \frac{\Delta T_b \times M_2 \times w_1}{K_b \times 1000}$$

$$= \frac{0.37 \times 342 \times 500}{0.52 \times 1000}$$

$$= 121.67 \text{ g (approximately)}$$

Hence, 121.67 g of sucrose is to be added.

Q. 7. **Calculate the mass of ascorbic acid (Vitamin C, $C_6H_8O_6$) to be dissolved in 75 g of acetic acid to lower its melting point by 1.5°C, K_f = 3.9 K kg mol^{-1}.**

Ans. Mass of acetic acid, w_1 = 75 g

Molar mass of ascorbic acid ($C_6H_8O_6$),

$$M_2 = 6 \times 12 + 8 \times 1 + 6 \times 16$$
$$= 176 \text{ g mol}^{-1}$$

Lowering of melting point, $\quad \Delta T_f = 1.5$ K

We know that:

$$\Delta T_f = \frac{K_f \times w_2 \times 1000}{M_2 \times w_1}$$

$$\Rightarrow \quad w_2 = \frac{\Delta T_f \times M_2 \times w_1}{K_f \times 1000}$$

$$= \frac{1.5 \times 176 \times 75}{3.9 \times 1000}$$

$$= 5.08 \text{ g (approx.)}$$

Hence, 5.08 g of ascorbic acid is needed to be dissolved.

Q. 8. **Calculate the osmotic pressure in Pascals exerted by a solution prepared by dissolving 1.0 g of polymer of molar mass 185,000 in 450 mL of water at 37°C.**

Ans. It is given that:

$$\text{Volume of water, V} = 450 \text{ mL} = 0.45 \text{ L}$$

$$\text{Temperature, T} = (37 + 273) \text{ K} = 310 \text{ K}$$

Number of moles of the polymer, $\quad n = \dfrac{1}{185000}$ mol

We know that:

$$\pi = \frac{n}{V} RT$$

Osmotic pressure,

$$= \frac{1}{185000} \text{mol} \times \frac{1}{0.45 \text{ L}} \times 8.314 \times 10^3 \text{ Pa L K}^{-1} \text{ mol}^{-1} \times 310 \text{ K}$$

$$= 30.98 \text{ Pa}$$

$$= 31 \text{ Pa (approximately).}$$

Q. 9. **Concentrated nitric acid used in the laboratory work is 68% nitric acid by mass in aqueous solution. What should be the molarity of such a sample of the acid if the density of the solution is 1.504 mL^{-1}?**

Ans. 8 g of HNO_3 is present in 100 g solution.

$$\therefore \quad \text{Volume of 100 g of solution} = \frac{\text{Mass}}{\text{Density}} = \frac{100}{1.504} = 66.489 \text{ mL}$$

$$= 0.0665 \text{ L}$$

$\therefore \qquad$ Number of moles of $HNO_3 = \dfrac{\text{Mass of } HNO_3}{\text{Mol. mass of } HNO_3} = \dfrac{68 \text{ g}}{63 \text{ g mol}^{-1}} = 1.079 \text{ mol}$

$\therefore \qquad$ Molarity of $HNO_3 = \dfrac{\text{No. of moles of } HNO_3}{\text{Volume of solution in L}}$

$$= \dfrac{1.079}{0.0665 \text{ L}} = 16.23 \text{ M.}$$

Alternative answer:

Molarity of the solution,

$$= \dfrac{\text{Percentage} \times d \times 10}{\text{Molar mass of } HNO_3}$$

$$= \dfrac{68 \times 1.504 \times 10}{63}$$

$$= \dfrac{1022.723}{63} = 16.23 \text{ M.}$$

Q. 10. **How many mL of 0.1 M HCl are required to react completely with 1 g mixture of Na_2CO_3 and $NaHCO_3$ containing equimolar amounts of the two?**

Ans. $\qquad\qquad Na_2CO_3 + 2HCl \longrightarrow 2NaCl + CO_2 + H_2O$

$\qquad\qquad$ 1 mol = 106 g $\quad$ 2 mol

$\qquad\qquad NaHCO_3 + HCl \longrightarrow NaCl + CO_2 + H_2O$

$\qquad\qquad$ 1 mol = 84 g $\quad$ 1 mol

Mass of a mixture containing 1 mol each of Na_2CO_3 and $NaHCO_3$ = (106 + 84) g = 190 g of mixture requires HCl = 3 mol

$$1 \text{ g of mixture requires HCl} = \dfrac{3}{190} \text{ mol}$$

$$\text{Moles of solute (HCl)} = M \times V(L)$$

$$\dfrac{3}{190} \text{ mol} = (0.1 \text{ mol L}^{-1}) \times V$$

$$V = \dfrac{3}{190} \times \dfrac{1}{0.1} L = \dfrac{3}{190} \times \dfrac{10}{1} \times 1000 \text{ mL}$$

$$= \dfrac{3000}{19} \text{ mL} = 157.89 \text{ mL} \approx 157.9 \text{ mL.}$$

Q. 11. **A solution is obtained by mixing 300 g of 25% solution and 400 g of 40% solution by mass.**

Ans. 300 g of 25% solution contains solute $= \dfrac{300 \times 25}{100} = 75 \text{ g}$

400 g of 40% solution contains solute $= \dfrac{400 \times 40}{100} = 160$

Total mass of solute = 160 + 75 = 235 g

Total mass of solution = 300 + 400 = 700 g

Percentage of solute in the resulting solution $= \dfrac{235}{700} \times 100 = 33.5\%$

Percentage of water in the resulting solution = 100 – 33.5 = 66.5%.

Q. 12. **A sample of drinking water was found to be severely contaminated with chloroform, $CHCl_3$, supposed to be carcinogen. The level of contamination was 15 ppm (by mass).**

$\quad$ (i) $\quad$ Express this in percent by mass.

$\quad$ (ii) Determine the molality of chloroform in the water sample.

Ans. 15 ppm means 15 parts in million (106) parts by mass in the solution.

$$\therefore \quad \text{Percentage by mass} = \frac{15}{10^6} \times 100$$

$$= 15 \times 10^{-4}$$

Taking 15 g chloroform in 10^6 g of the solution, mass of solvent 10^6 g = 1000 kg

$$\text{Molar mass CHCl}_3 = 12 + 1 + 3 \times 33.5 = 119.5 \text{ g mol}^{-1}$$

$$\therefore \quad \text{Moles of solute} = \frac{15 \text{ g}}{119.5 \text{ g mol}^{-1}} = 0.126 \text{ mol}$$

$$\text{Molality} = \frac{\text{Moles of solute}}{\text{Mass of solvent (kg)}}$$

$$= \frac{0.126 \text{ mol}}{1000 \text{ kg}}$$

$$= 1.26 \times 10^{-4} \text{ mol kg}^{-1} = 1.26 \times 10^{-4} \text{ m.}$$

Q. 13. The vapour pressure of water is 12.3 kPa at 300 K. Calculate vapour pressure of 1 molal solution of a non-volatile solute in it.

Ans. 1 molal solution means 1 mol of the solute is present in 100 g of the solvent (water).

Molar mass of water = 18 g mol^{-1}

$$\therefore \text{ Number of moles present in 1000 g of water} = \frac{1000}{18} = 55.56 \text{ mol}$$

Therefore, mole fraction of the solute in the solution is

$$x_2 = \frac{1}{1+55.56} = 0.0177$$

It is given that,

Vapour pressure of water,

$$p_1^0 = 12.3 \text{ kPa}$$

$$\frac{P_1^o - P_1}{P_1^o} = x^2$$

Applying the relation,

$$\Rightarrow \quad \frac{12.3 - P_1}{12.3} = 0.0177$$

$$\Rightarrow \quad 12.3 - P_1 = 0.2177$$

$$\Rightarrow \quad P_1 = 12.0823$$

$$= 12.08 \text{ kPa (approximately)}$$

Hence, the vapour pressure of the solution is 12.08 kPa.

Q. 14. If the density of some lake water is 1.25 g mL^{-1} and contains 92 g of Na$^+$ ions per kg of water, calculate the molality of Na$^+$ ions in the lake.

Ans. Number of moles present in 92 g of Na$^+$ ions $= \dfrac{92 \text{ g}}{23 \text{ g mol}^{-1}} = 4 \text{ mol}$

Therefore, molality of Na$^+$ ions in the lake $= \dfrac{4 \text{ mol}}{1 \text{ kg}} = 4 \text{ m.}$

Q. 15. If the solubility product of CuS is 6×10^{-16}, calculate the maximum molarity of CuS in aqueous solution.

Ans. Solubility product of CuS, $K_{sp} = 6 \times 10^{-16}$

Lets (S), be the solubility of CuS in mol L^{-1}.

$$\left(\underset{S}{CuS} \rightleftharpoons \underset{S}{Cu^{2+}} + \underset{S}{S^{2-}} \right)$$

Now,
$$K_{sp} = [Cu^{2+}] [S^{2-}]$$
$$= s \times s$$
$$= s^2$$

Then, we have, $K_{sp} = s^2 = 6 \times 10^{-16}$.

$\Rightarrow \qquad s = \sqrt{6 \times 10^{-16}} = 2.45 \times 10^{-8}$ mol L^{-1}

Hence, the maximum molarity of CuS in an aqueous solution is 2.45×10^{-8} mol L^{-1}.

Q. 16. Calculate the mass percentage of aspirin ($C_9H_8O_4$) in acetonitrile (CH_3CN) when 6.5 g of $C_9H_8O_4$ is dissolved in 450 g of CH_3CN.

Ans. 6.5 g of $C_9H_8O_4$ is dissolved in 450 g of CH_3CN.

Then, total mass of the solution $= (6.5 + 450)$ g $= 456.5$ g

Therefore, mass percentage of $C_9H_8O_4 = \dfrac{6.5}{456.5} \times 100 = 1.424\%$

Q. 17. Calculate the amount of benzoic acid (C_6H_5COOH) required for preparing 250 mL of 0.15 M solution in methanol.

Ans. 0.15 M solution of benzoic acid in methanol means,

1000 mL of solution contains 0.15 mol of benzoic acid

Therefore, 250 mL of solution contains $= \dfrac{0.15 \times 250}{1000}$ mol of benzoic acid

$$= 0.0375 \text{ mol of benzoic acid}$$

Molar mass of benzoic acid (C_6H_5COOH) $= 7 \times 12 + 6 \times 1 + 2 \times 16 = 122$ g mol^{-1}

Hence, required benzoic acid $= 0.0375$ mol $\times 122$ g mol$^{-1} = 4.575$ g.

Q. 18. Vapour pressure of water at 293 K is 17.535 mm Hg. Calculate the vapour pressure of water at 293 K when 25 g of glucose is dissolved in 450 g of water.

Ans. Here, $p^0 = 17.535$ mm, $w_B = 25$ g, $w_A = 450$ g.

For solute (glucose, $C_6H_{12}O_6$), $M_B = 180$ g mol^{-1}. For solvent (H_2O), MA $= 18$ g mol^{-1}.

Applying Raoult's law,
$$\frac{P^\circ - P_s}{P^\circ} = \frac{n_B}{n_A + n_B} \quad \text{or} \quad \frac{P^\circ - P_s}{P_s} = \frac{n_B}{n_A} = \frac{w_B/M_B}{w_A/M_A} \quad \text{or} \quad \frac{P^\circ}{P_s} - 1 = \frac{w_B M_A}{w_A M_B}$$

Substituting the given values, we get
$$\frac{17.535}{P_s} - 1 = \frac{25 \times 18}{450 \times 180} = \frac{25}{4500} \quad \text{or} \quad \frac{17.535}{P_s} = 1 + \frac{25}{4500} = \frac{4525}{4500}$$

or $$P_s = 17.535 \times \frac{4500}{4525} = 17.44 \text{ mm.}$$

Q. 19. Henry's law constant for the molarity of methane in benzene at 298 K is 4.27×10^5 mm Hg. Calculate the solubility of methane in benzene at 298 K under 760 mm Hg.

Ans. Here, $k_H = 4.27 \times 10^5$ mm

$$P = 760 \text{ mm}$$

Applying Henry's law
$$P = k_H x$$

$\therefore \qquad x = \dfrac{P}{k_H} = \dfrac{760 \text{ mm}}{4.27 \times 10^5 \text{ mm}} = 1.78 \times 10^{-3}$

i.e., mole fraction of methane in benzene $= 1.78 \times 10^{-3}$.

Q. 20. Benzene and toluene form ideal solution over the entire range of composition. The vapour pressures of pure benzene and toluene at 300 K are 50.71 mm Hg and 32.06 mm Hg respectively. Calculate the mole fraction of benzene in the vapour phase if 80 g of benzene is mixed with 100 g of toluene.

Ans. Molar mass of benzene (C_6H_6) $= 78$ g mol^{-1}

Molar mass of toluene (C_7H_8) $= 92$ g mol^{-1}

$$\therefore \qquad n_{C_6H_6} = \frac{80 \text{ g}}{78 \text{ g mol}^{-1}} = 1.026 \text{ mole}$$

$$n_{C_7H_8} = \frac{100 \text{ g}}{92 \text{ g mol}^{-1}} = 1.087 \text{ mole}$$

$\therefore$ In the solution

$$x_{C_6H_6} = \frac{n_{C_6H_6}}{n_{C_6H_6} + n_{C_7H_8}} = \frac{1.026}{1.026 + 1.087} = \frac{1.026}{2.113} = 0.486$$

$$x_{C_7H_8} = 1 - 0.486 = 0.514$$

$$P^o_{C_6H_6} = 50.71 \text{ mm}, \quad P^o_{C_7H_8} = 32.06 \text{ mm}$$

Applying Raoult's law

$$P_{C_6H_6} = x_{C_6H_6} \times P^o_{C_6H_6}$$

$$= 0.486 \times 50.71 \text{ mm} = 24.65 \text{ mm}$$

$$P_{C_7H_8} = x_{C_7H_8} \times P^o_{C_7H_8}$$

$$= 0.514 \times 32.06 \text{ mm} = 16.48 \text{ mm}$$

$\therefore$ Mole fraction of benzene in the vapour phase

$$= \frac{P_{C_6H_6}}{P_{C_6H_6} + P_{C_7H_8}}$$

$$= \frac{24.65}{24.65 + 16.48} = \frac{24.65}{41.13} = 0.60.$$

Q. 21. The air is a mixture of a number of gases. The major components are oxygen and nitrogen with approximate proportion of 20% is to 79% by volume at 298 K. The water is in equilibrium with air at a pressure of 10 atm. At 298 K, if the Henry's law constants for oxygen and nitrogen are 3.30 × 10^7 mm and 6.51 × 10^7 mm respectively, calculate the composition of these gases in water.

Ans. Total pressure of air in equilibrium with water = 10 atm

As air contains 20% oxygen and 79% nitrogen by volume,

$$\therefore \qquad \text{Partial pressure of oxygen } (p_{O_2}) = \frac{20}{100} \times 10 \text{ atm} = 2 \text{ atm} = 2 \times 760 \text{ mm} = 1520 \text{ mm}$$

$$\text{Partial pressure of nitrogen } (p_{N_2}) = \frac{79}{100} \times 10 \text{ atm} = 7.9 \times 760 \text{ mm} = 6004 \text{ mm}$$

$$k_H (O_2) = 3.30 \times 10^7 \text{ mm}, \quad k_H (N_2) = 6.51 \times 10^7 \text{ mm}$$

Applying Henry's law

$$p_{O_2} = k_H \times x_{O_2}$$

$$\text{or} \qquad x_{O_2} = \frac{p_{O_2}}{k_H} = \frac{1520 \text{ mm}}{3.30 \times 10^7 \text{ mm}} = 4.61 \times 10^{-5}$$

$$p_{N_2} = k_H \times x_{N_2}$$

$$x_{N_2} = \frac{p_{N_2}}{k_H} = \frac{6004 \text{ mm}}{6.51 \times 10^7} = 9.22 \times 10^{-5}$$

Q. 22. Determine the amount of CaCl$_2$ (i = 2.47) dissolved in 2.5 litre of water such that its osmotic pressure is 0.75 atm at 27°C.

Ans.

$$\pi = iCRT = i \frac{n}{V} RT$$

$$\text{or} \qquad n = \frac{\pi \times V}{i \times R \times T}$$

$$= \frac{0.75 \text{ atm} \times 2.5 \text{ L}}{2.47 \times 0.0821 \text{ L atm K}^{-1} \text{ mol}^{-1} \times 300 \text{ K}} = 0.0308 \text{ mole}$$

$$\text{Molar mass of CaCl}_2 = 40 + 2 \times 35.5 = 111 \text{ g mol}^{-1}$$

$$\therefore \quad \text{Amount dissolved} = 0.0308 \times 111 \text{ g} = 3.42 \text{ g}.$$

Q. 23. **Determine the osmotic pressure of a solution prepared by dissolving 25 mg of K_2SO_4 in 2 litre of water at 25ºC, assuming that it is completely dissociated.**

Ans.

$$K_2SO_4 \text{ dissolved} = 25 \text{ mg} = 0.025 \text{ g}$$

$$\text{Volume of solution} = 2 \text{ L}$$

$$T = 25°C = 298 \text{ K}$$

$$\text{Molar mass of } K_2SO_4 = 2 \times 39 + 32 + 4 \times 16 = 174 \text{ g mol}^{-1}$$

Since K_2SO_4 dissociates completely as $K_2SO_4 \longrightarrow 2K^+ + SO_4^{2-}$

i.e., ions produced 3,

$\therefore \ i = 3$

$\therefore$

$$p = i \text{ CRT} = i \frac{n}{V} \text{RT} = i \times \frac{w}{M} \times \frac{1}{V} \text{RT}$$

$$= 3 \times \frac{0.025 \text{ g}}{174 \text{ g mol}^{-1}} \times \frac{1}{2L} \times 0.0821 \text{ L atm K}^{-1} \text{ mol}^{-1} \times 298 \text{ K} = 5.27 \times 10^{-3} \text{ atm}.$$

Q. 24. **An antifreeze solution is prepared from 222.6 g of ethylene glycol $[C_2H_4(OH)_2]$ and 200 g of water. Calculate the molality of the solution. If the density of this solution is 1.072 g ml^{-1}, what will be the molarity of the solution?***

Ans.

$$\text{Molality } (m) = \frac{w_2}{M} \times \frac{1000}{w_1}$$

w_2 = Weight of solute in gram; M = Molar mass of solute

w_1 = Weight of solvent in gram

$\therefore$

$$m = \frac{222.6}{M} \times \frac{1000}{200}$$

[Molar mass of ethylene glycol: $(12 \times 2) + (1 \times 6) + (16 \times 2) = 62$ g/mol]

$$m = \frac{222.6}{62} \times \frac{1000}{200} = 17.95 \text{ mol/Kg}$$

Now

$$\text{molality} = 17.95 \text{ mol/kg}$$

$$\text{Density, } d = 1.072 \text{ g/ml, Density} = \frac{\text{Mass}}{\text{Volume}}$$

$$\text{Molarity} = \frac{\text{Moles of solute}}{\text{Litre of solution}}$$

$$= \frac{\dfrac{222.6}{62} \times 1000}{\text{Volume of solution}}$$

$$= \frac{222.6 \times 1000}{62 \times \dfrac{(222.6 + 200)}{1.072}}$$

$$= \frac{222.6 \times 1000 \times 1.072}{62 \times 422.6}$$

$$= 9.107 = 9.11 \text{ M}.$$

Q. 25. **Calculate relative lowering of vapour pressure for the below mentioned solution.**

   (i)   Vapour pressure of pure liquid at 25°C is 100 mm Hg and mole fraction of solvent is 0.8.

   (ii) Vapour pressure of water at 293 K is 17.51 mm Hg and lowering of vapour pressure of sugar solution is 0.0614 mm of Hg.

* are board exam questions from previous years

Ans. Relative lowering of vapour pressure is

$$\frac{P^O - P_s}{P^O} = x_2 \text{ (mole fraction of solute)}$$

P^O = Vapour pressure of pure solvent.

P_s = Vapour pressure of solution.

(i) Mole fraction of solvent = 0.8

Hence of solute (x_2) = 1 – 0.8 = 0.2

$$\therefore \qquad \frac{P^O - P_s}{P^O} = 0.2$$

(ii) P^o = 17.51 mm Hg, $P^o - P_s$ = 0.0614 mm Hg.

$$\therefore \qquad \frac{P^O - P_s}{P^O} = \frac{0.0614}{17.51} = 0.00351.$$

Q. 26. A 4.5% solution of cane sugar (sucrose) is isotonic with 0.87% solution of urea. Find the molecular mass of urea. *

Ans. Isotonic solutions have same osmotic pressure because of same concentration

$$C_1 \text{ (cane sugar)} = C_2 \text{ (urea)}$$

$$\pi_1 \text{ (cane sugar)} = \pi_2 \text{ (urea)}$$

$$C_1 = \frac{n_1 \text{ (moles of cane sugar)}}{V_1 \text{ (volume of cane sugar)}} = \frac{n_2 \text{ (moles of urea)}}{V_2 \text{ (volume of urea)}}$$

$$\therefore \qquad \frac{4.5}{M_1 \times V_1} = \frac{0.87}{M_2 \times V_2}$$

Molecular mass of sucrose ($C_{13}H_{22}O_{11}$) = 342.3 g/mol

4.5 % solution mean 4.5 moles in 100 ml of solution.

So both V_1 and V_2 are same 100 ml

$$\therefore \qquad \frac{4.5}{342.5 \times 100} = \frac{0.87}{M_2 \times 100}$$

$$\therefore \qquad M_2 = \frac{0.87 \times 100 \times 342.3}{4.5 \times 100} = 66.17 \text{ g/mol}$$

Molecular mass of urea = 66.17 amu.

Q. 27. Calculate the amount of KCl which must be added to 1 kg of water so that its freezing point is depressed by 2K. *

(K_f of water = 1.86 K kg mol^{-1}, K (Z) = 39, Cl (Z) = 35.5).

Ans.
$$KCl \longrightarrow K^+ + Cl^-$$

KCl dissociates to give two moles per mole of it so van't Hoff factor, i = 2.

ΔT_f = 2K, K_f = 1.86 K kg mol^{-1}

$\Delta T_f = i.K_f.m$, m = molality

$$\therefore \qquad m = \frac{\Delta T_f}{i.K_f} = \frac{2}{2 \times 1.86} = 0.54 \text{ mol kg}^{-1}$$

Thus, 0.54 mole of KCl should be added in 1 kg of water.

$$\text{Mass} = \text{Moles} \times \text{Molar Mass}$$

$$\text{Amount of KCl} = 0.54 \times (39 + 35.5) \text{ g/mol}$$

$$= 0.54 \times 74.5 = 40.23 \text{ g.}$$

Q. 28. The degree of dissociation of $Ca(NO_3)_2$ in a dilute aqueous solution containing 14 g of the salt per 200 g of water at 110°C is 80%. If the vapour pressure of water is 760 mm Hg. Calculate the vapour pressure of the solution.

Ans.
$$Ca(NO_3)_2 \longrightarrow Ca^{2+} + 2NO_3^-$$

Hence   No. of moles of solute, $n = 3$

For dissociation of a solute,

$$\alpha \text{ (Degree of dissociation)} = \frac{i-1}{n-1} \quad (i = \text{van't Hoff factor})$$

i.e.,
$$0.8 = \frac{i-1}{3-1}$$

$$\Rightarrow \quad i - 1 = 0.8 \times 2 = 1.6$$

$$\Rightarrow \quad i = 2.6$$

$$\frac{P_A^o - P_A}{P_A^o} = i \times x_B = \frac{i \times \dfrac{W_B}{M_B}}{\dfrac{W_A}{M_A} + \dfrac{W_B}{M_B}} = \frac{2.6 \times \dfrac{14}{164}}{\dfrac{200}{18} + \dfrac{14}{164}}$$

Now,

(Relative lowering of vapour pressure)

A = Pure solvent (H_2O)

B = $Ca(NO_3)_2$,

$$\text{Molecular mass} = [40 + (14 + 3 \times 16)2] = 164 \text{ g}$$

$$\Rightarrow \quad \frac{p_A^o}{p_A^o} - \frac{p_A}{p_A^o} = 2.6 \times \frac{14}{164} \times \frac{164 \times 18}{33052}$$

$$\Rightarrow \quad 1 - \frac{p_A}{p_A^o} = \frac{14 \times 18 \times 2.6}{33052} = \frac{665.2}{33052}$$

$$\Rightarrow \quad \frac{p_A}{p_A^o} = \frac{33052 - 655.2}{33052} = \frac{32396.8}{33052} = 0.9801$$

$$\Rightarrow \quad p_A = p_A^o \times 0.9801$$
$$= 760 \times 0.9801 = 744.87 \text{ mm Hg.}$$

Q. 29. Calculate the freezing point of an aqueous solution containing 10.50 g of $MgBr_2$ in 200 g of water. (Molar mass of $MgBr_2$ = 184 g/mol and K_f of water = 1.86 kg mol^{-1}).*

Ans.
$$MgBr_2 \text{ (aq)} \longrightarrow Mg^{2+} \text{ (aq)} + 2Br^- \text{ (aq)}$$

Hence, $i = 3$

$$\text{Weight of solvent } (W_2) = 10.50 \text{ g}$$
$$M_2 = 184 \text{ g/mol}$$
$$\text{Weight of solute } (W_1) = 200 \text{ g} = 0.2 \text{ kg}$$
$$K_f = 1.86 \text{ K kg mol}^{-1}, \Delta T_f = ?$$

Now,
$$\Delta T_f = i \times K_f \times \frac{W_2}{M_2} \times \frac{1}{W_1(\text{kg})}$$

$$= \frac{3 \times 1.86 \text{ K kg mol}^{-1}}{0.2 \text{ kg}} \times \frac{10.50 \times 10^{-3} \text{ kg}}{184 \times 10^{-3} \text{ kg/mol}}$$

$$= 1.59 \text{ K or } 1.59°C.$$

$$\text{Freezing point of water, } T_f = T_f^o - \Delta T_f$$
$$273 - 1.59 = 271.41 \text{ K.}$$

Q. 30. When 2.56 g of sulphur was dissolved in 100 g of CS_2, the freezing point is lowered by 0.383 K. Calculate the formula of sulphur.*

Given (K_f for CS_2 = 3.83 K kg mol^{-1}, Atomic mass S = 32 g/mol.)

Ans. $W_2 = 2.56$ g, $W_1 = 100$ g

$\Delta T_f = 0.383$ K, $K_f = 3.83$ K kg mol^{-1}

$M_2 = 32$ g/mol

Applying the formula :

$$\Delta T_f = \frac{K_f \times W_2 \times 1000}{W_1 \times M_2} = \frac{3.83 \text{ K kg mol}^{-1} \times 2.56 \text{ g} \times 1000}{100 \text{ g} \times M_2 \text{ gmol}^{-1}}$$

$$M_2 = \frac{3.83 \text{ K kg mol}^{-1} \times 2.56 \text{ g} \times 1000}{100 \text{ g} \times 0.383 \text{ K}} = 256 \text{ g/mol.}$$

Formula of Sulphur :

One mole atom has mass 32 g

Hence 256 gm has $\dfrac{256}{32} \approx 8$ atoms

So, sulphur exists as S_8.

Q. 31. Calculate the molarity of each of the following solutions :

(i)   30 g of $Co(NO_3)_2.6H_2O$ in 4.3 L of solution

(ii) 30 mL of 0.5 M H_2SO_4 diluted to 500 mL.

Ans. Molarity is given by :

$$\text{Molarity} = \frac{\text{Moles of solute}}{\text{Volume of solution in litre}}$$

(i)   Molar mass of $Co(NO_3)_2.6H_2O = 59 + 2(14 + 3 \times 16) + 6 \times 18 = 291 \text{ g mol}^{-1}$

$\therefore$ $\text{Moles of } Co(NO_3)_2.6H_2O = \dfrac{30}{291} \text{ mol} = 0.103 \text{ mol}$

Therefore, $\text{Molarity} = \dfrac{0.103 \text{ mol}}{4.3 \text{ L}} = 0.023 \text{ M}$

(ii) Number of moles present in 1000 mL of 0.5 M $H_2SO_4 = 0.5$ mol

$\therefore$ Number of moles present in 30 mL of 0.5 M $H_2SO_4 = \dfrac{0.5 \times 30}{1000} \text{ mol} = 0.015 \text{ mol}$

Therefore, $\text{Molarity} = \dfrac{0.015 \text{ mol}}{0.5 \text{ L}} = 0.03 \text{ M.}$

Q. 32. Calculate the mass of urea (NH_2CONH_2) required in making 2.5 kg of 0.25 molal aqueous solution.

Ans. $\text{Molar mass of urea } (NH_2CONH_2) = 2 (1 \times 14 + 2 \times 1) + 1 \times 12 + 1 \times 16$

$$= 60 \text{ g mol}^{-1}$$

0.25 molal aqueous solution of urea means :

1000 g of water contains 0.25 mol $= (0.25 \times 60)$ g of urea

$$= 15 \text{ g of urea}$$

That is, $(1000 + 15)$ g of solution contains 15 g of urea

Therefore, 2.5 kg (2500 g) of solution contains $= \dfrac{15 \times 2500}{1000 + 15} \text{ g} = 36.95 \text{ g}$

$$= 37 \text{ g of urea (approximately)}$$

Hence,   mass of urea required = 37 g.

Q. 33. H_2S, a toxic gas with rotten egg like smell is used for the qualitative analysis. If the solubility of H_2S in water at STP is 0.195 m, calculate Henry's law constant.

Ans. It is given that the solubility of H_2S in water at STP is 0.195 m, i.e., 0.195 mol of H_2S is dissolved in 1000 g of water.

$$\text{Moles of water} = \frac{1000 \text{ g}}{18 \text{ g mol}^{-1}}$$

$$= 55.55 \text{ mol}$$

$\therefore$ $\text{Mole fraction of } H_2S, x = \dfrac{\text{Moles of } H_2S}{\text{Moles of } H_2S + \text{Moles of water}}$

$$= \frac{0.195}{0.195 + 55.55}$$

$$= 0.0035$$

At STP, pressure $(p) = 0.987$ bar

According to Henry's law : $p = k_H x$.

$\Rightarrow \qquad k_H = \dfrac{p}{x}$ \hfill (where p is pressure and x is mole fraction)

$$= \frac{0.987}{0.0035} \text{ bar}$$

$$= 282 \text{ bar.}$$

Q. 34. **A solution of glucose in water is labelled as 10 percent w/w, what would be the molality and mole fraction of each component in the solution? If the density of the solution is 1.2 g mL^{-1}, then what would be the molarity of the solution?**

Ans. 10 g of glucose is present in 100 g solution i.e., 10 g of glucose has been dissolved in 90 g of water

$$\therefore \qquad \text{Volume of 100 g of solution} = \frac{\text{Mass}}{\text{Density}} = \frac{100}{1.2} = 83.3 \text{ mL} = 0.083 \text{ L}$$

$$\text{Number of moles of glucose} = \frac{10 \text{ g}}{180 \text{ g mol}^{-1}} = \frac{1}{18} \text{ mol}$$

$$\therefore \qquad \text{Molarity of solution} = \frac{\text{Mol. of solute}}{\text{Vol. of solution (L)}}$$

$$= \frac{(1/18 \text{ mol})}{0.083 \text{ L}} = 0.67 \text{ M}$$

$$\text{Mass of water} = 90 \text{ g} = 0.09 \text{ kg}$$

$$\therefore \qquad \text{Molality of solution} = \frac{\text{Number of moles of glucose}}{\text{Mass of solvent (kg)}}$$

$$= \frac{(1/18 \text{ mol})}{0.09 \text{ kg}} = 0.617 \text{ m}$$

To find mole fraction of each component

$$\text{Number of moles of glucose} = \frac{10}{180} = 0.055$$

$$\text{Number of moles of water} = \frac{90}{18} = 5$$

$$\text{Total number of moles} = 0.055 + 5 = 5.055$$

$$\therefore \qquad \text{Mole fraction of glucose} = \frac{0.055}{5.055} = 0.01$$

$$\therefore \qquad \text{Mole fraction of water} = \frac{5}{5.055} = 0.99.$$

Q. 35. **The partial pressure of ethane over a solution containing 6.56×10^{-3} g of ethane is 1 bar. If the solution contains 5.00×10^{-2} g of ethane, then what shall be the partial pressure of the gas?**

Ans. $\qquad$ Molar mass of ethane $(C_2H_6) = 2 \times 12 + 6 \times 1 = 30 \text{ g mol}^{-1}$

$\therefore$ Number of moles present in 6.56×10^{-2} g of ethane

$$= \frac{6.56 \times 10^{-2}}{30}$$

$$= 2.187 \times 10^{-3} \text{ mol}$$

Let the number of moles of the solvent be x.

According to Henry's law,

$$p = k_H x$$

$$\Rightarrow \qquad 1 \text{ bar} = k_H \cdot \frac{2.187 \times 10^{-3}}{2.187 \times 10^{-3} + x}$$

$$\Rightarrow \qquad 1 \text{ bar} = k_H \frac{2.187 \times 10^{-3}}{x} \qquad (\text{Since } x >> 2.187 \times 10^{-3})$$

$$\Rightarrow \qquad k_H = \frac{x}{2.187 \times 10^{-3}} \text{ bar}$$

Number of moles present in 5.00×10^{-2} g of ethane

$$= \frac{5.00 \times 10^{-2}}{30} \text{ mol}$$

$$= 1.67 \times 10^{-3} \text{ mol}$$

According to Henry's law,

$$p = k_H x$$

$$= \frac{x}{2.187 \times 10^{-3}} \times \frac{1.67 \times 10^{-3}}{(1.67 \times 10^{-3}) + x}$$

$$= \frac{x}{2.187 \times 10^{-3}} \times \frac{1.67 \times 10^{-3}}{x} \qquad (\text{Since, } x >> 1.67 \times 10^{-3})$$

$$= 0.764 \text{ bar}$$

Hence, partial pressure of the gas will be 0.764 bar.

Q. 36. **An aqueous solution of 2% non-volatile solute exerts a pressure of 1.004 bar at the normal boiling point of the solvent. What is the molar mass of the solute?**

Ans. Here, vapour pressure of the solution at normal boiling point (p_1) = 1.004 bar

Vapour pressure of pure water at normal boiling point (p_1°) = 1.013 bar = 1 atm

Mass of solute, (w_2) = 2 g

Mass of solvent (water), (w_1) = 98 g

Molar mass of solvent (water), (M_1) = 18 g mol^{-1}

According to Raoult's law,

$$\Rightarrow \qquad \frac{p_1^o - p_1}{p_1^o} = \frac{n_2}{n_1}$$

$$\Rightarrow \qquad \frac{p_1^o - p_1}{p_1^o} = \frac{w_2 \times M_1}{M_2 \times w_1}$$

$$\Rightarrow \qquad \frac{1.013 - 1.004}{1.013} = \frac{2 \times 18}{M_2 \times 98}$$

$$\Rightarrow \qquad \frac{0.009}{1.013} = \frac{2 \times 18}{M_2 \times 98}$$

$$\Rightarrow \qquad M_2 = \frac{1.013 \times 2 \times 18}{0.009 \times 98}$$

$$= 41.35 \text{ g mol}^{-1}.$$

Hence, the molar mass of the solute is 41.35 g mol^{-1}.

Q. 37. **Heptane and octane form an ideal solution. At 373 K, the vapour pressures of the two liquid components are 105.2 kPa and 46.8 kPa respectively. What will be the vapour pressure of a mixture of 26.0 g of heptane and 35 g of octane?**

Ans. Vapour pressure of heptane (p_1°) = 105.2 kPa

Vapour pressure of octane (p_2°) = 46.8 kPa

We know that,

Molar mass of heptane (C_7H_{16}) = $7 \times 12 + 16 \times 1 = 100$ g mol^{-1}

$\therefore$ $\qquad$ Number of moles of heptane $= \dfrac{26}{100}$ mol $= 0.26$ mol

$$\text{Molar mass of octane } (C_8H_{18}) = 8 \times 12 + 18 \times 1$$
$$= 114 \text{ g mol}^{-1}$$

$\therefore$ $\qquad$ Number of moles of octane $= \dfrac{35}{114}$ mol $= 0.31$ mol

$$\text{Mole fraction of heptane, } x = \dfrac{0.26}{0.26 + 0.31} = 0.456$$

and, $\qquad$ Mole fraction of octane, $x_2 = 1 - 0.456 = 0.544$

Now, $\qquad$ Partial pressure of heptane, $p_1 = x_1 p_1^{\circ}$
$$= 0.456 \times 105.2$$
$$= 47.97 \text{ kPa}$$

$$\text{Partial pressure of octane, } p_2 = x_2 p_2^{\circ}$$
$$= 0.544 \times 46.8$$
$$= 25.46 \text{ kPa}$$

Hence, $\qquad$ vapour pressure of solution $p_{total} = p_1 + p_2$
$$= 47.97 + 25.46$$
$$= 73.43 \text{ kPa}$$
$$= 73.43 \times 10^3 \text{ Pa} = 0.734 \times 10^5 \text{ Pa} = 0.734 \text{ bar.}$$

Q. 38. Calculate the mass of a non-volatile solute (molar mass 40 g mol^{-1}) which should be dissolved in 114 g octane to reduce its vapour pressure to 80%.

Ans. Let the vapour pressure of pure octane be, p_1^{o}

Then, the vapour pressure of the octane after dissolving the non-volatile solute is
$$p_1 = \dfrac{80}{100} p_1^{o} = 0.8 \, p_1^{o}$$

Molar mass of solute, $M_2 = 40$ g mol^{-1}
Mass of octane, $w_1 = 114$ g
Molar mass of octane, (C_8H_{18}), $M_1 = 8 \times 12 + 18 \times 1 = 114$ g mol^{-1}
Applying the relation,

$$\dfrac{p_1^{o} - p_1}{p_1^{o}} = \dfrac{n_2}{n_2 + n_1} \qquad\qquad (n = \text{no. of moles})$$

$\Rightarrow \qquad\qquad \dfrac{p_1^{o} - 0.8 p_1^{o}}{p_1^{o}} = \dfrac{w_2 \times 114}{40 \times 114}$

$\Rightarrow \qquad\qquad \dfrac{0.2 p_1^{o}}{p_1^{o}} = \dfrac{w_2}{40}$

$\Rightarrow \qquad\qquad 0.2 = \dfrac{w_2}{40}$

$\Rightarrow \qquad\qquad w_2 = 8$ g.

Q. 39. A 5% solution (by mass) of cane sugar in water has freezing point of 271 K. Calculate the freezing point of 5% glucose in water if freezing point of pure water is 273.15 K.

Ans. Here, $\Delta T_f = (273.15 - 271)$ K $= 2.15$ K

$\qquad$ Molar mass of sugar $(C_{12}H_{22}O_{11}) = 12 \times 12 + 22 \times 1 + 11 \times 16 = 342$ g mol^{-1}

5% solution (by mass) of cane sugar in water means 5 g of cane sugar is present in $(100 - 5)$ g $= 95$ g of water.

Now, $\qquad$ Number of moles of cane sugar $= \dfrac{5}{342}$ mol $= 0.0146$ mol

Therefore, $\qquad$ Molality of the solution, $m = \dfrac{0.0146 \text{ mol}}{0.095 \text{ kg}} = 0.1537$ mol kg^{-1}

Applying the relation,

$$\Delta T_f = K_f \times m$$

$$\Rightarrow \qquad K_f = \frac{\Delta T_f}{m}$$

$$= \frac{2.15\ K}{0.1537\ mol\ kg^{-1}}$$

$$= 13.99\ K\ kg\ mol^{-1}$$

Molar mass of glucose $(C_6H_{12}O_6) = 6 \times 12 + 12 \times 1 + 6 \times 16 = 180\ g\ mol^{-1}$

5% glucose in water means 5 g of glucose is present in $(100 - 5)\ g = 95\ g$ of water.

$$\therefore \qquad \text{Number of moles of glucose} = \frac{5}{180}\ mol = 0.0278\ mol$$

Therefore, Molality of the solution, $m = \dfrac{0.0278\ mol}{0.095\ kg}\ 0.2926\ mol\ kg^{-1}$

Applying the relation,

$$\Delta T_f = K_f \times m$$
$$= 13.99\ K\ kg\ mol^{-1} \times 0.2924\ mol\ kg^{-1}$$
$$= 4.09\ K\ (approximately)$$

Hence, the freezing point of 5% glucose solution is $(273.15 - 4.09)\ K = 269.06\ K$.

Q. 40. **At 300 K, 36 g of glucose present in one litre of its solution has an osmotic pressure of 4.98 bar. If the osmotic pressure of the solution is 1.52 bars at the same temperature, what would be its concentration ?**

Ans. Here, $T = 300\ K$

$$\pi = 1.52\ bar$$
$$R = 0.083\ bar\ LK^{-1}\ mol^{-1}$$

Applying the relation, $(\pi = CRT)$

$$\Rightarrow \qquad C = \frac{\pi}{RT}$$

$$= \frac{1.52\ bar}{0.083\ bar\ LK^{-1}\ mol^{-1}\ \times 300\ K} = 0.061\ mol$$

Or

I. Case :

Here, $\qquad \pi = CRT$

Molecular mass of glucose $= 180\ g/mol$

$$C = \frac{36}{180} = \frac{1}{5}\ M$$

$$\pi = \frac{\frac{1}{5} \times R \times 300\ K}{}$$

$$\Rightarrow \qquad 4.98 = 60R$$

$$\Rightarrow \qquad R = \frac{4.98}{60} = 0.083.$$

II. Case :

$$\pi = CRT$$
$$1.52 = C \times R \times 300$$

$$\Rightarrow \qquad C = \frac{1.52}{R \times 300} = \frac{1.52 \times 60}{300 \times 4.89} = 0.06\ mol.$$

Since the volume of the solution is 1 L, the concentration of the solution would be 0.061 M.

Q. 41. **Nalorphene $(C_{19}H_{21}NO_3)$, similar to morphine, is used to combat withdrawal symptoms in narcotic users. Dose of nalorphene generally given is 1.5 mg. Calculate the mass of 1.5×10^{-3} m aqueous solution required for the above dose.**

Ans. The molar mass of nalorphene ($C_{19}H_{21}NO_3$) is given as:

$$19 \times 12 + 21 \times 1 + 1 \times 14 + 3 \times 16 = 311 \text{ g mol}^{-1}$$

In 1.5×10^{-3} m aqueous solution of nalorphene,

1 kg (1000 g) of water contains 1.5×10^{-3} mol $= 1.5 \times 10^{-3} \times 311$ g $= 0.4665$ g (moles × molecular mass
$$= \text{mass in gm})$$

Therefore, total mass of the solution $= (1000 + 0.4665)$ g $= 1000.4665$ g

This implies that the mass of the solution containing 0.4665 g of nalorphene is 1000.4665 g.

Therefore, mass of the solution containing 1.5 mg of nalorphene is :

$$\frac{1000.4665 \times 1.5 \times 10^{-3}}{0.4665} = 3.22 \text{ g}$$

Hence, the mass of aqueous solution required is 3.22 g.

Q. 42. **100 g of liquid A (molar mass 140 g mol^{-1}) was dissolved in 1000 g of liquid B (molar mass 180 g mol^{-1}). The vapour pressure of pure liquid B was found to be 500 torr. Calculate the vapour pressure of pure liquid A and its vapour pressure in the solution if the total vapour pressure of the solution is 475 torr.**

Ans.
$$n_A = \frac{100 \text{ g}}{140 \text{ g mol}^{-1}} = \frac{5}{7} \text{ mole and } n_B = \frac{1000 \text{ g}}{180 \text{ g mol}^{-1}} = \frac{50}{9} \text{ mole}$$

$\therefore$
$$x_A = \frac{5/7}{5/7 \times 50/9} = \frac{5/7}{395/63} = \frac{5}{7} \times \frac{63}{395} = \frac{45}{395} = 0.114$$

$\therefore$
$$x_B = 1 - 0.114 = 0.886$$

Also, given $p_B° = 500$ torr

Applying Raoult's law.

$$p_A = x_A p_A^o = 0.114 \times p_A^o \qquad \text{...(i)}$$

$$p_B = x_B p_B^o = 0.886 \times 500 = 443 \text{ torr}$$

$$p_{total} = p_A + p_B$$

$$475 = 0.114 \ p_A^o + 443 \text{ or } p_A^o = \frac{475 - 443}{0.114} = 280.7 \text{ torr}$$

Substituting this value in equation (i), we get

$$p_A = 0.114 \times 280.7 = 32 \text{ torr.}$$

Q. 43. **The vapour pressure of pure liquids A and B are 450 and 700 mm Hg respectively, at 350 K. Find out the composition of the liquid mixture if total vapour pressure is 600 mm Hg. Also find the composition of the vapour phase.**

Ans. It is given that:

$p°_A = 450$ mm of Hg

$p°_B = 700$ mm of Hg

$p_{total} = 600$ mm of Hg

From Raoult's law , we have

$$p_A = p°_A x_A$$

Therefore total pressure,

$$p_{total} = p_A + p_B$$
$$p_B = p°_B x_B = p°_B(1 - x_A)$$
$\Rightarrow \qquad p_{total} = p°_A x_A = p°_B(1 - x_A)$

$\Rightarrow \qquad p_{total} = p_A^o x_A + p_B^o - p_B^o x_A)$

$\Rightarrow \qquad p_{total} = (p_A^o - p_B^o)x_A + p_B^o$

$\Rightarrow \qquad 600 = (450 - 700)x_A + 700$

$\Rightarrow \qquad -100 = -250 \ x_A$

$\Rightarrow \qquad x_A = 0.4$

$\qquad\qquad x_B = 1 - x_A$

$$\therefore \qquad x_B = 1 - 0.4 = 0.6$$

Now,
$$p_A = p_A^o x_A$$
$$= 450 \times 0.4$$
$$= 180 \text{ mm of Hg}$$
$$p_B = p_B^o x_B$$
$$= 700 \times 0.6$$
$$= 420 \text{ mm of Hg.}$$

Now, in the vapour phase : Mole fraction of liquid ,

$$Y_A = \frac{p_A}{p_A + p_B}$$
$$= \frac{180}{180 + 420}$$
$$= \frac{180}{600}$$
$$= 0.30$$

And, mole fraction of liquid B $= 1 - 0.30 = 0.70$ in vapour phase.

Q. 44. Vapour pressure of pure water at 298 K is 23.8 mm Hg. 50 g of urea (NH_2CONH_2) is dissolved in 850 g of water. Calculate the vapour pressure of water for this solution and its relative lowering.

Ans. It is given that vapour pressure of water, $P_1^o = 23.8$ mm of Hg

Weight of water taken, $w_1 = 850$ g
Weight of urea taken, $w_2 = 50$ g
Molecular weight of water, $M_1 = 18$ g mol^{-1}
Molecular weight of urea, $M_2 = 60$ g mol^{-1}
Now, we have to calculate vapour pressure of water in the solution. We take vapour pressure as p_1.
Now, from Raoult's law, we have : $p_1 = x_1 \times p_1^o$ and relative lowering of vapour pressure, is

$$\frac{p_1^o - p_1}{p_1^o} = \frac{n_2}{n_1 + n_2}$$

$$\Rightarrow \qquad \frac{p_1^o - p_1}{p_1^o} = \frac{\dfrac{w_2}{M_2}}{\dfrac{w_1}{M_1} + \dfrac{w_2}{M_2}}$$

$$\Rightarrow \qquad \frac{23.8 - p_1}{23.8} = \frac{\dfrac{50}{60}}{\dfrac{850}{18} + \dfrac{50}{60}}$$

$$\Rightarrow \qquad \frac{23.8 - p_1}{23.8} = \frac{0.83}{47.22 + 0.83}$$

$$\Rightarrow \qquad \frac{23.8 - p_1}{23.8} = 0.0173$$

$$\Rightarrow \qquad p_1 = 23.4 \text{ mm of Hg}$$

Hence, the vapour pressure of water in the given solution is 23.4 mm of Hg and its relative lowering is 0.0173.

Q. 45. Calculate (i) molality, (ii) molarity and (iii) mole fraction of KI if the density of 20% (mass/mass) aqueous KI is 1.202 g mL^{-1}.

Ans. (i)
$$\text{Molar mass of KI} = 39 + 127 = 166 \text{ g mol}^{-1}$$

20% (mass/mass) aqueous solution of KI means 20 g of KI is present in 100 g of solution.
That is,
20 g of KI is present in $(100 - 20)$ g of water $= 80$ g of water

$$\therefore \quad \text{Molality of the solution} = \frac{\text{Moles of KI}}{\text{Mass of water in kg}}$$

$$= \frac{\frac{20}{166}}{0.08} \text{ m} \left(\frac{20}{166} = 1.20 \text{ moles of KI} \right)$$

$$= 1.506 \text{ m}$$

$$= 1.51 \text{ m (approximately)}$$

(ii) It is given that the density of the solution = 1.202 g mL^{-1}

$$\therefore \quad \text{Volume of 100 g of solution} = \frac{\text{Mass}}{\text{Density}}$$

$$= \frac{100 \text{ g}}{1.202 \text{ g mL}^{-1}}$$

$$= 83.19 \text{ mL}$$

$$= 83.19 \times 10^{-3} \text{ L}$$

$$\therefore \quad \text{Molarity of the solution} = \frac{\frac{20}{166} \text{ mol}}{83.19 \times 10^{-3} \text{ L}} = 1.45 \text{ M}$$

(iii) Moles of KI $= \dfrac{20}{166} = 0.12$ moles

Moles of water $= \dfrac{80}{18} = 4.44$ moles.

$$\text{Mole fraction of KI} = \frac{\text{Moles of KI}}{\text{Moles of KI + Moles of Water}} = \frac{0.12}{0.12 + 4.44} = 0.0263 \text{ mole fraction}$$

Q. 46. Henry's law constant for CO$_2$ in water is 1.67 × 108 Pa at 298 K. Calculate the quantity of CO$_2$ in 500 mL of soda water when packed under 2.5 atm pressure at 298 K.

Ans. It is given that :

$$k_H = 1.67 \times 10^8 \text{ Pa}$$

$$p_{CO_2} = 2.5 \text{ atm} = 2.5 \times 1.01325 \times 10^5 \text{ Pa}$$

$$= 2.533125 \times 10^5 \text{ Pa}$$

According to Henry's law :

$$p_{CO_2} = k_H x$$

$$\Rightarrow \quad x = \frac{p_{CO_2}}{k_H}$$

$$= \frac{2.533125 \times 10^5}{1.67 \times 10^8}$$

$$= 0.00152$$

Now,

$$x = \frac{n_{CO_2}}{n_{CO_2} + n_{H_2O}} \approx \frac{n_{CO_2}}{n_{H_2O}}$$

We can write, n_{CO_2} is negligible as compared to

In 500 mL of soda water, the volume of water = 500 mL

[Neglecting the amount of soda present]

We can write :

$$500 \text{ mL of water} = 500 \text{ g of water}$$

$$= \frac{500}{18} \text{ mol of water}$$

$$= 27.78 \text{ mol of water}$$

Now,
$$\frac{n_{CO_2}}{n_{H_2O}} = x$$

$$\frac{n_{CO_2}}{27.78} = 0.00152$$

$$p_{CO_2} = 0.042 \text{ mol}$$

Hence, quantity of CO_2 in 500 mL of soda water $= (0.042 \times 44)$ g
$$= 1.848 \text{ g}$$

Q. 47. **A solution containing 30 g of non-volatile solute exactly in 90 g of water has a vapour pressure of 2.8 kPa at 298 K. Further, 18 g of water is then added to the solution and the new vapour pressure becomes 2.9 kPa at 298 K. Calculate :**

(i)   Molar mass of the solute

(ii) Vapour pressure of water at 298 K.

Ans. (i)   Let the molar mass of the solute be M g mol^{-1}

Now,   the no. of moles of solvent water, $n_1 = \dfrac{90 \text{ g}}{18 \text{ g mol}^{-1}} = 5 \text{ mol}$

And, the no. of moles of solute, $\qquad n_2 = \dfrac{30 \text{ g}}{M \text{ mol}^{-1}} = \dfrac{30}{M} \text{mol}$

$$p_1 = 2.8 \text{ kPa}$$

Applying the relation :

$$\frac{p_1^o - p_1}{p_1^o} = \frac{n_2}{n_1 + n_2}$$

$$\Rightarrow \qquad \frac{p_1^o - 2.8}{p_1^o} = \frac{\dfrac{30}{M}}{5 + \dfrac{30}{M}} \qquad \left[\text{as } \frac{30}{M} << 5 \text{ moles it can be ignored.}\right]$$

$$\therefore \qquad \frac{p_1^o - 2.8}{p_1^o} = \frac{\dfrac{30}{M}}{5} = \frac{30}{5\,M} = \frac{6}{M} \qquad \text{...(i)}$$

After the addition of 18 g of water :

$$n_1 = \frac{90 + 18 \text{ g}}{18} = 6 \text{ mol}$$

$$p_1 = 2.9 \text{ kPa}$$

Again, applying the relation :

$$\frac{p_1^o - p_1}{p_1^o} = \frac{n_2}{n_1 + n_2}$$

$$\Rightarrow \qquad \frac{p_1^o - 2.9}{p_1^o} = \frac{\dfrac{30}{M}}{6 + \dfrac{30}{M}}$$

As $\dfrac{30}{M} << 6$ moles, hence it can be neglected.

$$\Rightarrow \qquad \frac{p_1^o - 2.9}{p_1^o} = \frac{30}{6\,M} = \frac{5}{M} \qquad \text{...(ii)}$$

Divide equation (i) by (ii) we have,

$$\frac{p_1^o - 2.8}{p_1^o} \times \frac{p_1^o}{p_1^o - 2.9} = \frac{6}{M} \times \frac{M}{5}$$

$$\Rightarrow \qquad \frac{p_1^o - 2.8}{p_1^o - 2.9} = \frac{6}{5}$$

$$\Rightarrow \qquad 5p_1^o - 14 = 6p_1^o - 17.4$$

$$\Rightarrow \qquad p_1^o = 3.4 \text{ kPa Vapour pressure of water at 298 K}$$

To find molar mass of the solute:

Substitute the value of P_1^o in equation (i)

i.e.,
$$\frac{3.4\,kPa - 2.8\,kPa}{3.4\,kPa} = \frac{6}{M}$$

$$\Rightarrow \qquad \frac{0.6\,kPa}{3.4\,kPa} = \frac{6}{M}$$

$$\Rightarrow \qquad M = \frac{6 \times 3.4}{0.6} = 34 \text{ g/mol.}$$

Q. 48. **Two elements A and B form compounds having formula AB_2 and AB_4. When dissolved in 20 g of benzene (C_6H_6), 1 g of AB_2 lowers the freezing point by 2.3 K whereas 1.0 g of AB_4 lowers it by 1.3 K. The molar depression constant for benzene is 5.1 K kg mol^{-1}. Calculate atomic masses of A and B.**

Ans. We know that,

$$M_2 = \frac{1000 \times w_2 \times K_f}{\Delta T_f \times w_1}$$

Then,
$$M_{AB2} = \frac{1000 \times 1 \times 5.1}{2.3 \times 20} = 110.87 \text{ g mol}^{-1}$$

$$M_{AB4} = \frac{1000 \times 1 \times 5.1}{1.3 \times 20} = 196.15 \text{ g mol}^{-1}$$

Now, we have the molar masses of AB_2 and AB_4 as 110.87 g mol^{-1} and 196.15 g mol^{-1} respectively.

Let the atomic masses of A and B be x and y respectively.

Now, we can write:

$$x + 2y = 110.87 \qquad \qquad \text{...(i)}$$
$$x + 4y = 196.15 \qquad \qquad \text{...(ii)}$$

Subtracting equation (i) from (ii), we have

$$2y = 85.28$$
$$\Rightarrow \qquad y = 42.64$$

Putting the value of 'y' in equation (i), we have x

$$x + 2 \times 42.64 = 110.87$$
$$\Rightarrow \qquad x = 25.59$$

Hence, the atomic masses of A and B are 25.59 u and 42.64 u respectively.

Q. 49. **Calculate the depression in the freezing point of water when 10 g of $CH_3CH_2CHClCOOH$ is added to 250 g of water. $K_a = 1.4 \times 10^{-3}$, $K_f = 1.86$ K kg mol^{-1}.**

Ans. Molar mass of $CH_3CH_2CHClCOOH = 15 + 14 + 13 + 35.5 + 12 + 16 + 16 + 1 = 122.5$ g mol^{-1}

$\therefore$ No. of moles present in 10 g of $CH_3CH_2CHClCOOH$

$$= \frac{10\,g}{122.5\,g\,mol^{-1}}$$

$$= 0.0816 \text{ mol}$$

It is given that 10 g of $CH_3CH_2CHClCOOH$ is added to 250 g of water.

$\therefore \qquad$ Molality of the solution $= \dfrac{0.0186}{250} \times 1000$

$$= 0.3264 \text{ mol kg}^{-1}$$

Let (α) be the degree of dissociation of $CH_3CH_2CHClCOOH$.

$CH_3CH_2CHClCOOH$ undergoes dissociation according to the following equation:

$$CH_3CH_2CHClCOOH \rightleftharpoons CH_3CH_2CHClCOO^- + H^+$$

Initial conc.	C mol L^{-1}	0	0
At equilibrium	$C(1-\alpha)$	$C\alpha$	$C\alpha$

$\therefore$
$$K_a = \frac{C\alpha.C\alpha}{C(1-\alpha)} = \frac{C\alpha^2}{1-\alpha}$$

Since a is very small with respect to 1, $1 - \alpha \approx 1$

Now,
$$K_a = \frac{C\alpha^2}{1}$$

$\Rightarrow$
$$\alpha = \sqrt{\frac{K_a}{C}}$$

$$= \sqrt{\frac{1.4 \times 10^{-3}}{0.3264}} \qquad (\because K_a = 1.4 \times 10^{-3})$$

$$= 0.0655$$

Again,

$$CH_3CH_2CHClCOOH \rightleftharpoons CH_3CH_2CHClCOO^- + H^+$$

Initial moles	1	0	0
At equilibrium	$(1-\alpha)$	α	α

Total moles of equilibrium $= 1 - \alpha + \alpha + \alpha = 1 + \alpha$

$\therefore$
$$i = \frac{1+\alpha}{1}$$

$$= 1 + \alpha$$
$$= 1 + 0.0655 = 1.0655$$

Hence, the depression in the freezing point of water is given as :

$$\Delta T_f = i.K_f m$$
$$= 1.0655 \times 1.86 \text{ K kg mol}^{-1} \times 0.3264 \text{ mol kg}^{-1}$$
$$= 0.65 \text{ K.}$$

Q. 50. **19.5 g of CH_2FCOOH is dissolved in 500 g of water. The depression in the freezing point of water observed is 1.0°C. Calculate the van't Hoff factor and dissociation constant of fluoroacetic acid. K_f for water is 1.86 K kg mol^{-1}.**

Ans. It is given that :

$$w_1 = 500 \text{ g}$$
$$w_2 = 19.5 \text{ g}$$
$$K_f = 1.86 \text{ K kg mol}^{-1}$$
$$\Delta T_f = 1 \text{ K}$$

We know that :

$$\Delta T_f = K_f m \Rightarrow \Delta T_f = \frac{K_f \times w_2 \times 1000}{M_2 \times w_1}$$

$$M_2 = \frac{K_f \times w_2 \times 1000}{\Delta T_f \times w_1}$$

$$= \frac{1.86 \text{ K kg mol}^{-1} \times 19.5 \text{ g} \times 1000 \text{ kg}^{-1}}{500 \text{ g} \times 1 \text{ K}}$$

$$= 72.54 \text{ g mol–1}$$

Therefore, observed molar mass of CH_2FCOOH, $(M_2)_{obs} = 72.54$ g mol.

The calculated molar mass of

$$(M_2)_{cal} = 14 + 19 + 12 + 16 + 16 + 1 = 78 \text{ g mol}^{-1}$$

Therefore, van't Hoff factor is,
$$i = \frac{(M_2)_{cal}}{(M_2)_{obs}}$$

$$= \frac{78 \text{ g mol}^{-1}}{72.54 \text{ g mol}^{-1}}$$

$$= 1.0753$$

Let α be the degree of dissociation of CH_2FCOOH

$$CH_2FCOOH = CH_2FCOOH^- + H^+$$

Initial conc.	$C \text{ mol L}^{-1}$	0	0
At equilibrium	$C(1-\alpha)$	$C\alpha$	$C\alpha$

$$\therefore \quad i = \frac{C(1+\alpha)}{C}$$

$$\Rightarrow \quad i = 1 + \alpha$$

$$\Rightarrow \quad \alpha = i - 1$$

$$= 1.0753 - 1$$

$$= 0.0753$$

Now, the value of K_a is given as:

$$K_a = \frac{[CH_2FCOO^-][H^+]}{[CH_2FCOOH]}$$

$$= \frac{C\alpha.C\alpha}{C(1-\alpha)}$$

$$= \frac{C\alpha^2}{1-\alpha}$$

Taking the volume of the solution as 500 mL, we have the concentration :

$$\frac{19.5}{78} \times \frac{1000}{500} = 0.5 \text{ M}$$

Q. 51. **Calculate the degree of dissociation (α) of acetic acid if its molar conductivity (Λ_m) is 39.05 S cm^2 mol^{-1}. Given λ^o (H$^+$) = 349.6 S cm^2 mol^{-1} and λ^o (CH$_3$CHO$^-$) = 40.9 S cm^2 mol^{-1}.** *

Ans. Given : Molar conductivity (λ_m) for acetic acid = 39.05 S cm^2 mol^{-1}.

$$\lambda^o(H^+) = 349.6 \text{ S cm}^2 \text{ mol}^{-1}$$

$$\lambda^o(CH_3COO^-) = 40.95 \text{ S cm}^2 \text{ mol}^{-1}$$

We know that:

$$\lambda^o_m(CH_3COOH) = \lambda^o(H^+) + (CH_3COO^-)$$

$$390.5 = 349.6 + 40.9$$

$$390.5 = 390.5$$

also
$$\alpha = \frac{\lambda_m}{\lambda^o_m}$$

$$\alpha = \frac{39.05}{390.5}$$

$$\alpha = 0.1$$

Thus the degree of dissociation of acetic acid is 0.1.

Q. 52. **A 10% solution (by mass) of sucrose in water has freezing point of 269.15 K. Calculate the freezing point of 10% glucose in water, if freezing point of pure water is 273.15 K.** *

Given : (Molar mass of sucrose = 342 g mol^{-1})

(Molar mass of glucose = 180 g mol^{-1})

Ans. Given : Freezing point of = 269.15 K

10% solution of glucose

Freezing point pure water = 273.15 K

Molar mass of sucrose = 342 g mol^{-1}

Molar mass of glucose = 180 g mol^{-1}

We know that :

$$\Delta T_f = K_f \times m$$

also

$$m = \frac{W_2 \times 100}{M_2 \times M_1}$$

For the sucrose solution :

$$273.15 - 269.15 = \frac{k_f \times 10 \times 1000}{342 \times 90}$$

$$4 \times 242 \times 90 = K_f \times 100 \times 1000$$

$$\frac{4 \times 342 \times 90}{10 \times 1000} = K_f$$

$$K_f = 12.3 \text{ k kg/mol}$$

For the glucose solution :

$$\Delta T_f = k_f \times m$$

$$= \frac{12.3 \times 10 \times 1000}{180 \times 90}$$

$$\Delta T_f = 7.6 \text{ K}$$

thus

$$T_f = 273.15 - 7.6$$

$$T_f = 265.5 \text{ K}$$

The freezing point of 10% glucose in water is 265.5 K.

Q. 53. (i) Calculate the freezing point of solution when 1.9 g (of $MgCl_2$ (M = 95 g/mol) was dissolved in 50 g of water, assuming $MgCl_2$. Undergoes complete ionisation.*

(K$_f$ of water = 1.86 K kg mol^{-1})

(ii) (a) Out of 1 M glucose and 2 M glucose, which one has a higher boiling point and why?

(b) What happens when the external pressure of applied becomes more than the osmotic pressure of solution?

Ans. (i) $MgCl_2$ on ionisation gives 3 ions each mole.

$$MgCl_2(s) \longrightarrow Mg^{2+} \text{ (aq)} + Cl^-\text{(aq)}$$

Hence Vants Hoff factor, $i = 3$

$$\Delta T_f = Tf(\text{water}) - T_{f(MgCl_2)} = i \times K_f \times m$$

$$m(\text{molality}) = \frac{1.9 \text{ g} \times 1000 \text{ g}}{95 \text{ g mol}^{-1} \times 50 \text{ g}}$$

$\therefore$ $\quad T_g(\text{water}) = 273 \text{ K}$

Hence $\quad \Delta T_f = 273 \text{ K} - T_{f(MgCl_2)}$

$$= 3 \times 1.86 \text{ K.kg mol}^{-1} \times 0.4 \text{ mol kg}^{-1}$$

$$= 2.23 \text{ K}$$

$$T_{f(MgCl_2)} = (273 - 2.23) \text{ K} = 270.77 \text{ K}$$

(ii) (a) 2M glucose will have higher boiling point because boiling point of a solution of a non-volatile liquid increases with increase in concentration.

(b) When the external pressure exerted on the solution is higher than the osmotic pressure, pure solvent starts flowing out of the solution through the semi-permeable membrane. This process is known as reverse-osmosis.

Q. 54. **The electrical resistance of a column of 0.05 M NaOH solution of diameter 1 cm and length 50 cm is 5.55 × 10^3 ohm. Calculate its resistivity, conductivity and molar conductivity.***

Ans. $A = \pi r^2 = 3.14 \times (0.5)^2 = 0.785 \text{ cm}^2, l = 50 \text{ cm}$

$$R = \frac{\rho l}{A} \quad A = \frac{AR}{l} = \frac{5.55 \times 10^{-3} \times 0.785}{50}$$

$r = 87.18 \, \Omega \, \text{cm}$

Conductivity, $\kappa = \dfrac{1}{\rho} = 0.01147 \text{ Scm}^{-1}$

Molar Conductivity $= \dfrac{1000 \times \kappa}{C} = \dfrac{0.01147 \times 1000}{0.05}$

$\Lambda_m = 229.4 \text{S cm2 mol}^{-1}$.

Q. 55. **15.0 g of an unknown molecular material was dissolved in 450 g of water. The resulting solution was found to freeze at – 0.34°C. What is the molar mass of this material? (K_f for water = 1.86 K Kg mol^{-1}).***

Ans. Given : $W_2 = 15.0 \text{ g}, \Delta T_f = 0.34°C$

$W_1 = 450 \text{ g}, K_f = 1.86 \text{ K kg mol}^{-1}$

From the formula,

$$\Delta T_f = \frac{1000.K_f \times W_2}{W_1 \times m_2}$$

$$m_2 = \frac{1000 K_f \times w_2}{\Delta T_f \times w_1} = \frac{1000 \times 1.86 \times 15}{0.34 \times 450}$$

$$m_2 = 182.35 \text{ g/mol}.$$

Q. 56. **A solution of glycerol ($C_3H_8O_3$) in water was prepared by dissolving some glycerol in 500 g of water. This solution has a boiling point of 100.42°C. What mass of glycerol was dissolved to make this solution? (K_b for water = 0.512 K kg mol^{-1}).***

Ans. Given :

$$W_1 = 500 \text{ g}$$
$$K_b = 0.512 \text{ K kg mol}^{-1}$$
$$\Delta T_b = (100.42 - 100)°C$$
$$= 0.42°C$$
$$\Delta T_b = \frac{100 \times K_b \times W_2}{W_1 \times W_2}$$
$$W_2 = \frac{\Delta T_b \times W_1 \times m_2}{100 \times K_b}$$
$$W_2 = 37.7 \text{ g}.$$

Q. 57. **A 1.00 molal aqueous solution of trichloroacetic acid (CCl_3COOH) is heated to its boiling point. The solution has the boiling point of 100.18°C. Determine the Van't Hoff factor for trichloroacetic acid.**

(K_b for water = 0.512 K kg mol^{-1}).*

Ans. Given :

$$\Delta T_b = (373.18 - 373) \text{ K}$$
$$= 0.18 \text{ K}$$
$$K_b = 0.512 \text{ K kg mol}^{-1}$$
$$m = 1$$
$$\Delta T_b = k \, K_b \, m$$
$$k = \frac{\Delta T_b}{K_b m} = \frac{0.18}{0.512 \times 1} = 0.35.$$

Q. 58. **What mass of NaCl must be dissolved in 65.0 g of water to lower the freezing point of water by 7.50 °C? The freezing point depression constant (K_f) for water is 1.86° C/m, assume Van't Hoff factor for NaCl is 1.87. (Molar mass of NaCl = 58.5 g).***

Ans. Given : $m_2 = 58.5 \text{ g mol}^{-1}$

$w_1 = 65$ g, $\Delta T_f = 7.5\ °C$
$K_f = 1.86$ K kg mol^{-1}
$i = 1.87$

$$\Delta T_f = \frac{iK_f \times w_2 \times 1000}{w_1 \times w_2}$$

$$w_2 = \frac{\Delta T_f \times w_1 \times m_2}{i \times K_f \times 1000}$$

$$= \frac{7.5 \times 65 \times 58.5}{1.87 \times 1.86 \times 1000}$$

$$= \frac{28518.2}{3478.2}$$

$$= 8.1999$$

$\therefore$ Mass of NaCl to be dissolved

$$w_2 = 8.1999\ g$$
$$w_2 = 8.209\ g.$$

Q. 59. **Calculate the freezing point of a solution containing 60 g of glucose (Molar mass = 180 g mol^{-1}) in 250 g of water. (K_f of water = 1.86 K kg mol^{-1})***

Ans. Molality (m) of given solution of Glucose :

$$m = [(60/180\ \text{g mol}^{-1}/250\ \text{g}] \times 1000$$
$$= 1.33\ \text{mol kg}^{-1}$$

Now, depression in freezing point is given by,

$$\Delta T_f = K_f\, m$$

Putting the given values,

$$\Delta T_f = K_f\, m$$
$$= 1.86 \times 1.33 = 2.5$$

So, freezing point of the solution would be

$$273.15\ K - 2.5 = 270.65\ K.$$

Chapter 3. Electrochemistry

Q. 1. **The resistance of a conductivity cell containing 0.001 M KCl solution at 298 K is 1500 W. What is the cell constant if the conductivity of 0.001 M KCl solution at 298 K is 0.146 × 10^{-3} S cm^{-1}.***

Ans.
$$\text{Cell constant } (G^*) = K \times R$$
$$= 0.146 \times 10^{-3}\ S\ cm^{-1} \times 1500\ \Omega$$
$$= 0.219\ cm^{-1} \qquad\qquad (S = \Omega^{-1})$$

Q. 2. **How many grams of silver could be plated on a shield by electrolysis of a solution containing Ag$^+$ ions for a period of 2 hours at a current strength of 6.2 amperes?**

$$[1F = 96500\ C\ mol^{-1};\ \text{molar mass of Ag} = 107.8\ g]$$

Ans. Mass deposited, M

$$M = Z \times I \times t$$

Z = Electrochemical equivalent. For Ag$^+$ ion

$$Ag^+(aq) + e^- \longrightarrow Ag(s)$$

hence $n = 1$, so $Z = \dfrac{107.8}{F}$, 2 hrs = 2 × 60 × 60 sec.

$$M = \frac{107.8}{96500} \times 6.2 \times 2 \times 60 \times 60$$

$$= 49.867\ g\ \text{of Ag can be plated.}$$

Q. 3. **In the electrolysis of acidulated water, it is desired to obtain hydrogen at the rate of 1 cc per second at NTP condition. What should be the current passed?**

Ans. Discharging reaction of hydrogen

$$2H^+ + e^- \longrightarrow H_2$$

Thus, 1 mole of H_2, *i.e.*, 22400 ml/cc at NTP requires electricity $2\,F = 2 \times 96500$ C.

Hence 1 cc (ml) at NTP requires [At NTP, 1 mol = 22400 ml]

$$= \frac{2 \times 96500}{22400} \times 1 = 8.616 \text{ C.}$$

As $Q = It$

$$I = \frac{Q}{t} = \frac{8.616}{1s} = 8.616 \text{ ampere.}$$

Q. 4. **A current of 4 ampere was passed for 1.5 hrs through a solution of copper sulphate when 3.2 g of copper was deposited. Calculate the current efficiency.**

Ans.
$$Cu^{2+} + 2e^- \longrightarrow Cu \text{ (s)}$$

Hence to deposite one mole *i.e.*, 63.5 g of Cu, the charge required is 2F Coulomb (C).

Therefore, 3.2 g of Cu will require $\dfrac{2 \times 96500}{63.5} \times 3.2 = 9726$ coulomb charge.

Current passed

$$Q = It = 4 \times 1.5 \times 60 \times 60$$
$$= 21600 \text{ C}$$
$$\text{Current efficiency} = \frac{9726}{21600} \times 100 = 45\%.$$

Q. 5. **Calculate the potential of hydrogen electrode in contact with a solution whose pH is 10.**

Ans. For hydrogen electrode, $H^+ + e^- \longrightarrow \frac{1}{2}H_2$, it is given that pH = 10;

Also $E^o_{H^+/\frac{1}{2}H_2} = 0$

$\therefore$ $$[H^+] = 10^{-10} \text{ M}$$

Now, using Nernst equation:

$$E^o_{H^+/\frac{1}{2}H_2} = E^o_{H^+/\frac{1}{2}H_2} - \frac{0.0591}{1} \log \frac{1}{[H^+]}$$

From the reaction we see value of $n = 1$.

$$\Rightarrow \qquad E^o_{H^+/\frac{1}{2}H_2} = E^o_{H^+/\frac{1}{2}H_2} - \frac{0.0591}{1} \log \frac{1}{10^{-10}}$$
$$= 0 - 0.0591 \log 10^{10}$$
$$= -0.0591 \times 10 \log 10$$
$$= -0.591 \text{ V.}$$

Q. 6. **Calculate the emf of the cell in which the following reaction takes place:**

$$Ni(s) + 2Ag^+ (0.002 \text{ M}) \longrightarrow Ni^{2+} (0.160 \text{ M}) + 2Ag(s)$$

Given that ($E^\circ_{cell} = 1.05$ V)

Ans. Applying Nernst equation we have:

$$E_{(cell)} = E^o_{(cell)} - \frac{0.0591}{n} \log \frac{[Ni^{2+}]}{[Ag^+]^2}$$

$$= 1.05 - \frac{0.0591}{2} \log \frac{(0.160)}{(0.002)^2}$$

$$= 1.05 - 0.02955 \log \frac{0.16}{0.000004}$$

$$= 1.05 - 0.02955 \log 4 \times 10^4$$
$$= 1.05 - 0.02955 \, (\log 10000 + \log 4)$$
$$= 1.05 - 0.02955 \, (4 + 0.6021)$$
$$= 0.914 \text{ V.}$$

Q. 7. The cell in which the following reaction occurs:

$$2Fe^{3+} \text{ (aq)} + 2I^- \text{ (aq)} \longrightarrow 2Fe^{2+} \text{ (aq)} + I_2(s)$$

has $E°_{cell} = 0.236$ V at 298 K.

Calculate the standard Gibbs energy and the equilibrium constant of the cell reaction.

Ans. Here, $n = 2$, $E^o_{cell} = 0.236$ V, T = 298 K

We know that :

$$\Delta_r G° = -nFE^o_{cell}$$
$$= -2 \times 96487 \times 0.236$$
$$= -45541.864 \text{ J mol}^{-1}$$
$$= -45.54 \text{ kJ mol}^{-1}$$

Note : Generally we take value of F as 96500 C. Then

$$\Delta_r G° = -2 \times 96500 \times 0.236$$
$$= -45548.00 \text{ J mol}^{-1}$$
$$= -45.548 \text{ kJ mol}^{-1}.$$

Again, $\Delta_r G° = -2.303 \text{ RT} \log K_c$

$\Rightarrow$
$$\log K_c = -\frac{\Delta_r G°}{2.303 \text{ RT}}$$

$$= -\frac{-45.54 \times 10^3}{2.303 \times 8.314 \times 298}$$

$$= 7.981$$

$\therefore$
$$K_c = \text{Antilog } (7.981)$$
$$= 9.57 \times 10^7.$$

Or

$$\log K_c = \frac{nE^o_{eV}}{0.059}$$

$$= \frac{2 \times 0.236}{0.059}$$

$$= 8.0$$

$\therefore$
$$K_c = \text{Antilog } (8.0)$$
$$= 1 \times 10^8.$$

Q. 8. What is the quantity of electricity in Coulomb's is needed to reduce 1 mol of $Cr_2O_7^{2-}$?

Consider the reaction: $Cr_2O_7^{2-} + 14H^+ + 6e^- \rightarrow 2Cr^{3+} + 8 H_2O$

Ans. The given reaction is as follows :

$Cr_2O_7^{2-} + 14H^+ + 6e^- \rightarrow 2Cr^{3+} + 8H_2O$, the required quantity of electricity will be 6F.

Therefore, to reduce 1 mole of $Cr_2O_7^{2-}$ ions.

$$= 6 \times 96487 \text{ C}$$
$$= 578922 \text{ C}$$

or 6×96500 C $= 5.79 \times 10^5$ C quantity of electricity is required.

Q. 9. The conductivity of 0.20 M solution of KCl at 298 K is 0.0248 S cm^{-1}. Calculate its molar conductivity.

Ans. Given, $\kappa = 0.0248$ S cm^{-1} C

Molarity $= 0.20$ M

$$\therefore \qquad \text{Molar conductivity, } \Lambda_m = \frac{\kappa \times 1000}{C}$$

$$= \frac{0.0248 \times 1000}{0.2}$$

$$= 124 \text{ S cm}^2 \text{ mol}^{-1}.$$

Q. 10. **The resistance of a conductivity cell containing 0.001 M KCl solution at 298 K is 1500 W. What is the cell constant if conductivity of 0.001M KCl solution at 298 K is 0.146 × 10^{-3} S cm^{-1}.**

Ans. Given, Conductivity, $\kappa = 0.146 \times 10^{-3} \text{ S cm}^{-1}$

Resistance, $R = 1500 \ \Omega$

$$\therefore \qquad \text{Cell constant} = \kappa \times R$$

$$= 0.146 \times 10^{-3} \times 1500$$

$$= 0.219 \text{ cm}^{-1}$$

Q. 11. **How much electricity in terms of Faraday is required to produce**

(i)   20.0 g of Ca from molten $CaCl_2$.

(ii) 40.0 g of Al from molten Al_2O_3.

Ans. (i)   According to the question:

$$Ca^{2+} + 2e^- \longrightarrow Ca$$
$$40 \text{ g}$$

Electricity required to produce 40 g of calcium of 2 F

Therefore, electricity required to produce 20 g of calcium $= \dfrac{2 \times 20}{40} F = 1 F$

(ii) According to the question :

$$Al^{3+} + 3e^- \longrightarrow Al$$
$$27 \text{ g}$$

Electricity required to produce 27 g of Al = 3 F

Therefore, electricity required to produce 40 g of Al $= \dfrac{3 \times 40}{27} F = 4.44$ F.

Q. 12. **How much electricity is required in coulomb for the oxidation of:**

(i)   1 mol of H_2O to O_2

(ii) 1 mol of FeO to Fe_2O_3.

Ans. (i)   According to the question:

$$H_2O \longrightarrow H_2 + \frac{1}{2} O_2$$

Now, we can write:

$$O^{2-} \longrightarrow \frac{1}{2} O_2 + 2e^-$$

Electricity required for the oxidation of 1 mol of H_2O to O_2 = 2 F

$$= 2 \times 96487 \text{ C}$$

$$= 192974 \text{ C}$$

(ii) According to the question:

$$Fe^{2+} \longrightarrow Fe^{3+} + e^{-1} \ (e^-)$$

Electricity required for the oxidation of 1 mol of FeO to Fe_2O_3 = 1 F = 96487 C.

Q. 13. **A solution of Ni(NO$_3$)$_2$ is electrolysed between platinum electrodes using a current of 5 amperes for 20 minutes. What mass of Ni is deposited at the cathode?**

Ans. Given,

Current = 5 A

$$\text{Time} = 20 \times 60 = 1200 \text{ s}$$

$$\therefore \qquad \text{Charge} = \text{Current} \times \text{Time}$$

$$= 5 \times 1200$$
$$= 6000 \text{ C}$$

According to the reaction,

$$Ni^{2+}(aq) + 2e^- \longrightarrow Ni(s)$$
$$58.7 \text{ g}$$

Nickel deposited by 2×96487 C = 58.71 g (*i.e.*, by 2F charge is 58.7 g)

Therefore, nickel deposited by 6000 C = $\dfrac{58.71 \times 6000}{2 \times 96487}$ g = 1.825 g

Hence, 1.825 g of nickel will be deposited at the cathode.

Q. 14. Three electrolytic cells A, B, C containing solutions of $ZnSO_4$, $AgNO_3$ and $CuSO_4$, respectively are connected in series. A steady current of 1.5 amperes was passed through them untill 1.45 g of silver is deposited at the cathode of cell B. How long did the current flow? What mass of copper and zinc were deposited?

Ans. Given: Molar mass of Zn = 65.4 u

Molar mass of Cu = 63.54 u

Molar mass of Ag = 108 u

According to the reaction:

$$Ag^+ (aq) + e^- \longrightarrow Ag(s)$$
$$108 \text{ g}$$

i.e., 108 g of Ag is deposited by 96487 C.

Therefore, 1.45 g of Ag is deposited by = $\dfrac{96487 \times 1.45}{108}$ = 1295.43 C

Given,

Current = 1.5 A, Q = It

$\therefore$

$$\text{Time} = \frac{Q}{I}$$
$$= \frac{1295.43}{1.5} \text{ s}$$
$$= 863.6 \text{ s}$$
$$= 864 \text{ s}$$
$$= 14.40 \text{ min}$$

Again,

$$Cu^{2+} (aq) + 2e^- \longrightarrow Cu(s)$$
$$63.5 \text{ g}$$

i.e., 2×96487 C of charge deposited = 63.5 g of Cu

Therefore, 1295.43 C of charge will deposit = $\dfrac{63.5 \times 1295.43}{2 \times 96487}$ g = 0.426 g of Cu

$$Zn^{2+} (aq) + 2e^- \longrightarrow Zn(s)$$
$$65.4 \text{ g}$$

i.e., 2×96487 C of charge deposit = 65.4 g of Zn

Therefore, 1295.43 C of charge will deposit = $\dfrac{65.4 \times 1295.43}{2 \times 96487}$ g = 0.439 g of Zn

Or

The weight of Cu and Zn deposited can be calculated using Faraday's second law of electrolysis:

$$\frac{\text{Wt. of Ag}}{\text{Wt. of Cu}} = \frac{\text{Eq. wt. of Ag}}{\text{Eq. wt. of Cu}}$$

i.e.,
$$\frac{1.45}{W_2} = \frac{108}{63.5/2}$$

i.e.,
$$W_2 = \frac{1.45 \times 31.75}{108}$$

$\Rightarrow$ $W_2 = 0.426$ g

Similarly for zinc

$$\frac{Wt.\ of\ Ag}{Wt.\ of\ Zn} = \frac{Eq.\ wt.\ of\ Ag}{Eq.\ wt.\ of\ Zn}$$

$\Rightarrow$
$$\frac{1.45}{W_3} = \frac{108}{65.4/2}$$

$\Rightarrow$
$$W_3 = \frac{32.7 \times 1.45}{108} = 0.439 \text{ g}$$

Q. 15. **If a current of 0.5 ampere flows through a metallic wire for 2 hours, then how many electrons would flow through the wire?**

Ans.
$$I = 0.5 \text{ A}$$
$$t = 2 \text{ hours} = 2 \times 60 \times 60 \text{ s} = 7200 \text{ s}$$

Thus,
$$Q = It$$
$$= 0.5 \text{ A} \times 7200 \text{ s}$$
$$= 3600 \text{ C}$$

We know that 96487 C $= 6.023 \times 10^{23}$ number of electrons.

Then,

$$3600 \text{ C} = \frac{6.023 \times 10^{23} \times 3600}{96487} \text{ number of electrons}$$

$$= 2.25 \times 10^{22} \text{ number of electrons}$$

Hence, 2.25×10^{22} number of electrons will flow through the wire.

Q. 16. (i)   Calculate Λ_m^{∞} for AgCl; given that:

Λ_m^{∞} AgNO$_3$ = 133.4 ohm^{-1} cm^2 equiv^{-1}

Λ_m^{∞} KCl = 149.9 ohm^{-1} cm^2 equiv^{-1}

Λ_m^{∞} KNO$_3$ = 145.1 ohm^{-1} cm^2 equiv^{-1}.

(ii)   The molar conductance of ammonium hydroxide at two different concentrations of 0.1 M and 0.01 M are 3.6 and 10.4 ohm^{-1} cm^2 mol^{-1} respectively. Calculate the degree of dissociation of NH$_4$OH at these concentrations. Molar conductance for infinite dilution of NH$_4$OH is 271.1 ohm^{-1} cm^2 mol^{-1}.

Ans. (i)   According to Kohlrausch's law;

$$\Lambda_m^{\infty}[AgCl] = \Lambda_m^{\infty}[AgNO_3] + \Lambda_m^{\infty}[KCl] - \Lambda_m^{\infty}[KNO_3]$$
$$= [\,133.4 + 149.9 - 145.1\,] \text{ ohm}^{-1} \text{ cm}^2 \text{ equiv}^{-1}$$
$$= 138.2 \text{ ohm}^{-1} \text{ cm}^2 \text{ equiv}^{-1}.$$

(ii) (a) Degree of dissociation for 0.1 M solution of NH$_4$OH.

$$\alpha = \frac{\Lambda_m^c}{\Lambda_m^{\infty}} = \frac{3.6 \text{ ohm}^{-1} \text{ cm}^2 \text{ mol}^{-1}}{271.1 \text{ ohm}^{-1} \text{ cm}^2 \text{ mol}^{-1}} = 0.013$$

i.e., $0.013 \times 100 = 1.3\%$.

(b) Degree of dissociation for 0.01 M

$$\alpha = \frac{\Lambda_m^c}{\Lambda_m^{\infty}} = \frac{10.4 \text{ ohm}^{-1} \text{ cm}^2 \text{ mol}^{-1}}{271.1 \text{ ohm}^{-1} \text{ cm}^2 \text{ mol}^{-1}} = 0.038$$

i.e., $0.038 \times 100 = 3.8\%$.

Q. 17. **Conductivity of 0.00241 M acetic acid is 7.896×10^5 S cm^{-1}. Calculate the molar conductivity. If $\Lambda°$ for acetic acid is 390.5 S cm^2 mol^{-1}, what is the dissociation constant?***

Ans. Calculation of molar conductance (Λ_m^o).

$K = 7.896 \times 10^{-5}$ S cm^{-1}; C = 0.00241 M;

Now, $1\,M = mol\,L^{-1}$ *i.e.,* $\dfrac{1\,mol}{10^3\,cm^3}$

$$\Lambda_m^c = \dfrac{K}{C} = \dfrac{7.896 \times 10^{-5}\,S\,cm^{-1}}{0.00241 \times 10^{-3}\,mol\,cm^{-3}}$$

$$= 32.76\,S\,cm2\,mol\text{--}1.$$

Degree of dissociation $\alpha = \dfrac{\Lambda_m^c}{\Lambda_m^o} = \dfrac{32.76\,S\,cm^2\,mol^{-1}}{390.5\,S\,cm^2\,mol^{-1}} = 8.4 \times 10^{-2}$

$\therefore \qquad \Lambda_m^o = 390.5\,S\,cm^2\,mol^{-1}$

Dissociation constant Kc is related to degree of dissociation as:

$$CH_3COOH \rightleftharpoons CH_3COO^- + H^+$$
$$C(1-\alpha) \qquad Ca \qquad Ca$$

$$K_c = \dfrac{[CH_3COO^-][H^+]}{[CH_3COOH]} = \dfrac{Ca.Ca}{C(1-\alpha)} = \dfrac{Ca^2}{1-\alpha}$$

$$= \dfrac{0.00241\,mol\,L^{-1} \times (0.084)^2}{1-0.084} = 1.85 \times 10^{-5}\,mol\,L^{-1}$$

Q. 18. **Write the Nernst equation. Calculate EMF of the following cell at 25°C.** *

Pt (s) | Br$_2$(l) Br$^-$ (0.010 M) || H$^+$ (0.030 M) | H$_2$ (g) (1 bar) | Pt (s)

Given : $E^o_{Br_2/Br^-} = 1.08\,V$

Ans. The cell reaction is:

$$2Br^- (aq) + 2H^+ (aq) \longrightarrow Br_2 (l) + H_2 (g)$$

Using Nernst equation and substituting the values.

$$E_{cell} = [E^o_{H^+/H_2} - E^o_{Br2/Br^-}] - \dfrac{0.0591}{2}\log\dfrac{(P_{H_2})}{[Br]^2[H^+]^2}$$

$$= [0\,V - 1.08\,V] - \dfrac{0.0591}{2}\log\dfrac{1}{(0.01)^2(0.03)^2}$$

$$= -1.08\,V - \dfrac{0.0591}{2} \times \log\dfrac{10^8}{9}$$

$$= -1.08\,V - \dfrac{0.0591}{2}[\log 10^8 - \log 9]$$

$$= -1.08\,V - \dfrac{0.0591}{2} \times (8.000 - 0.9542)$$

$$= -1.08\,V - \dfrac{0.0591}{2} \times 7.0458$$

$$= -1.08\,V - 0.21\,V = -1.29\,V$$

$$E_{cell} = -1.29\,V.$$

Q. 19. **The molar conductivity of 0.025 mol L^{-1} methanoic acid is 46.1 S cm^2 mol^{-1}.**

Calculate its degree of dissociation and dissociation constant. Given $\lambda^o_{(H^+)} = 349.6\,S\,cm^2\,mol^{-1}$ and $\lambda^o_{(HCOO^-)}$

$= 54.6\,S\,cm^2\,mol.$

Ans.

$$C = 0.025\,mol\,L^{-1}$$
$$\Lambda_m = 46.1\,S\,cm^2\,mol^{-1}$$
$$\lambda^o_{(H^+)} = 349.6\,cm^2\,mol^{-1}$$
$$\lambda^o_{(HCOO^-)} = 54.6\,S\,cm^2\,mol^{-1}$$

---
* are board exam questions from previous years

$$\Lambda_m^o \text{ (HCOOH)} = \lambda^o_{(H^+)} + \lambda^o_{(HCOO^-)}$$

$$= 349.6 + 54.6$$

$$= 404.2 \text{ S cm}^2 \text{ mol}^{-1}$$

Now, degree of dissociation:

$$\alpha = \frac{\Lambda_{m(HCOOH)}}{\Lambda^o_{m(HCOOH)}} = \frac{46.1}{404.2}$$

$$= 0.114 \text{ (approximately)}$$

Thus, dissociation constant:

$$\kappa = \frac{c\alpha^2}{(1-\alpha)}$$

$$= \frac{(0.025 \text{ mol L}^{-1}(0.114)^2}{(1-0.114)}$$

$$= 3.67 \times 10^{-4} \text{ mol L}^{-1}.$$

Q. 20. If a current of 0.5 ampere flows through a metallic wire for 2 hours, then how many electrons would flow through the wire?

Ans.

$$I = 0.5 \text{ A}$$

$$t = 2 \text{ hours} = 2 \times 60 \times 60 \text{ s} = 7200 \text{ s}$$

Thus,

$$Q = It$$

$$= 0.5 \text{ A} \times 7200 \text{ s}$$

$$= 3600 \text{ C}$$

We know that $96487 \text{ C} = 6.023 \times 10^{23}$ number of electrons.

Then,

$$3600 \text{ C} = \frac{6.023 \times 10^{23} \times 3600}{96487} \text{ number of electrons}$$

$$= 2.25 \times 10^{22} \text{ number of electrons}$$

Hence, 2.25×10^{22} number of electrons will flow through the wire.

Q. 21. Conductivity of 0.00241 M acetic acid is 7.896×10^{-5} S cm^{-1}. Calculate the molar conductivity and if for acetic acid is 390.5 S cm^2 mol^{-1}, what is its dissociation constant?*

Ans. Given, $\kappa = 7.896 \times 10^{-5}$ S Cm^{-1} C

$$C = 0.00241 \text{ mol L}^{-1}$$

Then, molar conductivity,

$$\Lambda_m = \frac{\kappa}{C}$$

$$= \frac{7.896 \times 10^{-5} \text{ S cm}^{-1}}{0.00241 \text{ mol L}^{-1}} \times \frac{1000 \text{ cm}^3}{L}$$

$$= 32.76 \text{ S cm}^2 \text{ mol}^{-1}$$

$$\Lambda^o_m = 390.5 \text{ S cm}^2 \text{ mol}^{-1}$$

Again,

$$\alpha = \frac{\Lambda_m}{\Lambda^o_m} = \frac{32.76 \text{ S cm}^2 \text{ mol}^{-1}}{390.5 \text{ S cm}^2 \text{ mol}^{-1}} = 0.084$$

Now,

$$K_a = \frac{C\alpha^2}{(1-\alpha)}$$

$\therefore$ Dissociation constant,

$$= \frac{(0.00241 \text{ mol L}^{-1})(0.084)^2}{(1-0.084)}$$

$$= 1.86 \times 10^{-5} \text{ mol L}^{-1}.$$

---

* are board exam questions from previous years

Q. 22. (i) The standard electrode potential (E°) for the cell containing 0.1 M Ag^+ and 4.00 M Cu^{2+} at 298 K are $E^o_{Cu^{2+}/Cu} = +0.34V, E^o_{Ag^+/Ag} = +0.80$ V. *

Calculate the cell potential (E).

(ii) How many hours does it take to reduce 3 mol of Fe^{3+} to Fe^{2+} with 2.00 A current ?

$[R = 8.314$ J K^{-1} mol^{-1}, 1 F $= 96500$ C]

Ans. (i) Cell reaction.

$$Cu\ (s) + 2Ag^+\ (aq) \longrightarrow 2Ag\ (s) + Cu^{2+}\ (aq)$$

$n = 2$.

Using Nernst equation;

$$E_{cell} = E^o_{cell} - \frac{0.0591}{n}\log\frac{[Cu^{2+}]^1}{[Ag^+]^2} \qquad (T = 298\ K)$$

i.e.,

$$E_{cell} = (+\ 0.80\ V - 0.34\ V) - \frac{0.0591}{2}\log\frac{4}{(0.1)^2}$$

$$= \quad +0.46V - \frac{0.0591}{2}\{\log 400\}$$

$$= +\ 0.46\ V - 0.0295 \times 2.6021$$

$$= 0.46\ V - 0.0768\ V = 0.3832\ V$$

Hence, $E_{cell} = 0.3832$ V.

(ii) For 3 moles of Fe^{3+} to convert to Fe^{2+} we require 1 mol of electron charge per mol.

$$3\ Fe^{3+} + 3e^- \longrightarrow 3\ Fe^{2+}$$

hence 3 moles of electrons are required.

i.e., $Q = 3 \times 1$ F $= 3 \times 96500$ C.

as, 1 F $=$ charge of 1 mol of electron.

Also, $Q = It$

$\therefore$

$$t = \frac{Q}{I} = \frac{3 \times 96500}{2}\ second$$

$$= 144{,}750\ sec. \qquad [1\ hour = 3600\ second]$$

Hence, time in hrs $\frac{144750}{3600} = 40.20$ hrs.

Q. 23. (i) How many moles of mercury will be produced by electrolysing 1.0 M Hg $(NO_3)_2$ solution with a current of 2.00 A for 3 hours? $[Hg(NO_3)_2 = 200.6$ g $mol^{-1}]$. *

(ii) A voltaic cell is set up at 25°C with the following half-cells Al^{3+} (0.001 M) and Ni^{2+} (0.50 M). Write an equation for the reaction that occurs when the cell generates an electric current and determine the cell potential.

(Given : $E^o_{Ni^{2+}/Ni} = -0.25$ V, $E^o_{Al^{3+}/Al} = -1.66$ V).

Ans. (i)

$$Time = 3\ hrs. = 3 \times 60 \times 60 = 10800\ sec.$$

$$Current = 2A$$

$$Charge = Current \times Time\ (Q = It)$$

$$= 2 \times 10800 = 21600\ C.$$

1 mol of Hg $(NO_3)_2$ will produce 1 mol of mercury.

Molar mass $= 200.6$ g/mol.

$$Hg^{2+}\ (aq) \longrightarrow Hg.$$

Hence 2 mol electron charge is required.

i.e., for 63.0 of Hg we need 2 F charge.

Hence using 21600 C

$$= \frac{21600 \times 63.0}{2 \times 96500} = 7.051\ gram.$$

Therefore, moles of Hg $= \dfrac{7.1051}{63} = 0.112$ moles

(ii) Given:

$$E^o_{Ni^{2+}/Ni} = -0.25V, \quad E^o_{Al^{3+}/Al} = -1.66V$$

Half cell reactions:

$$Al \longrightarrow Al^{3+} + 3e^- \qquad \text{(Anode oxidation)}$$
$$Ni^{2+} + 2e^- \longrightarrow Ni \qquad \text{(Cathode reduction)}$$

Overall reaction cell representation.

$$2Al + 3Ni^{2+} \longrightarrow 2Al^{3+} + 3Ni$$

$Al \,|Al^{3+} \,||\, Ni^{2+} \,|\, Ni$

$$E^o_{cell} = E^o_{right} - E^o_{left}$$
$$= -0.25 - (-1.66)$$
$$= -0.25 + 1.66 \quad \Rightarrow \quad E^o_{cell} = 1.41 \text{ V}$$

Q. 24. Calculate the standard cell potentials of galvanic cells in which the following reactions take place:

(i) $2Cr(s) + 3Cd^{2+}(aq) \rightarrow 2Cr^{3+}(aq) + 3Cd$

(ii) $Fe^{2+}(aq) + Ag^+(aq) \rightarrow Fe^{3+}(aq) + Ag(s)$

Calculate the $\Delta_r G°$ and equilibrium constant of the reactions.

Ans. (i) $E^o_{Cr^{3+}/Cr} = -0.74$ (Given)

$E^o_{Cd^{2+}/Cd} = -0.40$ V

The galvanic cell of the given reaction is depicted as :

$Cr(s) \,|\, Cr^{3+}(aq) \,||\, Cd^{2+}(aq) \,|\, Cd(s)$

Now, the standard cell potential is

$$E^o_{cell} = E^o_R - E^o_L$$
$$= -0.40 - (-0.74)$$
$$= +0.34 \text{ V}$$
$$\Delta_r G° = -nFE^o_{cell}$$

In the given equation, n = 6

F = 96487 C mol^{-1}

$$E^o_{cell} = +0.34 \text{ V}$$

Then,
$$\Delta_r G° = -6 \times 96487 \text{ C mol}^{-1} \times 0.34 \text{ V}$$
$$= -196833.48 \text{ CV mol}^{-1}$$
$$= -196833.48 \text{ J mol}^{-1}$$
$$= -196.83 \text{ kJ mol}^{-1}$$

If value of F = 96500 C used then $\Delta_r G° = -196.86$ kJ/mol (Both are correct)

Again,
$$\Delta_r G° = -RT \ln K$$
$$\Rightarrow \qquad \Delta_r G° = -2.303 \ RT \log K$$
$$\Rightarrow \qquad \log K = -\dfrac{\Delta_r G}{2.303 \ RT}$$
$$= \dfrac{196.83 \times 10^3}{2.303 \times 8.314 \times 298}$$
$$= 34.496$$
$$\therefore \qquad K = \text{antilog} \ (34.496)$$
$$= 3.13 \times 10^{34}$$

(ii)
$$E^{o}_{Fe^{3+}/Fe^{2+}} = 0.77 \text{ V}$$

$$E^{o}_{Ag^{+}/Ag} = 0.80 \text{ V}$$

The galvanic cell of the given reaction is depicted as :

$$Fe^{2+} (aq) \mid Fe^{3+} (aq) \mid\mid Ag^{+} (aq) \mid Ag(s)$$

Now, the standard cell potential is

$$E^{o}_{cell} = E^{o}_{R} - E^{o}_{L}$$
$$= 0.80 - 0.77$$
$$= 0.03 \text{ V}$$

Here, $n = 1$.

Then,
$$\Delta_r G^\circ = -nFE^{o}_{cell}$$
$$= -1 \times 96487 \text{ C mol}^{-1} \times 0.03 \text{ V}$$
$$= -2894.61 \text{ J mol}^{-1}$$
$$= -2.89 \text{ kJ mol}^{-1}$$

Again,
$$\Delta_r G^\circ = -2.303 \text{ RT ln K}$$

$\Rightarrow$
$$\log K = \frac{-\Delta_r G}{2.303 \text{ RT}}$$

$$= \frac{2894.61}{2.303 \times 8.314 \times 298}$$

$$= 0.5073$$

$\therefore$
$$K = \text{antilog} (0.5073)$$
$$= 3.2 \text{ (approximately)}.$$

Q. 25. Write the Nernst equation and emf of the following cells at 298 K :

(i) $Mg(s) \mid Mg^{2+} (0.001M) \mid\mid Cu^{2+} (0.0001 \text{ M}) \mid Cu(s)$

(ii) $Fe(s) \mid Fe^{2+} (0.001M) \mid\mid H^{+} (1M) \mid H_2(g)(1 \text{ bar}) \mid Pt(s)$

(iii) $Sn(s) \mid Sn^{2+} (0.050 \text{ M}) \mid\mid H^{+} (0.020 \text{ M}) \mid H_2(g) (1 \text{ bar}) \mid Pt(s)$

(iv) $Pt(s) \mid Br_2 (l) \mid Br^{-} (0.010 \text{ M}) \mid\mid H^{+} (0.030 \text{ M}) \mid H_2(g) (1 \text{ bar}) \mid Pt(s).$

Ans. (i) For the given reaction, the Nernst equation can be given as :

Cell reaction $\qquad Mg(s) + Cu^{2+}(aq) \longrightarrow Mg^{2+}(aq) + Cu(s)$

$$E_{cell} = E^{o}_{cell} - \frac{0.0591}{n} \log \frac{[Mg^{2+}]}{[Cu^{2+}]}$$

$$= \{0.34 - (-2.36)\} - \frac{0.0591}{2} \log \frac{0.001}{0.0001}$$

$$= 2.7 - \frac{0.0591}{2} \log 10$$

$$= 2.7 - 0.02955$$

$$= 2.67 \text{ V (approximately)} \approx 2.7 \text{ V}$$

(ii) For the given reaction, the Nernst equation can be given as:

Cell reaction: $\qquad Fe(s) + 2H^{+}(aq) \longrightarrow Fe^{2+} (aq) + H_2(g)$

$$E_{cell} = E^{o}_{cell} - \frac{0.0591}{n} \log \frac{[Fe^{2+}]}{[H^{+}]^2}$$

$$= \{0 - (-0.44)\} - \frac{0.0591}{2} \log \frac{0.001}{1^2}$$

$$= 0.44 - 0.02955 (-3)$$

$$= 0.52865 \text{ V}$$
$$= 0.53 \text{ V (approximately)}$$

(iii) For the given reaction, the Nernst equation can be given as

Cell reaction:
$$Sn + 2H^+ \longrightarrow Sn^{2+} + H_2 \ (n = 2)$$

$$E_{cell} = E^o_{cell} - \frac{0.0591}{n} \log \frac{[Sn^{2+}]}{[H^+]^2}$$

$$= \{0-(-0.14)\} - \frac{0.0591}{2} \log \frac{0.050}{(0.020)^2}$$

$$= 0.14 - 0.0295 \times \log 125$$

$$= 0.14 - 0.062$$

$$= 0.078 \text{ V}$$

$$= 0.08 \text{ V (approximately)}$$

(iv) For the given reaction, the Nernst equation can be given as

Cell reaction:
$$2Br^- + 2H^+ \longrightarrow Br_2 + H_2$$

$$E_{cell} = E^o_{cell} - \frac{0.0591}{n} \log \frac{1}{[Br^-]^2[H^+]^2}$$

$$= (0-1.09) - \frac{0.0591}{2} \log \frac{1}{(0.010)^2(0.030)^2}$$

$$= -1.09 - 0.02955 \times \log \frac{1}{0.00000009}$$

$$= -1.09 - 0.02955 \times \log \frac{1}{9 \times 10^{-8}}$$

$$= -1.09 - 0.02955 \times \log (1.11 \times 10^7)$$

$$= -1.09 - 0.02955 (0.0453 + 7)$$

$$= -1.09 - 0.208$$

$$= -1.298 \text{ V.}$$

Q. 26. The conductivity of sodium chloride at 298 K has been determined at different concentrations and the results are given below:

Concentration/M	0.001	0.010	0.020	0.050	0.100
$10^{-2} \times \kappa /Sm^{-1}$	1.237	11.85	23.15	55.53	106.74

for all concentration and draw a plot between Λ_m and $C^{1/2}$. Find the value of Λ^0_m.

Ans. Given,

$\kappa = 1.237 \times 10^{-2} \text{ S m}^{-1}, C = 0.001 \text{ M}$

Then, $\kappa = 1.237 \times 10^{-4} \text{ S cm}^{-1}, C^{1/2} = 0.0316 \text{ M}^{1/2}$

$$\therefore \qquad \Lambda_m = \frac{\kappa}{C}$$

$$= \frac{1.237 \times 10^{-4} \text{S cm}^{-1}}{0.001 \text{ mol L}^{-1}} \times \frac{1000 \text{ cm}^3}{L}$$

$$= 123.7 \text{ S cm}^2 \text{ mol}^{-1} \qquad \qquad ...(i)$$

Given: $\kappa = 11.85 \times 10^{-2} \text{ S m}^{-1}, C = 0.010 \text{ M}$

Then, $\kappa = 11.85 \times 10^{-4} \text{ S cm}^{-1}, C^{1/2} = 0.1 \text{ M}^{1/2}$

$$\therefore \qquad \Lambda_m = \frac{\kappa}{C}$$

$$= \frac{11.85 \times 10^{-4}\,\text{S cm}^{-1}}{0.010\,\text{mol L}^{-1}} \times \frac{1000\,\text{cm}^3}{\text{L}}$$

$$= 118.5\,\text{S cm}^2\,\text{mol}^{-1} \qquad \qquad \text{...(ii)}$$

Given: $\kappa = 23.15 \times 10^{-2}\,\text{S m}^{-1}$, $C = 0.020\,\text{M}$

Then, $\kappa = 23.15 \times 10^{-4}\,\text{S cm}^{-1}$, $C^{1/2} = 0.1414\,\text{M}^{1/2}$

$\therefore$

$$\Lambda_m = \frac{\kappa}{C}$$

$$= \frac{23.15 \times 10^{-4}\,\text{S cm}^{-1}}{0.02\,\text{mol L}^{-1}} \times \frac{1000\,\text{cm}^3}{\text{L}}$$

$$= 115.8\,\text{S cm}^2\,\text{mol}^{-1} \qquad \qquad \text{...(iii)}$$

Given: $\kappa = 55.53 \times 10^{-2}\,\text{S m}^{-1}$, $C = 0.050\,\text{M}$

Then, $\kappa = 55.53 \times 10^{-4}\,\text{S cm}^{-1}$, $C^{1/2} = 0.2236\,\text{M}^{1/2}$

$\therefore$

$$\Lambda_m = \frac{\kappa}{C}$$

$$= \frac{55.53 \times 10^{-4}\,\text{S cm}^{-1}}{0.050\,\text{mol L}^{-1}} \times \frac{1000\,\text{cm}^3}{\text{L}}$$

$$= 111.11\,\text{S cm}^2\,\text{mol}^{-1} \qquad \qquad \text{...(iv)}$$

Given: $\kappa = 106.74 \times 10^{-2}\,\text{S m}^{-1}$, $C = 0.100\,\text{M}$

Then, $\kappa = 106.74 \times 10^{-4}\,\text{S cm}^{-1}$, $C^{1/2} = 0.3162\,\text{M}^{1/2}$

$\therefore$

$$\Lambda_m = \frac{\kappa}{C} = \frac{106.74 \times 10^{-4}\,\text{S cm}^{-1}}{0.100\,\text{mol L}^{-1}} \times \frac{1000\,\text{cm}^3}{\text{L}}$$

$$= 106.74\,\text{S cm}^2\,\text{mol}^{-1} \qquad \qquad \text{...(v)}$$

Now we have the following data:

	(i)	(ii)	(iii)	(iv)	(v)
$C^{1/2}/\text{M}^{1/2}$	0.0316	0.1	0.1414	0.2236	0.3162
$\Lambda_m\,(\text{S cm}^2\,\text{mol}^{-1})$	123.7	118.5	115.8	111.1	106.74

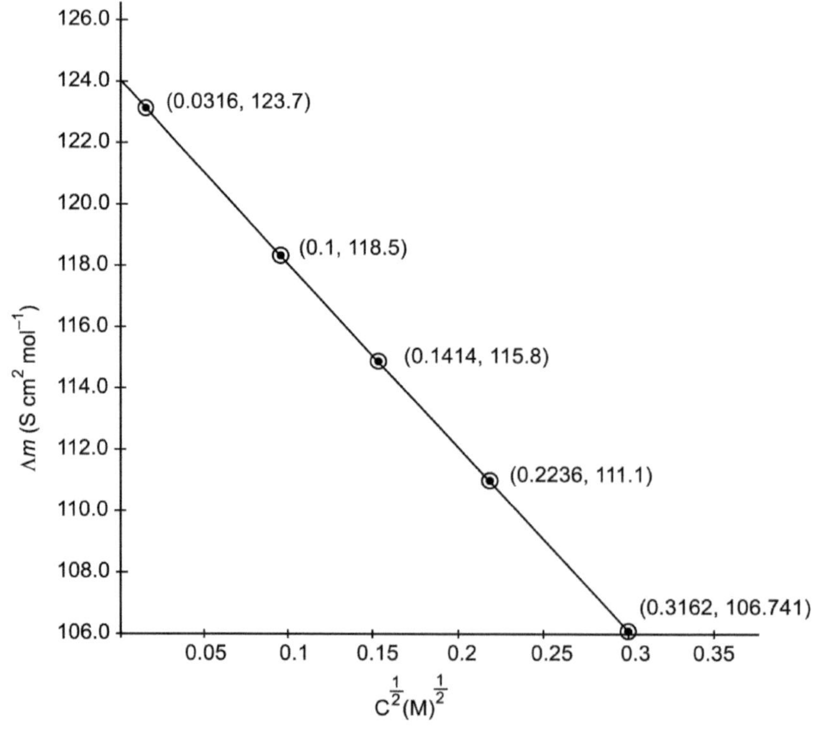

Since the line intercepts Λ_m at $124.0\,\text{S cm}^2\,\text{mol}^{-1}$, $\Lambda_m^0 = 124.0\,\text{S cm}^2\,\text{mol}^{-1}$.

Q. 27. (i) The cell in which the following reaction occur :*

$$2Fe^{3+}(aq) + 2I^-(aq) \rightarrow 2Fe^{2+}(aq) + I_2(s)$$

has E°_{cell} = 0.236 V at 298 K. Calculate the standard Gibbs energy of the cell reaction. (Given : 1F = 96,500 C mol^{-1}).

(ii) How many electrons flow through a metallic wire if a current of 0.5 A is passed for 2 hours? (Given: 1 F = 96,500 C mol^{-1}).

Ans. (i)
$$\Delta G^{\circ} = nF\,E^{\circ}\text{ cell}$$
$$= -2 \times 96500 \times 0.236$$
$$= -45.548 \text{ kJ/mol}$$

(ii) According to Faraday's first law the amount of metal deposited (w).
$$W = i \times t$$
$$= 0.5 \times 7200$$
$$= 3600 \text{ C}$$
$$1\,F = 96500 \text{ C mol}^{-1}$$

That is e^- flows from 96500 C = 1 mol

$$\therefore \qquad e^- \text{ flows from 3600 C} = \frac{1 \times 3600}{96500} \text{ mol}$$

$$= 0.037 \text{ mol.}$$
$$\text{No. of electrons} = 0.037 \times 6.023 \times 10^{23}$$
$$= 0.2246 \times 10^{23}$$
$$= 22.46 \times 10^{21} \text{ electrons.}$$

Q. 28. (i) Calculate the mass of Ag deposited at cathode when a current of 2 amperes was passed through a solution of $AgNO_3$ for 15 minutes.*

Given : Molar mass of Ag = 108 g mol^{-1}, 1F = 96500 C mol^{-1})

(ii) Define fuel cell.

Ans. (i) Given:
$$\text{Current} = 2 \text{ amperes}$$
$$\text{Time} = 15 \text{ minutes}$$
$$\text{Molar mass of Ag} = 108 \text{ g mol}^{-1}$$
$$1F = 96500 \text{ C mol}^{-1}$$
$$\text{Amount of metal deposited } (m) = ZQ$$
$$Q = It$$
$$= 2 \times 15 \times 60 = 1800 \text{ C}$$

Silver deposited
$$Ag^+ + 2e^- \rightarrow Ag(s)$$
$$\text{1 mole of electron or } 1 \times 96500 \text{ C of current deposit silver} = 108 \text{ g}$$
$$\text{1800 C of current will deposite} = 108 \times 1800 - 96500$$
$$\text{Amount of Ag deposited} = 2.01 \text{ g}$$

(ii) Fuel cell is the cell which converts the energy of combustion of fuels directly into electrical energy.

Q. 29. The standard electrode potential (E°) for Daniell cell is + 1.1 V. Calculate DG° for the reaction:*

$$\mathbf{Zn}(s) + \mathbf{Cu}^{2+}_{(aq)} \rightarrow \mathbf{Zn}^{2+}_{(aq)} + \mathbf{Cu}(s)$$

(1 F = 96500 C/mol)

Ans. $n = 2,$ E^{o}_{cell} = 1.1 volt, 1F = 96500 C mol^{-1}
$$\Delta_r G^{\circ} = -nFE^{\circ}_{cell}$$
$$= -2 \times 96500 \times 1.1$$
$$= -212.3 \text{ kJ mol}^{-1}$$

Q. 30. **Calculate the emf of the following cell at 25°C :**[*]

$$Ag(s)\,|\,Ag^+(10^{-3}M)\ PCu^{2+}(10^{-1}M)\,|\,Cu(s)$$

Given : $E^o_{cell} = +0.46\ V\ \&\ \log 10^n = n.$

Given cell notation is incorrect correct cell formula is
$$Cu^{2+}(10^{-1}M)\,|\,Cu(s)\ PAg^+(10^{-3}M)\ Ag(s)$$

Ans. I According to Nernst equation,

$$E_{cell} = E^o_{cell} - \frac{0.0591}{n}\log\frac{[Cu^{2+}]}{[Ag^-]^2}$$

$$= 0.46 - \frac{0.0591}{2}\log\frac{10^{-1}}{[10^{-3}]^2}$$

$$= 0.46 - \frac{0.591}{2}\log 10^5$$

$$= 0.46 - \frac{0.0591}{2}\times 5 = 0.46 - 0.14775$$

$$E_{cell} = 0.31\ V.$$

Q. 31. **The conductivity of 0.20 m solution of KCl at 298 K is 0.025 S cm^{-1}. Calculate its molar conductivity.**[*]

Ans. Given $\kappa = 0.025\ cm^{-1}$

Molarity, $m = 0.20\ m$

Molar conductiry

$$\lambda_m = \frac{\kappa \times 1000}{m} = \frac{0.025 \times 1000}{0.20}$$

$$\lambda_m = 125\ S\ cm^2\ mol^{-1}$$

Q. 32. **Calculate the emf of the following cell at 298 k:**[*]

Fe(s)|Fe^{2+} (0.001 m) || (1 m)|H$_2$(g) (1 bar), Pt(s)

Given $E^o_{cell} = +0.44\ V$

Ans. At anode: $\qquad\qquad Fe \longrightarrow Fe^{2+} + 2e^-$

At cathode: $\qquad 2H^+ + 2e^- \longrightarrow H_2$

So, total number of electrons (n) transferred = 2

Given that : $\qquad\qquad E^o_{cell} = +0.44\ V$

$$Temperature\ (T) = 298\ K$$

We know,

$$E_{cell} = E^o_{cell} - \left[\frac{2.303\,RT}{nF}\right]\log\frac{a_{oxi}}{a_{red}}$$

$$E_{cell} = E^o_{cell} - \left[\frac{0.05916\,V}{n}\right]\log\left[\frac{Fe^{2+}}{[H^+]^2}\right]$$

$$= 0.44 - \frac{0.5916}{2}\log\frac{0.001}{1}$$

$$= 0.44 - (0.02955 \times (-3))$$

$$= 0.44 + 0.8865$$

$$E_{cell} = 0.53\ V$$

Q. 33. **Conductivity of 2.5 $\times$ 10^{-4} M methanoic acid is 5.25 $\times$ 10^{-5} S cm^{-1}. Calculate its molar conductivity and degree of dissociation.**[*]

Given $\lambda_{(H^+)} = 349.5\ S\ cm^2\ mol^{-1}$ and

$$\lambda^0_{(HCOO^-)} = 50.5\ S\ cm^2\ mol^{-1}$$

Ans. We know molar conductivity

$$(\lambda_m) = \frac{1000 \times \text{conductivity } (\kappa)}{\text{concentration } (c)}$$

$\therefore$
$$\lambda_m = \frac{1000 \times 5.25 \times 10^{-5}}{2.5 \times 10^{-4}} = 210 \text{ cm}^2 \text{ mol}^{-1}$$

$$\lambda^{\circ}_{HCOOH} = \lambda^{\circ}_{(H^+)} + \lambda^{\circ}(HCOO^-)$$

$$= 349.5 + 50.5$$

$$= 400 \text{ S cm}^2 \text{ mol}^{-1}$$

$\therefore$
$$\lambda = \frac{\lambda_m}{\lambda^{\circ}} = \frac{210}{400} = 0.52$$

or
$$\lambda = 52.5\%$$

Q. 34. The reaction $N_2(g) + O_2(g) \rightleftharpoons 2NO(g)$ contributes to air pollution whenever a fuel is burnt in air at a high temperature. At 1500 K, equilibrium constant K for it is 1.0×10^{-5}. Suppose in a case $[N_2] = 0.80$ mol L^{-1} and $[O_2] = 0.20$ mol L^{-1} before any reaction occurs. Calculate the equilibrium concentrations of the rectants and the product after the mixture has been heated to 1500 K.*

Ans.

	$N_2(g)$	+	$O_2(g)$	$2NO(g)$
Initial conc.	0.80		0.20	0
at equilibrium	$0.80 - x$		$0.20 - x$	$2x$
Initial conc. at equilibrium :	$0.80 - x$		0.80	0.20 2x

$$K = \frac{[NO]^2}{[O_2][N_2]} = \frac{(2x)^2}{(0.8-x)(0.2-x)} = 10^5$$

$\Rightarrow$
$$\frac{(4x)^2}{0.16 - 1x + x^2} = 10^{-5}$$

$\Rightarrow$
$$400000x^3 = x^2 - x + 0.16$$

$\Rightarrow$
$$399999x^2 + x - 0.16 = 0$$

$$b^2 - 4ac = (1)^2 - 4(399999)(-0.16)$$

$$= 1 + 255999.36 = 256000.36$$

$\Rightarrow$
$$\sqrt{b^2 - 4ac} = \sqrt{256000.36} = 505.96$$

$$x = \frac{-1 \pm 505.96}{2 \times 399999} = \frac{504.96}{2 \times 399999}$$

$$= 0.63 \times 10^{-3}$$

$$[NO] = 2x = 2 \, Ô \, 0.63 \times 10^{-3} = 1.26 \times 10^{-3} \text{ mol/litre}$$

Q. 35. (i) What type of a battery is lead storage battery? Write the anode the cathode reactions and the overall cell reaction occurring in the operation of a lead storage battery.*

(ii) Calculate the potential for half-cell containing 0.10 M $K_2Cr_2O_7$ (aq), 0.20 MCr^{3+} (aq) and 1.0×10^{-4} M H^+ (aq). The half-cell reaction is and the standard electrode potential is given as $E^{\circ} = 1.33$ V.*

$$Cr_2O_7^{2-}(aq) + 14H^+(aq) + 6e^- \rightarrow 2Cr^{3+}(aq) + 7H_2O(l)$$

Ans. (i) Lead storage battery is a secondary cell (rechargable). The electrode reaction is as follows:

At anode : $Pb(s) + SO_4^{2-}(aq) \longrightarrow PbSO_4(s) + 2e^-$

At cathode : $PbO_2(s) + SO_4^{2-}(aq) + 4H^+(aq) + 2e^- \longrightarrow PbSO_4(s) + 2H_2O$

Overall reaction :

$$Pb(s) + PbO_2(s) + 4H^+(aq) + 2SO_4^{2-}(aq) \longrightarrow PbSO_4(s) + 2H_2O$$

(ii) $Cr_2O_7^{2-} + 14H^+ + 6e^- \longrightarrow 2Cr^{3+} + 7H_2O$

   0.1 M 10^{-4} M   0.2 M

$$E = E° - \frac{0.059}{6}\log\frac{[Cr^{3+}]^2}{[Cr_2O_7^{2-}][H^+]^{14}}$$

$$E = 1.33 - \frac{0.059}{6}\log\frac{(0.20)^2}{(0.10)(10^{-4})^{14}}$$

$$E = 1.33\ V - 0.55\ V$$
$$E = 0.78\ V$$

Q. 36. (i)   How many moles of mercury will be produced by electrolyzing 1.0 M $Hg(NO_3)_2$ solution with a current of 2.00 A for 3 hours? $[Hg(NO_3)_2 = 200.6\ g\ mol^{-1}]$

   (ii)   A voltaic cell is set up at 25°C with the following half-cells Al^{3+} (0.001 M) and Ni^{2+} (0.50 M). Write an equation for the reaction that occurs when the cell generates an electric current and determine the cell potential.

   (Given : $E°_{Ni^{2+}/Ni} = -0.25\ V, E°_{Al^{3+}|Al} = -1.66V$)

Ans. (i) $Hg^{2+} + 2e^- \rightarrow Hg$

Quantity of electricity (Q) $= I \times t = 2 \times 3 \times 60 \times 60 = 21600\ C$

2F (2×96500 C) deposit is Hg = 1 mole

$$1C\ deposit\ e\ Hg = \frac{1}{2 \times 96500}$$

∴ $$21600\ C\ deposit\ e\ Hg = \frac{1}{2 \times 96500} \times 21600 = 0.1119\ mole$$

(ii) $$2Al + 3Ni^{2+} \rightarrow 3Ni - 2Al^{3+}$$

$$E°_{cell} = E°_{cathode} - E°_{anode}$$

$$E_{cell} = E°_{cell} - \frac{0.0591}{n}\log\frac{[Al^{3+}]^2}{[Ni^{+2}]^3}$$

$$E_{cell} = -0.25 - (-1.66) - \frac{0.059}{6}\log\frac{[0.001]^2}{[0.50]^3}$$

$$E_{cell} = 1.41 - 0.00985\log\frac{1}{125}$$

$$E_{cell} = 1.41 - 0.00985 \times -2.0969$$
$$= 1.41 + 0.0206 = 1.43\ V$$

Chapter 4. Chemical Kinetics

Q. 1. **The rate constant for a first order reaction is 60 s^{-1}. How much time will it take to reduce the initial concentration of the reactant to its $1/10^{th}$ value?**[*]

Ans. First order reaction equation,

$$t = \frac{2.303}{k}\log\frac{[R_0]}{[R]}$$

$$= \frac{2.303}{k}\log\frac{[R_0]}{\left[\dfrac{R_0}{10}\right]}$$

$$\Rightarrow t = \frac{2.303}{60}\log 10 \Rightarrow t = \frac{2.303}{60} = 3.83 \times 10^{-2}\ sec$$

---

[*] are board exam questions from previous years

Q. 2. **Hydrogen per oxide, H_2O_2 (aq) decomposes to $H_2O(l)$ and $O_2(g)$ in a reaction that is first order w.r.t. H_2O_2 and has a rate constant; $k = 1.06 \times 10^{-3}$ min^{-1}.** *

    (i)   How long will it take for 15% of sample of H_2O_2 to decompose.

    (ii) How long will it take for 85% of the sample to decompose.

Ans. (i)   First order reaction

$$t = \frac{2.303}{k} \log \frac{[A]_0}{[A]}$$

$$k = 1.06 \times 10^{-3} \text{ min}^{-1}, \quad \frac{[A]_0}{[A]} = \frac{100}{85} \text{ for 15\%}$$

$$t = \frac{2.303}{1.06 \times 10^{-3} \text{ min}^{-1}} \log \frac{100}{85}$$

$$= \frac{2.303}{1.06} \times 10^3 [2 \log 10 - \log 85] \text{ min}$$

$$= \frac{2.303}{1.06}[2 - 1.9294] = \frac{2.303 \times 0.0706 \times 10^3}{1.06}$$

$$t = 153.39 \text{ min} = 153.4 \text{ min}$$

(ii)

$$t = \frac{2.303}{1.06 \times 10^{-3} \text{ min}^{-1}} \log \frac{100}{15}$$

$$= \frac{2303}{1.06}[2 \log 10 - \log 15] = \frac{2303}{1.06}[2 - 1.1761] \text{ min}$$

$$= \frac{2303 \times 0.8231}{1.06} \text{ min}$$

$$t = 1790 \text{ min.}$$

Q. 3. **For the reaction R $\rightarrow$ P, the concentration of a reactant changes from 0.03 M to 0.02 M in 25 minutes. Calculate the average rate of reaction using units of time both in minutes and seconds.**

Ans.

$$\text{Average rate of reaction} = -\frac{\Delta[R]}{\Delta t}$$

$$= -\frac{[R]_2 - [R]_1}{t_2 - t_1}$$

$$= -\frac{0.02 - 0.03}{25} \text{ M min}^{-1}$$

$$= -\frac{-0.01}{25} \text{ M min}^{-1}$$

$$= 4 \times 10^{-4} \text{ M min}^{-1}$$

$$= \frac{4 \times 10^{-4}}{60} \text{ M s}^{-1}$$

$$= 6.67 \times 10^{-6} \text{ M s}^{-1}.$$

Q. 4. **The conversion of molecules X to Y follows second order kinetics. If concentration of X is increased to three times how will it affect the rate of formation of Y?**

Ans. The reaction X $\rightarrow$ Y follows second order kinetics.

Therefore, the rate equation for this reaction will be:

$$\text{Rate} = k[X]^2 - (1)$$

Let $[X]$ = a mol L^{-1}, then equation (1) can be written as:

$$\text{Rate} = k.(a)^2 = ka^2$$

If the concentration of X is increased to three times, then $[X] = 3a$ mol L^{-1}

Now, the rate equation will be:

$$\text{Rate} = k(3a)^2 = 9(ka)^2$$

Hence, the rate of formation will increase by 9 times.

* are board exam questions from previous years

Q. 5. A first order reaction has a rate constant 1.15×10^{-3} s^{-1}. How long will 5 g of this reactant take to reduce to 3 g?

Ans. From the question, we can write down the following information :

Initial amount = 5 g

Final concentration = 3 g

Rate constant = 1.15×10^{-3} s^{-1}

We know that for a first order reaction,

$$t = \frac{2.303}{k}\log\frac{[R]_0}{[R]}$$

$$= \frac{2.303}{1.15\times10^{-3}}\log\frac{5}{3}$$

$$= \frac{2.303}{1.15\times10^{-3}}\times0.2219 = 444.38 \text{ s}$$

$$= 444 \text{ s (approximately)}.$$

Q. 6. Time required to decompose SO_2Cl_2 to half of its initial amount is 60 minutes. If the decomposition is a first order reaction, calculate the rate constant of the reaction.

Ans. We know that for a first order reaction,

$$t_{1/2} = \frac{0.693}{k}$$

It is given that $t_{1/2} = 60$ min

$\therefore$
$$k = \frac{0.693}{t_{1/2}}$$

$$= \frac{0.693}{60} = 0.01155 \text{ min}^{-1}$$

$$= 0.0115/6 \text{ sec}^{-1}$$

or
$$k = 1.925 \times 10^{-4} \text{ s}^{-1}.$$

Q. 7. In general, the rate of the chemical reaction doubles for an increase of 10 K in absolute temperature from 298 K. Calculate E_a.

Ans. It is given that $T_1 = 298$ K

$\therefore$
$$T_2 = (298 + 10) \text{ K} = 308 \text{ K}$$

We also know that the rate of the reaction doubled when temperature is increased by 10°.

Therefore, let us take the value of $k_1 = k$ and that of $k_2 = 2k$

Also, R = 8.314 J K^{-1} mol^{-1}.

Now, substituting these values in the equation :

$$\log\frac{k_2}{k_1} = \frac{E_a}{2.303\ R}\left[\frac{T_2-T_1}{T_1T_2}\right]$$

We get

$$\log\frac{2k}{k} = \frac{E_a}{2.303\times8.314}\left[\frac{10}{298\times308}\right]$$

$\Rightarrow$
$$\log 2 = \frac{E_a}{2.303\times8.314}\left[\frac{10}{298\times308}\right]$$

$\Rightarrow$
$$E_a = \frac{2.303\times8.314\times298\times308\times\log 2}{10}$$

$$= \frac{2.303\times8.314\times298\times308\times0.3010}{10}$$

$$= 52897.78 \text{ J mol}^{-1}$$

$$= 52.9 \text{ kJ mol}^{-1}.$$

Q. 8. For the reaction:

$$2A + B \rightarrow A2B$$

the rate $= k[A][B]^2$ with $k = 2.0 \times 10^{-6}$ mol^{-2} L^{2}s^{-1}. Calculate the initial rate of the reaction when $[A] = 0.1$ mol L^{-1}, $[B] = 0.2$ mol L^{-1}. Calculate the rate of reaction after $[A]$ is reduced to 0.06 mol L^{-1}.

Ans. The initial rate of the reaction is

$$\text{Rate} = k[A][B]^2$$
$$= (2.0 \times 10^{-6} \text{ mol}^{-2} \text{ L}^2 \text{ s}^{-1}) (0.1 \text{ mol L}^{-1}) (0.2 \text{ mol L}^{-1})^2$$
$$= 8.0 \times 10^{-9} \text{ mol}^{-2} \text{ L2 s}^{-1}$$

When $[A]$ is reduced from 0.1 mol L^{-1} to 0.06 mol^{-1}, the concentration of $[A]$ reacted

$$= (0.1 - 0.06) \text{ mol L}^{-1} = 0.04 \text{ mol L}^{-1}$$

Therefore, concentration of $[B]$ reacted $= \dfrac{1}{2} \times 0.04$ mol L$^{-1} = 0.02$ mol L^{-1}.

As $[B]$ used in reaction is 1/2 moles per 1 mole of A.

Then, concentration of $[B]$ available, $[B] = (0.2 - 0.02)$ mol L^{-1}.

$$= 0.18 \text{ mol L}^{-1}$$

After $[A]$ is reduced to 0.06 mol L^{-1}, the rate of the reaction is given by,

$$\text{Rate} = k[A][B]^2$$
$$= (2.0 \times 10^{-6} \text{ mol}^{-2} \text{ L}^2 \text{ s}^{-1}) (0.06 \text{ mol L}^{-1}) (0.18 \text{ mol L}^{-1})^2$$
$$= 3.89 \times 10^{-15} \text{ mol L}^{-1} \text{ s}^{-1}.$$

Q. 9. The decomposition of NH_3 on platinum surface is zero order reaction. What are the rates of production of N_2 and H_2 if $k = 2.5 \times 10^{-4}$ mol^{-1} L s^{-1}?

Ans. The decomposition of NH_3 on platinum surface is represented by the following equation.

$$2NH_3(g) \xrightarrow{\text{Pt}} N_2(g) + 3H_2(g)$$

Therefore,

$$\text{Rate} = -\frac{1}{2}\frac{d[NH_3]}{dt} = \frac{d[N_2]}{dt} = \frac{1}{3}\frac{d[H_3]}{dt}$$

However, it is given that the reaction is of zero order. Therefore, Rate = k.

$$\Rightarrow \qquad -\frac{1}{2}\frac{d[NH_3]}{dt} = \frac{d[N_2]}{dt} = \frac{1}{3}\frac{d[H_2]}{dt} = k$$
$$= 2.5 \times 10^{-4} \text{ mol L}^{-1} \text{ s}^{-1}$$

Therefore, the rate of production of N_2 is

$$\frac{d[N_2]}{dt} = 2.5 \times 10^{-4} \text{ mol L}^{-1} \text{ s}^{-1}$$

And, the rate of production of H_2 is

$$\frac{d[H_2]}{dt} = 3 \times 2.5 \times 10^{-4} \text{ mol L}^{-1} \text{ s}^{-1}$$
$$= 7.5 \times 10^{-4} \text{ mol L}^{-1} \text{ s}^{-1}.$$

Q. 10. Calculate the half-life of a first order reaction from their rate constants given below :

(i) 200 s^{-1}, (ii) 2 min^{-1}, (iii) 4 years^{-1}.

Ans. (i) Half life, $$t_{1/2} = \frac{0.693}{k}$$

$$= \frac{0.693}{200 \text{ s}^{-1}} = 3.47 \text{ s} \times 10^{-3} \text{ s}$$

(ii) Half life, $$t_{1/2} = \frac{0.693}{k}$$

$$= \frac{0.693}{2 \text{ min}^{-1}}$$

$$= 0.35 \text{ min (approximately) or } 3.5 \times 10^{-1} \text{ min}$$

(iii) Half life,

$$t_{1/2} = \frac{0.693}{k}$$

$$= \frac{0.693}{4 \text{ years}^{-1}}$$

$$= 0.173 \text{ years (approximately) or } 1.73 \times 10^{-1} \text{ year.}$$

Q. 11. The half-life for radioactive decay of ^{14}C is 5730 years. An archaeological artefact containing wood had only 80% of the ^{14}C found in a living tree. Estimate the age of the sample.

Ans. Here,

$$k = \frac{0.693}{t_{1/2}} \text{ for 1}^{st} \text{ order decay reactions of radioactive elements}$$

$$= \frac{0.693}{5730} \text{ years}^{-1}$$

It is known that, for 1st order reactions.

$$t = \frac{2.303}{k} \log \frac{[R]_0}{[R]}$$

$$= \frac{2.303}{\frac{0.693}{5730}} \log \frac{100}{80}$$

$$= 1845 \text{ years (approximately)}$$

Hence, the age of the sample is 1845 years.

Q. 12. The rate constant for a first order reaction is 60 s^{-1}. How much time will it take to reduce the initial concentration of the reactant to its 1/16th value?

Ans. It is known that,

$$t = \frac{2.303}{k} \log \frac{[R]_0}{[R]}$$

$$= \frac{2.303}{60 \text{ s}^{-1}} \log \frac{1}{\frac{1}{16}}$$

$$= \frac{2.303}{60 \text{ s}^{-1}} \log 16$$

$$= 4.6 \times 10^{-2} \text{ s (approximately)}$$

Hence, the required time is 4.6×10^{-2} s.

Q. 13. For a first order reaction, show that time required for 99% completion is twice the time required for the completion of 90% of reaction.*

Ans. For a first order reaction, the time required for 99% completion is

$$t_1 = \frac{2.303}{k} \log \frac{100}{100 - 99}$$

$$= \frac{2.303}{k} \log 100$$

$$= 2 \times \frac{2.303}{k}$$

For a first order reaction, the time required for 90% completion is

$$t_2 = \frac{2.303}{k} \log \frac{100}{100 - 90}$$

$$= \frac{2.303}{k} \log 10$$

$$= \frac{2.303}{k}$$

Therefore, $t_1 = 2t_2$.

Hence, the time required for 99% completion of a first order reaction is twice the time required for the completion of 90% of the reaction.

Q. 14. A first order reaction takes 40 min for 30% decomposition. Calculate $t_{1/2}$.

Ans. For a first order reaction,

$$t = \frac{2.303}{k} \log \frac{[R]_0}{[R]}$$

$$k = \frac{2.303}{40 \text{ min}} \log \frac{100}{100 - 30}$$

$$= \frac{2.303}{40 \text{ min}} \log \frac{10}{7}$$

$$= 8.918 \times 10^{-3} \text{ min}^{-1}.$$

Therefore, $t_{1/2}$ of the decomposition reaction is

$$t_{1/2} = \frac{0.693}{k}$$

$$= \frac{0.693}{8.918 \times 10^{-3}} \text{ min}$$

$$= 77.7 \text{ min (approximately).}$$

Q. 15. The rate constant for the decomposition of hydrocarbons is 2.418×10^{-5} s^{-1} at 546 K. If the energy of activation is 179.9 kJ/mol, what will be the value of pre-exponential factor.

Ans. $k = 2.418 \times 10^{-5}$ s^{-1} at 546 K.

$$T = 546 \text{ K}$$

$$E_a = 179.9 \text{ kJ mol}^{-1} = 179.9 \times 10^3 \text{ J mol}^{-1}$$

According to the Arrhenius equation,

$$k = Ae^{-E_a/RT}$$

$$\Rightarrow \qquad \ln k = \ln A - \frac{E_a}{RT}$$

$$\Rightarrow \qquad \log k = \log A - \frac{E_a}{2.303 \, RT}$$

$$\Rightarrow \qquad \log A = \log k + \frac{E_a}{2.303 \, RT}$$

$$= \log(2.418 \times 10^{-5} \text{ s}^{-1}) + \frac{179.9 \times 10^3 \text{ J mol}^{-1}}{2.303 \times 8.314 \text{ JK}^{-1} \text{ mol}^{-1} \times 546 \text{ K}}$$

$$= (0.3835 - 5) + 17.2082$$

$$= 12.5917$$

Therefore, $A = \text{antilog} (12.5917) = 3.9 \times 10^{12}$ s^{-1} (approximately)

Q. 16. Consider a certain reaction A $\rightarrow$ Products with $k = 2.0 \times 10^{-2}$ s^{-1}. Calculate the concentration of A remaining after 100 s if the initial concentration of A is 1.0 mol L^{-1}.

Ans. $k = 2.0 \times 10^{-2}$ s^{-1}, T = 100 s

$[A]_0 = 1.0$ mol L^{-1}

Since the unit of k is s^{-1}, the given reaction is a first order reaction.

Therefore,

$$k = \frac{2.303}{t} \log \frac{[A]_0}{[A]}$$

$$\Rightarrow \qquad 2.0 \times 10^{-2} \text{ s}^{-1} = \frac{2.303}{100 \text{ s}} \log \frac{1.0}{[A]}$$

$$\Rightarrow \qquad 2.0 \times 10^{-2}\ s^{-1} = \frac{2.303}{100\ s}(-\log[A])$$

$$\Rightarrow \qquad -\log[A] = \frac{2.0 \times 10^{-2} \times 100}{2.303}$$

$$\Rightarrow \qquad [A] = \text{Antilog}\left(-\frac{2.0 \times 10^{-2} \times 100}{2.303}\right)$$

$$= 0.135\ \text{mol L}^{-1}\ \text{(approximately)}$$

Hence, the remaining concentration of A is $0.135\ \text{mol L}^{-1}$.

Q. 17. Sucrose decomposes in acid solution into glucose and fructose according to the first order rate law, with $t_{1/2} = 3.00$ hours. What fraction of sample of sucrose remains after 8 hours?

Ans. For a first order reaction,

$$k = \frac{2.303}{t}\log\frac{[R]_0}{[R]}$$

It is given that, $t_{1/2} = 3.00$ hours

Therefore,

$$k = \frac{0.693}{t_{1/2}}$$

$$= \frac{0.693}{3}\ \text{h}^{-1}$$

$$= 0.231\ \text{h}^{-1}$$

Then,

$$0.231\ \text{h}^{-1} = \frac{2.303}{8h}\log\frac{[R]_0}{[R]}$$

$$\Rightarrow \qquad \log\frac{[R]_0}{[R]} = \frac{0.231\ \text{h}^{-1} \times 8h}{2.303}$$

$$\Rightarrow \qquad \frac{[R]_0}{[R]} = \text{Antilog}\ (0.8024)$$

$$\Rightarrow \qquad \frac{[R]_0}{[R]} = 6.3445$$

$$\Rightarrow \qquad \frac{[R]}{[R]_0} = 0.1576\ \text{(approx.)}$$

$$= 0.158$$

Hence, the fraction of sample of sucrose that remains after 8 hours is 0.158.

Q. 18. The decomposition of hydrocarbon follows the equation

$$k = (4.5 \times 10^{11}\ \text{s}^{-1})\ e^{-28000\ \text{K/T}}$$

Calculate E_a.

Ans. The given equation is

$$k = (4.5 \times 10^{11}\ \text{s}^{-1})\ e^{-28000\ \text{K/T}} \qquad \text{...(i)}$$

Arrhenius equation is given by,

$$k = Ae^{-E_a/RT} \qquad \text{...(ii)}$$

From equation (i) and (ii), we obtain

$$\frac{E_a}{RT} = \frac{28000\ \text{K}}{T}$$

$$\Rightarrow \qquad E_a = R \times 28000\ \text{K}$$

$$= 8.314\ \text{J K}^{-1}\ \text{mol}^{-1} \times 28000\ \text{K}$$

$$= 232792\ \text{J mol}^{-1}$$

$$= 232.792\ \text{kJ mol}^{-1}.$$

Q. 19. The rate of a reaction quadruples when the temperature changes from 293 K to 313 K. Calculate the energy of activation of the reaction assuming that it does not change with temperature. *

Ans. From Arrhenius equation, we obtain

$$\log\frac{k_2}{k_1} = \frac{E_a}{2.303\ R}\left(\frac{T_2 - T_1}{T_1 T_2}\right)$$

It is given that,
$$k_2 = 4k_1$$
$$T_1 = 293\ K$$
$$T_2 = 313\ K$$

Therefore,
$$\log\frac{4k_1}{k_1} = \frac{E_a}{2.303\times 8.314}\left(\frac{313 - 293}{293\times 313}\right)$$

$$\Rightarrow \qquad 0.6021 = \frac{20\times E_a}{2.303\times 8.314\times 293\times 313}$$

$$\Rightarrow \qquad E_a = \frac{0.6021\times 2.303\times 8.314\times 293\times 313}{20}$$

$$= 52863.33\ J\ mol^{-1}$$
$$= 52.863\ kJ\ mol^{-1}$$

Hence, the required energy of activation is 52.86 kJ mol^{-1}.

Q. 20. In a reaction, 2A → Products, the concentration of A decreases from 0.5 mol L^{-1} to 0.4 mol L^{-1} in 10 minutes. Calculate the rate during this interval?

Ans.

$$\text{Average rate} = -\frac{1}{2}\frac{\Delta[A]}{\Delta t}$$

$$= -\frac{1}{2}\frac{[A]_2 - [A]_1}{t_2 - t_1}$$

$$= -\frac{1}{2}\frac{(0.4 - 0.5)}{10}$$

$$= -\frac{1}{2}\frac{(-0.1)}{10} = 0.005\ mol\ L^{-1}\ min^{-1}$$

$$= 5 \times 10^{-3}\ M\ min^{-1}.$$

Q. 21. For a reaction, A + B → Product; the rate law is given by, What is the order of the reaction?

Ans.
$$\text{Rate law } (r) = k[A]^{1/2}\ [B]^2$$

$$\text{The order of the reaction} = \frac{1}{2} + 2 = 2\frac{1}{2} = 2.5.$$

Q. 22. The decomposition of dimethyl ether leads to the formation of CH$_4$, H$_2$ and CO and the reaction rate is given by

$$\text{Rate} = k[CH_3OCH_3]^{3/2}$$

The rate of reaction is followed by increase in pressure in a closed vessel, so the rate can also be expressed in terms of the partial pressure of dimethyl ether, i.e.,

$$\text{Rate} = k(p_{CH_3OCH_3})^{3/2}$$

If the pressure is measured in bar and time in minutes, then what are the units of rate and rate constants?

Ans. If pressure is measured in bar and time in minutes, then

$$\text{Unit of rate} = bar\ min^{-1}$$

$$\text{Rate} = k(p_{CH_3OCH_3})^{3/2}$$

$$\Rightarrow \qquad k = \frac{\text{Rate}}{(p_{CH_3OCH_3})^{3/2}}$$

Therefore, unit of rate constants, $\quad (k) = \dfrac{\text{bar min}^{-1}}{\text{bar}^{3/2}}$

$$= \text{bar}^{-1/2}\,\text{min}^{-1}.$$

Q. 23. A reaction is second order with respect to a reactant. How is the rate of reaction affected if the concentration of the reactant is (i) doubled (ii) reduced to half?

Ans. Let the concentration of the reactant [A] be $= a$

$$\text{Rate of reaction, R} = k[A]^2 = ka^2$$

(i) If the concentration of the reactant is doubled, *i.e.*, [A] $= 2a$, then the rate of the reaction would be

$$R' = k(2a)^2$$
$$= 4ka^2$$
$$= 4R$$

Therefore, the rate of the reaction would increase by 4 times.

(ii) If the concentration of the reactant is reduced to half, *i.e.*, $[A] = \dfrac{1}{2}a$, then the rate of the reaction would be

$$R'' = k\left(\dfrac{1}{2}a\right)^2$$
$$= \dfrac{1}{4}ka^2$$
$$= \dfrac{1}{4}\,R$$

Therefore, the rate of the reaction would be reduced to $\dfrac{1}{4}$th

Q. 24. The optical rotation of sucrose in acidic medium at different times is given below :

Using the table calculate the rate constant for the inversion of cane sugar.

Time (t) min	0	18	∞
Rotation (g)	+24.09	+17.7	−10.74

Ans. $\gamma_0 = $ Rotation at time $t = 0$

$\gamma_\infty = $ Rotation at time infinite

$\gamma_t = $ Rotation at time t

As rotation change is directly related to formation of product and forward movement of reaction, hence rotation can be used in place of concentration. As inversion of cane sugar (sucrose) is a pseudo first order reaction, hence the first order formula will hold good.

i.e., $$k = \dfrac{2.303}{t}\log\dfrac{\gamma_0 - \gamma_\infty}{\gamma_t - \gamma_\infty}$$

[Note] : The kinetics of the above reaction is studied by noting the angle of rotation at different intervals in the polarimeter.

Reading of polarimeter at zero time $= \gamma_0$

Reading of polarimeter at any time $= \gamma_t$

Reading of polarimeter at infinite time $= \gamma_\infty$

By looking carefully we can see,

Angle of rotation at any instant of time *i.e.,*

$(\gamma_0 - \gamma_t) \propto$ amount of sucrose hydrolysed (x)

Angle of rotation at infinite time *i.e.,*

$(\gamma_0 - \gamma_\infty)$ initial concentration of sucrose (a).

Therefore, $$a - x \propto (\gamma_0 - \gamma_\infty) - (\gamma_0 - \gamma_t)$$

$\Rightarrow$ $$a - x \propto (r_t - r_\infty)$$

Therefore, $$k = \dfrac{2.303}{18}\log\dfrac{24.09 - (-10.74)}{17.07(-10.74)}$$

$$= \frac{2.303}{18}[\log 34.83 - \log 27.81] \qquad \text{[use of log table]}$$

$$= \frac{2.303}{18}[1.5420 - 1.4442]$$

$$= \frac{2.303}{18} \times 0.0978 = 0.0125 = 1.2 \times 10^{-2} \text{ min}^{-1}.$$

Q. 25. The rate constants of a reaction at 500 K and 700 K are 0.02 s^{-1} and 0.07 s^{-1} respectively. Calculate the value of activation energy, $E_a°$, (R = 8.314 JK^{-1} mol^{-1}) and Arrhenius constant A.*

Ans. Given,
$$k_1 = 0.02 \text{ s}^{-1}; \text{ T}_1 = 500 \text{ K}$$
$$k_2 = 0.07 \text{ s}^{-1}, \text{ T}_2 = 700 \text{ K}.$$

The equation is,

$$\log \frac{k_2}{k_1} = \frac{E_a}{2.303 \times R}\left[\frac{(T_2 - T_1)}{T_2 \times T_1}\right]$$

Substituting the values,

$$\log \frac{0.07}{0.02} = \frac{E_a}{8.314 \times 2.303 \text{ (JK}^{-1} \text{ mol}^{-1})} \frac{(700 - 500)\text{K}}{700 \times 500 \text{ K}^2}$$

$$\Rightarrow \qquad \log 3.5 = \frac{E_a}{19.147} \times \frac{200}{350000 \text{ (mol}^{-1})}$$

$$\Rightarrow \qquad [\log 3.5 = 0.544] \; E_a = \frac{0.544 \times 19.147 \times 350000}{200} \text{ J mol}^{-1}$$

So
$$E_a = 18.228 \text{ kJmol}^{-1}$$

Since
$$k = Ae^{-E_a/RT}$$

So
$$0.02 = Ae^{-E_a/RT}$$

$$\therefore \qquad A = \frac{0.02}{e^{E_a/RT}}$$

or
$$\log A = \log 0.02 + \frac{E_a}{RT}$$

$$= -1.698 + \frac{18227.9}{8.314 \times 500}$$

$$= -1.698 + 4.385$$

$$= 2.687$$

$$\therefore \qquad A = \text{antilog } (2.687)$$

$$= 286.3.$$

Q. 26. The rate constant for the first order decomposition of H_2O_2 is given by the following equation:*

$$\log k = 14.2 - \frac{1.0 \times 10^4}{T} \text{ K.}$$

Calculate E_a for the reaction and rate constant k if its half life period be 200 minutes.

(Given : R = 8.314 JK^{-1} mol^{-1}).

Ans.
$$\log k = 14.2 - \frac{10^4 \text{ K}}{T}$$

According to Arrhenius equation : $k = Ae^{-E_a/RT}$

$$\Rightarrow \qquad \log k = \log A - \frac{E_a}{2.303 \text{ RT}}$$

Hence, comparing both the equations.

$$\frac{E_a}{2.303\,RT} = \frac{1.0\times 10^4\ K}{T}$$

$$\Rightarrow \quad E_a = 10^4 \times 2.303 \times R$$
$$= 10^4 \times 2.303 \times 8.314\ JK^{-1}\ mol^{-1}$$
$$E_a = 191.47\ kJ/mol$$

Also
$$k = \frac{0.693}{t_{1/2}}\ \text{for a 1st order reaction.}$$

So,
$$k = \frac{0.693}{200\times 60}\ sec^{-1} = 5.78 \times 10^{-5}\ sec^{-1}.$$

Q. 27. For the first order thermal decomposition reaction, the following data were obtained:*

$$C_2H_5Cl(g) \longrightarrow C_2H_4\ (g) + HCl\ (g)$$

Time/sec	Total Pressure/atm
0	0.30
300	0.50

Calculate the rate constant.

(Given : log 2 = 0.301, log 3 = 0.4771, log 4 = 0.6021).

Ans. If initial pressure is of C_2H_5Cl only.

If partial pressure of $C_2H_5Cl = P_A$

Let's partial pressure of $C_2H_4 = P_B$

Let's partial pressure of $HCl = P_C$, respectively at time t.

Suppose at time 300 sec, x atm pressure of C_2H_5Cl has decreased because of decomposition, then;

$$P_t = P_A + P_B + P_C \qquad\qquad \text{Now, from equation}$$
$$= (P_i - x) + P_B + P_C \qquad\qquad P_B = P_C = x$$
$$\Rightarrow \quad P_t = (P_i - x) + x + x$$
$$\Rightarrow \quad P_t = P_i + x$$
$$\text{or} \quad x = P_t - P_i \qquad\qquad\qquad\qquad\qquad\qquad \text{...(i)}$$
$$\text{Now,} \quad P_A = P_i - x$$
$$= P_i - (P_t - P_i)$$
$$\Rightarrow \quad P_A = 2P_i - P_t \qquad\qquad\qquad\qquad\qquad\qquad \text{...(ii)}$$

For 1st order kinetics :

$$k = \frac{2.303}{t}\log\frac{P_i}{P_A}$$

$$= \frac{2.303}{t}\log\frac{P_i}{2P_i - P_t}$$

Now, $P_i = 0.30$ atm at $t = 0$ sec.

$$\therefore \quad k = \frac{2.303}{300}\log\frac{0.30}{(2\times 0.30 - 0.50)} \qquad \text{and } P_t = 0.50 \text{ at time } t = 300 \text{ sec}$$

$$= \frac{2.303}{300}\log\frac{0.30}{0.10} = \frac{2.303}{300}\log 3$$

$$= \frac{2.303}{300}\times 0.4771 = 3.66\times 10^{-3}\ sec^{-1}.$$

Q. 28. (i) A reaction is second order in A and first order in B.*

    (a) Write the differential rate equation.

    (b) How is the rate affected on increasing the concentration of A three times ?

    (c) How is the rate affected when the concentration of both A and B are doubled ?

(ii) Rate constant 'k' of a reaction varies with temperature 'T' according to the equation :

$$\log k = \log A - \frac{E_a}{2.303\ R}\left(\frac{1}{T}\right)$$

where E_a is the activation energy. When a graph is plotted for log k vs $\frac{1}{T}$, a straight line with a slope of -4250

K is obtained. Calculate 'E_a' for the reaction. ($R = 8.314$ J K^{-1} mol^{-1}).

Ans. (i)   (a) The differential rate law

$$\text{Rate} = -\frac{d[R]}{dt} = k[A]^2[B]$$

   (b) When the concentrations of A is increased three times

$$-\frac{d[R]}{dt} = k[3A]^2[B]$$

$$= 9k\ [A]^2[B]$$

   Therefore, the rate of reaction will increase 9 times.

   (c) When the concentrations of both A and B are doubled,

$$-\frac{d[R]}{dt} = k[A]^2[B]$$

$$= k[2A]^2[2B]$$
$$= 8k\ [A]^2[B]$$

   Therefore, the rate of reaction will increase 8 times.

(ii) $$\log k = \log A - \frac{E_a}{2.303R}\left(\frac{1}{T}\right)$$

$\therefore$ $\dfrac{-E_a}{2.303R} = -4250$ K   as slope in plot $y = mx + C$ i.e., $m = \dfrac{-E_a}{2.303R}$

$\Rightarrow$ $E_a = 4250$ K $\times$ 2.303 $\times$ 8.314 JK^{-1}mol^{-1}

$\Rightarrow$ $E_a = 81375.35$ J mol^{-1} or 81.375 kJ mol^{-1}.

Q. 29. The rate constant is given by Arrhenius equation as :

$$k = Ae^{-E_a/RT}$$

Calculate the ratio of the catalysed and uncatalysed rate constants at 25°C, if the energy of activation of a catalysed reaction is 200 kJ mol^{-1} and for uncatalysed reaction, the value is 360 kJ mol^{-1}.

Ans. Let the rate constants for catalysed reaction $= k_1$

and rate constant for uncatalysed reaction $= k_2$

$$\log k_1 = \log A - \frac{(200 \times 10^3 \text{ J mol}^{-1})}{2.303\ RT} \qquad \text{...(i)}$$

and $$\log k_2 = \log A - \frac{(360 \times 10^3 \text{ J mol}^{-1})}{2.303\ RT} \qquad \text{...(ii)}$$

Subtract equation (ii) from (i).

$$\log k_1 - \log k_2 = \frac{360 \times 10^3 \text{ J mol}^{-1}}{2.303\ RT} - \frac{200 \times 10^3 \text{ J mol}^{-1}}{2.303\ RT}$$

$\Rightarrow$ $$\log\frac{k_1}{k_2} = \frac{160 \times 10^3 \text{ J mol}^{-1}}{2.303 \times 8.314 \text{ J K}^{-1}\text{ mol}^{-1} \times 298 \text{ K}}$$

$$\log\frac{k_1}{k_2} = 28.04$$

So, $$\frac{k_1}{k_2} = \text{antilog } 28.04 = 1.096 \times 10^{28}.$$

Q. 30. **The activation energy for the reaction**

$$2HI(g) \rightarrow H_2(g) + I_2(g)$$

is 209.5 kJ mol^{-1} at 581 K. Calculate the fraction of molecules of reactants having energy equal to or greater than activation energy?

Ans. In the given case:

$$E_a = 209.5 \text{ kJ mol}^{-1} = 209500 \text{ J mol}^{-1}$$
$$T = 581 \text{ K}$$
$$R = 8.314 \text{ JK}^{-1} \text{ mol}^{-1}$$

Now, the fraction of molecules of reactants having energy equal to or greater than activation energy is given as:

$$x = e^{-E_a/RT}$$

$\Rightarrow$
$$\ln x = -E_a/RT$$

$\Rightarrow$
$$\log x = -\frac{E_a}{2.303 \, RT}$$

$\Rightarrow$
$$\log x = \frac{-209500 \text{ J mol}^{-1}}{2.303 \times 8.314 \text{ JK}^{-1} \text{mol}^{-1} \times 581} = -18.8323$$

Now,
$$x = \text{antilog} \, (-18.8323)$$
$$= \text{antilog} \, \overline{19}.1677$$
$$= 1.471 \times 10^{-19}.$$

Q. 31. **In a pseudo first order hydrolysis of ester in water, the following results were obtained :**

t/s	0	30	60	90
[Ester] mol L^{-1}	0.55	0.31	0.17	0.085

(i)   Calculate the average rate of reaction between the time interval 30 to 60 seconds.

(ii)   Calculate the pseudo first order rate constant for the hydrolysis of ester.

Ans. (i)   Average rate of reaction between the time interval, 30 to 60 seconds,

$$\frac{d[\text{Ester}]}{dt} = \frac{0.31 - 0.17}{60 - 30}$$
$$= \frac{0.14}{30}$$
$$= 4.67 \times 10^{-3} \text{ mol L}^{-1} \text{s}^{-1}$$

(ii)   For a pseudo first order reaction,

$$k = \frac{2.303}{t} \log \frac{[R]_0}{[R]}$$

For $t = 30$ s,
$$k_1 = \frac{2.303}{30} \log \frac{0.55}{0.31}$$
$$= 1.911 \times 10^{-2} \text{ s}^{-1}$$

For $t = 60$ s,
$$k_2 = \frac{2.303}{60} \log \frac{0.55}{0.17}$$
$$= 1.957 \times 10^{-2} \text{ s}^{-1}$$

For $t = 90$ s,
$$k_3 = \frac{2.303}{90} \log \frac{0.55}{0.085}$$
$$= 2.075 \times 10^{-2} \text{ s}^{-1}$$

Then, average rate constant,
$$k = \frac{k_1 + k_2 + k_3}{3}$$

$$= \frac{(1.911 \times 10^{-2}) + (1.957 \times 10^{-2}) + (2.075 \times 10^{-2})}{3}$$

$$= 1.98 \times 10^{-2} \text{ s}^{-1}.$$

Q. 32. In a relation between A and B, the initial rate of reaction (r_0) was measured for different initial concentrations of A and B as given below:

A/mol L^{-1}	0.20	0.20	0.40
B/mol L^{-1}	0.30	0.10	0.05
r_0/mol L^{-1} s^{-1}	5.07×10^{-5}	5.07×10^{-5}	1.43×10^{-4}

What is the order of the reaction with respect to A and B?

Ans. Let the order of the reaction with respect to A be x and with respect to B be y.

Therefore,

$$r_0 = k[A]^x[B]^y$$
$$5.07 \times 10^{-5} = k[0.20]^x [0.30]^y \qquad \text{...(i)}$$
$$5.07 \times 10^{-5} = k[0.20]^x [0.10]^y \qquad \text{...(ii)}$$
$$1.43 \times 10^{-4} = k[0.40]^x [0.05]^y \qquad \text{...(iii)}$$

Dividing equation (i) by (ii), we obtain

$$\frac{5.07 \times 10^{-5}}{5.07 \times 10^{-5}} = \frac{k[0.20]^x[0.30]^y}{k[0.20]^x[0.10]^y}$$

$$\Rightarrow \qquad 1 = \frac{[0.30]^y}{[0.10]^y}$$

$$\Rightarrow \qquad \left(\frac{0.30}{0.10}\right)^0 = \left(\frac{0.30}{0.10}\right)^y$$

$$\Rightarrow \qquad y = 0$$

Dividing equation (iii) by (i), we obtain

$$\frac{1.43 \times 10^{-4}}{5.07 \times 10^{-5}} = \frac{k[0.40]^x[0.05]^y}{k[0.20]^x[0.30]^y}$$

$$\Rightarrow \qquad \frac{1.43 \times 10^{-4}}{5.07 \times 10^{-5}} = \frac{[0.40]^x}{[0.20]^x} \qquad \begin{bmatrix} \text{Since } y = 0, \\ [0.05]^y = [0.30]^y = 1 \end{bmatrix}$$

$$\Rightarrow \qquad 2.821 = 2^x$$
$$\Rightarrow \qquad \log 2.821 = x \log 2 \qquad \text{(Taking log on both sides)}$$
$$\Rightarrow \qquad x = \frac{\log 2.821}{\log 2}$$
$$= 1.496$$
$$= 1.5 \text{ (approximately) or } 3/2$$

Hence, the order of the reaction with respect to A is 1.5 and with respect to B is zero.

Q. 33. The reaction between A and B is first order with respect to A and zero order with respect to B. Fill in the blanks in the following table:

Experiment	A/mol L^{-1}	B/mol L^{-1}	Initial rate/mol L^{-1} min^{-1}
I	0.1	0.1	2.0×10^{-2}
II	......	0.2	4.0×10^{-2}
III	0.4	0.4	......
IV	......	0.2	2.0×10^{-2}

Ans. The given reaction is of the first order with respect to A and of zero order with respect to B.

Therefore, the rate of the reaction is given by,

$$\text{Rate} = k[A]^1[B]^0$$
$$\Rightarrow \qquad \text{Rate} = k[A]$$

From experiment I, we obtain

$$2.0 \times 10^{-2} \text{ mol L}^{-1} \text{ min}^{-1} = k(0.1 \text{ mol L}^{-1})$$
$$\Rightarrow \qquad k = 0.2 \text{ min}^{-1}$$

From experiment II, we obtain

$$4.0 \times 10^{-2} \text{ mol L}^{-1} \text{ min}^{-1} = 0.2 \text{ min}^{-1} [A]$$

$$\Rightarrow \qquad [A] = 0.2 \text{ mol L}^{-1}$$

From experiment III, we obtain

$$\text{Rate} = 0.2 \text{ min}^{-1} \times 0.4 \text{ mol L}^{-1}$$
$$= 0.08 \text{ mol L}^{-1} \text{ min}^{-1}$$

From experiment IV, we obtain

$$2.0 \times 10^{-2} \text{ mol L}^{-1} \text{ min}^{-1} = 0.2 \text{ min}^{-1} [A]$$

$$\Rightarrow \qquad [A] = 0.1 \text{ mol L}^{-1}.$$

Q. 34. During nuclear explosion, one of the products is ^{90}Sr with half-life of 28.1 years. If 1 µg of ^{90}Sr was absorbed in the bones of a newly born baby instead of calcium, how much of it will remain after 10 years and 60 years if it is not lost metabolically.

Ans. Here,

$$k = \frac{0.693}{t_{1/2}} = \frac{0.693}{28.1} y^{-1}$$

It is known that,

$$t = \frac{2.303}{k} \log \frac{[R]_0}{[R]}$$

$$\Rightarrow \qquad 10 = \frac{2.303}{\dfrac{0.693}{28.1}} \log \frac{1}{[R]}$$

$$\Rightarrow \qquad 10 = \frac{2.303}{\dfrac{0.693}{28.1}} (-\log[R])$$

$$\Rightarrow \qquad \log [R] = -\frac{10 \times 0.693}{2.303 \times 28.1}$$

$$\Rightarrow \qquad [R] = \text{antilog} (-0.1071)$$

$$= \text{antilog} (\bar{1}.8929)$$

$$= 0.7814 \text{ µg}$$

Therefore, 0.7814 mg of ^{90}Sr will remain after 10 years.

Again,

$$t = \frac{2.303}{k} \log \frac{[R]_0}{[R]}$$

$$\Rightarrow \qquad 60 = \frac{2.303}{\dfrac{0.693}{28.1}} \log \frac{1}{[R]}$$

$$\Rightarrow \qquad \log [R] = -\frac{60 \times 0.693}{2.303 \times 28.1}$$

$$\Rightarrow \qquad [R] = \text{antilog} (-0.6425)$$

$$= \text{antilog} (\bar{1}.3575)$$

$$= 0.2278 \text{ µg}$$

Therefore, 0.2278 µg of ^{90}Sr will remain after 60 years.

Q. 35. For the decomposition of azoisopropane to hexane and nitrogen at 543 K, the following data are obtained.

t (sec)	P (mm of Hg)
0	35.0
360	54.0
720	63.0

Calculate the rate constant.

Ans. The decomposition of azoisopropane to hexane and nitrogen at 543 K is represented by the following equation.

$$\underset{\text{Azoisopropane}}{(CH_3)_2CHN = NCH\,(CH_3)_2(g)} \longrightarrow \underset{\text{Nitrogen}}{N_2(g)} + \underset{\text{hexane}}{C_6H_{14}(g)}$$

At $t = 0$	P_0	0	0
At $t = t$	$P_0 - p$	p	p

After time t, total pressure,

$$P_t = (P_0 - p) + p + p$$

$\Rightarrow \qquad P_t = P_0 + p$

$\Rightarrow \qquad p = P_t - P_0$

Therefore,

$$P_0 - p = P_0 - (P_t - P_0)$$
$$= 2P_0 - P_t$$

For a first order reaction,

$$k = \frac{2.303}{t}\log\frac{P_0}{P_0 - p}$$

$$= \frac{2.303}{t}\log\frac{P_0}{2P_0 - P_t}$$

When time = 360 s,

$$k = \frac{2.303}{360\ s}\log\frac{35.0}{2\times35.0 - 54.0}$$

$$= 2.175 \times 10^{-3}\ s^{-1}$$

When $t = 720$ s,

$$k = \frac{2.303}{720\ s}\log\frac{35.0}{2\times35.0 - 63.0}$$

$$= 2.235 \times 10^{-3}\ s^{-1}$$

Hence, the average value of rate constant is

$$k = \frac{(2.175\times10^{-3}) + (2.235 + 10^{-3})}{2}\ s^{-1}$$

$$= 2.21 \times 10^{-3}\ s^{-1}.$$

Q. 36. The following data were obtained during the first order thermal decomposition of SO_2Cl_2 at a constant volume.

$$SO_2Cl_2(g) \longrightarrow SO_2(g) + Cl_2(g)$$

Experiment	Time/s^{-1}	Total pressure/atm
1	0	0.5
2	100	0.6

Calculate the rate of the reaction when total pressure is 0.65 atm.

Ans. The thermal decomposition of SO_2Cl_2 at a constant volume is represented by the following equation :

$$SO_2Cl_2(g) \longrightarrow SO_2(g) + Cl_2(g)$$

At $t = 0$	P_0	0	0
At $t = t$	$P_0 - p$	p	p

After time t, total pressure,

$$P_t = (P_0 - p) + p + p$$

$\Rightarrow \qquad P_t = P_0 + p$

$\Rightarrow \qquad p = P_t - P_0$

Therefore,

$$P_0 - p = P_0 - (P_t - P_0)$$
$$= 2P_0 - P_t$$

For a first order reaction,

$$k = \frac{2.303}{t}\log\frac{P_0}{P_0 - p}$$

$$= \frac{2.303}{t}\log\frac{P_0}{2P_0 - P_t}$$

When $t = 100$ sec, $k = \dfrac{2.303}{100 \text{ s}} \log \dfrac{0.5}{2 \times 0.5 - 0.6} = 2.231 \times 10^{-3} \text{ s}^{-1}$.

When $P_t = 0.65$ atm,

$$P_0 + p = 0.65$$

$$\Rightarrow \quad p = 0.65 - P_0$$

$$= 0.65 - 0.5$$

$$= 0.15 \text{ atm}$$

Therefore, when the total pressure is 0.65 atm, pressure of $SOCl_2$ is

$$p_{SOCl_2} = P_0 - p$$

$$= 0.5 - 0.15$$

$$= 0.35 \text{ atm}$$

Therefore, the rate of equation, when total pressure is 0.65 atm, is given by

$$\text{Rate} = k(p_{SOCl_2})$$

$$= (2.23 \times 10^{-3} \text{ s}^{-1})(0.35 \text{ atm})$$

$$= 7.8 \times 10^{-4} \text{ atm s}^{-1}.$$

Q. 37. The rate constant for the first order decompositon of H_2O_2 is given by the following equation :

$$\log k = 14.34 - 1.25 \times 10^4 \text{ K/T}$$

Calculate E_a for this reaction and at what temperature will its half-period be 256 minutes?

Ans. Arrhenius equation is given by,

$$k = Ae^{-E_a/RT}$$

$$\Rightarrow \quad \ln k = \ln A - \dfrac{E_a}{RT}$$

$$\Rightarrow \quad \log k = \log A - \dfrac{E_a}{2.303 \, RT} \qquad \qquad ...(i)$$

The given equation is

$$\log k = 14.34 - 1.25 \times 10^4 \text{ K/T} \qquad \qquad ...(ii)$$

From equation (i) and (ii), we obtain

$$\dfrac{E_a}{2.303 \, RT} = \dfrac{1.25 \times 10^4 \text{ K}}{T}$$

$$\Rightarrow \quad E_a = 1.25 \times 10^4 \text{ K} \times 2.303 \times R$$

$$= 1.25 \times 10^4 \text{ K} \times 2.303 \times 8.314 \text{ J K}^{-1} \text{ mol}^{-1}$$

$$= 239339.3 \text{ J mol}^{-1} \text{ (approximately)}$$

$$= 239.34 \text{ kJ mol}^{-1}$$

Also, when $t_{1/2} = 256$ minutes,

$$k = \dfrac{0.693}{t_{1/2}}$$

$$= \dfrac{0.693}{256} = 2.707 \times 10^{-3} \text{ min}^{-1}$$

$$= 4.51 \times 10^{-5} \text{ s}^{-1}$$

It is also given that, $\log k = 14.34 - 1.25 \times 10^4$ K/T.

$$\Rightarrow \quad \log (4.51 \times 10^{-5}) = 14.34 - \dfrac{1.25 \times 10^4 \text{ K}}{T}$$

$$\Rightarrow \quad \log (0.654 - 05) = 14.34 - \dfrac{1.25 \times 10^4 \text{ K}}{T}$$

$$\Rightarrow \quad \dfrac{1.25 \times 10^4 \text{ K}}{T} = 18.686$$

$\Rightarrow$

$$T = \frac{1.25 \times 10^4 \text{ K}}{18.686}$$

$$= 668.95 \text{ K}$$

$$= 669 \text{ K (approximately)}.$$

Q. 38. The decomposition of A into product has value of k as 4.5×10^3 s^{-1} at 10°C and energy of activation 60 kJ mol^{-1}. At what temperature would k be 1.5×10^4 s^{-1}?

Ans. From Arrhenius equation, we obtain

$$\log\frac{k_2}{k_1} = \frac{E_a}{2.303 \text{ R}}\left(\frac{T_2 - T_1}{T_1 T_2}\right)$$

Also, $k = 4.5 \times 10^3$ s^{-1}

$T_1 = 273 + 10 = 283$ K

$k_2 = 1.5 \times 10^4$ s^{-1}

$E_a = 60$ kJ mol^{-1} = 6.0×10^4 J mol^{-1}

Then,

$$\log\frac{1.5 \times 10^4}{4.5 \times 10^3} = \frac{6.0 \times 10^4 \text{ J mol}^{-1}}{2.303 \times 8.314 \text{ J K}^{-1} \text{ mol}^{-1}}\left(\frac{T_2 - 283}{283 \text{ T}_2}\right)$$

$\Rightarrow$

$$0.5229 = 3133.627\left(\frac{T_2 - 283}{283 \text{ T}_2}\right)$$

$\Rightarrow$

$$\frac{0.5229 \times 283 \text{ T}_2}{3133.627} = T_2 - 283$$

$\Rightarrow$

$$0.0472 \text{ T}_2 = T_2 - 283$$

$\Rightarrow$

$$0.9528 \text{ T}_2 = 283$$

$\Rightarrow$

$$T_2 = 297.019 \text{ K}$$

$$= 297 \text{ K (approximately)}$$

$$= 24°C$$

Hence, k would be 1.5×10^4 s^{-1} at 24°C.

Q. 39. The following results have been obtained during the kinetic studies of the reaction :

$$2A + B \longrightarrow C + D$$

Experiment	A/mol L^{-1}	B/mol L^{-1}	Initial rate of formation of D/mol L^{-1} min^{-1}
I	0.1	0.1	6.0×10^{-3}
II	0.3	0.2	7.2×10^{-2}
III	0.3	0.4	2.88×10^{-1}
IV	0.4	0.1	2.40×10^{-2}

Determine the rate law and the rate constant for the reaction.

Ans. Let the order of the reaction with respect to A be x and with respect to B be y.

Therefore, rate of the reaction is given by,

$$\text{Rate} = k[A]^x[B]^y$$

According to the question,

$$6.0 \times 10^{-3} = k[0.1]^x[0.1]^y \qquad \text{...(i)}$$

$$7.2 \times 10^{-2} = k[0.3]^x[0.2]^y \qquad \text{...(ii)}$$

$$2.88 \times 10^{-1} = k[0.3]^x[0.4]^y \qquad \text{...(iii)}$$

$$2.40 \times 10^{-2} = k[0.4]^x[0.1]^y \qquad \text{...(iv)}$$

Dividing equation (iv) by (i), we obtain

$$\frac{2.40 \times 10^{-2}}{6.0 \times 10^{-3}} = \frac{k[0.4]^x[0.1]^y}{k[0.1]^x[0.1]^y}$$

$$\Rightarrow \qquad 4 = \frac{[0.4]^x}{[0.1]^x}$$

$$\Rightarrow \qquad 4 = \left(\frac{0.4}{0.1}\right)^x$$

$$\Rightarrow \qquad (4)^1 = 4x$$

$$\Rightarrow \qquad x = 1$$

Dividing equation (iii) by (ii), we obtain

$$\frac{2.88 \times 10^{-1}}{7.2 \times 10^{-2}} = \frac{k[0.3]^x [0.4]^y}{k[0.3]^x [0.2]^y}$$

$$\Rightarrow \qquad 4 = \left(\frac{0.4}{0.2}\right)^y$$

$$\Rightarrow \qquad 4 = 2^y$$

$$\Rightarrow \qquad 2^2 = 2^y$$

$$\Rightarrow \qquad y = 2$$

Therefore, the rate law is

$$\text{Rate} = k[A][B]^2$$

$$\Rightarrow \qquad k = \frac{\text{Rate}}{[A][B]^2}$$

From experiment I, we obtain

$$k = \frac{6.0 \times 10^{-3} \text{ mol L}^{-1} \text{ min}^{-1}}{(0.1 \text{ mol L}^{-1})(0.1 \text{ mol L}^{-1})^2}$$

$$= 6.02 \text{ L}^2 \text{ mol}^{-2} \text{ min}^{-1}$$

From experiment II, we obtain

$$k = \frac{7.2 \times 10^{-2} \text{ mol L}^{-1} \text{ min}^{-1}}{(0.3 \text{ mol L}^{-1})(0.2 \text{ mol L}^{-1})^2}$$

$$= 6.0 \text{ L}^2 \text{ mol}^{-2} \text{ min}^{-1}$$

From experiment III, we obtain

$$k = \frac{2.88 \times 10^{-1} \text{ mol L}^{-1} \text{ min}^{-1}}{(0.3 \text{ mol L}^{-1})(0.4 \text{ mol L}^{-1})^2}$$

$$= 6.0 \text{ L}^2 \text{ mol}^{-2} \text{ min}^{-1}$$

From experiment IV, we obtain

$$k = \frac{2.40 \times 10^{-2} \text{ mol L}^{-1} \text{ min}^{-1}}{(0.4 \text{ mol L}^{-1})(0.1 \text{ mol L}^{-1})^2}$$

$$= 6.0 \text{ L}^2 \text{ mol}^{-2} \text{ min}^{-1}$$

Therefore, rate constant, $k = 6.0 \text{ L}^2 \text{ mol}^{-2} \text{ min}^{-1}$.

Q. 40. The experimental data for decomposition of N_2O_5

$$[2N_2O_5 \longrightarrow 4NO_2 + O_2]$$

In gas phase at 318 K are given below:

$t(s)$	0	400	800	1200	1600	2000	2400	2800	3200
$10^2 \times [N_2O_5]$ mol L^{-1}	1.63	1.36	1.14	0.93	0.78	0.64	0.53	0.43	0.35

(i) Plot $[N_2O_5]$ against t.

(ii) Find the half-life period for the reaction.

(iii) Draw a graph between log $[N_2O_5]$ and t.

(iv) What is the rate law?

(v) Calculate the rate constant.

(vi) Calculate the half-life period from k and compare it with (ii).

Ans. **(i)**

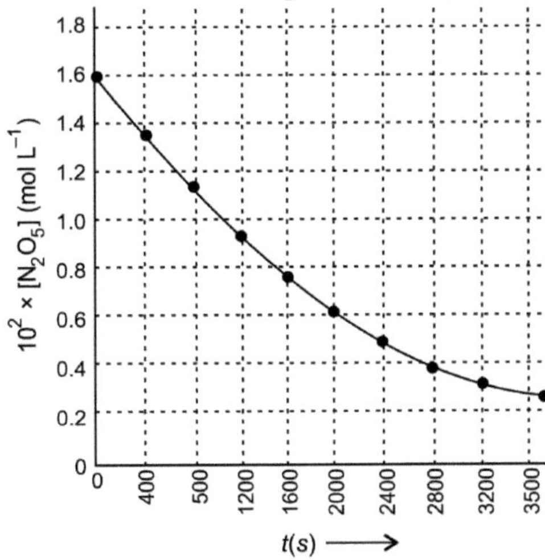

(ii) Time corresponding to the concentration, $\dfrac{1.630 \times 10^2}{2}$ mol L^{-1} = 81.5 mol L^{-1}, is the half life. From the graph, the half life is obtained as 1450 s.

(iii)

$t(s)$	$10^2 \times [N_2O_5]/\text{mol L}^{-1}$	$\log [N_2O_5]$
0	1.63	−1.79
400	1.36	−1.87
800	1.14	−1.94
1200	0.93	−2.03
1600	0.78	−2.11
2000	0.64	−2.19
2400	0.53	−2.28
2800	0.43	−2.37
3200	0.35	−2.46

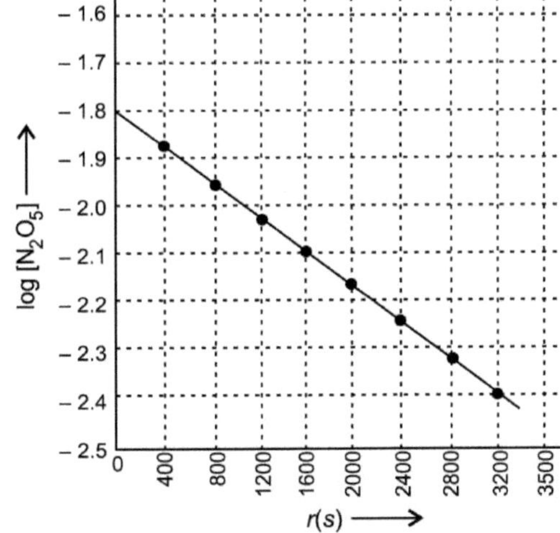

(iv) The given reaction is of the first order as the plot, $\log[N_2O_5]$ Vs./t, is a straight line.
Therefore, the rate law of the reaction is

$$\text{Rate} = k[N_2O_5]$$

(v) From the plot, $\log [N_2O_5]$

$$\text{Slope} = \frac{-2.46 - (-1.79)}{3200 - 0}$$

$$= -\frac{k}{2.303}$$

Again, slope of the line of the plot log $[N_2O_5]$ Vs. t is given by :

$$= -\frac{k}{2.303}$$

Therefore, we obtain,

$$-\frac{k}{2.303} = -\frac{0.67}{3200}$$

$$\Rightarrow \qquad k = 4.82 \times 10^{-4}\, s^{-1}$$

(vi) Half-life is given by,

$$t_{1/2} = \frac{0.639}{k}$$

$$= \frac{0.693}{4.82 \times 10^{-4}}\, s \;=\; 1.438 \times 10^3\, s$$

$$= 1438\, s$$

This value, 1438 s, is very close to the value that was obtained from the graph.

Q. 41. The rate constant for the decomposition of N_2O_5 at various temperatures is given below:

T/°C	0	20	40	60	80
$105 \times k/s^{-1}$	0.0787	1.70	25.7	178	2140

Draw a graph between ln k and 1/T and calculate the values of A and E_a.

Predict the rate constant at 30° and 50°C.

Ans. From the given data, we obtain

T/°C	0	20	40	60	80
T/K Kelvin	273	293	313	333	353
$\frac{1}{T}/K^{-1}$	3.66×10^{-3}	3.41×10^{-3}	3.19×10^{-3}	3.0×10^{-3}	2.83×10^{-3}
$10^5 \times k/s^{-1}$	0.0787	1.70	25.7	178	2140
k	7.87×10^{-7}	1.70×10^{-5}	2.57×10^{-4}	1.78×10^{-3}	2.14×10^{-2}
In $k(2.303 \log K)$	-14.06	-10.98	-8.27	-6.33	-3.85

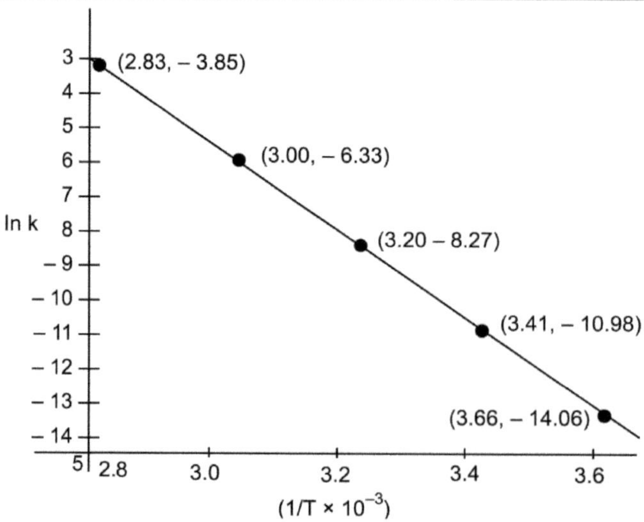

Slope of the line,

$$\frac{y_2 - y_1}{x_2 - x_1} = \frac{-10.98 - (-14.06)}{(3.41 - 3.66) \times 10^{-3}}$$

$$= -12.32 \times 10^3$$

According to Arrhenius equation,

$$\text{Slope} = -\frac{E_a}{R}$$

$\Rightarrow$
$$E_a = -\text{Slope} \times R$$
$$= -(-12.32 \times 10^3) \times (8.314 \text{ JK}^{-1} \text{ mol}^{-1})$$
$$= 102.43 \times 10^3 \text{ J K}^{-1} \text{ mol}^{-1} = 102.43 \text{ kJ K}^{-1} \text{ mol}^{-1}.$$

Intercept $= \ln A = -3.5$ (from graph)

$$\log A = \frac{\ln A}{2.303} = \frac{-3.5}{2.303}$$

$$= -1.5198$$

$\Rightarrow$
$$\log A = \bar{2}.4802$$

$$A = \text{antilog}\,(\bar{2}.4802)$$

$\Rightarrow$
$$A = 0.04802$$

Value of k from graph :

(i)
$$30°C = 303 \text{ K [T]}$$

$\therefore$
$$1/T = 3.33 \times 10^{-3}$$
$$\ln k = -9.9 \text{ (approx.) from graph.}$$
$$\log k = \frac{-9.9}{2.303} = -4.2987 \Rightarrow 5.027 \times 10^{-5} \text{ s}^{-1}$$

(ii)
$$50°C = 323 \text{ K (T)}$$

$\therefore$
$$1/T = 3.09 \times 10^{-3}$$
$$\ln k = -6.55 \text{ (approx.) from graph.}$$
$$\log k = \frac{-6.55}{2.303} = -2.8400$$

$$\text{antilog}\,(-2.8400) = 1.445 \times 10^{-3} \text{ s}^{-1}.$$

Q. 42. **The time required for 10% completion of a first order reaction at 298 K is equal to that required for its 25% completion at 308 K. If the value of A is 4×10^{10} s^{-1}, calculate k at 318 K and E_a.**

Ans. For a first order reaction,

$$t = \frac{2.303}{k} \log \frac{a}{a-x}$$

At 298 K,
$$t = \frac{2.303}{k} \log \frac{100}{90} = \frac{2.303}{k} \log 1.11 = \frac{2.303}{k} \times (0.0453)$$

$$= \frac{0.1044}{k}$$

At 308 K,
$$t' = \frac{2.303}{k'} \log \frac{100}{75} = \frac{2.303}{k'} \log 1.333 = \frac{2.303}{k'} \times (0.125)$$

$$= \frac{0.2875}{k'}$$

According to the question,

$$t = t'$$

$\Rightarrow$
$$\frac{0.1044}{k} = \frac{0.2875}{k'}$$

$\Rightarrow$
$$\frac{k'}{k} = 2.754$$

From Arrhenius equation, we obtain

$$\log \frac{k'}{k} = \frac{E_a}{2.303\,R}\left(\frac{T'-T}{TT'}\right)$$

$$\log(2.754) = \frac{E_a}{2.303 \times 8.314}\left(\frac{308-298}{298 \times 308}\right)$$

$$E_a = \log A - \frac{E_a}{2.303\ RT}$$

$$= 77319.32\ J\ mol^{-1}$$
$$= 77.32\ kJ\ mol^{-1}$$

To calculate k at 318 K.

It is given that, $A = 4 \times 10^{10}\ s^{-1}, T = 318\ K$

Again, from Arrhenius equation, we obtain

$$\log k = \log A - \frac{E_a}{2.303\ RT}$$

$$= \log(4 \times 10^{10}) - \frac{77.32 \times 10^3}{2.303 \times 8.314 \times 318}$$

$$= (0.6021 + 10) - 12.699$$
$$= -2.0969$$

Therefore, $k = \text{antilog}(-2.0969)$

$$= 8 \times 10^{-3}\ s^{-1}.$$

Q. 43. **For the reaction**

$$2NO_5(g) \longrightarrow 4NO_2(g) + O_2(g)$$

the rate of formation of $NO_2(g)$ is 2.8×10^{-3} Ms^{-1}. Calculate the rate of disappearance of $N_2O_5(g)$.*

Ans. Rate of reaction for the given reaction can be given as, $\text{Rate} = 1/2\{-\Delta[N_2O_5]/\Delta t\}$

or $\{-\Delta[N_2O_5]/\Delta t\} = 1/2\{[NO_2/\Delta t]\}$

So, rate of disappearance of N_2O_5 would be half of rate of production of NO_2 (given $2.8 \times 10^{-3}\ Ms^{-1}$). So,the rate of disappearance of N_2O_5 is $1.4 \times 10^{-3}\ Ms^{-1}$.

Q. 44. **W A first order reaction is 50% completed in 40 minutes at 300 K and in 20 minutes at 320 K. Calculate the activation energy of the reaction. (Given : log 2 = 0.3010, log 4 = 0.6021, R = 8.314 $JK^{-1}\ mol^{-1}$).***

Ans. Rate cosntant for a first order reaction is given by,

$$k = \frac{(2.303)}{t}\log\frac{[R_0]}{[R_1]}$$

So, at 300 K,

$$k_{300} = \frac{(2.303)}{40}\log\left(\frac{100}{50}\right)$$

$$= 0.058 \times \log 2$$
$$= 0.058 \times 0.301$$
$$= 0.017$$

$$k_{320} = \left(\frac{2.303}{20}\right)\log\left(\frac{100}{50}\right)$$

$$= 0.11 \times \log 2$$
$$= 0.11 \times 0.3010 = 0.034$$

Now, $$\log\frac{k_{320}}{k_{300}} = \left(\frac{E_a}{2.303R}\right)\left[\frac{T_2 - T_1}{T_1T_2}\right]$$

Putting the values,

$$\log\frac{0.034}{0.017} = \left(\frac{E_a}{2.303 \times 8.314 JK^{-1}mol^{-1}}\right)$$

* are board exam questions from previous years

$$= \left[\frac{320-300}{320\times200}\right]K$$

$$0.3010 = \frac{E_a}{19.14(0.0002)}$$

$$E_a = 28,805 \text{ J mol}^{-1}.$$

Q. 45. Following data are obtained for reaction: *

$$N_2O_5 \rightarrow 2NO_2 + 1/2O_2$$

t/s	0	300	600
$[N_2O_5]/\text{mol L}^{-1}$	1.6×10^{-2}	0.8×10^{-2}	0.4×10^{-2}

(i) Shows that it follows first order reaction.

(ii) Calculate the half-life.

(Given log 2 = 0.3010, log 4 = 0.6021)

Ans. (i)

$$k = 2.303/t \log [A_0]/[A]$$
$$= 2.303/300 \log 1.6 \times 10^{-2}/0.8 \times 10^{-2}$$
$$= 2.303/300 \log 2 = 2.31 \times 10^{-3} \text{ s}^{-1}$$
$$= \text{At } 600 \text{ s, } K = 2.303/t \log [A_0]/[A]$$
$$= 2.303/300 \log 1.6 \times 10^{-2}/0.4 \times 10^{-2}$$
$$= 2.303/600 \log 4 = 2.31 \times 10^{-3} \text{ s}^{-1}$$

Since K is constant when using first order equation therefore it follows order kinetics.

(ii)

$$t_{1/2} = 0.693/k$$
$$= 0.693/2.31 \times 10^{-3} = 300 \text{ s}$$

thus the half life of the reaction is 300s.

Q. 46. A first order reaction takes 20 minutes for 25% decomposition. Calculate the time taken when 75% of the reaction will be completed. *

Given : log 2 = 0.3010, log 3 = 0.4771, log 4 = 0.6021

Ans. T For first order reaction.

$$k = \frac{2.303}{t} \log \frac{a}{a-x}$$

$a - x \rightarrow$ amount left after time t

for 25% decomposition:

$$k = \frac{2.303}{20} \log \frac{100}{75} \qquad \qquad ...(i)$$

for 75% decomposition:

$$k = \frac{2.303}{t} \log \frac{100}{25} \qquad \qquad ...(ii)$$

K is constant throughout the process eq. (i) = eq. (ii)

Thus on comparing eq. (i) and eq. (ii) we have;

$$\frac{2.303}{20} \log \frac{100}{75} = \frac{2.303}{t} \log \frac{100}{25}$$

$$\frac{1}{20}(\log 100 - 75) = \frac{1}{t}(\log 100 - \log 25)$$

$$\frac{1}{2}[2 - 1.875] = \frac{1}{t}[2 - 1.398]$$

$$\frac{0.125}{2} = \frac{0.602}{t}$$

$$= \frac{1.204}{0.125}$$

$$t = 9.632 \text{ minutes.}$$

Q. 47. For a reaction A + B → P, the rate law is given by $r = k[A]^{1/2} [B]^{2*}$

    (i) What is the order of this reaction?

    (ii) A first order reaction is found to have a rate constant $k = 5.5 \times 10^{-14}$ s⁻¹. Find the half life of the reaction.

Ans. (i)   Order of reaction $= \dfrac{1}{2} + 2 = \dfrac{5}{2}$

    (ii) For first order reaction,

$$\text{Half life } (t_{1/2}) = \frac{0.693}{k}$$

$$= \frac{0.693}{5.5 \times 10^{-14}} = 1.25 \times 10^{13} \, s$$

Q. 48. The rate of reaction becomes four times when the temperature changes from 293 K to 313 K. Calculate the energy of activation (E_a) of the reaction assuming that it does not change with temperature.*

    [R = 8.314 J/K mol⁻¹, log 4 = 0.6021]

Ans. Given:

    $T_1 = 293$ K, $T_2 = 313$ K.

    $R = 8.314$ J K⁻¹ mol⁻¹

    $\log 4 = 0.6021$

$$E_a = \frac{2.303 R T_1 T_2}{T_2 - T_1} \log \frac{K_2}{K_1}$$

$$E_a = \frac{2.303 \times 8.314 \times 293 \times 313}{20} \times \log 4$$

$$E_a = 52.86 \text{ kJ mol}^{-1}.$$

□□

Test Your Knowledge

Q. 1. What is a unit cell?

Q. 2. Give an example of molecular solid and ionic solid?

Q. 3. What makes a glass different from solid such as quartz? Under what conditions could quartz be converted to glass?

Q. 4. Differentiate between isotropic and anisotropic solids.

Q. 5. Explain:
    (i)   The basis of similarities and differences between metallic and ionic crystals.
    (ii) Ionic solids are hard and brittle.

Q. 6. Answer the following questions:
    (i)   Why crystalline solids are called "anisotropic"?
    (ii) Name the three dimensional close packings generated from:
        (a) Two dimensional square closed packed layers,
        (b) Two dimensional hexagonal closed packed layers.
    (iii) Name the magnetic property of substances which are magnetised in a magnetic field in the same direction and lose their magnetism once the magnetic field is withdrawn. Give two examples.

Q. 7. Define the stoichiometric defects. How many types of stoichiometric defects are there, give examples also.

Q. 8. Answer the following questions:
    (i)   Atoms of element B from *hcp* lattice and those of element A occupy 2/3rd of tetrahedral voids. What is the formula of the compound formed by the elements A and B?
    (ii) Match the following figures with the name of deficiencies given below :
        (a) Interstitial defect,
        (b) Frenkel defect,
        (c) Schottky defect.

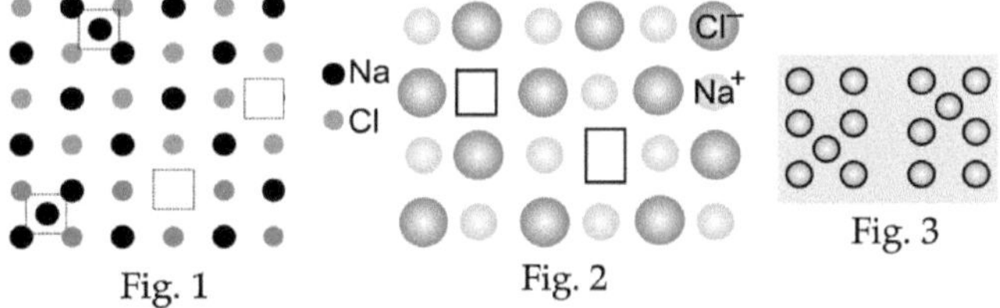

Q. 9. Answer the following questions:
    (i)   What fraction of each octahedral void belongs to one unit cell?
    (ii) What is the total number of atoms in a face centered cubic (*fcc*) unit cell?

Q. 10. Answer the following:
    (i)   Calculate the packing efficiency for body centered cubic (*bcc*) structures?
    (ii) Atoms of element X form *hcp* lattice and those of the element Y occupy 2/3rd of tetrahedral voids. What is the formula of the compound formed by these two elements ?

Q. 11. Answer the following questions:
    (i)   What is the total number of atoms in a face centered cubic (fcc) unit cell ? Show the calculation.
    (ii) What is dislocation defect?
    (iii) A substance X has its all the electrons paired. The substance is weakly magnetised in opposite direction in a magntic field, hence repelled weakly by the mgnetic field applied. Name the magnetic property being shown by the substance X.

Q. 12. Answer the following questions:
    (i)   Describe the types of stoichiometric defects with appropriate diagrams.

    (ii) An element crystallises in a body centered cubic structure. Its atomic mass is 93 μ. Calculate the atomic radius of this element if its density is 8.55 g/cm^3.

Q. 13. Give two examples each of:

    (i) Polar molecular solid   (ii) Covalent solid   (iii) Metallic solid

Q. 14. Krypton crystallises with a face centered cubic unit cell of edge 559 pm.

    (i) What is the density of solid krypton?

    (ii) What is the atomic radius of krypton?

    (iii) What is the volume of one krypton atom?

    (iv) What percentage of the unit cell is empty space if each atom is treated as a hard sphere?

Q. 15. We know that close packing in two dimensions can be of two types, square and hexagonal closed type packing. How can be they arranged in 'three dimensional' closed packing so as to obtain a 'primitive cubic cell' as the unit cell?

Q. 16. Silver forms *ccp* lattice and X-ray studies of its crystals show that the edge length of its unit cell is 408.6 pm. Calculate the density of silver (Atomic mass = 107.9 u).

Q. 17. Answer the following questions:

    (i) Provide the information in empty spaces:

S. No.	Crystal structure	Coordination number	Packing efficiency
1.	bcc		
2.	Simple cubic lattice		

    (ii) These are three dimensional arrangement of oppositely charged ions, bound by the strong coulombic forces. They are hard and brittle with high melting and boiling points. What type of solids are we talking about?

    (iii) This defect is shown by non-ionic solids and arises when some constituent particle occupies an interstitial site. What is the name of defect ? What effect this defect exerts on density of the substance ?

    (iv) Each electron has a permanent spin and an orbital magnetic moment associated with it. What is the magnitude of 'magnetic moment' of an electron?

    (v) What type of magnetic substances become paramagnetic on heating. Give an example.

Q. 18. Answer the following questions:

    (i) If the formula of a compound is A_2B, which sites would be occupied by A ions ?

    (ii) An element crystallises separately both in *hcp* and *ccp* structure. Will the two structures have the same density? Justify your answer.

Chapter 2. Solutions

Q. 1. Calculate molality of 2.5 g of ethanoic acid (CH_3COOH) in 80 g of benzene.

Q. 2. 36 g of glucose, $C_6H_{12}O_6$ is dissolved in 1 kg of water in a steel utensil. At what temperature will water boil at 1.013 bar? K_b for water is 0.52 K kg mol^{-1}.

Q. 3. What is de-icing agent ? How does it work?

Q. 4. Differentiate between osmosis and diffusion.

Q. 5. State the limitations of Henry's law.

Q. 6. Why scuba divers develop bends?

Q. 7. Why do gases always tend to be less soluble in liquids as the temperature is raised ?

Q. 8. Why is the vapour pressure of a solution of glucose in water lower than that of water ?

Q. 9. The density of 2.0 M solution of acetic acid (M_m = 60 g mol^{-1}) in water is 1.02 g m^{-1} or kg dm^{-3}. Calculate the mole fraction of acetic acid.

Q. 10. Answer the following questions:

(i) If in a nearly saturated solution the dissolution process is endothermic ($\Delta_{sol} H > 0$), what will be effect of increasing temperature on such solution ?

(ii) 1.00 g of non-electrolyte solute dissolved in 50 g of benzene lowered the freezing point of benzene by 0.40 K. The freezing point depression constant of benzene is 5.12 K Kg mol^{-1}. Find the molar mass of the solute.

Q. 11. Compound A and compound B form ideal solution over the entire range of composition. The vapour pressure of pure compound A at 300 K is 50.7 mm Hg and of pure compound B is 32.05 mm Hg. Now, calculate the mole fraction of compound A in vapour phase if 80 g of compound A is mixed with 100 g of compound B.

Q. 12. 20 g of ethylene glycol (C_2H_6O) is mixed with 700 g of ethanol ($K_f = 1.99$ K kg mol^{-1}; *f.p.* = 155.7 K). Calculate:
(i) the freezing point depression; (ii) the freezing point of the solution.

Q. 13. Answer the following questions:

(i) Interaction of solute molecules with solvent molecules is very crucial for dissolution of solute in that particular solvent. Arrange the following in order of increasing solubility in *n*-hexane :
Cyclohexane, NaCl, C_2H_5OH, CH_3CN

(ii) A solution containing 30 g of non-volatile solute and 90g of water has a vapour pressure of 2.8 kP$_a$ at 298 K. What happens to the magnitude of vapour pressure on adding 20 g of more water? Why?

Q. 14. Answer the following questions:

(i) Calculate the mole fraction of water in a mixture containing 9.0g of water, 120g acetic acid and 115g ethanol.

(ii) What is the sum of mole fractions of a mixture containing *i* no. of components?

Q. 15. Answer the following questions:

(i) Which area of work usually expresses concentration in 'mass percentage'?
What is the concentration of commercial bleaching solution in mass percentage of its constituents?

(ii) Give two examples of solid solutions.

Q. 16. A 0.5 percent aqueous solution of potassium chloride was found to freeze at 0.24 °C. Calculate the van't Hoff factor and the degree of dissociation of the solute at this concentration ($K_f = 1.86$ K kg mol^{-1}).

Q. 17. Answer the following questions:

(i) Which law primarily says that 'solubility of gas in a liquid is directly proportional to the partial pressure of the gas, at a given temperature'?

(ii) Name a membrane suitable for reverse osmosis of desalination of sea water. Why is it of use here?

(iii) Mountain climbers usually face a condition called 'anoxia'. Explain.

(iv) A litre of sea water (1038 g) contains about 6×10^{-3} g of dissolved oxygen (O_2). How is usually this small concentration expressed? Calculate and write.

Chapter 3. Electrochemistry

Q. 1. Write the cell reaction and calculate E° for the cell:
Zn, Zn^{2+} (1 M) | Fe^{2+}(1 M), Fe^{3+} (1 M); Pt

Given : $\qquad\qquad\qquad\qquad$ $Zn^{2+} + 2e^- \rightarrow$ Zn(s) (Standard electrode potential $= -0.76$ E°/V)
$\qquad\qquad\qquad\qquad\qquad\qquad$ $Fe^{3+} + e^- \rightarrow$ Fe^{2+} (Standard electrode potential $= +0.77$ E°/V)

Q. 2. Explain Faraday's law of electrolysis. What is the value of 1 F?

Q. 3. Give reasons for the following:

(i) The standard electrode potential for reduction of Zn^{2+} to Zn is highest (-0.76) among the first row transition elements.

(ii) Transition metals have catalytic activity.

(iii) Cu^{2+} ions are more stable in aqueous solutions that Cu^+ ions.

Q. 4. Given the standard electrode potentials (E°/V), write the following elements in their increasing order of reducing power:
$Al^{3+}/Al = -1.66$; $F_2(g)/2F^- = +2.87$; $K^+/K = -2.92$; $Ag^+/Ag = +0.80$.

Q. 5. The specific conductance of water is 7.6×10^{-2} S m^{-1} and the specific conductance of 0.1 M aqueous solution of KCl is 1.1639 S m^{-1}. A cell has a resistance of 33.20 Ω when filled with 0.1 M KCl solution and 300 Ω when filled with 0.1 M acetic acid solution. Calculate the molar conductance of acetic acid.

Q. 6. Give an equation to describe the relation between the change in Gibbs energy and reaction temperature. The value of ΔG_f° for formation of Cr_2O_3 is –540 kJ mol^{-1} and that of Al_2O_3 is –827 kJ mol^{-1}. Is the reaction of Cr_2O_3 possible with Al?

Q. 7. Answer the following questions:
    (i)   A solution of $CuSO_4$ is electrolysed for 20 min. with a current of 1 ampere. What is the mass of copper (63 g mol^{-1}), deposited at the cathode?
    (ii) Define the 'Kohlrausch law of independent migration of ions'.
    (iii) The most important secondary cell is the lead storage battery. It consists of a lead anode, lead dioxide cathode and sulphuric acid as electrolyte. Write the cell reaction when the battery is in use.

Q. 8. What are the factors on which 'cell constant' of a conductivity cell depends upon?

Q. 9. At 25 °C, the specific conductance of 0.01 M aqueous solution of an acid is 1.63×10^{-2} S M^{-1} and the molar conductance at infinite dilution is 390.7×10^{-4} S m^2 Mol^{-1}. Calculate the degree of dissociation of the acid.

Q. 10. Answer the following questions:
    (i)   What is molar conductivity?
    (ii) Show the variation in Λ_m with concentration for weak and strong electrolyte with the help of a plot.

Q. 11. What do you call a device which uses electrical energy for carrying non-spontaneous reactions?

Q. 12. Answer the following questions:
    (i)   Considering the electrochemical series, which substance do you think can be used for oxidising fluorides to fluorine ?
    (ii) Calculate the EMF of the following electrochemical cell at 25 °C :
        Cu, Cu^{2+} (c = 0. 1 M) | H^+ (c = 0.01 M), H_2 (1 atm); Pt
        (E°_{cell} for $2H^+$, $H_2(g)$; Pt = 0.00 V; Cu^{2+}, Cu(s) = + 0.34)

Q. 13. Some basic concepts of thermodynamics help us in understanding the theory of metallurgical transformations. Gibbs energy is the most significant term to be considered. The change in Gibbs energy is given by :

$$\Delta G = \Delta H - T\Delta S$$

Chapter 4. Chemical Kinetics

Q. 1. Define half-life of a reaction.

Q. 2. Identify the order of reaction from each of the following expressions:
    (i) 5.6×10^{-4} mol dm^{-3} s^{-1} (i) 4.5×10^{-3} dm^{3}mol^{-1} s^{-1} (i) 3.2×10^{-3} s^{-1}

Q. 3. What is the difference between 'Order' and 'Molecularity' of a reaction ?

Q. 4. Answer the following questions:
    (i)   Identify the order of reaction from below given formation :
        (a) Rate constant, $k = 3.5 \times 10^{-5}$ L mol^{-1} s^{-1} (b) Rate constant, $k = 5 \times 10^{-4}$ s^{-1}
    (ii) What is a pseudo first order reaction ?

Q. 5. All natural and artificial radioactive decay reactions follow which order of kinetics?

Q. 6. In a first order decomposition reaction, the initial concentration of A_2B_5 was 1.24×10^{-2} mol L^{-1} at 318 K, which reduces to 0.20×10^{-2} mol L^{-1} after 60 minutes. Calculate the rate constant of the reaction at 318 K. The reaction is as follows :

$$A_2B_5(g) \rightarrow 2AB_2(g) + \tfrac{1}{2}B_2(g)$$

Q. 7. Write the Arrhenius equation and indicate what do the terms used stand for in the equation.

Q. 8. Identify the order of reaction from the below given rate constants for that reaction:
    (i) L mol^{-1} s^{-1}, (ii) s^{-1}.

Q. 9. The gaseous decomposition of ozone, $2O_3 \rightarrow 3O_2$, obeys the rate law, $r = -d[O_3]/\,dt = k[O_3]^2/[O_2]$. Show that the following mechanism is consistent with the above rate law:
$$O_3 \underset{k}{\overset{k}{\rightleftharpoons}} \text{(fast equilibrium)}$$
$$O + O_3 \xrightarrow{\;k_1\;} 2O_2 \text{ (slow)}$$

Q. 10. Answer the following questions:
    (i)   What is the effect of adding catalyst on the free energy of a reaction?
    (ii) What is the order of reaction whose rate constant has the same units as the rate of reaction?
    (iii) Why is it difficult to find more number of reactions with higher order?

Q. 11. Write the rate expression for the below given reaction equation :
$$CH_3COOC_2H_5 + H_2O \text{ (excess)} \rightarrow CH_3COOH + C_2H_5OH$$

Q. 12. At 1100 K, the following data were obtained for the homogeneous reaction:
$$2NO\,(g) + 2H_2\,(g) \rightarrow N_2\,(g) + 2H_2O\,(g)$$

S. No.	[NO] (mol dm^{-3})	[H$_2$] (mol dm^{-3})	Rate, r ((mol dm^{-3}s^{-1})
1.	5.0×10^{-3}	2.5×10^{-3}	3.0×10^{-5}
2.	15.0×10^{-3}	2.5×10^{-3}	9.0×10^{-5}
3.	15.0×10^{-3}	10.0×10^{-3}	36.0×10^{-5}

    (i)   Calculate the order of the reaction with respect to NO, with respect to H$_2$ and overall reaction.
    (ii) Write the rate law expression for the reaction.

Chapter 5. Surface Chemistry

Q. 1. Use of powdered charcoal in place of charcoal chunks increases the extent of adsorption in a purification experiment, why?

Q. 2. Provide a comparison of 'chemisorption' and 'physisorption' while discussing at least six important criterias.

Q. 3. Define a 'shape selective catalysis' reaction.

Q. 4. Give reason for following:
    (i)   Physisorption decreases upon increasing temperature.
    (ii) Stability of colloidal solution is because of the presence of equal and similar charges on colloidal particles.
    (iii) Lyophobic sols show less stability than the lyophilic sols.

Q. 5. What is an 'Allosteric site'?

Q. 6. What is saponification?

Q. 7. State three characteristics each of chemisorption and physisorption.

Q. 8. Explain why:
    (i)   Physisorption decreases on increasing temperature.
    (ii) Lyophilic sols are more stable than lyophobic sols.
    (iii) Potassium chlorate decomposes slowly even after heating strongly, however it decomposes at considerably lower temperature when a little of manganese dioxide is added.

Q. 9. How would you define catalyst and catalysis?

Q. 10. What happens when :
    (i)   persistent dialysis of a sol is performed
    (ii) river water meets the sea water
    (iii) alum is applied on bleeding skin cuts

Chapter 6. General Principles and Processes of Isolation of Elements

Q. 1. Write a chemical reaction for each of the following statements involved in extraction of gold :
    (i)   The first step involves the leaching of metal with cyanide ion (CN$^-$), in presence of water and oxygen.
    (ii) The metal is later recovered by displacement method using zinc.

Q. 2. Answer the following questions:
    (i)   What is the principle behind hydraulic washing?
    (ii) Name the process which led to successful collection of copper from even low grade ores.
    (iii) In electrolytic refining of impure metal, what are the anode, cathode and electrolyte made up of?

Q. 3. Give a schematic diagram of iron extraction through blast furnace. Mention the chemical reactions occurring at each stage.

Q. 4. There may be two processes for obtaining aluminium from purified Al_2O_3. One is use of electrolytic cell for the reduction of Al_2O_3 as such and other is addition of cryolite in Al_2O_3 in the electrolytic cell to obtain aluminium.
    (i)   Which process will yield aluminium easily? Why?
    (ii) What is the role of graphite anode in the metallurgy of Al?

Q. 5. During reduction of metal oxide MO, the metal M is obtained in solid state whereas during reduction of metal oxide XO, metal X is obtained in liquid state, at the temperature of reduction. In which case reduction process will be easier? Why?

Q. 6. Answer the following questions:
    (i)   How is the choice of reducing agent for reduction of oxides is made in pyrometallurgy?
    (ii) What is the role of reducing agent in pyrometallurgy?
    (iii) Name a reducing agent in pyrometallurgy used commonly.

Chapter 7. *p*-Block Elements

Q. 1. Answer the following questions:
    (i)   Why interhalogen compounds are more reactive than the halogen molecules themselves? Predict the product of following reaction :

$$ICl + H_2O \longrightarrow ?$$

    (ii) A type of solid is hard and brittle in nature, it is high melting as well as high boiling and insulator of electricity. But become conductors of electricity in molten state or when dissolved in water. What type of solid is it?

Q. 2. Name one principle ore of each of these metals:
    (a) Copper,   (b) Iron.

Q. 3. Answer the following questions:
    (i)   Draw structures of :
       (a) XeF_2, (b) XeF_4, (c) XeF_6, (d) $XeOF_4$.
    (ii) Why is ICl more reactive than I_2 ?
    (iii) Complete the reactions :
       (a) $PCl_3 + 3H_2O \longrightarrow$
       (b) $NaNO_3 + H_2SO_4 \longrightarrow$

Q. 4. Copper (I) ion doesn't exist in solution, give reason.

Q. 5. Write structure of the compound XeF_6.

Q. 6. Why interhalogen compounds are more reactive than the halogen molecules themselves? Predict the product of following reaction :

$$ICl + H_2O \longrightarrow ?$$

Q. 7. Describe the manufacture of sulphuric acid through contact process.

Q. 8. Answer the following questions:
    (i)   Draw the structure of rhombic sulphur (S_8).
    (ii) Draw the two resonance structures of ozone, write the values of bond length and angles.
    (iii) Predominant species in lanthanoids are Ln(III), name a member of lanthanoids which is well known for its +4 state.
    (iv) Transition elements show a variety of oxidation states for a single element.
    (v) Halogens have the maximum negative electron gain enthalpy.

Q. 9. Answer the following questions:
   (i)   What is the hybridisation and geometry shown by tetrafluorides of S, Se and Te?
   (ii) State the thermodynamic factors which make fluorine a stronger oxidising agent than chlorine.

Q. 10. Answer the following questions:
   (i)   What is Deacon's process for manufacturing chlorine?
   (ii) Give two methods for formation of XeF_6.

Q. 11. Give reasons for following:
   (i)   Nitrogen exists as diatomic molecule whereas the other members of the group do not.
   (ii) PH_3 behaves as a base.

Q. 12. Explain why nitrogen does not form a pentahalide?

Q. 13. A single bond between two nitrogen atoms is weaker than two phosphorus atoms, why?

Q. 14. Why does nitrogen show less catenation properties than phosphorus and reacts with acids like HI?

Chapter 8. *d*- and *f*-Block Elements

Q. 1. Answer the following:
   (i)   Which property of potassium permanganate leads to its extensive use in textile fiber and oil industries as well as in preparative organic chemistry?
   (ii) The lanthanide elements occur together in nature and are difficult to separate from each other.

Q. 2. Answer the following questions:
   (i)   Why in case of Cr the electronic configuration is $3d^5 4s^1$ instead of $3d^4 4s^2$?
   (ii) Why Zinc is not regarded as a transition element in spite of its being a member of *d*-block elements?

Q. 3. Answer the following questions:
   (i)   Name a member of *f*-block elements which shows +4 oxidation state usually. Write its atomic number also.
   (ii) What is the general electronic configuration (outer orbital) for *d*-block elements?
   (iii) What is the oxidation state shown by actinoids in general?

Q. 4. A substance X has its all the electrons paired. The substance is weakly magnetised in opposite direction in a magnetic field, hence repelled weakly by the magnetic field applied. Name the magnetic property being shown by the substance X.

Q. 5. Give reasons for :
   (i)   Increase in ionisation enthalpy along each series of the transition elements.
   (ii) Chemistry of antinoids is complicated.
   (iii) Elements of group 18 exhibit very high ionisation enthalpy.

Q. 6. Answer the following:
   (i)   What is the disproportionation of an oxidation state?
   (ii) Why does nitrogen show less catenation properties than phosphorus?
   (iii) What is lanthanoid contraction?

Q. 7. Answer the following questions:
   (i)   Transiting from Sc to Zn in the first series of the transition metals, ionisation enthalpies vary from 631 KJ mol^{-1} to 906 KJ mol^{-1} (with some minor exceptions). Explain.
   (ii) Oxidation state of nickel and iron are zero in $Ni(CO)_4$ and $Fe(CO)_5$. Why?

Q. 8. Answer the following questions:
   (i)   It's difficult to separate the lanthanoid elements, why?
   (ii) Transition metal exhibit higher enthalpies of atomisation, why?
   (iii) Transition metals have high enthalpy of hydration, why?

Q. 9. Answer the following questions:

    (i)   Draw the structures of following homoleptic carbonyl coordination compounds.

        (a) $Ni(CO)_4$, (b) $Cr(CO)_6$.

    (ii) How is the magnetic moment of unpaired electron(s) calculated?

Q. 10. Complete the reactions:

    (i) $MnO^{4-} + Mn^{2+} + H_2O \rightarrow$

    (ii) $Cu^{2+} + 4I^- \rightarrow$

    (iii) What is the colour of Ce $+4$ ion? Given its atomic number is 58.

Q. 11. Answer the following questions:

    (i)   Comment why is magnetic moment of Sc^{3+} is 0 ?

    (ii) Calculate the magnetic moment of a divalent ion in aqueous solution, if its atomic number is 25.

Q. 12. Answer the following questions:

    (i)   What do we call the system where the central atom or ion is attached to the ligands and it may or may not bear an overall charge?

    (ii) Following observations are made with aqueous solutions of the below given compounds. Based on the observations assign secondary valences to the metals in the following compounds:

	Formula	Moles of AgCl precipitated per mole of the compounds with excess $AgNO_3$
1.	$CoCl_3.4NH_3$	1
2.	$PtCl_2.2NH_3$	0
3.	$NiCl_2.6H_2O$	2

Chapter 9. Coordination Compounds

Q. 1. Explain why $[Co(NH_3)_6]^{3+}$ is a homoleptic whereas $[Co(NH_3)_4Cl_2]^{3+}$ is heteroleptic complex.

Q. 2. Answer the following questions:

    (i)   The tetrahedral complex of $[NiCl_4]^{2-}$ shows paramagnetic behaviour while the tetrahedral complex of $[Ni(CO)_4]$ shows diamagnetic nature. Why ?

    (ii) Give the IUPAC name for following complexes:

        (a) $K_3[Al(C_2O_4)_3]$;   (b) $Hg[Co(SCN)_4]$.

Q. 3. Draw the geometrical isomers of coordination compound $[Co(NH_3)_4Cl_2]^+$.

Q. 4. Answer the following questions:

    (i)   Describe the hybridisation of $[CoF_6]^{3-}$ through diagram.

    (ii) Comment upon magnetic character and shape of $[CoF_6]^{3-}$.

    (iii) Why $[CoF_6]^{3-}$ is known as 'outer orbital' complex?

Q. 5. What is the shape of coordination compound $[Co(NH_3)_6]^{3+}$? Illustrate with drawing.

Q. 6. Consider a first row transition metal M. M^{2+} ion has a $3d^8$ configuration. Its M(II) chloride is dissolved in water to give hexahydrated green coloured complex A. On progressive addition of bidentate ligand, ethane-1, 2-diamine(en), three different compounds are formed:

en:M	Compound	Colour of compound
1 : 1	B	Pale blue
2 : 1	C	Blue/purple
3 : 1	D	Violet

What is the formula for compound A to D ? Provide the sequence of reactions to formation of compounds B to D as well.

$$[Ni(H_2O)_6]^{2+} \text{ (aq)} + en\text{(aq)} = [Ni(H_2O)_4(en)]^{2+} \text{ (aq)} + 2H_2O$$

            (Ethane-1, 2-   (Pale blue)

            diamine)

$$[Ni(H_2O)_4 (en)]^{2+} (aq) + en(aq) = [Ni(H_2O)_2(en)_2]^{2+} (aq) + 2H_2O$$
Blue/Purple

$$[Ni(H_2O)2(en)_2]^{2+} (aq) + en (aq) = [Ni(en)_3]^{2+} (aq)$$
Violet

Chapter 10. Haloalkanes and Haloarenes

Q. 1. When ethyl alcohol is reacted with sodium metal evolution of a gas is observed. Give the reason behind this observation.

Q. 2. Chlorobenzene does not undergo reaction through nucleophilic substitution reaction mechanism. Give any three reasons for this fact.

Q. 3. Give reasons for following:

(i) Free radical monochlorination of $(CH_3)_2CHCH_2CH_3$ gives a mixture of four different products.

(ii) The melting point of *para*-isomer of dihalobenzene is likely to be more than the *meta*- isomer.

(iii) The presence of a $-NO_2$ group at 2 and 4 positions increases the reactivity of a haloarene.

Q. 4. Arrange the following set of compounds in order of decreasing boiling points:
$$C_5H_{11}OH, C_4H_{10}, C_5H_{10}O, C_2H_5OC_2H_5.$$

Q. 5. Answer the following questions:

(i) Arrange in increasing order of reactivity towards S_N1 reaction:

(i)   (ii)   (iii)

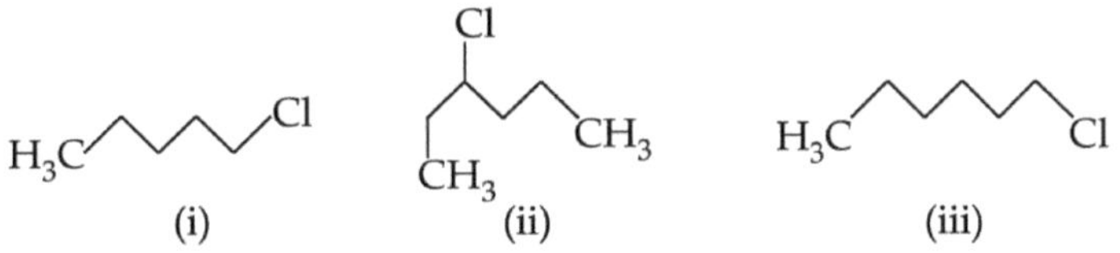

(ii) 'A mixture of alkyl halide and aryl halide gives alkylarene when treated with sodium in dry ether'— This statement fits to which named reaction? Give an example.

Q. 6. Answer the following questions:

(i) Give a reason for low reactivity of haloarenes compared to benzenes.

(ii) Why $C_6H_5CH(C_6H_5)$ Br is more reactive than in S_N1 reactions $C_6H_5CH(CH_3)Br$?

(iii) How does reactivity of a benzene ring vary with presence of a halogen atom on ring?

Q. 7. Define the following with examples (any two):

(i) Asymmetric carbon   (ii) Racemic mixture   (iii) Chirality

Q. 8. What would be the products in each case:

(i) $C_2H_2 + H - X \longrightarrow$

(ii) $CH_3CH_2Br + AgF \longrightarrow$

(iii) $CH_3COCl + C_2H_5OH \xrightarrow{\text{Pyridine}}$

(iv) $HCHO + R - Mg - X \xrightarrow{H_2O}$

(v) $C_2H_5OH \xrightarrow{\text{Conc. } H_2SO_4/180°C}$

Q. 9. Answer the following questions:

(i) Out of the four isomeric chlorobutanes, predict their order of reactivity towards S_N1 reactions.

(ii) What is the major product obtained when bromobenzene is reacted with conc. sulphuric acid under heating ? Give the complete reaction.

Q. 10. An optically active alkyl halide having molecular formula $C_7H_{15}Br$ reacts with aqueous KOH to give $C_7H_{15}OH$, which is optically inactive. Give mechanism for the reaction, why is the product optically inactive?

Q. 11. What is the effect of an alkoxy group present on the aromatic ring undergoing electrophilic substitution?

Q. 12. What happens when ethyl bromide undergoes Williamson's synthesis with sodium *tert*-butoxide? What happens when *tert*-butyl bromide is being taken as starting material and sodium ethoxide as base?

Chapter 11. Alcohols, Phenols and Ethers

Q. 1. Answer the following questions:
   (i)   Explain why the bond angle C–O–H in alcohols is slightly less than the tetrahedral angle (109°28′)?
   (ii) What is Williamson's synthesis of ethers?
   (iii) Give the chemical reaction for preparation of 'aspirin' starting from salicylic acid.

Q. 2. Answer the following questions:
   (i)   A compound is insoluble in water, gives an orange precipitate with 2, 4-DNP but fails to produce a silver mirror when heated with Tollen's reagent. What could be the functional group present in the unknown compound?
   (ii) Complete the following reactions :
   (a) $RCOOH + NH_3 \xrightarrow{\Delta} \text{........} CH_3CONH_2 + H_2O$
   (b) $(C_6H_5CH_2)_2 Cd + 2CH_3COCl \rightarrow$
   (iii) Give reasons why :
   (a)   Ketones are less reactive towards nucleophilic substitution reactions.
   (b)   Most carboxylic acids exists as dimer in the vapour phase or in the aprotic solvents.

Q. 3. Explain why:
   (i)   Carbonyl compounds have substantial dipole moments and are polar in nature.
   (ii) Boiling points of carboxylic acids are higher than corresponding aldehydes and ketones.
   (iii) Write the IUPAC names for following:
   (a) $(CH_3)_2C = CHCOCH_3$
   (b) 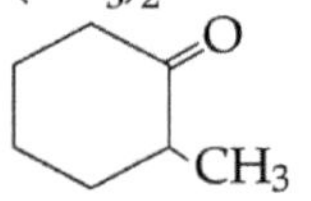   ![structure]
   (iv) How will you convert 4-Methylacetophenone to Benzene-1, 4-dicarboxylic acid? Give the reactions involved.

Q. 4. Give a method to convert propene to propan-2-ol.

Q. 5. Write the structures of the compounds whose names are given below:
   (a) 3-chloromethylpentan-2-ol, (b) *p*-nitroanisole.

Q. 6. Answer the following questions:
   (i)   Arrange the following in the increasing order of acidic strength:
         n-butanol, 2-methylpropan-l-ol, 2-methylpropan-2-ol and 2-methylpropan-2-ol.
   (ii) Give a chemical test to distinguish between butanol and 2-methylpropan-2-ol.
   (iii) Predict the products:

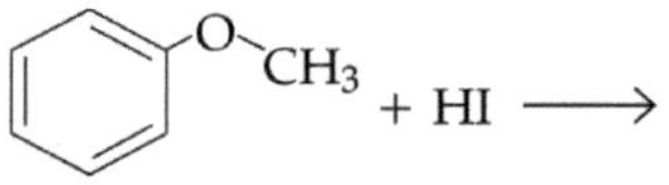

$$\text{(phenyl)}\!-\!O\!-\!CH_3 + HI \longrightarrow$$

Chapter 12. Aldehydes, Ketones and Carboxylic Acids

Q. 1. On warming an aldehyde with freshly prepared ammoniacal silver nitrate solution, a bright film of silver is deposited on the walls of test tube. Why?

Q. 2. Write the products obtained from following reactions:
   (i)   Reaction of propanone with ethylmagnesium bromide followed by hydrolysis.
   (ii) Ethoxy benzene is subjected to cleavage in presence of hydrogen chloride at high temperature.
   (ii) Phenol is subjected to react with concentrated nitric acid.

Q. 3. Answer the following questions:
   (i)   What is Cannizzaro reaction?
   (ii) Which of the following would undergo nucleophilic addition reaction faster than the other and why?
$$C_6H_5COCH_3 \text{ or } CH_3COCH_3$$

(iii) Carboxylic acid does not give reaction of carbonyl group, give reason.

(iv) What is the reaction called where aldehydes and ketones can be converted to alkanes on treatment with zinc and hydrochloric acid?

(v) Predict the product of following reaction:

$$C_2H_5COCH_3 \xrightarrow{\text{NaOI}}$$

Q. 4. Answer the following questions:

(i) What is aldol condensation?

(ii) Which organic compound is used for preserving biological specimens?

(iii) Arrange in decreasing order of acidity:

Benzoic acid, 4-Methoxy benzoic acid and 4-Nitrobenzoic acid.

(iv) Name a reagent which can distinguish between an aldehyde and a ketone.

Q. 5. Why is it that lower members of aldehydes and ketones are miscible with water?

Q. 6. Account for the following:

(i) Aldehydes are more volatile than alcohols.

(ii) Carboxylic acids do not give the characteristic reactions of carbonyl group.

Q. 7. Explain why:

(i) Carbonyl compounds have substantial dipole moments and are polar in nature.

(ii) Boiling points of carboxylic acids are higher than corresponding aldehydes and ketones.

Q. 8. Answer the following questions:

(i) Identify A and B in the below given reactions:

$$2\,RMgCl + CdCl_2 \longrightarrow A + 2MgCl_2$$
$$2R'CO - Cl + A \longrightarrow B + CdCl_2$$

(ii) Arrange the following compounds in decreasing order of their boiling points along with the reasons

$CH_3CH_2CH_2CHO$, $CH_3CH_2CH_2CH_2OH$, $C_5H_2-O-C_2H_5$, $CH_3CH_2CH_2CH_3$

(iii) Give two uses of formaldehyde.

(iv) Complete the reaction:

$$\text{C}_6\text{H}_5\text{CONH}_2 \xrightarrow[\Delta]{\text{H}_3\text{O}^+}$$

Q. 9. Compound A of molecular formula C_3H_6O is treated with Tollen's reagent to obtain a compound B. Compound B when reacted with aqueous sodium bicarbonate gives bubbles in solution and a compound C. The compound C when subjected to electrolysis gives a compound D and losses carbon dioxide (though it is trapped in the reaction mixture).

Identify the compounds A to D and give the complete reaction sequence for the above.

Q. 10. Complete the reactions:

(i) $\text{C}_6\text{H}_5\text{CH}_3 \xrightarrow[\text{Temp?}]{\text{Reagent?}} \text{C}_6\text{H}_5\text{CHO}$:

(ii) $CH_3MgCl + CO_2 \xrightarrow{\text{Dry ether}} A \xrightarrow{H_3O^+} B$

Q. 11. Answer the following questions:

(i) Which among the two is a stronger acid, give reason.

$CH_2FCH_2CH_2CO_2H$ (A) or $CH_3CHFCH_2CO_2H$ (B).

(ii) Draw structure for the ethylene glycol ketal of hexane-3-one.

(iii) Give three uses of compounds containing carbonyl compounds.

Q. 12. Answer the following questions:

(i) Give names of any two substances used in daily life made up of compounds containing —OH group.

(ii) Name the bonds holding together the polypeptides to give a fiber like structure.

(iii) When we say 'optically active polyhydroxy aldehydes or ketones or the compounds which produce such units on hydrolysis', which class of compounds are we referring to?

Chapter 13. Amines

Q. 1. Answer the following questions:
  (i)   Arrange the following amines in increasing order of their basic strength:

   NH_3, CH_3NH_2, $(CH)_3)_2NH$, $(CH_3)_3N$
  (ii) Predict the product in following reaction:

   $C_6H_5N_2^+X^- + CuCl_2/HCl \longrightarrow$
  (iii) Suggest a method to obtain Aniline from nitro benzene.

Q. 2. Answer the following questions:
  (i)   How will you convert 1-bromopropane to butane-1-amine.
  (ii) Aniline does not undergo Friedal-Craft's alkylation. Why?
  (iii) Illustrate the geometry or shape of ammonia through diagram.

Q. 3. Answer the following questions:
  (i)   Why amines are less acidic than alcohols of comparable molecular masses?
  (ii) Why are aliphatic amines stronger bases than aromatic amines?

Q. 4. Give reasons for the following:
  (i)   *O*-nitrophenol is more acidic than *m*-nitrophenol.
  (ii) Arrange the following in decreasing order of their basicity:

   $C_6H_5NH_2$, $(C_2H_5)_3N$, $(C_2H_5)_2NH$, $(C_2H_5)NH_2$.

Q. 5. Name a reagent which can selectively reduce nitriles to imines.

Q. 6. Write the compounds X and Y and also the chemical equation for the following reactions:
  (i)   One mole of benzyl chloride undergoes ammonolysis to give a product X and the product X is further reacted with two moles of ethyl chloride to give product Y.
  (ii) Aliphatic primary amine reacts with X and Y to give isocyanides.

Q. 7. Answer the following questions:
  (i)   In laboratory dinitrogen gas is obtained by treating an aqueous solution of ammonium chloride with sodium nitrite, but this brings few impurities as well. How can be dinitrogen prepared in laboratory in very pure form?
  (ii) Solution of NH_3 in water is a well-used base but solution of PH_3 in water is not stable. What happens to the solution in presence of light?
  (iii) Monohalides of group 16 elements are dimeric in nature, but they undergo disproportionation as well, explain with example of selenium chloride.
  (iv) Complete the reaction:

   $Cl_2 + 2Br^- \rightarrow$
  (v)   Name the gas used for providing inert atmosphere in high temperature metallurgical purposes and why?

Q. 8. Answer the following questions:
  (i)   At higher temperatures dinitrogen combines with metals readily to give ionic nitrides. But at room temperature dinitrogen is rather an inert gas, why?
  (ii) Interhalogen compounds of fluorine are very useful in fluorination. Complete the reaction below:

$$U(s) + 3ClF_3(l) \rightarrow$$

  (iii) Explain 'Brown ring test' in view of its use, principle and method of test.

Chapter 14. Biomolecules

Q. 1. Answer the following questions:
  (i)   Maltose is a disaccharide, write its structural formula.
  (ii) What are 'essential amino acid'? Give an example.
  (iii) 'Cheilosis' (fissuring around corners of mouth) can be caused due to deficiency of which vitamin?

Q. 2. Answer the following questions:
    (i) Define a peptide linkage.
    (ii) Classify proteins according to their molecular shape.
    (iii) What is glycosidic linkage? Give name of a biomolecule having glycosidic linkage.

Q. 3. Give two functions of protein in living organisms. State the difference between polypeptide and protein.

Q. 4. Explain the following:
    (i) Pyranose ring of glucose.
    (ii) Full form of DNA and RNA.
    (iii) Chemical name and source of vitamin C.

Q. 5. What is the difference between 'nucleoside' and 'nucleotide'?

Q. 6. Answer the following:
    (i) Name the type of bonding stabilising the α-helix structure of proteins.
    (ii) Draw a structure of illustrate glycosidic linkage, number the participating carbon atoms.
    (iii) How to enzymes facilitate a biochemical reaction?

Q. 7. Answer the following questions:
    (i) Explain the reason for following observation:
       When acidic solution of an amino acid is subjected to electrolysis, it migrates toward cathode. Whereas when electrolysis is performed in basic solution amino acid goes towards anode.
    (ii) What type of linkage holds together the monomers of DNA?

Chapter 15. Polymers

Q. 1. Which type of polymerisation process gives out a small molecule as a by product? Give an example of such type of reaction.
    (i) Bakelite is an "infusible" polymer. Why?
    (ii) What happens chemically to rubber when "vulcanisation process" is carried out?

Q. 2. Answer the following questions:
    (i) Name two copolymers.
    (ii) How is Nylon-6 prepared?
    (iii) Give examples of two biodegradable polymers.

Q. 3. Name the monomers used in preparation of Buna-S.

Q. 4. Classify the polymers based on their structure. Give a diagrammatic depiction and at least one example in each case.

Chapter 16. Chemistry in Everyday Life

Q. 1. Answer the following questions:
    (i) Why are synthetic detergents better than soaps?
    (ii) What are disinfectants? Name the disinfectant used for swimming pools.
    (iii) Name any bacteriostatic medicine.

Q. 2. Answer the following questions:
    (i) What is the use of Ranitidine (Zantac)?
    (ii) Why do receptors show selectivity towards the chemical messengers?
    (iii) Name two molecules which belong to 'barbiturates' class of tranquilizers.

Q. 3. Answer the following questions:
    (i) Name one natural and one synthetic commonly used food preservative.
    (ii) What is the common name of 2-3 percent solution of iodine in alcohol water mixture? What is it used for?
    (iii) What is the real active compound of antibacterial drug 'prontosil'?
    (iv) Aspirin is a well-known analgesic. Which class of analgesics it belongs to? Explain its mode of action.

Q. 4. What are synthetic detergents ? How are they classified? Give examples from each class.

❑❑

Topper's Answers - 2019

SECTION – A

1. Why are medicines more effective in colloidal state ?

OR

What is difference between an emulsion and a gel ?

> 1. In emulsion : physical state of dispersed phase :- liquid
> (e.g. milk, hair cream etc)
> physical state of dispersion medium :- liquid
> but, In gel : physical state of dispersed phase :- liquid
> (e.g. cheese, jellies etc). physical state of dispersion medium :- solid
> So, these colloids differ in physical states of their dispersion medium.

2. Arrange the following in increasing order of base strength in gas phase :
$(C_2H_5)_3N$, $C_2H_5NH_2$, $(C_2H_5)_2NH$

> 2. Increasing order of basic strength (gas phase)
> $C_2H_5NH_2 < (C_2H_5)_2NH < (C_2H_5)_3N$

3. Why conductivity of silicon increases on doping with phosphorus ?

> 3. Phosphorus is a pentavalent element. Therefore, when Silicon is doped with phosphorus one of the electron remains unbonded and is delocalised in the lattice. This electron can be easily excited to conduction band and move in the presence of external electric field. This way, doping Si with P increases the number of charge carriers and hence its conductivity.
>
> The semi-conductor thus formed is an extrinsic one (n-type).

4. What is the basic structural difference between glucose and fructose ?

OR

Write the products obtained after hydrolysis of lactose.

> 4. Products of hydrolysis of lactose :- β-D-galactose, β-D-glucose

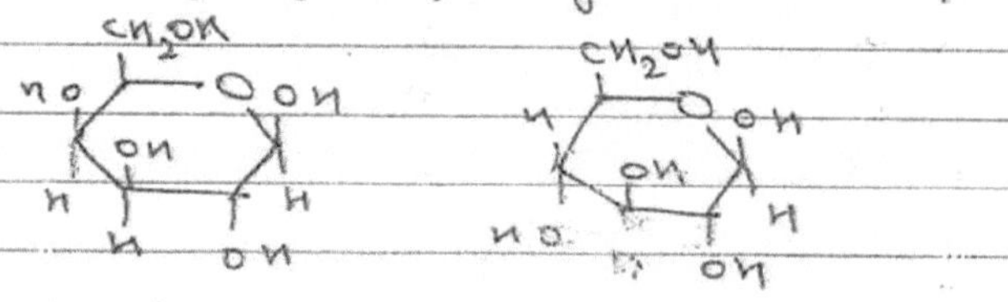

$$CH_2OH \quad\quad CH_2OH$$

β-D-galactopyranose   β-D-glucopyranose.

5. Write IUPAC name of the given compound :

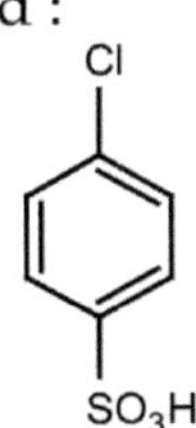

5. IUPAC name : 4-Chlorobenzene sulphonic acid

SECTION – B

6. Write structures of compounds A and B in each of the following reactions :

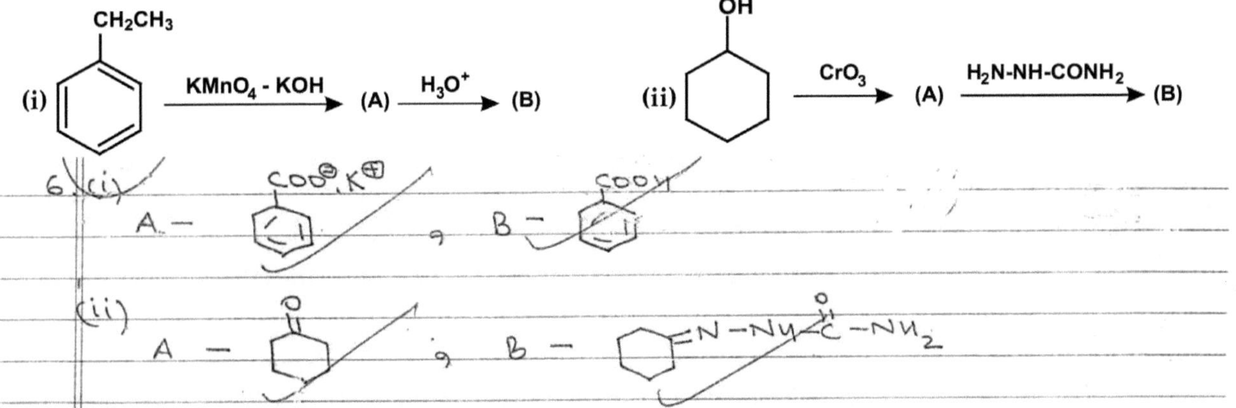

6 (i) A – [benzoate], B – [benzoic acid]

(ii) A – [cyclohexanone], B – [semicarbazone]

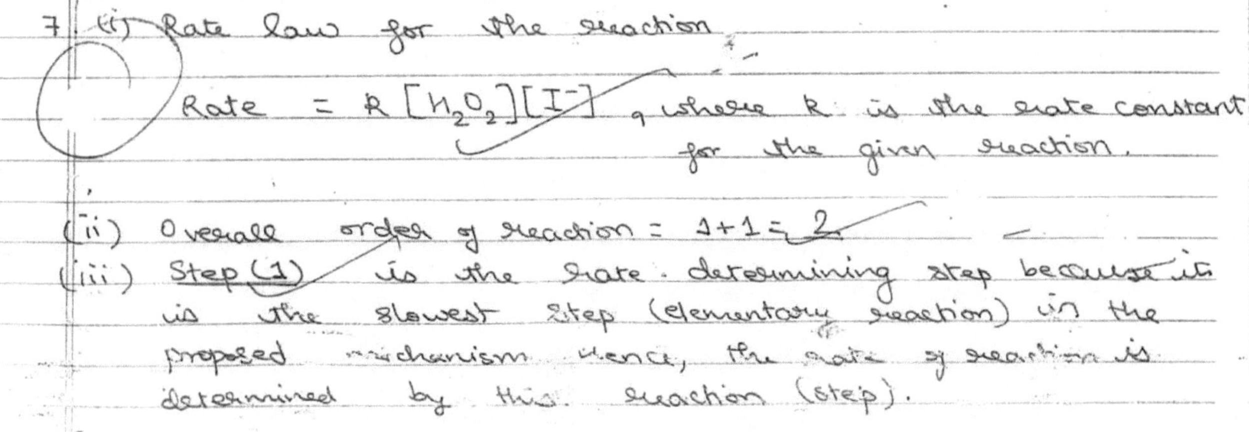

7. For a reaction

$$2H_2O_2 \xrightarrow[\text{Alkaline medium}]{I^-} 2H_2O + O_2$$

the proposed mechanism is as given below :

(1) $H_2O_2 + I^- \rightarrow H_2O + IO^-$ (slow)

(2) $H_2O_2 + IO^- \rightarrow H_2O + I^- + O_2$ (fast)

   (i) Write rate law for the reaction.

   (ii) Write the overall order of reaction.

   (iii) Out of steps (1) and (2), which one is rate determining step ?

7. (i) Rate law for the reaction

Rate $= k[H_2O_2][I^-]$, where k is the rate constant for the given reaction.

(ii) Overall order of reaction = $1 + 1 = 2$

(iii) Step (1) is the rate determining step because it is the slowest step (elementary reaction) in the proposed mechanism. Hence, the rate of reaction is determined by this reaction (step).

8. Write two differences between an ideal solution and a non-ideal solution.

Ideal Solution	Non-Ideal Solution
(a) The solution obeys Raoult's law over the entire range of concentration. The vapour pressure of solution is nearly equal to that predicted by Raoult's law.	(a) The solution does not obeys Raoult's law. The vapour pressure of the solution is either higher or lower than that predicted by Raoult's law.
(b) The intermolecular interactions between solute–solvent particles are of similar order to that of solute–solute particles and solvent–solvent particles. i.e. $\Delta_{mix}H = 0$ & $\Delta_{mix}V = 0$ e.g. Solution of n-hexane & n-heptane	(b) The intermolecular interactions between solute–solvent particles is either stronger or weaker than that existing between solute–solute particles & solvent–solvent particles. i.e. $\Delta_{mix}H > 0$, $\Delta_{mix}V > 0$ (+ve) OR $\Delta_{mix}H < 0$, $\Delta_{mix}V < 0$ (−ve) e.g. Solution of ethanol & acetone

9. When MnO_2 is fused with KOH in the presence of KNO_3 as an oxidizing agent, it gives a dark green compound (A). Compound (A) disproportionates in acidic solution to give purple compound (B). An alkaline solution of compound (B) oxidises KI to compound (C) whereas an acidified solution of compound (B) oxidises KI to (D). Identify (A), (B), (C), and (D).

A — K_2MnO_4
Potassium manganate.

B — $KMnO_4$
Potassium permanganate

C — KIO_3 (or IO_3^-)
Potassium iodate

D — I_2
Iodine

10. Write IUPAC name of the complex $[Cr(NH_3)_4Cl_2]^+$. Draw structures of geometrical isomers for this complex.

OR

Using IUPAC norms write the formulae for the following :

(i) Pentaamminenitrito-O-cobalt(III) chloride

(ii) Potassium tetracyanidonickelate(II)

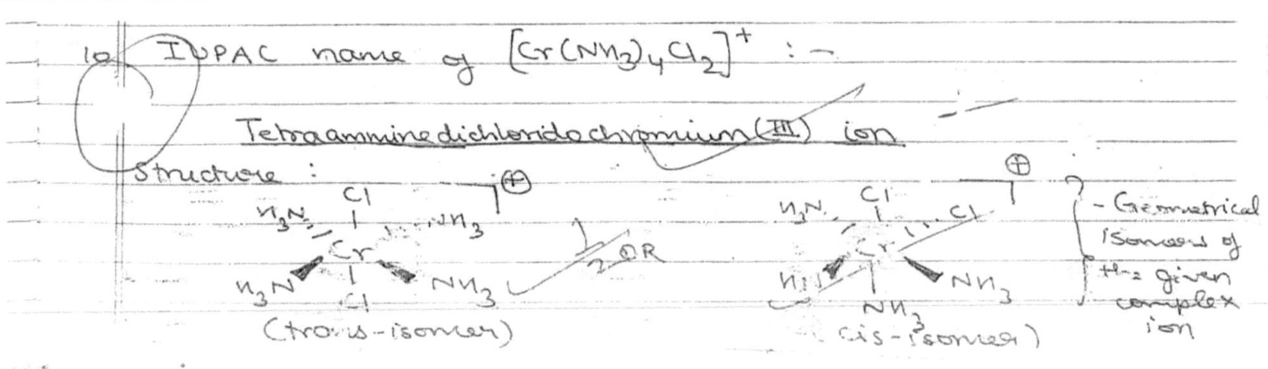

11. Out of $[CoF_6]^{3-}$ and $[Co(C_2O_4)_3]^{3-}$, which one complex is

(i) diamagnetic

(ii) more stable

(iii) outer orbital complex and

(iv) low spin complex ?

   (Atomic no. of Co = 27)

11. (i) Diamagnetic complex :- $[Co(C_2O_4)_3]^{3-}$

(ii) More stable complex :- $[Co(C_2O_4)_3]^{3-}$ (chelate effect)

(iii) Outer orbital complex :- $[Co\cdot F_6]^{3-}$

(iv) Low spin complex :- $[Co(C_2O_4)_3]^{3-}$

12. Write balanced chemical equations for the following processes :

(i) XeF_2 undergoes hydrolysis.

(ii) MnO_2 is heated with conc. HCl.

OR

Arrange the following in order of property indicated for each set :

(i) H_2O, H_2S, H_2Se, H_2Te – increasing acidic character

(ii) HF, HCl, HBr, HI – decreasing bond enthalpy

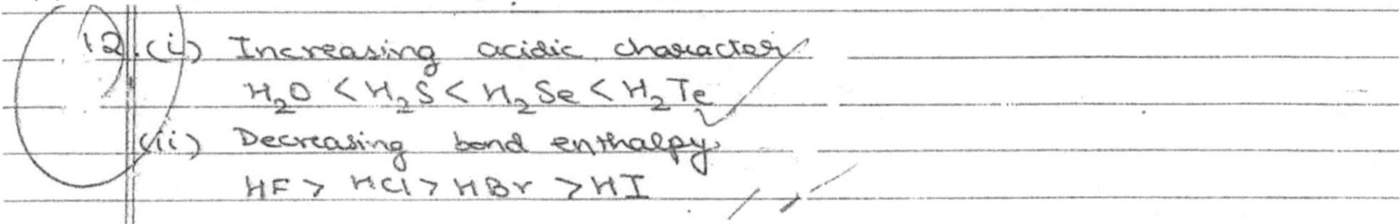

12. (i) Increasing acidic character

$H_2O < H_2S < H_2Se < H_2Te$

(ii) Decreasing bond enthalpy.

$HF > HCl > HBr > HI$

SECTION – C

13. An element crystallizes in fcc lattice with a cell edge of 300 pm. The density of the element is 10.8 g cm^{-3}. Calculate the number of atoms in 108 g of the element.

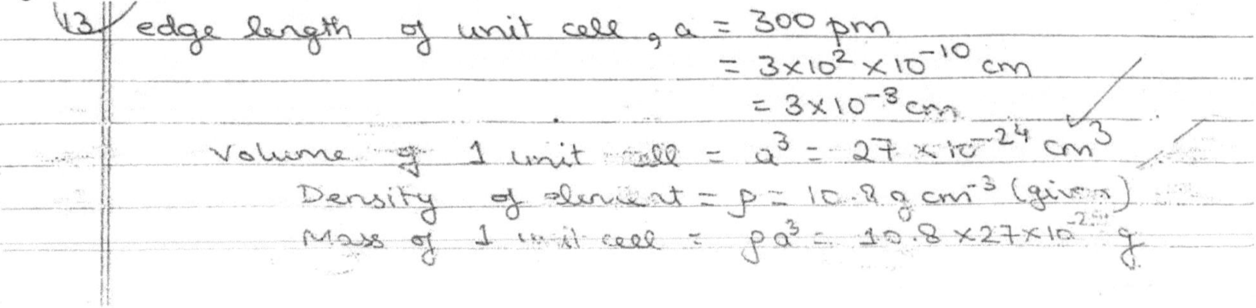

13. edge length of unit cell, a = 300 pm

$= 3 \times 10^2 \times 10^{-10}$ cm

$= 3 \times 10^{-8}$ cm

Volume of 1 unit cell $= a^3 = 27 \times 10^{-24}$ cm^3

Density of element $= \rho = 10.8$ g cm^{-3} (given)

Mass of 1 unit cell $= \rho a^3 = 10.8 \times 27 \times 10^{-24}$ g

Given mass of element = 108 g

So, Total number of unit cells in this mass of element

$$N = \frac{108 g}{\text{mass of 1 unit cell}} = \frac{108\ g}{10.8 \times 27 \times 10^{-24}\ g}$$

$$\text{OR}, \quad N = \frac{10 \times 10^{24}}{27}\ \text{unit cells}$$

Number of atoms present in one unit cell, $n = 4$ (fcc lattice)

So, total number of atoms $= nN = \frac{4 \times 10 \times 10^{24}}{27}$ atoms

$$= \frac{40 \times 10^{24}}{27}\ \text{atoms}$$

$$= 1.481481 \times 10^{24}\ \text{atoms}$$

Hence, a total of 1.481481×10^{24} atoms of element are present in 108 g of the given element.

14. A 4% solution(w/w) of sucrose (M = 342 g mol^{-1}) in water has a freezing point of 271.15 K. Calculate the freezing point of 5% glucose (M = 180 g mol^{-1}) in water.

(Given : Freezing point of pure water = 273.15 K)

14. Concentration of sucrose solution = 4% (w/w)

Considering 100 g of solution,

Mass of sucrose = 4 g (m_s)

Mass of water = 100 − 4 = 96 g (m_w)

Molar mass of Sucrose, $M_s = 342$ g mol^{-1}

Moles of Sucrose molecules

$$n_s = \frac{m_s}{M_s} = \frac{4}{342}\ \text{mol} = \frac{2}{171}\ \text{mol}$$

Molality of Solution = $\dfrac{n_s}{m_w (\text{in kg})}$

$$m = \frac{2 (1000)}{171 (96)}\ \text{mol kg}^{-1}$$

$$m = \frac{2000}{171 \times 96}\ \text{mol kg}^{-1}$$

Freezing point of solution = 271.15 K

Depression in freezing point = (273.15 − 271.15) K

$$= 2 K = \Delta T_f$$

Now, $\Delta T_f = K_f \, m$

where K_f = molal depression constant of water

Substituting values,

$$2 = K_f \times \frac{2000}{171 \times 96}$$

OR $K_f = \frac{2 \times 171 \times 96}{2000} = \frac{171 \times 96}{1000}$ K kg mol^{-1} ——①

Now, given 5% glucose solution.

Considering 100 g of solution.

Mass of glucose $= 5g = m_g$ [Mass of water = 95g]

Molar mass of glucose $= 180 \, g \, mol^{-1} = M_g$

moles of glucose, $n_g = \frac{m_g}{M_g} = \frac{5}{180}$ mol $= \frac{1}{36}$ mol

Molality of solution $= \frac{n_g}{\text{mass of water (in kg)}}$

$m = \frac{1}{36(95)} \times 1000$ mol kg$^{-1} = \frac{1000 \, mol}{36 \times 95 \, kg^{-1}}$

Using, $\Delta T_f = K_f \, m$

$\Delta T_f = \frac{171 \times 96}{1000} \times \frac{1000}{36 \times 95}$ (from ①)

$\Delta T_f = \frac{171 \times 96}{36 \times 95}$ K $= 4.8$ K

So, actual freezing point $= 273.15 K - 4.8 K$

$= 273.15$

$ \quad 4.80$

$ \quad \overline{268.35}$

$= 268.35$ K

Hence, the freezing point of 5% glucose solution in water is 268.35 K.

---

15. The decomposition of NH_3 on platinum surface is zero order reaction. If rate constant (k) is 4×10^{-3} Ms^{-1}, how long will it take to reduce the initial concentration of NH_3 from 0.1 M to 0.064 M.

15. Reaction: $NH_3(g) \rightleftharpoons \frac{1}{2} N_2(g) + \frac{3}{2} H_2(g)$

Rate of reaction $= -\frac{d[NH_3]}{dt} = k [NH_3]^0$

where $k = 4 \times 10^{-3}$ Ms^{-1} (given)

So, differential rate equation becomes,

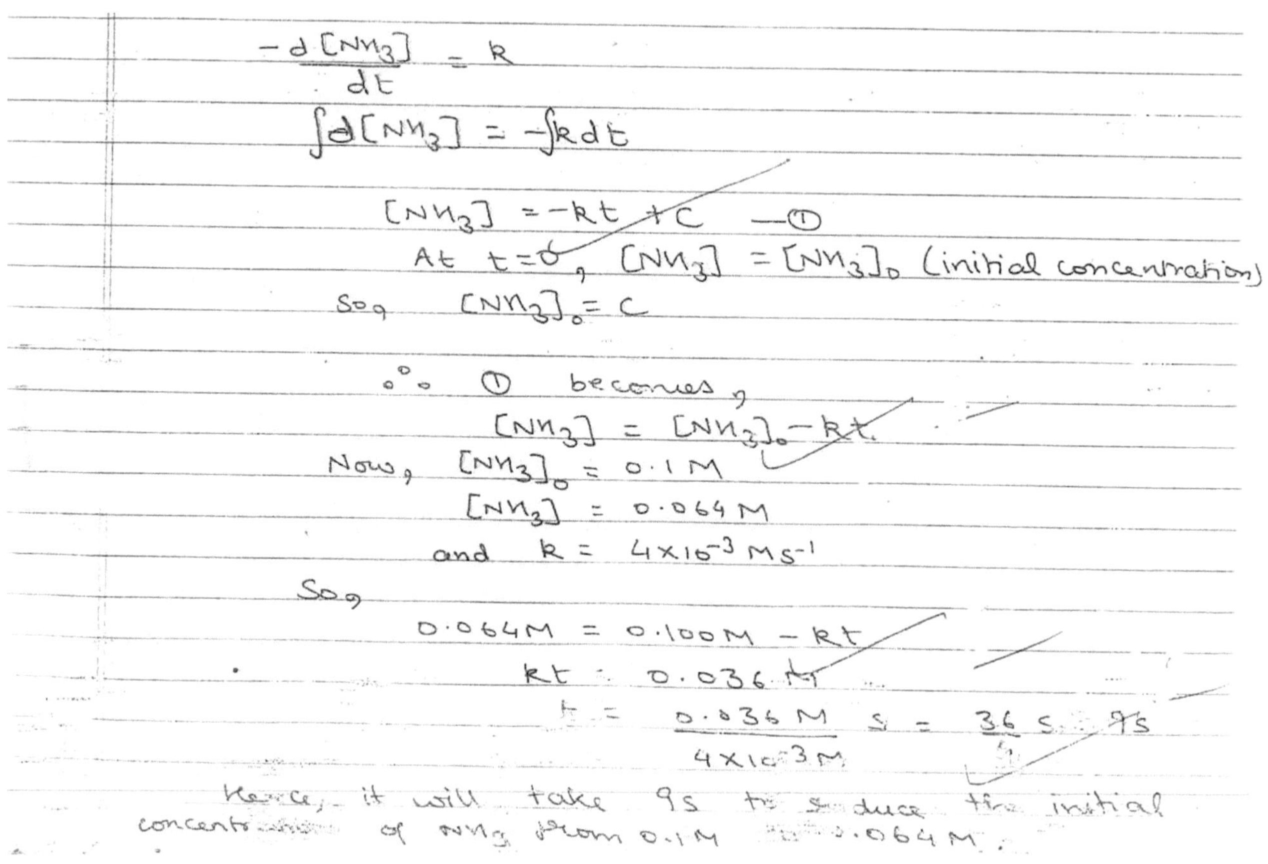

$$-\frac{d[NH_3]}{dt} = k$$

$$\int d[NH_3] = -\int k\, dt$$

$$[NH_3] = -kt + C \quad \text{—①}$$

At $t = 0$, $[NH_3] = [NH_3]_0$ (initial concentration)

So, $[NH_3]_0 = C$

∴ ① becomes,

$$[NH_3] = [NH_3]_0 - kt$$

Now, $[NH_3]_0 = 0.1\,M$

$[NH_3] = 0.064\,M$

and $k = 4 \times 10^{-3}\,Ms^{-1}$

So,

$$0.064\,M = 0.100\,M - kt$$

$$kt = 0.036\,M$$

$$t = \frac{0.036\,M}{4 \times 10^{-3}\,M} \quad s = 36\,s \quad 9s$$

Hence, it will take 9s to reduce the initial concentration of NH_3 from $0.1\,M$ to $0.064\,M$.

16. (i) What is the role of activated charcoal in gas mask ?

(ii) A colloidal sol is prepared by the given method in figure. What is the charge on hydrated ferric oxide colloidal particles formed in the test tube ? How is the sol represented ?

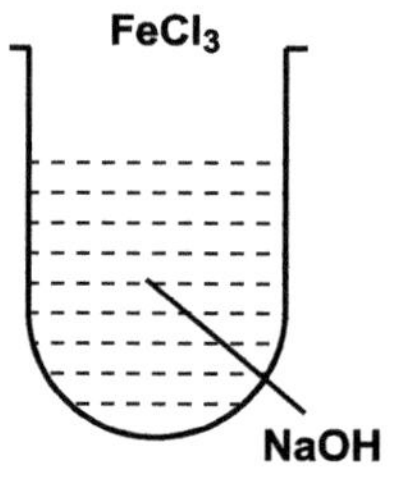

(iii) How does chemisorption vary with temperature ?

16. (i) Activated charcoal acts as an adsorbent in gas masks and adsorbs harmful and poisonous gases like SO_2, fumes of As etc on itself, thus, protecting the wearer of the mask from these gases.

(ii) The hydrated ferric oxide colloid is negatively charged in this case. (because it adsorbs OH^- ion from solution)

Sol can be represented as $\boxed{Fe_2O_3 \cdot xH_2O \,|\, OH^{\ominus}}$

OR $\quad Fe(OH)_3 \,|\, OH^{\ominus}$

(or extent)

(iii) The degrees of chemisorption increases with increasing temperature, as chemical bond - formation between the adsorbate and adsorbent molecules takes place in this case. Therefore, an appreciable amount of activation energy (E_a) is present, which can be easily overcome at high temperatures (according to Arrhenius $[k = Ae^{-\frac{E_a}{RT}}$ equation]). However, at even very high temperature, the extent of chemisorption decreases due to increasing thermal energy of gas particles (but that is very high temperature & not much perceptible).

---

17. (i) Write the role of 'CO' in the purification of nickel.

(ii) What is the role of silica in the extraction of copper ?

(iii) What type of metals are generally extracted by electrolytic method ?

---

17. (i) CO acts as a complexing agent and combines with Nickel atoms to form $[Ni(CO)_4]$ complex (volatile). This compound thus formed and is collected elsewhere and decomposed at higher temperature to give pure Ni is highly volatile in nature, which allows us to separate pure Nickel from the impurities present in crude nickel. Hence, helps in refining of Nickel metal.

$$Ni + 4CO \xrightarrow{350K} [Ni(CO)_4] \text{ (volatile)}$$

$$[Ni(CO)_4] \xrightarrow{450-470K} Ni(s) + 4CO\uparrow$$

$$\text{pure nickel metal.}$$

(ii) Silica (SiO_2) acts as an 'acidic flux' and combines with basic impurities (gangue – FeO) to form slag. The slag thus produced is a fusible component and immiscible with molten metal (Cu). Being lighter, Slag can be easily removed present pure molten Cu and helps in further purification and reduction of Cu metal.

$$2FeS + 3O_2 \longrightarrow 2FeO + 2SO_2$$

$$FeO(s) + SiO_2(s) \longrightarrow FeSiO_3(\ell)$$

$$\text{(slag)}$$

· This way, iron is removed from $CuFeS_2$ and other Cu ores containing iron.

(iii) Highly Electropositive elements such as Na, Mg, Al etc. are generally extracted through electrolytic method. This is so, because these metals are themselves the strongest ~~oxidising~~ reducing agent, therefore, no other element, compound can reduce these metals from their salts to metal form. Hence, electrolytic principles have to be used and external voltage is used to drive the non-spontaneous chemical reaction.

e.g. Extraction of Aluminium (Hall-Heroult Process)

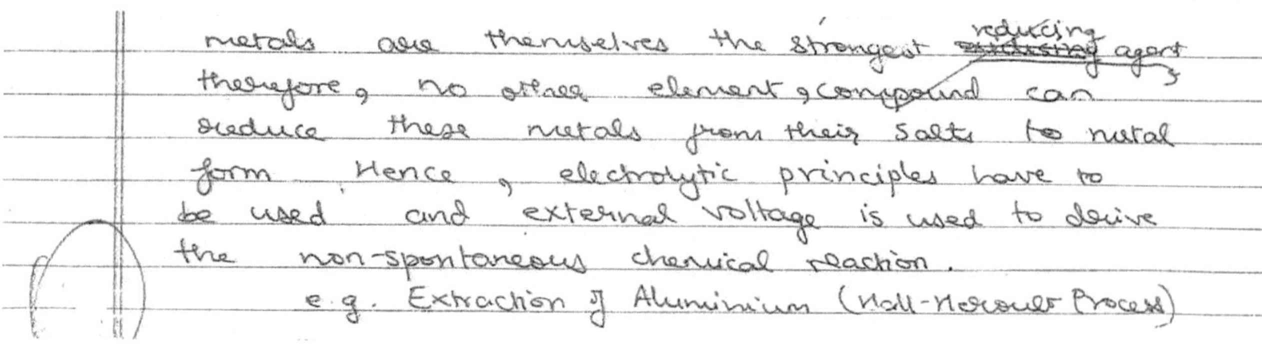

18. Give reasons for the following :

(i) Transition metals form alloys.

(ii) Mn_2O_3 is basic whereas Mn_2O_7 is acidic.

(iii) Eu^{2+} is a strong reducing agent.

18. (i) Transition metals have a large number of unpaired -d- electrons, are of small size and have vacant orbitals (d,sp) present for bonding (metallic bond). This makes the metals to homogeneously mix with one another (solid solution) leading to the formation of alloys. Also, in a period, the size of the elements are almost similar, and therefore, atoms of one element when present along with other elements do not interfere with corresponding metallic lattices and are able to fuse with one another quite effectively.
e.g. German Silver (Cu, Zn & Ni), Brass (Cu & Zn), Bronze (Cu & Sn).

(ii) In Mn_2O_3, Manganese is present in +3 oxidation state, whereas in Mn_2O_7, Manganese is present in +7 oxidation state. Since, higher the oxidation state, more is the polarising power of the metallic ion (Fajan's Rule), Mn–O bonds in Mn_2O_7 are more covalent as to those in Mn_2O_3. This increase in covalent nature and high oxidation state of Mn atom makes the solution of Mn_2O_7 in water more acidic as that of the solution of Mn_2O_3 in water. Hence, Mn_2O_7 is more acidic than Mn_2O_3.

(iii) Eu (Europium) belongs to the 4f-series (lanthanoids) and has a more stable oxidation state of +3, (+3 oxidation state for all lanthanoids is the most stable).
Hence, Eu^{2+} ion has a strong tendency to go to Eu^{3+} state (+3 oxidation state), and thus acts as a strong reducing agent.

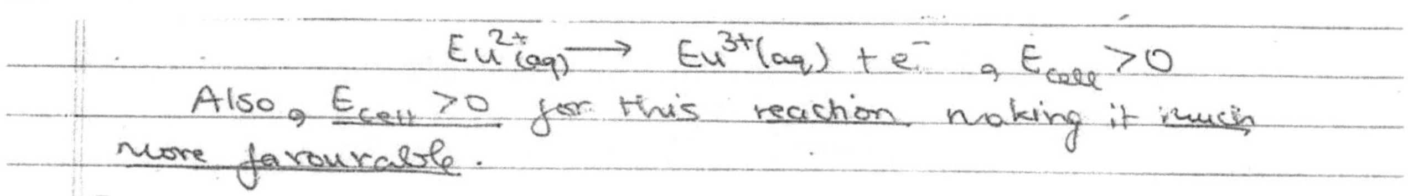

$$Eu^{2+}_{(aq)} \longrightarrow Eu^{3+}_{(aq)} + e^-, \quad E_{cell} > 0$$

Also, $E_{cell} > 0$ for this reaction making it much more favourable.

19. Write the structures of monomers used for getting the following polymers :

  (i)   Nylon–6,6

  (ii) Glyptal

  (iii) Buna-S

OR

  (i)   Is $\left[CH_2-\overset{\displaystyle CH_3}{\underset{|}{CH}}\right]_n$ a homopolymer or copolymer ? Give reason.

  (ii) Write the monomers of the following polymer :

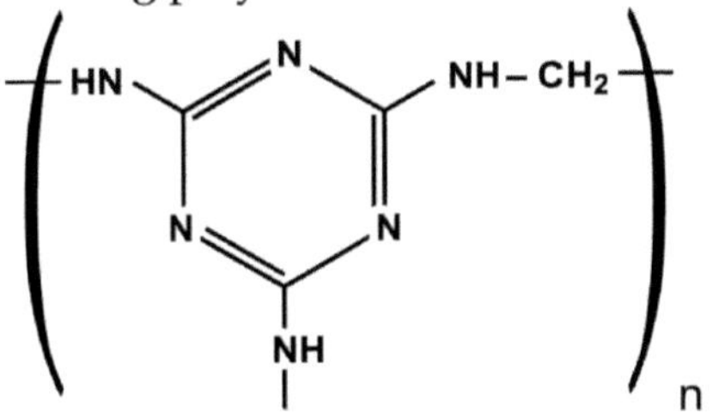

$$\left(HN-\underset{\underset{\underset{NH}{|}}{\triangle}}{\bigcirc}-NH-CH_2\right)_n$$

  (iii) What is the role of Sulphur in vulcani-zation of rubber ?

A. (i) Monomers of Nylon-6,6

$$HO-\overset{O}{\overset{||}{C}}-CH_2-CH_2-CH_2-CH_2-\overset{O}{\overset{||}{C}}-OH \quad \& \quad H_2N-CH_2-CH_2-CH_2-CH_2-CH_2-CH_2-NH_2$$

(Hexane-1,6-dioic acid)   (Hexane-1,6-diamine)

(ii) Monomers of Glyptal

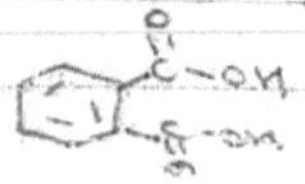

(benzoic acid) & $\underset{\underset{OH}{|}}{CH_2}-\underset{\underset{OH}{|}}{CH_2}$ (ethylene glycol)

(iii) Monomers of Buna-S

$$CH_2=CH-CH=CH_2 \quad \text{and} \quad \bigcirc-CH=CH_2$$

(Buta-1,3-diene)   (Styrene)

20. (i)   Why bithional is added in soap ?

    (ii) Why magnesium hydroxide is a better antacid than sodium bicarbonate ?

    (iii) Why soaps are biodegradable whereas detergents are non-biodegradable ?

OR

Define the following terms with a suitable example in each :

  (i)   Antibiotics

  (ii) Artificial sweeteners

  (iii) Analgesics

20. (i) Bithional is added to soap to impart to/its antiseptic properties to it.

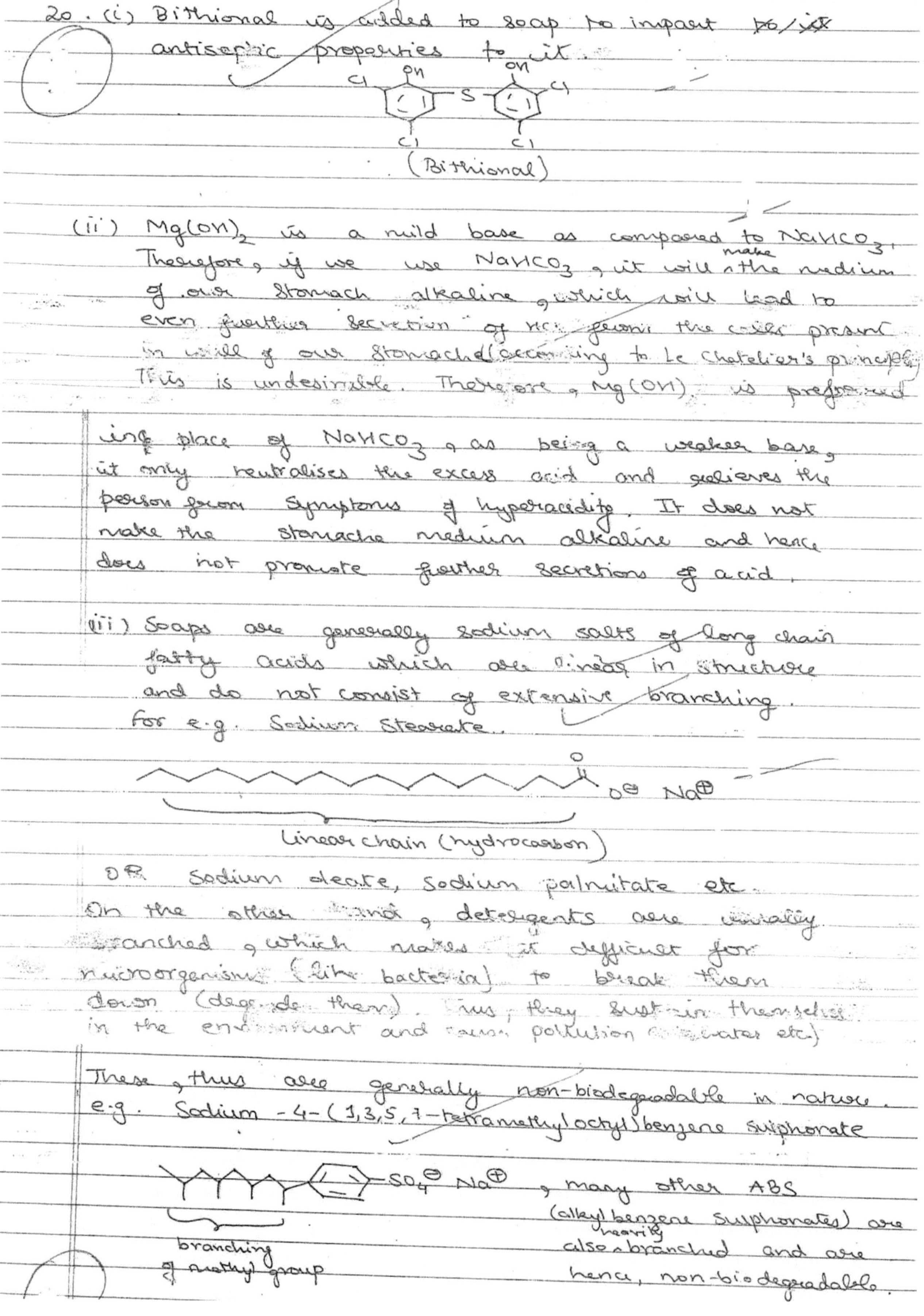

(ii) $Mg(OH)_2$ is a mild base as compared to $NaHCO_3$. Therefore, if we use $NaHCO_3$, it will make the medium of our stomach alkaline, which will lead to even further secretion of HCl (given the cells present in wall of our stomach) according to Le Chatelier's principle. This is undesirable. Therefore, $Mg(OH)_2$ is preferred

in place of $NaHCO_3$, as being a weaker base, it only neutralises the excess acid and relieves the person from symptoms of hyperacidity. It does not make the stomach medium alkaline and hence does not promote further secretions of acid.

(iii) Soaps are generally sodium salts of long chain fatty acids which are linear in structure and do not consist of extensive branching. For e.g. Sodium Stearate.

OR Sodium oleate, sodium palmitate etc. On the other hand, detergents are usually branched, which makes it difficult for microorganisms (like bacteria) to break them down (degrade them). Thus, they sustain themselves in the environment and cause pollution (of water etc.)

These, thus are generally non-biodegradable in nature. e.g. Sodium -4-(1,3,5,7-tetramethyloctyl)benzene sulphonate

, many other ABS (alkyl benzene sulphonates) are also heavily branched and are hence, non-biodegradable.

21. Write the structures of main products when benzene diazonium chloride reacts with the following reagents :

(i) CuCN

(ii) CH₃CH₂OH

(iii) KI

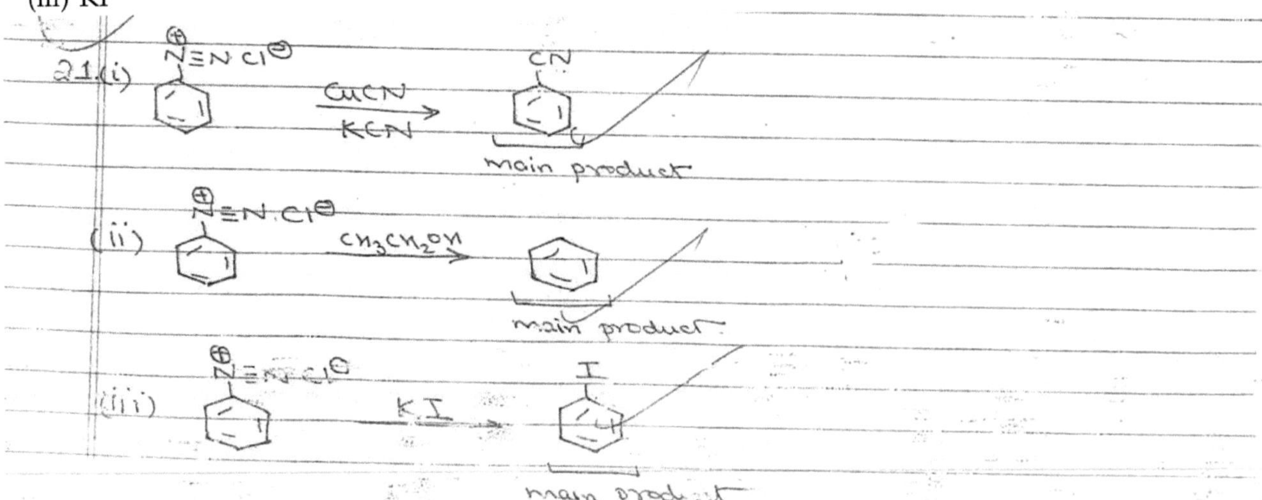

22. (i) Out of $(CH_3)_3C–Br$ and $(CH_3)_3C–I$, which one is more reactive towards S_N1 and why ?

(ii) Write the product formed when p-nitrochlorobenzene is heated with aqueous NaOH at 443 K followed by acidification.

(iii) Why dextro and laevo – rotatory isomers of Butan-2-ol are difficult to separate by fractional distillation ?

22 (i) $(CH_3)_3C-I$ is more reactive than $(CH_3)_3C-Br$ towards S_N1 reaction, because $I^\ominus$ is a better leaving group than $Br^\ominus$. Because of its larger size as compared to $Br^\ominus$, $I^\ominus$ is able to effectively stabilise the negative charge on itself, therefore, making the cleavage step more favourable.

Also, C–I bond is weaker than C–Br bond (i.e. C–I bond is longer than C–Br bond due to large size of $I^\ominus$ ion)

$$(CH_3)_3C-I \underset{\text{solvent}}{\overset{H^\oplus}{\rightleftharpoons}} (CH_3)_3C^\oplus + I^\ominus$$

$$(CH_3)_3C-Br \underset{\text{polar protic solvent}}{\overset{H^\oplus}{\rightleftharpoons}} (CH_3)_3C^\oplus + Br^\ominus$$

$I^\ominus$ is more stable and hence, cleavage takes easily

Also, we know that H–I is a stronger acid than H–Br, because of low bond–dissociation enthalpy of H–I bond as compared to H–Br.

∴ by Bronsted theory of acids and bases, the conjugate base $I^\ominus$ should be a weaker base than $Br^\ominus$, and we know that a stronger base can replace a weaker base more easily in a nucleophilic substitution reaction. Hence, $I^\ominus$ is more easily replaced by other nucleophiles as compared to Br⁻. Thus increasing the rate of reaction.

(ii)

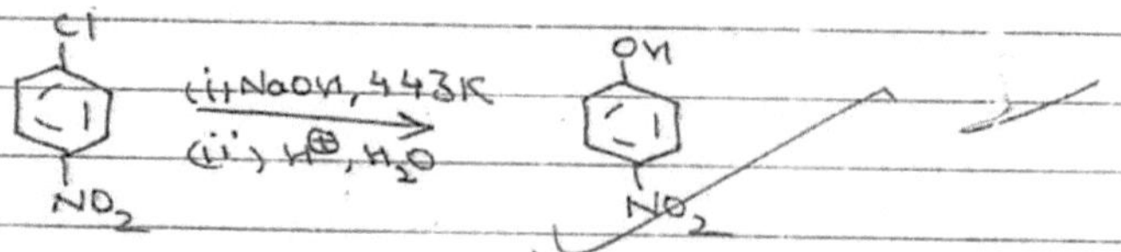

4-Nitrophenol

(iii) 'dextro' and 'laevo' rotatory forms of Butan-2-ol, mainly constitute the enantiomers of the same compound. i.e.

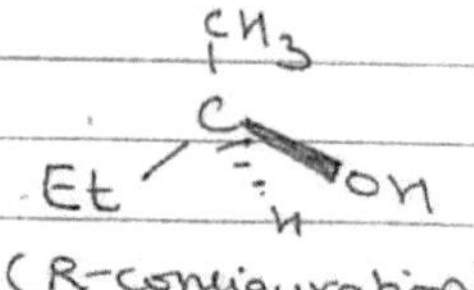

(R-configuration)   and   (S-configuration)

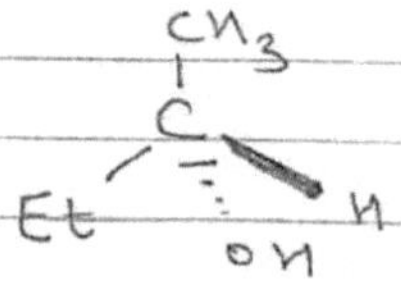

Key:
Et = ethyl group

These two forms of Butan-2-ol differ only in their spatial arrangement of molecules : Me, Et, H, OH around the chiral carbon, and therefore have the same physical properties like — melting point, boiling point, electrical conductivity, solubility etc.

Hence, it is difficult to separate these two isomers (optical stereoisomers) of Butan-2-ol by fractional distillation, as fractional distillation makes use of difference in boiling point of two substances (which should be greater than 20-25°C). But in this case, both the isomers have identical boiling points and thus these are not separable by this method.

23. Differentiate between the following :
   (i)   Amylose and Amylopectin
   (ii) Peptide linkage and Glycosidic linkage
   (iii) Fibrous proteins and Globular proteins

OR

Write chemical reactions to show that open structure of D-glucose contains the following :
(i)   Straight chain
(ii) Five alcohol groups
(iii) Aldehyde as carbonyl group

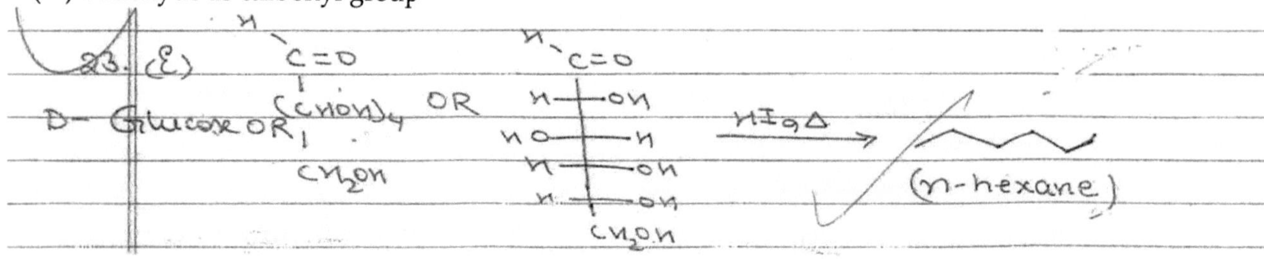

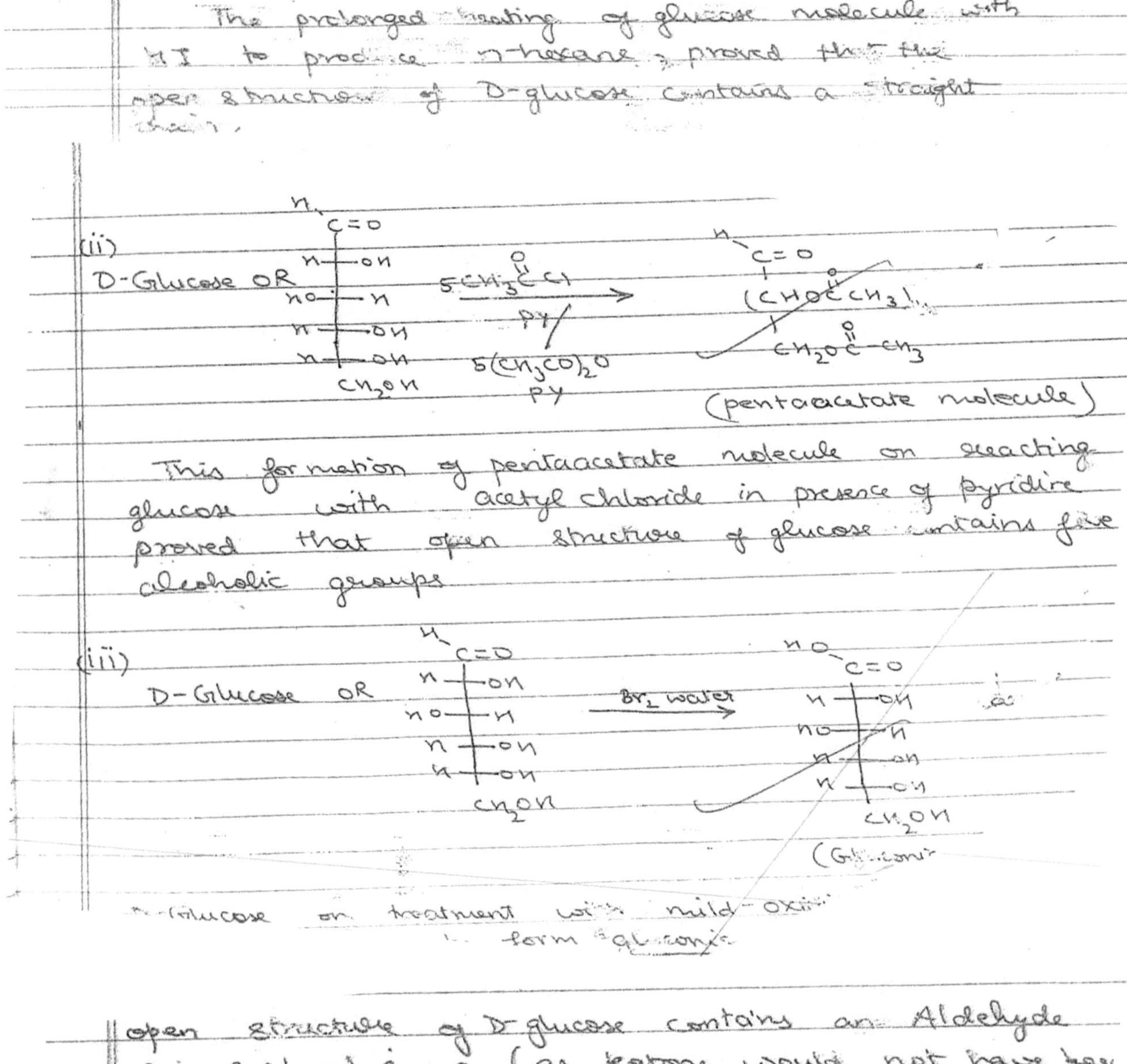

The prolonged heating of glucose molecule with HI to produce n-hexane, proved that the open structure of D-glucose contains a straight chain.

(ii) This formation of pentaacetate molecule on reacting glucose with acetyl chloride in presence of pyridine proved that open structure of glucose contains five alcoholic groups.

(iii) Glucose on treatment with mild oxidising agent form gluconic acid.

open structure of D-glucose contains an Aldehyde as carbonyl group (as ketone would not have been oxidised by Br_2 water).

24 *Ans.*

24. Complete the following reactions :

(i)

$$C_6H_5CHO \xrightarrow{\text{NaCN/HCl}}$$

(ii) $(C_6H_5CH_2)_2Cd + 2CH_3COCl$

(ii) $CH_3-\underset{\underset{CH_3}{|}}{CH}-COOH \xrightarrow[\text{(ii) } H_2O]{\text{(i) } Br_2/Red\ P_4}$

OR

Write chemical equations for the following reactions :
(i) Propanone is treated with dilute $Ba(OH)_2$.

(ii) Acetophenone is treated with Zn(Hg)/conc. HCl.
(iii) Benzoyl chloride is hydrogenated in presence of Pd/BaSO$_4$.

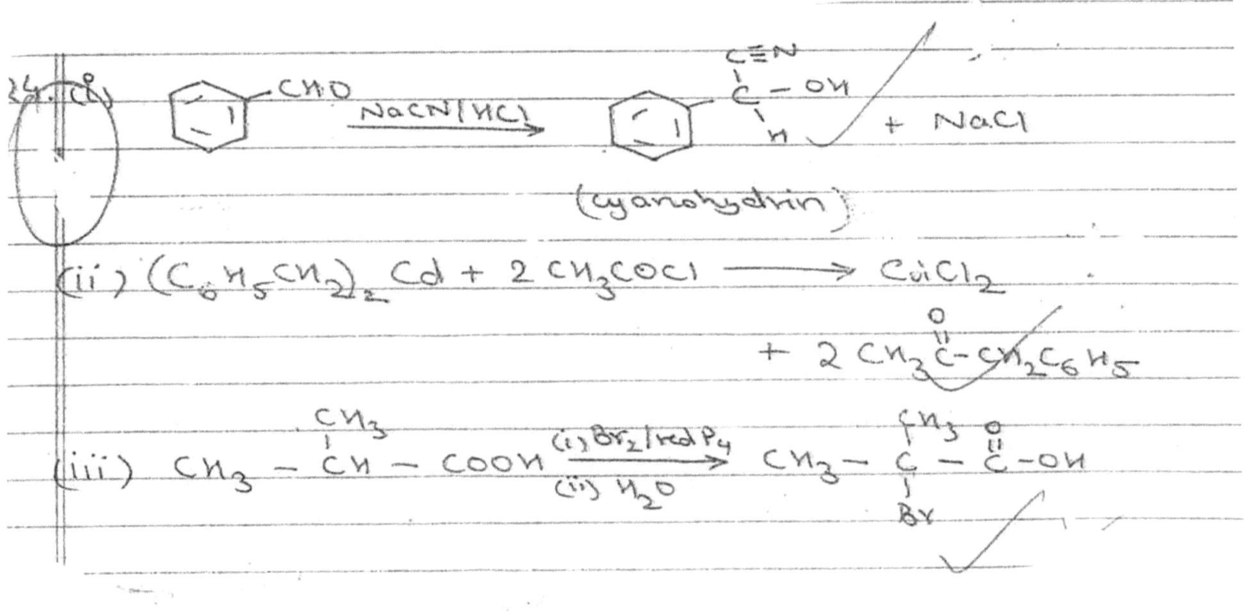

SECTION – D

25. (a) Give reasons for the following :
    (i) Sulphur in vapour state shows paramagnetic behaviour.
    (ii) N-N bond is weaker than P-P bond.
    (iii) Ozone is thermodynamically less stable than oxygen.
  (b) Write the name of gas released when Cu is added to
    (i) dilute HNO$_3$ and
    (ii) conc. HNO$_3$

OR

(a) (i) Write the disproportionation reaction of H$_3$PO$_3$.
    (ii) Draw the structure of XeF$_4$.
(b) Account for the following :
    (i) Although Fluorine has less negative electron gain enthalpy yet F$_2$ is strong oxidizing agent.
    (ii) Acidic character decreases from N$_2$O$_3$ to Bi$_2$O$_3$ in group 15.
(c) Write a chemical reaction to test sulphur dioxide gas. Write chemical equation involved.

25. (a) (i) Sulphur in vapour state exists as S$_2$ molecules. In S$_2$ like O$_2$, unpaired electrons are present in $\pi^*_{3p_x}$ and $\pi^*_{3p_y}$ orbital respectively. These unpaired electrons impart S$_2$ gas paramagnetic behaviour.

(ii) N-N bond length is shorter than P-P bond length (because of smaller size of nitrogen as compared to phosphorus). Due to this reason, the interelectronic repulsion between the non-bonding electrons in N-N is significantly higher as compared to that in P-P single bond. This makes the N-N bond weaker than P-P single bond.

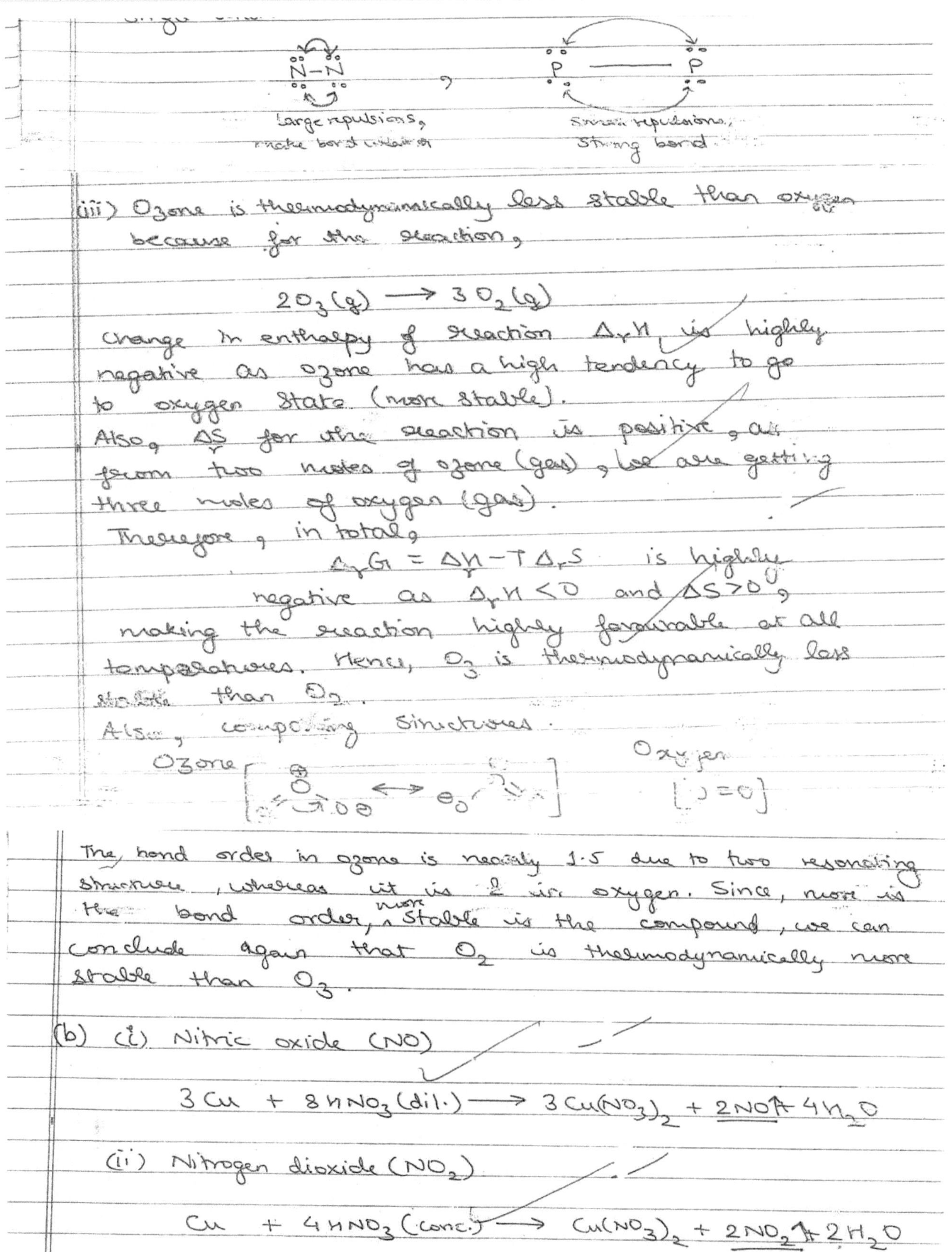

(iii) Ozone is thermodynamically less stable than oxygen because for the reaction,

$$2O_3(g) \longrightarrow 3O_2(g)$$

Change in enthalpy of reaction $\Delta_r H$, is highly negative as ozone has a high tendency to go to oxygen state (more stable).
Also, ΔS for the reaction is positive, as from two moles of ozone (gas), we are getting three moles of oxygen (gas).
Therefore, in total,

$$\Delta_r G = \Delta H - T\Delta_r S \quad \text{is highly}$$

negative as $\Delta_r H < 0$ and $\Delta S > 0$, making the reaction highly favourable at all temperatures. Hence, O_3 is thermodynamically less stable than O_2.

Also, comparing structures.

Ozone

Oxygen

The bond order in ozone is nearly 1·5 due to two resonating structure, whereas it is 2 in oxygen. Since, more is the bond order, more stable is the compound, we can conclude again that O_2 is thermodynamically more stable than O_3.

(b) (i) Nitric oxide (NO)

$$3\,Cu + 8\,HNO_3\,(dil.) \longrightarrow 3\,Cu(NO_3)_2 + 2\,NO\uparrow + 4\,H_2O$$

(ii) Nitrogen dioxide (NO_2)

$$Cu + 4\,HNO_3\,(conc.) \longrightarrow Cu(NO_3)_2 + 2\,NO_2\uparrow + 2\,H_2O$$

26. E_{cell} for the given redox reaction is 2.71 V $Mg_{(s)} + Cu^{2+}$ (0.01 M) $\to Mg^{2+}$ (0.001 M) $+ Cu_{(s)}$ Calculate E_{cell} for the reaction. Write the direction of flow of current when an external opposite potential applied is

(i) less than 2.71 V and

(ii) greater than 2.71 V.   [5]

OR

(a) A steady current of 2 amperes was passed through two electrolytic cells X and Y connected in series containing electrolytes $FeSO_4$ and $ZnSO_4$ until 2.8g of Fe deposited at the cathode of cell X. How long did the current flow ? Calculate the mass of Zn deposited at the cathode of cell Y.
(Molar mass : Fe = 56 g mol^{-1}, Zn = 65.3 g mol^{-1}, 1F = 96500 C mol^{-1})

(b) In the plot of molar conductivity (Λ_m) vs square root of concentration ($c^{1/2}$) following curves are obtained for two electrolytes A and B :

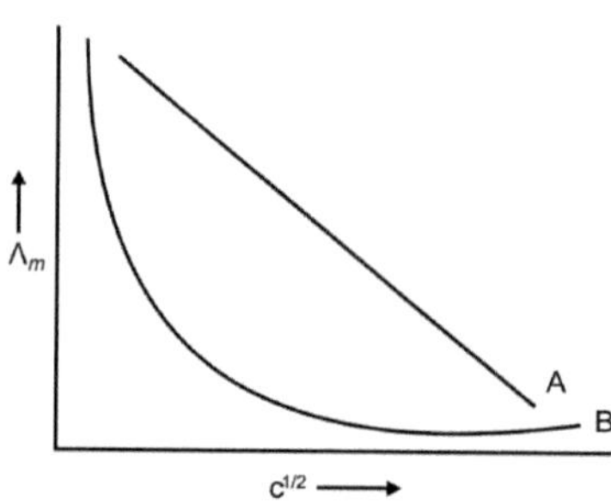

Answer the following :
(i) Predict the nature of electrolytes A and B.
(ii) What happens on extrapolation of Λ_m to concentration approaching zero for electrolytes A and B ?

---

26. Cell Reaction : $Mg(s) + Cu^{2+}(aq, 0.01 M) \longrightarrow Mg^{2+}(aq, 0.001M) + Cu(s)$

Anode Reaction :
$$Mg(s) \longrightarrow Mg^{2+}(aq, 0.001M) + 2e^-$$

Cathode Reaction :
$$Cu^{2+}(aq, 0.01M) + 2e^- \longrightarrow Cu(s)$$

Total Electrons exchanged during redox reaction = n = 2 mol

Reaction quotient of the reaction, $Q = \dfrac{[Mg^{2+}]}{[Cu^{2+}]} = \dfrac{0.001 M}{0.01 M}$

$$= \dfrac{1}{10} = 0.1$$

Using Cell Representation :

$$Mg(s) | Mg(aq, 0.001M) \| Cu^{2+}(aq, 0.01M) | Cu(s)$$

Standard potential, $E^{\circ}_{cell} = 2.71 V$ (given)

Using nernst's equation,

$$E_{cell} = E^{\circ}_{cell} - \dfrac{0.059}{n} \log Q \quad (at\ T = 298K)$$

Substituting the values,

$$E_{cell} = 2.71 - \dfrac{0.059}{2} \log (10^{-1})$$

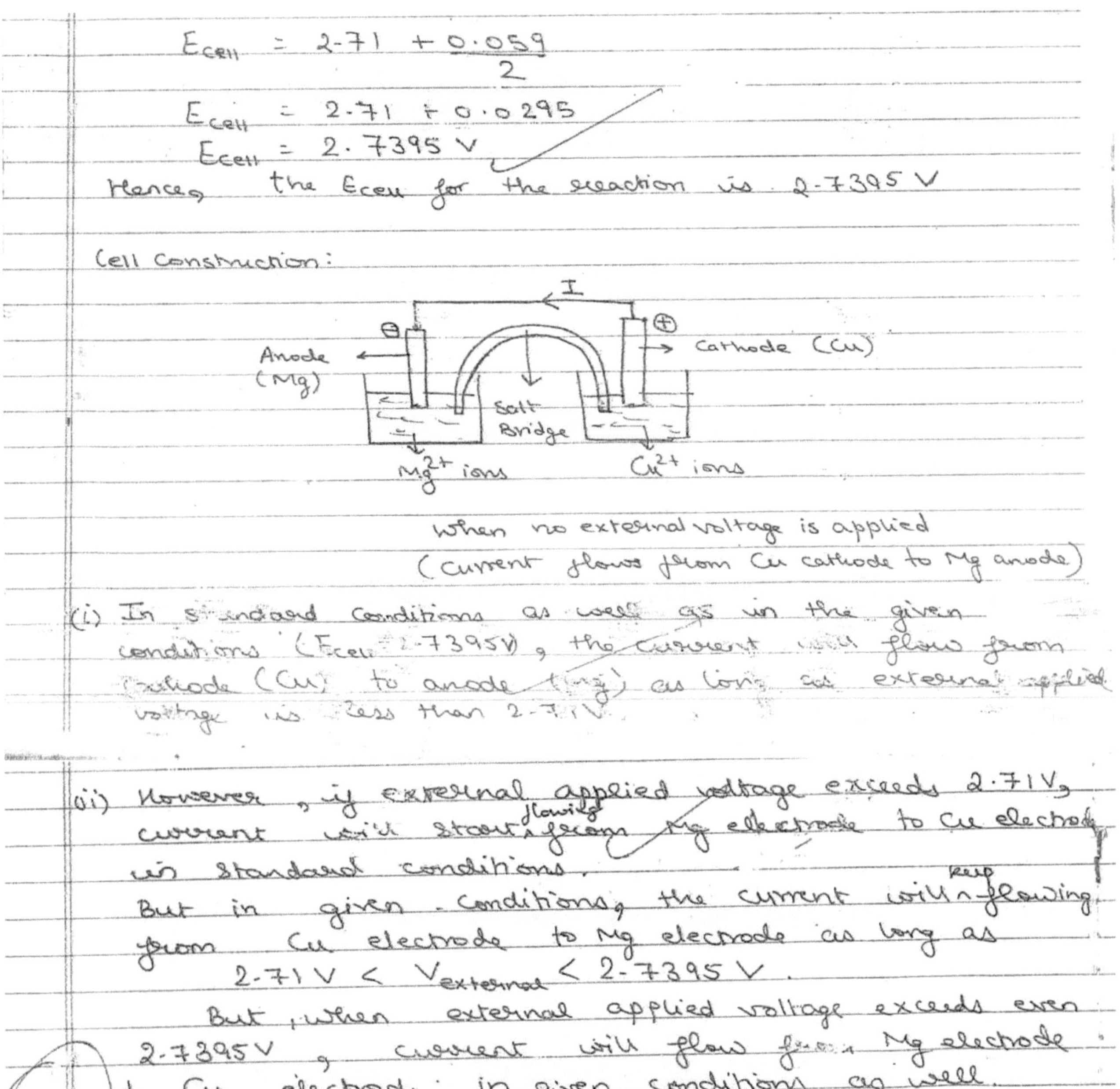

$$E_{cell} = 2.71 + \frac{0.059}{2}$$

$$E_{cell} = 2.71 + 0.0295$$

$$E_{cell} = 2.7395 \text{ V}$$

Hence, the E_{cell} for the reaction is 2.7395 V

Cell Construction:

when no external voltage is applied
(current flows from Cu cathode to Mg anode)

(i) In standard conditions as well as in the given conditions ($E_{cell} = 2.7395$V), the current will flow from cathode (Cu) to anode (Mg) as long as external applied voltage is less than 2.71 V.

(ii) However, if external applied voltage exceeds 2.71 V, current will start flowing from Mg electrode to Cu electrode in standard conditions.
But in given conditions, the current will keep flowing from Cu electrode to Mg electrode as long as
$$2.71 \text{ V} < V_{external} < 2.7395 \text{ V}.$$
But, when external applied voltage exceeds even 2.7395 V, current will flow from Mg electrode to Cu electrode in given conditions as well.

27. (a) How do you convert the following :
  (i) Phenol to Anisole
  (ii) Ethanol to Propan–2–ol
(b) Write mechanism of the following reaction :
$$CH_3OH \xrightarrow[443 \text{ K}]{H_2SO_4} CH_2 = CH_2 + H_2O$$
(c) Why phenol undergoes electrophilic substitution more easily than benzene ? [5]

OR

(a) Account for the following :
  (i) o–nitrophenol is more steam volatile than p-nitrophenol.
  (ii) t-butyl chloride on heating with sodium methoxide gives 2-methylpropene instead of t-butyl methylether.
(b) Write the reaction involved in the following :
  (i) Riemer Tiemann reaction
  (ii) Friedal Crafts Alkylation of Phenol
(c) Give simple chemical test to distinguish between Ethanol and Phenol.

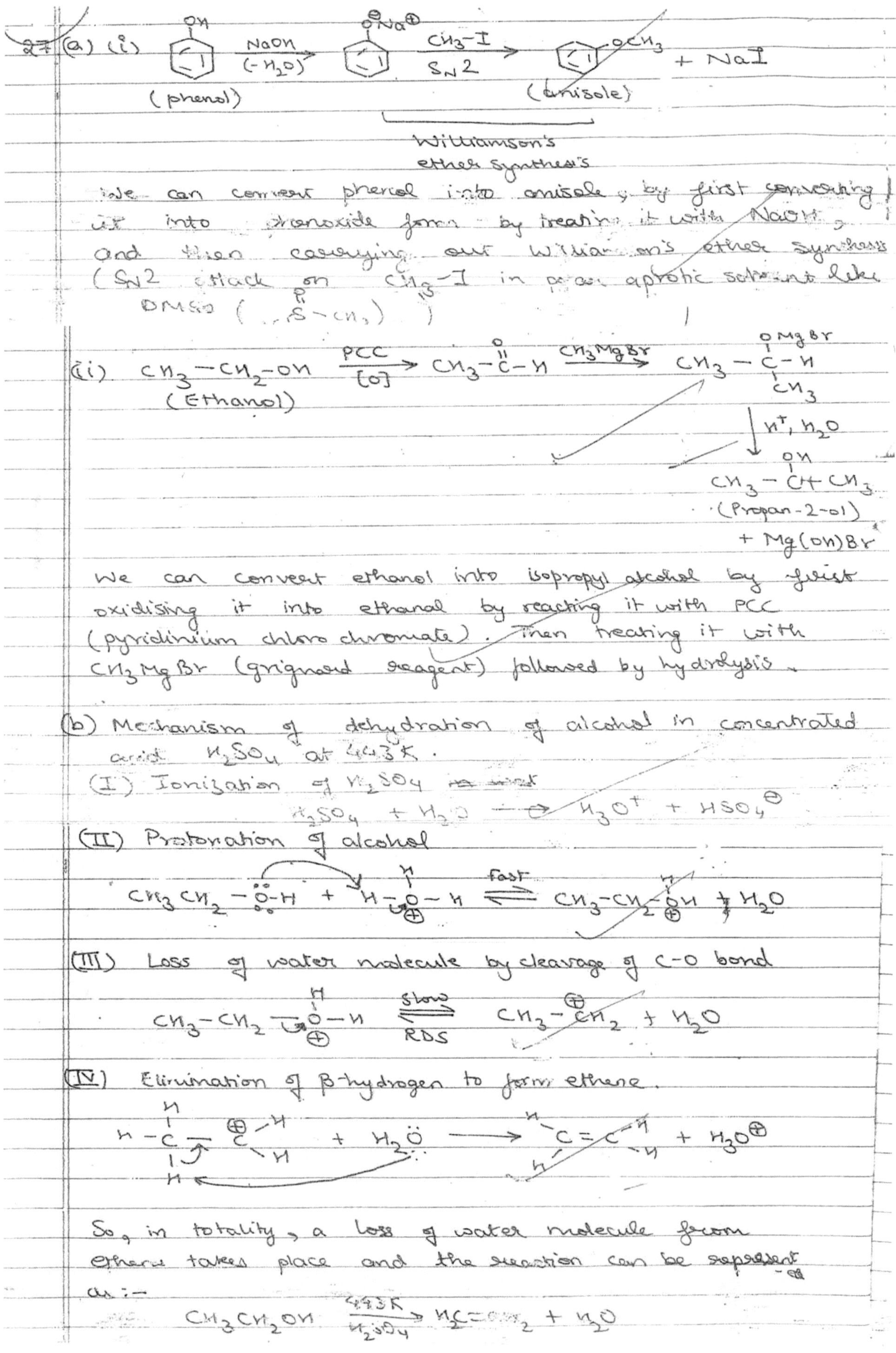

27 (a) (i)

phenol $\xrightarrow[(-H_2O)]{NaOH}$ sodium phenoxide (O^-Na^+) $\xrightarrow[S_N2]{CH_3-I}$ anisole ($-OCH_3$) $+ NaI$

(phenol) → (anisole)

Williamson's ether synthesis

We can convert phenol into anisole, by first converting it into phenoxide form by treating it with NaOH, and then carrying out Williamson's ether synthesis (S_N2 attack on CH_3-I in polar aprotic solvent like DMSO ($\overset{O}{\underset{..}{S}}-CH_3$)).

(ii)

CH_3-CH_2-OH (Ethanol) $\xrightarrow[[O]]{PCC} CH_3-\overset{O}{\overset{||}{C}}-H \xrightarrow{CH_3MgBr} CH_3-\underset{CH_3}{\overset{OMgBr}{\underset{|}{\overset{|}{C}}}}-H$

$\xrightarrow{H^+, H_2O}$

$CH_3-\overset{OH}{\overset{|}{C}H}-CH_3$ (Propan-2-ol) $+ Mg(OH)Br$

We can convert ethanol into isopropyl alcohol by first oxidising it into ethanal by reacting it with PCC (pyridinium chloro chromate). Then treating it with CH_3MgBr (grignard reagent) followed by hydrolysis.

(b) Mechanism of dehydration of alcohol in concentrated acid H_2SO_4 at 443 K.

(I) Ionization of H_2SO_4

$$H_2SO_4 + H_2O \longrightarrow H_3O^+ + HSO_4^-$$

(II) Protonation of alcohol

$$CH_3CH_2-\overset{..}{\underset{..}{O}}-H + H-\overset{H}{\underset{\oplus}{O}}-H \rightleftharpoons CH_3-CH_2-\overset{H}{\underset{\oplus}{O}}H + H_2O$$

(III) Loss of water molecule by cleavage of C-O bond

$$CH_3-CH_2-\overset{H}{\underset{\oplus}{O}}-H \underset{RDS}{\overset{slow}{\rightleftharpoons}} CH_3-\overset{\oplus}{C}H_2 + H_2O$$

(IV) Elimination of β-hydrogen to form ethene.

$$H-\overset{H}{\underset{H}{\overset{|}{\underset{|}{C}}}}-\overset{\oplus}{C}\overset{H}{\underset{H}{}} + H_2\overset{..}{\underset{..}{O}} \longrightarrow \overset{H}{\underset{H}{C}}=\overset{H}{\underset{H}{C}} + H_3O^{\oplus}$$

So, in totality, a loss of water molecule from ethanol takes place and the reaction can be represented as :-

$$CH_3CH_2OH \xrightarrow[H_2SO_4]{443K} H_2C=CH_2 + H_2O$$

(c) Phenol consists of −OH group attached to benzene ring which increases the electron density of the benzene ring due to +R-effect (strong) of −OH group, by virtue of presence of lone pair of electron on Oxygen atom.

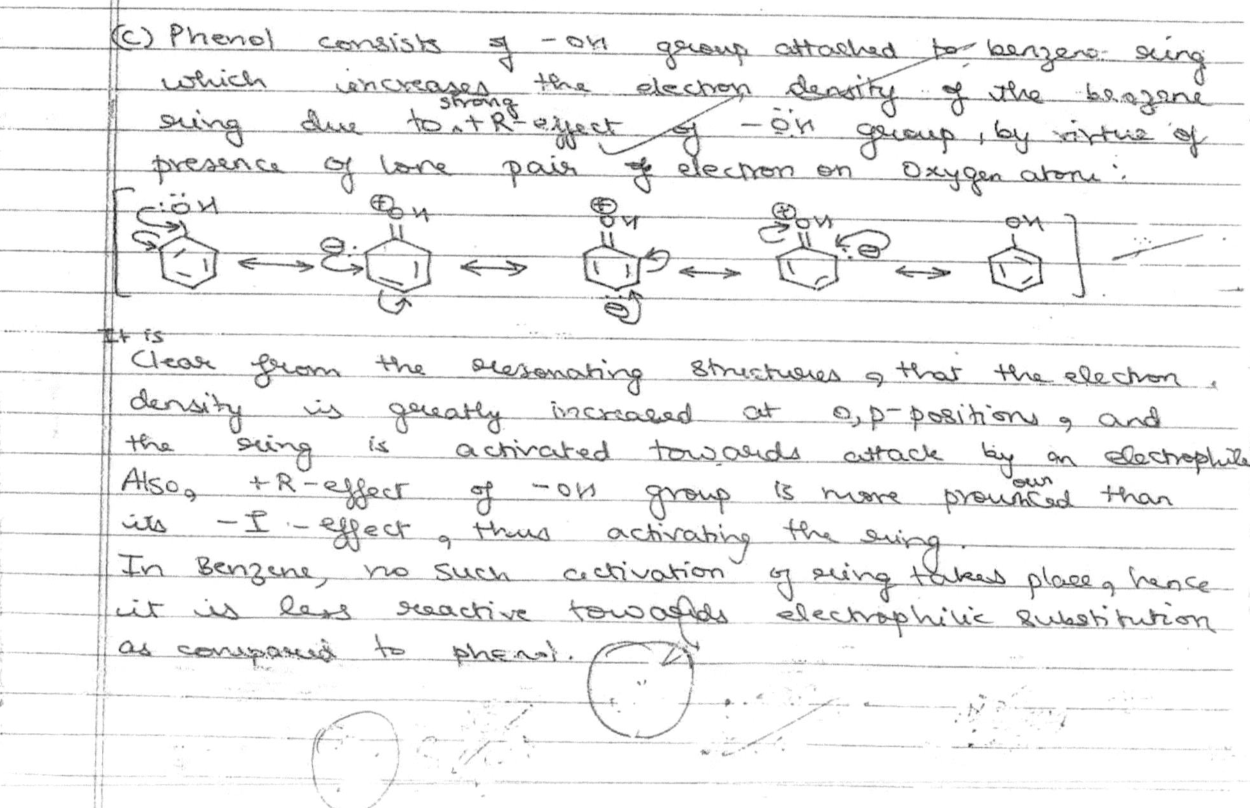

It is Clear from the resonating structures, that the electron density is greatly increased at o, p-positions, and the ring is activated towards attack by an electrophile. Also, +R-effect of −OH group is more pronounced (own) than its −I-effect, thus activating the ring.

In Benzene, no such activation of ring takes place, hence it is less reactive towards electrophilic substitution as compared to phenol.

Time allowed : 3 hours **Maximum marks : 70**

General Instructions :
Read the following instructions very carefully and strictly follow them :
(i) Question paper comprises four sections – **A, B, C and D.**
(ii) There are **37** questions in the question paper. **All questions are compulsory.**
(iii) **Section – A :** Q. No. **1** to **20** are very short answer type questions, carrying **1** mark each. Answer these questions in one word or one sentence.
(iv) **Section – B :** Q. No. **21** to **27** are short answer type questions, carrying **2** marks each.
(v) **Section – C :** Q. No. **28** to **34** are long answer type-I questions, carrying **3** marks each.
(vi) **Section – D :** Q. No. **35** to **37** are long answer type-II questions, carrying **5** marks each.
(vii) There is no overall choice in the question paper. However, an internal choice has been provided in **2** questions of **two** marks, **2** questions of **three** marks and all the **3** questions of **five** marks. You have to **attempt only one of the choices** in such questions.
(viii) In addition to this, separate instructions are given with each section and question, wherever necessary.
(ix) Use of calculators and log tables is **not** permitted.

SECTION – A

Read the given passage and answer the questions 1 to 5 that follow:

Colloidal particles always carry and electric charge which may be either positive or negative. For example, when $AgNO_3$ solution is added to KI solution, a negatively charged colloidal sol is obtained. The presence of equal and similar charges on colloidal particles provide stability to the colloidal sol and if, somehow, charge is removed, coagulation of sol occurs. Lyophobic sols are readily coagulated as compare to lyophilic sols.

1. What is the reason for the charge on sol particles?

Ans. Preferential adsorption of either positive or negative ions on surface of sol particles is the reason of the charge on them.

2. Why the presence of equal and similar charges on colloidal particles provide stability?

Ans. Due to the presence of similar and equal charges, the colloidal particles repel one another and are thus unable to combine together to form larger particles and coagulate. Hence, presence of equal and similar charge on colloidal particles provide stability to colloidal solution.

3. Why a negatively charged sol is obtained on adding $AgNO_3$ solution to KI solution?

Ans. When $AgNO_3$ solution is added to KI solution then negatively charged sol is formed due to the adsorption of iodide ions from KI which is disperse medium onto the precipitated AgI particles.

4. Name one method by which coagulation of lyophobic sol can be carried out.

Ans. The coagulation of the lyophobic sols can be carried out by electrophoresis.

5. Out of KI or K_2SO_4, which electrolyte is better in the coagulation of positive sol?

Ans. K_2SO_4 would be better in coagulation of positive sol due to higher flocculating power of SO_4^{2-}.

Questions 6 to 10 are one word answer:

6. Name the method applied for the concentration of Bauxite ore in the extraction of Aluminium.

Ans. Leaching or Baeyer's process

7. Out of ⬡—Cl **and** ⬡—CH_2–Cl, **which one is more reactive towards S_N1 reaction?**

Ans. ⬡—Cl.

8. Write an isomer of C_3H_9N which gives foul smell of isocyanide when treated with chloroform and ethanolic NaOH.

Ans. 1-Amino propane; $CH_3CH_2CH_2NH_2$

9. Which one of the following is an antidepressant drug?

Chloramphenicol, Luminal, Bithional.

Ans. Luminal

10. Write the name of component of starch which is water soluble.

Ans. Amylose

Questions 11 to 15 are Multiple Choice Questions:

11. How many ions are produced from the complex $[Co(NH_3)_5Cl]Cl_2$ in solution?
(a) 4 (b) 2
(c) 3 (d) 5

Ans. (c) 3

12. In a lead storage battery
    (a) PbO_2 is reduced to $PbSO_4$ at the cathode.
    (b) Pb is oxidised to $PbSO_4$ at the anode.
    (c) Both electrodes are immersed in the same aqueous solution of H_2SO_4.
    (d) All the above are true.
Ans. (d) All the above are true.

13. The slope in the plot of *ln* [R] Vs. time gives
    (a) +k
    (b) $\dfrac{+k}{2.303}$
    (c) – k
    (d) $\dfrac{-k}{2.303}$

    (where [R] is the final concentration of reactant.)
Ans. (c) – k

14. The pair $[Co(NH_3)_4 Cl_2] Br_2$ and $[Co(NH_3)_4 Br_2] Cl_2$ will show
    (a) Linkage isomerism
    (b) Hydrate isomerism
    (c) Ionization isomerism
    (d) Coordinate isomerism
Ans. (c) Ionization isomerism

15. An α-helix is a structural feature of
    (a) Sucrose
    (b) Polypeptides
    (c) Nucleotides
    (d) Starch
Ans. (b) Polypeptides

Questions 16 to 20 :
(A) Both Assertion (A) and Reason (R) are correct statements, and Reason (R) is the correct explanation of the Assertion (A).
(B) Both Assertion (A) and Reason (R) are correct statements, but Reason (R) is not the correct explanation of the Assertion (A).
(C) Assertion (A) is correct, but Reason (R) is wrong statement.
(D) Assertion (A) is wrong, but Reason (R) is correct statement.

16. **Assertion (A)** : F_2 is a strong oxidising agent.
    Reason (R) : Electron gain enthalpy of fluorine is less negative.
Ans. (B) As F_2 has low bond dissociation energy and high hydration energy than Cl_2 but less electron gain enthalpy due to its smaller size. Due to these factors F_2 wins in getting reduced fastly. Thus, both Assertion (A) and Reason (R) are correct statements but Reason (R) is not the correct explanation of the Assertion (A).

17. **Assertion (A)** : $(CH_3)_3 C—O—CH_3$ gives $(CH_3)_3 C—I$ and CH_3OH on treatment with HI.
    Reason (R) : The reaction occurs by S_N1 mechanism.
Ans. (A) SN^1 reaction occurs in compound that has steric hindrance and $(CH_3)_3—C—OCH_3$ has very much hindrance to attack by reagent.

Thus both Assertion (A) and Reason (R) are correct statements, and Reason (R) is the correct explanation of the Assertion (A).

18. **Assertion (A)** : Transition metals have low melting points.
    Reason (R) : The involvement of greater number of $(n – 1)d$ and ns electrons in the interatomic metallic bonding.
Ans. (D) Transition metals have high melting point. Thus, Assertion (A) is wrong, but Reason (R) is correct statement.

19. **Assertion (A)** : Hydrolysis of an ester follows first order kinetics.
    Reason (R) : Concentration of water remains nearly constant during the course of the reaction.
Ans. (A) Hydrolysis of an ester follows first order kinetics, because concentration of water remains constant during the course of the reaction. Both Assertion (A) and Reason (R) are correct statements, and Reason (R) is the correct explanation of the Assertion (A).

20. **Assertion (A)** : Benzoic acid does not undergo Friedal-Crafts reaction.
    Reason (R) : The carboxyl group is activating and undergo electrophilic substitution reaction.
Ans. (C) Benzoic acid does not undergo Friedal-crafts reaction due to deactivation of benzene ring by electron withdrawing effect of COOH group. Thus, Assertion (A) is correct, but Reason (R) is wrong statement.

SECTION-B

21. **What happens when**
    (i) a pressure greater than osmotic pressure is applied on the solution side separated from solvent by a semipermeable membrane ?
    (ii) acetone is added to pure ethanol ?
    [1 + 1 = 2]
Ans. (i) When a pressure greater than osmotic pressure is applied on the solution side, the solvent flows out to the solution through the semipermeable membrane. This is known as reverse osmosis.

(ii) Mixture of ethanol and acetone shows a positive deviation from Raoult's law and the vapour pressure over the solution increases. The acetone molecules weaken the hydrogen bonding between molecules of ethanol hence making escape of ethanol molecules easy.

22. **Write the principle of the following refining methods :**
    (a) vapour phase refining
    (b) chromatography
    [1 + 1 = 2]

OR

Write chemical equations involved to obtain:

(i) Cu from Cu_2S

(ii) Ag from $[Ag(CN)_2]^-$ complex   [1 + 1 = 2]

Ans. (a) In vapour phase refining the metal is converted into its volatile compound with a chemical reagent and is collected elsewhere. Then it is decomposed to give pure metal.

(b) Chromatography is a physical method of separation of different components of a mixture, that are partitioned differentially between the stationary and mobile phase, when mobile phase is run over the stationary phase loaded with the mixture at one point, they are adsorbed to different extent.

OR

(i) The sulphide ore is roasted to give oxide:

$$2Cu_2S + 3O_2 \rightarrow 2Cu_2O + 2SO_2.$$

The oxide is then reduced to metallic copper using coke:

$$Cu_2O + C \rightarrow 2Cu + CO$$

(ii) The silver cyanide complex is treated with zinc:

$$2[Ag(CN)_2]^-(aq) + Zn(s) \rightarrow 2Ag(s) + [Zn(CN)_4]^{2-}(aq).$$

23. Write the balanced chemical equations involved in the preparation of $KMnO_4$ from pyrolusite ore (MnO_2).   [2]

OR

Write the balanced ionic equations showing the oxidising action of acidified dichromate ($Cr_2O_7^{2-}$) solution with (i) Iron (II) Ion and (ii) tin (II) ion.   [1 + 1 = 2]

Ans. Potassium permanganate ($KMnO_4$) is prepared from pyrolusite ore (MnO_2). The finely powdered pyrolusite ore (MnO_2) is fused with an alkali metal hydroxide like KOH in the presence of air or an oxidising agent like KNO_3 to give the dark green potassium manganate (K_2MnO_4). Potassium manganate disproportionates in a neutral or acidic solution to give permanganate.

1. $2MnO_2 + 4KOH + O_2 \rightarrow 2K_2MnO_4 + 2H_2O$
2. $3MnO_4^{2-} + 4H^+ \rightarrow 2MnO_4^- + MnO_2 + 2H_2O$

OR

(i) With Iron (II) ion

$$Cr_2O_7^{2-} + 14H^+ + 6Fe^{2+} \rightarrow 2Cr^{3+} + 6Fe^{3+} + 7H_2O$$

(ii) With tin (II) ion

$$Cr_2O_7^{2-} + 14H^+ + 3Sn^{2+} \rightarrow 2Cr^{3+} + 3Sn^{4+} + 7H_2O$$

24. Write the IUPAC names and hybridisation of the following complexes:

(i) $[Ni(CN)_4]^{2-}$ **(ii) $[Fe(H_2O)_6]^{2+}$**

(Given : Atomic number Ni = 28, Fe = 26)   [1 + 1 = 2]

Ans. (i) $[Ni(CN)_4]^{2-}$

IUPAC name : Tetracyanonickelate (II).

Hybridisation : dsp^2

(ii) $[Fe(H_2O)_6]^{2-}$

IUPAC name : Hexaaquairon(II) ion.

Hybridisation : sp^3d^2

25. Define the following terms with a suitable example in each: [1 + 1 = 2]

(i) Antibiotics   **(ii) Antiseptics**

Ans. (i) Antibiotics: They are naturally occurring, semisynthetic, or synthetic anti-infective agents that destroys or inhibits the growth of microorganisms when ingested in low concentration. Example: Penicillin, Tetracycline etc.

(ii) Antiseptics: They are antimicrobial agents applied to the living tissues such as wounds, cuts, ulcers and other disease skin surfaces to destroy microbes or inhibit growth of microbes. These are not ingested as antibiotics. Example : Iodine solution, Dettol etc.

26. Write the reactions showing the presence of the following in the open structure of glucose :

(i) a carbonyl group   [1 + 1 = 2]

(ii) Straight chain with six carbon atoms

Ans. (i) Glucose reacts with hydroxylamine to form an oxime and adds hydrogen cyanide to give cyanohydrin. These reactions confirms the presence of carbonyl group in the glucose molecule.

$$\underset{\text{Glucose oxime}}{\overset{\begin{array}{c}CHO \\ | \\ (CH_2OH)_4 \\ | \\ CH_2OH\end{array}}{}} + NH_2OH \longrightarrow \overset{\begin{array}{c}CH=N-OH \\ | \\ (CHOH)_4 \\ | \\ CH_2OH\end{array}}{}$$

$$\underset{}{\overset{\begin{array}{c}CHO \\ | \\ (CHOH)_4 \\ | \\ CH_2OH\end{array}}{}} + HCN \longrightarrow \underset{\text{Glucose cyanohydrin}}{\overset{\begin{array}{c}CH(OH)CN \\ | \\ (CHOH)_4 \\ | \\ CH_2OH\end{array}}{}}$$

(ii) Glucose forms n-hexane on prolonged heating with HI, this shows that it has a linear structure.

$$\underset{\text{D-Glucose}}{\overset{\begin{array}{c}CHO \\ | \\ (CHOH)_4 \\ | \\ CH_2OH\end{array}}{}} \xrightarrow[\text{Reduction}]{HI, \Delta} \underset{\text{n-hexane}}{CH_3-(CH_2)_4-CH_3}$$

27. State Henry's law. Calculate the solubility of CO_2 in water at 298 K under 760 mm Hg. (K_H for CO_2 in water at 298 K is 1.25×10^6 mm Hg) [2]

Ans. Henry's law states that "at a constant temperature, The partial pressure of the gas in vapour phase (p) is directly proportional to the mole fraction of gas(x) in the solution".

Mathematically $p = K_H x$, where K_H is constant.

To calculate the solubility of CO_2 in water:

Given : $T = 298$ K; $K_H = 1.25 \times 10^6$ mm Hg; $p = 760$ mm Hg

We know by Henry's Law; $p = K_H x$, where x is mole fraction of the gas in the solution.

Substituting the given values:

$$760 = 1.25 \times 10^6 \times x$$
$$x = 760 / 1.25 \times 10^6$$
$$x = 608 \times 10^{-6}$$

Now, we know that mole fraction of gas is given

$$x = \frac{\text{moles of gas}}{(\text{moles of gas + moles of water})}$$

$$608 \times 10^{-6} = \frac{\text{moles of gas}}{\text{moles of gas} + 55.5}$$

(since number of moles of water in 1 L = 55.5)

As, moles of gas $<<<<$ moles of water

Moles of gas $= 608 \times 10^{-6} \times 55.5$ mol
$= 33744 \times 10^{-6} = 33.74 \times 10^{-3}$ mol.

Therefore, solubility of CO_2 in water is 33.74×10^{-3} mol/L.

SECTION C

28. The freezing point of a solution containing 5g of benzoic acid (M = 122 g mol^{-1}) in 35g of benzene is depressed by 2.94 K. What is the percentage association of benzoic acid if it forms a dimer in solution?

(K_f for benzene = 4.9 K kg mol^{-1}) [3]

Ans. Given:

Weight of benzoic acid (solute) = 5 g

Weight of benzene (solvent) = 35 g

$K_f = 4.9$ K Kg mol^{-1}

$\Delta T_f = 2.94$ K

We know that molecular weight of solute can be calculated as-

$$M_2 = \frac{(K_f \times W_2 \times 1000)}{\Delta T_f \times W_1}$$

Substituting the values –

$$M_2 = \frac{(K_f \times W_2 \times 1000)}{\Delta T_f \times W_1}$$

$$= \frac{(4.9 \times 5 \times 1000)}{2.94 \times 35}$$

$$= \frac{24500}{102.9}$$

$$= 238.09 \text{ g}$$

Now let us consider the following equilibrium for the benzoic acid :

$$2\,C_6H_5COOH \rightleftharpoons (C_6H_5COOH)_2$$

If x represents the degree of association of the solute then it would have $(1-x)$ mol of benzoic acid left in unassociated form and correspondingly $x/2$ as associated moles of benzoic acid at equilibrium. Therefore, total number of moles of particles at equilibrium is:

$$(1 - x) + x/2 = 1 - (x/2)$$

Thus, total number of moles of particles at equilibrium equals to van't Hoff factor i

But, $$i = \frac{\text{normal molar mass}}{\text{abnormal molar mass}}$$

So, van't Hoff factor, $i = \dfrac{122}{238.09} = 0.512$

Hence,

$$1 - (x/2) = 0.512$$
$$(x/2) = 0.512$$
$$= 0.488$$
$$x = 0.976$$

Hence, the percentage association is 97.6% for benzoic acid.

29. The rate constant for the first order decomposition of N_2O_5 is given by the following equation:

$k = (2.5 \times 10^{14} \text{ s}^{-1})\, e^{(-25000K)/T}$

Calculate E_a for this reaction and rate constant if its half-life period be 300 minutes. [3]

Ans. Arrhenius equation is given by:

$$k = Ae^{-E_a/RT}$$
$$k = (2.5 \times 10^{14} \text{ s}^{-1})\, e^{(-25000K/T)}$$

Comparing the two equations :

$$E_a / RT = \frac{25000 \text{ K}}{T}$$

$$E_a = 25000 \text{ K} \times 8.314 \text{ J K}^{-1}\text{mol}^{-1}$$
$$= 207850 \text{ J mol}^{-1}$$
$$E_a = 207.9 \text{ kJ mol}^{-1}$$

Now, for first order reactions, rate constant is given by:

$$k = \frac{0.693}{t_{1/2}}$$

Substituting the value of $t_{1/2}$:

$$k = 0.693 / 300$$
$$k = 2.3 \times 10^{-3}\text{s}^{-1}$$

30. Write the name and structures of monomer(s) in the following polymers: [1 + 1 + 1 = 3]

(i) Nylon-6 (ii) PVC (iii) Neoprene

Ans. (i) Caprolactum is monomer of Nylon–6.

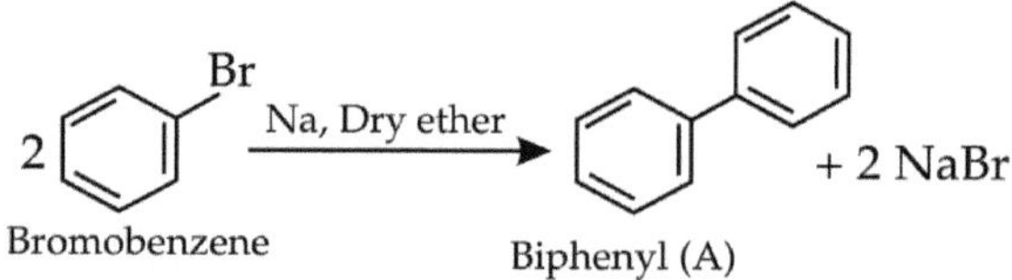

Caprolactum

(ii) PVC or Polyvinyl chloride is made up of Vinyl chloride (chloroethene) monomers.

Vinyl chloride → (Addition polymerisation) → Polyvinyl chloride

(iii) Chloroprene is the monomer of Neoprene.

$$n\ CH_2 = C\text{—}CH = CH_2 \xrightarrow{\text{Polymerisation}}$$

with Cl substituent — Chloroprene

$$\left(-CH_2\text{—}C = CH\text{—}CH_2\text{—}\right)_n$$
with Cl substituent — Neoprene

31. Following ions are given:

$$Cr^{2+}, Cu^{2+}, Cu^{+}, Fe^{2+}, Fe^{3+}, Mn^{3+}$$

Identify the ion which is

(i) a strong reducing agent.

(ii) unstable in aqueous solution.

(iii) a strong oxidising agent.

Give suitable reason in each. [1 + 1 + 1 = 3]

Ans. (i) Cr^{2+} is a strong reducing agent as it is very easily oxidised to more stable Cr^{3+} (d^3) where it attains a stable half-filled t_{2g}^3 configuration.

(ii) Cu^{+} is unstable in aqueous solution because it disproportionates in water to form Cu^{2+} and Cu.

(iii) Mn^{3+} is a strong oxidising agent because it gets reduced to Mn^{2+} (d^5) in the process and attains an extra stable half-filled d-orbital configuration.

32. (i) Write the structure of major alkene formed by β-elimination of 2, 2, 3–trimethyl–3–bromopentane with sodium ethoxide in ethanol.

(ii) Which one of the compounds in the following pairs is chiral?

(iii) Identify (A) and (B) in the following :

(A) ←[Na/dry ether]— Bromobenzene —[Mg/dry ether]→ (B)

[1 + 1 + 1 = 3]

OR

How can you convert the following?

(i) But-1-ene to 1-iodobutane

(ii) Benzene to acetophenone

(iii) Ethanol to propanenitrile   [1 + 1 + 1 = 3]

Ans. (i) 2,2,3-trimethyl-3-bromopentane will undergo elimination reaction in presence of sodium ethoxide and alcohol and will provide 2,2,3–Trimethylpent-3-ene as major production following Saytzeff's rule.

2, 2, 3 – trimethyl - 3 - bromo pentane —[Sodium ethoxide / Ethanol]→ 3,4,4–trimethylpent-2-ene

(ii) The following compound is chiral compound.

(Br substituted compound)

(iii) Compound A is biphenyl compound.

$$2\ \text{Bromobenzene} \xrightarrow{\text{Na, Dry ether}} \text{Biphenyl (A)} + 2\ NaBr$$

Compound B is Phenyl magnesium bromide

$$\text{Bromobenzene} + Mg \xrightarrow{\text{dry ether}} \text{Phenylmagensium bromide}$$

OR

(i) But-1-ene to 1-Iodobutane conversion

$$CH_3CH_2CH = CH_2 \xrightarrow{\text{HBr/Peroxide}} CH_3CH_2CH_2CH_2 – Br$$
$$\downarrow \text{NaI/dry acetone}$$
$$CH_3CH_2CH_2CH_2\text{—}I$$

(ii) Benzene to Acetophenone conversion

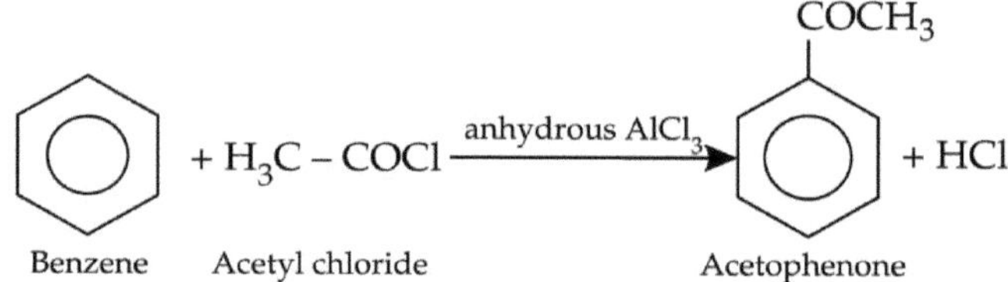

$$\text{Benzene} + H_3C – COCl \xrightarrow{\text{anhydrous } AlCl_3} \text{Acetophenone (}COCH_3\text{)} + HCl$$

Benzene   Acetyl chloride   Acetophenone

(iii) Ethanol to propane nitrile conversion : This can be carried out in two steps, first, conversion of ethanol to ethyl chloride by reacting with zinc chloride and then reacting ethyl chloride with KCN in aq. ethanol.

$$\underset{\text{Ethanol}}{C_2H_5OH} \xrightarrow{ZnCl_2} \underset{\text{Ethyl chloride}}{C_2H_5Cl}$$

$$\underset{\text{Ethyl Chloride}}{CH_3-CH_2-Cl} \xrightarrow[-KCl]{KCN/aq.ethanol} \underset{\text{Propane nitrile}}{CH_3-CH_2-CN}$$

33. Arrange the following compounds as directed:

(i) In increasing order of solubility in water:
$(CH_3)_2NH$, CH_3NH_2, $C_6H_5NH_2$

(ii) In decreasing order of basic strength in aqueous solution :
$(CH_3)_3N$, $(CH_3)_2NH$, CH_3NH_2

(iii) In increasing order of boiling point
$(C_2H_5)_2NH$, $(C_2H_5)_3N$, $C_2H_5NH_2$

[1 + 1 + 1 =3]

Ans. (i) Increasing order of solubility in water :
$C_6H_5NH_2 < (CH_3)_2NH < CH_3NH_2$

(ii) Increasing order of basic strength in aqueous solution :
$(CH_3)_3N < CH_3NH_2 < (CH_3)_2NH$

(iii) Increasing order of boiling point :
$(C_2H_5)_3N < (C_2H_5)_2NH < C_2H_5NH_2$

34. Write the product(s) of the following reactions: **[1 + 1 + 1 = 3]**

(i)
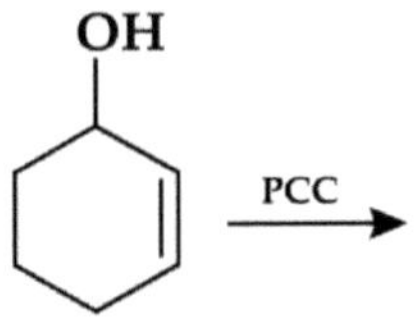

(ii)
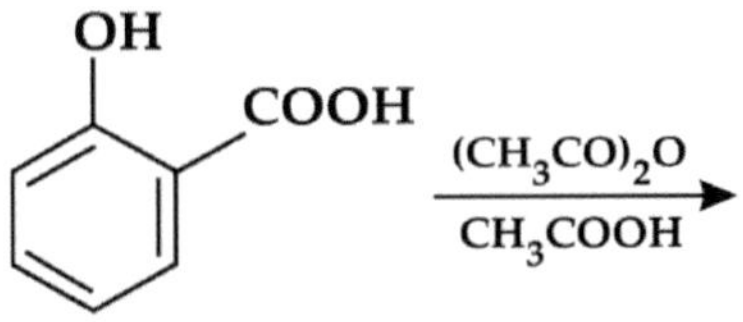

(iii)
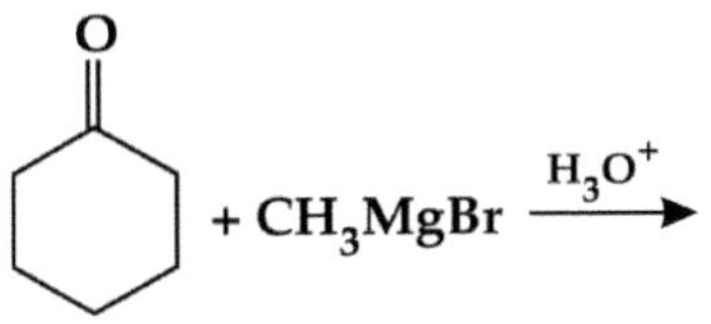

OR

(a) Write the mechanism of the following S_N1 reaction:

$$(CH_3)_3C-Br \xrightarrow{Aq.NaOH} (CH_3)_3C-OH + NaBr$$

(b) Write the equation for the preparation of 2-methyl-2-methoxypropane by Williamson synthesis. **[2 + 1 = 3]**

Ans.

(i)
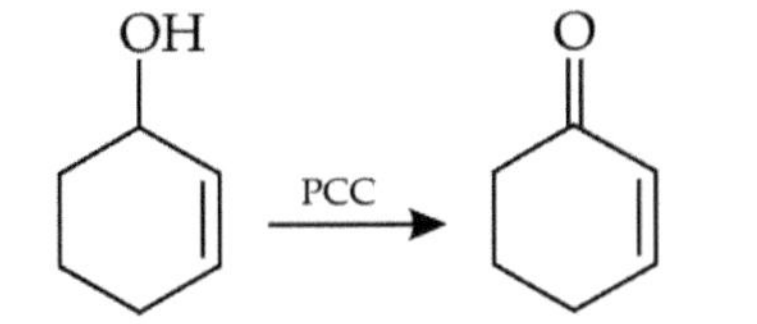

Cyclohexenol Cyclohexenone

(ii)
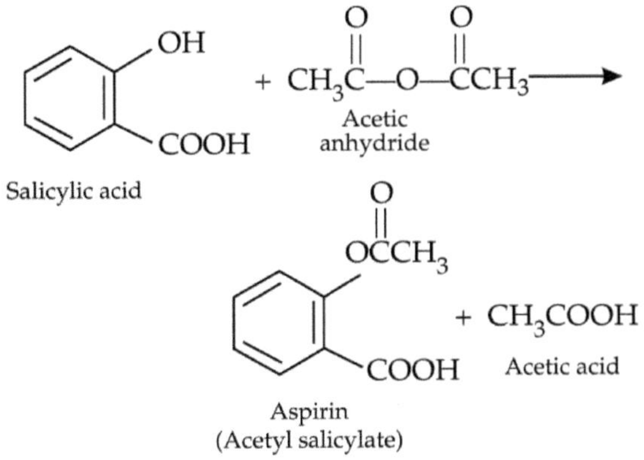

(iii)
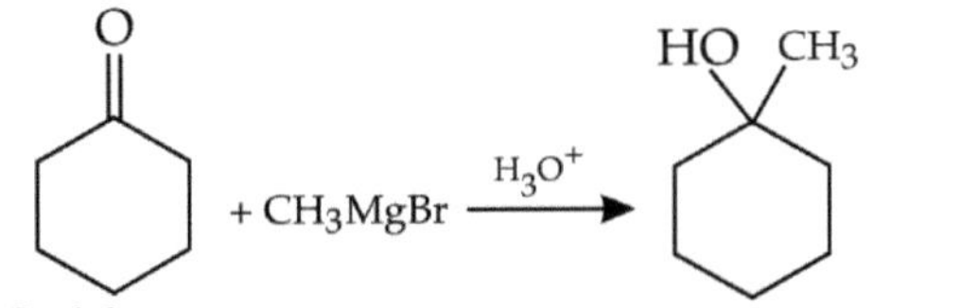

Cyclohexanone 1-methyl cyclohexanol

OR

(a) $(CH_3)_3Br \xrightarrow{Aq.\ NaOH} (CH_3)_3OH + NaBr$

The above S_N1 reaction happens in two stages:

Firstly a small proportion of halogenoalkane ionises to give a carbocation (carbonium ion) and a bromide ion.

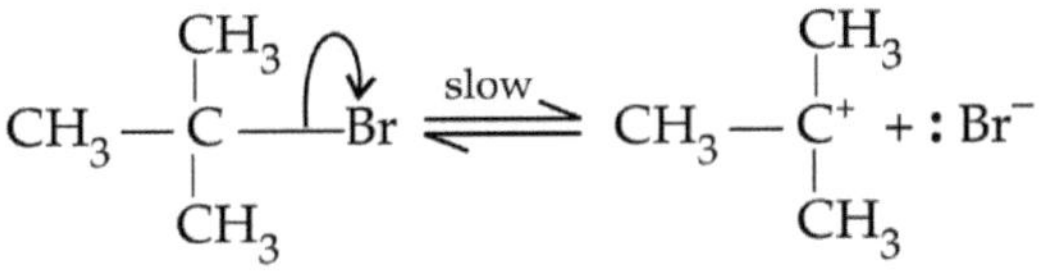

Once the carbocation is formed it would react immediately with an OH⁻ ion in the second stage of reaction. The lone pair on the nucleophile is strongly attracted towards the positive carbon, and moves towards it to create a new bond.

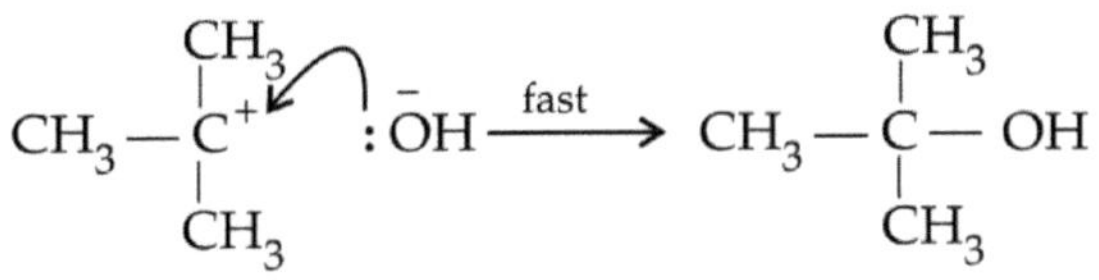

(b) Preparation of 2-methyl-2-methoxypropane can be done using sodium *tert*-butoxide and methyl chloride as starting materials:

$$H_3C \diagdown \diagup CH_3$$
$$H_3C \diagup \diagdown \underset{Sodium\ tert\text{-}butoxide}{\overset{..}{\underset{..}{O}}{}^- Na^+} + \underset{\underset{chloride}{Methyl}}{H_3C-Cl} \xrightarrow{\text{Williamson's synthesis}}$$

$$\underset{\underset{\text{2-methyl-2-methoxypropane}}{}}{H_3C \diagdown \underset{H_3C}{\diagup} \overset{CH_3}{\underset{..}{\overset{|}{\underset{..}{O}}}} \diagdown CH_3}$$

SECTION – D

35. (a) The electrical resistance of a column of 0.05 M KOH solution of length 50 cm and area of cross-section 0.625 cm² is 5×10^3 ohm. Calculate its resistivity, conductivity and molar conductivity.

(b) Predict the products of electrolysis of an aqueous solution of $CuCl_2$ with platinum electrodes.

(Given : $E°_{Cu^{2+}/Cu} = 0.34$ V, $E°_{(½\ Cl_2/Cl^-)} = +1.36$ V

$E°_{H^+/H_2\ (g),\ Pt} = 0.00V$, $E°_{(½\ O_2/H_2O)} = +1.23$ V)

OR

(a) Calculate e.m.f. of the following cell:
$$Zn(s)/Zn^{2+}\ (0.1\ M) \| (0.01\ M)\ Ag^+/Ag(s)$$
Given : $E°_{Zn^{2+}/Zn} = -0.76$ V, $E°_{Ag^+/Ag} = +0.80V$
[Given : $\log 10 = 1$]

(b) X and Y are two electrolytes. On dilution molar conductivity of 'X' increases 2.5 times while that Y increases 25 times. Which of the two is a weak electrolyte and why?

$$[3 + 2 = 5]$$

Ans. (a) Resistivity, $\rho = \dfrac{RA}{l}$ where, R is the electrical resistance; l is the length and A is the area of cross-section of the column.

$$\rho = \frac{RA}{l}$$

Substituting the given values :

$$\rho = \frac{RA}{l} = \frac{(5\times10^3\,\text{ohm} \times 0.625\ \text{cm}^2)}{50\ \text{cm}}$$

$$= 62.5\ \text{ohm cm}$$

The inverse of resistivity is called conductivity. Hence,

$$\kappa = \frac{1}{\rho} = \frac{1}{62.5\ \text{ohm}^{-1}\text{cm}^{-1}}$$

$$= 0.016\ \text{S cm}^{-1}$$

Now, the molar conductivity is given by :

$$\Lambda_m = \frac{\kappa}{c} \times 1000$$

Substituting the values:

$$\Lambda_m = \frac{0.016 \times 1000}{0.05}$$

$$= 320\ \text{S cm}^2\text{mol}^{-1}$$

(b) Reactions which will occur in the solution are:

$$CuCl_2(s) \leftrightarrow Cu^{2+} + 2Cl^-$$
$$H_2O \leftrightarrow H^+ + OH^-$$

Reaction at cathode:

$$Cu^{2+} + 2e^- \to Cu(s)$$

Because $E°_{Cu^{2+}/Cu} > E°_{H^+/H^2}$

Reaction at anode:

$$2Cl^- \to Cl_2 + 2e^-$$

This reaction occurs at the anode due to over potential of O_2 oxidation of Cl^- is preferred. Hence, Cu will deposit at cathode and Cl_2 gas will be liberated at anode.

OR

(a) The half-cell reactions can be written as:
$$Zn^{2+} + 2e^- \to Zn;\quad E_{el} = -0.76 + (0.0591/2)$$
$$(\log [Zn^{2+}])$$

Substituting the concentration value and calculating:

$$E_{el} = -0.76 + (0.0591/2)\ (\log 0.1)$$
$$= -0.76 - 0.0295$$
and $$= -0.789\ \text{V} \qquad ...(i)$$

$$Ag^+ + e^- \to Ag;$$
$$E_{el} = 0.8\ \text{V} + 0.0591\ (\log [Ag^+])$$

Substituting the concentration value and calculating:

$$E_{el} = 0.8 + 0.0591\ (\log 0.01)$$
$$= 0.8 - 0.1182$$
$$= 0.6818 \qquad ...(ii)$$

Here, Ag^+ will reduce and Zn will oxidise—
$$2Ag^+\ (aq) + Zn(s) \to Zn^{2+}\ (aq) + 2Ag(s)$$
will be the cell reaction

So, E_{cell} will be:

$$E_{cell} = 0.6818 - (-0.789)\ \text{V}$$
$$= 1.471\ \text{V}$$

(b) Y is weak electrolyte. On dilution weak electrolytes undergo complete dissociation and thus, there is a steep increase in molar conductivity observed. Whereas, in case of strong electrolytes, as they are already dissociated completely, dilution does not affect the conductivity very much. So, in this case X is a strong electrolyte.

36. (a) An organic compound **(A)** having molecular formula C_4H_8O gives orange red precipitate with 2, 4-DNP reagent. It does not reduce Tollens' reagent but gives yellow precipitate of iodoform on heating with NaOH and I_2. Compound **(A)** on reduction with $NaBH_4$ gives compound (B) which undergoes dehydration reaction on heating with conc. H_2SO_4 to form compound (C). Compound (C) on Ozonolysis gives two molecules of ethanal.

Identify (A), (B) and (C) and write their structures. Write the reactions of compound (A) with (i) $NaOH/I_2$ and (ii) $NaBH_4$.

(b) Give reasons:

(i) Oxidation of propanal is easier than propanone.

(ii) α-hydrogen of aldehydes and ketones is acidic in nature. **[3 + 2 = 5]**

OR

(a) Draw structures of the following derivatives.

(i) Cyanohydrin of cyclobutanone

(ii) Hemiacetal of ethanal

(b) Write the major product(s) in the following:

(i) $CH_3 - CH = CH - CH_2 - CN$

$$\xrightarrow[\text{(ii) } H_3O^+]{\text{(i) DIBAL} - H}$$

(ii) $CH_3 - CH_2 - OH \xrightarrow{CrO_3}$

(c) How can you distinguish between propanal and propanone? **[2 + 2 + 1 = 5]**

Ans (a) C_4H_8O (A) gives precipitate with 2, 4-DNP, it indicates that compound A contains a carbonyl ($>C = O$ group. It does not reduce Tollen's reagent so it is a ketone compound. It gives Iodoform test as it contains a methyl ketone group ($-COCH_3$). Let us assume tentative structure of A as $X-COCH_3$. Now, A gives compound B on $NaBH_4$ reduction, so the structure of compound B becomes $X-CHOH-CH_3$. Compound B further is subjected to dehydration which means the new compound C will contain a double bond. Compound C gives two molecules of ethanal on Ozonolysis, this tells us that compound C is symmetrical and the double bond divides the molecule in two equal parts.

Collating all the above given information, the reaction sequence can be formulated as:

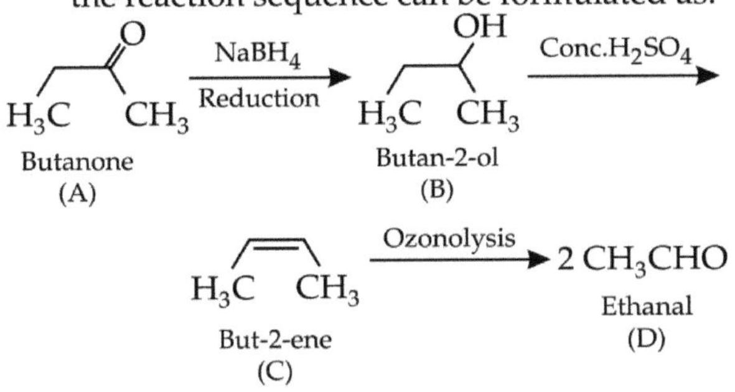

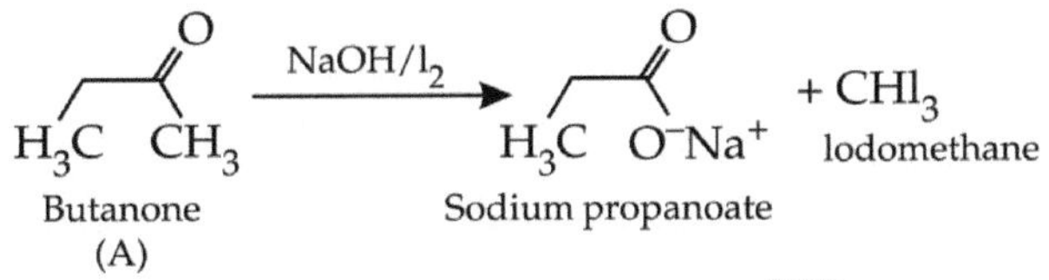

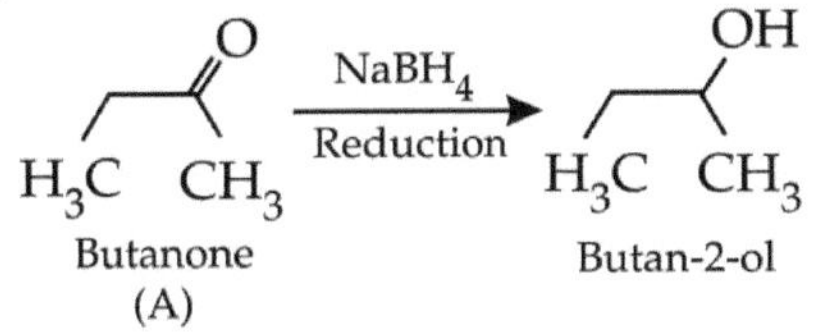

Butanone (A) $\xrightarrow[\text{Reduction}]{NaBH_4}$ Butan-2-ol (B) $\xrightarrow{Conc.H_2SO_4}$ But-2-ene (C) $\xrightarrow{\text{Ozonolysis}}$ $2\ CH_3CHO$ Ethanal (D)

Butanone (A) $\xrightarrow{NaOH/I_2}$ Sodium propanoate $+ CHI_3$ Iodomethane

Butanone (A) $\xrightarrow[\text{Reduction}]{NaBH_4}$ Butan-2-ol

(b) (i) Oxidation of aldehyde is easier than ketones as in propanal there is one oxidisable -H present attached to the carbonyl carbon whereas propanone being ketone does not have the oxidisable -H atom. Also, as the carbonyl carbon contains two alkyl groups attached to it in ketone, it becomes less reactive responsible for less reactivity of propanone compared to propanal

(ii) In aldehydes and ketone, α-hydrogen is the hydrogen atom attached to the alpha (α) carbon atom, which in turn is attached to the carbonyl carbon. After removal of α-hydrogen atom, conjugated base so obtained is resonance stabilised. Hence, it becomes easy to lose the α-hydrogen atoms in basic medium and thus aldehydes and ketones are acidic in nature. The phenomenon is shown below :

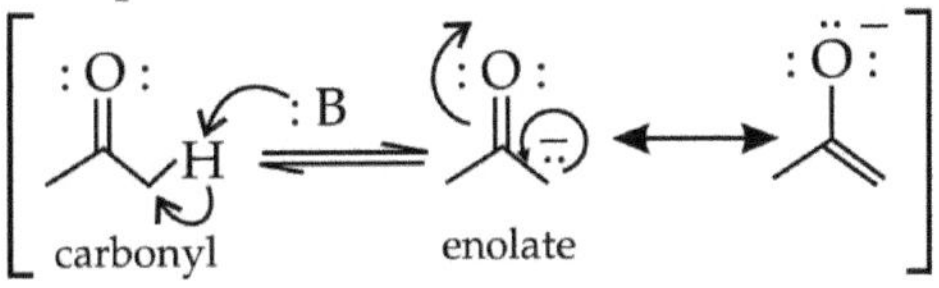

OR

(a) (i) Cyanohydrin of cyclobutanone

Cyclobutanone $\xrightarrow{HCN}$ Cyclobutane cyanohydrin

(ii) Hemiacetal of Ethanal

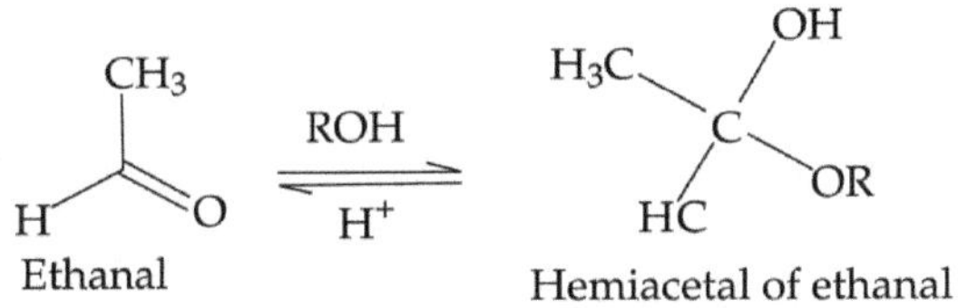

Ethanal $\xrightarrow[H^+]{ROH}$ Hemiacetal of ethanal

(b) (i)

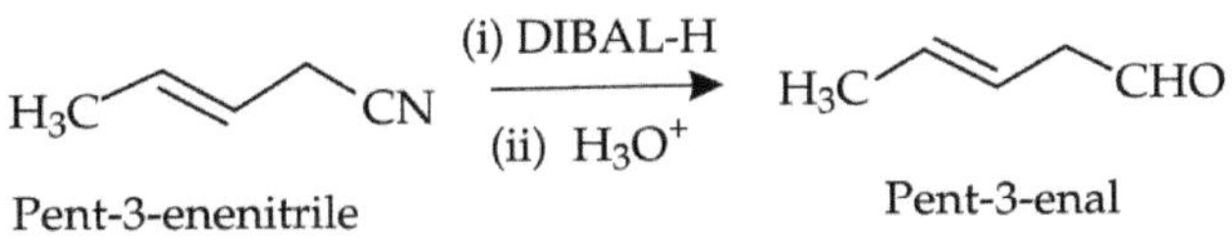

H_3C ⌇⌇ CN Pent-3-enenitrile $\xrightarrow[\text{(ii) } H_3O^+]{\text{(i) DIBAL-H}}$ H_3C ⌇⌇ CHO Pent-3-enal

(ii)
$$H_3C\text{—}CH_2\text{—}OH \xrightarrow[\text{Oxidation}]{CrO_3} H_3C\text{—}CHO$$
Ethanol → Ethanal

(c) Propanal and propanone can be distinguished by Iodoform reaction. When both are treated with NaOH and I_2, propanone (Acetone) gives a yellow precipitate of Iodoform whereas propanal does not react in these conditions.

$$CH_3\text{—}\overset{\overset{O}{\|}}{C}\text{—}CH_3 + 3I_2 + 4NaOH \longrightarrow$$
Acetone

$$CHI_3 + CH_3COONa + 3NaI + 3H_2O$$
Iodoform

$$\text{Propanal} + I_2 + NaOH \longrightarrow \text{No reaction}$$

37. (a) Account for the following:

    (i) Tendency to show –2 oxidation state decreases from oxygen to tellurium.

    (ii) Acidic character increases from HF to HI.

    (iii) Moist SO_2 gas acts an a reducing agent.

(b) Draw the structure of an oxoacid of sulphur containing S—O—S linkage.

(c) Complete the following equation:
$$XeF_2 + H_2O \rightarrow \qquad [3 + 1 + 1 = 5]$$

OR

(a) Among the hydrides of group 16, write the hydride

    (i) Which is a strong reducing agent.

    (ii) Which has maximum bond angle.

    (iii) Which is most thermally stable.

    Give situable reason in each.

(b) Complete the following equations:

    (i) $S + H_2SO_4 \longrightarrow$
    (Conc.)

    (ii) $Cl_2 + NaOH \longrightarrow$
    (Cold and dilute)   [3 + 1 + 1 = 5]

Ans. (a) (i) Tendency to show -2 oxidation states decreases from oxygen to tellurium due to increase in atomic size and decrease in electronegativity.

(ii) Acidic nature is determined by the ability to donate H^+ ion in solution. HI being the least stable due to its large size and its inability to form strong hydrogen bonds lose H^+ easily. Also, its bond enthalpy is least among the hydrogen halides, breakage of H-I bond becomes easy thus making it lose H^+ quickly and hence most acidic followed by HBr, HCl, HF due to their increasing order of stability. Thus the acidic character increases from HF to HI.

(iii) In SO_2, sulphur is in +4 oxidation state and can further get reduced to achieve +3 oxidation state. So, moist sulphur dioxide behaves as a reducing agent as shown in following reaction:
$$2Fe^{3+} + SO_2 + 2H_2O \rightarrow 2Fe^{2+} SO_4^{2-} + 4H^+$$

(b) Pyrosulphuric acid contains -S-O-S- linkage

$$HO\text{—}\overset{\overset{O}{\|}}{\underset{\underset{O}{\|}}{S}}\text{—}O\text{—}\overset{\overset{O}{\|}}{\underset{\underset{O}{\|}}{S}}\text{—}OH$$

(c) $2XeF_2(s) + 2H_2O(l) \rightarrow 2Xe(g) + 4HF(aq) + O_2(g)$

OR

(a) (i) H_2Te is the strongest reducing agent among all the hydrides of group 16 due to the low bond dissociation enthalpy for H-Te bond.

(ii) H_2O has maximum bond angle of 104.45°. This is because oxygen forms 2 covalent bonds with 2 hydrogen atoms, hence, 2 pairs of electrons are bonding pairs and 2 pairs of electrons are lone pairs (non-bonding pairs) around the central oxygen atom. The repulsion between lone pairs of electrons is greater than the repulsion between lone pairs and the bonding pairs, which is greater than the repulsion between the bonding pairs of electrons, so the bonding pairs of electrons are pushed even closer together. Hence, a tetrahedral distribution of electron pairs is there in water molecule.

(iii) Thermal stability of the hydrides of group 16 decrease on the decrease in enthalpy for the dissociation of H-E bond down the group. Hence, H_2O is thermally most stable.

(b) (i) Sulphur is oxidised to sulphur dioxide by conc. H_2SO_4.
$$S + 2H_2SO_4(Conc.) \rightarrow 3SO_2 + 2H_2O$$

(ii) Chlorine reacts with cold and dilute sodium hydroxide solution and forms the sodium chloride, sodium hypochlorite along with the water molecule in the solution.
$$Cl_2 + 2NaOH \text{ (cold and dilute)} \rightarrow NaCl + NaOCl + H_2O$$

●●

Outside Delhi [Set-II]

Note : Except for the following questions all the remaining questions have been asked in previous set.

SECTION-A

6. Name the depressant which is used to separate PbS and ZnS containing ore in forth floatation process.

Ans. NaCN

7. Out of (benzene)$-CH_2-Cl$ and (cyclohexene)$-CH_2-Cl$ which will react faster in S_N1 reaction with OH^-?

Ans. (cyclohexane ring)$\sim Cl$

8. Out of CH_3NH_2 and CH_3OH, which has higher boiling point?

Ans. CH_3OH

9. Which one of the following is a narcotic analgesic?
Penicillin, Codeine, Ranitidine.

Ans. Codeine

10. Write the name of linkage joining two monosaccharides.

Ans. Glycosidic linkage

11. The coordination number of 'Co' in the complex $[Co(en)_3]^{3+}$ is

(a) 3   (b) 6

(c) 4   (d) 5

Ans. (b) 6

12. An electrochemical cell behaves like an electrolytic cell when

(a) $E_{cell} = E_{external}$ (b) $E_{cell} = 0$

(c) $E_{external} > E_{cell}$ (d) $E_{external} < E_{cell}$

Ans. (c) $E_{external} > E_{cell}$

13. The half-life period for a zero order reaction is equal to

(a) $\dfrac{0.693}{k}$ (b) $\dfrac{2k}{[R]_0}$

(c) $\dfrac{2.303}{k}$ (d) $\dfrac{[R]_0}{2k}$

(Where $[R]_0$ is initial concentration of reactant and k is rate constant)

Ans. (d) $\dfrac{[R]_0}{2K}$

14. The crystal field splitting energy for octahedral (Δ_0) and tetrahedral (Δ_t) complexes is related as

(a) $\Delta_t = \Delta_0$ (b) $\Delta_t = \dfrac{5}{9}\Delta_0$

(c) $\Delta_t = \dfrac{4}{9}\Delta_0$ (d) $\Delta_t = 2\Delta_0$

Ans. (c) $\Delta_t = \dfrac{4}{9}\Delta_0$

15. α–D(+) glucose and (β–D(+) glucose are.

(a) Geometrical isomers   (b) Enantiomers

(c) Anomers   (d) Optical isomers

Ans. (c) Anomers

Questions 16 to 20:

(A) Both Assertion (A) and Reason (R) are correct statements, and Reason (R) is the correct explanation of the Assertion (A).

(B) Both Assertion (A) and Reason (R) are correct statements, but Reason (R) is not the correct explanation of the Assertion (A).

(C) Assertion (A) is correct, but Reason (R) is wrong statement.

(D) Assertion (A) is wrong, but Reason (R) is correct statement.

16. **Assertion (A) :** F_2 has lower bond dissociation enthalpy than Cl_2.

Reason (R) : Fluorine is more electronegative than chlorine.

Ans. (B) Fourine has low bond dissoiation enthalpy due to small atomic size number of electrons create large repulsion in bonded electron. Thus, Both Assertion (A) and Reason (R) are correct statements, but Reason (R) is not the correct explanation of the Assertion (A).

18. **Assertion (A) :** Transition metals have high melting point.

Reason (R) : Transition metals have completely filled d-orbitals.

Ans. (C) Transition metals have high melting point due to involvement of d and S orbitals in bonding. Thus, assertion (A) is correct, but Reason (R) is wrong statement.

SECTION-B

23. Write IUPAC name and hybridization of the following complexes:

(i) $[Ni(CO)_4]$ (ii) $[CoF_6]^{3-}$

(Atomic number Ni = 28, Co = 27) $[1 + 1 = 2]$

Ans. (i) **IUPAC name :** Tetracarbonylnickel (O)

Hybridisation : sp^3

(ii) **IUPAC name :** Hexa fluoridocobaltate (III) ion

Hybridisation : sp^3d^2

25. Define the following terms with a suitable example in each: $[1 + 1 = 2]$

(i) Tranquilizers   (ii) Anionic detergent

Ans. (i) **Tranquilizers:** They are a class of neurologically active chemical compounds used for treatment of stress and mild or even severe mental diseases. These relive anxiety by affecting the message transfer mechanism from nerve to receptor. Example: Chlordiazepoxide, Equanil etc.

(ii) Anionic detergent : They are sodium salts of sulphonated long chain alcohols or hydrocarbons. Alkyl hydrogen sulphates formed by treating long chain alcohols with concentrated sulphuric acid are neutralised with alkali to form anionic detergents. Example : Sodium lauryl sulphate.

26. Write the reactions showing the presence of following in the open structure of glucose.

(i) an aldehyde group (ii) a primary alcohol

$$[1 + 1 = 2]$$

Ans. (i) Glucose gets oxidised to six carbon carboxylic acid (gluconic acid) on reaction with mild oxidising agent like bromine water. This confirms the presence of an aldehyde group in glucose molecule.

$$\underset{\text{Glucose}}{\overset{\displaystyle CHO}{\underset{\displaystyle CH_2OH}{|\,(CHOH)_4\,|}}} + [O] \xrightarrow{Br_2/Water} \underset{\text{Gluconic acid}}{\overset{\displaystyle COOH}{\underset{\displaystyle CH_2OH}{|\,(CHOH)_4\,|}}}$$

(ii) On oxidation with nitric acid glucose yields a dicarboxylic acid, saccharic acid.

It indicates the presence of a primary alcoholic group (–OH) in glucose.

$$\underset{\text{Glucose}}{\overset{\displaystyle CHO}{\underset{\displaystyle CH_2OH}{|\,(CHOH)_4\,|}}} + [O] \xrightarrow{conc.HNO_3} \underset{\text{(Saccharic acid)}}{\overset{\displaystyle COOH}{\underset{\displaystyle CH_2OH}{|\,(CHOH)_4\,|}}}$$

SECTION - C

31. Write the name and structures of monomers in the following polymers : $\quad [1 + 1 + 1 = 3]$

(i) Nylon 6, 6   (ii) Terylene   (iii) PHBV

Ans. (i) Adipic acid and Hexamethylene dichloride are the monomers of Nylon 6,6 polymer.

Adipic acid + Hexamethylene diamine

Nylon 6,6

(ii) Ethylene glycol and Terephthalic acid are the monomers of Terylene polymer.

$$HO-CH_2-CH_2-OH + HOOC-\!\!\bigcirc\!\!-COOH$$

Ethylene glycol

Terephthalic acid

$$-H_2O$$

Polyethylene terephthalate or (Terylene)

(iii) 3-Hydroxybutanoic acid and 3-Hydroxy pentanoic acid are the monomers of PHBV polymer:

3-Hydroxy butanoic acid + 3-Hydroxy pentanoic acid

$$-H_2O$$

PHBV

Outside Delhi [Set-III]

Note : Except for the following questions all the remaining questions have been asked in previous sets.

SECTION-A

6. Name the method used for the refining of Zinc.

Ans. Electrolytic refining or Distillation

7. Out of $CH_3CH_2CH_2Cl$ and $CH_2 = CH - CH_2 - Cl$, which one is more reactive towards S_N1 reaction?

Ans. $CH_2 = CH - CH_2Cl$

8. Write an isomer of C_3H_9N which does not react with Hinsberg reagent.

Ans. $(CH_3)_3 N$; Trimethylamine

9. What type of protein is present in keratin?

Ans. Fibrous protein

10. Name the compound which is added to soap to provide antiseptic properties.

Ans. Bithional

11. Which of the following is the most stable complex?

(a) $[Fe(CO)_5]$ (b) $[Fe(H_2O)_6]^{3+}$

(c) $[Fe(C_2O_4)_3]^{3-}$ (d) $[Fe(CN)_6]^{3-}$

Ans. (c) $[Fe(C_2O_4)_3]^{3-}$

12. Which of the following is correct for spontaneity of a cell ?

(a) $\Delta G = -ve\ E° = +ve$

(b) $\Delta G = +ve\ E° = 0$

(c) $\Delta G = -ve\ E° = 0$

(d) $\Delta G = +ve\ E° = -ve$

Ans. (a) $\Delta G = -ve\ E° = +ve$

13. For a zero order reaction, the slope in the plot of [R] Vs. time is

(a) $\dfrac{-k}{2.303}$ (b) $-k$

(c) $\dfrac{+k}{2.303}$ (d) $+k$

(where [R] is the final concentration of reactant)

Ans. (b) $-k$

14. What type of isomerism is shown by the pair $[Cr(H_2O)_6]\ Cl_3$ and $[Cr(H_2O)_5\ Cl]\ Cl_2.H_2O$?

(a) Ionization isomerism

(b) Coordination isomerism

(c) Solvate isomerism

(d) Linkage isomerism

Ans. (c) Solvate isomerism

15. Which one is the complementary base of cytosine in one strand to that in other strand of DNA?

(a) Adenine (b) Guanine

(c) Thymine (d) Uracil

Ans. (b) Guanine

Questions 16 to 20:

(A) Both Assertion (A) and Reason (R) are correct statements, and Reason (R) is the correct explanation of the Assertion (A).

(B) Both Assertion (A) and Reason (R) are correct statements, but Reason (R) is not the correct explanation of the Assertion (A).

(C) Assertion (A) is correct, but Reason (R) is wrong statement.

(D) Assertion (A) is wrong, but Reason (R) is correct statement.

16. **Assertion (A):** F_2 has low reactivity.

Reason (R): F-F bond has low $\Delta_{bond}\ H°$

Ans. (D) F_2 is more reactive than other halogens because its valence electrons are more closer to nucleus and its more electronegative so, bonded electrons repel each other causing low bond dissociation enthalpy. Thus, assertion is wrong, but Reason is correct statement.

SECTION-B

23. Write the IUPAC name and hybridisation of the following complexes :

(i) $[Co(NH_3)_6]^{3+}$ (ii) $[NiCl_4]^{2-}$

(Given : Atomic number : Ni = 28, Co = 27)

$[1 + 1 = 2]$

Ans. (i) **IUPAC Name:** Hexamminecobalt (III) ion **Hybridisation:** d^2sp^3.

(ii) **IUPAC Name :** Tetrachloridonickelate (II) ion **Hybridisation** : sp^3.

25. Write the reactions showing the presence of the following in the open structure of glucose:

(i) five – OH groups (ii) a carbonyl group

$[1 + 1 = 2]$

Ans. (i) On acetylation with acetic anhydride, glucose gives glucose pentaacetate. This confirms presence of 5 –OH groups in glucose molecule.

$$\begin{array}{c} CHO \\ | \\ (CHOH)_4 \\ | \\ CH_2OH \end{array} + 5(CH_3CH)_2O \xrightarrow{\text{Acetic anhydride}} \begin{array}{c} CHO \\ | \\ (CHOCOCH_3)_4 \\ | \\ CH_2O-\overset{\overset{O}{\|}}{C}-CH_3 \end{array} + 5CH_3COOH$$

Glucose .... Glucose penta acetate

(ii) On reaction with hydroxylamine, glucose gives glucose oxime. This confirms presence of a $\overset{>}{C} = O$ group in glucose molecule.

$$\begin{array}{c} CHO \\ | \\ (CH_2OH)_4 \\ | \\ CH_2OH \end{array} + NH_2OH \longrightarrow \begin{array}{c} CH = N-OH \\ | \\ (CHOH)_4 \\ | \\ CH_2OH \end{array}$$

Glucose oxime

27. Define the following terms with a suitable example in each: $[1 + 1 = 2]$

(i) Antacids

(ii) Artificial Sweetener

Ans. (i) **Antacids:** They are used to relieve the symptoms of hyperacidity, heartburn or indigestion. Over production of acid in the stomach causes irritation and pain. By neutralising the acid in the stomach, they relieve the symptoms of hyperacidity.

Example: A mixture of aluminium and magnesium hydroxide.

(ii) **Artificial Sweetener :** They are substances which have no nutritive value and are used to provide sweetness to food with low calories. These do not increase the calorie intake values. **Example :** Aspartame.

SECTION-C

31. **Write the names and structures of monomers in the following polymers :**

   (a) **Buna-S**   **(b)** **Glyptal**

   (c) **Bakelite** $[1 + 1 + 1 = 3]$

Ans. (a) Butadiene and Styrene copolymerise to provide Buna-S polymer.

$$n CH_2 = CH - CH = CH_2 + n CH_2 = CH \xrightarrow{\text{Copolymerisation}}$$

1, 3-butadiene $\overset{|}{C_6H_5}$

                   Styrene

$$\left[CH_2 - CH = CH - CH_2 - CH_2 - \overset{\displaystyle |}{\underset{\displaystyle C_6H_5}{CH}} \right]_n$$

        Butadiene-Styrene copolymer
              (Buna -S)

(b) Ethylene glycol and Phthalic acid are the monomers of Glyptal polymer.

$$HOCH_2CH_2OH +$$

Ethylene glycol   Phthalic acid

$$\left[OCH_2 - CH_2OOC \qquad CO \right]_n$$

Glyptal

(c) Phenol and formaldehyde are the monomers of Bakelite-

Phenol   Formaldehyde   (many steps)

Bakelite

Time allowed : 3 hours   **Maximum marks : 70**

SECTION-A

Read the given passage and answer the questions 1 to 5 that follow:

The halogens have the smallest atomic radii in their respective periods. The atomic radius of fluorine is extremely small. All halogens exhibit –1 oxidation state. They are strong oxidising agents and have maximum negative electron gain enthalpy. Among halogens, fluorine shows anomalous behaviour in many properties. For example electronegativity and ionisation enthalpy are higher for fluorine than expected whereas bond dissociation enthalpy, m.p. and b.p. and electron gain enthalpy are quite lower than expected. Halogens react with hydrogen to give hydrogen halides (HX) and combine amongst themselves to form a number of compounds of the type XX', XX'_3, XX'_5 and XX'_7 called inter-halogens.

1. Why halogens have maximum negative electron gain enthalpy?

Ans. The outer electronic configuration of halogens is $ns^2\,np^5$, hence it completes its octet and gets stabilised by accepting one electron. So, halogens have maximum electron gain enthalpy.

2. Why fluorine shows anomalous behaviour as compared to other halogens?

Ans. Fluorine is the first element in halogen group, its atomic number is 9 and electronic configuration is $[He]2s^2\,2p^5$. The anomalous behaviour of fluorine is due to its small size, highest electronegativity, low F-F bond dissociation enthalpy, and non-availability of d orbitals in valence shell.

3. Arrange the hydrogen halides (HF to HI) in the decreasing order of their reducing character.

Ans. $HF < HCl < HBr < HI$

4. Why fluorine is a stronger oxidizing agent than chlorine?

Ans. Fluorine has high electronegativity low heat of dissociation, high heat of hydration and low electron affinity than chlorine which makes attraction of electrons towards fluorine more easy than chlorine, hence it is a better oxidising agent compared to oxygen.

5. What are the sizes of X and X' in the interhalogen compounds?

Ans. X is halogen of larger size and X' is halogen of smaller size.

Question 6 to 10 are one word answers.

6. Name the cell used in hearing aids and watches.

Ans. Mercury cell

7. How much charge in terms of Faraday is required to reduce one mol of MnO_4^- to Mn^{2+} ?

Ans. $5 \times 96500 = 482500F$

8. Write the slope value obtained in the plot of log $[R_0]/[R]$ Vs. time for a first order reaction.

Ans. Slope $= k/2.303$

9. Name the sweetening agent used in the cooking of sweets for a diabetic patient.

Ans. Sucralose

10. Name the polymer which is used for making electrical switches and combs.

Ans. Bakelite

Question 11 to 15 are multiple choice questions.

11. In the Mond's process the gas used for the refining of a metal is

(a) H_2 (b) CO_2
(c) CO   (d) N_2

Ans. (c) CO

12. The conversion of an alkyl halide into an alcohol by aqueous NaOH is classified as

(a) a dehydrohalogenation reaction
(b) a substitution reaction
(c) an addition reaction
(d) a dehydration reaction

Ans. (b) a substitution reaction

13. CH_3CONH_2 on reaction with NaOH and Br_2 in alcoholic medium gives

(a) $CH_3CH_2NH_2$ (b) CH_3CH_2Br
(c) CH_3NH_2 (d) CH_3COONa

Ans. (c) CH_3NH_2

14. The oxidation state of Ni in $[Ni(CO)_4]$ is

(a) 0   (b) 2
(c) 3   (d) 4

Ans. (a) 0

15. Amino acids are

(a) acidic   (b) basic
(c) amphoteric   (d) neutral

Ans. (c) amphoteric

Questions 16 to 20.

(A) Both Assertion (A) and Reason (R) are correct statements, and Reason (R) is the correct explanation of the Assertion (A).

(B) Both Assertion (A) and Reason (R) are correct statements, but Reason (R) is not the correct explanation of the Assertion (A).

(C) Assertion (A) is correct, but Reason (R) is wrong statement.

(D) Assertion (A) is wrong, but Reason (R) is correct statement.

16. Assertion (A) : Conductivity of an electrolyte increases with decrease in concentration.

Reason (R) : Number of ions per unit volume decreases on dilution.

Ans. (D) With increase in dilution, the number of ions in solution deceases. So, conductivity of electrolytic solution decease on dilution increasing. Thus, Assertion (A) is wrong, but Reason (R) is correct statement.

17. Assertion (A) : The C—O—C bond angle in ethers is slightly less than tetrahedral angle.

Reason (R) : Due to the repulsive interaction between the two alkyl groups in ethers.

Ans. (D) In ethers, bond angle around oxygen is not exactly 109° 28'. There is deviation in angle caused due to repulsive interactions between bulkier alkyl groups. Thus, Assertion (A) is wrong, but Reason (R) is correct statement.

18. Assertion (A) : Low spin tetrahedral complexes are rarely observed.

Reason (R) : Crystal field splitting energy is less than pairing energy for tetrahedral complexes.

Ans. (A) In tetrahedral complexes, none of the orbitals is pointing directly towards ligands due to which splitting is less such that the magnitude of crystal field spliting in field is quite small and is always less than pairing energy and consequently paring of electrons will never be energetically favourable. Thus, tetrahedral complexes are high spin complexes So, Both Assertion (A) and Reason (R) are correct statements, and Reason (R) is the correct explanation of the Assertion (A).

19. Assertion (A) : Elevation in boiling point is a colligative property.

Reason (R) : Elevation in boiling point is directly proportional to molarity.

Ans. (C) Elevation in boiling point is directly proportional to molarity. Thus, Assertion (A) is correct, but Reason (R) is wrong statement.

20. Assertion (A) : Oxidation of ketones is easier than aldehydes.

Reason (R) : C—C bond of ketones is stronger than C—H bond of aldehydes.

Ans. (D) Oxidation of aldehydes is easier than ketones. Thus, Assertion (A) is wrong, but Reason (R) is correct statement.

SECTION – B

21. State Raoult's law for a solution containing volatile components. What is the similarity between Raoult's law and Henry's law? [2]

Ans. Raoult's law states

For a solution of volatile liquids, the partial vapour pressure of each component of the solution is directly proportional to its mole fraction present in solution.

$$p_1 = p°_1 \, x_1$$

According to Henry's law, the partial vapour pressure of a gas (the component is volatile and exists as a gas) in a liquid is

$$p_1 = K_H \, x_1$$

If we compare the equations for Raoult's law and Henry's law, it can be seen that the partial pressure of the volatile component or gas is directly proportional to its mole fraction in solution. Thus, Raoult's law becomes a special case of Henry's law when $p°_1 = K_H$.

22. Write the role of

(a) Dilute NaCN in the extraction of Gold.

(b) CO in the extraction of Iron. [1 + 1 = 2]

OR

How is leaching carried out in the case of low grade copper ores? Name the method used for refining of copper metal. [2]

Ans. (a) Dilute NaCN is used to leach gold metal from its ore in presence of air–

$$4Au(s) + 8CN^-(aq) + 2H_2O(aq) + O_2\,(g) \rightarrow$$
$$4[Au(CN)_2]^-\,(aq) + 4OH^-(aq)$$

(b) CO acts as a reducing agent due to which iron in the ore reduces to iron metal.

$$3CO(g) + Fe_2O_3(s) \rightarrow 3CO_2(g) + 2Fe\,(l)$$

OR

Copper is extracted by hydrometallurgy from low grade ores. It is leached out using acid or bacteria. The solution containing Cu^{2+} is treated with scrap iron or H_2

$$Cu^{2+}\,(aq) + H_2\,(g) \rightarrow Cu(s) + 2H^+(aq)$$

Copper is refined by electrolytic refining method. Anodes are made up of impure copper and pure copper strips are taken as cathode.

23. Define adsorption with an example. What is the role of adsorption in heterogeneous catalysis? [2]

OR

Define Brownian movement. What is the cause of Brownian movement in colloidal particles? How is it responsible for the stability of Colloidal Sol? [2]

Ans. The accumulation of molecular species at the surface rather than in the bulk of a solid or a liquid is known as adsorption. It is essentially a surface phenomenon and the substance which concentrates at the surface is known as adsorbate and the material on the surface of which adsorption takes place is known as adsorbate. For example : Aqueous solution of raw sugar become colourless when passed through a bed of charcoal. Adsorption plays an important role in heterogenous catalysis. The catalyst adsorbs the reactants, forms an intermediate complex known as activated complex hence increases the concentration of reactant molecules. This increases the chances of reactant molecule coming close to each other for effective reaction. Heat of adsorption released is used in formation of activated complex and hence increases the rate of reaction.

OR

The continuous irregular and random zigzag motion of colloidal particles in the colloidal solution, when observed under an ultramicroscope, is called Brownian movement. Brownian movement is caused due to the collision between the molecules of dispersion medium and dispersed particles because of the unbalanced bombardment of the particles by the molecules of the dispersion medium. The Brownian movement gives a stirring effect to the colloidal solution, which does not permit the particles to settle and thus, is responsible for the stability of sols.

24. (a) **Write the IUPAC name and hybridisation of the complex [Fe(CN)₆]³⁻.**
   (Given : Atomic number of Fe = 26)
   (b) **What is the difference between an ambidentate ligand and a chelating ligand?**
   [1 + 1 = 2]

Ans. (a) $[Fe(CN)_6]^{3-}$

   IUPAC name - Hexacyanoferrate(III)

   Hybridisation- d^2sp^3

   (b) Ambidentate ligands are the ligand which can ligate through two different atoms such as $-NO_2$ ligand which can ligate through N atom as well as O atom as shown below:

nitro   nitrito

Whereas, ligands those bind *via* more than one atom are termed as chelating ligands. These are commonly formed by linking donor groups via organic linkers. The below given example explains the same:

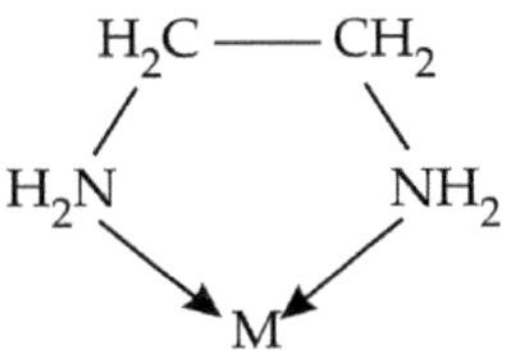

A chelating ligand forms a more stable complex as compared to an ambidentate ligand. Chelating ligand forms a cyclic complex while ambidentate ligand forms a non-cyclic complex.

25. How do antiseptics differ from disinfectants? Name a substance which can be used as a disinfectant as well as an antiseptic. [2]

Ans. Antiseptics are applied to the living tissues such as wounds, cuts, ulcers and other disease skin surfaces. These are not ingested as antibiotics. Disinfectants are applied to inanimate objects such as floors, drainage systems, instruments to sterilize. Same chemical can be used as antiseptic and disinfectant by varying concentration. Phenol is a substance which when used in 0.2 % concentration works as antiseptic whereas its 1 % solution is disinfectant.

26. Identify the monomers in the following polymers: [1 + 1 = 2]

(i) $\left[O-CH_2-CH_2-O-\overset{\displaystyle O}{\overset{\|}{C}}\underset{}{}CO\right]_n$

(ii) $\left[CH_2-\overset{\displaystyle CN}{\underset{|}{CH}}\right]_n$

Ans. (i) The given polymer is Glyptal and it is prepared from ethylene glycol and phthalic acid monomers.

$nHO-CH_2-CH_2-OH + nHO-\overset{\displaystyle O}{\overset{\|}{C}}\quad\overset{\displaystyle O}{\overset{\|}{C}}-OH$

Ethylene glycol   Phthalic acid

$\downarrow -2nH_2O$

$\left[O-H_2C-CH_2-O-\overset{\displaystyle O}{\overset{\|}{C}}\quad\overset{\displaystyle O}{\overset{\|}{C}}\right]_n$

(ii) The polymer is polyacrylonitrile and it is prepared through heating monomer acrylonitrile.

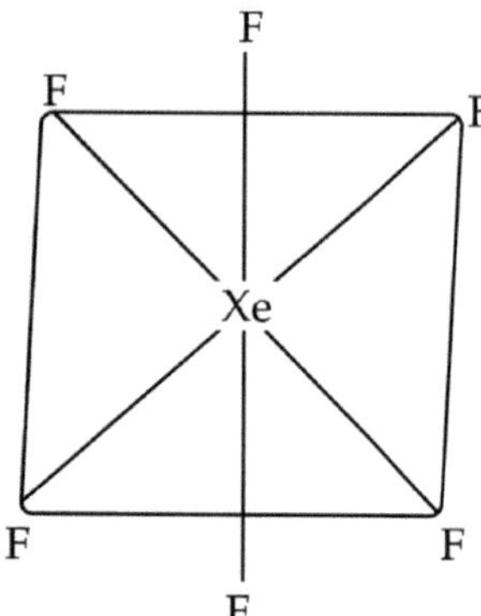

27. Draw the structures of the following:

(i) $H_2S_2O_8$ **(ii)** XeF_6 [1 + 1 = 2]

Ans. (i) Structure of $H_2S_2O_8$ (Peroxydisulphuric acid)

(ii) Structure of XeF_6 (Xenon hexafluoride)

SECTION – C

28. A 0.01 m aqueous solution of $AlCl_3$ freezes at −0.068°C. Calculate the percentage of dissociation. [Given : K_f for Water = 1.86 K kg mol⁻¹]   [3]

Ans. Given : K kg. mol⁻¹

$$\Delta T_f = 0.068, K_f = 1.86$$

Sustituting the values

$$\Delta T_f = iK_f m$$
$$0.068 = i \times 1.86 \times 0.01$$
$$i = 3.65$$

degree of dissociation = α

$$\alpha = \frac{i-1}{n-1}$$

$$\alpha = 0.883$$

or 88.3% is the percentage of dissociation of $AlCl_3$ in water.

29. When a steady current of 2A was passed through two electrolytic cells A and B containing electrolytes $ZnSO_4$ and $CuSO_4$ connected in series, 2 g of Cu were deposited at the cathode of cell B. How long did the current flow ? What mass of Zn was deposited at cathode of cell A ? [Atomic mass : Cu = 63.5 g mol⁻¹, Zn = 65 g mol⁻¹; 1F = 96500 C mol⁻¹]   [3]

Ans. For deposition of Cu, reaction is:

$$Cu^{2+} + 2e^- \rightarrow Cu$$

Thus, 1 mole, i.e., 63.5 g Cu is deposited by 2F = 2 × 96500 C

∴ 2 g of Cu will be deposited by (96500 / 63.5) × 2 C = 3039.37 ≈ 3039.4S

Now,   Charge Q = I × t

$$\frac{m_1}{m_2} = \frac{eq\ wt_1}{eq\ wt_2}$$

$$\frac{2}{m_2} = \frac{63.5/2}{65/2}$$

$$m_2 = 2.05\ g$$

2.05 g of Zn was deposited at cathode of cell A.

30. Differentiate between following:

(i) Amylose and Amylopectin

(ii) Globular protein and Fibrous protein

(iii) Nucleotide and Nucleoside   [1 + 1 + 1 = 3]

Ans. (i) Difference between Amylose and amylopectin

Amylose	Amylopectin
1. Straight chain polymer of D-glucose.	Branched chain polymer of D-glucose.
2. Constitutes about 20% of starch.	Constitutes about 80% of starch.
3. Amylose is water soluble component of starch.	Amylopectin is insoluble in water.
4. Gives a dark blue black colour with iodine.	Gives orange colour with iodine.

(ii) Difference between Globular protein and Fibrous protein:

Globular protein	Fibrous protein
1. Consists of coiled and folded polypeptide chains forming spherical shape. The structure is unstable.	Consists of long, parallel polypeptide chains forming helical structures or pleated sheets. The structure is linear and stable.
2. Soluble in water.	Insoluble in water.
3. Takes part in metabolite and chemical processes. Example : Enzymes and Haemoglobin.	Plays a major role in mechanical and structural functions. Example : Keratin and Collagen.

(iii) Difference between Nucleotide and Nucleoside:

Nucleotide	Nucleoside
1. Nucleotide is a compound formed by the union of a nitrogen base, a pentose sugar and phosphate.	Nucleoside is a compound formed by the union of a nitrogen base with a pentose sugar.
2. Nucleotide is formed through phosphorylation of nucleoside.	It is a component of nucleotide.
3. A nucleotide is acidic in nature. Example 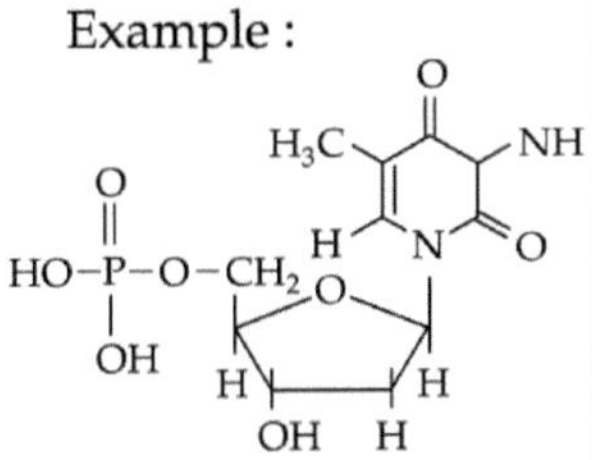 :	It is slightly basic in nature. Example 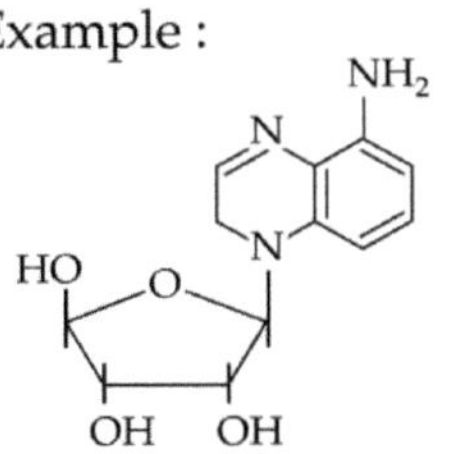 :

Thymidylic acid

Adenosine

31. Identify A, B, C, D, E and F in the following:

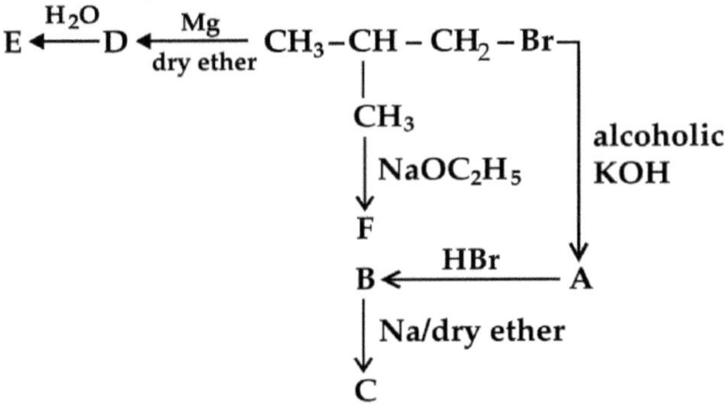

$$E \xleftarrow{H_2O} D \xleftarrow[\text{dry ether}]{Mg} CH_3-CH-CH_2-Br$$

(with CH_3 branch)

$NaOC_2H_5 \rightarrow F$

alcoholic KOH $\rightarrow$ A

$B \xleftarrow{HBr} A$

$B \xrightarrow{Na/dry\ ether} C$

$[6 \times \tfrac{1}{2} = 3]$

Ans.

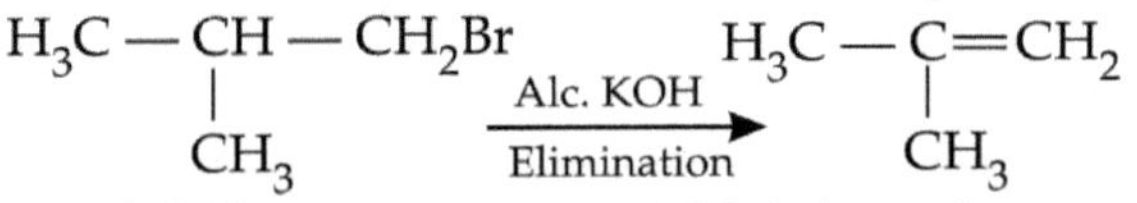

$H_3C-CH-CH_2Br$ (with CH_3), 2-Methyl-1-bromopropane $\xrightarrow[\text{Elimination}]{Alc.\ KOH}$ $H_3C-C=CH_2$ (with CH_3), 2-Methyl prop-1-ene (A)

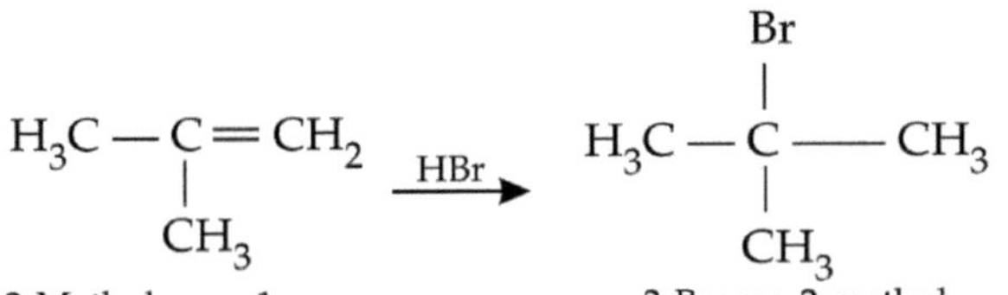

$H_3C-C=CH_2$ (with CH_3), 2-Methyl prop-1-ene (A) $\xrightarrow{HBr}$ $H_3C-C-CH_3$ (with Br and CH_3), 2-Bromo-2-methyl propane (B)

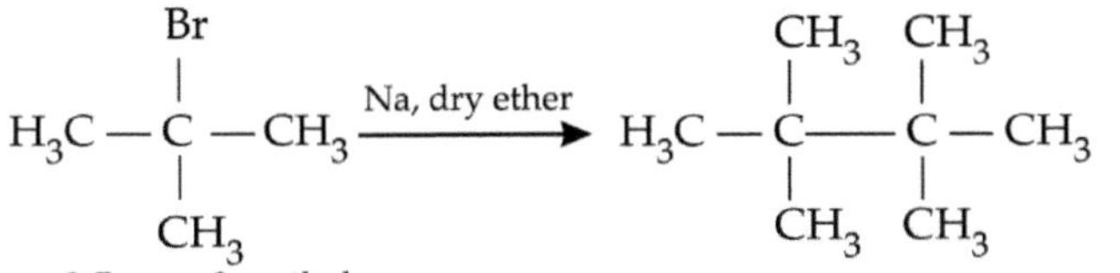

2-Bromo-2-methyl propane (B) $\xrightarrow{Na,\ dry\ ether}$ $H_3C-C-C-CH_3$ (with CH_3, CH_3, CH_3, CH_3), 2,2,3,3-Tetramethyl butane (C)

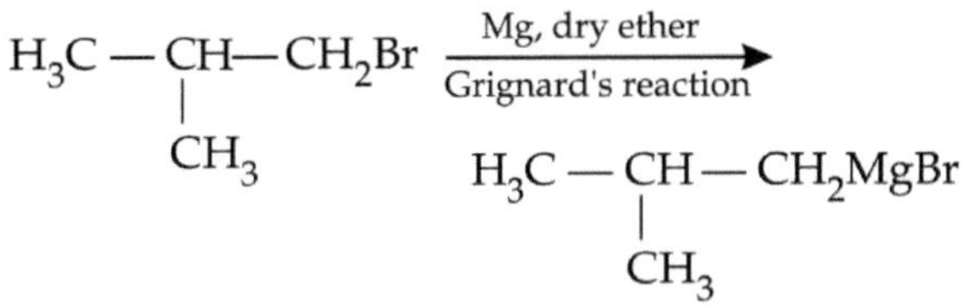

$H_3C-CH-CH_2Br$ (with CH_3) $\xrightarrow[\text{Grignard's reaction}]{Mg,\ dry\ ether}$ $H_3C-CH-CH_2MgBr$ (with CH_3), 2-Methylpropyl magnesium bromide (D)

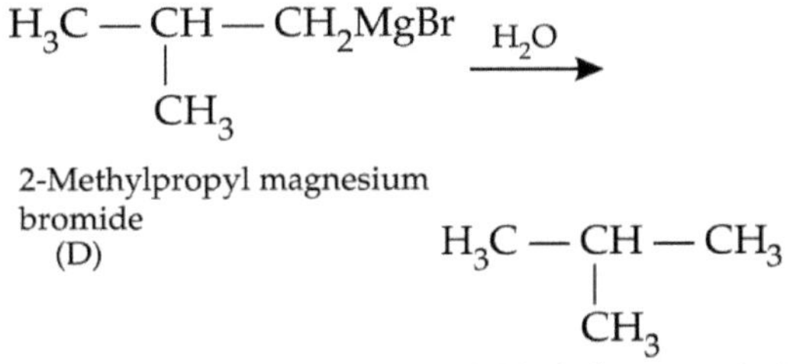

$H_3C-CH-CH_2MgBr$ (with CH_3), 2-Methylpropyl magnesium bromide (D) $\xrightarrow{H_2O}$ $H_3C-CH-CH_3$ (with CH_3), 2-Methylpropane-1 ol (E)

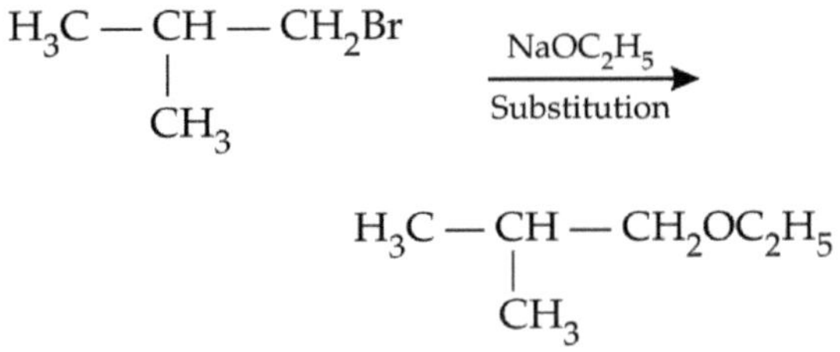

$H_3C-CH-CH_2Br$ (with CH_3) $\xrightarrow[\text{Substitution}]{NaOC_2H_5}$ $H_3C-CH-CH_2OC_2H_5$ (with CH_3), 1-Ethoxy-2-methylpropane (F)

32. Give the structures of final products expected from the following reactions:

(i) Hydroboration of propene followed by oxidation with H_2O_2 in alkaline medium.

(ii) Dehydration of $(CH_3)_3 C-OH$ by heating it with 20% H_3PO_4 at 358 K.

(iii) Heating of ⟨benzene⟩–CH_2—O–⟨benzene⟩ with HI. $[3 \times 1 = 3]$

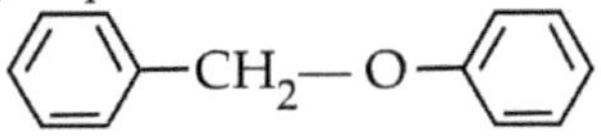

OR

How can you convert the following?

(i) Phenol to o-hydroxybenzaldehyde.

(ii) Methanal to ethanol

(iii) Phenol to phenyl ethanoate. $[1 + 1 + 1 = 3]$

Ans. (i) Propanol is obtained.

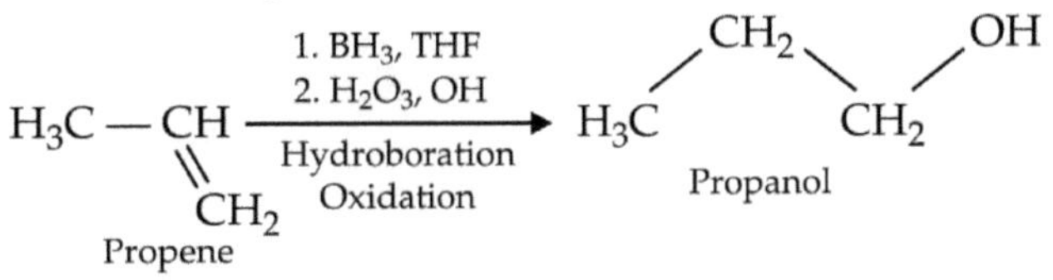

H_3C-CH (with CH_2, Propene) $\xrightarrow[\text{Oxidation}]{\substack{1.\ BH_3,\ THF \\ 2.\ H_2O_3,\ OH \\ \text{Hydroboration}}}$ Propanol

(ii) 2-Methyl propene is obtained.

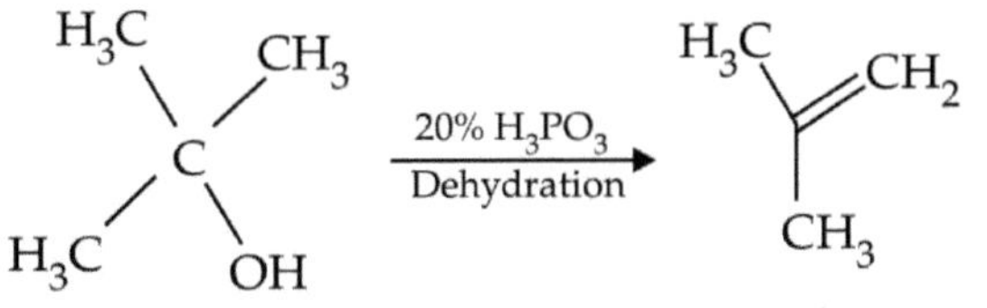

2-Methyl-propan-2-ol $\xrightarrow[\text{Dehydration}]{20\%\ H_3PO_3}$ 2-Methyl propene

(iii) Benzyl iodide is obtained along with phenol.

$$\text{C}_6\text{H}_5\text{CH}_2-\text{O}-\text{C}_6\text{H}_5 \xrightarrow{\text{HI}} \underset{\text{Benzyl iodide}}{\text{C}_6\text{H}_4\text{CH}_2\text{I}} + \underset{\text{Phenol}}{\text{C}_6\text{H}_5\text{OH}}$$

OR

(i) Reimer-Tiemann reaction will occur by electrophilic substitution reaction by reacting phenol with Chloroform in presence of aqueous alkali at 340K.

$$\underset{\text{Phenol}}{\text{OH}} \xrightarrow[\text{3 KOH}]{\text{CHCl}_3} \underset{\text{o-Hydroxy benzaldehyde}}{\text{OH} \ \text{O}}$$

(ii) Methanal reacts with Grignard's reagent to form products which on hydrolysis give alcohols.

$$\underset{\text{Methanal}}{\text{H}-\overset{\text{O}}{\underset{\|}{\text{C}}}-\text{H}} + \underset{\substack{\text{Methyl}\\\text{magnesium}\\\text{bromide}}}{\text{H}_3\text{C}-\text{Mg}-\text{Br}} \xrightarrow{\text{dry ether}}$$

$$\text{H}_3\text{C}-\overset{\text{H}}{\underset{\text{H}}{\text{C}}}-\text{O}-\text{Mg}-\text{Br}$$

$$\downarrow \text{H}_2\text{O}$$

$$\underset{\text{Ethanol}}{\text{H}_3\text{C}-\text{CH}_2-\text{OH}} + \text{Mg}\overset{\text{Br}}{\underset{\text{OH}}{}}$$

(iii) Phenol with acetic anhydrides in presence of H_2SO_4 react to give esters. This is called acylation.

$$\underset{\text{Phenol}}{\text{OH}} + \underset{\text{Acetic anhydride}}{(\text{CH}_3\text{CO})_2\text{O}} \xrightarrow{\text{H}^+} \underset{\text{Phenyl ethanoate}}{\text{OCO}-\text{CH}_3} + \text{CH}_3\text{COOH}$$

33. Give reasons:

(i) Aniline does not undergo Friedal-Crafts reaction.

(ii) Aromatic primary amines cannot be prepared by Gabriel's phthalimide synthesis.

(iii) Aliphatic amines are stronger bases than ammonia. **[3 × 1 = 3]**

Ans. (i) Aniline is basic in nature and AlCl3, the catalyst used in Friedal-Crafts reaction is a lewis acid and forms a salt with aniline.

$$\underset{\text{Aniline}}{\text{NH}_2} + \text{AlCl}_3 \longrightarrow \underset{\text{Salt}}{\overset{+}{\text{N}}\text{H}_2\bar{\text{Al}}\text{Cl}_3} + \text{HCl}$$

In this salt the N atom possesses a positive charge due to which the benzene ring is deactivated for electrophilic substitution and hence aniline does not undergo Friedal-Crafts reaction.

(ii) Gabriel phthalimide synthesis involves nucleophilic substitution (S_N2) of alkyl halides by the anion formed by the phthalimide as follows:

$$\underset{\text{Phthalimide}}{\text{N}-\text{H}} \xrightarrow{\text{KOH}} \overset{-}{\text{N}}\overset{+}{\text{K}}$$

$$\downarrow \text{R}-\text{X}$$

$$\underset{N-\text{Alkylphthalimide}}{\text{N}-\text{R}} \xleftarrow[\text{(aq)}]{\text{NaOH}} \underset{1° \text{ amine}}{\text{R}-\text{NH}_2} + \overset{-}{\text{C}}-\overset{+}{\text{O}}\text{Na}$$

Since, aryl halides do not undergo nucleophilic substitution with the anion formed by the phthalimide, aromatic primary amines cannot be prepared by this process.

(iii) Aliphatic amines are stronger bases than ammonia due to +I effect of the aliphatic group attached to $-\text{NH}_2$ group. The alkyl group increases electron density on N and thus renders the N atom as a more electron rich center, hence increasing the basicity.

$$\text{H}_3\text{C}\rightarrow\overset{\text{H}}{\underset{\text{H}}{\text{N}}}: \quad \begin{array}{l}\text{increase in electron}\\\text{density of nitrogen}\\\text{lone pair}\end{array}$$

34. Write three differences between lyophobic sol and lyophilic sol. **[3]**

OR

Define the following terms:

(i) Protective colloid

(ii) Zeta potential

(iii) Emulsifying agent **[1 + 1 + 1 = 3]**

Ans.

Lyophobic Sol	Lyophilic Sol
1. Interaction between dispersed phase and dispersion medium are weak.	Interaction between dispersed phase and dispersion medium are strong.
2. Irreversible	Reversible
3. Can be easily coagulated.	Cannot be easily coagulated

OR

(i) Lyophilic colloids have a unique property of protecting lyophobic colloids. When a lyophilic sol is added to the lyophobic sol, the lyophilic particles form a layer around lyophobic particles and thus protect the latter from electrolytes. Lyophilic colloids used for this purpose are called protective colloids.

(ii) A colloidal particle acquires charge by adsorbing a selective charge (either positive or negative). This potential difference between the fixed layer and the diffused layer of opposite charges is called the zeta potential by a colloid.

(iii) Emulsifying agent is a substance that help an emulsion to become more stable. They are added to an emulsion to prevent the coalescence of the globules of the dispersed phase.

SECTION-D

35. (a) Give reasons:

(i) Transition metals and their compounds show catalytic activities.

(ii) Separation of a mixture of Lanthanoid elements is difficult.

(iii) Zn, Cd and Hg are soft and have low melting point.

(b) Write the preparation of the following:

(i) $Na_2Cr_2O_7$ from Na_2CrO_4

(ii) K_2MnO_4 from MnO_2　　　$[3 + 2 = 5]$

OR

(a) Account for the following:

(i) Ti^{3+} is coloured whereas Sc^{3+} is colourless in aqueous solution.

(ii) Cr^{2+} is a strong reducing agent.

(b) Write two similarities between chemistry of lanthanoids and actinoids.

(c) Complete the following ionic equation:

$$3\,MnO_4^{2-} + 4H^+ \longrightarrow \qquad [2 + 2 + 1 = 5]$$

Ans. (a) (i) Transition metals and their derivatives show catalytic properties because they have partially filled d-orbitals which enables them to show variable oxidation states and form complexes with other chemical entities. Hence, they can adsorb other substances on their surface and activate them for reaction process.

(ii) In lanthanoid series, there is a regular decrease in the atomic and ionic radii with increase in atomic number. This steady but small decrease in the sizes of the atoms or ions of the Lanthanides is called lanthanide contraction. Lanthanides are difficult to separate because of their almost similar sizes which is a result of lanthanide contraction.

(iii) In Zn, Cd and Hg, all the electrons in outer d-subshell are paired. They have no unpaired electron. Hence the metallic bonds present in them are weak. That is why they are soft metals and have low melting and boiling points.

(b) (i) Preparation of $Na_2Cr_2O_7$ from Na_2CrO_4 is done by acidifying the solution of latter with sulphuric acid-

$$2Na_2CrO_4 + 2H^+ \rightarrow Na_2Cr_2O_7 + 2Na^+ + H_2O$$

(ii) Preparation of K_2MnO_4 from MnO_2 is done by using KOH solution-

$$2MnO_2 + 4KOH + O_2 \rightarrow 2K_2MnO_4 + 2H_2O$$

OR

(a) (i) Electronic configuration of Ti^{3+} ion is $[Ar]\,4s^0\,3d^1$ and Sc^{3+} $[Ar]\,4s^0\,3d^0$. As there is no unpaired electron in d orbitals of Sc^{3+} it does not show colour, while Ti^{3+} is coloured due to presence of one unpaired electron in $3d$ orbital.

(ii) Cr^{2+} is a strong reducing agent as by losing one more electron while reducing the other reacting species, it gains an oxidation state of +3 which is favourable and more stable.

(b) 1. Both lanthanoids and actinoids constitute the f-block of the periodic table, with the successive filling of the inner orbitals ($4f$ and $5f$ respectively). They both show f-f transitions.

2. Both lanthanoids and actinoids elements show a gradual decrease in atomic and ionic sizes with increase in atomic number. This effects the properties and reactivities of these elements to a large extent. They both show contration in atomic radii.

(c) $3MnO_4^{2-} + 4H^+ \rightarrow 2MnO_4^- + MnO_2 + 2H_2O$

36. (a) Write the products formed when benzaldehyde reacts with the following reagents:

(i) CH_3CHO in presence of dilute NaOH

(ii) $H_2N - NH -$ ⟨benzene ring⟩

(iii) Conc. NaOH

(b) Distinguish between following:

(i) $CH_3 – CH = CH – CO–CH_3$ and
$CH_3 – CH_2 –CO – CH = CH_2$

(ii) Benzaldehyde and Benzoic acid.

$$[3 + (1 + 1) = 5]$$

OR

(a) Write the final products in the following:

(i) $\begin{matrix} CH_3 \\ \\ CH_3 \end{matrix} \!\!>\!\! C = O \xrightarrow[\text{Conc. HCl}]{\text{Zn/Hg}}$

(ii) $\text{C}_6\text{H}_5\text{—COONa} \xrightarrow[\Delta]{\text{NaOH/CaO}}$

(iii) $CH_2 = CH – CH_2 – CN \xrightarrow[\text{(b) H}_3\text{O}^+]{\text{(a) DIBAL-H}}$

(b) Arrange the following in the increasing order of their reactivity towards nucleophilic addition reaction:

$$CH_3COCH_3, HCHO, CH_3CHO, \text{C}_6\text{H}_5\text{—COCH}_3$$

(c) Draw the structure of 2, 4 DNP derivative of acetaldehyde. $\quad [3 + 1 + 1 = 5]$

Ans. (a) (i) Cinnamaldehyde is formed when benzaldehyde reacts with acetaldehyde in presence of dil NaOH by Aldol condensation.

$$\underset{\substack{\text{Benzaldehyde}\\ \text{(no α-hydrogen)}}}{C_6H_5CHO} + \underset{\text{Aldol condensation}}{CH_3CHO} \xrightarrow{\text{dil NaOH}} \underset{\text{Aldol.}}{C_6H_5\overset{\overset{\textstyle OH}{|}}{C}HCH_2CHO}$$

$$\Big\downarrow \begin{matrix} H^+, \text{Heat} \\ -H_2O \end{matrix}$$

$$\underset{\text{Cinnamaldehyde}}{C_6H_5CH = CHCHO}$$

(ii) Benzaldehyde reacts with phenyl-hydrazine to give phenylhydrazone.

$$\underset{\text{Phenylhydrazine}}{\text{C}_6\text{H}_5\text{NHNH}_2} + \underset{\text{Benzaldehyde}}{\text{C}_6\text{H}_5\text{CHO}} \longrightarrow$$

$$\underset{\text{Phenyl hydrazone}}{\text{C}_6\text{H}_5\text{N(H)—N}=\text{CHC}_6\text{H}_5}$$

(iii) Benzaldehyde do not have α-hydrogen so on heating with concentrated KOH solution a mixture of alcohol and salt is formed this is Cannizzaro's reaction.

$$\underset{\text{Benzaldehyde}}{\text{C}_6\text{H}_5\text{CHO}} + \text{Conc.KOH} \longrightarrow \underset{\substack{\text{Potassium}\\ \text{benzoate}}}{\text{C}_6\text{H}_5\text{COOK}}$$

$$+ \quad \underset{\text{Benzyl alcohol}}{\text{C}_6\text{H}_5\text{CH}_2\text{OH}}$$

(b) (i) Among the two compounds given, $CH_3CH = CH–CO–CH_3$, has a terminal–CH_3 group attached to carbonyl carbon ($–CO–CH_3$) is present which will undergo Iodform reaction to give yellow coloured precipitate of triiodomethane.

$$CH_3CH = CH–CO–CH_3 + 4NaOH + 3I_2 \rightarrow$$
$$CH_3CH = CH – COO^-Na^+ + 3NaI + 3H_2O + \underset{\text{(Yellow solid)}}{CHI_3}$$

Whereas the other compound $CH_3 – CH_2 – CO – CH = CH_2$ will not give any such reaction.

(ii) Benzaldehyde when treated with ammoniacal silver nitrate gets oxidized and reduces Ag^+ ions to Ag (elemental) hence, a deposition of silver is obtained which is known as silver mirror, whereas benzoic acid does not undergo this reaction hence can be distinguished with the help of Silver mirror test from benzaldehyde.

$$\underset{\text{Benzaldehyde}}{\text{C}_6\text{H}_5\text{CHO}} \xrightarrow[\text{NH}_3/\text{H}_2\text{O}]{\text{AgO}_2} \underset{\substack{\text{Metallic silver is deposited}\\ \text{in a thin mirror coating}}}{\text{C}_6\text{H}_5\text{COOH} + Ag}$$

OR

(a) (i) Clemmenson reduction:

$$\underset{\text{Acetone}}{CH_3 — CO — CH_3} \xrightarrow[\text{Conc HCl}]{\text{Zn/Hg}}$$
$$CH_3 — CH_2 — \underset{\text{Propane}}{CH_3} + H_2O$$

(ii)

$$\underset{\text{Sodium benzoate}}{\text{C}_6\text{H}_5\text{COONa}} \xrightarrow[\Delta]{\text{NaOH + CaO}} \underset{\text{Benzene}}{\text{C}_6\text{H}_6} + Na_2CO_3 + H_2O$$

(iii)

$$\underset{\text{But-3-enenitrile}}{H_2C\!=\!\!\diagup\!\!\diagdown\text{CN}} \xrightarrow[\text{(b) } H_3O^+]{\text{(a) DIBAL H}} \underset{\text{But-3-enal}}{H_2C\!=\!\!\diagup\!\!\diagdown\text{CHO}}$$

(b) Reactivity in increasing order is–

$$C_6H_5COCH_3 < CH_3COCH_3 < CH_3CHO$$
$$< HCHO$$

(c)

(2, 4-dinitrophenyl) hydrazine

(1E)-acetaldehyde
(2-methyl-4dinitrophenyl) hydrazone

37. (a) A first order reaction is 25% complete in 40 minutes. Calculate the value of rate constant. In what time will the reaction be 80% completed?

(b) Define order of reaction. Write the condition under which a bimolecular reaction follows first order kinetics.

$$[3 + 2 = 5]$$

OR

(a) A first order reaction is 50% complete in 30 minutes at 300 K and in 10 minutes at 320 K. Calculate activation energy (E_a) for the reaction. $(R = 8.314 \text{ JK}^{-1} \text{ mol}^{-1})$

(b) Write the two conditions for collisions to be effective collisions.

(c) How order of reaction and molecularity differ towards a complex reaction?

[Given : log 2 = 0.3010, log 3 = 0.4771, log 4 = 0.6021, log 5 = 0.6991]   [3 + 1 + 1 = 5]

Ans. (a) For a first order reaction–

$$k = \left(\frac{2.303}{t}\right)\log\left(\frac{a}{a}-x\right)$$

When $\quad x = \left(\dfrac{25}{100}\right)a = 0.25\,a$

$$t = 40 \text{ minutes (given)}$$

Therefore, $\quad k = \left(\dfrac{2.303}{40}\right)\log\left(\dfrac{a}{a}-0.25a\right)$

$$k = \left(\frac{2.303}{40}\right)\log\left(\frac{1}{0.75}\right)$$

$$k = 0.00719 \text{ min}^{-1}$$

Hence the value of the rate constant is 0.00719 min^{-1}

Now, we need to find time for rest 50% reaction t =?, when $x = 0.50\,a$

From above, k = 0.00719 min^{-1}

Therefore, $\quad t = \left(\dfrac{2.303}{0.00719}\right)\log\left(\dfrac{a}{a}-0.50a\right)$

$$t = \left(\frac{2.303}{0.00719}\right)\log\left(\frac{1}{0.50}\right)$$

$$t = 230 \text{ min}$$

The time at which the reaction will be 50% complete is 230 min.

(b) Order of reaction for elementary reaction is the sum of the powers to which the reactant concentrations are raised in the rate law equation. It relates the rate of a chemical reaction with the concentrations of the reacting substances.

When concentration of one of the reactant is in excess and practically unchanged during the reaction for example when solvent used for reaction is one of the reactants, then the reaction follows first order kinetics as it depends on the concentration of only one reactant in practical sense.

OR

(a) The problem can be solved by using half-life equation–

by using half life equation, we get

$$K = \frac{0.693}{t_{1/2}}$$

$$K = \frac{0.693}{30\,\text{min}} = 0.0231 \text{ at } 300 \text{ K}$$

$$K = \frac{0.693}{10\,\text{min}} = 0.0693 \text{ at } 320 \text{ K}$$

From the Arrhenius equation

$$\log\frac{k_2}{k_1} = \frac{E_a}{2.303R}\left[\frac{T_2-T_1}{T_1T_2}\right]$$

$$E_a = \frac{2.303\times R\times T_1\times T_2}{T_2-T_1}\log\frac{k_2}{k_1}$$

$$= \frac{2.303\times 8.314\,\text{JK}^{-1}\text{mol}^{-1}\times 300\times 320\text{K}}{320\,\text{K}-300\text{ K}}\times i$$

$$\left(\log\frac{0.06935}{0.2315}\right) = 43.848 \text{ kJ mol}^{-1}$$

(b) Two conditions for collisions to be effective collisions are:

   1. Collisions must be sufficiently energetic to break chemical bonds; and it should be more than the threshold energy.

   2. The reacting particle must be properly oriented during collision, so as to confirm maximum interaction between the reacting particles for successful reaction.

(c) **1.** Order of reaction is an experimental quantity. It can be zero and even in fraction but molecularity cannot be zero or a non integer.

   2. Order is applicable to elementary as well as complex reaction where as molecularity is applicable only for elementary reactions.

   3. For complex reaction, order is given by the slowest step and molecularity of the slowest step is same as the order of overall reaction.

●●

Delhi [Set-II]

Note : Except for the following questions all the remaining questions have been asked in previous set.

SECTION-A

6. Out of

Cl

and

CH_2—Cl

, which will undergo $S_N 1$ reaction faster with OH^-?

Ans. $C_6H_5CH_2Cl$.

7. Write the IUPAC name of $CH_3—\underset{\underset{CH_3}{|}}{N}$—⟨phenyl⟩.

Ans. N, N-Dimethyl benzenamine.

8. What type of linkage is present in polysaccharides?

Ans. Glycosidic linkages.

9. Name an artificial sweetener whose use is limited to cold drinks.

Ans. Aspartame

10. Name the polymer which is used for making non-stick utensils.

Ans. Teflon or PTFE

11. Kohlrausch given the following relation for strong electrolytes:

$$\Lambda = \Lambda_0 - A\sqrt{C}$$

Which of the following equality holds ?

(a) $\Lambda = \Lambda_0$ as $C \longrightarrow \sqrt{\Lambda}$

(b) $\Lambda = \Lambda_0$ as $C \longrightarrow \infty$

(c) $\Lambda = \Lambda_0$ as $C \longrightarrow 0$

(d) $\Lambda = \Lambda_0$ as $C \longrightarrow 1$

Ans. (c) $\Lambda = \Lambda_0$ as $C \longrightarrow 0$

12. In an electrochemical process, a salt bridge is used.

(a) as a reducing agent.

(b) as an oxidising agent.

(c) to complete the circuit so that current can flow.

(d) None of these

Ans. (c) to complete the circuit so that current can flow.

13. In a chemical reaction $X \rightarrow Y$, it is found that the rate of reaction doubles when the concentration of X is increased four times. The order of the reaction with respect to X is

(a) 1   (b) 0

(c) 2   (d) 1/2

Ans. (d) 1/2

14. Which of the following will give a white precipitate upon reacting with $AgNO_3$?

(a) $K_2 [Pt(en)_2Cl_2]$ (b) $[Co(NH_3)_3Cl_3]$

(c) $[Cr (H_2O)_6]Cl_3$ (d) $[Fe (H_2O)_3Cl_3]$

Ans. (c) $[Cr (H_2O)_6]Cl_3$

15. Copper matte contains

(a) Cu_2S, Cu_2O and silica

(b) Cu_2S, CuO and silica

(c) Cu_2S, FeO and silica

(d) Cu_2S, FeS and silica

Ans. (d) Cu_2S, FeS and silica

Questions 16 to 20:

(A) Both Assertion (A) and Reason (R) are correct statements, and Reason (R) is the correct explanation of the Assertion (A).

(B) Both Assertion (A) and Reason (R) are correct statements, but Reason (R) is not the correct explanation of the Assertion (A).

(C) Assertion (A) is correct, but Reason (R) is wrong statement.

(D) Assertion (A) is wrong, but Reason (R) is correct statement.

16. Assertion (A) : 0.1 M solution of KCl has greater osmotic pressure than 0.1 M solution of glucose at same temperature.

Reason (R) : In solution, KCl dissociates to produce more number of particles.

Ans. (A) KCl can dissociates in water but glucose does not due to dissociation of ions, solution exhibit higher colligative property. Thus, Both Assertion (A) and Reason (R) are correct statements, and Reason (R) is the correct explanation of the Assertion (A).

18. Assertion (A) : Ortho and para-nitrophenols can be separated by steam distillation.

Reason (R) : Ortho isomer associates through intermolecular hydrogen bonding while Para isomer associates through intramolecular hydrogen bonding.

Ans. (C) Ortho and para isomers of nitro- phenol can be separated by steam distillation because of nearby same boiling point of both and Ortho isomers associate by intramolecular hydrogen bonding and Para isomers associate by hydrogen bonding. Thus, Assertion (A) is correct, but Reason (R) is wrong statement.

SECTION - B

23. Draw the structures of the following:

(i) $H_2S_2O_7$

(ii) BrF_5 [2]

Ans. (i) $H_2S_2O_7$ -Pyrosulphuric acid

(ii) BrF_5 - Bromine pentafluoride

25. Identify the monomers in the following polymers: [2]

(i)

(ii)

$$\left[-NH-(CH_2)_6-NH-\underset{\underset{O}{\|}}{C}-(CH_2)_4-\underset{\underset{O}{\|}}{C}-\right]_n$$

Ans. (i) The given polymer is Bakelite and the monomers are phenol and formaldehyde.

Bakelite polymer

(ii) The given polymer is Nylon 6,6. It's monomers are hexamethylene diamine and adipic acid-

$$nHO-\underset{\underset{O}{\|}}{C}-(CH_2)_4-\underset{\underset{O}{\|}}{C}-OH + nH_2N-(CH_2)_6-NH_2 \longrightarrow$$

Adipic acid　　　　Hexamethylene diamine

$$\left[-\underset{\underset{O}{\|}}{C}-(CH_2)_4-\underset{\underset{O}{\|}}{C}-NH(CH_2)_6-NH-\right]_n + 2nH_2O$$

Nylon 6,6

26. Discuss the nature of bonding in metal carbonyls. [2]

Ans. Nature of Bonding in Metal Carbonyls: CO ligands donate electron pair to metal atom to generate a σ bond. Also, they accept electron density from the metal into their π* orbitals which is known as back bonding. This back bonding stabilizes the complex further. The lower the formal charge on metal ion, more it is willing to donate electrons to π orbitals of the CO ligands. Hence, zero valent metal atoms easily form CO complexes compared to the positively charged metal ions.

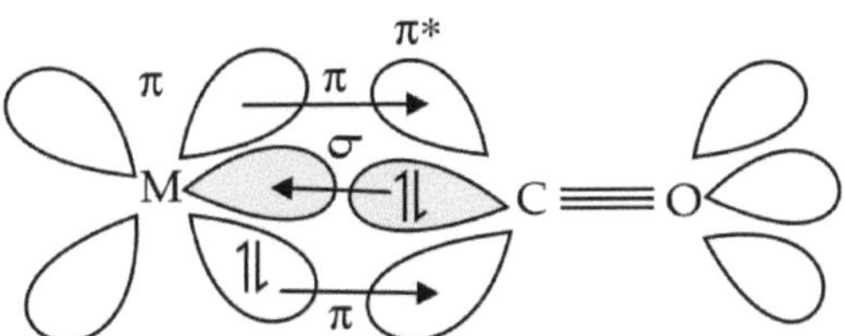

Synergic bonding in metal carbonyls

SECTION - C

30. Define the following terms with a suitable example in each :

(a) Polysaccharides

(b) Denatured protein

(c) Fibrous protein   [1 + 1 + 1 = 3]

Ans. (i) Polysaccharides–They contain large number of simple carbohydrate units joined together by glycosidic linkages. For example : Starch

(ii) Denatured proteins–When the protein molecules in their native form are subjected to physical changes like change in temperature, pH etc. the hydrogen bonds are disturbed within the structure of the proteins and they lose their tertiary structure resulting in loss of biological activity. This is known as denaturation of proteins. For Example: Hardening of egg upon boiling.

(iii) Fibrous protein–They are a fiber-like structure formed by the polypeptide chains. These proteins are held together by strong hydrogen and disulphide bonds and they run parallel to each other. It is usually insoluble in water. Fibrous proteins are usually used for structural purposes. For Example : Keratin present in nails and hair.

●●

Delhi [Set-III]

Note : Except for the following questions all the remaining questions have been asked in previous sets.

SECTION-A

6. A hydrocarbon C_5H_{12} gives only one monochloride on photochemical chlorination. Identify the compound.

Ans. The compound is 2, 2,-Dimethyl propane

$$H_3C\underset{\underset{\displaystyle H_3C \qquad CH_3}{|}}{\overset{\overset{\displaystyle H_3C \qquad CH_3}{|}}{C}}$$

2,2-Dimethyl propane

7. Out of $(CH_3)_3N$ and $(CH_3)_2NH$, which one is more basic in aqueous solution?

Ans. $(CH_3)_2NH$

8. Out of Cis–$[Pt(en)_2Cl_2]^{2+}$ and Trans $[Pt(en)_2Cl_2]^{2+}$, which one is optically active?

Ans. Cis-$[Pt(en)_2Cl_2]^{2+}$

9. Name the method of refining used to obtain semiconductor of very high purity.

Ans. Zone refining

10. Is $$-\left[CH_2-CH=CH-CH_2-CH_2-\underset{\underset{\displaystyle CN}{|}}{CH}\right]_n$$

a homopolymer or copolymer?

Ans. Copolymer

11. The amount of electricity required to produce one mole of Zn from $ZnSO_4$ solution will be:

(a) 3F   (b) 2F

(c) 1F   (d) 4F

Ans. (b) 2F

12. Zinc is coated over iron to prevent rusting of iron because

(a) $E^\circ_{Zn^{2+}/Zn} = E^\circ_{Fe^{2+}/Fe}$

(b) $E^\circ_{Zn^{2+}/Zn} < E^\circ_{Fe^{2+}/Fe}$

(c) $E^\circ_{Zn^{2+}/Zn} > E^\circ_{Fe^{2+}/Fe}$

(d) None of these

Ans. (b) $E^\circ_{Zn^{2+}/Zn} < E^\circ_{Fe^{2+}/Fe}$

13. The unit of rate constant depends upon the

(a) molecularity of the reaction.

(b) activation energy of the reaction.

(c) order of the reaction

(d) temperature of the reaction

Ans. (c) Order of the reaction

14. The formula of the complex triamminetri (nitrito-O) Cobalt (III) is

(a) $[Co(ONO)_3 (NH_3)_3]$

(b) $[Co(NO_2)_3 (NH_3)_3]$

(c) $[Co(ONO_2)_3 (NH_3)_3]$

(d) $[Co(NO_2)(NH_3)_3]$

Ans. (a) $[Co(ONO)_3 (NH_3)_3]$

15. Which of the following is a disaccharide?

(a) Glucose   (b) Starch

(c) Cellulose   (d) Lactose

Ans. (d) Lactose

Questions 16 to 20:

(A) Both Assertion (A) and Reason (R) are correct statements, and Reason (R) is the correct explanation of the Assertion (A).

(B) Both Assertion (A) and Reason (R) are correct statements, but Reason (R) is not the correct explanation of the Assertion (A).

(C) Assertion (A) is correct, but Reason (R) is wrong statement.

(D) Assertion (A) is wrong, but Reason (R) is correct statement.

16. Assertion (A) : An ideal solution obeys Henry's law.

Reason (R) : In an ideal solution, solute-solute as well as solvent solvent interactions are similar to solute-solvent interaction.

Ans. (D) An ideal solution obeys Raoults' law. Thus, Assertion (A) is wrong, but Reason (R) is correct statement.

18. Assertion (A) : Benzaldehyde is less reactive than ethanal towards nucleophilic addition reactions.

Reason (R) : Ethanal is more sterically hindered.

Ans. (C) Benzaldehyde is less electrophillic than ethanal due to resonance stability of benzaldehyde. Thus, Assertion (A) is correct, but Reason (R) is wrong statement.

SECTION - B

22. Draw the structures of the following :

 (i) $HClO_4$

 (ii) $XeOF_4$ **[1 + 1 = 2]**

Ans. (i) $HClO_4$ - Perchloric acid

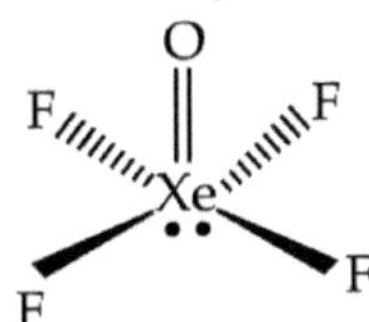

 (ii) $XeOF_4$ - Xenon oxytetrafluoride

24. Identify the monomers in the following polymers:

 (i)

 (ii)

          [1 + 1 = 2]

Ans. (i) The given polymer is Glyptal and it is prepared from ethylene glycol and phthalic acid monomers.

$$nHO-CH_2-CH_2-OH + nHO-C \cdots C-OH$$

Ethylene glycol

Phthalic acid

$-2nH_2O$

(ii) The given polymer is melamine polymer and it is prepared from melamine and formaldehyde monomers.

Melamine   Resin intermediate

Polymerisation

Melamine-formaldehyde polymer

27. Define the following terms with a suitable example in each :

 (i) Bacteriocidal antibiotics

 (ii) Food preservatives.   **[1 + 1 = 2]**

Ans. (i) Bacteriocidal antibiotics–They are the antibiotics which kill the bacteria. Example : Penicillin.

(ii) Food preservatives–They are added to food items to prevent spoilage of food due to microbial growth. Example : Sodium benzoate.

SECTION - C

31. (i) What are the hydrolysis products of DNA ?

(ii) What happens when D-glucose is treated with Bromine water ?

(iii) What is the effect of denaturation on the structure of proteins ? **[1 + 1 + 1 =3]**

Ans. (i) Complete hydrolysis of DNA yields a pentose sugar, phosphoric acid and nitrogen contaning heterocycles (nitrogenous bases). For example–

(ii) When D-Glucose is treated with bromine water, gluconic acid is obtained:

$$\underset{\text{Glucose}}{\begin{array}{c} CHO \\ | \\ (CHOH)_4 \\ | \\ CH_2OH \end{array}} \quad \xrightarrow[\text{[O]}]{Br_2/H_2O} \quad \underset{\text{(Gluconic acid)}}{\begin{array}{c} COOH \\ | \\ (CHOH)_4 \\ | \\ CH_2OH \end{array}}$$

(iii) When the protein molecules in their native form are subjected to physical changes like change in temperature, pH etc. the hydrogen bonds are disturbed within the structure of the proteins, this brings about denaturation of proteins due to which they lose their tertiary structure resulting in loss of biological activity. Example : Hardening of egg upon boiling.

●●

Printed by Libri Plureos GmbH in Hamburg,
Germany